INTERNATIONAL LAW AS SOCIAL CONSTRUCT

International Law as Social Construct

The Struggle for Global Justice

CARLO FOCARELLI

OXFORD
UNIVERSITY PRESS

OXFORD
UNIVERSITY PRESS

Great Clarendon Street, Oxford, OX2 6DP,
United Kingdom

Oxford University Press is a department of the University of Oxford.
It furthers the University's objective of excellence in research, scholarship,
and education by publishing worldwide. Oxford is a registered trade mark of
Oxford University Press in the UK and in certain other countries

First Edition published in 2012

Published in the United States of America by Oxford University Press
198 Madison Avenue, New York, NY 10016, United States of America

British Library Cataloguing in Publication Data
Data available

ISBN 978-0-19-958483-3

For Carla

Preface

This book touches upon a wide variety of themes which converge on what goes by the name of 'international law'. While some have been adequately developed, virtually all need further analysis and research. I hope to provide this in the coming years. For the time being, the book seeks to distil and articulate the essence and a systematization of international law through investigating some key concepts surrounding law in general (society, myth, and reason), in Part I, and international law in particular (its de- and remythologization, as well as players, rules, values, and remedies), in Part II.

What is, if any, the 'objective' reality of international law and how can international law be improved to further global justice? It is the argument of this book that a part of the answer can be found in considering law, including international law, as a socially constructed reality. The book does so by analysing the social foundations of law, its mythic essence, and its roots in practical and socially workable (as opposed to 'theoretical') reason. Prudence and social attunement, rather than scientific or philosophical reason, are seen as key to the understanding of law. The book reconceptualizes past and current doctrines of international law as strategies of concomitantly demythologizing and remythologizing international law. Key areas thereof, including subjects, sources, hierarchy, values, and remedies, are shown to be part of this process.

The book challenges, in many respects, popular ideas and will perhaps cause adverse reactions. I trust, however, that it is balanced and guided by good sense. Another inspiring sentiment is a combination of detachment from and engagement in human affairs. Although human history repeats itself indefinitely and one sees every day good and bad things which have already occurred myriad times, still every day is a new day and those who happen to live on this very day bear the responsibility to make it better than yesterday. I am confident that law can assist us to this end.

It would take too long to acknowledge the many people who have contributed to this book (including the publisher and the anonymous reviewers of the manuscript) and I am sure they will forgive me if I refrain from recalling them one by one, but I would like to express my deep gratitude to them all.

Carlo Focarelli

30 January 2012
Rome

Contents

II. THE CONSTRUCTION OF INTERNATIONAL LAW

EPILOGUE

Table of Cases

PERMANENT COURT OF INTERNATIONAL JUSTICE (PCIJ)

(<http://www.icj-cij.org/pcij/index.php?p1=9>)

INTERNATIONAL COURT OF JUSTICE (ICJ)

(<http://www.icj-cij.org/docket/index.php?p1=3>)

Judgments and Orders

Advisory Opinions

ICJ AD HOC CHAMBERS

WORLD TRADE ORGANIZATION (WTO) DSB INSTITUTIONS

(<http://www.wto.org/english/tratop_e/dispu_e/dispu_status_e.htm>)

GATT 1947

INTERNATIONAL TRIBUNAL FOR THE LAW OF THE SEA (ITLOS)

(<http://www.itlos.org/index.php?id=35&L=0>)

INTERNATIONAL LABOUR ORGANIZATION ADMINISTRATIVE TRIBUNAL (ILOAT)

(<http://www.ilo.org/dyn/triblex/triblexmain.advancedSearch?p_lang=en>)

EUROPEAN COURT OF HUMAN RIGHTS (ECTHR)

(<http://cmiskp.echr.coe.int/tkp197/search.asp?skin=hudoc-en>)

EUROPEAN COMMISSION OF HUMAN RIGHTS (ECOMMHR)

INTER-AMERICAN COURT OF HUMAN RIGHTS (IACTHR)

Advisory Opinions

Judgments and Orders

INTER-AMERICAN COMMISSION OF HUMAN RIGHTS (IACOMMHR)

AFRICAN COMMISSION OF HUMAN AND PEOPLE'S RIGHTS (ACOMMHPR)

(<http://www.achpr.org/english/_info/decisions_en.html>)

UN HUMAN RIGHTS COMMITTEE (HRC)

<http://www2.ohchr.org/english/bodies/hrc/comments.htm>

General Comments

Concluding Observations

Views

UN COMMITTEE ON ECONOMIC, SOCIAL, AND CULTURAL RIGHTS (CESCP)

INTERNATIONAL CRIMINAL TRIBUNAL FOR RWANDA

(<http://www.unictr.org/Cases/tabid/204/Default.aspx>)

INTERNATIONAL CRIMINAL COURT (ICC)

(<http://www.icc-cpi.int/Menus/ICC/Situations+and+Cases>)

SPECIAL TRIBUNAL FOR LEBANON (STL)

(<http://www.stl-tsl.org/sid/55>)

COURT OF FIRST INSTANCE (CFI) AND EUROPEAN COURT OF JUSTICE (ECJ)

(<http://curia.europa.eu/jcms/jcms/j_6>)
(<http://curia.europa.eu/jurisp/cgi-bin/form.pl?lang=en>)

ICSID ARBITRAL TRIBUNALS

(<http://icsid.worldbank.org/ICSID/FrontServlet?requestType=CasesRH&reqFrom=Main&actionVal=ViewAllCases>)

NAFTA ARBITRAL TRIBUNALS

IRAN–US CLAIMS TRIBUNAL

INTERNATIONAL CHAMBER OF COMMERCE COURT OF ARBITRATION

OTHER ARBITRAL TRIBUNALS

ERITREA–ETHIOPIA CLAIMS COMMISSION (EECC)

(<http://www.pca-cpa.org/showpage.asp?pag_id=1151>)

DOMESTIC COURTS

Denmark

France

Germany

Japan

Madagascar

Netherlands

Lesotho

Nigeria

Philippines

Poland

Singapore

Slovenia

South Africa

Spain

Switzerland

United Kingdom

United States

Table of Treaties and Other Instruments

UN SECURITY COUNCIL (UNSC) RESOLUTIONS

(<http://www.un.org/Depts/dhl/resguide/scact.htm>)

UN GENERAL ASSEMBLY (UNGA) RESOLUTIONS

(<http://www.un.org/documents/resga.htm>)

UN ECONOMIC AND SOCIAL COUNCIL (ECOSOC) RESOLUTIONS

(<http://www.un.org/en/ecosoc/docs/docs.shtml>)

INTERNATIONAL BANK FOR RECONSTRUCTION AND DEVELOPMENT (IBRD) AND INTERNATIONAL DEVELOPMENT ASSOCIATION (IDA) RESOLUTIONS

ORGANIZATION OF AMERICAN STATES (OAS) PERMANENT COUNCIL RESOLUTIONS

List of Abbreviations

General

a	answer
AB	Appellate Body
ACHPR	African Charter of Human and Peoples' Rights
ACHR	American Convention on Human Rights
ATS	Alien Tort Act
BIS	Bank for International Settlements
BITs	bilateral investment treaties
c	canon
CAT	Convention against Torture and Other Cruel, Inhuman or Degrading Treatment or Punishment, Committee Against Torture
CCPR	Committee on Civil and Political Rights
CEDAW	Convention on the Elimination of All Forms of Discrimination against Women
CESCR	Committee on Economic, Social and Cultural Rights
CIL	customary international law
CMR	Convention on the Contract for the International Carriage of Goods by Road
CMW	International Convention on the Protection of the Rights of All Migrant Workers and Members of Their Families
COE	Council of Europe
Comm	Communication
Cor	Letter of St Paul to the Corinthians
CRAs	credit rating agencies
CRC	Convention on the Rights of the Child
CSR	corporate social responsibility
d	distinctio
DSB	Dispute Settlement Body of the World Trade Organization
DSU	Understanding on Rules and Procedures Governing the Settlement of Disputes
ECAs	export credit agencies
ECHR	European Convention for the Protection of Human Rights and Fundamental Freedoms
ECJ	European Court of Justice
ECommHR	European Commission on Human Rights
ECOSOC	UN Economic and Social Council
ECtHR	European Court of Human Rights
Eph	Letter of St Paul to the Ephesians
FAO	Food and Agriculture Organization of the United Nations
FARC	Fuerzas Armadas Revolucionarias de Colombia (Revolutionary Armed Forces of Colombia)
FCAFC	Federal Court of Australia—Full Court
FCN	treaties of friendship, commerce and navigation
FDI	foreign direct investment
FRY	Federal Republic of Yugoslavia
GAL	global administrative law
GAOR	General Assembly Official Record
GATT	General Agreement on Tariffs and Trade

GC	Grand Chamber
GCI	Global Competitiveness Index
GDP	Gross domestic product
HCT	hybrid criminal tribunal
HR Council	Human Rights Council
IACHR	Series Inter-American Commission on Human Rights
IACommHR	Inter-American Commission on Human Rights
IACtHR	Inter-American Court of Human Rights
IAEA	International Atomic Energy Agency
ICs	crimes under international law
ICC	International Criminal Court
ICCPR	International Covenant on Civil and Political Rights
ICESCR	International Covenant on Economic, Social, and Cultural Rights
ICJ	International Court of Justice
ICSID	International Centre for Settlement of Investment Disputes
ICT	international criminal tribunal
ICTR	International Criminal Tribunal for Rwanda
ICTY	International Criminal Tribunal for the former Yugoslavia
IDI	Institut de Droit International
IG	Ius Gentium
IHL	international humanitarian law
IHRL	international human rights law
ILC	International Law Commission
ILO	International Labour Organization
ILOAT	International Labour Organization Administrative Tribunal
ILP	international legal personality
IMF	International Monetary Fund
IMT	International Military Tribunal Nuremberg
IMTFE	International Military Tribunal for the Far East
IOs	international organizations
IR	international relations
ITLOS	International Tribunal for the Law of the Sea
ITU	International Telecommunication Union
LAS	League of Arab States
MDGs	Millennium Development Goals
MNCs	multilateral corporations
MNEs	multinational enterprises
NAFTA	North American Free Trade Agreement
NAM	Non-Aligned Movement
NATO	North Atlantic Treaty Organization
NCPs	National Contact Points
NGOs	non-governmental organizations
NIEO	New International Economic Order
OAS	Organization of American States
OAU	Organization of African Unity
OECD	Organization for Economic Co-operation and Development
OIC	Organization of the Islamic Conference
PCA	Permanent Court of Arbitration
PCIJ	Permanent Court of International Justice
PKK	Kurdish Worker's Party, now Kongra-Gel
PLO	Palestine Liberation Organization
PPMs	processes and production methods

PSCs	private security companies
q	question
QB	Queen's Bench
QBD	Queen's Bench Division
Rom	Letter of St Paul to the Romans
RtoP	responsibility to protect
SCSL	Special Court for Sierra Leone
SPS Agreement	Agreement on Sanitary and Phytosanitary Measures
SRMs	social resistance movements (of the Third World)
STL	Special Tribunal for Lebanon
TBT Agreement	Agreement on Technical Barriers to Trade
TCL	transnational criminal law
TFEU	Treaty on the Functioning of the European Union
TNCs	transnational corporations
TNEs	transnational enterprises
TREMS	trade-related environmental measures
TWAIL	Third World Approach to International Law
USC	Code of Laws of the United States of America, at <http://www.gpoaccess.gov/uscode>
UDHR	Universal Declaration of Human Rights
UKHL	UK House of Lords
UN Doc	United Nations Document
UN HRC	United Nations Human Rights Committee
UNAT	United Nations Administrative Tribunal
UNCED	UN Conference on Environment and Development
UNCIO	United Nations Conference on International Organization
UNCLOS	United Nations Conference on the Law of the Sea
UNCTAD	United Nations Conference on Trade and Development
UNEP	United Nations Environment Programme
UNESCO	United Nations Educational, Scientific and Cultural Organization
UNGA	United Nations General Assembly
UNHRC	United Nations Human Rights Committee
UNODC	United Nations Office on Drugs and Crime
UNOSOM	United Nations Operation in Somalia
UNPROFOR	United Nations Protection Force
UNSC	United Nations Security Council
UNSG	United Nations Secretary-General
VCCR	Vienna Convention on Consular Relations
VCLT	Vienna Convention on the Law of Treaties
VCLT-IO	Vienna Convention on the Law of Treaties between States and International Organizations or between International Organizations
WEF	World Economic Forum
WEO	Western Europe Organization
WHA	World Health Assembly
WHO	World Health Organization
WTAM	World Trade and Arbitration Materials
WTO	World Trade Organization

Reports and publications

AC	Appeal Cases (England and Wales)
ADRPILC	Annual Digest and Reports of Public International Law Cases
AdV	*Archiv des Völkerrechts*
AFDI	*Annuaire Français de Droit International*
AGP	*Archiv für Geschichte der Philosophie*
AHRLR	African Human Rights Law Reports
AIDI	*Annuaire de l'Institut de Droit International*
AJCL	American Journal of Comparative Law
AJICL	American Journal of International and Comparative Law
AJIL	American Journal of International Law
AJJ	American Journal of Jurisprudence
Alb LR	Alberta Law Review
All ER	All English Reports
AMR	Academy of Management Review
APS	*Acta Psychiatrica Scandinavica*
APSR	American Political Science Review
Ariz SLJ	Arizona State Law Journal
ARS	*Archiv für Rechts- und Sozialphilosophie*
ASDI	*Annuaire Suisse de Droit International*
ASIL Proc	American Society of International Law Proceedings
Aus YBIL	Australian Yearbook of International Law
Boston Coll ICLR	Boston College International and Comparative Law Review
Brooklyn JIL	Brooklyn Journal of International Law
BSP	British and Foreign State Papers
BVerfGE	*Entscheidungen des Bundesverfassungsgerichts*, at <http://www.bundesverfassungsgericht.de/entscheidungen.html>
BYBIL	British Yearbook of International Law
Can JEPS	Canadian Journal of Economic and Political Science
Card LR	Cardozo Law Review
CETS	Council of Europe Treaty Series
Chic JIL	Chicago Journal of International Law
Chin JIL	Chinese Journal of International Law
CHRLD	Commonwealth Human Rights Law Digest
Col JTL	Columbia Journal of Transnational Law
Col LR	Columbia Law Review
Corn ILJ	Cornell International Law Journal
Corn LQ	Cornell Law Quarterly
CRIA	Cambridge Review of International Affairs
CTS	Clive Parry (ed), *Consolidated Treaty Series 1648–1919* (New York: Dobbs Ferry, 1969–81) 231 vols
CWR JIL	Case Western Reserve Journal of International Law
Den JILP	Denver Journal of International Law and Policy
Dig US PIL	Digest of United States Practice in International Law
DK	Hermann Diels and Walther Kranz, *Die Fragmente der Vorsokratiker* (Zurich: Weidmann, 1985)
Dodson, *Reports*	John Dodson, *Reports of Cases Argued and Determined in the High Court of Admiralty: Commencing with the Judgments of the Right Hon. Sir William Scott (Lord Stowell), Trinity Term 1811*, vol 2 (1815–22) (London: Strahan, 1828)
Duke JCIL	Duke Journal of Comparative and International Law
Duke LJ	Duke Law Journal

ECR	European Court Reports
ECtHR Rep	European Court of Human Rights Reports
EGZ	*Europäische Grundrechte-Zeitschrift*
EHRR	European Human Rights Reports
EIA	Ethics and International Affairs
EJIL	European Journal of International Law
EJLS	European Journal of Legal Studies
ELS	Encyclopedia of Law and Society: American and Global Perspectives
ER	English Law Reports
ESCOR	Economic and Social Council Official Record
ETS	European Treaty Series
Finn YBIL	Finnish Yearbook of International Law
Flo JIL	Florida Journal of International Law
Ford ILJ	Fordham International Law Journal
Ford LR	Fordham Law Review
GATS	General Agreement on Trade in Services
Geo Wash ILR	George Washington International Law Review
Ger LJ	German Law Journal
Ger YBIL	German Yearbook of International Law
GJA	The Global Jurists Advances
GPA	Government Procurement Agreement
GroJIL	Groningen Journal of International Law
GU	*Gazzetta Ufficiale della Repubblica Italiana*
Harv ILJ	Harvard International Law Journal
Harv LR	Harvard Law Review
HCR	James Brown Scott (ed), *The Hague Court Reports* (New York: OUP, 1916)
HRQ	Human Rights Quarterly
HRR	Human Rights Review
ICJ Rep	International Court of Justice Reports
ICLQ	International and Comparative Law Quarterly
ICLR	International Community Law Review
IHRR	International Human Rights Reports
IJLC	International Journal of Law in Context
IJP	International Journal of Psycho-Analysis
IJSL	International Journal of Sociology of Law
ILDC	International Law in Domestic Courts, at <http://www.oxfordlawreports.com>
ILM	International Legal Materials
ILR	International Law Reports
Ilsa JICL	Ilsa Journal of International and Comparative Law
Ind JGLS	Indiana Journal of Global Legal Studies
Indian JIL	Indian Journal of International Law
IOLR	International Organizations Law Review
Iran–US CTR	Iran–US Claims Tribunal Reports Awards and Decisions
IRRC	International Review of the Red Cross
Is YBHR	Israel Yearbook of Human Rights
ISQ	*International Studies Quarterly*
It YBIL	The Italian Yearbook of International Law
ITLOS Reports	International Tribunal for the Law of the Sea Reports
Jap AIL	Japanese Annual of International Law
JBM	Journal of Brand Management

JCSL	Journal of Conflict and Security Law
JDI	*Journal du Droit International*
JHIL	Journal of the History of International Law
JICJ	Journal of International Criminal Justice
JIEL	Journal of International Economic Law
JITE	Journal of Institutional and Theoretical Economics
JLR	Journal of Law and Religion
JPART	Journal of Public Administration Research and Theory
JPh	Journal of Philosophy
JWT	Journal of World Trade
JZ	*Juristen-Zeitung*
LBRA	Law and Business Review of the Americas
LCH	Law, Culture and the Humanities
LCP	Law and Contemporary Problems
LJIL	Leiden Journal of International Law
LLA ICLR	Loyola of Los Angeles International and Comparative Law Review
LNOJ	League of Nations Official Journal
LNTS	League of Nations Treaty Series
Lou LR	Louisiana Law Review
LPICT	The Law and Practice of International Courts and Tribunals
LQR	Law Quarterly Review
McGill LJ	McGill Law Journal
Mel JIL	Melbourne Journal of International Law
Mich JIL	Michigan Journal of International Law
Mich LR	Michigan Law Review
MLR	Modern Law Review
MP EPIL	Max Planck Encyclopedia of Public International Law
MP YBUNL	Max Planck Yearbook of United Nations Law
NC JILCR	North Carolina Journal of International Law and Commercial Regulation
Neth ILR	Netherlands International Law Review
Neth YBIL	Netherlands Yearbook of International Law
Nord JIL	Nordic Journal of International Law
NQHR	Netherlands Quarterly of Human Rights
Nw JIHR	Northwestern Journal of International Human Rights
Nw JILB	Northwestern Journal of International Law and Business
NwU LR	Northwestern University Law Review
NYU JILP	New York University Journal of International Law and Policy
NYU LR	New York University Law Review
OBHP	Organizational Behaviour and Human Performance
ODIL	Ocean Development and International Law
OJ	Official Journal of the European Communities
OJLS	Oxford Journal of Legal Studies
ONU	L'observateur des Nations Unies
ORIL	Oxford Reports of International Law
Pal YBIL	Palestine Yearbook International Law
PBPD	Place Branding and Public Diplomacy
PCIJ Series	Publications of the Permanent Court of International Justice (1922–46)
PEW	Philosophy East and West
PhR	Philosophical Review
Pol YBIL	Polish Yearbook of International Law
PPR	Philosophy and Phenomenological Research

RADIC	*Revue africaine de droit international et comparé*
RBDI	*Revue belge de droit international*
RD	Reports and Decisions (of the European Commission of Human Rights)
RdC	*Recueil des Cours de l'Académie de Droit International de la Haye*
RDI	*Rivista di Diritto Internazionale*
RDIPP	*Rivista di Diritto Internazionale Privato e Processuale*
RGDIP	*Revue Générale de Droit International Public*
RHDI	*Revue hellénique de droit international*
RIAA	Reports of International Arbitral Awards
RIFD	*Rivista Internazionale di Filosofia del Diritto*
RIP	*Revue Internationale de Philosophie*
RIS	Review of International Studies
RITD	*Revue internationale de la théorie du droit*
RTDH	*Revue trimestrielle des droits de l'homme*
S Cal LR	Southern California Law Review
SAIR	St Antony's International Review
SALR	South African Law Reports
Santa Clara JIL	Santa Clara Journal of International Law
SCOR	Security Council Official Record
SD ILJ	San Diego International Law Journal
Sri Lanka JIL	Sri Lanka Journal of International Law
Stan EP	Stanford Encyclopedia of Philosophy
Stan LR	Stanford Law Review
Tas ULR	Tasmanian University Law Review
TIAS	Treaties and Other International Acts Series
TLCP	Transnational Law and Contemporary Problems
TRIPS	Agreement on Trade Related Aspects of Intellectual Property Rights
UCLA LR	University of California in Los Angeles Law Review
UN YBILC	Yearbook of the International Law Commission
UNTS	United Nations Treaty Series
UTLJ	University of Toronto Law Journal
Van JTL	Vanderbilt Journal of Transnational Law
Virg JIL	Virginia Journal of International Law
Virg LR	Virginia Law Review
Wisc ILJ	Wisconsin International Law Journal
Yale JIL	Yale Journal of International Law
Yale LJ	Yale Law Journal
YBIHL	Yearbook of International Humanitarian Law
YBWA	Yearbook of World Affairs
ZaöRV	*Zeitschrift für ausländisches öffentliches Recht und Völkerrecht*

‘What is a mountain for?
For the moon to set behind’

Introduction

How much does international law contribute to solving today's global concerns affecting the lives of all humanity? Either law helps to ease practical problems or it is merely talk within professional circles. If 'very much' is definitely too optimistic an answer, 'not at all' is certainly excessively pessimistic. A good number of people expect international law to provide global responses to current global challenges and to bring about more justice in the world. This book argues that international law can contribute in some measure to global justice if it is seen as a social construct.

A. Purpose and Object

Today, international law is believed to be a global law of humankind and no longer a Westphalian, state-centred form of law. Non-state actors are given special emphasis in their participation in what is called 'global governance', and the centrality of states—in particular their consent to the rules of international law—is increasingly challenged. Yet, states are generally said to remain the 'principal' actors in global governance. Non-state actors matter more than in the past, but there is great uncertainty as to what role they play. International law in a globalized world shows two major breakthroughs: (a) to a significant extent, non-state actors shape, and are persuaded that they should shape, states' behaviour; and (b) the rules of international law govern how states must behave within their jurisdiction towards any individual, including their own citizens. It is the contention of this book that states as a whole (*uti universi*) remain central and that non-state actors, although being formally subject to each state, increasingly affect by all available means how states should behave towards both other states and any individual within their jurisdiction. While it is still made, unmade, and enforced by states, international law governs the lives of individuals within states.

It is notable that the reality and objectivity of international law has been seriously challenged, especially by Realists and Deconstructionists. While the objections to the legal character of international law are strong, the conclusion that international law is not real or objective law goes against the evidence. The view here presented is that international law, as any law, is law if and to the extent that its addressees as a whole believe that it is 'their' law. Law is law not because this or that academic has distilled the 'correct' notion of law which should serve as a paradigm. Law is law because it works among its addressees in their own perception. It is a social construct, not a scientific enterprise. As a social construct law is also a commitment, not a mere fact to be observed. Law is not only the law as it stands but also the law that there must be and the law that ought to come into being in the future, ie a matter of struggle. The law of today is the result of past struggles and the law of tomorrow will be the result of the struggles to be engaged today. And a struggle for law is ultimately a struggle for a just law, ie for justice. International law is part of this process. In this sense, the approach here adopted takes the realist and deconstructionist challenges seriously but attempts to go further, expose their flaws, and reclaim the reality and objectivity of international law by anchoring it to society.

Epistemologically, the construction of international law is indeed often thought to be a basically scientific enterprise. Outcomes of research are considered persuasive to the extent that they are scientifically reached. Quantitative analysis is believed to be particularly reliable and capable of generating sound legal arguments in contrast to personal idiosyncrasies and metaphysical preferences. By building on a particular version of social constructionism, the case is made here for the view that law is not so much a scientific project as an experience of social attunement and prudence. It does not necessarily reflect what is wise, or scientifically well-founded, but rather what 'works' in society in the perception of its addresses as a whole. This is not to say that the work of jurists is not, or should not be, 'scientific'. It may well be so, if and to the extent that the addressees of law believe in science and in its methods. The Western world is deeply infused with a confidence in science and the world is largely modelled on Western patterns. It is to this extent that scientific methods used when handling international law may be appropriate.

International law as the law of the global system is assumed to provide a 'world order' and this is often depicted in terms of a few models or 'paradigms', such as the Hobbesian (unsociability), the Grotian (inter-state sociability), and the Kantian (cosmopolitan sociability).[1] International jurists either place themselves, or are placed by others, within one or another of such (or still other) models. It is often asserted that a 'paradigm shift' in world order is under way and explanations abound about the possible shifts, with a marked preference for the process pulling from the Grotian to the Kantian paradigm.[2] Is this sort of categorizing exercise useful to legal discourse? Doubts are reasonable. After all there is little need to explain the 'model' of how the United States (or any other state) works as a 'whole order' to be able to determine whether a bank robbery which took place in New York yesterday is legal or illegal under US law. This book avoids forcing the whole material of international law into an a priori paradigm. It depicts international law as a social construct on the assumption that it is people and their beliefs that make the law, including international law, not the minds of theorists. People generally are varied and cultivate diverse beliefs which hardly fit into the paradigm of one mind. Readers might find this book as much Hobbesian (in that it is premised on the notion that human beings first of all do their best to survive), as Grotian (in that it retains the vision of a world governed by the system of states), or as Kantian (in that it presents states and non-state actors, including international organizations and primarily the United Nations, working together for a universal end). Indeed, much depends on the meaning assigned to such critical words as 'humanity', 'states system', 'international community', 'global governance', and the like. This book attempts to shed some light on them.

Also recurrent in today's international law discourse is the appeal to what is presented as the 'fundamental values' of the 'international community as a whole'.

[1] For a discussion of the IR English School's paradigms and an attempt to take their conceptions of international society forward, see A Hurrell, *On Global Order: Power, Values, and the Constitution of International Society* (Oxford: OUP, 2007).

[2] The term 'paradigm shift' was introduced by TS Kuhn, *The Structure of Scientific Revolutions* [1962] (Chicago and London: University of Chicago Press, 3rd edn, 1996) 85, 89, 104, 119, 150, to denote an essential shift in the sciences from one way of thinking to another, such as the transition in cosmology from the Ptolemaic cosmology to the Copernican one. Eventually, it has become a buzzword, frequently popularized as marketing speak. For criticism of the use of the expression, see R Fulford, *Globe and Mail*, 5 June 1999, at <http://www.robertfulford.com/Paradigm.html>.

These values are invariably translated into 'publicist' legal concepts like *jus cogens* and obligations *erga omnes* which tend to make international law shift from a horizontal 'private law "writ large"'[3] to a vertical, public (if not plainly constitutional) law of humankind. It is felt that certain 'values' deserve stronger protection because of their vital importance to the entire international community. The question of why they are important (while others are not) remains often unaddressed or undertheorized. The practice of states is not particularly illuminating since states, while accepting the above concepts, attach to them diverse effects which do not necessarily converge in practice. Domestic courts apply the concepts as a means of delivering justice and making them deviate from all other rules even when these rules are recognized as valid rules of international law by most states. It is suggested here that all these concepts should not be seen as incantations, but require analysis. Global values are seen with hope but also with caution. The global dimension itself is seen with caution, together with any totalizing vision of human affairs.

Few if any would deny that law, including international law, does and should reflect justice. However, the idea of justice is often accused of subjectivism and it is undoubtedly in the name of justice that extremely diverse acts have been carried out in history, wars fought by belligerents of any persuasion, and people exterminated. International law is expected today, perhaps more than ever, to bring about more justice on the planet at least in the form of eradication of extreme poverty and repression of the most abhorrent international crimes. Justice is here understood as the protection of the most vulnerable. It is argued that the most vulnerable are to be favoured when construing the law and when dealing with the way law should be changed. In fact, the justice achievable within the global states system is to be distinguished from the justice of the system itself, a system that has been imposed by the West on the rest of the world through dispossession and subjugation, and still is (in other forms) the product of Western prevalence. The struggle for global justice is first and foremost a struggle for some justice within the system rather than none. This justice is far from exhaustive. One has to take note of the injustice of the system itself to correct the inequities within the system and make the intra-systemic justice 'more just' even when it appears sufficiently just.

Whither international law? This question is diversely answered. The trend is towards giving as much weight as possible to the 'fundamental', common values of the international community and their legal corollaries. But there is no serious attempt to extract these values from the diverse peoples themselves (including tribal and indigenous peoples) as *they* perceive law, and hence possibly a law really common to all peoples. Values are inferred from certain attitudes, including 'pluralism', that are specifically Western. But there can be little hope for the construction of a credible international law without building on the legal traditions of all the peoples concerned. It is proposed here, as a further future project, to get out of the Western domination of the discipline, both epistemologically and politically, by starting a serious analysis of international law from a legal comparative perspective. Also extra-legal inputs from the arts and history of any civilization should be included to improve global social attunement and prudential judgment. This proposal is not so much aimed at new rules, more favourable to non-Western states and peoples, as on a new way to manage the discipline at the epistemological level in the first place. If international law is the law of all different peoples on earth and if these peoples have their own law and sense of

[3] TE Holland, *Studies in International Law* (Oxford: Clarendon Press, 1898) 152–3.

justice, then a 'working' global law in their perception cannot but be a reconciliation of all these traditions, to the fullest extent feasible.

B. Outline

A preliminary sketchy outline of the articulation and contents of the book may be helpful to clarify the argument.

Part I is devoted to the exploration of law in general as social construct. By developing Freud's insights into the origin and nature of law, Chapter 1 argues that law amounts to collective violence aimed at countering individual violence and that the distinction between law and non-law is relative to social context. Law is defined as a social phenomenon both because it is created and sustained by society and because its legal quality (in particular its possible distinction from, and hierarchical position towards, power and morality) depends on what its addressees as a whole in any particular society believe.

Chapter 2 proceeds by inquiring into the meaning of law as a socially constructed reality. It argues that law is a social construct ultimately founded in mythic belief. In any society law is what is seen as such by those who see themselves as its addressees. Thus defined, law, including international law, is real and objective to any member of the community as imposed by the community as a whole. Indeed, without a mythic sense of commonality there can hardly be law. A constant revival of the myth underlying law is essential for it to work. There can be no demythologization of law without remythologizing it in another direction. The fact that people are part of the process of law-making and unmaking creates a dynamic which both implies and calls for commitment and struggle. The struggle for law should be a struggle for justice, here understood as the protection of the most vulnerable. It may translate into a struggle for either more or less law depending on the circumstances. Progress is not necessarily towards more justice.

Chapter 3 concludes the analysis of law as social construct by showing that law is a process inspired by a 'working' reason operating in and for society. It argues that certain legal arguments are indeed better than others in society. Theoretical reason ultimately depends on the meanings prevailing in the particular society in which it operates. Also formal justice, notably epitomized in the maxim 'to everyone his due', is relative to social context and, like theoretical reason, used to appropriate universal truth and impose it on all. Practical reason is the reason that *works* in society. It mainly consists of common sense, social attunement, pre-comprehension, and consideration for the rules of the game prevailing in any particular society. It amounts to prudence.

In conclusion, Part I suggests that law as social construct is not necessarily a scientific enterprise and jurists are basically *juris prudentes* rather than theorists or scientists.

Part II applies the constructionist approach delineated in Part I to international law. Chapter 4 explores how international law is socially constructed through epistemology, doctrine, and communication. International law is seen as invariably thought of in accordance with Western categories and words. The chapter argues that legal doctrine constantly mythologizes, demythologizes, and remythologizes international law in various, often opposing directions, through Western categories and within a relatively closed circle of professionals. Nine theoretical models of international law are explored from this perspective, namely, naturalism, positivism, realism, axiologism, deconstructionism, sociologism, constitutionalism, administrativism, and third-worldism. The chapter also contends that the construction of international law by the media, today crucial, is far from being widespread and effective as expected and needed. This suggests that international law should be remythologized by investigating the legal traditions known in comparative legal analysis, rather than by continuing to analyse it according to Western jurisprudential categories, whether traditional or critical, such as 'law', 'order', 'system', and the like. In turn, its reality should be asserted, inter alia, in the sphere of media communication rather than being minutely debated, as is often the case, within a relatively closed circle of professionals.

Chapter 5 investigates who is engaged in constructing international law as a set of rules. It argues that states remain at the heart of global governance by exercising jurisdictional power in a partitioned and relatively coordinated way within a global state-centred system in which non-state actors constantly shape states' behaviour. The whole of such interaction denotes what is called the 'international community'. The traditional doctrine of international legal personality, once again inspired historically by the legal systems of a few European states, with its relatively closed list of 'international subjects', is exposed as an instrument of legal manipulation ultimately resting on the global states system. Today, not only is it a fact that the system is affected more than in the past by non-state actors and that states can no longer be taken as fixed entities; states are also required by the system itself to protect their own citizens and exercise sovereignty within their jurisdiction over any individual according to international legal standards. It is these two key features that mark the 'new' international law within the persisting inter-state model, suggesting that states are required today to protect, in a spatially partitioned way, all humanity according to the standards laid down by international law. The states system serves the purpose of providing governance to humankind so as to avoid its descent into chaos and to ensure its well-being to the fullest extent feasible. It is also true, though, that the states system as a global statist project is historically a product of the injustice committed by the European states and it is today increasingly unable to manage global concerns. However, the system is also the result of an irreversible historical process and no alternatives to states as the basic systemic political units at global level are in sight at the moment.

Chapter 6 turns to the law which the international community believes to be international law. It examines how the rules and other normative standards of international law are made, integrated, reconciled, changed, judicially applied, complied with, implemented within states, and enforced. It argues that all international law rules and judicial decisions are ultimately grounded in custom as a basic form of social, informal pressure by the states system and that no 'private affair' is conceivable in the system even when rules apply only to particular states, although this does not necessarily imply that rules apply also to non-consenting states solely by virtue of their importance. The identification of the rules of international law is loosely inspired by the doctrine of the sources of law originally developed in the domestic legal systems of a few Western states and by other criteria capable of ensuring a relatively systemic unity, coherence, and completeness. Unlike their domestic counterparts, international courts and tribunals are not available for any dispute, but when they are they can exercise the discretion which is inherent in their very creation and specify the content of the rules, as well as correcting, to some extent, inequities and legal fragmentation. Faced with doubts about the reality of international law, the degree of compliance and the possibility of enforcement are important, albeit not decisive, elements. Much of the credibility of international law rather depends on its domestic implementation by the states themselves.

Chapter 7 explores what 'values' are believed to be protected, or ought to be protected, by international law rules. Values make sense of existing rules and provide guidance for the rules to come. It is proposed to focus on five (although by no means exhaustive) basic global values: security, humanity, wealth, environment, and knowledge. Values tend to interact and do raise the question of whether and how separate legal rules and regimes underlying different, even opposing, values can be coordinated with one another. The analysis first focuses on the rules which protect, or ought to better protect, the above basic values and then turns to the interaction between rules, or classes of rules, protecting conflicting values. It will be argued that existing rules can be construed, to a certain degree, in accordance with presently demanded standards of justice and that social practices do impact on the interpretative process, especially by making new meanings emerge and impose on institutional interpreters, in addition to triggering social processes in favour of new rules aimed at improving justice and more consistency in cases where no clear rule exists to resolve conflicts.

Finally, Chapter 8 looks into the remedies against major breaches of international law in terms of sovereignty as responsibility. The focus will be on the fact that the 'new' international law is the law of the global states system in which, on the one hand, non-state actors are a key factor to shape states and their behaviour and, on the other hand, states have obligations on how to behave towards any individual within their jurisdiction. The question will thus be addressed as to what happens when states fail to observe these obligations. The concept of sovereignty as responsibility implies that it is primarily for states to protect the basic rights of individuals within their jurisdiction, and when they fail to do so, it is the international community that should intervene, in particular by collective and personal measures. The 'responsibility' of the international community is the consequence of the 'One World' now in the making. Collective measures—including collective standing in international courts, universal jurisdiction in domestic courts, collective countermeasures, and humanitarian intervention—are often based on the existence of obligations *erga omnes*. It is, however, difficult to draw definite legal conclusions from this concept. Humanitarian intervention is not permitted within the responsibility to protect doctrine, unless mandated on a case-by-case basis by the UN Security Council. Personal measures include targeted sanctions and criminal responsibility before international or hybrid courts. The case will be finally made for the operation of international courts as the best tool available, despite their shortcomings, to combat abuse of power by rulers and other state officials and to bring about more justice in and to the system.

PART I

LAW AS SOCIAL CONSTRUCT

1

Society

Any discussion about international law presupposes an underlying view on what law is, which is ultimately dependent on what is meant by human nature and social life. The purpose of Part I, specifically of Chapters 1 to 3, is to make such a view explicit. Chapter 1 analyses the social origins and nature of law and the consequences in terms of how law is discerned in society. It argues that law emerges as a form of collective violence against individual violence and that the distinction between law and non-law is relative to the social context. Law is viewed as a social phenomenon because it is created and sustained by society and its legal quality depends on what its addressees as a whole in any particular society so believe. Chapter 2 will then develop such insights to explore the socially constructed, mythic essence of law, and will focus on how law and justice are the subject of a daily struggle in any society. Finally, Chapter 3 will look into the rationality of law with a view to showing that law is indeed 'rational', but according to how reason is conceived in practice within any society.

A. The Origins of Law

The first, indeed the key question that a legal analyst (including the international legal analyst) is called upon to address is what is meant by 'law'. This section suggests that law is a form of collective violence against individual violence within a group.

(1) *'L'union fait la force'*

A helpful point of departure is offered by a well-known letter written by Sigmund Freud in reply to a letter from Albert Einstein in 1932 on the matter of a possible end of any war.[1] Apart from the point on war,[2] Freud developed a realist argument on the origins, nature, and conditions of law—drawing upon Charles Darwin and, presumably, Friedrich Nietzsche—which has not thus far been given sufficient attention and is worth reviewing and developing further.[3]

[1] A Einstein and S Freud, *Warum Krieg?* (Paris: Internationales Institut für Geistige Zusammenarbeit, 1933), English trans 'Why War?' [1933] in J Strachey (ed), *The Standard Edition of the Complete Psychological Works of Sigmund Freud* (London: Vintage, 1953) vol 22, 199–215. The translation used in the following pages is basically drawn from Strachey's Standard Edition, with some improvements by the present author.

[2] As a result of his analysis, Freud expressed himself rather sceptically regarding the possibility of an end of any war. He concluded his letter by asking Einstein's forgiveness for having 'disappointed you' (ibid 215). Freud's insights into war and death are especially found in his essay on war written some six months after the outbreak of World War I, 'Zeitgemäßes über Krieg und Tod' (1915) 4 *Imago* 1, English trans 'Thoughts for the Times on War and Death' in Strachey (ed) (n 1 above) vol 14, 275.

[3] For a critique of Freud's insights, see J Stevens, 'Sigmund Freud and International Law' (2006) 2 Law, Culture and the Humanities 201; in favour of Freud's realism, see R Schuett, *Political Realism, Freud, and Human Nature in International Relations: The Resurrection of the Realist Man* (London: Palgrave Macmillan, 2010).

(a) Freud's insights into the origins of law and justice

After noting that, like animals, human beings' conflicts of interests 'are resolved, in principle, by the recourse to violence'[4] and that muscular strength was replaced by the use of tools and weapons, Freud asked what was the path 'that led away from violence to law'. In his view, surely it issued from a single verity, namely, that 'the superior strength of a single individual could be rivalled by the union of many weaklings', according to the maxim '*l'union fait la force*'. In this way: 'Violence could be broken by union, and the power of those who were united now represented law in contrast to the violence of the single individual'. Thus 'law is the might of a community'. While 'It is still violence, ready to be directed against any individual who resists it, it works by the same methods and follows the same purposes, the only real difference lying in the fact that what prevails is no longer the violence of an individual but that of a community'. For the transition 'from violence to the new law', the psychological condition that 'The union of the many must be stable and enduring' is first to be met, otherwise 'The next person who thinks himself superior in strength would once more seek to set up a dominion by violence, and the game would repeat itself unendingly'. This implies that: 'The community must be maintained permanently, must organize itself, must enact provisions to anticipate the risk of revolts and must institute authorities to see that those provisions—the laws—are observed and that such acts of violence as the law demands are carried out'. It is 'the recognition of such a community of interests that leads to the growth of emotional ties and communal feelings between the members of a united group of people which constitute its real strength'. According to Freud, this was the very kernel of the matter and 'all the rest is details and repetitions'. To his eyes, 'from its very beginning the community comprises elements of unequal strength—men and women, parents and children—and soon, as a result of war and subjugation, victors and vanquished, who turn into masters and slaves'. From then on: 'The law of the community... becomes an expression of the unequal degrees of power obtaining within it; the laws are made by and for the stronger and stipulate few rights for the subjected'. As a result:

> From that time forward there are in the community two factors causing legal instability, but evolution in the law, too: first, the attempts by certain of the stronger to set themselves above the restrictions of law which apply to everyone, thus seeking to go back from the rule of law to the rule of violence; and, secondly, the constant efforts of the subjected to obtain more power and to have these changes in the law recognized, thus pressing forward from unequal law to equal law for all.[5]

Two years earlier, Freud had expressed a similar, even more illuminating view in *Civilization and its Discontents*.[6] There, he wrote that 'Human life in common is only made possible when a majority comes together which is stronger than any separate individual and which remains united against all separate individuals'. In Freud's view, 'The power of this community is then set up as "law" in opposition to the power of the individual, which is condemned as "brute force"'. This 'replacement of the power of the individual by the power of a community constitutes the decisive step of civilization'. Its essence 'lies in the fact that the members of the community restrict themselves in their

[4] Freud expressly stated at the outset that he preferred the term 'violence' (*Gewalt*) to 'might' (*Macht*) used by Einstein ('Why War?' (n 1 above) 203–4).

[5] ibid 204–6.

[6] S Freud, *Das Unbehagen in der Kultur* (Wien: Internationaler Psychoanalytischer Verlag, 1930), English trans 'Civilization and Its Discontents' in Strachey (ed) (n 1 above) vol 21, 64, 86–98.

possibilities of satisfaction, whereas the individual knew no such restrictions'. Therefore, 'the first requisite of civilization . . . is that of justice—that is the assurance that a legal order once made will not be broken in favour of an individual'. It was the first result of civilization that 'even a fairly large number of people were now able to live together in a community'. However, to Freud's mind, 'this implies nothing as to the ethical value of such a law'. The trend is then 'towards making the law no longer an expression of the will of a small community . . . which, in its turn, behaves like a violent individual towards other, and perhaps more numerous, collections of people' but instead, as a final outcome, towards 'a law to which all . . . have contributed by a sacrifice of their instincts, and which leaves no one . . . at the mercy of brute force'.[7]

This conception of the nature of law was a development of Freud's theory of the totemic origins of religion and civilization—both resulting from the Darwin-inspired killing of the primal-horde tyrannical father by his allied sons, who then established rules for equality among them—first developed in 1913 in *Totem and Taboo*.[8] Although Freud never abandoned this (indeed much critiqued)[9] theory, reiterated especially in 1923[10] and in 1939,[11] his account of the origins of law in 1913 and in the early 1930s sounds somewhat different. While in the 1913 'psychoanalytic' account the brothers kill their father and accept law *within themselves* out of a sense of guilt, in the early 1930s 'cultural' account the allied 'weak' (no longer the 'sons') do not necessarily kill the stronger (no longer the 'primal father'), and law emerges ambiguously not only within themselves but perhaps also in the relationship with the surviving stronger. It is also worth noting that the alliance of the weaker brings about not only civilization and law but also justice, and justice is conceived of as devoid of any ethical connotation.[12] Justice is simply equated with control of individual violence by a group. To Freud's eyes, arbitrariness is the violence of the individual against any other weaker individual. The key problem of law and justice is how to keep individual violence under control. Law is still violence, but by definition 'righteous' or 'just' violence, regardless of its content. The underlying assumption is that there is nothing else that can constrain

[7] ibid 95.

[8] S Freud, *Totem und Taboo* (Leipzig and Vienna: Heller, 1913), English trans 'Totem and Taboo: Some Points of Agreement between the Mental Lives of Savages and Neurotics' in Strachey (ed), *The Standard Edition* (n 1 above) vol 13, 1–161, IV, section 5, 140–6.

[9] See eg R Girard, *La violence et le sacré* (Paris: Grasset, 1972), English trans *Violence and the Sacred* (Baltimore: Johns Hopkins University Press, 1977) ch 8. Freud himself observed in his *Massenpsychologie und Ich-Analyse* (Leipzig, Vienna, and Zurich: Internationaler Psychoanalytischer Verlag, 1921), English trans 'Group Psychology and the Analysis of the Ego' in Strachey (ed), *The Standard Edition* (n 1 above) vol 18, 69, 122, that 'this is only a hypothesis, like so many others . . . a "Just-So Story", as it was amusedly called', however, a story that 'corresponds to a state of regression to a primitive mental activity' of individuals uniting in a group. Freud expounded here, inter alia, a theory of leadership whereby 'The leader of the group is still the dreaded primal father', the 'group ideal, which governs the ego in the place of the ego ideal' (ibid 127), building on the French sociologist and early social psychologist Gustav Le Bon, *La psychologie des foules* (Paris: F Alcan, 1895), English trans *The Crowd: A Study of the Popular Mind* (Mineola, NY: Dover Publications, 2002).

[10] Freud, 'Group Psychology and the Analysis of the Ego' (n 9 above) 122–8.

[11] S Freud, *Der Mann Moses und die monotheistische Religion: Drei Abhandlungen* (Amsterdam: Verlag Allert de Lange, 1939), English trans 'Moses and Monotheism: Three Essays' in Strachey (ed) (n 1 above) vol 23, I, sect D, 81–2, specifying that the brothers reached 'a sort of social contract', a 'recognition of mutual *obligations*, the introduction of definite *institutions*, pronounced inviolable (holy)' which marked 'the beginnings of morality and justice' (original emphasis).

[12] For Freud, moral conscience (*Gewissen*) is but 'social anxiety' (*soziale Angst*): see Freud, 'Group Psychology and the Analysis of the Ego' (n 9 above) 122; S Freud, 'Zur Einführung der Narzissmus' (1914) 6 *Jahrbuch der Psychoanalyse* 1, English trans 'On Narcissism: An Introduction' in Strachey (ed) (n 1 above) vol 14, 96; Freud, 'Thoughts for the Times on War and Death' (n 2 above) 280.

arbitrariness than a greater force and this force is only possible by a group against an individual. Once the group has gained this overarching force, this same force amounts to 'justice' in the group. Put differently, there can be no other justice in the group, since for this to occur another kind of group with another view of justice should prevail. At the same time, this 'collective arbitrariness' is indeed justice to the extent that all the members of the group are treated in an equal manner in that the individual who wants to be above the law is forced to obey the law by the group. Nothing can be done (in particular through law) against collective violence, except for the formation of a competitive group strong enough to impose a different notion of justice on the former. Law and justice are but a form of successful collective violence having the potential to have and dictate any content. On the other hand, the message is that only through forming a stronger group can injustice be overcome. Ethical appeals are helpless and useless unless ethics proves to be a successful weapon, as in fact it no doubt often is.

(b) Theoretical implications

Freud's narrative of the origins of law and justice is certainly open to various interpretations and depends, inter alia, on the text considered.[13] The most intuitive reading, if the early 1930s accounts in particular are considered, is perhaps that law emerges along with the 'balance of power' between the stronger and the many weak who unite to face the former. Once this balance materializes the weak may be thought to succeed in forcing the stronger to comply with legal rules.

The reading of Freud's insights favoured here is, however, different, perhaps somewhat more in line with his original view, and focuses on the need of the weak to unite and remain cohesively united by means of law against the stronger in order to avoid succumbing. The weak realize that a stable and effective resistance against the omnipotent stronger is only possible if all agree on legal rules which all will abide by. Legal rules within the group of the weaker allocate tasks, organize functions, keep cohesion. The community of interests among the members of the group, engendering 'a sentiment of unity and fraternal solidarity', gives rise to a political authority and permanent institutions—which are supposed, inter alia, to make and administer legal rules and, more generally, to act on behalf, and for the benefit, of all—as well as to the distinction between rulers and ruled. The arm wrestling, namely the balance of power, between the stronger and the (united) weak is, on this reading, still brute violence, not law. It is the need to defend themselves from the stronger that generates in the weak the pressing need for rules and for their observance. Law emerges *within* the group of the weaker rather than between them and their common challenger, although it may eventually evolve into law once the erstwhile stronger challenger enters the group and accepts its rules, an occurrence which will presumably materialize in the face of a new challenger common to both the former challenger and the original group.

Given the urge of human beings to survive and feel as good as possible in accordance with their biological structure and with their own view of the good life, if necessary to the detriment of the others' equal need, solidarity and responsibility appear only when it is felt that survival and prosperity would be better secured by offering loyalty to the group in exchange for protection. Obedience to the group and to its rules is felt to be necessary to obtain adequate protection from the group. Faced with an overwhelming

[13] It is not, of course, the purpose of this chapter to offer a 'correct' interpretation of Freud's thought, but rather to use it as a starting point for further theoretical analysis in so far as this may be relevant to international law.

challenge, all members of the united group feel that the protection received from the group outweighs the cost of obedience and forbearance of external pressure. What is gained in terms of chances of survival and better living is felt to be greater than what is sacrificed. This rather instinctive calculation also makes the stronger in the group accept the idea of law and actually comply with it. Violence authorized by the group as the 'law' becomes the expression of a common will which is distinct from violence from each member. Law is still violence in the end, presumably laid down by the stronger in the group, yet an 'organized' kind of violence. It is the violence, or the pressure, of the group towards each of its members, strong and weak alike. Put differently, it is the violence of the members acting *uti universi* (ie supposedly on behalf of the group as a whole) towards the members acting *uti singuli* (ie each per se).

Interestingly, Freud observed that the group is in any case never really and definitively united. It is in fact constantly challenged also from within by those members who are stronger in the group. The stronger unite because they feel themselves too weak compared to the original omnipotent challenger; still, they remain eager to impose their views and will within the group against those who are the weaker. Law tends to be made by the stronger in the group, but is also constantly challenged by the weaker, who seek to unite again in smaller groups against the newly formed stronger, once the original challenger has been tamed or forced to disappear. These 'internal' challenges may cause revolutions or secessions, and may change into 'external' threats as new groups emerge and secede. In any event, law emerges when a group is cohesive to the point where, on average, its members feel an overwhelming interest in making rules common to all and in abiding by them for fear of being destroyed by a common challenger. As long as the common challenger is sufficiently threatening and the cohesion of the group is urgent, the group succeeds in creating such a thing as 'law' and this may actually work. This departs from the conventional realist outlook by assuming that the stronger are bound by the law—even though they make the law and constantly try to bend it to their interests—because they need the weak and the group. They do pursue their self-interest, but, given the circumstances, their self-interest advises them that law and bounds (ie a protective community tied by rules) are better than no law.

The above reading of Freud's insights into the origin and essence of law have at least three implications that are worth clarifying.

First, not only can there be no law without a social group (as expressed by the old classical adage *ubi jus, ibi societas*), but also there can be no social group without a common challenger overwhelmingly stronger than each of all other members of the group, strong and weak alike. The common challenger may be any 'force' which is strong enough to make any member of the group perceive that the making of rules and their observance is in any case more advantageous than any advantage secured by denying any rules at all, or breaking existing rules, and thus being marginalized and placed at the mercy of the original challenger. Freud's insights may be generalized to apply to any human or non-human challenger, not necessarily a human 'enemy' in the traditional sense. It may be a natural disaster, a contagious disease, a dangerous Martian, anything (in a word) capable of threatening in any sense (physically as well as psychologically, for real or for purely imagined causes) one or more human beings or even all. Until a stronger common challenger emerges and, most importantly, is perceived as threatening by all potential members of a group, each individual or each group has a comparative advantage in avoiding uniting (or uniting too closely) with all others for such a common, universal cause. Different groups will unite simply to face other groups and alliances. At the global level, 'internal' conflicts and divergent views on the common good will constantly break up, dissolve, and transform into others. No ecumenical solidarity will really be plausible and any kind of free riding will be 'the rule'. Survival will actually prove better secured by free riding than by 'seriously' uniting and keeping united.

Secondly, law is a reflection not only of the stronger within a limited group which confronts an external challenger, but also of the relative force of the weaker. The stronger, in principle, respect the law that they have laid down (or have decisively contributed to laying down) for fear of dissolution of the group and fall at the mercy of the common challenger, while constantly trying to be above (even their own) law when this gives rise to more advantages than threats. The weak may use (and indeed do use) this condition to force the stronger to grant them more rights and equality.

It follows, thirdly, that law is dynamic. Although the few stronger constantly try to be above the law and avoid complying with even their own law, the weak (generally forming the majority) may claim rights, and threaten the strong that unless their demands are met they will spark off a rebellion and cause the dissolution of the group. To the extent that dissolution is more harmful to the stronger than facing the original (and supposedly still alarming) challenger, they are induced to grant the weak the rights claimed, thereby giving rise to an evolution of the law. This dynamic ensures what may appear at first sight hardly plausible to realists, although it constitutes the very essence of law: the stronger are being bound by the rules and forced to change them against their (at least short-term) interests by the weaker.

One could question the notion that communities and law emerge only as a result of fear of a common enemy or, more generally, of a perceived common danger. Other motivations may induce people to unite, such as generosity, sympathy, or love. The argument that only survival and fear lead people to unite seems to imply that all human relationships result in conflict and are but relationships of friend and enemy, or ally and foe, as Carl Schmitt insisted.[14] Thus construed, Freud's insights sound no less warmongering and disturbing than Schmitt's. However, one may embrace a notion of conflict broad enough to include any kind of competition (even verbal, speculative, or ideal-motivated) in any situation in which when someone wins someone else loses. Moreover, this view is neither for, nor against, conflict and lends itself to be used not only by those who are inclined to war, as it may appear at first sight, but also by those who are *against* war and try to prevent the former from engaging in war. Even pacifists are bound to defend pacifism by successfully confronting (possibly by peaceful means) warmongering forces. There is no necessity, at least for present purposes, to assume either that those in conflict are evil, or that 'human nature' itself is evil.[15] There are definitely individual persons who are prepared to live and sacrifice themselves for others and for the common good.[16] However, law is not a matter of individual or discrete persons or cases. It has to do with people who have to live together, for good or ill, and this, more often than not, means that what one gets is taken away from someone else in

[14] C Schmitt, 'Der Gegensatz von Parlamentarismus und moderner Massendemokratie' in C Schmitt, *Positionen und Begriffe im Kampf mit Weimar—Genf—Versailles 1923–1939* [1926] (Berlin: Duncker & Humblot, 1988) 52, 59; C Schmitt, *Der Begriff der Politischen* [1932] (Berlin: Duncker & Humblot, 1991) 26–7, English trans *The Concept of the Political* (New Brunswick: Rutgers University Press, 1976) 26–7.

[15] This chapter is not concerned with the question of determining whether human nature is good or evil, sympathetic or aggressive. A balanced view, critical of both Konrad Lorenz's neo-instinctivism and Burrhus F Skinner's behaviourism, is that proposed by Erich Fromm, *The Anatomy of Human Destructiveness* (London: Pimlico, 1973).

[16] For some empirical evidence of human sociability, see D Johnston, *A Brief History of Justice* (Chichester: Wiley-Blackwell, 2011) 9–14. See in addition F De Waal, *The Age of Empathy: Nature's Lessons for a Kinder Society* (New York: Harmony Books, 2009) 5.

the perception of those involved. Human beings may well be driven by generosity and a genuine sense of common good, but this seems to occur only on occasion, to certain persons, and under specific circumstances. For the purposes of law, what matters is what occurs at a *social* level *on average*. It is from this perspective that most humans pursue self-interest most of the time. They want to live in accordance with their view of the good life, whatever this means, including altruistic goals, and, to do so, they are inevitably prepared to fight for the realization of their view—by using force if necessary, but also by any other kind of effective strategy, including ethics, when this proves less costly and more effective—against all those who, rightly or wrongly, challenge them by embracing an opposite view.

(2) Law as a balance of balances

In the above narrative the three key figures (to use Freud's terms, the 'Giant', the 'Rulers', and the 'Ruled', the first outside and the latter within the 'Alliance') are driven by different and opposing forces.[17] Law derives from a combined balance of several balances between these several interacting forces, lasting a sufficient period of time to cause it to be perceived as reasonably stable and predictable. Let us have a quick look at a (no doubt oversimplified) possible dynamic within the narrative.

The Giant may be either annihilated or subjugated.[18] If the Giant is annihilated, the Alliance achieves its goal. This, paradoxically, causes the evaporation of its raison d'être at the very peak of its power.[19] The Alliance is then destined to weaken, perhaps even to collapse, unless a new Giant materializes or, more likely, unless a Giant is invented (it may even be, at least for a while, nothing more than a phantom of the old Giant) by the Rulers within the Alliance with a view to continuing to obtain obedience from the Ruled by leveraging the fear of the Ruled of annihilation by the Giant. If the Giant is subjugated, the members of the Alliance succeed in bridling the Giant under their rules and the Alliance finds itself, here again, without a common challenger and prone to grow weaker and possibly to collapse. The Giant may accept the option of simply surviving within the Alliance, possibly as a Ruler, once it becomes aware that the alternative is annihilation. In both scenarios, as the Giant weakens, the Alliance triumphs and starts waning at the same time. There is a point of equilibrium for the Alliance between strength and weakness, success against the Giant and failure in keeping internal cohesion to fight the Giant.

[17] Actually, Freud does not use the term 'Giant': he refers to 'the superior strength of a single individual' [*die größere Stärke des einen*] ('Why War?' (n 1 above) 205). Freud also refers to 'some overweening individual' [*Übermächtigen*] (ibid 205). The term 'Giant' is found in the translation by O Nathan and H Norden (eds), *Einstein on Peace* (New York: Schocken Books, 1960), and may be fruitfully used here for the sake of brevity. As for 'Rulers' and 'Ruled', the terms used by Freud are '*Herrschenden*'/'*Herren*' ('ruling'/'masters') and '*Unterdrückten*'/'*Unterworfenen*' ('oppressed'/'subjugated'). Freud also used the terms '*Führer*' ('leaders') and '*Abhängige*' ('followers', 'dependent') to point out that 'The latter constitutes the vast majority; they stand in need of an authority which will make decisions for them and to which they for the most part offer an unqualified submission' ('Why War?' (n 1 above) 212).

[18] A third scenario is that the Giant commits suicide so as to avoid falling into the hands of the enemies.

[19] In Freud's account the sons kill their father but remain united under the law because of their sense of guilt (n 8 above), an element which has a psychoanalytic plausibility but is less meaningful in the explication of power in general, and in the relations between states in particular. In fact, Freud avoided discussing the sense of guilt within the Alliance in the letter of 1932 to Einstein in which the question at hand concerned peace among nations (n 1 above).

The Rulers within the Alliance are under pressure by both the Giant and the Ruled. They cannot afford to exit the Alliance at their pleasure, whenever the Ruled request legal rules (sanctioning, in particular, equality) or their effective observance where rules are indeed in place, since the Rulers have joined the Alliance to avoid annihilation by the Giant. They cannot afford to be marginalized and are too weak to confront the Giant without the help of the whole Alliance, including the Ruled. They are stronger (perhaps even far stronger) than the weak in the Alliance, but not strong enough successfully to defeat the Giant. The Ruled are hardly unaware (or tend at least to become over time ever more aware, especially if keeping in touch) that the Rulers desperately need them and the Alliance. They know that at least a number of their requests will be met by the Rulers and that the Rulers will accept that relations within the Alliance must be governed by law. Against the spectre of the Giant, the Rulers need the cohesion and strength of the Alliance: as the Alliance grows weaker their fear of being annihilated by the Giant increases. It is reasonable to expect them to make legal rules and abide by them, at least up to the point where the Ruled do not threaten their withdrawal from participation in the Alliance and secession by uniting in a further sub-Alliance. The result is that the Rulers, who are by definition the strongest in the group and may in the abstract (ie as though the Giant were inexistent)[20] behave as they please, in fact agree to live under the law and to observe it. There is no 'inner solidarity' in the functioning of law within the Alliance. There can hardly be solidarity, as solidarity is generally understood, in a world of sentient beings who are under pressure to keep living, unless solidarity itself actually helps them to remain alive. Rulers and Ruled are basically pursuing what many would call their self-interest. Yet, in such circumstances, law is not only possible, it is inevitable. It is the result of two combined forces: the threat of the Giant outside and the request of the Ruled inside. The former provides the latter with the leverage to obtain law and its respect.

This is, however, not the whole story. The Rulers would, of course, prefer to remain unbound by the law, if this could ever be possible. Here again, everything depends on the relative strength over time of the Giant. While the Rulers are forced to make and observe law to keep cohesion and strength within the Alliance, they are also prepared to change their minds as soon as the Giant proves less strong, which may well be the effect of the correlative increased strength of the Alliance. As the Alliance grows stronger, the Giant grows weaker. There is a point of equilibrium for the Rulers between cohesion of the Alliance (hence law) and weakness of the Giant. When the Giant's force becomes affordable, the Rulers no longer have any interest in the Alliance (or, in any case, their interest tends to lessen) and this causes a weakening of the Alliance and of the bargaining power of the Ruled. The Rulers may now become the new Giant. This, however, exposes them to a new Alliance of the weak. The Rulers, or perhaps more likely the stronger among the former Rulers, will then pretend that the former Giant is still in place and/or is as threatening as ever and will try to control the Ruled by mobilizing them against a now-fictitious Giant in order to avoid their unmasking as the new Giant and the formation of a new Alliance. The tendency of the Rulers to be above the law is incessant. They understandably want to profit by their strength, while law forces them to obey rules just like any other is supposed to do. But until they do fear an actual Giant, they have no or little choice other than making and obeying the law. The

[20] This is the typical scenario of political realism: what is lacking is the spectre of the Giant and relationships are simply seen between strong and weak. Clearly, the weak will never, by definition, bend the stronger and law would remain inexplicable in these conditions. Without a Giant, in fact, there is no hope that the stronger will accept legal bounds towards the weak.

fact that they are the stronger within the Alliance plausibly helps them to make laws the content of which is closer to their interests than to the interests of the Ruled. They may also disregard the law far more easily than the weaker. Yet, although the Rulers are the stronger, they have no other choice than to live under the law. The weak succeed, despite their weakness, in forcing the stronger to make and obey the law common to all. This 'miracle', ie the miracle of law in a world of violence, is possible because of the Giant and of its relative strength.

The Ruled are under pressure by both the Giant and the Rulers. Their goal is to survive and their interest is to unite, possibly along with the stronger, against the Giant. Without the Rulers the Alliance is hardly feasible and the consequence is annihilation by the Giant. The Alliance is the result of the combined need of the Ruled by the Rulers and of the Rulers by the Ruled. However, the tendency of the Ruled to bridle the Rulers by the law is also incessant. The Ruled accept, and indeed welcome, the Rulers (as Rulers, ie as the stronger in the Alliance) only to the extent that the Rulers assist, lead, and protect them against the Giant. As the Giant grows weaker, possibly as a result of the success of the Alliance, the Ruled naturally tend to oppose the Rulers and request more law, more respect for law, and more equality. But if the Giant grows weaker, the Rulers have less interest in accepting law and granting equality since they can now successfully confront the Giant, or even become themselves a new unbound Giant. Thus, the Ruled can count on law only at a certain point of equilibrium where the Giant is still sufficiently strong to threaten the Rulers but not so strong as to annihilate the Alliance and destroy the Ruled themselves.

In conclusion, law is the result of a temporary balance of temporary balances which may (and often actually does) exist for a period sufficient to make it be perceived as reasonably stable and predictable. The key balance depends on the relative strength over time of the Giant. It is the Giant, at the heart of all scenarios from the very beginning, that provokes the creation of the Alliance and changes the dynamics within the Alliance. Subsequently, it is also the Alliance (in particular the mobilization of its internal forces, namely the Rulers and the Ruled) that affects the strength of the Giant. There is a 'miraculous' point of equilibrium at which: (a) the Giant is still strong but not so strong as to prevent the Alliance from forming; (b) the Rulers are sufficiently strong to lay down the law and ensure respect therefor within the Alliance but not so strong as to threaten their exit from the Alliance (in case the Giant has become affordable) if the Ruled insist on law; and (c) the Ruled can count on a Giant strong enough to terrorize the Rulers but not so strong as to annihilate the Alliance and the Ruled themselves. To the extent that this point of equilibrium is perceived by all (or virtually all) those concerned as reasonably stable over time and predictable, law is not only possible and actually at work within the Alliance, it is indeed inevitable.

(3) Defining the 'strong' and the 'collective' will

If law is 'collective' violence against the violence of each of the members of the group and if violence is always (nor can it be other than) the violence of the stronger, then the question arises of how the 'stronger' can be defined, and what is meant by the 'collective' will of the group.

Broadly speaking, the term 'collective' refers to the 'overwhelming majority' of the members of the group. Clearly, in principle, each member of a group is by far weaker than all other members of the group taken together. Few would doubt that the worst event that can happen to humans is being forced to aloneness. Unsurprisingly isolation is one of the most severe forms of punishment. Experience shows that people are constantly after social recognition, isolation being what they evidently fear the most.[21] Children seek their parents' and teachers' recognition; adults continue to do so along the course of their life and career. A human being alone is exposed to assault, defamation, and denial of basic resources by every group and other stronger individuals. From time immemorial, tyrants have controlled people by *divide et impera*, setting each against the other and preventing them from exchanging thoughts and feelings. Mafia bosses delegitimize their victims by first creating a social vacuum around them. Certain women were socially delegitimized as witches in sixteenth- and seventeenth-century Europe before being prosecuted and sentenced to death as criminals.[22] Even persons who live in solitude, like Buddhas, can do so because, and as long as, societies leave them alone and protect their solitude. Many people would desire to 'live in peace' like a Buddha and may follow the teachings of this or that Enlightened. However, they often fail under the terror of remaining vulnerably alone, helpless, powerless. Aspirant Buddhas are frequently after greater power than that of their competitors, but soon face aloneness. Some then give in, others transform the path into a business, a group of disciples, a new source of solidarity and power, a new circle, a strong group. The key challenge of a genuine Buddha is presumably to unveil that human beings are hopelessly alone and aloneness means bottomless frailty and constant exposure to attack and death. But most human beings want to live, cost what it may. Few if any escape learning and accepting over time that belonging to a group is vital, priceless. No individual achievement is possible without a supportive surrounding group. In most instances achievement is simply equivalent to a certain social recognition. Groups form and grow around an endless number of common motivations and founding reasons, ranging from religion to politics, profession, or sport. International law itself is one of the founding inspirations for a number of human beings who work in the field to partake (and be recognized by) the group of so-called experts and ward off isolation.

If 'collective' means the group as a whole (*uti universi*) set against its individual members (*uti singuli*), and if the group broadly means the overwhelming majority, then it is difficult (except for unanimity) to appreciate exactly what kind of 'majority' is necessary, or when a majority is 'overwhelming'. It may occur that a minority of overwhelmingly stronger members succeeds in imposing on each member of the group their will as the will of the group as a whole. In principle, a majority is stronger than a minority, but the larger the majority the higher the likelihood that the strength of the majority hinges on one or a few leaders who succeed in holding the majority united. It is then a minority within the majority that may be the stronger in the group. Divergences may also arise between sub-groups, each on behalf and for the benefit of its own members. Relationships may therefore concern not simply an overwhelming majority against the individual members, but different sub-groups or temporary (hence changing-in-time) alliances between the members of the group. Different sub-groups may succeed in having different laws, as is the case with federal states or with states with different laws for different people based on their ethnic origin or religious

[21] See RF Baumeister and MR Leary, 'The Need to Belong—Desire for Interpersonal Attachments as a Fundamental Human Motivation' (1995) 117 *Psychological Bulletin* 497.

[22] See HR Trevor-Roper, *The European Witch Craze of the Sixteenth and Seventeenth Centuries* (London: Penguin, 1967); BP Levack, *The Witch-hunt in Early Modern Europe* (Harlow: Pearson Education Ltd, 3rd edn, 2006).

belief. What matters is to what extent the group as a whole controls each of its members or, in reverse, to what extent each of its members is discouraged from evading the will of the group as a whole. The collective will of the group is the will of those who dominate the group as backed by the generality of its members. The term 'dominate' means that whoever should try to challenge the dominant forces is reasonably expected to lose and is seen as the 'deviant'. Of course there is nothing inherently deviant in the weaker. The deviant label depends on their weakness and on the power of the stronger to establish who is a good fellow in the group and who is not. The weaker naturally have their own ideas about who is a good fellow and who is not, but they cannot make their assessment effective. A hypothetical judge who is called upon to identify the law within the group is himself in the arena and proceeds by sensing and assessing the 'common feeling' prevailing in the group, which is inevitably imposed by the stronger unless there are meaningful signs of resistance by others.

Briefly, power in society always depends on the group, but may benefit—as is indeed most often the case—very few who 'use' the impact and power of an anonymous mass to their ends and exert this power. Without the 'mass' behind, there can be no tyrants, no dictators, no authority. The mass is decisive. In authoritarian regimes this is straightforward, while in democracy there is a (physiological, legitimate) constant fight between leaders of different parties who simply reflect, or are shown to reflect, the power of the relative 'masses' supporting each party. In constitutional regimes, institutions work according to 'checks and balances' that reflect different groups and their relative power. Distinctions can be made in social studies among different forms of groupings like hordes, herds, masses, multitudes, mobs, crowds, families, associations, societies, communities, and so on. Some, like hordes, are guided by a supreme chief, while others, like herds, simply behave and coordinate their members by mutual imitation. The point is the *overwhelming force* of the number (whether small or big) against individuals under particular circumstances and the impotence of the individual towards the group. In this sense law is grounded in the collective will, although this may emanate from very few who are in power.[23]

B. The Discernment of Law

If law is so entangled with violence, how can it be discerned as distinct from power? On the other hand, if law is distinct from brute force, how can it be dissected from morality? In order for law to be captured as distinctive, the relationships between law and power and between law and morality seem to need inspection. A number of different criteria of discernment have been suggested in various contexts and by numerous theorists. The debate has centred on the 'correct' criterion capable of defining law as such. This section is confined to showing, as a consequence of the above discussion, that all the criteria devised thus far to discern law as distinct from power and morality may be either correct or incorrect depending on whether and to what extent the addressees as a whole of the specific law considered believe and act upon it as their own law.

[23] On this point, but referring to Le Bon's 'crowds' and not to society as such, see Freud, 'Group Psychology and the Analysis of the Ego' (n 9 above) 74, 77, emphasizing that in a 'mass', individuals witness a sense of invincible force and of omnipotence (for the sole reason of the number) along with a sense of irresponsibility and lack of conscience (given the anonymousness of the mass itself).

(1) Law and power

The relationship between law and power is seen by realists as working one way, in the sense that power controls law. Most jurists, on the other hand, insist that the relationship also works the other way round. The two theses are not necessarily incompatible with each other. This section shows that law, although depending on power, may indeed exist as a distinct domain. A concise look at the contending theses (primacy of power versus primacy of law) is taken in the following two sub-sections before concluding that power prevails over law between individual members of a group (*uti singuli*), but law prevails over power when individual members face the group as a whole.

(a) Primacy of power

The realist stance that power creates and controls law—this ultimately being nothing other than an instrument of power or, more concretely, of the persons who have seized power in a community—is widespread. Many would concur that the stronger in society shape the law and use it to further their own interests and values. What is more, unlike the weaker, they are at liberty to observe the law or to disregard it without incurring serious consequences. Power comes 'before' and is above law: it precedes law both in time and in rank, and prevails over law whenever necessary. It is a fact that most people are constantly seeking to enter the 'ruling class', or the circle of the stronger in any group or sub-group, inter alia, to participate in the making of (or directly to lay down) the law and control it thereafter.

The perspective of power's primacy over law is a commonplace to the layman and has a long pedigree in Western political and legal thinking. In Plato's dialogues, the Sophists often argue that law is the means used by the stronger to bend the weaker. In the *Republic*, Thrasymachus famously claims that 'justice is nothing else than the advantage of the stronger'.[24] In the *Laws*, Clinias seems to agree with the Athenian interlocutor's assertions that 'justice is what benefits the stronger', that 'the laws in a state are always enacted by the stronger power', and that 'the lawgiver will style [laws] "justice", and will punish every transgressor as guilty of injustice'.[25] In the *Theaetetus*, Socrates observes that 'whatever laws a state makes, because they seem to it just, are just to the state that made them, as long as they remain in force'.[26] The idea that the ruling class legislates in its own interest, ie to keep itself in power and exploit all other people, is popular and well-documented. It is historically specially linked with positivism.[27] A qualification was introduced by Xenophon in the *Memorabilia*, when Pericles answers Alcibiades, who had asked what law is, that law is what is prescribed by the sovereign 'providing this is done with persuasion'.[28]

The notion that the stronger make the law, if they decide to do so, and use it as they please to pursue their self-interest is hard to deny. It is equally hard to deny, however, that the stronger often accept the idea of a law also binding on them. This seems counterintuitive because if they are really stronger than all others, they could simply make no law and prevail by force at any given moment. Why should the stronger make law and then use it as an instrument to get what they could directly get by brute force? Realists typically answer that there is no reason to suppose that the stronger would

[24] Plato, *The Republic*, I 338c.
[25] Plato, *Laws*, 714 c–d, 690b.
[26] Plato, *Theaetetus*, 177d.
[27] Ch 4 below, section B (2).
[28] Xenophon, *Memorabilia*, I, 2, 43–4.

behave 'ethically' or 'in accordance with the law' as though they would not be the stronger. The stronger are strong because they have actively pursued power and there is no reason why—apart perhaps from a few who may have happened to 'convert' to ethics or law—they should abandon power at the very moment when they can get what power offers. Realists insinuate that this unrealistic assumption is the typical weapon adopted by the weak when seeking to overthrow the powerful and become the stronger. It has already been shown why realists may be wrong. While it is true that the strong want to profit from their strength and that it is simply fanciful to expect them to sacrifice their interests for the sole benefit of others, it is also true that their calculations may lead them to both make and abide by the law as long as law abidance secures the cohesiveness of the group and the obedience of the weak against a common challenger. The pursuit of self-interest (however defined) is perfectly compatible with law. For example, the strong usually prefer to achieve their goals, all else being equal, by invoking law rather than displaying brute force. To act 'according to law' is perceived as being done on behalf and for the benefit of all members of society. Law, as the set of common rules in society, is assumed to accommodate the interests of all. The strong prefer, in their best interest, to present their actions as 'collective enforcement' of the law rather than arbitrary violence. Law is indeed one of the best instruments available to the stronger to subdue the weaker without instilling a feeling of injustice and revenge that could reduce the advantages gained. But if law is not equal to what the stronger please whenever they please, then it is distinct from power.

(b) Primacy of law

The reversed perspective is that law comes 'before' and is above power: law precedes, both in time and in rank, legitimate power (as opposed to brute force) and takes precedence over power in case of conflict.

Also the perspective of the primacy of law over power has a long pedigree in Western political and legal thinking and it can be found in the confidence of laymen on appealing to law and to the courts to solve their disputes. In Plato's *Gorgias* the Sophist Callicles asserts that laws are made by the weaker and more numerous 'with a view to themselves and their own interest'.[29] The typical conception of law designed to limit the power of the stronger is naturalism.[30] An example among many could be the eighteenth-century philosopher William Godwin, who held that society has no power to legislate absurdity and injustice, and that even universal consent cannot convert the unjust into the just.[31]

The advocacy of the primacy of law over power sounds noble but is often irremediably utopian. For example, when Godwin states that 'universal consent cannot convert the just into the unjust', the reader is left with a number of questions: 'What is meant by "just" and "unjust"?', 'Who decides on the meaning of such words?', 'How can a "universal" consent actually be resisted, and by whom?'. What is just or unjust may reasonably be agreed upon 'universally' within a homogenous society (such as, perhaps, the medieval *Respublica christiana*), but there is no one, save universal 'deviants' (such as heretics and infidels in that society) that could oppose universal consent. The 'higher authority' over human beings appealed to by Godwin is hard to discern, and if it is assumed that there

[29] Plato, *Gorgias*, 483b.

[30] Ch 4 below, section B (1).

[31] W Godwin, *Enquiry Concerning Political Justice and Its Influence on Modern Morals and Happiness* [1793] (Harmondsworth: Penguin, 1976) 196–7.

is one who expresses a super-human will (such as, perhaps, the Pope in the medieval *Respublica christiana*), then it is this authority that can do what it pleases. In a heterogeneous society, on the other hand, opposition is physiological, not necessarily deviant, but universality may easily be lacking. Even in a heterogeneous society, if a universal consent materializes on a certain question, the above difficulties resurface.

It is not by virtue of another-world law that law limits the stronger. It is self-evidently impossible that the weaker can make the strong abide by the law simply by appealing to another legal world, unless the appeal corresponds to power, as was the case with the medieval *Respublica christiana* when the Pope could excommunicate princes and immediately cause disobedience to the excommunicated prince by all believers. The law evoked by the Pope was highly effective because people believed in both the law and the Pope as his witness and messenger. If the weaker should make the stronger abide by the law, it would simply mean that the weaker are not as weak as supposed and the stronger are not as strong as supposed. Law limits the strong because it is (and as long as it is) in the interest of the stronger to have some law and to abide by it. In this sense, once again, law appears as collective violence, not an ideal that descends on earth and magically instils perfect moderation, wisdom, and harmony in all members of all communities.

(c) Law as collective power

To summarize, law exists as a balance of balances, ie as an equilibrium of several forces. It is collective violence, not an ideal parameter existing in the mind of this or that individual, lawyer, or theorist. Jurists may propose nice conceptions of law; however, the real law is the one which works in society and this can work only if it is backed by the stronger. It cannot be credibly created and enforced by the weaker. Law 'lives' in society as the result of power. But it is not the power of individuals; it is the power of the group. Law is distinct from (and actually above) power if power is understood as the power of individuals (*uti singuli*). From the perspective of *any* individual, including the stronger, law is indeed a limiting factor because any individual is impotent compared to the strength of the group taken as a whole, and law is the power of the group. At the same time, when power is understood as the power of the members of the group as a whole (*uti universi*), law is power, hence an instrument thereof.

This provides an explanation of the so-called 'is–ought problem', or 'naturalistic fallacy', ie the deduction of an 'ought' from an 'is'. The notion that one cannot derive an 'ought' from an 'is', or that no statement of fact by itself entails any statement of value, comes from a well-known passage in David Hume's *Treatise of Human Nature*,[32] and is typically defended by Hans Kelsen among the Positivists.[33] In particular sociologists of law tend, on the other hand, in their effort to treat law as being as close as possible to social realities, including power relationships, to infer the law from

[32] D Hume, *A Treatise of Human Nature* [1739] (Oxford and New York: Clarendon Press, 2007) 3.1.1.27, 302. The term 'naturalistic fallacy' was first introduced by GE Moore, *Principia Ethica* [1903] (Cambridge: CUP, rev edn, 1993) §§ 10, 12, 14, 22, excluding that a moral norm can be defined in terms of something else, such as pleasure or utility, which is verifiable as a fact. For a collection of essays on the topic, see WD Hudson, *The Is–Ought Question: A Collection of Papers on the Central Problem in Moral Philosophy* (London: Macmillan, 1969).

[33] H Kelsen, *General Theory of Law and State* [1945] (New Brunswick and London: Transaction Publishers, 2007) 37. See J Wróblewski, 'Kelsen, The Is–Ought Dichotomy and Naturalistic Fallacy' (1981) 35 RIP 508, noting that in Kelsenian normativism the dichotomy serves to critique (albeit in different ways) traditional legal positivism, legal realism, and natural law theories.

social facts.[34] The dichotomy, also described as one between 'apology' and 'utopia',[35] serves to ensure normativity to law, but risks picturing law as an ideal detached from realities. The reverse occurs (namely, law as mirroring realities, but losing normative drive) with the overlap of the 'is' and the 'ought'.[36] However, once the distinction between individuals *uti singuli* and individuals *uti universi* is made, both 'ought' and 'is' prove to be nothing more than 'facts', although behind the 'ought' there is collective force and behind the 'is' there is individual force. The two concepts are interrelated in the sense that collective force is an 'ought' in relation to individual force while individual force is an 'is' in relation to both collective and individual force. The dichotomy is thus perfectly justified when referring to the relation of individuals vis-à-vis the group as a whole. In contrast, it is unjustified when it refers to the conduct of individuals towards either the group as such or other individuals.[37]

(2) Law and morality

The foregoing discussion can be helpful in shedding some light also on the relation between law and morality.[38] This point raises a number of difficult questions concerning, inter alia, the very notion of morality. Many theories have been advanced concerning such a concept, especially in connection with the perennial controversy over naturalism versus positivism[39] and such typically positivist positions as the 'separation thesis'[40] or Hart's 'incorporation thesis'.[41] Etymologically, the word comes from the Latin *mores*. It may either describe the social practices of a specific society or people, or prescribe what is 'good' and 'evil' and how people must behave in every society.[42] It is often said that the hallmark of morality is its 'inner' dimension, while law relates to external conduct. In fact, while individuals *uti singuli* are impotent vis-à-vis all members *uti universi* as a matter of law, they maintain an inner moral freedom from the group. Many argue that morality serves as a factor capable of inspiring changes in the law, or as a set of values that at least in part must be found in the law, or as the basis of obligation of law.[43] Others add (while still others deny) that morality is the criterion of validity of law.[44] Yet another view is that there is an 'inner' morality serving as the condition that makes law possible.[45]

[34] Ch 4 below, section B (6).
[35] ibid section B (5).
[36] For a recent revisitation within a 'planning theory' of law, see SJ Shapiro, *Legality* (Cambridge, Mass and London: Harvard University Press, 2011) 45–50, 188.
[37] For two attempts to bridge the gap between the 'is' and the 'ought', from a philosophical and from a biological perspective respectively, see JR Searle, 'How to Derive "Ought" from "Is"' (1964) 73 PhR 43–58; H Gommer, 'From the "Is" to the "Ought"' (2010) 96 ARS 449.
[38] For the often-related concept of justice, see Ch 2 below, section B (1).
[39] See MH Kramer, *Where Law and Morality Meet* (Oxford: OUP, 2004).
[40] J Austin, *The Province of Jurisprudence Determined* [1832] (Cambridge: CUP, 1995) 217, n 20, stating that 'no *positive* law is *legally* unjust' in commenting on Hobbes' proposition that 'no law can be unjust'; Kelsen (n 33 above) 20.
[41] HLA Hart, 'Postscript', in *The Concept of Law* (Oxford: OUP, 2nd edn, 1994) 250, famously observing that 'the rule of recognition [ie the rule by which the validity of other rules in the legal system are determined] may incorporate as criteria of legal validity conformity with moral principles or substantive values'.
[42] For an overview, see B Gert, 'The Definition of Morality', in Stan EP, at <http:www.//plato.stanford.edu/archives/fall2008/entries/morality-definition>.
[43] Hart (n 41 above) 185.
[44] ibid.
[45] LL Fuller, *The Morality of Law* (New Haven and London: Yale University Press, rev edn, 1969).

However, morality is a concept that must first be placed in context. One should first determine in relation to what social group morality is evoked. The question is what is believed to be 'morality', as a factor operating in one or another of the directions just mentioned (or still others), in any particular group. It may be that what is 'moral' coincides in different groups, and even that one and the same morality is found in all humanity, and performs the same function in relation to law. However, there can be no abstract morality to be 'applied' to a group. If the group distinguishes law and morality, it has its own reasons to do so. If it overlaps the two concepts, it has again its own reasons to do so. Any concept of morality extrapolated by way of abstract theorizing, and then generalized, is the mere projection of the vision of morality shared in the group from which the theorist comes. This is not to espouse moral relativism. Even relativism is equivalent to that particular notion of 'relativism' that prevails in the mind of the theorist. Relativism is the view of a particular group from the standpoint of what *that* group assumes to be morality in absolute terms. Since there is no chance that any particular notion of morality can prevail without being supported by the stronger in any particular group (ranging from a tribe to humankind), morality, just like law, is what is collectively deemed to be treated as morality, and to perform certain functions affecting the law, such as its validity, the reason why it should be obeyed, and so on. In addition to 'social morality', the group may either prohibit, or tolerate, or even praise 'individual moral enlightenment' in order for this to influence the developments of the law. This prohibition, or toleration, or praise cannot but be the result of the struggle of a certain class of individuals vis-à-vis others. Different moralities, even inspired by opposing ideas, may co-exist in a group as a reflection of different views of different sub-groups in the principal group. The option itself between the morality of one pervasive morality concerning all and the plurality of moralities within a more general tolerant morality is itself an option that reflects the relative force of the competing forces in any group.

Just as power and law are distinct in the perception of society, and theories on their distinction are but 'frozen' generalizations of what peoples have perceived here and there at different times, the same holds true for the distinction between law and morality. Certain societies need to keep law and morality distinct, while others do not. Peoples may have different ideas about what morality is and about whether and how morality should relate to law. For example, according to a classical approach, both law and morality are thought to pursue the common good, but morality is deemed to be based on enduring and perhaps ubiquitous principles, while law is thought to change in both space and time, unless natural law is espoused. On this account, it seems that law is basically man-made and depends on power as exercised by specific human beings in a particular temporal and spatial context, whereas morality is the result of 'reason' and points to what is good or bad 'per se'. However, even assuming that morality is related to the good or bad 'per se', this 'per-se' dimension is itself the result of what the stronger in a group judge as good from their viewpoint, which may well include a sincere desire to pursue this good for the benefit of all. If all the members of the group believe that a per-se-based definition of morality is meaningful and serves as, say, a test to judge the 'validity' of law or as a trigger to promote the conviction that the law made in that group is to be obeyed, then this 'explanation' of morality will work in the group as both distinct and relevant to law. It will also happen that this group, confident of its own vision of morality and of the positive function that morality is expected to perform as a test for the validity of law, will seek to 'export' it to other groups, which may have other ideas in this respect. This attempt may or may not succeed; if it does, this particular notion of morality, emerging within a certain group to solve certain specific problems of this group, will be found acceptable by other groups and, little by little, will be believed as 'universal' by more and more people and groups. This will happen because people will believe in it, not necessarily because it is 'true'. It is certainly true for those who have reasons to believe in it, but not necessarily for the others. No doubt what is generally believed may be true, but may well also be untrue, and the question remains from whose viewpoint 'true', or 'truth' in itself, should be thought of.

From the perspective here adopted there is little difference in how to treat the relationship of power and morality to law. Both power and morality are the manifestation of the stronger in any particular society, which may also be humankind. Both are introduced to make distinctions useful to solve specific problems emerging in the group taken as a reference point. The fact that they are conceived of as different, or that among certain peoples they are conceived as distinct (if not opposed) while among certain others they are completely overlapped (as is the case with 'fundamentalist' regimes), is of course meaningful, but it is not the key point, at least for present purposes. The fact is that only the stronger are actually capable of proving that their morality is the best and imposing it on dissidents. Morality has no 'inner' force capable of imposing itself on the attention of human beings if human beings are not interested in it. The notion of what morality is for this or that moral philosopher or jurist is of consequence in society only if it is backed by most people. Lacking inner force, morality (or one or another notion of morality and ensuing functions to be performed in relation to law) can 'triumph' to the extent that physical human beings successfully promote it in the real world where other human beings are likely to compete for a different morality, or for a different function that morality should perform in relation to law, or even for no morality at all (presumably in the name of an implied 'counter-morality'). Moralism and realism tend to overlap. History and experience teaches that it is always the stronger who have acted (not only as lawgivers, but also) as moralizers and civilizers in every society.

(3) Criteria for discernment

If law is collective violence, possibly distinct from both (individual) power and morality, it is necessary to look into the criteria which allow the determination of when a certain proposition is law rather than a mere reflection of power or of a moral imperative (or any other kind of 'norms', including those based on religion, magic, social expectation, etc). Historically, a number of criteria have been developed in various contexts, at different times and in different places. They are generally called criteria of validity, or legality, or legitimacy, depending on the general approach to law taken. Today, their need is at times rejected as unnecessary, or irrelevant, or even ideological, by some anti-formalist theorists and jurists.[46] The best known criteria for law discernment include procedure, content, purpose, compliance, inherentness, sanction, and convention. The analysis will now succinctly focus on them to show that none can be assumed as valid, regardless of the particular group whose law is considered.

[46] See eg B de Sousa Santos, *Toward a New Legal Common Sense* (London: Butterworths, 2nd edn, 2002); PS Berman, 'Global Legal Pluralism' (2007) 80 S Cal LR 1155, 1177; G Anderson, *Constitutional Rights after Globalization* (Oxford: Hart, 2005).

(a) Procedure

Law can be tested by appealing to the procedure followed in its creation. *Who* makes the rules and/or *how* rules are made are the key questions. Only the rules made by certain 'authorities' (law-makers) or in accordance with a certain prescribed 'procedure', regardless of their content and function, count as legal rules. What matters is not the content but rather the origin of the rules, either their factual 'derivation from' the proper authority,[47]or their normativistic 'flowing from' the proper legal procedure for law-creation,[48] in a word their 'source'.[49] The identification of the law and its distinction from non-law is conceived as a neutral, technical operation consisting in checking whether the requirements of the sources are met. The political process is apparently detached from the applicative moment of the rules. These are supposed to be identified without any political involvement just by verifying whether the prescribed procedure has been duly followed. The morality and justice of the rules are regarded as issues 'already' dealt with 'up-stream' in the political (or constitutional) process. It is assumed that it is the sovereign who makes justice and no other justice exists beyond what is stated by the political authority within a group. It is also assumed that law can and should be 'objectively' found and proved in individual instances by empirically verifiable and inter-subjectively acceptable 'facts' so as to enhance legal certainty.[50]

The key objection to this 'positivist' approach is that any prescription, even the most absurd or odious, may count as law if adopted by the prescribed authority according to the prescribed procedure.[51] Disobedience is allowed only when permitted by the law itself as an 'exception' to the rule. Law appears as the instrument of the sovereign or the lawgiver, whether a monarch or an assembly or other, designed to serve its will and interests. Legal certainty and empirical basis is thought to limit arbitrariness in the application of law in particular cases by individual legal officials, but law as such tends to coincide with the arbitrariness of the law-maker. A bulwark is constructed in constitutional states by positing a constitution (at a sort of timeless 'constitutional moment', outside the ordinary temporal dimension of legislation) at a higher level than standard law and making the validity of the latter dependent also on certain intangible contents sanctioned in the constitution.

The debate is largely misplaced when intended in absolute terms. If a group values the idea of the 'source', along with the concomitant ideas of 'technical production'—suggesting that the 'outcome' of the law productive process will be good if the procedure has been carefully followed—and of unlimited trust in the law-maker, there can be little doubt that the law thus defined is the law in that group. It may even be the law of the group against the constitution itself, which can do little, however 'sacred', to avoid what the majority of the moment wants as their law. Even less relevant are individual critics when faced with the overarching power of the addressees of the law

47 For the view that 'Every positive law, or law simply and strictly so called, is set by a sovereign person, or a sovereign body of persons, to a member or members of the independent political society wherein that person or body is sovereign or supreme', see Austin (n 40 above)16.

48 For the well-known Kelsenian critique of Austin's command positivism by contending that law is law not because it has been created by the sovereign but because the sovereign is authorized by the law (and ultimately by a *Grundnorm*) to create the law, see Kelsen (n 33 above) 30–2. In turn, Hart (n 41 above) 59–60, 110–11, 116–17, criticized Kelsen's theory of the *Grundnorm* and grounded his 'rules of recognition' in the social practice of the law-applying authorities captured, inter alia, from their 'internal point of view'.

49 The doctrine of legal sources is specifically addressed in Ch 6 below, section A (1).

50 A Ross, *On Law and Justice* (London: Stevens & Sons, 1958) 258–67.

51 Positivism is addressed below in Ch 4 below, section B (2).

taken as a whole. At best, their efforts may work as a strategy to seek change in the way in which law is perceived by its addressees, an attempt that might either succeed or fail.

(b) Content

The arbitrariness of the law-maker can be avoided, at least in principle, by assessing law by its contents. Law then hinges on what a rule states, not on how it has been produced. The key imagery surrounding the rule is here self-evidence, not the 'factory' typical of the procedure approach. On this criterion, rules having certain contents—usually a morally unacceptable or logically untenable content, such as commanding the impossible—do not count as valid law. This substantive, often naturalist approach is supposed to work negatively as a limit to man-made law, rather than positively as a creating factor of law. It does not say what contents law must have, but rather what contents it cannot have.[52]

Also substantivism, although aimed at remedying the defects of proceduralism, has raised objections. As experience abundantly shows, different people have regarded as required by law thus defined the most extravagant behaviour, and the risk of arbitrariness is thus hardly avoided. Moreover, unjust or immoral behaviour, albeit prohibited in general, may be justified under particular circumstances for a worthy cause, such as in a state of necessity or as a reaction to an unlawful conduct. It may also happen that a rule with a different, more acceptable content in moral or logical terms may prove difficult (or even impossible) to be adopted or complied with. Finally, even assuming that certain acts are evil everywhere to all, this may imply in a certain group a moral prohibition distinct from what is required by the law.

It seems that substantivism can reasonably work among people who share common basic values. The justice, morality, or truth of legal rules are then generally held as self-evident. Everyone in the group immediately agrees that a certain rule is a legal rule and cannot be otherwise in order for the group to hold together. The substantive approach is typical of one-dimensional societies in which values are perceived by all as self-evident, although it is also invoked in multi-dimensional societies to *promote* common values. But if law is collective violence, then there is nothing that can prevent it from proving arbitrary (or contrary to morality, justice, or logic) in the perception of some insider or outsider, including natural law, in cases where its addressees as a whole support it as their law.

(c) Purpose

Both the arbitrariness of procedure and contents could be overcome by assessing law on the basis of its purpose. A given rule is then assumed to be a legal rule in that it meets the desired purpose and achieves the corresponding outcome. Purposes are often meant as 'values' that the community is willing to pursue, ranging from the coexistence of its members to the effectiveness of institutions, their accountability, protection of basic rights, and so on. This functionalist approach is generally set against the positivistic appeal to the 'sources' of law and procedure. However, in addition, moderate Positivists may be influenced by functionalism when they prefer certain sources (such as general principles of law) to others for their instrumental potential to achieve the purposes and values of the system, such as humanitarian values. What matters here is, however, the

[52] Naturalism is addressed in Ch 4 below, section B (1).

outcome of the rules, not their origin, although their origin may reveal their underlying purpose. It is believed that either law 'works' for the purposes for which it has been made or it is irrelevant, or no law at all. Functionalism is often espoused by constitutionalists with a view to realizing the values informing national constitutions.[53]

The problem with functionalism is that purposes and values are either selected by interpreters in accordance with their preferences or are 'logically' deduced from general statements of the law that may be arbitrary, or at least remote from the language of the law. Moreover, from the same general value or principle different and even conflicting statements of the law may equally plausibly be deduced. Another problem is that the 'thing' which is supposed to achieve the desired outcome is 'law' and this needs to be identified beforehand. Not everything is law for the sole reason that it can contribute to the performance of a certain social function or to the achievement of a certain desired outcome in the community. Nor is every rule a legal rule operating 'here and now' for the sole reason that it ought to be law. It is notably dynamic societies that may prefer a functionalist approach to law with a view to enabling a detached (rather than a literal) reading of the rules and ensuring legal solutions along the lines of the rules' basic, persistent function during social change without the need continuously to introduce formal amendments to the law.

(d) Compliance

Another move towards avoiding being stuck to the letter of the law is to assess it by its compliance record. What matters is here how and to what extent law affects the behaviour of its addressees. It is assumed that either law is complied with or is irrelevant, or no law at all. Its possible origins and basis in the formally accepted legal 'sources' is irrelevant. Law 'on paper' cannot be law. The factors pulling towards compliance, such as legitimacy or clarity, are crucial.

This behaviouralist approach presupposes that the question of what counts as 'law' to be complied with is already solved somehow. Clearly, it is one thing to identify a legal rule as such, it is quite another to comply with it.[54] Not everything is law for the sole reason that it is complied with, just as not everything is non-law simply because it is not observed. People may abide by many types of rules or standards for a variety of reasons without acknowledging (or even thinking of) them as legal rules. There may be particular rules which are still regarded as the law in force to be obeyed although most people in most instances do not actually comply with them. Moreover, some rules may be complied with more than others but it may be difficult to see the former as 'less' legal than the latter, or as no law at all, on this sole ground. Behaviourism takes for granted that legal rules are defined otherwise than by their compliance record, but this remains key to their legal characterization.

The problem with behaviourism is that, while legal rules are certainly expected to be actually complied with, law works to 'inform' people how the others expect them to behave in the group and what sanctions they may expect in case of transgression.[55] Compliance tests may indeed contribute to find that certain legal rules (as defined by other criteria) are not complied with and their respect is scarcely 'expected' (or

53 M Loughlin, 'The Functionalist Style in Public Law' (2005) 55 UTLJ 361, 372–3.

54 H Kelsen, *Allgemeine Theorie der Normen* (Vienna: Manz, 1979), English trans *General Theory of Norms* (Oxford: Clarendon Press, 1991) 44.

55 Hart (n 41 above) 86–8; CC Wendehorst, 'The State as a Foundation of Private Law Reasoning' (2008) 56 AJCL 567.

sanctioned) in particular instances by the other members of the group, or that their existence has ceased because of desuetude. However, it is by the standard of existing law that desuetude is measured. Another difficulty is that if law hinges on compliance one should 'wait and see' to what degree each particular rule is complied with. Furthermore, measuring compliance is extremely difficult and easily manipulable, open to questionable methodologies and to different results depending on the particular rule examined, and different people may have different opinions thereon, with a resulting loss of legal certainty. Finally, people would be left at liberty to decide whether to adhere and respect a rule or not, at least initially when no one knows what is the degree of obedience to the rule, and hence whether the rule is to be treated as a 'legal' rule at all.

The compliance approach is diffused in pragmatic societies in which people want to see the immediate effects of law and expect the law to be somehow 'created', or administered, if not negotiated, by themselves in their daily life. The law-making process is still necessary to have some rule to abide by; however, it is the daily and conspicuous observance of the rules that makes them 'legal' in the perception of their addressees as a whole. Less pragmatic societies may find this approach rather anarchic, even contrary to the essence of law, in that it seems to allow people to manage at liberty what is the law made by the formal, generally recognized law-making authority.

(e) Inherentness

In order to reject 'odious' man-made law (or odious interpretations thereof) as non-law without taking a plain substantive approach, law may be defined in terms of 'inherentness', ie in terms of what is believed to be its inherent structure. If this approach is adopted, only what meets the requirements deemed to be inherent in the concept of law qualifies as law.

Lon Fuller famously developed a sort of procedural version of natural law termed 'positive natural law' by combining content and procedure.[56] He identified eight 'intrinsic', procedural (rather than substantive) requirements of legality (or of 'fidelity' to law) which cannot be ignored by human law-makers without depriving law of its inherent quality and legal validity, namely: generality, promulgation, non-retroactivity, clarity, non-contradiction, not asking the impossible, constancy, and congruence between rules and official action.[57] These requirements constitute what Fuller called the 'internal' or 'inner' morality of law, along with its cognates 'interstitial law' and 'implicit law'. In his view, when such requirements are met it is extremely unlikely that an 'immoral' or 'odious' law (in short a law at odds with natural law) may pass or be considered valid law. Everyone would feel a deep sense of injustice if one or more of these standards are not met. Law is not seen as 'immoral' because it is directly in conflict with the content of a certain moral vision, but rather because it has been made in a way that is incompatible with the very concept of law, no matter what its content may be.

The identification of Fuller's requirements with law is open to question. There may be odious laws, at least for some people, which do fulfil his eight requirements. Moreover, odious laws may in fact be imposed even where they do not fulfil the

[56] Fuller (n 45 above). For analysis, see K Rundle, 'The Impossibility of an Exterminatory Law: Law and the Holocaust' (2009) 59 UTLJ 65.

[57] ibid 39.

requirements. It has also been suggested that Fuller's criteria are concerned with the rule of law—which is certainly a virtue of law, but not necessarily a moral virtue of law—and fail to prove a necessary connection between law and morality.[58] There may be law without any rule of law. Canon law apparently qualifies as law without respecting the rule of law in a broad sense, the Pope actually enjoying unlimited powers. Inherentness works within the particular society whose basic values it reflects, not in others where the proposed inherent requirements are felt to be spurious.

Fuller's notion that 'immoral law' is not law is exemplarily expressed in the well-known 'Radbruch's formula' of 1946,[59] named after the German philosopher Gustav Radbruch who converted to natural law after World War II. The formula, which is endorsed by some theorists and fiercely attacked by others,[60] was applied by the post-war German courts to deny the application of Nazi laws and, years later, for the purposes of judgment of German Democratic Republic injustice in the trials over the Berlin wall shootings. It famously stirred a controversy between Hart and Fuller in the 1950s.[61] Whatever its moral value,[62] the formula remains rather laconic as to where exactly the 'intolerable degree' of 'justice' starts, to whose viewpoint of justice it refers, and what are its 'legal' effects, whether nullity *ab initio*, post-fact invalidation, or justice-orientated interpretation.[63] It is hard to expect the courts to deny the application of the law in force *at the moment* on grounds that it is immoral. It is quite another thing for the courts at a later stage (as German post-war courts) to deny the application of previously existing laws as 'invalid from the outset', which may be straightforward, if not compulsory, in the context of a radically different legal and constitutional order, regardless of their 'inherent' unjustness.

[58] J Raz, *The Authority of Law: Essays on Law and Morality* (Oxford: OUP, 2009) 223–6.

[59] The English translation of the formula reads as follows: 'The conflict between justice and legal certainty may well be resolved in this way: The positive law, secured by legislation and power, takes precedence even when its content is unjust and fails to benefit the people, unless the conflict between statute and justice reaches an intolerable degree that the statute, as "flawed law", must yield to justice'. An alternative formulation is as follows: 'It is impossible to draw a sharper line between cases of statutory lawlessness and statutes that are valid despite their flaws. One line of distinction, however, can be drawn with utmost clarity: Where there is not even an attempt at justice, where equality, the core of justice, is deliberately betrayed in the issuance of positive law, then the statute is not merely "flawed law", it lacks completely the very nature of law'. See G Radbruch, 'Gesetzliches Unrecht und übergesetzliches Recht' (1946) 1 *Süddeutsche Juristen-Zeitung* 105–8, English trans 'Statutory Lawlessness and Supra-Statutory Law (1946)' (2006) 26 OJLS 1, 7.

[60] See SL Paulson, 'On the Background and Significance of Gustav Radbruch's Post-War Papers' (2006) 26 OJLS 17; G Vassalli, *Formula di Radbruch e diritto penale: note sulla punizione dei delitti di Stato nella Germania postnazista e nella Germania postcomunista* (Milan: Giuffrè, 2001). See in addition 'Symposium: The Hart-Fuller Debate At Fifty' (2008) 83 NYU LR 993; P Cane (ed), *The Hart-Fuller Debate in the Twenty-first Century* (Oxford: Hart, 2010).

[61] HLA Hart, 'Positivism and the Separation of Law and Morals' (1958) 71 Harv LR 593, 615–21; LL Fuller, 'Positivism and Fidelity to Law: A Reply to Professor Hart' (1958) 71 Harv LR 630, 648–57.

[62] For a classical non-positivist defence of the formula, see R Alexy, 'A Defence of Radbruch's Formula' in D Dyzenhaus (ed), *Recrafting the Rule of Law: The Limits of Legal Order* (Oxford: Hart, 1999) 15–39; R Alexy, *Begriff und Geltung des Rechts* [1992] (Freiburg and Munich: Alber Karl, 2nd edn, 2002), English trans *The Argument from Injustice: A Reply to Legal Positivism* (Oxford: Clarendon Press, 2002). For a comment, see B Bix, 'Robert Alexy, Radbruch's Formula, and the Nature of Legal Theory' (2006) 37 *Rechtstheorie* 139. See in addition F Haldemann, 'Gustav Radbruch vs. Hans Kelsen: A Debate on Nazi Law' (2005) 18 Ratio Juris 162.

[63] Arguing for the invalidity from the outset, see eg German Constitutional Court, Decision of 14 February 1968, 23 BVerfGE (1968) 98, 106.

(f) Sanction

However law is discerned, one could believe that it cannot be called law unless its breaches are punished by a sanction.[64] Also this approach is aimed at excluding that the law on paper is valid law, although the compliance test rests on the voluntary observance of law by its addressees and sanctions are instead directed to force to compliance those who are not willing to do so. It is assumed that it makes no sense to state that a rule is a binding rule when nothing negative happens to its transgressor. It is also generally assumed that sanctions must be *external* to the transgressor (ie applied by others) and *legal* (ie subject to legal rules) so as to distinguish legal rules from moral and social norms, which are backed by internal and social sanctions, respectively. Sanctions variously understood seem to be empirically found in any legal system, whether primitive or not, although their form and degree of effectiveness may vary with the context and the rule involved.

Also this imperative approach, albeit widespread, is open to serious objections.[65] It is a fact that every legal system is effective pre-eminently because and to the extent that it is voluntarily complied with by most of its addressees. While sanctions may discourage few transgressions, they are impotent to ensure obedience to law as a whole. It is simply impossible to punish all transgressions when these become the rule. Sanctions make sense only when transgressions are the exception, but this presupposes that the vast majority of rules are observed for reasons other than the threat of a sanction. As is well known, compliance may be induced by several factors (including consent, belief, calculation, custom, habit, inertia, morality, and sense of justice), not necessarily by the fear of a sanction. Experience shows that no one can obtain obedience by brute force only: even the cruellest authoritarian regimes or dictators at the peak of their power invest much of their energies and resources in manufacturing consensus, especially through propaganda. It is also objected that man is by nature free and human beings can always resist obedience to law. Even torturers can never be completely sure that the tortured will obey their requests. It is argued, moreover, that there are many 'legal rules', unquestionably recognized as such, whose breach does not implicate a sanction. While some are occasionally found in private law, most of them are found in public law, notably in constitutional law. Finally, while compliance with legal rules may be encouraged by sanctions, sanctions themselves are in turn subjected to legal rules and also these rules can be breached. Further sanctions would pose the same problem, giving rise to an endless process, unless an *Ur*-rule is admitted which is backed by no sanction. But this implies that there must be at least one rule not backed by sanctions in every legal system and, significantly, that *it is the system itself* that excludes the indispensability of sanctions.

The diffused impression that people at any latitude and in any circumstances rely on sanctions to define law is clearly excessive. People may believe themselves to be governed by the law even when they are perfectly aware that the breach thereof does not entail any significant sanction. Just as there may be people who call for sanctions for

[64] Austin (n 40 above) 22–5, 118, 136, 151; Kelsen (n 33 above) 15–24; EA Hoebel, *The Law of Primitive Man: A Study in Comparative Legal Dynamics* (Cambridge, Mass: London, 1954) 28.

[65] For the view that sanctions are not a requisite of law, See eg E Ehrlich, *Grundlegung der Soziologie des Rechts* (Munich and Leipzig: Duncker & Humblot, 1913), English trans *Fundamental Principles of Sociology of Law* (New Brunswick, NJ: transaction reprint, 2002) 20–4; Hart (n 41 above) 218; M Barkun, *Law without Sanctions: Order in Primitive Societies and the World Community* (New Haven and London: Yale University Press, 1968) 59–65; MDA Freeman, *Lloyd's Introduction to Jurisprudence* (London: Sweet and Maxwell, 7th edn, 2001) 215.

the purposes of law credibility and working, other people may well show an opposite attitude and focus on how law can be made to work at the level of immediate compliance rather than expecting sanctions (and hence force) to 'remedy' its breaches. Sanctions are valuable to those who esteem that the prospect of a cost associated with a transgression has an impact on behaviour, and hence in utilitarian societies in which the relationships between members are typically assessed in terms of costs and benefits. To people sharing this vision, costs and benefits have a universal import, but experience shows that the same does not apply to other societies, such as 'fundamentalist' societies, in which evidently a different view of law must be in operation.

(g) Convention

Law may also be considered, in Hart's words, simply as a set of rules that are 'thought of, spoken of, and function as such' in social practice.[66] Brian Tamanaha has developed such an approach by defining law as being 'whatever we attach the label *law* to',[67] meaning by 'social practice' that of legal officials 'as socially defined'.[68] Tamanaha rejects as 'myths' the typically Western ideas of progressive evolution and social contract underlying the theses that (a) law mirrors society; and (b) it contributes to social order, ie what he calls the 'mirror thesis' and the 'social order thesis', respectively.[69] This conventionalist, or anti-essentialist, view favours legal pluralism in that it elevates to law any practice that is regarded as law by its addressees, regardless of its origins, contents, purpose, procedure, essence, and so on. On this account, the rules prevailing in non-Western and stateless societies, and even those existing within criminal gangs, may qualify as law depending on their 'ability to exert an influence in given social arenas'.[70] This view also favours a notion of law that changes over time with people's beliefs and prevailing social opinion.

Conventionalist pluralism seems to accept that law coincides with what is treated as law by its addressees as a whole.[71] While there can be little doubt that law is far from being an exclusive product of the state, legal pluralism raises the problem that many 'private' rules (such as parents' orders addressed to their children or mafia injunctions) can hardly be seen as legal rules. In contrast, the view of law as collective violence depicted here means that law is made and applied, in the (right or wrong) perception of its members as a whole, on behalf and for the benefit of all, ie in *latu sensu* 'public' terms. If law is rooted in collective violence against individual violence, then there must be a 'public' sphere in any society, whatever the name and the form. Individuals are not permitted as such to make the law, unless the group as a whole grants (or delegates to) them a legitimate authority, to use common terms, to exercise such a power. There is a difference between the injunction of a gunman and the injunctions made by the group as a whole as 'law' in the perception of its members, including those who claim to have

66 Hart (n 41 above) 231, 235.

67 BZ Tamanaha, *A General Jurisprudence of Law and Society* (Oxford: OUP, 2001) 193 (original emphasis).

68 ibid 142, defining a legal official as 'whomever, as a matter of social practice, members of the group (including legal officials themselves) identify and treat as "legal" officials' (original emphasis omitted).

69 ibid 52–65.

70 ibid 225.

71 For other recent pluralist approaches to law, see E Melissaris, *Ubiquitous Law: Legal Theory and the Space for Legal Pluralism* (Farnham and Burlington: Ashgate, 2009); K Culver and M Giudice, *Legality's Borders: An Essay in General Jurisprudence* (Oxford and New York: OUP, 2010).

their 'own' law.[72] If mafia bosses want to 'lay down the law' beyond the sphere of their activities, they have to secede from the state (so long as the national community believes that only the state is their political organization) and successfully create another political (hence 'public') entity. Until then, their commands are not law at all, although they may happen to work within the mafia clans and guide their behaviour.[73] Mafia bosses themselves in fact count on the law of the state every day as the 'true' law common to all, which they simply 'break' for their gain, just as do those who obey their commands. Another difficulty is that law may well work based on one or another 'myth', including Western myths, and it may even *require* myth to work.[74] Yet another difficulty is that Tamanaha himself defines a 'core concept' of law, purportedly immune from state-based and Western-biased myths, but still conceived of in terms of (typically Western) *general* (ie universal) jurisprudence, and this claim *itself* is open to confutation when tested against the practice of certain particular groups.[75]

Conclusion

This chapter started by noting that any discourse on international law presupposes a given conception of law, and ultimately one or another approach to human nature and social life, from which certain conclusions rather than others about law are derived. This implicit, unreflected conception of law 'as such' is autonomous and should be brought into light before investigating the particularities of international law. The chapter addressed two questions concerning law in general which are invariably involved in any discourse on international law, namely, 'What is the nature of law?' and 'How can law be distinguished from non-law?'. By developing Freud's insights into the social origins and nature of law and justice, this chapter argued that law is a form of collective violence against individual violence and that the distinction between law and non-law is relative to social context. Law is a social phenomenon both because it is created and sustained by society and because its legal quality depends on what its addressees as a whole in any particular society believe. The above analysis is aimed at introducing the view developed in this book that law in general, and international law in particular, is to be seen as a social construct.

72 cf Hart (n 41 above) 6–7; Kelsen (n 33 above) 31.

73 For a critique of Tamanaha's 'labeling test', see W Twining, 'A Post-Westphalian Conception of Law' (2003) 37 Law and Society Review 199, 223–31.

74 Ch 2 below, section A (3)(d).

75 Ch 2 below, n 78.

2

Myth

Chapter 1 set out from a realist stance the origins and nature of law, based on Freud's notion that law amounts to collective violence against individual violence, and developed, against conventional realism, that law is conceivable as a relatively stable balance of balances. Chapter 2 seeks, against legal deconstructionism,[1] to found the objective reality of law. It does so by discussing law as a social construct, consisting of both social aggregation and psychological belief, ultimately grounded in a mythic sense of commonality within any particular group. Law is defined as what is believed by a group as a whole to be their law. Its objectivity is created and imposed by the group on any member. At the same time, far from being a static field of observation from without, law depends on social change and calls for struggle. It is argued that the 'reality' of law, including international law, is a function of the degree to which those who fight for law prevail over their opponents at any given moment. The struggle may be for either more or less law, or for progress or not, but should ultimately be for more justice in favour of the most vulnerable.

A. In Quest of Objectivity

What is, if any, the 'objective' reality of law? This section answers that law is objective as a socially constructed reality. It explores the notion of social construct and investigates how the reality of law is 'objectively' constructed in society and ultimately grounded in a mythic sense of commonality. Several possible objections are then countered. Finally, the argument is extended to international law.

(1) Social construct

What constitutes a 'social construct' or a 'social construction' is anything but clear.[2] A great many things are said to be socially constructed.[3] Philosophy, sociology, and psychology have developed different views from different perspectives on socially constructed objects. While the widely used passive 'socially constructed' may underlie both 'construct' and 'construction', these two terms remain conceptually distinct. Both seem to involve a human artifact, but a construct may refer either to 'an object of perception or thought' or to 'a concept specially devised to be part of a theory',[4] while a construction relates to the building of things and more generally to the process through which something becomes real. A social construct may be seen in particular as the product or resultant of the process of social construction, ie as the outcome of social construction moment after moment. The word 'construction' itself, though, may refer

[1] Ch 4 below, section B (5).
[2] I Hacking, *The Social Construction of What?* (Cambridge: Harvard University Press, 1999).
[3] ibid 1, for a list made out of titles from a library catalogue.
[4] cf *Oxford English Dictionary*, at <http://www.oed.com>.

to both process and product.[5] Even the use of the verb 'construct' rather than others (such as invent, produce, build, assemble, make, cause, control, structure, construe, manufacture) is obscure,[6] if not induced by publishers in the belief that it would sell more copies of a book.[7] The qualifier 'social', for its part, adumbrates that the 'construct' or the 'construction' is an act of imagination and symbolic representation underpinned by the living experiences and practices of all those concerned within a group, not a discrete individual act. It can also allude to the fact that people are (active) part of the process of its construction, as opposed to uninfluential (passive) observers. The word 'social' may also ambivalently refer both to *how* construction occurs or *what* is constructed: a non-social entity (eg an inner attitude of an individual) may be constructed socially, when society affects its formation, whereas a social entity (eg a group of protesters) may be constructed non-socially, when each has only a personal motivation. Further, social constructionism and social constructivism, although both concerned with the process of creation of reality by humans in society, are at times considered to be distinct,[8] and other variations are possible, such as constructionalism.[9] To complicate matters, the difference between 'social construction of reality'[10] and 'construction of social reality'[11] may raise difficulties. A 'weak' version of constructionism is often set against a 'strong' version thereof. While the former claims that social reality is built upon natural (ie human-independent reality), the latter contends that even natural reality is socially constructed, irrespective of whether natural reality exists or not.[12] Applied to IR theory, constructivism argues that international relations are historically and socially contingent, rather than inevitable consequences of human nature or other essential structures of world politics.[13] IR theory's constructivism has also been sharply distinguished from Kantian moral constructivism.[14]

To claim that a certain reality is a 'social construct', or a 'social construction', or 'socially constructed', basically means that it is a product of human social interactions rather than existing independent of human beings. To show the contingency, or non-inevitability, of taken-for-granted realities, often also implying or conveying an agenda

[5] Hacking (n 2 above) 36–8.

[6] ibid 49–50, noting that literally the term 'construction' refers to building or assembling things of the real world, such as a five-string banjo, not to metaphors, as it is recurrently used.

[7] ibid 18.

[8] For a table sorting out variations on the use of the terms 'constructionism' and 'constructivism', see B Kim, 'Social Constructivism', at <http://projects.coe.uga.edu/epltt/index.php?title=Social_Constructivism>.

[9] Hacking (n 2 above) 44–9.

[10] PL Berger and T Luckmann, *The Social Construction of Reality: A Treatise in the Sociology of Knowledge* (New York: Anchor Books, 1966).

[11] See n 21 below.

[12] R Mallon, 'Naturalistic Approaches to Social Construction', in Stan EP, at <http://plato.stanford.edu/entries/social-construction-naturalistic/index.html>.

[13] A Wendt, 'Anarchy is What States Make of It: The Social Construction of Power Politics' (1992) 46 *International Organization* 391; A Wendt, *Social Theory of International Politics* (Cambridge: CUP, 1999); JG Ruggie, 'What Makes the World Hang Together? Neo-utilitarianism and the Social Constructivist Challenge' (1998) 52 *International Organization* 855; M Finnemore and K Sikkink, 'International Norm Dynamics and Political Change' (1998) 52 *International Organization* 887. For a critical appraisal, see JT Checkel, 'The Constructivist Turn in International Relations Theory' (1998) 50 *World Politics* 324, noting that IR constructivism lacks a theory of agency and 'overemphasizes the role of social structures and norms at the expense of the agents who help create and change them in the first place'.

[14] See J Rawls. 'Kantian Constructivism in Moral Theory' (1980) 77 JPh 515; O O'Neill, *Constructions of Reason: Explorations of Kant's Practical Philosophy* (Cambridge: CUP, 1990).

for change, is the core matrix of social construction.[15] How 'real' such reality is depends on how *humans see* it in *society*. That is, it depends on how human beings believe that something is real as a result of their interaction. This has a number of implications. First, to say that something is socially constructed may mean that its existence is not based on some timeless essence or inherent qualities, such as 'nature' or 'biological structure', and hence that it can indeed be changed by human practice. Reality is no longer assumed or taken as given, fixed, or immutable, but rather negotiated out of interactions within specified communities.[16] At the same time, communities are seen as an active part of the process of reality construction and not only as uninfluential observers or passive receivers. Secondly, it may mean that a certain reality is the product of what people within a community believe or are made to believe (for example through the media) either to 'deconstruct' such beliefs as non-genuine or to 'construct' and reproduce them as genuine. Thirdly, it may mean that reality is not necessarily based on criteria of scientific validity and that even unscientific truth may fully count as reality to the people who believe it as their reality. What matters is what people believe, not what is scientifically well-founded, and the two notions may not coincide. Fourthly, it may mean that a certain reality is created and makes sense in a group of individuals, rather than within the inner sphere of single individuals, thereby implying that what single individuals believe in, within or without the group, is irrelevant with regard to what reality is within the group. Social construction is thus assumed to be different from individual psychological construction, although it may be the sum of individual psychological constructions.[17] Fifthly, it may mean that research should focus on the practices of social construction in order to better understand both why a certain reality is as it is today, as a result of past practices, and how it can be changed for tomorrow, as a result of current and future practices. Thus defined, a social construct or construction emphasizes the process of changing that reality constantly undergoes. Sixthly, it may mean that this reality is constructed on behalf and for the benefit of certain people or groups and to the detriment of others. In this sense, a claim that a certain reality is socially constructed may not only indicate that reality can be changed but also that it should be, by way of reform or revolution. It is a fact that individuals and subgroups are always struggling with one another to make their own construction of reality prevail and be the one accepted by all as the 'objective' reality in the group. Seventhly, it may mean that reality does not come 'for free', or for the sole reason that it is the 'reality'. It is thus assumed that a struggle is to be engaged in to control and change people's hearts and minds against others who are struggling in the opposite direction. Finally, it may mean that the actors themselves who construct reality are socially constructed rather than 'givens'. What the actors believe as the reality of their surroundings is thus taken as susceptible of change as a direct result of the change in their very essence. For example, states may make decisions more responsive to moral considerations, rather than to realpolitik, if their calculations about their self-interest are changed through social interactions from within or without.[18] All these meanings are clearly interconnected and, therefore, are assumed here.

[15] Hacking (n 2 above) 6–7, 12, noting that social constructionism usually holds, on the precondition that (0) *X* is taken for granted; that (1) *X* is not inevitable; (2) *X* is quite bad as it is; and (3) we would be much better off if *X* were done away with or at least radically transformed. He also points out, however, that not all constructionists go as far as thesis (3) or even (2).

[16] TJ Bierstecker and C Weber, *State Sovereignty as Social Construct* (Cambridge: CUP, 1996) 11.

[17] G Kelly, *The Psychology of Personal Constructs* (New York: Norton, 1955) 2 vols.

[18] Ch 5 below, n 153.

The key criticism of social constructionism, especially in the 'strong' variation, is relativism and subjectivism.[19] It appears anti-naturalistic and anti-scientific on the one hand, and anti-religious on the other. The same 'thing' can be either real or unreal to different people in different places at different times. It is the notion itself of the 'thing' (namely, of the 'essence') that social constructionism challenges. As hinted earlier, this relativism may conceal or convey an underlying agenda, ie how and towards which direction undesired realities can and should be changed. If reality is what we make of it, then we can always make it differently. Any suggested change, in turn, aims at favouring people or groups other than those who are believed to benefit from the current 'reality', and social constructionism often sounds emancipatory. It can, however, also be used in a conservative, if not in a reactionary, sense since when opinions are as good as any other there appears to be no ground for criticizing oppressive ideas, historical revisionism, religious fundamentalism, and the like.[20] It is thus necessary to address the question of whether and in what sense the reality which is socially constructed (such as law) is 'objective'.

(2) Constructing social reality

In *The Construction of Social Reality* John R Searle, while defending 'the idea that there is a reality which is totally independent of us' (so-called 'brute facts', like a mountain or the sun), argued that 'institutional facts', ie facts involving human institutions, such as money, property, governments, and marriages, depend on (or exist by) human agreement and are thus a construction of social reality.[21] For example, 'the bits of paper in my pocket are money only because we believe it is money'.[22] It is necessary, for paper to be money, that it works as money in most cases among most people, regardless of individual instances and persons.[23] It is also necessary that money exists in some physical form, such as paper: the paper exists even if no one believes it is paper and is a 'brute fact', but this does not prevent this same paper from working as money in so far as it is believed to be money.[24] A planet exists in a sense that is different from a dollar bill.[25] Three elements are required for the construction of social reality, namely: (a) assignment of a function to facts or objects, whether naturally occurring or created especially to perform the assigned function (on the assumption that functions and purposes are socially assigned, as opposed to being intrinsic, to facts); (b) collective intentionality (ie beliefs, desires, and intentions shared by people and different from singular intentionality and mere cooperative behaviour); and (c) constitutive rules (as opposed to regulative rules).[26]

[19] See eg JA Rabkin, *Law without Nations?: Why Constitutional Government Requires Sovereign States* (Princeton, NJ: Princeton University Press, 2005) 14–16. For a critique of the 'moral relativism' and 'purely social construct' understanding of reality and law by legal postmodern deconstructionism (on which see Ch 4 below, section B (5)) from a behavioural biological and neuro-scientist perspective based on the derivation of all human behaviour and legal systems from objective brain physical processes at individual level, see ES Fruehwald, *Law and Human Behavior: A Study in Behavioral Biology, Neuroscience, and the Law* (Lake Mary: Vandeplas Publishing LLC, 2011) 43–85.

[20] Hacking, (n 2 above) 3–5.

[21] JR Searle, *The Construction of Social Reality* (New York: Free Press, 1995) 1–2. More recently, see JR Searle, *Making the Social World: The Structure of Human Civilization* (Oxford: OUP, 2010), expounding a more general theory of which the previous one is seen as a special aspect and implementation.

[22] Searle (1995) (n 21 above) 3, 32, 42–3 ('If everybody always thinks that this sort of thing is money, and they use it as money and treat it as money, then it is money. If nobody ever thinks this sort of thing is money, then it is not money').

[23] ibid 32–3. [24] ibid 34–5. [25] ibid 36. [26] ibid 13–57.

There is no need here to dwell on the philosophical question about the 'reality' of what Searle calls 'brute facts'.[27] Suffice it to assume that law belongs to what Searle calls 'institutional facts'—at least as far as it is managed and 'lived' by human beings for social purposes—and can be viewed as an objective reality in so far as those involved, particularly its addressees as a whole, such as laymen and judges, 'believe' that it is the law and act upon such a belief.

(a) Objectivity in society

Most people believe that 'facts' are 'objective' in the sense that their existence is 'given' and not dependent on what we may think or believe. The 'facts come first' imagery of empiricism or positivism asserts that there is an 'objective reality'. Friedrich Nietzsche famously remarked that 'the factual is always stupid and has at all times resembled a calf rather than a god' until people give it a meaning and the meanings given by different people are often divergent, thus spurring conflicts the winner of which will 'certify' *which* facts count as 'real'.[28] The essentialistic confidence in an 'objective essence' of the things that populate our world is based on transcendentalism, ie on a parallel confidence in an 'essence' of things transcending all our subjective opinions and judgment. Essentialism tends then to present itself as neutral, apolitical, uncontroversial, totalizing (in antithesis to the particular, partial, opinion of certain individuals or groups), independent of gender, religion, culture, ideology, etc. Things are deemed to exist not because I say so but because they are so, regardless of whether I say so or not. The essence is generally self-explanatory or self-evident and is assumed to 'speak for itself'. Legal deconstructivists insist that essentialism and transcendentalism, far from being 'neutrally' grounded in the things themselves, are profoundly ideological and serve the interests of the dominating classes and individuals in society. This debate is to be taken seriously and requires us to analyse the concept of objectivity, beginning with objectivity in society.

The term 'objectivity' is used in several different meanings and every answer to the question of whether there is anything 'objective' in society and what is objective social reality may vary accordingly. Different answers (either positive or negative) may be given to the same question as a function of what is meant by the very question. Something (including law) may be 'objective' in one respect but not in another. To critique law for lack of objectivity is of little help if objectivity has different meanings, unless persuasive articulation is provided about the respect in which law is not objective.

Searle usefully distinguishes between epistemic objectivity, ontological objectivity, and intrinsic objectivity. *Epistemic* objectivity refers to *judgements* about facts (as distinct from facts themselves) if truth or falsity can be settled regardless of the feelings of their makers or hearers.[29] For example, a judgement such as 'Rembrandt is a better artist than Rubens' (or 'I am better than you') is generally perceived as subjective, while a

[27] ibid xii–xiii, 2, 55–6, 149–97. For a recent, in-depth discussion on objectivity, see T Burge, *Origins of Objectivity* (Oxford: Clarendon Press, 2010).

[28] FW Nietzsche, *Unzeitgemässe Betrachtungen*, II, *Vom Nutzen und Nachteil der Historie für das Leben* (Leipzig: EW Fritzsch, 1874) 265 ('das Faktum immer dumm ist und zu allen Zeiten einem Kalbe ähnlicher gesehen hat als einem Gotte'), English trans *Untimely Meditations* (Cambridge: CUP, 1997) 106.

[29] Searle (1995) (n 21 above) 8.

judgement like 'Rembrandt lived in Amsterdam during the year 1632' (or 'I was born in Rome') is perceived as objective. Searle aptly points out that the distinction is anything but settled and a matter of degree. The assertion 'I am better than you' usually sounds *less* objective than the assertion 'I was born in Rome'. The key factor to draw and 'measure' the distinction is the degree of 'objective' ascertainment. This, in turn, depends on the existence of a commonly agreed test of truth: if you and I trust empirical verification as a test of truth (rather than, say, a certain reading of a sacred book or the word of a reputed sorcerer), then we may have a look at the Registry Office (in which we trust), find that I 'really' was born in Rome, and conclude that what I asserted was an objective judgement. Likewise, my claim that 'I am better than you' sounds less objective because it is generally more difficult to prove and is exposed to contestations of comparable dignity. In reverse, if my test of truth is empirical verification and yours is the word of a reputed sorcerer, and if the truths flowing from these two different tests happen to be different, then you and I will never reach an unequivocal conclusion about which of the two claims is 'objective'. It is worth noting that only by a commonly agreed objectivity standard, such as empirical verification, or the word of a reputed sorcerer, or other, can epistemic objectivity be demonstrated. Objectivity (of someone's judgement) is then defined in terms of objectivity (of the test of truth) commonly shared by a circle of unidentified subjects covering at a very minimum the two interlocutors. When the circle extends to society as a whole, the shared test of truth (whether empirical verification, or the word of a reputed sorcerer, or other) 'certifies' objectivity within the group, in the sense that it makes the disputed fact 'certain' for social purposes.

Ontological objectivity refers to *facts* themselves when their existence is independent of their perception by some sentient being.[30] For example, pains are subjective in so far as their existence depends on their perception by someone, whereas mountains are objective in that their mode of existence is independent of any perceiver. While a mountain is thought to exist even without any sentient being living on earth, pains cannot exist without sentient beings who experience them. Interestingly, the objectivity of a mountain is imagined as existing even when no human being lives on earth and can talk or think about it, a rather extravagant *subjective* hypothesis: when there are no human beings on earth, ontological objectivity will be pointless, but until human beings live on earth, such objectivity can hardly be seen as really independent of human beings. Be that as it may, when dealing with ontological objectivity facts are perceived or stated as independent of what 'anyone' might think, believe, or sense. This 'anyone' may refer either to particular trustworthy individuals, or to groups, or to the whole human race, with a variety of possible different meanings attachable to objectivity. The car I am driving can be said to exist 'objectively' either because it exists independently of what *I* believe about its existence (which may be successfully challenged by others if I am mentally insane or currently under the influence of drugs), or because it exists independently of what *all human beings* believe about its existence, or both. The same fact, like a car, can thus be objective in some respects (it may exist *despite my particular belief* in its inexistence because all my friends believe it exists) and subjective in others (it may not exist *despite my friends' belief* that it exists because all human beings on earth other than my friends believe that it does not exist): what is 'objective' in the first context turns out to be subjective in the second context.

[30] ibid 8–9.

Intrinsic objectivity relates to the intrinsic features of an object (like its mass or chemical composition) and is contrasted by Searle with *intentional* subjectivity, which is understood as dependent on the attitudes of observers and users. It is to be noted that observation and use are themselves also intrinsic features of the perceiver, although they become agent-relative only when referred to other agents and to objects or facts existing outside the perceiver. They can thus be viewed as a manifestation of (intentional) subjectivity or of (intrinsic) objectivity depending on the respect in which they are considered. For example, the assertion 'this object is a stone' (or 'this is a piece of timber') is objective in terms of the intrinsic features of the stone (or of the timber), while the assertion 'this object is a paperweight' (or 'this is a table'), referring to the very same stone (or piece of timber), is subjective in terms of the use of the stone (or of timber) which is created by the mental phenomena of the user, which in their turn are intrinsic to the user. Such mental phenomena are ontologically subjective (in that they exist because sentient beings perceive them) and may also be epistemically subjective (in that the judgement about them is not objectively ascertainable). The assertion 'this object is a paperweight' is epistemically objective (in that its truth is objectively ascertainable), while the assertion 'the moon is beautiful tonight' is epistemically subjective (in that its truth cannot be objectively ascertained), although both are observer- or user-relative (in that they are considered from someone's viewpoint rather than based on their intrinsic features). Inevitably, for the distinction between intrinsic and observer-relative to make sense, there must be a commonly shared test of intrinsicness.[31] The belief that mass or chemical composition are 'intrinsic' properties may be correct, but the fact is that people may well come to share and give more weight to a different belief. History shows that many different tests of intrinsicness have taken over and supplanted others.

All the above distinctions and examples show that the question of whether an assertion or an object (including law and legal statements) is 'objective' or not is incredibly multilayered and makes little sense when posed in general terms. The various notions of objectivity cut across each other and it is difficult to see what counts as 'objective reality' in society.[32] One can plausibly claim both that objectivity is impossible and that it is inescapable.

It seems that 'objectivity' is what is seen from a hypothetical 'external point of view', external to our subjective perception and judgement, a sort of God's eye view, or of some Super Mind floating somewhere outside the human world, a perspective which does not suffer from any defective or biased human attitude. In this sense 'objective' means non-humanly biased. But we know no one other than humans in a position to tell us what a non-human could capture about human life. Our problem is that every point of view we take is irremediably our own, hence 'internal'. We can split, by our imaginative force, reality into external and internal and believe in this opposition as real. In so far as all of us share and act upon this belief, this belief is our reality and the opposition itself is absolutely real. There is no way to prove that it is unreal, *unless one changes the whole viewpoint* and becomes dissident within the group. Human beings can *always* split the matters believed until then as objective into (a) what is seen 'from within'; and (b) what is seen 'from without', or into (a) what is seen from an 'insider's viewpoint' (referred to

[31] See eg S Yablo, 'Intrinsicness', at <http://www.mit.edu/~yablo/intrinsicness.html>.

[32] Not only objective facts (like 'Mt Everest is 8848 meters high') but also subjective facts (like 'My backache is unbearable') may be the subject of either objective judgements (like 'I have a backache') or subjective judgements (like 'Mt Everest is more beautiful than Mt Whitney'), clearly a subjective judgement about objective entities. cf Searle (1995) (n 21 above) 8–9.

one or more individuals or groups); and (b) what is seen from an 'outsider viewpoint' (referred to 'other' individuals or groups, and ultimately to God as the Outsider *par excellence* in respect of human bias). It is sufficient to imagine and campaign for a view divergent from that which prevailed until then. This, however, implies that objectivity itself—apart from the objectivity of this or that matter—is dependent on our imaginative force and ability to raise and successfully publicize questions. It depends *in concreto* on the emergence of disputes about the existence or the mode of existence of anything, including statements about objectivity. Put differently, objectivity is a context-relative, multilayered dimension, and subjectivity is in turn objectivity relative. Everything is objective in a sense (or to some people) and subjective in another (or to other people).

It is always possible for human beings to invent an 'external' (supposedly disinterested) viewpoint, thus creating also a parallel 'internal' (supposedly biased) viewpoint, and to sell the former as the 'objective' view. This is, in fact, a typical strategy for groups wishing to credit themselves with righteousness and great care for all. Human beings actually struggle to the death for what should be seen as objective. Objectivity does not really exist until it is actually questioned: before being challenged, it coincides with 'normality', a dimension in which there is neither objectivity nor subjectivity: what is 'normal', ie universally unquestioned, is objective and subjective at the same time because what is believed by anyone is also believed by all. Objectivity emerges as a challenge to normality by someone in the flesh, not as a pure concept in the speculative mind of some disinterested academics. The challengers claim to be 'objective'—thus identifying and taking an outsider's viewpoint towards all those who continue to believe in the 'normal' standpoint—and accuse those who now appear as the opponents of subjectivity. At this juncture, with the emerged objectivity–subjectivity dichotomy, the advocates of the earlier normal view cannot but accuse the challengers of subjectivity by presenting themselves as objective. While this occurs and produces a layer of discourse, an endless number of other aspects of life remain unchallenged: what is now objective (or subjective) in the matter challenged can be subjective (or objective) in other matters.

In summary, objectivity is 'objectively' what is believed to be so by all those concerned in a community, ranging from a small community of two people to all humanity. Both what is believed to be objective and the 'objectivity test' used depend on universal belief. It is for the appropriation of the 'objectivity test' that people compete every day with one another. The objectivity of those who prevail is objectivity in the group, whatever dissenters or members of other groups may think or believe.

(b) Objectivity in law

When rejecting the objectivity of law, deconstructionists contend that there can be no objective ascertainment of law. This may derive from a lack of objectivity both in the existence of law and in its ascertainment. If law 'itself' is not objective (in that it exists only if it is perceived by at least one human being), then whatever is said of it can always be said to be dependent on the perception and bias of the perceiver. Divergences over law 'as it is' would endlessly multiply if there is no test of independence of reality from the perception structure of the perceiver generally shared in the group. Divergences will give rise to indeterminacy and conflicts between different stakeholders, such as defendants, plaintiffs, lawyers, judges, law scholars, etc over what should qualify as law. Moreover, the perceiver may make judgements about law that are not objective (in that they are not objectively ascertained) and there can be no common test of truth generally shared in the group. Both ontological and epistemic objectivity may be missing when law is regarded as observer- or user-relative and cannot be defined in terms of its 'intrinsic' features due to the absence of a generally agreed test of determining what counts as 'intrinsic'. Deconstructionists claim that law is neither ontologically objective (in that it does not exist without humans, unlike mountains), nor intrinsically objective (in that it has no 'intrinsic' features dissectible from the observer or user), nor epistemically objective (in that all judgments about law are impossible to ascertain objectively). These assertions evidently presuppose that there are no universally accepted tests of independence, intrinsicness, and truth in the group involved. Behind all this lies the assumption that law 'is not a mountain', ie a 'fact' in positivistic terms, that 'the fact is always stupid', as Nietzsche warned,[33] and that meanings attached to law are always the result of ongoing conflicts.

However, whether such tests are, or are not, available and what kind of test should be trusted to make this determination is the point to be demonstrated. It may be that truth, independence, and intrinsicness do not pass a test based on the scientific method, but it may also be the case that the addressees of law (laymen, judges, lawyers, etc) in a particular community generally share another kind of test of truth, independence, and intrinsicness, such as the word of God, as distilled by a number of clergymen or internally perceived by the single faithful, or flowing directly from the word of a supreme sorcerer. Of course, this kind of test may be philosophically questioned as false, idiotic, or dangerous by this or that critic, but law is different from philosophical speculation precisely because it is something that is deemed to *work* in society and society is made up of all kinds of people with very different inclinations and resources, whether physical or intellectual. An unfathomable word of God or the esoteric teachings of a supreme sorcerer may well work better in society than a law 'scientifically' demonstrated in the perception of the people concerned, as experience largely shows. Criticisms of such approaches from the outside, or from a dissident insider, may appear fully justified to other observers, including the present writer, but law is not what this or that critic argues, it is what the community as a whole believes it to be. It is only *this* law that the people concerned will obey as law. Any other law is speculation and, at best, an input for change in the law as part of a plan of action for a better law in the future, once society has changed its attitude and belief. After all, it is not a mystery that people, deconstructionists included, use and profit from law in any society, whatever its indeterminacy. This suggests that there must be something else to be accounted for when law is considered, and that it would not be surprising if law turned out to be, on closer examination, an 'objective' experience, despite its denounced indeterminacy and lack of objectivity.

Six different conceptions of objectivity of law (along with a few 'ancillary conceptions') have been usefully proposed in the literature,[34] of which three are ontological (mind independence, determinate correctness, and uniform applicability), two are epistemic (transindividual discernibility and impartiality) and one is semantic in its orientations (truth-aptitude). From this analysis, objectivity in law may take on a variety of different meanings and what is objective in one respect may not be objective

[33] See n 28 above.

[34] MH Kramer, *Objectivity and the Rule of Law* (Cambridge: CUP, 2007). See in addition K Greenwalt, *Law and Objectivity* (New York and Oxford: OUP, 1992); N Stavropoulos, *Objectivity in Law* (New York and Oxford: Clarendon Press, 1996); B Leiter (ed), *Objectivity in Law and Morals* (Cambridge: CUP, 2001); CS Rosati, 'Some Puzzles about the Objectivity of Law' (2004) 23 *Law and Philosophy* 273.

in another. For example, as to mind interdependence, law can be said to be objective in the sense that (a) separate individuals' opinions or preferences are irrelevant in respect of what judges will state as the law; or (b) separate judges' opinions are irrelevant in respect of the previous jurisprudence, and further instances in the same proceedings, or in respect of the law-maker; or (c) the law-maker's opinion itself is irrelevant in respect of certain principles of public morality or of natural law. Determinate correctness implies that there is only one correct answer to a problematic legal question. Thus defined, the objectivity of law has been particularly challenged by legal deconstructionists by reliance on divergences among courts in hard cases. The reply has been that law is in most cases determinate, although it may be neither demonstrable nor predictable, and that absolute determinacy is impossible.[35] Uniform applicability refers to the application of law alike to everyone, irrespective of their preferences and inclinations. Everyone is judged by reference to the same criteria, although the outcomes may be more favourable to certain people. To say that law is not objective because it is not 'neutral' is different from saying that law is not objective because it is not uniformly applied. No law is absolutely neutral, but certain forms of law are uniform in application, whatever they prescribe. Transindividual discernibility refers to the ability of all (or nearly all) those concerned to concur on what is the law. It is argued that when there is such concurrence the tastes of individuals are not dispositive touchstones for what can warrantedly be affirmed. Impartiality refers to disinterestedness, absence of prejudice, and favouritism, as opposed to bias and partisanship. Truth-aptitude relates to the possibility of asserting meaningful statements endowed with truth-values, ie values of 'true' or 'false'. To the extent that law is susceptible to being described by such statements, it is semantically objective.

Overall, it is difficult to deny that people more often than not perceive law as objective in at least one of the above meanings and that law generally works as objective despite its alleged indeterminacy.

(3) Mythic foundations

Social constructivism, focused as it often is on unmasking the contingency of current realities, generally fails to explore and explain the 'reality' of social constructs. This section suggests that the process of the social construction of law is ultimately founded in myth.

The relationship between social construct and myth is hard to grasp in social science terms. On one view the two notions are deeply opposed. While myth refers to the sphere of the archaic, obscurantist, circular, passively received, backward-looking, conservative (if not downright reactionary), and politically manipulative, social construction sounds modern, linear, self-empowering, future-orientated, liberating, progressive, possibly democracy-driven. On a second view myth is just one form of social construction among many others. Societies, it is argued, construct a large variety of 'realities', and myths are those constructs which do not reflect 'reality' in a scientific sense, but are irrational beliefs socially induced by such means as propaganda, misinformation, fake, fraud, and the like. This conception is reflected in a wide range of essays entitled 'the social construction of the *X* myth', implying that *X* is false and needs to be demystified. It is not in this restrictive and indeed popular sense that it is here proposed to deal with myth. It is, rather, suggested that the process of social

[35] Kramer (n 34 above) 16–18.

construction, and all social constructs, whether true or untrue in scientific terms, are part of a mythic vision and shared sense of commonality within those who believe themselves to be part of the same community. For present purposes, therefore, the commonly accepted relationship is reversed: it is not myth that is the product of social construction, but rather it is social construction that is the product of myth.

The question of defining myth is clearly to be addressed first, before addressing the question of the relationship between myth and reality, in particular how myth has historically been repeatedly 'overcome' by other non-mythic visions, as is manifestly the case with metaphysics taking over mythology in ancient Greece and science taking over metaphysics in modern times. Myth then appears as an all-pervasive dimension of human life which materializes only at the moment of demythologization, this being possible by way of a remythologization in another direction. This section argues that law is a social construct that needs collective mythic belief to work. There can be no law without a shared myth of law, and no law can be expected to work effectively without a surrounding myth.

(a) Defining myth

The term 'myth' comes from the Greek *mythos*, meaning etymologically 'word' or 'story'. In early Greek literature its meaning developed from a 'true story', 'an account of facts', to an 'invented story', a legend, fairy story, fable, or poetic creation. In later Greek thought *mythos* came to stand in antithesis both to *logos* (reason) and *historia* (historical account) and so came to denote 'what cannot really exist'.[36] In nineteenth-century Western Europe, the term was generally given the 'classical' meaning of something opposed to reality: a fabulous, untrue story about gods (or demi-gods) set at the dawn of time. It has been suggested that 'In popular usage the term "myth" is almost always intended pejoratively', as 'erroneous beliefs clung to against all evidence'.[37] In everyday language myth is more frequently associated with a range of experiences including illusion, lie, childish credence, fabrication, manipulation, subjective opinion, utopian ideal, expression of naive religious (if not animistic and magical, in any case emotional) feelings, authoritarianism, irrationalism, ideology, unfounded or unproven but fashionable conviction, legend, saga, folk tale, fairy tale, deceit, and prejudice. A scientific definition of myth is extremely difficult.[38] Myth has been the subject of several opposing theories, and is variously studied by several disciplines.[39] For the sake of simplicity and convenience, attention will be concentrated here on three key conceptions of myth, namely: (a) myth as a false or imperfect truth; (b) myth as an autonomous form of truth; and (c) myth as a technique of social control.

Defined as an imperfect, inferior form of knowledge compared to rational knowledge, myth can be traced back to ancient Greek thought. The conventional account is that philosophers' *logos* supplanted poets' *mythos* at the dawn of Western philosophical thinking.[40] Xenophanes claimed that the myths of the poets had nothing to do with the

[36] J-P Vernant, *Mythe et société en Grèce ancienne* (Paris: Librairie François Maspero, 1974), English trans *Myth and Society in Ancient Greece* (New York: Zone Books, 1990) 203–26.

[37] PS Cohen, 'Theories of Myth' (1969) 4 *Man* 337–53.

[38] A Dundes (ed), *Sacred Narrative: Readings in the Theory of Myth* (Berkeley, Los Angeles, and London: University of California Press, 1984).

[39] eg seven theories have been proposed by Cohen (n 37 above).

[40] See KA Morgan, *Myth and Philosophy from the Presocratic to Plato* (Cambridge: CUP, 2000); R Buxton (ed), *From Myth to Reason? Studies in the Development of Greek Thought* (Oxford: OUP, 2001).

true religion.[41] Plato set myth against truth,[42] stating that myth attains verisimilitude rather than truth, but also recognizing that verisimilitude occasionally is the sole possible knowledge available to human beings.[43] Myth is presented by Plato as 'old wives' chatter'[44] which, while indemonstrable, has anyway some moral or religious weight in guiding conduct.[45] A similar approach was adopted by Aristotle, who at times opposed myth to truth,[46] and at other times regarded myth as an approximate or imperfect form of truth.[47] Crates defined myth as 'a representation of what has not happened and is not true'.[48] Plutarch noted that '*mythos* means a false *logos* similar to a true one'.[49] St Paul contrasted Jesus's message of salvation as the truth with the myths of the heathens.[50] At the turn of the nineteenth century the dominant view among European anthropologists was that myth expressed some truth of primitive man,[51] such as his speculation about the heavens and the annual cycle of nature and fertility, his handling of fears of the unknown (particularly death and beyond), his conceptualization of the mysterious in his present experience (gods, demons, spirits), and his attempts to control and manipulate these powers by ritual magic. Myths are thus frequently related to religion and to beliefs concerning the origin of the universe, salvation, and the ultimate destiny of humanity in the forms of cosmogonic, soteriological, and eschatological narratives.

Myth has also been defined in terms of an original, autonomous form of knowledge which, although different in nature, has the same dignity as rational knowledge or intellectual truth. It was the Italian philosopher Giambattista Vico who first explicitly developed this concept, suggesting that myth fully attains truth, although in a fantastic and poetic manner.[52] Friedrich WJ Schelling, a nineteenth-century German Idealist philosopher, took this concept one step further by regarding myth as the natural religion of the human race and an integral part of God's process of self-revelation.[53] His notion that myths are not the product of a rational mind but that of a much earlier unconscious activity—hence the expression of the subconscious, the archetypal images rising from the depths of human beings, often drawing on the psychic heritage of centuries—has been seen as a precursor to Carl G Jung's archetypes.[54] Mircea Eliade also spoke of myth as 'a living thing' which, far from indicating a fiction, reveals the truth *par excellence* and absolute reality,[55] still present but camouflaged in the banalities of everyday life within the modern desacralized Western world.[56] A leading exponent of

[41] Xenophanes, B 11 DK. [42] Plato, *Gorgias*, 523a.
[43] Plato, *Timaeus*, 29c–d; Plato, *The Republic*, 377a.
[44] Plato, *Theaetetus*, 176b. [45] Plato, *Gorgias*, 526a–b.
[46] Aristotle, *Historia Animalium*, VIII, 12, 597a 7. [47] ibid VI, 35, 580a 18.
[48] Crates, fr 18 Mette.
[49] Plutarch, *De Gloria Atheniensium*, English trans *On the Fame of Athenians*, 4, 348b.
[50] St Paul, 2 Tim 4:4; Titus 1:14; 1 Tim 4:7; 2 Pet 4:16.
[51] JG Frazer, *Folklore in the Old Testament* (London: Macmillan, 1918) vol 1, 362–87; EB Tylor, *The Origins of Culture* (New York: Harper, 1958) 368–416.
[52] G Vico, *New Science: Principles of the New Science Concerning the Common Nature of Nations, Third edition Thoroughly Corrected, Revised, and Expanded by the Author* [1744] (London: Penguin Books, 2001) IV; ibid VI, X, IX, arguing that myth is true narration (*vera narratio*), a 'mental language common to all nations'. For an insightful analysis, see J Mali, *The Rehabilitation of Myth: Vico's 'New Science'* (Cambridge: CUP, 1992).
[53] FWJ Von Schelling, *Philosophie der Mythologie—in drei Vorlesungsnachschriften* [1842] (Munich: Fink 1996), English trans *Historical-Critical Introduction to the Philosophy of Mythology* (Albany: State University of New York Press, 2007).
[54] CG Jung, *Memories, Dreams and Reflection* (London: ET, 1963) 343.
[55] M Eliade, *The Quest: History and Meaning in Religion* (Chicago: University of Chicago Press, 1969) 73; M Eliade, *Myth and Reality* (New York: Harper and Row, 1963) 139.
[56] M Eliade, *The Sacred and the Profane: The Nature of Religion* (New York: Harper and Row, 1961) 201–13.

the conception of myth as an autonomous form of truth is the twentieth-century neo-Kantian German philosopher Ernst Cassirer, who basically defined mythical thought in terms of an absent or imperfect distinction between the symbol and the symbolized, ie as absent or imperfect awareness of the symbol as a symbol.[57] In the *Essay on Man*, he focused on the emotional or sentimental (as opposed to intellectual) foundations of myth, the coherence of which was supposed to flow from a sentimental unit rather than from logical rules.[58] Myth as poetic truth capable of expressing a whole area of human experience and awareness that can only be presented in symbolic language was also evoked by the twentieth-century German psychiatrist and philosopher Karl Jaspers by hinting at 'the cipher language of myth',[59] based on images and analogy, without wishing to define the 'beyondness' or 'moreness' to life than eating, sleeping, working, or loving.[60] Advocates of myth as a non-intellectual expression of truth may also be found among sociologists like Emile Durkheim and Lucien Lévy-Bruhl. The former regarded myth as a form of maintaining and expressing solidarity and cohesion in society.[61] The latter defined mythical thought as pre-logical, typical as such of the primitive mind, in contrast to rational thinking, based on logic and inference, which was seen as typical of the civilized mind.[62]

Finally, myth has been conceived in terms of the function of social control it performs in society. Thus defined, myth is said to be found in any society, both primitive and modern. According to Bronislaw Malinowsky, myth is a form of legitimizing social institutions and practices by reinforcing tradition, and works in any culture 'as a justification by precedent' supplying 'a retrospective pattern of moral values, sociological order, and magical belief'.[63] His cultural theory of myth was thought to account for myth's 'intimate relation to belief... showing the close connection between ritual and tradition'.[64] A step forward in this perspective was Claude Levi-Strauss's work on the structure of myth and his comparative analysis of myths in different societies, as well as his view that myth is not a re-presentation of facts, a depiction of the real, but a justification of the shortcomings of reality.[65]

[57] E Cassirer, *Philosophie der symbolischen Formen. Zweiter Teil: Das mythische Denken* [1925] (Hamburg: Meiner, 2010), English trans *Philosophy of Symbolic Forms: Volume 2: Mythical Thought* (New Haven and London: Yale University Press, 1955).

[58] E Cassirer, *An Essay on Man: An Introduction to a Philosophy of Human Culture* [1944] (New Haven and London: Yale University Press, 1972). In *The Myth of the State* [1946] (New Haven and London: Yale University Press, 1977) the emphasis was on the dreadful resurrection of myth by the Nazis as something 'lurking in the dark and waiting for its hour and opportunity', a 'new thing' which is 'manufactured... as any other modern weapon' (at 280, 282).

[59] K Jaspers, 'Myth and Religion' in H-W Bartsch (ed), *Kerygma and Myth: A Theological Debate* (London: ET, 1962) 145.

[60] M Grant, *Myths of the Greeks and Romans* (London: Weidenfeld and Nicolson, 1962) xvii.

[61] E Durkheim, *Les formes élémentaires de la vie religieuse: le système totémique en Australie* [1912] (Paris: Les Presses universitaires de France, 1968), English trans *The Elementary Forms of Religious Life* (Mineola, New York: Dover Publications, 2008) 375.

[62] L Lévy-Bruhl, *La mentalité primitive* [1922] (Paris: Les Presses universitaires de France, 1960), English trans *Primitive Mentality* (New York: AMS Press, 1978); L Lévy-Bruhl, *L'âme primitive* [1927] (Paris: Les Presses universitaires de France, 1963), English trans *The 'Soul' of the Primitive* (New York: Macmillan, 1928).

[63] B Malinowski, 'Myth in Primitive Psychology' in *Magic, Science and Religion and Other Essays 1948* (Boston: Beacon Press, 1948) 78–9, 120, 122.

[64] ibid 120.

[65] C Lévi-Strauss, 'The Structural Study of Myth', in *Structural Anthropology* (New York: Basic Books, 1963); C Lévi-Strauss, 'The Story of Asdiwal', in E Leach (ed), *The Structural Study of Myth and Totemism* (London: Tavistock Publications, 1967) 29–30.

(b) Myth and reality

It thus seems that the hallmark of myth is elusiveness, beyondness, visibility, or relevance only from 'outsiders', enshrouding and involving any possible layer of supposed reality.

Myth has been mostly studied in respect of 'other' peoples by modern European scientists. The 'other' was the primitive in contrast to the modern and the non-Western in contrast to the Western. The popular idea that myth is a false truth invariably refers to the account of a certain reality that is 'lived' as true by others and taken by the observer as untrue. Myth is never 'ours', it is always 'theirs'. It seems inexorably to reflect the view of the *outsider*. Even in their inner sphere people live their present as non-mythic but find eventually, when looking at their past as outsiders, that they lived in what they can now call a mythic dimension, such as childhood. The unveiling of the past mythic 'truth' of what was non-mythic at the material time puzzlingly occurs from a further potential mythic dimension bound to remain invisible until it is unveiled as mythic. The unveiling of the myth that takes place when reality is seen from outside flies in the face of present self-evidence and common sense, proving disturbing and no longer acceptable. Myth invariably reveals 'another' truth (of another person, another community, another myself) as a false truth from the outside, while this truth is 'lived' as real and absolutely 'normal' from the inside. Myth is disentangled from reality by outsiders, but their outside is invariably the inside of a further outside. When myth appears, reality is lost, yet it indeed *was* reality. And the non-reality now unveiled appears in the name of (and thanks to) a current, obvious 'reality' that has the full potential of being in turn unveiled as mythic and non-real when the insider observer is displaced by the outsider. It seems that there can be no demythologizing without remythologizing. In short, myth is a narrative which refers to a per se non-mythic reality by unveiling it as mythic from the viewpoint of another lived reality that is potentially capable of being further unveiled as mythic. The relationship of myth to reality is thus fourfold: myth is the narrative of the (1) unreality of a (2) reality from the viewpoint of (3) another reality, in turn capable of being unveiled as (4) unreal.

Thus defined, myth goes beyond, or lies behind, both truth and untruth. Statements about truth and untruth presuppose some faith in the criteria used to measure truth and untruth. I can say that something is true or untrue because I trust the test I use which enables me to make the statement, such as empirical verification. I 'trust' the test, I cannot provide any explanation thereof in any form. If I introduce criteria to 'prove' that my test is better than others, and hence the result of a 'reasonable' trust, then it is these criteria that I trust 'unreasonably' unless I introduce further criteria, and so forth in an endless circle. Myth is lived 'before' any conscious making sense of the world as a whole, inclusive of tests of truth. It always unconsciously precedes any kind of account of the world in both logical or pre-logical terms, and is destined to be 'unmasked', sooner or later, inevitably as emotion and unreflected faith. It constantly generates a shift from reality to non-reality, from what is lived as absolutely real to what is uncovered as absolute imagery. This imagery, once emerged, may also be conceptually kept distinct from other beliefs, such as superstition, legend, magic, or dream, in order to create a reliability scale of beliefs.

Myth is also a social phenomenon for social purposes. So-called 'personal' myths have a meaning only within a surrounding society. Myths are shared and gain their strength from the physical and psychological strength of the group. In this sense, myths are always ritual, ie 'the spoken part of a ritual, the story which the ritual enacts',[66] or 'a reality lived',[67] within the group. Rituals are inherently collective either because enacted by the group or because they take such a meaning from the group. Myth, however, lies beyond ritual. Myth is the underlying, unreflected belief and confidence in both the ritual and in its social and personal effects.

In summary, myth is the underlying, all-pervasive dimension of human life and imagery. It emerges whenever a certain reality is 'unveiled' as false on the basis of a new reality, ie when a social group challenges a certain 'normal' condition as 'non-normal' (hence arbitrary, unjustified, unproven, inequitable, authoritarian, etc) by using a strategy (whether intellectual, or philosophical, scientific, moral, emotional, fideistic, sectarian, superstitious, etc) which actually works in uniting people and inducing them both to accept the new truth and struggle for it against those who share what appears now an outdated myth. But the process is endless. This is crucial. There is no reason why the generation of myths should cease. *Any* reality can be challenged and change, if successful, at that very moment into myth.

(c) Myth, philosophy, and science

People seem to live in the midst of an indefinite number of myths conflicting with one another. Typical in this respect is the process involving the (initially Aristotelian) attempt of 'philosophers' to 'unveil' pre-philosophical mythic cosmologies and, later on, the (initially Baconian, then Enlightenment-driven) attempt of science to 'unveil' or 'dispel' pre-scientific, ie philosophical and theological, myths.[68]

Philosophy was presented by Plato and Aristotle as a 'rational' form of knowledge in antithesis to the ancient, 'primitive' mythic tales or 'explanations' of the world. In fact, ancient myths had no claim to 'explaining' the world, at least as Plato and Aristotle conceived of 'explanation' in their days; still they arguably did help people to live together. It has been suggested that a new mythic account displaced the previous one because the latter was worse at living up to the expectations of the former.[69] Ironically, a similar displacement occurred against philosophy itself at the beginning of the modern age in Europe. Several 'metaphysical' propositions made in the name of philosophy began to appear detached from reality. What was supposed to be the key tool to unveil myth came under attack as itself being a set of mythical propositions. A new strategy, which was called 'scientific' and given an explicit anti-Aristotelian flavour, was devised and developed progressively. Science offered to humankind (specifically to European powers) a method to better control and subdue both the natural and human world.

Today science proudly claims to be anti-mythic *par excellence*. The scientific method is valued as a procedure capable of securing the highest level of inter-subjective 'objectivity' humanly attainable by means of standardized testing based on empirical verification of hypotheses. Scientists hold that science works as a trustful procedure which constantly unveils untrue or unproven beliefs. This scientific thrust, however, is

[66] SH Hooke (ed), *Myth and Ritual* (Oxford: OUP,1933) 3.

[67] Malinowsky (n 63 above) 70, 72, 98.

[68] See n 40 above.

[69] For the view that, with Plato and Aristotle, 'Into the place of magic and religion now stepped philosophical metaphysics' and 'Narrative myths and poems were replaced by philosophic-metaphysical speculations, that is, an intellectual activity which in its logical and systematic construction imitates disciplined cognition, but which is in reality more than a new mythology', being 'everyone . . . at liberty to maintain what he likes' or 'empty vessels that can be filled as one pleases', see A Ross, *On Law and Justice* (London: Stevens & Sons, 1958) 237–9.

also criticized on moral, philosophical, religious, or poetic grounds by arguing that scientists 'believe' quite unscientifically in the scientific method. Among their more problematic 'articles of faith' instrumental reason[70] and disciplinary fragmentation[71] are often mentioned. Hans Blumenberg has argued that the very opposition, and boundary, between *mythos* and *logos* is imaginary.[72] This would imply that not only is *logos* somehow mythic but also the distinction itself is mythic as a post hoc product of *logos*.[73]

A radical critique of science as 'myth' was famously engaged by Paul Feyerabend in the first edition of his *Against Method*, published in 1975.[74] In Chapter 18 of this work Feyerabend contended that 'science is much closer to myth than a scientific philosophy is prepared to admit', that 'science and myth overlap in many ways', that science was not necessarily superior to astrology, voodoo, and alternative medicine as a form of knowledge, and that the scientific message is a 'little fairy tale' presented 'not [as] mere ideology, but [as] an objective measure of all ideologies' purporting that *extra scientiam nulla salus* ('there is no salvation outside science'). In his view, far from being neutrally committed to truth, 'modern science *overpowered* its opponents, it did not *convince* them' and 'took over by *force*, not by argument', its rise coinciding, inter alia, 'with the suppression of non-Western tribes by Western invaders'. This argument—along with the idea that the procedures to attain truth had to be decided by vote,[75] on the assumption that in science 'anything goes' as far as method is concerned—was not reiterated by Feyerabend in later editions of the book, where he shifted, much less radically, from science as myth towards scientific pluralism.[76]

Feyerabend's thesis has been sharply criticized. His notion that truth should be 'decided by vote', in particular, reflects an exceedingly anarchistic mood typical of the 1970s in the West. Moreover, Feyerabend's pejorative use of the term 'myth' corresponds to the popular, only negative, meaning of myth previously rejected. His account is accurate, however, at least in one respect. Science is not value-free, unbiased, disinterested, or neutral as is generally presented. It is itself a system (made up of

[70] M Horkheimer, *Eclipse of Reason* (New York: OUP, 1947), eventually published in German as *Zur Kritik der instrumentellen Vernunft* (Frankfurt am Main: S Fischer, 1967) ('On the Critique of Instrumental Reason'); M Horkheimer and TW Adorno, *Dialektik der Aufklärung* (Amsterdam: Querido, 1947), English trans *Dialectic of Enlightenment* (Stanford: Stanford University Press, 2002), significantly arguing that 'Enlightenment mythic terror springs from a horror of myth' (at 22). For a critical analysis, see S Cochetti, *Mythos und 'Dialektik der Aufklärung'* (Königstein: Taunus, 1985).

[71] I Wallerstein, *World-Systems Analysis: An Introduction* (Durham and London: Duke University Press, 2004) 1–22.

[72] H Blumenberg, *Arbeit am Mythos* (Frankfurt am Main: Suhrkamp Verlag, 1979), English trans *Work on Myth* (Cambridge, Mass, and London: The MIT Press, 1988). For a critical comment, see B Yack, 'Myth and Modernity: Hans Blumenberg's Reconstruction of Modern Theory' (1987) 15 *Political Theory* 244.

[73] See n 40 above.

[74] P Feyerabend, *Against Method* (London: New Left Books, 1975) ch 18, at <http://www.marxists.org/reference/subject/philosophy/works/ge/feyerabe.htm>.

[75] Feyerabend (n 74 above): 'the manner in which we accept or reject scientific ideas is radically different from democratic decision procedures. We accept scientific laws and scientific facts, we teach them in our schools, we make them the basis of important political decisions, but without ever having subjected them to a vote. *Scientists* do not subject them to a vote—or at least this is what they say—*and laymen* certainly do not subject them to a vote... Scientists, especially physicians, frequently come to different results so that it is up to the relatives of the sick person (or the inhabitants of a certain area) to decide *by vote* about the procedure to be adopted' (original emphasis).

[76] P Feyerabend, *Against Method* (London: Verso, 4th edn, 2010).

very many proven truths, until falsified) of ultimately unproven beliefs.[77] This is not, of course, to suggest that science should not be pursued, nor that its myths have the same quality as those unmasked by science itself as myths, but rather to indicate that also the scientific path is in some sense mythic in a world in which myth is unavoidable and different mythologies—or, more specifically, different individuals and groups who promote their myths—compete for appropriating 'truth' in society. The upshot of the competition is uncertain. The advocates of science will prevail if they prove stronger than the advocates of voodoo, astrology, religion, poetry, contemplation, and the like, by attracting more people to their side than their competitors. The purported methodological truth of science may be insufficient to make it win. The competition is inevitably between different mythic visions of the human world.

(d) The mythic dimensions of law

Law is what all or most of those who see themselves as its addressees believe objectively to be their law, regardless of how questionable this objectivity may be to individual members of the group or to this or that enlightened scholar. All theories about what law is and how law can be distinguished from other dimensions of human life capture what law has been at some point in time, in some places, among some people. The more credited theories reflect better than others *this* context-relative law, but can hardly be universalized without losing their explicative force.[78]

Law is not like a mountain. It exists and works (or it does not exist and work) to the extent that people believe that it exists and works (or fails to do so) as a result of this collective adherence (or dismissal). The attitude that we take towards law is constitutive thereof and of the very process through which it 'becomes' law, however law is defined. If a mountain exists objectively because it is independent of the subjective attitude of any human being living on earth and it would exist even in a world where no human being were still alive, law exists objectively because it is so accepted by those human beings who are (and collectively think of themselves as being) its addressees here and now. This 'objectivity' of law is quite different from the objectivity of a mountain—unless one applies the yardstick used for mountains to law—but it is still objectivity when compared to unilateral claims of this or that individual or group, such as 'I am right' because 'it is so' whatever you or others may think. Without a shared mythic vision in society there can be no law. The rejection of myth as 'irrational' will create a myth of rationality as a base for law. When law works, it is because there is a mythic vision shared by the community, whether rational or emotional or other. In reverse, when law does not work, it is because it is actually *not* part of the mythic belief of its addressees as a whole, in which case the development of theories arguing for its 'legal nature' makes no difference. All 'rational', enlightenment-guided attempts to expel myth from the realm of law once and for all are destined to fail and are bound to create and provide support for new myths. People are an integral part of the legal process; it is

[77] See M Midgley, *The Myths We Live By* (London and New York: Routledge, 2004) 9–15.

[78] For attempts to see law 'from a global perspective' as based on social practice beyond the traditional Western state blueprint, but still pointing to a *general* jurisprudence basically constructed according to Western categories of thought, see BZ Tamanaha, *A General Jurisprudence of Law and Society* (Oxford: OUP, 2001); W Twining, *Globalisation and Legal Theory* (London, Edinburgh, and Dublin: Butterworths, 2000); W Twining, *General Jurisprudence: Understanding Law from a Global Perspective* (Cambridge: CUP, 2009).

impossible to define law without considering the *we* who *believe* in, and act upon, this law as their own law.[79]

The mythic dimension of law basically implies that the observer is part of the law that s/he is trying to describe and her/his description is part, like it or not, of the collective myth of law.[80] When a certain reality is challenged as myth, a novel belief in another reality is immediately and desperately needed in society in order to keep on going rather than dissolving. New mythologists, such as politicians and moralists, then come to the fore to construct new tales capable of impressing as many people as possible. When law is demythologized, it must immediately be differently remythologized. Remythologization is naturally lived as the truth against the untruth of the past. However, this truth is open to further challenge and demythologization in favour of other future truths. People are simply more at ease with the new truth, and experience the past untruth as now evidently false and intolerable, often disturbing. Priests of any stripe, scientists, philosophers, poets, jurists, and many others have created throughout history countless new myths in any society to hold people together. Law and institutions have thus been established and made enduring.

(4) Countering objections

Apart from the critique of irrationalism, which will be specifically discussed in Chapter 3, an objection to law as here presented is immanentism, on grounds that—echoing Protagoras' Man as 'measure of all things'[81]—human beings are left 'imprisoned' within the earthly, often arbitrary world failing any 'superior' value in which firmly to anchor. Many feel that *there must be* 'something else' *beyond* the human world, both individual and collective, and its arbitrariness and abuses. One could reply that both transcendence and immanence hardly avoid the mythic dimension of human life. The 'reality' of both depends on whether and to what extent people gathered in a homogenous group are prepared to give credence to them and to live accordingly. What society understands as transcendent (ie as human-independent) in contrast to immanent is indeed distinct from what society understands as immanent, yet it is still the subject of social construction. Different societies may make different constructions of transcendent and immanent reality to better serve their goals, just as different religious orders within Christianity (like Dominicans and Franciscans) have a different sense of what they see as one and the same God. Different peoples share the belief in a transcendent God but their Gods irremediably differ from one another. History shows that the spectre of human arbitrariness may nestle in both transcendence and immanence to the extent that both are social constructs for social ends.

A second objection is political totalitarianism when the argument made here is taken to suggest that individuals are totally dominated by society. The response is that the argument applies to every sort of political regime, including liberal regimes. It claims that what matters is the will and relative force of the generality of the members of the

[79] See P Fitzpatrick, *The Mythology of Modern Law* (London and New York: Routledge, 1992).

[80] This is different from the 'internal point of view' described by HLA Hart, *The Concept of Law* (Oxford: OUP, 2nd edn, 1994) 88–91, whereby for insiders in a group the violation of a rule 'is not merely a basis for the prediction that a hostile reaction will follow', as the external observer might state, 'but a *reason* for hostility' (original emphasis). In the sense here advanced, 'internal' means involvement as part of the ongoing process of law-making and unmaking.

[81] H Diels and W Kranz, *Die Fragmente der Vorsokratiker* (Zurich: Weidmann, 1985) 80b1 ('Of all things the measure is man, of the things that are, that they are, and of things that are not, that they are not').

group. Liberalism can prevail if it wins the competition with those who fight for authoritarianism. The argument, far from being totalitarian, can actually help to unmask totalitarianism and make people fight against it. It is unwise to hope for a liberal regime to materialize one of these days for the sole reason that it is the 'right' regime and to assume simplistically that people know what is right.

The assertion that law is a social construct having a mythic dimension is open to a third, antithetical objection by charging it with individualism. It seems to depict life as a Hobbesian or Darwinian arena in which war of all against all is the rule and life is but a *sauve qui peut* enterprise. However, the 'social nature' of man is far from being denied. Quite to the contrary, the argument can serve as a spur for reversing the status quo and bring about more communitarianism, including a stronger sense of commitment to law and justice. If a society believes in common values and in law as a set of rules common to all, then this is indeed the reality of the community. But such a reality is not carved in stone: it is contingent, fragile. It is conquered by struggle and is constantly under threat by opposing forces. The idea and hope that communitarianism, along with law and justice, will work by the force of its own truth is unrealistic, especially when this truth has lost its grip in society. A group may concede a greater or lesser margin of freedom to individuals, yet individuals' freedom of action ultimately depends on society. Individualism *in society* is possible only if it is supported *by society*. It is not in the power of each individual member of society to impose individualism.

A fourth objection may be raised by accusing the argument of nihilism because it seems to obscure moral issues, notably the moral basis of law. Once denied morality, it is difficult to maintain justice, and without justice law can be seen as nothing other than the abuse of the stronger.[82] However, there is no need to reject ethics or the morality of law. The point is that morality is the morality that people succeed in defending against both other conflicting views of morality and nihilism as well. There would be no Catholic Church or Buddhism on earth if all Catholics or all Buddhists were killed by anti-Catholics or anti-Buddhists. This means that whatever the answer to the question of whether morality exists, the defenders of morality are in any case expected to fight fiercely enough at the very least to survive against those who would like them to disappear.

Finally, the charge of promoting incommunicability may also be made. If people are abandoned to conflict, most of them will feel helplessly incapable of engaging in the struggle for what they feel is right. There is then no point in human communication, except for the use of communication as a weapon by which to prevail, with no regard to any 'truth' whatsoever. However, law as here understood does not imply that conflict is inevitable. It assumes that less conflict (or even no conflict at all) is indeed possible, but in doing so, it also assumes that less conflict, and perhaps a better functioning of law, is possible as a result of the daily prevalence of those who fight for less conflict against opponents, not as a 'grace' coming down from heaven on the sole ground that less conflict is 'obviously' better than more conflict for many human beings.

(5) The 'reality' of international law

Although international law will specifically be the subject of Part II, it is convenient at this juncture to ask whether it is 'true' law, and why. This question is traditionally known as that of the 'reality' of international law, since the investigator is called upon to

[82] Ch 1 above, n 24, and section B (2); and section (1) below.

determine whether international law is or is not 'real' law, hence whether it is actually 'legal' in nature and worthy of its name.[83] The question is linked to that of the 'basis of obligation' of international law, ie 'why' international law is binding and to be obeyed as 'law'.[84]

The answer clearly depends on what is assumed to be 'real law' as a yardstick. The question has rarely been analysed in terms of giving an explicit and satisfactory answer to the preliminary question of what counts as 'real law' in the first place, as this book attempts to do. The most common assumption has been that 'real law' is what is known as the law of the state or, to be more accurate, the law of an average modern Western state. Contrasted to, and measured by such a model or ideal type, with the aid of Western-based general jurisprudence, international law has invariably appeared 'primitive' and 'too political',[85] thereby raising the question of its 'reality'.[86] It is only on this often instinctive comparison and on the perceived certainty about the reality of domestic law that the question could be asked. Theoretical exercises of various kinds have been engaged to counter sceptics, critics, and deniers—basically political realists,[87] statist positivists,[88] and epistemological deconstructionists[89]—to 'prove', one way or another, that international law is indeed 'real', binding law and 'hence' must be obeyed.[90] Jurists have anchored international law's bindingness, just to name a few well-known theories, in the sociality of man,[91] in a self-limitation of states,[92] in the 'collective will' of states,[93] in a 'basic norm',[94] in social institutions,[95] in 'spontaneous'

[83] See eg PC Jessup, 'The Reality of International Law' (1939–40) 18 *Foreign Affairs* 244; W Friedmann, 'The "Reality" of International Law—A Reappraisal' (1971) 10 Col JTL 46; I Brownlie, 'The Reality and Efficacy of International Law' (1981) 52 BYBIL 1; A D'Amato, 'Is International Law Really "Law"?' (1985)79 NwUR 1293. For an overview of the whole spectrum of theories, see A Truyol y Serra, *Doctrines sur le fondement du droit des gens* (Paris: Pédone, 2007, rev edn by R Kolb).

[84] See eg J Brown Scott, 'The Legal Nature of International Law' (1907) 1 AJIL 831; WW Willoughby, 'The Legal Nature of International Law' (1908) 2 AJIL 357; JL Brierly, 'Le fondement du caractère obligatoire du droit international' (1928) 23 RdC 467; JL Brierly, *The Basis of Obligation in International Law and Other Papers* (Oxford: Clarendon Press, 1958) 1, 64–7; GG Fitzmaurice, 'The Foundations of the Authority of International Law and the Problem of Enforcement' (1956) 19 MLR 1; O Schachter, 'Towards a Theory of International Obligation' (1968)8 Virg JIL 300.

[85] Y Dinstein, 'International Law as a Primitive Legal System'(1986–87) 19 NYU JILP 1.

[86] M Koskenniemi, 'The Fate of Public International Law: Between Technique and Politics' (2007) 70 MLR 1, 1.

[87] T Hobbes, *De cive* [1642], XIV, 4; T Hobbes, *Leviathan, or the matter, forme and power of a commonwealth ecclesiasticall and civill* [1651] I, 15; ibid II, 17, 30.

[88] J Austin, *Lectures on Jurisprudence or the Philosophy of Positive Law* (London: John Murray, 5th edn, 1885) 86–103; GWF Hegel, *Grundlinien der Philosophie des Rechts* [1821] (Berlin: Akademie Verlag, 2005), English trans *Elements of the Philosophy of Right* (Cambridge: CUP, 1991) paras 330–335.

[89] M Koskenniemi, *From Apology to Utopia. The Structure of International Legal Argument* (Cambridge: CUP, reissue with new epilogue, 2005).

[90] For a recent résumé, see S Besson and J Tasioulas (eds), *The Philosophy of International Law* (Oxford: OUP, 2010) 6–13.

[91] H Grotius, *De Jure Belli ac Pacis Libri Tres* [1625], English trans *On the Law of War and Peace Three Books* (Washington, DC, Oxford, and London: Carnegie Institution, Clarendon Press, and Humphrey Milford, 1925), 'Prolegomena', paras 3, 5, 6, 8.

[92] G Jellinek, *Die Rechtliche Natur Der Staatenverträge: Ein Beitrag Zur Juristischen Construction Des Völkerrechts* [1880] (Whitefish: Kessinger, 2010) 7, 46.

[93] H Triepel, *Völkerrecht und Landesrecht* (Leipzig: Hirschfeldt, 1899).

[94] H Kelsen, *Principles of International Law* (New York: Rinehart & Co, 1952); H Kelsen, *General Theory of Law and State* [1945] (New Brunswick and London: Transaction Publishers, 2007).

[95] S Romano, *Corso di diritto internazionale* (Padua: Cedam, 4th edn, 1939) 6–7; S Romano, *L'ordinamento giuridico* (Florence: Sansoni, 2nd edn, 1962) paras 10, 12–13, 17, 28–30.

behaviour,[96] in the power of the strongest acting on behalf of the international community as a whole,[97] in the general treatment as law in social practice,[98] in actual compliance,[99] in legitimacy,[100] and in norm internalization.[101] However, no argumentative trick can really convince sceptics that international law is 'real' law *despite* its difference from domestic law, if the basic assumption that domestic law is 'real' law continues to represent the background of the whole debate. Faced with these problems, in recent decades a tendency to 'skip', or to address in pragmatic terms, the 'philosophical' question of the reality of international law, has generally prevailed,[102] inevitably raising criticisms of positivism and managerialism.[103]

Few have investigated—rather than dwelling on the 'flaws' of international law compared to domestic law—the mythic imagery that surrounds domestic law itself, and law in general. One key reason is that domestic law is critical to cementing national societies, and nation states relentlessly construct and re-construct the nation myth to ward off internal chaos and dissolution.[104] People grow up in national societies with a strong feeling, instilled daily in countless forms through routine symbols and habits of language often operating mindlessly, that the law of their community must be obeyed. Any challenge to the reality of domestic law is immediately felt as damaging and strongly discouraged by national authorities. All responsible people in national societies feel that there *must* be a law and this law *must* work in everyday life as far as possible. Even sceptics of the reality of domestic law cannot avoid profiting from (and counting on) the law in their daily life, whatever their theories. A similar discouragement is understandably absent in international law because there is no political unity at global level to be preserved, no immediate perception of the urgency of law in everyday life, no authority which might react to challenges to the reality of international law, this being, inter alia, a result of a greater competitive loyalty placed by people on their own nation state. In fact, domestic law is as primitive and political (or as much 'a balance of balances')[105] as international law, but the need to cement national societies is apparently (though by no means necessarily) far stronger than the need to cement global society. The point is not that international law is not real law compared to domestic law, or any other law, but that domestic law itself (as any other law) is based on myth.

Both domestic and international law are 'more or less' real as a function of how deep and diffused is the belief in their reality by their addressees taken as a whole. The key factor of law is not, in particular, centralization, but diffused belief. Centralization of the processes of law creation, adjudication, and enforcement is only one among a number of factors which influence (or have been specially devised to influence) this

[96] R Ago, *Scienza giuridica e diritto internazionale* (Milan: Giuffrè, 1950); R Ago, 'Positive Law and International Law' (1957) 51 AJIL 691.

[97] R Quadri, 'Le fondement du caractère obligatoire du droit international public' (1952-I) 80 RdC 579; R Quadri, *Diritto internazionale pubblico* (Naples: Liguori, 5th edn, 1968), 25–33, 119–29, 275–8.

[98] Hart (n 80 above) 208–31, arguing that international law is 'law' but not a 'legal system' (at 231, 235–6). See further Ch 1 above, n 66, as well as Ch 6 below, n 65 and accompanying text.

[99] L Henkin, *How Nations Behave: Law and Foreign Policy* (New York: Columbia University Press, 2nd edn, 1979) 25–7, 88–98.

[100] TM Franck, *The Power of Legitimacy Among Nations* (Oxford: OUP, 1990).

[101] HH Koh, 'Why Do Nations Obey International Law?' (1996–97) 106 Yale LJ 2599.

[102] cf JL Brierly, *The Law of Nations: An Introduction to the International Law of Peace* (Oxford: Clarendon Press, 6th edn, 1968) 69.

[103] M Koskenniemi (n 86 above) 1.

[104] See M Billig, *Banal Nationalism* (London: Sage, 1995).

[105] Ch 1 above, section A (2).

belief and the ensuing behaviour. There can indeed be 'true' law without centralization, and there can be no 'true' law even with formal centralization. International law may be 'more' law than the domestic law of a weak state.[106] A tribe may be governed by law more or better than a well-functioning state. The yardstick is whether and to what extent this law is believed to be the law by its addressees taken as a whole, just as the compliance rate itself is a function of its collective perception. The same holds true for other types of law. For example, the 'reality' of canon law—including its prescriptions of divine and natural law—depends on whether its addressees as a whole believe in it, are committed to it, and actually obey it. That there is no authority that can 'really' enforce canon law (in particular by physical and external sanctions) is irrelevant if clergymen and the faithful 'believe' that this is their law. In all of these cases law needs the support of the respective communities since law, as previously seen, is the power of the group towards its individual members, whatever the form given to it by the group, whether centralized, decentralized, backed up by external or internal sanctions, and so on.

There can hardly be a 'real' international law without the support of its addressees as a whole, whatever the comparison with domestic law or any other types of law. Since support or adherence is essential to law as mythic belief, what counts in law is whether and to what extent people are prepared to support it, rather than whether law is 'in itself' real law. Those who argue that international law is not law are expressing their disbelief in it and, since law depends on collective belief, are in fact contributing (negatively) to the reality of international law.[107] This very acknowledgement tends to weaken international law, making it less real, in real time. What seems at first sight value-free judgement deriving from impartial observation is in fact a definite stance against the reality of international law. Law cannot be reduced to an observational fact in scientific terms. It is not like a mountain. Its reality, whether domestic or international or other, depends on how its addressees as a whole, as opposed to each of them, see it. The point is thus whether we want international law—or a certain international law rather than another—or not. Its reality will flow from how deep and widespread support for it is and to what extent those who fight for it prevail at any moment over those who oppose it, which is exactly what also occurs in national (as in any other) society. The 'reality' of international law is the outcome of a struggle in society, not merely the scientific finding of individual theorists, although their descriptions of law (along with its desirability) may be well-founded and may also affect realities.

B. The Struggle for Justice

Law is not like a mountain. If law is a social construct ultimately founded in mythic belief, there must be a constant struggle engaged by different groups to control the generation and prevalence of beliefs about its reality. While science looks for truth in the world 'before us', like mountains, law is 'among us'. Scientists are not part of the process of creating mountains, but jurists and people do participate in the making and

[106] For the view that when it comes to institutional facts, because the whole system works only by collective acceptance, 'it all looks very fragile, as if the whole system might just collapse at any time', see Searle (1995) (n 21 above) 90.

[107] For a reiteration of the realist argument see eg JR Bolton, 'Is There Really "Law" in International Affairs?' (2000) 10 TLCP 1. For a critical view of international law from the rational choice perspective, see JL Goldsmith and EA Posner, *The Limits of International Law* (Oxford: OUP, 2005) 15, 185–203.

unmaking of law. Law is mythic because we are *part thereof.* When dealing with law 'observers' become 'agents', whether they like it or not. The 'we' who make or unmake law is in constant struggle, whether actively or tacitly, to shape the law one way or another. Law as it stands is always one side of the coin, the other side being law as it is being shaped at any given moment and law as it ought to be in the future, ie justice. The struggle is at least threefold, between the stronger and the weaker, between the stronger themselves, and between the weaker themselves. If law is ultimately founded in a mythic sense of commonality, then what matters is how relentlessly this myth is revived every day. Those who critique law as inadequate or irrelevant fail (or are unwilling) to realize that law is the result (also) of their belief and (lack of) commitment. Realists and deconstructionists end up working against law when they—in exercising abstract rationality—break both the belief and the hope in the law without caring that belief and hope are a vital part of any law. This section explores the dynamics of law by looking into the well-known 'struggle for law' debate, which is ultimately a struggle for justice, and by examining the meaning of 'progress' when dealing with law.

(1) Defining justice

There is absolutely no clear answer to what should be meant by 'justice', let alone 'global' justice.[108] Countless different views have been given in the course of history in different contexts and disciplines, including legal theory. It is well known that in the name of justice all kinds of heinous acts and wars have been carried out, either justified or condemned, at all times. What is called an 'elementary sense of justice' appears to be extraordinarily diverse in different peoples, places, times, legal traditions, and civilizations.[109]

In the Western tradition, Thrasymachus, the interlocutor of Socrates in Plato's *Republic*, famously stated that justice is 'nothing else than the advantage of the stronger',[110] a view expressed to counter Polemarchus' notion that 'justice . . . consists in restoring to every man what is his due',[111] before inspiring Glaucon to form a mid-path notion of justice as a strictly human artifact concocted through an agreement,[112] and then paving the way for Socrates' (and Plato's) own view of justice as a proper, harmonious relationship between the three warring components of either the person or the city-state. In *Ecclesiastes* it is said that 'there is not a just man upon earth, that doeth good, and sinneth not',[113] rather suggesting that justice and injustice cannot be separated and that it is in the name of justice that injustice is done. In legal theory, by taking up the Hobbesian suggestion that in a community in which each member can invoke its own view of justice there can be only social chaos to the disadvantage of all, positivist rationalists are persuaded that justice either cannot be properly defined or can properly be defined as plain respect for the law as it stands. They reject justice as nothing other than natural law in disguise, or the reverse, while denying the problem that the law as made by the law-maker of the day may be unjust and as such invalid, and

[108] For a discussion of the practical difficulties in defining justice in general, see MJ Sandel, *Justice: What's the Right Thing to Do?* (New York: Ferrar, Straus and Giroux, 2009).

[109] For an insightful collection of essays from diverse perspectives, see RD Masters and M Gruter (eds), *The Sense of Justice: Biological Foundations of Law* (Nesbury Park, London, and New Delhi: Sage Publications, 1992).

[110] Ch 1 above, n 24.

[111] Plato, *Republic*, 331e.

[112] ibid 358e–359a.

[113] *Ecclesiastes*, 7:20.

describe justice as merely 'banging on the table',[114] or as an empty formula, a meaningless tautology, or ideology, an 'irrational idea', ultimately nothing more than 'legality'.[115] Legal deconstructionists insist that justice is merely subjective opinion which is passed off as objective in any legal discourse, including international law discourse, and is no different in this respect from all reasoning about natural law.[116] To complicate matters, there are several perspectives, sometimes in opposition with each other, from which justice can be addressed (global,[117] criminal,[118] distributive,[119] random,[120] contractarian fairness-centred,[121] transcendental institutional or realization-focused comparative,[122] utilitarian or deontological,[123] just-order-based and inherent-rights based,[124] and so on). What is just in one sense may thus not be just, or equally just, in another sense.[125]

This uncertainty suggests that justice, including global justice, is fatally subjective, either because it is established by society (and society may consider 'just' even extermination camps if need be) or by any individual according to her/his taste. Against this nihilistic scenario, one could object that it is impossible to live without some sense of justice. We all feel that certain acts are profoundly unjust and must be discouraged as far as possible. We all feel that the law should conform to this sense of justice, however difficult the definition of justice may be. This can hardly be ignored or simply relegated to a 'subjective' feeling that has nothing to do with law and nothing to say to jurists. Justice may indeed be 'only' subjective, but this may reveal more than what deniers of the objectivity of justice claim. Dismissers of justice in the name of a 'scientific' approach to law are unsatisfactory. They may throw justice away from the door and justice will soon reappear at the window. It is thus vital to better articulate, although succinctly, what is this thing called 'justice'. The position adopted here could be summarized as follows.

First, justice cannot, and should not, be defined in the abstract. A general definition of justice is not only either impossible or empty,[126] but also undesirable and dangerous. It is actually in the name of justice as defined in general terms that injustices have

[114] Ross (n 69 above) 274.

[115] Kelsen (2007) (n 94 above) 10–13; H Kelsen, *Was ist Gerechtigkeit?* (Wien: Franz Deuticke, 1953); H Kelsen, *What is Justice?: Justice, Law, and Politics in the Mirror of Science* (Berkeley and Los Angeles: University of California Press, 1957).

[116] See C Douzinas and A Gearey, *Critical Jurisprudence: The Political Philosophy of Justice* (Oxford: Hart, 2005).

[117] See T Nagel, 'The Problem of Global Justice' (2005) 33 *Philosophy and Public Affairs* 113–47; and the collection of seminal essays found in T Pogge and D Moellendorf (eds), *Global Justice: Seminal Essays* (St Paul: Paragon House, 2008) vol 1.

[118] Ch 7 below, section A (2)(c), and Ch 8 below, section B (4).

[119] See H Bull, *The Anarchical Society: A Study of Order in World Politics* (Houndmills and New York: Palgrave, 3rd edn, 2002) 74–94; R Foot, JL Gaddis, and A Hurrell (eds), *Order and Justice in International Relations* (Oxford: OUP, 2003).

[120] N Duxbury, *Random Justice: On Lotteries and Legal Decision-Making* (Oxford: OUP, 2002).

[121] J Rawls, *A Theory of Justice* (Cambridge, Mass: The Belknap Press of Harvard University Press, rev edn, 1999); for its extension to the international community, pointing to 'how a world Society of liberal and decent Peoples might be possible', see J Rawls, *The Law of Peoples* (Cambridge, Mass and London: Harvard University Press, 1999).

[122] A Sen, *The Idea of Justice* (London: Allen Lane, 2009) 5–18, 67–72, 91–105.

[123] D Johnston, *A Brief History of Justice* (Chichester: Wiley-Blackwell, 2011) 1–2.

[124] N Wolterstorff, *Justice: Rights and Wrongs* (Princeton and Oxford: Princeton University Press, 2008) 21–43.

[125] For the view that disagreement about justice is but a reflection of disagreement about which rationality should be followed, see A MacIntyre, *Whose Justice? Which Rationality?* (London: Duckworth, 1988).

[126] For an analysis of formal justice, see Ch 3 below, section A (2).

always been committed. In this sense, there is no 'objective' justice that can be validly argued by way of abstract reason. It is submitted that only a *personal* view of justice may honestly be provided, without any claim to universality or to rational adherence by others, but still open to sympathetic feeling. This is far from implying, from a constructivist perspective, that justice is only 'subjective', and hence irrelevant, as commonly intended by those who deny any objectivity of justice.

Secondly, justice needs to be distinguished in a 'collective' sense of justice and an 'inner' sense of justice. In a sense, justice certainly is, just like law and morality, what is so defined in any particular community.[127] However, justice also refers to what any individual may think thereof. The sense of collective justice is dictated by society to any of its members and is 'objective' in the sense that what society as a whole succeeds in imposing on any of its members is objective in their life. The inner sense of justice lives in the psychological sphere of any individual and is certainly 'subjective' from the viewpoint of society as a whole. Yet, unlike law, justice is not only what is imposed by society on its members. It is also constantly what single individuals feel as justice in their living together. While law cannot work as law without the collectivity, justice may well inspire how law ought to be from within the inner sphere of any individual. This may not be enough to change the law; still it is valuable and no one can avoid taking due account thereof. Most individuals have no idea of the law to be brought about, but have a sense of what is just and should be reflected in the law.

Thirdly, justice in the inner sense is the dynamic engine of (social construction, and hence of) collective justice and law. To say that justice is a social construct not only means that it is established by society towards (or against) individuals, but also that it is established by individuals who can *inspire others* to change the prevailing sense of justice (and possibly law) in society. Someone, by personal inspiration, must start the process. It is the individual who can do so, not society *en bloc* instantly. This dynamic, constant process inspired by the inner sense of justice of any member in society is vital to the process of constructing objectivity. There is something 'objective' in the subjective view of justice and this is both a *personal commitment* and a *direction in action*, two dimensions neglected by rationalists. If law is not like a mountain, but rather the actual result (in combination with that of all other members of society) of my supportive or unsupportive attitude, then my attitude is an integral part of the objective law *right now*. My commitment to law, or lack thereof, is part of the law as well as what I actually do, or do not do, for the law. I am always 'within' the constructing process and the outcome depends, inter alia, on the notion of justice which I have personally embraced. People need to act 'in the meantime', ie before objectivity is irrefutably found or denied, as well as to feel themselves to be living objectively, whatever this may mean. I need to know *what to do next* in my daily life and this requires of me a commitment, regardless of having yet to achieve any objective 'justice' and regardless of feeling that no real objective justice will ever be achieved.

Fourthly, justice is a 'sense' or a 'sentiment' which surfaces when experiencing its opposite, ie *injustice*, rather than the reflection of a rational idea or a speculative process through demonstrations, let alone a result of instrumental reason,[128] or communicative action.[129] This 'emotional sense' is not necessarily equal to 'instant emotional reaction', but may refer to the emotionally stable structure of an individual's personality as a

127 This is, eg, Freud's understanding of justice (see Ch 1 above, nn 7 and 12, and accompanying text).
128 Horkheimer (n 70 above).
129 Ch 4 below, n 179.

whole shared in the community.[130] Emotion is, inter alia, a mode of knowledge enabling individuals to take a stance in their life.[131] It is difficult to see human beings and even their rationality without emotion.[132] True, this shift from abstract reason to intelligent emotion, and from the idea of justice to the experience of injustice, typically raises at least three objections: (a) emotional reaction to injustice presupposes a rule prescribing equality and this rule is extracted by way of reason; (b) emotional reactions to injustice are arguably as diverse as the rational theories of justice themselves, even within one and the same society; and (c) from an emotional reaction to injustice, which is a fact, one cannot derive a normative value ('naturalistic fallacy').[133] However, objections (a) and (c) presuppose that reason should unreservedly prevail over emotion in case of conflict, but this very conflict is questioned here in the first place by stressing the need to shift from abstract reason to reason informed by emotion. As to objection (b), it is assumed that there is an elementary level of injustice beyond all diversity and it is at *this* level that a sense of injustice makes sense. If a society fails to reach a level of a shared sense of justice in emotional terms, no justice will ever prevail and mere speculative arguments will fail. Not surprisingly, in the Nazi extermination camps emotion and the elementary sense of the just and the unjust, together with an inner force of resistance and revolt, was harshly and systematically discouraged. Humanity was annihilated basically by denying emotional life.[134]

Finally, justice as proposed here, and in particular global justice, as will be discussed elsewhere in this book,[135] reflects a very elementary aspect of human life, however difficult to articulate, namely the protection of the most vulnerable.[136] To put it negatively, injustice is to treat people (or other living beings) in such a way that they experience absolute, or manifest out-of-proportion impotence vis-à-vis an overwhelming power, or manifestly exercised omnipotence, of other human beings, which generally amounts to deprivation of human basic needs.[137] Thus defined, injustice is exemplarily epitomized in the experience of torture: the tortured is completely in the hands of the torturer, who even controls the ability of the tortured to commit suicide in order to bring the torment to an end.[138] What matters is the individual here and now, not society as an aggregate some time in the future. No doubt it is difficult to make sense of 'vulnerability'. Different people may be equally vulnerable for opposite reasons and justice cannot be done to all at the same time. Furthermore, the protection of an individual who is vulnerable today may amount to doing injustice to several individuals equally vulnerable tomorrow. It is submitted that whenever somebody faces more

[130] G Zagrebelsky, *Intorno alla legge: Il diritto come dimensione del vivere comune* (Turin: Einaudi, 2009) 50–81.

[131] DP Goleman, *Emotional Intelligence: Why It Can Matter More Than IQ* (New York: Bantam Books, 1997).

[132] MC Nussbaum, *Upheavals of Thought: The Intelligence of Emotions* (Cambridge: CUP, 2001). See in addition A Damasio, *Descartes' Error: Emotion, Reason and the Human Brain* [1994] (London: Vintage Books, rev edn, 2006); A Damasio, *Self Comes to Mind: Constructing the Conscious Brain* (New York: Pantheon Books, 2010).

[133] Ch 1 above, section B (1)(c).

[134] See B Bettelheim, *Surviving and Other Essays* (New York: Alfred A Knopf, 1979) 48–83. For the view that public and objective 'Reasoning is central to the understanding of justice even in a world which contains much "unreason"', while acknowledging the 'complementary role' of emotion, see Sen (n 122 above) xix, 4–5, 31–51.

[135] Ch 4 below, section B (4), and Ch 7 below.

[136] For this notion of justice since antiquity, see Johnston (n 123 above) 16, 23.

[137] This notion of justice, in so far as it coincides with 'inequality' only to the extent that basic human needs are threatened, has a somewhat more restricted meaning than the one generally endorsed of any 'balance' or 'proportion': see eg Hart (n 80 above) 159.

[138] See E Peters, *Torture* (Philadelphia: University of Pennsylvania Press, exp edn, 1996).

vulnerability than another in *any* particular society according to how life is lived *there*, then the sense of justice suggests that the former must be protected against the latter. What 'vulnerability' means in any society varies (just deserts, merits, ability, need, bargaining power, equal treatment, reciprocity, fairness, equal distribution of wealth, retribution for misdeeds, etc)[139] and only social attunement, as discussed in Chapter 3, may ultimately provide the answer. This is not to recommend a just society.[140] It is suggested that whatever the type of society (Franciscan, communist, liberal, tribal, etc), the most vulnerable therein, according to the sense of vulnerability therein prevailing, are to be protected. Thrasymachus may be reassured and may well retain his stance that justice is the 'advantage of the stronger', but he *may also* start to struggle for the protection of the most vulnerable rather than struggling for the stronger or simply staying idle and letting justice be shaped by the stronger. The point is clearly *who* should be the stronger. The protection of the most vulnerable is only possible when most of the members of society want society to be protective of the vulnerable and successfully resist opponents. The apparent paradox is that in order successfully to contain the stronger one has to be even stronger but then the vulnerable become the stronger and no longer deserve protection. This suggests that a struggle for justice is not a project for some specified individual or group at present, but rather for whoever becomes vulnerable over time. Justice to be promoted, as here understood, refers to the protection of the most vulnerable *whoever they may be at any time*.

To argue for justice as the engine of law is not to say that law 'as it stands' should be bent at will and manipulated in the name of justice, let alone along the lines of what is felt as justice by one or another member of society. Law is what is recognized as such by society as a whole, whatever the inner sense of justice of its individual members. The personal sense of justice may help to construe the law as it stands, according to the interpretative criteria recognized in society, and also to struggle for a new (future) law which is non-existent at the moment. This is certainly part of the legal process. *My* commitment to the law as it stands and *my* struggle for the law as I think it ought to be in the future, is vital to law. If law is socially constructed and I am part of society, then I am also part of the legal process. What is subjective in myself has the potential to become objective in society, since social reality is a combination of the beliefs and acts of its members, including myself. I am *right now* committed (or uncommitted) to, and constructing (or letting others construct) the law as an *objective* reality in society, based on my inner sense of justice.

(2) Struggling for law

In the widely held view, at least in the Western tradition,[141] that law is directed to peace and order, law is depicted as the antithesis of (and a remedy to) violence, conflict, social chaos, and anarchy. In *Der Kampf ums Recht*, published in 1872,[142] Rudolph von Jhering argued that: 'The life of law is a struggle . . . a warfare . . . to overcome

[139] See R Norman, 'Criteria of Justice: Desert, Needs And Equality' (2001) 7 *Res Publica* 115.

[140] For a non-institutional idea of justice, see Sen (n 122 above) 8–10.

[141] See eg Tamanaha (n 78 above) 11–50.

[142] R von Jhering, *Der Kampf ums Recht* [1872] (Frankfurt am Main: Klostermann, 2003), English trans *The Struggle for Law* (Chicago: Callaghan and Co, 1915). The English title is misleading: 'ums' in German should be translated as 'around' rather than 'for'; besides, Jhering's argument refers to 'rights' rather than to 'law'. A better translation is 'the struggle around law' or 'the battle for rights', as rightly suggested by Roger Cotterrell, 'The Struggle for Law: Some Dilemmas of Cultural Legality' (2008) 4 IJLC 373, 373.

opposition... a struggle in which, as in every struggle, the issue is decided not by the weight of reason, but by the relative strength of opposing forces'.[143] Confrontation thus appears as the essence of the very law that is supposed to ban violence, manage conflicts, and secure order. Violence is not only necessary to enforce law and make it effective; it is also unavoidable to have or to transform law in the first place. Law is presently as it is because of a struggle engaged in the past, and it may be different in the future because of a struggle to be engaged in the present. While from a static perspective law appears to be aimed at securing order, dynamically it appears as 'the result of pain, uninterrupted effort' and constant strife. Jhering was concerned with the struggle for interest-based change in law. He opposed Puchta's and Savigny's conservative Historical School,[144] as well as his own previous works inspired by the so-called 'jurisprudence of concepts',[145] by proposing a progressive new 'jurisprudence of interests' to be used for the further advancement of the moral and social interests of mankind.[146] In particular, he focused on the duty of every person, both to himself and to society, to assert and strive for his own rights as a way ultimately to make law and justice concretely work and triumph.

For the sake of clarity, a distinction should be made between the struggle for law *as such* and the struggle for a *certain* law rather than another. The first is the struggle of those who defend law against those who want no law at all, while the second is typically the struggle between those who defend either existing or a certain future law against those who strive for a new law or for an alternative future law. Another helpful distinction is between the struggle for law and the struggle for justice. Jhering's analysis primarily concerned the struggle for a new law, not necessarily for justice, although he regarded the former as a reflection of the latter. His trust in the equation between law and justice, common to many jurists,[147] needs to be treated with caution since law can be, and is often, used to commit injustice, at least in the sense here proposed of the protection of the most vulnerable. Order secured by law is often better than chaos, but when order is secured by systematic abuse sanctioned by law, the reverse may be true. It follows, going beyond Jhering's account and the common idea that a struggle for law is always a good thing, that the focus needs to be turned to three different forms of 'struggle for law': (a) struggle for less law (or social chaos); (b) struggle for more law (or legal order); and (c) struggle for justice (or just law).

[143] Jhering (n 142 above) 1, 3, 6, 11.

[144] The book was written to counter what von Jhering himself called 'the Savigny-Puchta theory of the origin of the law' whose 'principles of jurisprudence [call] for no strife, no struggle' and 'are nothing but the quiet working power of truth which, without any violent effort, slowly but surely makes its way' (ibid at 8). Jhering insisted that 'the new has to undergo a struggle to force its way into the world' and that 'The law can renew its youth only by breaking with its own past' (ibid at 11, 13). His claim was to legislation as a means to new law against immemorial custom defended by Savigny and Puchta and, more generally, by the Historical School of law (ibid at 15). In Jhering's opinion 'Not mere custom, but sacrifice, forges the strongest bond between a people and their principles of legal right', thus concluding that 'The struggle needed by laws to fight their way into existence is not a curse, but a blessing' (ibid at 19).

[145] cf R von Jhering, *Scherz und Ernst in der Jurisprudenz Eine Weihnachtsgabe für das juristische Publikum* (Göttingen: Breitkopf und Härtel, 1884) 7.

[146] Hence the theory of law as 'a means to and end' developed by von Jhering in *Der Zweck im Recht* (Leipzig: Breitkopf und Härtel, 1877–1883, 2 vols), English trans of the first volume, originally published in 1877, of the 4th German edition published in 1903, *Law as a Means to an End* (Kila: Kessinger, 1914). Also this translation is misleading: the literal translation is 'Purpose in Law'. For a recent, more general exploration of the question of legal instrumentalism, see BZ Tamanaha, *Law as a Means to an End: Threat to the Rule of Law* (Cambridge: CUP, 2006) 3–4.

[147] See eg GG Fitzmaurice (n 84 above) 12–13, stating that 'obeying the law serves justice'.

People may, first, struggle for less or less effective law. This struggle is apparently towards chaos, and against law and order, at least in some areas of social intercourse, and may sound at first implausible. It does take place, however, to varying degrees when those who benefit from social chaos or freedom of action seek to impose less law as 'normal' on all others in a group. One could think that few if any would benefit from chaos in society, but experience shows that the stronger can profit significantly therefrom. When this struggle succeeds, law invariably consists of very few and less effective rules. The most vulnerable are then exposed to the arbitrariness of the stronger with little or no margin of predictability. Society is thought by the stronger to function well enough in this state of 'equal freedom' left to everyone. The vulnerable of course experience equal freedom as a Darwinian arena, where in principle all participants are given the chance to win, but in practice no one other than the stronger can actually do so. It is obvious that the stronger are unlikely to surrender part at least of their power. Some of them may easily come to believe that their success depends on their merits tested on the ground. Few are fully aware that the system is made and carefully maintained to select and reward precisely the stronger. Apart from external factors, only a counter-struggle engaged by the vulnerable for law and order can bring about more justice. In this scenario, the counter-struggle for law is also a struggle for justice, although the stronger themselves will invoke justice (and will no doubt critique 'legalistic' views of the law) to justify their privileges and, ultimately, their abuses. Both sides will thus invoke justice, but only the vulnerable will invoke more (or more effective) law and justice as here understood.

It may also occur, to turn to a second scenario, that it is the stronger who invoke more (and more effective) law, clearly a law different from that possibly invoked by the vulnerable, ie a law which sanctions their privileges and abuses on the one hand, and severely punishes transgressors and rebels on the other. Totalitarian regimes tend obsessively to make and rely on law. In tyrannies legal rules, especially prohibitive in character, mushroom and 'freeze' every aspect of the lives of people. Now there is apparently 'law and order' to the benefit of all, but this state of affairs serves once again the interests of the stronger. It is to protect *their* freedom that law is made and inflexibly applied. The vulnerable are completely subjected to the law made by the stronger and experience the severest consequences thereof. Life to them is again a Darwinian arena where the winners are always the stronger and the key strategy for survival is to circumvent the law by any means. Law tends to be applied one way only, towards the vulnerable, and wherever possible on a case-by-case basis. It is generally lived as 'flexible' towards the stronger and merciless towards the vulnerable. Flexibility is claimed by the stronger to be necessary to secure law and order, and law and order are for the benefit of all. It is then in the name of law that the most heinous and intolerable crimes are committed by the rulers and their lackeys. It is law that provides the stronger with an inexorable machine which renders them virtually invincible. The confrontation is not on a 'free terrain', as in the first scenario, but on a highly regulated ground. Resistance of the vulnerable against the stronger is illegal and illegality is socially stigmatized, internally banned, and legally punished. The struggle for law in this scenario is engaged by the stronger, while the way out for the vulnerable towards justice is a counter-struggle *against* the law. Less law, and less effective law, is the goal to attain for more justice to be brought about. Law is the problem. As a result, an *illegal* revolt is the way out. Only by 'illegal' acts can the vulnerable obtain justice. No legal means to justice is allowed by the regime. There is little doubt that the law in force in such a society is what this society has enacted as law, until the regime changes. Justice is only a prospect of the vulnerable and a banner under which they draw inspiration and strength to fight for a change. No confusion is to be made between the two spheres, the 'is' and the 'ought'. It is in the full awareness that there is no law other than the one that armours the ruling class in its legalized bunkers that the revolt is understood as the only way out. The struggle for law, understood as 'just' law, is then a struggle against the (existing) law.

It thus follows, as a third scenario, that the 'struggle for law', understood as a struggle for justice, may be both for more (or more effective) law and for less (or less effective) law, depending on the circumstances. The proposition that a struggle for more law or for more effective law is always a good thing is misconceived, unless justice is thought of as coincident with the law in force at any given moment. In reverse, the critique that a certain law, including international law, is unsatisfactorily 'not really law' because there are too few or too ineffective rules, may be (at least in some measure) wide of the mark. More law, or more effective law, may be the problem, and a solution to global justice as here understood may not necessarily follow either from more international law, or from more effective international law, or from particular international law rules constructed as higher in rank than others or endowed with an on-paper wider range of reactions to their breach.[148]

(3) Progress in law

Is the struggle for justice also a struggle for 'progress' in law? Many would answer affirmatively and assume that the above discussion on the struggle for justice coincides with a struggle for progress. However, the answer depends on what is meant by progress.[149]

In everyday language, and often in scientific circles, the word 'progress' has a positive connotation, meaning improvement over time. The underlying idea, closely connected to the notion of civilization,[150] is that the world goes along a linear path for the better, at least if a given course of action is taken (generally a science-driven path). This idea, which can be traced back to the Enlightenment and perhaps to the Judaic-Christian linear eschatological vision of human life, rejects the circular approach to time and history whereby the world basically endlessly repeats itself in apparently different forms without any real improvement and direction.[151] Once the circular outlook is dismissed, 'progress' tends to coincide with what is valuable, and 'change for the sake of change' tends to hold the stage. Dynamics towards an 'end of history', or ultimate goal, are then preferred to a static acknowledgement of the eternal nature of the things. Progress is always towards the better. For present purposes, if the better is assumed to be the protection of the most vulnerable, then it seems to go without saying that the struggle

[148] It is alluded to in the notions of *jus cogens* and obligations *erga omnes* discussed in Ch 6 below, section B (4)(f), and Ch 8 below, section B (1).

[149] For a classic work on the idea of progress see JB Bury, *The Idea of Progress: An Inquiry Into Its Origin and Growth* (London: Macmillan, 1920). More recently, see Y Burgess, *The Myth of Progress* (Glasgow: Cromwell Press, 1996); and AM Melzer, Jerry Weinberger, and MR Zinman (eds), *History and the Idea of Progress* (Ithaca, NY: Cornell University Press, 1995).

[150] Ch 6 below, n 169.

[151] The circular approach to human life is typically associated with conservatism. For an insightful analysis of the three principal conservative (or 'reactive-reactionary') theses against progressive calls for change, see AO Hirschman, *The Rhetoric of Reaction: Perversity, Futility, Jeopardy* (Cambridge, Mass and London: The Belknap Press of Harvard University Press, 1991).

for justice is also a struggle for progress. The following equations are made: justice is equal to value and value is equal to progress, hence justice is equal to progress.[152]

The problem with this 'progressistic', but not necessarily progressive, attitude is that it takes for granted that change is always for the better. Experience shows that change can be either for the better or for the worse (in terms of a certain goal, such as the protection of the vulnerable) depending on the circumstances. Change can be for the worse when it is the stronger themselves who use the 'progress' approach to change things towards a certain goal in their interest and for their exclusive benefit. Progress is actually a reflection of an idea of the good life projected onto the past from the present by the stronger, whatever both the present and the process towards the present may be. What is 'truly' progressive depends on who is winning the daily struggle for establishing what is good and worth pursuing. Those who lose have no chance to prove that their goals would have been towards the better. It is necessarily for the winners to dictate what is 'progress', to tell the story of this progress, and to suggest what should be seen as progressive. It is true that one could reasonably expect the vulnerable to call for change, rather than those who are currently taking advantage of the status quo. However, in modern societies the stronger have learned that when change is called for by the vulnerable the best course of action is to endorse change, rather than resisting it, so as to control and channel it for their benefit. Another reason for caution when equating justice with progress is that even when it is the vulnerable who spur change for their benefit and change meets the demands of justice, it is still possible that those who are the most vulnerable today will become the oppressors tomorrow as a result of their success. That is, those who are on the just side today may well be on the unjust side tomorrow, although they are the same people and are pursuing the same cause. Rebels against oppressors have often become oppressors in turn once their rebellion has succeeded.

Briefly, progress or change in law is not necessarily towards justice. People and jurists committed to justice, as here intended, do not need the label of being progressive. Beyond labels and fashion trends, what matters is what is in the interest of the most vulnerable at any given moment in any given place and this may or may not require a change in the law. Stability in law is a value just like change. A 'conservative' stance can on occasion be more in the interest of the most vulnerable than a progressive attitude. Analysis is necessary to reduce arbitrariness in the uses of such ambivalent attitudes as conservative and progressive in order to avoid injustice in disguise.

Conclusion

This chapter argued that law is a social construct ultimately founded in mythic belief. It is not like a mountain. Its reality depends on our making and unmaking thereof. In any society law is what those who believe themselves to be addressees of a certain set of rules also believe to be their law. This law is objective to any member of the community as imposed on each of them by the community as a whole. International law, in particular, is 'real' law to the extent that it is so believed by its addressees. That law has a mythic dimension which means that it can cease to be objectively the law of a certain group

[152] On progress in international law, see RA Müllerson, *Ordering Anarchy: International Law in International Society* (The Hague: Nijhoff, 2000) 69–84; DJ Bederman, *The Spirit of International Law* (Athens: University of Georgia Press, 2002) 204–20; RA Miller and RM Bratspies (eds), *Progress in International Law* (Leiden: Nijhoff, 2008); T Skouteris, *The Notion of Progress in International Law Discourse* (The Hague: TMC Asser Press, 2010).

only through a remythologization in another direction. Without a mythic sense of commonality there can be no law. To revive the underlying myth is essential in order for law to work. This does not yet prescribe what myths law should embrace. They may be immanent or transcendent, totalitarian or liberal, communitarian or individualistic, nihilist or value-laden, communication-driven or stuck to incommunicability. The fact that we are part of the process of making and unmaking of law creates an inherent dynamics which implies and calls for struggle. This struggle for law must specifically be for justice, understood here as the protection of the most vulnerable, and this may imply either more or less law. Justice is also independent of progressivism and conservatism in law, since change in the law may or may not be for the benefit of the most vulnerable.

3

Reason

The previous chapters argued that law is a form of collective violence that is socially constructed and ultimately founded in myth. This chapter is designed to articulate the social dimension of law, against legal deconstructionists, in the further sense that law is basically inspired by reason operating in society. It is argued that law embodies common meanings that ensure people live in a communal world, ie in a 'rational' world rooted in common sense and social attunement where certain claims count as arguments while others do not, and certain arguments are better than others. Although often structured according to formal deduction and justice, law works as practical reason and prudential judgement. What matters in law is not what is logically irresistible, but what 'works in practice' in any particular society. Law is not the scientific, philosophical, or aesthetical enterprise of an individual. It must work in people's daily life as *they* see their own life rather than in the minds of single individuals, no matter how enlightened or learned.

A. Theoretical Reason

In *Legal Reasoning and Legal Theory*, Neil MacCormick suggested that 'The idea that reason has a part to play in the ordering of human affairs has a long history', it being 'associated with the view that some things are "by nature" right for human beings' or that 'some actions . . . are always wrong simply in virtue of the nature of human beings—or, more generally, the "nature of things"', actions which can and should be disclosed by the exercise of reason.[1] He recalled Lord Stair's remark that: 'Law is the dictate of reason determining every rational being to that which is congruous and convenient for the nature thereof'.[2] This reason-based view of law, however, has not gone unchallenged and MacCormick aptly recalls David Hume's scepticism about the limits of reason in practical affairs, conceding that 'our faculty of reasoning can operate only upon given premisses' which 'are not themselves provable, demonstrable, or confirmable in terms of further or ulterior reasons'.[3] MacCormick has framed the question by asking 'how far the determination of order in human affairs is a matter of reason'.[4] His answer is 'up to a point', in the sense that 'our ultimate premises are not reasoned', but there are reasons that 'can be given for adhering to such ultimate normative premises', even though these reasons 'are not in their nature conclusive,

[1] N MacCormick, *Legal Reasoning and Legal Theory* (Oxford: Clarendon Press, 1978) 1–2. For critical comments, see PD White, 'Philosophy and Law: Some Observations on MacCormick's Legal Reasoning and Legal Theory' (1979–80) 78 Mich LR 736; A Wilson, 'The Nature of Legal Reasoning: A Commentary with Special Reference to Professor's MacCormick's Theory' (1982) 2 *Legal Studies* 273. For a reply, stressing that 'the syllogism plays a fundamental structuring part in legal thought, though not all of such thoughts is exhausted by the structure alone', see N MacCormick, *Rhetoric and the Rule of Law: A Theory of Legal Reasoning* (Oxford: OUP, 2005) 33, 69–70.

[2] James, 1st Viscount Stair, *Institutions of the Law of Scotland* [1893] (New Haven: Yale University Press, 1981) I.1.i, cited by MacCormick (1978) (n 1 above) 1–2, 39–40.

[3] ibid 2–3, 5. [4] ibid 5.

nor equally convincing to everyone'. To his eyes, adherence to such premises is not a 'mere reaction to stimuli in the environment', as behaviourists would contend, nor 'simple emotional or animal reactions to immediate circumstances' (ie irrational), and: 'At least at the formal level, there are worthwhile analogies to be drawn between "practical" and "pure" reason'.[5] This section examines theoretical reason based on formal deduction and justice to see how 'reason' operates in legal contexts 'at its purest'. It argues that formal deduction and justice ultimately hinge on the meanings prevailing in any given society.

(1) Deduction

A typical line of argument used in everyday life and in law is deduction. Deductive reasoning proceeds syllogistically by drawing a conclusion from a major and a minor premise.[6] Syllogism is formal in the sense that the truth of the conclusion derives from the truth of the premises independent of their contents. As noted, 'it would be self-contradictory for anyone to assert the premises and at the same time to deny the conclusions'.[7] For example, if 'all men are mortal' and 'Socrates is a man', then it must necessarily follow that 'Socrates is mortal'. A typical hypothetical syllogism proceeds by arguing that 'if it rains, then the road is wet', and when 'it rains' it must necessarily follow that 'the road is wet'. Adverbs like 'therefore', 'hence', 'then', 'as a result', 'consequently', and the like, crowd everyone's talk. They abound also in the realm of law, in judicial decisions and in scholarly legal arguments. A typical legal rule is drafted in terms of 'if *X*, then *Y*', implying that when *X* occurs (eg a murder), then *Y* must follow (eg sentencing to life imprisonment).[8] Adverbs like 'therefore' are clearly intended to provide a 'bridge', from one sentence or a number of sentences to another, and are felt to be particularly forceful in persuading interlocutors. The question of whether, or to what extent, syllogism and reason-giving apply to legal reasoning is much debated.[9] Attention is confined here to the social implications of formal reasoning applied to law.

In everyday life syllogism is often used fallaciously. For example, a proposition like 'this food is natural, therefore it cannot be harmful' may be shorthand for the implied syllogism 'non-natural food is (often) harmful, this is natural, therefore it is not harmful'. Of course, the fact that non-natural food is (often) harmful does not imply that natural food is always non-harmful. Many adult human beings have apparently internalized the inexorability of the syllogistic process and tend to associate its structure

[5] ibid 6.

[6] Aristotle, *Prior Analytics*, 24b 18–20, defining a syllogism as 'a discourse in which, certain things having been supposed, something different from the things supposed results of necessity because these things are so'. For syllogism in non-Western cultures, see eg J Ganeri, 'The Hindu Syllogism: Nineteenth-Century Perceptions of Indian Logical Thought' (1996) 46 PEW 1.

[7] MacCormick (1978) (n 1 above) 21–2.

[8] In Kelsenian terms, the hypothetical statement in which a legal rule consists reads 'if an individual A behaves in a certain way, then another individual B *ought* to behave in a certain other way' (emphasis added), unlike statements of natural science in which the condition is connected with the consequence by an 'is'. See H Kelsen, *General Theory of Law and State* [1945] (New Brunswick and London: Transaction Publishers, 2007) 45–9, 164.

[9] Seminal in American legal realism against deductivism in legal reasoning is J Dewey, 'Logical Method and Law' (1924–25) 10 Corn LQ 17, 26, arguing for 'a logic of prediction of probabilities rather than one of deduction of certainties'. For a comprehensive treatment of the topic, see eg A Soeteman, *Logic in Law: Remarks on Logic and Rationality in Normative Reasoning, Especially in Law* (Dordrecht: Kluwer, 1989).

with the generation of logically irresistible conclusions. Once drawn by way of syllogism, a proposition is felt to be 'rational' and to count as a reasoned argument preferable to the less reasoned arguments of antagonists.[10] It has also been noted that schizophrenics use distorted syllogisms by identifying predicates, such as when from the major premise 'men die' and the minor premise 'grass dies' the conclusion is drawn that 'men are grass'.[11]

But even when it is used validly, syllogism is far from being as forceful and definitive as it claims to be. The point is that syllogisms are always used by human beings in a human world in which what matters is always the *contents* of the premises, and contents always refer to social interaction, conflicting meanings given by different groups which defend opposing interests. Divergences always arise between conclusions reached through different syllogisms, although each contending party claims that its own syllogism is the only correct one. While the dispute is apparently about the only correct deduction to make, and hence on the very formal validity of syllogism, in fact it is about different premises. The contending parties seek to show that *their own* syllogism is *the* formally correct syllogism. The formal structure of the syllogism is used instrumentally to impose in terms of formal (and hence universal) validity a certain content as opposed to another. References to the meanings prevailing in society are found both when proving the premises of a syllogism and when breaking the otherwise endless circle of questioning and giving reasons in which syllogisms consist.

The formal structure of any syllogism implies that the conclusion must be fully contained in the premises. What is at stake in a syllogism is not the deduction, but the premises themselves. In every syllogism the question to be asked is whether the premises are true, on the basis of what criteria, and for the benefit of whom. For example, the proposition 'Socrates is mortal' presupposes that the interlocutors share a common understanding of 'what' the words 'Socrates' and 'mortal' mean. This shared understanding may be, as it is in the classic example that Socrates is a 'man', ie an entity like all those that the interlocutors call 'men', and that 'mortal' is everything that ceases to 'exist'. To state persuasively that 'Socrates is mortal' means that the audience *already* knows and has a common understanding of what is meant by Socrates and by mortal. This presupposed understanding is not dependent on the syllogism, but is crucial to the conclusion drawn therefrom. Even where the premises are the conclusions of other antecedent syllogisms, these latter cannot but ultimately rest on extra-syllogistic understandings. The always-presupposed common understanding of any term of all syllogisms is found in 'living' social interaction. The meaning which is to be attached to the terms of a syllogism is what any particular society so considers. In the legal context, premises may consist either in statements of propositions of law assumed to be true for legal purposes, or in findings of fact taken to be true for legal purposes, or intermediate conclusions derived from such premises. All these elements are usually anything but straightforward. Propositions of law are normally susceptible of disparate interpretations (about their very existence, scope of application, and content). This holds true also for their relevance in the instant case, the classification of the facts, any inference

[10] See RMI Byrne, J St BT Evans, and SE Newstead, *Human Reasoning: The Psychology of Deduction* (Hove: Lawrence Erlbaum Associates, 1993) 211–42; K Manktelow and MC Chung (eds), *Psychology of Reasoning: Theoretical and Historical Perspectives* (Hove and New York: Psychology Press, 2004).

[11] E von Domarus, 'The Specific Laws of Logic in Schizophrenia' in JS Kasanin (ed), *Language and Thought in Schizophrenia* (New York: Norton, 1944) 104, 111. The example is taken from G Bateson, *Steps to an Ecology of Mind* [1972] (Chicago and London: University of Chicago Press, 2000) 205, equating Domarus' formulation with metaphors and arguing that metaphors are indispensable tools for all human communication, even for that of the scientist.

drawn from the 'evidence' of facts available, their coherence and plausibility, the choice between two rival coherent versions of prima facie similar past cases, and includes also the methods used (whether scientific, or based on common sense, or other).[12] It is society that supplies the contents presupposed by any syllogism. This means that, behind the universally valid structure of syllogisms, in the real world (a) identical syllogisms may lead to different conclusions in different societies or in the same society at different points in time; and (b) the conclusion of any syllogism depends on the struggle in society between different groups which aspire to impose their own preferences as the 'common understanding', possibly the universal understanding, of the society as a whole.

One should also consider that a syllogism is a form of giving reasons by a process of explicitation. If somebody states that 'Socrates is mortal' and somebody's else asks 'why', a possible reasoned answer is 'because Socrates is a man and all men are mortal', which amounts to a syllogism. The interlocutor may be either satisfied with the answer or further ask 'why Socrates is a man' or 'why all men are mortal'. Many answers are possible thereto based on scientific evidence or other criteria, such as the Word of God or the teachings of a reputed sorcerer. This process of 'asking why' and giving reasons is potentially endless. It is always possible for human beings to question everything, including why one should question everything. However, human beings cannot afford in their real world to proceed endlessly by asking questions and giving reasons. They are pressed by quite a few other things, beginning with fulfilling their basic needs every day. They have to break at some convenient point the process of questioning and giving reasons (and hence of making syllogisms) by a decision, that is by an act of will, not of cognition. In the abstract there is no reason why one should stop at one point or at another. If I state 'God exists', my interlocutor may either be satisfied with this proposition or may challenge it by asking 'why'. I could try to give a reason such as 'because He spoke to humans through Jesus Christ'. This may count as a 'reason' to some but not to others. The process may either stop or go on endlessly, depending on how the interlocutor is prepared or willing to raise further questions and challenge the answers given. It will presumably be stopped at the point when the interlocutor is satisfied with the reason (or the entire string of reasons) given or when there is no longer interest in pursuing the argument. A common understanding of what 'level' of reason-giving is supposed to be satisfactory can only be found in society. Logic does not suggest what amount of reasons is satisfactory (and hence what syllogistic intensity is needed) to make a case with success. Certain arguments count as 'good reasons' in one environment but may be felt pedantic, artificial, pointless, or manifestly manipulative in others. The process evidently stops at the point which is judged 'sufficient' to counter possible counter-arguments in the circumstances. An argument appears 'more reasoned' than another when more reasons have been made explicit in its favour than the opposite argument, ie when more presuppositions have been unveiled. While certain arguments are stronger than others in any given society at any given point in time, all possible arguments are arbitrary in the sense that it is always possible to make stronger arguments in the same society at a different point in time or in other societies. It follows that (a) while certain reasons are better than others, no reason is better than all possible others; and (b) what counts as a better reason, also for legal purposes, depends on any particular society at any given point in time. The desirability of an identical standard of

[12] MacCormick (1978) (n 1 above) 90–2.

'better reasons' everywhere in all societies is matched by the current Western project to have the 'Western way' to truth count as the global, ultimate truth for all.

(2) Formal justice

Another technique used to apply 'reason' to law is the appeal to the 'logic' of 'formal justice', as opposed to substantive justice. Formal justice is commonly defined as 'to treat like cases alike, and different cases differently, and give to everyone his due',[13] whatever the content. It is also defined, in the context of the common law tradition, as a technique to 'suppl[y] one good reason for following judicial precedents',[14] and to 'universalize' the instant case,[15] by following earlier similar cases and by thinking of the instant decision as potentially applicable to future similar cases with a view to avoiding the irrationality and arbitrariness of 'the uncertainty and insecurity of an arbitrarily run society, in which decisions of all kinds are settled on somebody's whim or caprice of the moment, without reference to past or future decision making'.[16]

Reason is thus contrasted with 'somebody's whim and caprice of the moment', ie to single persons making decisions at their caprice moment by moment, thus equating reason (and *formal* justice) with decisions made by one or more 'authorized' persons in accordance with some rules of general application and continuity in time. This concept is inherent in the view that law is ultimately 'general and abstract' so as to guarantee both equality and certainty. Law is law (ie formally just) only when its propositions are universalized or capable of being rendered universal. This seems to be a typical view of the law in the Western tradition. Others elsewhere may have a different outlook. Of course, it is reasonable to suppose that 'somebody's whim and caprice of the moment' would be felt to be 'unjust' by every human being everywhere, but the point is that the form this may take on in practice varies with people and divergences focus on *these* forms rather than on the general formula. If forms vary with the people involved, then also 'reason' and 'justice' vary in their conceptualization and contents, even where all people follow the same rules of logic, including the logic of formal justice. A particular society, no doubt different from English or Scottish society, to take MacCormick's preferred field of inquiry, may feel that what is sensed as arbitrariness and caprice by the Englishman or the Scotsman is to them perfectly 'rational', or simply 'normal'. What may provoke revulsion to the English or the Scots, or to the present writer, may be absolutely 'normal' in other peoples, and what is felt by the English or the Scottish as a threat to certainty and security (two issues they no doubt most value) may be felt as sufficiently certain and secure by other peoples (or two issues even unworthy of wasting time and energy over). People elsewhere may have no 'humiliating feeling' of being discriminated against, but rather of being valued as unique, while they may indeed experience humiliation in completely different circumstances. It seems reasonable to expect that certain people feel as highly threatening and upsetting certain situations which are felt by the English or the Scottish as perfectly reassuring and far from arbitrary. In a tribe, what the sorcerer decides on a case-by-case basis as a function of the person in question may be far more reassuring, given the faith in the sorcerer's infallibility, than general and abstract rules which 'treat like cases alike, and different cases differently, and give to everyone his due'. The much-celebrated maxim *suum cuique tribuere*—along with its derivatives 'to each what he deserves' or 'to each

[13] MacCormick (1978) (n 1 above) 73.
[14] ibid 74. [15] ibid 81, 84. [16] ibid 77.

according to his merits'—is found in the ancient Western wisdom[17] and in human rights,[18] but was also placed over the Buchenwald concentration camp's main entrance gate ('Jedem das Seine').[19]

What is thought to be 'reason' and 'formal justice' may well be common to all peoples and, indeed, inherent in the human being. It is not implausible, however, to think that reason and formal justice have been actually invoked and used differently to reach different outcomes. This being the case, what really matters is not whether 'reason' or 'formal justice' are common to all peoples and inherent in the human being—a statement that, even if true, does not affect the outcome of any reasoning, unless it is used to appropriate the supposed 'only' truth and impose it on all—but rather what kinds of different uses of reason are made by human beings living in the real world through their social interaction.

B. Practical Reason

When propositions like Lord Halsbury's 'Every lawyer must acknowledge that the law is not always logical at all',[20] or Oliver Wendell Holmes' 'the life of the law has not been logic, it has been experience',[21] are contrasted with Lord Stair's warning that 'Law is the dictate of reason determining every rational being to that which is congruous and convenient for the nature thereof',[22] it is difficult to avoid a deep sense of puzzlement. If reason has to do with law but only 'up to a point', what is its role and what room should be left to 'experience' or 'non-logical' considerations? Was Franz Kafka right in the closing lines of *The Trial* in asserting that 'Logic may be unshakeable, but it cannot hold out against a human being who wants to live'?[23] What is known as 'practical reason' is often supposed to be the appropriate ground in which law operates and is to be placed, somewhere in between 'pure' reason and no reason at all.[24]

The term 'practical reason' refers to both 'reason' and 'action' (this latter from the Greek *praxis*) and may denote either reason that 'guides action',[25] or reason that 'can be

[17] Plato, *The Republic*, IV, 433a–b; Cicero, *De Natura Deorum*, III, 38; Cicero, *De Finibus, Bonorum et Malorum*, V, 67; Ulpian, in *Digest*, 1, 1, 10pr. See N Wolterstorff, *Justice: Rights and Wrongs* (Princeton and Oxford: Princeton University Press, 2008) 21–6.

[18] MacCormick (2005) (n 1 above) 115.

[19] To be intended in the sense that 'everyone gets what he deserves'. For memorial footage of the Buchenwald concentration camp, see <http://www.youtube.com/watch?v=OWV-Gp2IrEY&feature=related>.

[20] UK House of Lords, *Quinn v Leatham* Judgment of 5 August 1901, [1901] AC 495, 506.

[21] OW Holmes, *The Common Law* (Boston: Little Brown, 1881) 1.

[22] See n 2 above.

[23] F Kafka, *Der Prozeß*, 1 *Gesammelte Werke* (Frankfurt am Mein: S Fischer, 1950) 194 ('Die Logik ist zwar unerschütterlich, aber einem Menschen, der leben will, widersteht sie nicht'), English trans *The Trial* (Oxford: OUP, 2009) 164.

[24] RJ Wallace, 'Practical Reason', in Stan EP, at <http://plato.stanford.edu/entries/practical-reason>.

[25] See eg Plato, *Statesman*, 258d–e, dividing 'all science into two arts, . . . the one practical, and the other purely intellectual', the former 'possessed by the arts relating to carpentering and to handicraft in general [being] inherent in their application, and with its aid [creating] objects which did not previously exist' and the latter 'which merely furnish knowledge', like 'arithmetic and certain other kindred arts' independent of 'practical application'; Aristotle, *Metaphysics*, VI, 1, 1025b 22, arguing that 'practical' is what is produced, hence 'willed' by human decision; Aristotle, *Nicomachean Ethics*, I, 2, 1094b, stating that practical reason concerns ethics, economics, oratory, strategy, and politics. This meaning was later revived in defining theology as a practical science: cf Thomas Aquinas, *Summa Theologiae*, I, q 1, a 4; Duns Scotus, *Opus Oxoniense*, Prol q 4, n 31. The Aristotelian notion was

translated into action',[26] or 'what is rational in action'.[27] In relation to law, practical reason has been defined as comprising 'principles for action' articulated 'in the realm of reasoning concerning the practical affairs of life', working as the 'guidance of decisions, judgments, appraisals' and engaging rationality as well as affectivity.[28] The domain of law being both reasoned and practical, lawyers and judges are called upon to give reasons for their statements,[29] assuming that we 'distinguish between good and bad, more sound and less sound, relevant and irrelevant, acceptable or unacceptable arguments', which 'is possible only given some criteria', including the rules of formal logic.[30] Acceptance 'as good reasons within the system', ie as both persuasive and justificatory reasons, is said to be vital.[31] But if so, one is led to conclude that even the rules of formal logic 'work' successfully *if* and *to the extent* that the community accepts them as persuasive and justificatory, or better than others. This shifts the problem from formal logic or theoretical reason to 'what is accepted' as logic or theoretical within the community, including the *criteria* to identify what is acceptable. Practical reason is, therefore, here defined as reason operating in society, counting as 'reason' to society and capable of guiding daily social action enabling people to live together. Thus defined, practical reason is not necessarily what is true to one or a few scholars, logicians, theorists, or outsiders. Practical reason amounts to what 'works in practice' within the community, whatever its theoretical or logical soundness from the perspective of the single observer.

Reason does accompany every act of human existence. Even the 'anything goes' thesis is an argument presented as being better than others. Yet, as previously observed, it is no less true that all 'reasoned' arguments between human beings are inexorably contingent on what people believe and understand as an 'argument' and as a 'good' argument. Excellent arguments in one group may well sound very bad, unpersuasive, or be no argument at all, in another. While it is possible to identify good arguments, in practical reasoning it is misleading to identify them regardless of the social context in which such arguments actually operate. Even a completely unsound notion of law may 'work in practice', and fully operate as law in a group that elevates it to 'the law', irrespective of what a few dissenters, members of other groups, or future generations within the same group, may think. Reasons within a group may be completely 'illogical' or 'irrational' from the perspective of an out-group or dissenters and yet work perfectly well within the group. To accuse law of being contradictory, as deconstructionists typically do, makes little sense because law, as a social phenomenon rather than a speculative or an aesthetical enterprise, does not aspire, nor does it have any need, to be logical or non-contradictory, but rather to 'work' in the perception of those concerned. If they are mad, their law will (and 'should') reflect their madness in order to be 'working', and no other law will presumably work in such a community. This is not to argue that this 'law for the mad' is 'in reality' not mad, but only that it is the only law that can be expected to work within the mad community. As explained in Chapter 1,

endorsed in the modern age, in particular, by C Wolff, *Philosophia Practica Universalis, Methodo Scientifica Pertracta* [1738–1739] (Hildesheim and New York: Georg Olms, 1979) § 3.

[26] This is the meaning prevailing in the ordinary language, such as when it is said that a person has 'practical ideas', meaning that s/he has ideas easily realizable with a high chance of success.

[27] cf I Kant, *Kritik der reinen Vernunft* [1781] (Berlin: De Gruyter, 1968) 520 ('Praktisch ist alles, was durch Freiheit möglich ist'), English trans *Critique of Pure Reason* (London: Penguin, 2007) 632, referring to all that which relates to free will, both as a principle and as a consequence ('all that is possible by means of freedom').

[28] MacCormick (1978) (n 1 above) 7.

[29] ibid 17. [30] ibid 12. [31] ibid 14–15.

law emerges as a balance of balances to hold together a group and help it to face a common overpowering challenger. Law works when it helps to perform this function. The need for cohesion in the group may require that emphasis be placed on security, or disciplinary order, or ethics, or physical training, or culture, or religion, or compassion; briefly on whatever the group thinks it most valuable to attain cohesion given the peculiarities of its members and what best works to that end in their perception as a group.

In summary, practical reason is reason used in a social context, rather than solipsistically. It has not to face personal tastes and logic, but rather to come to terms with very disparate people, as well as with the limitations of the physical and social world that may make everyday life difficult. The reasoner is immersed in the reality reasoned, and reasoning is in real time an integral part of what is reasoned. While the 'theoretical' thinker may perhaps remain detached from the reality observed, the practical thinker can hardly do so and must be mindful that her/his thinking will immediately affect the reality thought of. This section investigates practical reason thus understood by exploring the role played by common sense and prudence in legal reasoning.

(1) Common sense

Practical reason should be meant, first and foremost, in accordance with 'common sense', a term that sometimes overlaps with 'good sense' or 'sound judgement', especially in languages other than English.[32] Law works in society when the people who believe in it as their law share an unreflected and pervasive 'common sense'. Most of the law 'in force' in any community operates 'invisibly' as common sense. Explicit law, whether voluntarily posited or found in human nature or in the nature of things, is always a very tiny portion of the rules actually in operation. Even the rules 'posited' or 'found' work (to a great extent and in most societies) implicitly as common sense, ie as a sense of being somehow 'in tune' with one another. People perceive law as a matter of common sense, law-makers usually test the feasibility of laws against common sense, judges seek to interpret laws in the light of common sense, scholars endeavour to articulate theories of law possibly in accordance with common sense. It is indeed difficult to adopt and hold for long a stance that is radically antithetical to common sense in any given society. However, what people, law-makers, judges, and law scholars, intend by common sense

[32] eg in the Italian language, good sense (*buon senso*) and common sense (*senso comune*) have a somewhat different meaning and the difference may amount to sharp opposition in certain contexts. The best illustration is a splendid sentence found in Alessandro Manzoni's *I promessi sposi* [1840–1842] (Roma: Newton Compton, 2004) 489 ('il buon senso c'era; ma se ne stava nascosto, per paura del senso comune'), English trans *The Betrothed* (London and New York: Penguin Books, 1972) 603, in which Manzoni notes that at the time of the plague in 1630 in Milan 'Good sense [*buon senso*] still existed; but it was kept concealed, for fear of the popular sense [*senso comune*]' (this is a more accurate English translation found at <http://manzoni.classicauthors.net/IPromessiSposiOrTheBetrothed/IPromessiSposiOrTheBetrothed37.html>). It is adumbrated here that good sense means some personal, balanced, tactful, 'sound understanding' which is in tune with the most elementary demands of humanity, while common sense is the (presumably false, manipulative, or manipulated) sense shared by the community. The English-speaking world tends, to the contrary, to praise, rather than to view with suspicion, common sense, evidently on the reasonable belief that personal idiosyncrasies are more frequent and dangerous than those shared in society. In German two expressions are found (*gemeiner Verstand* and *gesunder Menschenverstand*), whose relationship is complex in Kant's thought (as will be seen in nn 57 and 58 below). Common sense and good sense are synonyms also in Thomas Reid's thinking (n 53 below). In the French language Henry Bergson significantly used the term 'bon sens' to mean something overlapping both common sense and good sense (n 64 below). For a philosophical analysis of good sense, see E Weil and JG Labadie, 'Good Sense or Philosophy' (1955) 3 *Diogenes* 29.

varies widely. Its definition and reliability is indeed highly contentious and, ironically, far from being itself accepted as a matter of common sense. People generally understand it as practical, self-evident, and socially inherited. Its meanings range from a physical unifier of the senses, to a cement which holds society together, to a set of empirical cause-and-effect relationships useful for practical orientation in everyday actions, to an array of scientifically untested or unfounded (although normally 'working') commonplaces mistakenly used in everyday life, to a preconceptual attunement with what is 'common' in any group, and to a mutual 'understanding' of social reality useful to its practical decipherment.

This section will discuss the Western intellectual background surrounding the notion of common sense in its key orientations, the tremendous importance in everyone's life of common sense as exemplarily illustrated by those who have lost it on account of schizophrenia, the pre-comprehension which invariably precedes any legal statement in accordance with what is known as the hermeneutic circle, and the vital role played by the 'rules of the game' working in a practical way in any social environment.

(a) Commonsensism

In the Western philosophical and legal tradition the term 'common sense' appears in Aristotle's *De anima* and *De somno* (*koiné aisthesis* in Ancient Greek), meaning common perception, ie what is common in the human senses (beyond their peculiarities) and what allows individuals to be conscious of sensation (namely, the 'feeling to feel').[33] Aristotle's *koiné aisthesis* is a sensory, embodied (pre-reflexive) act comparable to touch,[34] not a noetic (reflexive) act.[35] *Koiné aesthesis* is, first, the common root of the outer senses that allows the integration of different modalities of specific senses (seeing, hearing, etc) and the direct perception of 'common sensibles' (movement, rest, shape, number, unity) without any ad hoc sense organ, hence perceptual unity;[36] and, secondly, the consciousness of the sensation itself which cannot reside in any specific sense organ, hence self-consciousness, ie 'the common power accompanying all the senses, by which we perceive that we are seeing and hearing'.[37] This meaning was taken up by the Stoic Stobaeus in his *Eclogues* (*koiné ennoia*)[38] and by Aristotelian theologians such as Avicenna[39] and Thomas Aquinas[40] in the Middle Ages. Besides this Greek strand of thinking, there is a (partially Stoic-orientated) Latin tradition that links common sense (*sensus communis*) to habit, taste, common lifestyle, shared fashion of talking, hence self-evident, commonly shared truths, knowledge that connects individuals to society. Cicero held that it was a major defect for an orator 'to abhor from the vulgar form of the discourse and from the custom of common sense'.[41] Seneca's philosophy was explicitly driven by the development of *sensus communis*.[42] In the

[33] Aristotle, *De somno et vigilia*, 2, 455a 13; Aristotle, *De anima*, III, 1, 425a 14 ff.

[34] Aristotle, *De somno et vigilia*, 455a 22–4.

[35] CH Kahn, 'Sensation and Consciousness in Aristotle's Psychology' (1966) 48 AGP 41; CH Kahn, 'Aristotle on Thinking' in MC Nussbaum and AO Rorty (eds), *Essays on Aristotle's* De Anima (Oxford: Clarendon Press, 1992) 343–79.

[36] Aristotle, *De anima*, III, 1, 425a 14.

[37] ibid 425b, 427a; Aristotle, *De Somno*, 455a 13, 15.

[38] Stobaeus, *Eclogarum Physicarum et Ethicarum Libri Duo*, English trans *Physical and Moral Extracts* ('Eclogues'), I, 50.

[39] Avicenna, *Liber de anima seu sextus de naturalibus* (Leiden: Simone van Riet, 1972) III, 30.

[40] Thomas Aquinas, *Summa Theologiae*, I, q 78, a 4, ad 1; and I, q 1, a 3, ad 2.

[41] Cicero, *De oratore*, I, 3, 12; II, 16, 68; II, 9, 36.

[42] Seneca, *Epistulae morales ad Lucilium*, 5, 4 ('hoc primum philosophia promittit, sensum commune, humanitatem et congregationem').

Latin tradition, Aristotle's naturalistic explanation evolved into a humanistic outlook with a strong social and political connotation.[43]

A communitarian, Latin-inspired analysis of common sense was developed by the Italian philosopher Giambattista Vico. In *The New Science* (1744) he famously defined common sense as 'an unreflecting judgment shared by an entire social order, people, nation, or even all humankind'.[44] His was a thorough critique of René Descartes' geometrical method (*mos geometricus*)[45] and scientific-demonstrative ideal, later to be upheld by the Enlightenment and Jansenism, and a revival of the wisdom of the ancient and humanistic rhetoric in order to ground and maintain common good and justice based on a somewhat instinctive sense of natural law. Vico's concept of common sense was thus conspicuously different from Aristotle's and Thomas Aquinas'. Deeply rooted in the rejection of the exclusivity of the scientific method, it had an unquestionably moral and communitarian flavour. According to Vico it is 'from our common sense about what is necessary and useful to humankind', necessity and utility being 'the two sources of the natural law of nations', that human judgement (*umano arbitrio*), 'by nature uncertain', gains certainty.[46] This common sense consists of 'uniform ideas' which arose 'in entire nations . . . unknown to each other' which 'must have a common basis in truth'. It followed that 'mankind's common sense is a criterion which divine providence teaches peoples to aid them in defining what is certain in the natural law of nations' by 'looking beyond local variations in this law to recognize its essential unities, on which they all agree'. It was Vico's contention—against 'all previous ideas about the natural law of nations, which was believed to have originated first in one nation, from which it was later adopted by others'—that 'the natural law of nations arose separately among various peoples who knew nothing of each other' and that: 'Only later, on occasions involving wars, embassies, pacts, and trade, was it recognized as common to all humankind'.[47] He believed that 'Popular traditions always have a public basis in truth, which explains their birth and their preservation for many years by entire peoples' so that a 'great task' of his New Science was 'to discover these bases in truth, even when the passage of time and the subsequent changes in languages and customs have enveloped the truth in falsehood'.[48] To this end: 'Vernacular expressions are invaluable witnesses to the customs current among ancient peoples as their languages were forming'.[49] As is well known, Vico's key assumption was that: 'The *nature* of an institution is identical with its *nascence* at a certain time and in a certain manner'.[50]

[43] For the view that 'Aristotle's *koiné aisthesis* expresses both embodiment and attunement to the social world, self-consciousness and other-consciousness, today visible in the light of developmental psychology and neurobiology, see G Stanghellini, *Disembodied Spirits and Deanimated Bodies: The Psychopathology of Common Sense* (Oxford: OUP, 2004) 121.

[44] G Vico, *New Science: Principles of the New Science Concerning the Common Nature of Nations, Third edition Thoroughly Corrected, Revised, and Expanded by the Author* [1744] (London: Penguin Books, 2001) book 1, section 2, No 12, 80.

[45] However, in his *Discours de la méthode: Pour bien conduire sa raison, et chercher la vérité dans les sciences* [1637] (Paris: Flammarion, 2000), English trans *Discourse on the Method of Rightly Conducting the Reason, and Seeking Truth in the Sciences* (Oxford: OUP, 2008), Descartes himself used the terms 'good sense' and 'common sense' by referring 'good sense' to the man of sound judgment and to 'the power of judging aright and of distinguishing truth from error', ie 'reason' (ibid parts 1, 2, 3, and 6) and 'common sense' to what is received from tradition and ought to be followed (ibid parts 5 and 6).

[46] Vico (n 44 above) book 1, section 2, No 11, 79.

[47] ibid No 13, 80–1.

[48] ibid No 16, 81.

[49] ibid No 17, 81.

[50] ibid No 14, 81 (emphasis in the translated text, absent in the original).

A similar strong reliance on common sense was developed a few years later by Shaftesbury in his *Characteristicks of Men* specifically as the 'sense of the common' or 'the human aptitude for community and civility'.[51] His concept of common sense refers to 'wit' and 'humour', and more generally to 'love of the community or society, natural affection, humanity, obligingness', in a word 'sympathy'. Also Francis Hutchenson referred to common sense in his *A System of Moral Philosophy* (1755) as an instinctive capacity of moral assessment and infallible guide.[52] The Scottish School elevated the concept of common sense to the ultimate criterion of judgement and the basic principle to solve any philosophical doubt against metaphysics and the inevitable scepticism deriving therefrom. In his *An Inquiry Into the Human Mind* Thomas Reid referred 'common sense' and 'good sense' to traditional beliefs of humankind.[53] In his view:

> ... several original forces for belief... serve to direct us in the everyday affairs of life, where our reasoning faculty would leave us in the dark. They are a part of our constitution, and all the discoveries of our reason are based on them. They make up what is called 'the common sense of mankind'; and what is plainly contrary to any of them is what we call 'absurd'. Their strength is 'good sense', which is often found in people who are not highly intelligent. A remarkable deviation from them, arising from a disorder in the person's constitution, is what we call 'lunacy'.[54]

He thus called for 'A clear listing and explanation of the principles of common sense' as 'one of the chief things that logic should provide'.[55]

Pietism also accepted the guiding value of common sense. In particular, M Friedrich C Oetinger contrasted *sensus communis*—translated as 'heart' (*Hertz*)—with reason. To his eyes, common sense 'is concerned only with things that all men see daily before them, things that hold an entire society together' and reflects 'the vivid and penetrating perception of objects evident to all human beings, from their immediate contact and intuition, which are absolutely simple'. Here, Aristotle's notion of perceptual unity is combined with a sense of divine mystery of life and simplicity.[56]

This strand of thought was resolutely opposed by Immanuel Kant, who provided an epistemological and aesthetical concept of common sense, stripping it of its peculiar moral and communitarian connotations relied upon by Vico, Shaftesbury, Hutchinson, Reid, and Oetinger. In the *Prolegomena to Any Future Metaphysics* (1783) Kant argued that metaphysics as a science of pure reason is confined to speculative understanding and does not extend to 'gemeiner Verstand' or 'gemeiner Menschenverstand' (literally 'common understanding' or 'common human understanding') and 'gesunder Verstand' (literally 'healthy understanding').[57] He thought that *gemeiner Verstand* was

[51] AA Cooper, Earl of Shaftesbury, *Characteristics of Men, Manners, Opinions, Times* [1711] (Cambridge, CUP, 1999) 29, note A.

[52] F Hutchenson, *A System of Moral Philosophy* [1755] (London and New York: Thoemmes Continuum, 2006).

[53] T Reid, *An Inquiry Into the Human Mind* [1794] (Edinburgh: Edinburgh University Press, 2010).

[54] ibid ch 7, Conclusion, para 4.

[55] ibid.

[56] MFC Oetinger, *Inquisitio in sensum commune et rationem* [1753] (Stuttgart: Bad Cannstatt, 1964); MFC Oetinger, *Die Wahrheit des sensus communis oder des allgemeinen Sinnes, in den nach dem Grundtext erklärten Sprüchen und Prediger Salomo oder das beste Haus- und Sittenbuch für Gelehrte und Ungelehrte* [1753] (Stuttgart: Ehmann, 1861). See GA Magee, *Hegel and the Hermetic Tradition* (Ithaca: Cornell University Press, 2001) 67.

[57] I Kant, *Prolegomena zu einer jeden künftigen Metaphysik, die als Wissenschaft wird auftreten können* [1783] (Hamburg: Meiner, 1957) 6, 27, 138–9, 141, English trans *Prolegomena to Any Future*

'only of use so far as it can see its rules (though they actually are a priori) confirmed by experience', but 'to comprehend them a priori, or independently of experience, belongs to the speculative understanding, and lies quite beyond the horizon of common sense [*liegt ganz außer dem Gesichtskreise des gemeinen Verstandes*]'. To his mind, *gemeiner Menschenverstand* was to be 'shown practically, by well-considered and reasonable thoughts and words, not by appealing to it as an oracle, when no rational justification can be advanced'. He regarded the appeal to common sense (*die Berufung auf den gemeinen Menschenverstand*) as 'an appeal to the opinion of the multitude [*eine Berufung auf das Urteil der Menge*], of whose applause the philosopher is ashamed, while the popular charlatan glories and confides in it', a witness 'whose authority depends merely upon rumor [*dessen Ansehen nur auf dem öffentlichen Gerüchte beruht*]', an accommodation 'to personal peculiarities [*nach persönlichen Eigenschaften*]', nothing but 'normal good sense, so far it judges right [*der gemeine Verstand, sofern er richtig urteilt*]', which in turn 'is the faculty of the knowledge and use of rules *in concreto*, as distinguished from the speculative understanding, which is a faculty of knowing rules *in abstracto*', and, finally, something to which appeal should never be made except 'when we are forced to... renounce all purely speculative cognition [*Metaphysik, als einer spekulativen Wissenschaft der reinen Vernunft*]'. A few years later, in *The Critique of Judgment* (1790), Kant defined 'gesunder Verstand' as what makes a judgement of taste possible. In his view 'This differs essentially from common understanding [*vom gemeinen Verstande*], which is also sometimes called common sense [*Gemeinsinn*] (*sensus communis*)' in so far as 'the judgement of the latter is not one by feeling, but always one by concepts, though usually only in the shape of obscurely represented principles'.[58] Kant's critique, whose roots are traceable to the very beginning of philosophy in ancient Greece as a 'scientific' project against *doxa* (false opinion),[59] was echoed by George FW Hegel,[60] perhaps Martin Heidegger,[61] Gilles Deleuze,[62] and others.[63]

Metaphysics (Forgotten Books, 2008) 5–6, 25, 128–129, 131, also available at <http://philosophy.eserver.org/kant-prolegomena.txt>.

[58] I Kant, *Kritik der Urteilskraft* [1790] (Hamburg: Meiner, 1959) § 20, 79–80, English trans *The Critique of Judgement* (Oxford: OUP, 2007) 68–9.

[59] cf eg Heraclitus' fragment whereby 'Though the logos is common, the many live as if they had a wisdom of their own' (DK B2), as well as Plato's picture of the philosopher detached from populace and practical life, unbiased, 'pay[ing] no attention to his next door neighbour' and 'derided by the common herd', or of philosophy as private (albeit universal) knowledge as opposed to public, manipulated knowledge (*Theaetetus*, 174a–b, 175b). This picture was revived, in other circumstances and for different purposes, in the Renaissance by Francis Bacon's four classes of idols which beset men's minds, discussed in his *Novum Organum* [1620], English trans *The New Organon* (Cambridge: CUP, 2000) para 39.

[60] GWF Hegel, *Phänomenologie des Geistes*, in *Werke* (Hamburg: Meiner, 1980) 47, English trans *Phenomenology of Spirit* (Oxford: Clarendon Press, 1977) 42, para 69, observing that 'when philosophizing by the light of nature [*das natürliche Philosophieren*] flows along the more even course of sound common sense [*im ruhigeren Bette des gesunden Menschenverstandes*], it offers at its very best only a rhetoric of trivial truths [*eine Rhetorik trivialer Wahrheiten*]'.

[61] M Heidegger, *Sein und Zeit* [1927] (Frankfurt am Main: Klostermann, 1977) 222–6, English trans *Being and Time* (Oxford: Blackwell Publishing, 2005) § 35, 211–14. It is controversial whether Heidegger's depiction of 'Idle Talk' or 'Chatting' (*Gerede*), which he defined as 'the possibility of understanding everything without previously making the thing one's own' (at 213), without necessarily having disparaging connotations (at 211), can be linked to common sense.

[62] G Deleuze, *Différence et répétition* (Paris: Presses Universitaires de France, 1968), English trans *Difference and Repetition* (New York: Columbia University, 1994) 131. For a comment, see J Reynolds, 'Common Sense and Philosophical Methodology: Some Metaphilosophical Reflections on Analytic Philosophy and Deleuze' (2010) 41 *Philosophical Forum* 231.

[63] See eg n 65 below.

A rediscovery of the communitarian connotation of common sense is owed to Henry Bergson, who invoked 'good sense' in *Ecrits et paroles* (1895). He stressed that 'le bon sens préside à nos relations avec les personnes', as 'un sens délicat, une vision ou plutôt un tact de la vérité pratique', thanks to its 'sens social'.[64] A few decades later, the inevitability of common sense was emphasized by Alfred N Whitehead in *The Organization of Thought* (1929), observing that 'science is rooted in ... the all apparatus of common sense thought', ie 'the *datum* from which it starts, and to which it must recur' in that 'You may polish up common sense, you may contradict it in detail, you may surprise it. But ultimately your whole task is to satisfy it'.[65] After a few years, John Dewey highlighted the practical character of common sense in his *Logic* (1938).[66] He defined common sense as 'the conceptions and beliefs that are currently accepted without question by a given group or by mankind in general'. Such conceptions and beliefs are deemed to 'have something of the same ultimacy and immediacy for a group that "sensation" and "feeling" have for an individual in his contact with surrounding objects'. Dewey maintained that 'every cultural group possesses a set of meanings which are so deeply embedded in its customs, occupations, traditions and ways of interpreting its physical environment and group-life, that they form the basic categories of the language-system by which details are interpreted'.[67] As a result, common sense problems and inquiries are thought to form 'a system but the system is practical rather than intellectual', constituted as such 'by the traditions, occupations, techniques, interests, and established institutions of the group' and composed by meanings 'carried in the common everyday language of communication between members of the group'.[68]

Finally, a reading of common sense as a set of social constructs was proposed in 1953 by the sociologist Alfred Schutz.[69] He suggested that common-sense constructs are forms of organization of thought shared by a group which are from the outset intersubjective, or socialized, a sort of 'syntax', 'constructed' to decipher the other and enabling mutual understanding and communication, 'needed to grasp [typify] the other [and the self] and his behaviour'. Such constructs help the understanding of the world as a 'treasure house of ready-made pre-constituted types' and make socialization of knowledge possible since common sense overcomes the difference in individual perspectives through the idealization of both the interchangeability of the standpoints and the congruency of the system of relevances.

(b) Attunement

People experience their involvement in communities by the act of intuitively 'attuning' with one another. Attunement amounts to feeling 'in tune' (or 'in body resonance') with others, a two-part process going beyond empathy by metaphorically feeling to be 'in their skin'. As Daniel N Stern has shown in *The Interpersonal World of the Infant*, attunement is the cornerstone of intersubjectivity, originating in the mother–infant

[64] H Bergson, *Ecrits et paroles* [1895] (Paris: Presses universitaires de France, 1957) I, 84, 84–5, 88–9, noting that 'le bons sens consiste en partie dans une disposition active de l'intelligence, mais en partie aussi dans une certaine défiance toute particulière de l'intelligence vis-à-vis d'elle-même'.

[65] AN Whitehead, *The Organization of Thought: Educational and Scientific* (London: Williams and Norgate, 1929) 110. For a partial criticism from a scientific perspective, see LP Thiele, *The Heart of Judgment: Practical Wisdom, Neuroscience, and Narrative* (Cambridge: CUP, 2006) 103–4.

[66] J Dewey, *Logic: The Theory of Inquiry* (New York: Holt, Rinehart and Winston, 1938).

[67] ibid IV, 62.

[68] ibid VI.6, 115.

[69] A Schutz, 'Common-sense and Scientific Interpretation in Human Action' (1953) 14 PPR 1.

relationship.[70] It is the ability to recognize and join with the other through the same common meaning structures, affectivity, and emotional life.[71] It is not a set of cognitive beliefs forming the content of consciousness, nor a stock of reflective knowledge, nor an act of theoretical cognition. Attunement makes intersubjectivity and a communal real world possible. As common sense, it is 'the ability to see things in the appropriate perspective, an implicit non-conceptual grip of the "rules of the game", a sense of proportion, a taste for what is adequate and appropriate, likely and relevant',[72] an experience of belonging that makes one feel 'one of them' who share a common world. The exposition to the absence of such a feeling means the loss of reality, the reality of both self and other, and the abnormal experience of depersonalization (self-disorders) and desocialization (autism).

Schizophrenics are prone to lose common sense.[73] They seem to lack or reject common-sense constructs, such as the cause-and-effect relationships in the physical realm and motivational ones in society, that are normally used for practical orientation in everyday action. As noted, 'our literal survival depends upon a finely tuned knowledge of the causal texture of the world'.[74] This detachment, or hypo-connectedness, or 'out-of-tune' state, from common sense is particularly revealing of the centrality of common sense to everyone's life, both as an individual and as a social being.[75] From this perspective, common sense is understood as 'the constitutive element of the perception of reality, and as such, the true pillar of normal mental life', a 'set of interpretative procedures or "account practices" shared in a tacit and implicit manner by everyone belonging to the same cultural context... built on the edge of the great abyss of the doubt that reality is *not* how it is usually represented', covering, concealing, and preventing access to the abyss of doubt.[76] Schizophrenics' loss of common sense amounts to lack of attunement and a damaged network of social knowledge. Their capacity to accurately typify the mental states of others is impaired because of 'an incapacity to be involved in their mental life', and their background knowledge useful for organizing everyday experiences is damaged.[77]

Nothing shows better that schizophrenia how people, even the most self-professed individualist or anarchic, rely on common meaningful rules in society. Law can hardly be made sense of if one does not take account of this disorientating, indeed devastating, experience of total absence of common rules capable of indicating how one should behave minute after minute. Human beings count on, and ask for, rules far more than

[70] DN Stern, *The Interpersonal World of the Infant* (New York: Basic Books, 1985). For a comment, see TW Downey, book review (1988) 69 IJP 139.

[71] M Scheler, *Wesen und Formen der Sympathie: Die Deutsche Philosophie der Gegenwart* [1923] (Bern and Munich: Francke, 1973), English trans *The Nature of Sympathy* (New Brunswick and London: Transaction Publishers, 2008).

[72] J Parnas, P Bovet, and D Zahavi, 'Schizophrenic Autism: Clinical Phenomenology and Pathogenetic Implications' (2002) 1 *World Psychiatry* 131; P Bovet and J Parnas, 'Schizophrenic Delusions: A Phenomenological Approach' (1993) 19 *Schizophrenia Bulletin* 579, 583.

[73] W Blankenburg, 'Ansätze zu einer Psychopathologie des "common sense"' (1969) 12 *Confinia Psychiatrica* 144, holding 'lack of common sense' as the essential feature of autism; W Blankenburg, *Der Verlust der natürlichen Selbstverständlichkeit: ein Beitrag zur Psychopathologie symptomarmer Schizophrenien* (Stuttgart: Enke, 1971).

[74] HC Plotkin, *Evolution in Mind: An Introduction to Evolutionary Psychology* (London: Penguin, 1997) 195.

[75] Stanghellini (n 43 above), arguing that the 'crisis of common sense' is probably the main root of schizophrenia and the origin of full-blown psychotic symptoms.

[76] ibid 67–8.

[77] G Stanghellini, 'At Issue: Vulnerability to Schizophrenia and Lack of Common Sense' (2000) 26 *Schizophrenia Bulletin* 775–87, 783.

is usually conceded by both theorists and laymen. And, unfortunately, the lack of acknowledgement of law impacts on its reality and makes it less relevant in real time. It is part of the reality of law to be hoped for and strongly willed. To state that law *is* inadequate or irrelevant amounts to saying that law *must* be so.

(c) Pre-comprehension

The concept of common sense is central to philosophical hermeneutics, as evidenced by the special attention devoted to it by Hans-Georg Gadamer in *Method and Truth*, published in 1960.[78] In this connection Joseph Esser, a German scholar concerned with civil law and legal methodology, sought to critique positivism—along with the claim that law should be reduced to a legalistic subsumption of facts into norms without considering extra-positive factors—by appealing to the notion of the 'hermeneutical circle' and 'pre-comprehension' in the interpretation and application of law. He did so in his *Vorverständnis und Methodenwahl in der Rechtsfindung*, which first appeared in 1970.[79] Hermeneutical thinking assumes that the inquirer is always involved in interpretations of the world that do not grow out of nothing, but are born 'already framed' according to pre-existing interpretative patterns, both objective and subjective. In the hermeneutical circle the inquirer finds new meanings which are invariably based on others already given. Comprehension occurs always within a 'pre-comprehension' and, at the same time, it constitutes the pre-comprehension for a new, further comprehension. Comprehension is thus seen as interpretation, and interpretation unfolds as a circular (rather than unilinear) phenomenon.

In transposing the concepts of the hermeneutical circle and pre-comprehension to law, Esser contended that interpreters, in particular judges, operate within a pre-existing normative horizon comprising not only their subjective or 'private' judgement but also, and pre-eminently, 'objective' judgements reflecting the 'expectations' (or expected outcomes) of sense shared by the community in which they operate. The whole of these objective expectations is epitomized in such legal techniques as 'general clauses' and principles 'open' to interpretation (meta-normative and all-embracing in character), basically converging on the principles of fairness and reasonableness. The decision of the judge is, in effect, expected to be 'reasonable' (or 'fair') to its addressees, ie 'convincing, or at least acceptable' as 'the statement of objective law'. However, reasonableness is not, and cannot be 'posited' in legalistic terms, since it reflects the objective whole of expected outcomes of the community within which the interpretative process takes place. Legal interpretation thus represents a continuum with the making of rules, although the two operations remain distinct and there is no room for any 'free law'.[80] The legal material to be interpreted enters the interpretative process as a pre-comprehensive *objective* given, which makes it possible, at the same time, to generate the production of *further* meanings. The 'application' of law by the judge is then not to be reduced—unlike what positivists are traditionally said to contend—to the mechanical subsumption of a fact into a norm, since the interpretation of both facts

[78] H-G Gadamer, *Wahrheit und Methode: Grundzüge einer philosophischen Hermeneutik* (Tübingen: JCB Mohr, 1960, rev edn 1975), English trans *Truth and Method* (London and New York: Continuum, rev translation, 2004) 17–27.

[79] J Esser, *Vorverständnis und Methodenwahl in der Rechtsfindung: Rationalitäts-Garantien der Richterlichen Entscheidungspraxis* (Frankfurt am Main: Athenäum-Fischer-Taschenbuch-Verlag, 1970, 2nd edn, 1972).

[80] See Ch 4 below, n 107.

and norms already occurs in a given framework which objectively pre-orientates the interpreter, based on principles (such as reasonableness) which lie 'before' every principle or norm 'posited' by the law-maker. The principle of reasonableness itself, were it to be posited or clarified by the law-maker in a written norm, would be affected by a broader, still presupposed sense of reasonableness. Reasonableness required by a law-maker would still be required to be 'reasonable', and this can occur only on the basis of criteria that the law-maker has not, and could not, 'posit' by explicit norms. Posited norms invariably refer to presupposed norms. There can be no stated meaning without an unstated, yet decisive, meaning.

The application of the hermeneutical circle to law has been critiqued—especially when used in constitutional law—as leaving too much room for the courts' discretion, legal uncertainty, and the possibility of manipulating existing law. It has also attracted criticism for its rehabilitation of prejudices and tradition as part of the pre-comprehensive horizon which provides the meanings enabling the interpreter to proceed in the interpretation of the law. As Gadamer wrote: 'If we want to do justice to man's finite, historical mode of being, it is necessary to fundamentally rehabilitate the concept of prejudice and acknowledge the fact that there are legitimate prejudices', rooted in tradition.[81] Critics accuse this approach of being conservative and, at least potentially,[82] obscurantist. It indeed seems to imply that people can understand one another and share a common world only if they share a set of historically determined prejudices and preconceptions (amounting to what is known as common sense), whereas prejudices (intended as unfounded judgments) do obstruct rather than facilitate communication and mutual understanding. Gadamer replied that 'The overcoming of all prejudices, this global demand of the Enlightenment, will itself prove to be a prejudice' and 'we are always situated within traditions'.[83]

The point of philosophical hermeneutics is to re-position inquirers in society and throw them out of their ivory towers from which—in their personal, solitary, idiosyncratic eyes—truth is believed to be accessible, then 'proclaimed' to the populace and contrasted with the false or unfounded 'opinion' (*doxa*). It is in effect for society, within society, and by way of society that inquirers can pursue their activity. Once in society, the inquirer cannot avoid *attuning* with the surrounding people and exploring truth as part of this ensemble of people for whom truth is looked for and must be meaningful. If this is true for the philosopher, it is all the more so for the jurist, whose subject-matter is law, and law is what works as such in society, whatever the society, not in the mind of a single person, however learned. Only by grasping common sense in a particular society at a particular time in a particular place and by attuning with such society can the jurist get the 'code' which allows the 'real' law to be identified. This law is objective to the extent that it is the 'objective law' for the people concerned. The charge with too broad a margin of discretion and legal uncertainty for the judges falls if account is taken of the fact that attunement is aimed at grasping law as believed in its objectivity in society, as opposed to objectivity in the solitary mind of the jurist. Gadamer's 'legitimate prejudices' are nothing other than the *impact of society* on the inquirer who is trying to

[81] Gadamer (n 78 above) 273–85, 273, 278.

[82] In distinguishing 'legitimate prejudices' from all others and in reframing the question in terms of 'what distinguished legitimate prejudices from the countless others which it is the undeniable task of critical reason to overcome', ibid 278, in effect, Gadamer seems to retain the distinction between what may be called prejudices and biases.

[83] ibid 277, 283.

capture truth and finds that s/he has to come to terms with all those for whom truth will be meaningful.

The 'presupposed' meaning underlying any posited norm is the social impact on single individuals, including inquirers. The attempt of the inquirer to be 'above the community' in the search of truth is a strategy that may succeed, but this does not detract from the fact that it is actually used as a tool in the daily struggle for what should count as truth and, ultimately, justice in the group. The inquirer seeks to make proselytes and cause her/his truth, rather than another, to be imposed by the group on its members. It is the attempt of the inquirer to occupy the status of a 'ruler' who lays down the truth supposedly against all injustices that occur in the group. S/he is not simply presenting her/his truth as 'the' truth, but *fighting* to make this truth, against competing truths, become the truth in the group, sustained as such by the force of the group. Legal inquirers are part of the struggle, it is also for them to strive and transform the world, not just to 'discover' a 'real' truth that 'is there' waiting to be discovered.

(d) Rules of the game

In his famous essay *A Defence of Common Sense*, George E Moore assigned to 'truisms', which he understood as beliefs ascribable to common sense, the character of intuitive and irrefutable ontological certainties rooted in human nature.[84] He argued that such simple perceptual statements as 'this is a hand' are a certainty, and their denial—typical of sceptics—leads to inconsistency in beliefs and behaviour, as well as to even less certain propositions.

In *On Certainty*, a compilation of notes published posthumously in 1969, Ludwig Wittgenstein, while nowhere expressly mentioning the term 'common sense', replied that Moore's truisms are grammar rules presiding over the linguistic articulation of experience,[85] perhaps, as noted, 'the relics of that stable Victorian world that mistook its logical and grammatical points of view for cognitive certainties'.[86] Wittgenstein asked 'Why *am* I so certain that this is my hand? Doesn't the whole language-game rest on this kind of certainty? Or: isn't this "certainty" (already) presupposed in the language-game?', answering: 'Namely by virtue of the fact that one is not playing the game, or is playing it wrong, if one does not recognize objects with certainty'.[87] The picture of the world represented by common sense is deemed to be received as a form of socially derived, cultural imprinting, as opposed to the natural quality of common-sense knowledge claimed by Moore, as 'the inherited background against which I distinguish between true and false'.[88] It is described by propositions that 'might be part of a kind of mythology', and 'their role is like that of rules of a game; and the game can be learned purely practically, without learning any explicit rules'.[89] People understand one another and share a communal world because they have learnt to play the same game—including a variety of language games (*Sprachspiele*) embedded in what Wittgenstein called 'forms of life' (*Lebensformen*)—as the others are playing. He emphasized that 'The child learns to believe a host of things', ie 'to act according to

[84] GE Moore, 'A Defence of Common Sense' in JH Muirhead (ed), *Contemporary British Philosophy (2nd series)* (London: Allen and Unwin, 1925) 193. For a comment, see AF Holmes, 'Moore's Appeal to Common Sense' (1961) 58 *Journal of Philosopy* 197; AR White, 'Moore's Appeal To Common Sense' (1958) 33 *Philosophy* 221.

[85] L Wittgenstein, *Über Gewissheit*, English trans *On Certainty* (Oxford: Basil Blackwell, 1969).

[86] A Gargani, 'Introduzione' in L Wittgenstein, *Della certezza. L'analisi filosofica del senso comune* (Turin: Einaudi, 1978) xxv (English trans by the author).

[87] Wittgenstein (n 85 above) § 446. [88] ibid § 94. [89] ibid § 95.

these beliefs' and 'Bit by bit there forms a system of what is believed, and in that system some things stand unshakeably fast and some are more or less liable to shift'; however: 'What stands fast does so, not because it is intrinsically obvious or convincing; it is rather held fast by what lies around it'.[90] Games have rules, but no foundational basis thereof. It is not that truisms have an ungrounded conceptual presupposition; it is rather that their 'way of acting' is ungrounded.[91] The process of 'Giving grounds . . . justifying the evidence, comes to an end' and 'the end is not certain propositions' striking us immediately as true, ie it is not a kind of *seeing* on our part; it is our *acting*, which lies at the bottom of the language-game'.[92]

If sociality is based on playing by the same rules, it is necessary for human beings to be acquainted with the rules. This is possible only by entering the realm of society and capturing what 'works' as rules and how rules work. Law is part of this 'living' embedding in the game. There is no game without emotional participation therein. No one can learn the game by mere observation from an assumed privileged viewpoint detached from the game. The network of the games operating in a group forms the reality for the group, including the reality of law. It is for the jurist to grasp the rules of the game in the group as a precondition for identifying those particular rules that, according to the game, are supposed to work as legal rules. What matters is that law 'works' in the particular network of games in operation within the group. Reason is an element to make it work in so far as it accommodates the theoretical demands of what the group needs and acknowledges as its own law.

(2) Prudence

Although law is not equal to informal attunement, social attunement still grounds intersubjectivity and represents the 'horizon of sense' of the law prevailing in a group. Law constantly and implicitly refers to its meta-dimension in a variety of ways. It presupposes a pre-reflexive meta-narrative of law, inexplicable in terms of law, that is socially derived—namely, socially constructed, daily exchanged, and re-negotiated.[93] This *Ur*-law invariably 'preceding' and constantly 'surrounding' law has been given several names and meanings in jurisprudence, such as natural law or the 'nature of the things', *Grundnorm*, and so on. Legal officials and jurists are called upon to 'attune' themselves to the community and settle the meta-legal questions constantly raised by the law as it is formally understood. This exercise is traditionally known as 'prudence', from the Latin *juris prudentia*.

Prudentia is the translation of the ancient Greek word *phronesis*, usually translated in English as 'prudence' or 'practical wisdom'. Aristotle distinguished *phronesis* from *sophia* understood as theoretical science (later to be translated as *sapientia* in Latin, hence 'wisdom' in English). The distinction was apparently unknown before Aristotle. Plato used the two terms *phronesis* and *sophia* quite interchangeably. He defined *sophia* as the science (*epistéme*) that presides over just and honourable (*dikaían kaì kalèn*) action (*praxei*) capable of preserving and helping to produce a condition of the soul marked by harmony between self-mastery and inner, beautiful order,[94] while he stated with reference to *phronesis* that 'by far [its] highest and fairest part . . . is that which

[90] ibid § 144. [91] ibid §§ 109–110. [92] ibid § 204 (original emphasis).

[93] See L Gies, *Law and the Media: The Future of an Uneasy Relationship* (Abingdon and New York: Routledge-Cavendish, 2008) 4, arguing that 'law is a formidable construct to which we respond through quiet resignation, vociferous contestation and active negotiation' in our everyday routines.

[94] Plato, *The Republic*, IV, 443d–e.

concerns the regulation of cities and habitations... called sobriety [*sophrosúne*] and justice [*dikaiosúne*]'.[95] Aristotle defined *phronesis*, in opposition to *sophia*, as 'a truth-attaining rational quality, concerned with action in relation to things that are good and bad for human beings',[96] a knowledge not only 'of general principles' but also taking into account 'particular facts, since it is concerned with action, and action deals with particular things',[97] notably 'concerned with the affairs of men, and with things that can be the object of deliberation', a good deliberator being 'a man who can arrive by calculation at the best of the goods attainable by man' about 'variable things that are... a means to some end, and that end a good attainable by action'.[98] Thus defined, *phronesis* was highly praised by Epicurus, who described it as 'sober reasoning, searching out the grounds of every choice and avoidance, and banishing those beliefs through which the greatest tumults take possession of the soul' which is 'a more precious thing even than philosophy',[99] as well as by the Stoics,[100] whereas Plotinus revived the primacy of *sophia*.[101] Thomas Aquinas took up Aristotle's distinction and defined *prudentia* as 'good counsel about matters regarding man's entire life, and the end of human life',[102] a virtue 'most necessary for human life'.[103] In modern times, prudence was still associated with practical knowledge, such as Descartes' statement that 'philosophy signifies the study of wisdom' and that:

> ...by wisdom is to be understood not merely prudence in the management of affairs, but a perfect knowledge of all that man can know, as well for the conduct of his life as for the preservation of his health and the discovery of all the arts, and that knowledge to subserve these ends must necessarily be deduced from first causes.[104]

In recent times, Gadamer has stressed the distinction of Aristotle's *phronesis*—as 'practical' moral knowledge concerning 'action' in communal life (*praxis*), as opposed to individually 'making' things (*poiesis*)—from both theoretical and technical knowledge, ie from science (*episteme*) and technique (*techne*). Unlike acquiring an objective skill, *phronesis* cannot be learned or chosen, since 'we are always already in the situation of having to act'. Applying law itself entails 'refrain[ing] from applying the full rigor of the law, thereby 'finding the better law' corresponding to the 'nature of the thing' determined in each case.[105]

It is submitted that jurists are first and foremost *juris prudentes*, not scientists.[106] The observational standpoint of the scientist makes little sense with regard to law, unless the people concerned value science to the point of elevating it to the status of a general legal 'horizon of sense'. The scientific method may be helpful to law, but not necessarily, and can prove misleading and mistaken. In fact, the scientific vision of life typical of the

[95] Plato, *Symposium*, 209a.

[96] Aristotle, *Nicomachean Ethics*, VI, 1140b 4. See MT Thornton, 'Aristotelian Practical Reason' (1982) 41 *Mind* 57.

[97] Aristotle, *Nicomachean Ethics*, 1141b 7.

[98] ibid 1141b 6.

[99] Epicurus, *Letter to Menoeceus*, 132.

[100] Diogenes Laertius, *Lives of Eminent Philosophers*, VII, 1, *Zeno*, 125–6.

[101] Plotinus, *The Six Enneads*, V, 8, 4.

[102] Thomas Aquinas, *Summa Theologiae*, II, 1, q 57, a 4 ('prudentia est bene consiliativa de his quae pertinent ad totam vitam hominis, et ad ultimum finem vitae humanae').

[103] ibid a 5 ('prudentia est virtus maxime necessaria ad vitam humanam').

[104] R Descartes, *Principia Philosophiae* [1644], preface to French edn, English trans *The Philosophical Writings of Descartes* (Cambridge: CUP, 1985) vol 1, 179.

[105] Gadamer (n 78 above) 310–21.

[106] For the opposite view, see eg Kelsen (n 8 above) xxxix, advocating: 'The ideal of an objective science of law and State, free from all political ideologies'.

Western world and any attempt to conceive of law in universal terms based on the scientific model is an attempt to universalize the Western way to truth and conception of law. If law is not a mountain, as contended in the previous chapter, then legal reasoning is not a scientific enterprise.

Law implies some sense of the fairness and reasonableness (however understood) expected by and within the group concerned.[107] It is the group, with its constant, informal, internal interaction and its overwhelming force, that creates such an ungraspable (albeit 'living') horizon of sense that the jurist is expected to sense and capture. This cannot be done without 'living within' the group. Social attunement cannot take place intellectually from an observational standpoint. No one can learn how to behave better in a party without having ever participated in any party, merely relying on readings and thinking. Law is always the law of a certain group, whether the village or the universal community. Social attunement of course, although being per se an informal process, may well include formalism, or more precisely a certain level of formalism, when this degree of formalism is valued and required by the group. To object that the idea of reasonability or reasonableness is too vague and leaves law too widely indeterminate is a good point only when one refers to and reflects societies whose members as a whole require exactness and determinacy of law or, far more likely, *a certain way* of understanding exactness and determinacy, often something close to the scientific method.[108] But not all peoples have the same understanding of how determinate a legal statement must be in order to work in practice among them. The indeterminacy of law in this or that society is often measured by *outsiders* according to the law prevailing in *their* societies and by standards grown in their individual minds, including deconstructionist minds. It is, indeed, a claim to impose one's own conception of law on societies sharing another sense of law and another degree of determinacy needed to enable their law to work.

Law reflects a wide range of social interactions constantly in need of tuning, such as empathy, sympathy, attunement, sharing common-sense social constructs of typicality, but also ignorance, desire, panic, enthusiasm, idiocy, love, and many other nuances of human experience. As meaningful to any particular group, law has to accommodate this mix of persons, feelings, constructs, expectations, anticipations. To say that law is based on practical reason means that it tackles all the disparate beliefs found in a group. Thus it makes little sense to accuse law, from a speculative viewpoint, of not being 'logical' or 'well founded' enough. The law which operates in the solipsistic mind of the critic does not work in the group, and has no reason to work within the critic's mind, either. To take a 'theoretical' approach and assess how far a certain law is 'well founded', amounts

107 The meaning of 'reasonableness' and its difference from 'rationality' is notoriously elusive. Augustine argued that 'reasonable' (*rationabilis*) is he who can use reason, while 'rational' (*rationalis*) refers to what is done or said by reason (*De ordine*, XI, 31). However, the human being was also called 'rational' in antiquity (cf eg Quintilian, *Institutes of Oratory*, V, 10, 56). John Dewey defined the reasonable as the proportion of means to its ends, in the sense that the means are reasonable when with all probability they will produce the expected effects (*Logic* (n 66 above) 1). Thus defined, reasonableness implies a limitation to rationality, in particular the exclusion of the infallibility of reason and the taking into account of the concrete circumstances in which reason finds itself to operate. For an insightful discussion of the topic, see A Gewirth, 'The Rationality of Reasonableness' (1983) 57 *Synthèse* 225, arguing that rationality is a matter of means–end calculation pertaining to egoism and self-interest and reasonableness refers to morality and justice.

108 See eg T Van Doan, *Reason, Rationality, and Reasonableness* (Washington, DC: The Council for Research in Values and Philosophy, 2001). Similar observations apply to the 'rationality' of rational choice theory—see SL Quackenbush, 'The Rationality of Rational Choice Theory' (2004) 30 *International Interactions* 87—and to political realism.

to retreating to an ivory tower, observing the game from above, and proclaiming in total isolation the 'truth' of law as seen from the tower. It is of course easier to adjust things within the mind of one single theorist as s/he thinks fit than accommodating the variety of people and human experiences found in society.

In summary, prudence is key to practical reason and to law. Those who handle law are called upon to exercise prudence, of which the scientific process is at best a component. Law is not a construction aimed at truth, coherence, contradiction-proof propositions. It is not the creation of a single mind, however skilled or learned. It is what is believed by a group to be their law. Prudence presupposes a contact with the group, including its shared idiosyncrasies. It is often feared that a non-scientific method reduces certainty and increases arbitrariness in the identification, interpretation, and application of law. This may be true in a society which strongly believes in science. In other societies, however, faith in God or in a reputed sorcerer may provide much more certainty than the scientific method and its reliance on 'facts'. In other societies legal certainty may not even be a value.

Conclusion

This chapter has argued that (a) law is based on reason in the sense that certain legal arguments are better than others; and (b) the process of capturing this reason is basically a matter of prudence. Law is socially founded not only as a form of collective violence aimed at countering individual violence and as a mythic social construct, but also as a process inspired by a 'working' reason operating in and for society. Theoretical reason ultimately depends on the meanings prevailing in the particular society in which it operates. Identical syllogisms may thus reach different conclusions in different social contexts and any syllogism expresses a struggle between different groups aspiring to impose their preferences on society as a whole. Since deductive reasoning is both inescapable and potentially endless, in any society certain reasons are indeed better than others but no reason is better than all others. Also formal justice, notably epitomized in the maxim 'to everyone his due', is social-context-relative and, like syllogism, is used to appropriate a universal truth and to impose it on all. Practical reason is reason operating and working within any society. It consists of common sense, social attunement, pre-comprehension, and consideration for the rules of the game. It amounts to prudence. The whole discourse on the social foundations of law discussed in Part I of this book suggests that law is not necessarily a scientific enterprise and that jurists are, first and foremost, *juris prudentes* within the community.

PART II

THE CONSTRUCTION OF INTERNATIONAL LAW

4

De- and Remythologizing International Law

Having discussed law as a social construct in Part I, it is now possible to inquire how international law is socially constructed. This chapter addresses the way in which the construction of the reality of international law depends on its epistemological presuppositions, doctrinal diversity, and communicative strategies. It is argued that the processes through which international law is made known, problematized, and disseminated are part of its 'reality'. Epistemology, while challenging knowledge, cannot avoid ontological reality and reveals the Western analytical categories and words invariably used to *think* international law, whatever its contents. Doctrine has constantly mythologized, demythologized, and remythologized international law within a relatively closed circle of professionals. Communication is the key to spreading belief in international law worldwide but is far from being effective. Part II of the book will then address, in Chapters 5 to 8, the questions of who directly constructs international law, what international law is constructed, which values inspire international law and interact with one another, and, finally, what remedies are available against major breaches of international law.

A. Epistemology

How do we know what we know about international law? This key epistemological question, which affects the whole narrative of international law, articulates in other questions, such as: 'Who decides how we know what we know about international law?', 'Has what we know about international law some connection with the "reality" we believe we know?', 'Is there a "reality" of international law at all?', 'How can we know we are right, or *who* is right and *why*?', 'Is epistemological awareness of international law relevant after all?'. The question of the reality of such a thing as international law can hardly avoid being questioned by first of all asking how we know that international law is 'real', or at least what we mean by supposing so. This involves asking whether and how we can hope to understand our mental processes in capturing international law, whether there is a method or a methodology in understanding international law, and whether and to what extent language is influential in our representation of international law. This section argues that (a) while it is true that reality depends on knowledge and knowledge is knower-relative, still there is a level of 'reality' that is constantly 'beyond' critical epistemological reach; (b) this apparently inescapable 'ultimate' reality is the reality as viewed by the stronger; (c) since law is a social construct, there is no universal method or methodology of law other than prudential judgment; and (d) language, specifically English today, indeed shapes what we know as international law.

(1) How we know what we know

Posing the epistemological question of how we know what we know about international law basically amounts to challenging essentialism.[1] The premise is that international law does not exist 'in itself', regardless of the knowers and their idiosyncrasies and interests. The process signals a shift from the 'being' to the 'knowing', from the world 'out there' to the world represented 'within' the (individual or collective) knower, from reality to mind.[2] Deconstructionists have notably challenged classical international law by understanding epistemology as the process of uncovering its veiled biases.[3] Their project is often similar to the unmasking of (bourgeois) ideologies in Marxist thought.[4]

The point to make here is that, once the known and the knower are believed to be distinct, the epistemological exercise is both inevitable and ultimately impossible. It seems obvious that the known is the result of the way the knower knows and that knowers vary in their way of knowing. This process, on the other hand, is intrinsically endless since any level of knowledge is inexorably open to uncovering its underlying, unstated presuppositions. If we are to explore international law as it is currently known, then we can hardly avoid looking into whether and why our knowledge of international law is trustworthy at any stage of knowing. But unless we are prepared to get involved in an unending search for whatever imaginable further precondition of knowledge, we are forced to stop somewhere and we usually call this somewhere 'reality'.

In this sense the epistemological project is ultimately impossible, and ontology (together with essentialism) proves as inescapable as epistemology itself. We cannot avoid reality, whatever this may be. The knower can move 'backwards' in the search for the preconditions of knowledge but cannot go 'out' of reality. There is always an ontological 'reality' that can be challenged epistemologically and there is always some epistemological precondition of knowledge that must be (that *is* indeed) taken as *the* reality. Discussing epistemology in international law amounts not only to exploring how *any* 'reality' of international law can be challenged by investigating how knowledge occurs and for whose benefit, but also to take note that at some point in the epistemological exercise the knower must and *will* stop. The key question is *at exactly what point* the process should stop, or actually stops, and why stopping there rather than elsewhere is better or even inevitable in the circumstances as a matter of law, as opposed to personal taste or theory.

A corollary is that the entire epistemological project is ultimately ontological and Western in inspiration even when it is aimed at demystifying ontological and Western thought.[5] Epistemology found its way in the West as a strategy to take issue with (a certain) Western ontology by emphasizing such classical oppositions as those between 'subject' and 'object', 'being' and 'knowing', 'reality' and 'mind', and so on.

[1] It is indeed difficult to define what is meant by 'legal epistemology'. In Western thinking epistemology refers to the study of the nature, sources, value, and limits of knowledge. If the knowledge of law is regarded as a scientific endeavour, then legal epistemology is part of the epistemology of science. Often, however, what passes for legal epistemology coincides with the presuppositions of this or that legal theory. For legal epistemology in general, see C Atias, *Epistémologie juridique* (Paris: Dalloz-Sirey, 2002); G Samuel, *Epistemology and Method in Law* (Aldershot: Ashgate, 2003); P Dubouchet, *Droit et épistémologie: L'Organon du droit* (Paris: L'Harmattan, 2008).

[2] See n 178 below.

[3] See section B (5) below.

[4] See G Frankenberg, 'Critical Theory' MP EPIL (October 2010 update).

[5] See M Williams, *Problems of Knowledge: A Critical Introduction to Epistemology* (Oxford: OUP) 4–5.

While apparently designed to uncover the process of knowing and its 'subjective' influences—such as Kant's transcendentalism, whereby human knowledge of the world depends on how humans experience it according to the universally shared structure of mind in terms of space, time, and categories including cause and effect, substance, unity, plurality, necessity, possibility, and reality[6]—all epistemologies have always reiterated and reinforced their Western presuppositions by remythologizing Western thought in another direction. Epistemology has actually worked just like ontology for the Western domination of the world. It is, in the end, a Western ontology in disguise in so far as it invites deconstruction and stops deconstructing knowledge at a certain point rather than proceeding further. Unsurprisingly, this apparently candid, truth-orientated exploration of the preconditions of knowledge is systematically conducted in one way. Few today are prepared to take the lifestyle of this or that indigenous tribe as a valid global 'epistemological' framework in the quest for reality, including that of international law, nor have indigenous tribes been successful in globalizing their own approach to reality.

(2) A method for international law?

Is there a reliable 'method' or 'methodology', or a multiplicity of methods and methodologies, in international law?[7] This question needs to be discussed as part of the epistemological inquiry into international law because 'method' and 'methodology' may not be as neutral as their use is generally thought to imply.[8] Method and methodology may turn out to be an epistemological strategy to assert a certain construction of international law against others.[9]

The question of 'method' was the subject of lively debate during the European Renaissance,[10] and crucially theorized by René Descartes in his *Discourse on the Method* in which he sought to identify the 'true method' to arrive at truth against sceptics.[11] Within this Western tradition, the term 'method' refers either to *research* or to a *particular technique* of research consisting of an ordered, repeatable, self-correcting procedure, capable of ensuring valid outcomes. The distinction between the process through which an outcome is achieved and the contents of the outcome is key. Today the second, procedural, machine-like meaning prevails: an outcome is presumed valid if the machine has worked correctly. Any theory of truth may thus be seen as pertaining to method when its procedural protocol to attain truth is taken into consideration as a decisive element. The appeal to 'method' is an attempt to place the quest for truth on an apparently 'neutral' terrain and to replace the concept of truth as 'inherent' (in somebody's unchecked wisdom) by truth as 'correctly reached' by objective checks, generally scientific evidence and reasoning, whatever the outcome. It is procedure that

[6] P Guyer, *Kant and the Claims of Knowledge* (Cambridge: CUP, 1987); HE Allison, *Kant's Transcendental Idealism: An Interpretation and Defense* (New Haven: Yale University Press, rev expanded edn, 2004).

[7] For an overview, see O Corten, *Méthodologie du droit international public* (Brussels: Editions de l'Université de Bruxelles, 2009).

[8] For Feyerabend's 'anything goes' theory advanced against the purported neutrality of the scientific method, see Ch 2 above, section A (3)(c).

[9] P Allott, 'Language, Method and the Nature of International Law'(1971) 45 BYBIL 79.

[10] See NW Gilbert, *Renaissance Concepts of Method* (New York, Columbia University Press, 1960).

[11] R Descartes, *Discours de la méthode: Pour bien conduire sa raison, et chercher la vérité dans les sciences* [1637] (Paris: Flammarion, 2000), English trans *Discourse on the Method of Rightly Conducting the Reason, and Seeking Truth in the Sciences* (Oxford: OUP, 2008).

generates truth. The struggle for what should count as truth to all the members of a community shifts from the plain assertion of truth to the control of what should count as the valid procedure to follow in pursuing truth. Methodology, as distinct from method, has historically been understood as logic or as that part of logic concerned with methods. Methodology may also refer to certain scientific procedural techniques (such as analysis, synthesis, induction, deduction, experiment, etc) designed to reach valid outcomes.

In the legal domain, method and methodology pertain to how law is created, ascertained, and applied to particular facts. In law-making, as seen earlier, procedure is thought to work as a 'criterion of validity' when a certain proposition is regarded as a 'legal' rule because it has been (correctly) created according to a predefined procedure.[12] In law ascertainment, procedure is thought to work as the best way to identify the rule to be applied in a particular case.[13] The two contexts may not coincide. For example, a rule of natural law may not have been 'made' by anyone, yet it may be ascertainable by a standardized modus operandi, such as a philosophical or theological procedure based on the 'correct' manner to inquire into human nature or God's will. In international law, 'method' and/or methodology are often associated with the sources or with the interpretation and application of law,[14] and occasionally with the construction of a legal argument either in judicial reasoning or in academic work.[15] Method is also associated with one or another theory of international law.[16] By understanding international law as 'an argumentative practice', Martti Koskenniemi suggested that 'What passes for method . . . has to do with what counts as persuasive arguments' in international law ('how to convince *this audience, here and now*') as determined by 'the consensus in the profession'.[17] He seems to assume that international law is detached from the reality of 'ordinary people' and lives only (or predominantly) in the minds, thoughts, and debates of professionals and their circles.[18]

Most theorists conceive of legal analysis as a scientific endeavour and suppose that the scientific method, at least in principle, should be adopted when investigating law. The view here taken is that law is far from necessarily requiring the scientific method or any method at all. Since the community may prefer either no method, or one particular method, or a variety of methods, prudential judgement is the best approach to law in general, as already discussed in Chapter 3, and to international law in particular.

[12] See Ch 1 above, section B (3)(a).

[13] See J D'Aspremont, *Formalism and the Sources of International Law: A Theory of the Ascertainment of Legal Rules* (Oxford: OUP, 2011).

[14] cf F Castberg, 'La méthodologie du droit international public' (1933–I) 43 RdC 313; A Bleckmann, *Grundprobleme und Methoden des Völkerrechts* (Freiburg: Alber, 1982); M Bos, *A Methodology of International Law* (Amsterdam: North-Holland, 1984); S Rosenne, *Practice and Methods of International Law* (London: Oceana Publications, 1984); Corten (n 7 above) 137–262.

[15] ibid 263–77; Rosenne (n 14 above) 94–7.

[16] cf A-M Slaughter and SR Ratner (eds), 'Symposium on Method in International Law' (1999) 93 AJIL 291, selecting seven 'methods' defined as 'the application of a conceptual apparatus or framework—a theory of international law—to the concrete problems faced in the international community' (at 292). It is worth recalling Martti Koskenniemi's critique of the format adopted by the editors as a 'shopping mall approach to method' assuming the 'styles of legal writing' like 'brands of detergent' to be 'put on display alongside one another' before being 'picked up by the customer according to his/her idiosyncratic preferences' (at 352).

[17] M Koskenniemi, 'Methodology of International Law' MP EPIL (November 2007 update) paras 1 and 25 (original emphasis).

[18] For a critique of this approach, see section B (5) below.

(3) The Importance of language

In so far as international law is a matter of verbal discussion between interlocutors, including legal officials and scholars, it needs a common language. Every discussion presupposes some common understanding between the interlocutors. What the sender of a message has in mind is supposed to be identical, or at least as close as possible, to what reaches the mind of the receiver. The language used is thus essential. Not only thinking, as in epistemology, but also words presuppose a cultural background and a direction in researching, orientating interlocutors to a certain truth rather than another. Clearly, those who are more familiar with the dominant language are far more capable of making their points and having their arguments accepted.

Language is particularly critical in today's post-decolonization, multicultural world. If a common language is indispensable, and if any language is crucial to the relative strength of the interlocutors, then the question arises of possible misunderstandings and differing persuasive force between peoples of different cultural backgrounds. A linguistic hierarchization is little in tune with a world in which different cultural codes are supposed to enjoy equal dignity, yet speaking in all existing languages may frustrate any communication. There was apparently no such problem when international law was expressed by a language common to all the interlocutors in the European landscape, as Latin was at the time, a Western, sufficiently common understanding that can no longer be taken for granted at global level.[19]

The adoption of a certain language amounts to adopting a distinctive logic and world image. Language is key to the construction of reality, including the reality of international law. The fact that the *lingua franca* today is English implies that the English logic, worldview, and preferences are more likely to prevail and shape what 'reality' is taken to mean.[20] The dominance of the English language forces the international law debate into a specific mode of thought, which is far from being as universal as English itself apparently is,[21] and reinforces the Western bias in its Anglo-American variant.

B. Doctrines

The image of international law is relentlessly made and unmade by scholars. New theories demythologize past ones in the name of new approaches that remythologize international law in another direction.[22] All theories, beyond their variety and

[19] AB Bozeman, *The Future of Law in a Multicultural World* (Princeton: Princeton University Press, 1971) xi–xii, arguing that the word 'law' itself is 'overworked and overstretched' and that 'this Western verbal symbol does not really cover the non-Western substance of which it speaks'.

[20] R Phillipson, 'Lingua franca or lingua frankensteinia? English in European Integration and Globalisation' (2008) 27 *World Englishes* 250.

[21] For the dominance of English in international law institutions and journals, see sections B (9) and C (3) below.

[22] For the inevitability of theorizing international law, without espousing the methods of natural science but rather inter-disciplinarity and inter-subjective theoretical diversity and complementarity, see RA Müllerson, *Ordering Anarchy: International Law in International Society* (The Hague: Nijhoff, 2000) 9–48. Against theory in international law, see I Brownlie, 'International Law at the Fiftieth Anniversary of the United Nations: General Course on Public International Law' (1995) 255 RdC 13, 30, noting that theory 'provides no real benefits' and rather 'obscure[s] the more interesting questions'. For a recent theoretical and historical overview of international law, see A Orakhelashvili (ed), *Research Handbook on the Theory and History of International Law* (Cheltenham: Elgar, 2011).

variations, tend to converge on two antagonistic attitudes: trust and distrust.[23] People who trust international law appear ideal-orientated, humanitarian, ethics- and solidarity-driven, disinterested, basically optimistic about humanity. Their critics, by contrast, appear sceptical, down-to-earth, self-interest- and order-driven, instrumentalist, basically pessimistic about humanity. The former insist that international law is absolutely necessary and must be supported, developed, and improved. The latter insist that international law is a pure ideal that fails to affect (and/or should be prevented from affecting) the real world. This section analyses nine major theories of international law which could be held to be sufficiently representative (although by no means exhaustive) of the repertoire of intellectual constructions of international law. All are, one way or another, Western or Western-inspired. Since each has several variants, the analysis is confined to exploring some of their basic tenets to the extent that this is useful for present purposes. It is argued that (a) all theories are valid if and to the extent that their addressees as a whole so believe, this varying in time and place; and (b) any theory contains both demythologizing and remythologizing elements rather than being either trust- or distrust-driven.

(1) Naturalism

The 'mother' of all alleged mythologizations of international law is natural law. International law was actually born out of natural law as understood in the Western philosophical, theological, political, and legal tradition,[24] and continues to be at centre stage in current 'global law' projects which place the person at the heart of international law,[25] in line, inter alia, with the Roman sources.[26] The fundamental role played by natural law within the Western-Christian globalizing project of world control under a universal law could hardly be underestimated and needs historical contextualization.

The notion of a *societas omnium inter omnes* and of a *ius humanae societatis*—contrasted with civil law applying to the citizens of local communities—and the penchant to overlap *jus gentium* with *jus naturae* is first found in Cicero, reflecting his education in the Stoic cosmopolitan ideal.[27] In providing the bridge to modernity,[28] as the only political thinker accessible to the Christian West after the collapse of the

[23] See JL Kunz, 'The Swing of the Pendulum: From Overestimation to Underestimation of International Law' (1950) 44 AJIL 135, 140, arguing for the golden middle way equidistant from both 'superficial optimism' and 'cynical minimizing'.

[24] This is not to suggest that the core of natural law did not already exist in the Ancient Near East and elsewhere well before the 'Western' civilization flourished, but only that the West appropriated it and developed it into international law as we know it. For the view that natural law already existed in the early Jewish faith, see P Weil, 'Le judaïsme et le développement du droit international' (1976-III) 151 RdC 253, 276–7. The question of whether there is a natural law tradition in Islam is contentious: see AM Emon, 'Natural Law and Natural Rights in Islamic Law' (2004–05) 20 JLR 351–95; AM Emon, *Islamic Natural Law Theories* (Oxford: OUP, 2010).

[25] See, recently, R Domingo, *The New Global Law* (Cambridge: CUP, 2010) 49–50; R Domingo, 'Gaius, Vattel, and the New Global Law Paradigm' (2011) 22 EJIL 627.

[26] cf *Digest*, 1, 5, 2 ('cum igitur hominum causa omne ius constitutum sit'); *Institutes*, 1, 2, 12 ('nam parum est ius nosse si personae quarum causa statutum est ignorentur').

[27] Cicero, *De officiis*, III, 17, 69; I, 7, 21; III, 5, 23; *Tusculanae Disputationes*, I, 13, 30; *De Partitione Oratoria*, 37, 130. It is controversial whether a citation made by Gellius of Cato the Elder in which *jus gentium* is mentioned is truly Cato's, in which case the latter would be the first known user of the term in the Latin literature: cf Gellius, *Noctes Atticae*, VI, 3, 45.

[28] See JC Rolfe, *Cicero and His Influence* (New York: Longmans, Green & Co, 1928). For the view that 'Cicero was the architect of modern Enlightenment' and he 'who founded the political and ethical foundations of contemporary international law', see DM Johnston, *The Historical Foundations of World Order: The Tower and the Arena* (Leiden and Boston: Nijhoff, 2008) 220–1.

Roman empire,[29] Cicero has unquestionably exerted a special influence on the construction of international law as a global law, although the Stoic cosmopolitan ideals (including the notion of an 'eternal cosmic law') were seen as dreamlike even at the time.[30]

Aristotle had previously distinguished natural justice (*physikón díkaion*), applicable everywhere (*pantachoû*) from legal justice (*nomikón díkaion*), applicable only to the specific communities in which it had been enacted or 'posited' (hence positive law) by an authority.[31] This basic distinction, the origin of which is apparently unknown,[32] is also found in the earlier Xenophon's *Memorabilia*[33] and in Sophocles' *Antigone*.[34] In Plato's *Protagoras* Hippias contrasted law (*nomos*), as a 'tyrant of human beings' with nature (*physis*), this latter being said to be common to human beings: what law commands is often in conflict with what is commanded by nature and, in such cases, it would be shameful of those who have knowledge of 'the nature of things' to defy it.[35] While it is difficult to define the hierarchical relationship between natural law and positive law in ancient Greece, Plato's Hippias evidences that some thinkers were inclined to opt for the prevalence of nature based on some 'moral' considerations with regard to 'unjust laws' against those who took the view that positive law was to be observed unconditionally. Nature and law over time probably converged in a Hellenic customary law (*hellenika nomina*) common to all Greek city-states, as hinted at by Thucydides.[36] Herodotus relates that the killing of Darius' ambassadors by Athens and Sparta was considered by Xerxes to be a violation of 'the usages of all mankind'.[37] Even earlier the pre-Socratics had insisted on the unity or totality of the being as captured by the *logos*.[38]

As a result of Cicero's writings, inter alia, the Roman sources tend to treat natural law and *jus gentium* similarly. While there is no definitive agreement about the meaning of Roman *jus gentium*, three texts eventually gave rise to highly influential traditions. One is Gaius' definition of *jus gentium* at the beginning of his *Institutes*, whereby 'what natural reason establishes among all men and is observed by all peoples alike, is called

[29] See CJ Nederman, 'Nature, Sin and the Origins of Society: The Ciceronian Tradition in Medieval Political Thought' (1988) 49 JHI 3–26, 6.

[30] M Schofield, *The Stoic Idea of the City* (Chicago and London: University of Chicago Press, 1999) 147–8.

[31] Aristotle, *Nicomachean Ethics*, V, 7, 1134b 19–20; Aristotle, *Rhetoric*, I, 10, 3, and I, 13, quoting Sophocles' *Antigone*, line 456 (n 34 below). For the view that Aristotle referred to natural justice in the *polis* rather than to natural law, see D Johnston, *A Brief History of Justice* (Chichester: Wiley-Blackwell, 2011) 78–83.

[32] In *On Sophistical Refutations*, 173a 7–18, Aristotle states that 'all the men of old' accepted the *topos* (ie the common-place argument) based on the opposition between 'the standards of Nature and of the Law', as Callicles did in Plato's *Gorgias*. Whether 'the men of old' (explicitly contrasted by Aristotle with 'the men of today') refers to precursors of the Sophists or to the Sophists (like Callicles himself) is controversial. GB Kerferd, *The Sophistic Movement* (Cambridge and New York: CUP, 1981) 113–14, inclines towards the second alternative.

[33] Xenophon, *Memorabilia*, IV, 4, 19–24. Although in this passage Hippias states that general unwritten laws are of divine origin and does not mention natural law, most commentators argue that such laws can be traced to natural law: see M Untersteiner, *I sofisti* [1949] (Milan: Bruno Mondadori, 1996) XV, 430, note 38, English trans *The Sophists* (Oxford: Basil Blackwell, 1954) 281, note 38.

[34] Sophocles, *Antigone*, line 456. As observed by Kerferd (n 32 above) 113, Antigone does not mention natural law, but rather the God-inspired unwritten laws, as opposed to man-made laws, and it is actually Aristotle who interprets her God-inspired laws as what is 'just by nature' (n 31 above).

[35] Plato, *Protagoras*, 337d.

[36] Thucydides, *History of the Peloponnesian War*, III, 67.

[37] Herodotus, *The History*, VII, 136.

[38] Heraclitus, DK B114.

the *jus gentium*, as being the *jus* which all nations employ'.[39] Here *jus gentium* and *jus naturale* are virtually synonyms, as confirmed by Gaius elsewhere,[40] and the key division of law is bipartite between *jus gentium* and *jus naturale* on the one hand, and *jus civile* on the other. In another text, Ulpian stated that 'natural law is that which nature teaches to all animals' while '*jus gentium* is that used by the human race'.[41] Here *jus gentium* and *jus naturale* are distinct, the former applying only to human beings and the latter also to animals, and the key division of law is tripartite among *jus gentium*, *jus naturale*, and *jus civile*. A third description of *jus gentium* was offered by Hermogenian, who stated that:

> By this *jus gentium* wars were introduced; races were distinguished; kingdoms founded; rights of property ascertained; boundaries of land established; buildings constructed; commerce, purchases, sales, leases, rents, obligations created, such being excepted as were introduced by the civil law.[42]

This passage suggests a number of historically situated *jus gentium* institutions rather than an abstract reason-based concept.

In the Middle Ages Christianity took up the tradition of natural law and *jus gentium*. The assertion *lex iniusta non est lex*, which is the ultimate guiding principle of natural law and today of human rights, arose out of the Christian claim that universal order is created and ultimately maintained by God, not by temporal rulers, although Christians are subject to these as long as their laws do not contradict the commands of God. In his *Epistle to the Romans* St Paul alluded to natural law as a 'law written in [Gentiles'] hearts'.[43] Commenting on this passage, the Church Fathers constantly evoked natural law as a (now Christianized) law inspired by God in the hearts of people.[44] Ambrose regarded natural law as a path leading to God.[45] Augustine argued that natural law is written by God in the hearts of men as eternal law (*lex aeterna*) and prevails over temporal law (*lex temporalis*).[46] Isidore of Seville revived both *jus gentium* and natural law from the Roman sources in his *Etymologies* [47] and served as a key source of Gratian's *Decretum* (c 1140), which 'officially' grounded natural law in God's revelation and, quite significantly, expressly elevated it to a higher rank than any other law.[48] In Thomas Aquinas' *Summa Theologiae*, natural law (*lex naturalis*) is defined as 'nothing else than the rational creature's participation of the eternal law' and as 'an imprint on us of the Divine light' whose function is to help us to 'discern what is good and what is evil'.[49] Assuming that *lex humana* derives from *lex naturalis*, Thomas had no doubt that

[39] Gaius, *Institutes*, 1, 1, 1. Gaius' definition was inserted in the 6th century AD in Justinian's *Institutes*, 1, 2, 1, and reiterated in *Digest*, 1, 1, 9, however, suppressing the word *populus*.

[40] Gaius, *Institutes*, 1, 56; 2, 65; 2, 73.

[41] Ulpian, *Institutes*, in *Digest*, 1, 1, 1, 2–4 and 6 *principium* Ulpian definition was inserted in the 6th century AD in Justinian's *Institutes*, 1, 2, 2, and *Digest*, 1, 1, 1, 2.

[42] Hermogenian, *Liber Primus Iuris Epitomarum*, in *Digest*, 1, 1, 5. A similar definition is that provided by Marcianus, ibid 1, 2, 2.

[43] St Paul, 2 Rom 14–15.

[44] See eg Lactantius, *Divine Institutes*, VI, 8, 6–9.

[45] Ambrose, *In Epistolam Beati Pauli Ad Romanos*, 2, 14.

[46] Augustine, *Confessiones*, III, 8; Augustine, *De civitate Dei*, XIX, 21; Augustine, *Commentary on the Sermon on the Mount*, 2, 9, 32; Augustine, *On Eighty Three Diverse Questions*, 53(2); Augustine, *On the Free Choice of the Will*, 1, 16, 15; Augustine, *On the Trinity*, 14, 15, 21; Augustine, *Sermon on Psalm*, 118, 25, 4; Augustine, *Epistolae*, 157.

[47] Isidore of Seville, *Etymologies*, V, 4.

[48] *Decretum Gratiani*, d I, c 7; d V, pars 1, para 1; d VII, pars 2. As regards *jus gentium*, see d I, c 11.

[49] T Aquinas, *Summa Theologiae*, *Prima Secundae*, q 91, a 2; Aquinas, ibid q 94; Aquinas, ibid *Secunda Secundæ*, q 57, a 3.

in case of conflict human law 'is no longer a law but a perversion of law' (*legis corruptio*) and natural law prevails.[50] *Jus gentium* itself was said to comprise 'those things which are derived from the law of nature'.[51]

The medieval Church developed the idea of the universal community under one common law, intertwined with the law of local communities, a nexus that persists today and directly or indirectly inspires global law projects, especially those informed by the principle of subsidiarity.[52] The scriptural sources of the idea that the Church is a universal body were found in St Paul's doctrine of the Church as the mystical body of Christ (*corpus mysticum Christi*).[53] This doctrine conceded diversity (many limbs and organs) in unity (one body), the ordering of difference within a unitary, hierarchical community. In turn, as has been suggested, the 'Oneness and Universality of the Church must manifest itself in a unity of law'.[54] Natural law, together with the doctrine of just war,[55] fuelled the Christian universalizing project based on a global community to which all human beings, both Christian and non-Christian, belong by their very nature. How the process unfolded is especially revealed by the theological debate on the applicability of natural law first to infidels and later, after the discovery of the New World, to Amerindians.[56]

Pivotal was Pope Innocent IV's 'moderate' stance adopted in his commentary on Pope Innocent III's papal decretal *Quod super his* on the question, concerning the Crusades, of whether it was 'licit to invade a land that infidels possess or which belongs to them'. Innocent IV answered negatively in principle, thereby following Thomas Aquinas against those (notably Alanus Anglicanus) who had contended that Christians had the absolute right to rule non-Christians.[57] Innocent IV argued that in principle 'Men can select rulers for themselves' and 'sovereignty, possessions and jurisdiction can exist licitly, without sin, among infidels', but he also noted that 'if a gentile, who has no law except the law of nature, does something contrary to the law of nature [such as the worship of idols, assuming that "it is natural for man to worship the one and only God"], the pope can lawfully punish him'. The pope can also 'order and command that [infidel rulers] not molest unjustly the Christians who are their subjects' and if they fail to obey he 'can deprive them of the jurisdiction and sovereignty they possess over Christians by judicial sentence'. Moreover, although 'Infidels should not be forced to become Christians' (this being 'left to their own free will'), the pope 'can order infidels to admit preachers of the Gospel in the lands that they administer, for every rational creature is made for the worship of God'. Finally, 'if infidels prohibit preachers from

50 ibid q 95, a 2. 51 ibid q 95, a 4.

52 Domingo (2010) (n 25 above) 176–81.

53 St Paul, 1 Cor 12:12 and 27, and 6:15; Eph 4:4, 16, 25, and 5:30.

54 O von Gierke, *Political Theories of the Middle Ages* (Boston: Beacon Press, 1958) 18–19.

55 See eg JB Elshtain, 'The Just War Tradition and Natural Law' (2005) 28 Ford ILJ 742; as well as Ch 7 below, section A (1)(a).

56 See eg LC Green and OP Dickason, *The Law of Nations and the New World* (Edmonton: The University of Alberta Press, 1989), arguing that all early 'fathers' of international law 'are of opinion that it is just to wage war and so conquer those who reject the basic tenets of Christianity or behave in a way that Christians consider to be contrary to nature' (at 56); RA Williams, *The American Indian in Western Legal Thought: The Discourses of Conquest* (New York and Oxford, OUP, 1990). The point will be further pursued in nn 61–71 below and accompanying text.

57 Also Henry of Segusia, known as Hostiensis, a student of Innocent IV, chose not to follow his master's teachings. In his view, 'with the coming of Christ every public office and every government... was taken from infidels and given over to the faithful through Him who has the highest power and cannot err', thereby deducing that 'by law infidels ought to be subject to the faithful and not the reverse'. See Hostiensis, *Lecture quinque decretalium* [1512], in J Muldoon (ed), *The Expansion of Europe. The First Phase* (Philadelphia: University of Pennsylvania Press, 1977) 192.

preaching, they sin' and, in this as in other cases, 'they ought to be compelled by the secular arm and war may be declared against them by the pope and not by anyone else'.[58]

In practice, Innocent IV claimed that natural law applied to all human beings including non-Christians, that consequently non-Christians were subject to punishment for breaching natural law, that natural law derived exclusively from the Christian revelation, and that the pope was the only or ultimate authority empowered to punish (by either prosecution or war) anyone who broke natural law. While conceding that non-Christians had the right to choose their own rulers without interference, Innocent IV asserted the pope's ultimate 'jurisdiction over all men and power over them in law' (although 'not in fact' as the vicar of Jesus Christ, Christ having power 'over all men'). While granting natural-law rights to non-Christians, the pope retained the right to enforce natural law outside Christianity. It was assumed that natural law, as understood under the Christian Revelation, was 'universal' and God-inspired, and that the pope could impose it on all peoples on earth. The accordance of natural-law 'rights' actually masked an imposition of natural-law *duties* on non-Christians and on their rulers. It was apparently to protect non-Christians' rights that the pope could intervene to enforce them. This process was of course unthinkable in the reverse. Since every 'rational creature' was 'made for the worship of God' and the pope was God mandated to protect also non-Christians' natural and spiritual well-being, there was no room for holding an alternative view as to what had to count as 'nature', 'natural law', and 'well-being'. Those who took a different view were seen as irrational and in error. Innocent IV specified that infidels could not be accorded reciprocal rights to proselytize in Europe 'because they are in error and we are on the righteous path'.[59]

This globalizing attitude is exemplarily epitomized by the letters sent by Innocent IV to the Mongol Khan Güyük in the years 1245–48. In the first, of 1245, Innocent IV asked the Khan to stop his attacks on Europe and the killing of Christians. After having instructed the Khan in the rudiments and truths of Christian doctrine, in particular why the pope 'though unworthy' had become 'by the Lord's disposition, the successor of this vicar [Peter]' on earth who was designated by the consubstantial-with-God Savior-Son Jesus Christ, Innocent IV informed the Khan that he, as pope, was bound 'to lead those in error into the way of truth'. In the second letter, again of 1245, Innocent accused the Khan of violating the divine natural law, the law which unites all men, even 'irrational animals', with the 'very elements which go to make up the world machine'. He then enjoined the Khan to desist in this 'breaking the bond of natural ties' and cease his persecutions of Christians. The Khan Güyük answered by noting that God had blessed the Mongols' successes at war, which could not have occurred if these had been 'contrary to the command of God'. Innocent's reply was that God was losing patience with the Mongols, especially now that they could no longer claim ignorance of the true faith on Judgment Day. Here, one and the same word 'God' clearly referred to two quite different entities. The one-and-only Christian God was challenged by another God, invoked by non-Christians apparently to support anti-Christian claims.[60]

[58] Innocent IV, *Commentaria doctissima in Quinque Libros Decretalium* [1581], in Muldoon (ed) (n 57 above) 191–2.

[59] J Muldoon, *Popes, Lawyers, and Infidels: The Church and the non-Christian World, 1250–1550* (Philadelphia: University of Pennsylvania Press, 1979) 14.

[60] Some of Innocent IV's letters are available at the Wikisource website: *Cum non solum*, 13 March 1245, at <http://en.wikisource.org/wiki/Cum_non_solum>; *Dei Patris Immensa*, 5 March 1245, at <http://en.wikisource.org/wiki/Dei_Patris_Immensa>; *Viam Agnoscere Veritatis*, 22 November 1248, at <http://en.wikisource.org/wiki/Viam_agnoscere_veritatis>. The letters are published in C Dawson

Natural law made sense if only one God, within a monotheistic faith, dominated all human beings. Two competing Gods meant two opposing totalizing projects and conceptions of universality and natural law.

Innocent IV's doctrine was eventually reiterated by the Scholastic Spanish School at the time when the question arose of whether Amerindians were true possessors of their goods and had dominion over their lands. *Jus gentium* was equated with the natural law of the *totus orbis*, this latter being understood as diversity in unity, or a universal unity of local authorities, traceable to the doctrine of the Church as the mystical body of Christ.[61] In his lectures *De Indiis* (1539) Francisco de Vitoria took up Gaius' nature-based definition of *jus gentium*, replacing Gaius' *homines* with *gentes* (*quod naturalis ratio inter omnes gentes constituit*) and using the term *gentes* as a synonym for *nationes*,[62] a substitution that has generally been considered a breakthrough that paved the way for the 'law of nations'.[63] He also argued for the legitimacy of the Spanish conquest of the New World as a just war (or self-defence against a wrong) in cases where natural law was broken by Amerindians, notably the natural rights to travel, to sojourn, to trade, and to preach the Gospel in their lands, as well as when Amerindians were ruled by tyranny.[64] Francisco Suárez, in his *De legibus ac Deo legislatore* (1612),[65] depicted the mystical body conception of the universal community as a 'a certain unit' (*aliqua unitatem*) embracing all humanity, despite the division of humankind into complete communities, such as republics and kingdoms, which need 'some law' (*aliquod iure*), this being *jus gentium*.[66] Suárez also delineated the difference—which had remained ambiguous in the past—between *jus gentium* as a body of law *inter gentes* and *jus gentium* as a body of law which most peoples observe *intra se*, pointing out that *jus gentium* proper ('*propriissime*') is the former, ie 'the law which all peoples and the various *gentes* must comply with in their mutual relations'.[67] In *De Triplici Virtute Theologica* (1621) Suárez followed Vitoria in admitting, as 'just defense', coercion when the Christians' natural right to preach and to make the unbelievers listen to the Gospel was broken by the Amerindians.[68] A few years earlier, the Italian Protestant jurist Alberico Gentili had restated, in his *De Iure Belli* (1598), that *jus gentium* amounts to

(ed), *The Mongol Missions: Narratives and Letters of the Franciscan Missionaries in Mongolia and China in the Thirteenth and Fourteenth Centuries* (New York: Sheed and Ward, 1955).

[61] SJ Brown Scott, *The Spanish Origin of International Law: Francisco de Vitoria and his Law of Nations* (London: Humphrey Milford, 1934).

[62] F de Vitoria, *De Indis et De Jure Belli Relectiones* [1539], English trans in *The Reflections in Moral Theology of the Very Celebrated Spanish Theologian, Franciscus De Victoria* (Washington, DC: Carnegie Institution, 1917) 151, 257, arguing that *jus gentium* 'either is natural law or is derived from natural law'.

[63] See A Nussbaum, *A Concise History of the Law of Nations* (New York: Macmillan, 1954) 81, for the view that Vitoria's expression might have been just a slip of the memory; and, for a detailed discussion, P Haggenmacher, *Grotius et la doctrine de la guerre juste* (Paris: Presses Universitaires de France, 1983) 338–40.

[64] Vitoria (n 62 above) 151–62, discussing the 'lawful titles' (*tituli legitimi*) and the conditions of the Spanish conquest. See J Catry, 'La liberté du commerce international d'après Vitoria, Suarez et les Scholastiques' (1932) 39 RGDIP 193; Green and Dickason (n 56 above) 39–47.

[65] F Suárez, *De Legibus ac Deo Legislatore* [1612], English trans in *Selections from Three Works of Francisco Suarez* (Oxford: Clarendon Press, 1944) vol 2, chs 17–20.

[66] ibid ch 19, para 9, at 348. For a comment, see C Focarelli, 'Customary Foundations of *jus gentium* in Francisco Suárez's Thought and the Concept of International Community in Contemporary International Law' (2006) 16 It YBIL 41.

[67] Suárez (n 65 above) ch 19, para 8, at 347.

[68] F Suárez, *De Triplici Virtute Theologica* [1621], in *Selections from Three Works of Francisco Suarez* (note 65 above) XVIII, at 749 and 756.

natural law,[69] as the British philosopher Thomas Hobbes would also do a few decades later.[70] Gentili further pointed out, in keeping with Vitoria, that a denial of the right to trade by the Amerindians or their commission of 'sins against human nature' and 'other sins recognized as such by all except haply by brutes and brutish men', such as cannibalism, could be a just ground for war.[71] Around the same time Richard Zouche, successor of Gentili to the chair at Oxford, reiterated that *jus gentium* was a law 'inter gentes' and that war was lawful against breaches of natural law.[72] Hugo Grotius proposed, in his *De jure belli ac pacis* (1625), a voluntary *jus gentium* founded on the consent of all or many peoples and ultimately on the natural law *pacta sunt servanda* principle.[73] He endorsed the view that war against those who have broken natural law, such as by consuming human flesh, was lawful.[74] Grotius is also known as the secularizer of natural law (after it had been christianized by Gratian) due to his statement that this law would exist even *etsi Deus non daretur*.[75] In his *Elementa jurisprudentiae universalis* (1660), Samuel Pufendorf reduced *jus gentium* to natural law.[76] In 1661 he obtained the chair of *De jure naturae et gentium* at the University of Heidelberg, the first ever chair in international law, a commitment that led him to write a few years later the treatise *De iure naturae et gentium* (1672) in which he articulated a completely deductive natural and international law.[77] Christian Wolff, in his *Ius gentium methodo scientifica perpetractatum* (1749), distinguished a necessary and immutable *jus naturae ad gentes applicatum* from a 'positive', voluntary *jus gentium* arising from covenants (*pacta*) or customs (*consuetudines*) and issuing from the *civitas maxima* into which peoples were thought to be organized.[78] The worldview of a law applicable to all human beings evolved into a law obtaining between nation-states in Emmerich de Vattel's *Le droit des gens* (1758), which conceived of *jus gentium* as a natural law 'qui a lieu entre les nations ou l'Etat', specifically a universal law adjusted to the peculiarities of states.[79] A few decades later, however, in his (first ever) history of international law,

[69] A Gentili, *De Iure Belli Libri Tres* [1598], English trans *Three Books on the Law of War* (Oxford and London: Clarendon Press and Humphrey Milford, 1933) book I, ch I, at 5. See C Focarelli, 'Le *jus gentium* dans la pensée d'Alberico Gentili', in P Haggenmacher, V Mainetti and D Campanelli (eds), *Alberico Gentili and International Law* (Leiden and Boston: Nijhoff, forthcoming 2012).

[70] T Hobbes, *De cive* [1642] ch 14, para 4; Hobbes, *Leviathan* [1651] ch XXX.

[71] Gentili (n 69 above) book I, ch XXV, at 122, 126.

[72] R Zouche, *Iuris et Iudicii Fecialis, sive, Iuris Inter Gentes, et Quaestionum de Eodem Explicatio* [1650], English trans *An Exposition of Fecial Law and Procedure, or of Law Between Nations and Questions Concerning the Same* (Washington, DC: Carnegie Institution, 1911) 116.

[73] H Grotius, *De Jure Belli ac Pacis Libri Tres* [1625], English trans *On the Law of War and Peace Three Books* (Washington, DC, Oxford, and London: Carnegie Institution, Clarendon Press, and Humphrey Milford, 1925) book I, ch I, para 14, at 44, and book III, ch XIX, para 2(2), at 794.

[74] ibid book II, ch XX, para 40, at 505–6.

[75] ibid 'Prolegomena', para 11, at 13. Alf Ross noted that the *etsi Deus non daretur* formula 'in itself would not have amounted to much' in that 'it makes little difference in the interpretation of the commands of nature whether God is added or subtracted'. What was novel was Descartes' deductive or geometrical method by which natural law 'was deduced from human nature'. As a result, 'a comprehensive system of legal rules was deduced, often down to the minutest details'. See A Ross, *On Law and Justice* (London: Stevens & Sons Limited, 1958) 246–7.

[76] S von Pufendorf, *Elementa Jurisprudentiae Universalis Libri Duo* [1660], English trans *The Elements of Universal Jurisprudence Two Books* (Oxford and London: Clarendon Press and Humphrey Milford, 1931).

[77] S von Pufendorf, *De Iure Naturae et Gentium Libri Octo* [1672], English trans *Of the Law Of Nature And Nations, Eight Books* (Oxford and London: Clarendon Press and Humphrey Milford, 1934), book II, ch 3, paras 7–9, at 188–94; and para 23, at 226–9.

[78] C von Wolff, *Ius Gentium Methodo Scientifica Perpetractatum* [1749], English trans *The Law of Nations Treated According to a Scientific Method* (Oxford and London: Clarendon Press and Humphrey Milford, 1934), 'Prolegomena', at 9–19.

[79] E de Vattel, *Droit des gens; ou, Principes de la loi naturelle appliqués à la conduite et aux affaires des nations et des souverains* [1758] (Boston: Adamant Media, 2001), English trans *The Law of Nations or*

Robert Ward, noting that history shows that 'men had the most opposite opinions of their duties towards one another' due to the 'varieties of religion and the moral systems which governed them', admitted that 'we expected too much when we contended for the *universality* of the duties laid down by the Codes of Law of Nations' and 'what is commonly known as the Law of Nations, falls very short of *universality*', it being 'not the Law of *all* nations, but only of particular classes of them'.[80] He concluded that 'the Law of Nations is not to be considered as the Law of the World, but only of particular classes of Nations, united by familiar religious and moral systems, and influenced by particular local institutions', thereby endeavouring 'to prove, that *Christianity* is the only *certain* foundation for that code which is observed by Christian, in other words, by European nations'.[81]

The foregoing discussion shows that natural law, as a universal law prescribed and enforced by a self-professed universal but de facto non-universal authority, is far more ambiguous than is commonly acknowledged. Its definition can only be grasped with extreme difficulty. There are several traditions of natural law reflecting the various meanings given to 'nature' or to the 'nature of the things'.[82] Apart from the innumerable variations, including those of recent decades,[83] natural law theories are generally based on a few basic beliefs: (a) human beings share a common nature; (b) this common nature can be reasonably identified through our means of knowledge; (c) once identified, it can be communicated to and can be understood by others; (d) normative prescriptions can be derived therefrom; and (e) in case of apparent conflict with one another, such prescriptions—having a hidden harmony between them—can ultimately be reconciled.[84] In practice, natural law is often invoked either as the basis of the validity of man-made law, or as the basis for the limits to the validity of specific man-made rules, or as a background fall-back resource in the absence of man-made rules. The apparent basic *raison d'être* of naturalism is to make law ultimately independent of society's arbitrariness vis-à-vis individuals. Natural law is presented as the ultimate (universal, necessary, non-derogable) measure of right and wrong, capable of warding off intolerable local and voluntary human laws, a sort of law of last resort which is over and above human law-makers.[85] It is deemed to reflect a justice that human authority

the Principles of Natural Law Applied to the Conduct and to the Affairs of Nations and of Sovereigns (Washington, DC: Carnegie Institution, 1916). The application of natural law to states as 'moral persons' had already been maintained by Wolff (see Ch 5 below, n 518).

[80] RP Ward, *An Enquiry Into the Foundation and History of the Law of Nations in Europe from the Time of the Greeks and Romans to the Age of Grotius* (London: Strahan and Woodfall, 1795) xiii–xv (original emphasis).

[81] ibid xi–xii (original emphasis).

[82] For a broad analysis of human nature in various civilizations, see L Stevenson and DL Haberman, *Ten Theories of Human Nature* (New York: OUP, 5th edn, 2009).

[83] Besides the advocates of the Radbruch formula (Ch 1 above, nn 59–63), see eg the classical work of J Finnis, *Natural Law and Natural Rights* (Oxford and New York: Clarendon Press, 2nd edn, 2011) and RP George (ed), *Natural Law Theory: Contemporary Essays* (Oxford and New York: Clarendon Press, 1992) for a (mostly critical) collection of essays. Natural law has been recently developed from a biological perspective by H Gommer, *A Biological Theory of Law: Natural Law Theory Revisited* (Seattle: CreateSpace, 2011), anchoring law in genes and the 'chemical laws of nature' presiding gene biological replication. It is worth noting that what is argued here applies also to biological natural law since everything depends on whether this kind of law attracts enough people who believe to be its addressees and who take biology seriously as a matter of law. The fact that belief itself depends on genes is immaterial, the question arising *within* the biological structures of human beings and bearing upon the margin allowed of human belief and behaviour among those who share such a margin.

[84] A Passerin D'Entrèves, *Natural Law: An Introduction to Legal Philosophy* [1951] (New Brunswick and London: Transaction Publishers, 1994) 17.

[85] E Barker, *Traditions of Civility: Eight Essays* (Cambridge: CUP, 1948) 312.

may fail to follow or may even defy through the imposition of an 'unjust law' by force. Naturalism assumes that there must be some human-independent limitation to human law-making, powerful enough to prevail over society and rulers however powerful society and rulers may be. Natural law is thus designed to ban the use of law by the stronger of the day to their own advantage.

However, natural law has been systematically used by tyrants to legitimize their oppressive behaviour against the vulnerable, for example to legitimize 'natural slavery', drawing from Plato and Aristotle.[86] It has been noted that 'natural law has served the interests of those in power to perpetuate their power, to freeze the law, to avoid change in the law in accordance with change in society'.[87] As illustrated above, it was natural law and the just war doctrine that provided a legal ground for colonialism.[88] The Nazis made an appeal to 'nature' to justify the killing of the 'unfit'.[89] Natural law, on the other hand, has also been invoked and successfully used for the protection of the vulnerable against oppressors. The anti-slavery movement of the eighteenth century was inspired and driven by the idea of natural law. It was in the name of natural law that 'unjust laws' were challenged, resisted, and possibly removed according to the maxim *lex iniusta non est lex*. An explanation generally given for this ambivalence is that natural law is open to 'manipulation' or 'perversion' when used to serve authoritarian or imperialist purposes.[90] But it is in the very essence of natural law to serve *any* purpose and its perverted use is merely the other side of the same coin when the coin is viewed by those who have a different perception of what human nature is or should be. Naturalism is apparently designed to prevent the stronger from abusing power but, in fact, it is only the stronger who are in a position to moralize (or civilize) the others. Positivism, as explained below, is the project aimed precisely at demythologizing abusive recourse to human nature for oppressive purposes. Naturalism can thus be either progressive or conservative, and its advocates can be conservative despite their self-proclaimed progressivism, and vice versa.

The key problem with natural law is that in a world populated by human beings, no law can be expected to be 'really' extra-human as natural law advocates claim. Whatever human beings may think of natural law and no matter what natural law is 'of itself', the fact is that natural law is destined to work in human minds and relationships. It is a 'higher law', capable of superseding 'ordinary' man-made law, if and to the extent that its addressees as a whole so believe. People may have excellent reasons to believe in natural law, and critics of legal naturalism are wrong in rejecting natural law unconditionally. If a group believes in some natural law, whether Christian-inspired or other, then this is the true law of the group. But excellent reasons may not be sufficient to make natural law work when those who do not believe in it—or who believe in a different form of it—prove stronger. And even assuming that natural law is not man-made, it is in any case identified by man (whether theologians, philosophers, or other) in a human world. If only human law exists, whether humanly made or humanly found

[86] cf among the many relevant passages, Plato, *The Republic*, IV, 435a–6a; Aristotle, *Politics*, I, 1252a. Against slavery was Hippias of Elis, whose opinion is related by Plato, *Protagoras*, 337c.

[87] W Friedmann, *The Changing Structure of International Law* (London: Stevens and Sons, 1964) 77–80.

[88] See n 56 above.

[89] 'By killing the weak, we merely obey the orders of nature, which "sides with the strong, the good, the victorious."' See H Arendt, 'The Image of the Hell' [1946] in *Essays in Understanding, 1930–1954: Formation, Exile, and Totalitarianism* (New York: Schocken Books, 1994) 197, 204.

[90] See eg A Orakhelashvili, 'Natural Law and Justice', MP EPIL (August 2007 update) paras 7, 17–21. This opinion is based on Thomas Aquinas' doctrine of *legis corruptio* (n 50 above).

in nature, only human law can limit the intolerableness of the law made or found by human beings. It is the *responsibility* of human beings *here in this world* to ensure that a just law is made or found. The struggle for 'just' law, as opposed to unjust man-made law, in the name of a certain conception of 'human nature', is not any different from the struggle for a certain man-made law which reflects another conception of 'human nature'.

Natural law as we know it is the globalist product of the West used to *unite and control* humankind as a whole. Its historical opposition to man-made law, which constitutes its *reason d'être*, is internal to the Western ability to construct the opposition and use it for total control. Both can be said to be man-made (or used by humans for human ends) and both may work to the extent that people believe in either. The conceptualization of international law as natural law, just like any globalizing project, is invariably the product of a circle of self-professed enlightened who seek to guide humankind to the best, as seen from their viewpoint. Naturalism is the *particular* vision of the universal that succeeds in prevailing over antagonist visions, whether local or aspiring to globalization.[91] It is now on the rise, especially following the end of the Cold War, concomitant with globalization. But from the (tautological) notion that all human beings fall into the concept of humanness, it does not follow that all human beings must form one and the same community and live under one and the same law. The logical, moral, and empathic unity of all humanity is in itself perfectly compatible with discrete communities living each under their own law. Nor does a universally labelled community automatically avoid conflicts. A global international law is only one among many possible visions of international law, very deep rooted in the West, and a dangerous vision because global law is an instrument for global control and for global enforcement, necessarily (in one or another form) by the stronger, at a time when there is no effective way to check and prevent global abuse.

(2) Positivism

Positive law is deemed to be 'posited' by human beings rather than found in human nature and is accordingly also called 'conventional' or man-made.[92] As noted, the notion of a 'positive' law in opposition to natural law goes back to antiquity.[93] Beyond

[91] For the view that there are today three main candidates in a race to globalize, and three globalizations (understood as world dominations) under way, ie westernization, islamization, and easternization, see HP Glenn, *Legal Traditions of the World: Sustainable Diversity in Law* (Oxford: OUP, 4th edn, 2010) 52–4.

[92] This was clearly stated in what appears to be the first reference in history to 'positive law': P Abelard, *Dialogus inter philosophum, judaeum et christianum*, English trans 'Dialogue between a Philosopher, a Jew and a Christian', *Abélard's* Collationes: *Text and Translation* (Oxford: OUP, 2003) ('Jus quippe aliud naturale, aliud positivum dicitur', this latter being 'quod ab hominibus institutum ad utilitatem scilicet vel honestatem tutius muniendam vel amplificandam aut sola consuetudine aut scripti nititur auctoritate'). This definition is found in subsequent medieval writers, whether theologians, philosophers, or canonists. In particular, Thomas Aquinas' *lex humana*—deemed to derive from *lex naturalis* either *per conclusionem* (ie through logical deduction) or *per determinationem* (ie through specification of broader principles)—in its second mode has binding force only on the basis of the law-maker who has created it: see Thomas Aquinas, *Summa Theologiae*, *Prima Secundae*, q 95, a 2.

[93] The first known reference to 'positive', as opposed to natural, justice, is found in a translation and commentary of Plato's *Timaeus* by Calcidious, which was the only source of knowledge of Plato in the Latin West until the 12th century ('non positivae, sed naturalis illius justitiae atque aequitas') <http://image.ox.ac.uk/show?collection=bodleian&manuscript=msdigby23a>. Previously, a reference to 'positive' language, again in opposition to 'natural', was made by Aulus Cornelius Gellius, *Noctes Atticae*, X, 4.

its several doctrinal variations,[94] positive law has been contrasted with natural law as: (a) particular or local in space;[95] (b) mutable in time;[96] (c) grounded in *potestas* or in *populus*;[97] (d) knowable through a statement of will (*voluntas*) made by an authority, namely promulgation;[98] (e) governing any kind of conduct, which thus becomes commanded or prohibited only after promulgation;[99] and (f) driven by utility.[100] Legal positivism as the doctrine specifically holding positive law as the only valid law is a modern Western product. Few apparently asserted in antiquity that positive law is the only valid law and that natural law is no law at all.[101] Positivism can be traced back to the process of monopolization of law-making in the European modern state and notably to the Enlightenment's rational systematization of law and its codification, which started in France in the early nineteenth century, at a time when, faced with the ambiguity and possible abuse of natural law, the need for certainty, clarity, uniformity, effectiveness, and strict legality began to gain currency.

In England, Thomas Hobbes conceived of law as independent of content and purpose, assuming that what matters is who makes it (*aucoritas non veritas facit legem*).[102] In so doing, he could argue, against Edward Coke, that the (English) monarch was not limited by the common law, and statutes made by the monarch were the only law in force in the realm.[103] In France, Jean-Baptiste Colbert, minister of Louis XIV of France, could assert that 'all the legislative power of this kingdom resides in the person of the sovereign'.[104] The Enlightenment inspired Montesquieu to defend, in his *Esprit des lois* (1748), the separation of powers, to avoid their abuse, and in an attempt to overcome the legal uncertainty flowing from several sources of law.[105] In Italy, in his *Dei delitti e delle pene* (1764), Cesare Beccaria insisted on strict legality and syllogistic judicial reasoning so as to reduce the arbitrariness not only of the executive but also of the courts, which were not allowed to interpret the law, let alone convict anyone other than on the clear letter of the legislation. He trusted general and abstract laws as prescriptions made by 'society united by a social contract'.[106] Positivism was thus seen as a guarantee against abuse of power by the executive and the courts in any particular case. Codification reinforced the power of the legislature (monarch or

[94] See eg HLA Hart, 'Positivism and the Separation of Law and Morals' (1958) 71 Harv LR 593, 601, identifying five different meanings of positivism in jurisprudence; J Salmon (ed), 'Positivisme juridique', *Dictionnaire de droit international public* (Brussels: Bruylant, 2001) 852–4.

[95] cf Aristotle, *Nicomachean Ethics*, V, 7, 1134b 19–20; Justinian, *Institutes*, I, 1, 2, 1.

[96] cf Justinian, *Institutes*, I, 1, 2, 11; Paul, in *Digest*, 1, 1, 11. Aristotle, *Nicomachean Ethics*, V, 7, 1134b 19–20, recognized that also natural law can change in time.

[97] cf Justinian, *Institutes*, I, 1, 2, 11; Grotius, *De Jure Belli ac Pacis* (n 73 above) book I, ch 1, paras 10.

[98] Aristotle, *Nicomachean Ethics*, V, 7, 1134b 19–20; and 14, at 38 and 44, referring to volitional human (municipal) law.

[99] ibid.

[100] Paul, in *Digest*, 1, 1, 11.

[101] Aristotle, *Nicomachean Ethics*, V, 7, 1134b 19–20, recalls that: 'Some people think that all rules of justice are merely conventional'.

[102] T Hobbes, *Leviathan* [1651], II, 26, holding as 'manifest' that 'law in general is not counsel, but command; nor a command of any man to any man, but only of him whose command is addressed to one formerly obliged to obey him'. The sentence 'autoritas non veritas facit legem' is found in the Latin edition of 1668.

[103] See E Campbell, 'Thomas Hobbes and the Common Law' (1958) 1 Tas ULR 20.

[104] J Gilissen, *Les sources du droit en Europe occidentale (XIIe–XX siècle)* (Brussels: Presses Universitaires de Bruxelles, 1978) 49.

[105] C-L De Secondat, Baron de la Brède et de Montesquieu, *De l'esprit des lois* [1748] (Paris: Gallimard, 1995–1999) 2 vols, English trans *The Spirit of the Laws* (New York: Macmillan, 1949).

[106] C Beccaria, *Dei delitti e delle pene* [1764] (Milan: Feltrinelli, 2008), English trans *On Crimes and Punishments* (Indianapolis: Hackett, 1986).

assembly) by centralizing law-making in one single supreme authority and by forcing the courts to apply only the law made and controlled by the ruler rather than customary law, natural law, or other non-statutory types of law. According to the French School of Exegesis, the only valid law was thought to be that which was created by the legislature, thereby provoking, at the turn of the eighteenth century, a reaction towards a creative role for judges by the 'free law' movement.[107] In early positivism, international law (still deeply associated with natural law) ceased to be regarded either as a law common to states, but was seen rather as an 'external domestic public law' of each state (äuβeres Staatsrecht), or as a law 'properly so called', as George FW Hegel in Germany[108] and John Austin in England[109] exemplarily theorized.[110]

During the emergence of positivism, natural law survived by filling the 'gaps' in positive law. Hobbes observed, in the *De cive* (1642), that 'seeing it is impossible to prescribe such universal rules, whereby all future contentions, which perhaps are infinite, may be determined' there was nothing else to be done other than assuming that:

> . . . in all cases not mentioned by the *written laws*, the *law of natural equity* is to be followed, which commands us to distribute equally to equals; and this by the virtue of the *civil law*, which also punisheth those who knowingly and willingly do actually transgress the *laws of nature*.[111]

Similarly, Gottfried W Leibniz noted, in *Nova methodus discendae docendaeque jurisprudentiae* (1667), that: 'In those cases, on which the law is not declared applicable, it is on the basis of natural law that one must judge'.[112] Gottfried Achenwall explained in his *Jus naturae in usum auditorium* (1752) that natural law applied 'naturally' (*naturaliter*) to the relations between states and to the relations between the prince and his subjects, while it applied 'subsidiarily' (*subsidiarie*) in case of gaps in positive law.[113] Article 7 of the Austrian Civil Code of 1811 expressly provided that in cases which could not be decided by the usual means of interpretation, the case 'must be decided, with regard to the carefully collected and well considered circumstances according to the precepts of natural law'.[114] The notion that natural law supplements positive law and may explain or reinforce positive law is often defended in contemporary

[107] H Kantorowicz (under the pseudonym of Gnaeus Flavius), *Der Kampf um die Rechtswissenschaft* [1906] (Baden-Baden: Nomos, 2002), arguing that a 'free law' [*Freirecht*] directly drawn from social life, ie independently of state legal sources, was the 'new' natural law in the sense that it performed the function of the old natural law but, unlike old natural law, was contingent and based on will. A precursor was F Gény, *Méthode d'interprétation et sources du droit positif* (Paris: Librairie générale de droit et de jurisprudence, 1899; 2nd edn, 1919), contrasting the School of Exegesis with the 'scientific free search' (*libre recherche scientifique*) for the rule to be applied in social 'living law'.

[108] GFW Hegel, *Grundlinien der Philosophie des Rechts* [1821] (Berlin: Akademie Verlag, 2005), English trans *Elements of the Philosophy of Right* (Cambridge: CUP, 1991) paras 330–360.

[109] J Austin, *The Province of Jurisprudence Determined* [1832] (Cambridge: CUP, 1995) 157 ('The existence of law is one thing; its merit and demerit another. Whether it be or be not is one enquiry; whether it be or be not conformable to an assumed standard, is a different enquiry.').

[110] For the topic of the 'reality' of international law, see Ch 2 above, section A (5).

[111] T Hobbes, *De cive*, XIV, 14 (original emphasis).

[112] GW Leibniz, *Nova Methodus Discendae Docendaeque Jurisprudentiae* (Francofurti: Zunnerus, 1667) para 71 ('In iis casibus, de quibus lex se non declaravit, secundum jus naturae esse judicandum.').

[113] G Achenwall, *Jus Naturae in Usum Auditorium* [1752] (Göttingen: Sumtibus Victorini Bossigelii, 7th edn, 1774) 2, at <http://catalog.hathitrust.org/Record/003867738> ('vero ad dijudicandas actiones et terminandas lites etiam illorum omnium, qui certo Iuri Humano subsunt, . . . ubi hoc Ius Humanum plane deficit, quippe tum, si opus fuerit, ad Ius Naturale est recurrendum').

[114] Austrian Civil Code of 1811, Art 7.

international law doctrine.[115] It has also historically provided the theoretical framework to explain that 'general' law (such as customary international law), while in case of conflict giving way to 'special' law (such as treaty law), 're-surfaces' when the special regime for some reason fails.[116]

With the positivistic turn, possible abuses of power shifted from executives and courts on a case-by-case basis to the legislatures and those who controlled law-making themselves. The new approach had the potential to give rise to abuses on a massive scale, based on the general will of society, as embodied in the legislation enacted by a charismatic leader—a danger emerged in the twentieth-century totalitarian inter-war regimes which shed a sinister light on positivism and suggests that positivism is inherently authoritarian.[117] However, just as naturalists may be conservative despite their apparent progressivism, so positivists may be progressive. It is a fact that authoritarian regimes have made systematic appeals both to natural law and to positive law to justify their misdeeds, depending on the circumstances.

While natural law is relevant to international law for its inherent universalistic connotations, positive law is relevant in that the positivistic techniques of analysis of law used in assessing positive national law have been extended to international law and still largely form part of the 'repertoire' of the international jurist's professional skills.[118] This extension presupposed that only the law of the state—*rectius*, of the modern European state, or better, of an efficient modern European state, like the few that were stronger at the time—was law proper.[119] Hence the need to credit international law as 'true' law by proving that it could be handled intellectually and practically in a way similar to the way in which domestic law was treated. The basic structures of domestic law were transplanted into the universal domain and generated a variety of 'national schools' of international law.[120] Since natural law also has always been a projection of a particular worldview on the global domain, the opposition between positivism and naturalism is largely a Western invention. The whole positivistic debate centred on the allocation of power between the sovereign and other state officials, notably the courts, and on how abuse of power and injustice by either could be reduced within the state. The transposition to international law of these concerns indeed makes little sense since the sovereign, the key figure of the debate whose power had to be allocated and limited, is absent in international affairs.

It is this transposition, involving a more or less blind (although no doubt technically sophisticated) use of categories of domestic law, or better, of the domestic law of a few Western states serving as a model, that means that today international legal positivists

115 See eg Orakhelashvili (n 90 above) para 33.

116 See Ch 6 below, n 332 and accompanying text.

117 D Dyzenhaus, 'Why Positivism is Authoritarian'(1992) 37 AJJ 83–112.

118 See eg P Weil, 'Towards Relative Normativity in International Law'(1983) 77 AJIL 413; R Ago, 'Positivism', MP EPIL, 1st edn, 1984, vol 7, 385; AP Rubin, *Ethics and Authority in International Law* (Cambridge: CUP, 1997); B Simma and AL Paulus, 'The Responsibility of Individuals for Human Rights Abuses in Internal Conflicts: A Positivist View' (1999) 93 AJIL 302, distinguishing 'classic' positivism (marked by centrality of state will, separation of law from non-law and merely desirable or soft law based on the sources, completeness of the legal system, and relevance of states only as unitary actors) from 'modern' or 'enlightened' positivism (retaining only 'normativity and the prescriptive force of law' based on the formal sources as the 'core of international legal discourse' against 'arbitrariness or post-modern relativism').

119 See n 109 above, and Ch 2 above, n 88.

120 See section C (2) below.

are often accused of being 'legalist',[121] or too 'rule-based'.[122] The problem, however, does not lie so much in legalism and rules, as in the insistence of international positivists on mirroring the administration of domestic law, notably the domestic law of Western states—if not only of a few conveniently or impliedly selected Western states—without considering the peculiarities of the international environment and the implications of the absence of a global sovereign. International positivism demythologizes natural law by ignoring the differences between the global and the local spheres, by using local law as a model, by preferring states among the local legal systems available, and by selecting Western states (if not certain specific Western states) as the model. In doing so, it remythologizes international law as a sort of universalized domestic law of an ideal type of Western state, to be handled with the professional techniques successfully applied in Western states.

(3) Realism

Realism in international relations (IR) may be seen as a demythologization of either the reality, or the relevance, or the desirability of international law.[123] Beyond its variations, IR realism typically claims that: (a) states, notably great powers, are the principal actors in world politics failing a global supreme authority; (b) their behaviour is influenced mainly by the external environment, in particular by the structure of the international system, rather than by their internal features (such as their form of government) or institutional articulations; and (c) they are constantly pursuing their self-interest in competing for scarce resources so as to maximize their power at the expense of other states. It is assumed that the driving force of human beings and institutions is the quest for survival and security. Since in an anarchical world states are potentially dangerous to each other, they fear each other, and there is no impartial and effective '911' to which they could turn for help in case of threat from other states.[124] Admittedly, IR realism rarely even mentions international law, its goal being to analyse what affects international relations and what course of action governments or other non-state actors should take, or can be reasonably expected to take, but its overall implication is generally unsupportive of international law. Accepting international law as a guide for foreign policy is generally seen by Realists as 'legalistic-moralistic',[125] or idealistic and ultimately dangerous, even immoral,[126] or as intolerably urging states to let law destroy their way of life.[127]

[121] See EA Posner, *The Perils of Global Legalism* (Chicago and London: University of Chicago Press, 2009).

[122] In this context, positivism is equated with 'rules' and opposed to 'principles', soft law, standards, and other prescriptions of law other than rules. For a typical rule-based approach, see HLA Hart, 'Postscript' in *The Concept of Law* (Oxford: OUP, 2nd edn, 1994) 254–68. This point will be discussed in greater detail in Ch 6 below, sections A (2)(b) and B (2).

[123] Reference is made here to 'political realism', not to the 'legal realism' that is typical of a strand of thinking (with differences) in American and Scandinavian jurisprudence (for the former, see n 157 below). For the dismissive attitude of political realism to the 'reality' of international law, see Ch 2 above, section A (5).

[124] JJ Mearsheimer, *The Tragedy of Great Power Politics* (New York and London: WW Norton, 2001) 32.

[125] GF Kennan, *American Diplomacy, 1900–1951* (Chicago: University of Chicago Press, 1951) 95–9.

[126] H Morgenthau, 'Diplomacy' (1946) 55 Yale LJ 1067, 1078, 1080.

[127] cf Dean Acheson's famous remarks on the Cuban missile crisis (1963) 57 ASIL Proc 14, and on international lawyers in 'The Arrogance of International Lawyers' (1968) 2 International Lawyer 591–9.

Realists may concur with positivists such as John Austin that in a world devoid of any global authority there can be no 'true' international 'law'.[128] However, Realists may accept in the abstract that international law is 'true' law, yet deny that it affects reality or that it should be applied when respect therefor is likely to lead to undesirable goals, whether national or global. While descriptive realists generally believe that international law is irrelevant, prescriptive realists might think that international law is true and effective law but advise that it should not be adopted by a state in a particular instance or as a matter of principle.[129] For realists international law apparently works as long as there is no serious dispute, ie where states would behave in accordance with what international law requires even if there were no international law at all, but would be quick to depart from it if to do so would make them better off. States of course may (and do) defend international law in principle, but this is assumed to occur only for reasons of self-interest: international law offers a reassuring picture of apparent order in a chaotic world, this order is in the end the order sustained and used by the stronger to pursue their interests, law can always be invoked to make apparently legitimate claims (whatever their real grounds) or to resist the undesired claims made by competitors. In short, international law is supported as 'true' law by the generality of states only *in the abstract* as a matter of general applicability in hypothetical cases. States are guided by 'a limitless lust for power' which is largely unresponsive to law.[130] International law 'works' when one does not need it and fails to work when one needs it. In both cases it is pointless,[131] or, as recently argued from the perspective of the 'rational-choice' theory, of little relevance.[132]

The IR realist demythologization of international law is grounded in a set of beliefs which are worth bringing to light: (a) international law can easily be violated by states without incurring effective sanctions, assuming that sanctions are essential elements of 'law'; (b) respect for international law depends only on states and their calculations, all other actors being substantially uninfluential; (c) the calculations of states depend only on their self-interest; (d) states' self-interest is fundamentally fixed and can be identified a priori; (e) the pursuit of self-interest is considered 'rational' according to a means–end or cost–benefit definition of rationality; (f) states are indeed rational under this definition; (g) the realist or the rational choice account is better than others to explain reality; and (h) law should not be read formalistically. Jurists may counter that law is by no means exclusively a matter of sanctions, that non-state actors have always been and are today especially influential in altering perceived state self-interest and decisions, that states do include in their calculations elements other than (at least short-term and

128 For the Austinian stance, see n 109 above and Ch 2 above, n 88.

129 For the distinction between descriptive and prescriptive realism, see C Beitz, *Political Theory and International Relations* (Princeton: Princeton University Press, 1999) 20.

130 H Morgenthau, *Scientific Man vs Power Politics* (Chicago: University of Chicago Press, 1946) 194; H Morgenthau, *Politics among Nations: The Struggle for Power and Peace* (New York: Knopf, 5th edn, 1973) 208.

131 In other words, a high rate of compliance may not prove that international law affects state behaviour, as against Louis Henkin's famous adage whereby 'almost all nations observe almost all principles of international law and almost all of their obligations almost all the time'. cf L Henkin, *How Nations Behave: Law and Foreign Policy* (New York: Columbia University Press, 2nd edn, 1979) 47. On compliance with international law, see Ch 6 below, section D.

132 For a general overview, see JL Goldsmith and EA Posner, *The Limits of International Law* (Oxford: OUP, 2005); AT Guzman, *How International Law Works: A Rational Choice Theory* (Oxford and New York: OUP, 2008). Similar observations also hold true, *mutatis mutandis*, for the 'economic analysis' of law, on which see JL Dunoff and JP Trachtman, 'Economic Analysis of International Law' (1999) 24 Yale JIL 1, and, for a recent analysis, AL Paulus, 'Potential and Limits of the Economic Analysis of International Law: A View from Public International Law' (2009) 165 JITE 170.

narrowly understood) self-interest and are involved in factors that can hardly be reduced to calculation, that the rationality ascribed to states is not necessarily based on means–end or cost–benefit analysis, that reality can be seen in other ways than that adopted by realists, and that law values and affects reality precisely as a result of its formalities.

What international law 'is' should be kept distinct from both 'how it works' and 'how it can be used' as a means to an end, as realists usually contend.[133] While law needs ultimately to be meaningful to people in their real lives, what constitutes the 'real' life of people is extremely varied. Law may work simply because people believe in it, as is the case with divine or natural law. Realists evidently share a different view of what beliefs count as reality and of what should be meant by 'count'. But even assuming that the reality of the people concerned is the same as the reality viewed by Realists, law is not simply a matter of 'if and how law affects behaviour'. If the addressees of law as a whole do not believe in a law as their law, this law will not work even though it is backed by sanctions. Moreover, if the law of a group is what is believed to be the law by the group, then the reality and relevance of law is closely intertwined with such belief. When realists assert that international law is unreal or irrelevant they are not so much stating a 'detached truth' about international law as directly shaping it to the effect that international law *must* be unreal or irrelevant.[134] Law is not only what is thought to be observable from a scientific perspective, but first and foremost what *must* be in play and requires constant *support*. Further, states constantly need to know how to behave according to what is expected by all other states as a matter of law. To say that states behave in keeping with international law only when there is no need for such law, since they would behave in the same way even with no international law at all, ignores the fact that international law provides states with information about how to behave in the perception of all others and that all states constantly need this information. If in most cases states behave in conformity with international law, this occurs because there is an international law in the first place. Even when a state is willing to breach international law because it gains a comparative advantage if it does so, it has an interest in knowing whether its planned behaviour is really a 'breach' and will be perceived as such by all other states.

All the above considerations are straightforward to communitarians. Realists, by contrast, tend to consider international law from the viewpoint of a single state that has to make a decision in a particular case concerning (compliance with or defiance of) a particular rule. Theirs is often the viewpoint of the decision-maker who has to consider a number of factors in order to make the decision and may decide, after due consideration of all (political, strategic, moral, legal) pertinent factors, that to breach the law would be the best decision in the circumstances. However, *what* is the law which is breached by a decision of this kind is another question. It is one thing to determine whether respect for individual rules of international law by any individual states in individual cases is *convenient* from the unilateral perspective of such a state; it is quite another to determine which rules of international law *must* be respected in the conviction of the generality of states whatever the calculations of any particular state in particular instances. The fact that the members of a group pursue their self-interest does not disprove that their relations are, or can be, governed by law. By way of example, leaving aside for the moment the peculiarities of national law, US or Swiss law

[133] Legal instrumentalism is discussed by BZ Tamanaha, *Law as a Means to an End: Threat to the Rule of Law* (Cambridge: CUP, 2006).

[134] See Ch 2 above, section A (5).

are not denied the quality of law based on the self-interest calculations of every single American or Swiss citizen, although every single American or Swiss citizen does make calculations about whether to obey or disobey single rules in single instances. US or Swiss law continues to be and work as law even where one or another rule is broken in one or another case by one or another American or Swiss citizen, who may well also be the stronger in society. Law is first and foremost what every member of a community expects from any other member of the community as the law binding on all. Unless law is seen from this social perspective, as the structural and silently working cement of a community as a whole, what is dealt with is not really law but either the politics of law, concerning what better law should be made for the future, or individual strategies towards evading existing law. One may of course argue that the two notions coincide, but the people concerned (such as American or Swiss citizens *as a whole*) may well think otherwise and keep them distinct, as is usually the case.

If most people believe in the particular 'reality' seen by realists, then there is little chance, as Realists predict, for international law to be real or relevant. But if most people disbelieve realism, ie the particular reality seen by realists, then international law may be very real and relevant indeed. Belief and disbelief depend on a wide variety of perceptions of current realities and hopes for the future. The reality and relevance of international law cannot be argued and fixed once and for all. People may change their minds and either abandon or endorse IR realism. Political realism usually spreads when major crises break out and justice is patently denied. In periods of relative stability realism is strongly critiqued by most people. Human life relentlessly oscillates between compliance and abuse, activism and fatalism. Those who experience massive abuse are inclined to realism and cynicism, whereas those who happen to live in places and times in which power is not intolerably abused generally find that realism is too pessimistic and, what is worse, ends up fulfilling its own prophecy and sparking escalating conflict and further arbitrariness. When IR realism demythologizes international law, it does so in the name of other myths, among which the belief that human nature is ultimately aggressive is the most deep rooted, a belief that while certainly inspired by wise watchfulness may also prove itself devastating for human coexistence.[135]

(4) Axiologism

The word 'values' is extensively used in the contemporary discourse on international law to denote its 'moral' foundation, either as it stands or as it ought to be. This general trend can be termed as 'axiologism' when considering that axiology is the philosophical study of value (from the Greek *axios*).[136] Since ethics investigates what is valuable to humankind, axiologism pertains to the nexus between international law, global justice, and morality.

In *Justice, Legitimacy, and Self-Determination* Allen Buchanan has challenged on moral grounds 'not only . . . some central features of the existing legal order, but also . . . the dominant ways in which theorists conceive of international law and international relations'.[137] Taking note that international law has proved fairly unresponsive to serious problems, such as secession crises, ethnic conflicts, failed states, and global terrorism, because of a failure of commitment and will of the states, Buchanan rejects

[135] See Ch 1 above, n 15.

[136] See eg N Rescher, *Value Matters: Studies in Axiology* (Frankfurt: Ontos Verlag, 2005).

[137] A Buchanan, *Justice, Legitimacy, and Self-Determination: Moral Foundations for International Law* (Oxford: OUP, 2004) 5, 9.

the assumption that international law is and ought to be the law of a society of equal sovereign states grounded in their consent (rather than in justice), as well as the dogma that the proper goal for the international legal system is peace among states (rather than justice for individuals). He has thus developed 'a coherent, systematic vision of international law that takes the protection of human rights seriously, while anchoring that vision in moral reasoning' by assuming that 'sovereignty is conditional on the protection of human rights'. In his view, existing international law 'can and ought to be evaluated from the standpoint of moral principles, including, pre-eminently, principles of justice', and should also be the subject of proposals of 'new principles [and institutions in some cases] or modifications of existing ones that are more consonant with the demands of justice', meaning by justice the protection of 'the most basic human rights and obligations that persons have'.[138] The project is designed morally and holistically to evaluate certain fundamental existing international law rules with a view to proposing new norms and practices which, if implemented with reasonable care, 'would make the system more just'.[139] Its concern is therefore with 'what the law should be', 'without embracing a naturalistic view of what international law is', or being concerned with what the law is.[140] Proposals for reform include the abandonment of effectiveness (which would be replaced by legitimacy, namely, the meeting of certain minimal standards of justice) as a criterion for statehood and the prohibition of recognition of entities that do not meet the appropriate minimal standards of justice, hence a serious erosion of sovereignty, the support or even the mandate by international legal institutions of intrastate autonomy regimes, the obligation (rather than merely the discretion) to participate in an international legal order, and the partial admissibility of humanitarian intervention.[141]

The goal of Buchanan's theory is apparently similar to naturalism, since both evaluate existing law 'from outside' and fault unjust or immoral law.[142] However, the moral theory is confined to evaluating existing law in order for a new, more just law to be created, while naturalism evaluates existing law, inter alia, for validity purposes. Axiologism suggests that when existing law is unjust, a more just law should be made, and aspires to work as a pacesetter. In axiologism unjust law remains valid, but it is pressured for change. It needs belief supportive of change and to this effect it demythologizes pervasive 'dogmas' such as realism, moral minimalism, and legal nihilism.[143]

Axiologism ultimately demythologizes existing international law by remythologizing it as a moral enterprise. Buchanan argues for new beliefs to be shared in support of a new, better international law. His is a personal vision and articulation of how international law ought to be. Since the theory is based on what the law ought to be, ie on a set of reasoned desiderata, competing desiderata may be argued with no less cogency. The moral theory avoids facing the reasons why reality is as it is at the moment rather than otherwise, and why its desiderata may reasonably fail. It contends that existing international law rules are insufficient, inadequate, ambiguous, and incoherent. Little is said

138 ibid 1–2.

139 cf S Besson and J Tasioulas (eds), *The Philosophy of International Law* (Oxford: OUP, 2010) 13. See in addition S Besson, 'The Authority of International Law: Lifting the State Veil', 31 Sydney Law Review (2009) 343–80; S Wheatley, *The Democratic Legitimacy of International Law* (Oxford: Hart, 2010).

140 Buchanan (n 137 above) 4, 21.

141 ibid 6–8.

142 For an earlier moral theory of international law based on Kant's idea of perpetual peace ensured by a free league of independent republics (n 212 below), see F Tesón, *A Philosophy of International Law* (Boulder, CO: Westview Press, 1998).

143 Buchanan (n 137 above) 29–53.

about the reasons why they are so and what (and whose) interests lie behind them. The risk that a 'guiding' theory may actually and successfully be refused by those concerned is minimized, if not left unaddressed. It is likely, for example, that people abhor humanitarian catastrophes but the existence and effectiveness of a ban on humanitarian intervention to stop them derives from *their* interests as *they* perceive them, whatever the global moral philosopher may think. What is offered is a banner under which it is worth fighting rather than a 'foundation' of international law, ie a vision concerning the 'politics' of international law.[144] In order to 'think' a different future (or to mythologize 'the' future), axiologism is inevitably compelled to bracket (or to demythologize) the present in its working operation in the current circumstances, apart from what goes wrong, and invites reform.

(5) Deconstructionism

An explicitly stated, demythologizing project is that pursued by the jurists ('Crits') who have espoused the Critical Legal Studies (CLS) movement.[145] Despite their significant variations, they may all be called 'deconstructionists' since they tend to prove that the typical arguments used in orthodox legal reasoning are flawed. The CLS demythologization project has not spared any 'mainstream' theory or assumption, including legal liberalism, value neutrality, formalism, determinacy, and objectivity. CLS appeared in the late 1970s, showing little or no interest in international law. When it began to gain currency in international law around the 1990s, it had almost disappeared (after having attracted strong criticism)[146] in the other fields of law. Whether this occurred because deconstructionism is particularly fit for international law or because international legal theory had failed to tune up at the relevant time is unclear. It is a fact, however, that ever since that time international law scholars have engaged in a wave of writings which continue to ignore, or at least underemphasize, the major criticisms that deconstructionism has encountered in general jurisprudence.[147]

While other CLS-inspired or deconstructionist works in international law had been already produced,[148] the spread of deconstructionism began after the publication, in 1989, of *From Apology to Utopia* by Martti Koskenniemi.[149] This book has been analysed in possibly every detail by quite a few commentators, and revisited by its

[144] No wonder the 'policy-orientated' approach of the Yale Law School, equally based on the central concept of 'human dignity', has always been critiqued as politically orientated and, more specifically, US-orientated. See eg Henkin (n 131 above) 40.

[145] Among the seminal pieces of CLS literature, see RM Unger, *Knowledge and Politics* (New York: The Free Press, 1975); D Kennedy, 'Form and Substance in Private Law Adjudication' (1976) 89 Harv LR 1685.

[146] For a recent critique, see MH Kramer, *Objectivity and the Rule of Law* (Cambridge: CUP, 2007) 15–33; and, from a biologist's perspective, ES Fruehwald, *Law and Human Behavior: A Study in Behavioral Biology, Neuroscience, and the Law* (Lake Mary: Vandeplas Publishing LLC, 2011) 55–72.

[147] For a critical analysis, see N Purvis, 'Critical Legal Studies in Public International Law' (1991) 32 Harv ILJ 81–127.

[148] See eg A Carty, *The Decay of International Law? A Reappraisal of the Limits of Legal Imagination in International Affairs* (Manchester: Manchester University Press, 1986); D Kennedy, *International Legal Structures* (Baden-Baden: Nomos Verlag, 1987).

[149] M Koskenniemi, *From Apology to Utopia: The Structure of International Legal Argument* (Helsinki: Lakimiesliiton Kustannus, 1989); M Koskenniemi, 'Letter to the Editors of the Symposium' in Slaughter and Ratner (n 16 above) 351, 351, for Koskenniemi's rejection of the classification of his work as representing 'CLS'.

author himself on the occasion of its reissue in 2005.[150] It may, however, be considered here succinctly as a highly representative deconstructionist exercise. Its thesis is grounded in a radical dichotomy between 'apology' and 'utopia', which reflects the perennial divide between sceptics and idealists, or more broadly, between those who do not trust international law and those who do, as well as the 'is' and the 'ought', politics and morals, and similar oppositions. The focus is not, however, on an 'essence' of international law in which to believe or not to believe (ie in the 'objective' existence of the *thing* called international law), but rather on the 'structure of argument' conducted around international law by all those concerned, especially professionals. Once the objective essence is abandoned, there remains nothing other than what is *said* of international law, and its analysis changes into a sort of argumentative exercise carried out against opposite arguments. In this verbal, infinite game international law appears as either apologetic or utopian, constantly oscillating between these two extremes without stabilizing in a definite, ultimate, essence. It is apologetic when it *reflects* (empirically verifiable and demonstrable) facts and realities; it is utopian when it *guides* facts and realities towards how they ought to be (other than how they are). When discussed apologetically, international law is redundant, since it is confined to legitimizing what has already been done by those who have the power to do so, hence reflecting or 'following' power and politics; when discussed utopianly, international law is irrelevant, since it proves powerless in guiding the conduct of those who have the power to resist any attempt to do so, hence its inability to use moral inputs to affect realities. This causes a pervasive contradiction in the 'argumentative strategies' used by orthodox theory. Apologetic and utopian arguments are continually assembled in different degrees according to the 'right' (ie the *desired*) conclusion to be reached, apparently developing a 'neutral' line of reasoning, but in fact promoting a certain vision of 'justice' that is never demonstrated. Behind 'objective' arguments in favour of a certain legal solution always lies a strategy to impose a 'subjective'—in any sense, not only 'personal' to the arguer—idea of justice. Subjective feelings of what is just are always claimed to be objective, to enable them to be more easily sold and imposed on others. Arguments are always the manifestation of a will to dominate and international law has lent itself to being used for imperialistic purposes. Both apologetic and utopian arguments end up being politics in disguise, either to justify actions taken regardless of law or to promote value-laden goals. The substance of the entire argument is very close to the realist account of international law. The stronger can always render it either redundant or irrelevant.

In Koskenniemi's thought between apology and utopia *tertium non datur*.[151] Any *tertium* argument is, in his view, contradictory and untenable, yet most international law scholars, so he argues, continue to treat international law as a 'hybrid' being which keeps in contact with reality without being totally absorbed by it. Law is thought to be both 'within' and 'outside' the world just like natural law, which has always been thought to work in this world while being inspired by an 'outer', extra-human world. In Koskenniemi's view the 'tertium' constantly alluded to by orthodox international law scholars is an illusion that must be demystified.[152] The result is, literally, a 'de-spirited'

[150] M Koskenniemi, *From Apology to Utopia. The Structure of International Legal Argument* (Cambridge: CUP, 2005, reissue with new epilogue).

[151] ibid 59, excluding a 'middle position' between state behaviour and normative codes, the two extremes being 'both exhaustive and mutually exclusive'.

[152] ibid 535.

international law, an empty vessel condemned to be reasoned with insurmountable contradictions and exposed only to political instrumental use and manipulation.

Koskenniemi's typical way of proceeding is to assume two extremes and then to prove that they are extremes, as such excluding each other with nothing else as a result. Most jurists would reply that law is precisely a *tertium* between any couple of extremes (which are nothing other than abstractions of the mind) and that this *tertium* can indeed be captured objectively. The denial of this *tertium* by the force of logic leads to the denial of law and, ultimately, to the denial of any objective reality. It sounds like Zeno's paradox of Achilles and the tortoise related by Aristotle, whereby Achilles logically never reaches the tortoise although we all know that Achilles *will* reach it.[153] Unlimited critique and 'unmasking' of law may sound fascinating but it proves destructive while people have a pressing need for law in their daily lives. People have to live here and now and cannot either wait for an irresistibly logical argument for objectivity nor feel at ease with a perennial struggle of all against all. Crits fail to suggest how law would work positively and practically in this sort of world. To most people law *does* exist and *must* exist, whatever its flaws. Crits downplay the fact that people (including themselves) live in society and society constantly establishes what counts as objectivity. The point is not logical and calls for common sense and emotional attunement in the group to be given due weight. Crits cannot avoid contradiction when they assert the impossibility of objectivity while inevitably assuming the objectivity of everyday life, such as the validity of their marriages or copyrights. The way out of their labyrinth is to conclude that law is nothing other than a struggle of all against all, verbally or by any other means, just like Realists but on epistemological grounds.

Deconstructionists' demythologization of 'objective reality' is in fact a remythologizing project pulling in a different direction. They seek to induce people to believe in ideas other than those presented by 'mainstream' scholars. If deconstructionism gains the belief by most people in a group, this group will live accordingly. Its members will presumably live together by sharing an objective trust in the impossibility of reaching objectivity, a lifestyle which might appear bizarre and contradictory to outsiders, but not to the group. Among deconstructionists, in other words, law works just as it does in any other group which shares other views of objectivity and of whether objectivity is detectable. Deconstructionism demythologizes what it calls 'orthodoxy', which it invariably 'challenges', by promoting 'another' (mythic vision of) international law whose fascination lies in never being what is 'orthodox' and which is destined to remain 'another' for good.

(6) Sociologism

Sociological approaches to international law are no doubt in vogue but their vast variety raises perplexities as to their scientific delimitation, objectives, and outcomes.[154] Little clarity exists as to whether the 'sociology of law', whose disciplinary origins are often traced back to Eugen Ehrlich's *Grundlegung der Soziologie des Rechts*, published in 1913,[155] is a sub-discipline of sociology, or a branch of legal studies, or a field of

[153] Aristotle, *Physics*, VI, 239b 15.

[154] For a general overview, see A Carty, 'Sociological Theories of International Law', MP EPIL (March 2008 update).

[155] E Ehrlich, *Grundlegung der Soziologie des Rechts* (Munich and Leipzig: Duncker & Humblot, 1913), English trans *Fundamental Principles of Sociology of Law* (New Brunswick, NJ: Transaction Reprint, 2002); E Ehrlich, 'The Sociology of Law' (1922) 36 Harv LR 130. For a critical analysis, see

research in its own right within a broader social science tradition.[156] As noted by Roscoe Pound in 1911, sociological jurists, beyond their diversity, tend to 'look more to the working of the law than to its abstract content'; to 'regard law as a social institution which may be improved by intelligent human effort, and hold it their duty to discover the best means of furthering and directing such effort'; to lay 'stress upon the social purposes which law subserves rather than upon sanction'; and to 'urge that legal precepts are to be regarded more as guides to results which are socially just and less as inflexible molds'.[157]

The common denominator of all sociological approaches seems then to lie in the analysis of the social and political underlying conditions of law,[158] ie what may compendiously be called its 'sociological substratum', and, more specifically, 'the relations between the law and the social, political, economic, and psychological facts to an understanding of its origins, and stability, change and breakdown in its development'.[159] The link between law and society in fact may be framed in different sociological theories and produce different outcomes. To put it differently, the end results of legal sociological studies depend on what kind of sociological approach is adopted in the first place, and different sociological approaches lead to completely different outcomes in terms of international law. Legal sociologism may be grounded (at the very least) in two opposite schools of thought about law, depending on whether the sociological approach adopted is systemic (or 'structural-functional') or interactional ('symbolic-interactionist').[160] The systemic approach—traceable to Emile Durkheim, Talcott Parsons, and Robert Merton[161]—tends to picture society as an all-pervasive 'system' and present the inter-dependence of the elements of society, their cooperation and integration within shared values, stability, and equilibrium. The interactional approach—traceable to Max Weber, Herbert Blumer, and Harold Garfinkel[162]—rather tends to stress asystemic social conflict, agency, capacity of the individual to challenge society, social change, inequality, and disorder. In sociology, the latter approach has today apparently taken over the former, the shift being known as 'from structure to agency' or from macro- to micro-sociology.[163] In the interactional approach, the individual is seen as an active social agent (capable of resisting,

KA Ziegert, 'The Sociology behind Eugen Ehrlich's Sociology of Law' (1979) 7 IJSL 225; D Nelken, 'Eugen Ehrlich, Living Law, and Plural Legalities' (2008) 9 TIL 443.

[156] For a general overview, see R Cotterrell, *The Sociology of Law: An Introduction* (Oxford: OUP, 1992); R Cotterrell, 'Sociology of Law' in ELS (Thousand Oaks: Sage, 2007).

[157] R Pound, 'The Scope and Purpose of Sociological Jurisprudence' (1911) 25 Harv LR 489. American Legal Realism, largely inspired by the pragmatist motto 'truth is what works best' defended, for example, by W James, 'Pragmatism: A New Name for some Old Ways of Thinking' in W James, *Writings 1902–1910* (New York: The Library of America, 1987) 479, 522, has particularly attacked legal formalism understood as neutral adjudication by rejecting its 'mechanical jurisprudence' and 'abuse of logic'. See R Pound, 'Mechanical Jurisprudence' (1908) 8 Col LR 605, noting that 'law must not become too scientific for the people to appreciate its workings' and warning that 'The effect of all systems is apt to be petrifaction of the subject systematized'.

[158] M Huber, 'Die soziologischen Grundlagen des Völkerrechts' in M Huber, *Gemischte Schriften: Gesellschaft und Humanität* (Zürich: Atlantis, 1948) vol 3, 49–162.

[159] J Stone, 'Problems Confronting Sociological Enquiries Concerning International Law' (1956) 89 RdC 65, 65.

[160] For this analysis, see M Hirsch, 'The Sociology of International Law: Invitation to Study International Rules in their Social Context' (2005) 55 UTLJ 891. For an insightful discussion of the 'agent-structure' debate from an IR constructivist perspective, see AE Wendt, 'The Agent-Structure Problem in International Relations Theory' (1987) 41 *International Organization* 335–70, and M Finnemore, *National Interests in International Society* (New York: Cornell University Press, 1996) 14–33.

[161] Hirsch (n 160 above) 897–902. [162] ibid 902–6. [163] ibid 931.

challenging, and changing social structures) rather than the product (or the victim) of the social system.[164] However, it appears that the systemic approach is still prevalent in international law discourse basically because of the need to regard international law as a 'system' (rather than a haphazard collection of rules) which ensures stability and integration.[165]

International legal sociologism in fact often adopts either a 'realist' (statist and anti-normativist) approach, stressing power-political relations between states as the essential substratum of international law,[166] or an (rule-sceptic and anti-statist) 'spontaneist' or interactional perspective, placing emphasis on the social realities which underlie the 'formalism' of law and the state as the only formal source of legal rules.[167] While both tend to critique positivist-styled 'black-letter rules' in favour of a more 'fluid' or 'flexible' understanding of the law, the latter, to which the analysis may be limited here,[168] focuses especially on factors ranging from the 'living law' in opposition to the 'law in the books',[169] to 'legitimacy' rather than legality,[170] 'socialization' and 'internalization' of law,[171] non-hierarchical social construction of the law 'from below' or in interaction between the rulers and the ruled,[172] pulls towards law compliance,[173] and use of the law as a means to an end for a change in society towards desired goals, such as human dignity.[174] The stress generally is on what positivists would call 'pre-legal' behaviour leading to the making of the law but not coincident with the law.[175] In so doing, this legal sociologism tends to confuse law with facts lest law remains too distant from society with too little credibility, thus making the 'is' prevail over the 'ought', although at times the reverse is also the case, such as in McDougal's doctrine, which elevates 'human dignity' to the general and absolute 'ought' to which law should conform.[176] In any case, either the 'is' absorbs the 'ought' or the 'ought' absorbs the 'is'. A spontaneist or interactional thrust is found in other sociological and constructivist accounts of international law, such as those grounded in Herbert Hart's theory of law based on social practice and the 'internal aspect' of norms,[177] Philip Allott's constructivism of the mind,[178] Jürgen Habermas's theory of 'communicative

[164] Hirsch (n 160 above) 902.

[165] ibid 932. For the systemic view of international law, see Ch 6 below, section A (3).

[166] See eg PE Corbett, *Law and Society in the Relations of States* (New York: Harcourt Brace & Co, 1951); PE Corbett, 'Social Basis of a Law of Nations' (1954) 85 RdC 471; G Schwarzenberger, 'Jus Pacis Ac Belli?: Prolegomena to a Sociology of International Law' (1943) 37 AJIL 460, 478–9, characterizing international law as 'a type of social law which does not condition, but is conditioned, by the rule of force'; G Schwarzenberger, 'International Law and Society' (1947) 1 YBWA 159; C de Visscher, *Théories et réalités en droit international public* (Paris: Pédone, 4th edn, 1970), English version *Theory and Reality in International Law* (Princeton: Princeton University Press, 1968).

[167] See B Landheer, 'Contemporary Sociological Theories and International Law' (1957) 91 RdC 1. For an analysis of the various meanings of legal formalism, see Ch 6 below, n 19.

[168] For the realist arguments, see section B (3) above.

[169] See nn 107 and 155 above.

[170] See Ch 6 below, section A (2)(a).

[171] HH Koh, 'Why Do Nations Obey International Law?' (1996–97) 106 Yale LJ 2599.

[172] See Ch 5 below, section C (4) (d).

[173] See Ch 6 below, n 559.

[174] MS McDougal, 'International Law, Power, and Policy: A Contemporary Conception' (1953) 82 RdC 137, 257.

[175] cf H Kelsen, *General Theory of Law and State* [1945] (New Brunswick and London: Transaction Publishers, 2007) 24–8, 162–78.

[176] cf GJH van Hoof, *Rethinking the Sources of International Law* (Deventer: Kluwer, 1983) 42.

[177] Recently, see eg d'Aspremont (n 13 above) especially 75–6, for other Hart-inspired international law scholars; and Ch 6 below, n 78.

[178] P Allott, *Eunomia: New Order for a New World* [1990] (Oxford: OUP, 2001), arguing that 'the international system itself is nothing other than a structure of ideas' (at xiv); P Allott, *The Health of*

action',[179] Harold Koh's notion of transnational legal process,[180] as well as the systems theory developed by Niklas Luhmann[181] and Gunther Teubner,[182] alone or with Andreas Fischer-Lescano,[183] towards law as 'autopoiesis'.

Two sociological approaches particularly espoused today are worth examining, namely, solidarism and constructivism. This will also allow a discussion of the difference between widespread current sociological ideas about international law and the approach adopted in this book.

The champion of the use of solidarism in approaching international law is undoubtedly Georges Scelle.[184] His theory of international law is well known and needs no detailed description. Scelle's theory was built on Léon Duguit's institutionalist theory,[185] which also inspired several other scholars and schools of thought in the twentieth century and beyond, notably in Italy, with such authors as Santi Romano,[186] Rolando Quadri,[187] and Roberto Ago.[188] In Scelle's view, there are two basic 'laws'

Nations: Society and Law beyond the State (Cambridge: CUP, 2004), calling for 'a revolution not in the street but in the mind' (at 399–422) on the assumption that 'if we can change our consciousness of the world, we can change the world' (at 406).

179 J Habermas, *Theorie des kommunikativen Handelns* (Frankfurt am Main: Suhrkamp, 1981), English trans *Theory of Communicative Action* (Boston: Beacon Press, 1984–87) 2 vols; J Habermas, *Moralbewußtsein und kommunikatives Handeln* (Frankfurt am Main: Suhrkamp, 1983), English trans *Moral Consciousness and Communicative Action* (Cambridge, Mass: MIT Press, 1990) 66, famously arguing that 'Only those norms can claim to be valid that meet (or could meet) with the approval of all affected in their capacity as participants in a practical discourse'.

180 HH Koh, 'Transnational Legal Process (1996) 75 Nebraska Law Review 181, describing transnational legal process as 'the theory and practice of how public and private actors—nation-states, international organizations, multinational enterprises, non-governmental organizations, and private individuals—interact in a variety of public and private, domestic and international fora to make, interpret, enforce, and ultimately, internalize rules of transnational law', thus 'embrac[ing] not just the descriptive workings of a process, but the *normativity* of that process' and 'focus[ing] not simply upon how international interaction among transnational actors shapes law, but also on how law shapes and guides future interactions: in short, how law influences why nations obey' (original emphasis).

181 N Luhmann, *Das Recht der Gesellschaft* (Frankfurt am Main: Suhrkamp, 1993), English trans *Law As a Social System* (Oxford: OUP, 2004). For an assessment, see J Mingers, 'Can Social Systems be Autopoietic? Assessing Luhmann's Social Theory' (2002) 50 *Sociological Review* 278.

182 G Teuber (ed), *Autopoietic Law: A New Approach To Law and Society* (Berlin: de Gruyter, 1988); G Teuber, '"Global Bukowina": Legal Pluralism in the World Society' in G Teuber (ed), *Global Law Without a State* (Aldershot: Dartmouth, 1997) 3–22. For a critical analysis, see D Michailakis, 'Review: Law as an Autopoietic System' (1995) 38 *Acta Sociologica* 323.

183 A Fischer-Lescano and G Teubner, 'Regime Collisions: The Vain Search for Legal Unity in the Fragmentation of Global Law' (2004) 25 Mich JIL 999; A Fischer-Lescano and G Teubner, *Regime-Kollisionen: zur Fragmentierung des globalen Rechts* (Frankfurt am Main: Suhrkamp, 2006).

184 G Scelle, *Précis de droit des gens: principes et systématique* (Paris: Sirey, 1932–34) vol 1, at 1; G Scelle, *Théorie du gouvernement international* (Paris: Presses Universitaires de France, 1934); G Scelle, *Manuel de droit international public* (Paris: Domat-Montchrestien, 1948) 6; G Scelle, *Manuel élémentaire de droit international public* (Paris: Domat-Montchrestien, 1943) 403 and 504; G Scelle, 'Le phénomène juridique du dédoublement fonctionnel' in W Schätzel and H-J Schlochauer (eds), *Rechtsfragen der internationalen Organisation: Festschrift für Hans Wehberg zu seinem 70. Geburtstag* (Frankfurt am Main: Klostermann, 1956) 324–42.

185 L Duguit, *L'Etat, le droit objectif et la loi positive* (Paris: Fontemoing, 1901) 12; L Duguit, *Traité de droit constitutionnel* (Paris: Fontemoing, 2nd edn, 1921) vol 1, 478. See G Scelle, 'La doctrine de L. Duguit et les fondements du droit des gens' (1932) 2 *Archives de Philosophie du Droit et de Sociologie Juridique* 83.

186 Romano (n 213 below), advancing a pluralistic theory of legal systems linking law to 'institutions' and denying that the state is the only legitimate source of law.

187 Quadri (n 214 below): 'Le fondement du caractère obligatoire du droit international public', ibid proposing a 'realist' approach based on the 'vertical' relationship between states *uti universi* vis-à-vis states *uti singuli* guaranteed by the 'intervention' of states *uti universi* against transgressions of the law.

188 R Ago, 'Positive Law and International Law' (1957) 51 AJIL 691, developing a theory of customary international law as 'spontaneous law', devoid as such of any formal source, and hence 'non-positive'. For a critical comment, see JL Kunz, 'Roberto Ago's Theory of a "Spontaneous" International

common to all legal systems, including international law: (a) the origin of law in society according to the principle *ubi societas ibi jus*; and (b) the expansion of societies beyond their spatial borders according to the principle of 'material solidarity'.[189] The principle *ubi societas ibi jus* was intended in the sense that there can be no society without law. Law is thought to emerge and remain effective 'spontaneously' from society (as opposed to being voluntarily posited by a sovereign) as a result of a 'biological necessity'. This necessity includes an endless number of social constraints going well beyond human will (climatic, physical, psychic, linguistic, religious, imitative, etc), thus suggesting that human beings are the product of their milieu. The principle of 'material solidarity' between different societies is believed to generate an 'inter-societal' law which hierarchically overarches the law of any single society and individual, just as in federal states federal law trumps state law. The inter-societal law emerges 'spontaneously' from the human desire to meet needs of various kinds. It then becomes a law prevailing over the law of each society on logical grounds, capable as such of automatically abrogating conflicting local or national laws, hence Scelle's monism.[190] It is on the above two 'laws' that Scelle built his famous theory of 'dédoublement fonctionnel' whereby public officials set up in a certain legal system are deemed to exercise public functions also in other legal systems when in these latter systems a public function is not (or not adequately) performed by other public officials. Scelle's examples refer to French administrative law and colonial law. In international law, the principle was allegedly prevailing and described by Scelle as 'an instinctive tendency of the ecumenical society towards the integration of the law that it generates', beyond 'state feudalism'.[191] Critics are seen as still being imbued with 'the old ideology of tribal nationalism' expressed by the idea of sovereignty which, by rejecting the two basic laws, was the cause of the lack of institutions of the international legal system. International law, as any law, was regarded as 'the natural product of an increasing human solidarity' which could avail itself, at that time, only of the 'imperfect' mechanism of 'dédoublement fonctionnel'. State officials who made treaties were seen as 'veritable international organs' who create an international 'legislation' (or 'conventional laws'). International law could thus be seen as 'true law' despite its lack of organs of its own. What mattered was the law as it derived from society. Central to this account was the distinction between 'formal' and 'material' competences. Law as based on society referred to the 'material' sphere of law as opposed to its 'formal' dimension, if necessary.

Scelle's theory, although self-proclaiming as 'sociological', and hence presumably empirical, is actually driven by the theoretical idea that international law is indeed real law based on societal solidarity which, as such, trumps domestic law. When historically contextualized, the theory is clearly aimed at opposing the (totalitarian) state of the inter-war period by intellectually building an overpowering international law based ('from below') on society against the will 'from above' of the sovereign. Whatever its merits and usefulness to the struggle against totalitarian regimes and states' abuses, it was somewhat paradoxically too distant from realities, and still is. Scelle himself noted that the primacy of international law was actually resisted by states 'despite the absurdity of their conception'.[192] And there is little or no sign that domestic law is

Law' (1958) 52 AJIL 85, rightly observing that Ago's theory is 'a typical pseudonatural law construction' (ibid 90). See further Ch 6 below, n 103.

[189] The following summary is basically drawn from Scelle (1956) (n 184 above).

[190] See Ch 6 below, section D (2).

[191] Scelle (1956) (n 184 above) 342 (trans by the author).

[192] ibid 333–4 (trans by the author).

automatically 'abrogated' when conflicting with international law. Historically, international law performed very poorly in terms of containing dictators in their will to wage World War II, and Scelle's theory did not succeed in avoiding the war and catalysing solidarity among the peoples rather than hostility. It is also apparent that state officials act on behalf of and in the interests of (as well as in obedience to) their own law and state.[193] They do not claim to act for the international community, save occasionally in the attempt to justify acts the legality of which is contentious at best. Scelle's federalist appraisal of international law finds no evidence in reality and sounds like the perennial dream of an at-last unified, harmonious, universal community whose features are, hardly surprisingly, typically Western. Scelle's notion of the 'material' sphere, as opposed to being formal, goes well beyond what society may really imply in its actual behaviour and ends up in a mystical justification of his own theory without supporting evidence. It also downplays formalism when formalism itself can well be the result of what people and society demand of law. His is, in the end, a natural law theory in disguise. The 'social' element was assumed or constructed in his mind and then he expected social reality to adjust to his mind, not the other way round. It was clearly a theory with a goal and a mission. It demythologized international law, as resulting from 'absolute' statehood and sovereignty, by remythologizing it in terms of 'social necessity', or even biological inevitability. But solidarity is only one among many other drives of human behaviour and social necessity based on the maxim *ubi societas ibi jus* simply means that there must be some law in any society; it says nothing about what kind of law or which specific rules prevail in this or that society, let alone whether a certain number of individuals or other entities form a 'society' as supposed.

Also social constructivism takes the recent 'pro-agency' trend in sociology seriously and seeks to apply it to international law. While this trend has been quite successful in IR theory,[194] it has met more resistance in the construction of international law, in which, as previously noted, systemic and even formalistic considerations are often compelling.[195] Notably, Jutta Brunnée and Stephen J Toope have developed a form of 'interactional' constructivism grounded in Lon Fuller's inherent requirements of law.[196] Also Benedict Kingsbury, in the context of global administrative law (GAL)

[193] For a telling confutation of Scelle's claim, assuming that respect for international law is one thing and the strict duty of the courts to apply domestic law (even where conflicting with international law) is quite another whatever the consequences on the international plane, see US Court of Appeals for the District of Columbia Circuit, *United States v Yunis*, Judgment of 29 January 1991, 924 F2d 1086, at <http://law.justia.com/cases/federal/appellate-courts/F2/924/1086/224419>, para 19, holding that 'Yunis seeks to portray international law as a self-executing code that trumps domestic law whenever the two conflict. That effort misconceives the role of judges as appliers of international law and as participants in the federal system. Our duty is to enforce the Constitution, laws and treaties of the United States, not to conform the law of the land to norms of customary international law.' This point will be discussed at length, and the *Yunis* approach in turn criticized, in Ch 6 below, section D (2).

[194] See Ch 2 above, n 13.

[195] For a description of international law as 'what those who handle it believe it to be' as opposed to 'something that is objectively given like laws of nature', from the perspective of its objectivity as intersubjectivity built in particular on the writings of J Coulter, J Habermas, R Rorty, K Popper, and A Wendt, see Müllerson (n 22 above) 46–8, rejecting 'pure' normativism in favour of an appropriate consideration of political, economic, historical, social, humanitarian, moral, and other factors shaping international affairs.

[196] J Brunnée and SJ Toope, 'International Law and Constructivism: Elements of an International Theory of International Law' (2000) 39 Col JTL 19; J Brunnée and SJ Toope, *Legitimacy and Legality: An Interactional Account* (Cambridge: CUP, 2010) especially 1–125, laying emphasis on the 'perception of international law's role among people on the street' and claiming that 'there is law in the jungle . . . made through the interactions of a variety of actors, including elites, the media, NGOs and "ordinary" citizens' (at 4–5). For a summary of Lon Fuller's theory, see Ch 1 above, section B (3)(e).

studies,[197] is to some extent involved, although apparently more based on Hart's foundation of law in social practices.[198] Brunnée and Toope claim that IR constructivism misses the explanation of how norms shape identities and actors' behaviour due to its positivist understanding of law.[199] Even self-professed non-positivists, such as Nicholas G Onuf and Friedrich Kratochwil,[200] are said to be affected by a positivist bias endorsing an essentially vertical understanding of the operation of legal rules.[201] In contrast, Brunnée and Toope take up Fuller's 'interactive', non-hierarchical understanding of law as 'a creative activity' which can be constructed as legal 'by degrees', rather than in terms of an all-or-nothing proposition, and cannot be understood as 'a fully realized system sprung full-born from the head of a sovereign', but rather as a 'construction dependent upon the mutual generative activity and acceptance of the governing and the governed', even 'in seemingly hierarchical state systems'.[202] Legal rules are seen as 'persuasive' and 'legitimate' when rooted in 'thick' acceptance by the citizenry. Law is authoritative only when it is mutually constructed, and hence legitimate, ie in accordance with Fuller's famous criteria of 'internal morality'. Brunnée and Toope thus argue that 'law's existence is best measured by the influence it exerts, and not by formal tests of validity', assuming that 'Pre-legal normativity is valuable in itself, and is not purely a set of instruments on the road to law', and conclude that when legal norms 'are perceived to be legitimate, because of their adherence to an internal morality, and their congruence with a normative inheritance, past and present social practice and contemporary aspirations, they generate adherence'.[203]

Brunnée and Toope's constructivism is directed to demythologize international law as a 'fixed' number of fixed rules flowing from the formal sources, with a view to laying the stress on agency, interaction, dynamics, and impact on behaviour. In doing so, they remythologize international law as a dynamic and interactive social phenomenon at the risk of downplaying its formal and systemic dimension. Basically, they rely on social practice to further Fullers' concept of law with its 'inherent' (hence pre-established, society-independent) morality. This concept is elaborated in the mind of the theorist, not in or by society. It is the theorist who claims to know what counts in society as law. This constructivism accepts social construction only to the extent that this allows the development of a concept of law which is relatively independent of the sovereign, the state, and its formal sources. Once this notion is built, constructivists either abandon society as a factor of the analysis or assume that 'society' attaches to law certain 'inherent' features no differently from the natural law tradition. Their two-tier reasoning is based first on reliance on society in order to dismiss the notion that the

[197] See section B (8) below.

[198] B Kingsbury, 'The Concept of "Law" in Global Administrative Law'(2009) 20 EJIL 23, 26–31, noting that a claim to 'law' in GAL 'is a claim that diverges from, and can be sharply in tension with the classical models of consent-based inter-state international law and most models of national law', notably with positivist command theories, and arguing for law as 'a social practice' consisting of Hartian primary and secondary rules—indeed 'a modern positivist approach' that has made 'a decisive break from the Hobbesian (and Austinian) dependence of the concept of law on sovereignty'—and (beyond Hart's positivism, somewhat inspired by Fuller) of 'intrinsic' or 'immanent' publicness requirements evidenced through comparative materials.

[199] Brunnée and Toope (2000) (n 196 above) 33, 37.

[200] F Kratochwil, *Rules, Norms and Decisions: On the Conditions of Practical and Legal Reasoning in International Relations and Domestic Affairs* (Cambridge: CUP, 1989); NG Onuf, *World of Our Making: Rules and Rule in Social Theory and International Relations* (Columbia, SC: University of South Carolina Press, 1989).

[201] Brunnée and Toope (2000) (n 196 above) 38–43.

[202] ibid 47–8.

[203] ibid 65, 70.

sovereign is the only law-maker and then on the 'inherent' features of this society-based concept of law so as to dismiss also the notion that law ultimately depends on society, on the understandable ground that society may be as dangerous as the state itself. This reasoning is inextricably contradictory. Fuller tries to reconcile 'social interaction' with 'inner morality', presumably supposing that the inner morality is the outcome of social interaction, but there is no certainty about such relationship. His insistence on social interaction is used to smuggle its inner morality tests for a practice stemming 'from below', but there is an insuperable contradiction between the 'inherent' morality of law and social interaction. If social interaction is the ultimate criterion, then it must be followed wherever it leads and be tested in any kind of society, not just against the background of Western societies or, more specifically, of the Anglo-American tradition of democracy and rule of law. The ultimate goal of this interactional theory is to conceive of law as *independent of both the sovereign and society* and to leave law to the 'interaction' of individuals as such. But if individuals themselves should not see this as law, then this is simply not their law, whatever the theory. And it is likely that people do not see this as law because people need law as a set of formal, authoritative statements capable of being enforced in society. A concept of law that aspires to be ultimately free from both the sovereign and society is precisely natural law. And natural law is often created (or invented, or identified) by the mind of the theorist, regardless of (or against) society, this precisely being its function. For a natural law advocate such as Fuller the theory may hold. Problems arise, however, when seeking to build on Fuller's ideas about interaction a 'constructivist' or 'interactional' theory of law without discarding Fuller's inner morality and any 'inherent', pre-conceived, extra-societal (or intra-mental constructed) criterion of law.

Law as social construct as here understood differs from the above theories in two key respects. First, it is founded on conflict and force since law is seen as collective violence imposed by the group on each of its members rather than in cooperative activities between the rulers and the ruled or between the ruled themselves. It presupposes hierarchy, however informal, and heteronomy, in the sense that the individual is subjected to the *whole* of individuals making up society but not vis-à-vis *each* of the others. From the viewpoint of any individual, law comes from outside and from above in so far as it is made and enforced by society as a whole rather than autonomously by the individual or through a mere 'horizontal' interaction with other individuals. Law is not equal to social practice. Social practice between members of society each vis-à-vis each is one thing; social practice consisting of the relationship between each member vis-à-vis the whole of the others is quite another. But the distinction between law and social practice does not mean that the 'is' and the 'ought' are distinct either.[204] The force of society as a whole, while being an 'is' of itself, translates into (or is lived as) an 'ought' for any member of society. That law is ultimately founded in society does not imply that it must be confused with the social practice of any consociate vis-à-vis any other. Hierarchy and heteronomy do not necessarily require a formal superior authority, much less statehood, as classical command theorists claim. Still, such elements are needed for law to work as law. Non-hierarchical pictures of law resemble children's games, not the law that people *themselves* expect to be operative in order to protect them from abuses by others (possibly including public authorities). On the other hand, each individual certainly contributes (both actively and passively) to the shaping of society as

[204] See Ch 1 above, section B (1)(c).

a whole and its rules.[205] Secondly, the approach here adopted furthers the 'record' of what *any* society sees as its law without providing a general definition of law based on a view of one and the same idea of society taken as the paradigm. Commitment, social attunement, and prudence are preferred to pure science of law, including a social science of law as developed by constructivists. Myth is here valued while prospects of 'definitive' scientific demythologizations of the law are disbelieved. Natural law and divine law may also be included in the notion of law *if the people involved so believe*, not because this is demanded by a particular theory in general terms. People in a group may well accept as law a set of rules on which they have no power at all, such as divine law and even the law of an absolute monarch or an unfathomable sorcerer. Law is what 'is lived' as law among its addressees as a whole, not what is elaborated in general terms in the mind of the jurist. Law is thus differently constructed in different societies.

The key problem with legal sociologism, especially the interactional version, is that social norms tend to be equated with legal rules on the basis of intellectual considerations, overlooking the elementary fact that people in one or in another society may want to differentiate social norms from legal rules and see legal rules work as such, whatever theorists may see as 'inherent' in law. Sociality is not necessarily equal to law and law is not a simple mirror of society, as Kelsen warned.[206] In fact, states appear to appreciate the difference between social norms and legal rules and to be clear when a rule is legally required as opposed to when it is socially expected. The overlap of social norms and legal rules reflect the expectation, no less than the naturalist dream, of a harmonious society in which all people spontaneously 'negotiate and accept' the rules by way of interaction. This image recalls the Western democratic ideal. But if law has a function, this is first of all to seek to coordinate the disharmonies in society (whether democratic or not) which individuals vis-à-vis themselves cannot solve without the assistance of formal legal statements and their enforcement under the community's control.

(7) Constitutionalism

The 'constitutional' construction of international law dates back to Hans Kelsen's *Grundnorm* and its development by Alfred Verdross.[207] The underlying premise was structural in character in that the appeal to an international constitution was thought to enable the jurist to make sense of the unity, coherence, and completeness of international law as a 'system'.[208] This allowed the identification of general principles of international law capable of being applied in the absence of specific rules, to solve antinomies between rules by the establishment of a hierarchy of values, and to fill the gaps in the law. Verdross progressively gave to Kelsen's 'pure', epistemologically inspired *Grundnorm* a 'moral', content-based foundation grounded in the Western philosophical and constitutionalist tradition, embodied in Aristotle's concept of

205 As previously discussed, see Ch 2 above, section B (2).

206 See n 175 above.

207 H Kelsen, *Reine Rechtslehre: Einleitung in die rechtswissenschaftliche Problematik* (Leipzig: Deuticke, 1934) 147–54; A Verdross, *Die Einheit des rechtlichen Weltbildes auf Grundlage der Völkerrechtsverfassung* (Tübingen: JCB Mohr, 1923); A Verdross, *Die Verfassung der Völkerrechtsgemeinschaft* (Wien: Springer, 1926). On Verdross, see E Lagrange, 'Retour sur un classique: A. Verdross, *Die Verfassung der Völkerrechtsgemeinschaft*, 1926' (2008) 112 RGDIP 973–84.

208 cf E Benvenisti, 'The Conception of International Law as a Legal System' (2007) 50 Ger YBIL 393; AL Paulus, 'The International Legal System as a Constitution' in JL Dunoff and JP Trachtman (eds), *Ruling the World? Constitutionalism, International Law, and Global Governance* (Cambridge: CUP, 2009) 69, 82–7, 107–9.

politeia,[209] Stoic *cosmopolis*,[210] medieval *Respublica christiana*,[211] Immanuel Kant's project for a perpetual peace, and the ideals of the American and French revolutions.[212] The constitutional idea was taken up and further developed by other scholars in subsequent decades, both in the 'social-institutionalist' and in the 'realist' doctrines of international law. International constitutional principles were seen as forming a 'material' constitution reflecting either the social, immanent foundations of international law,[213] or the ultimate shaping of international law by the 'prevailing forces' operating on the international scene.[214] This idea, drawn from national law, thus lent itself to meeting demands that could (ambiguously) be either systemic, or ethical, or realist.

The end of the Cold War witnessed the resurrection and the progressive rise of a 'new' world constitutionalism.[215] The debate has focused on the (substantive and procedural) limitations to international power by international organs by appealing to monitoring, transparency, participation of the addressees in law-making and decision-making, accountability, rule of law, due process, human rights, democracy, and judicial review of acts adopted by international bodies.[216] The new global constitutionalism is sometimes thought to 'compensate' for the allegedly ongoing, parallel deconstitutionalization of domestic legal systems.[217] It is not confined to ensuring the systemic unity, coherence, and completeness of international law. It extends to the substance of international norms and decisions, pointing to their legitimacy. It is a prescriptive constitutionalism, rather than being merely descriptive of principles deemed to be 'immanent' in the system (as was the old constitutionalism). It is, also, a multi-dimensional and pluralist constitutionalism, as opposed to the old constitutionalism based on the basic values of the Christian-European tradition embodied in natural law. It is, finally, a 'prospective' constitutionalism, presented as a 'perspective', an 'approach', a 'mindset', and the like, concerning how to see reality rather than a technique useful to identify norms and principles 'in force' or a search for the ultimate foundations of international law.[218] Its main purpose is to constitutionalize (or to 'constitute' as reality) global governance and the role of *non-state* actors and rules for the benefit of peoples (ie of the ruled rather than the rulers) in apparent detachment from the so-called Westphalia model based on the centrality of states and the *raison d'Etat*. Its ambition is to signal a major shift from a state-centred to a people-centred

[209] CH McIlwain, *Constitutionalism, Ancient and Modern* (Ithaca, NY: Cornell University Press, 1940); J Frank, 'Aristotle on Constitutionalism and the Rule of Law Critical Modernities: Politics and Law beyond the Liberal Imagination' (2007) 8 TIL 37.

[210] See M Schofield (n 30 above).

[211] See eg WG Grewe, *Epochen der Völkerrechtsgeschichte* (Baden-Baden: Nomos, 1984) 72–82, English trans *The Epochs of International Law* (Berlin and New York: Walter de Gruyter, 2000) 51–9.

[212] cf I Kant, *Zum ewigen Frieden. Ein philosophischer Entwurf* [1795] (Stuttgart: Reclam, 1984), English trans *To Perpetual Peace: A Philosophical Sketch* (Indianapolis, Hacket, 2003); along the same lines, recently, see J Habermas, *Die gespaltene Westen* (Frankfurt am Main: Suhrkamp, 2004), English trans *The Divided West* (Cambridge: Polity, 2006).

[213] See eg S Romano, *Corso di diritto internazionale* (Padua: Cedam, 4th edn, 1939) 31–3.

[214] See eg R Quadri, *Diritto internazionale pubblico* (Naples: Liguori, 5th edn, 1968) 109–12, 119–29, 275–8; R Quadri, 'Le fondement du caractère obligatoire du droit international public' (1952-I) 80 RdC 579.

[215] B Ackerman, 'The Rise of World Constitutionalism' (1997) 83 Virg LR 771–97.

[216] For the reasons in favour of global constitutionalism, see critically C Focarelli, book review (2010) 104 AJIL 557.

[217] A Peters, 'Compensatory Constitutionalism: The Function and Potential of Fundamental International Norms and Structure' (2006) 19 LJIL 579.

[218] See eg M Koskenniemi, 'Constitutionalism as Mindset: Reflections on Kantian Themes about International Law and Globalization' (2007) 8 TIL 9–36.

international law. Thus defined, global constitutionalism tends to oppose the old realist constitutionalism.

International constitutionalism refers today either to specific treaty regimes (such as those established by the United Nations,[219] the World Trade Organization,[220] the European Union,[221] or the human rights treaties, both universal and regional)[222] or to international law as a whole. Quite a few uncertainties surround both strands of thinking. For example, against the view that the UN Charter is (not so much a treaty like any other, as) the constitution of the international community, several objections can be raised.[223] Even stronger objections can be made to the constitutional character of sector or regional systems like the WTO, human rights treaties, and the EU itself. As regards international law as a whole, global constitutionalism can be challenged on several grounds.[224]

A first objection is that the term 'constitution' is used by global constitutionalists with great generosity, but its meaning often remains obscure. A 'core', unquestionable, essence of a constitution is usually taken for granted. It is generally presented as intuitive and self-evident, ie as an indication of the 'mode of being' of international law. This 'mode of being', despite its descriptive appearance, invariably contains prescriptive overtones and tends to allude to what 'must' be, or to what 'is already' there, albeit *in nuce*. The difference between what 'is already' in act, what 'is already' in potency, and what 'is not yet' (either in act or in potency) but may anyway come to light in the future, is often vague.[225] The distinction between the 'is' (or the 'constituted') and the 'ought' (or the 'constituent') is blurred, presumably with a view to 'anticipating' as law what at best is future law.[226] The risk is to construct, as a formally superior constitutional international (or quasi-constitutional)[227] law, a law that in fact

[219] See B Fassbender, *The United Nations Charter and the Constitution of the International Community* (Leiden and Boston: Nijhoff, 2009). For a critical view, see B Conforti and C Focarelli, *The Law and Practice of the United Nations* (Leiden and Boston: Nijhoff, 4th rev edn, 2010) 9–21. See further Ch 6 below, n 326.

[220] For a critical view, see JL Dunoff, 'The Politics of International Constitutions: The Curious Case of the World Trade Organization' in Dunoff and Trachtman (eds) (n 208 above) 178.

[221] See eg N Walker, 'Reframing EU Constitutionalism' in Dunoff and Trachtman (eds) (n 208 above) 149; G De Búrca and JHH Weiler (eds), *The Worlds of European Constitutionalism* (Cambridge: CUP, 2011).

[222] See Ch 6 below, n 123.

[223] Such as the following: (a) absence of separation of powers; (b) absence of checks and balances between the UN organs; (c) absence of any relationship of confidence between the General Assembly and the Security Council; (d) absence of a Bill of Rights applicable to UN organs; (e) absence of courts entrusted to adjudicate breaches of human rights by UN organs; (f) absence of judicial review of UN organs' binding resolutions; (g) functioning of UN organs in formal isolation from one another; (h) detachment of public opinion from UN activities, these being carried out, inter alia, by representatives of *states* who are *governmental* delegates belonging to the *majorities* in each member state.

[224] For a different recent critique, see N Krisch, *Beyond Constitutionalism: The Pluralist Structure of Postnational Law* (Oxford and New York: OUP, 2010).

[225] D Kennedy, 'The Mystery of Global Governance' in Dunoff and Trachtman (eds) (n 208 above) 37, 60–1, observing that 'current constitutionalist discussions of global governance, although they begin as description, end up sounding far more like proposals to remake the world's political order by sacralizing the institutional forms with which they are most familiar'.

[226] For the distinction, see M Loughlin and N Walker, *The Paradox of Constitutionalism: Constituent Power and Constitutional Form* (Oxford: OUP, 2007).

[227] See eg L Condorelli and L Boisson de Chazournes, 'Common Article 1 of the Geneva Conventions Revisited: Protecting Collective Interest' (2000) 82 IRRC 67; and, critically, C Focarelli, 'Common Article 1 of the 1949 Geneva Conventions: A Soap Bubble?' (2010) 21 EJIL 125.

is not even 'ordinary' law, but rather a value that is worth striving for in order to bring about a new law that may or may not conform thereto in the future.[228]

Secondly, the model of global constitutionalists is invariably (either expressly or impliedly) the national constitution, ie the constitution of the Western nation state in its evolution subsequent to the American and the French revolutions. The transplantation of the domestic model of constitution to the international plane is encouraged by the historical 'positive' connotations of the former.[229] However, differences are fairly numerous and deep rooted. Domestic constitutions vary greatly with states and it is difficult to extract a common core. They work, when they do, because of the existence in the state of a politically legitimate authority that succeeds in making itself obeyed by the addressees of the rules. In international law such an authority is missing. A world state does not exist, and even the most powerful state is not powerful enough to be able to enforce the alleged global constitution. Clearly, if the international constitution is to be seen strictly in terms of a national constitution, then there can be no international constitution at all. At best, the evocation of a global constitution can be instrumental in creating an atmosphere more prepared to accept the constitutional project for something to be brought about in the future. Global constitutionalists are mindful of this, of course, and generally propose a model conveniently 'adjusted' to the international reality. The adjustments proposed vary considerably with the context and often appear tailored *ex post* to label international law (as a whole or in particular areas) as 'constitutional' without making it clear to what end and with what legal effects.

Thirdly, the ambiguity of the term 'constitution' raises doubts when it is used in its derivatives, such as 'constitutionalism', 'constitutionalization', 'constitutional moment', and so on. These terms are not necessarily interchangeable. Constitutionalism is a historical-legal and institutional process typical of Western states and of their liberal-democratic evolution within which the 'constitution' basically denotes the limitations to sovereign power. When the term is used in the context of international law, the implication is that the term 'constitution' is used with the same meaning, but the problem with this is that a world sovereign to limit does not exist. True, there are international powers, but their nature is significantly different from that of the sovereign state which has emerged in Europe in the modern age. Alternatively, if constitutionalism is meant to refer to a concept of constitution broader than the Western liberal-democratic one, for example as the 'mode of being' of any legal system reduced to its basic structures, then it may refer also to authoritarian states or to states dominated by Islamic fundamentalism, a conclusion that few if any global constitutionalists would endorse. If the content of the constitution is taken away and if 'anything goes' as a constitution, then the very idea of a constitution seems to fade. How can a legal system that does not safeguard fundamental rights, as understood today, be called 'constitutional'?[230] Similar doubts arise when speaking of a 'constitutionalization' of international law,[231] or of a 'constitutional moment' as a fundamental change in the world *Grundnorm*.[232]

[228] See Ch 6 below, section B (4)(f).

[229] See DZ Cass, *The Constitutionalization of the World Trade Organization* (Oxford, OUP, 2005) 208, 234–36.

[230] See C Focarelli, 'Costituzionalismo internazionale e costituzionalizzazione della "global governance": alla ricerca del diritto globale' (2011) 42 *Politica del Diritto* 207.

[231] J Klabbers, A Peters, and G Ulfstein, *The Constitutionalization of International Law* (Oxford: OUP, 2009).

[232] A-M Slaughter and W Burke-White, 'An International Constitutional Moment' (2002) 43 Harv ILJ 1.

A fourth criticism is that the state serving as a model is nothing other than (and cannot be anything other than) the Western state. It is in Europe that statehood was born and it is from Europe that the model (including its constitutional form) has been spread (and imposed) elsewhere in the world. To speak of a 'constitution' to indicate the 'basic law' of an indigenous tribe makes little sense. It may even be the case that in the tribe—unlike in the mind of the Western analyst—the words 'law' and 'basic' do not exist at all. To constitutionalize international law means to see and judge the law of peoples markedly different from the model of the Western constitutional state. Any 'adjustment' to international realities cannot erase this background model which represents the yardstick of the adjustments themselves. Global constitutionalists retort that, although it is true that constitutionalism arose in Europe and in the United States in the eighteenth and nineteenth centuries, it 'was asserted against the dominant culture and the establishment, and can thus hardly be called a product of that culture'. Today's global constitutionalism, on the other hand, is said to be aimed at 'constitutionalizing global (polyarchic and multi-level) governance' by taking into due account the interests and needs of developing countries and of their populations, rather than creating a centralized world government by imitation of one or another of existing national constitutions.[233] The problem with this view is that Western constitutionalism may well have been a reaction to domination, but this does not detract from the fact that it is a product of the Western civilization and reflects a liberal-democratic logic. It is a fact that when global constitutionalists cite some national constitutions, the constitution of a Western state is invariably evoked, typically that of the United States.

Fifthly, from a practical viewpoint it is often hard to grasp what the constitutional perspective adds to international law as non-constitutionally understood.[234] Constitutionalism would be useful if it plausibly led to legal outcomes that could not be reached otherwise. However, the effort to present global constitutionalism as an approach more reflective of today's world (in particular of what is being called global governance) is rather reticent when it comes to concrete evidence. Put differently, global constitutionalism appears either redundant, when it leads to outcomes that could be reached even without endorsing it, or overloaded, when it offers a vision of the good capable of guiding political action. If constitutionalism is a plan of action for changing the world, a call for uniting forces in one direction and realizing certain values, then it situates itself in the battleground of political struggle in competition with other world views and, inter alia, with other global constitutionalisms. This is in keeping with the constructionist approach here adopted; still, there remains to be understood what international law a judge, either domestic or international, has to apply in the meantime. Existing law is socially constructed too.

Finally, global constitutionalists tend to present constitutionalism as a perspective that helps to solve the question of 'fragmentation' of international law.[235] International law is today far richer than in the past. Yet its norms are still scarce compared to the number and gravity of the global problems that international law is expected to govern. Further, these few norms are often rather generically formulated and their underlying values compete with one another, nor it is clear which should prevail in case of conflict. It is difficult to imagine how a formula like constitutionalism can solve such problems overnight, which are rooted in opposing interests within the system. An alternative

[233] Klabbers, Peters, and Ulfstein (n 231 above) 346.

[234] For a succinct affirmative answer, see T Franck, 'Preface: International Institutions: Why Constitutionalize?' in Dunoff and Trachtman (eds) (n 208 above) xi–xiv.

[235] See Ch 6 below, section A (3)(b), and section C (3).

strategy, adopted by a number of constitutionalists,[236] is to conceive of constitutionalism in pluralistic terms and to admit more than just one form of constitutionalism. However, in so doing, not only does fragmentation remain in practice, it is also theoretically radicalized.

Global constitutionalism is a construction of international law aimed at creating a new mythology sustaining legitimacy, the mythology (known under the Greek name of *ethos*) which national constitutions constantly need. This remythologizing project is accompanied by the contextual demythologization of the Westphalian, state-centric international law by advancing, in particular, the cause of non-state actors and rules. It is 'constituent' far more than 'constituted' or 'constitutive', a plan of action for a supposedly better world under global, possibly pluralistic, governance and law, a projection onto the global sphere of what is seen as the best achievements of Western political and institutional history and theory.

(8) Administrativism

A strand of scholarship especially developed in the 1920s and 1930s, called at the time 'international administrative law',[237] has been revitalized in recent years as a theory of global governance, under the name of 'global administrative law' (GAL).[238] At the core of GAL lies the opinion that 'the decisions of domestic administrators are increasingly constrained by substantive and procedural norms established at the global level' and, conversely, that 'the global administrative bodies making... decisions in some cases enjoy too much de facto independence and discretion to be regarded as mere agents of states'.[239] Global regulators include, for example, Organization for Economic Co-operation and Development (OECD) networks and committees, World Trade Organization (WTO) committees and the Dispute Settlement Body's (DSB's) Panels and Appellate Body, the G-7 and G-8, national antitrust authorities, the Basel Committee on Banking Supervision, the Financial Action Task Force, the Clean Development Mechanism devised in the Kyoto Protocol, the UN Security Council and its committees, the International Atomic Energy Agency (IAEA), the supervision mechanism of the Chemical Weapons Convention (CWC), and many others at various levels. Areas of regulation include government procurement, international investment, supervision of commercial banks, urban water services, Security Council sanction administration, international management of refugees, and so forth. The basic propositions of the administrativist approach are that 'much of global governance can be understood as regulation and administration', that 'the strict dichotomy between domestic and international has largely broken down' and that 'regulation may be highly effective despite its predominantly non-binding forms'.[240]

[236] Klabbers, Peters, and Ulfstein (n 231 above) 43; A Stone Sweet, 'Constitutionalism, Legal Pluralism, and International Regimes' (2009) 16 Ind JGLS 621.

[237] See C Tietje, *Internationalisiertes Verwaltungshandeln* (Berlin: Duncker & Humblot, 2001).

[238] For a general overview, see B Kingsbury, N Krisch, and RB Stewart, 'The Emergence of Global Administrative Law' (2005) 68 LCP 15. For a collection of 14 essays devoted to GAL and IOs, see (2009) 6 IOLR 315–673. On the 'concept of law' (Hart-inspired 'social practice' plus Fuller-inspired 'publicness requirements') underlying GAL, see n 198 above. Further information is found at the GAL Project Website, at <http://iilj.org/GAL>.

[239] Kingsbury, Krisch, and Stewart (n 238 above) 26.

[240] N Krisch and B Kingsbury, 'Introduction: Global Governance and Global Administrative Law in the International Legal Order' (2006) 17 EJIL 1, 1.

Underlying the administrativist approach is the vast increase in the reach and forms of transgovernmental regulation and administration,[241] by now deemed to be enough to justify a new approach compared to the traditional inter-state one, and the need for accountability—more specifically, for transparency, participation, reasoned decision, legality, and judicial review—of such global administrative bodies. GAL furthers a 'global administrative space', built on (and at the same time transcending) both inter-state and domestic spaces, in which various entities (international, national, transnational, private) interact. Administrativism concerns all law governing the effects in the forum state of foreign states' administrative acts, stretching to 'all rules and procedures that help ensure the accountability of global administration'.[242]

Global administrativism calls for international controls because internal controls are increasingly ineffective. But international controls remain extremely limited in many respects. Many different sources, bodies, and regimes, are assembled together in GAL without any unifying formal structure. Administrativists themselves note that the landscape is 'by no means uniform or coherent' since administrative law mechanisms and principles 'operate in some areas and not in others, many are not more than embryonic, and they diverge widely in their forms'.[243] Despite the emphasis put on administrative regulators, on their effective impact even when they have no legally binding decision-making powers, and on the interpenetration between domestic and international, global administrativism leaves states at the heart of the system. Borders remain critical, law-making and law enforcement is reserved to each state within its borders, all states and other actors are assumed to respect other states' borders and accept local law as the 'law in force' therein, international law and administrative regulators continue to be created by states, and all non-state actors are presumed to accept and rely on the effectiveness and political legitimacy of states.

Like global constitutionalists, global administrativists begin with the insight that Westphalian classical international law is increasingly challenged, and that challenges—including the breaking down of the distinction between private and public spheres as well as between international and domestic realms, the spreading of soft (yet highly effective) law, the erosion of the equality of states and of their consent for rules to be created, and the overall legitimacy of international law—are not merely quantitative but qualitative, marking a paradigm shift that only a new theoretical model can capture. Global administrativists, no differently from constitutionalists, contend that many functions which in the past were performed within states are today carried out in a global context, although in a great number of different forms and by different organs (international, domestic, internal to international organizations, and transnational). Domestic legal officials are today particularly struck by so many 'external' norms affecting virtually every branch of domestic law, and particularly public and administrative law. As hinted, this supranational regulation is deemed to evade domestic controls and to require supranational ones. Here again, like global constitutionalists, global administrativists unquestionably use, as their basic model, the Western liberal-democratic state.

In other respects global constitutionalism and administrativism are rather different and betray a different approach to the problem of global governance from a Western perspective, the former insisting on *non-state* actors (albeit retaining the state as a

241 A-M Slaughter, *A New World Order* (Princeton and Oxford, Princeton University Press, 2004).
242 Kingsbury, Krisch, and Stewart (n 238 above) 28.
243 Krisch and Kingsbury (n 240 above) 2.

unitary legal and political entity) and the latter disassembling the state into its *internal articulations* (but retaining it as the key international actor). While constitutionalism is systemic, theoretical, prospective, and possibly politically orientated in the quest for a legitimate global order, administrativism is operational, pragmatic, descriptive of changes in positive law, a political, driven by a domestic law perspective projected onto global rule- and decision-making, somewhat more marketable to domestic practitioners. GAL applies the typical administrative law safeguards found in Western domestic legal systems to international bodies. It generally fails to unveil the political realities underlying such bodies, whether public or private, and takes for granted that their control through transparency, participation, and review is a feasible and in many respects desirable path to global governance. GAL proposes a view from within the state as struck by an increasing number of international decisions that penetrate its administrative structures far more than in the past, without much attention to how the whole mechanism works and what lies behind it politically, ie who decides on this system rather than another, on what ultimate legitimacy, and for whose benefit. The silence surrounding the political sphere behind international administrative regulators, or better, the caution taken towards a global democratic project in a pluralist order,[244] together with the confidence on the working of international bodies according to the administrative model, seems to presuppose that there exists a world government capable of providing political (and not only administrative) legitimacy to administrative regulators. However, in the formal absence of such a government, GAL ends up *concealing* the sphere of political power. The political dimension of administrative regulators is downgraded to the administrative and provided with internal bounds. Controls operate downstream while nothing works to check power upstream. GAL thus turns into a technocratic project. It demythologizes international law as a Westphalian state-centric law through remythologizing it in post-Westphalian (although still plainly Western-rooted) pragmatic, managerial, and technocratic terms.[245]

(9) Third-worldism

Deconstructionism has generated a number of 'critical studies' questioning the 'objectivity', 'neutrality', and 'fairness' of the conventional narrative of international law, and taking the side of marginalized subjects ('the Other').[246] In this context, the Third World Approach to International Law (TWAIL) is central in current world order as a critical understanding of international law—often using a Marxist vocabulary[247]—from the perspective of third world states and social movements, and as a project

[244] ibid 46, 48–9.

[245] See M Koskenniemi, 'Constitutionalism, Managerialism and the Ethos of Legal Education' (2007) 4 EJLS, at <http://www.ejls.eu/1/3UK.pdf>; M Koskenniemi, 'The Fate of Public International Law: Between Technique and Politics' (2007) 70 MLR 1; M Koskenniemi, 'The Politics of International Law—20 Years Later' (2009) 20 EJIL 7.

[246] For an engaging discussion from a Derrida-inspired deconstructionist perspective of 'the many forms of relation to the other, as it is figured, performed, inscribed and imagined in the discipline of international law', see A Orford (ed), *International Law and Its Others* (Cambridge: CUP, 2006), reviewed by R Falk (2010) 104 AJIL 543–8.

[247] Although often Marxist, Third-worldism is not necessarily so: it may also be critical of the Marxist linear, universal, and ultimately Eurocentric view of history and development and of the fact that Marxism is in the end another Western theory. On Marxism in international law, see C Miéville, *Between Equal Rights: A Marxist Theory of International Law* (London: Pluto Press, 2006); S Marks (ed), *International Law on the Left: Re-examining Marxist Legacies* (Cambridge: CUP, 2008).

aiming to bring into existence an international law of emancipation.[248] The term 'Third World', far from being anachronistic, is meant by TWAIL to refer to all countries of Asia, Africa, and Latin America sharing a common history of subjection to colonialism and still underdeveloped and marginalized, beyond their differences and the plurality of their possible practices of collective resistance to hegemonic policies.[249] It has been said that 'TWAIL scholars seek to transform international law from being a language of oppression to a language of emancipation' aimed at promoting 'truly global justice'.[250] TWAIL is generally engaged in analyses of the colonial past by challenging the history of international law as a product of European Christian civilization written by Western scholars, claiming that modern international law was born in the sixteenth century as an offspring of colonialism and the civilization/barbarian or European/non-European divide.[251]

Leaving aside variations, including the difference between a first-generation and a second-generation strand,[252] TWAIL insists on 'recolonization' and on the imperialist structure of international law since the Conquest of the New World. Globalization is routinely seen as a new form of imperialism imposed by Western states. International law is accused of playing 'a crucial role in helping legitimize and sustain the unequal structures and process that manifest themselves in the growing north–south divide' and has been used by the Western dominating capitalist forces to subdue the peoples of the South.[253] It is argued that in the globalization era 'the ruling elite in the third world is coming to be an integral part of an emerging transnational ruling elite that seeks to establish the global rule of transnational capital on the pretext of pursuing "national interests"'.[254] In seeking 'to unify the world market through the instrument of international law' the emerging transnational capitalist class is producing alienation of human beings from nature (for example, global warming), from labour (for example, labour flexibility), from their 'species being' (for example, consumerism), and from each other (for example, *refoulement* of asylum seekers).[255] Moreover, this new unity is 'slowly transforming international law into [the] internal law' of a Global State

248 A Anghie, BS Chimni, K Mickelson, and O Okafor (eds), *The Third World and International Legal Order: Law, Politics and Globalization* (Leiden: Nijhoff, 2003). For a Marxist approach, see recently BS Chimni, 'Prolegomena to a Class Approach to International Law' (2010) 21 EJIL 57.

249 BS Chimni, 'Third World Approaches to International Law: A Manifesto' (2006) 8 ICLR 3, 4–7.

250 A Anghie and BS Chimni, 'Third World Approaches to International Law and Individual Responsibility in Internal Conflict' (2003) 77 Chin JIL 77, 79.

251 See A Anghie, *Imperialism, Sovereignty and the Making of International Law* (Cambridge: CUP, 2005). A critical approach to 'West-centrism' for the purposes of providing 20th-century international law and global justice with transcivilizational (in addition to international and transnational) legitimacy, without using the Marxist vocabulary, has been significantly advanced by Y Onuma, 'Eurocentrism in the History of International Law' in Y Onuma (ed), *A Normative Approach to War: Peace, War and Justice in Hugo Grotius* (Oxford: Clarendon Press, 1993) 371–86; Y Onuma, 'When Was the Law of International Society Born? An Inquiry of the History of International Law from an Intercivilizational Perspective' (2000) 2 JHIL 1–66; Y Onuma, *A Transcivilizational Perspective on International Law: Questioning Prelevant Cognitive Frameworks in the Emerging Multi-polar and Multi-civilizational World of the Twenty-first Century* (Leiden: Nijhoff, 2010) 179–86. While several of Onuma's insights can be readily shared (such as the persisting prevalence of Western doctrine and media in the handling of international law, ibid 156–60, 177–9), others seem to go a bit too far as a matter of existing law, such as his (admittedly central in the theory) criticism of customary international law (ibid 134–9, 206–44).

252 Anghie and Chimni (n 250 above) 79–87.

253 Chimni (n 249 above) 3.

254 ibid 6, 7, 15, 17, 18, 24, 26.

255 BS Chimni, 'The Past, Present and Future of International Law: A Critical Third World Approach', 8 Mel JIL (2007) 499, 504–8.

reflecting 'an imperialist global law' or an 'international law of empire'.[256] Human rights discourses are seen with suspicion since their omnipresence 'has coincided with increasing pressure on third world States to implement neo-liberal policies'. The right to private property is systematically privileged to social and economic rights, although the globalization of human rights is recognized as per se offering 'an important basis for advancing the cause of the poor and the marginal in third world countries'.[257] The vocabulary of human rights 'has been co-opted and deployed by global capital to promote a conception of "good life" that furthers its interests'.[258] TWAIL is generally critical of statehood itself and, consequently, not only of human rights, but also of self-determination (aimed at ensuring statehood to peoples who have always lived otherwise) and development (aimed at conditioning politically how statehood should be).

The alienation of international law has produced an alienation of the discipline itself, with the dominant majority of international lawyers formalistically 'not speaking on behalf of subaltern peoples'. It is assumed that there is, in fact, an 'ideological domination of Northern academic institutions' and, in particular, 'Third World students of international law tend to take their cue from books and journals published in the North' with the risk of 'unquestioningly reproduc[ing] scholarship that is suspect'.[259] Critical international lawyers have to revisit the history of international law so as to prevent 'what is now called global history, which promotes and projects the ongoing capitalist globalisation process into the future' and 'global capitalism's worst effect'; to engage with issues of global justice beyond the anachronistic model of 'global order in a sovereign state system' and for an 'egalitarian Global Law of Peoples'; to preserve alternative notions of 'good life' according to a 'diversity of diversity' model, as opposed to 'diversity of unity'; and to mobilize the resources of international law against violence to humans or nature as 'the only way of creating a just world under law'.

TWAIL's charge that international law is the expression of the interests of the stronger is one that mutatis mutandis may be addressed to any legal system. It is the argument of this book that any kind of law reflects the interests of the stronger. Those who critique law because it is the expression of the stronger simply state the obvious, or use the critique simply to change the law in their favour. But to the extent that TWAIL attacks current international law as 'unjust', its claim means something different. The charge is that international law favours the stronger of the moment, not the weaker, and assumes that this is unjust and worth struggling against. Criticisms that TWAIL is too rudimentary or wide of the mark are usually conducted by Western theorists according to Western legal categories. It is true that Western thought has informed international law as we know it and *this* is, for good or ill, international law. But it is also true, if law is a social construct as here maintained, that international law and its intellectual structures may be changed towards more justice. Clearly, when struggling for a new law there is little or no interest in detailing existing law, this being the law to be swept away. There can also be an interest in showing that the future law for which to struggle is already in place.[260] When doing this with non-existent law, however undesirable existing law may be, TWAIL smuggles for legal what is a political claim. As a political

[256] ibid 509–10; BS Chimni, 'International Institutions Today: An Imperial Global State in the Making' (2004) 15 EJIL 1.

[257] ibid 11, 17.

[258] Chimni (n 255 above) 508.

[259] Chimni (n 249 above) 3–4, 15.

[260] In this sense the trenchant criticism made by C Tomuschat, 'World Order Models: A Disputation with B.S. Chimni and Yasuaki Onuma' (2006) ICLR 71, 71–6, sounds somewhat out of tune with the TWAIL's charges.

claim, one can sympathize with TWAIL; as a legal analysis, it is simply misconceived. TWAIL demythologizes international law as imperialistic and Western-biased by appealing to its remythologization in favour of third world peoples. It invites people to join the fight for this new vision of international law.

C. Communication

Together with thought, language, and doctrine, communication plays a key role in socially constructing (by both demythologizing and remythologizing) international law. If international law is poorly covered in the media, the belief in it remains weak and scepticism spreads. Once it is assumed that law is what is socially believed to be law, then the role of the media may be seen as even more crucial than the role of doctrine. The media shape public opinion and extensively contribute to the construction of social reality, including the reality of law. The internet and new media technologies, in particular, are key to the growth of transnational civil society. As was suggested as early as at the beginning of the twentieth century, the media encourage interconnection in international society and create new opportunities for the growth of international law.[261] Despite today's centrality of communication, however, the mediatization of international law is still underresearched.[262] Among the many channels through which international law is socially constructed, attention is given here only to a few, ie mass media, national schools of thought, specialized journals and blogs, and official strategies of 'visibility'. This section argues that: (a) the coverage of international law by the mass media is rather feeble and selective; (b) national schools compete with one another to construct a picture of international law ultimately in line with the structures of their respective law; (c) specialized journals and blogs affect what counts as international law only among the relatively closed circle of professionals; and (d) strategies for visibility are increasingly pursued by all actors concerned with international law to call attention to and exert pressure for their causes.[263]

(1) Media coverage

Various approaches are possible to the relationship between the coverage of international law by the mass media.[264] One is to check if and how newspapers and news magazines have covered events involving international law.[265] Another is to see how

[261] See E Root, 'The Need of Popular Understanding of International Law' (1907) 1 AJIL 1, 1; AP Higgins, *The Binding Force of International Law* (Cambridge: CUP, 1910) 41.

[262] See C Harland, 'The Impact of the Media on International Law and Relations' (1995) 89 ASIL Proc 119–27; L Reed, 'The Media's Portrayal of International Law' (2001) 95 ASIL Proc 216, noting that 'The American media has given short shrift to international law, even front-page news raises international legal issues' and asking 'What are the structural and other causes of this lack of media attention?'; D Joyce, 'Human Rights and the Mediatization of International Law' (2010) 23 LJIL 507, 507, taking note that the media are increasingly translating international law 'for global audiences, and this is changing the character of the discipline' (at 516).

[263] The relationship between the media and international law can be viewed either from the perspective of the impact of international law on the media, or, in reverse, from the perspective of the impact of the media on international law. While the first aspect will be treated in Ch 7 below, section A (5)(b), the second is discussed in this section.

[264] See generally L Gies, *Law and the Media: The Future of an Uneasy Relationship* (Abingdon: Routledge-Cavendish, 2008).

[265] JK Gamble and NL Dirling, 'Mass Media Coverage of International Law: (Benign) Neglect?, Distortion?' (2006) 18 Flo JIL 211, focusing on 13 major international law-related events from the

selectively the media cover international law.[266] Still another is to analyse how the media influence the international legal process.[267] A further approach is to measure if and how the media affect governments in complying with international law. Yet another is to analyse what idea of international law the media convey to audiences, an idea that may possibly put some pressure on governments.

A diffused perception is that the media either plainly omit international law or treat it inadequately. The media often emphasize that a certain action, especially when taken by a foreign country against their home country or its allies, is contrary to international law without giving details of what international law is and what can realistically be expected from it. Governments directly or indirectly tend to use the media to have them say that their actions are 'legal' and promote their foreign policy decisions.[268] Even when an indisputably *legal* concept specifically defined by international law is concerned, the issue is, more often than not, about its political use. For example, in reviewing the public debate on possible intervention by the United States to halt the mass killings occurring in Darfur in 2004, Scott Strauss has talked about the 'magic' use of the word genocide and shown that 'much of the public debate in the United States and elsewhere . . . focused not on how to stop the crisis, but on whether or not it should be called a "genocide" under the terms of the Genocide Convention' since 'Such a designation, it was long thought, would inevitably trigger an international response'.[269] He stressed that 'The term grabs attention', although in fact no action followed,[270] and in the end it 'diverts attention from the most difficult questions', such as the substantial deployment of troops that Darfur requires and, in particular, the complicated but enduring problems that have given rise to the violence in the first place.[271] A double standard in the use of terms describing atrocities is very frequent, typically 'genocide' being used when atrocities are committed by an enemy and 'repression' when similar actions are taken by allies.[272] The media generally find this attitude to be in accordance with their pressing need to sell the news, since national audiences as a whole inevitably prefer to be told that the government or its allies are doing the right thing to protect them. Only rarely are front pages and columnists critical of the official position of national governments. Lengthy legal analyses are systematically avoided, while faster consumable information is subject to political manipulation. Debating political conjectures generally proves far more appealing to audiences than carefully scrutinizing facts. The media generally focus on consumer-driven topics capable of emotionally gripping audiences by affecting their daily lives, such as fear, pride, love stories, and

Korean War (1950) to Camp X-Ray/Guantanamo Bay (2002) assessed based on coverage provided in five news magazines in the first two weeks of news.

[266] H Friel and R Falk, *The Record of the Paper: How the New York Times Misreports US Foreign Policy* (London and New York: Verso, 2004), critiquing the *New York Times'* systematic refusal to consider international law arguments against the legality of the 2003 Iraq War.

[267] M Hakimi, 'The Media as Participants in the International Legal Process' (2006) 16 Duke JCIL 1.

[268] See P Robinson, 'The CNN Effect: Can the News Media Drive Foreign Policy?' (1999) 25 RIS 301; E Gilboa, 'The CNN Effect: The Search for a Communication Theory of International Relations' (2005) 22 *Political Communication* 27; J Der Derian, *Virtuous War: Mapping the Military–Industrial–Media–Entertainment Network* (New York and London: Routledge, 2nd edn, 2009).

[269] S Strauss, 'Darfur and the Genocide Debate' (2005) 84 *Foreign Affairs* 123, 123.

[270] ibid 131.

[271] ibid 133.

[272] ES Herman and N Chomsky, *Manufacturing Consent: The Political Economy of the Mass Media* (New York, Pantheon Books, 2002) xix–xxiv.

celebrities. Complexity and possible answers arguing that no ready-made solutions exist to a given front-page issue are unfit for the market.

The adage 'good news is no news' inevitably applies also to international law.[273] TV journals cannot simply report all the infinite 'normal' occurrences that happen in everyday life to everyone. People are induced to believe that the world is fraught with disputes and conflict, enemies and dangers, although this is only a partial (if not consciously selective) truth. The countless times every day each of the countless treaties in force in the world are complied with in silence is simply no news. A single treaty breached only once by a major power, the behaviour of which at a particular time strikes a sufficient audience, typically triggers discussions about whether and to what extent international law is 'true' and 'effective' law. People get the impression that what is worth discussing about international law is whether this law is really law, since it appears to be 'always' broken whenever the stronger of the day so wish. The media do not, and actually cannot, waste time and energy on reporting how many times most rules are observed by most states, including the stronger.

Indeed, it seems that one of the key reasons why international law lacks media attention is that 'it is so rarely enforced'.[274] Media focus is greater when international institutions make enforceable decisions and especially when international crimes, in particular certain criminal proceedings[275] and violations of international humanitarian law,[276] are concerned.[277] Public opinion is most shaped by humanitarian activism, such as naming and shaming, advocacy and lobbying, presentation of evidence, victim narratives, investigation, publicity, witnessing, NGOs' news campaigning, multimedia flash sites, documentary new-media formats, and the like.[278] It has been suggested that the International Criminal Tribunal for the former Yugoslavia (ICTY) 'gets media attention... because rape, murder, genocide, and ethnic cleansing are universally despised as well as violations of international law'.[279]

Media coverage has a hardly deniable effect on what is perceived as 'customary' international law, especially in shaping what is known as *opinio juris ac necessitatis*.[280] Appropriate coverage and campaigning may encourage domestic and international courts to argue that certain 'soft law' norms are 'hard' rules that reflect customary international law. Also *usus*, the other element of custom, may depend on the media. Well-known cases weigh more than others and unknown practice is, of course, irrelevant. To contend that the identification of customary international law is virtually impossible because we do not know many cases and inevitably overemphasize the few we know is hardly tenable.[281] Law is the resultant of what is known and meaningful to

[273] cf Henkin (n 131 above) 46–7.

[274] cf Reed (n 262 above), Summary of Remarks by Stuart Taylor, at 216.

[275] See eg M Steinitz, '"The *Milošević* Trial—Live!": An Iconical Analysis of International Law's Claim of Legitimate Authority' (2005) 2 JICJ 103; DL Altheide, 'The Mass Media, Crime and Terrorism'(2006) 4 JICJ 982.

[276] RW Gutman, 'Spotlight on Violations of International Humanitarian Law: The Role of the Media' (1998) 80 IRRC 619.

[277] See D Kennedy, *The Dark Sides of Virtue: Reassessing International Humanitarianism* (Princeton and Oxford: Princeton University Press, 2004) 22–3, 276–7, 280, 295, 311.

[278] D Rieff, *A Bed for the Night: Humanitarianism in Crisis* (New York: Simon & Schuster, 2002); Z Pearson, 'NGOs and International Law: New Mechanisms for Governance?' (2004) 23 Aus YBIL 73, 97–8.

[279] Reed (n 262 above) Summary of Remarks by Stuart Taylor, at 217.

[280] See Ch 6 below, section B (1)(a).

[281] A Carty, 'Distance and Contemporaneity in Exploring State Practice: The British Archives in Relation to the 1957 Oman and Muscat Incident' in M Craven, M Fitzmaurice, and M Vogiatzi (eds), *Time, History and International Law* (Leiden: Nijhoff, 2007) 231–46, arguing that it is impossible

the people concerned. It needs to be workable, not necessarily true, coherent, or complete in the abstract. Only the cases known and believed to be 'relevant' are legally relevant, and rightly so. What is unknown remains outside of the awareness and expectations of those addressed by the law.

It is perhaps no exaggeration to state that the 'reality' of international law, on which so much ink has been spilt as a 'theoretical' question,[282] depends very much on whether and to what extent international law is sold on the market. It is the absence of international law in the media and in the awareness of people in their daily life, rather than abstract reasons exchanged among specialists in their books and journals, that affects its reality and relevance. There can be little hope for international law to be 'true' law if most people do not believe this to be the case, and the media are today the key tools that make people form their beliefs.

(2) Schools of thought

It is striking to note how international law is constructed by scholars as a function of how national law is structured.[283] In a sense this is inevitable because jurists' training in the university system is for the most part concerned with domestic law. This dependence mirrors the legal and institutional history of each particular country, a preferred branch of law (such as constitutional law or civil law), and generally the domestic law of a few Western states. The overall picture is that the struggle for international law as global law is also a struggle for this or that vision of international law as constructed on the basis of the national law of very few countries and legal traditions.

Another key domestic factor to the construction of international law is connected with the scope of the foreign policy of any particular country. International law is differently viewed, for good or ill, in countries which are more involved in global politics, such as the United States, compared to those which play a minor role. While in the former security is generally central, in the latter a 'legalist' and 'humanitarian' view of international law—as a law to be applied by the courts in a way similar to domestic law—may appear more correct. No less important is the need of governments for international law scholars who defend their decisions in legal terms and provide specialized assistance. Although scholars may well preserve their independence and express criticism towards their governments, as Gerald Fitzmaurice did in the 1956 Suez crisis,[284] on occasions this may not be appropriate to their position within the government. On balance, cases of resignation are rare and it is fair to state that most lawyers tend to align with their government's view and to make a case for its action.[285] The 'use' of 'embedded' international lawyers by governments, even when a given

without comprehensive access to the governmental policy-making process 'to determine exactly how international law is being interpreted, applied, followed or ignored'. For a critical comment, see C Focarelli, book review (2009) 11 JHIL 357.

[282] See Ch 2 above, section A (5).

[283] See D Kennedy, 'The Disciplines of International Law and Policy' (1999) 12 LJIL 9, 17–18, (critically) noting that usually 'when European international lawyers defend a methodological formalism, a focus on the state, or a fetish for courts, they can think of themselves as protecting European cultural patrimony against the cowboys', ie the 'United Statesean political project to jettison the welfare state in the name of un unrestrained market' (ibid 34).

[284] cf G Marston, 'Armed Intervention in the 1956 Suez Canal Crisis: The Legal Advice Tendered to the British Government' (1988) 37 ICLQ 773.

[285] One honourable exception, for example, is the resignation of Elizabeth Wilmshurst, the Deputy Legal Adviser at the UK Foreign and Commonwealth Office, on 20 March 2003 in relation to the Iraq War in 2003. cf <http://news.bbc.co.uk/2/hi/uk_news/politics/4377605.stm>.

decision is hardly defendable in legal terms, inevitably causes a trend in doctrine in favour of certain (nationalistic) positions rather than others.

National variations overlap with regional, continental, transcontinental, and even local ones. While on occasion 'American' and 'European' law are considered similar as both belonging to the Western legal tradition, at other times they are strongly contrasted.[286] On one account, for example, the US legal tradition has been depicted as 'less formalist in method, more interdisciplinary, less court focused, less state focused, less philosophical, and more pragmatic', more based on norm application and enforcement than on norm generation, more rule-sceptics and policy wonks, than its European counterpart.[287] Other sufficiently unitary strands may have a transcontinental scope, such as TWAIL.[288] At the other extreme of the spectrum there are sub-national, local variations associated with this or that university or research centre within the same country.

What may appear paradoxical is the countless variations in a law that is deemed to be 'common' to all peoples. Fragmentation and conflict resurfaces even in the very meaning of a 'law common to all' among specialists belonging to the same legal tradition. Doubtless, a variety of views is frequent in all human affairs and does not preclude international law from forming a common set of rules. However, if international law is socially constructed, this social construction is the combination and the result of a variety of very different perceptions, each of which have a different weight in the end result. Inevitably, some are 'more equal than others' and inevitably all tend to find themselves constantly engaging in a struggle for prevalence over what international law is to be seen as 'the' international law in force worldwide.

(3) Journals and blogging

What is known about international law is daily constructed by specialized journals and, today ever more, by blogging on the internet.[289] The number of journals devoted to international law throughout the world is impressive and on the rise. Journals are windows enabling scholars to make themselves known and be admitted to the pre-existing circle of specialists. Articles dealing with international law are produced on a massive scale as a result, inter alia, of the trend in university systems to request professors and lecturers to meet 'performance' standards, not dissimilarly from an assembly plant, ie as many published scientific works as possible, thereby discouraging time-consuming reflection aimed at higher quality and independence (but propelling the market). Journals also serve as windows for those who provide financial resources with a view to entering and influencing the market of ideas, the public debate, events, and raising further funds. Journals are formally or informally ranked, based on a number of criteria which inevitably tend to standardize outcomes, and have a varying

[286] See, in this vein, RH Pildes, 'Conflicts Between American and European Views of Law: The Dark Side of Legalism' (2003–04) 44 Virg JIL 145–67, contrasting European legalism with American realism in relation to the post-9/11 events. See in addition E Jouannet, 'French and American Perspectives on International Law: Legal Cultures and International Law' (2006) 58 Maine Law Review 291; G Verdirame, '"The Divided West": International Lawyers in Europe and America' (2007) 18 EJIL 553.

[287] See Kennedy (n 283 above) 19, 25–6, especially note 21, and 29.

[288] BS Chimni, 'Is there an Asian Approach to International Law?' (Tokyo: ASIL Conference, 2009), at <http://asiansil.web.fc2.com/PlenarySessionI/chmni.pdf>.

[289] cf eg <http://www.ejiltalk.org> and <http://www.echrblog.blogspot.com>. In defence of legal blogging, see J D'Aspremont, 'In Defense of the Hazardous Tool of Legal Blogging' (2011), at <http://www.ejiltalk.org/in-defense-of-the-hazardous-tool-of-legal-blogging>.

impact on the scientific ranking of their authors, their careers within the universities where they work, and the ranking of their universities themselves.

Editorial policies depend on the persons who form the board of editors and on the editor-in-chief of the moment. It is in the interest of any journal to have the most prestigious figures on its board of editors so as to raise its reputation and income. It is, at the same time, in the interest of scholars to enter the boards of editors of the most respected journals. As a result, the boards of editors of the most influential journals tend to be made up of a limited circle of renowned scholars who cannot avoid forming an elite with great powers in the scholarly world. The selection of articles for publication is made by anonymous peer-reviewing and other (less predictable) editorial policies. The citation-based 'impact factor' (IF) in which journals take great pride inevitably channels the selection of articles towards those which offer more chances of being cited in the short-term, the only ones whose 'impact' is detectable and measurable within a market-meaningful span of time, with no evidence (and even no need for evidence) that they will prove the best in the long term. Citations should serve purposes other than casting or denying a vote for this or that colleague, or for oneself, or for this or that journal, but the trend is irresistibly towards making a citation market blossom. Arthur Schopenhauer would have found it very difficult, had the scientific world of his days been imbued with the market-impact tests prevailing today, to publish *Die Welt als Wille und Vorstellung*, given its near-zero immediate impact. Peer-reviewers, for their part, include this activity in their curriculum vitae as an achievement. The selection of peer-reviewers is based on expertise and on several other factors, including personal sympathy and scientific affinities. Peer-reviewing is very difficult because, beyond a certain threshold, no one really knows why a certain piece of research is better than another, apart from personal taste, system of values, and scientific inclinations. Experience shows countless examples of articles or books which have become landmarks by pure chance and there is no certainty that another reviewer, as learned as the one who accepted the piece and in perfectly good faith, would have refused publication. Anonymity helps the avoidance of bias, but leaves open the doubt that the reviewer may not be as qualified as supposed, and may even be less qualified than the reviewed, or simply less available than other potential reviewers to accept seemingly eccentric paths, the reviewed having no possibility of verification. Peer-reviewing is certainly invaluable between peers, but which individuals are 'peers' remains open to question. Giving policy reasons publicly to justify 'objectivity' in the selection of articles sounds a hopeless endeavour and one can ask why overt subjectivity, ie the statement of the mission and policy of the journal in the pursuit of a selected line of research, should not in the end prove sharper and more transparent.[290] Moreover, scholars who prefer to work in relative solitude, as in-depth intellectual work generally demands, tend to remain distant from boards of editors, committees of advisers, and peer reviewers in any journal. The peer-reviewing system also tends to standardize research outcomes, despite policies open to pluralism, which can itself become highly standardized, and to generate enormous and fast-passing quantities of vogue scholarship. Standardization, under cover of pluralism and creativity, in turn is contingent on market demand.

Although many journals are still published in the 'local' language, the language increasingly dominant is English.[291] Authors are thus encouraged to write in English to reach out to a larger audience and make themselves known. National journals are still

[290] For a recent *rationem reddere* approach, see J Weiler, 'Demystifying the EJIL Selection and Editorial Process: How Does One Get Published in EJIL?' (2011) 22 EJIL 1.

[291] See section A (3) above.

on the market, but endeavour to survive by going global through the use of English. Journals are sold to universities, research centres, single researchers, and law firms around the world. Subscriptions to both paper and online versions are typical means to make profit. The turnover is high. English-written journals are dominant on the market and can rely on millions of potential readers and purchasers, while journals published in other languages may count only on local markets and, as such, are destined to perish in a globalized economy.[292] Overall, the impact of this mass of scientific production on people in general in their daily lives throughout the world is marginal and one occasionally gets the impression that the whole machine works within the circle of the specialists to coordinate their own lives and careers.[293]

(4) Visibility strategies

International law is also the subject of constant communication by governments, international organizations, and international courts. States which can afford it publish their practice in order to have the internationally relevant conduct of their organs publicly known to third parties for scientific purposes, but also, by providing material sources in which practice is found, to contribute to a customary international law that is more in keeping with their behaviour and preferences.[294] Press corps are found in all government offices. International courts may take due account of the possible media effect of their decisions. This is indeed part of their work, to some degree, as social constructors of international law within the international community.

Little known and worth discussing in some greater detail is the media activity of the United Nations (as well as all other international organizations (IOs)) to gain more currency and credit. In fact, the extent to which the United Nations can pursue international law depends on the way the organization is capable of becoming 'visible' through media coverage.[295] The organization evidently has a strong interest in controlling how it is portrayed worldwide and in reaching out to both people and (print, broadcasting, online) journalists, in addition to the governments of member states. Nothing can help it to carry out its responsibilities and to reinforce the idea of a rule of law in world affairs more than a widespread sense of legitimacy 'from below', and nothing can possibly work better to this end than an effective communication strategy. UN News and information are made available to the public and to the press through a large number of institutions and sources.[296]

However, despite the efforts made by the United Nations, it is editors, publishers, and TV producers who work as 'gatekeepers' and who decide what to tell the public. The world's media organizations, typically private global conglomerates, have little

[292] For a strongly critical appraisal of the dominance of Western academic institutions and journals, within a Marxist version of TWAIL, cf n 259 above and accompanying text.

[293] For the somewhat idealized role of the 'invisible college' of international law scholars, see Ch 6 below, section B (4)(d). For their modest impact, see ibid n 414.

[294] L Ferrari Bravo, 'Méthodes de recherche de la coutume internationale dans la pratique des états' (1985-III) 192 RdC 233.

[295] The information offered in this section is essentially drawn from B Crossette, 'Media' in TG Weiss and S Daws (eds), *The Oxford Handbook on the United Nations* (Oxford: OUP, 2007) 275–84.

[296] The UN 'image' is in charge of the UN Department of Public Information (DPI). The Secretary-General's spokesman's office is responsible for the Secretary-General. A communications strategy group headed by a Director of Communications also works in the field. Sources of information include the main UN website (at <http://www.un.org>), the UN News Centre website (at <http://www.un.org/News>), the Companion Multimedia Center, the UN Radio (at <http://www.un.org/radio>), and UN TV (at <http://www.un.org.av/tv>).

interest in international institutions. They want reporters to focus on 'human interest' or celebrity-focused stories. Some important issues may thus prove 'unsexy' and remain uncovered, whereas others may be covered only as far as they are attention-grabbing as either entertainment or human drama. Media attention also varies with the place of consumption. The media pick and choose UN stories as a function of perceived key national problems and national foreign policy debates. Such issues as poverty alleviation, development aid, reproductive health, gender empowerment, the Millennium Development Goals (MDGs), and regional problems (like AIDS in Uganda, desertification in the Sahel, child soldiers in the Democratic Republic of Congo) get much more attention in developing countries' newspapers and news magazines than in North America and Europe. In contrast, the Western media are much more interested in security and on what the Security Council does. Most information in developing countries still depends on mainstream Western news agencies. Thus the UN efforts to supply worldwide and comprehensive information appear to be very much frustrated.[297]

A major difficulty is that the competition for world media attention is fierce and the UN is poorly equipped to play to the forefront. UN Secretary-General Kofi Annan reportedly stated in 2005 that 'There is a sort of auto-sanction on ourselves' in that the UN cannot reveal to the press a lot of confidential information; besides, competitors 'have resources that we don't have, and they are relentless, and they are organized'.[298] One may add that in an information market dominated by those who unrelentingly 'make news' and 'set agendas' the United Nations may even find the task to be incompatible with its mission.[299] The Organization is not there to construct its 'brand', but to do things. The dilemma is that the UN either sells its 'brand' and then perhaps does things, or avoids doing so and then remains with no work at all.

A similar activity is carried out by the UN when drafting or commissioning to experts the preparation of reports on key issues.[300] The purpose of these reports is to attract the attention of world public opinion and, inter alia, to propose or affirm basic principles of international law. Experience shows, however, that this marketing strategy—despite the torrents of ink spilt by legal scholarship dissecting every possible word of such reports—more often than not fails because states, and their peoples, refrain from endorsing the principles written on paper.

Conclusion

While Part I discussed law in general as a social construct, Part II is specifically designed to apply such an approach to international law. This chapter has explored the way international law is socially constructed through epistemology, doctrine, and communication. It argued that (a) international law is invariably thought of according to Western analytical categories and words, whatever its contents, beginning with the very word 'law'; (b) doctrine constantly mythologizes, demythologizes, and remythologizes

297 IA Lehmann, *Peacekeeping and Public Information: Caught in the Crossfire* (London: Frank Cass, 1999).

298 cf F Eckhard (ed), *Speaking for the Secretary-General—A History of the UN Spokesman's Office* (New York: United Nations, 2005), quoted by Crossette (n 295 above) at 280.

299 The suggestion that the United Nations should make news and set agendas, rather than only reacting, is made by Crossette (n 295 above) 284.

300 Among the most famous reports, see Ch 5 below, nn 7, 9, and 305; Ch 6 below, nn 18 and 247; Ch 7 below, nn 78 and 419; and Ch 8 below, n 102.

international law in various, often opposing, directions, here again through Western standards of theoretical analysis and within a relatively closed circle of professionals; and (c) the construction of international law by the media, today crucial, is far from being effective. This suggests that international law should be remythologized by investigating all the legal traditions known in comparative legal analysis, rather than on (Western) jurisprudential grounds, and its reality in the sphere of communication. However, as far as *existing* international law is concerned, legal analysis should be confined to the criteria currently prevailing, whatever their vices.

5

Players

If international law is socially constructed, *who* is 'directly' engaged in its construction? This chapter addresses the issue of identifying international actors as the 'players' involved in the process of constructing international law and the role they play in global governance. Constructing international law includes the construction of the players themselves as those who believe in international law as 'their' law and who expect compliance therewith from all others. The chapter argues that states remain key to global governance—although their global system is the historical product of injustice and is increasingly unable to manage global concerns—by exercising jurisdictional power in a partitioned and relatively coordinated way within a global system in which non-state actors shape states' behaviour. The chapter first explores the meaning of global governance, public and private authority, and international community. States and a variety of non-state players are then discussed. Finally, the concept of international legal personality is explored and disaggregated in different meanings and legal consequences, concluding that it is often used as a tool for manipulation to favour one or another 'deserving' player.

A. Global Governance

In the 1927 *Lotus* Judgment the PCIJ famously stated that: 'International law governs relations between independent States. The rules of law binding upon states therefore emanate from their own free will... Restrictions upon the independence of States cannot therefore be presumed'.[1] This historic dictum has been generally understood as implying that (a) states are the makers ('emanate') and subjects ('binding') of international law based on their sovereignty and independence; (b) international law norms emanate from the 'free will' of states; and (c) states retain freedom of action unless there is a positive law restriction. Non-state actors and non-consensual rules are excluded, while state conduct is automatically permitted if a prohibitive rule does not exist or cannot be proved in judicial proceedings.[2] This chapter is concerned with the first of such questions, leaving the other two for discussion in the next chapter.

The PCIJ's dictum appears to be at odds with current realities. Many other entities participate today, in various forms, in international relations and decision-making. This complex of (both formal and informal) interactions, when referring to the entities which 'govern' the world, is routinely called 'global governance'. The issue is 'who governs whom' at global level. It is generally assumed that the world is governed today by both state and non-state actors through norms based not only on state consent but also independent of state consent in pursuit of basic common values of humankind. The way in which these actors 'govern' the world is not described as a 'government', in

[1] PCIJ, *The Case of the SS Lotus (France v Turkey)* Judgment of 7 September 1927, PCIJ Series A No 10, at 18.

[2] For a comment, see eg H Handeyside, 'The Lotus Principle in ICJ Jurisprudence: Was the Ship Ever Afloat?' (2007–08) 29 Mich JIL 71.

the same sense as in the state context, since a world government manifestly does not exist, and, for most scholars, cannot or should not exist.[3] This chapter discusses the concepts of global governance, public and private authority, and international community, and argues that global governance is best viewed as state governance constantly sustained by global mindfulness as constructed by non-state actors.

(1) Defining 'global governance'

Since the end of the Cold War the term 'global governance', together with the idea of a 'New World Order',[4] has gained great currency as a description of globalization.[5] In 1992 James N Rosenau suggested that 'governance is not synonymous with government', although both 'refer to purposive behaviour, to goal-oriented activities, to systems of rule', and that it was 'possible to conceive of governance without government'.[6] The Commission on Global Governance, in the 1995 *Our Global Neighborhood* report, defined global governance as 'the sum of many ways individuals and institutions, public and private, manage their common affairs'.[7] Other definitions of global governance were offered that same year by an assortment of scholars and practitioners in the newly founded journal *Global Governance*.[8] UNDP's *Human Development Report 1999* reiterated that 'Governance does not mean mere government', but rather 'the framework of rules, institutions and established practices that set limits and give incentives for the behaviour of individuals, organizations and firms'.[9] In attempting to sharpen this definition it was recently argued that while in a national

[3] For the view in favour of a world government, see A Wendt, 'Why a World State Is Inevitable' (2003) 9 EJIR 491; DH Deudney, *Bounding Power: Republican Security Theory from the Polis to the Global Village* (Princeton: Princeton University Press, 2006). For a comprehensive discussion of the topic, see C Lu, 'World Government', Stan EP, at <http://plato.stanford.edu/entries/world-government>; C Craig, 'The Resurgent Idea of World Government' (2008) 22 EIA 133.

[4] A decisive step towards a new world order was the landmark speech given by Mikhail Gorbachev to the UN General Assembly on 7 December 1988, at <http://www.writespirit.net/inspirational_talks/mikhail_gorbachev_talks/united_nations_address>. The term 'New World Order' was soon taken up by US President George Bush Sr, on 11 September 1990, in a speech to the Congress relating to the military response to Iraq's invasion of Kuwait, at <http://www.cryan.com/war/speech>.

[5] For the measurement of globalization according to its economic (ie long-distance flows of goods, capital and services, as well as information and perceptions that accompany market exchanges), social (ie spread of ideas, information, and images and people), and political dimension (ie diffusion of government policies), see the KOF Globalization Index, at <http://globalization.kof.ethz.ch>; A Dreher, N Gaston, and P Martens, *Measuring Globalisation: Gauging its Consequences* (New York: Springer, 2008).

[6] JN Rosenau, 'Governance, Order, and Change in World Politics' in JN Rosenau and E-O Czempiel (eds), *Governance Without Government: Order and Change in World Politics* (Cambridge: CUP, 1992) 1, 4–5, pointing out that governance 'embraces governmental institutions, but it also subsumes informal, non-governmental mechanisms' and 'is always effective' as 'a system of rule that works only if it is accepted by the majority (or, at least, by the most powerful of those it affects), whereas governments [defined in turn as 'activities backed by formal authority'] can function even in the face of widespread opposition to their policies'. In a later definition, Rosenau referred global governance to 'mechanisms for steering social systems toward their goals': cf JN Rosenau, 'Toward an Ontology for Global Governance' in M Hawson and T Sinclair (eds), *Approaches to Global Governance Theory* (Albany: State University of New York Press, 1999) 287, 296.

[7] Commission On Global Governance, *Our Global Neighborhood* (Oxford: OUP, 1995), at <http://www.sovereignty.net/p/gov/ogn-front.html>, pointing out that it was 'not proposing movement towards world government'.

[8] See, in particular, L Finkelstein, 'What is Global Governance?' (1995) 1 *Global Governance* 367.

[9] United Nations Development Programme (UNDP), *Human Development Report 1999* (Oxford and New York: OUP, 1999) 8.

context 'governance is government plus additional nongovernmental mechanisms that contribute to order and predictability in problem-solving', at global scale governance is 'the sum of nongovernmental mechanisms but minus an input from a central authority because there is none', and hence a *faute de mieux*, a 'surrogate for transnational authority' rather than a global government.[10]

Several theories of global governance have been developed in the past two decades, depending on the political actors placed at its core, namely, the United States as the sole hegemonic superpower after the end of the Cold War,[11] multinational enterprises operating in a borderless global market,[12] non-governmental organizations (NGOs) pursuing 'public goods' and protesters fighting against multinational enterprises,[13] great powers,[14] the United Nations in pursuit of a Kant-inspired cosmopolitan project,[15] a global 'Empire' substituting for the sovereignty of nation states,[16] peoples and social movements fighting against Western neo-imperialism,[17] transgovernmental networks of internal agencies and bodies of different states or international organizations (IOs) and NGOs,[18] international or transnational administrative regulators active in virtually every issue area of private and public life,[19] private social systems capable of generating their own legal norms,[20] and humanity.[21] It is indeed a patchwork of actors, norms, and theories that justifiably conveys a sense of 'mystery'.[22]

Global governance is linked to a world order without a world government and with a significant, both formal and informal, contribution being made by non-state actors in addition to (or even in substitution for) states and state-centric institutions.[23] By non-state actors is meant supra-, sub-, non-, and counter-state actors. Global governance is often depicted as a sort of apolitical, problem-solving, somewhat technocratic 'invisible hand' governing a unified, post-Cold War world in need of some common management through handling power and law at a diffused level by a multitude of both public or private entities in competition with one another to capture loyalty, get media visibility, and confer identity on as many people as possible. Its ultimate goal—if a

[10] TG Weiss and S Daws (eds), *The Oxford Handbook on the United Nations* (Oxford: OUP, 2007) 10.

[11] See M Byers and G Nolte (eds), *United States Hegemony and the Foundations of International Law* (Cambridge: CUP, 2003).

[12] See eg JE Stiglitz, *Freefall: Free Markets and the Sinking of the Global Economy* (New York: Norton, 2010).

[13] See DC Korten, *When Corporations Rule the World* (Sterling and San Francisco: Kumarian Press and Berrett-Koeler Publisher, 2nd edn, 2001).

[14] See DW Drezner, *All Politics is Global. Explaining International Regulatory Regimes* (Princeton and Oxford: Princeton University Press, 2007).

[15] See eg D Monazahian, *Vergleich der UNO-Charta mit Immanuel Kant's "Zum ewigen Frieden" und John Rawls "Das Recht der Völker"* (Hamburg: Diplomica-Verlag, 2008).

[16] M Hardt and A Negri, *Empire* (Cambridge, Mass: Harvard University Press, 2002).

[17] See Ch 4 above, section B (9).

[18] A-M Slaughter, *A New World Order* (Princeton and Oxford: Princeton University Press, 2004).

[19] See Ch 4 above, section B (8).

[20] G Teuber (ed), *Autopoietic Law: A New Approach To Law And Society* (Berlin: de Gruyter, 1988).

[21] See recently AA Cançado Trindade, *International Law for Humankind: Towards a New Jus Gentium* (Leiden and Boston: Nijhoff, 2010).

[22] D Kennedy, 'The Mystery of Global Governance' in JL Dunoff and JP Trachtman (eds), *Ruling the World? Constitutionalism, International Law, and Global Governance* (Cambridge, CUP, 2009) 38.

[23] Advocates of global governance are generally against a world government, as both undesirable and infeasible, although a few other scholars have taken the opposite view, such as DR Griffin, 'Objections to World Government Considered', at <http://www.dwfed.org/pp_objections_world%20govt_considered.htm>.

goal can be assigned to an order which by definition has no centralized power—is to 'overcome global problems with global solutions'.

Is this picture a reliable representation of current world affairs? Four different levels of globalization should be kept distinct: psychological, social, political, and legal. It is submitted that the process of globalization that is under way involves the psychological sphere of *individual* mindfulness of a world common to all human beings. More and more people across the world are aware of being part of a community much larger than their local communities. While necessary in the construction of the global, this individual sense of globality is different from the existence of a *social* global reality, let alone of a *political* global institutional framework and of a global *law*. The first is actually in the making, whereas the others are still far from being real.

(2) Public and private authority

There is general agreement that global governance deals with the question of 'who governs the globe' and this amounts to asking who exerts 'authority' in the globe, whether a prospective world sovereign, or the states system, or major states, or private actors acting transnationally. The notion of 'authority' is evoked today in various contexts with different meanings, often without in-depth discussion.[24] Authority may refer, inter alia, either to persons or to norms. The authority of a head of state is different from the authority of law, although the latter depends, inter alia, on the authority of law-makers.

A much-cited notion of 'authority' is that provided by Max Weber as 'the probability that a command with a given specific content will be obeyed by a group of persons'.[25] For Weber, 'legitimate' authority is an authority which is obeyed, at least in part, 'because it is in some appreciable way regarded by the [subordinate] actor as in some way obligatory or exemplary for him'.[26] The classical locus of legitimate force, thus defined, is the modern state, which is characterized by its 'monopoly of the legitimate use of physical force within a given territory'.[27] Similarly, it has been suggested that, while power is 'the ability to compel compliance, either through the use or the threat of force', authority is 'the right to command, and correlatively, the right to be obeyed'.[28] On this account, authority can only be 'public'. Private entities may of course unilaterally claim (and also be perceived by others) as authorities, under one or another definition of authority, but they do not and cannot really act as authorities, or better, as *ultimate* authorities, thereby assuming that a 'real' authority is in fact the authority of last resort in a group, not every sub-authority being followed in sub-groups.

Since the end of the Cold War a growing number of 'new' non-state, non-state-based, and non-state-legitimated actors have emerged and been given 'authoritative' functions which in the past fell within the exclusive authority of states. Former states' 'public services' have been privatized and are today offered by businesses and NGOs. International relations (IR) scholars, in particular, have been quick to investigate the

[24] See RB Friedman, 'On the Concept of Authority in Political Philosophy' in J Raz (ed), *Authority* (New York: New York University Press, 1990) 56, 73–5.

[25] M Weber, *Economy and Society: An Outline of Interpretive Sociology* (Berkeley: University of California Press, 1978) vol 1, 55.

[26] ibid 31.

[27] ibid 78. See in addition M Weber, 'Politics as a Vocation' reprinted in HH Gerth and C Wright Mills (eds), *From Max Weber: Essays in Sociology* (New York: OUP, 1958) 77, 78.

[28] RP Wolff, 'The Conflict between Authority and Autonomy', in J Raz (ed), *Authority* (New York: New York University Press, 1990) 20, 20.

emergence of 'private authority' in global governance as 'institutionalised forms or expressions of power',[29] such as 'market authority' (transnational enterprises (TNEs)), 'moral authority' (NGOs), and 'illicit authority' (mafias, Colombian drug cartels, and the like). On this view, authority differs from power because it is legitimate, and legitimacy implies that 'there is some form of normative, uncoerced consent or recognition of authority on the part of the regulated or governed'.[30] A more recent, quite loose definition of private authority refers to 'the ability to induce deference in others'.[31] While 'there must be some public way of identifying the persons whose utterances are to be taken as "authoritative"',[32] and 'the social recognition of authority should be publicly expressed',[33] states are no longer considered the sole, and often not even the principal, source of authority. This recognition may occur within or without a state. Advocates of private authority insist that authority should not be about coercion, but 'deference', which may well be uncoerced. As regards law, they hold that law generally works irrespective of sanctions and legitimacy, on the ground that support 'from below' is far more important than strict legality.

The problem with this view is that the fact that private entities may perform functions which were carried out 'authoritatively' by states in the past does not necessarily transform them into 'authorities'. They still need states (ie state laws, judgments, officials, etc) to enforce their alleged authority. The so-called 'public' functions performed today by private actors are actually mandated by states and remain under state formal oversight. States may be in actual fact weaker than in the past, but in any event non-state actors cannot do without them. Quite to the contrary, they do count on states. When private actors are spontaneously obeyed, they are indeed 'authorities', but to the extent that they need the state for the enforcement of their authority they are not *ultimate* authorities. For example, parents do exercise 'authority' over their children, but when it comes to enforcing mutual rights and duties the state, as their common ultimate authority, is needed. To say that 'Private authority is a form of "governance without government"',[34] amounts to saying that global governance is realized, inter alia, by all parents on earth in respect of the authority exercised over their children. In a sense this is true, but it is certainly neither novel, nor explicative, nor relevant as far as law is concerned. In political analyses it may be of utmost importance to identify who exerts real influence and to discover that the behaviour of children is much more dependent on the commands of their parents than those of the state. However, legally speaking, the point is what both parents and children can do when they want to challenge either how children obey or how parents command. A society without an 'ultimate' authority, but rich in a multitude of authorities placed at the same level, is either anarchical or, much more likely, silently driven by invisible and unchecked powers apparently leaving all actors free to participate in the game. The issue is thus: *cui bono*? No doubt both the public and private actors directly or indirectly involved in the private business make the most of this representation of global governance and push for its global dissemination as a process that is both inevitable

[29] RB Hall and TJ Bierstecker (eds), *The Emergence of Private Authority in Global Governance* (Cambridge: CUP, 2002) 4.

[30] ibid 4–5.

[31] DD Avant, M Finnemore, and SK Sell (eds), *Who Governs the Globe?* (Cambridge: CUP, 2010) 9.

[32] Friedman (n 24 above) 64.

[33] Hall and Bierstecker (eds) (n 29 above) 5.

[34] AC Cutler, V Haufler, and T Porter (eds), *Private Authority and International Affairs* (Albany: State University of New York Press, 1999) ix.

and beneficial to all. But whether the process is really beneficial to all, rather than to a few, as well as inevitable and irreversible, remains to be seen, as will be discussed below.

The notion that states and state officials should be checked 'from below' at global level is quite reasonable, but it does not necessarily imply that the state and its public institutions should be thrown away or be left (by a decision of the public authorities themselves) at the mercy of private 'authorities'. If the problem is that state officials behave irresponsibly, it is difficult to see why, once the idea of authority has been shifted to the private sphere and has gained more trust than public authority, one should not find that such officials favour convenient private authorities or directly operate within private businesses (but now with no legal checks at all).[35] It seems much more sensible, should the state prove defective, to either change it or replace state officials and seek to have the new ones work better for the public good, or, alternatively, seek out new political organizations, other than states, as ultimate authorities which could work better for the public good.

(3) Discerning the 'international community'

Global governance refers to both who governs (ie who exerts authority over) the globe and, by implication, who is governed. Their complex forms what is called 'international community'.[36] However, the meaning of the expression 'international community' is uncertain and requires close scrutiny. In *Imagined Communities*, Benedict Anderson defined a 'community' as 'a deep, horizontal comradeship' sharing a sense of 'fraternity', observing that in a national community 'the members of even the smallest nation will never know most of their fellow-members, meet them, or even hear of them, yet in the minds of each lives the image of their communion'.[37] Is this also the case with the global community? Anderson seems to incline towards the negative when he states that 'No nation imagines itself as coterminous with mankind'.[38] An accurate answer is undoubtedly very difficult. Several terms are used to denote international aggregation with many different meanings.

The word 'community' is no doubt used to convey a stronger sense of togetherness than 'society', according to the well-known dichotomy between *Gesellschaft* (society) and *Gemeinschaft* (community) introduced in the nineteenth century by Ferdinand Tönnies.[39] It has been noted, however, that 'Invoking the international community is a lot easier than defining it'.[40] Kenneth Boulding's image of the 'spaceship earth' may

[35] From an economic perspective against neo-liberals, see H-J Chang, *Bad Samaritans: The Guilty Secrets of Rich Nations & and the Threat to Global Prosperity* (London: Business Books, 2007) 118.

[36] See G Abi-Saab, 'Whither the International Community?' (1998) 9 EJIL 248; B Simma and AL Paulus, 'The "International Community": Facing the Challenge of Globalization' (1998) 9 EJIL 266; DR Mapel and T Nardin (eds), *International Society: Diverse Ethical Perspectives* (Princeton: Princeton University Press, 1999); AL Paulus, *Die internationale Gemeinschaft im Völkerrecht: Eine Untersuchung zur Entwicklung des Völkerrechts im Zeitalters der Globalisierung* (Munich: Beck, 2001); D Kritsiotis, 'Imagining the International Community' (2002) 13 EJIL 961; A Alkoby, 'Three Images of "Global Community": Theorizing Law and Community in a Multicultural World' (2010) 12 ICLR 35.

[37] B Anderson, *Imagined Communities: Reflections on the Origin and Spread of Nationalism* (London and New York: Verso, rev edn, 1991) 6, specifying that 'nation-ness, as well as nationalism, are cultural artefacts' (at 4) and defining a nation as 'an imagined political community—and imagined as both inherently limited and sovereign' (at 6–7).

[38] ibid 7.

[39] F Tönnies, *Gemeinschaft und Gesellschaft: Grundbegriffe der reinen Soziologie* [1887] (Darmstadt: Wissenschaftliche Buchgesellschaft, 2005), English trans *Community and Society: Gemeinschaft und Gesellschaft* (Minneapolis: Michigan State University Press, 1957).

[40] A Gowers, 'The Power of Two' (2002) 132 *Foreign Policy* 32.

be taken as a good approximation to the idea of a 'closed' globalized community resulting from the factual disappearance of any 'open frontier'.[41] On this view, the term is meant to express a conservationist ethical principle 'postulating identity of the individual with some human community or society which extends not only back into the past but forward into the future'.[42] The notion that all human beings form a social and moral unity can be traced back to Judaic monotheism and a sense of brotherhood among human beings as sons of one and the same God,[43] as revived by Christian theology in Western Europe. It survived the fall of the Roman Empire as *Respublica Christiana*[44] when the Christian *ecclesia* meant a 'mystical body' as opposed to a mere aggregate of persons and states.[45] Traces are also found in the Stoic idea of *Cosmopolis*,[46] especially in Cicero,[47] and in the subsequent developments by the 'founders' of international law, including Francisco de Vitoria, Francisco Suárez, Hugo Grotius, Samuel Pufendorf, up to Christian Wolff's *Civitas Maxima*,[48] as well as in the secularized concept of *fraternité* in vogue during the French revolution.[49] The idea of a unity of all human beings is not of course exclusive to Western civilization, but it is the Western notion of international community that has historically informed international law as we know it.

The problem with all visions of world community lies in its organic, mystical, and all-encompassing (hence often imperial) nature and ensuing potential for justifying oppression against dissenters to secure the unity of the 'social body'. This is presumably one of the reasons why the international community is so frequently evoked nowadays. A specific problem with the global community is that a community is defined by what it is not, and if none is left outside of it, its concept dissolves.[50] However, while it seems that there can be no 'we' without a 'they', the 'they' no doubt includes also non-human threats, such as pandemics.[51]

(a) Levels of international aggregation

Although the term 'international community' is highly popular, its precise meaning and distinction from other similar expressions is very uncertain. In *The Anarchical Society*, Hedley Bull famously distinguished different degrees of international aggregation, calling them 'international system', 'international society', 'international order',

41 KE Boulding, 'The Economics of the Coming Spaceship Earth' in H Jarrett (ed), *Environmental Quality in a Growing Economy* (Baltimore: John Hopkins University Press, 1966) 3–14.

42 ibid 11.

43 P Weil, 'Le judaïsme et le développement du droit international' (1976-III) 151 RdC 253, 272–7.

44 See eg W Levi, *Contemporary International Law: A Concise Introduction* (Boulder: San Francisco and Oxford: Westview Press, 2nd edn, 1979) 7–8.

45 See G Vismara, '"Impius Foedus": Le origini della Respublica Christiana' in *Scritti di storia giuridica. 7. Comunità e Diritto Internazionale* (Milan: Giuffrè, 1989) 8–13, 21, 24–5, 29–31, 35, 64; J Bartelson, *Visions of World Community* (Cambridge: CUP, 2009) 48.

46 cf eg Plutarch, *Alexander* 329 A-B.

47 Cicero, *De legibus*, 1, 23 ('universus <sit> hic mundus una civitas communis deorum atque hominum').

48 See Ch 4 above, section B (1).

49 See Bartelson (n 45 above) 108–14, 142–3.

50 ibid 19, observing that 'a community cannot be fully inclusive and still have boundaries'.

51 See A Etzioni, *From Empire to Community: A New Approach to International Relations* (New York and Houndmills: Palgrave Macmillan, 2004) 195–6.

and 'world order'. This progression, although contingent on an IR theory developed during the Cold War, is still a valid starting point for analysis.[52]

Bull defined the 'international system' or a 'system of states' as being 'formed when two or more states have sufficient contact, and have sufficient impact on one another's decisions, to cause them to behave—at least in some measure—as parts of a whole' and 'to make the behaviour of each a necessary element in the calculations of the other'.[53] The term is used to keep this condition distinct from the one of two or more states which exist without exchanging any (or sufficiently relevant or impactful) mutual contacts. The notion of a 'system' as an interactional unity among sufficiently autonomous component units appears to have been first introduced in Europe by Samuel Pufendorf in 1675, referring to the German states within the Holy Roman Empire after the Peace of Westphalia and furthering a shift from the Empire towards a system of confederates or allies (*systema foederatorum* or *sociorum*) united in an unequal league and finally to a true 'system of states' (*systema civitatum*).[54] It was later used specifically to denote the 'European system of states', among others, by Arnold Heeren.[55] He defined a states system as 'the union of several contiguous states, resembling each other in their manners, religion and degree of social improvement, and cemented together by a reciprocity of interests'.[56] Heeren's notion of a state system is far more demanding than Bull's in so far as it requires a common culture or civilization. If one accepted Heeren's meaning, there would be no other term to describe Bull's condition of two or more states entertaining sufficient contacts to make the behaviour of each a necessary element in the calculations of the other without going so far as to share a common civilization. It seems anyway little questionable that states do form today what Bull called a 'system', especially as a result of the current world interconnectedness. While indisputable, this is not, however, to imply, unlike in Heeren's definition, that all existing states share a common culture, much less that people do.

To Bull's eyes it is presumably 'international society' (or a 'society of states'), what Heeren called a system, namely, 'a group of states, conscious of certain common interests and common values' which conceive themselves 'to be bound by a common set of rules in their relations with one another, and share in the working of common institutions'.[57] It is thus only in a 'society', in which certain common interests and

[52] For a discussion of the English School's paradigms and an attempt to take their conceptions of international society forward, see A Hurrell, *On Global Order: Power, Values, and the Constitution of International Society* (Oxford: OUP, 2007).

[53] H Bull, *The Anarchical Society: A Study of Order in World Politics* (Houndmills and New York: Palgrave, 3rd edn, 2002) 9–10. The notion of a states system is further discussed at section B (3) below.

[54] S Pufendorf, *De Systematibus Civitatum*, in *Dissertationae Accademicae Selectiores* (Uppsala, 1677) ('Systemata Civitatum nobis appellantur plures una civitates, vinculo aliquot ita inter se connexae, ut unum corpus videantur constituere; quarum singulae tamen summum in sese imperium retineant'). 'Thus States appear to constitute one body, but each none the less retains sovereign power.' See further S Da Monzambano [ie Samuel Pufendorf], *De Statu Imperii Germanici* (1667, rev edn 1684) I, 8, 12–15, and VI, 9, English trans *The Present State of Germany, or an Account of the Extent, Rise, Form, Wealth, Strength, Weaknesses and Interests of that Empire* (London: Chiswell, 1690) 1–13, 18–24, 152–4, arguing that the Empire was a constitutional 'monster'. On this issue, see J Robertson, 'Empire and Union: Two Concepts of the Early Modern European Political Order' in J Robertson (ed), *A Union for Empire: Political Thought and the British Union of 1707* (Cambridge: CUP, 1995) 3–36, 26–7.

[55] AHL Heeren, *Handbuch der Geschichte der Staaten des Alterthums, mit besonderer Rücksicht auf ihre Verfassungen, ihren Handel und ihre Colonien* (Göttingen: Rower, 1809), English trans from the 5th German edn, *A Manual of the History of the Political System of Europe and its Colonies, from its Formation at the Close of the Fifteenth Century, to its Re-establishment upon the Fall of Napoleon* (Oxford: Talboys, 1834).

[56] ibid vol 1, vii–viii.

[57] Bull (n 53 above) 13.

perhaps some common values are recognized by the generality of states, that common rules—such as respect for independence, abidance by agreements, limitation in exercising force, cooperation in the working of common institutions like international law, diplomacy, international organizations, and the laws of war—are possible. According to Bull, states may form a society only if they already form a system, but they may well form a system without forming a society by simply communicating, exchanging envoys, and entering into agreements. It is conceded that in borderline instances a sense of common interest or values may be only tentative and inchoate, common rules may be perceived as too vague and ill-formed, unworthy perhaps of the name 'rules', and common institutions are only implicit and embryonic. By 'common culture or civilisation' Bull meant at least some of the typical elements of a civilization, such as a common language, a common epistemology and understanding of the universe, a common religion, a common ethical code, a common aesthetic or artistic tradition.[58] On this view, the classification of the current states system as a 'society' is far more problematic than it may appear at first. Whether all existing states share a common sense of interests and values or at least some of the elements of a common culture or civilization is indeed doubtful. It is self-evident that there is no common language, no common epistemology, no common religion, no common ethical code, no common aesthetic tradition among the innumerable peoples living on earth. In certain moments in time and in certain subject-matters of states' interaction it would seem that this sense is tentative at best, while in other moments and in other subject-matters of interaction a stronger sense of commonality may exist.[59]

In Bull's view the international society can evolve into an 'international order', this being understood as 'a pattern or disposition of international activity that sustains those goals of the society of states that are elementary, primary or universal', such as the higher goal of preserving the states system itself (from challenges by state, supra-state, sub-state or trans-state actors), the subordinate goal of preserving the independence of individual member states, the further subordinate goal of preserving peace in terms of absence of war as the normal (as opposed to a permanent) condition of the relationships among states, and the goals of limiting violence, keeping promises, and stabilizing possession.[60] The word 'order' is not taken to mean an order defined in terms of obedience to rules of law, but rather 'a pattern of human activity that sustains elementary, primary or universal goals of social life' the fulfilment of which is in some measure a condition of social life as such.[61] There may be order without legal rules and, in reverse, there may be regularity, recurrent patterns in behaviour, and predictability without there being an order, let alone legal rules. People may behave in conformity with some recurrent patterns and yet define their condition as a condition of disorder, while in reverse they may perceive very little regularity and predictability where an order, and even legal rules, actually exist. Order is not any pattern but a particular kind of pattern which places emphasis on certain goals and values. When goals and values change, what was order before the change may become disorder thereafter, and vice versa. Similarly, someone's order may be someone else's disorder.

[58] ibid 15.

[59] Bull himself, admittedly in the Cold War period when his book was written, was sceptical (ibid 14).

[60] ibid 15–19.

[61] ibid 6–7.

While the word 'system' stresses 'some diversity in some unity' and the word 'society' denotes awareness of common interests and values, the word 'order' means a particular pattern of regularity from the perspective of certain goals or values. None of these concepts implies in itself law, although all of them are (at least to some extent) found when law is felt as existent in a social group.

Finally, a 'world order' was viewed by Bull as an order consisting in 'patterns or dispositions of human activity that sustain the elementary or primary goals of social life among mankind as a whole' or 'in the great society of all mankind'. It is, in a word, an order between all human beings on earth not limited to relationships between states or peoples, regardless of their being grouped into states or other kinds of political communities.[62] Until the latter half of the nineteenth century this 'great society of all mankind' to which canonists and naturalists had made allusion 'was a notional society that existed in the sight of God or in the light of the principles of natural law' rather than an actual political system.[63] Eventually a genuinely 'global' political system has arisen and world order has taken the form of a global system of states, spanning the world as a whole as a result of the expansion of the European states system all over the globe. This global states system has evolved as part of an emerging world political system. World order among mankind as a whole is wider, more fundamental, and primordial than (even morally prior to) order among states. It seems that in Bull's terminology 'global' simply means 'spanning the world as a whole' (as opposed to being limited to certain areas of the world), while 'world' refers to 'all mankind'. On this premise, globalization may refer to the spread of the Western model of statehood over the whole planet, without any implication for the role that non-state actors should play on the international scene.

In the above progression from a minimum to a maximum of involvement among those who are supposed to form or to participate in the 'whole' of human affairs, whatever this is called, the threshold which divides each category from the next remains largely indeterminate and probably a matter of taste. Pessimists would find the ties within a group still to be too loose to elevate internal interactions to the higher, more integrated level, while optimists would more readily be impressed by the opposite perception. Evidence could be found in both directions but the reading thereof might vary dramatically. Many would probably agree that the existence of a 'system' is easier to detect and prove than the existence of a 'society', since in order to claim that there is a system it is sufficient to show that a number of states (or other entities) are in contact with each other and interact in such a way that they are necessary factors in each other's calculations. Contacts and calculations are facts that can be ascertained without raising significant objections. Still, their number and intensity, as well as their weight in making decisions, may be differently assessed by different observers, who may thus reach different plausible conclusions. Thus, to detect and to prove a 'sense' of common interests and values, let alone a common 'culture', is much harder and open to question than just measuring the number and intensity of contacts and calculations. If law required a society in Bull's sense, it would be likely that no certainty could ever be reached as to the social basis and sound foundations of international law. Many would be content with proving the existence of an international 'system', ie of much less than a society in Bull's sense, and presumably even less than a community as commonly intended.

62 ibid 19.

63 See Ch 4 above, section B (1).

(b) The international community in operation

What there must be 'in common' for an international community to be in place is highly indeterminate. One could refer, for example, to a 'planetary space', a 'demos', a 'discent', or even 'Christ'.[64] In international practice at least seven different meanings of 'international community' can be identified.

One first, traditional meaning is 'the community of states', an expression that can be understood as implying either that *all* states (to which international law applies) form a community[65] or that *only* states form the international community.[66] Article 53 of the Vienna Convention on the Law of Treaties (VCLT) defines *jus cogens* by referring to the 'international community of states as a whole'.[67] The term 'as a whole' seems to hint at a 'organic whole' in a sense similar to a biological organism or a mystical body and to place emphasis on the fact that the community of states has to be understood as the *indivisible unity* of states, as opposed to a 'mere' arithmetical sum of them taken individually.[68]

A second meaning includes all international 'subjects' or 'legal persons', among which international organizations and possibly also individuals are included.[69] For example, the International Court of Justice (ICJ) *Barcelona Traction* Judgment and Article 5 of the Statute of the International Criminal Court (ICC Statute) mention 'the international community as a whole', thus suggesting that the international community is larger than only states.[70] Here 'as a whole' may mean either that the international community is an organic whole or that the international community is more inclusive than only states, or both.

In a third, even larger meaning, the international community is assumed to be the community of 'actors' participating in international relations, including non-governmental organizations (NGOs), multinational enterprises (MNEs), and the International Committee of the Red Cross (ICRC).[71] For example, in 1995 the UN General Assembly recognized that the United Nations would be more successful 'if it is supported by all concerned actors of the international community, including non-governmental organizations, multilateral financial institutions, regional organizations and all actors of civil society'.[72] Likewise, the International Law Commission (ILC) pointed out that the expression 'the international community as a whole' refers to non-state actors such as the United Nations, the European Community, and the ICRC, and is thus preferable to 'the international community of states as a whole'.[73]

[64] cf Bartelson (n 45 above) 13, 24, 48.

[65] PCIJ, *The Case of the SS Lotus* (n 1 above) 16, observing that '"principles of international law"... can only mean international law as it is applied between all nations belonging to the community of States'.

[66] B Cronin, *Community Under Anarchy: Transnational Identity and the Evolution of Cooperation* (New York: Columbia University Press, 1999), arguing that states can indeed form a community by sharing common identities and that the term community is not necessarily linked to people.

[67] See Ch 6 below, section B (4)(f).

[68] cf the statement of Mr Yasseen, in *United Nation Conference on the Law of Treaties*, First Session (Vienna, 26 March–24 May 1968), *Official Records*, Summary Records of the Plenary Meetings of the Committee of the Whole, 472, para 12, noting that 'as a whole' meant 'a very large majority' of states, the position of 'one State in isolation' or 'a very small number of States' being irrelevant.

[69] International legal personality is discussed at section D below.

[70] ICJ, *Barcelona Traction, Light and Power Co Ltd (Belgium v Spain) (Second Phase)* Judgment of 5 February 1970, [1970] ICJ Rep 3, para 33.

[71] See sections C (3)(a)(b) and (5)(c) below.

[72] UNGA Res 50/6 of 24 October 1995, para 17.

[73] cf J Crawford, *The International Law Commission's Articles on State Responsibility: Introduction, Text and Commentaries* (Cambridge: CUP, 2002) 40–1, and commentary to Art 25, para 18.

Under a fourth definition, the international community means the universal community of individuals, ie humankind regardless of its political partition in a multiplicity of states. The concept of humankind is often associated with that of humanity but it is necessary to avoid confusion. It is one thing to mean the total number of *physical* human beings living on earth; it is quite another to refer to the *psychological* or *moral* sense of sharing a common destiny with any other human being; it is yet another to have regard to the *legal* centrality of the human person as a value pursued by certain norms.[74] To state that international law pursues the interests and values of humanity may mean either that it protects the interests and values of *all* human beings on earth, or that it protects the *moral* values of humanity (as identified through philosophical, not legal, inquiry), or that it places at the heart of its norms the human person as opposed to states or other abstract entities. The temptation to equalize all these interconnected (albeit not necessarily coincident) meanings should be resisted, at least in first approximation.

A fifth meaning of international community refers to the participation of all actors in a supportive 'family' capable of assisting its members wherever this is necessary. It comprises whoever can help human beings in need, such as people stricken by natural disasters or humanitarian catastrophes, famine, drought, poverty, etc, and embraces states, peoples, national and transnational private associations, NGOs, transnational enterprises (TNEs), individuals, and any other participating to support the political aims of the actor. For example, former UN Secretary-General Kofi Annan spoke of the international community in such terms in a speech delivered in 1999.[75]

Under a sixth meaning, the international community is understood as an entity capable of enforcing international obligations *erga omnes* aimed at protecting its most fundamental values.[76] Under this meaning, the sense of community is found in the power conferred on all states to support the victims of a particularly serious international unlawful act which is deemed to strike all members of the community—although it has been directed at one or even none of them (as is the case when a state commits an abuse of human rights against its own citizens)—and to uphold the 'public' protection of an alleged common fundamental value of all states, similar to the operation of criminal law in domestic legal systems.

Finally, a seventh meaning of international community is the one which results from the representation made by certain states or international organizations which proclaim to act 'on behalf' of the international community.[77] For example, on 23 March 1999 the Secretary-General of the North Atlantic Treaty Organization (NATO) announced the NATO decision to initiate a military campaign against the Federal Republic of Yugoslavia (FRY), as a response to the egregious violations of human rights committed

[74] For a discussion of the meaning of 'humanity' for international law purposes, see Ch 7 below, section A (2)(a).

[75] Address of the Secretary-General Kofi Annan entitled 'The Meaning of International Community', as delivered to the fifty-second DPI/NGO Conference in New York on 15 September 1999, at <http://www.un.org/News/Press/docs/1999/19990915.sgsm7133.doc.html>.

[76] On obligations *erga omnes*, see Ch 8 below, section B (1). For the view that the most powerful states *uti universi* enforce international law acting on behalf of the international community, see R Quadri, 'Le fondement du caractère obligatoire du droit international public' (1952-I) 80 RdC 579.

[77] For the view that the concept of international community is typically used to 'tame' and subjugate the 'other', see M Chibundu, 'The Other in International Law: Community and International Legal Order', SSRN (University of Maryland Working Paper Series No 2004–03), at <http://papers.ssrn.com/sol3/papers.cfm?abstract_id = 504782>.

there against Kosovars, 'to support the political aims of the international community'.[78] Whatever the assessment of the legality of the war,[79] it was clear that most states did not share the view of NATO and that NATO was thus not acting on behalf of the international community.[80] It had no mandate from the international community, however defined, nor did it have any authorization from the UN Security Council. As most states opposed the war, one could imagine that NATO intended the term international community in a sense unlinked to the opinion of states, or of states alone, such as the second or the third meanings among those mentioned above. Another possible reading is that NATO was referring to humanity in a moral sense and could act 'on behalf' of humanity, despite the fact that most states opposed the war, on grounds that in that case war was necessary for moral reasons affecting the values of human dignity, regardless of the attitude of states. However, the 'proper' meaning of international community was assumed by NATO *states* in a *unilateral* way, and at least in this respect NATO was not acting in the name and on behalf of the international community.

(c) Sovereignty for the global community

All of the above meanings of international community reflect realities, except for the last one, which is a unilateral claim by a few states of what should count as universal.

There can be little doubt about the existence of a system of states which shares common identities, interests, and values, beyond their differences. 'The destiny of any state, weak and strong alike, depends on all others.' Nor can it be credibly denied, on the other hand, that a multitude of non-state actors participate in this system by influencing states and shaping their behaviour from both 'outside' and 'inside', 'above' and 'below', through a network of interactions amounting to a 'global community'. States remain the ultimate 'regulators', while all other actors shape their calculations. Even the sense of a universal community of individuals beyond the partition of the world into a number of states reflects realities and emotional attunement among human beings whatever their nationality, identity, or loyalty. There is no inevitable opposition between statehood and humanity. States as a whole (*uti universi*) can well pursue the values of humanity and can do so better than any universal community of individuals devoid of any political authority and left to the steering power of alleged private authorities. Individuals and their associations can and should push states 'from below', through their political consent or dissent, towards pursuing global justice and the protection of the most vulnerable. Also IOs can (and indeed do) push states 'from above' towards adopting a more solidarity-orientated behaviour in their networked relations. The rules of international law protecting state sovereignty exist in the interest of humanity, no less than any others, and sovereignty can be constructed and exercised in many ways. Sovereignty is what we make of it and nothing prevents it from being used in the service of humanity, except for those who do not think that this pursuit is worth engaging.

[78] cf the Press Statement of Mr Javier Solana, Secretary General of NATO, at <http://www.nato.int/docu/pr/1999/p99-040e.htm>.

[79] See Ch 8 below, section B (2).

[80] cf UN Doc S/PV.3989 at 16. For the equally critical position taken by non-aligned countries see the Final Communique of 23 September 1999, at <http://www.nam.gov.za/minmeet/newyorkcom.htm>.

If the international community is defined as a network of mutual influences relevant to the protection of the most vulnerable, then anyone who makes a contribution thereto is part of the international community. International law then appears to be the law of an international community in which different actors perform partly different functions: states govern individuals through jurisdictional power grounded in political legitimacy—although this latter's degree varies considerably with the state—while all other actors dynamically influence states in such a way as to exercise authority for the benefit of all and in particular of the most vulnerable. Thus defined, international law is the law that governs the community of states with a view to governing the community of all humankind. Whether this prospect is to be seen as an illusory dream, or a plan of action, or a reality already in place depends on us and on what we are able and willing to make of international law.

B. States

It has been noted that 'the worst fate that can befall a human being is to be stateless'.[81] State authorities undoubtedly believe in international law as their law. They hold international law as the law to which their state is expected to conform. Participation in the creation of, and compliance with, international law is established in the domestic legislation, and often in the constitutional provisions, of virtually every state. This section argues that states emerged in Europe at the beginning of the Modern Age and have been imposed on all other peoples as the key political organizations exercising supreme authority over individuals within a defined territory. This model of statehood eventually spread globally and has been upheld by international law. It is also contended that, by current standards, the global states system is historically the product of injustice, and is today often unable to manage global problems, yet it continues to ensure intra-systemic order and justice through a partitioned and coordinated exercise of state jurisdiction which is not necessarily at odds with the pursuit of global values.

(1) The modern European state

By defining the state in terms of class division of society and the advent of a permanent and institutionalized leadership in society and by assuming that the state is a form of political organization whose hallmark is the monopoly of the legitimate use of force by an elite,[82] the origins of statehood have been traced back to the Neolithic and Urban Revolutions (so-called 'Early State').[83] The 'modern' state, however, emerged in Western Europe at the beginning of the Modern Age, or earlier in the late Middle Ages, or still earlier.[84] In the course of their historical development, modern European states have: (a) displaced the medieval feudal order;[85] (b) won the competition with

[81] JR Strayer, *On the Medieval Origins of the Modern State* (Princeton and Oxford: Princeton University Press, 1970) 3.

[82] This is the well-known notion of 'authority' endorsed by Max Weber (n 27 above).

[83] HJM Claessen and P Skalnik (eds), *The Early State* (The Hague: Mouton, 1978); HJM Claessen and JG Oosten (eds), *Ideology and the Formation of Early States* (Leiden: Brill, 1996); M Frangipane, *La nascita dello Stato nel Vicino Oriente: Dai lignaggi alla burocrazia nella Grande Mesopotamia* (Roma-Bari: Laterza, 2nd edn, 2005).

[84] See Strayer (n 81 above). For a discussion of the problem of the origins of the modern state, see WG Grewe, *Epochen der Völkerrechtsgeschichte*, (Baden-Baden: Nomos, 1984) 194–204, English trans *The Epochs of International Law* (Berlin and New York: Walter de Gruyter, 2000) 163–71; Q Skinner, 'The State', in T Ball, J Farr, and RL Hanson (eds), *Political Innovation and Conceptual Change* (Cambridge: CUP, 1989) 90–131.

[85] Strayer (n 81 above).

other political competitors[86] and progressively monopolized legitimate international violence;[87] (c) expanded oversees and displaced Aboriginal forms of rule concomitant with the colonization of non-European territories,[88] thus absorbing, eclipsing, or extinguishing rival states systems;[89] (d) changed their internal structure from absolutist to others, among which the liberal-democratic one is noteworthy;[90] and (e) imposed statehood on all peoples on the planet.[91]

The modern state emerged as a sovereign, territorial, and exclusive system of rule. Sovereignty implied a claim to (internal) final authority, ie a denial of any higher source of governmental power. Territoriality meant that sovereignty was exercised over a fixed territorial space delimited by mutually recognized linear (rather than zonal) borders. Exclusivity denoted that sovereignty was exercised within a fixed territory with the exclusion of any other authorities. The modern state was not *dominus mundi* and advanced no superiority over other states. It conceived of itself from the very beginning as being part of a wider system made up of other states, although not as an organ of a superior authority. It defined individuals by spatial markers, regardless of kin, tribal affiliation, or religious beliefs. Identity was given by, and loyalty depended on, physical location. Its key features were built up by policing the territory and raising revenue by means of monopolies, customs duties, the sale of offices, tax farming, imposts, and levies of various kinds. It has been suggested that the modern state was born as a unitary, secularized, centralized organization (differentiated from other organizations operating in the same territory) whose divisions are coordinated with one another, which exercised last-resort coercive control and supreme exclusive authority over a population occupying a definite territory.[92] Eventually, the modern state was also marked by legal personality[93] and nationhood.[94]

When modern states emerged, other modes of rule system were possible and actually existed.[95] In clans, tribes, and kinship groups, where rule was exercised by clan leaders or tribal elders over the members of the collectivity, it was the membership of the group, not space, that defined the sphere of rule. In nomadic peoples, among which

[86] H Spruyt, *The Sovereign State and Its Competitors* (Princeton: Princeton University Press, 1994).
[87] JE Thomson, *Mercenaries, Pirates, & Sovereigns: State Building and Extraterritorial Violence in Early Modern Europe* (Princeton: Princeton University Press, 1994).
[88] A Anghie, *Imperialism, Sovereignty and the Making of International Law* (Cambridge: CUP, 2005).
[89] C Tilly, *Coercion, Capital, and European States, A.D. 990–1992* (Cambridge: Blackwell, 1990) 4.
[90] G Poggi, *The Development of the Modern State: A Sociological Introduction* (London: Hutchinson, 1978); G Poggi, *The State, Its Nature, Development and Prospects* (Cambridge: Polity Press, 1990) 34–68.
[91] H Bull and A Watson (eds), *The Expansion of International Society* (Oxford: OUP, 1983).
[92] C Tilly, 'Reflection on the History of European State-Making' in C Tilly (ed), *The Formation of National States in Western Europe* (Princeton: Princeton University Press, 1975) 70. See further Strayer (n 81 above) 5–10, suggesting as 'signs' of the emergence of the modern state, ie as its key initial features, 'persist[ence] in time and fix[ity] in space, development of permanent, impersonal institutions, agreement on the need for an authority which can give final judgments, and acceptance of the idea that this authority should receive the basic loyalty of its subjects'.
[93] M van Creveld, *The Rise and Decline of the State* (Cambridge: CUP, 1999) 1, 416. For state international legal personality, see section D below.
[94] Poggi (1990) (n 90 above) 26–7.
[95] JG Ruggie, 'Territoriality and Beyond: Problematizing Modernity in International Relations' (1993) 47 *International Organization* 139, 149. For the evolution of political structures in Western civilization and a critique of the state as a 'timeless [inescapable] marker of civilization', see A Osiander, *Before the State: Systemic Political Change in the West from the Greeks to the French Revolution* (Oxford and New York: OUP, 2007). On nomadic peoples in international law, see M Moretti, *Le Droit international public et les peuples nomades* (Paris: Editions Publibook, 2006).

rule was exercised over a particular spatial area variable with the seasons or trade routes, space defined the sphere of rule but in a fluctuating way.[96] The medieval order, basically made up of feudal lords, the Church, and the Empire, was considerably different. A variety of authorities claimed to govern over the same space and cross-cutting (rival) jurisdictions overlapped. Feudal lords were not sovereign (supreme authority being disputed at best), their authority was not based on spatial location but on personal bonds (since they exercised authority over specific persons wherever these were in space) and was not exclusive (other lords could exercise authority over the same subjects and there was no clear hierarchy in case of conflict between competing loyalties). The Church did claim sovereignty, but a universal one as opposed to sovereignty over a defined territory as states did, its authority extended to all Christians wherever they were, and was exclusive in the sense that, unlike states' claim to exclusivity only within their territory and recognition of other equal states exercising an equal exclusive authority within their territory, no other authority was recognized. The Empire conceived itself as universalistic as the Church, the Emperor claiming to be *dominus mundi*, with exclusive authority not limited to a defined territory. In the feudal order there were no spatial 'borders' and there could thus be no 'international' sphere, as opposed to 'domestic', this being possible only in a states system in which *more* authorities claim supreme power but only within their borders while acknowledging themselves as part of *one and the same* broader, all-encompassing system.[97]

(2) Statehood under international law

A world of states is an oversimplified world, specifically a rationalization of the European mind, since all political formations other than states are either forced into statehood or excluded from legal relevance (and hence reduced to be 'subjected' to, and at the mercy of, existing states) and all states are supposed to fit into an abstract model of statehood while states themselves, including Western states, vary in space and time. The former effect of global Western etatization raises serious concerns about the justice of the statist model itself, which will be discussed below. As to its latter effect, there is little doubt that once put in historical and geographical context statehood appears considerably diversified.[98] As noted, 'the European experience does not provide a template for state-making in other regions of the world'.[99] While retaining its original European name, the state is not the same everywhere, just as its history is different from place to place.[100] Yet statehood as defined by international law and promoted by international institutions, such as the United Nations through international administrations and state-building, reflects the Western model. This statist rationalization may of course be helpful to the governability of the world, but there was no compelling reason why the world should be governed as a global unity in the first place. If this is

[96] Spruyt (n 86 above) 34.

[97] ibid 34–57.

[98] For statehood in Africa, see C Clapham, *Africa and the International System: The Politics of State Survival* (Cambridge: CUP, 1996). For statehood in Asia, see A Rabo and B Utas (eds), *The Rule of the State in West Asia* (Stockholm: Swedish Research Institute in Istanbul, 2005); J Bautista and F Khek Gee Lim (eds), *Christianity and the State in Asia: Complicity and Conflict* (London and New York: Routledge, 2009). For statehood in the Islamic world, see N Feldman, *The Fall and Rise of the Islamic State* (Princeton and Oxford: *Princeton University Press, 2008). For the standardization brought about by the state,* see JC Scott, *seeing like a State: How Certain Schemes to Improve the Human Condition Have Failed* (New Haven and London: Yale University Press, 1998).

[99] J Herbst, *States and Power in Africa: Comparative Lessons in Authority and Control* (Princeton: Princeton University Press, 2000) 21–2.

[100] ibid 13–21.

today the case, it is because the West has historically globalized its own type of political organization. It is only *within* this model, once accepted, that human rights, self-determination, the protection of minorities and indigenous peoples, the rule of law, constitutional restraints to abuse of power, rule on behalf and for the benefit of the ruled, and the like, make sense. The model, as recognized in state and international practice, is based on the 'three-elements' doctrine first developed in domestic constitutional law, precisely in the construction of the constitutional law of a few Western states, in particular Germany. The doctrine requires territory, people, and government for a political entity aspiring to statehood to be treated as a state and to acquire international legal personality. No other requirements, such as a democratic form of government or the recognition from pre-existing states, are necessary. A succinct illustration of the practice bearing upon the definition of the state may be helpful for present purposes.

(a) The three-element doctrine

The *Drei-Elementen Lehre*, expounded by the German public law scholar Georg Jellinek for constitutional purposes,[101] has proved successful in international practice. In the 1929 *Deutsche Continental Gas-Gesellschaft* Award a Mixed Arbitral Tribunal held that 'a state does not exist unless it fulfils the conditions of possessing a territory, a people inhabiting that territory, and a public power which is exercised over the people and the territory'.[102] Article 1 of the 1933 Montevideo Convention on the Rights and Duties of States defines a state as 'a person of international law' that 'should possess . . . (a) a permanent population, (b) a defined territory, (c) government, and (d) capacity to enter into relations with the other states'.[103] A similar definition is found in the US Restatement (Third) of Foreign Relations (1987).[104] In its 1991 Opinion No 1 on the dissolution of the former Yugoslavia, the Badinter Arbitration Committee considered that 'the state is commonly defined as a community which consists of a territory and a population subject to an organized political authority'.[105] Domestic courts generally concur.[106] The competing view that statehood consists of the

[101] G Jellinek, *Allgemeine Staatslehre* (Berlin: O Häring, 3rd edn, 1914) 396.

[102] Germano-Polish Mixed Arbitral Tribunal, *Deutsche Continental Gas-Gesellschaft v Polish State* Award of 1 August 1929, (1929) 5 ILR 11, 13.

[103] Montevideo Convention on the Rights and Duties of States (signed at Montevideo on 26 December 1933, entered into force on 26 December 1934, reaffirmed by Protocol on 23 December 1936). For the view that the requirement of capacity to enter into relations with other states represents the concept of independence, see eg English Special Commissioners, *Caglar v Billingham (Inspector of Taxes) and Related Appeals*, Decision of 7 March 1996, (1998) 108 ILR 510, para 168, and in the literature eg I Brownlie, *Principles of Public International Law* (Oxford: OUP, 7th edn, 2008) 71.

[104] *Restatement of the Law, Third, Foreign Relations Law of the United States* (Washington, DC: The American Law Institute, 1987) § 201.

[105] Arbitration Commission of the Peace Conference on the former Yugoslavia, Opinion No 1 of 29 November 1991, at <http://ejil.oxfordjournals.org/content/3/1/178.full.pdf>.

[106] See eg Italian Court of Cassation, *Re Yasser Arafat* Judgment of 28 June 1985 No 1981, (1986) 69 RDI 885; Italian Court of Cassation, *Re: Djukanovic* Judgment of 28 December 2004 No 49666, (2006) 89 RDI 569, 572, 18 ItYIL (2004) 342, ILDC 74 (IT 2004); Quebec Supreme Court, *Parent et al v Singapore Airlines Ltd and Civil Aeronautics Administration*, Decision of 22 October 2003, (2008) 133 ILR 264, ILDC 181 (CA 2003), para 54; Singapore Court of Appeal, *Civil Aeronautics Administration v Singapore* Judgment of 14 January 2004, (2008) 133 ILR 371, para 30; Swiss Federal Supreme Court, *Wang et al v Switzerland* Judgment of 3 May 2004 No 1A.3/2004, ILDC 90 (CH 2004), para 5.2; US Court of Appeals for the First Circuit, *Ungar et al v Palestine Liberation Organization and Palestinian Authority, Estate of Efrat Ungar et al v Palestine Liberation Organization and Palestinian Authority* Judgment of 31 March 2005, ILDC 124 (US 2005), paras 56–59; Israeli

government alone,[107] often based on the assumption that the hallmark of statehood is force and force is exercised by the government, is disproved by a number of facts observable in international legal practice, including the continuity of the state after a revolution and the persistence of the state even where there is no longer effective government, or the government is in exile abroad, or there is a protracted civil war.[108] Also, the view that the existence of a state hinges on legal criteria and not only effectiveness—assuming that international law precedes statehood[109] against the positivists who defend the 'state-as-a-mere-fact' conception[110]—needs some qualification. It is certainly true that international law as made and sustained by states *uti universi* precedes states *uti singuli* and makes their legal existence conditional on legal requirements; it is also true, however, that states *uti universi* precede and determine the rules of international law which apply to any individual state.[111]

For a state to exist under international law there must therefore be (a) a territory, (b) a people; and (c) a government that is both (i) effective and (ii) independent. Territory is inherent in statehood. The state is defined as the form of political organization which can politically and legally manage all that occurs within its borders. Modern states' borders are generally linear (as opposed to zonal) and exclude interstitial vacuums (or 'grey zones') of authority: where the territory of one state ends, the territory of another state immediately begins. Uncertain or disputed borders seem not to affect statehood, as the international practice largely attests and the ICJ reiterated in the 1969 *North Sea* Judgment.[112] The dimension of territory is also irrelevant and 'micro-states' have been admitted as 'states' to the United Nations. The territory of a state must be 'natural', ie not artificially created by man. According to the Administrative Court of Cologne, in its 1978 *Re Duchy of Sealand* Judgment:

> A man-made artificial platform, such as the so-called Duchy of Sealand, cannot be called either 'a part of the earth's surface' or 'land territory' and only structures which make use of a specific piece of the earth's surface can be recognised as State territory within the meaning of international law.[113]

People are also implied in statehood. A completely uninhabited territory cannot be a state, although uninhabited territories belonging to inhabited states can be regarded as parts thereof. The possession of citizenship of all those forming the people of a state is the rule. The size of the population is irrelevant. Even Nauru, with about 9,000 inhabitants, is a state which joined the United Nations. However, the people of a state must form a 'community' in the sense aptly described, once again, in the *Re Duchy*

District Court of Jerusalem, *Basha, Association of the Elon Moreh College v Israel et al* Judgment of 23 April 2006 No 4049/02, ILDC 453 (IL 2006), para 9.

[107] See eg DP O'Connell, *State Succession in Municipal Law and International Law* (Cambridge: CUP, 1967) vol 1, 5–6; R Quadri, *Diritto internazionale pubblico* (Naples: Liguori, 5th edn, 1968) 425.

[108] J Crawford, *The Creation of States in International Law* (Oxford: Clarendon Press, 2nd edn, 2006) 34–5.

[109] ibid 97–107. See further H Kelsen, 'La naissance de l'Etat et la formation de sa nationalité: les principes; leur application au cas de la Tchécoslovaquie' (1929) 4 RDI 613, 617–18; J Dugard, *Recognition and the United Nations* (Cambridge: CUP, 1987) 123.

[110] See eg A Cavaglieri, 'Règles générales du droit de la paix' (1929) 26 RdC 315, 321, claiming that 'Ce n'est pas l'Etat qui est le produit de droit, mais le contraire'.

[111] This point will be further pursued in sections B 2(c) and D below.

[112] ICJ, *North Sea Continental Shelf (Federal Republic of Germany v Denmark and Federal Republic of Germany v Netherlands) (Merits)* Judgment of 20 February 1969, [1969] ICJ Rep 4, para 46.

[113] Administrative Court of Cologne, *Re Duchy of Sealand* Judgment of 3 May 1978, (1978) 80 ILR 683, 685.

of Sealand Judgment, namely, that the state's duty to promote community life 'does not merely consist of the promotion of a loose association aimed at the furtherance of common hobbies and interests', as was the case with Sealand in that particular instance, but 'rather it must be aimed at the maintenance of an essentially permanent form of communal life in the sense of sharing a common destiny'.[114]

The government is a most salient element of statehood.[115] It is the government that holds together territory and people and combines them into a unity legally meaningful from the outside. The government must be effective. Effectiveness means the capacity of the government to make itself obeyed, ie the capacity to have laws, judicial decisions, administrative acts observed by the ruled by, inter alia, threatening and applying coercion. No other international player claims to exercise governmental powers on a par with states. Uncertainty surrounds the identification of the degree of effectiveness required of state governments. It is sometimes said that the reference point is an 'average' state, assuming as a yardstick a typical Western state in its historical development. The degree of effectiveness required seems to be context-related: it operates differently in respect of the acquisition of a new territory (when allowed) and continuation of the title over time,[116] or of the legal relevance of an insurgent government,[117] or as evidence of disputed sovereignty over a portion of territory between two or more states.[118] A nice illustration of what is meant by the effectiveness of a government was given in the 1998 *Sierra Leone Telecommunications* Judgment by the High Court QBC.[119] By checking whether political institutions were functioning in Sierra Leone, the court extended the standards of a typical Western state to a non-Western state. It assumed that a government which is incapable of ensuring those basic services could not be regarded as the government of a state.

Governments that are no longer effective, as a result of an international or internal conflict, or for any other reason, have been termed 'failed' and presumed to be in need of being 'saved'.[120] Since effectiveness is required to become a state, logic would suggest that failed states are no longer states. International practice, however, shows that failed states continue to be considered states, remaining, inter alia, members of the United Nations. The 1992 *Woodhouse Drake and Carey* Judgment by the High Court QBD, for example, did not suppose that Somalia was no longer a state, despite the clear lack of effectiveness of its provisional government.[121] This continuity is sometimes explained by saying that if a failed state ceased to be a state, it would presumably become a *terra nullius* which could be occupied and acquired, in breach of the principle of self-determination, by any power. But this would only mean that the acquisition is prohibited. It is more likely that the persisting statehood of failed states means a sort of 'promotion' by the international community of their returning to full effectiveness. The notion that failed states are 'quasi-states' or 'juridical states', created artificially in

[114] ibid 687.

[115] cf US Court of Appeals for the First Circuit, *Ungar v Palestine Liberation Organization* (n 106 above) para 57.

[116] PCA Arbitral Tribunal, *Island of Palmas Case (Netherlands v United States)* Award of 4 April 1928, 2 RIAA 829, 838–40.

[117] Sole Arbitrator, *Anguilar-Armory and Royal Bank of Canada Claims (Great Britain v Costa Rica)* Award of 18 October 1923, 1 RIAA 369, 379.

[118] Sole Arbitrator, *Affaire de l'Ile de Clipperton* Award of 28 January 1931, 2 RIAA 1105, 1109–10.

[119] UK High Court, Queen's Bench Division, *Sierra Leone Telecommunications Co Ltd v Barclays Bank plc* Judgment of 6 February 1998, (1999) 114 ILR 466, 476–7.

[120] GB Helman and SR Ratner, 'Saving Failed States' (1992–93) 89 *Foreign Policy* 3.

[121] UK High Court, QBD, *Republic of Somalia v Woodhouse Drake and Carey (Suisse) SA et al* Judgment of 13 March 1992, (1994) 94 ILR 608, 619–21.

the name of self-determination of people despite their obvious lack of effectiveness, is untenable.[122] It may help to explain decolonization and failed states in political terms, but does not reflect current international law and is open to abuse, especially when state failure is invoked to justify (otherwise unjustifiable) military interventions or the termination of treaties. It is a fact that the identification of the threshold which transforms a state into a failed state is difficult to assess due to the variety of degrees of ineffectiveness of existing states;[123] moreover, the yardstick of effectiveness is provided by Western states and these are, at the same time, those which accuse other states of having 'failed', as well as the very states which in the colonial past created the causes of present failures and also the states which have pushed in recent decades for global privatization of state functions and thus the weakening of the state.

The government of a state must also be independent. No state of course is absolutely independent from the others and clearly the weaker are more dependent on the stronger that the reverse. However, states maintain a certain autonomy and exclusiveness. Independence required for statehood is not factual, but legal. The authority of the state must be *legally supreme*: laws, judicial decisions, executive acts must not be carried out on the basis of decisions made by others who do not enjoy political legitimacy from the addressees of such acts taken as a whole. As Judge Anzilotti stated in his individual opinion appended to the 1931 *Customs Regime* Advisory Opinion of the PCIJ, 'the state has over it no other authority than that of international law'.[124] In other words, states are independent from each other, although each depends on (or, better, is bound by) international law as the law common to all. Member states of federal states are not, therefore, states in the sense of international law.[125] As specified in Article 2 of the 1933 Montevideo Convention: 'The federal state shall constitute a sole person in the eyes of international law', its member states not being independent, as domestic courts have often stated.[126] The power occasionally conferred by national constitutions on state sub-units to enter into international agreements with foreign states or foreign states' sub-units does not transform them into states under international law. Unlike federations, confederations of states are not states since their member states, while associating for common goals, retain independence. Puppet governments are formally independent, but actually totally depend on another state. Their formal independence is often considered irrelevant in international practice. For example, in 1976 the UN General

[122] RH Jackson, *Quasi-states: Sovereignty, International Relations and the Third World* (Cambridge: CUP, 1990).

[123] For a measurement of the degree to which states are failing, see the Fund for Peace's Failed States Index (2011), at <http://www.fundforpeace.org/global/?q = fsi-grid2011>.

[124] PCIJ, *Customs Regime between Germany and Austria*, Advisory Opinion of 5 September 1931, [1931] PCIJ Series A/B No 41, individual opinion of Judge Anzilotti, at 57.

[125] See J Trone, 'Sovereign Immunity of the Member States of a Federation' (2008) 11 International Trade and Business Law Review 279.

[126] cf UK High Court QBD, *Chloride Industrial Batteries Ltd et al v F & W Freight Ltd* Judgment of 13 October 1989, (1991) 86 ILR 152, affirmed by the Court of Appeal, Judgment of 12 June 1989, (1991) 86 ILR 157–60, arguing that for the purposes of the Convention on the Contract for the International Carriage of Goods by Road (CMR) (signed 19 May 1956, entered into force 2 July 1961, 399 UNTS 189), as enacted into English law, the UK 'is to be regarded as a single state' and Jersey was not a separate country from the UK; US Court of Appeals for the Second Circuit, *Morgan Guaranty Trust Company of New York et al v Republic of Palau* Judgment of 4 February 1991, (1992) 87 ILR 647, 653–5, holding that Palau (a trust territory under US authority) was not a foreign state under the meaning of the Foreign State Immunity Act (FSIA); Italian Court of Cassation, *Re: Djukanovic* (n 106 above) 574–6, ruling that Djukanovic was not head of a sovereign state (Montenegro, which was at the time a part of the Federal Republic of Yugoslavia of Serbia and Montenegro) and, therefore, enjoyed no right to jurisdictional immunity.

Assembly declared invalid, for lack of independence, the proclamation by South Africa of the independent State of Transkei.[127] In the 1995 and 1996 *Loizidou* Judgments the ECtHR treated the Turkish Republic of Northern Cyprus (TRNC) as a sort of puppet government whose acts fall within the jurisdiction of (and are attributable to) Turkey as an (unlawful) occupier.[128]

(b) Constitutionality and democracy

Statehood is not affected by the illegality under domestic law of the way the state has come into existence.[129] Several states have been created despite the unconstitutional takeover of governments by way of revolution or coup. There is a trend, however, whereby the UN Security Council declares who is the 'legitimate authority' within a state—as a rule the one which has been democratically elected, especially when the election has been monitored internationally—and condemns the other contending party.[130]

Nor is statehood affected by the form of government of the state, whether democratic or other. The notion that democracy is required for statehood captures a trend in international practice especially since the end of the Cold War, namely, the process of democratization in many states (also as a result of UN-driven state-building) and the practice of requiring democracy as a condition for obtaining benefits, such as recognition by other states, admission to IOs, loans, and other forms of assistance.[131] The justification to list democracy among the requirements for statehood often lies in the wish to deny statehood to those political entities which commit massive violations of human rights. A similar attitude has been taken towards so-called 'rogue' or 'outlaw' states accused of sponsoring international terrorism, or other threats to the security of this or that great power, if not to the international system itself, such as the former US President George W Bush's doctrine of the 'axis of evil'.[132] However, there are still several states which are considered undemocratic the statehood of which is absolutely uncontested. The accusers themselves entertain relations with such states on an equal footing. Cases of total isolation are extremely rare. The example of Southern Rhodesia in the 1960s for its apartheid policy[133] has little import when considering that in those same years and afterwards South Africa, which was equally accused of apartheid, was far from being isolated by the whole international community. Finally, the meaning itself of the 'democracy' that should work as a yardstick is uncertain and reflects, once again, the form of government of Western states.

[127] UNGA Res 31/6 A of 26 October 1976, referring to Transkei's 'sham independence' as 'invalid' and calling upon 'all Governments to deny any form of recognition to the so-called independent Transkei'.

[128] ECtHR, *Loizidou v Turkey (Preliminary Objections)* Judgment of 23 February 1995, App 15318/89, Series A No 310, 20 EHRR (1995) 99, para 62; *Loizidou v Turkey (Merits)* Judgment of 18 December 1996, ECtHR Rep 1996-VI 2216, 23 EHRR (1996) 513, para 56. See further English Special Commissioners, *Caglar v Billingham (Inspector of Taxes) and Related Appeals* (n 103 above) para 182, holding that the TRNC 'does not have functional independence as it cannot enter into relations with other states'.

[129] Sole Arbitrator, *Anguilar-Armory and Royal Bank of Canada Claims* (n 117 above) 381–2.

[130] See section C (4)(a) and (b) below.

[131] See A Duxbury, *The Participation of States in International Organisations: The Role of Human Rights and Democracy* (Cambridge: CUP, 2011).

[132] cf State of the Union Address of 29 January 2002, labelling Iran, Iraq, and North Korea as the axis of evil for helping terrorism and seeking weapons of mass destruction, at <http://georgewbush-whitehouse.archives.gov/news/releases/2002/01/print/20020129-11.html>.

[133] cf UNSC Resolutions 232 (1966) of 16 December 1966 and 253 (1968) of 29 May 1968.

(c) Recognition

Statehood is not contingent on the recognition by other individual states. The constitutive theory of recognition was apparently upheld in Article VII of the 1856 Peace Treaty of Paris which, at the end of the Crimean War, ambiguously 'admitted' the Ottoman Empire to the advantages of the public law of Europe, even though the Ottoman Empire had had quite extensive treaty relations with European states well before.[134] A similar attitude is apparently found in the EU directives of 1991 on the recognition of European Eastern states emerged from the dissolution of the USSR and Yugoslavia.[135] It is today generally agreed that recognition from individual states is a voluntary act with only declaratory effect.[136] Palestine, for example, is recognized by many states, but is not considered a state by domestic courts,[137] whereas Taiwan is often considered a state by domestic courts although its statehood is not recognized by most states.[138] The declaratory theory of recognition was formulated in the 1923 *Tinoco* Arbitral Award[139] and, more recently, in Opinion No 10 of the Badinter Committee,[140] and in domestic jurisprudence.[141] While states as a rule are free not to proceed to recognition, an obligation not to recognize a new entity as a state may derive from a UN Security Council binding resolution, such as resolutions 216 (1965), 541 (1983), and 662 (1990) concerning Northern Rhodesia, the TRNC, and the Iraqi annexation of Kuwait.[142] Article 41(2) of the ILC Articles on State Responsibility provides an obligation of non-recognition of situations deriving from the serious

[134] See A Orakhelashvili, 'The Idea of European International Law' (2006) 17 EJIL 315, 337.

[135] EU, Declaration on the 'Guidelines on the Recognition of New States in Eastern Europe and in the Soviet Union' and Declaration on Yugoslavia of 16 December 1991, both at <http://www.ejil.org/pdfs/4/1/1227.pdf>.

[136] See eg Supreme Court of Bophuthatswana, *S v Banda et al* Judgment of 6 February 1989, (1990) 82 ILR 388, 410–12, arguing for the declaratory theory of recognition in order to conclude, quite untenably, that Bophuthatswana met the Montevideo Convention statehood requirements (although it was recognized only by South Africa and was not a member of the UN).

[137] See eg US Court of Appeals for the Second Circuit, *Klinghoffer et al v SNC Achille Lauro et al* Judgment of 21 June 1991, (1994) 96 ILR 69, 73–4, arguing that 'It is quite clear that the PLO meets none of the [Montevideo Convention's] requirements' since it 'has no defined territory' and hence 'it cannot have a permanent population', it 'is unable to demonstrate that the State of Palestine is under the control of its own government', and, finally, it 'lacks the ability actually to implement the obligations that normally accompany formal participation in the international community'; US Court of Appeals for the First Circuit, *Ungar v Palestine Liberation Organization* (n 106 above) para 73. For the view that the Palestinian National Authority had a quasi-sovereign power over at least some of the territories, see Israeli District Court of Jerusalem, *Basha, Association of the Elon Moreh College v Israel* (n 106 above) paras 8–9.

[138] See eg US Court of Appeals for the Second Circuit, *New York Chinese TV Programs Inc v UE Enterprises Inc* Judgment of 24 January 1992, (1994) 96 ILR 81, 88; Superior Court of Quebec, *Parent et al v Singapore Airlines Ltd and Civil Aeronautics Administration* (n 106 above) para 56; Swiss Federal Supreme Court, *Wang et al v Switzerland* (n 106 above) para 5.2. In *Civil Aeronautics Administration v Singapore* (2008) 133 ILR 371, para 43, the Court of Appeal of Singapore held that Taiwan is not a state for jurisdictional immunity purposes, although it might be a state for other purposes.

[139] Sole Arbitrator, *Anguilar-Armory and Royal Bank of Canada Claims* (n 117 above) 380–1.

[140] Arbitration Commission of the Peace Conference on the former Yugoslavia, Opinion No 10 of 4 July 1992, at <http://www.ejil.org/pdfs/4/1/1227.pdf>.

[141] See eg Italian Court of Cassation, *Re: Yasser Arafat* (n 106 above) 887; Italian Court of Cassation, *Re: Djukanovic* (n 106 above) 572; Superior Court of Quebec, *Parent et al v Singapore Airlines Ltd and Civil Aeronautics Administration* (n 106 above) para 58, holding that 'recognition is principally, but not exclusively, linked to the presence of constituent elements of the State'; Swiss Federal Supreme Court, *Wang et al v Switzerland* (n 106 above) para 5.3; Israeli District Court of Jerusalem, *Basha, Association of the Elon Moreh College v Israel* (n 106 above) para 9.

[142] UNSC resolutions 216 (1965) of 12 November 1965, 541 (1983) of 18 November 1983, and 662 (1990) of 9 August 1990.

violation of a peremptory norm of international law.[143] When dealing with private law disputes domestic courts are uncertain about whether they should acknowledge the statehood of new entities regardless of recognition on the part of their own government. A judicial trend to be approved, however, is to recognize laws and acts of effective foreign bodies even where their state has not been recognized by the government of the forum 'in regard to the laws which regulate the day to day affairs of the people'.[144]

It is a fact that pre-existing states have always 'judged' whether a new entity could become a state and enter their circle. This was more apparent in the nineteenth century when non-European states were assessed for admission to the 'club' of 'civilized nations'.[145] But it persists today for the simple reason that the issue of who is part of the decision-making table (notably with reference to its reliability) is vital to all participants. The fact that certain entities have become states (such as East Timor) and others have not (such as Palestine and Tibet) cannot be said to be independent of the attitude of pre-existing states. However, it is equally apparent that an entity does not become a state only because it has obtained some recognition from this or that pre-existing state, irrespective of its effectiveness, nor that it does not become a state only because one or another state opposes. Recognition is thus to be situated in the context of the whole *system* of states and be seen from a *dynamic* perspective. Recognition from individual states exactly at the moment when it is formulated is irrelevant and does not create statehood. However, it certainly contributes in some way to fulfilling the classical requirements of statehood, namely, territory, people, and government. Admission to the United Nations, as an informal recognition from the international community as a whole, tends to work as a 'certification' of statehood by embodying the attitude of pre-existing states as a whole.[146] Recognition is thus an attempt (from a single state) dynamically to *influence* the creation of a new state, just as non-recognition's purpose

[143] See Ch 8 below, n 49 and accompanying text.

[144] With regard to the German Democratic Republic, see UK Court of Appeal, *Carl-Zeiss-Stiftung v Rayner and Keeler Ltd* Judgment of 18 May 1966, (1971) 43 ILR 23, 66, viewing as an open question in English law that 'where private rights, or acts of everyday occurrence, or perfunctory acts of administration are concerned ... the courts may, in the interest of justice and commonsense, where no consideration of public policy to the contrary has to prevail, give recognition to the actual facts or realities found to exist in the territory in question' (*per* Lord Wilberforce); UK Court of Appeal, *Hesperides Hotels Ltd and anor v Aegean Turkish Holidays Ltd and Muftizade* Judgment of 23 May 1977, (1987) 73 ILR 9, 15, holding, in relation to the Turkish Federated State of Cyprus (forerunner of the TRNC), 'unhesitatingly ... that the courts of this country can recognize the laws or acts of a body which is in effective control of a territory even though it has not been recognized by Her Majesty's Government de jure or de facto: at any rate, in regard to the laws which regulate the day-to-day affairs of the people, such as their marriages, their divorces, their leases, their occupations, and so forth: and furthermore that the courts can receive evidence of the state of affairs so as to see whether the body is in effective control or not' (*per* Lord Denning MR); Court of Appeal, *Gur Corp v Trust Bank of South Africa Ltd (Government of the Republic of Ciskey, third party)* Judgment of 22 July 1986, [1987] 1 QB 599, 622, seeing, in relation to Ciskey, 'great force in this reservation, since it is one thing to treat a state or government as being "without the law", but quite another to treat the inhabitants of its territory as "outlaws" who cannot effectively marry, beget legitimate children, purchase goods on credit or undertake countless day-to-day activities having legal consequences' (*per* Sir Donaldson MR). For the (unacceptable) view that the 'so-called' German Democratic Republic was not a state since Italy had not recognized it, and its 'so-called' laws and judicial decisions could not be regarded as legally existent in a divorce case, see Tribunal of Bolzano, *Kweton v Ullmann* Judgment of 21 May 1971, (1972) 16 RDIPP 288–9.

[145] For a classical expression of this trend, see J Westlake, *Chapters on the Principles of International Law* (Cambridge: CUP, 1894) 136–8; WE Hall, *A Treatise on International Law* (Oxford: Clarendon Press, 8th edn, 1924) 47–8; LFL Oppenheim, *International Law* (London and New York: Longmans, 3rd edn, 1920) 134–5.

[146] Dugard (n 109 above).

is to make this creation more difficult. The sum of recognitions or non-recognitions is an integral part of the collective and informal recognition (from states as a whole) capable of making it possible (or alternatively very difficult, if not impossible) for a new entity to meet the requirements of statehood.

(3) The states system

The modern European state emerged as a *part of a system* of 'equal' states and has developed as the *only* system ruling the world by both displacing competitors in Europe and by universalizing the system worldwide. The world states system is ambivalent. On the one hand, it prevents a world tyrant and holds together the variety of existing peoples by enabling states to exercise jurisdiction over them in a partitioned way, thus avoiding global anarchy. On the other hand, it is structurally unjust as a product historically imposed by Western states on all other peoples. Moreover, due to its inherent fragmentation for anti-hegemonial purposes it has always—and not merely today—proved to have scant ability to solve global problems.[147] No better alternative device, however, is at the moment in sight and the state remains the key jurisdictional player in global governance. This section explores how the system of states contributes to world order and the functioning of international law despite its inherent injustice inherited from the past and current inability satisfactorily to manage global concerns.

(a) Structure

Although history may have known other systems of states (broadly defined)[148] in the past, such as the Indian Kautilya system and the system of the Greek city-states, the current world states system emerged together with the state at the beginning of the Modern Age in Europe.[149] Among the many theories on the origins of the European states system, Garrett Mattingly's view that the system emerged in Italy between 1340 and 1450 AD and then spread to the rest of Europe around 1500 AD (before further spreading globally) has proved particularly persuasive.[150] The global states system is premised on a number of key understandings between states: (a) every human being must be under the jurisdiction of a state; (b) every state must control its territory and avoid the risk that private individuals may use its territory to do harm in other states; (c) there must be no territory on earth devoid of state jurisdiction; and (d) states are responsible *inter se* for the conduct of individuals within their territory. The system

[147] For the 'anti-hegemonial' character of the 'Westphalian system', see A Watson, *The Evolution of International Society: A Comparative Historical Analysis* (London and New York: Routledge, 1992) 182–97.

[148] For a thorough critique of IR studies which espouse the position that states, and states systems, are as old as civilization itself, see Osiander (n 95 above) 14–6.

[149] CH Alexandrowicz, 'Kautilyan Principles and the Law of Nations' (1965–66) 41 BYBIL 301; M Wight, *Systems of States* (Leicester: Leicester University Press, 1977); A Osiander, *The States System of Europe, 1640–1990: Peacemaking and the Conditions of International Stability* (Oxford: Clarendon Press, 1994); B Buzan and R Little, *International Systems in World History: Remaking the Study of International Relations* (Oxford: OUP, 2000); FR Bridge and R Bullen, *The Great Powers and the European States System 1815–1914* (London and New York: Longman, 2nd edn, 2005).

[150] G Mattingly, *Renaissance Diplomacy* (Boston: Houghton Mifflin, 1955; repr New York: Dover Publications, 1988) 47–60; Watson (n 147 above) 152–8; Tilly (n 89 above) 164. JL Abu-Lughod, *Before European Hegemony: The World System A.D. 1250–1350* (New York and Oxford: OUP, 1989) pushes the origins of the European states system back to 1250.

ensures that all humanity is under jurisdictional control (and presumably legal protection) without being subjected to a universal authority.

A 'system' of states means both cooperation and competition, harmony and conflict.[151] While putting states under pressure to comply with the rules, the system cannot prevent inequalities of power, weak institutions, societal differences, cultural divergences, insurmountable disagreement on vital common issues, diffidence, fear, and rivalry for power and scarce resources. Within the system, states pursue their self-interest to the fullest extent possible in the circumstances and only occasionally their self-interest converges towards a common interest to make and obey common rules. Despite states' pursuit of self-interest within the system, one cannot explain what holds states together, including international law, unless the informal, pervasive pressure of the system is given due weight. In the states system it may be sufficient that one or a few states enact rules legalizing a certain conduct (such as, today, gay marriages, abortion, or on-line gambling) or making it possible and profitable for foreign businesses to invest locally (by reducing cross-border trade barriers, corporate taxes, and financial controls) so that other states are induced to follow suit in order to avoid their legislation being bypassed. The trend may become compelling even without any formal rule imposing it at international level. Systemic and informal pressure on individual states, strong and weak alike, is the necessary (although possibly not a sufficient) condition for international law to be created and observed. There are several reasons for this.

First, the states system is inescapable for all states. Even strong states cannot escape from the system, and the system has evolved thus far in such a way that attempts to dominate it (as is the case with Charles the Fifth, Napoleon, and Hitler) have failed.[152] The system does not contemplate 'empty' spaces to which those states that are willing to retain their total freedom of action can retreat. Strong states constantly experience virtually insurmountable hurdles in forcing the system as a whole to obey their will, although they certainly have more success in their attempts than other less powerful states. This state of affairs forces them to concede that in most instances it is in their own interest to obey rather than defy the restraints prescribed by international law.[153] To argue that, were this the case, it is not international law that affects their behaviour but their self-interest, simply overlooks the fact that they would not behave in this way if there were no international law at all. The fact itself that a certain behaviour is 'contrary' to international law makes calculations change because formally unlawful conduct is perceived by other states as being a great deal worse than hostile but lawful conduct.

Secondly, membership of the system is vital to all states and comes at a price. Even the stronger need recognition in the system and some rules against tyrannies of the weak or other competing strong states. In an interconnected system, by definition, the strongest state is not strong enough to dominate all other states and needs membership, ie help from all or most other states. Help may come from imports of certain desirable goods or services, military alliances, support in an international institution, etc. This

[151] Poggi (1990) (n 90 above) 83–4, stating that the states system 'only exists as the product of the self-activating, self-interested interactions of its constituent units . . . This essential, constitutive feature of the modern states system . . . imparts to the modern states system a particular turbulence and restlessness, and a potential destructiveness'.

[152] cf Bull (n 53 above) 16.

[153] M Finnemore, *National Interests in International Society* (New York: Cornell University Press, 1996) 5–6, arguing from a constructivist perspective (Ch 2 above, n 13) that the system 'changes state action, not by constraining states with a given set of preferences from acting, but by changing their preferences'.

means that within the system even strong states are vulnerable, at least to some extent, and eager to obey the rules when their vulnerability can be protected with the assistance of others.

Thirdly, in a system observance of the rules common to all is often far more profitable than violations. States generally have a strong interest in safeguarding their reputation as reliable partners. True, the stronger may decide to breach the law when in their calculations the reputational cost is lower than the benefit from the breach, an attitude that is precluded to the weaker, but breaches necessarily constitute exceptions even for the stronger. No state within the system can afford to breach the law at its pleasure and with no costs. It is in the nature of the system to generate costs for deviant behaviour.[154]

Fourthly, breaches of law in a system have a cost not only for the injured party, but also (often especially) for other states. As in a small village, all states generally know what other states do and are well aware of their compliance record. States avoid breaking the law whenever possible so as not to be burdened by the inevitable costs which will flow from the fact that the breach will become immediately known to all states. It may be that other states are impotent to react and compel the transgressor to observe the law in particular instances, but the knowledge they acquire of the breach will automatically produce adverse effects that the transgressor would well do without if it could. As a result, any mechanism in the system capable of making state behaviour known worldwide—for example through NGOs and the media—is essential to channel state behaviour into compliance with the law.

Fifthly, breaches of international law within the system also generate costs and other problems *within* states. In democratic states voters may penalize rulers for the breach of international law and all the costs flowing from such a breach. Voters may have little interest in foreign affairs, as is often noted, but the internal repercussions of foreign policy and their partial attribution to the critical reaction of the international community to a manifest breach of international law may be relevant. Even in undemocratic states these costs may have an impact, if only because to stay in power tyrants need the support (or at least the tolerance) of the global community. Domestic law often takes note that the state is an integral part of a wider system of states and makes provision that international law must be applied.[155] There is clearly a fear that state officials could unjustifiably undermine the state by isolating it within the system.

Finally, states tend to observe even rules they do not want in order to have other rules they want observed by others. There is a connection between different rules, and the state system tends to translate into international law as a rule system. If a strong state breaks a rule, no sanction may follow, but other states will be suspicious from then on also in regard to other rules they value more, and the transgressor may thereafter find it more difficult to have them observe other rules it especially values.

(b) Injustice

A state-centric world governed by the states system is historically a product of injustice since it has been imposed by Europe on all other peoples, displacing their forms of

[154] For the 'high cost of America's post-September 11 international law violations', see ME O'Connell, 'Crying War' in TJ Biersteckcr, PJ Spiro, CL Sriram, and V Raffo (eds), *International Law and International Relations: Bridging Theory and Practice* (London and New York: Routledge, 2007) 93, 103–4.

[155] See Ch 6 below, section D (2).

social order and lifestyle.[156] Few European states have dispossessed and embedded peoples, tribes, and other human associations within their structures in the colonial enterprise. Many aboriginal peoples have remained *encased* in, and subjected to, one or another state, while a number of colonized peoples have attained 'independence' by becoming *states* under the principle of self-determination.[157] The former have been forced to lose their natural freedom and to obey the encasing state; the latter have been forced to become a state and adjust their original lifestyle to this alien structure. Both have arguably lost their distinctive character for the sake of a more easily governable and more rational global order imagined and built by the European powers for the benefit of those powers. The reasons for the European expansion were exemplarily described by John Westlake when he observed that 'When people of the European race come into contact with American or African tribes, the prime necessity is a government under the protection of which the former may carry on the complex life to which they have been accustomed in their homes'.[158] Tribal peoples have never been asked whether they wished to be transformed into a European-style government to ensure security to the Europeans who had decided to travel and stay there, nor has their own social order ever been thought to expand to Europe. The state was considered the 'most advanced' form of political organization and 'civilization' that all peoples on earth were supposed to adopt by a sort of 'catching up' effort.[159]

Once embedded in a state or once having attained statehood, non-Western peoples become part of the global states system and are pressed to meet all the requirements of membership, such as, today, the protection of human rights and democracy. There is no option to exit the states system, nor is there any room on earth left for social organizations other than states to live 'out of the global' dimension. Even those who would like not to live 'globalized' are compelled to do so. There can be no vacuum of power on earth, all humankind must be subjected to one or another state, and all states must be able to rely on others in their ability to carry out what are regarded as the 'typical' functions of a state. Traditional practices at odds with human rights, for example, appear objectively intolerable, while they could be seen as 'physiological' in their original local context and surrounding world environment. The system cannot tolerate 'dysfunctional' states. Once in place, the system needs trust among all its members, hence their basic homogeneity. When a member does not live up to the expectations of all the others, the system necessarily must react for the common good. In so doing, the system seeks to ensure efficiency and justice within itself by limiting the freedom of action of its members on the basis of common rules applying in principle equally to all members. In practice, however, dysfunctional behaviour is far more likely

[156] H Rae, *State Identities and the Homogenisation of Peoples* (Cambridge: CUP, 2002). For the devastation and genocidal practices of the early European contact with non-European peoples in Latin America, see eg D Batstone, *From Conquest to Struggle: Jesus of Nazareth in Latin America* (Albany: State University of New York Press, 1991). See further B Kiernan, *Blood and Soil: A World History of Genocide and Extermination from Sparta to Darfur* (New Haven and London: Yale University Press, 2007)

[157] See section C (4)(c) below.

[158] Westlake (n 145 above) 141–3.

[159] Francisco Vitoria adumbrated that the Indians might be 'unfit to found and administer a lawful State up to the standard required by human and civil claims' but did not 'dare' to either affirm or condemn it. See F de Vitoria, *De Indis et De Jure Belli Relectiones* [1539] (Washington, DC: Carnegie Institution of Washington, 1917) 160–1. In *Leviathan* [1651], I, 13, Thomas Hobbes stated, more explicitly, that 'the savage people in many places of America, except the government of small Families, . . . have no government at all; and live at this day in that brutish manner' with 'no common Power to feare'.

in those members that have been forced to become states regardless of their original features based on geographical morphology, local climate, etc. Collective reactions by the system may reflect justice within the system itself, yet they find fault with peoples that prove incapable (or less capable than others) of being a state after statehood has being imposed on them. The problem is not with the state in itself, but with the system of states as a global, rational project to bring all humanity under control.

A struggle for justice should pursue not only justice *within* the system but also the justice *of* the system itself. Most intra-system inequities are ultimately based on the injustice of the global, all-encompassing states system. Hence the stress on non-state actors, subsidiarity, and pluralism, in the global governance debate as participation in the global decision-making process beside and beyond statehood. The debate is often inspired by human rights as demands for justice but human rights pursue justice *within* the system and do not dare to challenge the very states system itself. However, there is no way to go back to the past (for instance as a world of tribes) and there is no viable political alternative to the state for the imminent future. The struggle for the justice of the system itself is rather difficult and uncertain for a variety of reasons: the process of state globalization is, at this stage, hardly reversible to the modern pre-statehood status (given the size and density of world population, the human interconnectedness of cyberspace, etc) and today it is not possible for any people to live without participating in the states system in one way or another; existing states are not willing to create a new global system based on structures other than states, especially those which most gain therefrom, notably the great powers; critics of the present-day system *as such* will presumably be seen and fought as 'global terrorists' who threaten the order and justice that the system secures; the struggle for the justice of the system is a leap in the dark, as long as there is no credible substitute in sight; non-state actors remain fully dependent on, and presuppose, states in many respects; subsidiarity and pluralism are, once again, thought of in global terms, while 'genuine' pluralism is diversity not embedded in any global project aimed at regulating the autonomy of the local; and even tribal and indigenous peoples might now be reluctant to abandon the states system.

The short- and medium-term justice under the circumstances is *within* the states system, although the injustice of the system itself should always be given due weight in order for the root causes of intra-systemic injustice to be identified and better remedies devised.[160] In this sense, international law as the law of the globalized states system can be credited as a law which ensures *justice within the system*, although it is historically the product of injustice and perpetuates this broader sense of injustice by forcing all peoples on earth to adjust to a system (at least initially) congenial to others. Non-state actors, far from challenging the states system itself, in fact take for granted and operate within the states system.

(c) Inability

Today the state is often said to be weakening as a result, inter alia, of political denationalization,[161] institutional disaggregation,[162] and economic globalization.[163]

[160] B Rajagopal, *International Law from Below: Development, Social Movements and Third World Resistance* (Cambridge: CUP, 2003) 189–94.

[161] M Horsman and A Marshall, *After the Nation State: Citizens, Tribalism and the New World Disorder* (London: Harper Collins, 1994) 23.

[162] Slaughter (n 18 above).

[163] S Strange, *The Retreat of the State: The Diffusion of Power in the World Economy* (Cambridge: CUP, 1996).

After the end of the Cold War, some observers declared the 'end of the nation-state',[164] soon opposed by others who replied that states were well and safe and just transforming.[165] Most states can sufficiently control people or goods within their territory but are increasingly unable to control cross-border flows of information, capital, pollution, terrorism, organized crime, drug trade, currency crises, AIDS, and other diseases.

The state's power to control national macro-economic policy—including taxation, industrial policy seeking to have an impact on corporate strategies, monetary policy—is drastically diminished. A global economy coincides with an open marketplace free of institutional or locational constrains and the displacement of national networks by transnational economic networks. National measures can be bypassed by simply moving elsewhere. International decision-making, especially from the WTO and financial institutions, affects domestic legal systems and constitutionally protected rights, and reduces the ability of the state to protect welfare rights. Human rights tend to weaken the sense of 'nationality' and allegiance towards one's own state in favour either of cosmopolitanism or of local empowerment of ethnic groups, indigenous peoples, and other identity formations—hence claims to federalism, self-government, self-determination within existing states potentially leading to their dissolution. It is difficult for states to retain their authority in such conditions. Further, international human rights courts' and court-like institutions' decision-making penetrates domestic legal systems, affects national constitutions, and provokes a deconstitutionalization of states. The global environment is in need of global action and here too national measures can easily be bypassed by moving and polluting elsewhere, yet states are reluctant to agree on effective common rules and then to comply with them. Even where a number of states are capable of managing the environment within their jurisdiction, a few others unable or unwilling to do so may cause global environmental problems. Finally, information technology has created a borderless virtual space which it is hard (albeit not impossible) for states to control. True, events occurring in cyberspace can be traced to physical space and subjected to the physical jurisdiction of one or another state, or more states, but no individual state, however powerful, can ultimately affect the global interconnectedness achieved through the internet. Censorship or measures protective of copyright introduced by one state can, here again, relatively easily be bypassed through other states and channels.

In the globalized world the state still retains jurisdiction but is also compelled to be efficient and to compete with all other public and private actors. It is subjected, on a par with private businesses, to efficiency and solvency ratings developed by private businesses. There has always been a close tie between the globalization of statehood and economic capitalistic globalization carried out by states.[166] The very birth and consolidation of states has been made possible by the accumulation of capital and wealth, as attested, inter alia, by the innumerable studies on the 'wealth of nations' (or, perhaps more accurately, on how to increase the wealth of one's own nation) in Western European modern history which saw the confrontation between mercantilist, physiocratic, and free-market economic theories. In this sense, the state has always been an actor in the marketplace and there is little novelty in present-day globalization; or, to put it differently, economic globalization is—far from being an economic drive

[164] See eg K Ohmae, *The Borderless World: Power and Strategy in the Interlinked Economy* [1991] (New York: HarperCollins Publishers, 1999 rev edn); K Ohmae, *The End of the Nation-State: The Rise of Regional Economies* (New York: Simon and Schuster Inc, 1995).

[165] See eg L Weiss, *The Myth of the Powerless State* (Ithaca, NY: Cornell University Press, 1998).

[166] Tilly (n 89 above) 16–20.

dominating politics and states, as is routinely depicted by neo-liberals—nothing more than a by-product of the (political, Western) globalization of the state. While outsourcing 'public' functions to private actors, such as MNEs and NGOs, states themselves seem increasingly to be operating in the system as private actors in that they provide 'services'—limited to the 'typical' core state services such as legislation, adjudication, and enforcement—on the same footing (and possibly in competition) with all other economic actors, managing to sell their 'brand'.[167] One may even ask whether the state is changing into a 'mere' service provider like any other working in the global marketplace according to corporate standards. States' competitiveness is increasingly crucial to their survival and wealth.[168] States, and notably politicians, use advertisement and communication strategies like any MNE and seek to sell political services to voters.[169] They are also being forced more and more to migrate to the internet in order to be more competitive in a world in which most people (including businesses, scholars, purchasers, and voters) are pressed to move thereto as well.

Critics reply that states retain centrality in the system since all non-state actors are dependent on both individual states and the states system as a whole. National policies are deemed to remain viable, indeed essential, since the state retains a pivotal, if changing, role. It is noted that globalization has been advanced by states, although to a different degree depending on the state, and states have exhibited considerable adaptability and a variety of responses to face it. The idea of a 'powerless state' has been dismissed as a myth.[170] It is presumably aimed at persuading people that neo-liberal policies are both inevitable (according to Margaret Thatcher's famous slogan 'there is no alternative', or 'TINA', later to be endorsed by the WTO)[171] and irreversible (there is no way back to the state-centred past). It has been contested, however, that states are really unable to control MNEs;[172] and the irreversibility of the globalization process is doubtful, if not suspect, from a historical perspective.[173] It is not 'states'

[167] See S Anholt, *Competitive Identity: The New Brand Management for Nations, Cities and Regions* (Houndmills: Palgrave Macmillan, 2007); J Yan, 'Branding and the International Community' (2003) 10 JBM 447; G Szondi, *Public Diplomacy and Nation Branding: Conceptual Similarities and Differences* (The Hague: Netherlands Institute of International Relations, 2008); K Dinnie (ed), *Nation Branding: Concepts, Issues, Practice* (Oxford: Butterworth-Heinemann, 2008); K Dinnie, 'The Impact on Country Image of the North Africa and Middle East Uprisings' (2011) 6 PBPD 79. For the measure of states' 'image' or 'brand' on the market, see <http://en.wikipedia.org/wiki/Nation_ Brands_Index# Nation_Brands_Index>.

[168] In the 2010 World Economic Forum's competitive rankings, based on the Global Competitiveness Index (GCI), based in turn on 12 pillars of competitiveness (institutions, infrastructure, macroeconomic environment, health and primary education, higher education and training, goods market efficiency, labour market efficiency, financial market development, technological readiness, market size, business sophistication, and innovation), Switzerland is ranked first. The WEF's 2010 rankings are at <http://www.weforum.org/issues/global-competitiveness>. Other indices of state competitiveness are those resulting from credit rating agencies (CRAs), such as Standard & Poor's, Moody's Investor Service, and Fitch Ratings (see further n 345 below).

[169] C Leys, *Market Driven Politics: Neoliberal Democracy and the Public Interest* (London: Verso, 2001).

[170] See n 165 above.

[171] WTO, '10 Benefits of the WTO Trading System', at <http://www.wto.org/english/res_e/doload_e/10b_e.pdf>, 9–10.

[172] See eg Chang (n 35 above) 98–100. For the impact on states and global governance of CRAs, see n 345 below.

[173] R Findlay and KH O'Rourke, *Power and Plenty: Trade, War, and the World Economy in the Second Millennium* (Princeton and Oxford: Princeton University Press, 2007) 535. For the view that globalization is a cyclical phenomenon, hence 'not inevitable, and also quite reversible', see DJ Bederman, *Globalization and International Law* (New York: Palgrave Macmillan, 2008) at x (see in addition n 194 below and accompanying text).

generally understood, as is routinely claimed, but *certain* states that find globalization profitable or disastrous. While some states are stronger as a result of globalization, others are certainly weaker, and for a few others globalization may be fatal and decisively contribute to their failure. Moreover, what especially matters, in addition to *state* winners and losers, are the domestic redistributive effects of globalization, ie who gains and who loses *within* each state. It is of course in the interest of those who gain that the push towards the globalization in the policies of their states comes first and foremost. It is they who seek to picture globalization, together with 'less state', as an inevitable and irreversible process driven by economic laws and technological progress.[174] In reverse, it is (or it should be) in the interest of those who lose from globalization within each state to picture the same process as neither inevitable nor irreversible and as being *more than ever* under the full control of politics and the state, or, more accurately, the stronger states. Thus seen, globalization is simply the covert *political* strategy (although overtly presented as apolitical or even anti-political so as to conceal the true winners) of those (individual, groups, and states) who most gain from it to the detriment of those who lose, nothing more than the strategy of the stronger at both intra- and inter-state level to retain, and possibly increase, their power and wealth.[175]

It is the states system, rather than 'the' state, that is increasingly under strain. The system is premised on the ability of states sufficiently to coordinate themselves, and to make and observe common rules. This presupposes adequate homogeneity and common understanding among states. However, while homogeneity has been attained at the level of political organization by globalizing statehood, with decolonization state heterogeneity has increased and the current need for competition leads states to pursue as much profit as possible. Global problems cannot be solved unless *all* states converge on common rules which establish a threshold to be observed in any circumstances. But failing a world authority capable of imposing rules and compliance therewith on states from above, states remain at liberty to accept or reject rules. If a world government is undesired and/or unfeasible, global convergence is rather difficult and in most cases proves impossible. The system is thus unable to manage the world, unless the people of the world request it to work differently.

(4) Jurisdiction

The peculiarity of statehood is jurisdiction. Deriving from the Latin *iurisdictio* used by medieval jurists, jurisdiction is broadly understood as the power to make, adjudicate, and enforce legal rules.[176] In the sense of *jus dicere*, or adjudication, jurisdiction is thus only one aspect of state jurisdiction as a whole. No other international player, even when stronger than a state in terms of capacity to influence international relations or in terms of budgetary resources, can, or claims to, exercise jurisdiction over people. All non-state global actors presuppose states and their legislatures, courts, and enforcement organs. The states system is structured to ensure that state jurisdiction is exercised in

[174] For a critique of the neo-liberal conception of the state, see R Plant, *The Neo-liberal State* (Oxford and New York: OUP, 2009); D Harvey, *A Brief History of Neoliberalism* (Oxford and New York: OUP, 2007).

[175] For a recent discussion on the preservation of states' centrality and diversity in a sustainable, 'moderate' globalization to turn to in the future, see D Rodrik, *The Globalization Paradox: Why Global Markets, States, and Democracy Can't Coexist* (Oxford and New York: OUP, 2011).

[176] *Restatement of the Law, Third, Foreign Relations Law of the United States* (n 104 above) vol 1, 230, § 401.

such a partitioned way that all persons, wherever they are, fall within the authority of at least one state and can be held responsible for their behaviour before state organs. Only in a world in which all persons are under the jurisdiction of one or another state, failing a world government, can all persons be protected. Pirates have been regarded as 'enemies of humankind' (*hostes humani generis*) precisely because they do not fall within the jurisdiction of one or another state and undermine all other human beings. This section briefly discusses the legal allocation of jurisdiction and its spatial delimitation among states. It argues that globalism and statism are not necessarily at odds with each other. States remain central to the system as they continue vitally to ensure some 'law and order' on a global level.

(a) Allocation

In the current states system the exercise of state jurisdiction is basically spatial.[177] In principle, each state exercises its jurisdiction within its borders over people and resources by enacting laws, delivering judicial decisions, and enforcing both laws and judicial decisions. State jurisdiction is allocated among all states. While the jurisdiction to enforce is exclusive and cannot be exercised on the territory of another state without its consent,[178] the jurisdiction to prescribe and the jurisdiction to adjudicate can occasionally be exercised even when it produces effects on the territory of other states. This system implies mutual trust among states, since any state is confident that, at a least on average, other states will be able and willing to enforce laws and judicial decisions in their territory, thereby ensuring that their territory is not used by individuals to do harm elsewhere in the territory of other states.[179] The jurisdiction to prescribe is allocated according to territoriality, personality, and security. Exceptionally it may extend to all states when piracy and international crimes are involved.[180]

For a variety of reasons, including expediency and effectiveness, states do not usually enact laws that apply to all human beings living on earth wherever they are and whatever their nationality, nor do they prescribe the exercise of adjudicative jurisdiction by their courts to everyone under any circumstances. In particular, states do not exercise legislative and adjudicative jurisdiction over aliens when they do not want other states to do the same towards their own citizens. This has brought about a relatively stable equilibrium in terms of the 'allocation' of state jurisdiction among all states. In principle, each state is allowed to make laws applicable to persons, goods, and events in its territory or on board its ships and aircraft. States do not usually apply their laws to aliens to the same extent as to their citizens, but exempt aliens from the laws that they do not want other states to apply to their own citizens abroad. For example, military service, or taxes unjustified by commercial or professional activities carried out in the territory of the receiving state are generally not imposed on aliens. Although territoriality is an efficient criterion for the partitioned protection of people worldwide in the absence of a universal sovereign, it is uncertain what law applies to an event that

[177] See FA Mann, 'The Doctrine of Jurisdiction in International Law' (1964) 111 RdC 1; FA Mann, 'The Doctrine of International Jurisdiction Revisited After Twenty Years' (1984) 186 RdC 9; WM Reisman (ed), *Jurisdiction in International Law* (Aldershot: Ashgate, 1999); C Ryngaert, *Jurisdiction in International Law* (Oxford: OUP, 2008).

[178] PCIJ, *The Case of the SS Lotus* (n 1 above) 23.

[179] See Ch 7 below, section A (4)(b).

[180] See note 280 below, Ch 7 below, section A (2)(c), and Ch 8 below, section B (1)(b).

takes place in more than one state, such as an explosion on a train occurring in one place due to a bomb loaded aboard the train in another state. Both the state in which the bomb has been loaded aboard the train and the state on whose territory the bomb has exploded generally claim legislative and adjudicating jurisdiction and legal proceedings may be brought in their courts. Exceptionally states have claimed jurisdiction over events that occurred entirely in another state, or in any case outside their territory, but produced direct and unlawful effects within their territory, either on their citizens or markets, especially in criminal and antitrust matters.[181] This 'extra-territorial' application of legislation has been contested,[182] although it may prove useful in certain circumstances to cope with common values (notably with anti-competitive practices abroad keeping prices high to the detriment of consumers).[183] Today 'cyberspace' is a problem since, in principle, any act carried out therein produces immediate effects worldwide, save where filtering devices and bans are in place, and justifies the jurisdiction of all states. The trend in domestic courts is to apply the traditional principle of territoriality, with adjustments inspired by the effect doctrine.[184]

However, many people and their goods usually move from one state to another, if only for commerce. States tend to 'follow' their citizens when going abroad and apply their laws to them, especially when they are the perpetrators of wrongs, although at the same time their citizens instantly fall within the legislative reach of the territorial state when they enter another state. If the two legislations are incompatible, people may find themselves forced to breach either one or another law. States prefer to retain full control over anyone, including aliens, found in their territory at the price of 'losing' control of their nationals when they are victims of wrongs abroad. This confirms that the current global states system gives more weight to spatial than to personal links. However, jurisdiction based on passive personality has often been invoked against terrorism, due to the reluctance of territorial states to prosecute perpetrators and award damages, and is generally envisaged in anti-terrorism treaties.[185] Occasionally, states have claimed

[181] The effects doctrine was first adopted by the US Court of Appeals for the Second Circuit, *United States v Aluminium Co of America* Judgment of 12 March 1945, 148 F 2d 416, 796. holding that it was 'well-established by now that the [US] Sherman Act [1890] applies to foreign conduct that was meant to produce and did in fact produce some substantial effect in the United States'. The doctrine has been cautiously endorsed in *Restatement of the Law, Third, Foreign Relations Law of the United States* (n 104 above) vol 1, §§ 402(1)(c) and 415, only when the effects are 'substantial' and jurisdiction is not 'unreasonable' (which implies some 'balancing' of the factors and interests involved). The UE Commission too has upheld the doctrine in anti-trust matters, but the ECJ seems to prefer the somewhat different 'implementation test' which gives weight to the place where the anti-competitive practice is implemented (cf ECJ, *Åhlström Osakeyhtiö et al v Commission of the European Communities* Judgment of 27 September 1988, Case 89/85, [1988] ECR 5193, paras 16–18. The ambiguity of the UE policy results, inter alia, from the strong reaction against the application of the doctrine by the US, as for example was the case with Council Regulation 2271/96 of 22 November 1996 (see [1996] OJ L309/).

[182] See eg District Court of The Hague, *Compagnie Européenne des Petroles v Sensor Nederland* Judgment of 17 September 1982, (1983) 22 ILM 66, para 7.3.4. In the Note of 27 July 1978 No 196 to the US Department of State, the UK observed that 'in the present state of international law there is no basis for the extension of one country's antitrust jurisdiction to activities outside that country by foreign nationals' (1978) 49 BYBIL 390.

[183] cf R Higgins, *Problems and Process: International Law and How we Use it* (Oxford: Clarendon Press, 1994) 77.

[184] See M Hayashi, 'The Information Revolution and the Rules of Jurisdiction in Public International Law' in M Dunn, SF Krishna-Hensel, and V Mauer (eds), *The Resurgence of the State: Trends and Processes in Cyberspace Governance* (Haldershot: Ashgate, 2007) 59–83.

[185] cf Higgins (n 183 above) 66.

jurisdiction based on the nationality of goods, or parts thereof, rather than of people, raising protests by other states.[186]

States also claim to exercise jurisdiction over persons, goods, or events found or occurring outside of their territory for the 'protection' of their 'vital interests'.[187] What should be meant by 'vital interests' is uncertain, but it seems reasonable that they are limited to the security and credibility of the state and do not extend to any interest pertaining to its foreign policy.[188]

(b) Spaces

The globe is 'mapped' according to a complex grid of legal lines (both 'horizontal' on the planisphere and 'vertical' moving upwards from the planet) and 'spaces' encased therein which divide the jurisdiction of states as regulated by international law. This being the outcome of historical development, there is no inevitability in this sort of world legal regulation and one should marvel at this, for good or ill, rather than taking it for granted, as is usually the case. Although the single 'lines' are occasionally defied, no doubt the grid as a whole is respected and works in day-to-day global business, preventing global chaos. Just a cursory look at the whole is sufficient for present purposes.

The *land*—with the exception of Antarctica—is virtually entirely ruled by states and partitioned along their (linear) borders, although some of the latter are disputed or difficult to assign to one particular state. States can exercise all their powers on land within their borders unless this is prohibited by international law. While certain borders or territories may be disputed, overall the planet appears sufficiently ordained. Trains, aircraft, merchandise, and people constantly travel with relative certainty within the global states system. The *sea* is unavailable to human settlement and subject to different legal regimes. The greater portion of the sea (the high seas) is 'international', ie not subject to the jurisdiction of any individual state. States retain control over areas of sea adjacent to their coasts for different purposes depending on the area, and with less and less intensity as one moves farther from their coasts. The territorial sea, extending up to 12 nautical miles from the baseline, is subject to their full jurisdiction regardless of effectiveness, except for innocent passage and jurisdictional immunity of foreign ships. The contiguous and the archaeological zones extend up to 24 nautical miles from the baseline, providing coastal states with limited, functional powers for the prevention and punishment of any infringement of their customs, fiscal, immigration, or sanitary regulations within their territory or territorial sea, or for the recovery of objects of an archaeological and historical nature found at sea. Other areas, such as the continental shelf and the exclusive economic zone (EEZ) extend up to 200 nautical miles from the baseline, or (the former) even more under certain conditions, providing coastal states with 'sovereign rights' (as distinct from sovereignty as such) over the exploitation of natural resources. Other new, legally uncertain areas, such as the ecological zone, have been instituted by some states of late.[189] Finally, beyond all these areas the sea is left to

[186] District Court of The Hague, *Compagnie Européenne des Petroles v Sensor Nederland* (n 182 above) para 7.3.2.

[187] See eg District Court of Jerusalem, *Attorney-General of the Government of Israel v Adolf Eichmann* Judgment of 12 December 1961, (1962) 36 ILR 5, para 30.

[188] District Court of The Hague, *Compagnie Européenne des Petroles v Sensor Nederland* (n 182 above) para 7.3.3.

[189] A Del Vecchio, 'In maiore stat minus: A Note on the EEZ and the Zones of Ecological Protection in the Mediterranean Sea' (2008) 39 ODIL 287–97.

freedom as regards the use of the water but subject to an international regime as to the exploitation of natural resources. The *airspace* above the territory and the territorial sea of each state is subjected to the state's full sovereignty, while the airspace above all other land spaces is left to freedom of use, with the exception of Air Defence Identification Zones (ADIZs), which allow coastal states to take measures against approaching foreign aircraft even in the international airspace on national security grounds. *Outer space* is left to freedom of use, whether 'above' a state or international land and sea spaces. Jurisdiction and control over a space object, and over any personnel thereof, while in outer space or on a celestial body is (under Article VIII Outer Space Treaty) retained by the state party 'on whose registry [the] object [is] launched'.[190] Finally, in *Antarctica* there is an international regime providing for the jurisdiction of national states.[191]

(c) *Global values*

The concept of state jurisdiction is today strongly criticized by globalists and humanitarians as an expression of state sovereignty understood as brute coercion and of the state-centred 'Westphalian' system.[192] Likewise, the 'old' Westphalian international law is under attack as a mere 'inter-jurisdiction' law, ie 'as a law governing interstate relations by delimiting their jurisdictions'. It is claimed that 'the new world order... must move beyond the idea of the state',[193] or a law which is confined to allocate (basically) spatially (state) power on earth,[194] rather than a personal and value- or justice-based law. The jurisdictional world 'grid' devised in early European history and governed by international law through the allocation of state power across the world is said to be merely limited to the 'co-existence' of states without any regard to cooperation and solidarity,[195] uncommitted as such to how states and state officials should exercise jurisdiction. States are increasingly seen as being 'not ends in themselves, but merely instrumental for the rights and needs of individuals'.[196] State sovereignty, once unbound, is now thought to be 'legalized', ie 'defined by international law', notably by the ban on the use of force and the protection of human rights.

This view is certainly correct in depicting as 'old' the international law of the past which did not bind the behaviour of rulers and state officials towards people's

190 Art VIII Treaty on Principles Governing the Activities of States in the Exploration and Use of Outer Space, Including the Moon and Other Celestial Bodies (signed 27 January 1967, entered into force 10 October 1967) 610 UNTS 205. Similarly, cf Art 12(1) Agreement Governing the Activities of States on the Moon and Other Celestial Bodies (adopted 5 December 1979, entered into force 11 July 1984) 1363 UNTS 3.

191 Art VIII Antarctic Treaty (signed 1 December 1959, entered into force 23 June 1961) 402 UNTS 71. In *Smith v United States* Judgment of 8 March 1993, 507 US 197, 201, the US Supreme Court equated Antarctica with a 'foreign country', even though Antarctica has no recognized government, for the purposes of the application of the Federal Tort Claims Act (FTCA).

192 Globalists and humanitarians often refer to global justice studies, on which see the essays collected by T Pogge and D Moellendorf (eds), *Global Justice: Seminal Essays* (St Paul: Paragon House, 2008) vol 1.

193 cf R Domingo, *The New Global Law* (Cambridge: CUP, 2010) 39, 41.

194 See eg CW Jenks, *The Common Law of Mankind* (London, Stevens & Sons, 1958) 2; HJ Berman, 'World Law' (1995) 18 Ford ILJ 1617; HJ Berman, 'World Law: An Ecumenical Jurisprudence of the Holy Spirit', Emory Public Law Research Paper No 05–4 (February 2005), at <http://papers.ssrn.com/sol3/papers.cfm?abstract_id=666143>. For a historical, sceptical account of the relationship between international law and legal globalism, see Bederman (n 173 above).

195 This terminology, recurrently repeated, dates back to W Friedmann, *The Changing Structure of International Law* (London: Stevens and Sons, 1964) 60–1.

196 See eg J Klabbers, A Peters, and G Ulfstein, *The Constitutionalization of International Law* (Oxford: OUP, 2009) 179–201.

behaviour within the state, but only dealt with the external relations of the state with other states. It does not follow, however, that state jurisdiction is an 'old' concept which has nothing to do with the needs and values of individuals. States have always served the interests and values of individuals.[197] State sovereignty was originally thought to protect people, both within and outside the state.[198] States have outplayed their competitors since their inception as better providers of security and welfare to individuals. On the other hand, it is precisely this perceived virtue of the state that has inspired the notion that statehood is a sign of civilization and a 'point of arrival' for non-Western peoples through an ethnocentric vision of what should count as the 'well-being' to be secured.[199] Sovereignty has also always been defined by international law.[200] The *point* is that today sovereignty is extensively limited by rules governing how state power is to be exercised by states within their jurisdiction towards *any individual* who is there, including of course their own citizens. It is still state jurisdiction, after all, that ensures the observance and enforcement of international law, including the (apparently pro-non-state or even counter-state) rules on human rights, and in particular the duty to protect people within it, ie the values allegedly pointing to global values.[201] This confusion leads many today to fault 'strong' states and sovereignty while at the same time shouldering states with duties of every sort concerning the protection of people, a rather schizophrenic approach—resembling what has been termed the 'double bind' in psychology[202]—capable of resulting in impotence, lack of protection, and chaos.

C. Non-state Players

While states exercise jurisdiction based on political legitimacy worldwide in a partitioned way, non-state players compete with, and influence, state behaviour.[203] This section explores non-state actors by dividing them into five categories: supra-state

[197] cf T Hobbes, *Leviathan* [1651], II, 30, observing that 'The Office of the Soveraign, (be it a Monarch, or an Assembly,) consisteth in the end, for which he was trusted with the Soveraign Power, namely the procuration of the Safety of the People' and pointing out that 'by Safety here, is not meant a bare Preservation, but also all other Contentments of life, which every man by lawfull Industry, without danger, or hurt to the Common-wealth, shall acquire to himselfe'. See futher E de Vattel, *Droit des gens; ou, Principes de la loi naturelle appliqués à la conduite et aux affaires des nations et des souverains* [1758] (Boston: Adamant Media, 2001), English trans *The Law of Nations or the Principles of Natural Law Applied to the Conduct and to the Affairs of Nations and of Sovereigns* (Washington, DC: Carnegie Institution of Washington, 1916) 13, para 15, noting that the end of the 'perfect' state is 'to procure for its citizens the necessities, the comforts, and the pleasures of life, and in general their happiness; to secure to each the peaceful enjoyment of his property and a sure means of obtaining justice; and finally to defend the whole body against all external violence'.

[198] See Strayer (n 81 above) 10, noting that 'The state gave greater peace and security, more opportunity for the good life, than loose associations of communities'.

[199] See n 159 above and accompanying text.

[200] Bounds to sovereigns were accepted even by the theorists of the absolute state, including Jean Bodin, *Les six livres de la République* [1576] (Paris: Fayard, 1986) I, 8, arguing that sovereigns are 'sujets aux lois de Dieu, & de la nature, & à plusieurs lois humaines communes à tous les peuples'), English trans *On Sovereignty: Six Books of The Commonwealth*, at <http://www.constitution.org/bodin/bodin_.htm>; and T Hobbes, *Leviathan* [1651], II, 30 (n 197 above). For a theoretical discussion of sovereignty, see J Bartelson, *A Genealogy of Sovereignty* (Cambridge: CUP, 1995); TJ Bierstecker and C Weber, *State Sovereignty as Social Construct* (Cambridge: CUP, 1996); SD Krasner, *Sovereignty: Organized Hypocrisy* (Princeton: Princeton University Press, 1999).

[201] See Ch 7 below, section A (2)(d).

[202] See Ch 7 below, n 333.

[203] See, recently, J D'Aspremont (ed), *Participants in the International Legal System: Multiple Perspectives on Non-state Actors in International Law* (London: Routledge, 2011).

players (international organizations), sub-state players (individuals), trans-state players (non-governmental organizations and multinational enterprises), counter-state players (insurgents and terrorists, peoples fighting for self-determination, indigenous peoples and minorities), and *sui generis* players (Holy See, Sovereign Military Order of Malta, and International Committee of the Red Cross). It is argued that non-state players, far from eroding or displacing states, presuppose and need them, and aspirations regarding their ability to oversee states' behaviour raise the question of 'who will guard the guardians themselves'.[204] Yet they play, and should play, a major role in pushing towards overcoming the inequities and the inability of the states system to manage global problems.

(1) International organizations (IOs)

The states system seeks to ensure the co-existence of all human beings living on earth by mutually coordinating their partitioned authority. Coordination may take place in a variety of forms (including bilateral negotiations, and multilateral conferences) which can go as far as establishing organized associations of states called 'international organizations' (IOs). The constituent instrument, whatever its official name and impact on global affairs, is no different from any other treaty.[205] While there is no universally agreed-upon definition of IOs,[206] there are a few unquestioned features of most entities regarded as IOs. As a rule IOs are created by an international treaty to which states and/or other IOs may be parties,[207] and operate through their own organs whose acts are attributed to the organization rather than to their member states, and in accordance with international law. These features distinguish them in theory from NGOs and MNEs, whose local affiliations or subsidiarities are created by an act of domestic law and are made up of private individuals or entities, as well as from international conferences, the acts of which are attributed to the organs of the participating states rather than to the conference as such, and from 'intergovernmental corporations of private

[204] Juvenal, *Satirae*, VI, 347–8 ('Sed quis custodiet ipsos custodies?').

[205] ICJ, *Legality of the Use by a State of Nuclear Weapons in Armed Conflict*, Advisory Opinion of 8 July 1996, [1996] ICJ Rep 66, para 19, stating that 'From a formal standpoint, the constituent instruments of international organizations are multilateral treaties, to which the well-established rules of treaty interpretation apply'. A number of founding treaties carry the official title of 'constitution', such as those of UNESCO, WHO, ILO, FAO, and ITU, without implying that they are different from any other treaty. The term 'constitution' is frequently used in the context of the EU, especially since the ECJ stated that 'the EEC Treaty, albeit concluded in the form of an international agreement, none the less constitutes the constitutional charter of a Community based on the rule of law' in its Opinion No 1/91 of 14 December 1991, *European Economic Area I*, [1991] ECR I-6079, para 21. Despite attempts to regard the WTO in constitutional terms, the WTO Appellate Body argued that the WTO Agreement is 'a treaty—the international equivalent of a contract' in WTO, *Japan—Taxes on Alcoholic Beverages*, AB Report of 4 October 1996, WT/DS8/AB/R, WT/DS10/AB/R, WT/DS11/AB/R, at 15. See Ch 4 above, nn 219–221.

[206] cf Art 2(1)(i) VCLT-IO, defining an IO as 'an intergovernmental organization', and Art 2 UN ILC 'Draft Articles on the Responsibility of International Organizations' adopted in 2011, at <http://untreaty.un.org/ilc/texts/instruments/english/draft%20articles/9_11_2011.pdf>, defining an IO as 'an organization established by a treaty or other instrument governed by international law and possessing its own international legal personality' which 'may include as members, in addition to States, other entities'. Both definitions are only for the purposes of the instruments which contain them and do not claim to necessarily state a general legal definition of IOs.

[207] Certain IOs are considered international organizations even though they have not been created by a formal treaty, such as the Organization for Security and Cooperation in Europe (OSCE) and the Arctic Council. The term 'soft' (reminiscent of 'soft law') referred to IOs has been often used in recent times. See J Klabbers, 'Institutional Ambivalence by Design: Soft Organizations in International Law' (2001) 70 Nord JIL 403.

law',[208] such as the Bank for International Settlements (BIS) and the European Company for the Financing of Railroad Rolling Stock (Eurofima), which were created by international treaty but are governed (apart from the founding treaty) by the domestic law of the host state.[209] Despite their strong dependence on states since their establishment, there is little doubt that by their policies and decision-making, covering today virtually every aspect of human life, IOs have become significant actors of global governance.[210]

(a) Autonomy

IOs are often said to be 'eroding' the traditional selfish attitude of states in the name of solidaristic values. It is a fact, however, that IOs presuppose states and depend on them. They are voluntarily created by states, persist in life as long as states so wish, and dissolve when their members states so decide.[211] IOs do not govern in principle any territorial community, as states do, nor do they enjoy any political support comparable to that which empowers states to rule. On the contrary, their 'democratic deficit' is frequently criticized, inter alia, in the European Union,[212] and also the dominant role played within them by great powers. There is neither 'separation of powers' nor appropriate 'checks and balances' between an IO's organs, let alone a relationship of 'confidence' and accountability between the plenary body (save for some control through its budgetary powers) and the executive body.[213] Not having a territory of their own in a world in which there is no space left for systems of rule other than states, IOs are compelled to establish their headquarters in the territory of one or another state with the ensuing, inevitable risks of being under its pressure. It is states that, as a rule, participate in IO's decision-making. When IOs engage in the 'administration' of a territory, as has recently been the case with the United Nations, they cannot but 'delegate' powers, which have in turn been delegated to them by the member states, to willing states, ie in practice to the states which have an interest in carrying out their mandate. Nor do IOs operate to change the current states system into one which is not centred on states. In the United Nations, only states may be admitted as members, only states may be parties in disputes before the ICJ, only representatives of states are

[208] See Brownlie (n 103 above) 66–7.

[209] On the BIS, see JF Williams, 'The Legal Character of the Bank for International Settlements' (1930) 24 AJIL 665; DJ Bederman, 'The Unique Legal Status of the Bank for International Settlements Comes into Focus' (2003) 16 LJIL 787. In *Dr Horst Reineccius, First Eagle SoGen Funds, Inc, Mr Pierre Mathier and La Société de Concours Hippique de la Châtre v Bank for International Settlements*, Partial Award of 22 November 2002, at <http://www.pca-cpa.org/showfile.asp?fil_id=415>, the PCA Arbitral Tribunal held that 'the essential international character of the Bank is apparent from its treaty origin', its functions 'were essentially public international in their character' (paras 108–114), and it was recognized as an international organization in three host country agreements (para 115). The Tribunal concluded that, although 'obviously, the Bank is not a state', it is 'a *sui generis* creation which is an international organization' (para 118) and 'thus, subject to international law' (para 172).

[210] See JE Alvarez, *International Organizations as Law-Makers* (Oxford: OUP, 2005). For IOs' decision-making, see Ch 6 above, section B (1)(c).

[211] C Martini, '"States" Control over New International Organization' (2006) 6 GJA 1.

[212] German Federal Constitutional Court, *Lisbon Treaty Case* Judgment of 30 June 2009, paras 264, 272, ILDC 1364 (DE 2009).

[213] ICTY, *Prosecutor v Tadić, Decision on the Defence Motion for Interlocutory Appeal on Jurisdiction*, Decision of 2 October 1995, Case No ICTY-94-1, para 43, noting that clearly 'the legislative, executive and judicial division of powers which is largely followed in most municipal systems does not apply to the international setting nor, more specifically, to the setting of an international organization such as the United Nations'.

granted places in the General Assembly and in the Security Council, only state-building is pursued when the international administration of territories is set up, and non-state actors are accorded rights of participation in discussion and decision-making to obtain, at best, rules made by states.

However, IOs do participate in global governance as relatively autonomous players capable of affecting state behaviour.[214] It would certainly be excessive to infer from their dependence on states, notably on great powers and on the states system as a whole, that they make no difference. While IOs are unquestionably dependent on their member states as a whole (*uti universi*), they generally succeed in affecting, to various degrees, the behaviour of their member states taken individually (*uti singuli*), including the stronger. It is from the viewpoint of any individual member state that one can perceive the impact of IOs on the behavior of the member states, not from that of the members states as a whole. In this sense, to argue that IOs 'depend' on member states is both true and false depending on whether member states are regarded as a whole or individually vis-à-vis the IO. In any event, the ability of IOs to impose their collective will on any individual member thereof suggests that IOs are 'supra-state' (and not merely 'inter-state') players. More specifically, IOs' autonomy is greater when: (a) their organs are made up of independent individuals; (b) they have the power to adopt legally binding resolutions; (c) which are adopted by majority; and (d) are given 'direct effect' within the legal systems of the member states; (e) their legality is scrutinized by a mechanism of judicial or quasi-judicial review capable of annulling them (or stating them to be inapplicable in the actual instance) if illegal; (f) membership and voting in the body having binding decision-making powers are based on equal weight; (g) at least one of their organs directly represents the peoples of the member states and has meaningful powers; (h) their functioning is funded by their 'own' resources; and (i) have their own 'legal order'.[215] The more an IO possesses these features, the greater its ability to evade the control of its member states. But, leaving aside the European Union,[216] all IOs, including the United Nations, lack one or more (if not all) of the above features. Most IOs are made up of governmental representatives, have no power to adopt binding resolutions, and when they do these resolutions are not given direct effect within the legal system of the member states, nor are they subject to judicial review,[217] no organ directly representing the peoples of the member states is envisaged,

[214] ICJ, *Legality of the Use by a State of Nuclear Weapons in Armed Conflict* (n 205 above) para 19, noting that the WHO is 'endowed with a certain autonomy'. Recently, see R Collins and ND White (eds), *International Organizations and the Idea of Autonomy: Institutional Independence in the International Legal Order* (Abingdon and New York: Routledge, 2011).

[215] For the EU, cf ECJ, *Van Gend en Loos v Netherlands Inland Revenue Administration* Judgment of 5 February 1963, Case No 26/62, [1963] ECR 1, 12.

[216] For the view that even in the EU the Member States remain the 'masters of the Treaties', see German Constitutional Court, Judgment of 30 June 2009 (n 212 above) para 231, 298, 334.

[217] A notable exception is the EU (Arts 263–4 TFEU). As regards the UN, in the 1992 *Lockerbie* Orders, the ICJ abstained from determining 'definitely the legal effect of Security Council resolution 748 (1992)': cf ICJ, *Questions of Interpretation and Application of the 1971 Montreal Convention arising from the Aerial Incident at Lockerbie (Libyan Arab Jamahiriya v United Kingdom) (Provisional Measures)*, Order of 14 April 1992, [1992] ICJ Rep 3, 15, para 40; *Questions of Interpretation and Application of the 1971 Montreal Convention arising from the Aerial Incident at Lockerbie (Libyan Arab Jamahiriya v United States)*, Order of 14 April 1992, [1992] ICJ Rep 114, 126, para 43. On the legality of acts within the UN, see B Conforti and C Focarelli, *The Law and Practice of the United Nations* (Leiden and Boston: Nijhoff, 4th rev edn, 2010) 422–9. In the 1995 *Tadić* Decision the ICTY denied its power to review the acts 'of the other organs of the United Nations, particularly those of the Security Council' (para 20), yet it proceeded to assess its proper establishment and concluded in the affirmative (paras 47–48) (n 213 above). Domestic courts might also assess the legality of IOs' binding decisions (Ch 6 below, section A (2)).

and their continuing existence depends on the financial contributions of the member states. Faced with these problems, today IOs are strongly engaged, within their administrative autonomy and the unregulated discretion left by their constituent treaties, in reaching out to as many people as possible, inter alia, by using visibility strategies in the media.[218]

(b) Personality

For international law purposes an IO exists as a legal entity distinct from its member states when it has international legal personality (ILP). The ILP of IOs is especially inferred by their capacity to make international treaties with member states (such as headquarters agreements and conventions on the privileges and immunities of the organization's personnel) and third states, including other IOs. It is commonly understood that such treaties are neither contracts of domestic law nor international treaties to which the states members of the IO, rather than the IO itself, are parties. The capacity of IOs to enter into treaties with states or other IOs is often set out in the founding treaty, or may be inferred impliedly by resorting to the 'implied powers' doctrine on an IO-by-IO basis.[219] IOs are also entitled to immunity from civil jurisdiction in domestic courts.[220] While unqualified autonomy is a matter of degree and depends on the various factors already examined, ILP is an on/off concept referring to the *legal* autonomy and distinctiveness of IOs.[221]

By laying a legal veil between IOs and their member states, ILP does enhance IOs' autonomy and ability to entertain legal relations with states and other IOs, but has the effect of exempting member states from their own obligations. Member states can 'transfer' to IOs some of their sovereign powers and let IOs do what states are not allowed to do. This process, far from 'eroding' state sovereignty in favour of IOs' more trustworthy powers, as is often enthusiastically claimed, actually widens states' (or, perhaps more accurately, certain states') freedom of action. Since IOs have no jurisdictional authority, they cannot but 'delegate' to states the implementation of their acts adopted in furtherance of the powers transferred to them by member states. Accountability is transferred to IOs only in theory because there are few mechanisms, if any, entrusted to hold IOs accountable, and when IOs are made to account the bill is paid by all member states and their peoples. The risk is that neither IOs nor their member states are held accountable and the outcome of the combined game is the total freedom of action of states.

While it was dismissed in the past, at a time when only states were regarded as international law subjects, the notion that IOs do possess ILP is currently popular. It was first explicitly affirmed by the Italian Court of Cassation in the 1931 *Profili* Judgment, referring to the International Institute for Agriculture, the predecessor of the FAO,[222] and soon reiterated by the same Court in 1935 in respect of the League of

[218] See Ch 4 above, section C (4).

[219] See Ch 6 below, section B (2)(c).

[220] See A Reinisch, *International Organizations Before National Courts* (Cambridge: CUP, 2000).

[221] See T Gazzini, 'The Relationship between International Legal Personality and Institutional Autonomy', in Collins and White (n 214 above) 196–212.

[222] Italian Court of Cassation, *International Institute for Agriculture v Profili* Judgment of 26 February 1931, (1935) ADRPILC Years 1929–30 (Case No 254) 413, 415. In this case, the Court of Appeal of Rome had dismissed the appeal by ruling, in the then traditional terms, that the International Institute for Agriculture 'was not a subject of international law seeing that it did not exercise sovereignty over a fixed territory and a population' and concluding that 'It therefore had not

Nations,[223] despite the acknowledgement that this organization 'is neither a State, nor a Super-State, nor a Confederation of States'.[224] As is well known, during the post-war period the ICJ has greatly contributed to the topic. In the 1949 *Reparation for Injuries* Advisory Opinion the Court affirmed the ILP of the United Nations without implying that the organization is either a state or a super-state, or that it had the same rights and duties as a state.[225] In the Court's view, the enjoyment of ILP meant that the United Nations was capable of possessing international rights and duties,[226] and no doubt: 'Fifty States, representing the vast majority of the members of the international community, had the power, in conformity with international law, to bring into being an entity possessing objective international personality, and not merely personality recognized by them alone'.[227] Along the same lines, the ECtHR, in the 2007 *Behrami* Decision, considered it 'clear that the UN has a legal personality separate from that of its member states', and as such that it was capable of being held accountable (instead of its member states) for violations of international law, in particular of human rights by its 'international presence' in Kosovo under the mandate of the UN Security Council.[228] In the 1980 *Interpretation of the WHO–Egypt Agreement* Advisory Opinion the Court went further, stating that: 'International organizations are subjects of international law and, as such, are bound by any obligations incumbent upon them under general rules of international law, under their constitutions or under international agreements to which they are parties'.[229] In the 1996 *Nuclear Weapons* Advisory Opinion the Court pointed out that 'international organizations are subjects of international law which do not, unlike States, possess a general competence', this justifying the principle of speciality.[230] Domestic courts also generally recognize the international personality of IOs to the extent of their official functions.[231]

the character of a State' enjoying jurisdictional immunity 'at least in regard to controversies with respect to which each of those States [which had created it] recognised in its own internal law the competence of its own tribunals'. The Court of Cassation responded that 'Following the better and more widely held doctrine', the Institute was 'an international legal person', this 'ruli[ng] out all State interference and all authority of its laws, substantive or procedural'. The view in favour of the ILP of the Institute was previously maintained in Italian scholarship, against the majority of other writers, by Guido Fusinato, 'La personalità giuridica dell'Istituto Internazionale d'Agricoltura' (1914) 3 RDI 149.

223 On the widely discussed (but never really settled) question of the international legal personality of the League of Nations, see JL Brierly, 'The Covenant and the Charter' (1946) 23 BYBIL 83.

224 Italian Court of Cassation, *Nanni et al v Pace and the Sovereign Order of Malta* Judgment of 13 March 1935, (1941) ADRPILC Years 1935–37 (Case No 8) 2, 5.

225 ICJ, *Reparation for Injuries Suffered in the Service of the United Nations*, Advisory Opinion of 11 April 1949, [1949] ICJ Rep 174, 179.

226 ibid.

227 ibid 185. For a reading of the Opinion favourable to the 'objective' ILP of IOs in general (drawing legal 'consequences' from the fulfilment of 'certain objective preconditions'), see M Rama-Montaldo, 'International Legal Personality and Implied Powers of International Organizations' (1970) 44 BYBIL 111.

228 ECtHR, *Agim Behrami and Bekir Behrami v France and Ruzhdi Saramati v France, Germany and Norway* Decision of admissibility of 2 May 2007 [GC], Apps 71412/01 and 78166/01, 45 EHRR SE10, para 144.

229 ICJ, *Interpretation of the Agreement of 25 March 1951 between the WHO and Egypt*, Advisory Opinion of 20 December 1980, [1980] ICJ Rep 73, para 37.

230 ICJ, *Legality of the Use by a State of Nuclear Weapons in Armed Conflict* (n 205 above) para 25; *Case concerning Pulp Mills on the River Uruguay (Argentina v Uruguay)* Judgment of 20 April 2010, at <http://www.icj-cij.org/docket/files/135/15877.pdf>, para 89, applying the principle of speciality 'of course to organizations, which ... only have two member States'.

231 eg Italian courts apply the *par in parem non habet iudicium* doctrine and equate, in this respect, IOs with states. cf Italian Court of Cassation, *Cristiani v Istituto-italo-latino-americano* Judgment of 23 November 1985 No 5819, (1986) 69 RDI 147; Italian Court of Cassation, *Nacci v Istituto di Bari del*

Whether *every* IO possesses ILP for any purpose is doubtful, but no satisfactory criteria exist to draw the line between organizations which possess it and others which do not. The ILC assumes IOs' ILP for its own purposes.[232] In the *Interpretation of the WHO–Egypt Agreement* Opinion, the ICJ seems to have implied that *all* IOs are 'subjects of international law', but, even conceding that this was what the Court intended, the question remains as to the difference, if any, between ILP and the mere (legally relevant) definition of IOs. One could say that 'all' IOs 'proper' possess ILP, but IOs 'proper' are precisely those which are treated as legal entities independent of their member states, ie those which possess ILP. The ILP question might thus simply coincide with that of the definition. A different matter is to ask whether an IO possesses *domestic* legal personality, as generally prescribed by constituent instruments and other agreements.[233] In domestic law the courts have generally treated IOs as juridical persons endowed with legal personality and separate responsibility from their member states.[234] While this jurisprudence is often taken as reflective of the ILP of IOs and of their distinct international responsibility,[235] the two planes are not to be confused. The fact that an IO is, for any reason, either domestic or international, treated as a legal person within this or that municipal legal system, does not imply that it is an international legal person. The constituent instrument, in particular, is per se insufficient to prove the possession of international legal personality since it has an *internal* import and cannot establish how a particular IO is treated by the whole international community 'from the outside'. Exceptionally, treaties provide for 'international legal

Centre International hautes études agronomiques méditerranéennes Judgment of 8 June 1994, (1994) 77 RDI 838.

[232] See n 206 above.

[233] cf eg Art 104 UN Charter.

[234] See Swiss Court of Justice of Geneva, *Arab Organization for Industrialization v Westland Helicopters Ltd* Judgment of 23 October 1987 No 443, (1989) 80 ILR 622, 642–3, ruling that the Arab Organization for Industrialization (AOI) was endowed with legal personality under its establishment documents and was 'a legal entity under public international law', also noting that in the silence of its Statute the member states were not liable for its financial obligations, contrary to the opinion expressed in the Interim Award rendered on 5 March 1984 by the International Chamber of Commerce Court of Arbitration on the *Jurisdiction in the Arbitration between Westland Helicopters Ltd and the Arab Organization for Industrialization, United Arab Emirates, Saudi Arabia, Qatar, Egypt, Arab British Helicopter Co* (1989) 80 ILR 595, 613–14; Federal Supreme Court, *Arab Organization for Industrialization v Westland Helicopters Ltd* Judgment of 19 July 1988, (1989) 80 ILR 652, 658, affirming the 'total legal independence' of the AOI in relation to the founding states as a result of public international law; UK House of Lords, *Maclaine Watson & Co Ltd v Department of Trade and Industry* Judgment of 26 October 1989, (1990) 81 ILR 670, 677–9, holding that the International Tin Council (ITC) was a juridical person separate and distinct from its members and these were not liable for the ITC's debts since they were not parties to the contracts made by the ITC; UK House of Lords, *Arab Monetary Fund v Hashim (No 3)* Judgment of 21 February 1991, (1991) 85 ILR 1, 9–13, ruling that the Arab Monetary Fund was to be treated as a juridical person in the UK since it enjoyed legal personality under the law of the host state (United Arab Emirates) and this was recognized by the UK.

[235] It was notably on the basis of this domestic case law that Art 6(a) of IDI Res 'The Legal Consequences for Member States of the Non-fulfilment by International Organizations of their Obligations toward Third Parties' of 1 September 1995 was drafted, to the effect that, in principle, the member states of IOs are not liable (either concurrently or subsidiarily) for failure of the IO to fulfil its international obligations, at <http://www.idi-iil.org/idiE/resolutionsE/1995_lis_02_en.pdf>. A similar approach was taken by the ILC in its Draft Art 62 on the responsibility of international organizations (n 206 above), except for cases—which add to other instances of state derivative responsibility envisaged in Draft Arts 58–61 or relevant as *lex specialis* under Draft Art 64—where the state has accepted responsibility for the act towards the injured party or it has led the injured party to rely on its responsibility (in which case there is a presumption for subsidiary, rather than concurrent, responsibility).

personality', such as Article 4(1) ICC Statute,[236] but this can only be interpreted as an internal engagement of member states. Quite naturally, the larger the membership of an IO, the greater the presumption that what its member states have agreed upon (including its ILP) is established by international law at global level. The question is far more uncertain when an IO is regional in scope, or made up of a few members. In such a case, what its members have established in the constituent instrument is of little consequence, while how the organization is treated by all other actors is decisive.

When an IO is treated as an international legal person, it is supposed to possess its own rights and/or obligations and to account for the breach of the latter. A crucial point is that the alleged ILP of IOs is generally not accompanied by adequate remedies and tends to favour unaccountability. When this entails the exclusion also of the accountability of the member states, as hinted earlier, IOs' ILP may be *used* by the member states to create legal vacuums, ie situations in which obligations exist only on paper and no one is ultimately accountable for their breach. The issue of IOs' international responsibility has come to the fore in recent years, notably in the ILC work[237] and in relation to the alleged breach of human rights by UN peacekeeping and territorial missions or through sanctions.[238] In fact, the prospects of successfully suing an IO before domestic courts remain modest, due to their jurisdictional immunity, which is often understood in absolute terms.[239] Even less likely are the prospects of successfully suing an IO before international courts, in particular in human rights monitoring bodies for lack of jurisdiction *ratione personae*.[240] In response, in recent times some domestic and international courts have reviewed the (domestic or EU) rules implementing UN sanctions[241] and the failure of

[236] Statute of the International Criminal Court (adopted 17 July 1998, entered into force 1 July 2002) 2187 UNTS 90.

[237] See n 206 above.

[238] See PJ Kuyper, 'Introduction to the Symposium on Responsibility of International Organizations and of (Member) States' (2010) 7 IOLR 9; G Hafner, 'Is the Topic of Responsibility of International Organizations Ripe for Codification?' in U Fastenrath, R Geiger, D-E Khan, A Paulus, S von Schorlemer, and C Vedder (eds), *From Bilateralism to Community Interest: Essays in Honour of Judge Bruno Simma* (Oxford: OUP, 2011) 695–717.

[239] Recently, see Dutch District Court of The Hague, *Association of Citizens 'Mothers of Srebrenica' v State of the Netherlands and the United Nations* Judgment of 4 July 2008, Case No 295247/HA ZA 07–2973, (2008) 55 Neth ILR 428, para 5.26; US Court of Appeals for the Second Circuit, *Brzak v United Nations* Judgment of 2 March 2010, (2010) 49 ILM 1016, 1018–19; Dutch Court of Appeal of The Hague, *Mothers of Srebrenica v Netherlands and United Nations* Judgment of 30 March 2010, Case No 200.20.151/01, (2010) 49 ILM, 1021, paras 4–6.

[240] See ECtHR, *Behrami* (n 228 above) paras 127 and 143, attributing the conduct of participating state forces within UNMIK and KFOR in Kosovo to the UN and not to the states. The ECtHR subsequently affirmed *Behrami* in other cases concerning Kosovo (see *Kasumaj v Greece* Decision of 5 July 2007, App 6974/05, para 4 of 'The Law'; *Gajic v Germany* Decision of 28 August 2007, App 31446/02, para 1 of 'The Law', and extended it also to Bosnia-Herzegovina (see *Berić and 25 Others v Bosnia and Herzegovina* Decision of 16 October 2007, App 36357/04 *et al*, paras 27, 29). It was espoused by the District Court of The Hague, *M, M-M, DM and AM (Mustafic) and HN (Hasan Nuhanovic) v The Netherlands* Judgment of 10 September 2008, Case No 265615 (2008) 55 Neth ILR 440, paras 4.8 and 4.11; District Court of The Hague, *Association of Citizens 'Mothers of Srebrenica' v State of the Netherlands and the United Nations* (n 239 above) para 5.22. However, the *Nuhanovic* decision was quashed on 5 July 2011 by the Court of Appeal of The Hague holding that the decisive question about attribution to an IO was who has 'effective control' and the UNPROFOR Dutchbat's conduct challenged was directly linked to the decisions and instructions of (and thus attributable to) the Dutch government, at <http://zoeken.rechtspraak.nl/detailpage.aspx?ljn=BR5388>, para 5.19. For a comment, see A Nollkaemper, 'Dual Attribution: Liability of the Netherlands for Removal of Individuals from the Compound of Dutchbat', at <http://www.sharesproject.nl/dual-attribution-liability-of-the-netherlands-for-removal-of-individuals-from-the-compound-of-dutchbat>.

[241] See Ch 7 below, nn 564–6.

IOs to guarantee an 'equivalent protection' (compared to that ensured by a state) of human rights.[242] The overall picture suggests that states remain essential even where the ILP and the international responsibility of IOs are recognized. It is domestic courts, when lawsuits may successfully be brought against an IO within a municipal legal system, that can hold the IO responsible and produce the correlative legal effects, such as the annulment of IO decisions deemed to be illegal or *ultra vires*. Even when international courts are seised, it is again domestic courts that can ultimately enforce international decisions through the enforcement authorities of the state. Finally, it is still domestic courts that can assert the responsibility of the participating state (including their own state) by adopting a dual or multiple attribution test, or on other grounds, including 'circumvention' of international obligations.[243]

(2) Individuals

The states system, in its purest form, contemplates only states as legally relevant component units, any other entity being the subject of one or another state. In the past, individuals (natural and juridical persons) have thus not enjoyed a legal status under international law. However, today they are at centre stage.[244] Their relevance in international law—as international legal persons, if not the sole international legal persons—has, in particular, been defended against the totalitarianisms of the inter-war period (together with Hegel's concept of absolute statehood, Rousseau's *volonté générale*, and the positivist assumption of state will as the only source of international law) by a number of international law scholars such as Alejandro Alvarez,[245] Hugo Krabbe,[246] Louis Le Fur,[247] Nicolas Politis,[248] Maurice Bourquin,[249] Georges Scelle,[250] Hans Kelsen,[251] James Brierly,[252] and Hersch Lauterpacht,[253] and was stated by the Nuremberg Tribunal in 1946.[254] The pro-individual theory, despite its diverse intellectual roots (in particular naturalist, sociological, psychological, and normativist), basically assumes that the individual is antecedent and superior to the state and, consequently, that the state and its rulers have to behave in the service of the ruled

[242] Recently, see G Verdirame, *The UN and Human Rights: Who Guards the Guardians?* (Cambridge: CUP, 2011) 359–86. For the application by domestic courts of the doctrine of 'equivalent protection' to deny jurisdictional immunity to IOs when they lack adequate internal mechanisms of redress, see Ch 7 below, section B (1)(b).

[243] See UN ILC Draft Art 61 'Draft Articles on the Responsibility of International Organizations' (n 206 above). For the 'dual' attribution test, see ECtHR, *Al-Jedda v United Kingdom* Judgment of 7 July 2011 [GC], App 27021/08, paras 76–86, and n 240 above and Ch 7 below, section A (1)(d).

[244] See O Dörr, 'Privatisierung des Völkerrechts' (2005) 60 JZ 905–16; PK Menon, 'The Legal Personality of Individuals' (1994) 6 Sri Lanka JIL 127; K Parlett, *The Individual in the International Legal System: Continuity and Change in International Law* (Cambridge: CUP, 2011).

[245] A Alvarez, *La codification du droit international: ses tendances, ses bases* (Paris: Corp, 1912) 83–4.

[246] H Krabbe, *Die moderne Staats-Idee* (Haag: Nijhoff, 2nd edn, 1919) 275–6.

[247] L Le Fur, 'La théorie du droit naturel depuis le XVIIIe siècle et la doctrine moderne' (1927-III) 18 RdC 263, 404.

[248] N Politis, *Les nouvelles tendances du droit international* (Paris: Hachette, 1927) 55.

[249] M Bourquin, 'Règles générales du droit de la paix' (1931-I) 35 RdC 5, 42–7.

[250] G Scelle, *Précis de droit des gens: principes et systématique* (Paris: Sirey, 1932–4) 42, arguing that only individuals are legal subjects in international law.

[251] H Kelsen, 'Théorie générale du droit international public: problèmes choisis' (1932-IV) 42 RdC 121, 142.

[252] JL Brierly, 'Règles générales du droit de la paix' (1936-IV) 58 RdC 5, 47.

[253] H Lauterpacht, 'The Subjects of the Law of Nations' (1947) 63 LQR 438.

[254] See JE Nijman, *The Concept of International Legal Personality. An Inquiry into the History and Theory of International Law* (The Hague: TMC Asser Press, 2004) 85–243.

and their original, 'fundamental' rights. The theory often plainly revives natural law, with which it shares its state-transcendent universalism,[255] by conceiving the individual as 'the ultimate unit of all law, international and municipal'.[256] It suggests that a 'paradigm shift' of international law as a whole from an inter-state law to a humankind law is under way.[257] Advocates of individuals' international legal personality (ILP) invoke a number of international rights and obligations found in existing international law rules addressed to individuals, as well as the participation of individuals in international law- and decision-making.[258] However, individual rights and obligations, just like participation in international law- and decision-making, are provided for by states and have a relatively limited impact. Individuals hardly believe that international law is 'their' law, although many arguably accept that international law is the law addressed to states, including their own national states, and may provide for rights and duties affecting them. When occasionally the courts acknowledge the ILP of individuals, they often point out that it is 'partial' and does not imply directly enforceable rights.[259]

(a) International rights and duties of individuals

In its 2001 *LaGrand* Judgment,[260] reiterated in the 2004 *Avena* Judgment,[261] the ICJ held that the 'rights' to consular assistance granted to any detained alien by Article 36 (1) of the 1963 VCCR[262] are '*his rights* under this sub-paragraph', hence 'individual rights for the detained person in addition to the rights accorded by the sending state',[263] but refrained from holding them to be 'human rights'.[264] In a 1999 Advisory Opinion the IACtHR had previously ruled that the right to communicate with and to have access to consular officers, and to be informed about the former rights provided for by Article 36 VCCR fell within the human right to a fair trial.[265] The ICJ pointed out in *LaGrand* that the 'individual rights' in Article 36 VCCR 'by virtue of Article I of the Optional Protocol, may be invoked in this Court by the national *State* of the arrested person'.[266] The Court may have meant 'individual right' as an actionable right in domestic courts.[267] In a Judgment handed down in 2006 the German Constitutional

[255] See Ch 4 above, section B (1).

[256] H Lauterpacht, 'The Grotian Tradition of International Law' (1946) 23 BYBIL 1, 27. For the ancient Roman sources of this conception, see Ch 4 above, n 26.

[257] See A Emmerich-Fritsche, *Vom Völkerrecht zum Weltrecht* (Berlin: Duncker & Humblot, 2007).

[258] The individualistic approach to international law is today particularly heralded by AA Cançado Trindade, *International Law for Humankind: Towards a New Jus Gentium* (Leiden and Boston: Nijhoff, 2010).

[259] German Constitutional Court, *Bombing of the Bridge of Varvarin* Judgment of 2 November 2006, at <http://lexetius.com/2006,2924>, see n 542 below.

[260] ICJ, *LaGrand Case (Germany v United States) (Merits)* Judgment of 27 June 2001, [2001] ICJ Rep 466, paras 77–78.

[261] ICJ, *Case concerning Avena and Other Mexican Nationals (Mexico v United States)* Judgment of 31 March 2004, [2004] ICJ Rep 12, para 124.

[262] Vienna Convention on Consular Relations (concluded 24 April 1963, entered into force 19 March 1967) 596 UNTS 261.

[263] ICJ, *LaGrand Case* (n 260 above) paras 77 and 89 (original emphasis).

[264] ibid para 78.

[265] IACtHR, *The Right to Information on Consular Assistance in the Framework of the Guarantees of the Due Process of Law*, Advisory Opinion No OC-16/99 of 1 October 1999, at <www.corteidh.or.cr/docs/opiniones/seriea_16_ing.pdf>, paras 124, 129, 137.

[266] ICJ, *LaGrand Case* (n 260 above) para 77 (emphasis added).

[267] For the opposite view, see previously eg Canadian Alberta Court of Appeal, *The Queen v Van Bergen* Judgment of 26 July 2000, at <http://www.albertacourts.ab.ca/jdb%5C1998-2003%5Cca%5CCriminal%5C2000%5C2000abca0216.pdf>, 261 AR 387, para 15 ('The Vienna Convention

Court held that the rights in Article 36 VCCR are individual 'subjective rights' directly applicable in German criminal procedure law.[268] The opposite view, however, was adopted in 2008 by the US Supreme Court in the *Medellín* case.[269]

Substantive rights are apparently conferred on individuals by human rights treaties, and may be envisaged by particular rules of international humanitarian law, such as Articles 7, 7, 7, and 8 respectively of the 1949 Geneva Conventions. Human rights treaties may also provide individuals with a right to a remedy within domestic legal systems and to a right to reparation in case of breach of their rights. Article 41 ECHR, just like similar provisions found in other human rights treaties, provides that the ECtHR may find against contracting states, granting a reparation in favour of the victim.[270] Article 25 ICC Statute requires the Court to establish principles relating to the reparation in favour of victims of international crimes.[271]

It is debated whether individuals have an international right to diplomatic protection. Although diplomatic protection is discretionary and governments may renounce 'their' right to exercise it for political reasons,[272] there is a trend to interpret both constitutional provisions and the 'duty to protect' under international law to the effect that states have an obligation to exercise diplomatic protection in favour of their citizens.[273] Correlative to this obligation of the state is the right of the ill-treated individual to have the state exercise diplomatic protection. The ILC stated in its draft Article 19 on Diplomatic Protection that states 'should . . . give due consideration to the possibility of exercising diplomatic protection, especially when a significant injury has occurred'.[274] International practice, however, offers little support for this. Some national constitutions do provide for an obligation of the state to exercise (or at least to consider possible recourse to) diplomatic protection in favour of its nationals, such as the constitutions of Croatia (Article 10), Hungary (Article 69(3)), Estonia (Article 13(1)),

creates an obligation between states and is not one owed to the national'); Ontario Superior Court of Justice, *R v Partak* Judgment of 31 October 2001, at <http://www.canlii.org/en/on/onsc/doc/2001/2001canlii28411/2001canlii28411.html>, para 25 (stating that 'the Vienna Convention appears to deal with obligations between states as opposed to obligations owed to nationals', but proceeding 'with this analysis on the basis that art. 36 does create, within the countries that have ratified the convention, an obligation on the authorities to advise a foreign national of his or her right to have them notify the appropriate consulate or embassy').

[268] German Constitutional Court, *F, T, S, S, D* Judgment of 19 September 2006, 33 EGZ (2006) 684, at <http://www.bundesverfassungsgericht.de/entscheidungen/rk20060919_2bvr211501.html>.

[269] US Supreme Court, *Medellín v Texas* Judgment of 25 March 2008, 552 US 491, 498–9. In *Leal Garcia v Texas* 564 US___(2011), the Supreme Court denied an application for stay of execution on the ground that Congress had not yet enacted legislation in order for Art 36 VCCR to apply, holding that 'the bare introduction of a bill in a single house of Congress' could not justify stay of execution, all the more so considering that 7 years had elapsed since the ICJ *Avena* Judgment and three years since the *Medellín* decision without the Congress progressing further.

[270] For the widespread view that human rights treaties place on states obligations vis-à-vis individuals rather than states, see eg Ch 6 below, n 125. The point is discussed at section D (3)(a) below.

[271] See E Dwertmann, *The Reparation System of the International Criminal Court: Its Implementation, Possibilities and Limitations* (Leiden: Nijhoff, 2010).

[272] PCIJ, *The Mavrommatis Palestine Concessions (Greece v Great Britain) (Objection to the Jurisdiction of the Court)* Judgment of 30 August 1924, PCIJ Series A No 2, at 12.

[273] Critically, see V Pergantis, 'Towards a "Humanization" of Diplomatic Protection?' (2006) 66 ZaöRV 351.

[274] ILC Report, Fifty-eighth session (1 May–9 June and 3 July–11 August 2006), GAOR, Sixty-first session, supplement No 10 (A/61/10) 94. See JR Dugard, 'Commentary on Article 19', ibid 96–7, arguing that 'international law already recognizes the existence of some obligation on the part of a state to consider the possibility of exercising diplomatic protection on behalf of a national who has suffered a significant injury abroad'.

and the Russian Federation (Article 61). An obligation to give due consideration to exercising diplomatic protection, and/or to give the reasons why it has not been exercised, has also been endorsed by a few national decisions, among which the 2002 *Abbasi* Judgment of the UK Court of Appeal[275] and the 2004 *Kaunda* Judgment by the Constitutional Court of South Africa[276] stand out. However, the *Kaunda* decision is grounded in domestic constitutional law and expressly denies that international law imposes obligations on the matter, while the *Abbasi* decision—after accepting the justiciability of the question but denying the existence of a duty of the state to exercise diplomatic protection—only accepted that legitimate expectations could arise in this context. In the international jurisprudence, notable in this respect is the 2004 *Ilascu* Judgment of the ECtHR,[277] in which the Court stated that 'Moldova had a positive obligation under Article 1 of the Convention to take the diplomatic, economic, judicial or other measures that it is in its power to take . . . to secure to the applicants the rights guaranteed by the Convention'.[278]

While typically listing a series of rights of individuals, human rights treaties are often silent on duties. Article 29(1) of the Universal Declaration of Human Rights (UDHR) and Articles 27 to 29 of the African Charter on Human and Peoples' Rights (ACHPR) are important exceptions, albeit having little impact. It is worth noting that in human rights treaties, duties of individuals cannot be claimed in international monitoring bodies, nor can individuals be tried for their breaches.

Individuals may be deemed to bear international obligations in international criminal law if they can be held accountable for their breach regardless of any intermediating domestic rule. Piracy *jure gentium* is often recalled as the antecedent of present-day international crimes.[279] The better view, however, is that piracy was only 'a special ground of state jurisdiction—of jurisdiction in every state' and not 'a crime under the law of nations'.[280] In allowing universal jurisdiction, assuming that pirates were *hostes humani generis* (enemies of the human race) who 'have thrown off their [state] allegiance and are acting in defiance of law',[281] international law merely provided the definition of piracy,[282] this not necessarily implying that international obligations were

[275] UK Supreme Court of Judicature—Court of Appeal, Civil Division, *Abbasi v Secretary of State for Foreign and Commonwealth Affairs* Judgment of 6 November 2002, (2003) 42 ILM 358, paras 99–100, 105.

[276] South-African Constitutional Court, *Samuel Kaunda et al v President of the Republic of South Africa et al* Judgment of 4 August 2004, (2005) 44 ILM 173, para 192.

[277] ECtHR, *Ilaşcu et al v Moldova and Russia* Judgment of 8 July 2004 [GC], App 48787, ECtHR Rep 2004-VII 179, (2005) 40 EHRR 1030, para 331.

[278] See F Flauss, 'Vers un aggiornamento des conditions d'exercice de la protection diplomatique', in *La protection diplomatique: Mutations contemporaines et pratiques nationales* (Brussels: Bruylant, 2003) 29, 53.

[279] cf G Komarow, 'Individual Responsibility under International Law: The Nuremberg Principles in Domestic Legal Systems' (1980) 29 ICLQ 21, 22.

[280] cf 'Harvard Research Draft on Piracy' (1932) 26 AJIL Supp 739, 757, 759–60. See recently Parlett (n 244 below) 232. In Res 1976 (2011) of 11 April 2011, para 14, the UN Security Council has recently recognized that piracy is 'a crime subject to universal jurisdiction' and reiterated its call on states 'to favourably consider the prosecution of suspected, and imprisonment of convicted, pirates apprehended off the coast of Somalia, consistent with applicable international human rights law'.

[281] See 'Harvard Research Draft on Piracy' (n 280 above) 823.

[282] See US Supreme Court, *United States v Smith* Judgment of 25 February 1820, 18 US 153, 162, defining piracy as 'an offence against the law of nations', ie 'robbery upon the sea', and noting that 'the general practice of all nations in punishing all persons, whether natives or foreigners, who have committed this offence against any persons whatsoever, with whom they are in amity, is a conclusive proof that the offence is supposed to depend, not upon the particular provisions of any municipal code, but upon the law of nations, both for its definition and punishment'.

imposed on the pirates themselves.[283] In fact, pirates were tried by national courts under domestic law.[284] Still, the Nuremberg Tribunal famously stated in 1946 that 'individuals have international duties which transcend the national obligations of obedience imposed by the individual State'.[285] Despite this clear-cut statement, not only pre-Nuremberg international law but also subsequent treaties, such as (notably) the 1949 Geneva Conventions, do not directly impose on individuals obligations not to commit international crimes. Rather, they impose on *states* obligations to enact domestic criminal law and to try alleged perpetrators of international crimes in domestic criminal courts.[286] The CAT stated in General Comment No 2 that the 1984 Torture Convention imposes obligations only on states parties and not on individuals.[287] Existing rules on international crimes thus hardly 'transcend the national obligations of obedience' in the words of the Nuremberg Tribunal. It is, however, true that the Nuremberg Tribunal referred to its own Charter[288] and was not a standard national tribunal. Moreover, the 'transcendence' of the Charter over domestic law was perfectly in line with its international character. The same applies today to existing international criminal tribunals, since they may try alleged criminals for breaches of international obligations regardless of the domestic law of any state. It is when the statement of the Nuremberg Tribunal is used by a national court that the 'transcendence' of the national obligation of obedience becomes problematic. National courts may, however, exceptionally be induced to apply international law 'directly' when the crime is so intolerable as to lead them to believe that no court under any kind of law could abstain from adjudicating and punishing it as a matter of justice.[289]

(b) Participation in law-making

While individuals may be addressees of certain international rights and obligations created by states through the making of international treaties and other rules of international law, they are not normally international law-makers. Individuals' international rights and obligations are not self-created and depend on states. What individuals do amounts to 'participation' in international law-making, especially through NGOs and as members of communities or groups affected by international law rules. While

[283] See 'Harvard Research Draft on Piracy' (n 280 above) 754.

[284] See AP Rubin, *The Law of Piracy* (Irvington-on-Hudson, NY: Transnational Publishing, 2nd edn, 1998); D Heller-Roazen, *The Enemy of All: Piracy and the Law of Nations* (New York: Zone Books, 2009).

[285] IMT, *Trial of the Major War Criminals* Judgment of 1 October 1946, (1947) 41 AJIL 172, 221. The IMT statement was revived by the ICTY beginning with *Prosecutor v Tadić (Opinion and Judgment)* Judgment of 7 May 1997, Case No ICTY-94-1, para 665. The 'Nuremberg tradition' has been endorsed by the US courts in the interpretation of the Alien Tort Claims Act (ATCA) with regard to natural persons, while doubts exist as to its application to juridical persons, such as TNEs (see n 367 below and Ch 6 below, n 590).

[286] M Bothe, 'The Role of National Law in the Implementation of International Humanitarian Law' in C Swinarski (ed), *Studies and Essays on International Humanitarian Law and Red Cross Principles in Honour of Jean Pictet* (Dordrecht: Nijhoff, 1984) 301, 302.

[287] CAT, 'General Comment No 2: Implementation of Article 2 by States Parties' (UN Doc CAT/C/GC/CRP.1/Rev. 4 of 23 November 2007) para 15.

[288] At <http://avalon.law.yale.edu/imt/imtconst.asp>.

[289] cf IMT, *Trial of the Major War Criminals* (n 285 above) 219, appealing to the 'general principles of justice applied by jurists and practised by military courts'. Domestic courts may need to ground their decisions on practice more closely than international criminal tribunals set up specifically to try perpetrators of international crimes, unless applying 'general principles of law recognized by civilized nations', on which see Ch 6 below, section B (1)(d).

individuals cannot be properly said to participate 'directly' in the formation of international customary law and treaties or other rules of international law, they may and should play a key role in influencing the behaviour of their and others' states with regard to what rules of international law are made.

(c) Participation in decision-making

Reviving a trend followed in post-World War I minority treaties, since the end of World War II individuals have been conferred rights to initiate judicial or quasi-judicial international proceedings against states. This has occurred in human rights treaties, both regional and universal, as well as in international investment law.

A right to claim rights in international monitoring bodies is envisaged in the field of human rights, at both universal (for example, UN human rights committees) and regional level (for example, the European Court of Human Rights); of international investment law (for example, the ICSID Tribunals); and of international environmental law (for example, the Compliance Committee set up by the Aarhus Convention on environmental information).[290] As regards international financial law, the IBRD and IDA resolutions regulating the World Bank Inspection Panel provide that two or more natural persons who believe themselves to be adversely affected by a World Bank-financed project can request an inspection and have participatory rights.[291] Also of interest was the Focal Point set up in 2006 by the Security Council enabling individuals listed as terrorists to request delisting.[292] The legal effects of such mechanisms may be either binding (as in the case of judgments of human rights courts and ICSID awards) or non-binding (as in the case of committees). Some decisions may not be addressed either to the individuals or the states concerned, as in the case of the IBRD Inspection Panel, which is an in-house review system. The Security Council Focal Point was not an independent review mechanism and, after having attracted strong criticisms, has recently been replaced by an Ombudsperson.[293]

In other venues, while not entitled to file complaints, individuals may participate in the proceedings, as is the case for victims in the ICC proceedings.[294]

(3) Trans-state players

MNEs and NGOs make all affordable efforts to operate transnationally and have an impact on global governance in ways that further their goals, alongside or even as substitutes for states. Their traditional legal status is no different from that of the individual as such. In particular, their local sections or subsidiaries are generally set up under, and thus subjected to, the domestic law of the host state. Despite their transnational operations, which may be absent in the individual in general, all rules

[290] Convention on Access to Information, Public Participation in Decision-Making and Access to Justice in Environmental Matters (done 25 June 1998, entered into force 30 October 2001) 2161 UNTS 447.

[291] IBRD Executive Directors, Res No 93–10 of 22 September 1993 establishing the Inspection Panel, (1995) 34 ILM 520; IDA Executive Directors, Res No 93–6 of 22 September 1993 establishing the Inspection Panel, ibid.

[292] UNSC Resolutions 1730 (2006) of 19 December 2006 and 1735 (2006) of 22 December 2006.

[293] UNSC Res 1904 (2009) of 17 December 2009. See Ch 8 below, section B (3).

[294] C Stahn, H Olásolo, and K Gibson, 'Participation of Victims in Pre-trial Proceedings of the ICC' (2006) 4 JICJ 219.

of international law dealing with them (in most cases not even binding) are made by states and, even where these accord them international rights or duties, their overall role in constructing international law is limited. They no doubt often exert a considerable influence over people's beliefs and lifestyles. This influence, however, is focused on attaining specific, non-legal outcomes and rarely if ever affects international law, which they do not believe to be 'their' law.

(a) Non-governmental organizations (NGOs)

Failing a universally accepted definition of transnational non-governmental organizations (NGOs), the set of Fundamental Principles of the Council of Europe, of 2002, may provide some guidance. They define NGOs as 'essentially voluntary self-governing bodies... not therefore subject to direction by public authorities'. NGOs are said to include 'associations, charities, foundations, funds, non-profit corporations, societies and trusts', with the exclusion of 'bodies which act as political parties',[295] encompassing 'bodies established by individual persons (natural and legal) and groups of such persons' that 'may be national or international in their composition and sphere of operation'.[296] Their primary aim is not to make a profit and distribute profits to members or founders, but to use profits 'for the pursuit of their objectives'.[297] Finally, NGOs 'can be either informal bodies or organisations which have legal personality' and 'enjoy different statuses under national law'.[298] There are a large number of international treaty rules enabling NGOs to engage in diverse forms of involvement in international affairs. However, very few international law rules regulate the NGOs' international status in general. The 1986 European Convention on the Recognition of the Legal Personality of International Non-Governmental Organisations is made by and directed to states.[299]

NGOs generally perform advocacy and service functions, ranging from providing information to offering expertise, vocalizing interests, adopting norms, lobbying transnationally, naming and shaming other actors (in particular states and MNEs), and attracting media coverage through mass protests. NGOs are often pictured as the 'moral' private authority in the international arena and they often claim to speak and act on behalf of 'the oppressed' or 'the excluded', thus pursuing 'public goods' in global governance, as opposed to states' and MNEs' self-interest. It is debated whether in carrying out these functions NGOs enjoy international rights and obligations, notably the right to participate in international law- and decision-making.

The participation of NGOs in international law-making has boomed since the UN Conference on Environment and Development (UNCED) of 1992. What is to be meant by 'participation' remains unclear. Advocates of NGOs tend to present it as 'quasi' law-making. In practice, NGOs activities include informal lobbying during the negotiations between states, holding parallel forums, and preparing codes of conduct, guidelines, memoranda, and standards for incorporation into treaties entered into by

[295] COE, *Fundamental Principles on the Status of Non-governmental Organisations in Europe and Explanatory Memorandum* of 13 November 2002, Principle 1.

[296] ibid Principle 2.

[297] ibid Principle 4.

[298] ibid Principle 5.

[299] COE, European Convention on the Recognition of the Legal Personality of International Non-governmental Organisations of 24 April 1986 (entered into force on 1 January 1991 and, as of 9 October 2011, binding upon 11 states), ETS No 124. For the NGOs Conference website, see <http://www.coe.int/T/NGO/default_en.asp>.

states. There is little evidence that the 'agreements' they make, especially with IOs, are 'international treaties' governed by international law.[300] Nor can the 'duty' to consult NGOs, often envisaged in legal instruments of various kinds, be interpreted in terms of their 'right' to be consulted.[301] To stress the impact of NGOs' on (inter-state) treaty-making, it is often recalled—albeit also contested[302]—that NGOs were decisive in the conclusion of the 1984 Torture Convention, the 1997 Landmine Convention, and the 1998 ICC Statute, as well as in the failure of the Wellington Mineral Convention on Antarctica in 1989 and the Multilateral Agreement on Investment (MAI) in 1998.[303]

It is a fact that several IOs, international conferences, committees, and other bodies allow for the accreditation of NGOs and lay down in treaty or other provisions a procedure for accreditation or admission. Important exceptions are, among others, the WTO[304] and the United Nations as a whole.[305] The existing accreditation procedures vary considerably from forum to forum. Accreditation generally confers on NGOs a 'consultative', or an 'observer', or a 'participatory', or a 'cooperative' status. The accreditation procedure to the UN Economic and Social Council (ECOSOC), based on Article 71 of the UN Charter and specified in ECOSOC Resolution 1996/31,[306] has served thus far as a model for other international bodies. It is debated whether NGOs possess an unconditional right to participate; and if not, whether they possess at least a right to be accredited or admitted according to the conditions established by each international forum; or, even more loosely, whether they possess a minor right to apply for admission and have their application duly considered. Some correctly deny that NGOs have any general right of access at all, at least for the time being.[307] Not only would accreditation and unconditional access be simply unworkable, but there are instances of denial of accreditation. It is also not difficult to imagine sound reasons for refusing admission to one or another self-professed NGO in one or another international forum. The right to due consideration of the application makes sense if the reasons given for refusal are reviewable, but there is no body entrusted with reviewing denial of access. If one looks at the texts, the plainer explanation of the 'right' to participation found in treaties is that the international body concerned (such as ECOSOC) which may have an obligation to admit NGOs, or at least to consider their applications, does so according to the conditions in force regarding member states or other international bodies rather than the NGOs themselves.

How accreditation and screening, and the suspension and withdrawal procedure unfolds is self-evidently quite a sensitive issue. States tend to control and politicize the

[300] A Peters, 'Treaty-Making Power', MP EPIL (March 2009 update) paras 77–79.

[301] For the view that 'A duty to consult NGOs can . . . be characterized as a right of NGOs to speak (their conception of) truth to power', see S Charnovitz, 'Nongovernmental Organizations and International Law' (2006) 100 AJIL 348, 370.

[302] See eg Drezner (n 14 above) 21–2. See further Ch 6 below, n 419.

[303] For a detailed analysis of these instances, see A Boyle and C Chinkin, *The Making of International Law* (Oxford: OUP, 2007) 67–77.

[304] See P van den Bossche, 'NGO Involvement in the WTO: A Comparative Perspective' (2008) 11 JIEL 717.

[305] Apart from ECOSOC (n 306 below), NGOs participate in UN activities, in particular in those of the General Assembly and of the Security Council, on an ad hoc basis. The proposal in the so-called 2004 'Cardoso Report' for a general participation has not been put into practice. cf 'We the People: Civil Society, the United Nations and Global Governance, Report of the Panel of Eminent Persons on United Nations-Civil Society Relations', UN Doc A/58/817, 11 June 2004, paras 123–128, and proposal 19.

[306] ECOSOC, Res 1996/31 of 25 July 1996, 'Consultative Relationship between the United Nations and non-governmental organizations', UN Doc A/RES/1996/31.

[307] Boyle and Chinkin (n 303 above) 57.

procedure and to decide which NGO should be involved, and have a voice, based on their national interests. The Council of Europe has shifted the accreditation procedure to the Secretariat,[308] whereas a similar proposal made in the UN was rejected.[309] A number of accreditation criteria to be assessed by the international institutions themselves rather than by states have been proposed concerning NGOs' independence from governments, transparency, even-handed application, due process guarantees, expertise, and a sufficient degree of representativeness, but their standardization, national registration, international character, accountability, internal democracy, and statement of adherence to certain policies have been reputed to be inappropriate.[310] All of these recommendations are no doubt sensible, but remain indeterminate, open to question, and often unrealistic. States may be right to exclude certain NGOs and the secretariats' independence from member states may be dubious. Too much openness is undesirable and in any case unworkable, but selective criteria presuppose a selection of the best policy and who should call the shots. The suggestion that the 2002 Council of Europe's Principles may work as a model for the elaboration of a universal minimum on accreditation procedures is not convincing.[311] Acceptance of the Principles by forty-seven states is far from proving that those principles may work universally for a variety of reasons: first, they only amount to one-quarter of the total number of states and even less of the world population as a percentage; secondly, the Council of Europe, as a regional organization, reflects European policy and outsiders may find no reason to follow it; thirdly, the Council of Europe lacks binding powers even within itself and the Principles remain exhortatory even within it. What is certain is that, once accredited, the alleged rights and obligations of NGOs vary with the accrediting body, but in no case are NGOs given voting rights. Attempts have been made to extrapolate general principles applicable to situations in which no written rules of procedure exist.[312] The suggestion was made that NGOs enjoy a 'legitimate expectation' to prior notification of meetings and agenda items, automatic and continuous admission to meetings, the option to distribute documents, and the opportunity to address the conference upon explicit permission.[313] A review mechanism, such as an NGO ombudsman, has also been recommended to sanction undue refusals, as well as abuse of participatory status by NGOs. All these practices remain fragmentary and largely relegated to the sphere of case-by-case convenience rather than law, let alone of general international law.

NGOs usually also participate in international judicial and quasi-judicial proceedings, treaty monitoring, and verification processes.[314] The participation of a given NGO in judicial proceedings may be direct, as a party to the dispute, or indirect, as an intervener (or *amicus curiae*). NGOs generally lack standing (or *jus standi*) in international courts and tribunals. Provisions such as Article 34 ECHR allow groups to file complaints but on condition that they are 'victims' of the alleged violation of the Convention, and NGOs as a rule are not the victims of the violation but rather assistants of the victims. An *actio popularis* in defence of others' interests, or of the public at large, is actually envisaged in some provisions found in constituent

[308] COE, Res 2003(8) of 19 November 2003, 'Participatory status for international non-governmental organisations with the Council of Europe', paras 12–14.

[309] Cardoso Report (n 305 above) paras 120–2.

[310] Klabbers, Peters, and Ulfstein (n 196 above) 223–5.

[311] ibid 239.

[312] R Sabel, *Procedure at International Conferences* (Cambridge: CUP, 2nd edn, 2006) 57–8.

[313] cf Klabbers, Peters, and Ulfstein (n 196 above) 226–7.

[314] T Treves, M Frigessi di Rattalma, A Tanzi, A Fodella, C Pitea, and C Rani (eds), *Civil Society, International Courts and Compliance Bodies* (The Hague: TMC Asser Press, 2005).

instruments of IOs, such as Article 24 ILO Constitution, Article 44 ACHR, and Article 5(3) of the 1998 Protocol establishing the African Court on Human and Peoples' Rights. In the European Union, the EU CFU denied standing to *Greenpeace* in defence of others' interests in the 1995 *Greenpeace* Order.[315] In contrast, the EU Council Directive on Racial Discrimination of 2000 provides that member states shall ensure that NGOs may act on behalf of or in support of complainants.[316] Like any kind of *actio popularis*, the standing of third-party NGOs in international bodies entails an overburdening risk. Besides, victims who count on stronger NGOs may enjoy an advantage as compared to others.

In their practice, international treaties, as well as courts, tribunals, and monitoring bodies, increasingly admit NGOs to submit briefs as *amici curiae*. Such briefs are not binding but may influence the decision, it is to be hoped for the better. The participation of NGOs in the proceedings, albeit indirectly, may contribute to the legitimacy of the decision-makers. For example, the ECtHR has considered NGOs' briefs under Article 36(2) ECHR.[317] The ICC prosecutor can request information from NGOs under Articles 15(2) and 44(4) ICC Statute. The ICJ can request information or comments in advisory proceedings.[318] NAFTA[319] and ICSID[320] tribunals have admitted NGOs' briefs on several occasions. The WTO Appellate Body has admitted NGOs briefs since the *Shrimps/Turtles* Report under Article 13(2) DSU, attracting strong criticism from member states.[321] However, NGOs have no right to submit briefs in international bodies under general international law, since each tribunal acts according to its own Statute and Statutes vary considerably.[322] In addition, NGOs often have the power to trigger non-compliance proceedings envisaged by treaties and are allowed to submit information to courts and court-like institutions.

NGOs, as trustworthy 'global governors', can give rise to a considerable number of problems that should not be overlooked.[323] First, NGOs as a whole are far from being a coordinated network pursuing a clear-cut goal. On the contrary, they often have different, even opposing, views on critical issues. Different humanitarian NGOs may campaign for opposite outcomes: typically, some may be in favour of humanitarian intervention with a view to protecting people whose basic rights are being violated by their own governments, whereas others may campaign against the same intervention by invoking the protection of civilians from military action. Even one and the same NGO may be hampered by internal disagreements, as was the case with Human Rights

[315] EU CFI, *Greenpeace v Commission* Order of 9 August 1995, Case T-585/93, [1995] ECR II–2205, paras 48–52.

[316] Council Directive (EC) 2000/43 of 29 June 2000 implementing the principle of equal treatment between persons irrespective of racial or ethnic origin [2000] OJ I 180/22.

[317] N Vajic, 'Some Concluding Remarks on NGOs and the European Court of Human Rights' in Treves, Frigessi di Rattalma, Tanzi, Fodella, Pitea, and Rani (eds) (n 314 above) 97–102.

[318] cf Arts 15(2) and 44(4) ICJ Statute.

[319] cf NAFTA Tribunal, *Methanex Corp v United States*, Decision on Authority to Accept Amicus Submissions of 15 January 2001, at <http://www.naftaclaims.com/disputes_us_methanex.htm>.

[320] cf ICSID Tribunal, *General de Aguas de Barcelona SA and Interagua Servicios Integrales de Agua SA v Argentina* Order in Response to a Petition for Participation as Amicus Curiae of 17 March 2006, Case No ARB/03/17.

[321] cf WTO, *United States—Import Prohibition of Certain Shrimp and Shrimp Products*, AB Report of 12 October 1998, WT/DS58/AB/R, paras 79–110.

[322] See Ch 6 below, section C (1)(c).

[323] cf E Rebasti, 'Beyond Consultative Status: Which Legal Framework for an Enhanced Interaction Between NGOs and Intergovernmental Organizations?' in P-M Dupuy and L Vierucci (eds), *NGOs in International Law: Efficiency and Flexibility* (Northampton: Edward Elgar, 2008) 21, 32.

Watch on the occasion of the Kosovo War.[324] Opposition may arise not only between NGOs that pursue a similar goal, but also between NGOs that pursue diametrically opposite goals, as evidenced by anti- and pro-light weapon NGOs.[325] This variety is often seen as a beneficial pluralism, which may be the case, but the whole picture is far from being reassuring as a form of governance unless states are considered central and centralizing units in the system. Secondly, NGOs are increasingly in need of financial resources to stay in the marketplace and to succeed in achieving their missions. NGOs sponsored and controlled by governments ('quangos') are spreading.[326] The suspicion that governments (or, more accurately, great powers) use NGOs to attain their goals by exploiting NGOs' reputation with the public is anything but fanciful. NGOs have to invest huge resources to gain a reputation for independence, but their need for such resources makes them vulnerable to funders, including private donors. To avoid dependence on governments, NGOs might seek financing from the for-profit private sector, in addition to donors and members, but then funds are inevitably raised in proportion to each NGO's relative 'visibility' in the media. Like for-profit firms, NGOs basically have to sell a 'brand' and, albeit not profit-driven, they may be media-driven. Certain fields are more welcome in the marketplace than others and NGOs which are willing to operate in fields where there is no immediate or large-scale gain, such as in research on rare diseases, might find themselves discouraged by the market. Thirdly, NGOs are neither accountable for their internal structure nor for their external activities. This is obvious where private operators are concerned, but less acceptable when these operators claim to operate for the public good in competition with others, such as states. Whether and to what extent NGOs are 'legitimate' is contentious.[327] Stronger NGOs have an across-the-board advantage to the weaker, beginning with accreditation, and the 'representation' of different segments of global civil society accommodates the relative force of the NGOs concerned. Paradoxically, NGOs are expected to enhance the legitimacy of other global actors while they are as a rule undemocratic and lack legitimacy by their own standards.[328] They contribute to the accountability of other global actors, by acting as a sort of 'global opposition',[329] without being accountable themselves. It has been suggested that what matters is their *legalist* legitimacy through international accreditation, their *moral* legitimacy according to the worthiness and credibility of their aims and mission, and their *social* legitimacy derived from acceptance and visible in a large membership and broad donorship.[330] In fact, accreditation is politicized, worthiness and credibility are volatile concepts, and acceptance can be manipulated or fabricated just as consent can be manipulated by governments within states. The 'brand' of an NGO in the marketplace depends on its legitimacy, and this depends on public opinion, but public opinion is

[324] cf M Kaldor, *Human Security: Reflections on Globalization and Intervention* (Cambridge: Polity, 2007) 52.

[325] Clifford Bob, 'Packing Heat: Pro-Gun Groups and the Governance of Small Arms' in Avant, Finnemore, and Sell (eds) (n 31 above) 183.

[326] Cardoso Report (n 305 above) para 127.

[327] MT Kamminga, 'What Makes an NGO "Legitimate" in the Eyes of States?' in A Vedder (ed), *The Involvement of NGOs in International Governance and Policy: Sources of Legitimacy* (Leiden: Nijhoff, 2007) 175. For the concept of 'legitimacy', see Ch 6 below, section A (2)(a).

[328] eg the UN attracts NGOs in an attempt to increase its legitimacy directly from public opinion, besides from member states. This may ensure a higher level of autonomy and more room for the pursuit of their institutional goals. As a result, NGOs act as a parameter of 'good governance' for IOs. cf E Rebasti (n 323 above) 66.

[329] Klabbers, Peters, and Ulfstein (n 196 above) 236, 315–18.

[330] ibid 236.

easily manipulated.[331] If governments can manipulate people, it is difficult to see why people should be able to resist manipulation from NGOs themselves, notably from the 'media effect' on which they strongly depend in a globalized world in which (unlike the village) what one does is known only because it has been made public globally through powerful, anonymous media conglomerates. In turn, while having no unquestioned legitimacy, NGOs may indeed be very harmful to others (rightly or wrongly) by their use of the media. Fourthly, NGOs are generally based in Western countries and inevitably promote, for good or ill, the Western worldview, including what should count globally as global justice and pluralism itself. The bigger and stronger Northern NGOs are more readily selected and accredited internationally and observers insist that Southern NGOs should be given additional financial and technical support, for example through a trust fund,[332] but meet insurmountable resistance. This clearly shows that NGOs, whatever their good intentions and valuable missions, are functional and in the end instrumental to Western states, whether they want it or not. Fifthly, no objective criteria exist to determine which NGO, in the inhomogeneous galaxy they form, is or is not 'genuinely' representative of 'public opinion' or 'global civil society'. Accreditation is strategically sought by NGOs to this very end, but this risks making accreditation procedures suspect of politicization. The concept of 'public opinion' itself is highly uncertain and particularly hard to grasp at global level. Most of the world's people actually support their governments. There is something missing in asserting that NGOs represent public opinion better than people's own governments. NGOs no doubt represent themselves, and their claim to represent public opinion as a whole is obviously an extrapolation. This is not to suggest that such extrapolation may not be benign, but only to take note that what is a benign extrapolation in one case (or today, or in regard to a certain NGO) may become arbitrariness in another (or tomorrow, or in regard to another NGO). Sixthly, NGOs have no effective 'authority' to enforce their rights without the assistance of states and they answer for their duties before state authorities. To say that they subrogate states in market and state failures is true, but it does not follow that states are really replaced. NGOs need entities that have jurisdictional power, if only in order to be set up. Significantly, although very frequently bringing complaints before domestic prosecutors against alleged perpetrators of international crimes on the basis of universal jurisdiction, NGOs have had very little success and domestic courts have shown no deference (let alone impotence) towards them.[333] Finally, NGO participation in law- and decision-making is costly and time-consuming, and may weaken rather than strengthen global governance.[334]

(b) Multinational enterprises (MNEs)

Alarming messages have been broadcast in recent years stating that today, 'corporations govern our lives' and 'now govern society, perhaps more than governments themselves

331 See Ch 6 below, section B (4)(e).

332 Cardoso Report (n 305 above) para 143.

333 cf M Langer, 'The Diplomacy of Universal Jurisdiction: The Political Branches and the Transnational Prosecution of International Crimes' (2011) 105 AJIL 1, showing that only in a very tiny percentage of cases raised by NGOs have domestic courts brought the case to trial (never, in any event, when the accused was a 'high-cost' defendant), and even fewer have reached a conviction. One might presume that if NGOs really reflected public opinion, domestic courts would take them more seriously as representatives thereof.

334 Cardoso Report (n 305 above) para 25.

do',[335] or that 'corporations rule the world'.[336] The question is very complex, beginning with terminology. The appropriate name for global corporations, as they are often termed in the media, varies with the context, ranging from transnational corporations (TNCs),[337] to multinational corporations (MNCs),[338] transnational enterprises (TNEs),[339] multinational enterprises (MNEs),[340] businesses,[341] and still others. The definitional issue hinges on the variety of their possible organization structures (distribution or franchising or licensing agreements, public private partnerships, holdings, joint ventures, etc) and local legal forms ('enterprise', 'company', 'partnership', corporation', etc). This diversity suggests that there is little reason, for definitional purposes, to assume the more commonly studied organization consisting of a pyramid-structured 'parent' company in the 'home' state and one or more 'subsidiaries' in other states.[342] The term 'MNEs' will be used here to include the widest possible spectrum of businesses having a transnational impact, independently of local legal forms, in line with a widespread trend in all soft law norms adopted thus far.

MNEs operate today in full competition with states and other global players such as NGOs. As is well known, the revenues of major MNEs are higher in terms of value-added sales than the GDPs of many states.[343] Their size is constantly growing as a result of ever bigger and more numerous mergers, and their activities include the delivering of 'public goods' outsourced by states, such as the management of prisons, public welfare programmes, public utilities, and wars, thus significantly shaping states' behaviour and impacting on global governance.[344] Credit rating agencies (CRAs) are, in particular, routinely mentioned as private actors capable of deciding the fate of states (and today even of the European Union as a whole).[345] The words 'public' and 'public goods' are

[335] J Bakan, *The Corporation: The Pathological Pursuit of Profit and Power* (London: Constable and Robinson Ltd, 2004) 5, 25.

[336] Korten (n 13 above).

[337] cf UN Code of Conduct on Transnational Corporations (1988), UN Doc E/1988/39/Add.1, para 1(a). The term 'transnational corporation' has also been adopted by UNCTAD and in the UN Norms on the Responsibility of Transnational Corporations and Other Business Enterprises with Regard to Human Rights of 26 August 2003 (cf UN Doc E/CN.4/Sub.2/2003/12/Rev.2 (2003) paras 20 and 21).

[338] cf UN ECOSOC Res 1721 (LIII) of 28 July 1972.

[339] cf UN Department of Economic and Social Affairs, *The Impact of Multinational Corporations on Development and on International Relations* (New York: United Nations, 1974, UN Doc E/5500/Rev1, ST/ESA/6, using the term 'multinational corporation' ('in accordance with common usage', not 'as a legal term') to align with ECOSOC (n 338 above) but recommending that 'the word "enterprise" should be substituted for "corporation"' and that 'the word "transnational" would better convey the notion that these firms operate from their home bases across national borders', at 25, n 2.

[340] ILO, *Tripartite Declaration of Principles Concerning Multinational Enterprises and Social Policy*, 16 November 1977, para 6; OECD, *Declaration on International Investment and Multinational Enterprises: Guidelines for Multinational Enterprises, OECD, Declaration on International Investment and Multinational Enterprises: Guidelines for Multinational Enterprises?* [for the fifth 2011 update, see <http://www.oecd.org/dataoecd/43/29/48004323.pdf>]. The term 'multinational enterprise' was also adopted by the *Institut de droit international* (IDI), Resolution on Multinational Enterprises of 7 September 1977, Art 1, (1978) 2 AIDI 341.

[341] UN Global Compact, at <http://www.unglobalcompact.org/index.html>.

[342] See PT Muchlinski, *Multinational Enterprises and the Law* (Oxford: OUP, 2007) 45–79.

[343] For making comparisons between states' GDP and TNEs' sales, see <http://www.imf.org/external/ns/cs.aspx?id=28> and <http://www.forbes.com/lists/2010/18/global-2000-10_The-Global-2000_Rank.html>.

[344] See section B (3)(c) above, and Ch 7 below, section A (3)(d).

[345] See T Kubota, 'Regulation of Rating Agencies: Current and Future' in M Giovanoli and D Devos (eds), *International Monetary and Financial Law: The Global Crisis* (Oxford: OUP, 2010) 251–61. For the EU November 2011 proposal of stricter rules on CRAs, see <http://www.bbc.co.uk/news/business-15739234>, the EU internal market commissioner acknowledging that rating agencies

often used to mean that private authorities may be outsourced by states to provide public services and pursue public goals. The 'common good' allegedly governed, however, may be public when it is in the hands of the state, but once it is outsourced to a private entity it becomes instrumental to private gains. Partnerships with NGOs, and even trilaterally with governments, are often recommended to compensate for possible 'private' excesses, but one should be mindful that NGOs are also 'condemned' to follow the rules of the game in the marketplace to accomplish their missions.[346] It is also often unclear whether the 'common good' at stake is that of the host state, of the home state, or of the international community as a whole, three concepts that do not necessarily coincide. MNEs appear more powerful than most states also in terms of market shares, of ability to avoid regulations, taxes, public scrutiny, and mobility of capital. They are increasingly capable of influencing the political debate and to exercise a key political role within states, through lobbying and rent-seeking, campaign and party financing, public body-financing (so-called 'policies for sale'), agenda-setting by punishing and rewarding governments for their policy choices through moving investments and jobs, state official-bribing, self-regulation, and self-policing,[347] quasi regulation through rating and standard setting, and even campaigning against IOs.[348]

MNEs have a considerable effect, both positive and negative, on the rights and lives of employees, consumers, taxpayers, contractors, and all other people throughout the world. Beneficial-perceived 'spill-over' effects for the public include lower prices and alleged better quality of goods and services for consumers, employment for households, and perhaps less poverty for some people. When the impact is negative, states appear ever more incapable of making decisions in favour of those affected and of relieving themselves of the MNEs' factual control. Allegations against MNEs include corruption, discrimination, child and forced labour, violation of regulations and basic standards concerning health and safety, restrictions to the freedom of association, the application of lower wages and longer working hours, harsh disciplinary practices, logging, massive pollution, complicity in international crimes committed by states or state officials, such as apartheid, and even masquerading as NGOs to be accredited under Article 71 UN Charter.[349] It is true that MNEs are careful today (even competing with one another) to display certifications that they do not engage in such practices, but the observer is left with their globally mediatized messages and with

have 'a serious and widespread effect on individuals' and their ratings 'a direct impact on the markets and the wider economy and thus on the prosperity of European citizens'.

[346] cf the Forest Stewardship Council (FSC), at <http://www.fsc.org>; the Ethical Trade Initiative (ETI), at <http://www.ethicaltrade.org>; the Kimberly Process (cf UNGA Res 55/56 of 1 December 2001, para 5; UNSC Res 1306 (2000) of 5 July 2000, paras 10, 11, 13; UNSC Res 1343 (2001) of 7 March 2001, para B.16).

[347] MNEs compete for consumers and investors by voluntarily adopting and conforming to standards, codes of conduct, and right-sensitive certifications and branding initiatives (C.A.F.E., Ethical Banana, SA 8000, etc), these being in line with international human rights instruments, made by and for states, including the 1948 Universal Declaration, the ILO Conventions, and the UN Child Convention. Certified MNEs thus differentiate themselves from their uncertified competitors and better pursue their goal to make profits. MNEs also wish such constraints to remain voluntary, so that they can be accommodated to the needs of the market. See eg the Global Reporting Initiative (GRI), at <http://www.globalreporting.org>; and, for analysis, RG Steinhardt, 'Soft Law, Hard Markets: Competitive Self-Interest and the Emergence of Human Rights Responsibilities for Multinational Corporations' (2007–08) 33 Brooklyn JIL 933.

[348] cf WHO, *Tobacco Company Strategies to Undermine Tobacco Control Activities at the World Health Organisation: Report of the Committee of Experts on Tobacco Industry Documents* (Geneva, 2000).

[349] Klabbers, Peters, and Ulfstein (n 196 above) 250.

certifiers who are themselves in the marketplace seeking to sell their own brand and make profits, whatever the cost.

MNEs can relatively easily evade the jurisdiction of any single state and, more often than not, play states against one another. How they succeed in doing so depends on a variety of factors that are worth briefly reviewing to understand why state jurisdictional power is today weak and is constantly weakening. First, MNEs consist of separate legal entities in different states and have no unitary legal personality. It is thus not possible to sue an MNE as a whole, but only its local subsidiaries. This means that while one subsidiary may be held accountable for abuses, others may remain untouched, although the abuses may well have been the result of a strategy of the whole MNE. The parent company is generally not liable under domestic law for wrongs committed by a subsidiary, unless the subsidiary is its agent. Moreover, when MNEs outsource their activities to third companies, they can hardly be held responsible for the abuses committed by the outsourced company. Secondly, host states may lack legislation to make MNEs respect human rights and may not be parties to human rights treaties which can bind them to have rights respected by MNEs within their jurisdiction. MNEs may choose to invest in these states for this very reason, the host state may fail to enact adequate legislation or to accede to human rights treaties precisely to attract foreign MNEs, and there is no international authority which can force a state to enact appropriate laws (especially if the enactment is not required by international law) or to accede to an appropriate treaty. But even when a host state does have adequate legislation and has acceded to one or more human rights treaties, it may lack the institutional capacity to enforce its own laws which punish human rights abuses by MNEs, especially when it comes to developing countries. Lack of state effectiveness, on the other hand, is not a problem for MNEs, which may hire private security companies (PSCs). Courts of the host state may lack a jurisdictional basis in domestic law or experience problems with enforcement. Host states may be discouraged from protecting human rights within their jurisdiction due to their desperate need to compete internationally for investment. They can attract MNEs by offering better conditions than other states, such as exemptions from legal and regulatory requirements or failure to adopt stricter labour, tax, or environmental standards. Thirdly, home states on their part may be reluctant to apply their legislation to national MNEs operating overseas to avoid being accused of applying their laws extra-territorially, to prevent national MNEs from losing investment opportunities, or relocating their headquarters. Bilateral investment treaties (BITs) and host government agreements may expose host states to challenges (including lawsuits) by foreign investors claiming that the investment regime has been violated as a result of measures aimed at protecting human rights. Export credit agencies (ECAs) do not usually require insured MNEs to respect human rights in the host country. In the home state's courts victims may incur prohibitive costs, or may lack legal standing, or be barred by statutes of limitations, or the absence of a jurisdictional basis (for example, as a result of the *forum non conveniens* doctrine), or be barred by the political question doctrine, in addition to experiencing difficulties in enforcing the law. Finally, when investment cases are submitted to international arbitration they are generally treated as commercial disputes, with no consideration for human rights, and are often conducted in strict confidentiality.

Faced with the overall impotency of individual states—to varying degrees, depending on the state—to make MNEs account for their abuses, it has been proposed that MNEs should be subject to international responsibility and this, in turn, requires them to be recognized as international legal persons, assuming that an entity can be held to account provided that it exists legally in the first place. The abstract question of personality is thus closely linked to the very practical need for international responsibility. As far as MNEs are concerned, international obligations are far more at centre stage than international rights. However, the international legal personality of MNEs would also entail, as an undesired side-effect, that the latter are independent of any state and can legally evade responsibility under domestic law.

Few scholars hold that MNEs possess international legal personality.[350] In their view, agreements between MNEs and states, such as concession and investment agreements, are 'international treaties' governed by international law rather than 'contracts' subject to domestic law or to the law (including international law) referred to by the parties. The inference is thus made that MNEs have a treaty-making power and 'therefore' are international legal persons. Once this conclusion is reached, the door is open to make MNEs accountable internationally. However, the circularity of this argument is obvious: MNEs are said to be legal persons because they make 'international treaties', but such agreements are actually 'international treaties' (rather than contracts)[351] because of the qualification of MNEs as international legal persons.[352] Furthermore, MNEs are economically unitary, but legally fragmented. Their legal status is dependent on the law of the state where they have been incorporated (home state) or actually operate (host state) and cannot be referred to as a unitary legal entity.

In fact, no international treaty exists providing MNEs with rights or obligations susceptible to violations on their part, nor have MNEs any access to WTO dispute settlement.[353] There are a few treaty rules apparently providing for the rights or obligations of legal entities, such as Article 137(1) UNCLOS, prohibiting 'juridical persons' from appropriating the Area,[354] International Investments Agreements (IIAs) and, in particular, Bilateral investment treaties (BITs), providing for both the substantive and procedural rights of 'investors', typically defined as both natural and juridical persons,[355] and an allegedly emerging customary international law prohibiting core international crimes also when committed by juridical persons.[356] Some also argue that UN Security Council resolutions sanctioning various 'entities' are addressed, inter

[350] V Lowe, 'Corporations as International Actors and International Law Makers' (2004) 14 It YBIL 23; K Nowrot, *Normative Ordnungsstruktur und private Wirkungsmacht: Konsequenzen der Beteiligung transnationaler Unternehmen an der Rechtssetzungsprozessen im internationalen Wirtschaftssystem* (Berlin: Berliner Wissenschaftsverlag, 2006) 562; K Nowrot, 'New Approaches to the International Legal Personality of Multinational Corporations: Towards a Rebuttable Presumption of Normative Responsibilities', at <http://www.esil-sedi.eu/fichiers/en/Nowrot_513.pdf>.

[351] Sole Arbitrator Dupuy, *Texaco Overseas Petroleum Company/California Asiatic Oil Company v Government of the Libyan Arab Republic* Award on the Merits of 19 January 1977, (1979) 53 ILR 422, 457, para 47, arguing—by expressly referring to the ICJ's *Reparation for Injuries* Opinion (n 225 above)—for a treaty-making power of private persons limited to the rights deriving from a contract made with a state; Sole Arbitrator Cavin, *Sapphire International Petroleums Ltd v National Iranian Oil Company* Award of 15 March 1963, (1967) 35 ILR 136, 175–6; Arbitral Tribunal, *Sandline International Inc v Papua New Guinea*, Interim Award of 9 October 1998, (2001) 117 ILR 552, para 10.1 ('An agreement between a private party and a state is an international, not a domestic, contract. This Tribunal is an international, not a domestic, arbitral tribunal and is bound to apply the rules of international law.').

[352] Peters (n 300 above) paras 72–76.

[353] As is well known, the issue is much debated doctrinally. See eg Klabbers, Peters, and Ulfstein (n 196 above) 253.

[354] Under Art 137(1) UNCLOS no juridical person 'shall . . . appropriate any part' of the Area and 'such appropriation shall [not] be recognized'.

[355] See Ch 7 below, section A (3)(d).

[356] See V Nerlich, 'Core Crimes and Transnational Business Corporations' (2010) 24 JICJ 895. See further RC Slye, 'Corporations, Veils, and International Criminal Liability' (2007–08) 33 Brooklyn JIL 955.

alia, to MNEs.[357] However, these rules apply to juridical persons and not specifically to MNEs. While they may apply to MNEs, they do not prove that MNEs as such possess international legal personality. Moreover, in international criminal law there are no substantive rules applicable to MNEs and no international criminal tribunal has jurisdiction over juridical persons.[358] UN Security Council targeted sanctions are clearly addressed to states by requesting them to adopt a number of measures against the private individuals listed.[359]

What does exist is a set of non-binding norms and codes of conduct,[360] and there can be no responsibility for 'defiance' of norms that are not binding. The *OECD Guidelines (2000)*, for instance, describe themselves as '*recommendations* addressed by governments to multinational enterprises' providing '*voluntary* principles and standards for responsible business conduct consistent with applicable laws'.[361] *OECD Council Decision (2000)* provides for the establishment of National Contact Points (NCPs) for the review of specific cases dealing with MNEs' respect for the Guidelines. In the 2008 *Global Witness v Afrimex* Statement the UK NCP found that Afrimex had breached the OECD Guidelines by failing to contribute to sustainable development in a war-torn region of the Democratic Republic of Congo (DRC) and by applying insufficient due diligence to the supply chain, sourcing minerals from mines that used child and forced labour.[362] There have been more than 200 requests since 2000.[363] However, NCPs depend on national governments, their procedures are in principle confidential, and MNEs have no legal obligation to conform to NCPs' Statements.

The responsibility of *states* for activities carried out by MNEs, either because such activities are attributable to one or another state or because the state has failed to fulfil its duty to protect people within its jurisdiction from MNEs' encroachment, is a different question.[364] Yet another question is the possibility for victims to request a remedy against MNEs' abuses in domestic courts under domestic law of either the host state,[365] or the home state,[366] or even a third state on the basis of domestic laws such as the US Alien Tort Claims Act (ATCA).[367]

[357] See Ch 8 below, section B (3).

[358] cf eg Art 6 ICTY Statute, Art 5 ICTR Statute, and Art 25(1) ICC Statute.

[359] Conforti and Focarelli (n 217 above) 252.

[360] See nn 337, 340, and 341 above.

[361] OECD, *Declaration on International Investment and Multinational Enterprises* (n 340 above) 'Preface', para 1 (emphasis added), and 'Concepts and Principles, para 1 ('Observance of the Guidelines by enterprises is *voluntary* and *not legally enforceable*') (emphasis added).

[362] Final Statement by the UK National Contact Point for the OECD Guidelines for Multinational Enterprises, *Afrimex (UK) Ltd*, 28 August 2008, at <http://www.berr.gov.uk/files/file47555.doc>.

[363] cf Report by the Chair of the 2010 Meeting of the National Contact Points, at <http://www.oecd.org/dataoecd/15/23/46385752.pdf>. For an archive of specific instances considered by NCPs as of June 2009, see <http://www.oecd.org/dataoecd/15/43/33914891.pdf>. For some 52 Statements adopted by NCPs thus far, see <http://www.oecd.org/document/59/0,3746,en_2649_34889_2489211_1_1_1_1,00.html>.

[364] See Ch 7 below, section A (2)(d).

[365] See eg Nigerian Federal High Court (Benin Judicial Division), *Gbemre v Shell Petroleum Development Company of Nigeria and Nigerian National Petroleum Corp* Judgment of 14 November 2005, Case No FHC/B/CS/53/05, (2005) AHRLR 151, para 4, ruling that Shell had breached the right to life and the right to human dignity set out in the Nigerian Constitution and in the ACHPR.

[366] See eg the *Probo Koala* case decided by the District Court of Amsterdam in July 2010, fining the oil trader Trafigura around €1m for illegally exporting tonnes of hazardous waste to Côte d'Ivoire, in *The Guardian* 23 July 2010, and at <http://www.business-humanrights.org>. On this case, see NMCP Jagers and M-J van der Heijden, 'Corporate Human Rights Violations: The Feasibility of Civil Recourse in the Netherlands' (2007–08) 33 Brooklyn JIL 833.

[367] cf 28 USC § 1350. See recently US Court of Appeals for the Second Circuit, *Kiobel et al v Royal Dutch Petroleum Co at al* Judgment of 17 September 2010, No 06-4800-cv, 06-4876-cv, 2010 WL

The UN Special Representative working on human rights and transnational corporations and other business enterprises has proposed a 'responsibility to respect' human rights *directly* incumbent on MNEs based on due diligence, but only as a 'standard of expected conduct'.[368] Non-binding norms embodying the so-called 'corporate social responsibility' (CSR), ie responsibility not only towards stakeholders but also towards society at large,[369] may be effective, but MNEs are designed to maximize profits. They can consider social benefits only to the extent that these help them to do so. CSR is merely one strategy among many others designed to win the competition in the marketplace, one which can indeed work if and to the extent that customers are or become attracted, for whatever reason, to humanitarian or other (stereotyped) 'public' causes. Such social responsibility can of course be inspired by 'moral' concerns, but the goal is just how to stay in the market and make profits. It is thus quite unwise to hope that CSR will inject 'morality' and concern for the public good in human affairs. It is also injudicious to allow issues that are critical to vulnerable people, such as their basic needs, to be negotiated in the marketplace and used to gain more wealth and power.

(4) Counter-state players

With the advent of the modern European state and its expansion worldwide, 'peoples' of any sort have been forced either to become an 'element' of statehood or to fight for statehood. Any emancipatory project is assumed to take place within the state frame by either becoming a state or by acquiring rights within a state. There are actors who fight against a particular state, but few if any fight against the states system itself. This confirms that states as political organizations are still central to the system, the key issue being how they (or, more accurately, their governments) behave, in particular towards their own citizens. Identity formations and groupings which aspire either to become a state or to acquire more rights within a state (notably a right to self-government) include insurgents, peoples fighting for self-determination, social resistance movements, indigenous peoples, and minorities. In so far as they use violence to subvert the state, they are generally seen as 'terrorists' in their state. This section argues that

3611392, at <http://caselaw.findlaw.com/us-2nd-circuit/1538603.html>, 43, stating that 'imposing liability on corporations for violations of customary international law has not attained a discernible, much less universal, acceptance among nations of the world in their relations inter se'. The Court based its reasoning on the jurisprudence of international criminal courts suggesting that juridical persons, unlike natural persons, are not convicted for international crimes. Significantly, it is assumed that at least natural persons have international obligations which they may violate. A contrary approach has been subsequently adopted by the US Court of Appeals for the District of Columbia Circuit, *John Doe VIII v Exxon Mobil Corp* Judgment of 8 July 2011, at <http://www.leagle.com/xmlResult.aspx?xmldoc=In%20FCO%2020110708139.xml&docbase=CSLWAR3-2007-CURR>, noting that 'corporate liability is consistent with the purpose of the ATS, with the understanding of agency law 1789 and the present, and with sources of international law'; and by the US Court of Appeals for the Seventh Circuit, *Boimah Flomo et al v Firestone Natural Rubber Co LLC* Judgment of 11 July 2011, at <http://caselaw.findlaw.com/us-7th-circuit/1573873.html>, holding that 'The factual premise of the majority opinion in the Kiobel case [wa]s incorrect' and concluding that corporations are not immune from suit in US courts under the ATCA (but excluding that the defendant corporation had violated international law in the instant case).

[368] cf <http://www.ohchr.org/EN/Issues/Business/Pages/Reports.aspx>.

[369] cf EU, European Commission, *Green Paper on Promoting a European Framework for Corporate Social Responsibility*, 18 July 2001, COM(2001) 0366, para 20 ('a concept whereby companies integrate social and environmental concerns in their business operations and in their interaction with their stakeholders on a voluntary basis'). On CRS and the UN Global Compact, see OF Williams (ed), *Peace through Commerce: Responsible Corporate Citizenship and the Ideals of the United Nations Global Compact* (Notre Dame: University of Notre Dame Press, 2008).

counter-state players, on the one hand, seek international support in their fight against a particular state but, on the other hand, enhance the states system and the centrality of states in international law since they do not fight for freedom from statehood and for equal standing in the system as political entities other than states. If they have legal relevance during the fight it is because they may become states or are potential states. The conversion of any emancipation project into a human rights claim—apparently directed against 'the state', but in fact aimed at a particular government—has decisively contributed thus far to conceal the globalization of state-centrism, ie the 'nothing-outside' of statehood currently shaping the world politically. The rules of international law governing the fight against the state by the above peoples and grouping are, unsurprisingly, those made and ultimately enforced by the states.

(a) Terrorists

Insurgents within one or another state are typically called 'terrorists' by the 'legitimate' or 'constitutional' government and often also by outsiders and international bodies. What systematically goes unnoticed is that most existing states have emerged and consolidated through acts (such as a conquest, a revolution, a coup, or a secession) which might have been regarded as terrorist at the time they were carried out or would be called terrorist should they be carried out today. Formerly alleged terrorists have often been the leaders of identity formations and it is difficult to see how such formations might have come into existence (and they have indeed come into existence, today enjoying full recognition and legitimacy) without a rebellion against those who, rightly or wrongly, opposed their project.

While numerous international law rules are today concerned with international terrorism,[370] what constitutes 'terrorism' and, specifically, 'international terrorism' for international law purposes is anything but clear.[371] A good number of writers has denied that customary international law provides a universally shared definition of international terrorism.[372] Certain organizations (such as Hezbollah,[373] the

[370] See further Ch 7 below, section A (1)(c) and (e), and section B (2)(a).

[371] See A Cassese, 'The Multifaceted Criminal Notion of Terrorism in International Law' (2006) 4 JICJ 933; GP Fletcher, 'The Indefinable Concept of Terrorism' (2006) 4 JICJ 894; B Saul, *Defining Terrorism in International Law* (Oxford: OUP, 2006); R Young, 'Defining Terrorism: The Evolution of Terrorism as a Legal Concept in International Law and its Influence on Definition in Domestic Legislation' (2006) 29 Boston Coll ICLR 23; R Lavalle, 'A Politicized and Poorly Conceived Notion Crying Out for Clarification: The Alleged Need for a Universally Agreed Definition of Terrorism' (2007) 67 ZaöRV 89; UD Acharya, 'War on Terror or Terror Wars: The Problem in Defining Terrorism' (2009) 37 Den JILP 653; CM Díaz-Barrado, 'The Definition of Terrorism and International Law', in PA Fernández Sánchez (ed), *International Legal Dimension of Terrorism* (Leiden: Nijhoff, 2009) 27; JJ Paust, 'Terrorism's Proscription and Core Elements of an Objective Definition' (2010) 8 Santa Clara JIL 51.

[372] cf Y Dinstein, 'Terrorism as an International Crime' (1989) 19 Is YBHR 55, 55; S Zeidan, 'Desperately Seeking Definition: The International Community's Quest for Identifying the Specter of Terrorism' (2003–04) 36 Corn ILJ 491, 491; A Schmid, 'Terrorism: The Definitional Problem' (2004) 36 CWR JIL 375, 394; E Corthay, 'Le concept de terrorisme ou la définition d'un monstre polycéphale' (2006) 20–21 ONU 111, 131; Saul (n 371 above) 270; Young (n 371 above) 65; Acharya (n 371 above) 678.

[373] The Hezbollah are regarded as 'terrorist' by the United States (see <http://www.state.gov/s/ct/rls/other/des/123085.htm>), Canada (see <http://www.publicsafety.gc.ca/prg/ns/le/cle-eng.aspx>), Australia (see <http://www.nationalsecurity.gov.au/agd/WWW/NationalSecurity.nsf/Page/What_Governments_are_doingListing_of_Terrorism_Organisations>), the UK (only Hezbollah's Military Wing, see <http://www.homeoffice.gov.uk/publications/counter-terrorism/proscribed-terror-groups>) but not by the European Union (see EU Council Decision 2009/1004/CFSP of 22 December

PKK,[374] and FARC[375]) are labelled as 'terrorist' by some governments but not by others. The viewpoints of the so-called 'terrorist' groups themselves are rarely considered to check their possible differences.[376] The debate about terrorism often avoids the scientific task of establishing what terrorism is, struggling instead for a simple, all-purpose condemnation of all alleged forms of 'terrorism', no matter who against whom, for what goals, and from whose perspective. General definitions of international terrorism are found in several international instruments, either universal[377] or regional in character,[378] including resolutions of the UN Security Council[379] and the UN General Assembly,[380] while regional conventions often prefer to list the crimes to be regarded as terrorist for their purposes.[381] Certain crimes commonly associated with terrorism are specifically defined by ad hoc multilateral treaties: for such crimes a general, universally accepted definition of terrorism is not needed.[382] Nor is a definition of international terrorism necessary when the UN Security Council expressly defines as terrorist *for its purposes* a certain incident[383] or a certain organization (for example, Al Qaeda) or certain persons (Osama bin Laden or the Taliban) when committing certain acts.[384] It seems plain that a general definition is needed in all other cases where a *special* legal regime, other than that which would otherwise apply to the crime, is set up in

2009, at <http://eur-law.eu/EN/Council-Decision-2009-1004-CFSP-22-December-2009,402354,d>) and the Russia Federation (see <http://rg.ru/2011/07/06/extremism-dok.html>).

374 The PKK are regarded as 'terrorist' by the US, Canada, Australia, the UK, and the EU, but not by the Russia Federation (same sources as in n 373 above).

375 The FARC are regarded as 'terrorist' by the US, Canada, Australia, and the EU, but do not appear in the UK's list of proscribed terror groups (the same sources as at n 373 above) and are apparently not regarded as terrorist by Nicaragua and Venezuela (see <http://www.elnuevodiario.com.ni/politica/5856>).

376 For an analysis from the perspective of the terrorist groups themselves, see FM Moghaddam, *From the Terrorists' Point of View: What They Experience and Why They Come to Destroy* (Westport and London: Praeger Security International, 2006).

377 cf Art 2 (1)(b) International Convention for the Suppression of the Financing of Terrorism (signed 9 December 1999, entered into force 10 April 2002) 2178 UNTS 197.

378 cf Art 1(3) OAU Convention on the Prevention and Combating of Terrorism (adopted 14 July 1999, entered into force 6 December 2002) 2219 UNTS 179; Art 1(2) OIC Convention on Combating International Terrorism (adopted 1 July 1999, entered into force 7 November 2002), at <http://www.unhcr.org/refworld/publisher,OIC,,,3de5e6646,0.html>; Art 1(2) Arab Convention on the Suppression of Terrorism (adopted 22 April 1998, entered into force 7 May 1999), at <http://www.unhcr.org/refworld/publisher,LAS,,,3de5e4984,0.html>.

379 UNSC Res 1566 (2004) of 8 October 2004 (para 3).

380 UNGA Res 49/60 of 9 December 1994 (para 3), later reiterated eg in Res 50/53 of 11 December 1995 (para 2); Res 51/210 of 17 December 1996 (para 2); Res 52/165, of 15 December 1997 (para 2); Res 53/108 of 8 December 1998 (para 2); Res 54/110 of 9 December 1999 (para 2); Res 55/158 of 12 December 2000 (para 2); Res 56/88 of 12 December 2001 (para 2); Res 57/27 of 19 November 2002 (para 2); Res 58/81 of 9 December 2003 (para 2); Res 59/46 of 2 December 2004 (para 2); Res 60/43 of 8 December 2005 (para 2); Res 61/40 of 4 December 2006 (para 4); Res 62/71 of 6 December 2007 (para 4); Res 63/129 of 11 December 2008 (para 4); Res 64/118 of 16 December 2009 (para 4), and Res 65/34 of 6 December 2010 (para 4).

381 cf OAS, Inter-American Convention to Prevent and Punish the Acts of Terrorism Taking the Forms of Crimes against Persons and Related Extortion That Are of International Significance (adopted 2 February 1971, entered into force 16 October 1973), (1971) 10 ILM 255; COE, European Convention on the Suppression of Terrorism (concluded 27 January 1977, entered into force 4 August 1978) 1137 UNTS 93; SAARC Regional Convention on Suppression of Terrorism (signed 4 November 1987, entered into force 22 August 1988), at <http://www.saarc-sec.org/SAARC-Conventions/63>.

382 cf <http://treaties.un.org/Pages/DB.aspx?path=DB/studies/page2_en.xml&menu=MTDSG>.

383 See n 400 below.

384 cf eg UNSC Resolutions 1267 (1999) of 15 October 1999 and 1333 (2000) of 19 December 2000.

regard to 'international terrorism' without providing its definition, as is the case with several UN Security Council resolutions,[385] or the qualification of terrorism as an autonomous international crime.[386] However, states still find it difficult to converge on a general definition, as evidenced by the persisting failure to finalize a Comprehensive Convention on international terrorism because of the disputed distinction between terrorists and freedom fighters.[387] Article 3 of the OAU Convention on the Prevention and Combating of Terrorism significantly points out that 'the struggle waged by peoples in accordance with the principles of international law for their liberation or self-determination, including armed struggle against colonialism, occupation, aggression and domination by foreign forces shall not be considered as terrorist acts'.[388] One might also ask whether international terrorism has just one and the same meaning in the various legal contexts in which it is relevant (extradition, UNSC measures, military response, domestic or international prosecution, jurisdiction based on passive personality, universal jurisdiction, specific effects attached to terrorism by individual treaties on terrorism, such as *aut dedere aut judicare*, cooperation, etc). Nothing prevents a certain act from being 'terrorist' for one purpose and not for another. For instance, a certain act could be 'terrorist' for the purposes of denying its 'political' nature in an extradition context, or of triggering a duty of criminal cooperation under a given treaty, or of falling within the obligation to implement UN Security Council sanctions, although not as a ground for military intervention.[389] Several other combinations may be easily imagined along these lines.[390]

That a group operating against a government in blatant violation of the local constitution is labelled as 'terrorist' by the government and the laws in force in the state goes without saying. This, however, from an international law perspective is only a *unilateral* definition of terrorism (accompanied by a *special*—typically aggravated—legal regime in terms of possible responses as compared to those applied to ordinary crimes) which varies with place and time. As is well known, what is terrorism here may

[385] cf eg UNSC Res 1373 (2001) of 28 September 2001 adopted in the aftermath of the 9/11 attack on the US.

[386] For the view that international terrorism amounts to a distinct international crime in peacetime under customary international law, see STL, 'Interlocutory Decision on the Applicable Law: Terrorism, Conspiracy, Homicide, Perpetration, Cumulative Charging' of 16 February 2011, Case No STL-11-01/I, at <http://www.stl-tsl.org/x/file/TheRegistry/Library/CaseFiles/chambers/20110216_STL-11-01_R176bis_F0010_AC_Interlocutory_Decision_Filed_EN.pdf>.

[387] cf Report of the *Ad Hoc* Committee established by General Assembly Resolution 51/210 of 17 December 1996, Fifteenth session, 11 to 15 April 2011, UN Doc A/66/37, para 10, at <http://www.un.org/law/terrorism/index.html>.

[388] OAU Convention on the Prevention and Combating of Terrorism (n 378 above). A similar clause is also found in Art 2(a) of the Arab Convention on Suppression of Terrorism and in the preamble to the Convention of the Organization of the Islamic Conference on Combating International Terrorism (n 378 above).

[389] eg the 13 existing counter-terrorism treaties (n 382 above) are confined to criminalizing terrorism-related crimes and establishing the *aut dedere aut judicare* rule, a domestic matter for the states parties, without saying anything about (and presumably without allowing) cross-border military responses to violations. The law applicable in principle is international human rights law where available—imposing a duty on the use of lethal force only when 'absolutely necessary'—as opposed to international humanitarian law. See eg ECtHR, *Isayeva v Russian Federation* Judgment of 24 February 2005, App 57950/00, 41 EHRR (2005) 791, para 173.

[390] For the view that terrorism is to be seen not only as a security threat justifying military response but also (and primarily) as 'a tool in political struggle' requiring 'regulatory response' through inter-state cooperation, see FB Adamson, 'International Terrorism, Non-State Actors, and Transnational Political Mobilization: A Perspective from International Relations', in Bierstecker, Spiro, Sriram, and Raffo (eds) (n 154 above) 79.

well be heroism there, and what was terrorism yesterday may well be heroism today in the same place. History is rich in examples. Whether terrorists are 'right' or 'wrong' is often a matter of perspective. Many fear that a 'relativist' approach may favour terrorists who are serious criminals and deserve punishment. But history teaches that certain unreservedly terrorist individuals of yesterday have later been praised as pursuers of *justice* even by those who labelled them as terrorists previously. Taking the example of the African National Congress (ANC) in South Africa, today few would deny that violence was needed to bring apartheid to an end faced with the firm resistance of the elite in power (which, of course, believed in its right to continue with apartheid).[391] All dictators invoke the need to fight terrorism to maintain (or seize more) power and oppress political competitors. Even within the same class of people, such as advocates of democracy, certain acts (otherwise called terrorist) may be felt to be right if they are strictly necessary in order to overthrow a brutal tyrant and to bring about democracy. Briefly, the *point* in terrorist matters is always what the 'right cause' is, and how to make it prevail against its opponents. No doubt it is for every state to define the 'right cause' from its own perspective and no state may be assumed to allow its own destruction. But states may have different views of the 'right cause'. It is thus quite a different matter to capture what is meant by international terrorism from a perspective transcending that of one or more individual states or local communities.

Terrorists seem to be those who spread terror basically because they assault the existing constitutional order of a community. The order threatened may be that of one or more states or that of the whole globe. Great powers try to present terrorism against them as an attack on the global order. To some extent this equation may be accurate because by definition great powers have interests in the whole globe. Global terrorism proper is conceivable as an attack on the very statist structure of the world since *this* is the 'constitutional' order currently prevailing. Such an attack is obviously also an attack on those major powers which are particularly interested in retaining their supremacy in this structure unless and until *they* opt for a new structure. Al Qaeda may be thought to fight against the statist global order, although a correct assessment of this hypothesis is rather difficult because of its elusive, still opaque nature.[392] While global anti-systemic terrorism, thus defined, should be kept distinct from terrorism fighting against this or that state, such as typically insurrectional groups,[393] the states system may indirectly and occasionally be undermined also by spill-over, destabilizing effects of intra-systemic terrorism. Clearly, no one in the system can operate with an unconditioned freedom since what occurs in one state may have significant repercussions in another and mutual reliability of all the system's units is paramount. But no general answer can be given once and for all. The international legal regime of terrorism depends on who has done what against whom from the perspective of the legal rules that are relevant in the instant case.

[391] For the suggestion that 'the violence used to suppress terrorism is the price paid to maintain the status quo' and that terrorism has different forms and motives, against those who assert that all terrorism is alike and requires the same response everywhere at any time, see V Held, *How Terrorism Is Wrong: Morality and Political Violence* (Oxford and New York: OUP, 2008) 13, 21–2.

[392] For a collection of annotated key texts of Al Qaeda leaders and excerpts from their speeches, internet postings, and published writings, see G Kepel and J-P Milelli (eds), *Al Qaeda in Its Own Words* (Cambridge, Mass: Belknap Press of Harvard University Press, 2010). See in addition BK Berner, *The World According to Al Qaeda* (New Delhi: Peacock Books, 2006); R Ibrahim, *The Al Qaeda Reader: The Essential Texts of Osama Bin Laden's Terrorist Organization* (New York: Broadway Books, 2007); B Riedel, *The Search for Al Qaeda: Its Leadership, Ideology, and Future* (Washington, DC: Brookings Institution Press, 2nd edn, 2010).

[393] See Ch 7 below, nn 96 and 97.

(b) Insurgents

Most states have emerged out of successful insurrections. Under 'classical' international law, third states were not allowed to 'recognize' insurgents when the insurrection was under way, this amounting to an interference in the internal affairs of the state in which the insurrection was taking place. However, insurgents are accorded international legal personality to the extent that they 'resemble' states, ie to the extent that they exercise effective control over a part of the territory.[394] This legal regime presupposes that (a) only states make up the system; (b) states could not be challenged internally; (c) if challenged, the challengers are internationally legally relevant to the extent that they exercise the functions of a state in a part of the territory; and (d) if successful, the challengers have to become the new government of the state or secede and form a new state. *Tertium non datur.*

The international legal personality of insurgents is by definition temporary. The challengers are 'given' the opportunity of becoming the new government of the state or of creating a new state by secession as a result of their capacity to defeat the legitimate government on the ground. There is no 'intermediate' *stably defined* status between insurgents (operating *within* the state to form a different state or a new government) and the 'legitimate government' of the state. As prospective exponents of a new state or a new government of the same state, insurgents are often accorded immunities, regarded as capable of making treaties,[395] and held accountable for the treatment of aliens in the territory under their control and for violations of international humanitarian law, today including the rules on international crimes.[396]

The current trend is towards determining *internationally* who is on the 'right' side in internal conflict, taking as a basic point of reference the democratic form of government and the prohibition on international crimes. The UN Security Council ever more overtly takes the side of one of the conflicting parties in internal conflict, claiming to express the position of the 'international community as a whole' about what constitute the genuine 'legitimate aspirations' of the people and who is entrusted to represent them.[397] When this occurs the 'old' international law regime still remains in the background, but profoundly challenged. For example, in the Libyan crisis of 2011, a number of governments 'recognized' the Libyan National Transitional Council (NTC) as 'the legitimate representative of the Libyan people', as distinct from the state of 'Libya', while actual support among the Libyan people was unclear,[398] and the Security Council authorized 'any means', including the use of force, necessary for the protection

[394] See eg South African General Division of Bophuthatswana, *Mangope v Van Der Walt et al NNO* Judgment of 18 April 1994, (1996) 103 ILR 6, 24; Court of Appeal of Lesotho, *Makenete v Lekhanya et al* Judgment of 5 June 1992, (1996) 103 ILR 27.

[395] cf eg Common Art 3(2) Geneva Conventions on the Protection of the Victims of War, which reads: 'The Parties to the conflict [not of an international character] should further endeavour to bring into force, by means of special agreements, all or part of the other provisions of the present Convention'.

[396] See Ch 7 below, section A (2)(c).

[397] See eg UNSC presidential statement S/PRST/2008/30 of 19 August 2008, condemning 'the Mauritanian military's overthrow of the democratically elected Government of Mauritania' and thus rejecting the claim by Mauritania's representative that the people of Mauritania had massively supported 'the corrective change' since the deposed President, although he had won the elections the previous year, had entered into conflict with the majority in Parliament and was no longer supported by the people.

[398] See S Talmon, 'Recognition of the Libyan National Transitional Council' (16 June 2011) 15 ASIL Insights, at <http://www.asil.org/insights110616.cfm>.

of civilians in the internal conflict under way, imposing sanctions on the regime and referring the Libyan situation to the ICC.[399] Although the Security Council intervention was not expressly a stance in favour of insurgents, including their recognition as the representative of the state of 'Libya' after the overthrow of the Kaddafi government, it turned out to be so. One can hardly maintain that the intervening states under the UN mandate were unlawfully 'interfering' in the domestic affairs of Libya (as the case would have been treated in the past or would presumably be treated in the absence of a mandate from the Security Council) since they were authorized to take 'enforcement measures' adopted by the Security Council under Chapter VII and such measures expressly, and understandably, do not fall within the 'domestic jurisdiction' of states under Article 2(7) UN Charter. On the other hand, the Security Council often condemns specific acts and their perpetrators as 'international terrorism',[400] thus apparently making specific attacks fall under its counter-terrorism legal regime and indicating who is not the representative of the legitimate aspirations of the people.

(c) Peoples fighting for self-determination

In modern international law, 'peoples' are but one of the elements of statehood. What matters is states, whether already existing or to be created, not peoples in themselves. Certain peoples, however, are apparently given the 'right' to freely determine their political status in the system. The fact that these peoples have a 'right' may suggest that such peoples are also endowed with international legal personality and have international standing on a par with states. However, self-determination may be understood in a wide variety of legal meanings.

The doctrine of popular sovereignty defended by the French Revolutionaries implied a renunciation of all wars of conquest and contemplated, in the name of the self-determination of all peoples, annexations of territory to France only after plebiscites. Self-determination meant that peoples had to be given the option to decide in which state to live. In the nineteenth century, self-determination was thought to imply (as a 'principle of nationalities') a right of 'nations' to become independent states. Accordingly, only nationally homogenous states were considered legitimate. In his theses on *The Socialist Revolution and the Rights of Nations to Self-Determination*, published in 1916,[401] Vladimir I Lenin provided a broad definition of self-determination as an entitlement of ethnic or national groups to decide whether to secede and form a new state or to demand autonomy within the state where they lived. Shortly thereafter, in his Fifth Point, US President Woodrow Wilson championed self-determination as a right of peoples freely to choose their government.[402] While self-determination was not envisaged in the Covenant of the League of Nations, Wilson's proposal inspired a number of plebiscites held by the Allies in disputed areas and was

[399] See Ch 8 below, n 127.

[400] See eg the presidential statements S/SPRT/2006/30 of 12 July 2006 (India), S/PRST/2008/19 of 2 June 2008 (Islamabad), S/PRST/2008/35 of 22 September 2008 (Islamabad), S/PRST/2008/41 of 30 October 2008 (Somalia), S/PRST/2009/22 of 17 July 2009 (Jakarta). Similar expressions are found in UNSC Resolutions 1516 (2003) of 20 November 2003 (Istanbul), 1611 (2005) of 7 July 2005 (London), and 1618 (2005) of 4 August 2005 (Iraq). For the legal characterization of UNSC presidential statements, see S Talmon, 'The Legal Character of Statements by the President of the Security Council' (2003) 2 Chin JIL 419.

[401] At <http://www.marxists.org/archive/lenin/works/1916/jan/x01.htm>.

[402] At <http://avalon.law.yale.edu/20th_century/wilson14.asp>. For a comment, see J Schwietzke, 'Fourteen Points of Wilson (1918)', MP EPIL (March 2007 update).

inserted in minority treaties. The League mandates system itself was a compromise between self-determination and the interests of the administrative powers. The 'principle of nationalities' was relied upon for the dismemberment of the Austro-Hungarian, Russian, and Ottoman Empires.[403]

During World War II the principle of self-determination of peoples was included, inter alia, in Principles 2 and 3 of the Atlantic Charter banning 'territorial changes that do not accord with the freely expressed wishes of the peoples concerned' and welcoming 'the right of all peoples to choose the form of government under which they will live'.[404] After the war, the principle was expressly mentioned in Articles 1(2), 55, and 56 UN Charter, and impliedly referred to in Articles 73 and 76(b) UN Charter in relation to dependent territories. It is commonly thought that the principle reflects general international law and amounts to an 'essential', peremptory international law norm,[405] contemplating an obligation *erga omnes*.[406] There is little certainty as to the addressees and to the contents of the principle. In the abstract, it may confer a 'right' either on individuals belonging to a people, or on peoples as such, possibly in tension with the same right conferred on its individual members, or on states, thus susceptible of translating into an individual right towards the state, or a collective right towards states, or a state right to non-interference from other states.[407] These different legal meanings may easily be at odds with one another.[408] It is equally obscure who is the bearer of the correlative obligation and whether the principle implies a right of secession *from* an existing state, or only a right to self-government *within* an existing state, or *any form* of political organization a people promotes for itself, including remaining part of the colonial power.

Despite the uncertainties about the definition of a people,[409] it seems relatively uncontroversial that peoples subjected to colonial domination, apartheid, and foreign military occupation have a right to 'external' self-determination if they so wish, namely, the right either to become a state, or to associate or integrate to a pre-existing state, as specified in the 1971 *Namibia* and 1975 *Western Sahara* Advisory Opinions by

[403] See A Cassese, *Self-Determination of Peoples: A Legal Reappraisal* (Cambridge: CUP, 1995) 11–33.

[404] Declaration of Principles, Known as the Atlantic Charter (signed and entered into force 14 August 1941) 204 LNTS 381.

[405] See Ch 6 below, section B (4)(f).

[406] ICJ, *East Timor (Portugal v Australia)* Judgment of 30 June 1995, [1995] ICJ Rep 90, para 29; *Legal Consequences of the Construction of a Wall in the Occupied Palestinian Territory* Advisory Opinion of 9 July 2004, [2004] ICJ Rep 136, para 156.

[407] For a variety of meanings of self-determination, see ACommPHR, *Katangese Peoples' Congress v Zaire* Report of October 1995, Comm No 75/92, AHRLR (2000) 72, para 4, referring to 'independence, self-government, local government, federalism, confederalism, unitarism or any other form of relations that accords with the wishes of the people' in keeping, however, with 'other recognised principles such as sovereignty and territorial integrity'.

[408] J Crawford (ed), *The Rights of Peoples* (Oxford: Clarendon Press, 1988).

[409] See UNESCO, Final Report and Recommendations, International Meeting of Experts on Further Study of the Concept of the Rights of Peoples, 27–30 November 1989, UNESCO Doc SHS-89/CONF.602/7, para 22. The (very broad) concept of 'people' defined therein was accepted 'as a guide' by the ACommPHR in *Kevin Mgwanga Gunme et al v Cameroon* Report of 27 May 2009, Comm No 266/2003, para 170, at <http://www.achpr.org/english/Decison_Communication/Cameroon/Comm.266-03.pdf>, finding that the people of Southern Cameroon could legitimately claim to be a 'people' for ACPHR purposes (ibid paras 178–179); as well as in the joint cases *Sudan Human Rights Organisation v The Sudan* Comm No 279/03, and *Centre on Housing Rights and Evictions v The Sudan* Comm No 296/05 (Sudan cases), Report of 13–27 May 2009, ACHPR (2009–10), at <http://www.achpr.org/english/Decison_Communication/Sudan/Comm.%20279-03.pdf>, para 220, finding that the people of Darfur constitute a 'people' for ACPHR purposes (ibid para 223).

the ICJ.[410] The UN General Assembly's Declaration on the Granting of Independence to Colonial Countries and Peoples of 1960[411] and Friendly Relations Declaration of 1970 affirmed respect for state sovereignty, ie the unity and integrity of statehood, and condemned only colonial states.[412] The 1993 Vienna Declaration and Program of Action reiterated that 'All peoples have the right of self-determination', namely, 'peoples under colonial or other forms of alien domination or foreign occupation'.[413] The identically worded Articles 1(2) ICCPR and ICESCR attribute such a right to 'all peoples'.[414] Also Article 20 ACHPR provides for the right to self-determination.[415] Article 1(4) of 1977 Geneva Protocol I Additional to the 1949 Geneva Conventions stipulates the applicability of international humanitarian law to conflicts for self-determination, provided that the oppressive government has ratified the Protocol and the Representative Authority of the people makes a unilateral declaration under Article 96(6) containing a commitment to respect the Protocol. The legal effect of the right to self-determination is that the peoples falling under the above three categories have a right to secession.

The right of external self-determination, unlike insurrection in general, implies an international obligation of the colonial power, or the state practicing apartheid, or of the occupying state, not to use force to prevent the exercise of self-determination of the people, as well as the prohibition on third states to assist the oppressing state, while humanitarian assistance to the people is generally allowed. The oppressing state is also arguably precluded from concluding treaties relating to the extension of the territory (such as an agreement on maritime boundaries) from the moment when the activity of the national liberation movement 'has acquired an international impact', namely, from the moment when its activities 'constitute, in the institutional life of the territorial State, an abnormal event which compels it to take exceptional measures, ie, when in order to control, or try to control events, it is obliged to resort to means which are not those used normally to deal with occasional disturbances'.[416] The trend of the international community to favour peoples fighting for a valuable cause such as anti-colonialism and to take sides with one of the parties in an internal conflict is liable to be extended to other situations, but international practice (except in some measure for the determinations of the UN Security Council)[417] is rather reluctant to endorse this.

The right to internal self-determination denotes a right to political participation and representation, or even to self-government and to a democratic form of government,

[410] ICJ, *Legal Consequences for States of the Continued Presence of South Africa in Namibia (South West Africa) notwithstanding Security Council Resolution 276 (1970)*, Advisory Opinion of 21 June 1971, [1971] ICJ Rep 16, para 52; *Western Sahara*, Advisory Opinion of 3 January 1975, [1975] ICJ Rep 12, paras 54–59.

[411] UNGA Res 1514 (XV) of 14 December 1960, 'Declaration on the Granting of Independence to Colonial Countries and Peoples', GAOR 15th Session Supp 16, 66.

[412] UNGA Res 2625 (XXV) of 24 October 1970, 'Declaration on Principles of International Law concerning Friendly Relations and Co-operation among States in Accordance with the Charter of the United Nations', GAOR 25th Session Supp 28, 121, Principle 5.

[413] 'Vienna Declaration and Programme of Action', UN World Conference on Human Rights (25 June 1993) UN Doc A/CONF.157/23.

[414] UN International Covenant on Civil and Political Rights (adopted 19 December 1966, entered into force 23 March 1976) 999 UNTS 171; International Covenant on Economic, Social and Cultural Rights (adopted 16 December 1966, entered into force 3 January 1976) 993 UNTS 3.

[415] African Charter on Human and Peoples' Rights (adopted 27 June 1981, entered into force 21 October 1986) 1520 UNTS 217.

[416] Arbitral Tribunal, *Determination of the Maritime Boundary (Guinea-Bissau v Senegal)* Award of 31 July 1989, 20 RIAA 119, para 51.

[417] See nn 399 and 400 above, and accompanying text.

within an existing state. It is associated with human rights, but a tension exists between individual and collective rights. Minorities and indigenous peoples may have this right under specific treaty rules.[418] These rules may provide for the possibility of bringing a case before an international monitoring body, such as the UN Human Rights Committee.[419] It has been suggested that massive violations of human rights against a minority give rise to a right of secession (so-called 'remedial secession'), similarly to the right to external self-determination, or even to humanitarian military intervention to allow secession to take place against the oppressor government.[420] In its 1998 *Secession of Quebec* Opinion, the Supreme Court of Canada stated that the right to self-determination 'is normally fulfilled through internal self-determination' and enables a people to secede from a state only exceptionally when the rights of the members of the people are violated in a grave and massive way.[421] No new light has been cast by the ICJ in the 2010 *Kosovo* Advisory Opinion.[422] Although the ACommPHR seems to have admitted remedial secession in the abstract,[423] international state practice hardly supports this, whatever its aspirational merits.[424]

As regards international legal personality, the question is whether the 'right' to self-determination is a right conferred on the people as distinct from a state and its individual members. If so, peoples fighting for self-determination (specifically, their representative organizations) would possess international legal personality regardless—unlike insurgents in general—of any effective control of the territory. If not, the apparent right of the peoples would in fact be a right of all other states having an obligation *erga omnes* as a counterpart and legal relationships would be entertained among states, the people only being an 'object' or a 'beneficiary' of the principle of self-determination.

418 See section C (4)(e) below.

419 The Human Rights Committee has repeatedly stated that Art 1(2) refers to 'all peoples', not only to peoples subjected to colonial domination, but has always declined its jurisdiction to review cases submitted by groups of persons who held that they were a 'people' under Art 1(2). According to the Committee, Art 1(2) may serve for the interpretation of other provisions of the Covenant, in particular Arts 25, 26, and 27, concerning the rights to political participation, the right to non-discrimination, and the right to cultural identity of ethnic, religious, and linguistic minorities, respectively. cf HRC, *Ominayak, Chief of the Lubicon Lake Band v Canada* Views of 26 March 1990, Comm No 167/1984, GAOR 45th Session, Supp 40, vol 2, 1, paras 13.3–13.4; 'General Comment No 23: The Rights of Minorities (Art. 27)' of 8 April 1994, GAOR 49th Session Supp 40, vol 1, 106, para 3.1.

420 See J Summers, 'Relativizing Sovereignty: Remedial Secession and Humanitarian Intervention in International Law' (2010) 6 SAIR 16.

421 Supreme Court of Canada, *Reference re Secession of Quebec*, Opinion of 20 August 1998, (1998) 37 ILM 1340, para 126.

422 ICJ, *Accordance with International Law of the Unilateral Declaration of Independence in Respect of Kosovo*, Advisory Judgment of 22 July 2010, at <http://www.icj-cij.org/docket/files/141/15987.pdf>, para 83, abstaining from pronouncing on 'remedial secession'.

423 cf ACommPHR, *Katangese Peoples' Congress v Zaire* (n 407 above) para 6 ('In the absence of concrete evidence of violations of human rights to the point that the territorial integrity of Zaire should be called to question and in the absence of evidence that the people of Katanga are denied the right to participate in government as guaranteed by Article 13(1) of the African Charter, the Commission holds the view that Katanga is obliged to exercise a variant of self-determination that is compatible with the sovereignty and territorial integrity of Zaire'); ACommPHR, *Kevin Mgwanga Gunme et al v Cameroon* (n 409 above) paras 190, 199–200 ('the people of Southern Cameroon cannot engage in secession [in the absence of proof of massive violation of human rights under the Charter], since secession is not recognised as a variant of the right to self determination within the context of the African Charter').

424 See A Tancredi, 'Neither Authorized nor Prohibited? Secession and International Law after Kosovo, South Ossetia and Abkhazia' (2009) 18 It YBIL 37, 78–9.

Evidence that the right to self-determination is a right of the peoples, rather than of states, is thin. Article 1(4) Additional Protocol I has been denied the status of general international law.[425] It also makes the applicability of the Protocol conditional on rather unlikely requirements, and national liberation organizations are, quite significantly, not admitted to accede to the Protocol, which remains an inter-state treaty. The request made in 2009 by the Palestine Liberation Organization (PLO) to initiate an ICC investigation on the Israeli military action in Gaza is based on the rules of the Court allowing anyone to bring a case to the attention of the Prosecutor and does not in itself imply the international legal personality of the PLO. Domestic courts have only occasionally recognized a 'limited' international legal personality of national liberation movements but, significantly, have refused to grant international immunities to their representative organizations and leaders.[426] National liberation organizations often enter into agreements with both the oppressive government and third states on whose territory they operate, but the nature of such agreements as 'international treaties' governed by international law is contested,[427] and their invocation involves the circularity already noted when dealing with MNEs.[428] Nor is the participation of national liberation committees in certain works of international organizations and conferences conclusive, since such participation is also open to entities that no one considers to be international legal persons.

(d) Social resistance movements

Social movements are defined as networks of informal interactions between a plurality of individuals, groups, and/or organizations, engaged in political or cultural conflicts, on the basis of shared collective identities.[429] As such, they are distinguished from interest groups, political parties, protest events, and coalitions.

In *International Law from Below*, published a few years after the 'anti-globalization' protests in Seattle, Washington, DC, and Genoa, Balakrishnan Rajagopal contended that international law—by focusing on states, institutional non-state actors, and individuals—has ignored the non-institutional spaces where most people in the Third World live and interact. Among non-state actors, local and transnational Third World social resistance movements (SRMs), as catalysing agents of popular discontent or disaffection, are deemed to challenge the authority and legitimacy of international law. A theory of resistance, not only one of governance, is reputed to be necessary to make the voice of the ordinary people, who are increasingly marginalized in the current global order, properly heard; to rethink international law 'from below',[430] beyond Liberalism and Marxism; and to ensure that legitimate protests are not labelled as

[425] South-African Cape Provincial Division, *S v Petane* Judgment of 3 November 1987, 3 SALR (1988) 51, at <http://www.icrc.org>.

[426] Italian Court of Cassation, *Re: Yasser Arafat* (n 106 above) 886–7.

[427] US Court of Appeals for the First Circuit, *Ungar v Palestine Liberation Organization* (n 106 above) para 71.

[428] See n 352 above, and accompanying text.

[429] M Diani, 'The Concept of Social Movement' (1992) 40 *Sociological Review* 1. For a more general overview, see C Tilly and LJ Wood, *Social Movements, 1768–2008* (Boulder: Paradigm Publishers, 2nd edn, 2009); S Staggenborg, *Social Movements* (New York and Oxford: OUP, 2nd edn, 2010).

[430] See further R Falk, *Law in an Emerging Global Village: A Post-Westphalian Perspective* (Ardsley, NY: Transnational Publishers: 1998).

'terrorism'.[431] Social movements and so-called civil society are seen as distinct from NGOs, although the latter may form a part of specific social movements.[432] Members of social movements include an 'eclectic mix' of Western labour activists worried about the loss of jobs, unions pushing for protectionism, environmental activists concerned about the ecological damage of global business practices, human rights activists exposing the unaccountability of corporations and IOs, governments which exploit these fears to promote geopolitical interests, Third World social movements (made up of urban poor, peasants, workers in the informal sector, illiterate women, and indigenous peoples whose resources are being destroyed) struggling in alliance with those of the West just to live, and many others. Social movements are said to be willing to abandon the nation-state as the collectivity that guarantees autonomy and allow a multiplicity of arenas as political actors, offering a 'pluriversal' defence of local communities. They emerge, inter alia, as a remedy against the inability and unwillingness of Third World states—accused of colonizing all life spaces in civil society and championing the interests of the global elite that controls the world economy—to act as effective guarantors of the democratic aspirations of the masses in the Third World.

The global resistance to globalism outside the institutionalized spaces proposed by Rajagopal seems to refer to a constant opposing movement within the states system and not to a project of restructuring the whole system anew. It is a fact that social resistance movements, although important and necessary in order to bring about more justice in the system in favour of the most vulnerable at a global level, have a limited impact on world affairs and their action is often lacking in power. Most of the members of such movements are from the West rather than from the Third World, or in any event those of the West take the lead. While it is true that social movements are different from NGOs, most concerns about NGOs apply *a fortiori* to social movements. There is no method, in particular, to ascertain 'who' social movements really represent in the global context and why their voice, once heard, should be given more weight than that of others, which may be equally worth taking seriously. Their impact could possibly be greater if, while globally constructed, they were channelled domestically.

(e) Indigenous peoples and minorities

Before modern states came into existence, the earth was populated by countless 'peoples'. After subjugation by the European colonial powers, these peoples became 'indigenous' (or 'native', or 'aboriginal') peoples.[433] The story of indigenous peoples is the story of the dispossession of their lands, ie the history of colonialism, most notably (but not limited to) European colonialism, and of the rights reclaimed by these peoples today under international and constitutional law.[434] Many existing states were born out of the extermination of native inhabitants on their territories.[435] While indigenous peoples do raise the problem of colonialism, on a par with decolonized states, most of

[431] B Rajagopal, 'International Law and Social Movements: Challenges of Theorizing Resistance' (2003) 41 Col JTL 397, 400.

[432] SG Tarrow, *Power in Movement: Social Movements, Collective Action and Politics* (Cambridge: CUP, 1994) 15, arguing that 'bimodal relationship between leaders and followers... is absent from movements'.

[433] SJ Anaya, *Indigenous Peoples in International Law* (Oxford: OUP, 2nd edn, 2004) 3. For a recent comprehensive overview, see B Kingsbury, 'Indigenous Peoples', MP EPIL (July 2011 update).

[434] P Keal, *European Conquest and the Rights of Indigenous Peoples: The Moral Backwardness of International Society* (Cambridge: CUP, 2003).

[435] Rae (n 156 above).

them do not claim 'decolonization' or secession from the states where they are enclosed, but rather self-government. In fact, indigenous peoples generally do not pursuit statehood because they do not conceive of the state in the first place. What is claimed is the right to control of 'their' ancestral land, to the exploitation of natural resources, to cultural identity and to their own way of life, to representation in the United Nations and on the international stage at large, and to compensation and moral restitution.[436] In recent years the indigenous movement has come under attack on grounds that indigeneity is a construction, since the populations concerned no longer live the way they claim they lived in the pre-colonial period.[437]

A workable, albeit non-binding, definition of indigenous peoples was provided in 1983 by UN Special Rapporteur José Martinez Cobo, whereby indigenous communities, peoples, and nations are those which 'having a historical continuity with pre-invasion and pre-colonial societies' that developed on their territories, 'consider themselves' distinct from other sectors of the societies now prevailing in those territories or parts of them and form at present non-dominant sectors of society.[438] A definition of tribal and indigenous peoples is also provided by the ILO 1957 Indigenous and Tribal Populations Convention No 107[439] and the ILO 1989 Indigenous and Tribal Peoples Convention No 169.[440] Tribal and indigenous peoples are clearly regarded here as part of independent states and their rights as rights conferred by the states which embed them. No right to independence is granted, as is manifestly envisaged in Article 1(3) ILO Convention No 169, where the term 'people' is denied 'any implications as regards the rights which may attach to the term under international law'.[441] The 2007 UN General Assembly Declaration on Indigenous Peoples even avoids defining indigenous peoples.[442] Terms like indigenous and aboriginal denote different meanings, since some indigenous peoples have subjugated aboriginal peoples. Also the term 'land' of indigenous peoples is difficult to define. Indigenous peoples were neither 'sovereign' nor 'owner' of the land where they used to live, since sovereignty and ownership are typical Western concepts. Moreover, their claim to ancestral lands is challenged by other indigenous peoples who contend that they have lived there before.[443]

From the sixteenth to the eighteenth centuries indigenous peoples concluded numerous agreements with colonial powers whose status as 'international treaties' has

[436] Anaya (n 433 above) 8–9, arguing for a human rights approach to indigenous peoples within the states in which they are embedded.

[437] A Kuper, 'The Return of the Native' (2003) 44 *Current Anthropology* 389; A Kuper, 'Discussion' (2006) 14 *Social Anthropology* 21. For a critical comment, see J Friedman, 'Indigeneity: Anthropological Notes on a Historical Variable' in H Minde (ed), *Indigenous Peoples: Self-determination Knowledge Indigeneity* (Delft: Eburon, 2008) 29, 42–6.

[438] UN, *Study of the Problem against Indigenous Populations, Conclusions, Proposals and Recommendations*, 30 September 1983, in UN Doc E/CN.4/Sub.2/1983/21, Add 8, paras 379, 381.

[439] ILO Convention (No 107) concerning the Protection and Integration of Indigenous and Other Tribal and Semi-Tribal Populations in Independent Countries (adopted 26 June 1957, entered into force 2 June 1959) 328 UNTS 247. The Convention has been ratified by only 17 states so far (see <http://www.ilo.org/ilolex/cgi-lex/ratifce.pl?C107>).

[440] ILO Convention (No 169) concerning Indigenous and Tribal Peoples in Independent Countries (signed 27 June 1989, entered into force 5 September 1991). The Convention has been ratified by only 22 states so far (see <http://www.ilo.org/ilolex/cgi-lex/ratifce.pl?C169>).

[441] For further details, see Ch 7 below, section A (2)(e).

[442] UNGA Declaration on the Rights of Indigenous Peoples of 13 September 2007, UN Doc A/Res/61/295.

[443] For possible criteria for identifying indigenous peoples, see the 2005 Report of the ACommHPR's Working Group of Experts on Indigenous Populations/Communities, 89–104, at <www.pro169.org/res/materials/en/identification/ACHPR%20Report%20on%20indigenous%20populations-communities.pdf>.

remained controversial.[444] In *Worcester v Georgia* the US Supreme Court characterized the treaties concluded between the United States and the Cherokee as 'international'[445] and described the Cherokee as 'a distinct community, occupying its own territory, with boundaries accurately described'.[446] One year earlier, in *Cherokee Nations v State of Georgia*, the Court likened the Indian tribes to 'domestic dependent nations' whose relationship to the United States resembled 'that of a ward to its guardian'.[447] Internationally, in the 1926 *Cayuga Indians* Award, the Arbitral Tribunal stated that the '"Cayuga Nation", an Indian tribe... is not a legal unit of international law' because 'The American Indians have never been so regarded'.[448] In the 1928 *Island of Palmas* Award the Arbitrator famously stated that: 'As regards contracts between a State... and native princes or chiefs of peoples not recognized as members of the community of nations, they are not, in the international law sense, treaties or conventions capable of creating rights and obligations'.[449] In the 1933 *Eastern Greenland* Judgment the PCIJ acknowledged the indigenous Inuit population in Eastern Greenland but the Court considered the territory's legal status to be a matter confined to the competing claims made by Norway and Denmark.[450]

A reverse tendency has emerged in recent decades, especially following the decolonization process in the 1960s. In the *Western Sahara* case the ICJ found that agreements between colonizing states and local rulers were 'to be regarded as derivative roots of title, and not original titles obtained by occupation of terra nullius'.[451] In *Land and Maritime Boundary between Cameroon and Nigeria*, Nigeria argued that the pre-colonial city-states in the contested region of Nigeria had enjoyed international treaty-making power.[452] In its 2002 Judgment, however, the ICJ held that the agreements between representatives of Great Britain and local chiefs of the Niger Delta near the end of the nineteenth century were not inter-state treaties.[453] The IACtHR has insisted, since 2001 by relying upon the ILO Conventions on indigenous peoples under Article 29 ACHR, that the right to property under Article 21 ACHR also applies (and needs to be balanced against possible conflicting rights to property of single individuals) to indigenous peoples' communal property, lands, and resources,[454] a position recently upheld by the ACommPHR in the 2009 *Centre for Minority* Report.[455] The preamble to the

[444] AD McNair, *The Law of Treaties* (Oxford: Clarendon Press, 2nd edn, 1961) 53–4.

[445] US Supreme Court, *Worcester v Georgia* [1832] 31 US 515, 559–60. Previously, in *Johnson v M'Intosh* Judgment of 10 March 1823, 21 US 543, the Supreme Court had described the Indians as 'fierce savages, whose occupation was war, and whose subsistence was drawn chiefly from the forest', hence 'To leave them in possession of their country was to leave the country a wilderness' (at 590).

[446] ibid 556.

[447] US Supreme Court, *Cherokee Nations v State of Georgia* [1831] 30 US 1, 17.

[448] American and British Claims Arbitration Tribunal, *Cayuga Indians (Great Britain) v United States* Award of 22 January 1926, 6 RIAA 173, 176.

[449] PCA Arbitral Tribunal, *Island of Palmas Case (Netherlands v United States)* Award of 4 April 1928, 2 RIAA 829, 858.

[450] PCIJ, *Legal Status of Eastern Greenland (Denmark v Norway)* Judgment of 5 April 1933, PCIJ Series A/B No 53, 146–7.

[451] ICJ, *Western Sahara* (n 410 above) 39.

[452] ICJ, *Case concerning the Land and Maritime Boundary between Cameroon and Nigeria (Cameroon v Nigeria: Equatorial Guinea Intervening)* Judgment of 10 October 2002, [2002] ICJ Rep 303, 403.

[453] ibid 405–6.

[454] IACtHR, *Mayagna (Sumo) Awas Tingni Community v Nicaragua* Judgment of 31 August 2001, IACtHR Series C No 79, para 148; *Yakye Axa Indigenous Community v Paraguay* Judgment of 17 June 2005, IACtHR Series C No 125, para 143; *Sawhoyamaxa Indigenous Community v Paraguay* Judgment of 29 March 2006, IACtHR Series C No 146, para 120.

[455] ACommPHR, *Centre for Minority Rights Development (Kenya) and Minority Rights Group International on behalf of Endorois Welfare Council v Kenya* Report of 11–25 November 2009,

2007 Declaration on the Rights of Indigenous Peoples asserts 'the urgent need to respect and promote the rights of indigenous peoples affirmed in treaties, agreements and other constructive arrangements with States', and Article 37(1) provides that indigenous peoples 'have the right to the recognition, observance and enforcement of treaties, agreements and other constructive arrangements concluded with States or their successors'.[456] In the 2007 *Pueblo Saramaka* Judgment, concerning logging and mining concessions awarded by Suriname on territory possessed by the Saramaka people without their full and effective consultation, the IACtHR conceded that Suriname could grant concessions, but had to avoid undermining the Saramaka's survival as a tribal people and provide effective consultations, prior and informed consent, benefit-sharing, and prior and independent environmental and social impact assessment.[457] In the 2007 *Aurelio Cal* Judgment the Supreme Court of Belize found that the right of indigenous peoples to their lands and natural resources is embodied, in addition to treaty obligations binding on Belize, in customary international law and general principles of international law.[458] In the 2009 *Raposa Serra do Sol* Judgment the Brazilian Supreme Court ruled that the Raposa Serra do Sol reservation had to be maintained as a single continuous territory exclusively for use by the indigenous population and perpetuation of their livelihoods, subject to conditions such as the need to realize specific infrastructure projects on indigenous lands in the national interest without the prior and informed consent of indigenous communities.[459]

On balance, the limited number of states which have ratified the ILO 1989 Indigenous and Tribal Peoples Convention, the resistance of several states, and the compromissory language (legally non-binding) adopted by the 2007 Declaration on the Rights of Indigenous Peoples suggest that the legal relevance of indigenous peoples remains basically a matter for the domestic constitutional law of the states concerned and, as regards international law, of human rights to be protected within the frameworks of existing states.

It seems that the same applies to minorities, the protection of which is provided by a large number of bilateral treaties and by a few multilateral treaty rules among which Article 27 ICCPR stands out.[460] The 1995 European National Minorities Convention is of little help in delineating what a national minority is and what role it plays in the world system.[461] The Convention fails to provide a definition of national minorities and sets out rights attributed only to 'persons belonging to national minorities' rather

Comm 276/2003, para 190, at <http://www.achpr.org/english/Decison_Communication/Kenya/Comm.%20276-03.pdf>.

456 Declaration on the Rights of Indigenous Peoples (n 442 above) preamble, para 14; see in addition Art 37.

457 IACtHR, *Pueblo Saramaka v Suriname* Judgment of 28 November 2007, IACtHR Series C No 52, para 129.

458 Supreme Court of Belize, *Aurelio Cal et al v Attorney General of Belize* Judgment of 18 October 2007, at <http://www.elaw.org/node/1620>, para 127.

459 Supreme Court of Brazil, *Raposa Serra do Sol* Judgment of 19 March 2009, at <http://www.stf.jus.br/portal/jurisprudencia/listarJurisprudencia.asp?s1=Raposa+Serra+do+Sol&base=baseAcordaos>.

460 See n 419 above. For the view that Art 27 ICCPR does not reflect general international law, see Italian Constitutional Court, *Servizio Riscossione Tributi per la Provincia di Trieste v Pahor et al* Judgment of 29 January 1996 No 15, (1996) 79 RDI 505, 508. See generally M Weller (ed), *Universal Minority Rights: A Commentary on the Jurisprudence of International Courts and Treaty Bodies* (Oxford: OUP, 2007).

461 COE, Framework Convention for the Protection of National Minorities (opened for signature 1 February 1995, entered into force 1 February 1998) 2151 UNTS 243.

than to national minorities as such. The Convention remains an inter-state treaty and embodies obligations that states have undertaken to respect in their mutual relations.[462]

(5) *Sui generis* players

There have always been 'discordant voices' in the states system, ie entities which are not states proper but are treated like states by all states. The system only *tends* to state uniformity, but there is always room for occasional *sui generis* players.[463] Leaving aside past experiences, such as Free Cities, three *sui generis* entities are worth discussing. The Holy See has been historically considered an international legal person by modern states in the name of their common Christian values. The Order of Malta (SMOM), the oldest Christian chivalry order, was sovereign in the past over Rhodes and Malta and is still considered an international legal person, although it does not rule any territory. Finally the International Committee of the Red Cross (ICRC), created in 1863 to assist the victims of war, enjoys a unique position with regard to the tasks assigned to it by the 1949 Geneva Conventions and its 1977 Additional Protocols. This section argues that, while the international legal personality of the Holy See is generally recognized, that of the SMOM and the ICRC are highly doubtful.

(a) Holy See

The Holy See is the only religious organization in the world held as an international legal person by the generality of states. The reason is historical and lies in the 'universal' power of the Christian Church in Western history since the Middle Ages from which the 'international community' of today derives. The Holy See is the central authority of the Catholic Church and, at the same time, the supreme political authority of the State of the Vatican City, established by the 1929 Treaty of Lateran between the Holy See and Italy, and before of the Papal States which ruled Middle Italy until their annexation by Italy in 1870.[464] The international legal personality of the Holy See was recognized even during the period between 1870 and 1929 when it had no territory.[465] This suggests that the Holy See, unlike states, is an international legal person regardless of any territorial control, which may justify its description as a 'sui generis' international subject. In any event, since 1929 the Holy See has also had a territory in the form of the Vatican State, in Rome, the smallest state in the world (with an area of 0.44 km^2, 556 citizens, 249 residents, and 476 inhabitants as of October 2007). Its official form of government is absolute monarchy headed by the Supreme Pontiff, who has full legislative, judicial, and enforcement powers. Law and order are ensured by the Corps of the Pontifical Swiss Guard (founded in 1506) and by the Gendarme Corps

462 For further details, see Ch 7 below, section A (2)(e).

463 While lacking determinacy, the term 'sui generis' is commonly used in the literature to mean, at least as a first approximation, entities other than states which are neither composed of nor created by states. In the practice, a reference to the 'unique character' of the Holy See is found in the Council of Europe's decision accepting the grant to the Holy See of observer status (see n 472 below), noting also that in view of 'its specific nature' the decision 'could not be invoked as a precedent'.

464 According to canon 361 of the Code of Canon Law, by 'Holy See' is meant 'not only the Roman Pontiff but also the Secretariate of State, the Council for the Public Affairs of the Church and other institutions of the Roman Curia'. Under canon 360 the Pope 'usually conducts the business of the universal Church by means of the Roman Curia'.

465 RA Graham, *The Rise of the Double Diplomatic Corps in Rome: A Study in International Practice (1870–1875)* (The Hague: Nijhoff, 1952); G Arangio-Ruiz, 'On the Nature of the International Personality of the Holy See' (1996) 29 RBDI 354.

(founded in 1816), while the police forces of the Italian state control access to St Peter's Square under Article 3 of the 1929 Lateran Treaty.[466]

The international legal personality of the Holy See results, first, from the making of treaties, both bilateral and multilateral, with states. Among bilateral treaties, Concordats establish the treatment of the Catholic Church in the territory of the contracting state. Of special importance are the 1929 Lateran Pacts, three agreements (Lateran Treaty, Concordat, and Financial Convention) entered into by the Kingdom of Italy and the Holy See.[467] The Lateran Treaty's preamble found it 'necessary to create under special conditions Vatican City' in order 'to assure the absolute and visible independence of the Holy See', as well as its 'indisputable sovereignty even in the international realm'. Under the terms of the Treaty, Italy 'recognizes the sovereignty of the Holy See in the international realm as an attribute inherent in its nature in conformity with its tradition and with the requirements of its mission to the world', as well as 'the full ownership and the exclusive and absolute power and jurisdiction of the Holy See over the Vatican as it is presently constituted, together with all its appurtenances and endowments'.[468] The Concordat was replaced in 1984 by an Agreement of Revision.[469] The multilateral treaties to which the Holy See is a party include the 1949 Geneva Conventions I–IV for the Protection of War Victims and their Additional Protocols, the 1961 Vienna Convention on Diplomatic Relations, the 1968 Treaty on Non-Proliferation of Nuclear Weapons, the 1961 Vienna Convention on the Law of Treaties, and the 1989 Convention on the Rights of the Child. Secondly, the Holy See is accorded immunity from civil jurisdiction and all other privileges granted to foreign states.[470] It also participates in conferences and international organizations (for example, as an observer without voting rights in the United Nations[471] and in the Council of Europe)[472] and entertains diplomatic relations with the vast majority of states.

(b) Sovereign Military Order of Malta (SMOM)

The Sovereign Military Order of Malta (SMOM), or 'Sovereign Military Hospitaller Order of Saint John of Jerusalem of Rhodes and of Malta', is an organization linked to the Holy See and committed to medical, humanitarian, and charitable assistance. In the past the Order ruled over Rhodes (1310–1522) and Malta (1530–1798); today it does not rule over any territory. The term 'sovereign', therefore, is not to be taken literally and should not lead anyone to believe that the Order is a state under international law, or in any case a 'sovereign' over a territory. The headquarters of the Order is in two buildings in Rome, Italy, Palazzo Malta in Via dei Condotti 68 and Villa Malta on the Aventine.[473]

[466] See n 467 below.

[467] Treaty between Italy and the Holy See (signed 11 February 1929, entered into force 7 June 1929). An English version of the Lateran Pact is available at <http://www.vaticanstate.va/NR/rdonlyres/3F574885-EAD5-47E9-A547-C3717005E861/2528/LateranTreaty.pdf>.

[468] ibid Arts 2 and 3.

[469] Agreement of Revision of the Lateran Concordat of 18 February 1984, Italian text at <http://www.internetsv.info/Concordato.html>.

[470] cf Italian Court of Cassation, *Capitolo della patriarcale arcibasilica di San Giovanni in Laterano v Zammerini* Judgment of 17 November 1989 No 4909, (1991) 27 RDIPP 489.

[471] UNGA Res 58/314 of 1 July 2004.

[472] The Holy See has been an observer in the Council of Europe since 7 March 1970 (see <http://www.coe.int/lportal/web/coe-portal/country/holy-see>).

[473] C D'Olivier Farran, 'The Sovereign Order of Malta in International Law' (1954) 3 ICLQ 217; AC Breycha-Vauthier and M Potulicki, 'The Order of St John in International Law: A Forerunner of

The Order entertains relations with several states, besides Italy,[474] and since 1994 has been a permanent observer at the UN General Assembly.[475] Its relations with Italy are based on an Exchange of Notes made in 1960, which accords 'sovereign prerogatives' to the Order's Grand Master as a 'foreign head of state' and 'diplomatic immunities' to the Roman headquarters, as well as the legal personality of the Order's institutions as 'entities of public law' and fiscal and customs exemptions.[476] Other agreements between Italy and the Order were entered into in 1966, 1981, 1991, and 2000, this latter (concerning the management by the Order of hospitals and ambulatories in Italy) duly authorized by Parliament and ratified by the head of state under Article 80 of the Italian constitution.[477] These agreements are apparently regarded by the Italian courts as international treaties proper.[478]

Given its particularities, unsurprisingly the pertinent 'international practice' as to the Order's international status comes predominantly from Italian jurisprudence. Italian courts recognize the Order as an international subject enjoying the prerogatives and immunities that are usually accorded to foreign states under international law. For example, in the 1935 *Nanni and Pace* Judgment, the Italian Court of Cassation held that the Order was 'an international legal person, existing apart from the national sovereignty of the [Italian] State'.[479] More recently, in the 1991 *Amministrazione delle finanze dello Stato* Judgment, the Court of Cassation recognized that the Order, as 'the holder of a system of its own', possesses a 'peculiar international subjectivity that is instrumental to the realization of its institutional goals'.[480] In practice, this means, inter alia, that the Order is accorded, similarly to foreign states, immunity from both civil jurisdiction in labour disputes between the Order and its workers (those who are deprived of their right of access to justice), except for acts *jure gestionis*,[481] and exemption from taxation concerning immovables and movables that the Order possesses in Italy.[482] Judgments of the Order's courts are treated as decisions of a foreign

the Red Cross' (1954) 48 AJIL 554; HP Scicluna, *A Short History of the Knights Hospitaller of St John, of Jerusalem, of Rhodes, and of Malta* (Floriana: Catholic Institute, 1970); HJA Sire, *The Knights of Malta* (New Haven and London: Yale University Press, 1994).

474 See <http://www.orderofmalta.org/diplomatic-relations/862/bilateral-relations-with-countries/?lang=en>.

475 UNGA Res 48/265 of 24 August 1994, considering 'the long-standing dedication of the Sovereign Military Order of Malta in providing humanitarian assistance and its special role in international humanitarian relations'.

476 Exchange of Notes, done in Rome on 11 January 1960 between Italy and Order of Malta, (1967) 50 RDI 545 (note 52).

477 Agreement between Italy and the Sovereign Military Order of Malta concerning their mutual relations on sanitary matters (signed in Rome on 21 December 2000, entered into force on 1 August 2003), Law No 157 of 9 June 2003, 144 GU of 4 July 2003 No 153.

478 See n 486 below.

479 Italian Court of Cassation, *Nanni et al v Pace and the Sovereign Order of Malta* (n 224 above) 4.

480 Italian Court of Cassation, *Sovrano Militare Ordine di Malta v Amministrazione delle Finanze dello Stato* Judgment of 5 November 1991 No 11788, (1992) 75 RDI 176 (trans by the author).

481 Italian Court of Cassation, *Sovereign Order of Malta v Brunelli, Tacali et al* Judgment of 17 December 1931, (1958) ADRPILC Years 1931 and 1932 (Case No 46) 88, 89, allowing Italian jurisdiction to the extent that the case bore upon a 'private law relationship'; Tribunal of Rome, *Sovereign Order of Malta v Société Anonyme Commerciale* Judgment of 3 November 1954, (1958) 22 ILR 1, 2, 5, allowing Italian jurisdiction on grounds that the Order of Malta (albeit 'a subject of international law having the characteristics of a sovereign State' or 'more precisely' of Governments-in-exile) had accepted it and appeared as a subject of the Italian legal system.

482 Italian Court of Cassation, *Ministry of Finance v Association of Italian Knights of the Order of Malta* Judgment of 3 May 1978 No 2051, (1984) 65 ILR 320, 323, deriving fiscal immunity in respect of activities directed at the realization of institutional objectives (although by way of a contract

state.[483] Occasionally, fiscal immunity has apparently been accorded to an even greater extent than that usually granted to foreign states, as the Court of Cassation did in the above-mentioned 1991 Judgment when stating—by assuming that the Order enjoys a 'functional subjectivity'—that the immunity extends to all acts exclusively directed at the realization of institutional objectives of the Order regardless of the private law nature of the means adopted.[484] More recently, however, the Italian Court of Cassation has applied the *jure imperii* limitation to the Order,[485] and has gone as far as denying jurisdictional immunity in the absence of a treaty rule prescribing the same.[486]

Some Italian scholars have criticized the Italian courts' attitude with regard to recognizing the Order as an international legal person and, more specifically, the consequences that this entails, ie the exemption from jurisdiction and taxation accorded to the Order in tension with either the right of access to justice (prescribed by Article 24 of the Italian constitution and by several human rights treaties binding on Italy, such as Article 6 ECHR) or the principle of equality of citizens (under Article 3 of the Italian constitution).[487] It is argued that the Order is dependent on the Holy See, as held by a Cardinals' Tribunal of the Holy See in 1953,[488] hence it lacks independence (besides territory) as a requirement for statehood. It is also contended that privileges are granted to the Order as a matter of either *comitas gentium*, rather than international law, or simply of domestic law. It is further observed that the status of observer at the United Nations is not conclusive since, as is well known, UN observer status is often conferred on entities whose international legal personality is universally excluded. An additional argument is that the 'agreements' made with Italy are not 'international treaties' governed by international law, but rather agreements of various kinds falling within domestic law, not dissimilar from many others made by Italy with other associations and entities committed to humanitarian and medical assistance. Besides, the fact that Article 3(1) of the Order's Constitutional Charter states that the Order is 'a subject of international law' and 'exercises sovereign functions' is hardly of relevance since international legal personality is no doubt independent of self-profession.[489] These

of private law nature) from the fact that 'The Order is in all things equal to a State, even though it is deprived of territory and, as such, it is to be accorded the legal treatment which is due to States'.

[483] Italian Court of Appeal of Rome, *Piccoli v Association of Italian Knights of the Order of Malta* Judgment of 23 January 1978, (1988) 77 ILR 613, 615.

[484] Italian Court of Cassation, *Sovrano Militare Ordine di Malta v Amministrazione delle Finanze dello Stato* (n 480 above) 177–8. See previously Italian Court of Cassation, *Ministry of Finance v Association of Italian Knights of the Order of Malta* (n 482 above) 322–4.

[485] Italian Court of Cassation, *ACISMOM v Santini* Order of 2 October 2003 No 17087, at <http://www.olir.it/documenti/?documento=2787>.

[486] Italian Court of Cassation, *Associazione dei Cavalieri del Sovrano Militare Ordine di Malta (ACISMOM) v Di Alesio* Order of 9 August 2010 No 18481, (2011) 47 RDIPP 459, noting that although 'the recognition of international legal personality to ACISMOM is confirmed by Article 13 of the Agreement of 21 December 2000' and the activity of the Order 'is governed on the international plane . . . by agreements made by the Italian State and the Order' (ibid para 2.5), this 'does not imply, *ex se*, the immunity from domestic jurisdiction' (ibid para 2.6), thereby excluding immunity 'in the absence of a specific treaty rule' applicable to the case (ibid para 2.8) (English trans by the author). See, previously, *ACISMOM v Alba et al* Judgment of 18 March 1992 No 3360, (1992) 75 RDI 178, holding, inter alia, that the Order's workers are fully subject to the Italian sanitary legislation and courts' jurisdiction.

[487] B Conforti, 'Sui privilegi e le immunità dell'Ordine di Malta' (1990) 113 *Foro Italiano* 2597; B Conforti, *Diritto internazionale* (Naples: Editoriale Scientifica, 8th edn, 2010) 30–1.

[488] Holy See, Tribunal of Cardinals, Judgment of 24 January 1953, (1955) 38 RDI 39 (note 1).

[489] For the English 'free translation' of the official Italian text, this latter prevailing in case of conflict, see <http://www.orderofmalta.org.uk/downloads/Constitution_Charter_and_code.pdf>;

criticisms have not remained confined to the doctrinal sphere. In an Advisory Opinion rendered in 2000, the Council of State, Italy's highest court in administrative matters, argued that the Order is not relieved from payment of social security contributions since 'in fact ... the recognition of its subjectivity in the international community is not undisputed, it is actually denied by many subjects, also European, and therefore it cannot be said that it corresponds to the international practice "*generally* recognized"', hinting here at Article 10 of the Italian constitution whereby 'The Italian legal system conforms to the generally recognized principles of international law'.[490]

The general impression is that the whole debate revolves around the issue of immunities, exemptions, and privileges of the Order to be 'logically' derived from its alleged international legal personality. What seems hardly disputable is that international legal personality cannot be drawn from the 'moral' nature of the activities carried out by the Order, as Italian courts occasionally adumbrate. Such activities are carried out also by several other transnational associations which are denied both international legal personality and immunities. If a state (such as Italy) is willing to favour and promote the Order's activities on grounds of their moral and humanitarian nature, it can do so without the need to appeal to international law, provided that this is in accordance with both Italian constitutional law and international human rights binding on Italy. Advocates of the Order's international legal personality, and the ensuing right to immunities, insist that the Order (in addition to its observer status at the United Nations) has made numerous agreements and entertains 'diplomatic relations' with several countries. However, relations with other states are not necessarily 'diplomatic relations' capable of proving that the Order is globally considered an international legal person, and the agreements made by the Order are all bilateral in character. Unlike the Holy See, the Order is not a party to any multilateral treaty. The Order might certainly be seen as a 'relief society' under the terms of the 1949 Geneva Conventions,[491] but it is not, unlike the Holy See, a party to such Conventions. The Order may be recognized by this or that state, for one or another reason and for certain ends, but it is far from being recognized by the generality of states as an international legal person. The possibility of abusing international legal personality in order to enjoy exemptions or other privileges is conspicuous in the 1978 *Bacchelli* Judgment. Here, the Italian Court of Cassation rightly denied both international legal personality and immunities to the plaintiff, who claimed to be entitled to tax exemption as 'prince of Lluchmager, sovereign and Grand Master of the Most Serene Military Order of the Glorious Saint Mary', with arguments partly similar to those of the Order of Malta.[492]

N Cox, 'The Acquisition of Sovereignty by Quasi-States: The Case of the Order of Malta' (2002) 6 Mountbatten Journal of Legal Studies 26, 40–1.

[490] Italian Council of State, Opinion of 23 February 2000 No 294/97 on the social security and assistance regime applicable to the SMOM, at <http://www.giustizia-amministrativa.it/novita/sec_sez/sez.294-97.htm> (original emphasis) (English trans by the author).

[491] cf Art 18 (I) Geneva Convention, Arts 14, 24, and 25 (II) Geneva Convention, Arts 123 and 125 (III) Geneva Convention, and Arts 39, 63, 140, and 142 (IV) Geneva Convention, as well as Art 18 (II) Additional Protocol.

[492] Italian Court of Cassation, *Bacchelli v Comune di Bologna* Judgment of 20 February 1978 No 804, (1979) 23 RDIPP 689. While denying the plaintiff's international legal personality and fiscal immunity, the Court distinguished this case from the status of the Order of Malta and affirmed that the Order of Malta, unlike the Order of the Glorious Saint Mary, was an international legal person.

(c) International Committee of the Red Cross (ICRC)

The International Committee of the Red Cross (ICRC) was established in 1863 in response to a proposal made by a Swiss citizen, Henry Dunant, who happened to witness the aftermath of the 1859 Battle of Solferino.[493] It has neither historical connection to territory nor aspiration to statehood. It defines itself as 'an impartial, neutral and independent organization whose exclusively humanitarian mission is to protect the lives and dignity of victims of war and other situations of violence and to provide them with assistance'.[494] Legally, the ICRC is a private, non-profit, Geneva-based association set up under, and governed by, Swiss law. It has its own statutes and legal personality under Swiss law.[495] Its members are fifteen to twenty-five persons, all of Swiss nationality, chosen by co-option. The permanent staff consists of around 12,500 persons, of which around 10,000 are local staff (mostly non-Swiss), operating in some eighty countries. The ICRC is financed through voluntary financial contributions, about 90 per cent of which are from states and the European Commission. The United States, the European Commission, the United Kingdom, and Switzerland are the larger donors.

The 1949 Geneva Conventions for the Protection of War Victims and their Additional Protocols assign to the ICRC a number of functions to be performed during an armed conflict. Article 81(1) Additional Protocol I stipulates 'the humanitarian functions assigned to [the ICRC] by the Conventions and this Protocol' during international armed conflict and points out the commitment of states parties to humanitarian treaties, particularly those engaged in an armed conflict, to grant the ICRC 'all facilities within their power' to enable it to carry out its tasks as specified in other treaty provisions, including visiting civilian places of detention or POW camps, organizing relief operations, or protecting the rights of those living in occupied territories. The ICRC may serve as a substitute for a Protecting Power, under common Articles 10 and 11 Geneva Conventions, and take any humanitarian initiative that it deems necessary, under common Articles 9 and 10 Geneva Conventions, although states remain at liberty not to accede to them. It may also 'offer its services' to the parties to a non-international armed conflict under Common Article 3 Geneva Conventions, without this being understood as interference in the internal affairs of the state concerned or a recognition of the insurgents.[496]

A number of scholars hold that the ICRC possesses international legal personality, although limited to what is required to carry out its mandate as set out in the 1949 Conventions and 1977 Additional Protocols, and in its Statutes. It is argued that most

[493] H Dunant, *A Memory of Solferino* (Geneva: ICRC, 1986).

[494] For a general overview, see Y Sandoz, *International Committee of the Red Cross: The International Committee of the Red Cross as Guardian of International Humanitarian Law* (Geneva: ICRC, 1998); DP Forsythe, *The Humanitarians: The International Committee of the Red Cross* (New York: CUP, 2005); DP Forsythe and BAJ Rieffer-Flanagan, *The International Committee of the Red Cross: A Neutral Humanitarian Actor* (Abingdon and New York: Routledge, 2007); H-P Gasser, 'International Committee of the Red Cross (ICRC)', MP EPIL (April 2009 update); SR Ratner, 'Law Promotion Beyond Law Talk: The Red Cross, Persuasion, and the Laws of War' (2011) 22 EJIL 459.

[495] Statutes of the International Committee of the Red Cross (adopted 8 May 2003, entered into force 8 May 2003) in ICRC and IFRC (eds), *Handbook of the International Red Cross and Red Crescent Movement* (Geneva: ICRC, 14th edn, 2008) 549.

[496] Previously, see Arts 79 and 88 of the Convention relative to the Treatment of Prisoners of War (signed 27 July 1929, entered into force 19 June 1931) 118 LNTS 343. See in addition Arts 123, 125, and 129 of 1949 Geneva Convention (III), Arts 140 and 143 of 1949 Geneva Convention (IV), and Art 5 of Additional Protocol (I).

states and IOs grant immunities and privileges to the ICRC; that the ICRC concludes agreements with states (including headquarters agreements),[497] IOs, insurgents, and other entities;[498] and finally, that the ICRC enjoys the observer status at the United Nations,[499] at various UN agencies and regional governmental organizations. Other scholars deny that the ICRC has the power to make international treaties proper governed by international law.[500] The ICTY held in the 1999 *Simic* Decision that 'It is widely acknowledged that the ICRC, an independent humanitarian organization, enjoys a special status in international law, based on the mandate conferred to it by the international community' and that 'the ICRC has a right under customary international law to non-disclosure of the information', adding in a footnote that 'It is generally acknowledged that the ICRC, although a private organization under Swiss law, has an international legal personality'.[501] This rule has been taken up in Article 73 (4) ICC Rules of Procedure and Evidence whereby the information or documents 'which [the ICRC] came into the possession of in the course, or as a consequence, of the performance by ICRC of its functions under the Statutes of the International Red Cross and Red Crescent Movement' are to be treated as privileged communications and information, and not subject to disclosure unless the ICRC waives its privilege or the information is included in public statements and documents.[502]

It is hardly questionable that the ICRC 'has a pivotal [as well as "unique"] role in the regime established by the Geneva Conventions and their Protocols'.[503] However, to state that the ICRC's right to non-disclosure is embodied in customary international law, resulting from state practice and *opinio juris*, as the ICTY stated, is far from necessarily implying that the ICRC has a 'right' under international law, and can also be read in the sense that criminal tribunals are not given by the states (in furtherance of *their* obligation under customary international law) the power to compel the ICRC to disclose information in court. The ICRC legal structure is in some respects similar to that of NGOs, but unlike NGOs the ICRC is called upon to perform important functions in situations of armed conflict as set out in the Geneva Conventions and

[497] Agreement between the International Committee of the Red Cross and the Swiss Federal Council to Determine the Legal Status of the Committee in Switzerland (signed 19 March 1993), 33 IRRC (1993) 152. Under this Agreement, Switzerland guarantees the ICRC's 'independence and freedom of action', assures the inviolability of its premises, and grants immunity from legal process and execution, not only to the institution, but also to its staff in the exercise of their official functions.

[498] C Dominicé, 'La personnalité juridique internationale du CICR' in Swinarski (n 286 above) 663, 668; P Reuter, 'La personnalité juridique internationale du Comité international de la Croix-Rouge' in Swinarski (n 286 above) 783, 789; Parlett (n 244 above) 35–6, stressing, however, the monopolistic role of states as gatekeepers of the entry of legal persons in the international legal system (see in addition n 567 below).

[499] UNGA Res 45/6 of 16 October 1990, GAOR 45th Session Supp 49, 15, considering 'the special role carried on . . . by the International Committee of the Red Cross in international humanitarian relations'. Observer status was also given in 1994 to the International Federation of the Red Cross and Red Crescent Societies by UNGA Res 49/2 of 19 October 1994.

[500] E David, *Principes de droit des conflits armées* (Brussels: Bruylant, 3rd edn, 2002) 579.

[501] ICTY, *Prosecutor v Simic et al*, Decision on the Prosecution Motion under Rule 73 for a Ruling concerning the Testimony of a Witness of 27 July 1999, Case No IT-95-9, paras 46, 72–74, finding that the ICRC could only discharge its mandate if it could maintain its practice (that the parties to the Geneva Conventions must be taken as having accepted) of not testifying before courts. For comments, see S Jeannet, 'Recognition of the ICRC's Long-Standing Rule of Confidentiality' (2000) 82 IRRC 403; G Rona, 'The ICRC Privilege not to Testify: Confidentiality in Action' (2002) 84 IRRC 207. See in addition *Prosecutor v Radoslav Brdjanin and Momir Talić* Decision on Interlocutory Appeal of 11 December 2002, Case No ICTY-99-36, para 34.

[502] ICC, Rules of Procedure and Evidence (adopted 9 September 2002) Doc ICC-ASP/1/3 (Pt II-A).

[503] ICTY, *Prosecutor v Simic et al* (n 501 above) para 72.

Additional Protocols.[504] While it is thus inaccurate to regard the ICRC as an NGO, it is also inappropriate to qualify it as an IO, if only because of its private membership and establishment under Swiss law. It is true that the headquarters agreements concluded by the ICRC do provide for its exemption from jurisdiction and taxation, as well as for the inviolability of its premises and archives, but only as a matter of domestic law. Given its unique position, every effort to deduce its international legal personality from other international subjects is unwarranted. The better view is to see it as a private association like any other that states have mandated to perform on their behalf certain functions. However important such functions may be, and certainly are, it is states as a whole that 'use' the ICRC as an independent body to carry out the legal rules contained in the Geneva Conventions and Protocols, to which the ICRC is not a party. Rights and obligations exist between the states which are parties to the Conventions, not between states and the ICRC, and the ICRC supplies its specialized and reputed services as any other state-mandated private association may do.

D. Disaggregating International Legal Personality

The term 'international legal personality' (ILP) has recurrently surfaced in the preceding sections. It is helpful now to explore how ILP as a general concept accommodates all the various internationally relevant activities of the players reviewed above. One might expect that ILP provides a unitary conceptualization of them all, but this is hardly the case.[505] The present section argues that ILP is a construction which is open to disaggregation in a variety of different meanings in different contexts (as to both its requirements and practical legal consequences) and to manipulative use to favour 'deserving' actors. A given entity may be an 'international legal subject' in one sense and not in another, for one legal effect and not for another, with little or no general reason to prefer one sense rather than another, and even the often alleged positive/progressive or negative/conservative impact of ILP depends on the circumstances. That is, behind one and the same word or concept lies a large number of different legal realities that call for analytical scrutiny. All meanings of ILP ultimately end up referring, in one way or another, to 'who ultimately decides who decides' in global affairs, which is states.

(1) Legal personality in international law

Unlike in domestic law, there is no centralized law of persons in the international legal system. No principle or norm in international law provides clear indications concerning what is meant by ILP (or international subjectivity), what entities are international legal persons (or subjects) on the basis of what criteria or requirements, and which legal consequences flow from their qualification as legal persons (or subjects).[506] The

[504] See Forsythe and Rieffer-Flanagan (n 494 above) 2, also noting that the ICRC's secrecy policy stands in contrast to the work of many NGOs (at 99–101), and assuming anyway that the ICRC is a 'rather unique' NGO; Ratner (n 494 above) 472.

[505] For the view that 'there is no definition of personality in international law which is sufficiently comprehensive to apply in some constructive or realistic way to all the different types of entities which operate in the international field', see E Lauterpacht, 'The Development of the Law of International Organization by the Decisions of International Tribunals' (1976-IV) 152 RdC 377, 403.

[506] The terms 'subject' and 'person' are today routinely used interchangeably (see n 508 below), although the two terms have sometimes been given different meanings (cf *Restatement of the Law, Third, Foreign Relations Law of the United States* (n 104 above) vol 1, 70).

classical doctrine is that only states are international legal persons, or that only states 'form part' of the international realm, or that international law solely 'emanates' from states and exclusively 'applies' to (or can bind) states, specifically those states that have consented to it.[507] This implies that entities other than states (in particular individuals) do not form part of the international realm, and do not make and cannot be bound by international law. It also implies that international law cannot bind the states themselves in cases where they have not consented to this.

In the 1949 *Reparation for Injuries* Advisory Opinion the ICJ held that the United Nations was an 'international legal person', meaning that 'it is a subject of international law and capable of possessing international rights and duties', including the right to bring international claims.[508] ILP was defined in terms of capacity to possess rights and duties deriving from international law. The Opinion added that 'The subjects of law in any legal system are not necessarily identical in their nature or in the extent of their rights, and their nature depends upon the needs of the community'.[509] While most writers accept, on this basis, a more inclusive range of international legal persons extended to non-state actors, a few have discarded ILP altogether by replacing it—along with its implied traditional subject–object dichotomy[510]—with the concept of active 'participation' in international relations, or in the international decision-making process, by non-state actors,[511] or by other notions such as legal capacities,[512] international legal relationships,[513] or actual or preferable exercise of functions.[514]

International and domestic practice shows that ILP is evoked in different contexts, in different terms, with regard to different players (raising uncertainties even within one and the same category of players), and for different purposes. States are 'naturally' regarded as international legal persons. IOs are considered to be international legal persons in the sense that they exist legally and can be held responsible as separate entities from the member states. Individuals are regarded as international subjects in particular to emphasize their position as ultimate holders of fundamental *rights* antecedent and superior to the state in order to conclude that the state has a (non-state-contingent) duty to protect individuals. When international *obligations* are placed on individuals, this is generally premised on the notion that powerholders have duties (and personally account for their breaches) vis-à-vis those other individuals who are subjected to their power, ie as an implication of the *rights* conferred on any individual vis-à-vis the state and possibly those who *pro tempore* exert power on its behalf. NGOs may be held to be international legal persons in order to provide them with international rights to participate in global governance. By contrast, MNEs' ILP is grounded in the need for their subjection to international duties and exposition to international responsibility for their gravest abuses. The ILP of insurgents is premised on their effectiveness on the ground, while claims to ILP by national liberation movements prescinds from effectiveness and hinges on the very cause of their fight for self-determination. Finally,

[507] cf PCIJ, *The Case of the SS Lotus* (n 1 above). For a lucid overview of Heinrich Triepel's, Dionisio Anzilotti's, and Lassa Oppenheim's doctrinal insights along these lines, see R Portmann, *Legal Personality in International Law* (Cambridge: CUP, 2010) 42–7.

[508] ICJ, *Reparation for Injuries Suffered in the Service of the United Nations* (n 225 above) 179.

[509] Ibid 178.

[510] See G Manner, 'The Object Theory of the Individual in International Law' (1952) 46 AJIL 428.

[511] Higgins (n 183 above) 50.

[512] DP O'Connell, *International Law* (London: Stevens and Sons, 2nd edn, 1970) vol 1, 82–3.

[513] C Walter, 'Subjects of International Law', MP EPIL (May 2007 update) paras 20–31.

[514] C Schreuer, 'The Waning of the Sovereign State: Towards a New Paradigm for International Law?' (1994) 4 EJIL 447, 453.

the ILP of the Holy See, of the Order of Malta, and of the ICRC is based on historical considerations, on their role, tasks, and general recognition from states.

To complicate matters, the requirements and the consequences of ILP vary with the player and/or the category of players involved. For some players (for example, states themselves, IOs, the Holy See, and the Order of Malta) the possession of ILP implicates in practice jurisdictional and fiscal immunities in foreign courts and/or within the domestic jurisdiction of the forum state, although this is not generally the case for other players (for example, individuals, NGOs, and MNEs). While for certain players effectiveness is decisive (for example, states, insurgents, and MNEs at least in terms of power exerted in global governance), for others different factors, including justice, appear more weighty (for example, individuals). The ILP of certain players (for example, IOs, national liberation movements, MNEs, and the Order of Malta) is often justified in terms of treaty-making power, while others apparently have less or no need to display such a capacity (for example, individuals). For some players the possession of international duties and the exposition to international responsibility is crucial (for example, MNEs), while for others it is rights and the capacity to invoke international responsibility that appears central (for example, individuals).

(2) Defining a legal 'persona'

The term 'person' comes from the Latin *persona*, meaning 'mask'. A legal person is defined as an entity that exists as a matter of law, or as viewed from the standpoint of law, similar to a masked person on stage or an actor viewed as such from the audience's perspective. Slaves of the past were not legal persons, or 'subjects' of law, but rather 'objects' of their masters. A group of people who are legal persons when taken one by one, may lack legal personality if taken as a group. The notion of legal personality, first built in domestic private law, concerned individual human beings in their mutual relations and then juridical persons. It was subsequently applied to the (modern European) state in order to keep state officials and the ruled distinct from the state for domestic law purposes. Eventually, the doctrine was extended to the relations between states, at first European and subsequently any other state, as distinct entities from both the ruler and the ruled for international law purposes. Finally, the doctrine has been applied to players acting on the international scene other than states.

Throughout this process, every shift from one stage to another has caused a partial change in the meaning of legal personality. At the *first stage*, legal personality was invoked for those who did not exist as a matter of law, and whose life, legally speaking, depended entirely on other people who were recognized as persons by the law, as is typically the case with slaves and masters. Thus defined, legal personality means 'emancipation'. It means that those who do not legally exist may come into legal existence and handle their lives autonomously. Of course, the recognition of legal personality means that the person recognized is attributed not only rights but also obligations. But even obligations, in so far as they are established and limited by the law, are a sign of emancipation compared to legal non-existence, ie compared to existing as a mere 'object' and being legally at the complete mercy of others.

At the *second stage*, when applied to the state itself, the notion of legal personality changed in meaning. To assert that the state is a legal person means that the state itself is the holder of rights and the bearer of obligations regardless of the natural persons who are members thereof, whether rulers, state officials, or citizens. The state comes to be seen, in particular, as a permanent institution separated from its *pro tempore* rulers.

Absolute monarchical power yields to liberal constitutionalism. Rulers are deemed to 'administrate' the state on behalf of the ruled, who acquire 'rights' vis-à-vis the state. Thus defined, legal personality means 'rule of law', ie less arbitrariness on the part of the state through the acts of its rulers and state officials. At the same time, however, the legal personality of the state means that rulers and state officials, while acting on behalf of the state and the ruled, are legally separate from the state and basically not responsible for their official acts. Only the 'state' can be brought to account, but the state as distinct from the rulers means the collectivity and the collectivity ultimately means the ruled themselves taken as a whole. Rights may remain on paper, while the correlative obligations may shift from the ruler and state officials to the state as an abstract entity behind which one finds once again the ruled, who end up facing the consequences of what rulers and state officials do. Briefly, the legal personality of the state implies a legal personality of the ruled, who now have rights and duties towards the state, while the rulers tend to disappear behind the state veil.

At the *third stage*, the legal separation of the state from rulers, state officials, and the ruled extends to inter-state relations. The concept of ILP (*persona jure gentium*) was apparently first introduced by Gottfried Leibniz in 1693 to legitimize the participation of the German princes in the international life of eighteenth-century Europe,[515] although the term 'moral person' had previously been used by Thomas Hobbes, meaning the multitude becoming 'One Person' embodied in the Sovereign, and by Samuel Pufendorf, referring to the state,[516] and Leibniz himself appears to have referred the concept of *persona juris gentium* still to the ruler, not to the state.[517] The concept was later developed by Christian Wolff, arguing that nations could have rights and duties, under *jus gentium*, that were not necessarily rights and duties of their members, thereby implying that individuals (including state officials) were no longer responsible for violations of *jus gentium* but only states were, whereas states could not be judged like individuals and their relations were ultimately dominated by war.[518] The process from an inter-ruler to an inter-state *jus gentium* was completed by Emmerich de Vattel, who rejected Wolff's idea of a *civitas maxima* and endorsed the notion that international law was a law between states as 'moral persons'.[519] It only applied to states, all other entities (in particular individuals) being subjected to one or another state. It is towards the end of the seventeenth century that treaties began to refer to states as parties.[520] The ILP of the state now meant that rulers, state officials, and the ruled had to be treated under international law as distinct from the state by other states. It has been suggested that this state-centric theory was historically and conceptually developed mainly by the nineteenth-century German public law doctrine concomitant with the formation of a national German state emancipated by the Imperial legacy—ruler and citizens now tied under the banner of the 'nation'—and was unsurprisingly in line with German

[515] ED Dickinson, 'The Analogy between Natural Persons and International Persons in the Law of Nations' (1917) 26 Yale LJ 564, 568–74; Nijman (n 254 above) 77–80; Portmann (n 507 above) 35–8.

[516] See Nijman (n 254 above) 50–8, excluding that Hobbes referred the term to the state as such and that Pufendorf (who did refer it to the state as such) used it to mean ILP.

[517] ibid 77–9. For Leibniz's notion of *persona juris gentium*, see n 558 below and accompanying text.

[518] Nijman (n 254 above) 80–3.

[519] De Vattel (n 197 above) 1, § 2, observing that '[l'Etat] devient une personne morale, qui a son entendement et sa volonté propre, et qui est capable d'obligations et de droits'.

[520] See Grewe (n 84 above) 196, 361; R Lesaffer, 'The Grotian Tradition Revisited: Change and Continuity in the History of International Law' (2002) 73 BYBIL 103, 130–1.

imperialist projects and military action abroad as a way of 'settling' legal disputes.[521] International law was progressively used to force all polities and peoples other than states either to become a state or to disappear and be absorbed into an existing state. Not only were individuals irrelevant to international law, but also every people was either irrelevant or downgraded to an 'element' of statehood. While individuals and peoples were governed by the domestic law of one or another state, states were governed by international law.[522] Thus defined, ILP meant 'emancipation' from subjection to colonial powers when certain pre-existing (European) 'standards of civilization' were met.[523] Non-European peoples who acquired ILP could deal with the pre-existing legal persons on an equal footing in the global system, at least formally.[524]

Finally, at the *fourth stage*, when the question of international legal status arose in respect of new international entities like the League of Nations,[525] the International Institute for Agriculture,[526] the Bank for International Settlements (BIS),[527] as well as in respect of minorities (or their individual members) and the individual in general,[528] in a context strongly critical of state legal personality,[529] ILP has been progressively attached to 'non-state' entities, some indeed aspiring to become a state (for example, national liberation movements), others having no such aspirations (for example, individuals, IOs, MNEs, NGOs, and the ICRC). With regard to the former, the question is pre-eminently one of emancipation, as for ancient slaves and modern colonized peoples. In respect of the latter, as hinted earlier, the matter is more intricate. When referred to IOs, ILP is often evoked in terms of both emancipation (to stress that an IO is independent from its member states) and state irresponsibility (to note that states may recognize and use the ILP of IOs to enable IOs to do what they are not allowed to do directly). As for MNEs, ILP has an almost opposite meaning, the key issue being how states can make MNEs account at the international level. The problem with MNEs is not to 'elevate' their status to a higher degree of (legal) autonomy, but rather to contain their (factual) autonomy and make them account for their abuses. When it comes to individuals and NGOs, the point is generally how to grant them more rights, going so far (with regard to individuals serving as state organs charged with international crimes) as to pierce the veil of the state and punish rulers and state officials for the breach of international obligations directly placed on them, regardless of their legal separateness from the state.

(3) Disaggregating international legal 'personae'

The notion that ILP amounts to the possession of international rights and duties, as endorsed by the ICJ in the *Reparation for Injuries* Opinion, is far from satisfactory. On the one hand, it allows the identification of international subjects other than states, as was the case with the United Nations at the time; on the other hand, it does not address

[521] Portmann (n 507 above) 47–64.

[522] On 'dualism' in the relationship between international law and domestic law, see Ch 6 below, section D (2)(a).

[523] See Ch 6 below, n 169.

[524] See Anghie (n 88 above) 32–114.

[525] See n 223 above.

[526] See n 222 above.

[527] See n 209 above.

[528] See nn 245–53 above.

[529] See eg N Politis, *The New Aspects of International Law* (Washington: Carnegie Endowment for International Peace, 1928) 13–14. For Kelsen's view, see n 534 below.

the question of who makes the rules containing such rights and duties and who decides who should make the rules. If the rules are made exclusively by states, ILP may indeed extend to non-state actors, but still within a state-centric system. If a different notion of ILP is endorsed, either individuals or states are not international subjects, depending on the theory accepted: the first conclusion is undesirable, the second is unrealistic.

(a) Possession of rights and duties

If international subjects are those which hold rights and bear duties stemming from international law, according to the *Reparation for Injuries* Opinion, then individuals may be international subjects. According to this view individuals are international subjects only under *one* meaning of ILP. But if ILP is defined in terms of law-making,[530] then individuals are not international subjects since they do not generally make international law: the rights and duties of individuals are those so recognized by states.[531] While there is no particular difficulty in describing individuals as international subjects as bearers of international rights and duties, there remains to be determined in what specific sense states also are international subjects. The answer cannot be homogenous. States *uti singuli* may be international subjects because states *uti universi* make rules addressed to any of them. States are legally relevant both because they make international law and, most importantly, because they successfully reserve only for themselves the ultimate authority to decide 'who decides' in international affairs. This latter meaning of ILP is self-evidently different from the one applied to individuals. It thus seems that one and the same term ('ILP') means two different things when applied to two different entities like individuals and states. Moreover, the same term 'ILP' is apparently used to draw different legal consequences, such as the jurisdictional immunity of foreign states and prosecution for international crimes, respectively. It is true that the ICJ specified in the *Reparation for Injuries* Opinion that the subjects of law, including international subjects, are 'not necessarily identical in their nature or in the extent of their rights', their nature depending on 'the needs of the community' and international law being influenced by 'the requirements of international life'.[532] However, it is difficult to see what purpose the concept of ILP can serve (including what weight can plausibly be given to such elusive criteria as 'the needs of the community' and 'the requirements of international life')[533] when in practice it splits into various, unrelated or even counter-related, meanings.

Particularly congenial to the definition of legal personality as possession of rights and duties is Hans Kelsen's theory of legal personality as a mere 'construction of juristic thinking' referring to a substance which 'is not a separate entity besides "its" duties and rights, but only their personified unity', just as 'The leaf is not a new entity in addition to all [its] qualities'.[534] Thus defined, legal personality is nothing other than the sum of individual rights and/or duties of any particular entity, to which legal rules refer, as resulting from the interpretations of the relevant rules, without any premise or

530 See section D (3)(c) below.

531 For insights into Karl Strupp's, Arrigo Cavaglieri's, and Georg Schwarzenberger's theorization of this 'recognition conception' of ILP and for the surrounding historical and doctrinal context, see Portmann (n 507 above) 80–99.

532 See n 509 above.

533 See section D (3)(h) below.

534 H Kelsen, *General Theory of Law and State* [1945] (New Brunswick and London: Transaction Publishers, 2007) 93–109. Kelsen's theory of legal personality is defined (and basically endorsed, with an exception in favour of individuals' ILP in certain circumstances) as 'formal' by Portmann (n 507 above) 173–207.

consequences. The problem with Kelsen's theory is precisely his normativist hallmark and, in particular, his equations of the state with the legal system and of the legal person with the single rules of which it consists. To say that an entity is a legal person because it has (or, more accurately, because 'it is') rights and duties says nothing in itself about who makes the rules in such a way as to envisage this entity as a holder of rights and/or duties. If this entity is a legal person, what is the (different) legal status of the other entity which makes the rules? Since in Kelsen's theory a rule is a (valid) rule because there is another rule stating so—the process culminating in the (legally undefined and indefinable) 'basic norm'—no one is 'properly' the law-maker except for the law itself. This 'purely normativist' existence of rules and legal persons is hardly satisfactory in making sense of law in our material world. Another difficulty with Kelsen's theory is that once one accepts that legal personality is a 'construction of juristic thinking' which adds nothing to rights and/or duties attached to an entity, then one wonders why the concept is retained. It only generically means that an entity has one or more rights and/or duties for one or another purpose, but it is of no avail to know exactly what rights or duties for what purpose.

The criterion of possession of rights and duties for defining legal personality is in particular accepted in international legal doctrine when arguing that also entities other than states may possess ILP *if states so agree*. For example, it is frequently argued today that individuals are 'international subjects', although they do not make the law, in so far as they are accorded international rights and/or duties by states.[535] This view is rooted in the sociological approach to international law, notably in the realist variant.[536] While acknowledging the ILP of non-state actors, it presupposes the centrality of states, which remain the 'primary' international law subjects. Non-state actors may be holders of international rights and/or duties to the extent that these are conferred by states when they so wish. States are thus clearly seen as the supreme authorities in international relations.[537] As such, not only do they make the rules; they also establish who else may make the rules and to whom the rules apply. All that occurs in international relations, including the ILP of single states and of non-state actors, depends on the states as a whole.

Another theory which may match the notion of ILP as possession of rights and duties is the one based on international law as an 'open system'.[538] The system is thought to be open to any entity, state and non-state alike, which possesses international rights and/or duties according to the interpretation of the relative rules, including individuals in line with the 'basic premises' of contemporary international law. While the concept of openness of the system is clear, it remains less clear what kind of openness is upheld, which criteria are to be used to identity to whom exactly the system is open and why, and who makes the rules in such a way as to confer this or that right and/or obligation on this or that entity. To argue that the system's openness is simply a function of the 'basic premises' of contemporary international law amounts to grounding ILP—and

[535] See n 531 above. For the view that states occasionally confer upon individuals 'international rights *stricto sensu*, i.e. rights which they acquire without the intervention of municipal legislation and which they enforce in their own name before international tribunals', and that individuals are subjects of international law when states treat them as directly endowed with international rights and duties, see R Jennings and A Watts, *Oppenheim's International Law* (Harlow: Longman, 9th edn, 1992) 16–17, 506–8, 847.

[536] See Ch 4 above, section B (6).

[537] See section D (3)(d) below.

[538] See Portmann (n 507 above), 271–2, referring to JR Crawford, *International Law as an Open System: Selected Essays* (London: Cameron May, 2002) 27–8.

possible rights and/or duties of non-state actors, notably individuals—in abstractions (or intellectual constructions) which may equally justify several different, if not opposing, outcomes.

If, by espousing one or another of the above theories, non-state actors are regarded as international subjects in that they possess international rights and duties, a number of other problems arise. The fact that a rule of international law provides for a right or a duty does not necessarily mean that the apparent holder of the right or the apparent bearer of the duty are the 'real addressees' of the rule.

One difficulty is that considerable ambiguity lies in the language used in the 'rights' debate surrounding the ILP of individuals.[539] It is often said that the international law of human rights provides for 'rights' of individuals and the conclusion is drawn that individuals must then be international subjects (as opposed to objects) endowed with ILP. But the association of the word 'right' with a certain entity in an international instrument does not necessarily mean that such a right is an international right of that entity. By way of illustration, a Universal Declaration on Animal Rights (UDAR) proclaimed in Paris on 15 October 1978 at the UNESCO headquarters mentions a number of 'rights' to which animals are said to be entitled.[540] Under Article 1 'All animals have equal rights to exist within the context of biological equilibrium'; Article 4 stipulates that 'Wild animals have the right to live and to reproduce in freedom in their own natural environment', etc. Leaving aside the UDAR's non-binding nature, few would conclude from this rights-based language that all animals on earth are 'international legal persons' on the ground of the language of UDAR. Many would read such provisions in the sense that human beings should treat animals in accordance therewith. It may well be that animals have 'rights' under one or another theory of human or animal rights,[541] but the term is used in UDAR as a shorthand to indicate that *others* have correlative duties. Since it is apparently an international instrument, the most obvious meaning of UDAR is that *states* have an obligation to see to it that within their jurisdiction human beings are compelled to treat animals accordingly. This construction is supported by other provisions of UDAR, such as those found in Article 3 providing that 'Animals must not be subjected to bad treatments or to cruel acts', that 'If it is necessary to kill an animal, it must be instantaneous, painless and cause no apprehension', and that 'A dead animal must be treated with decency'. The reading here proposed, despite the language used, presupposes that it is states *in their relations* that have mutual obligations and are international legal persons in the sense of possession of rights and duties. Despite the language used, it is not animals who are given substantive rights let alone procedural rights to file petitions.

Another source of ambiguity of the ILP theory based on the possession of international rights and duties is the 'domestic' aspect of the rights-based language. When international instruments accord 'rights' to this or that entity, it is generally left unanswered whether these rights are designed to work internationally or domestically.[542] When a 'right' is apparently granted to an individual, this right may be

[539] The same uncertainty surrounds the debate on treaty-conferred rights to individuals dating back to the PCIJ's 1928 Advisory Opinion on the *Jurisdiction of the Courts of Danzig* (n 543 below).

[540] cf <http://www.shahmai.org/udar.html>.

[541] CR Sunstein and MC Nussbaum (eds), *Animal Rights: Current Debates and New Directions* (Oxford and New York: OUP, 2004); R Garner, *The Political Theory of Animal Rights* (Manchester: Manchester University Press, 2005); GL Francione and R Garner, *The Animal Rights Debate: Abolition or Regulation?* (New York: Columbia University Press, 2010).

[542] See German Constitutional Court, *Bombing of the Bridge of Varvarin* Judgment of 2 November 2006, at <http://lexetius.com/2006,2924>, arguing that individuals are today international subjects,

understood in a variety of different legal meanings. Individuals may formally have 'substantive rights' flowing from a (state-made) treaty, yet be deprived of the legal power to invoke them in national or international courts. Or they may have the legal power to invoke their rights in an international court or other monitoring body, but not in national courts. Or they may have the power to invoke their rights before a monitoring body which, however, is not allowed to adopt binding decisions or before an international court which is indeed entrusted to adopt binding decisions but lacks enforcement mechanisms. Even when an international right can be exceptionally invoked by individuals in domestic courts without any incorporating legislation, the fact remains that the right has been created by the states, is recognized by state courts, and will possibly be enforced by state authorities. Consider a provision in an international treaty whereby workers have a 'right to holiday'. This provision may mean either that the *states* parties are required to accord workers such a right within their legal systems,[543] or that *workers* themselves have the right and are entitled to invoke it before domestic courts without any further domestic legislation.[544] In the first scenario, workers appear as *domestic* legal persons in so far as the state creates their right domestically, while the state may be held internationally responsible towards the other states parties to the treaty for non-performance of its treaty obligations. In the second scenario, workers are given a right directly enforceable in domestic courts, ie a right that the worker can invoke in domestic courts on the basis of the treaty without any need for domestic entitlement and regardless of the attitude of national executive and legislatives bodies. Even in this second scenario, however, the worker may still appear as a *domestic* legal person who invokes a right that is part of the domestic law to the extent that the treaty itself has become 'the law of the land' as a result of domestic (constitutional or standard) law. While in the first scenario the word 'right' translates into an *obligation of the state* to create and respect it within its legal system, in the second scenario the term indeed denotes a right of the individual, but *a domestic right*, not an international one, although created at the international level. The fact that the 'right' is set out in an international instrument is in this respect irrelevant. Direct enforceability of a rule of international law is not equal to ILP, although it does give individuals more opportunities *in the domestic legal system*. That international law governs (or is routinely construed in such a way as to govern) relations between individuals within states is one thing; the fact that individuals possess *international* rights is quite another. Evidence of ILP may derive only from those rights, whether substantive or procedural,

although 'partial', on the basis of a 'pre-statehood' element of human dignity and of the fact that international law 'may attribute rights and obligations directly to individual persons' (§§ 9–10). This does not imply, however, that every legal regime concerned with individuals provides for individual rights (§ 11).

[543] PCIJ, *Jurisdiction of the Courts of Danzig* Advisory Opinion of 3 March 1928, PCIJ Series B No 15, at 17–18, holding that 'an international agreement cannot, as such, create direct rights and obligations for private individuals', but this does not exclude the possibility that 'the very object of an international agreement, according to the intentions of the contracting Parties, may be the adoption by the Parties of some definite rules creating individual rights and obligations enforceable by the national courts'. For the opposing readings of this dictum in legal doctrine, see Parlett (note 244 above) 17–26.

[544] Italian Court of Cassation, *Armenio et al v Società Caramar* Judgment of 10 September 1993 No 9459, (1995) 78 RDI 807, ruling that Art 3(3) of the ILO Seafarers' Annual Leave with Pay Convention of 29 October 1976 No 146 (whereby 'The leave shall in no case be less than 30 calendar days for one year of service' to be read in combination with Art 3(1) whereby 'Every seafarer to whom this Convention applies shall be entitled to annual leave with pay of a specified minimum length') is not self-executing, does not 'enter' the domestic legal system, and thus does not provide for a right of seafarers to annual leave with pay of no fewer than 30 calendar days.

that individuals can claim either internationally towards the state or domestically in cases where the internationally created right prevails over contrary domestic law, *not* on the basis of domestic law itself (the same applying also to international duties). Even so, not only do international rights and duties of individuals require and presuppose the states for their very creation, but state courts and enforcement authorities are still needed to have them recognized and enforced. Once the question is reduced to these terms, the likelihood of the conclusion that an individual is an international legal person on the basis of the possession of international rights and duties is very low indeed and the ILP of individuals seems to be shorthand pre-eminently to indicate a wider range of *domestic* rights and duties of international origin, and hence, more accurately, *a domestic empowerment* of the individual *as a result of international law*.

A further problem in defining ILP in terms of possession of international rights and duties is circularity.[545] When courts are called upon to decide whether a certain entity is, or is not, an international person in order to provide an answer to specific questions, such as the granting of jurisdictional immunities to IOs or the classification of agreements made by national liberation movements as 'international treaties' proper, ILP works as a precondition for a legal consequence. For example, a given IO may be accorded jurisdictional immunity or its agreements may be classified as international treaties depending on the determination that it is an international legal person. But in order to determine whether this IO is an international legal person reliance is often placed on the fact that courts generally accord it jurisdictional immunities or capacity to make international treaties. Briefly, an entity is recognized as an international legal person if it is accorded a certain right, but it is accorded a certain right if it is recognized as an international legal person. The problem of circularity is inherent in the conception of ILP as the possession of international rights and duties and tends to lead the theorist to do away with ILP altogether. If what matters is rights and duties, then all that is needed is rights and duties. ILP appears as a manipulative 'super-structure' usable to reach desired outcomes by conveniently selecting the premise. Circularity may apparently be avoided if at least two different meanings of ILP are devised: one works as the premise and the other as the consequence. For example, an entity may be an international legal person according to one meaning of ILP (for instance because it is generally recognized to have the capacity to make international treaties) in order to draw the desired consequence (for example, 'therefore' it enjoys jurisdictional immunity). This, however, exposes the concept of ILP to instability and arbitrariness: the decision as to which premise works for which consequence is a matter of taste at best. The various meanings of ILP could be combined in several ways and offer the opportunity to reach virtually any desired outcome. They can of course also be reversed, using the consequence as the premise.

Finally, the often-cited distinction between 'primary' (or 'full', 'direct', 'active') ILP ascribed to states and 'partial' (or 'indirect', 'specially adapted', 'passive') ILP ascribed to non-state international actors is largely misleading. In the *Reparation for Injuries* Opinion the ICJ pointed out that, presumably unlike other international subjects, 'a state possesses the *totality* of international rights and duties recognized by international

[545] See J Klabbers, 'The Concept of Legal Personality', 11 *Ius Gentium* (2005) 35, 49; and, more in general, for the ambivalences of subjects doctrine, J Klabbers, '(I Can't Get No) Recognition: Subjects Doctrine and the Emergence of Non-state Actors' in J Petman and J Klabbers (eds), *Nordic Cosmopolitanism: Essays in International Law for Martti Koskenniemi* (Leiden: Nijhoff, 2003) 351; P Sands and P Klein, *Bowett's Law of International Institutions* (London: Sweet & Maxwell, 6th edn, 2009) 476. Against the circularity argument, see Rama-Montaldo (n 227 above) 116.

law' and that international subjects other than states possess ILP precisely because states so wish.[546] While the underlying idea is that states are still the 'central' international subjects, 'some' weight is also given to other entities. However, the role attributed to 'partial' international subjects remains unclear. This partiality, inter alia, could presumably be differently understood depending on the subject (or the category of subjects) concerned.

(b) Legal relevance

ILP may also refer, more generically, to the 'legal relevance' of a certain entity by attaching to it further deontic modes other than rights and duties or prohibitions, such as capacities, competences, or permissions to act in a legally relevant way, for example by entering into contracts or committing torts, the consequence of both acts being determined by the legal system.[547] If the concept of ILP is understood in terms of 'legal relevance', the circle of subjects may become larger than only possessors of rights and duties: even animals could be thought to be 'legal subjects' to the extent that the law provides other entities with rights and duties for their protection. It is generally in this broad sense that certain 'deserving' entities are considered to be legal 'subjects', meaning that the law is not completely silent on them and indeed protects them.

It is difficult, however, to see the protected entities as being other than 'objects' of the law, unless one is prepared to accept a notion of 'subject' so loose to make no difference between those entities who may (and must) actually do something for the protection of the protected entities and these latter. Put differently, to reiterate the previous example, it seems that the position of states within UDAR is not exactly the same as that of the animals. If the 'traditional' dichotomy between subjects and objects is to be discarded, as many today claim,[548] there is still the question of deciding if and how the above difference should be signalled.[549] A variation of both the 'legal relevance' and the 'rights and duties' approach is ILP of either states or non-state actors deriving from explicit or implicit recognition by pre-existing states.[550]

(c) Law-making capacity

Another frequent meaning associated with ILP is the capacity to make international law. It is those who make international law that are often described as 'international subjects'.[551] In so far as international law is created on the basis of powers or competences conferred on the law-making entities by other rules of international law itself (evidently made by others previously) this meaning tends to overlap with possession of international rights and duties and legal relevance. Once ILP is understood in these terms, the circle of international legal persons shrinks, since presumably only states and a few IOs, specifically those having the power to adopt legally binding decisions and to make treaties autonomously, may be said to make international law. Non-state actors do not generally make international law and are, thus, not

[546] ICJ, *Reparation for Injuries Suffered in the Service of the United Nations* (n 225 above) 180.
[547] See Portmann (n 507 above) 8.
[548] See n 510 above, and n 557 below.
[549] Parlett (n 244 above) 352–3, ends up introducing the dichotomy in terms of 'active subjects' (states) and 'passive recipients' of international rights and obligations (individuals).
[550] ibid 13, 80–125.
[551] ibid 3 and 8.

international subjects in the sense of law-making, although—as seen earlier—they may indeed be international subjects because of possession of rights and duties under (state-made) international law.[552] Entities such as MNEs and national liberation movements do make agreements, but these are rarely regarded as international treaties governed by international law. Even entities that make treaties proper may not necessarily participate in the formation of customary international law.[553]

It is worth noting that the entities which are international subjects as law-makers are also those which determine who is a subject as addressee of the law, ie as a holder of rights and/or a bearer of duties, or who should be considered legally relevant and to be protected. It is law-makers who decide to whom the law they make applies or is designed to protect. In this sense, the entities that make the law are *decisive* and 'antecedent' to both the addressees and the protected entities of the law. Even more decisive in turn are the entities that make the law which confers the power to make rules of international law on other entities. It could be said that those who are the 'very first' sources of the law are 'original' or 'primary' subjects and those who make the law as a result of law-making powers conferred upon them by the former, as well as those who receive the law, are 'derivative' or 'secondary' subjects.[554] ILP could then be defined as the status (traditionally reserved to states) of possessing free discretion to allocate personality, directly or indirectly, to other entities.[555]

It is also to be noted that *on this basis* a certain entity may be regarded as an international legal person and be accorded certain rights and duties, such as the right to jurisdictional immunity. An IO, for example, may be granted the right to jurisdictional immunity as an international legal person by assuming that it makes international law. In so doing, the IO is an international subject because it makes international law and this operates as a precondition for its right to jurisdictional immunity. But also the reverse reasoning could be made by assuming that an IO is an international subject because it is generally accorded jurisdictional immunity, thereby drawing the consequence that the 'agreements' it makes must be 'international treaties' governed by international law. This same finding could then be used as a manifestation of the ILP of the IO and used as a precondition of a further consequence, such as the right to fiscal immunities, and so forth.

(d) Exercise of authority

A further meaning of ILP refers to the entities which exert ultimate 'authority' in the international system. As previously discussed, the notion of 'authority', whether public or private, is uncertain.[556] However, this meaning is often adumbrated by IR theorists and jurists who embrace the notion of ILP as participation in the international decision-making process.[557] Leibniz himself referred the concept of *persona juris*

[552] Brownlie (n 103 above) 67, arguing that 'the individual is in certain contexts regarded as a legal person, and yet it is obvious that he cannot make treaties'.

[553] For the view that individuals do not directly contribute to the formation of customary international law, see Ch 6 below, n 106 and accompanying text.

[554] See Friedmann (n 195 above) 213, grounding the 'basic primacy of the State as a subject of international relations and law' in the fact that 'States are the repositories of legitimated authority over peoples and territories'. In other words, unlike any other actor on the international scene, states take the responsibility of governing people in any respect and in cooperation with one another.

[555] Portmann (n 507 above) 3.

[556] See section A (2) above.

[557] See PC Jessup, 'The Subjects of a Modern Law of Nations' (1947) 45 Mich LR 383, 384; Higgins (n 183 above) 50; JR Dugard, 'First Report on Diplomatic Protection', UN Doc A/CN.4/506, para 24; R McCorquodale, 'An Inclusive International Legal System' (2004) 17 LJIL 477, 481,

gentium to 'He... who represents the public liberty, such that he is not subject to the tutelage of the power of anyone else, but has in himself the power of war and of alliances', although 'he may perhaps be limited by the bonds of obligation towards a superior' (as was actually the case with the German princes vis-à-vis the Empire), so that 'If his authority is sufficiently extensive, it is agreed to call him a potentate, and will be called a sovereign or a sovereign power' including those 'who can count on sufficient freedom and power to exercise some influence in international affairs'.[558] A similar approach is taken by the courts when they assert that a given entity (such as IOs or the Order of Malta) possess ILP either in that they are treated as 'peers' by the states or somehow deserve to be treated as such given their otherwise found ILP.[559] If what matters is staging or participation, then the concept of personality becomes contingent on the degree of participation, this latter—especially from a realist perspective—amounting to the influence successfully exerted in practice.

If this approach were to be adopted, states would clearly fall within the range of 'international subjects', although perhaps the weakest states would be excluded. It is a fact, however, that even micro-states are regarded as subjects of international law and have been admitted to the United Nations. Less powerful states are considered international legal persons just like the more powerful ones. By contrast, other non-state entities, such as MNEs, which are thought to exert more power than several states, would deserve the status of international subjects even though formally they might have no rights and duties under international law and make no international law. Different classes of insurgents would perhaps enjoy a different international status (ie more or less rights and duties, or no rights and duties at all), depending on the kind and degree of 'participation' in international relations of each of them. The Holy See would perhaps not qualify as an international 'subject' because of the lack of 'hard power' of the Vatican State, although the Holy See does take part in international relations and is usually said to exert a considerable 'soft power'. According to this approach the ILP conferred on the Order of Malta appears hardly comprehensible. Difficult questions of comparing different kinds and degrees of participation would arise. This realist, anti-formalistic approach tends to drive the jurist to the conclusion that 'relevant actors' are simply those who call the shots with regard to who is a 'legitimate' legal person under other meanings.

The 'actor conception' has the merits of capturing the elementary fact that there must be 'upstream' some entity which 'ultimately decides who decides' and acts as 'supreme authority' in the system. This systemically supreme position is obviously dependent on the outcome of a constant competition (and hence of a decision-making process) among diverse actors (state and non-state alike) which participate in the struggle for conquering supreme (or at least higher) authority over the system *as such*. But this competition is nothing else than the competition for power. Law, including legal personality, possibly comes afterwards. Either the concept of ILP means something *within* the system or it simply reflects the relative power of those engaged in the

arguing that Higgins' argument for considering individuals as participants in the international legal system is compelling, without necessarily adopting her broader conception of international law as process rather than rules.

[558] GW Leibniz, *Codex Juris Gentium Diplomaticus* [1693], English trans '*Codex Iuris Gentium (Praefatio)*' in P Riley (ed), *Leibniz: Political Writings* (Cambridge: CUP, 2nd edn, 1988) 175. See Nijman (n 254 above) 58–76.

[559] eg in the *Société Anonyme Commerciale* Judgment (n 481 above) 2–3, the Tribunal of Rome held that the Order of Malta 'as a sovereign entity' enjoying ILP had the 'right to be treated by other States as *par inter pares*'.

struggle for *one or another* system (and dominant entities therein) moment after moment. The latter meaning, often linked to a constitutional reading of the system, is useless in legal terms and constitutional theories end up mirroring the prevalence of the stronger of the day. The former is potentially suited for law, although the question of whether and to what extent it is practically relevant to reach outcomes which cannot be reached otherwise remains to be seen.

(e) Membership of the international community

It is occasionally argued that the 'members' of the international community are the legal persons within this community.[560] ILP is then defined in terms of 'belonging' (whether formally or informally) to a pre-defined community, whatever the functions carried out therein. It is assumed that who is part of the international community is self-evident, or easily determinable; that the concept of international community is as such clear; and that 'membership' implies a number of obvious legal consequences. Unfortunately, all of these issues are far from being incontrovertible, as is supposed.

To be a member of a community is one thing, it is quite another to have rights and duties, or to make the law, or to participate in the community. An entity may well be a 'member' of the international community in one sense but not in another. For example, natural persons or national liberation movements may be international subjects as holders of rights under international law, yet they may not be regarded as members of the international community, at least in certain circumstances. On the other hand, the view that ILP hinges on membership of the international community can easily lead to the denial of the ILP of individuals on grounds that the internationally community is clearly not made up of individuals,[561] regardless of possible (state-created) international rights and duties of individuals. If the concept of membership is expanded to include as many 'actors' as possible, it tends to become coterminous with participation and to meet with the difficulties already seen. But if the concept of membership is narrowed to the addressees of the law or to the law-makers, then it turns out to be redundant.

The point is that an entity may be a 'member' of a community in a variety of ways. The generic idea that an entity is 'accepted' within the community may capture the essence of this approach but the problem is that it still remains to be seen what exactly is accepted, whether participating in law-making or being the addressee of rights and duties created by others, etc, and what is their legal difference, if any, from those who accept. Yet another difficulty is that the concept of 'membership' is used to include and exclude, ie to ostracize the demonized 'other', or simply to include only certain pre-determined 'deserving' categories of relevant actors, such as states (or only some states having certain features, such as the 'civilized' states of the past) and perhaps IOs. The same concept is understandably also used by those who seek to enter the 'circle' and become members somehow, such as NGOs and social resistance movements. The

[560] See eg LFL Oppenheim, *International Law: A Treatise* (London: Longmans, 1st edn, 1905) 99, para 63, arguing that 'As this law is the body of rules which the civilised States consider legally binding in their intercourse, every State which belongs to the civilised States, and is, therefore, a member of the Family of Nations, is an International Person' and that only sovereign states were international persons or subjects of international law.

[561] See M Giuliano, T Scovazzi, and T Treves, *Diritto internazionale, Parte generale* (Milan, Giuffrè, 2nd edn, 1983) 541–3.

question of who is the 'gatekeeper' and forms the 'circle' in the first place, and why there should be this circle rather than another, remains unanswered.

(f) Enforcement capability

Lawyers who have a strong sanction-based inclination to law tend to shift the problem of personality from law-making to law enforcement. They would typically claim that it is pointless to contend that certain entities formally enjoy rights and duties, or that they participate in the law-making process, if their rights and duties are not enforceable and their participation does not affect realities. On this account, natural persons would hardly be regarded as 'international subjects'. Even assuming that formally they have rights under international law, individuals can do very little to enforce such rights in case of transgression. True, they may in certain contexts seise an international body (such as international courts and monitoring bodies in the field of human rights) to have their rights determined. Yet they have very little capacity to force states into compliance, and if states do enforce international decisions this occurs because they have given undertakings to do so to the other states parties to the relevant treaties and are possibly monitored by international (inter-state) bodies.

Were enforcement's capacity decisive in possessing ILP, then there would arguably be no international legal person other than states, but also weak states would hardly qualify. NGOs might succeed in influencing one or more governments to enforce their rights to a far greater degree than weak states. Thus this approach would be likely to lead to the conclusion that only the great powers are international legal persons, and perhaps only a few of them. On the other hand, if the perspective is changed, weaker states may also qualify as international subjects according to this approach. For example, however powerful they may be, in the end MNEs need a state, even a micro-state, to have their rights and duties enforced locally. MNEs count on the enforcement mechanisms found in the states and assume that it is for states to enforce the law. They can of course use private security companies (PSCs) and state institutions themselves, but this takes place within the legal order of the local state. They may even 'steer' the host state at their pleasure, given their overarching power, but they still need the formal structure of a state. In this sense even a weak state (compared to strong states) may be considered stronger than an MNE.

(g) Historical pedigree

ILP is occasionally inferred also from the historical pedigree of a particular entity, as is the case with the Holy See, or from the quality of the activities carried out, as is the case with the Order of Malta and perhaps also with the ICRC.

Apart from the existence of the Vatican State, it is pre-eminently for historical reasons—the very fact that the global states system was born in Western Europe out of the dissolution of the medieval, universally conceived Christian power of the Christian Church—and their persisting repercussions that the Head of the Catholic Church is the only religious leader in the world who is recognized by all states as the supreme authority of an international legal person. The Order of Malta is also recognized, particularly by Italian courts, as an international legal person for reasons other than the effectiveness required of states. Italian courts somehow adumbrate that the Order deserves an international status both for historical reasons, linked, inter alia, to those of the Holy See, and for the charitable activities carried out by the Order, while lack of effectiveness is considered of no import.

However, the historical pedigree and the quality of the activities performed are not applied to other potential international subjects, which may reasonably be regarded as worthy of equal consideration. The recognition of ILP has a practical importance in that it works as a premise allowing courts to accord both the Holy See and the Order of Malta jurisdictional and fiscal immunities. One may suppose that in such cases what matters is the ad hoc 'recognition' by the generality of states, a sort of reversed process compared to the medieval practice whereby it was the Pope who approbated the Emperor and somehow recognized princes and kings.[562] The question remains, in any event, why the criteria applied to these two entities do not apply to other candidates for ILP.

(h) Conformity to the nature and purpose of international law

Finally, ILP may actually be made dependent on the conformity of an entity to the nature and purpose of international law in general.[563] Personality may accordingly be granted or denied to individuals and NGOs, or to IOs, based on what meaning and weight are given to the 'nature' and 'purpose' of international law.[564] At the same time, the global states system may suggest that, despite apparent signs to the contrary, only states possess (or deserve) ILP since the nature and purpose of international law is to govern *their* system and people are ultimately expected to receive better protection from states than from 'private' authorities or other entities (such as IOs) which present a lower degree of political legitimacy than that enjoined on average by the states themselves. According to this approach, international and national practice and jurisprudence concerning the ILP of individuals, or any other candidate for ILP, may easily be differently construed as a function of the general theory of international law endorsed. While a given theory *as a whole* may indeed be preferable to another, the fact remains that there is no apparent reason automatically to suppose that *specific* logical consequences drawn in the field of ILP from a general theory are as such plausible, or even desirable.

(4) Avoiding manipulation of international personality

The key lessons to be learned from the foregoing analysis are that: (a) what matters is whether this or that entity has this or that specific right or obligation for this or that specific purpose under international law as (essentially) made by states; (b) the ILP of individuals is largely and in many respects dependent on states contrary to the presuppositions of the whole conception of international law whereby the individual 'comes before' (although it is unclear whether historically, or logically, or morally) any society or political organization, notably the state.

The first point implies that states remain at the heart of the system, even accepting the international personality of non-state actors (including individuals), and that one has to see on a case-by-case basis whether the entity (or the category of entities) at hand have or do not have the particular international right and obligation for the purposes which are relevant in the instant case (or possibly in similar cases). What is to be avoided is the instrumental use of the concept of international personality as the 'logical

[562] Grewe (n 84 above) 75–82.

[563] Portmann (n 507 above) 10–12.

[564] For the ICJ's reference to 'the needs of the community' and 'the requirements of international life', see n 532 above and accompanying text.

premise' from which mechanically to draw any sort of legal rights and duties for any purpose. This clearly exposes the entire reasoning to personal taste and different outcomes even in similar cases. As argued elsewhere in this book, law in general and international law in particular do not necessarily need to be as 'logical' as the observer would expect or desire them to be. Logic itself may well lead to socially unsatisfactory outcomes, despite its ambition to provide law with clarity and systematization. As a general pattern, ILP lends itself to manipulative uses inspired, inter alia, by its original transplantation to international law from domestic law, or, more accurately, from the domestic law of a few Western states. Even critical analyses of ILP are ultimately concerned with the 'right' conception thereof, often drawing from what is believed to be the key systemic features of contemporary international law.[565] Thus understood, no doubt ILP has the potential to extend to any subject, including individuals, but it is still conceived as having one and the same meaning for all of those which possess it. The above discussion has shown, however, that no plausible abstract reasons exist to favour one or another general and unitary meaning (or conception) of ILP based either on international practice, or on theoretical preferences, or on the alleged overall features of contemporary international law. A given entity may well be seen and treated as possessing ILP, but it still remains to be seen what purpose ILP serves in order to have which specific legal rights and/or obligations and for the ultimate benefit of which 'deserving' actor from whose viewpoint.

The second point is that the international rights and obligations of individuals are made and enforced by states and that their international personality is more often than not an empowered *domestic* legal personality which results from international law but is different from international personality. This domestic empowerment as a result of international law indeed corresponds to the idea underlying the whole debate favouring individual empowerment.[566] However, far from eroding statehood and moving towards the emergence of a 'global community' of individuals at last 'freed' from state bounds, such an empowerment does presuppose statehood, and hence a world of states.[567] To imagine the individual as an 'original', 'pre-state' entity which enjoys 'fundamental rights' to be recognized by any 'later' society and political organization amounts to saying that the individual can be conceived of as detached from any group. It is a contention of this book, however, that such an idea exists only in the minds of theorists. The individual is always found in a group for the elementary reason that it has no chance to survive otherwise. It seeks protection in the group in return for obedience to (and hence as a contribution to the cohesion and enforcing capabilities of) the group. Individuals barely have 'fundamental rights' or any 'original' international or universal 'legal personality' merely because they are imagined 'to come first'. They have international legal rights and duties if and to the extent that the group (ie society and its

565 This is basically the ('minimal') approach adopted by Portmann (n 507 above) 271–83, who concludes, in the light of 'the basic premises of the contemporary international legal order', in favour of a combination of the formal and the individualistic conceptions of ILP so that they 'can temper their respective shortcomings'.

566 For an insightful analysis on the topic, see TM Franck, *The Empowered Self: Law and Society in the Age of Individualism* (Oxford: OUP, 2001).

567 For the accurate conclusion that 'individuals have no control over the way in which they receive rights and obligations' and that 'an inter-state normative framework may be more effective and result in better protection of individuals... than an individual rights framework', assuming that 'no doubt... individuals can have rights and obligations conferred on them by international treaties and by general international law', as evidenced by 'normalised practice' since 1945, although without questioning the distinction between 'active subjects' and 'passive recipients' (n 549 above), see Parlett (n 244 above) 347–9, 353, 357, 360, 363, 370.

political organization, whether the state or other) recognizes and enforces them. The individual has no chance to 'enforce' in any meaningful sense any 'right' against the group. It is rather the group that has the power to enforce rights and obligations recognized by its members. Escapes to 'original', pre-society states of nature, so pervasive in today's rhetoric of liberal globalization and the ILP of individuals, end up leaving individuals at the mercy of the stronger individuals and bringing about *less* rather than more individual empowerment. This is not to imply that individuals have no original, natural rights, and much less that liberalism or cosmopolitanism is to be discarded. The philosophical question of whether individuals are 'original' and have fundamental rights and obligations may still be answered affirmatively. Yet, what counts in this world of human beings for legal purposes is whether such rights and obligations will or will not be enforced with sufficient predictability and political legitimacy. This is a question of collective force, not of truth, although the purported truth of the antagonists may also be successfully used as a weapon to prevail. It is the state, and the states system as a whole, that do so at present, and it is from the states that people daily expect protection.

Conclusion

If international law is a social construct, it is vital to know who is engaged in its official construction, ie who plays what role in global governance. This chapter argued that the globalized states system is central, although it is the historical product of injustice and increasingly unable satisfactorily to manage global concerns. The injustice *of* the system as a global project is, however, irreversible and, at least in the short and medium term, justice should be basically pursued *within* the system, giving due consideration to the inherited injustice of the system itself. The inability of the system to solve common problems is inbuilt and can be remedied to some extent only 'from below' by non-state players. International law remains the law of the global states system with two important innovations: the system is increasingly influenced by non-state actors and states are required by the system itself to protect any individual within their jurisdiction, including their own citizens, and to exercise sovereignty in accordance with international legal standards. This mix of states and non-state players, the former exercising jurisdiction over the world in a partitioned and coordinated way and the latter shaping states hopefully to pursue global justice and protect the most vulnerable, form the international community and foster global governance. International legal personality, far from conceptually unifying the players, disaggregates itself in a variety of meanings which allow manipulative strategies to favour this or that actor and ultimately rests on the constitutive centrality of the global states system.

6
Rules

After having identified in Chapter 5 the community which believes in international law as 'its' law, it is now possible to see what is the law that this community believes to be international law. This chapter investigates how the rules and other normative standards of international law are made, integrated, reconciled, changed, judicially applied, complied with, implemented within states, and enforced. It argues that all international law rules and judicial decisions are ultimately grounded in custom as a basic form of social informal pressure by the states system and that no 'private affair' is conceivable in the system even when rules apply only to particular states, although rules are not necessarily always applicable to all states. The identification of the rules of international law is loosely inspired by the doctrine of the sources of law originally developed in the domestic legal systems of Western states and on other criteria capable of ensuring a relative systemic unity, coherence, and completeness of all the rules of international law. Only rarely, compared to all possible disputes, are international courts and tribunals seised and thus have the opportunity to specify the law in particular cases, but when they do they can exercise the discretion inherent in their very establishment to provide an impartial specification of the content of the rules and to remedy, to some extent, the inequities and fragmentation of international law. Of vital importance is the implementation of international law within domestic legal systems.

A. Sources of Law

What classes of international law rules are believed to be 'valid' within the international community? The doctrine of the sources of law articulates how international law rules are created and how they can be ascertained. According to the doctrine the only valid rules are those 'flowing' from the authorized sources.[1] As noted, 'there must be some criteria settling what counts as "rule of law"' and the doctrine of the legal sources is deemed to provide formal criteria to draw the line between law and non-law.[2] The authorities entrusted to apply the law are expected to use this test of validity without asking the ultimate reason why the law applied is binding, assuming that the ultimate basis of obligation of law is extra-legal and falls under legislative power. The doctrine thus claims to be, at least in principle, anti-foundationalist, apolitical, and made up of objective parameters capable of separating the mere 'application' of law in particular cases from its 'creation' in the political process. This section shows how problematic the transplantation of the doctrine from domestic law to international law is. It then turns to a number of techniques enabling the interpreter somehow to go 'beyond' the rules as

[1] A good description of the term is provided by C Du Pasquier, *Introduction à la théorie générale et à la philosophie du droit* (Neuchâtel and Paris: Delachaux et Niestlé, 1948) 47: 'Ce terme de source crée une métaphore assez juste, car remonter à la source d'un fleuve, c'est rechercher l'endroit où ses eaux sortent de terre; de même s'enquérir de la source d'une règle juridique, c'est rechercher le point par lequel elle est sortie des profondeurs de la vie sociale pour apparaître à la surface du droit'.

[2] N MacCormick, *Legal Reasoning and Legal Theory* (Oxford: Clarendon Press, 1978) 54.

mechanically flowing from the formal sources of law in general. Finally, the ability of the doctrine to ensure some systemic unity, coherence, and completeness to international law is analysed.

(1) The doctrine of the sources of law

The doctrine of the sources of law was notably developed in Europe in the age of absolutism and after the Enlightenment-inspired codification process, at a time when the notion that all valid law was made (or recognized) by the sovereign took hold. The 'sources' were theorized as a closed, formal, and universal list of law-making methods. The doctrine was a reflection of the relative force of sub-groups within the modern state. Each group pushed for the insertion in the list, possibly at the highest rank, of the sources which it controlled. The law thus 'flowing' from the 'authorized' sources was deemed to exist independently of its contents and to apply equally to all 'subjects' of law in the realm. The doctrine was later transplanted to international law but a number of problems arose due to the absence of an international sovereign and a radically different type of social conflict. This section argues that behind the sources lie people, groups, and interests competing with one another, and that, when dealing with international law, one should be very careful about making mechanical parallels with the doctrine developed in domestic law and general jurisprudence.

(a) Origins in domestic law

Before the codification process in Europe, many different kinds of rules, often dating back to ancient Roman and medieval law, were applied by the courts in different legal contexts. In the course of time, the sense of justice which these rules had inherited from the past progressively shrank. A rationalization and standardization of the law, a 'method' to make and to identify the rules by formal, procedural, scientific-like standards, applicable by all in all cases to all subjects was perceived as urgent.[3] With the French Revolution, all pre-existing sources of law—such as the orders of the king and customary rules, which favoured the monarch, the nobility, the Church, and the corporations—were reduced to the sole (general and abstract) statutes enacted by the assembly which represented the people. The doctrine was introduced in the first place to establish who *makes* the law of the realm, whether the king or an assembly, and what margin of discretion all other state officials had to enjoy in administering the law. It reflected a balance of power between state authorities, social groups, and individuals. It served the purpose to have the rules made by the dominant group applied to the largest possible extent and to set aside any other rule unless it was compatible with the former. Unwelcome sources of law were expunged from the list, or relegated to the lower rank, while the rules the creation of which was controlled by those who were dominant were included in the list and placed at the highest rank. The concept of sources also reflected an 'industrialist' imagery. What counted was the process of production: if the process is correct, the rule is valid regardless of its contents. Rules are thus identified through a 'technical' (as opposed to a moral, wise, or enlightened) judgment. Judges become technicians of the rules. The identification of the rules is believed to be 'objective', ie independent of the subjective qualities of the interpreter.

[3] On method and methodology in legal analysis, see Ch 4 above, section A (2).

There was no justice beyond what the sovereign sanctioned as justice, and judges were called upon to deliver *this* justice, the sole justice admitted in the realm. All kinds of standards other than the 'rules' flowing from the sources as devised by the sovereign were placed outside the notion of justice. It seemed that judges could not attain justice without 'certainty' if they were left, as in the past, at liberty to interpret maxims and practices by attuning with what the community felt to be just. This process was felt as granting judges an arbitrary power capable of undermining the centralization of the state and the security of citizens. Standardization and guarantees for the accused, as Cesare Beccaria exemplarily expounded,[4] intercepted genuine needs and met with approval. The struggle of the sovereign, whether monarch or assembly, to reduce the area of 'penumbra' of the law, however, was basically a struggle between the sovereign and its competitors carried out, inter alia, through the apparently technical standardization of the sources of the law. Personal and class conflicts underlay the apparently neutral, technical question of the sources. The sovereign first *created the idea* of the 'list' of the sources with its 'rationalizing' benefits, then *closed* the list, and finally *hierarchized* the list by placing at the top its own law. The official list, its (ideal) exhaustiveness, and its hierarchization are the quintessence of the doctrine of the sources of law. It is the sovereign that has an interest in inventing, closing, and hierarchizing the list to acquire and retain total control of the law of the realm.

(b) Transplantation to international law

The doctrine of the sources of law as a jurisprudential construction of potentially universal validity was then extended to international law. The nineteenth-century positivist schools of a few European states, pre-eminently Germany, transplanted the doctrine to international law. National needs, such as the push towards creating a German nation-state, were projected onto the international domain. The transplantation appeared as a merely 'technical' improvement in constructing a better and more rational international law. It would have led to a 'rule of law' in international affairs similar to the 'rule of law' which emerged in nation-states. When after World War I both positivism and naturalism, at least in their extreme variants, were rejected, the sources theory was disentangled from the question of the basis of obligation of law by preferring pragmatism.[5] Article 38 PCIJ Statute 'officialized' a list of classes of international law rules that sounded like the sources of international law and became 'the founding moment of sources discourse'.[6] Since the 1920s the word 'source' has been increasingly used in international law, although the PCIJ used it for the first time in the 1927 *Danube Commission* Advisory Opinion.[7]

The transplantation of the doctrine of the sources of law to international law immediately met with a number of grave difficulties. The key problem was that the doctrine was instrumental to the sovereign and there was no sovereign in international affairs. At the same time, the social conflict underlying the doctrine was often overlooked or misrepresented. While in its domestic sphere the doctrine was instrumental to establishing who was the sovereign between competing groups and what law was to

[4] See Ch 4 above, section B (2).

[5] T Skouteris, *The Notion of Progress in International Law Discourse* (The Hague: TMC Asser Press, 2010) 118–19.

[6] ibid 126.

[7] PCIJ *Jurisdiction of the European Commission of the Danube between Galatz and Braila* Advisory Opinion of 8 December 1927, PCIJ Series B No 14, at 22.

count as the only (or ultimate) valid law in the realm, in international law it took the form of a mechanical technique of apparent legal rationalization. Many shortcomings followed.

First, in the absence of a universal law-maker, custom remained central to international law while in the domestic law of the relevant European states (for reasons that presented no parallel in international law) sovereign possibly relegated custom to the lowest rank of the sources since custom consisted of the practices prevailing in the realm from time immemorial of the people other than the sovereign. Secondly, there was little reason to transpose to international law what in domestic law was the primacy of the sovereign over the courts (transforming the latter into a mere *bouche de la loi* made by the law-maker), since international law courts are relatively few, separate, subjected to no hierarchy, and operative only with the consent of the disputing states, each under the terms of its own statute.[8] Thirdly, treaties were equated with domestic statutes (as opposed to unwritten custom), since they are generally written and adopted after a procedure that may be compared to the approval of a statute in domestic law. However, statutes are of general application and grounded in a national political pact among all citizens, whereas treaties (similarly to contracts in domestic law) are made by individual states, have no general application, and produce only rights and obligations between the parties. Unsurprisingly, on the assumption that a legal source implicates a 'community' and a 'general law' common to all its members, the view was soon held that international treaties could not be considered sources of law but only of rights and obligations.[9] Fourthly, international 'sources' of law have often been confused with a 'delegation' of law-making power.[10] Many would exclude the suggestion that international judicial decisions and arbitral awards are sources of international law, although they do contain international obligations binding on states.[11] Fifthly, what may be satisfactory when applied within a state, in its Western form, as was the case at the time, may not be so in international law among non-Western peoples. Finally, in international law there is no superior authority entrusted to list the sources and provide their definition, possible hierarchy, and implications in terms of interpretation. This implies that entities other than states (in particular individuals) do not form part of the international realm, do not make, and cannot be bound by international law. It also implies that international law cannot bind the states themselves without their consent.

The above discussion shows that caution is never enough when speaking of the 'sources' of international law in terms of domestic law and general jurisprudence modelled on the practices of law followed in a few Western states.

(2) Beyond the sources?

Since what flows from the sources are 'rules' which are far from covering all possible cases and can prove 'unjust' as brutal expressions of the law-maker's force, other

[8] See section C below.

[9] PE Corbett, 'The Consent of States and the Sources of the Law of Nations' (1925) 6 BYBIL 20; GG Fitzmaurice, 'Some Problems Regarding the Formal Sources of International Law' in *Symbolae Verzijl* (The Hague: Martinus Nijhoff, 1958) 153–76.

[10] cf H Kelsen, *General Theory of Law and State* [1945] (New Brunswick and London: Transaction Publishers, 2007) 131–2.

[11] Fitzmaurice (n 9 above) 170–3, observing that international judicial decisions are 'quasi-formal sources', more than material but less than formal sources since they end up being followed in the subsequent practice by all.

normative ideas (such as 'legitimacy') and methods (such as 'principles' and 'standards') are commonly evoked in the law discourse and administration as possible channels to go 'beyond' the sources and the 'rules' flowing therefrom. The trend today is to distrust 'rules' as flowing from the sources and to prefer other looser standards of conduct. This trend is often confusing. Sources may be criticized when applied to international law, but this has little to do with the validity of the rules. The international community may not accept the doctrine of the sources as developed in domestic law (ie as a closed and hierarchized list of classes of rules) but it accepts rules. This section argues that in any legal context, domestic and international alike, legal sources call for integration by a number of devices traceable to interpretation. Some of them, such as legitimacy as opposed to legality, may lead to unacceptable results, whereas others are not only useful but also inevitable.

(a) Legality and legitimacy

While 'legality' often refers to strict conformity to the 'rules' as identified from the sources, 'legitimacy' usually implies general acceptability by the people and going 'beyond' conformity to the rules, such as conformity to the 'spirit' as opposed to the 'letter' of the law.[12] Legitimacy has received a variety of different meanings[13] and has always been used ambivalently. The Nazi regime justified its arbitrary power at times by invoking the rules 'in force' (ie legality) and at other times by invoking the common belief of the German people, allegedly supremely embodied in the *Führer*, against the formal rules in force (ie legitimacy).[14] This ambivalent use in turn has induced opponents to invoke either legitimacy or legality, respectively, depending on which was relied on by the abusers. Thus both legality and legitimacy have the potential for both abusing power and contesting power abusers. The diffused view that legitimacy is inherently 'corrective' of what goes wrong with strict legality is untenable. Recourse to legitimacy may lead to even worse results.

When legitimacy is understood in 'procedural' terms, it tends to coincide with 'legality', unless legality itself is understood in substantive terms, as may be the case with natural law. It may also be seen as a significant factor of compliance with the law,[15] or as a yardstick to evaluate the morality of the law.[16] A diffused tendency holds that decisions are legitimate when 'stakeholders' have been represented and the decision-making process has been transparent, in particular when those affected have had a chance to have their say ('input' legitimacy). However, in decisions adopted by

[12] For a recent analysis extending Lon Fuller's conception of fidelity to law to international law, see J Brunnée and SJ Toope, *Legitimacy and Legality: An Interactional Account* (Cambridge: CUP, 2010). The question was famously addressed by C Schmitt, *Legalität und Legitimität* (Munich: Duncker & Humblot:, 1932), English trans *Legality and Legitimacy* (Durham and London: Duke University Press, 2004). For an analysis of Schmitt's concept of legitimacy, see H Hofmann, *Legitimität gegen Legalität: Der Weg der politischen Philosophie Carl Schmitts* (Berlin: Hermann Luchterhand, 1964); D Dyzenhaus, *Legality and Legitimacy: Carl Schmitt, Hans Kelsen, and Hermann Heller in Weimar* (Oxford: OUP, 1997).

[13] AP D'Entrèves, 'Legality and Legitimacy' (1963) 16 RM 687.

[14] C Schmitt, 'Der Führer schützt das Recht. Zur Reichstagrede Adolf Hitlers vom 13. Juli 1934', (1 August 1934, issue No 15) *Deutsche Juristen-Zeitung* 1. In the speech of 13 July 1934 Hitler proclaimed himself 'supreme judge' (*oberster Gerichtherr*) of the German people, over and above ordinary courts, and defender, as Schmitt noted, of substantive Justice—namely, 'law at its purest', the ultimate source of all other law, the direct expression of the right to existence of the German people in a state of necessity—as opposed to mechanical Legalism instrumentally usable by 'criminals'.

[15] TM Franck, *The Power of Legitimacy Among Nations* (Oxford: OUP, 1990) 24–5.

[16] S Besson and J Tasioulas (eds), *The Philosophy of International Law* (Oxford: OUP, 2010) 13–19.

majority, some stakeholders are inevitably outvoted and outvoting should itself be perceived as legitimate. In other contexts, decisions are believed to be legitimate when they are actually obeyed and apparently effective ('output' legitimacy). Legitimacy may be bestowed by consent, expertise, effectiveness, rational discourse, and several other factors. In international law, state consent is traditionally viewed as playing a strongly legitimizing role in securing procedural legitimacy.[17]

That law is more than 'strict rules' is hardly deniable, but the question remains of how to identify the law, and the concept of legitimacy is of little assistance. The law of a community is what the community believes to be 'its' law. This may let one suppose that when a certain rule is seen by the community as 'legitimate', then 'this' is the 'true' law. But such a conclusion is too hasty. The community may accept a given rule as a matter of legitimacy, yet not as a matter of law. If the community accepts that the law is made up of the rules flowing from what the community itself sees as the authorized sources, then *this* is the law, and what the community simultaneously sees as 'legitimate' pertains to legitimacy, this being understood by the community itself evidently differently from what the same community sees as the law. Of course, the fact that legitimacy, appropriately defined (for example, acceptance by stakeholders and/or legal doctrine, or embodied in soft law, etc), may increase the prospect of observance of the law or provide a push for the formation of new and better rules, is a different matter.

The assertion 'illegal, yet legitimate' that is occasionally adopted in international practice and doctrine is rather unfortunate, albeit politically intriguing.[18] An action is either legal or illegal. It can also be either legitimate or illegitimate, or 'more or less' legitimate. It is often noted that legality is an on/off matter, whereas legitimacy is a matter of degree. However, either the two concepts coincide, but then the phrase 'illegal, yet legitimate' is a contradiction in terms; or they do not coincide and have different meanings, in which case the two meanings are incommensurate and 'legitimacy' can hardly 'cure' 'illegality', and vice versa. To say that a given conduct is 'illegal' because it is at odds with the 'letter' of the law but, at the same time, it is 'legitimate' because it is in keeping with the 'spirit' of the law, amounts to saying (contradictorily) that the 'spirit' of the law is somehow relevant to the law even though it lies outside the law. The point is, however, whether the 'spirit' of the law is or is not 'incorporated' in the law as it stands.

Legitimacy seems to refer to some undefined, non-rule-based 'law beyond the sources', a law which is deemed to be less formalistic and more supported by social practices. Legitimacy is one among many strategies aimed at skipping the law as a set of formal rules, assuming that the main defect of law is formality and people generally live informally in their daily lives. It apparently serves to bridge the gap between rules and real life. However, formal law is often *supported* by its addressees precisely because it *is* formal, although occasionally and individually they may feel that informality is more reflective of justice than formal law.[19] People know that formal boundaries may work to reduce abuse of power or, at least, somehow to contain the stronger. A formally fixed

[17] J Klabbers, A Peters, and G Ulfstein, *The Constitutionalization of International Law* (Oxford: OUP, 2009) 37–43.

[18] Famously, the 2000 'Kosovo Report' of the Independent International Commission on Kosovo, chaired by Mr Goldstone, concluded that the Kosovo War was an 'illegal, yet legitimate' humanitarian intervention. cf *The Kosovo Report: Conflict, International Response, Lessons Learned* (Oxford: OUP, 2000) 186. For a discussion on the 'legitimacy' of the Kosovo War, see F Francioni, 'Of War, Humanity and Justice: International Law after Kosovo' (2000) 4 MP YUNL 107. For its legality, see Ch 8 below, n 96.

[19] For the diverse meanings of legal 'formalism', see recently J D'Aspremont, *Formalism and the Sources of International Law: A Theory of the Ascertainment of Legal Rules* (Oxford: OUP, 2011) 12–37.

percentage of favourable votes required in decision-making for the validity of the rules adopted (such as a two-thirds majority, unanimity, etc), is one way to avoid leaving the stronger to do as they please and to pressure them either to participate in the voting (and accept its results) or to make the whole regime (together with its gains for the stronger themselves) collapse. To set 'formalistic' law against informal legitimacy is plainly misleading at best. At worst, it is a strategy to propagandize an objectively unlawful conduct as acceptable and just, or even lawful, despite all evidence to the contrary.

(b) Prescriptions other than rules

Critics of the sources often argue that law not only consists of rules but also of other 'more or less' binding and effective standards, variously denominated.

Among them, 'principles' are doubtless the most recurrent in legal reasoning. It is not necessary here to review the debate on rules and principles engaged by Herbert Hart and Ronald Dworkin in the past few decades.[20] The only point to stress is that Dworkin relied on 'principles', besides rules, as being part of every legal system, hence binding on judges. This brought him to believe that there is 'one right answer' even in hard cases and that law is inherently gapless. A mid-path position has been taken by Neil MacCormick, who accepts both Hart's positivism and Dworkin's principles[21] by holding that law inevitably presents gaps and suggests that these are filled 'by extrapolation from what is already there'.[22] A position closer to Dworkin's is that of Robert Alexy, who sees principles—as opposed to rules defined as norms which demand a complete fulfilment—as 'optimization commands' establishing that something must be carried out to the greatest possible degree, this degree depending on both factual and legal possibilities.[23]

The term 'principle' actually refers to a variety of meanings which are very difficult to unravel. First, the term is used to denote elusive, non-binding, general principles inspiring the law, or very general rules which underlie classes of rules. In this sense, what is binding are the rules, not the principles, although principles may give rules a systematic meaning and rationale.[24] Secondly, general principles of law are systematically drawn from the whole of existing rules as identified from the sources by way of abstraction (*analogia juris*). In embodying the 'underlying reasons' of more specific rules, principles provide some glue and coherence to the system, yet they are hardly distinguishable from very general rules.[25] Thirdly, constitutional principles of law are drawn from the basic, or immanent, values informing the law and have the proprieties of principles in Dworkin's sense. They can assist the balancing of values and their consideration may profoundly differ from the mere application of 'hard-and-fast' rules. Thus defined, they also 'inform' existing rules and give them a 'direction' when they are applied in particular cases.[26] Fourthly, meta-normative principles of law are 'presupposed' by the law, rather than 'posited' by the law-maker.[27] They underlie all other

[20] R Dworkin, *Taking Rights Seriously* (London: Duckworth, 1978) 22–8, noting in particular that a principle is 'a standard . . . to be observed . . . because it is a requirement of justice or fairness or some other dimension of morality'; HLA Hart, 'Postscript' in *The Concept of Law* (Oxford: OUP, 2nd edn, 1994) 238–76.

[21] MacCormick (n 2 above) 244.

[22] ibid 246.

[23] R Alexy, *Theorie der Grundrechte* (Frankfurt: Suhrkamp, 3rd edn, 1996), English trans *A Theory of Constitutional Rights* (Oxford: OUP, 2002).

[24] MacCormick (n 2 above) 152.

[25] ibid especially 152–3, 156, 232.

[26] See n 20 above.

[27] See Ch 3 above, section B (1)(c).

rules and principles but cannot solve any legal problem. They may also conceptually overlap with constitutional principles, depending on the conception of the term 'constitutional'.[28]

Besides rules and principles, other normative prescriptions are often hinted at, such as norms, guidelines, practices, doctrines, and usages. These terms are very recurrent, but mostly with little accuracy, leaving a great deal of indeterminacy which adds to the indeterminacy of the rules themselves. Critics favour a sharp division between 'hard rules' (ie binding rules) and non-law, while advocates insist that law cannot be made up only of rules. Legal texts actually contain a variety of terms that denote apparently different types of prescriptions. The term 'standard' is generally deemed to be vaguer than 'rules'. For example, it was suggested that 'the only distinction between rules and standards is the extent to which efforts to give content to the law are undertaken before or after individuals act'.[29] Others have observed that standards are vaguer because of 'their use of evaluative terms about which there is disagreement or uncertainty'.[30]

All prescriptions other than rules cannot be considered as law unless some evidence can be given that they are regarded as law, as opposed to mere recommendations, by their addressees as a whole. A critical point is whether courts are involved. As clarified below, while in domestic legal systems jurisdiction is compulsory and courts are hierarchized, with the consequence that standards of any kind can be considered by courts in the very process of applying the rules, in international law any recourse to standards beyond the cases brought before the courts is not certain. It is difficult to see as law standards those prescriptions that the states themselves make as non-law, although these may have an impact on the rules proper.

(c) Deontic modes of juridical concern

Even when a rule is 'valid' because it 'flows' from an authorized source, or more generally because it is regarded as a rule in force by its addressees as a whole, its 'deontic mode' may be difficult to grasp. The analysis of the deontic modes of the rules is often overlooked by international law scholars, yet it deserves attention because international law 'rules' are often the result of intellectual construction and are susceptible of manipulative strategies. Moreover, as will be shown, the deontic modes are key to the question of the completeness of international law and to its construction as a 'system'.

It is generally supposed that 'all laws command or prohibit or permit some form of conduct'.[31] Legal rules are thus usually divided into obligatory, prohibitory, or permissive rules, depending on the fact that they contemplate a 'must', a 'must not', or a 'may' deontic mode. Prohibition ('must not') means impermissibility or commanded omission. Obligation ('must') means commanded action. Prohibitions may also be seen as negative obligations. In international law, for example, the ban on the use of force or on torture is a negative obligation, while the duty of states to carry out an investigation in cases of torture is a positive obligation. As will be shown in Chapter 7, in the law of international human rights negative obligations are often 'expanded' by implication to

[28] See Ch 4 above, section B (7).

[29] L Kaplow, 'Rules versus Standards: An Economic Analysis' (1992) 42 Duke LJ 557, 560–2, arguing that: 'A rule might prohibit "driving in excess of 55 miles per hour on expressways." . . . A standard may entail leaving both specification of what conduct is permissible and factual issues for the adjudicator. (A standard might prohibit "driving at an excessive speed on expressways.")'.

[30] L Alexander and E Sherwin, *Demystifying Legal Reasoning* (Cambridge: CUP, 2008) 14.

[31] See eg MDA Freeman, *Lloyd's Introduction to Jurisprudence* (London: Sweet & Maxwell, 7th edn, 2001) 205.

include also correlative 'positive obligations', as the example of torture just given shows. Permission ('may') is more complex. The term 'may' can refer to different deontic modes, namely, permission (or authorization), discretionary power, *de jure* freedom (ie freedom protected by the law through a correlative prohibition imposed on transgressors, also known as legal 'indifference'), and *de facto* freedom (ie freedom not protected by the law, also known as legal 'irrelevance'). It is often underrated that the vast majority of potential cases occurring in life are legally unregulated (such as 'killing butterflies'), or perhaps regulated as just indifferent. People can generally direct their behaviour in coordination with one another and settle their divergences through means other than law, such as comity, amicable accommodation, and, most importantly, 'up-stream' self-restraint. No legal system can be expected to work if it is not assisted by a strong sense of self-restraint on the part of its individual addressees.

In most cases, when a rule stipulates that its addressees 'may' behave in a certain manner, their behaviour is either 'permitted' or discretionary. An example in point drawn from international law is found in the advisory competence of the ICJ. Article 65(1) ICJ Statute stipulates that the Court 'may' give an advisory opinion on any 'legal question' at the request of whatever body may be authorized by or in accordance with the UN Charter to make such a request. The term 'may' in Article 65 is routinely understood to the effect that the Court may or may not render the Opinion. The Court, as is known, usually gives the Opinion requested unless 'compelling reasons' exist not to do so. Thus understood, the term 'may' refers to a *discretionary power* conferred on the Court to opt for one or another response to the request and excludes a duty on the Court to give the Opinion. However, the term 'may' in Article 96 is susceptible of another equally plausible meaning when it is understood as *permitting* the Court to give the Opinion *on condition* that the request relates to a 'legal question'. Under this meaning nothing in Article 96 would prevent an *obligation* on the Court to give the Opinion when requested, thus enhancing the duty of cooperation between the Court and the requesting bodies, provided that it is on a 'legal question' and not on others. Thus understood, the term 'may' refers to a *permission* (or authorization), rather than to a discretion, conferred on the Court to behave in a way that is otherwise prohibited.[32]

Deontic modes are often abused to reach desired goals and need careful scrutiny. Two further examples drawn from international law may be instructive. Article 103 UN Charter provides that the 'obligations' deriving from the Charter shall prevail over any other treaty obligations binding on the parties. This provision has been construed, both in legal doctrine and in jurisprudence, as also covering (for systemic reasons) UN Security Council 'authorizations' of member states to use force, and has in practice served as a tool to justify acts inconsistent with human rights treaties binding on the authorized UN member states. On the other hand, the states which opt to take up the authorization tend to present their action as 'compelled' by a UN international obligation with a view to persuading domestic audiences that the deployment of troops abroad is 'required' by the United Nations and 'therefore', as an 'international police action', does not qualify as 'war' in terms of both constitutional and international requirements.[33] Common Article 1 of the 1949 Geneva Conventions contains the 'undertaking' of the parties to do what is in their power to 'respect and ensure respect' of the Conventions, a typical 'positive obligation', but it has frequently been construed

[32] See B Conforti and C Focarelli, *The Law and Practice of the United Nations* (Leiden and Boston: Nijhoff, 4th rev edn, 2010) 388.

[33] On Art 103 UN Charter, see section B (3)(d) below.

as providing a discretionary power, inter alia, to react against states which violate the Conventions so as to avoid the conclusion that when the Geneva Conventions are breached by one party, all other parties which have not taken all the measures in their power (in practice virtually all parties, since no state generally reacts) are in turn responsible for a violation of Common Article 1.[34] In the first case a 'permission' is arbitrarily transformed into on obligation, while in the second case an obligation is equally arbitrarily, transformed into a discretionary power.

Obligatory, prohibitory, and permissive rules must be distinguished from recommendations and advices ('should'). These latter do not generate any prohibition, obligation, or permission. The addressees of recommendations and advices remain free to conform their behaviour to the recommendation or the advice. The point is that they are informed that, all else being equal, conforming to the recommendation or to the advice would be viewed more favourably by the adviser or the community at large. This information is vital to enable the members of any group to know and to decide how to behave in the innumerable unregulated acts of their daily lives. Unlike permissions (or authorizations), a recommendation encourages a behaviour that is per se lawful, because it is permitted or indifferent or irrelevant: it provides for discretion to adopt a behaviour that, if adopted, would be lawful even without the recommendation. Permissions (or authorizations), on the other hand, make a behaviour lawful where it would otherwise be unlawful. Recommendations are also to be distinguished from a 'delegation' of powers. While recommendations and permissions (or authorizations) imply that those who behave in accordance therewith act on their own behalf, and their acts are thus attributed to them, a delegation implies that the delegated acts are performed on behalf of the delegator, and its acts may be attributed to the latter within the terms of the delegation. Authorized subjects exercise their own powers, while delegated subjects exercise (and may only exercise) powers that are possessed by the delegator.[35]

(d) Argumentative techniques

Sources are far from covering (and offering a solution to) all possible cases which occur in real life. In most instances a solution must be found outside the law expressly flowing from the sources, either by stretching the scope of existing rules or by creating (more or less formally) new rules for the instant case, a sort of 'implicit' or 'interstitial' law.[36] The line between the 'interpretation' of pre-existing rules and the 'creation' of new rules is anything but clear cut but, however blurred and even circular,[37] it must be retained. Interpretation involves some reasoning around 'something' which pre-exists it. In every community there is a threshold beyond which something becomes something else. The exact point where the line lies is often very uncertain and questionable, but the extremes of the spectrum are no doubt perceived as radically different and there must be a turning point in between. There is a point beyond which a rule is no longer 'interpreted' but re-created from scratch in the perception of the community. The rules flowing from the sources are thus as much necessary as insufficient in the daily

[34] See C Focarelli, 'Common Article 1 of the 1949 Geneva Conventions: A Soap Bubble?' (2010) 21 EJIL 125.

[35] See Ch 7 below, section A (1)(d).

[36] L Fuller, *The Anatomy of Law* (Westport, Conn: Greenwood Press, 1968); for a comment, see GJ Postema, 'Implicit Law' (1994) 13 Law and Philosophy 361.

[37] For the 'hermeneutical circle', see Ch 3 above, section B (1)(c).

administration of law. A set of argumentative techniques or strategies is inevitable in any law and at any level of legal discourse.[38] These techniques are basically drawn, once again, from Western general jurisprudence and interpretative criteria.[39] What especially matters here is that persuasiveness and social attunement may help to solve such issues more than pure logic.[40]

The argument *a contrario* allows the inference (from an existing rule prohibiting, commanding, or permitting a certain conduct) of an opposite rule in accordance with the adage *ubi lex voluit, dixit; ubi noluit, tacuit*. If the rule prohibits murder, it may be assumed to prohibit only murder and nothing else; if it commands charity, it may be assumed to command only charity and nothing else; and if it permits overtaking on a motorway, it may be assumed to permit only overtaking and nothing else. The argument thus prevents inclusion of the cases not regulated into the same deontic mode and is silent about the legal status of the unregulated cases left outside. It justifies narrow interpretation and proves particularly persuasive where special importance is assigned either to the letter of the rules or to the law-maker.

While the argument *a contrario* excludes from the rule, by implication, all the cases which are not expressly and clearly included in its scope, the argument *a simili* (analogy) allows the inference from an existing rule (prohibiting, commanding, or permitting a certain conduct) either of another rule or an extension of the meaning of the former rule (this latter also prohibiting, commanding, or permitting a conduct) which is similar (ie partly identical and partly different) in its legal regime to the regime falling within the scope of the former rule. The analogical argument favours inclusion of the cases not regulated into the same deontic mode and/or the creation of an analogized rule from the original one (*lex minus dixit quam voluit*). The underlying rationale is that like cases have to be treated alike, which is generally highly persuasive and enables legal officials to extend existing rules to many expressly unregulated cases, especially by broad interpretation.[41] Since the analogy between the regulated case and the unregulated case must be felt *relevant* by the audience, and this is a matter of further argumentation and social attunement, the analogical argument needs other arguments to persuade that audience that the two cases are similar for the purposes of extending the original rule.

The argument *a fortiori* allows an inference from an existing rule prohibiting, commanding, or permitting a given conduct another rule (or an extension of the meaning of the former rule), in turn prohibiting, commanding, or permitting a conduct which *deserves* 'all the more so' the same legal regime. The argument thus, like analogy, favours inclusion of the cases not regulated into the same deontic mode and justifies broad interpretation of existing rules (*lex minus dixit quam voluit*). However, unlike analogy, it is not necessarily based on likeliness, but on how an unregulated case 'deserves' to be regulated like a regulated case, the sense of 'deserving' being largely dependent on social attunement. The argument can be either *a minori ad maius* or *a maiori ad minus*. The first applies to disadvantageous deontic modes (such as

[38] The term 'strategy' may appear excessive for arguments that often appear logical or quasi-logical. But even assuming that they pertain to logic, it is their use that is invariably instrumental to one or another preferred end.

[39] N MacCormick, *Rhetoric and the Rule of Law: A Theory of Legal Reasoning* (Oxford: OUP, 2005) 121–42.

[40] For the rhetorical approach to law, see C Perelman and L Olbrechts-Tyteca, *Traité de l'argumentation. La nouvelle rhétorique* (Paris: Presses universitaires de France, 1958), English trans *The New Rhetoric: A Treatise on Argumentation* (Notre Dame: University of Notre Dame Press, 1991); C Perelman, *Logique juridique, nouvelle rhétorique* (Paris: Dalloz, 1976).

[41] LL Weinreb, *Legal Reason: The Use of Analogy in Legal Argument* (Cambridge: CUP, 2005).

prohibitions), while the second applies to advantageous deontic modes (such as permissions). For example, a rule that prohibits murder *a fortiori* may be understood as prohibiting also extermination (*a minori ad maius*); and a rule that permits overtaking on the motorway *a fortiori* may be understood as permitting overtaking also in a playground (*a maiori ad minus*). The argument is, however, likely to be abused especially when it is applied to numbers. For example, permission to sell 'two bottles of wine to each customer' does not necessarily imply (*a maiori*) that the sale of one bottle is also permitted since the rationale of the rule may be to discourage the sale of wine at least to those who cannot afford two bottles. Like in part the analogical argument and unlike the argument *a contrario*, the argument *a fortiori* is a typical device to 'create' rules and fill lacunae.

The argument *ab absurdo* leads to the exclusion of any meaning that would lead to giving a rule a contradictory or impossible meaning. The underlying assumption is that the law-maker is rational enough and avoids absurdities when making the law. The argument *ab absurdo* is frequently used together with other arguments, especially those based on purpose and equity. It usually suggests that one meaning of the rules is preferable to another, which would render the rule absurd. It thus favours the exclusion of 'absurd' perceived meanings and, consequently, the cases which such meanings would have otherwise covered. Its employment is often problematic because the notion of 'absurdity' is to a large extent historically relative. The argument is also weak because where the rule is absurd to all the members of a community the argument appears useless, since no one would even imagine that the rule might be construed in such terms, and when the rule is absurd to only a few it cannot but yield to alternative meanings supported by the majority. There is also ambiguity as to what is to be assessed as absurd, whether the application of the rule to a particular case or its extrapolation to an entire class of cases, or the effects produced by its application in the particular case or by its extrapolation to an entire class of cases.

The argument *ab exemplo*, largely used since antiquity, leads to a preference for the meaning that has been suggested by someone in the past (courts or doctrine) who was deemed to be 'authoritative'. It is on this basis that judicial precedents or legal doctrine are followed as authoritative. The argument's compelling persuasiveness rests on the principle of authority and on the belief that such authority knows better than others what is the most suitable legal answer in a given case. Other legal systems could also be taken on as 'authorities' from a comparative law perspective when a sufficiently common social and cultural background is shared. The argument ensures the continuity of legal systems, and hence certainty, predictability, and equal treatment of cases worthy of being governed similarly. It favours the inclusion of all the cases already regulated or those expected to be in keeping with the authorities recognized, and the exclusion of all other cases. Its use presents a number of difficulties, however. First, when faced with divergences in judicial and doctrinal opinions, no doubt greater weight must be given to precedents of higher courts but there is no clear criterion as regards doctrine. Formulae like 'most writers' or 'the better view' may remain obscure, fixed in a remote past, or simply untenable. Secondly, while doctrine is often clear and internally coherent enough, judicial decisions may not be so and different parts of the same decision may be open to different meanings or have a different weight, such as obiter dicta as compared with *ratio decidendi*. The argument can easily be abused to persuade addressees that a desired rule exists based on certain selected sections (in particular obiter dicta), while other less supportive sections have been omitted. This same manipulability obviously holds true for doctrinal opinions.

The 'historical' argument presumes the continuity of the law to the effect that a new rule is preferably to be given the same meaning as that of an old rule (if not of an 'archetypal' rule held as the ultimate foundation of the whole law obtaining in the community) which governs the same subject-matter. Novelties in the rules are thus reduced to the minimum. The 'core' of a legal regime is believed to remain unchanged and changes in the law are construed as specifications and relative updates of that core. This argument favours the exclusion of new meanings and, consequently, of the cases that such meanings would have otherwise covered. It sounds decreasingly persuasive today at a time when innovative, even bizarre, constructions of the law are more likely to find their way in the marketplace.

The argument based on the law-maker's will implies that a rule should be given the meaning which results from the intention of its author—the legislature in domestic legal systems, notably found in the 'preparatory work'. This ancient argument is clearly grounded in the view that law is a command from the sovereign addressed to its subjects. It may be found especially in the European theorists of the absolute state of the seventeenth and eighteenth centuries. To ensure that judges do not engage in 'creative' or 'politicized' interpretation, they have occasionally been expressly required to make appeal to the legislature for an authentic interpretation of the rules to be applied.[42]

The teleological argument leads to a preference for the meaning that corresponds to the purpose for which the rule has been made. The purpose of the rule does not need to coincide with the law-maker's motives and is deemed to be found, at least in principle, in the law as it has been adopted, regardless of the preparatory work. Its use is increasingly frequent, especially to extend an existing rule to new cases, usually against the argument *a contrario* and/or in concurrence with analogy. It clearly favours the inclusion of new cases. However, its functioning is different from analogy: what matters here, in order for a rule to be extended to new cases, is not likelihood but the realization of the rule's purpose to the full. The argument lends itself easily to abuse since it enables the operation of alleged rules which have no basis whatsoever in existing law, whatever their desirability.

The economical argument is aimed at avoiding redundancy and at specifically excluding meanings that already derive from other (pre-existing, or hierarchically superior, or more general) rules. Its persuasiveness is rooted in the belief (or better, in the ideal) that the law-maker is not repetitive and does not make two or more identical rules. In fact, law-makers often repeat rules in various forms and formulations over time and in diverse contexts. It is then for interpreters to rationalize the law and approximate it to an ordained 'system', as defined below.[43]

The naturalistic argument, typical of natural law theorists, is based on the 'nature' either of human beings or of things in general. The law made by the law-maker tends to be regarded as non-law (or as invalid law) in cases where it conflicts with nature. What has been meant by 'nature' in history is extremely diverse, as already shown.[44] The argument excludes all meanings contrary to nature, and hence all cases which would have been covered by the meanings excluded.

[42] See eg the *référé législatif* provided for by Law 16–24 August 1790, at Title II, Art 12, stating that courts 'ne pourront point faire de règlements, mais ils s'adresseront au Corps législatif toutes les fois qu'ils croiront nécessaire, soit d'interpréter une lois, soit d'en faire une nouvelle'. On this provision see Y-L Hufetau, *Le référé législatif et les pouvoirs du juge de silence de la loi* (Paris: Presses universitaires de France, 1965).

[43] See section A (3)(a) below. [44] See Ch 4 above, section B (1).

The argument for equity (or fairness) prefers the meaning which is less at odds with what is generally felt to be the 'better' outcome of the application of the law to a particular case in terms of perceived justice or the settlement of conflicting interests. The underlying assumption is that law may be applied inequitably or too rigidly and that its 'application' is (or should be) never purely mechanical or neutral.[45] Since even in the most uncontroversial and routine applications of the law there is a margin of uncertainty which allows more than one plausible solution, equity (or fairness) is thought to help to identify the better outcome within this margin. It favours the exclusion of all meanings (and relative cases) at odds with equity (or fairness). Its persuasiveness is greater in homogenous societies, whereas it is rather weak in divided societies—which could describe most societies (and all the more so the international community) today.

The 'systemic' argument leads to a preference for the meaning which appears to be more in keeping with all or most other rules belonging to the 'system'. It may imply a preference for the *sedes materiae* expressly selected by the law-maker (the rule is given the meaning in keeping with all rules belonging to the same section of the law as decided by the law-maker), or for the recurrent language (the rule is given the meaning that it has in other occurrences in the law, preferably in the same legal text, such as a statute or a treaty), or for the ensemble of the legal concepts within the system (as constructed by legal doctrine). The argument seems logically sound but depends heavily on how the legal system is defined.[46]

The completeness argument implies that in the absence of a rule applicable to a case there must be an existing rule capable of somehow providing a legal answer and avoiding either a lacuna or a *non liquet*. This argument, positivist in nature, is rather persuasive because of the diffused belief that law does or should always give a solution, all the more so when there are judges with compulsory jurisdiction. This belief is often anything but disinterested and tends to be used to reach certain desired results rather than others. It favours the inclusion of all possible cases through the use of further arguments (such as analogy, general principles, etc) designed to close lacunae or avoid a *non liquet*.

The argument for coherence (*a coherentia*) implies that there must be no antinomies in existing rules and that in case of conflict between rules there must always be a rule or principle capable of resolving the conflict and eliminating the antinomy. If antinomies remained, no legal solution could be given and this would coincide with the existence of a lacuna. Unlike the argument of completeness, however, the argument of coherence is often regulated in domestic legal systems by specific rules. It generally works by forcing the interpreter to choose the interpretation of one or both of the potentially conflicting rules which eliminates the conflict. It calls for further arguments capable of eliminating the conflict. Courts often lean towards this argument because it leads to keeping as many rules as possible alive.

Finally, general principles of law are applied so as to fill all possible gaps in the law. When a legal solution is apparently unavailable in existing law, general principles may assist in finding a solution which is coherent with the entire system. While analogy (*analogia legis*) pertains to the extension of the scope of one rule to an unregulated case on grounds of the similarity between the regulated and the unregulated cases, general principles (*analogia juris*) fill the gap by devising a solution which is in accordance with

[45] See Ch 2 above, section B (1); Ch 3 above, section B (2); Ch 7 below, note 507.
[46] See section (3)(a) below.

the structure and basic values of all the rules belonging to the same system.[47] Domestic legal systems not infrequently provide for the application of 'general principles' of the legal system when a specific rule for the case at hand is not found. As noted, general principles of law may be given a variety of different meanings.[48] Traditionally, general principles have been found in the principles of natural law, in the principles of civilized nations, or in the whole set of positive rules belonging to a particular system, or in the principles informing the political regime or the constitution of a given state. The argument obviously favours the inclusion of all possible circumstances in the legal system and is well received by jurists since it permits a legal (presumably the 'just') solution to be found in every case. The objection is that the solutions reached are at best on paper, at worst arbitrarily extrapolated, and more often than not ideologically driven.

(3) International law as a legal system

The question of whether the sources ensure systemic unity to international law does not allow a 'yes or no' answer. Everything depends on what is meant by 'legal system' and many different definitions can be (and have indeed been) provided thus far. The assertion that international law is a legal system is deemed to allow a variety of inferences aimed at remedying its 'imperfections', such as gaps, inconsistencies, indeterminacies, inequities, or undesired outcomes,[49] and is often relevant also to uphold (or deny) the 'reality' of international law.[50] This section argues that international law is undoubtedly—and can be treated, at least to some degree, as—a legal system, ie as a collection of rules which not only flow from certain authorized sources but are also interconnected with one another in the perception of the system's addressees as a whole.

(a) Defining a 'legal system'

A 'legal system' denotes a 'unitary' body of legal rules, possibly 'logically clear, internally consistent... gapless'.[51] It refers to 'a coherently organized assortment' of a set of *elements* arranged in an order characterized by the *interaction* between the elements and possessing a certain degree of *unity* or cohesiveness.[52] A 'system' refers neither to an undivided totality, nor to a collection of unrelated elements. There must be 'sufficient' interrelation between 'sufficiently' autonomous component units. How 'sufficient' both interrelation and autonomy are can be determined only through social attunement, depending on the community concerned.

Diverse definitions of 'legal system' have been proposed in legal theory. In John Austin's view, a legal system is the set of rules created by the same sovereign.[53] Hans

[47] The difference between the application of a principle and the application of analogy, given that the latter seems to imply or even consist in a principle, is, however, difficult to grasp. See MacCormick (n 2 above) 186; N MacCormick, 'In Praise of Theory' (1997) 29 Ariz SLJ 353, 371.

[48] See nn 20–23 above.

[49] See eg E Benvenisti, 'The Conception of International Law as a Legal System' (2007) 50 Ger YBIL 393.

[50] See Ch 2 above, section A (5).

[51] cf M Weber, *Economy and Society: An Outline of Interpretive Sociology* (Berkeley: University of California Press, 1978) 656.

[52] Y Shany, *The Competing Jurisdictions of International Courts and Tribunals* (Oxford: OUP, 2003) 87.

[53] J Raz, *The Concept of a Legal System: An Introduction to the Theory of Legal Systems* (Oxford: Clarendon Press, 2nd edn, 1980) 5.

Kelsen held that a multiplicity of rules forms a single legal system if their validity can ultimately be traced back, through a 'chain of validity', to (or derive from) a 'superior', common basic norm (*Grundnorm*), provided that the system as a whole (as opposed to its individual rules) is also effective.[54] Herbert Hart defined law as 'a system of rules' in terms of a union of primary and secondary rules and argued that the existence of a legal system is proved 'so long as the laws which are valid by the system's tests of validity are obeyed by the bulk of the population'.[55] Joseph Raz argued that norms forming a 'legal system' enjoy 'genetic relations' (hierarchical in character) and 'operative relations' (substantive in character), comprising coercion.[56] The latter, in particular, comprise coercion.[57] This implies a minimal institutional structure[58] and a minimal substantive content.[59] According to a sociological account, while 'law' refers only to rules and norms (and to their *internal* analysis), a legal system comprises also the *social background* (and the external analysis of rules), namely, 'how and why rules are made' (ie the 'social and legal forces that, in some way, press in and make "the law"') and 'what effect they have on people's lives' (ie 'the impact of law on behaviour in the outside world').[60]

From the system concept three types of inferences are generally drawn: the system is 'unitary' (ie there is one single rule on which depends the validity of all other inter-related rules), 'coherent' (ie there is always a method to resolve antinomies), and 'complete' (ie there is a legal solution to every possible case). Assuming that a set of rules forms a 'system', as many affirm and others deny, it therefore remains to be seen whether they constitute (a) a *unitary* system and how legal *hierarchies* are organized; (b) a *coherent* system and how *antinomies* are solved; and (c) a *complete* system and how lacunae are filled up.

Unity of the rules belonging to a system means that all such rules depend on one basic rule or source of law. No historical legal system simply consists of one sole source of law. Rules usually derive from a variety of sources. Even in theologically grounded systems of law only some basic principles derive from God, while many man-made rules are accepted. When all possible sources, and ensuing rules, are ultimately justified by one and the same source, then the collection of rules is unitary and the rule on which all others depend is regarded as hierarchically 'superior', ie prevailing over the others in case of conflict (*lex superior*).

Coherence is one of the most compelling reasons why legal rules are generally seen as part of a 'system' rather than existing separately. Two rules commanding and prohibiting one and the same conduct undermine both. Systematic interpretation is based on the view that logical coherence strongly militates for a meaning in line with the 'spirit' of the system or of the 'reasonable' law-maker's will. Two rules belonging to the same system and having partially or totally the same scope of applicability, may be in conflict either (a) because one imposes an obligation and the other a prohibition; or (b) because one imposes an obligation and the other a permission; or (c) because one imposes a prohibition and another a permission. The traditional criteria applied by courts and often laid down by law-makers for the solution of antinomies between rules having the same rank are *lex posterior* and *lex specialis*. But if the two conflicting rules not only have an equal rank but may also have emerged at the same moment and

[54] Raz has criticized Kelsen's basic norm by contending that the basic norm may derive from a different legal order, such as the law of a colonial power (ibid 102–5).

[55] Hart (n 20 above) 114.

[56] Raz (n 53 above) 183–5

[57] ibid 185–6, 192–4.

[58] ibid 212.

[59] ibid 141.

[60] LM Friedman, *The Legal System: A Social Science Perspective* (New York: Russell Sage Foundation, 1975) 2.

are both general, then neither *lex posterior*, nor *lex specialis*, nor *lex superior* applies and the system tends to destabilize.

Completeness often appears as a compelling condition for a system of law. It is assumed that every case has a rule or a legal answer in the law. The rejection of completeness implies that judges will be authorized to deny justice in cases where no applicable rules exist. Conversely, the acceptance of completeness implies that (a) judges are obliged to decide *every* case (*non liquet* is thus prohibited); and (b) judicial decisions must be based on a legal rule of the system rather than on other normative standards. As noted, it is impossible, for a variety of reasons, for all possible cases to be covered by the rules expressly existing in a legal system. Lacunae in the law are inevitable. However, what constitutes a 'lacuna' is anything but clear.[61] A lacuna is a 'missing' rule, a rule which is *expected* but not found in the law. There are at least three strategies to tackle lacunae, traceable to the practice of filling lacunae in positive law by applying natural law.[62] One focuses on the *interpretation* of an existing rule in such a way as to cover a prima facie unregulated case: for example, a rule which explicitly applies to 'aircraft and jets' is interpreted to the effect that it also applies to spaceships, assuming that spaceships are a type of aircraft. In consequence, lacunae may be detected either easily or rarely according to how far interpreters are willing to 'stretch' existing rules by way of interpretation, and there are generally no rules instructing interpreters to this end. It could be said that a lacuna is an 'invention' of the judge to open a legal space *for justice* (limited to the instant case) against the legislative will of the law-maker. Another strategy concerns the *integration* of the system by resorting to ad hoc criteria for the regulation of the apparently unregulated cases, such as analogy and general principles of law. Conflicts, however, may arise between different criteria (for example, between analogy and general principles of law) or between different forms of the same criterion (for example, between different general principles of law). In such cases, if the system does not provide a *further* criterion to resolve these conflicts, the system is left with a lacuna that cannot be eliminated. A third strategy is to imply the existence of a *'closing' (implied) principle* providing for a residual general principle of law to be applied in case of lacunae, either 'what is not permitted is prohibited' (ie every behaviour is prohibited unless specifically permitted) or 'what is not prohibited is permitted' (ie every behaviour is permitted unless specifically prohibited). The latter approach is evidently much more viable. When a general (implied) exclusive clause conflicts with analogy or a general principle of law whose application to unregulated cases is expressly stipulated by the law itself, once again the system remains stuck because the lacuna cannot be eliminated.

Finally, it should be noted that the definition of law as a system is based on some circularity between description and prescription. The assertion that a set of rules is a 'system' *presupposes* that there is some (already determined) unity, coherence, and completeness among the rules. Once the system is defined, however, from the *fact* that the rules do form a system (the 'is' dimension) certain *consequences* are drawn in terms of unity, coherence, and completeness (the 'ought' dimension). The description of the system tends to translate into a prescription. On the description side the system may possess a certain degree of unity or coherence; on the prescription side a *higher* degree of unity or coherence is inferred, no longer reflecting the system exactly as it is, but pushing it somehow to change into a more unitary or coherent one.

61 For the view that lacunae are fictions, see Kelsen (n 10 above) 146–9.

62 See Ch 4 above, section B (1).

(b) Unity and fragmentation in international law

The question of 'fragmentation' in international law, to be discussed in greater detail elsewhere in this book,[63] invites the question of whether international law is a unitary, coherent, and complete 'legal system'.[64] A simplistic operation consists in determining whether international law squares with one or another of the jurisprudential definitions of legal system illustrated above. The answer may be positive or negative, optimistic or pessimistic, according to the definition selected. For example, as is well known, Hart conceded that international law is law, but denied that it is a 'legal system' in accordance with his general theory of law and of a 'legal system'.[65]

The view that international law is 'unitary' and does form a 'legal system', ie a systemic unity/totality, has been largely accepted as axiomatic in the past and can be traced to the (Western) doctrines of natural law.[66] Many modern international law theorists argue for the unity of international law by holding general custom as an all-encompassing, unifying source providing for a set of interpretative rules and a fall-back regime, serving a purpose similar to that performed by natural law in the past relative to positive law. They defend the 'unity' of international law as a condition for its reality.[67] To reinforce unity they often mention as 'pillars' of the construction such 'special' rules as *jus cogens* and obligations *erga omnes*.[68] Critics retort that international law is an irremediably fragmented law of a deeply fragmented states system.[69] They argue that custom is either no longer relevant or is itself fragmented and that interpretative rules are far from securing unity and consistency. Their attitude to *jus cogens* and obligations *erga omnes* is sceptical. For its part, the ILC Study Group, as is well known, has extensively explored the topic and concluded that 'international law is a legal system'.[70]

Both sides impliedly endorse the idea that the Western state is the yardstick of systemic unity. Both imagine a world regulated (or unregulated) by a law similar, as far as possible, to state law, ie a world similar to a Western state rather than, say, a tribe. The debate seems rather overstated. International law is a 'system' simply because there

63 See section B (3) below, and Ch 7 below, section B.

64 On the systems theory, see A Kiss and D Shelton, 'System Analysis of International Law: A Methodological Inquiry' (1986) 17 Neth YBIL 45; SA Kocs, 'Explaining the Strategic Behaviour of States: International Law as a Systems Structure' (1994) 38 ISQ 535, arguing against neo-realists that international law is the principal structure of the international system in that it embodies the self-interest of states.

65 Hart (n 20 above) 231, 235–6, arguing that international law is 'law' (ie a 'set of rules') but not a 'system' since 'there is no basic rule providing general criteria of validity for the rules of international law'. See in addition n 55 above, and Ch 2 above, n 98. On Hart from an international law perspective, see J D'Aspremont, 'Hart et le positivisme postmoderne en droit international' (2009) 113 RGDIP 635; M Payandeh, 'The Concept of International Law in the Jurisprudence of H.L.A. Hart' (2010) 21 EJIL 967.

66 For a recent discussion of five possible meanings of 'unity' when applied to international law, see M Prost, *The Concept of Unity in Public International Law* (Oxford: Hart, forthcoming).

67 See eg C Dominicé, 'Methodology of International Law', MP EPIL, 1st edn, 1984 vol 7, 334, 334, arguing that international law does exist, as evidenced by 'a mere observation of reality and is expressed by the maxim *ubi societas ibi ius*', and hence 'there exists a system of legal rules'.

68 P-M Dupuy, 'L'unité de l'ordre juridique international: Cours général de droit international public' (2002) 297 RdC 9. For *jus cogens* and obligations *erga omnes*, see section B (4)(f) below; and Ch 8 below, section B (1).

69 A Carty, *The Decay of International Law? A Reappraisal of the Limits of Legal Imagination in International Affairs* (Manchester: Manchester University Press, 1986) 1, 10, 15. See previously A Zimmern, *The League of Nations and the Rule of Law (1918–1935)* (London: Macmillan, 1936) 98.

70 Report of the International Law Commission on the Work of its Fifty-eighth Session (2006), in GAOR, Sixty-first Session, Supp No 10, A/61/10, at 407.

are certain entities (both states and non-state actors) which see themselves as direct or indirect addressees of such a unitary thing called international law. They appear to be able to recognize to a sufficient degree which rules belong to the domain of international law and which do not. This very basic attitude may presumably be found in every social group, not only in states and in the states system, including tribes. If there is a system of addressees of international law, and there certainly is,[71] then there must also be some systemic unity in what they see as their law. To argue, for instance, that the thing called international law is made up only of treaties applicable to different sets of parties completely detached from one another, like unrelated islands in a totally unknown and limitless ocean, is clearly divorced from reality. This 'international law' is believed to be a set of a certain number of rules which are—arguably to a different degree depending on the issue area, entities involved, etc—mutually related. A different, crucial question is the critical passage from the *description* of international law as a system to the *prescription* that *there must be* a certain level of systemic unity thereof. International law may well be a system, albeit not the *desired* system.

B. Law-making

Article 38 ICJ Statute, just like its predecessor Article 38 PCIJ Statute,[72] is the *locus classicus* where the sources of international law are deemed to be listed.[73] The routine reference to Article 38 as a 'source rule' raises many difficulties, however. Article 38 does not expressly mention the word 'sources', but simply indicates the rules that the ICJ shall apply in its decisions.[74] Moreover, Article 38 is a treaty rule, binding only on the states parties thereto, and cannot establish the sources of international law as a whole. Nor does Article 38 imply any built-in hierarchy between the classes of norms it lists. As Lord Phillimore pointed out during the preparatory work of the PCIJ Statute, 'the order mentioned simply represent[s] the logical order in which these sources would occur to the mind of the judge'.[75] Article 38 does not even specify whether the list is exhaustive or open-ended. For example, the ICJ has apparently recognized rules of international law not mentioned in the list, such as unilateral declarations, in the 1974 *Nuclear Tests* Judgment,[76] confirmed in the 1986 *Frontier Dispute* Judgment,[77] unless unilateral declarations are seen as treaties. In summary, not only does Article 38 avoid establishing the sources of international law, it seems not to be exhaustive and mandatory for the ICJ itself. Reference to Article 38 tends often to perpetuate the untenable notion that international law possesses a set of 'sources' approximately similar to those of domestic law. This section examines how the rules are made,

[71] See Ch 5 above, section B (3).

[72] Statute of the Permanent Court of International Justice (adopted 16 December 1920, entered into force 20 August 1921) 6 LNTS 389.

[73] Statute of the International Court of Justice (adopted 26 June 1945, entered into force 24 October 1945) 145 BSP 832.

[74] For a critique of Art 38 ICJ Statute, see Y Onuma, *A Transcivilizational Perspective on International Law: Questioning Prevalant Cognitive Frameworks in the Emerging Multi-polar and Multi-civilizational World of the Twenty-first Century* (Leiden: Nijhoff, 2010) 206–25.

[75] Advisory Committee of Jurists, *Procès-verbaux of the Proceedings of the Committee, 16th June–24th July 1920, with Annexes* (The Hague: Van Langhuysen, 1920) 333.

[76] ICJ, *Nuclear Tests Case (Australia v France)* Judgment of 20 December 1974, [1974] ICJ Rep 253, para 43; *Nuclear Tests Case (New Zealand v France)* Judgment of 20 December 1974, [1974] ICJ Rep 457, para 46.

[77] ICJ Chamber, *Case concerning the Frontier Dispute (Burkina Faso/Republic of Mali)* Judgment of 22 December 1986, [1986] ICJ Rep 554, para 40.

integrated, reconciled, and changed. It argues that they are ultimately grounded in custom, ie in a social phenomenon sustained by a constant informal pressure of the states system on individual states, strong and weak alike. Custom means that states *uti universi* press states *uti singuli* within the system.

(1) Rules

While the case for the transplantation of the legal sources doctrine to international law is debatable,[78] there is little doubt that certain distinct classes of rules are believed to be part of international law by their (direct and indirect) addressees as a whole.[79] Custom, treaties, and general principles of law recognized by civilized nations form part of international law. Each class has its own distinctive features as regards their coming into being, objective and subjective scope, and effects. They are also mutually interrelated to some extent, certainly not at a level comparable to the rules of an efficient state. At the same time, all rules of international law are ultimately grounded in custom, ie in the informal pressure of the system on its individual members. This section argues that: (a) international law includes only 'rules', even when it endorses 'principles', deriving from custom, treaties, IOs' decisions, and general principles of law recognized by civilized nations; (b) all such rules are of general concern in the global states system but do not necessarily need be thought to apply to all states on account of their importance in a globalized world.

(a) Custom

The term 'customary international law' (CIL) refers to a category of international law rules that, although strongly attacked in the past and particularly in recent times, no one can seriously deny, whatever its shortcomings. CIL is constantly evoked and applied by international and national courts in innumerable decisions as *unwritten* law created by the *generality* of states (not necessarily the totality thereof), binding on *all* states, regardless of the attitude of individual dissenting states.[80] Despite several

[78] For a Hart-inspired revisitation of formalism, see J D'Aspremont, *Formalism and the Sources of International Law: A Theory of the Ascertainment of Legal Rules* (Oxford: OUP, 2011), advocating—against current processes of deformalization of international law—the identification (as distinct from the creation) of international legal rules based on 'some elementary' formal standards rooted in the social practice of law-applying authorities, notably international courts and tribunals (in particular the ICJ) and their 'cross-fertilization' practices, domestic courts, the International Committee of the Red Cross, and, although indirectly, international legal scholars.

[79] See eg US Court of Appeals for the Second Circuit, *Vietnam Association for Victims of Agent Orange et al v Dow Chemical Company et al* Judgment of 22 February 2008, ILDC 1040 (US 2008), para 25; Slovenian Constitutional Court, *Elizabeta Dolenc et al* Judgment of 9 November 2006 No U-I-266/04, ILDC 570 (SI 2006) para 12, specifying that 'generally valid principles of international law' embrace 'rules of international customary law and general legal principles recognized by civilized nations' as 'sources of international law'.

[80] See ICJ, *North Sea Continental Shelf (Federal Republic of Germany v Denmark and Federal Republic of Germany v Netherlands) (Merits)* Judgment of 20 February 1969, [1969] ICJ Rep 4, para 63, arguing that, while 'it is a characteristic of purely conventional rules and obligations that, in regard to them, some faculty of making unilateral reservations may, within certain limits, be admitted ... this cannot be so in the case of general or customary law rules and obligations which, *by their very nature*, must have *equal force* for *all* members of the international community, and cannot therefore be the subject of any right of *unilateral exclusion* exercisable *at will* by *any one* of them in its own favour' (emphasis added). Significantly, in *United States Diplomatic and Consular Staff in Tehran (United States v Iran)* Judgment of 24 May 1980, [1980] ICJ Rep 3, para 86, the ICJ seems to have acknowledged the 'intercivilizational' character of CIL as a 'common' law when it held that 'the principle of the

theoretical and practical difficulties, in practice states have a precise sense of what CIL prescribes in most cases and courts do not seem to find it insurmountable to identify and apply CIL rules to particular cases.

Like customary law in general,[81] a CIL rule emerges, and can thus be ascertained as existent, when it is supported by a generalized, uniform, and constant state practice (*usus*) accompanied by a sense of legal obligation or of necessity (*opinio juris sive necessitatis*).[82] This dualistic conception of CIL has been contested in the past either by denying *opinio juris* on grounds of logic[83] or by downplaying *usus*,[84] but it is firmly supported in the international and domestic case law. The ICJ famously upheld it in the 1969 *North Sea* Judgment,[85] in the 1985 *Continental Shelf (Libya v Malta)* Judgment,[86] in the 1986 *Nicaragua* Judgment,[87] and in the 1996 *Nuclear Weapons* Advisory Opinion.[88] In the domestic jurisprudence, it was endorsed, among countless others, by the Italian Court of Cassation in the 1955 *Dobre* Judgment,[89] by the German Administrative Tribunal in 1971 *Privileges on the Parking of Diplomats* Judgment,[90] by the South African Cape Provincial Division in the 1987 *Petane* Judgment,[91] by the High Court of Australia in the 1991 *Polyukhovich* Judgment,[92] by the South African Competition Tribunal in the 2001 *American Natural Soda Ash*

inviolability of the persons of diplomatic agents and the premises of diplomatic missions is one of the very foundations of [a] long-established régime, to the evolution of which the traditions of Islam made a substantial contribution'. For the 'persistent objector' doctrine, see n 105 below and accompanying text. For a transcivilizational perspective to universal international law, see Onuma (n 74 above) 203–65.

[81] See A Perreau-Saussine and JB Murphy (eds), *The Nature of Customary Law: Legal, Historical and Philosophical Perspectives* (Cambridge: CUP, 2007); DJ Bederman, *Custom as a Source of Law* (Cambridge: CUP, 2010).

[82] See eg M Akehurst, 'Custom as a Source of International Law' (1974–75) 47 BYBIL 1; MH Mendelson, 'The Subjective Element in Customary International Law' (1995) 66 BYBIL 177, 204–7, arguing that in standard cases (when uniform practice exists) *opinio* is superfluous.

[83] H Kelsen, 'Théorie du droit international coutumier' (1939) 1 RITD 253, 263–4, arguing that if *opinio* is accepted, CIL would result from an erroneous belief. As is well-known, while this view was espoused by other writers, such as M Sørensen, 'Principes de droit international public: cours général' (1960-III) 101 RdC 6, 50, Kelsen himself later changed his mind in 'Théorie du droit international public' (1953-III) 84 RdC 1, 123. The 'monistic' view based on the sole *usus* has found little if any support in international and national jurisprudence.

[84] See recently BD Lepard, *Customary International Law: A New Theory with Practical Applications* (Cambridge: CUP, 2010) 23–5, 77–94, 122–39, arguing for state practice as evidence of *opinio juris*, this latter inspired by a number of 'fundamental ethical principles'.

[85] ICJ, *North Sea Continental Shelf Cases* (n 80 above) paras 73–74. See further, more recently, ICJ, *Jurisdictional Immunities of the State (Germany v Italy: Greece intervening)* Judgment of 3 February 2012, at <http://www.icj-cij.org/docket/files/143/16883.pdf>, para 55.

[86] ICJ, *Case Concerning the Continental Shelf (Libyan Arab Jamahiriya/Malta)* Judgment of 3 June 1985, [1985] ICJ Rep 13, para 27, regarding as 'axiomatic that the material of customary international law is to be looked for primarily in the actual practice and *opinio juris* of States'.

[87] ICJ, *Case concerning Military and Paramilitary Activities in and against Nicaragua (Nicaragua v United States) (Merits)* Judgment of 27 June 1986, [1986] ICJ Rep 14, paras 183–186.

[88] ICJ, *Legality of the Threat or Use of Nuclear Weapons* Advisory Opinion of 8 July 1996, [1996] ICJ Rep 226, paras 70–73.

[89] Italian Court of Cassation, *Re Dobre* Judgment of 28 May 1955, 107 GI (1955) II, 365, 367.

[90] German Federal Administrative Court, *Parking Privileges for Diplomats* Judgment of 22 January 1971, (1986) 70 ILR 396, 401–3.

[91] South-African Cape Provincial Division, *S v Petane* Judgment of 3 November 1987, (1988) 3 SALR 51, at <http://www.icrc.org>.

[92] High Court of Australia, *Polyukhovich v Commonwealth of Australia et al ('War Crimes Act Case')* Judgment of 14 August 1991, [1991] HCA 32, at <http://www.austlii.edu.au/au/cases/cth/HCA/1991/32.html>, para 28 (*per* Brennan J).

Corp Judgment,[93] by the Canadian Supreme Court in the 2007 *Hope* Judgment,[94] and by the High Court of the Special Administrative Region of Hong Kong in the 2008 *C* Judgment.[95] Article 38(1)(b) seems to be in line therewith when it defines international custom as 'evidence of a general practice accepted as law'. While *usus* ensures effectiveness by avoiding taking paper rules as CIL, however desirable, *opinio juris* ensures legal quality by avoiding taking non-legal rules (in particular, comity, convenience, or tradition) as CIL.[96]

In recent years CIL has attracted strong criticism, often out of domestic concerns and taking domestic law as a yardstick.[97] A well-known study published in 2000 by J Patrick Kelly may be taken as a good example and a useful basis for discussion.[98] Kelly stated that both the formation and the content of CIL are contentious and that the theory of CIL is indeterminate and manipulable, in practice a matter of taste in 'a world of many cultures and values' in which 'general acceptance is neither ascertainable nor verifiable' since 'the international society of nation-states is not an organic community'. He emphasized that CIL lacks procedural legitimacy because 'the less powerful nations and voices are ignored', in defiance of 'the basic notion of democratic governance among states', and that it is determined 'by the academic and judicial elites'. It is thus no wonder that CIL is considered to be too ineffective 'to generate substantive norms that will command compliance'. The only 'empirical' CIL rules in place are 'fundamental structural norms', such as diplomatic immunities, which 'place few limits to state action'. He concluded that CIL 'cannot function as a legitimate [and relatively objective] source of substantive legal norms in a decentralized world of nations without a broad base of shared values', and proposed that it 'should be eliminated . . . and replaced by consensual processes' that permit wide state participation.[99] This conclusion was specified by observing that: 'The U.S. and many other nations will not accept norms that limit their sovereign prerogatives without specific agreement'.

While the above objections to CIL present a certain plausibility, they are still untenable, all the more so where international law is viewed as a social construct.

First, from the lack of unanimous agreement it does not follow that CIL is a matter of taste. There is disagreement on virtually everything in the world, but this does not mean that everything is a matter of taste in one and the same sense and with the same consequences. Writers and states may disagree with one another on the matter of CIL, but this is far from proving that CIL is not law, let alone that it should be discarded. What Kelly calls the 'custom-speak' does exist, but it is distinct from CIL itself. Courts may also disagree on this or that CIL norm, and they often do, but this is not enough to dismiss CIL as a class of rules sharing certain features. Even domestic courts disagree

[93] Competition Tribunal of South Africa, *Competition Commission v American Natural Soda Ash Corp* Judgment of 30 November 2001, Case Nos 49/CR/Apr00 and 87/CR/Sep00, at <http://www.comptrib.co.za/assets/Uploads/Case-Documents/49CRAAPR00-2pdf.pdf>, at 14.

[94] Supreme Court of Canada, *R v Hope* Judgment of 7 June 2007, [2007] 2 SCR 292, at <http://scc.lexum.org/en/2007/2007scc26/2007scc26.html>, para 46.

[95] Hong Kong, High Court of the Special Administrative Region, *C et al v Director of Immigration* Judgment of 18 February 2008, ILDC 1119 (HK 2008) para 68.

[96] cf ICJ, *North Sea Continental Shelf Cases* (n 80 above) para 77, noting that 'The frequency, or even habitual character of the acts is not in itself enough' given that 'many international acts, e.g., in the field of ceremonial and protocol, . . . are performed almost invariably, but . . . are motivated only by considerations of courtesy, convenience or tradition, and not by any sense of legal duty'.

[97] See eg PR Trimble, 'A Revisionist View of Customary International Law' 33 (1986) UCLA LR 665, 718–23.

[98] JP Kelly, 'The Twilight of Customary International Law' (1999–2000) 40 Virg JIL 449.

[99] ibid 451–2.

with one another on this or that point of national law and several issues remain 'open' despite their hierarchization, but to conclude from this that the disputed law is no law at all or should be discarded would be an obvious exaggeration.

Secondly, the world may be not 'as one' to the degree desired, but still it is 'one world' despite all its intra-differences. The notion that states do not share today a sense of belonging to one and the same world sounds indeed unreal. A certain degree of difference is simply physiological, even desirable, in any society, including small tribes. While differences in the world population are patent, this is far from proving that there are absolutely no common interests and values to prevent CIL as such from working appropriately, let alone indicating that it should be discarded.

Thirdly, CIL has nothing to do with the 'democratic governance' known within certain specific states, such as the United States. It is true, of course, that in the formation and transformation of CIL the stronger play a much greater role, but law in general (including domestic law, whether democratic or not), as here understood, is *always* the expression of the stronger. On the other hand, CIL can emerge only if the generality of states participate in its formation, meaning that a CIL rule does not emerge if it is supported only by few major powers, and for this sole reason.[100] The fact that they impose the purported rule as a legal rule by way of brute force is another question. Robberies occur and may succeed, yet they remain prohibited as far as law is concerned, at least until the whole legal system collapses. Rather, consent-based treaty law may be viewed as being even more anti-democratic than custom, as individual treaties may well be imposed by the (individual) stronger on the (individual) weaker. Only advocates of the negotiating parties which have a stronger bargaining power may praise treaties as democratic.

Fourthly, the ascertainment of CIL may be, and certainly is, very difficult and open to question and manipulation. Courts often abstain from attempting any systematic inquiry into international practice and show little inclination to offer a fully fledged theory of CIL. However, CIL is not the outcome of a scientific enterprise. It hardly needs 'evidence' in the scientific sense. It must work to allow people to live together in their local and national communities, as well as in the global community. The practice needed as evidence is the one which is persuasive enough to its addressees as a whole, not to a circle of scientists. Courts cannot be expected to write treatises and fill up their decisions with cases, dicta, and all relevant material available as though they should provide evidence of a scientific truth. This would paradoxically weaken their authority, and courts are set up and called upon to state the law authoritatively. Judges are entrusted to identify and apply the law first and foremost as *reliable* persons who are, rightly or wrongly, deemed capable of 'feeling' and articulating the prevailing sense of justice and law in the community, in addition to competence, integrity, and expertise requirements. No one would expect a judge to be a scientist or a mathematician. The ultimate basis of their persuasiveness is the possible reaction of those which have conferred on them the power to make authoritative decisions. Scientific evidence may be of help, but it is by no means conclusive if the addressees of the law count it as less valuable than other factors.

Fifthly, it is true that 'Much of state practice is unavailable',[101] but this is not really the point. The relevant material is *inevitably* the material *known*, and of course which

[100] UK House of Lords, *Jones v Ministry of Interior Al-Mamlaka Al-Arabiya AS Saudiya (the Kingdom of Saudi Arabia) et al* Judgment of 14 June 2006, [2006] UKHL 26, para 22 ('one swallow does not make a rule of international law', *per* Lord Bingham of Cornhill).

[101] Kelly (n 98 above) 472.

material is made known and by whom is strategically crucial. To complain that there is a great deal of other material, often unknown, or even classified, is of little interest to state the law as it stands, although it may be helpful to struggle for more publicity and a less-biased law in the future. Once again, law is not a scientific enterprise. It has to work in practice and it could do so even on the basis of few precedents, so long as all (possibly divergent) others remain unknown or even little known, if its addressees as a whole see them as key to identify the law. The frequent charge that CIL is 'incomprehensible' or 'enigmatic' and logically implausible misses the mark.[102] Everything in this world is enigmatic, in theory, but not everything is as enigmatic as everything else. When it comes to CIL, logic is to a large extent out of place. Social attunement is far more suitable. Customary law is ultimately based on the social nature of human beings. They cannot survive without joining groups, but uniting entails subjection to the group. Custom is the informal pressure of the group on each of its members.[103] It has nothing to do with democratic processes. It precedes any political arrangement and legal formal process simply because every arrangement and process is the result of how the group presses its members in the first place, whether towards democracy or not. Individual members in individual cases in regard to individual rules may dislike this state of affairs, yet they generally *accept* and *defend* this *same* state of affairs when it comes to others, ie to all members in all cases with respect to all rules. This is why CIL is accepted as binding on *all* states, including dissenters. It is states as a whole that want each of them to be under the control and pressure of the whole, although they may understandably contest a CIL rule in particular cases in which they get involved. The price that a state must pay in order to have all others in the system under collective control is to be subjected to collective control.

Finally, nothing is said in Kelly's account of *who* is entitled to 'eliminate' CIL. Kelly concludes that: 'Only a consensual process will permit nations with diverse values and interests to negotiate standards that reconcile differences and meet common needs'.[104] He fails to discuss whether these 'standards' are themselves based on CIL and how they can work as 'law' once CIL has been 'eliminated'.

The key problem with the critics of CIL is that they completely misunderstand, or refuse to accept, the social foundations of law, ie law as social construct, including the law of the world system. Their perspective of the 'global' is focused on how the world is seen from the angle of one single state, whether their own or another. They assume that individuals and states create their autonomy by themselves and agree to enter groups on certain conditions that they are completely free to either accept or refuse. The group

[102] Kelly (n 98 above) 542.

[103] The idea of CIL here presented is different from that of the 'sociological' schools of international law which insist either on solidarity, such as Scelle (see Ch 4 above, nn 184–92 and accompanying text), or on realistic power-politics, like Corbett, De Visscher, and Schwarzenberger (ibid n 166), or on legal change towards a desired goal, as occurs with McDougal (ibid n 174), or on constructivism rooted in legal inherentness, such as Brunnée and Toope (ibid nn 196–203 and accompanying text), or in spontaneism, as is the case with Ago (ibid n 188). It is argued that CIL is a *formal* source made by *states* as distinct from social practice as such, although it rests on social practice, and that custom itself is a *heteronomous* legal source imposed by a *hierarchically superior* (in the sense of overpowering) authority embodied in the global states system *as constantly shaped by non-state actors*. In other words: (a) every single state participates in the CIL formation by exercising its authority over any natural and juridical person within its jurisdiction, and (b) the generality of states (*uti universi*) exerts a social pressure as a whole towards individual states (*uti singuli*). In this picture there is little 'spontaneism', if spontaneism is meant as a process of law creation devoid of any formal recognition (whether called 'source' or otherwise) by its addressees as a whole.

[104] Kelly (n 98 above) 542.

and the degree of involvement in the group is believed to be optional. But groups are not an option. Individuals have little choice but to join a group, although they may have an option to join one group rather than another; and so do states. Within the group individuals are expected by all other members to behave in the same way as both they and the generality of the members of the group have behaved up to then. Repetition is a basic expectation of human beings as a defence against the prospect of social chaos. A repeated gesture creates of itself a 'norm' in the human psychology. Repetition gives rise to certain expectations that are viewed by the group as the law, while others are characterized differently. This also occurs with states and other entities, both because states act through individuals and because it is human beings that perceive and interpret in human terms the behaviour of states and other entities. Even the 'persistent objector' doctrine, when admitted, rests on two requirements in order for the objector to opt out of the emergent CIL rule it has opposed, ie the objection must have been raised at the very beginning and it must run constantly to the present, two conditions which are not set out by the objector itself and can be identified only by referring to *general* state attitudes.[105]

The relevant expected 'behaviour' within the international community is basically the behaviour of states. To assume that CIL is 'directly' made also by non-state actors, in particular by private individuals, would be to go too far.[106] Non-state actors may (and should) press states and shape their behaviour so as to give rise to new CIL rules, but it is not for them directly to create CIL. First, there is no way to know the actual position of the whole humankind on this or that (existing or future) CIL rule. Massive worldwide demonstrations against war, for example, are hardly sufficient. Even millions of demonstrators are still a very tiny portion of all humanity. The fact that most governments are in favour of a given war and are not overthrown due to this invites the presumption that the majority of the world population is not as hostile to the war as protesters are. Secondly, even assuming that people's behaviour contributes to the formation of CIL, this CIL would remain a dead letter if by hypothesis most governments were not prepared to enforce it, unless of course governments were pressed to do so, but this is a matter of domestic law and policy and how far people succeed in shaping states *from within*. People live under the constraints and laws of their states and rulers. They should be able either to change the rulers and how their state behaves or to form a new state headed by better rulers, with the help of foreign actors if need be. Thirdly, excessive confidence in people's wishes may be a cure worse that the illness. One should never overlook the fact that it is the people that generally support dictators, and there is no reason why people should not do so when dealing with world affairs.[107] People 'in the street' may indeed and should contribute to the change of their governments, inter alia, by asking for help abroad, but this request for help cannot

[105] JI Charney, 'The Persistent Objector Rule and the Development of Customary International Law' (1985) 56 BYBIL 1 In the opposite sense, see MH Mendelson, 'The Formation of Customary International Law' (1998) 272 RdC 155, 227–44. For a recent discussion, see Lepard (n 84 above) 229–42.

[106] See eg IR Gunning, 'Modernizing Customary International Law: The Challenge of Human Rights' (1991) 31 Virg JIL 211, 227–34, 244–7; C Ochoa, 'The Individual and Customary International Law Formation' (2007–08) 48 Virg JIL 119–86.

[107] Unpersuasive in this respect is the constructivist effort made by Jutta Brunnée and Stephen J Toope, in *Legitimacy and Legality*, to ground international law in 'legitimacy' in terms of Lon Fuller's conception of fidelity to law, and his notion that 'law is the work of its everyday participants ... to construct and sustain a common institutional framework to meet the exigencies of social life', as opposed to strict legality (Brunnée and Toope (n 12 above) 22). See further Ch 4 above, nn 196–206 and accompanying text.

be mistaken for CIL. Their effort may or may not be successful. A better international law is possible on condition that people assume their responsibility and this can first be done towards their own rulers.

Critics of CIL are right, however, in detecting manipulative strategies to further (rightly or wrongly) desired outcomes. CIL is often used as a stratagem to impose international legal obligations on dissenting (or at least reluctant) states and their peoples in the name (or under the pretext) of common universal values. CIL is then conceived of as a sort of natural law and its universality is plainly deduced from the alleged universality of globalist needs,[108] regardless of *usus*, either invoking 'principles',[109] or giving *opinio juris* more weight than *usus*.[110] The mechanical finding of such elements of custom is hastily made, even when there is little or nothing in its support, in order to conclude that a CIL rule exists and 'therefore' applies to all states, including dissenting states. Another method to manipulate custom is to suppose that since CIL applies to 'all' states, then it must necessarily apply to all 'international subjects', and hence also to relevant non-state actors, such as IOs. But the fact that states have created a rule applicable to their relations does not necessarily mean that they want the rule to apply to others, or that the rule applies to others regardless of states' attitudes. While there is little doubt that CIL may apply to international organizations (IOs),[111] the *automatic* application of *all* CIL rules (including those on human rights) to their full extent to IOs (as distinct from their member states), let alone to other non-state actors,

[108] In its Partial Award of 19 December 2005, 'Western Front, Aerial Bombardment and Related Claims Eritrea's Claims 1, 3, 5, 9–13, 14, 21, 25 & 26', the Eritrea–Ethiopia Claims Commission (EECC) held that the prohibition of attacks on water reservoirs laid down in Art 54 Geneva Protocol I additional to the 1949 Geneva Conventions on the Protection of the Victims of War reflected CIL because of its 'compelling humanitarian nature' together with the fact that it 'had not been questioned by any statements of reservation or interpretation and [was] not inconsistent with general State practice in two decades since the conclusion of the treaty', at <http://www.pca-cpa.org/upload/files/FINAL%20ER%20FRONT%20CLAIMS.pdf>, para 105.

[109] See B Simma and P Alston, 'The Sources of Human Rights Law: Custom, *Jus Cogens* and General Principles' (1988–89) 12 Aus YBIL 81, arguing for the universality of human rights even where 'tangible State conduct ... does not live up' to general recognition (ibid 104) on the basis of general principles of law. Contrary to what is asserted by the authors (ibid 105–6), the ICJ has indeed characterized the 'elementary considerations of humanity' as being part of CIL. For example, in the 1986 *Nicaragua* Judgment, the Court expressly referred to CIL (n 87 above) 147–8, No 8 of the operative part. Even assuming the existence of a general principle of law, it is difficult to see how such a principle could credibly set aside a CIL rule strongly rooted in state practice. The authors themselves concede that 'general principles have not fared too well as a source of international law', but note that 'in the development of human rights law principles have always preceded practice'. But it is one thing to *promote* human rights through the appeal to general, unspecified principles of law (a struggle that may or may not be successful, depending on several factors) in order for the law to conform over time thereto; it is quite another to regard as existing law the principles appealed to at a moment when by hypothesis realities do not reflect desires.

[110] A Cassese, 'The Martens Clause: Half a Loaf or Simply Pie in the Sky?' (2000) 11 EJIL 187, 214. The same view was taken in *Prosecutor v Kupreškić* Trial Chamber Judgment of 14 January 2000, Case No IT-95-16, para 527, Judge Cassese presiding, who recently reiterated it in relation to *jus cogens* in STL, *El Sayed*, 'Order assigning Matter to Pre-Trial Judge' of 15 April 2010, Case No CH/PRES/2010/01, para 30. In favour of this view, see recently R Portmann, *Legal Personality in International Law* (Cambridge: CUP, 2010) 262.

[111] See eg *Interpretation of the Agreement of 25 March 1951 between the WHO and Egypt* Advisory Opinion of 20 December 1980, [1980] ICJ Rep 73, para 37, referring to 'general rules of international law'; ECJ, Case C-162/96 *Racke v Hauptzollamt Mainz* [1998] ECR I-3655, paras 45–51, Judgment of 16 June 1998, according CIL a direct position in the EC/EU legal order above secondary law and confirming its invocability by individuals for the review of the legality of EC/EU acts within the limits of 'fundamental rules of customary international law'.

needs caution.[112] In the *Gulf of Maine* Judgment an ICJ Chamber observed that customary rules must be tested by a process of 'induction', based on an analysis of general practice accepted as law, 'and not by deduction from preconceived ideas'.[113] The approach of some judges and scholars in presenting as CIL certain alleged universal (humanitarian or other) values to be applied to all states or even to all international actors is in fact 'promotional' (and as such it may well be worth supporting) but cannot be understood as stating the law until it is accepted by the generality of states according to the recognized sources.[114]

(b) Treaties

There is no doubt that the provisions found in international treaties are part of international law. Leaving aside particular aspects of the law of treaties that will be examined elsewhere in this book, it is necessary to elucidate, on the one hand, the social nature of treaties (ie their foundation in customary international law) and, on the other hand, the untenability of the attempts often made to widen the subjective and objective scope of a few 'special' treaties beyond what is ordinarily established by international law.

Unlike customary international law, treaties are generally *written* law created by *two or more* states, or other international actors endowed with international treaty-making power, binding only on the *parties* thereto. These features are thought to be sufficient to see treaties as a distinct 'source' of international law. Treaties do not apply as a rule to third parties,[115] although great power concerts have always attempted to impose their will on all others by appealing to a purported *ultra partes* effect of *certain* treaties of theirs.[116] It is also assumed that certain 'objective' legal regimes apply to third parties,[117] as well as 'constitutional' treaties such as the UN Charter.[118] The notion that in today's globalized world it is vital that all states are compelled to respect the rules protecting global values embodied in multilateral (sometimes even 'constitutional') treaties, induces many to suppose that: (a) certain special treaties, at least in particular circumstances, are binding even on third parties; (b) they may be higher in rank than all other treaties; and (c) respect for their authority may be supervised and enforced by international bodies with which even non-injured states may file a complaint against an alleged transgressor. However wise on paper, such attempts to overcome state consent—evidently through the consent of other (non-state) actors—by labelling a treaty as 'special' for some reason are far from reflecting realities.[119] In fact, states and their

[112] See G Verdirame, *The UN and Human Rights: Who Guards the Guardians?* (Cambridge: CUP, 2011) 71–2.

[113] ICJ Chamber, *Case concerning Delimitation of the Maritime Boundary in the Gulf of Maine Area (Canada/United States)* Judgment of 12 October 1984, [1984] ICJ Rep 246, para 111.

[114] See, exemplarily, AA Cançado Trindade, *International Law for Humankind: Towards a New* Jus Gentium (Leiden and Boston: Nijhoff, 2010).

[115] Vienna Convention on the Law of Treaties (concluded 23 May 1969, entered into force 27 January 1980) 1155 UNTS 331 (Arts 34–38).

[116] cf 'Report of the International Committee of Jurists entrusted by the Council of the League of Nations with the Task of giving a Advisory Opinion upon the Legal Aspects of the Aaland Islands Question' of October 1920, LNOJ Special Supplement, No 3, at 17.

[117] B Simma, 'The Antarctic Treaty as a Treaty Creating an "Objective Regime"' (1985–86) 19 Corn ILJ 189.

[118] See Conforti and Focarelli (n 32 above) 148–55.

[119] For the traditional, cautious approach, see P Weil, 'Towards Relative Normativity in International Law' (1983) 77 AJIL 413, 433–40.

peoples as a whole generally do not accept that they should be the addressees of bilateral or multilateral treaty obligations entered into by others who are perhaps on the other side of the world.

Treaties, even bilateral treaties, are not ultimately a 'private affair' of the parties and depend on the international community as a whole. The rule whereby 'treaties must be kept' by the parties (*pacta sunt servanda*)[120] may lead to the assumption that treaties, unlike custom, are left to the autonomy of the parties, unless perhaps they conflict with some 'core' general rule belonging to *jus cogens*.[121] This approach invites scholars such as Patrick Kelly to prefer treaties to custom and possibly to any other kind of international legal source. However, the rule *pacta sunt servanda* is a rule of customary international law that holds together all treaties made by all states, although each treaty binds only the parties and is in a sense a world unto itself. Treaty obligations must be met because all states within the system have an interest in each state abiding by the treaties entered into with one or more other states. The *generality* of states, whether parties or third parties, demands that *any* state respects its treaties towards the other parties. It is not just the parties that 'create' their treaty-making power, although it is only the parties that formally enter into the treaty and are thereafter the only entities which are bound thereby. If states are 'autonomous', ie free to make the treaties they like when they like, it is also true that this autonomy is accorded to them by the international community as a whole and is crystallized in CIL.

By way of illustration, the 'contract' made by two shipwrecked persons on a desert island is an arrangement that is left entirely to the relative force of the parties from day to day. There is nothing that induces the parties to compliance other than their individual force and, perhaps, prudential calculation. A contract made within a state, say the United States, is something rather different. It is still a private affair of the two parties, but now there is a surrounding social and legal framework. This framework is decisive in characterizing the contract as 'legal' in this kind of society and many people will agree that the two situations are completely different, although the imagined terms of the contract may be just the same. In the US scenario, all the people around the two parties have an interest in finding that most contracts made by others (regardless of this or that particular contract) are complied with. This interest produces an informal, albeit strong and constant pressure to compliance. Moreover, this society will support (inter alia, by providing financial resources) the work of judges and state officials entrusted to enforce the law and will give each of the parties the opportunity to address all their disputes to judges rather than having to count only on their individual force and prudence. Judges will presumably decide a given case on the basis of a bulk of precedents and other material obtained from previous similar cases between other people of the same community. The collectivity will assist the parties in ascertaining who is right and who is wrong and use its overwhelming force to have justice delivered to the parties. On the desert island there are of course no courts, no precedents, and no support for arriving at the truth if a dispute arises between the two contractors in respect of the performance of the contract. States are said to be part of a 'system' precisely because, inter alia, they do not make treaties as two shipwrecked persons on a desert island. Put differently, the world is very far from being a myriad separated desert islands (ie as many as the treaties made by any state with any other state), although it is equally far from being a unitary, harmonic heaven. A world of desert islands was presumably possible (or only more likely) in the past, when the world population

[120] Art 26 VCLT. [121] See section B (4)(f) below.

was not as dense as it is today and polities could live without entertaining relations with many others, perhaps far away or even completely unknown. This is no longer possible in today's planet. In this sense, even to make a bilateral treaty is a 'public' affair, authorized and *informally* monitored by the international community.

However, if it is true that treaties bind the parties as a matter of common interest within the global states system, it does not follow that treaties may also bind third parties, or states parties beyond what they have actually accepted, on the sole basis of the importance of the common value they protect. States as a whole want the treaties made by any of them to be respected by their parties, but they also want treaties to remain *res inter alios acta* as regards third parties or the parties themselves beyond their consent. The non-effect of treaties on third parties as well is a rule of CIL which reflects the position of the entire international community. The fact that the accession to a treaty, as well as the respect and enforcement thereof, is the expression of the interest of the global community does not necessarily imply that treaties should also bind third parties, nor that certain 'special' treaties are higher in rank than 'standard' treaties, nor that their violation can be invoked by all states on grounds of the 'common' values protected. These aspects are distinct from one another and evidence supporting one does not in itself also prove the other.

A recurrent question—traceable to the 'objective' law-making treaties (as opposed to contract treaties) developed by nineteenth-century German public law scholarship[122]—is whether human rights treaties have a 'special character' which permits them to derogate from the rules of international law applicable to any other treaty, notably from the rules strictly requiring state consent for a treaty provision to be binding. In the 1995 *Loizidou* Judgment the ECtHR referred to the 'special character of the Convention as a treaty for the collective enforcement of human rights', indeed 'a constitutional instrument of European public order'.[123] Previously, in the 1978 *Ireland v United Kingdom* Judgment, the Court had held that the Convention 'comprises more than mere reciprocal engagements between Contracting States' in that it 'creates, over and above a network of mutual, bilateral undertakings, and of objective obligations which . . . benefit from a "collective enforcement"'.[124] The IACtHR applied this line of reasoning—going as far as noting that in human rights treaties the states 'assume . . . obligations, not in relation to other States, but towards all individuals within their jurisdiction'—to 'modern human rights treaties in general' in the 1982 *Effect of Reservations* Advisory Opinion.[125] The notion that human rights obligations are not merely reciprocal, although without referring to any collective enforcement mechanism, was first introduced by the ICJ in the 1951 *Reservations* Advisory Opinion.[126]

122 CM Brölmann, 'Law-Making Treaties: Form and Function in International Law' (2005) 74 Nord JIL 383.

123 ECtHR, *Loizidou v Turkey (Preliminary Objections)* Judgment of 23 February 1995, App 15,318/89, Series A No 310, (1995) 20 EHRR 99, paras 70–72, 75; taken up, eg in *Al-Adsani v United Kingdom* Judgment of 21 November 2001 [GC], App 35763/97, ECtHR Rep 2001-XI 79, (2002) 34 EHRR 273, para 55; and *Bankovic et al v Belgium et al* Decision of 12 December 2001 [GC], App 52207/99, ECtHR Rep 2001-XII 333, para 57.

124 ECtHR, *Ireland v United Kingdom* Judgment of 18 January 1978, App 5310/71, Series A No 25, (1979–80) 2 EHRR 25, para 239. See, previously, ECommHR, *Austria v Italy* (*Pfunders Case*), Decision of 11 January 1961, App 788/60, (1962) 7 RD 23, 41–3.

125 IACtHR, *The Effect of Reservations on the Entry into Force of the American Convention on Human Rights (Articles 74 and 75)* Advisory Opinion of 24 September 1982 No OC-2/82, IACHR Series A No 2, paras 29–33.

126 *Reservations to the Convention on the Prevention and Punishment of the Crime of Genocide* Advisory Opinion of 28 May 1951, [1951] ICJ Rep 15, 23.

There is no doubt that a few human rights treaties, such as the European Convention for the Protection of Human Rights and Fundamental Freedoms (ECHR) and the American Convention on Human Rights (ACHR), provide for collective mechanisms of supervision over compliance, but this is expressly stipulated in the treaties and there is little evidence that their special character entails conspicuous derogations from general international law going beyond what the treaty itself (expressly or impliedly) provides.[127]

One field in which the special character of the ECHR has allegedly produced special effects by widening the scope of obligations of the states parties without their consent is that of reservations. In the 1988 *Belilos* Judgment the ECtHR held that inadmissible reservations are to be taken, for the purposes of the legal consequences of their inadmissibility, as not having been made rather than as invalidating the accession of the reserving state to the treaty, regardless of the fact that the reserving state (Switzerland) considered the disputed reservation to be 'essential' to its accession to the ECHR.[128] The Court assumed that Switzerland was bound by a certain interpretation of Article 6 ECHR to which Switzerland had never consented, and was free not to accept, although Switzerland had indeed accepted the then Article 64 ECHR that regulated the admissibility of reservations to the ECHR and the ECHR rules concerning the adjudicative function of the Court. This jurisprudence was upheld by the UN Human Rights Committee in its 1994 General Comment No 24[129] and in the 1999 *Kennedy* Views,[130] raising protests from a few states (France, the United Kingdom, and the United States) and the denunciation of the ICCPR in 2000 by the defendant state (Trinidad and Tobago).[131] However, the ICJ failed to endorse it in the 1998 *Fisheries* Judgment in relation to reservations made to a declaration of acceptance of its jurisdiction,[132] and the attitude of UN human rights committees seems recently to have moved towards greater cooperation with the reserving states. It is thus difficult to see the *Belilos* jurisprudence as a reflection of CIL (not even within the limited field of human rights) and as evidence of the 'special character' of human rights treaties.

Another critical field is treaty interpretation, in particular the 'evolutionary' approach taken in recent decades by human rights monitoring bodies. According to this approach—apparently at odds with intertemporal law[133]—between equally plausible meanings that can be given to a treaty rule, the one which is current at the moment of interpretation is to be preferred to that prevailing at the time when the treaty was made. This approach leads, once again, to the imposition on the parties of obligations that

[127] See MT Kamminga and M Scheinin (eds), *The Impact of Human Rights Law on General International Law* (Oxford: OUP, 2009).

[128] ECtHR, *Belilos v Switzerland* Judgment of 29 April 1988, App 10,328/83, Series A No 132, (1988) 10 EHRR 466, paras 60 and 73.

[129] UNHRC, 'General Comment No 24: Issues relating to reservations made upon ratification or accession to the International Covenant on Civil and Political Rights or the Optional Protocols thereto, or in relation to declarations under article 41 of the Covenant' of 2 November 1994, UN Doc CCPR/C/21/Rev.1/Add.6, GAOR 50th Session, Supp 4, vol 1, 119, para 18.

[130] UNHRC, *Kennedy v Trinidad and Tobago (Admissibility)* Views of 2 November 1999, Comm No 845/1999, UN Doc CCPR/C/67/D/845/1999, para 7.

[131] cf GAOR 50th Session, Supp 40, vol I, 104, 130, 126; see in addition <http://www.unhchr.ch/html/menu3/b/treaty6_asp.htm>.

[132] ICJ, *Fisheries Jurisdiction (Spain v Canada) (Jurisdiction of the Court)* Judgment of 4 December 1998, [1998] ICJ Rep 432, paras 40–1, 44.

[133] Arbitral Tribunal, *Determination of the Maritime Boundary (Guinea-Bissau v Senegal)* Award of 31 July 1989, 20 RIAA 119, para 54, referring to PCA Arbitral Tribunal, *Island of Palmas Case (Netherlands v United States)* Award of 4 April 1928, 2 RIAA 829, 845. With regard to state responsibility, see ICJ *Jurisdictional Immunities of the State* Judgement (n 85 above) para 58.

they had apparently not accepted, and were free not to accept, at the moment of ratifying or acceding to the treaty. The ECtHR has often construed the ECHR in evolutionary terms, assuming that the Convention is a 'living instrument' to be interpreted 'in the light of present-day conditions',[134] just like the IACtHR.[135] Indeed, it is impossible to accept the notion that human rights treaties should remain anchored in the meanings prevailing at the time of their conclusion. One of the leading decisions of the ECtHR, the 1979 *Marcks* Judgment,[136] is illuminating: according to the Court the term 'family' in Article 8 ECHR could not be understood as including only 'legitimate' children, as was typical of the 1950s when the Convention was concluded, but had to be intended to include also 'illegitimate' children in line with most European legislation in the 1970s when the case was to be decided. In several cases the Dispute Settlement Body (DSB) of the World Trade Organization (WTO) has also endorsed this approach in the economic field,[137] as well as the ECJ.[138] The ICJ had cautiously acknowledged an evolutionary approach in the 1971 *Namibia* Advisory Opinion in relation to self-determination of peoples.[139] In the 1997 *Gabčíkovo-Nagymaros* Judgment the Court noted that 'by inserting certain evolving provisions' in a treaty 'the parties recognized the potential necessity to adapt the Project' provided therein: 'Consequently, the Treaty is not static, and is open to adapt to emerging norms of international law'.[140] In the 2009 *Navigational and Related Rights* Judgment the Court, called upon to interpret a bilateral treaty on free navigation, stated that an evolutionary interpretation of a treaty is permissible either when the parties' original intent was, or may be presumed to have been, to give the terms used a meaning or content capable of evolving in time, or in accordance with their subsequent practice resulting in a tacit agreement to depart from the original intended meaning.[141] The Court, thus, grounded the evolutionary interpretation in the consent of the parties as substantiated either in their original intent or in their subsequent practice. The ICJ approach seems quite reasonable in general terms and is capable of both explaining and limiting the more extensive attitude of other international bodies, although different standards might be justified in different contexts. In any event, the evolutionary approach cannot be held as evidence of any major derogation from the consent requirement as an alleged result of the special character of human rights treaties, since it has also been adopted in other fields of international law, and in so far as it is confined within the 'ordinary' limits established by the ICJ.

Finally, suggestions of the 'speciality' of human rights treaties have also been made in relation to the succession of states in respect of treaties. It has been claimed that, in

[134] See eg, recently, ECtHR, *Serkov v Ukraine* Judgment of 7 July 2011, App 39766/05, para 39; *RR v Poland* Judgment of 26 May 2011, App 27617/04, para 186.

[135] IACtHR, *Mayagna (Sumo) Awas Tingni Community v Nicaragua* Judgment of 31 August 2001, IACtHR Series C No 79, paras 146, 148.

[136] ECTHR, *Marckx v Belgium* Judgment of 13 June 1979, App 6833/74, (1979–80) 2 EHRR 330, para 41.

[137] WTO, *United States—Import Prohibition of Certain Shrimp and Shrimp Products*, AB Report of 12 October 1998, WT/DS58/AB/R, para 130.

[138] ECJ, *Srl CILFIT and Lanificio di Gavardo SPA v Ministry of Health* Judgment of 6 October 1982, Case 283/81, [1982] ECR 3415, para 30.

[139] ICJ, *Legal Consequences for States of the Continued Presence of South Africa in Namibia (South West Africa) notwithstanding Security Council Resolution 276 (1970)* Advisory Opinion of 21 June 1971, [1971] ICJ Rep 16, para 53.

[140] ICJ, *Gabčíkovo-Nagymaros Project (Hungary/Slovakia)* Judgment of 25 September 1997, [1997] ICJ Rep 7, para 112.

[141] ICJ, *Dispute regarding Navigational and Related Rights (Costa Rica v Nicaragua)* Judgment of 13 July 2009, [2009] ICJ Rep 213, paras 63–64.

derogation from the *tabula rasa* principle, for human rights treaties the continuity rule applies. This implies that such treaties are immediately and automatically binding on new states without any need for the new state to accede to them or notify their succession. In its General Comment No 26 the UN Human Rights Committee affirmed that the 'rights enshrined in the Covenant belong to the people' and that:

> . . . once the people are accorded the protection of the rights under the Covenant, such protection devolves with territory and continues to belong to them, notwithstanding change in government of the State party, including dismemberment in more than one State or State succession or any subsequent action of the State party designed to divest them of the rights guaranteed by the Covenant.[142]

It is a fact, however, that except for the states seceding from the former Yugoslavia as well as the Czech and Slovak Republics, all the states of the Commonwealth of Independent States (CIS) and the three Baltic States have acceded to the International Covenant on Civil and Political Rights (ICCPR). The practice is, therefore, uncertain and insufficient to lead to the conclusion that this trend proves the special character of human rights treaties in CIL.[143]

The above discussion shows that despite several efforts to overcome state consent, international practice is in fact far from endorsing them, even where human rights treaties (no doubt the stronger candidates today) are considered.

(c) Decisions of IOs

Treaties establishing IOs occasionally provide for their organs to adopt, by majority, decisions which are binding on all the member states.[144] These decisions produce international obligations on the basis of the power conferred on the enacting bodies by the constituent instrument (typically a treaty) and are thus ultimately grounded in the CIL rule *pacta sunt servanda*.[145] Whether they are a mere reflection of the treaty or an autonomous source of international law rules is open to question.[146] The first reading would suggest that such decisions are included in the Article 38 ICJ Statute list under the treaties heading, while the latter would confirm that Article 38 is open-ended. The ICJ has recognized UN Security Council binding decisions adopted under Article 25 and Chapter VII UN Charter as a source of legal obligations, for example in the 1971

[142] UNHRC, 'General Comment No 26: Continuity of obligations' of 8 December 1997, UN Doc CCPR/C/21/Rev.1/Add.8/Rev.1, para 4.

[143] A Rasulov, 'Revisiting State Succession to Humanitarian Treaties: Is There a Case for Automaticity?' (2003) 14 EJIL 141.

[144] For a thorough analysis, see JE Alvarez, *International Organizations as Law-Makers* (Oxford: OUP, 2005). See further AJP Tammes, 'Decisions of International Organs as a Source of International Law' (1958) 94 RdC 265; R Sonnenfeld, *Resolutions of the United Nations Security Council* (Dordrecht: Nijhoff, 1987).

[145] Besides the binding resolutions of the UN Security Council, discussed at greater length in this section, also worth mentioning are WHA Res 58.3, 'Revision of the International Health Regulations' (adopted 23 May 2005, entered into force 15 June 2005); and the 18 ICAO Annexes, at <http://www.icao.int/icaonet/anx/info/annexes_booklet_en.pdf>.

[146] If nominally 'binding decisions' of international organs are regarded—at least in certain circumstances—as in fact executive agreements (or agreements concluded 'in simplified form') binding on all states which have cast their positive vote regardless of their legal value as institutional acts, critical problems arise at the *domestic* level since, given their equal rank at the international level to that of the constituent instrument, they would presumably require further, ad hoc implementing legislation and would prevail as *lex posterior* over the constituent instrument rather than being subjected to it (see n 605 below and accompanying text).

Namibia Advisory Opinion,[147] in the 1992 *Lockerbie* Orders,[148] and in the 2010 *Kosovo* Advisory Opinion.[149] It seems that when an IO's decision is adopted unanimously—or in any case with the concurrence of the parties to a later dispute—its difference from a treaty (in particular, from an executive agreement concluded by voting) is difficult to grasp.[150] Under certain conditions, even decisions and non-binding resolutions adopted by majority can be viewed as agreements between the members which have voted in their favour.[151] Like the distinction between general and treaty international law, the distinction between constituent treaties and binding decisions is critical to the 'hierarchy' of legal sources, both internationally and domestically.[152] In the 2010 *Kosovo* Advisory Opinion, the ICJ held that for the purposes of interpretation of UN Security Council resolutions, while Articles 31 and 32 VCLT may 'provide guidance', 'other factors' are to be taken into account—such as the statements by representatives of members of the Security Council made at the time of adoption, and other Security Council resolutions on the same issue, as well as the subsequent practice of relevant UN organs and of states affected by such resolutions—so as to give due weight to the fact that 'Security Council resolutions are issued by a single, collective body and are drafted through a very different process than that used for the conclusion of a treaty' and are binding on all member states.[153]

The social, systemic import of IOs' decisions is similar to that of the constituent instrument, with a further stress on community interests when the IO is a universal organization such as the United Nations. Here again, however, this does not justify extrapolations of obligations, and notably what has gone by the name of 'legislative' or 'adjudicatory' powers of the Security Council. In particular, after the adoption by the Council of Resolution 1373 (2001) against international terrorism and Resolution 1540 (2004) against proliferation of weapons of mass destruction among terrorists,[154] it has been argued that a decision made by majority by an international body which also binds the minority amounts to an act of international 'legislation'. The term 'legislation' is taken to mean the adoption of rules binding on entities which have not consented to be bound by them, thereby departing from traditional international consent-based law-making. As a result, not only treaties, as already seen, but also IO decisions tend to be used instrumentally to place obligations on third parties in an effort

147 ICJ, *Legal Consequences for States of the Continued Presence of South Africa in Namibia* (n 139 above) paras 113–114, 116.

148 ICJ, *Questions of Interpretation and Application of the 1971 Montreal Convention arising from the Aerial Incident at Lockerbie (Libyan Arab Jamahiriya v United Kingdom) (Provisional Measures)*, Order of 14 April 1992, [1992] ICJ Rep 3, para 39; *Questions of Interpretation and Application of the 1971 Montreal Convention arising from the Aerial Incident at Lockerbie (Libyan Arab Jamahiriya v United States)*, Order of 14 April 1992, [1992] ICJ Rep 114, para 42.

149 ICJ, *Accordance with International Law of the Unilateral Declaration of Independence in Respect of Kosovo* Advisory Opinion of 22 July 2010, para 85, at <http://www.icj-cij.org/docket/files/141/15987.pdf>.

150 cf PCIJ, *Railway Traffic between Lithuania and Poland (Railway Sector Landwarów-Kaisiadorys* Advisory Opinion of 15 October 1931, PCIJ Series A/B No 42, at 116, noting that 'Lithuania and... Poland participated in the adoption of th[e] Resolution of the [League of Nations] Council' and they were thus 'bound by their acceptance of the Council's Resolution'.

151 Conforti and Focarelli (n 32 above) 414–18.

152 See section B (3) below.

153 ICJ, *Accordance with International Law of the Unilateral Declaration of Independence in Respect of Kosovo* (n 149 above) paras 94, 117, quoting the *Namibia* Advisory Opinion ((n 139 above) para 114). Similarly, cf STL, 'Interlocutory Decision on the Applicable Law: Terrorism, Conspiracy, Homicide, Perpetration, Cumulative Charging' of 16 February 2011, Case No STL-11-01/I, paras 26–27, at <http://www.stl-tsl.org/index.php?option=com_k2&view=item&task=download&id=447>.

154 UNSC Res 1373 (2001) of 28 September 2001 and Res 1540 (2004) of 28 April 2004.

to find 'global solutions to global problems'. These 'legislative' decisions are increasingly directed to target individuals mentioned by name.[155] They are general and abstract, ie they apply to an undefined class of addressees and/or cases. By contrast, judicial or arbitral decisions are deemed to be concerned with specific disputes. They also contemplate an open-ended range of addressees over time, ie a binding effect for the future rather than on an ad hoc basis.[156]

This construction captures some elements of reality but is exaggerated and misleading.[157] The model for 'legislation' is invariably the legislative power of a state, and the state thought of is clearly a Western state. But legislation within a state makes sense within a broader political context that is totally absent in IOs. In the 1995 *Tadić* Decision the ICTY observed that: 'There is . . . no legislature, in the technical sense of the term, in the United Nations system . . . That is to say, there exists no corporate organ formally empowered to enact laws directly binding on international legal subjects'.[158] It is true that the expression 'legislative powers' has been used in relation to decisions which actually provide for 'new' powers compared to the past, for example when imposing on all UN member states obligations corresponding to those found in treaties that the addressees of the decision had not ratified and were free not to ratify, such as the 1999 Convention for the Suppression of the Financing of Terrorism (not yet in force at the time) as regards Resolution 1373 (2001).[159] In any event, Resolution 1540 (2004) in particular has been criticized by several UN member states, precisely for its 'legislative' features, for 'destabilizing' international relations. States have observed that a *specific* consent is necessary for new general and abstract obligations to arise through binding decisions, the one given 'originally' to Article 41 UN Charter being insufficient to this effect. They have also noted that the Charter does not give the Security Council a power to 'legislate' (in particular by 'creating treaties' of universal application) on behalf of the international community. The measures envisaged by Article 41 have been described as being temporary and of exceptional character, aimed at supplementing (rather than replacing) existing treaties.[160] Equally misleading, for the same reasons, is the view that the committees set up by the Security Council when adopting sanctions have 'judicial' or 'quasi-judicial' powers in so far as they deal with specific cases rather than with general and abstract rules.[161]

(d) Principles

Article 38(1)(c) ICJ Statute stipulates that the Court 'shall apply', in deciding the disputes submitted to it, 'the general principles of law recognized by civilized nations'. In the 1984 *Gulf of Maine* Judgment an ICJ Chamber stated that:

[155] See Ch 8 below, section B (3).

[156] See eg S Talmon, 'The Security Council as World Legislature' (2005) 99 AJIL 175.

[157] For a critical view of the 'domestic analogies' often surrounding the 'constitutional interpretation' of the UN Charter and the Security Council's alleged legislative powers, see Alvarez (n 144 above) 66–108, especially 68–9.

[158] ICTY, *Prosecutor v Tadić, Decision on the Defence Motion for Interlocutory Appeal on Jurisdiction*, Decision of 2 October 1995, Case No ICTY-94-1, para 43.

[159] International Convention for the Suppression of the Financing of Terrorism (signed 9 December 1999, entered into force 10 April 2002) 2178 UNTS 197.

[160] For a detailed discussion, see Conforti and Focarelli (n 32 above) 240–2.

[161] I Johnstone, 'Legislation and Adjudication in the UN Security Council: Bringing down the Deliberative Deficit' (2008) 102 AJIL 275.

... the association of the terms 'rules' and 'principles' [found in the Special Agreement grounding the jurisdiction of the Court] is no more than the use of a dual expression to convey one and the same idea ... the use of the term 'principles' may be justified because of their more general and more fundamental character.[162]

There is much uncertainty about general principles of law recognized by civilized nations. Little is known about their nature and effects, although they were in the past, and continue to be today, frequently applied by arbitral tribunals. For example, in the 1905 *Antoine Fabiani* Award, the arbitrator applied 'the general principles of the law of nations on the denial of justice', defining them as 'the rules common to most legislations or taught by doctrines'.[163] The ICJ, just like the PCIJ earlier, has been very reluctant to apply 'principles' of international law—unlike individual ICJ judges in their separate opinions—and, when referring to principles, it has generally taken them into account *ad abundantiam*. Only in the 1951 *Reservations* Advisory Opinion did the ICJ use a similar expression ('principles which are recognized by civilized nations') to indicate the principles which underlie the 1948 Genocide Convention and are binding on states 'even without any conventional obligation'.[164] If the ICJ tends to avoid applying these principles, the question arises of whether they are part of international law at all. Article 38(1)(c) simply assumes that such principles are part of the 'international law' that the Court 'shall apply'.

As is well known, the category was first introduced in Article 38(3) PCIJ Statute, later to be reproduced with slight variations in Article 38 ICJ Statute. The basic reason for this insertion by the Committee of Jurists entrusted to draft the PCIJ Statute was the observation that the PCIJ should have applied extra-state rules reflecting 'the law of objective justice, at any rate in so far as it has twofold confirmation of the concurrent teachings of jurisconsults of authority and of the public conscience of civilised nations', and avoided a *non liquet* when applicable custom and treaty rules were not found.[165] It was apparently agreed that these principles were 'those which were accepted by all nations *in foro domestico*, such as certain principles of procedure, the principle of good faith, the principle of *res judicata*, etc'.[166] The ambivalence of international law as *jus inter gentes* and *jus intra gentes* is inherent in *jus gentium* and was theorized in a masterly manner by Francisco Suárez.[167] Ironically enough, the best description of such principles was perhaps that of one of their stronger critics, Judge Anzilotti, in his individual opinion appended to the PCIJ 1937 *Diversion of Water from the Meuse* Judgment, observing that the principle *inadimplenti non est adimplendum* 'is so just, so equitable, so universally recognized, that it must apply to international relations also' and 'In any case, it is one of these "general principles of law recognized by civilized nations" which the Court applies in virtue of Article 38 of its Statute'.[168] The term 'civilized', historically traceable to the 'standard of civilization' of the European powers,[169] has

162 ICJ Chamber, *Case concerning Delimitation of the Maritime Boundary in the Gulf of Maine Area* (n 113 above) para 79.

163 Arbitral Tribunal, *Antoine Fabiani* Award of 31 July 1905, 10 RIAA 83, 117.

164 ICJ, *Reservations to the Convention on the Prevention and Punishment of the Crime of Genocide* (n 126 above) 23.

165 Advisory Committee of Jurists, *Procès-verbaux* (n 75 above) 324.

166 ibid 335.

167 See Ch 4 above, section B (1).

168 PCIJ, *The Diversion of Water from the Meuse (Netherlands v Belgium)* Judgment of 28 June 1937, PCIJ Series A/B No 70, dissenting opinion of Judge Anzilotti, at 50.

169 See GW Gong, *The Standard of 'Civilization' in International Society* (Oxford: Clarendon Press, 1984; B Bowden, 'The Colonial Origins of International Law: European Expansion and the Classical Standard of Civilization' (2005) 7 JHIL 1. For the view that general principles of law recognized by civilized nations typically leads to the application of Western law, see A Anghie, *Imperialism,*

been strongly criticized in the past few decades[170] and states have avoided using it in recent treaties.[171]

The doctrinal debate surrounding the nature of the principles referred to by Article 38(1)(c) involves the fundamental questions of international law and ranges from legal irrelevance to top ranking in the hierarchy of the international law sources. As hinted earlier, the key points are the avoidance of *non liquet* and the admissibility of rules that are not posited by states or, at least, do not stem from state practice (such as treaties and CIL). Of the two points, the second is the crucial one. Once natural law is excluded from the sources, and Article 38(1)(c) meaningfully avoids it, the issue is how to justify the consideration for international law purposes of the most elementary and universal demands of justice and humanity. These demands are, within a state, presumably dictated or at least inspired by the sovereign, but international law has to do with all humanity.

It seems that, in the light of the above, the principles referred to by Article 38(1)(c) should meet the following four requirements: (a) they are to be found in most domestic legal systems, regardless of their cultural and legal tradition; (b) with the exclusion of those states that the international community as a whole (for example, through resolutions of the UN General Assembly) does not regard as 'civilized' in the specific sense that they do not pursue values that are generally perceived as common to humanity, as was the case with South Africa at the time of apartheid;[172] (c) to the extent that they can actually be transposed to the international realm and applied as international law despite their domestic origin; and (d) provided that they do not conflict with applicable CIL and treaty rules. Requirement (a) distinguishes general principles under Article 38(c) ICJ Statute from the 'sense of universal justice', a generic notion that—in line with the objections made within the Committee of Jurists entrusted to draft the PCIJ Statute to the proposed reference to the 'legal conscience of civilized nations'—is open to the subjectivism of the interpreter and, in the end, to the arbitrariness of the stronger. Requirement (b), while today it sounds anachronistic, can be meant to refer to 'human civilization' rather than to certain self-professed 'superior' civilizations or cultures against others, to the extent that they can objectively be detected in the international community as a whole. Requirement (c) distinguishes any unqualified uniformity in domestic legal systems from the principles of domestic law which can actually work at the international level in terms of their contents and support from the international community as a whole. Finally, requirement (d) avoids the prevalence of general principles under Article 38(c) ICJ Statute, which by definition are applied by each state for domestic legal purposes, over the norms that the states directly establish as the norms governing their relations. International practice, especially arbitral practice, supporting the application of such principles suggests that, when fulfilling these four requirements, they are part of international law and should be applied by both international and domestic courts. It is within *this* category, in particular, that the 'elementary considerations of humanity' appealed to on various occasions by the

Sovereignty and the Making of International Law (Cambridge: CUP, 2005) 229. For a recent, insightful inquiry into the idea and ideal of civilization, see B Bowden, *The Empire of Civilization: The Evolution of an Imperial Idea* (Chicago: University of Chicago Press, 2009).

170 ICJ, *North Sea Continental Shelf Cases* (n 80 above) 132–3, separate opinion of Judge Ammoun.

171 While it is still found in Art 7(2) ECHR, it is absent in Art 15(2) ICCPR, and in Art 21(1)(c) ICC Statute.

172 In accordance with the ICJ's Opinion on the *Reservations to the Convention* (n 126 above) 23, referring to the 'purely humanitarian and civilizing purpose' for which the Genocide Convention in particular has been adopted.

ICJ are to be situated in cases where no practice is available and no rule of CIL is demonstrable.[173] Similar considerations apply *mutatis mutandis* to the Martens Clause when referring 'in cases not included' in the treaty containing it to 'the laws of humanity and the requirements of the public conscience'.[174]

No other 'principles', other than rules in the ICJ's 'more general' sense, as construed according to the interpretative criteria generally accepted, are part of international law, nor is any 'balancing' of principles or values recognized in international law going beyond the interpretation of existing rules.[175] There is no legal basis for any other construction of 'principles' as clearly distinct from rules, let alone for any balancing of values, although courts do have some useful margin of discretion, as will be shown below.[176] Principles cannot be inferred 'from the system' for the sole reason that international law is a 'legal system', since the fact that international law is (to some extent) a system does not in itself authorize the assumption that it must generate principles as distinct from rules or certain principles rather than others. The stark opposition between the 'just-rules' and the 'entire decision-making process' approaches is overstated.[177] Briefly, detached from rules—in a system devoid of a sovereign which establishes and enforce the values to be pursued—principles are to be excluded as destabilizing factors, except when (a) used promotionally for a change in international law; or (b) falling within the margin of the discretion of courts and arbitral tribunals.[178]

(2) Lacunae

Lacunae, or 'gaps' in the law, are 'missing rules', ie rules which are *expected* but not found in the law.[179] Their occurrence depends on whether it is felt that an absent rule is needed and on how existing rules are construed or integrated by general principles. To state that international law is just 'rules', flowing from the recognized sources and expressly created by states, means that new cases will constantly fall outside the law. Given that the cases occurring in real life are overwhelmingly more numerous than those covered by existing rules, however many of these there may be, such a rigid attitude is untenable. In international law the 'gaps' in the law may be filled, in addition to a standard interpretation of existing rules,[180] by applying the so-called 'Lotus

[173] See n 109 above, and Ch 7 below, n 186. In the 2012 *Jurisdictional Immunities of the State* Judgement (n 85 above) paras 52 and 81, the ICJ noted that certain 'acts perpetrated by German armed forces and other organs of the German Reich' during their military occupation of Italy during World War II 'can only be described as displaying a complete disregard for the "elementary considerations of humanity"' and 'no doubt... [constituted] a serious violation of the international law of armed conflict applicable in 1943–1945' amounting to 'crimes under international law'. The Court assumed, for the purpose of the instant case, that such violations were also breaches of *jus cogens*, there being no need to ascertain whether the assumption made was sound since it found no conflict between the rule assumed to be peremptory and the state immunity rule involved in the case (ibid paras 93 and 94). See P-M Dupuy, 'Les "considérations élémentaires d'humanité" dans la jurisprudence de la Cour internationale de justice' in R-J Dupuy (ed), *Mélanges en l'honneur de Nicolas Valticos. Droit et justice* (Paris: Pédone, 1999) 117; NHB Jørgensen, *The Responsibility of States for International Crimes* (Oxford: OUP, 2000) 123–30.

[174] See n 110 above.

[175] See, in particular, Ch 7 below, section B (4).

[176] For the opposite view, taking up Dworkin's principles (n 20 above), see V Lowe, *International Law* (Oxford: Clarendon Press, 2007) 101.

[177] R Higgins, *Problems and Process: International Law and How we Use it* (Oxford: Clarendon Press, 1994) 1–12.

[178] See sections B (4) and C (2) and (3) below.

[179] See section A (3)(a) above.

[180] cf Japanese District Court of Tokyo, *Ryuichi Shimoda et al v The State* Judgment of 7 December 1963, English trans (1964) 8 Jap AIL 212. The Court, after acknowledging that there was a gap in the law in 1945 with regard to nuclear weapons, applied the then-existing law on the aerial bombing of

principle', or by resorting to analogy, or by extracting the 'implied powers' of an international organization vis-à-vis its member states. This section assumes that while international courts and tribunals may fill lacunae to some extent as a matter of judicial discretion, as explained in greater detail below, most international disputes are not decided judicially, and lacunae can hardly be bridged at the level of inter-state relations without the risk of destabilization and/or manipulation. The better view is that international law, whatever may be said of domestic law, is very far from regulating all possible cases.

(a) The Lotus principle

The 'Lotus principle' says that 'what is not prohibited is allowed'. It seems to provide a legal qualification of all possible cases of life by framing as permitted all cases which are not prohibited by existing rules, thus filling all lacunae of the legal system and avoiding a *non liquet* when the case is to be decided by a court.[181] The principle is rooted in the 1927 *Lotus* Judgment in which the PCIJ held that 'Restrictions upon the independence of States cannot . . . be presumed', and perceived 'the prohibition of exercising State power in the territory of another State as "the first and foremost restriction imposed by international law upon a State"'. In addition the Court held that:

> Far from laying down a general prohibition to the effect that States may not extend the application of their laws and the jurisdiction of their courts to persons, property and acts outside their territory, it leaves them in this respect a wide measure of discretion which is only limited in certain cases by prohibitive rules; as regards other cases, every State remains free to adopt the principles which it regards as best and most suitable.[182]

The Court concluded that there was no rule of international law which restricted the discretion or freedom of Turkey to exercise criminal jurisdiction over the French official who was allegedly responsible for a collision which occurred on the high seas.[183]

The principle has been understood as reducing the sphere of international law only to the rules to which states have strictly consented,[184] and in particular as prescribing a restrictive interpretation of treaties.[185] It is thus deemed to favour absolute sovereignty and less international law, briefly a move 'to take the law backward in time' to the nineteenth century.[186] Assuming that any presumption of freedom is no longer tenable in contemporary international law and an interconnected world, the opposite presumption in favour of law has been proposed whereby 'normative utterances should be presumed to give rise to law, unless and until the opposite can somehow be proven', a

defenceless cities. It then found a rule applicable to the case by stretching the meaning of an existing rule and without resorting to general principles.

[181] On *non liquet*, meaning 'it is not clear' and leading courts to dismiss the case, see section C (2) (d) below.

[182] PCIJ, *The Case of the SS Lotus (France v Turkey)* Judgment of 7 September 1927, PCIJ Series A No 10, at 18–19.

[183] ibid 29.

[184] See, more recently, ICJ, *Case concerning Military and Paramilitary Activities* (n 87 above) para 269, stating that 'in international law there are no rules, other than such rules as may be accepted by the State concerned, by treaty or otherwise'.

[185] The ICJ rightly rejected the correlation in the *Dispute regarding Navigational and Related Rights* (n 141 above) para 48, observing that 'While it is certainly true that limitations of the sovereignty of a State over its territory are not to be presumed, this does not mean that treaty provisions establishing such limitations . . . should for this reason be interpreted a priori in a restrictive way'.

[186] ICJ, *Fisheries (United Kingdom v Norway)* Judgment of 18 December 1951, [1951] ICJ Rep 116, separate opinion of Judge Alvarez, ibid 152, stating: 'This principle, formerly correct, in the days of absolute sovereignty, is no longer so at the present day'.

solution thought to 'revers[e] what seems to be the current [*Lotus*] presumption ... of non-law'.[187] The rationale of the principle is controversial. Many insist that the principle is positivist in that it is firmly based on states' sovereignty.[188] Others argue that it is naturalist since it refers to the state of nature.[189] Another frequent interpretation is that the principle is basically liberal.[190] It is a fact, though, that if it reflects a residual general principle aimed at regulating (as either prohibited or permitted) all possible cases of life, the opposite principle, 'what is not permitted is prohibited', is far less viable, regardless of any ideological underpinning. In any legal system it is a great deal easier to permit any act and prohibit only a few, than to prohibit any act and permit a few. In the second scenario, countless acts of everyday life ought to be specifically prohibited, an occurrence that has some plausibility, if any, only in very small societies. In courts the principle translates into a problem of burden of proof with regard to which party has to prove the absence of a prohibition.

In the 1996 *Nuclear Weapons* Advisory Opinion the ICJ seems to have rejected the conventional reading of the principle with a view to excluding the permissibility of the threat and use of nuclear weapons once it was realized that there was no prohibition thereon in international law,[191] as argued by Judge Bedjaoui, whereby the Court upheld the principle 'neither prohibited nor permitted'.[192] More inclined to the opposite principle 'if not permitted then prohibited', so as to conclude that the threat and use of nuclear weapons were prohibited, was Judge Shahabudden;[193] while Judge Higgins insisted that the decision was an unacceptable *non liquet*.[194] The principle was also invoked by Belgium in the 2002 *Arrest Warrant* Judgment as a basis for its claim to universal jurisdiction over war crimes and crimes against humanity, noting that in the absence of any prohibitive rule it was entitled to confer upon itself a universal jurisdiction *in absentia*,[195] but the Court did not address the question.[196]

Of great interest is the 2010 *Kosovo* Advisory Opinion on whether the unilateral declaration of independence (UDI) of Kosovo of 2008 was 'in accordance' with international law.[197] The ICJ argued that the UDI (a) was not prohibited; and hence (b) its making was not a violation of international law. One could impliedly infer, when considering the language of the question submitted by the General Assembly, that according to the Court (c) the making of the UDI was 'in accordance' with

[187] Klabbers, Peters, and Ulfstein (n 17 above) 115. For a critical comment, see Carlo Focarelli, book review (2010) 104 AJIL 559.

[188] H Handeyside, 'The Lotus Principle in ICJ Jurisprudence: Was the Ship ever Afloat?' (2007–08) 29 Mich JIL 71, 77–8.

[189] A Peters, 'Does Kosovo Lie in the Lotus-Land of Freedom?' (2011) 24 LJIL 95, 101.

[190] ICJ, *Arrest Warrant of 11 April 2000 (Democratic Republic of the Congo v Belgium)* Judgment of 14 February 2002, [2002] ICJ Rep 3, joint separate opinion of Judges Higgins, Kooijmans, and Buergenthal, ibid 78, para 51, stating that the principle 'represents the high water mark of laissez-faire in international relations, and an era that has been significantly overtaken by other tendencies'. See in addition M Koskenniemi, *From Apology to Utopia. The Structure of International Legal Argument* (Cambridge: CUP, reissue with new epilogue, 2005) 255–72, noting that the Lotus principle is 'nothing else than a restatement of the pure fact approach' leaving unanswered all cases in which a conflict of freedoms arises unless one assumes—but then going beyond the pure fact approach—the presence of a material (and hence a 'legal') criterion enabling the interpreter to prefer one freedom to another.

[191] ICJ, *Legality of the Threat or Use of Nuclear Weapons* (n 88 above) para 21.

[192] Declaration of Judge Bedjaoui, ibid paras 11–18.

[193] Dissenting opinion of Judge Shahabuddeen, ibid 394–7.

[194] Dissenting opinion of Judge Higgins, ibid paras 2, 29–30, 38.

[195] ICJ, *Arrest Warrant of 11 April 2000* (n 190 above) Counter Memorial of the Kingdom of Belgium of 28 September 2001, paras 3.3.29–3.3.31, at <http://www3.icj-cij.org/docket/files/121/8304.pdf>.

[196] ICJ, *Arrest Warrant of 11 April 2000* (n 190 above) para 43.

[197] See n 149 above.

international law, although nowhere in the Opinion did the Court state this. Passage from (a) to (b) is plain: for example, if smoking is not prohibited, one who smokes does not violate any rule. Passage from (b) to (c), carefully avoided by the Court, is ambiguous: for example, one who smokes may be believed to do so 'in accordance' with the law either (i) because the law authorizes smoking in certain circumstances while smoking is otherwise prohibited; or (ii) because the law regulates smoking as 'legally indifferent' (*de jure* freedom) and protects smokers from others' encroachment; or (iii) because the law simply does not regulate smoking in any way and smoking is 'legally irrelevant', ie 'neither prohibited nor allowed' (*de facto* freedom).[198] Meanings (i) and (ii) are *within* international law, while meaning (iii) is outside it. If the UDI is assumed to be 'allowed' under meaning (iii), then its making is *not* 'in accordance' with international law, although at the same time it does not violate it either. Even the fact that it is not 'in violation' of international law would not mean that it is 'lawful' since for a conduct to be lawful it must conform to the applicable law, but in this hypothesis there is no applicable law at all. This shows that a conduct may be 'not prohibited' (or 'allowed') in the sense of meaning (iii), but also 'not in accordance' with international law because it is simply not regulated by it.[199] These apparent sophisms show that the principle may be manipulated to reach one desired outcome rather than another: under meaning (iii) the Court had to conclude that there was no legal answer from international law, and hence that the UDI was an 'act of force' outside the law. This favoured Serbia by presenting the authors of the UDI as 'revolutionaries', against whom Serbia was presumably allowed to take some counter-insurrectional measures. However, as hinted, the Court avoided the passage from (b) to (c) and concluded that the UDI 'did not violate' international law, without going as far as to state that the UDI did not violate international law simply because international law did not regulate the matter at all,[200] as suggested by a number of states.[201]

Misunderstandings of the Lotus principle unfortunately abound and it is advisable to keep it at some distance when dealing with international law. First, as noted, in its original formulation the principle concerned the allocation of criminal jurisdiction between two states for an event that occurred on the high seas. It was not conceived of as a general principle applicable to any area of international law. It is true that it builds on the general premise that (arguably all) international law restrictions to state sovereignty cannot be 'presumed', which justifies the commentator in supposing that the principle is designed to work as a 'presumption of freedom' or as a 'residual principle' in which all cases not regulated by existing rules automatically fall and receive legal qualification. However, in the specific field of jurisdiction the notion that there is a rule granting states 'in principle' a right to exercise jurisdiction within their territory over foreign nationals with regard to events that occurred abroad was, and still is, straightforward. The Court noted that, unlike the strict territoriality of the jurisdiction to enforce, the 'extra-territorial' jurisdiction to prescribe and adjudicate was routinely

[198] See section A (2)(c) above.

[199] For critical remarks, see Declaration of Judge Simma to the *Kosovo* Advisory Opinion (n 149 above) paras 8–9, arguing for 'possible degrees of non-prohibition, ranging from "tolerated" to "permissible" to "desirable"'.

[200] For this view, see C Focarelli, 'Tanto rumore (quasi) per nulla: lo status del Kosovo e la strategia argomentativa della Corte Internazionale di giustizia nel parere del 22 luglio 2010' (2011) 76 *Il Politico* 59.

[201] eg the US held that 'international law does not generally authorize or prohibit declarations of independence', a statement that 'merely recognizes that international law does not regulate every human event', such as a 'political act' like declaring independence. cf (2010) 104 AJIL 102.

endorsed in international practice.[202] The issue was about delimiting the spheres of jurisdiction of the two states concerned. The Court concluded that there was no exception to the jurisdiction applicable to the instant case and admitted that the two states had the same 'discretion' or 'freedom' to exercise, if they so wished, jurisdiction over the collision. In summary, the Court did not presume 'freedom of action' of states, nor did it state a 'residual principle' covering the whole of international law, but simply accepted that Turkey was allowed to exercise criminal jurisdiction within its borders in its courts over an event that had occurred abroad involving a foreign national, failing evidence to the contrary for cases like the instant case. It did not presume that there were no rules; rather, it stated that there was a clear rule on state jurisdiction—*limiting* sovereignty to *all* states *equally*—the scope of which was to be determined in allocating jurisdiction between the two states. The rule suffered no restriction (except for the permission of the local sovereign) when applied to the jurisdiction to enforce, while it might have suffered one as far as the jurisdiction to prescribe and to adjudicate was concerned, which was not found.

Secondly, the principle is often confusedly deemed to mean both 'less law' limiting state sovereignty and 'narrower scope of the deontic modes of existing rules'. In fact, when the Court referred to restrictions to state sovereignty which could not be presumed, the presumption did not necessarily relate to 'freedom' in the sense of lack of rules, but rather to the deontic mode 'permission' as opposed to the deontic mode 'prohibition' of rules that are assumed to exist. The Lotus principle requires that *prohibitive* rules in the specific field under examination are as few as possible, not that rules *as such* should be as few as possible. It is one thing to conclude that there are no rules at all applicable to a case, it is quite another to state that an applicable rule does exist and is permissive (rather than prohibitory) in its deontic mode. Once the rule is established as existing, the permission contained therein may limit the sovereignty of other states if and to the extent that the rule entails a right whose counterpart is a prohibition imposed on other states not to encroach it. While a rule, if existing, applies equally to all, the deontic mode of a certain rule may be different depending on the addressee of the rule. A rule either exists, and applies to all, or it does not exist, and applies to none. The deontic mode of a rule may be permission for some and prohibition for others. That is to say, more permissions does not necessarily mean fewer prohibitions. It may well mean more permission for some and more prohibitions (hence restrictions to sovereignty) for others. Freedom resulting from the absence of any rule and freedom resulting from a deontic mode of an existing rule are different freedoms. The former is 'freedom of action' corresponding to absolute sovereignty, ie sovereignty not limited by any legal rule whatsoever, a 'state of nature',[203] in practice a potential or actual war of all against all. The latter is freedom within the law. The PCIJ itself, just four years earlier in the 1923 *Nationality Decrees* Advisory Opinion, held that the domestic jurisdiction of the League of Nations' member states under Article 15(8) of the League Covenant was wider or narrower in scope according to the development of international law, which means that international law was understood by the Court as a limiting factor of sovereignty.[204]

Finally, when the Lotus principle is understood as being capable of 'closing' the international legal system by way of either legal presumption or the application of a

[202] PCIJ, *The Case of the SS Lotus* (n 182 above) 20. See Ch 5 above, section B (4)(a).

[203] See n 189 above.

[204] PCIJ, *Dispute between France and Great Britain as to the Nationality Decrees issued in Tunis and Morocco (French Zone)* Advisory Opinion of 7 February 1923, PCIJ Series B No 4, at 23–4.

residual general principle favourable to permission as opposed to prohibition, it is open to ambiguity and manipulation. The operation of the principle in the service of systemic completeness refers to the existence of rules, not to their deontic modes, and implies that all cases of life not covered by expressly existing rules, as appropriately construed, must be assumed to be either covered by an implied rule whose deontic mode is permission for some and prohibition for others (*de jure* freedom) or unregulated freedom of all (*de facto* freedom). It assumes an extrapolation of the argument *a contrario*: if a conduct is expressly prohibited by a rule, by implication this same rule does not prohibit (and hence 'permits') any other conduct. But the principle 'what is not prohibited is permitted' does not specify the meaning to be attached to 'permitted', whether authorization or discretion or indifference or irrelevance. If one adopts the 'irrelevance' meaning, then the principle does not make all possible cases of life fall within the sphere of law. The opposite conclusion holds if one of the other three possible meanings is selected. The *a contrario* reasoning underlying the Lotus principle as a tool for the systemic completeness has little to do with the argument *a contrario*. This, in fact, works *against* completeness by saying that any existing rule does not apply to cases outside its expressly stated scope.[205] Rather, the argument prevents existing rules from expanding their scope of application to all possible cases of life, these latter simply remaining unregulated by the law and in any case unaffected by the argument *a contrario*.

The Lotus principle is invoked by those who have an interest in a permission and is criticized by those who in the same subject-matter prefer a prohibition. The latter often consider themselves to be more progressive, accusing the principle of blessing the 'old' international law which allowed unrestricted freedom of action to states in the name of absolute sovereignty. It is highly debatable that in the past international law left states completely free to behave as they pleased: it either was no law at all or it was law and could only restrict state sovereignty. That major powers usually broke international law as a matter of fact is a different question, and this occurs also today under the 'new' international law. What has changed is that sovereignty is today limited *differently* than in the past, not that it limits (or ought to limit more extensively) state sovereignty while it failed to do so formerly. The novelty, as already noted (and as will be discussed in greater detail in Chapter 8), is that under current international law sovereignty is restricted also in the way rulers are supposed to rule over any individual within their jurisdiction. The critical point with the Lotus principle does not pertain so much to the existence of rules, nor does it really concern the deontic mode (prohibition or permission) per se of existing rules, but rather to *what* is being, or is to be, prohibited or permitted. In *Nuclear Weapons* the Lotus principle was criticized because it militated for the permissibility of the threat and use of nuclear weapons and this was perceived as 'unjust' in that it favoured the stronger. In *Arrest Warrant* the principle was invoked by Belgium to justify universal jurisdiction over international crimes, this time to further an apparently 'just' cause.[206] It is far from unrealistic to suppose that critics of the principle in *Nuclear Weapons* would have been its advocates in *Arrest Warrant*. The same principle has the potential to lead to the (undesired) permissibility of nuclear weapons and to the (desired) permissibility of universal jurisdiction over international crimes. Both

[205] See section A (2)(d) above.

[206] ICJ, *Arrest Warrant of 11 April 2000* (n 190 above) Dissident Opinion of Judge Van Den Wyngaert, ibid para 51, arguing that 'There is ample evidence in support of the proposition that international law clearly permits States to provide extraterritorial jurisdiction' for war crimes and crimes against humanity committed abroad.

advocates and critics use the principle to further their (opposite) goals. Which goals are more valuable is a different question that has nothing to do with the alleged ability of the principle to fill the gaps in the law.

On balance, international law is far from regulating all possible cases and, in fact, most cases fall within the 'neither required nor prohibited' area. Any attempt to construct a systemically totalizing approach to international law unduly pushes for a law to be understood as a 'perfect machine' which may work perhaps in a world of machine-like human beings, or in the insulated minds of a few academics, or in a fully standardized society, but not in the many, admittedly 'imperfect', actual societies currently known. International practice and jurisprudence generally pull in the direction favoured here whereby most cases are 'neither required nor prohibited' by international law.[207]

(b) Analogy

If there is no 'residual' general principle in international law covering all possible cases of life beyond those covered by existing rules flowing from the sources, individual existing rules may still be integrated (or duly interpreted) by expanding *each* by way of analogy. It is controversial whether analogy in international law amounts to mere interpretation or veritable law-making, or both. Analogy used to create new rules, if admitted, would constitute an autonomous source of international law. Article 38 ICJ Statute makes no mention of this, although it refers to general principles of law recognized by civilized nations and these may be (and indeed have been) seen as forms of 'private law analogies'.[208] As general principles of law under Article 38(1)(c) ICJ Statute, so-called private law analogies have been discussed already. The specific question to be addressed here is whether analogy can be used starting from an existing rule of *international law* (as opposed to a rule of another legal system) applicable to a class of cases in order to find an international legal solution for a case prima facie unregulated by all the rules flowing from the international law sources, including general principles of law recognized by civilized nations. Unlike when framed as an autonomous source, analogy used as a means of interpretation of existing rules provides a basis for a legal solution of prima facie unregulated cases limited to the instant case (as opposed to a new rule applicable also in future cases).

The key objection to analogy is that the extension of the meaning of a pre-existing rule or the 'automatic' creation by implication of a new rule from analogy is not, by hypothesis, backed up by states. It seems reasonable to presume that when states make a rule which applies to a class of cases, they are not willing to apply the rule to other cases, otherwise they would have shaped the rule accordingly. On the other hand, life usually moves faster than law and one cannot expect the law-maker to be able and/or willing constantly to have a say on what law is in force at any given moment. It may well accept, at least provisionally, that an existing rule devised for a given class of cases may be immediately applied also to a new class of cases in need of regulation, at least until a specific regulation is expressly made. Critics sometimes deny the use of analogy in

[207] See eg nn 191, 192, 201 above.

[208] H Lauterpacht, *Private Law Sources and Analogies (With Special Reference to International Arbitration)* (London and New York: Longmans, Green and Co, 1927). For the parallel of the analogy between domestic and international legal persons with the analogy between domestic and international law, see ED Dickinson, 'The Analogy between Natural Persons and International Persons in the Law of Nations' (1917) 26 Yale LJ 564.

CIL;[209] others allow analogy in CIL, based on a general principle of law recognized by civilized nations or on CIL itself, but deny it in treaty law;[210] still others allow analogy only as a tool of interpretation, not as a source of law;[211] exponents of legal positivism generally deny analogy altogether, unless expressly accepted by the parties.[212] Advocates argue that analogy is vital to the legal 'system' since it ensures consistency, justice, and rationality, unless special limitations are exceptionally necessary,[213] as is typically the case with criminal international law.[214] They note that through analogy new cases will often find some, at least provisional, legal answer and, while perhaps lacking direct and specific states support in itself, analogy presents a certain degree of plausibility to audiences.[215]

International courts and tribunals have resorted to analogy on several occasions in different legal contexts. In the past, analogy was especially mentioned or resorted to as a private law source, as is the case with the 1912 *Affaire de l'indemnité russe* Arbitral Award in relation to moratory and compensatory interests,[216] and the 1923 *Wimbledon* Judgment of the PCIJ in relation to servitudes.[217] As regards arbitral practice, in the 1905 *Affaire des boutres de Mascate* Arbitral Award the Tribunal held that analogy 'had always been recognized as a means to complete the very deficient written regulations of capitulations as far as circumstances are analogous', which was not found to be the case in that instance.[218] In the 1941 *Trail Smelter* Award the Tribunal analogized air pollution to water pollution in order to identify rules applicable to the former from those governing the latter and, in the absence of international law rules in the field of water pollution as well, further found it:

> ... reasonable to follow by analogy, in international cases, precedents established by [the US Supreme Court] in dealing with controversies between States of the Union or with other controversies concerning the quasi-sovereign rights of such States, where no contrary rule prevails in international law and no reason for rejecting such precedents can be adduced from the limitations of sovereignty inherent in the Constitution of the United States.[219]

The ICJ has also used analogy, beginning with the 1950 *Namibia* Advisory Opinion, in which the Court excluded any analogy between the mandate system of the League of

[209] cf WH von Heinegg, 'Die weiteren Quellen des Völkerrechts' in K Ipsen (ed), *Völkerrecht* (Munich: Beck, 5th edn, 2004) 210, 246.

[210] M Giuliano, 'Il problema dell'analogia nell'ordinamento giuridico internazionale' (1941) 20 RDI 69, 117–20.

[211] R Quadri, *Diritto internazionale pubblico* (Naples: Liguori, 5th edn, 1968) 214–15.

[212] D Anzilotti, *Corso di diritto internazionale* [1928] (Padua: Cedam, 1964) 106; K Strupp, 'Les règles générales du droit de la paix' 47 RdC (1934) 263, 337; H Kelsen, *Principles of International Law* (New York: Holt, 2nd edn, 1967) 527.

[213] G Schwarzenberger, *International Law as Applied by International Courts and Tribunals* (London: Stevens, 3rd edn, 1957) vol 1, 63–6; A Bleckmann, *Grundprobleme und Methoden des Völkerrechts* (Freiburg: Alber, 1982) 241–3.

[214] cf Art 22(2) ICC, prohibiting analogy in accordance with the principle *nullum crimen nulla pena sine lege*.

[215] Weinreb (n 41 above) 9.

[216] Arbitral Tribunal, *Affaire de l'indemnité russe (Russie, Turquie)* Award of 11 November 1912, 11 RIAA 421, 441, 446.

[217] PCIJ, *Case of the SS 'Wimbledon' (Government of His Britannic Majesty v German Empire)* Judgment of 17 August 1923, PCIJ Series A No 1, at 24, abstaining from deciding the 'very controversial' question of whether in international law there really existed servitudes analogous to the servitudes of private law.

[218] Arbitral Tribunal, *Affaire des boutres de Mascate (France, Grande-Bretagne)* Award of 8 August 1905, 11 RIAA 83, 94.

[219] Arbitral Tribunal, *Trail Smelter Case (United States v Canada)* Award of 11 March 1941, 3 RIAA 1905, 1963–4.

Nations and the mandate in national law but accepted by analogy that the procedure to be followed to amend the Mandate over Namibia was applicable to any modification of the international status of a territory under Mandate which would not have for its purpose the placing of the territory under the Trusteeship System.[220] In the 1984 *Nicaragua* Judgment the Court extended by (good faith-inspired) analogy the law of treaties to unilateral declarations under Article 36(2) ICJ Statute, thus requiring a reasonable time for the termination of declarations with indefinite duration.[221] In the 1986 *Nicaragua* Judgment the Court analogized countermeasures taken by third states to collective self-defence, the former being in principle less grave.[222] In the 1998 *Land and Maritime Boundary between Cameroon and Nigeria* Judgment the Court qualified the application by analogy of the law of treaties to declarations under Article 36(2) ICJ Statute by excluding analogy to the deposit of declarations on grounds that while withdrawal ends existing consensual bonds, deposit establishes such bonds, and concluded that no time period is required for the establishment of a consensual bond following deposit.[223] Analogy has also been resorted to 'in exceptional cases' by the ECJ, such as in the 1985 *Krohn* Judgment[224] and in the 2004 *Krings* Judgment.[225] Also the tendency of international courts and tribunals to follow their own and others' precedents, albeit not compulsory,[226] involves analogical reasoning.[227]

In international practice existing rules have also in various circumstances been applied by analogy to new cases without causing significant protests. For example, when aircraft and balloons were invented, the rules applicable to maritime navigation were thought to apply by analogy before the conclusion of an ad hoc treaty;[228] jurisdictional immunity of foreign heads of state, heads of governments, and ministers of foreign affairs have sometimes been applied by analogy from the rule granting such immunity to foreign diplomats;[229] diplomatic protection by an international organization in favour of its employees operating in the territory of a state may be admitted to some extent by analogy from the rule granting such power to states in relation to their citizens;[230] rules on land warfare can be applied by analogy to air warfare.[231] Perhaps more grounded in the *a fortiori* argument than in analogy is the proposition that restrictions applicable in wartime can be applied in peacetime.[232]

The line between 'extensive interpretation', 'analogical interpretation', and 'creation' of new law by analogy is difficult to draw. Conceptually, everything seems to depend on how relevant the identical element in the two allegedly similar cases is perceived to be

220 ICJ, *International Status of South West Africa* Advisory Opinion of 11 July 1950, [1950] ICJ Rep 128, 132, 142.

221 ICJ, *Case concerning Military and Paramilitary Activities in and against Nicaragua (Nicaragua v United States) (Jurisdiction and Admissibility)* Judgment of 26 November 1984, [1984] ICJ Rep 392, para 63.

222 ICJ, *Case concerning Military and Paramilitary Activities* (n 87 above) para 210.

223 ICJ, *Land and Maritime Boundary between Cameroon and Nigeria (Cameroon v Nigeria: Equatorial Guinea intervening)* Judgment of 11 June 1998, [1998] ICJ Rep 275, paras 30, 34.

224 ECJ, *John Friedrich Krohn (GmbH & Co KG) v Bundesanstalt für landwirtschaftliche Marktordnung* Judgment of 12 December 1985, Case 165/84, [1985] ECR 3997, paras 13–14.

225 ECJ, *Krings GmbH v Oberfinanzdirektion Nürnberg* Judgment of 4 March 2004, Case C-130/02, [2003] ECR 2121, paras 35–38.

226 See section C (3)(c) below.

227 For this view in general, see MacCormick (n 39 above) 80.

228 cf A Bleckmann, 'Analogie im Völkerrecht'(1977–78) 17 AdV 161, 161.

229 Tribunal of Rome, *In re Bigi* Judgment of 28 February 1987, (1988) 24 RDIPP 359, 360.

230 Conforti and Focarelli (n 32 above) 132–7.

231 cf Bleckmann (n 228 above) 165.

232 ICJ, *Corfu Channel (United Kingdom of Great Britain and Northern Ireland v Albania) (Merits)* Judgment of 9 April 1949, [1949] ICJ Rep 4, 22. See further n 173 above.

by the decision-maker and the surrounding community. For example, a rule prohibiting a foreign 'vessel' from entering the territorial waters of a state may reasonably be thought to apply also to a 'lifeboat' (extensive interpretation) but not to aircraft (analogy). This depends only on the fact that a boat is perceived in the community as nearly identical to a vessel, while an aircraft is different, although an aircraft might pose similar problems to those of a vessel or a lifeboat as far as transportation is concerned. Since 'analogue' means 'in part equal, in part different' and analogy is based on the 'equal' element, the element chosen to count as 'equal' is obviously critical and ultimately depends on common sense and social attunement. States as a whole support case-by-case analogy, except when it is expressly excluded,[233] as an interpretative tool or as a further tool of legal integration (after standard interpretation has been made of the rule to be analogized), focused on the similarity of the two cases analogized and the relevance of the analogy as perceived by the international community.

(c) Implied powers

The doctrine of 'implied powers' derives from the jurisprudence of the US Supreme Court concerning the allocation of constitutional powers between the federal state and the federated states. Applied to international law, it provides that the organs of IOs possess not only the powers expressly attributed to them by the constituent instrument, but also those 'implied' powers that are essential to the performance of their duties, or to the exercise of the powers expressly granted, or to the fulfilment of one of the stated purposes of the IO. The doctrine has been applied, by endorsing one or another of the above criteria, to broaden the powers of the United Nations against those of the member states by the ICJ in a number of advisory opinions, notably in *Reparation for Injuries*,[234] *Effect of Awards*,[235] and *Certain Expenses*.[236] In the 1996 *Nuclear Weapons* Advisory Opinion, while reaffirming it in general, the Court applied the principle of 'speciality' and gave greater weight to expressly stated powers, thus denying that the WHO had the power to request an advisory opinion of the ICJ on the matter of the legality of nuclear weapons.[237] Writers are divided, ranging from those who have argued for 'inherent' powers allowing any act which is not expressly prohibited by the constituent instrument,[238] to those who only admit the powers which enable the IO involved to function effectively,[239] to those who remain adherent to an 'objective' interpretation of the constituent instrument within the ambit of the members' consent.[240]

233 See n 214 above. For the view that analogy cannot be used to reach an outcome incompatible with *jus cogens*, see S Vöneky, 'Analogy in International Law', MP EPIL (February 2008 update) para 21.

234 ICJ, *Reparation for Injuries Suffered in the Service of the United Nations* Advisory Opinion of 11 April 1949, [1949] ICJ Rep 174, 180.

235 ICJ, *Effect of Awards of Compensation made by the United Nations Administrative Tribunal* Advisory Opinion of 13 July 1954, [1954] ICJ Rep 47, 57.

236 ICJ, *Certain Expenses of the United Nations (Article 17, Paragraph 2, of the Charter)* Advisory Opinion of 20 July 1962, [1962] ICJ Rep 151, 168.

237 ICJ, *Legality of the Use by a State of Nuclear Weapons in Armed Conflict* Advisory Opinion of 8 July 1996, [1996] ICJ Rep 66, para 25.

238 F Seyersted, 'International Personality of Intergovernmental Organizations: Do Their Capacities Really Depend upon Their Constitutions?' (1964) 4 Indian JIL 1, 20–5; F Seyersted, *Common Law of International Organizations* (Leiden: Nijhoff, 2008) 29–33, 65–70; N White, *The Law of International Organisations* (Manchester: Manchester University Press, 2nd edn, 2005) 87–9.

239 For a critical account, see J Klabbers, *An Introduction to International Institutional Law* (Cambridge: CUP, 2002) 36–9, 63–81, noting in any case that 'the doctrine has passed its heyday' (at 79).

240 GL Tunkin, 'The Legal Nature of the United Nations' (1966-III) 119 RdC 6, 22; RJ Araujo, 'Objective Meaning of Constituent Instruments and Responsibility of International Organisations' in

The doctrine of 'implied powers' often presupposes a special character of treaties establishing IOs and builds on the analogy between federal states and IOs. It replicates the relations between the federal state and the federated states to the level of the relations between IOs and the member states. The goal of the doctrine is obviously to increase the powers of IOs to the detriment of the member states. However, the 'federal analogy' surrounding the doctrine is barely tenable.[241] As noted, IOs are profoundly different from states. They do not govern a community and when administering a territory they cannot but 'authorize' states to carry out the functions of a state.[242] The ICJ pointed out that the United Nations, although endowed with international legal personality, is neither a state nor a super-state.[243] There are few if any mechanisms of redress against IO abuses.[244] Nowhere in the 1969 VCLT, which applies to treaties establishing IOs under Article 5, does one find the possibility of departing from the common rules of interpretation when such treaties are involved.

The doctrine does not, therefore, seem justified beyond the criteria of extensive interpretation commonly applied to any treaty.[245] It cannot, in particular, be used to create implied powers from the generic *purposes* of an IO rather than from its expressed *powers*. IOs' powers cannot be 'enlarged', let alone created, but only interpreted to the full extent of their potential. It is one thing to interpret a *specific* provision *already existing*; it is quite another to bring a *new* provision into being merely because it allegedly serves the same *generic* purpose as an existing provision. Powers not expressly set out in the constituent instrument, or not inferable by the ordinary rules of interpretation applicable to any treaty, may also be extracted when a special customary rule has developed within the organization without raising objections, as is the case with the rule derogating from Article 27(3) UN Charter whereby abstentions by permanent members do not prevent resolutions from being validly adopted.[246] As a technique of pressure on member states to coordinate their behaviour along the directives of IOs the doctrine is understandable, but this does not imply that it can be used as an automatic legal justification for the transfer of powers from states to IOs.

(3) Conflicts

International law, as any other law, suffers from inconsistencies, gaps, indeterminacies, hard and borderline cases. The ideal remedy is often thought to be hierarchization. If certain rules are 'higher in rank' than others, all shortcomings could be solved by simply applying the former and ignoring the latter, at least after unsuccessful dissolution of the conflict by way of interpretation. Prioritarization is basically attained through the ancestral *lex posterior* and the *lex specialis* principles, the nature of which oscillates between 'interpretative' tools (or mere reasoning strategies) or genuine rules governing

M Ragazzi (ed), *International Responsibility Today: Essays in Memory of Oscar Schachter* (Leiden: Nijhoff, 2005) 343, 346.

[241] G Arangio-Ruiz, 'The "Federal Analogy" and UN Charter Interpretation: A Crucial Issue' (1997) 8 EJIL 1.

[242] See Ch 5 above, section C (1)(a).

[243] See Ch 5 above, n 224.

[244] See Ch 5 above, nn 239–43, and n 329 below.

[245] See PCIJ, *Jurisdiction of the European Commission of the Danube* (n 7 above) 64, stating that 'the European Commission is not a State, but an international institution with a special purpose' which 'has power to exercise these functions [bestowed upon it by the Statute with a view to the fulfilment of that purpose] to their full extent, in so far as the Statute does not impose restrictions upon it'.

[246] This is one possible reading of the ICJ 1971 *Namibia* Advisory Opinion. For this view, see Conforti and Focarelli (n 32 above) 76–9.

rule conflicts. This section explores a few techniques of prioritization between the sources of international law (*lex posterior*, *lex specialis*, customary and treaty rules on rule conflict, in particular Article 103 UN Charter, and systemic integration), and argues that whatever the theoretical reasons in favour of formal hierarchies, hierarchization as understood in domestic law is not generally established in existing international law. Rather, as explained in the next section, what is often seen as 'superior' law (such as *jus cogens*) should be situated in the dynamics of international law.

(a) Lex posterior *and* lex specialis

The *lex posterior* principle (*lex posterior priori derogat*), found in the Roman sources, was revived by the 'founders' of international law[247] and is considered to be of universal application. In *Mavrommatis* the PCIJ affirmed the prevalence of a subsequent protocol over a previous treaty by generically stating that 'in cases of doubt, the Protocol, being a special and more recent agreement, should prevail'.[248] The rationale of *lex posterior* is self-evident: when two or more states create a legal rule which conflicts with a previous one having the same rank, the later in time must prevail, otherwise the creation of the later rule would make no sense.

The *lex specialis* principle (*lex specialis generalibus derogat*) is also considered to be of universal application and can be found in the Roman sources as well as in the 'classics' of international law.[249] It has been endorsed by international courts, such as in *Chemin de fer Zeltweg*,[250] *Mavrommatis*,[251] *Chorzów*,[252] *European Commission of the Danube*,[253] *Rights of Passage*,[254] and *Navigational and Related Rights*.[255] Its basic rationale is that where states have made special provision, in the absence of any indication to the contrary, it must be supposed that they intended this special provision—and not some more general rule otherwise applicable to their relations—to be applied. It is presumed that states would have not made the special provision if they had intended to apply in their relations the already existing, background general rule. When combined with *lex posterior*, of course, *lex specialis* makes sense in order to have an earlier rule prevail over a later one, not vice versa. However, despite its general acceptance, it raises several problems, beginning with what is meant by 'special'.[256] There are actually different kinds of speciality, the best known being *ratione materiae* and *ratione personarum*, and they also may conflict with each other. A treaty may be special *ratione materiae* but not *ratione personarum* in

[247] cf ILC, 'Fragmentation of International Law: Difficulties Arising From the Diversification And Expansion of International Law', *Report of the Study Group on the Fragmentation of International Law, finalized by Martti Koskenniemi*, UN Doc A/CN.4/L.682, 13 April 2006, para 225.

[248] PCIJ, *The Mavrommatis Palestine Concessions (Greece v Great Britain) (Objection to the Jurisdiction of the Court)* Judgment of 30 August 1924, PCIJ Series A No 2, at 31.

[249] cf ILC, *Report of the Study Group on the Fragmentation of International Law* (n 247 above) 24 and 37, paras 56 and 61.

[250] Arbitral Tribunal, *Affaire des chemins de fer Zeltweg-Wolfsberg et Unterdrauburg-Woellan (Autriche et Yougoslavie, Société des Chemins de fer Zeltweg-Wolfsberg et Unterdrauburg-Woellan)* Award of 7 October 1933, 3 RIAA 1798, 1803.

[251] PCIJ, *Mavrommatis Palestine Concessions* (n 248 above) 30–1.

[252] PCIJ, *Chorzów Factory (Jurisdiction)* Judgment of 26 July 1927, PCIJ Series A No 9, at 30.

[253] PCIJ, *Jurisdiction of the European Commission of the Danube* (n 7 above) 23.

[254] ICJ, *Case concerning Right of Passage over Indian Territory (Portugal v India) (Merits)* Judgment of 12 April 1960, [1960] ICJ Rep 6, 44.

[255] ICJ, *Dispute regarding Navigational and Related Rights* (n 141 above) para 35.

[256] See A Lindroos, 'Addressing Norm Conflicts in a Fragmented Legal System: The Doctrine of *Lex Specialis*' (2005) 74 NJIL 27.

relation to a certain legal regime deemed to be more general, and vice versa.[257] International humanitarian law, for example, is 'special' in relation to international human rights law *ratione materiae* but the latter may well be special *ratione personae*.[258] Moreover, more often than not, two opposite approaches to speciality are claimed by the parties in a dispute in order to reach (opposite) desired outcomes: speciality as an 'exception' to a general rule, this latter continuing to apply in the absence of any conflict between the two rules, and speciality as a 'whole regime' *exclusively* governing the matter.[259] The first approach, which keeps the general regime 'in the background' ready to 'resurface' whenever the conflict dissolves, is more intuitive and indeed correct. A 'general' rule is necessarily a rule which *applies* (also) to the parties, only 'exceptionally' and 'provisionally' put aside when a conflicting special rule emerges so long as the conflict persists.

(b) Inter-source prioritizations and self-contained regimes

While in domestic legal systems *lex specialis*, just like *lex posterior*, concerns conflicts between rules flowing from the same sources, ie between rules of equal rank according to the legislature, in international law it is common to apply the *lex specialis* principle to conflicts between rules flowing from different sources. The typical case is the relationship between general and particular international law: a treaty is 'special' vis-à-vis general custom, particular custom is special vis-à-vis general custom,[260] and so forth.

The prevalence of treaties over general international law based on speciality is uncontroversial, at least in principle.[261] Prevalence is generally grounded in speciality *ratione personarum*, since the parties to a treaty are less numerous than the whole circle of existing states bound by general international law. It may also derive from speciality *ratione materiae* when a treaty regulates a narrower subject-matter than that regulated by general law. Article 38(1) ICJ Statute, as noted, suggests that the ICJ should first of all look for and apply treaties when deciding a case, a clear reflection of their speciality. In the 1969 *North Sea* Judgment the ICJ stated that, apart from *jus cogens*, 'it is well understood that, in practice, rules of international law can, by agreement, be derogated from in particular cases, or as between particular parties'.[262] In the 1982 *Continental Shelf* Judgment the Court held that states can agree on specific rules by declaring that 'in their bilateral relations in the particular case such rules should be binding as *lex specialis*'.[263] In the 1987 *AMOCO* Award the Iran–United States Tribunal asserted that 'As a *lex specialis* in the relations between the two countries, the Treaty supersedes the

[257] ILC, *Report of the Study Group on the Fragmentation of International Law* (n 247 above) para 112.

[258] See Ch 7 below, n 192.

[259] cf WTO *EU—Conditions for the Granting of Tariff Preferences to Developing Countries*, AB Report of 7 April 2004, WT/DS246/AB/R, paras 14, 39, 90, affirming the Panel's view that the Enabling Clause is an 'exception' to Art I(1) GATT 1994 which does not exclude the application of Art I(1) 'only to the extent of any conflict between the two rules'. For a similar opposition in the relationship between international human rights law and humanitarian international law, see Ch 7 below, n 694 and accompanying text.

[260] E Olufemi, 'The Relationship Between General and Particular Customary International Law' (1996) 8 AJICL 67.

[261] See eg US Supreme Court, *The Paquete Habana* [1900] 175 US 677, 700, stating that 'where there is no treaty and no controlling executive or legislative act or judicial decision, resort must be had to the customs and usages of civilized nations'; ICJ, *Gabčíkovo-Nagymaros Project* (n 140 above) para 132.

[262] ICJ, *North Sea Continental Shelf Cases* (n 80 above) para 72.

[263] ICJ, *Case concerning the Continental Shelf (Tunisia/Libyan Arab Jamahirya) (Merits)* Judgment of 24 February 1982, [1982] ICJ Rep 18, para 24.

lex generalis, namely customary international law', although at the same time 'the rules of customary law may be useful in order to fill in possible *lacunae* of the Treaty, to ascertain the meaning of undefined terms in its text, or, more generally, to aid the interpretation and implementation of its provisions'.[264] Also the IDI stated, in 1995, that 'There is no *a priori* hierarchy between treaty and custom' and that, apart from *jus cogens*, 'relevant norms deriving from a treaty will prevail between the parties over norms deriving from customary law'.[265]

A particularly 'strong form' of *lex specialis* goes by the name of 'self-contained regime'.[266] The concept has been given, in both practice and doctrine, different meanings in different contexts. It was first mentioned by the PCIJ in the 1923 *Wimbledon* Judgment, holding that the 'The provisions relating to the Kiel Canal in the Treaty of Versailles are . . . self-contained', to the effect that they could not be interpreted or supplemented by other rules.[267] In the 1980 *Hostages* Judgment the ICJ maintained that 'the rules of diplomatic law . . . constitute a self-contained regime' in the sense that they provide for their own means of redress in case of breach.[268] The term 'self-contained' appeared also in the 1999 *Tadić* Decision, in which the ICTY stated that 'In international law, every tribunal is a self-contained system', meaning that its competences are only those established in its own Statute.[269] Article 55 ILC Articles on State Responsibility provides for the prevalence of *lex specialis* over the rules of general international law allegedly codified therein.[270] The concept of 'self-contained regime' is discussed especially in relation to the admissibility of counter-measures under general international law when a treaty regulates them differently. *Lex specialis* requires that when a treaty admits countermeasures on certain conditions, as WTO law does, then these provisions are to be followed. The same applies to treaties which apparently prohibit countermeasures in all circumstances, such as EU law. The question of whether a 'fall-back' on general international law is permitted as *ultima ratio* despite the apparent contrary will of the parties to the treaty is to be answered affirmatively.[271] The fall-back is not so much dependent on the respect for *jus cogens*[272] as on the social context of treaties in the international community. The parties can make a valid treaty because of general international law. Not only is it difficult to presume that they have contracted out of it,[273] it is even more difficult to suppose that they can really insulate themselves within their treaty in terms of law. States are generally given the power to opt out of general international law by the international community, as *lex specialis* holds, on the assumption that treaties work, but a stalemate between the parties is exactly the opposite. In any event, no trace of

[264] Iran–US Claims Tribunal, *Amoco International Finance Corp v Islamic Republic of Iran* Award of 14 July 1987 No 310-56-3, (1987-II) 15 Iran–US CTR 189, para 112.

[265] IDI, Resolution on 'Problems Arising from a Succession of Codification Conventions on a Particular Subject', Conclusion 11, Session of Lisbonne (1995), at <http://www.idi-iil.org/idiE/resolutionsE/1995_lis_01_en.pdf>.

[266] See eg B Simma and D Pulkowski, 'Of Planets and the Universe: Self-contained Regimes in International Law' (2006) 17 EJIL 483.

[267] PCIJ, *Case of the SS 'Wimbledon'* (n 217 above) 23–4.

[268] See n 672 below and accompanying text.

[269] ICTY, *Prosecutor v Dusko Tadić*, Appeal Judgment of 15 July 1999, No ICTY-94-1-A, para 39.

[270] UN ILC, 'Draft Articles on Responsibility of States for Internationally Wrongful Acts, with Commentaries' (2001) GAOR 56th Session Supp 10, 43.

[271] ILC, *Report of the Study Group on the Fragmentation of International Law* (n 247 above) paras 56–122. See further Ch 8 below, nn 43, 62.

[272] E Klein, 'Self-contained Regime', MP EPIL (November 2006 update) para 13.

[273] J Pauwelyn, 'The Role of Public International Law in the WTO: How Far Can We Go?' (2001) 95 AJIL 535, 537.

genuine self-contained regimes is found in actual practice and states are hardly inclined to remain closed in one or another treaty regime.[274]

In case of conflict between a binding decision of an IO and the founding treaty, the treaty prevails as *lex superior*. However, binding decisions could be seen as subsequent treaties, especially when adopted unanimously. A treaty may well provide the possibility of concluding agreements on the matter it regulates. For example, it is difficult to determine whether the acts adopted under Article IX of the 1959 Antarctic Treaty are 'decisions' subordinated to the treaty or subsequent agreements that, as such, prevail over the Antarctic Treaty based on *lex posterior*.[275] This question has important repercussions in domestic legal systems since treaties and IOs' binding decisions may have, within states, a different method of becoming 'the law of the land' and, once incorporated in domestic law, a different rank. Their adoption may also raise constitutional issues when falling within the areas governed by treaties for which the Constitution requires parliamentary approval.

(c) Incompatibility between treaty rules

The proliferation of treaties witnessed in the twentieth and twenty-first centuries has exacerbated the question of conflicts between treaty rules. Are there rules stating which of two conflicting treaty rules must be given preference? Are certain treaties ranked higher than others? If all treaties enjoy the same rank with no exception whatsoever, then priority is determined by the *lex posterior* and *lex specialis* criteria; if not, the *lex superior* criterion would rule. Although far from novel, the question has held the stage in recent decades as a manifestation of the fragmentation of international law and even as a purposive strategy pursued by certain groups of states to resist—by concluding a multilateral treaty (such as a treaty on environmental protection or on cultural diversity)—the construction and application of another (such as a free trade treaty).

The relevant scenarios of conflicting treaty rules can be set out in diagram form as follows: AB:AB, ABC:ABC (same parties to the treaty, whether bilateral or multilateral); AB:AC (different parties to a bilateral treaty), AB:ABCD or ABCD:AB, ABCD: ABEF (different parties to a multilateral treaty).[276] The classical solutions, inspired by a combination of the *pacta sunt servanda*, *lex posterior*, and *pacta tertiis* principles, are the following: in the AB:AB or ABC:ABC scenarios, the later treaty applies to all parties; in the AB:AC scenario, A can choose to apply either treaty but cannot avoid violating the other treaty towards the party to this latter (ie if A applies the earlier treaty with B, it will violate the later treaty with C, and vice versa); in the AB:ABCD scenario, A and B will apply the later treaty (as a result of the last-in-time rule in their relations) in full compliance also towards C and D; in the ABCD:AB scenario, A and B will again apply the later treaty (as a result of the last-in-time rule in their relations), but in so doing they will violate the earlier treaty towards C and D; finally, in the ABCD:ABEF scenario, A and B will apply the later treaty (as a result of the last-in-time rule in their relations) and in so doing they will be in compliance with the later treaty towards E and F, but will be in violation of the early treaty towards C and D.

274 A Lindroos and M Mehling, 'Dispelling the Chimera of "Self-contained Regimes" International Law and the WTO' (2005) 16 EJIL 857, 877.

275 See C Focarelli, 'The Legal Nature of the Acts Adopted Under Article IX of the Antarctic Treaty and their Implementation in Italy' in F Francioni and T Scovazzi (eds), *International Law for Antarctica* (The Hague: Kluwer, 1996) 505.

276 The diagrams concept is borrowed from CJ Borgen, 'Resolving Treaty Conflicts' (2005) 37 Geo Wash ILR 573, 582–3.

The question is governed along these lines by Article 30 VCLT.[277] Most commentators maintain that this rule codifies CIL.[278] However, its drafting history shows that there was little agreement about the solution to be upheld and the final outcome fails to provide a solution for the most complex and relevant cases. The ILC Special Rapporteurs took different views: initially, Waldock's first draft proposal contained no explicit mention of conflicts, on the assumption that any would-be conflict 'shall be resolved on the basis of the general principles governing the interpretation and application of treaties';[279] then, Lauterpacht favoured the invalidity of the later colliding treaty (*lex prior* approach),[280] but eventually Fitzmaurice contended that both treaties were valid but applicability depended upon whether a party had joined the later treaty or was a party only to the earlier agreement (*lex posterior* approach).[281] Article 30 expressly refers only to 'successive treaties relating to the same subject-matter'. What is meant by 'relating to the same subject-matter' is unclear.[282] Treaties dealing with different subject-matters may actually prove incompatible, for instance a treaty on free trade and a treaty on environmental protection, although one may argue that the particular colliding provisions do concern the same subject-matter *in concreto*.[283] In any event, a conflict arises when in a particular case one and the same subject is bound and compelled to apply two treaty rules pulling in the opposite direction in such a way that there is no margin for the subject to avoid applying one rule and incurring responsibility for violating the other. Being the rules binding by hypothesis, it is up to the subject concerned to avoid, by interpretation or any other means, incompatibility and hence responsibility.

Today a great many treaties provide for some regulation of their relationship with other (either pre-existing or later) treaties relating to the same matters through an ad hoc conflict clause.[284] These clauses are designed to derogate from the general rules applicable to conflicts between treaties set out in Article 30 VCLT. They may establish either priority or subordination of the treaty in which they are found in case of conflict with another treaty, the latter being far more common.[285] They may also combine priority and subordination by qualifying subordination, as is the case with Article 22 (1) Biodiversity Convention.[286] A different clause is the one that prohibits the parties

[277] RD Kearney and RE Dalton, 'The Treaty on Treaties' (1987) 64 AJIL 495, 517.

[278] See eg A Aust, *Modern Treaty Law and Practice* (Cambridge: CUP, 2nd edn, 2007) 228.

[279] ILC, 'Second Report on the Law of Treaties, by Sir Humphrey Waldock, Special Rapporteur' (1963) II UN YBILC 36, 53.

[280] ILC, 'Report by Mr H. Lauterpacht, Special Rapporteur' (1953) II UN YBILC 90, 137–41; 'Second Report by H. Lauterpacht, Special Rapporteur' (1954) II UN YBILC 123, 133–9. See, previously, H Lauterpacht, 'The Covenant as the "Higher Law"' (1936) 17 BYBIL 54.

[281] ILC, 'Third Report by G. G. Fitzmaurice, Special Rapporteur' (1958) II UN YBILC 20, 41–5.

[282] IR Sinclair, *The Vienna Convention on the Law of Treaties* (Manchester: Manchester University Press, 2nd edn, 1984) 93.

[283] A common interpretation of the provision understands it in the sense that Art 30 VCLT shall not apply when a general treaty contradicts a particular provision of an earlier agreement. Yet, this restrictive understanding does not define any further what constitutes the subject-matter of a treaty, when a *lex specialis* relationship is irrelevant.

[284] For a definition by the ILC, see 'Report of the International Law Commission on the Work of its 18th Session' (4 May–19 July 1966) UN Doc A/CN.4/191, at 214, para 2.

[285] For an example of subordination clause, see Art XIII of the Convention on the Prevention of Marine Pollution by Dumping of Wastes and Other Matter (done 13 November 1972, entered into force 30 August 1975) (1972) 11 ILM 1294; typical priority clauses are Art 20 of the League of Nations Covenant and Art 103 UN Charter, this latter is specifically discussed in the next sub-section.

[286] 'The provisions of this Convention shall not affect the rights and obligations of any Contracting Party deriving from any existing international agreement, except where the exercise of those rights and obligations would cause a serious damage or threat to biological diversity.'

from entering into later inconsistent treaties, such as Article VIII NATO Treaty.[287] Yet another, such as Article 351 TFEU Treaty, requires that the states parties to the treaty should do what is in their power to eliminate incompatibilities. Being part of a treaty, such clauses do not create any general hierarchy of treaties opposable even to third parties and may themselves yield to other treaties as a result of criteria such as *lex posterior*. However, as between the parties of both conflicting treaties, the conflict clause dictates which treaty is to be applied. When two conflict clauses collide there is no solution available and presumably the only applicable rules are those found in Article 30 VCLT.

(d) Article 103 of the UN Charter

Among conflict clauses Article 103 UN Charter stands out. It stipulates that: 'In the event of a conflict between the obligations of the Members of the United Nations under the present Charter and their obligations under any other international agreement, their obligations under the present Charter shall prevail'.[288] While it is clear that Article 103 provides for the priority of the UN Charter over any other (existing and future) treaties, several questions arise which converge on the following two, which are often unjustifiably confused: (a) What is its meaning as a treaty rule?; (b) Is it reflective of either a general, or a constitutional, or even a peremptory norm of international law?

The first question arises because Article 103 is first and foremost a treaty rule.[289] Quite a few commentators regard it as a 'special' treaty rule, on the ground that the United Nations plays a crucial role in world order. They are, however, reticent when it comes to specifying the special legal status of the Charter *in concreto*.[290] As a treaty rule, Article 103 is binding only on UN member states and can be derogated by other treaty rules. The *ultra partes* effect is excluded: states remain free not to ratify the Charter and there is little doubt that their legal position is different from that of states which have acceded to it. It is of course a different issue that virtually all existing states are UN members and have the power to put any non-member state under overwhelming pressure. As a treaty rule, there is nothing preventing all UN member states from concluding another treaty rule incompatible with the UN Charter despite Article 103. The most likely case is, however, that few UN member states conclude one or more treaty rules contrary to the UN Charter (or, more plausibly, to a UN Security Council resolution). In such a case, assuming that Article 103 is 'only' a treaty rule, the rules governing the incompatibility between treaties apply.[291]

By 'any' other international agreement is meant an agreement both between UN member states and between a member state and a non-member state, as the preparatory work evidences.[292] With regard to agreements between member states and third states, while member states violate Article 103 in case of conflict, third states do not.[293]

[287] 'Each Party declares that none of the international engagements now in force between it and any other of the Parties or any third State is in conflict with the provisions of this Treaty, and undertakes not to enter into any international engagement in conflict with this Treaty.'

[288] Charter of the United Nations (adopted 26 June 1945, entered into force 24 October 1945) 892 UNTS 119.

[289] Conforti and Focarelli (n 32 above) 10–13.

[290] See on this P-M Dupuy, 'The Constitutional Dimension of the Charter of the United Nations Revisited' (1997) 1 MP YBUNL 1, 13–15.

[291] See section B (3)(c) above.

[292] 13 UNCIO, at 696.

[293] LM Goodrich and E Hambro, *Charter of the United Nations: Commentary and Documents* (New York: Columbia University Press, 3rd edn, 1969) 615; A Toublanc, 'L'article 103 et la valeur juridique de la Charte des Nations Unies' (2004) 108 RGDIP 439, 457; J-M Thouvenin, 'Article 103' in J-P

Turning to substantive issues, the term 'any' is perplexing when it leads to making the UN Charter prevail over human rights treaties. To avoid this undesired result, one could argue that human rights treaties are not covered by Article 103, despite its language, because the Charter itself protects human rights and it cannot allow their violation by the United Nations itself. This approach, however, is at odds with the fact that, although the Charter may protect human rights, its key goal is the maintenance of international peace and security and in case of conflict between this goal and human rights it is difficult to argue that the latter should prevail. This would turn a treaty centred on international peace and security into a humanitarian treaty, a consequence hardly traceable to the drafters and states parties to the Charter. In the 2007 *Al-Jedda* Judgment the UK House of Lords stated, concerning the purported 'special character' of the ECHR, that 'reference in article 103 to "any other international agreement" leaves no room for any excepted category'.[294] Interestingly, in its 2011 Judgment delivered in the same case the ECtHR found that, since the UN Charter protects human rights, there is a presumption that the Security Council does not place on member states any obligation to violate human rights.[295] This presumption, which the Council may apparently rebut only by specifically compelling member states to perform acts in violation of human rights, prevents a conflict under Article 103 from arising at all.

The term 'shall prevail' may have a variety of different meanings. Since Article 103, unlike Article 20 of the League Covenant, does not contain any reference to the 'abrogation' of conflicting treaties,[296] most commentators argue for the mere non-application being limited to the particular case at hand and for the validity of the conflicting agreement,[297] although the thesis of the invalidity *ab initio* was adopted in the past,[298] as well as that of temporary suspension.[299] The former reading is more in line with the ordinary meaning of the term and is supported by the preparatory work in which the word 'abrogation' was expressly rejected.[300] In *Al-Jedda* Baroness Hale stated that Article 103 merely 'qualifies' the conflicting obligations, in the sense that: 'The right is qualified but not displaced... The right is qualified only to the extent required or authorized by the [UNSC] resolution. What remains of it thereafter must be observed'.[301] The 1969 VCLT does mention Article 103 in Article 30(1), concerning conflicts between treaty provisions, but does not include Article 103 among the grounds of invalidity and termination of treaties.

Cot, A Pellet, and M Forteau (eds), *La Charte des Nations Unies: Commentaire article par article* (Paris: Economica, 3rd edn, 2005), vol 2, 2133, at 2136.

294 UK House of Lords, *R (on the application of Al-Jedda) (FC) (Appellant) v Secretary of State for Defence (Respondent)* Judgment of 12 December 2007, [2007] UKHL 58, para 35.

295 ECtHR, *Al-Jedda v United Kingdom* Judgment of 7 July 2011 [GC], App 27021/08, para 102.

296 cf 13 UNCIO, at 604, for the rejection of the term 'abrogation' in the preparatory work of the UN Charter.

297 See eg T Flory, 'Article 103' in J-P Cot and A Pellet (eds), *La Charte des Nations Unies: Commentaire article par article* (Paris: Economica, 2nd edn, 1991) 1381, 1384; Toublanc (n 293 above) 453.

298 H Kelsen, *The Law of the United Nations: A Critical Analysis of its Fundamental Problems* (London: Stevens, 1950, with supplement 1951) 113; R Bernhardt, 'Article 103' in B Simma (ed), *The Charter of the United Nations: A Commentary* (New York: OUP, 1994) 1116, 1122.

299 C Dominicé, 'L'article 103 de la Charte des Nations Unies et le droit international humanitaire' in L Condorelli, A-M La Rosa, and S Scherrer (eds), *The United Nations and International Humanitarian Law* (Paris: Pédone, 1996) 175, 179.

300 See n 296 above.

301 UK House of Lords, *R (on the application of Al-Jedda)* (n 294 above) para 126.

Article 103 stipulates that the Charter prevails over any other 'international agreement' but fails to specify what kinds of agreements are covered. In the 1986 *Nicaragua* Judgment, the ICJ expressly stated that Article 103 applies to bilateral, regional, and 'even' multilateral treaties.[302] It has been suggested that by 'agreement' for the purposes of Article 103 should also be meant contractual arrangements made by states with other states and with private entities, notably MNEs.[303] In the preparatory work it was only stated that Article 103 would have made the Charter prevail over previous treaties as between the parties.[304] In his separate opinion appended to the ICJ 1971 *Namibia* Advisory Opinion Judge Ammoun argued for the application of Article 103 to both previous and subsequent conflicting agreements.[305] It goes without saying that previous agreements are superseded by the Charter, as between the parties to both the conflicting treaties, pursuant to the *lex posterior* principle.[306] Conversely, there is no certainty as to the prevalence over *subsequent* treaties, which is indeed the heart of the question.

In prioritizing the Charter over 'obligations under any other international agreement', Article 103 apparently excludes all other kinds of international law sources. The exclusion of general international law is attested to by the preparatory work,[307] and was asserted by Judges Bedjaoui and Rezek in their dissenting opinion in *Lockerbie* appended to the 1992 Orders[308] and the 1998 Judgments.[309] The prevalence of the Charter over general international law derives from the *lex posterior* principle in respect of general rules which emerged *before* the entry into force of the Charter and by virtue of the *lex specialis* rule with regard to general rules emerging *after* its entry into force. Article 103 is thus meaningful only where it is taken to imply the prevalence of the Charter over an agreement enabling the parties to apply general international law, rather than the Charter, in derogation from either *lex posterior* or *lex specialis*. This effect would be precluded if the general law rule were peremptory, and the problem would become even more complicated if Article 103 were also regarded as peremptory, as some theorists believe.[310] While there is general agreement on the prevalence of peremptory norms over ordinary norms, there is no guidance on dealing with instances where two alleged peremptory norms conflict with each other.

The question of whether the expression 'the obligations of the Members of the United Nations under the present Charter' includes special customary norms developed within the UN system—such as, arguably, that relating to abstention in the voting in the Security Council under Article 27(3) and perhaps that concerning *litis pendence* before the Security Council and the General Assembly under Article 12 UN Charter—is unclear, depending, inter alia, on how to read the practice in the

[302] ICJ, *Case concerning Military and Paramilitary Activities* (n 221 above) para 107.

[303] R Liivoja, 'The Scope of the Supremacy Clause of the United Nations Charter' (2008) 57 ICLQ 583, 598–601.

[304] 13 UNCIO, at 671.

[305] ICJ, *Legal Consequences for States of the Continued Presence of South Africa in Namibia* (n 139 above), separate opinion of Judge Ammoun, at 87.

[306] See in addition 13 UNCIO, at 671.

[307] 19 UNCIO, at 376. See Liivoja (n 303 above) 602–5.

[308] ICJ, *Questions of Interpretation and Application of the 1971 Montreal Convention* (n 148 above), dissenting opinion of Judge Bedjaoui, at 47 and 157, para 29.

[309] ICJ, *Questions of Interpretation and Application of the 1971 Montreal Convention arising from the Aerial Incident at Lockerbie (Libyan Arab Jamahiriya v United Kingdom) (Preliminary Objections)* Judgment of 27 February 1998, [1998] ICJ Rep 9, separate opinion of Judge Rezek, at 61, para 2; *Questions of Interpretation and Application of the 1971 Montreal Convention arising from the Aerial Incident at Lockerbie (Libyan Arab Jamahiriya v United States) (Preliminary Objections)* Judgment of 27 February 1998, [1998] ICJ Rep 115, separate opinion of Judge Rezek, at 152, para 2.

[310] See eg B Conforti, *Diritto internazionale* (Naples, Editoriale Scientifica, 8th edn, 2010) 178.

organization as mere evolutionary interpretation, or interpretation by subsequent practice, or emergence of new special customary rules.[311] On the other hand, the question of whether 'the obligations of the Members of the United Nations under the present Charter' include Security Council resolutions is generally answered affirmatively. The expression is clear in extending to all obligations flowing from the Charter, whether directly or by way of 'specification' in Security Council resolutions. This is confirmed by the preparatory work of the Charter, in which reference was made to possible conflicts of 'economic sanctions' decided by the Security Council with other agreements.[312] The practice of the Security Council points in the same direction, as evidenced by Resolution 670 (1990)[313] and Resolution 748 (1992),[314] among many others.[315] The same view was taken by the ICJ in the 1992 *Lockerbie* Orders.[316] Commentators generally agree that Article 103 also applies to Security Council resolutions, with few exceptions.[317] Much less clear is, however, whether Article 103 covers only binding resolutions, whether contemplating positive or negative obligations, or also authorizing resolutions, or even recommendations.[318] In referring to 'obligations' Article 103, taken literally, clearly excludes recommendations and authorizations. In fact, in the 2007 *Behrami* Decision, the ECtHR, followed by the UK House of Lords in the 2007 *Al-Jedda* Judgment,[319] took the opposite view, adhering to a number of commentators while not taking due account of others who argued against.[320] In the 2011 *Al-Jedda* Judgment the ECtHR spoke only of 'obligations' mentioned in Article 103 and its silence on authorizations is not conclusive regarding the exclusion of authorizations from the scope of Article 103. Security Council recommendations are not binding, even though they are made under Chapter VII, and do not impose any 'obligation' on member states, as the ICJ held in 1998.[321] The broader interpretation is clearly aimed at prioritizing the Security Council and its primary responsibility in the maintenance of international peace and security, apparently a persuasive policy consideration. It sounds, though, less persuasive when the conflicting treaty is a human rights treaty. An authorization means that states remain free to carry out what has been authorized by the Security Council, and if it is in their

[311] Conforti and Focarelli (n 32 above) 20–1, 76–9.

[312] 13 UNCIO, at 717.

[313] UNSC Res 670 (1990) of 25 September 1990, paras 1 and 3.

[314] UNSC Res 748 (1992) of 31 March 1992, para 7.

[315] See eg UNSC Res 713 (1991) of 25 September 1991 on the former Yugoslavia; Res 724 (1991) of 15 December 1991, Res 727 (1992) of 8 January 1992, and Res 733 (1992) of 23 January 1992 on Somalia; Res 743 (1992) of 21 February 1992 and Res 748 (1992) of 31 March 1992 on Libya; Res 787 (1992) of 16 November 1992 and Res 788 (1992) of 19 November 1992 on Liberia; Res 820 (1993) of 17 April 1993 and Res 1132 (1997) of 8 October 1997 on Sierra Leone; Res 1173 (1998) of 12 June 1998 on Angola; Res 1267 (1999) of 15 October 1999 on Afghanistan; and Res 1298 (2000) of 17 May 2000 on Ethiopia and Eritrea.

[316] ICJ, *Questions of Interpretation and Application of the 1971 Montreal Convention* (n 148 above) 15, para 39, and 126, para 42. Previously, in his separate opinion attached to the *Namibia* Advisory Opinion, Judge Ammoun had stated that the obligations contemplated by Art 103 'clearly include obligations resulting from the provisions of the Charter and from its purposes, and also those laid down by the binding decisions of the organs of the United Nations' ((n 305 above) para 18).

[317] One exception is Flory (n 297 above) 1383.

[318] For the difference between Security Council recommendations, authorizations, and delegations, see Ch 7 below, section A (1)(d).

[319] UK House of Lords, *R (on the application of Al-Jedda)* (n 294, above) para 33.

[320] For the two positions, see R Kolb, 'Does Article 103 of the Charter of the United Nations Apply Only to Decisions or Also to Authorizations Adopted by the Security Council?' (2004) 64 ZaöRV 21, siding with the broader view.

[321] ICJ, *Questions of Interpretation and Application of the 1971 Montreal Convention* (n 309 above) para 44.

power to avoid violating human rights treaties binding on them, there is no reason why they should not do so. The restrictive approach is more in line with the language of Article 103 and with the notion that states cannot be assumed to have been given the liberty to join a UN-authorized military operation without incurring any responsibility with regard to possible violations of human rights. Admittedly, there is an alternative theory by which to arrive at the result of preventing Article 103 from blessing such an unacceptable result when at least certain core human rights are seen as *jus cogens* and this is understood as a limit to the Security Council, in which case *jus cogens* would trump . . . the trumping function of Article 103.[322] This theory, however, is very baroque indeed (suggesting that certain peremptory rules are more peremptory than others) and meets with the objections which will be discussed below when specifically dealing with *jus cogens*. Another, softer theory capable of leading to the exclusion of human rights from the operation of Article 103 is to take the Charter as embodying the protection of human rights and regard these latter as 'internal' limits to the action of the Security Council. But it is very difficult to determine what human rights are protected by the Charter to this end. In any event, an 'internal' limit simply makes a Security Council resolution *ultra vires* and presumably invalid. Conflicting (external) human rights treaties would then apply simply because there is no longer any valid resolution providing for their violation and any conflict at all. Briefly, while applying to sanctions *decided* under Article 41 UN Charter, Article 103 hardly extends to measures (either peaceful or forcible) authorized by the Security Council. A middle-path solution may be to take the authorization as authorizing all acts *connected* to the conduct specifically authorized on a case-by-case basis, ie contingent on *any* authorization and with regard to *specific* conflicting treaties, such as a bilateral treaty prohibiting the use of force or hostile acts,[323] without triggering the operation of Article 103.

Turning now to the second (and indeed crucial) question of whether Article 103 reflects general international law, virtually all existing states are today members of the United Nations, but occasionally new states may remain for a period outside the organization, in which case the issue is relevant. It is also relevant for the purposes of determining whether Article 103 is a constitutional or a peremptory norm, since these types of rules are normally seen as rules of general international law. It is often argued that the references to the Charter contained in many other treaties signal a 'centrality' of the UN Charter.[324] However, while it is true that some treaties prioritize the Charter, it is also true that the overwhelming majority of existing treaties fail to do so. It has also been suggested that in reproducing the language of Article 103, the 1970 UN Declaration on Friendly Relations confirms its general character,[325] but, of course, the Declaration is not only per se non-binding but is also incapable alone of creating general international law. What is needed to state that Article 103 reflects general international law is *usus* and *opinio juris*, and these elements are scarce. The vague impression that the world would be better off if the Charter prevailed over any other

[322] cf ICJ, *Case concerning Application of the Convention on the Prevention and Punishment of the Crime of Genocide (Bosnia Herzegovina v Yugoslavia (Serbia and Montenegro))*, Order of 13 September 1993, [1993] ICJ Rep 3, separate opinion of Judge *ad hoc* Elihu Lauterpacht, at 439–40, paras 99–100. The same view was later upheld by the EU Court of First Instance (CFI) in the 2005 *Kadi* and *Yusuf* Judgments, but the ECJ failed to endorse it (see n 437 below).

[323] A case in point are Arts 3 and 4(2) of the Benghazi Treaty on Friendship, Partnership and Cooperation between Italy and Libya of 30 August 2008 in connection with the military operations, in which Italy took part, authorized by UNSC Res 1973 (2011) of 17 March 2011.

[324] cf eg Art 30(1) and (6) VCLT, Art 7 NATO Treaty, Art VI WEU Treaty, Art 131 OAS Charter, Art 21(c) GATT 1994, Art 14*bis* GATS, and Art 73(c) TRIPS.

[325] Toublanc (n 293 above) 459.

obligations is not evidence of CIL, nor does it necessarily guarantee a better world in all circumstances.

A few commentators have maintained that the UN Charter is (not only the founding treaty of the United Nations, but also) the constitution of the international community.[326] They are inclined to see Article 103 as a principle establishing the superiority of the Charter over any other norm of international law. This, however, goes well beyond what Article 103 expressly stipulates, and presupposes a constitutional reading of the Charter as a whole. While there certainly are elements showing that the Charter is somehow different from other treaties, what special legal effects this difference entails remains unclear. The term 'prevalence', already discussed when dealing with Article 103 as a treaty rule, has inspired a few commentators to argue that Article 103 is not only a treaty rule but more specifically a rule of general international law belonging to *jus cogens*.[327] Article 103, however, mentions 'prevalence'—presumably meaning non-application of the conflicting obligation on a case-by-case basis and affecting only the conflicting part of the sole conflicting provision, without affecting the rest of the treaty—while *jus cogens* is defined in Article 53 VCLT in terms of non-derogability and specifically of *invalidity* or *termination* of the conflicting treaty taken *as a whole*.[328] The concept of *jus cogens* that would lie behind Article 103, if this approach were to be taken, would be different from that of Article 53. As a result, two different notions of *jus cogens* would emerge, which is hardly consistent with its alleged absolute character. Once again, one would be called upon to decide which *jus cogens* rule 'is more peremptory than the other' and enjoys, as such, a super-trumping effect.

To sum up, in practice, Article 103 has almost always been relied upon to assert the priority of Security Council resolutions (rather than the Charter itself) over conflicting treaty rules, especially those touching upon human rights. As a result, Article 103 has served hitherto, in practice, the purpose of prioritizing security over humanity, an outcome that has left many humanitarians rather dissatisfied, such dissatisfaction reaching a peak with the ECtHR *Behrami* Decision. Perplexities are justifiably fuelled by the fact that the United Nations does not have any judicial review mechanism and the control of the conformity of Security Council resolutions to the Charter—a clear prerequisite for considering them as falling within the scope of Article 103—is left to individual states.[329] This, inter alia, shows that giving a 'constitutional' meaning to Article 103 may well lead to an opposite outcome from that expected, with security concerns (and the will of the five permanent members of the Security Council) prevailing over the protection of human rights. In any case, with the 2011 *Al-Jedda* Judgment, by assuming that UN Security Council resolutions are (in the absence of explicit evidence to the contrary) presumed to be in keeping with human rights, the ECtHR has wisely considerably reduced, in practice, the likelihood of rule conflicts requiring the operation of Article 103 where human rights are involved.

(e) Systemic integration

Conflicts arise as a result of the way potentially conflicting rules are interpreted. Is there a general rule compelling states to interpret treaty provisions is such a way as to render

[326] B Fassbender, 'The United Nations Charter as Constitution of the International Community' (1998) 36 Col JTL 529, 590; R Bernhardt, 'Article 103' in B Simma (ed), *The Charter of the United Nations: A Commentary* (New York: OUP, 2nd edn, 2002) vol 2, 1292, 1302. See further Ch 4 above, n 219.

[327] See n 310 above. [328] See n 427 below.

[329] Conforti and Focarelli (n 32 above) 423–9.

them as compatible as possible with any other, or even imposing a certain type of 'systemic' interpretation?[330] Article 31(3)(c) VCLT provides that in the interpretation of treaties 'There shall be taken into account, together with the context . . . any relevant rules of international law applicable in the relations between the parties'. This provision has recently been 'rediscovered' for the purposes of interpreting the rules of a legal sub-system, such as a WTO regime, in the light of (and possibly in harmony with) other treaty systems or general international law.[331]

The notion that a treaty should be read in principle against the background of general international law is obvious and classically stated in the 1928 *Georges Pinson* Decision.[332] It has been reiterated on innumerable occasions by various international courts and tribunals, including the ICJ,[333] the Iran–US Claims Tribunal,[334] PCA Arbitral Tribunals,[335] the ECtHR,[336] and WTO panels and the Appellate Body.[337] As a matter of fact, many technical terms found in treaties, such as typically 'state', are usually taken for granted as 'incorporated by reference' by the parties to the treaty. Significantly, in the 2003 *Oil Platforms* Judgment, the ICJ excluded the suggestion that a clause in a bilateral treaty binding on the parties to the dispute 'was intended to operate wholly independently of the relevant rules of international law on the use of force', thereby applying CIL on the use of force to the United States, although the Court's jurisdiction was formally limited to disputes concerning the interpretation or application of the treaty.[338]

More problematic is the reading of a treaty in the light of other treaties, whether binding on all the parties to the treaty being interpreted or only to the parties to the dispute.[339] While minor doubts arise when the agreement to be interpreted

[330] N Matz-Lück, 'Harmonization, Systemic Integration, and "Mutual supportiveness" as Conflict-solution Techniques: Different Modes of Interpretation as a Challenge to Negative Effects of Fragmentation?' (2008) 17 Finn YBIL 39.

[331] C McLachlan, 'The Principle of Systematic Integration and Article 31(3)(C) of the Vienna Convention' (2005) 54 ICLQ 279; U Linderfalk, 'Who are "the Parties"? Article 31, Paragraph 3(c) of the 1969 Vienna Convention and the "Principle of Systemic Integration" Revisited' (2008) 55 Neth ILR 343.

[332] French-Mexican Claims Commission, *Georges Pinson (France) v United Mexican States* Decision No 1 of 19 October 1928, 5 RIAA 327, 422, para 50(4).

[333] ICJ, *Case concerning the Right of Passage over Indian Territory (Portugal v India) (Preliminary Objections)* Judgment of 26 November 1957, [1957] ICJ Rep 125, 142; ICJ, *Legal Consequences for States of the Continued Presence of South Africa in Namibia* (n 139 above) para 47; *Case concerning Elettronica Sicula SpA (ELSI) (United States v Italy)* Judgment of 20 July 1989, [1989] ICJ Rep 15, para 50.

[334] Iran–US Claims Tribunal, *Amoco International Finance Corp v Islamic Republic of Iran* (n 264 above) para 112; *Esphahanian v Bank Tejarat*, Award of 29 March 1983 No 31-157-2, 2 Iran–US CTR (1983–I) 157, 161.

[335] PCA Arbitral Tribunal, *Dispute concerning Access to Information Under Article 9 of the OSPAR Convention (Ireland v the United Kingdom)*, Final Award of 2 July 2003, 23 RIAA 59, para 84.

[336] The ECtHR typically recalls that the ECHR, despite its 'special character' (nn 123, 124 above), 'cannot be interpreted in a vacuum' and other international law rules need to be considered. See n 346 below.

[337] The Appellate Body typically recalls that WTO agreements cannot be read 'in clinical isolation' from general international law.

[338] *Oil Platforms (Islamic Republic of Iran v United States)* Judgment of 6 November 2003, [2003] ICJ Rep 161, para 41.

[339] In the first sense, see WTO, *EC—Measures Affecting the Approval and Marketing of Biotech Products*, Panel Report of 7 February 2006, WT/DS291-293/INTERIM, paras 7.70–7.72, stating that only non-WTO agreements binding on all WTO members could be taken into account in the interpretation of a WTO agreement under Art 31(3)(c) VCLT. See B McGrady, 'Fragmentation of International Law or "Systemic Integration" of Treaty Regimes: EC-biotech Products and the Proper Interpretation of Article 31(3)(c) of the Vienna Convention on the Law of Treaties' (2008) 42 JWT 589.

implements another, as was the case in the 1937 *Tardieu-Jaspar* Award,[340] perplexities arise when the agreement in the light of which the interpretation takes place seems to be selectively chosen to arrive at a desired outcome.[341] It is true, of course, that 'the normative environment cannot be ignored' when interpreting a treaty.[342] However, it is also true that in most instances the parties are bound by a very large number of international obligations and 'parallel treaties' bearing upon the dispute,[343] possibly pulling in opposite directions, and the discretionary selection of those relevant to the case is critical. In this sense the principle of systemic integration, despite being presented as a tool of coherence and meaningfulness, may be used as a tool to reach desired outcomes that could not be reached otherwise. For example, in the 2004 *Rhine River* Award, the Arbitral Tribunal, called upon to apply Article 31(3)(c) VCLT by the Netherlands, held that the polluter pays principle 'se situe a des niveaux d'effectivité variables', is not part of general international law, and was not pertinent to the case.[344] In the 2001 *Al-Adsani*, *Fogarty*, and *McElhinney* Judgments the ECtHR appealed to Article 31(3)(c) VCLT to make sovereign immunity prevail over the right of access to justice impliedly embodied in Article 6 ECHR.[345] Intriguingly, in the 1975 *Golder* Judgment, the ECtHR had argued that the right of access to justice was a general principle of law recognized by civilized nations under Article 38(1)(c) ICJ Statute and this latter had to be taken into account on the basis of Article 31(3)(c) VCLT.[346] In the 2003 *Mox Plant* Award a PCA Tribunal decided not to apply the instruments invoked by Ireland (the 1992 Rio Declaration[347] and the 2001 Aarhus Convention[348]) because these were not 'rules of law applicable between the parties' but only 'evolving international law'.[349]

While taking into account that general international law can hardly be excluded when interpreting a treaty, except when it has been expressly contracted out by the

[340] Sole Arbitrator, *Différend concernant l'accord Tardieu-Jaspar (Belgium/France)* Award of 1 March 1937, 3 RIAA 1701, 1713.

[341] VP Tzevelekos, 'The Use of Article 31(3)(C) of the VCLT in the Case Law of the ECtHR: An Effective Anti-fragmentation Tool or Selective Loophole for the Reinforcement of Human Rights Teleology? Between Evolution and Systemic Integration' (2009–10) 31 Mich JIL 621.

[342] ILC, Report of the Study Group, 'Fragmentation of International Law: Difficulties Arising from the Diversification and Expansion of International Law' (Analytical Study), (2006) UN Doc A/CN.4/L.682, at 211, para 419.

[343] cf Arbitral Tribunal Constituted under Annex VII UNCLOS, *Southern Bluefin Tuna Case (Australia and New Zealand v Japan)* Award on Jurisdiction and Admissibility of 4 August 2000, (2000) 39 ILM 1359, para 52.

[344] Arbitral Tribunal, *Case concerning the auditing of accounts between the Kingdom of the Netherlands and the French Republic pursuant to the Additional Protocol of 25 September 1991 to the Convention on the Protection of the Rhine against Pollution by Chlorides of 3 December 1976 (Netherlands/France)* Award of 12 March 2004, 25 RIAA, 267, para 103.

[345] ECtHR, *Al-Adsani* (n 123 above); *Fogarty v United Kingdom* Judgment of 21 November 2001 [GC], App 37,112/97, ECtHR Rep 2001-XI 137; and *McElhinney v Ireland* Judgment of 21 November 2001 [GC], App 31253/96, ECtHR Rep 2001-XI 37.

[346] ECtHR, *Golder v United Kingdom* Judgment 21 February 1975, App 4451/70, Series A (1975) No 18, (1979–80) 1 EHRR 524, paras 27–31, 35.

[347] UN Conference on Environment and Development, 'Rio Declaration on Environment and Development' of 14 June 1992, UN Doc A/CONF.151/26/Rev 1, vol I, 3.

[348] Convention on Access to Information, Public Participation in Decision-Making and Access to Justice in Environmental Matters (done 25 June 1998, entered into force 30 October 2001) 2161 UNTS 447.

[349] PCA Arbitral Tribunal, *Dispute concerning Access to Information Under Article 9 of the OSPAR Convention* (n 335 above) paras 99, 101–105.

parties,[350] the pertinence of treaties other than the one being interpreted is open to question. As will be shown when discussing the abuse of rights doctrine, some 'principles' of systemic integration can work within the margin of discretion of international courts and tribunals. There is no other basis for this, the limit being the risk of the court or tribunal losing legitimacy when the use of it is perceived as an abuse of power.

(4) Change

It is one thing to state the law as it stands, it is quite another to identify how the law is changed. The dynamics of law are of utmost importance in explaining both why there is a certain law today, as a result of what has been done in the past, and how current law can be changed in the future, as a result of what is being done today. Put differently, the law as it is today is the outcome of past struggles; therefore, only a struggle engaged today can make the law change for tomorrow. This is all the more so where law—for example, international law—is grounded in custom, since custom changes every day as a function of the attitudes adopted within the international community. To 'apply' a given CIL rule amounts to reinforcing the rule, adding a further case to the practice of the past; by contrast, to avoid 'applying' the rule amounts to weakening it, adding a further case to those deviating from the practice of the past.[351] This process is profoundly different from the law of states in which written legislative law is the core of law. In domestic law, all that precedes the adoption of a statute (in particular the political competition among different groups and parties to have one or another bill approved) is legally irrelevant for the purposes of its legal existence, although it may be relevant later in view of its interpretation. In a law grounded in custom, by contrast, what 'precedes' the formation of a rule is *already* an integral part of the rule, although the rule comes into existence only when a sufficient level of support is reached. All international actors are *constantly* involved in the making and unmaking of international law. This is not to say that international law cannot be determined as sufficiently objective at a given moment. While every actor influences individual rules at every moment, there exists an international law objectively detectable at any given moment involving the attitude of the states as a whole adopted in the course of adequate time. This section will investigate how international law is changed by equity, soft law, judicial decisions, legal doctrine, and appeals to *jus cogens*. Its purpose is to show that not only should international law be changed, but that it also changes anyway as a (direct or indirect) result of the behaviour of all global actors and, in particular, of state organs.

(a) Equity

As the ICJ stated in the 1982 *Continental Shelf* Judgment: 'Equity as a legal concept is a direct emanation of the idea of justice'.[352] In international law equity has a variety of

[350] cf eg WTO, *United States—Standards for Reformulated and Conventional Gasoline*, AB Report of 29 April 1996, WTO Doc WT/DS2/AB/R, at 17; *Korea—Measures Affecting Government Procurement*, Panel Report of 1 May 2000, WT/DS163/R, para 7.96.

[351] There is no possibility for a state of changing customary international law other than by deviating from it in particular cases in the hope that other states will follow suit and a new rule will emerge. Statements may prove insufficient since custom does not emerge only by way of *opinio*. This deviation is objectively an unlawful act but its motivation makes it different from unlawful acts performed with no intent to change the law. Here the transgressor is prepared to accept that what it claims for itself also should apply to others.

[352] ICJ, *Case concerning the Continental Shelf (Tunisia/Libyan Arab Jamahiriya)* (n 263 above) para 71.

different meanings. The classical distinction, suggested by the ICJ in the *Frontier Dispute* Judgment,[353] is between equity *infra legem* or *secundum legem* (within the law), equity *praeter legem* (beyond the law) and equity *contra legem* (against the law).

Equity *infra legem* is interpretative in character and aimed at adjusting the law to the specific circumstances of the case in terms of 'individualized' justice. It is thus not an autonomous source of international law since its consideration is justified within the limits of what is permitted by the standard criteria used in international interpretation and stipulated in ad hoc legal rules, such as Articles 31 to 33 VCLT. Thus defined, equity was frequently resorted to in early arbitration settlements[354] and was endorsed by the Institut de Droit International (IDI) in 1937.[355] The ICJ noted in the 1969 *North Sea* Judgment that 'it is not a question of applying equity simply as a matter of abstract justice, but of applying a rule of law which itself requires the application of equitable principles',[356] and reiterated in the *Fisheries Jurisdiction* cases decided in 1974 that: 'It is not a matter of finding simply an equitable solution, but an equitable solution derived from the applicable law'.[357] In the 1986 *Frontier Dispute* Judgment an ICJ Chamber held that it could 'have regard to equity *infra legem*, that is, that form of equity which constitutes a method of interpretation of the law in force, and is one of its attributes', although it did so in regard to equity *infra legem* 'which both Parties have recognized as being applicable'.[358] As already held by the Court in the *Continental Shelf* case,[359] the Chamber argued that 'to resort to the concept of equity in order to modify an established frontier [inherited from the colonial powers] would be quite unjustified', especially in the African context, and declined to alter the frontier to reflect equity. However, where the boundary did not delimit in any precise manner an important water pool, the Court stated that 'the [boundary] line should divide the pool . . . in two, in an equitable manner' and '"equity does not necessarily imply equality"; where there are no special circumstances the latter is generally the best expression of the former'.[360] In the 2007 *Diallo* Judgment, however, the Court avoided considering equity *infra legem* and denied diplomatic protection on this basis in favour of shareholders of a company. It preferred to undertake a careful examination of 'State practice and decisions of international courts and tribunals' as evidence of CIL rather than relying on equity.[361]

353 ICJ Chamber, *Case concerning the Frontier Dispute (Burkina Faso/Republic of Mali)* (n 77 above) para 28.

354 See eg American and British Claims Arbitration Tribunal, *Cayuga Indians (Great Britain) v United States* Award of 22 January 1926, 6 RIAA 173, 179–83; Arbitral Tribunal, *Norwegian Shipowners' Claims (Norway v United States)* Award of 13 October 1922, 1 RIAA 307, 330–1. See further PCIJ, *The Diversion of Water from the Meuse (Netherlands v Belgium)* Judgment of 28 June 1937, PCIJ Series A/B No 70, individual opinion of Judge Hudson, at 73.

355 IDI 'La compétence du juge international en équité' (1937) 40 AIDI 132, 140.

356 ICJ, *North Sea Continental Shelf Cases* (n 80 above) para 85.

357 ICJ, *Fisheries Jurisdiction (United Kingdom v Iceland) (Merits)* Judgment of 25 July 1974, [1974] ICJ Rep 3, para 78; *Fisheries Jurisdiction (Federal Republic of Germany v Iceland) (Merits)* Judgment of 25 July 1974, [1974] ICJ Rep 175, para 69.

358 ICJ Chamber, *Case concerning the Frontier Dispute (Burkina Faso/Republic of Mali)* (n 77 above) paras 28 and 149; *Land, Island And Maritime Frontier Dispute (El Salvador/Honduras: Nicaragua Intervening)* Judgment of 11 September 1992, [1992] ICJ Rep 351, para 262.

359 See n 352 above.

360 ICJ Chamber, *Case concerning the Frontier Dispute (Burkina Faso/Republic of Mali)* (n 77 above) para 149.

361 ICJ, *Ahmadou Sadio Diallo (Republic of Guinea v Democratic Republic of the Congo) (Preliminary Objections)* Judgment of 24 May 2007, at <http://www.icj-cij.org/docket/files/103/13856.pdf>, para 89. A similar attitude has been adopted by the Court in its 2012 *Jurisdictional Immunities of the State* Judgment (n 85 above).

Equity *praeter legem* has an integrative character and is aimed at filling gaps in the law. It has been resorted to in the field of the delimitation of continental shelves, beginning with the ICJ 1969 *North Sea* Judgment. The Court ambiguously held that it 'was not applying equity simply as a matter of abstract justice, but applying a rule of law which itself requires the application of equitable principles'.[362] Judge Morelli suggested in his dissenting opinion that the Court acted as if there were a gap in the law to be filled by a reference to equity.[363]

Equity *contra legem* cannot, by definition, be a source of law.[364] Although both equity *infra legem* and equity *praeter legem* can spur a change in the law, it is specifically equity *contra legem* that is of particular importance for the purposes of changing international law. By way of illustration, it was on grounds of equity that, in the second half of the nineteenth century, Italian courts started to exercise their jurisdiction over acts of foreign states performed *jure gestionis*, as opposed to *jure imperii*, setting in motion the 'restrictive' doctrine of sovereign immunity, and it is apparently on this ground that they have sought in recent years to introduce a 'humanitarian exception' to foreign state jurisdictional immunity.[365] Equity *contra legem* can be used by a state to signal, expressly or impliedly, that a breach on its part of a given existing CIL rule is designed to set a precedent in the hope that other states will follow suit and current CIL will be changed. If the generality of states do so, the 'proposed' rule will come into being. In these instances, equity operates as *opinio necessitatis* for the purposes of the formation of a new future rule of CIL.

Article 38(2) ICJ Statute empowers the Court to decide a case *ex aequo et bono*, ie according to equity as opposed to according to law, provided that the parties to the dispute so agree. A similar provision is found in Article 293(2) UNCLOS. By contrast, Article 4(2) of the 2000 Algiers Agreement establishing the Eritrea–Ethiopia Boundary Commission provides that the Commission 'shall not have the power to make decisions *ex aequo et bono*'.[366] The WTO Panels and Appelate Body are not granted the power to judge *ex aequo et bono* either. Decisions *ex aequo et bono* are necessarily made 'in good conscience' and notwithstanding existing law. A rule is being created 'beyond the law' by the court or tribunal upon authorization of the parties. Its prevalence over other rules of international law as between the parties is based on the speciality of the treaty conferring on the court or the tribunal the power to adopt it.[367] It might also have an impact on the development of general international law should it be followed on account of its justness by the whole international community. In nineteenth- and twentieth-century arbitrations payments of interest and compensation for damages were often quantified *ex aequo et bono*, such as in the 1910 *Orinoco* Award[368] and in the 1922 *Norwegian Shipowners' Claims* Award.[369] However, the courts approach the issuance of decisions *ex aequo et bono* very cautiously. As the PCIJ held in an Order of 1930 in the *Free Zones* case, the power given to the Court 'to prescribe a settlement

[362] ICJ, *North Sea Continental Shelf Cases* (n 80 above) para 85.

[363] ibid dissenting opinion of Judge Morelli, [1969] ICJ Rep 198, para 19.

[364] ICJ Chamber, *Case concerning the Frontier Dispute (Burkina Faso/Republic of Mali)* (n 77 above) para 28.

[365] See Ch 7 below, section B (1)(a).

[366] Agreement between the Government of the State of Eritrea and the Government of the Federal Republic of Ethiopia of 12 December 2000, UN Doc A/55/686–S/2000/1183, at 2.

[367] On the speciality of treaties in respect of general international law, see section B (3)(b) above.

[368] Arbitral Tribunal, *Orinoco Steamship Co Case (United States v Venezuela)* Award of 25 October 1910, 11 RIAA 227, 240.

[369] Arbitral Tribunal, *Norwegian Shipowners' Claims* (n 354 above) 341.

disregarding rights recognized by it and taking into account considerations of pure expediency only' is 'of an absolutely exceptional character' and 'could only be derived from a clear and explicit provision to that effect'.[370] A restrictive interpretation was also given by the ICJ in the 1992 *Land, Island and Maritime Frontier Dispute* Judgment.[371] As is well known, to date no case has been submitted to both the ICJ and ITLOS in which the parties have authorized the Court or the Tribunal to decide *ex aequo et bono*. In the 1969 *North Sea* Judgment the ICJ insisted that its delimitation decisions were not *ex aequo et bono*.[372] In a sense this confirms that states trust international law as being sufficiently objective law distinct from equity.

(b) Soft law

The term 'soft law' is in vogue and often attached to the notion that its effectiveness 'on the ground' is greater than that of 'hard' (ie legally binding) international law. In a system where no effective and legitimate enforcer exists on a global level, states appear to be at liberty either to respect or disrespect any sort of norm, whether binding or not. Thus it seems only reasonable to suppose that non-binding norms (such as recommendations adopted by international bodies, UN General Assembly declarations of principles, codes of conduct, plans of action, findings of non-compliance by international mechanisms, various determinations by financial institutions, and the like) may work even better than those which are formally binding. The reasons why states may be more inclined to follow non-binding law are numerous and have been extensively studied, including speediness of drafting and adoption, the ease with which they can be changed, susceptibility to avoiding domestic constitutional procedures of control, and effective mutual pressure.[373] However, it is one thing to see how effective a certain standard is, but quite another to determine whether a standard amounts to law. All international players have a strong need to know what standards are expected to be the law in the international community. The fact that they may decide to defy the law, while conforming to soft law, pertains to their *individual* calculations, not to the law as their *common* framework. The assertion that the 'law' has been defied presupposes that one is able to discern what the law is, and this law cannot be anything other than 'hard' law. The suggestion that soft law can be 'in some sense' a law equivalent to (or even more effective and useful than) hard law is misleading. It is, once again, an attempt to smuggle for law applicable to all states what (rightly or wrongly) is merely the desired law of one or another circle of self-professed enlightened (either states, non-state actors, judges, or scholars).

Undoubtedly current international law and state behaviour are 'influenced' by non-state actors and their 'soft law', or 'informal law',[374] or even law made 'by

[370] PCIJ, *Case of the Free Zones of Upper Savoy and the District of Gex (France v Switzerland)* Order of 6 December 1930, PCIJ Series A No 24, at 10.

[371] ICJ Chamber, *Land, Island and Maritime Frontier Dispute (El Salvador/Honduras: Nicaragua Intervening)* Judgment of 11 September 1992, [1992] ICJ Rep 351, para 47.

[372] ICJ, *North Sea Continental Shelf Cases* (n 80 above) para 88.

[373] For a résumé, see D Shelton, 'Normative Hierarchy in International Law' (2006) 100 AJIL 291, 319–21. See extensively D Shelton (ed), *Commitment and Compliance: The Role of Non-binding Norms in the International Legal System* (Oxford: OUP, 2000).

[374] For the project named 'Informal International Law-Making: Mapping the Action and Testing Concepts of Accountability and Effectiveness', see <http://nilproject.org>. For an overview, see eg RA Wessel, 'Informal International Law-Making as a New Form of World Legislation?' (2011) 8 IOLR 253.

subterfuge'.[375] Besides IOs' agencies and transgovernmental bodies, as conceptualized in particular in terms of 'global administrative law'[376] or of 'a new world order',[377] of special interest are more or less 'confidentially operating' bodies in which high-ranking state organs participate in a private capacity, such as the Trilateral Commission,[378] the Council on Foreign Relations (CFR),[379] the Committee of 300,[380] and the Bilderberg Commission.[381] The arrangements of such bodies may be implemented by their members in the exercise of domestically granted formal powers, bypassing the traditional mechanisms of incorporation of international law within domestic legal systems and constitutional controls.[382] One may be tempted to call them 'law' even before they become domestic law and conclude that *this* increasingly *is* today *real* international law. It is true that this soft law may be more effective than hard law. It is also true that hard law may well prove unsuitable or unable to regulate certain areas of human behaviour. Yet, to argue that soft law is 'law' is hardly less than discarding law proper and leaving human relationships to the haphazard nature of informal standards which no one sees as legal rules to be observed. The game may work for some time but with no certainty (other than that based on personal trust, and perhaps gain) for any participant in the game, which in practice means with reasonable certainty only for the stronger on the ground. Pressures of any kind 'impacting' on the formal creation of law have always existed. Earthquakes and corruption also have an impact on the law, but are not the law. The recurrent idea that today international soft or informal law is more important than international hard law may well be reflective of realities, but this simply means that law is, for good or ill, more and more *absent* from realities.

This is not to deny that soft law has an important systemic role to play in international law.[383] While incapable of generating 'instant' custom,[384] soft law may express the *opinio juris* of the international community and thus have an effect on the formation of CIL, as noted (in respect of UN General Assembly resolutions) in the 1986 *Sedco* Award by the US–Iran Tribunal[385] and in the 1996 *Nuclear Weapons* Advisory Opinion by the ICJ.[386] It may, of course, reflect CIL when its contents correspond to both the generalized practice and *opinio juris* of the international community. It may also catalyse the consent of states in view of the conclusion of a treaty having the same content, as was the case with the principles governing outer space.[387] Most importantly, soft law is crucial to the dynamics of international law. It

375 Alvarez (n 144 above) 217. For the notion of 'Global Governance Organizations' (GGOs) formally and informally interacting on a regular basis and creating linkages as well as 'a web of transnational rules and regulations', see JGS Koppell, *World Rule: Accountability, Legitimacy, and the Design of Global Governance* (Chicago: University of Chicago Press, 2010).

376 See Ch 4 above, section B (8).

377 See Ch 4 above, n 241.

378 See <http://www.trilateral.org>. See S Gill, *American Hegemony and the Trilateral Commission* (Cambridge: CUP, 1990).

379 See <http://www.cfr.org>.

380 See <http://www.whale.to/b/300.html>.

381 See <http://www.bilderbergmeetings.org/index.html>.

382 See section D (2) below, especially notes 586–7 and accompanying text.

383 For a defence of UN General Assembly resolutions as a 'cognitive basis' of international law from a transcivilizational perspective for universal legitimacy purposes, see Onuma (n 74 above) 238–44.

384 B Cheng, 'United Nations Resolutions on Outer Space: "Instant" International Customary Law?' (1965) 23 Indian JIL 23.

385 Iran–US Claims Tribunal, *SEDCO Inc v National Iranian Oil Co & Islamic Republic of Iran* Award of 27 March 1986, No ITL 59-129-3, Case No 129, (1986) 84 ILR 521, 533–4.

386 ICJ, *Legality of the Threat or Use of Nuclear Weapons* (n 88 above) paras 70–71.

387 UNGA Res 1962 (XVIII) of 13 December 1963, 'Declaration of Legal Principles Governing the Activities of States in the Exploration and Use of Outer Space' GAOR 18th Session Supp 15, 15, paving the way for the 1967 Treaty on the Outer Space (see Ch 5 above, n 190).

constantly informs all international actors about what behaviour is recommended (although not sanctioned as law) by the generality of other actors and about the direction of the law in its progress towards likely future changes. This kind of information, which may be of minor relevance in domestic legal systems, is vital in a world of 'peers' devoid of a universal superior government.

When soft law does not reflect existing law, it is still important to *promote* a future law which is believed, rightly or wrongly, to be better and fitter for the international community as a whole. This holds particularly true for UN General Assembly declarations of principles adopted with the vote of the vast majority of states. In promoting future hard law, soft law in a sense makes the former come into being since soft law 'posits' the first elements that, together with others, could indeed give rise to a future hard law rule. Advocates of soft law have their sights on new law, rightly assuming that a new law needs pressure from the present and that future law will necessarily have the contents which have won the earlier competition. International and domestic courts should not apply international soft law as the law 'in force', but, supreme domestic courts in particular, should consider soft law when making decisions aimed at innovating international law on grounds of greater global justice, as this is objectively found in practice rather than merely being inspired by subjective or unilateral impressions. A change in international law is not only inevitable but also much more likely to occur—and its violation is much less likely to be perceived as a 'pure' unlawful act—if evidence is given that some universal, objectively verifiable consensus exists.

(c) *Judicial decisions*

International law is far from being the law stated by the courts.[388] In most cases international law has no chance to progress to being discussed and stated by international courts.[389] Domestic courts, for their part, are called upon to decide international law issues relatively often, but they do so also in accordance with domestic law and their decisions have formal legal effects only within their legal systems.

Article 38(1)(d) of the ICJ Statute provides that the Court, the function of which is to decide in accordance with international law the disputes submitted to it, shall apply, 'subject to the provisions of Article 59', among other things, the 'judicial decisions... as subsidiary means for the determination of rules of law'. Article 59 stipulates that the decisions of the Court 'have no binding force except between the parties and in respect of that particular case', thus confirming that they cannot be sources of international law applicable to any other state in any other case. Judicial decisions do not qualify as sources of international law, but may contribute to identifying the norms of international law as they derive from the sources. The silence of Article 38(1)(d) ICJ Statute on whether it refers only to decisions of international courts or also to decisions of domestic courts could easily be intended in the broader sense.

Leaving aside their formal consent-based bindingness vis-à-vis the parties to the dispute, such as those delivered by the ICJ itself, international courts' and tribunals' judicial decisions not only 'apply' international law as it stands but also contribute to the formation of general international law as an expression of *opinio juris*—particularly authoritative when it comes from the ICJ as 'the principal judicial organ of the

[388] See eg JC Gray, *The Nature and Sources of the Law* (New York: Columbia University Press, 1909) 125, arguing that 'all the Law is judge-made Law'.
[389] See section C (1)(c) below.

United Nations' under Article 1 ICJ Statute[390]—sustained by the states which are parties to their particular statutes. In this respect there is no significant difference between (binding) judgments and (non-binding) advisory opinions since both have the same chance to develop general international practice. One or a few decisions may be insufficient to prove the existence of a norm of general international law, especially if they are not accompanied by the actual practice of states. The tendency in legal doctrine to quote this or that decision or passage as 'evidence' of *existing* norms should be treated with caution. It may, however, work as a strategy to accelerate a *change* in the law. Advisory opinions may be even more effective than judgments in expressing an *opinio necessitatis* when they argue for the necessity of a new international law which is non-existent at that time, thus seeking to spur a change in the practice and hence in the law, as evidenced, for example, by the developments in the field of reservations to treaties following the 1951 *Reservations* Advisory Opinion.[391]

Domestic judicial decisions come from individual states and cannot *a fortiori* qualify as sources of international law. However, they can and do influence the making and unmaking of international law as an expression both of *opinio necessitatis*, when they propose new norms deemed to be more in line with social needs,[392] and as direct state practice, especially in those areas of international law, such as jurisdictional immunity, in which they play a prominent role. As the House of Lords held in the 2006 *Jones* Judgment 'one swallow does not make a rule of international law',[393] which means that domestic judicial decisions—in the instant case the target being the *Ferrini* decision adopted by the Italian Court of Cassation in 2004[394]—are relevant only if they reflect a generalized and uniform practice concerning courts of several states and cases. Domestic supreme courts naturally have a greater weight than lower courts as an expression of the ultimate position of the state as a whole, at least from the perspective of its judicial branch. In the absence of a universal law-maker, domestic courts are key factors in the making and unmaking of international law also when, as is generally the case, they construe and apply international law 'as it stands'. When they 'apply' international law, they reinforce the rule applied; in reverse, when they refrain from applying international law for any reason, including on grounds of their (interpretation of) domestic law, they weaken the rule potentially applicable.[395]

Domestic courts should be mindful of their role in reinforcing or weakening the norms of international law and assume the responsibility of performing their function from the more general perspective of the global system which they affect *in any case*, whether they apply or refuse to apply international law. This is no longer a 'political'

[390] It is also to be considered that international decisions have a different weight as a function of the support they presumably have from states. For example, the decisions of the ICJ must be deemed to have much more weight than the decisions delivered by arbitral tribunals because the former are far more likely to reflect the overall view and attitude of states (with a concomitant prudence to avoid dicta manifestly unacceptable even to third states which are potential parties), while the latter basically rest on the support and 'legitimacy' conferred thereon by the parties in bilateral agreements or relationships.

[391] ICJ, *Reservations to the Convention on the Prevention and Punishment of the Crime of Genocide* (n 126 above).

[392] This is how the 2004 *Ferrini* decision of the Italian Court of Cassation denying jurisdictional immunity to Germany for alleged commission of international crimes should be understood. cf Italian Court of Cassation, *Ferrini v Federal Republic of Germany* Judgment of 11 March 2004 No 5044, (2004) 128 ILR 658. On this question, see Ch 7 below, section B (1)(a).

[393] UK House of Lords, *Jones v Ministry of Interior Al-Mamlaka Al-Arabiya AS Saudiya* (n 100 above) para 22 (*per* Lord Bingham of Cornhill).

[394] See n 392 above.

[395] It is in this sense that the House of Lords' *Jones* decision (n 393 above) should be read.

role to be reserved to the executive branch as in the past. Today, international law broadly governs the lives of individuals within national communities, and domestic courts can no longer strip themselves of the duty to apply it and to deliver justice to individuals also in accordance with global standards.

(d) Scholarship

Article 38(1)(d) of the ICJ Statute provides that the Court shall apply, among other things, the 'teachings of the most highly qualified publicists' of the various nations, as a 'subsidiary means' for the determination of rules of law.[396] Like judicial decisions, the teachings of the most highly qualified publicists, ie scholarship or doctrine, do not qualify as sources of international law, but may contribute to identifying the norms of international law. Unlike judicial decisions, however, scholarship unrelated to states does not formally contribute to the formation of general international law.

Legal doctrine includes not only individual scholars, but also private (national and transnational) associations committed to the study and elaboration of international law, such as the American Society of International Law (ASIL), the European Society of International Law (ESIL), the Asian Society of International Law (AsianSIL), the Institut de Droit International (IDI),[397] national 'task forces',[398] and so on. Their work may carry special weight in the light of the authority and reputation of their members and the level of academic analysis.[399] The IDI adopts 'resolutions' which may have some weight in legal argumentation but clearly lack legal force. The ILC, which could also be viewed as legal doctrine,[400] often relies heavily on academic writings. International and domestic courts have frequently referred to ILC drafts, especially the Articles on State Responsibility, as 'evidence' of general international law.[401] The tendency to regard such resolutions and documents as evidence of international law should be treated cautiously since they are not in themselves sources of legal rules and their makers are unable to ensure their effectiveness.

The view that the work of jurists is relevant to the identification of international law has been generally accepted, although with vigilance. As early as 1778 the English Court of Admiralty in *The Renard* held that: 'A pedantic man in his closet dictates the law of nations; and who shall decide, when doctors disagree? Bynkershoek, as is natural to every writer or speaker who comes after another, is delighted to contradict Grotius'.[402] In 1826 James Kent, however, acknowledged that: 'In cases where the principal jurists agree, the presumption will be very great in favour of their maxims'.[403] A reference to 'the works of jurists and commentators' as 'evidence' of the 'customs and

[396] See generally 'Scholars in the Construction and Critique of International Law' (2000) 94 ASIL Proc 317; JL Dunoff, 'International Legal Scholarship at the Millennium' (2000) 1 Chic JIL 85–92; WJ Aceves, 'Symposium Introduction: Scholarship as Evidence of International Law' (2003) 26 LLA ICLR 1.

[397] G Fitzmaurice, 'The Contribution of the Institute of International Law to the Development of International Law' (1973) 138 RdC 203.

[398] See eg the Genocide Prevention Task Force, launched on 13 November 2007, and its report released to the public on 8 December 2008, at <http://www.ushmm.org/genocide/taskforce>.

[399] see Onuma (n 74 above) 190–1, arguing for 'a plurality of active academic societies that can compete with each other'.

[400] For a critical appraisal, see M Koskenniemi, 'International Legislation Today: Limits and Possibilities' (2005) 23 Wisc ILJ 61.

[401] J Crawford and S Olleson, 'The Continuing Debate on a UN Convention on State Responsibility' (2005) 54 ICLQ 959; J Crawford, A Pellet, and S Olleson, *The Law of International Responsibility* (Oxford: OUP, 2010).

[402] English High Court of Admiralty, *The 'Renard'* Judgment of 9 December 1778, [1778] 165 ER 51, 52.

[403] cf J Kent, *Commentaries on American Law* [1826–1830] (New York: Da Capo Press, 1971) vol 1, 18.

usages of civilized nations' was made by the US Supreme Court in the 1900 *The Paquete Habana* Judgment.[404] As Chief Justice Fuller, dissenting, stated in the same case, however: 'Their lucubrations may be persuasive, but not authoritative'.[405] A rather critical approach to scholarship was taken by Judge Robb in his concurring opinion appended to the 1984 *Tel Oren* Judgment.[406] Still, it is a fact that more often than not judges take inspiration and knowledge from doctrinal writings, whether they quote publicists or not, when they apply international law.

In the 1927 *Lotus* Judgment the PCIJ referred to the 'teachings of publicists', but left open 'the question as to what their value may be from the point of view of establishing the existence of a rule of customary international law'.[407] The ICJ has very rarely expressly mentioned specific publicists, an exception being the 1992 *Land, Island and Maritime Frontier Dispute* Judgment.[408] Other international courts have been far more prone to rely on scholarship. The ECtHR has often done so, as occurred, just to name a few well-known cases, in the 2001 *Bankovic* Decision,[409] in the 2007 *Jorgic* Judgment,[410] and in the 2007 *Behrami* Decision.[411] A similarly receptive attitude has been exhibited by the ICTY and the ICTR, as well as by the WTO Appellate Body.

A key role of legal doctrine has always been the promotion of new norms in the light of the analysis of social realities and flaws in existing international law. Legal doctrine provides the more general framework within which individual cases and rules should be seen to make sense and be operative in practice.[412] This promotional role of legal doctrine dates back to Grotius, who wrote in his *De Jure Belli ac Pacis* of 1625 that a general treatment of the rules applicable to armed conflicts, ie what is today known as

[404] US Supreme Court, *The Paquete Habana* (n 261 above) 700. [405] ibid 720.

[406] Court of Appeals for the District of Columbia Circuit, *Tel-Oren v Libyan Arab Republic* Judgment of 3 February 1984, (1988) 77 ILR 252.

[407] PCIJ, *The Case of the SS Lotus* (n 182 above) 26.

[408] ICJ Chamber, *Land, Island and Maritime Frontier Dispute* (n 371 above) para 394.

[409] ECtHR, *Bankovic et al v Belgium et al* Decision of 12 December 2001 [GC], App 52,207/99, ECtHR Rep 2001-XII 333, paras 35–36.

[410] ECtHR, *Jorgic v Federal Republic of Germany* Judgment of 12 July 2007, App 74,613/01, ECtHR Rep 2007-IX, paras 36, 107, 111.

[411] ECtHR, *Agim Behrami and Bekir Behrami v France and Ruzhdi Saramati v France, Germany and Norway* Decision of admissibility of 2 May 2007 [GC], Apps 71412/01 and 78166/01, 45 EHRR SE10, para 130.

[412] O Schachter, 'The Invisible College of International Lawyers' (1977) 72 NwU LR 217. For criticisms, see J Goldsmith, 'Sovereignty, International Relations Theory, and International Law: Sovereignty: Organized Hypocrisy' (2000) 52 Stan LR 959, 982; J Goldsmith, 'Remarks' in 'Scholars in the Construction and Critique of International Law' (n 396 above) 319, arguing that 'international law scholarship is characterized by normative rather than positive argument, and by idealism and advocacy rather than scepticism and detachment'. This is true and certainly there may be some undue exaggeration in 'advocacy' by self-professed legal analysts who are expected to be less influenced by their desired goals than, say, NGOs and MNEs' marketing strategies. It is also true that, once it is conceded that jurists may work for what each of them sees as the 'better' law, no matter how anchored in actual realities and interests, the international law discourse becomes a Babel of conjectures at best, in which opinions inflate and all end up losing their value. Equally true is the observation that generally 'international law scholars view themselves as a source of law' which they certainly are not. This same book argues that international law as social construct has to be a law actually found in society rather than in the minds of this or that expert or professional. However, it is also a contention of this book that jurists (presumably unlike IR theorists) are not scientists, although they may fruitfully use scientific methods, and cannot but deal with justice, policy, and what IR realists see as 'idealism', 'bias', 'normativism', and, in the final analysis, engagement. In this sense there is nothing wrong with idealism, contrary to what IR realists would have people believe, and law promotion is indeed a due task of jurists. On the other hand, even realism is a doctrine with its own presuppositions and goals, ie an 'ideal' which is thought to be better than others in describing 'reality' and in directing action for the (supposed) better.

international law, were urgently needed to bring about peace in Europe at the time.[413] Today, scholars (together with states and non-state actors) are particularly committed to promoting 'new' norms, pre-eminently by stating that existing rules must be read in line with the fundamental values of the international community. Their impact beyond the circle of the specialists and some courts is limited, however.[414] Domestic courts, although not bound to follow doctrinal opinions, should consider legal doctrine with reference to its endeavour to clarify existing international law and, most importantly, to keep international law 'in motion' to ensure that it keeps up with the changes in global social realities.[415]

(e) Public opinion and epistemic communities

People can influence the behaviour of both states and non-state actors, in particular by modifying their interest recalculation.[416] While states and other organizations are necessary in order to catalyse and strengthen public opinion and avoid leaving individuals alone in the fight, they are at the same time influenced by public opinion.[417] To say that it is 'states' that essentially handle international law is by no means to imply that people are not involved in international affairs. States are constantly shaped (for good or ill) by the people. Even in authoritarian regimes can one reasonably suppose that people count in terms of whether the ruler remains in power. The same applies of course *a fortiori* in democratic regimes. Everything depends on how people as a whole, within and outside states, conceive of states and the way states should behave. Nothing prevents people from believing in states which operate in the service of humankind to the fullest extent feasible while retaining their sovereignty as limited by the common rules of international law. The perception that states are 'egoistic' is often real, but this reality is socially constructed just like any other and can be changed if most people were to take the opposite attitude, whether voluntarily or forcefully as a result of the prospect of global catastrophes or other adverse consequences affecting all.

The term 'public opinion', just like 'civil society', let alone 'global civil society',[418] is very broad indeed. It may comprise single individuals and groups capable of mobilizing other people and state authorities for a given cause,[419] transnational NGOs, NGO

[413] H Grotius, *De Jure Belli ac Pacis Libri Tres* [1625], English trans *On the Law of War and Peace Three Books* (Washington, DC, Oxford, and London: Carnegie Institution, Clarendon Press, and Humphrey Milford, 1925), 'Prolegomena', paras 28–30.

[414] Suffice it to recall the letter 'War would be Illegal' written by a number of distinguished international law scholars which was published in *The Guardian* on 7 March 2003, available at <http://www.guardian.co.uk/politics/2003/mar/07/highereducation.iraq> and the 'Appel de juristes de droit international concernant le recours à la force contre l'Iraq', reprinted in (2003) 36 RBDI 266, both remained unheard among policy-makers and public opinion as well as in the media themselves.

[415] Courts and tribunals may also adopt regressive views based on scholarship. For example, in *Cayuga Indians (Great Britain) v United States* (n 354 above), 176, the American and British Claims Arbitration Tribunal relied on Hyde to state that the '"Cayuga Nation", an Indian tribe . . . is not a legal unit of international law' because 'The American Indians have never been so regarded'.

[416] See n 423 below.

[417] See S Odugbemi and T Lee (eds), *Accountability through Public Opinion: From Inertia to Public Action* (Washington, DC: The World Bank, 2010).

[418] See J Keane, *Global Civil Society?* (Cambridge: CUP, 2003).

[419] A case in point is the mobilization sparked by Henri Dunant (after having witnessed the inhumane consequences of the battle of Solferino of 1959), which led to the creation of the Red Cross in 1863 (see Ch 5 above, section C (5)(c)) and the conclusion of the Geneva Convention for the Amelioration of the Condition of the Wounded in Armies in the Field (signed 22 August 1864, entered into force 22 June 1865) 129 CTS 361. For insights into these events from a IR constructivist

networks, and coalitions,[420] as well as resistance movements.[421] Another source of influence on state behaviour are 'epistemic communities', defined as 'communities of shared knowledge', of scientists and experts who share similar beliefs and act as informally coordinated lobbying groups, as such distinct from interest groups, popular mass opinion, and international law scholarship itself.[422] The epistemic communities of ecologists and marine scientists, for example, have been found to play a significant role in promoting and monitoring environmental treaties, while other factors, such as coercion, public opinion, and anticipation of benefits, have proved less influential. Following the involvement of epistemic communities, state interests and behaviour (including domestic implementation of international rules) have come more and more to reflect their view in diverse policy domains, such as environmental protection and nuclear non-proliferation.

One may object that the impact of public opinion and epistemic communities on international law is minimal, at best. Constructivists generally counter that neither states' not individuals' interests are fixed. It is assumed here, however, that even such an assertion is open to construction, in the sense that states' and individuals' interests *may well* be fixed *if people so believe*.[423] This means that anti-constructivists may be perfectly right when claiming that states' and individuals' interests are in fact far more fixed than constructivists admit. The key point is what the people involved believe. Even assuming that anti-constructivists were to be right in respect of what occurs in a certain place among certain people today, this proves nothing as to the possibility of changing not only the law but (so to speak, 'upstream') the very idea that interests are fixed and cannot be changed for a new law tomorrow. This belief itself is subject to social construction, and social construction may operate in both directions (either fixity or change) or, more plausibly, more towards one than the other.

Another diffused, related objection is that statehood and humankind are incompatible because states by nature pursue their self-interest, and in this real world what is in

perspective, see M Finnemore, *National Interests in International Society* (New York: Cornell University Press, 1996) 68–88. Other well-known civil-society movements include that against the slave trade and those for peace, worker solidarity, free trade, international law, and NGO promotion. On the anti-slave movement, see J Jennings, *The Business of Abolishing the British Slave Trade, 1783–1807* (Abingdon and New York: Routledge, 1997); Keane (n 418 above) 153, noting that 'the campaign to abolish the slave trade . . . was arguably the first moral entrepreneur to emerge out of the structures of civil society, to play a prominent role in world politics by pressing for new prohibition laws that would apply globally'; and the sceptical remarks by I Clark, *International Legitimacy and World Society* (Oxford: OUP, 2007) 47–58. For a valuable historical account, see S Charnovitz, 'Two Centuries of Participation: NGOs and International Governance' (1997) 18 Mich JIL 183, arguing for a 'cyclical pattern' of ONG involvement apparently depending on governments' needs and suggesting that 'in some ways NGO penetration into international organizations is no deeper than it was seventy years ago' (ibid 190).

420 See Ch 5 above, section C (3)(a).

421 See Ch 5 above, section C (4)(d).

422 PM Haas, 'Do Regimes Matter? Epistemic Communities and Mediterranean Pollution' (1989) 43 *International Organization* 377; PM Haas, 'Epistemic Communities and International Policy Coordination' (1992) 46 *International Organization* 1; E Adler, 'The Emergence of Cooperation: National Epistemic Communities and the International Evolution of the Idea of Nuclear Arms Control' (1992) 46 *International Organization* 101; JK Sebenius, 'Challenging Conventional Explanations of International Cooperation: Negotiation Analysis and the Case of Epistemic Communities' (1992) 46 *International Organization* 323; E Adler and PM Haas, 'Conclusion: Epistemic Communities, World Order, and the Creation of a Reflective Research Program' (1992) 46 *International Organization* 367; TW Craig, 'Public Management as Interagency Cooperation: Testing Epistemic Community Theory at the Domestic Level' (1997) 2 JPART 221.

423 For IR constructivism, see Ch 2 above, n 13. For the specific constructionist approach developed in this book, see the final critical observations in Ch 4 above, section B (6).

the interest of one state is inevitably and inextricably against the interest of another. But, here again, nothing prevents people from believing otherwise. Indeed, civil society cannot be set against the state, as was done in the nineteenth century,[424] nor can it replace the state in its essential function of governing people. The function of civil society is to be explained precisely in the context of the state and, at the global level, of the states system. The universal community of human beings needs states, or other political organizations yet to come. For the time being it is for states, the authority of which is grounded in their respective national communities, to use their authority to administer international law. It is thus vital to foster a global social climate 'from below' which demands that states manage and change international law for the benefit of all. States are not necessarily 'egoistic' entities detached from their (or other) populations. Rather, they are the expression of their populations (whether egoistic or solidaristic) and can be transformed and made to operate in the service of the global system. Briefly, public opinion and epistemic communities have no direct *legal* character, but have an indirect one that is *crucial* to the reality, effectiveness, change, and justice of international law.

It is true, at the same time, that public opinion and expert technocracies may turn out to be as dangerous as states themselves. In so far as states reflect public opinion it is unsurprising that the risks associated with states can also be found in public opinion itself. In the post-World War I debate about the role of public opinion in international law for a 'new international order' shifting from state authoritarianism towards individual empowerment, triggered in particular by US President Woodrow Wilson as early as July 1918 in his 'Four Points' address at Mount Vernon, several leading European writers who were favourable in principle to democracy and individual empowerment took a very cautious attitude.[425] It was obvious that mass public opinion was pushing states like Italy and Germany towards totalitarianism. For this reason it is necessary to side with, and struggle for, one sense of justice as opposed to others. This book suggests that public opinion is to be hailed when it pushes for the protection of the world's most vulnerable.[426]

(f) Jus cogens

Article 53 VCLT stipulates that 'A treaty is void if, at the time of its conclusion, it conflicts with a peremptory norm of general international law' and defines such a 'jus cogens' norm for the purposes of the Convention as 'a norm accepted and recognized by the international community of States as a whole as a norm from which no derogation is permitted and which can be modified only by a subsequent norm of general international law having the same character'. In the event of the emergence of a new peremptory norm of general international law, Article 64 VCLT provides that 'any existing treaty which is in conflict with that norm becomes void and terminates'.[427] *Jus cogens* is thus conceived of as a ground for invalidity or termination of conflicting

[424] M Kaldor, *Global Civil Society: An Answer to War* (Cambridge: Polity Press, 2003) 15–49; T Toyoda, 'Influence of Public Opinion on International Law in the Nineteenth Century' 46 Alb LR (2009) 1099.

[425] JE Nijman, *The Concept of International Legal Personality. An Inquiry into the History and Theory of International Law* (The Hague: TMC Asser Press, 2004) 100, 123–6.

[426] See Ch 2 above, section B (1).

[427] Other auxiliary VCLT provisions dealing with *jus cogens* are Art 44(5), Art 66, and Art 71, concerning non-separability of the treaty conflicting with *jus cogens*, submission to the ICJ of disputes over *jus cogens*, and effects of invalidity and termination of conflicting treaties, respectively.

treaties. No mention of which norms are peremptory is made. Scholars have often drawn from a variety of sources, including state statements; lists of peremptory norms which generally include those prohibiting aggression, genocide, torture, slavery, racial discrimination, apartheid, as well as the principle of self-determination of peoples; and the fundamental norms of humanitarian international law.[428]

Article 53 was adopted with the strong support of Third World and Socialist states and some scepticism, if not opposition, from Western states.[429] *Jus cogens* was regarded by non-Western states as a technical tool to supersede traditional (European, colonialist, and capitalist) international law by new principles worked out by the whole of states,[430] or at least (from the Soviet perspective) to protect the principles underlying the doctrine of peaceful coexistence.[431] Eventually, *jus cogens* was accepted by Western states on condition that the ICJ be given jurisdiction over its determination, a clause that was included in Article 66(a) VCLT.

The language of Article 53 leaves a variety of questions open. It is apparent that *jus cogens* can only relate to 'general' norms of international law and should enjoy 'acceptance and recognition' by the 'international community of states as a whole' as a body of rules 'from which no derogation is permitted' and which can be 'modified' only by a subsequent norm of general international law having the same character. A treaty 'is void' if it conflicts with *jus cogens* thus defined. The uncertainty of the meaning to be given to those expressions raises confusion as to what exactly the states parties are bound to. For a norm to be 'general', as a precondition of *jus cogens*, it must be supported by the generalized *usus* and *opinio juris*, or else it must meet the requirements of general principles of law recognized by civilized nations. But a general principle of law recognized by civilized nations can apply only in the absence of relevant CIL and cannot prevail over contrary CIL.[432] On the other hand, if a generalized practice exists and supports a given CIL rule, it is difficult to see how another equally general international law rule belonging to *jus cogens* may exist *at the same time*. General practice cannot be on both sides if the two sides are in conflict. Nor is it tenable to argue that *jus cogens* requires only a generalized *opinio juris* about the peremptory character of the rule, whatever the *usus*, since if the practice is manifestly at odds with the purported *jus cogens* rule there is no reason why the latter should be seen as generally 'accepted and recognized' against all evidence to the contrary.[433] For similar reasons the view that *jus cogens* needs to give more importance to *opinio juris* than when establishing ordinary custom is also untenable.[434] What Article 53 states is only that while an 'ordinary' general international law can be derogated from by way of treaty, this is not possible when the law which is derogated from belongs to *jus cogens*.[435]

[428] For a more detailed analysis and further references, see C Focarelli, 'Promotional *Jus Cogens*: A Critical Appraisal of *Jus Cogens*' Legal Effects' (2008) 77 Nord JIL 429.

[429] The major opponent to *jus cogens* was France (in *United Nations Conference on the Law of Treaties*, First Session (Vienna, 26 March–24 May 1968), *Official Records*, Summary Records of the Plenary Meetings of the Committee of the Whole, at 309–10, paras 26–34). Doubts were also cast by Switzerland (ibid 323–4, paras 25–31). Other Western states were more accommodating, especially considering that *jus cogens* was bound to protect basic human rights that were deemed to be in common with Socialist and Third World states.

[430] See eg the statement at the Vienna Conference of Sierra Leone, ibid 300, para 9.

[431] See eg the statements of Romania and Ukraine, ibid 312–13, paras 55–63, and 322, para 6.

[432] See section B (1)(d) above.

[433] See the discussion on 'opinio juris No 2' by K Kawasaki, 'A Brief Note on the Legal Effects of *Jus Cogens* in International Law' (2006) 34 Hitotsubashi Journal of Law and Politics 27, 29–31.

[434] See n 110 above.

[435] U Linderfalk, 'The Creation of *Jus Cogens*: Making Sense of Article 53 of the Vienna Convention' (2011) 71 ZaöRV 359.

Jus cogens has been predominantly conceptualized in terms of the identification of peremptory norms. The main reason is that the 1969 Vienna Convention, while defining *jus cogens* and contemplating invalidity and termination as special effects affecting incompatible treaties, fails to enumerate what norms are to be considered peremptory. In recent times *jus cogens* has been invoked and applied 'beyond' the Vienna Convention in legal contexts other than the law of treaties (such as state responsibility, state creation, international crimes, etc) with a variety of other effects. Courts and writers have progressively assumed that *jus cogens* must bring about a virtually unlimited number of 'overriding', if not 'constitutional', effects. Concomitantly, other definitions of *jus cogens* have been proposed with a view to conveying the idea that *jus cogens* is a 'higher-in-rank' law or a law 'taking precedence' over all other international norms, as is the case with the 1998 *Furundžija* Judgment[436] and the 2005 *Yusuf* and *Kadi* Judgments[437] delivered by the ICTY and by the EU Court of First Instance, respectively. Underlying this reasoning is the notion that *jus cogens* constitutes a sort of an 'insurmountable minimum'—aimed at protecting the fundamental interests and values of the international community as a whole—from which no deviation, for any reason, is permitted.[438] Unfortunately this notion may be given a virtually endless variety of equally plausible legal meanings. Mere knowledge that an international norm is 'peremptory' or 'non-derogable' does not help much in determining exactly *what* legal effects are produced. It does not seem sufficient today to know that a norm is peremptory; what is also necessary is to know what special effect it brings about, since *not all* conceivable special effects seem to be brought about at one time and in any area of international law. Certain effects have been excluded in national and international jurisprudence, some are in competition with one another, and others are so far-reaching in their efforts to put into practice the overriding character of *jus cogens* as to raise serious doubts regarding their very feasibility (notably the retrospective application of the present-day legal regime of international crimes as a 'special effect' derogating from intertemporal law).[439]

[436] ICTY, *Prosecutor v Furundžija* Trial Chamber Judgment of 10 December 1998, Case No IT-95-17/I-T, (1999) 38 ILM 317, paras 153–154, stating that *jus cogens* 'enjoys a higher rank in the international hierarchy than treaty law and even "ordinary" customary rules' in that it corresponds to an 'absolute value from which nobody must deviate' thereby specifying that it 'cannot be derogated from by States through international treaties or local or special customs or even general customary rules not endowed with the same normative force'.

[437] EU CFI, Case T-306/01 *Yusuf and Al Barakaat International Foundation v Council of the European Union and Commission of the European Communities and United Kingdom (intervening)* [2005] ECR II-3533, para 227, Judgment of 21 September 2005; Case T-315/01 *Kadi v Council of the European Union and Commission of the European Communities and United Kingdom (intervening)* [2005] ECR II-3649, para 226, Judgment of 21 September 2005. In 2008 the ECJ reversed the *Kadi* and *Yusuf* decisions of first instance without taking a stance on the point of *jus cogens*. cf ECJ, Case C-402/05 P *Kadi v Council of the European Union and Commission of the European Communities* [2008] ECR I-6351, Appeal Judgment of 3 September 2008, para 329.

[438] For a recent example, among many others, see the 2010 *Habib* Judgment (n 632 below) paras 8 and 9, in which the Federal Court of Australia held that 'Torture offends the ideal of a common humanity and the Parliament has declared it to be a crime wherever outside Australia it is committed', thus reflecting 'the status of the prohibition against torture as a peremptory norm of international law from which no derogation is permitted and the consensus of the international community that torture can never be justified by official acts or policy' (*per* Black CJ).

[439] See Focarelli (n 428 above) 439–44. Of particular interest is the recent *Jurisdictional Immunities of the State* Judgement of the ICJ (n 85 above) paras 95–96. After having defined a *jus cogens* rule as 'one from which no derogation is permitted', the Court held that, even assuming that the rules allegedly breached by Germany were peremptory (paras 93 and 97), 'the rules which determine the scope and extent of jurisdiction [of foreign states in domestic courts] and when that jurisdiction may be exercised do not derogate from those substantive rules which possess *jus cogens* status, nor is there

A criterion is vital in order to determine which effects are produced and which are not. Most scholars tend to adopt a deductive approach,[440] ie to infer a variety of 'special' or 'derogatory' effects which are deemed to be virtually unlimited, not unlike the way constitutional norms operate within domestic legal systems, or the very notion of *jus cogens*, or the need to effectively safeguard basic human rights or the global inter-state system.[441] The 'deductivist' doctrine does not ignore practice and underlines that it is precisely in the practice, especially in recent years, that *jus cogens* can objectively be found. However, as already remarked, there is no point in ascertaining whether a specific norm is 'peremptory' if the special legal effect that one would draw from this label is neither certain nor automatic. It seems that the only sufficiently objective criterion to this end, as in international law in general, is states' practice and *opinio juris ac necessitatis* concerning the *specific derogatory effect* rather than the generic classification of the norm at issue as 'peremptory' or 'non-derogable'—two terms which clearly bear a variety of different legal meanings. According to this approach no special effect of *jus cogens* can be syllogistically drawn from any premise, whether conceptual or empirical. But if international practice is always necessary, even to confirm inferences, then the 'surviving' notion of *jus cogens* overlaps with 'ordinary' general international law. Either the specific effect ascribed to *jus cogens* reflects generalized practice and *opinio*, in which case it is 'ordinary' international law, or it does not, but then there can be no 'general' international law supporting the effect ascribed to *jus cogens* and *jus cogens* is appealed to in the hope that the desired effect will become part of general international law in the future. In the second case *jus cogens* is invoked provisionally as long as it acquires the status of general international law. Once the new norm is established, there is no longer any need to invoke *jus cogens*.

The question is, thus, whether *jus cogens* has a specificity and a rationale other than denoting 'higher-in-rank' international law. Thus defined, *jus cogens* does have a specificity, although this is not concerned with existing law but rather with the process of bringing into existence a different international law in the future. In other words, *jus cogens* is inherently *promotional* and is to be properly situated in the *dynamics* (rather

anything inherent in the concept of *jus cogens* which would require their modification or would displace their application'. The Court cited the 2006 *Armed Activities* Judgment, concerning its own jurisdiction (see Ch 8 below, n 56 and accompanying text) and the 2002 *Arrest Warrant* Judgment (n 190 above), concerning the immunity of a foreign minister before domestic courts, and observed that the same reasoning applies to the CIL rule on foreign state jurisdictional immunity. It thus concluded that 'even on the assumption that the proceedings in the Italian courts involved violations of *jus cogens* rules, the applicability of the customary international law on State immunity was not affected' (para 97). While apparently endorsing the notion of *jus cogens*, the Court: (a) ruled that the overriding effect of substantive *jus cogens* does not go as far as producing consequences on the procedural avenues against its violation; (b) excluded the existence of a procedural immunity rule having the status of *jus cogens*, presumably in the face of almost completely contrary state practice; (c) held that nothing can be logically deduced as 'inherent' in the concept of *jus cogens* in order to modify or displace the application of the procedural rules on jurisdiction; (d) asserted that *jus cogens* does not entail of itself the means for its enforcement 'even in the absence of a direct conflict' with another rule such as the state immunity rule, regardless of this rendering one means of enforcement unavailable; and (e) ruled that contrary state practice, notably the rejection by domestic courts of the *jus cogens*' overriding effect sought and the silence of national legislations on the matter, is relevant to rule out this overriding effect. All these propositions are perfectly in line with the argument made here.

[440] For an illustration of the deductive line of reasoning, see the joint dissenting opinion appended to the Judgment of the ECtHR in *Al-Adsani* (n 123 above). A radically deductive (at times indeed apodictic) approach was taken by Alexander Orakhelashvili, *Peremptory Norms in International Law* (Oxford: OUP, 2006) 8, whose view is that peremptory norms apply (as 'intrinsically superior') 'whatever the attitude of States'.

[441] On the 'constitutional' theory of *jus cogens*, see R Kolb, *Théorie du* ius cogens *international: Essai de relecture du concept* (Genève: Presses Universitaires de France, 2001) 98–124.

than in the statics) of international law, ie in the ways the creation of a new international law can be triggered. In this process of norm generation courts fulfil (or purport to fulfil) the 'deontological' function of 'educating' states by pushing them to make their behaviour conform to values which need to be presented as 'superior' to the extent that they are felt as 'foreign' to current state behaviour and worthy of superseding currently existing norms. *Jus cogens* is 'applied' as *jus necessarium*, as the law that 'there must be', ie as the law that if it does not exist currently, must be in place in future and steps have to be taken to this end. This promotional, provisional, and ultimately deontological function is patently fulfilled when the alleged *jus cogens* special *effect* (as distinct from the generic notion of *jus cogens*) is at odds with state practice and *opinio juris*, as in the *Ferrini* jurisprudence,[442] but it may also take place when international practice is scarce or contentious or contradictory. In these cases courts may want to reinforce the dubious norm in order to make state practice develop and become firmer, more coherent, and generalized.

In summary, *jus cogens* is a tool to set aside existing law in the name of 'superior values'. Of necessity, such values do not support the specific effect ascribed to *jus cogens* as resulting from existing rules: were this the case, there would be no need for *jus cogens* since the rules corresponding to the desired effect would already be in place. There must be a gap between existing law and the value deemed to be protected for *jus cogens* to make sense. Faced with unquestionably existing rules precluding the desired effect, the only strategy to avoid their application is to imagine the existence of a 'superior' law which has the potential to set them aside. *Lex superior* prevails over any other norm, including the *lex posterior* and *lex specialis* principles. Its superiority is explained in terms of values and tends to meet with sympathy in so far as it evokes a similarity with domestic constitutional norms, thus ignoring the radical difference between the international and the national political environments and even the frailty of national constitutions themselves. The subsequent passage is to deduce from this superiority a potentially unlimited (but in actual fact far from being really unlimited) number of 'special' effects, ie effects which are thought to succeed in avoiding the application of the undesired law flowing from the 'traditional' sources. Only certain effects which appear to be in line with a certain perception of 'justice' and 'fundamental values' are drawn. Thus defined, *jus cogens* is invariably and unsurprisingly defended by those—the Third World and Socialist states before the end of the Cold War, and today in particular the Western states and their standard-bearers—who think of themselves as the depositaries of the best 'fundamental values' and 'justice' to which humanity should conform. It may well be that certain values (Western or other) are really the best values to be pursued for the good of humankind. It is quite another thing to state the law as it stands. It is still another to protect the vulnerable. In respect of these, *jus cogens* may be as much favourable as unfavourable, with some likelihood that it will be used unfavourably by the stronger.[443]

C. Judicial and Quasi-judicial Decision-making

Having discussed international law-making, it is now convenient to explore international judicial and quasi-judicial decision-making. This section seeks first to dispel the

[442] See n 392 above.

[443] See C Chinkin, '*Jus Cogens*, Article 103 of the UN Charter and Other Hierarchical Techniques of Conflict Solution' (2006) 17 Finn YBIL 63, 68–70.

confusion about the difference between law-making and judicial (or quasi-judicial) decision-making, to provide some guidance on what is meant by an international court, and to make it clear that international adjudication is profoundly different from domestic adjudication. It will then consider certain aspects of international courts' and tribunals' exercise of discretionary power in both substantive matters, involving abuse of rights, good faith, reasonableness, and *non liquet*, and procedural matters touching upon current courts' fragmentation by an examination of *lis alibi pendens*, *res judicata*, and *stare decisis*. It is argued that international courts and tribunals may arrive at a point where the rules of international law in themselves do not, using the discretionary power inherent in their very establishment, and in common sense and social attunement as to the boundaries of discretion to be used 'within the law' and not '*ex aequo et bono*'.

(1) International adjudication

The role of courts is impartially to apply and specify the law in particular cases, as well as participating, to some extent, in the law-making process by adding precedents and reinforcing the rules through their systematic application. International courts and tribunals are created to perform similar functions in an environment which is profoundly different from that of domestic legal systems. This section is designed to trace the differences between law-making and judicial decision-making in international law, to provide a basic definition of 'international' courts, and to signal the key features of international adjudication in contrast with domestic adjudication. The purpose is to show that most inferences about international adjudication are mistakenly modelled on domestic adjudication and in particular on adjudicatory mechanisms typical of the Western state.

(a) Law-making and judicial decision-making

The term 'decision-making' is open to question. By using it, reference is made here to how international courts, tribunals, and other court-like institutions make decisions and apply the law. The expression 'applying the law' means that there is some pre-existing law and this law is applied in a particular case. It does not imply that the sole role of courts and tribunals is 'mechanically' to apply the law previously made by other (law-making) entities. What courts do, even when they go beyond mere application of the law and play some 'creative' role, cannot be seen as law-making. The difference is that courts basically consider the law made by others as 'the law' to be applied to the case at hand in order to resolve a given dispute. Although there certainly are borderline cases, communities generally share a sense of what is to be seen as the law and what its application is to a particular case. Judicial decision-making takes place within a pre-existing, general legal framework in the perception of its addressees as a whole, however indeterminate or uncertain. An indeterminate pre-existing legal framework is not the same as no legal framework at all.

The diffused tendency today to characterize international courts as law-making institutions is misleading.[444] It seems designed to shift the law-making function from states to other entities. That law is indeterminate and requires identification and

[444] See eg A Boyle and C Chinkin, *The Making of International Law* (Oxford: OUP, 2007) 268–9; Klabbers, Peters, and Ulfstein (n 17 above) 127.

specification when settling a dispute is straightforward. No law is so indeterminate as not to provide some guidance, and no law is so detailed as not to need specification by the courts or other legal officials. Legal 'activism' by courts is, to a certain extent, in their very nature: courts are set up to apply the law by exercising discretion within predetermined boundaries. Were this not the case, machines would be preferred to judges. It is a fact that international courts and tribunals have always asserted that it is not for them to make the law, but only to 'apply' the law as they find it. For example, in the 1974 *Fisheries* Judgment the ICJ said of itself that it, 'as a court of law, cannot render judgment *sub specie legis ferendae*, or anticipate the law before the legislator has laid it down'.[445] Even more clearly, in the 1996 *Nuclear Weapons* Advisory Opinion the Court held that 'It is clear that the Court cannot legislate, and, in the circumstances of the present case, it is not called upon to do so', but 'Rather its task is to engage in its normal judicial function of ascertaining the existence or otherwise of legal principles and rules applicable.' In its view, the Court 'states the existing law and does not legislate . . . even if, in stating and applying the law, the Court necessarily has to specify its scope and sometimes note its general trend'.[446]

While they are distinct, law-making and judicial decision-making share a lack of capacity to enforce decisions. Since courts typically intervene to settle disputes, and the disputes submitted to courts usually concern the alleged breach of a 'primary' rule of international law, it could be supposed that international courts deal with the 'secondary' rules and hence 'enforce' the law.[447] This view may be inspired by domestic legal systems where there is almost always a court for any dispute and any decision will be enforced by ad hoc authorities. This is not the case, however, with international law. In international law there is no court for most disputes, and even when a court exists and has jurisdiction over a case there can be no enforcement. The equation between courts and enforcement makes sense in domestic law, but not in international law. The decisions made by international courts lack enforcement just like the rules created by international law-makers. What international courts and tribunals do is to posit a (one would hope) less indeterminate concrete rule than the law to be applied and to sustain this rule with the blessing of impartiality, thus making its contestation less justifiable. This also suggests that the notion that international courts and tribunals are 'dispute settlement' bodies may be misleading. The chances of them deciding a case and then, in case of non-compliance, enforcing the decision or having the decision enforced by other bodies are very low indeed. What they do amounts to a sort of *specification* of the rules in relation to *particular cases* from a *third-party institution*. This is much more than a 'rough' rule, but much less than a 'settlement' of the dispute. A settlement is secured with the enforcement where the losing party fails to comply with the decision. Until the losing party fails to comply, the case remains unsettled whatever the decision has prescribed. Of course determinacy and impartiality are, quite reasonably, expected to increase the degree and likelihood of compliance, and hence the effectiveness of international law. It is in *this* sense that judicial decision-making enhances international law and represents a determinative continuum with law-making. Adjudication makes a

[445] ICJ, *Fisheries Jurisdiction* (*United Kingdom v Iceland*) *(Merits)* Judgment of 25 July 1974, [1974] ICJ Rep 3, para 53; ICJ, *Fisheries Jurisdiction* (*Federal Republic of Germany v Iceland*) *(Merits)* Judgment of 25 July 1974, [1974] ICJ Rep 175, para 45.

[446] ICJ, *Legality of the Threat or Use of Nuclear Weapons* (n 88 above) para 18.

[447] On the distinction between international 'primary' and 'secondary' rules, see critically U Linderfalk, 'State Responsibility and the Primary–Secondary Rules Terminology: The Role of Language for an Understanding of the International Legal System' (2009) 78 Nord JIL 53.

rule more workable. But the central problem of how to force transgressors to comply with the law against their will remains intact. A state that is unwilling to abide by a rule can also refuse to abide by a judicial decision.

(b) What is meant by an international court?

The identification of a general definition of international courts and tribunals is not merely a theoretical issue; it has a number of legal implications and is relevant to the generation of certain legal effects. For example, the characterization of international courts and tribunals as 'international' is relevant in relation to international *litis pendence*, which applies only between 'international' courts, not between international and national courts;[448] the rule of complementarity under Article 17 ICC Statute applies only in the relations between the ICC and domestic courts; and, according to the ICJ 2002 *Arrest Warrant* Judgment, jurisdictional immunity may be admitted only before 'certain international criminal courts', where they have jurisdiction.[449]

There are no universally accepted criteria to determine when a court or tribunal is 'international'. In principle, every element of internationality is pertinent but in practice certain elements may be more weighty than others and national elements are also often present to complicate matters, notably in so-called hybrid criminal tribunals.[450] It has been suggested that a court is international when it is permanent, has been established by an international legal instrument, applies international law and rules of procedure that cannot be modified (or derogated from) by the parties, and makes binding decisions.[451] A more recent approach has proposed five, partly different criteria, by requiring that the court should be permanent, made up of independent judges, adjudicates disputes between two or more entities one of which is a state or an IO, works on the basis of predetermined rules of procedures, and makes binding decisions.[452] It is apparent that the requirements tend to vary with the purpose for which the characterization is made and the court or tribunal taken as a model.

(c) Hallmarks of international adjudication

Some further confusion surrounds the nature of international adjudication and its distinction from domestic adjudication. It is often supposed that international courts and tribunals work approximately like domestic courts, assuming that the 'judicial function' is an essence that cannot change (at least significantly) according to the legal context. This belief generates a series of unsound deductions. To clarify the point for a better understanding of the following analysis, the key differences between domestic and international adjudication are worth discussing.

[448] See section C (3)(a) below.

[449] ICJ, *Arrest Warrant of 11 April 2000* (n 190 above) para 61. See E Cimiotta, 'Immunità personali dei Capi di Stato dalla giurisdizione della Corte penale internazionale e responsabilità statale per gravi illeciti internazionali' (2011) 94 RDI 1083.

[450] For a discussion on the 'international' character of hybrid criminal tribunali, see E Cimiotta, *I tribunali penali misti* (Padua: Cedam, 2009) 40–122. The 'international' character of the STL was affirmed by the STL itself in the 2011 'Interlocatory Decision on the Applicable Law' (n 273 above), para 15.

[451] C Tomuschat, 'International Courts and Tribunals with Regionally Restricted and/or Specialized Jurisdiction' in H Mosler and R Bernhardt (eds), *Judicial Settlement of International Disputes: International Court of Justice, Other Courts and Tribunals, Arbitration and Conciliation: An International Symposium* (Heidelberg and New York: Springer, 1974) 285, 299–312.

[452] C Romano, 'PICT Synoptic Chart', at <http://www.pict-pcti.org>.

First, unlike domestic courts, international courts may be simply non-existent to settle certain disputes. This occurs whenever states, for any reason, have not set up courts, an occurrence that is certainly the rule despite the recent 'proliferation' of international courts and tribunals. While domestic courts are permanent and prepared at all times to accept new litigants, international tribunals—with a few exceptions, such as the ICJ and ITLOS—are generally established by the parties at the very moment when a dispute arises, but at that point in time the parties may find it difficult to agree on the establishment thereof. Most international disputes simply have no forum where they may be addressed. This means that in most cases international law rules work regardless of any court entrusted to settle disputes over their scope, interpretation, or application.[453] In such situations there is no settlement dispute body that can make rules more determinate or less disputable in a particular case. Understandably, rules that are either too subtle or too indeterminate barely work in this milieu and are destined to be manipulated by the stronger or to remain a dead letter. This also explains why diplomatic methods of dispute settlement may be seen as (and indeed be) more fruitful than judicial proceedings, and doctrinal subtleties end up adding obscurity.

Secondly, while domestic courts 'have plenary jurisdiction' in the sense that virtually all possible claims which can be formulated under the laws of the forum state can be brought before one court or another, international courts and tribunals have limited and selective jurisdiction. There are many possible claims which could be formulated in the abstract under international law but which in fact cannot be submitted to any existing international court for lack of *ratione materiae* jurisdiction.

Thirdly, in domestic legal systems there is a legal obligation upon persons to submit the case to the jurisdiction of courts independently of the will of the litigants. In international law consent of the parties to the dispute is always necessary. As a result, even when an international court exists to adjudicate a particular case and has *ratione materiae* jurisdiction, it may lack jurisdiction for want of consent of the defendant. Many would think that a judicial function which works only when transgressors give their consent to be judged is very far from being what a legal system worthy of this name requires.

Fourthly, while domestic judges are usually professionals selected by way of technical competition, international judges are typically selected politically. For example, in the ICJ the five permanent members of the UN Security Council permanently retain a judge. All other states may have a judge on rotation based on a geographical distribution, or a judge *ad hoc* in any particular disputes in which no national judges of the parties are part of the Court. Some non-permanent states seem to be preferred to others (for example, Germany and Japan), and certain states may have never had a judge in the Court. As to the impact of this state of affairs on the decisions of the Court, it appears that 90 per cent of the time ICJ judges vote in favour of 'their' appointing or national state, and judges of states uninvolved in the case tend to prefer the case of states whose economy and political system is closer to those of the judges' home states.[454]

Fifthly, while decisions by national courts are binding on citizens and others whether they like it or not as part of their larger political duty of obedience supported by the legitimacy and effectiveness of the government, international courts generally lack

[453] For a critique of excessive judicial-centrism from a transcivilizational perspective of international law, see Onuma (n 74 above) 167, 244–52.

[454] For this criticism from a realist perspective, see EA Posner, *The Perils of Global Legalism* (Chicago and London: University of Chicago Press, 2009) 144–5.

political legitimacy and enforcement mechanisms, nor is there a world executive endowed with world legitimacy capable of enforcing their decisions.

Sixthly, international courts work each within its own legal regime (established by its Statute) and are not governed by a unitary set of rules dealing with their relationships, division of labour, competence, hierarchy, and so forth.[455] International appellate courts operate *within* their (more or less) 'self-contained' regime and, rather than contributing to the unity of the system, may indeed exacerbate fragmentation by reinforcing their own primacy and jurisprudence.

Seventhly, while domestic courts can rely on funds from the state to a level that is in most states sufficient to ensure their functioning, international courts are diversely financed and resources are not always available to the extent that is needed. It is also reasonable to suppose that states and other actors which provide funds, do so for a gain, whether direct or indirect. It is difficult to imagine a state financing a court in the absence of any gain, just for the sake of justice.

Finally, although domestic courts need to appear legitimate and credible, this is far more necessary to international courts. One of the main reasons for this is that international courts do not generally enjoy any enforcement mechanism and are aware of the likelihood that their decisions will remain a dead letter if they are not sufficiently accepted by all the parties. They are also aware that a certain number of dead-letter decisions might lead to them losing their authority. Domestic judges know that even their 'unacceptable' decisions will in the end be enforced and this because domestic adjudication is compulsory and courts are assisted by the enforcement machine of the state. Every suggestion, so frequently made today, that international courts should innovate the law thus appears to be based on a parallel with domestic adjudication and should be viewed with caution and sense of reality, as most international judges know well. It is also true that activists push for creative jurisprudence also in the hope that courts might provide some help in 'legitimizing' causes which deserve to be furthered by any means.

(2) Substantive discretion

International courts and tribunals settle disputes by applying international law, but precisely what international law they are expected to apply is often unclear. Article 38 ICJ Statute lists the classes of rules that the ICJ 'shall apply' in deciding disputes, and similar provisions are found in the statutes of a few other international courts, such as Article 293(1) UNCLOS combined with Article 23 ITLOS Statute.[456] Other court-like institutions may fail to mention the applicable law, as is the case with the WTO DSU. WTO panels and the Appellate Body have interpreted this silence to the effect that they are expected to apply international law as a whole since WTO agreements cannot be applied 'in clinical isolation from public international law'.[457] Does the applicable law require courts and tribunals to 'consider' other 'general principles' such as abuse of rights, good faith, reasonableness, and *non liquet*? This section argues that

[455] cf ICTY, *Prosecutor v Tadić, Decision on the Defence Motion for Interlocutory Appeal on Jurisdiction*, Decision of 2 October 1995, Case No ICTY-94-1, para 11, stating that: 'In international law, every tribunal is a self-contained system (unless otherwise provided)'.

[456] ITLOS Statute, Annex VI of the UN Convention on the Law of the Sea (concluded 10 December 1982, entered into force 16 November 1994) 1833 UNTS 3, at <http://www.itlos.org/fileadmin/itlos/documents/basic_texts/statute_e.pdf>.

[457] See n 350 above.

these doctrines, while not being 'sources', should be taken into due consideration by international courts and tribunals, on the basis (and within the limits) of the applicable law, as part of the margin of discretion conferred on them at the moment of their establishment. Such discretion is ultimately founded on and limited by the degree of credibility, reputation, and ultimately legitimacy gained by the court in the perception of the states parties to its statute as a whole.

(a) Abuse of rights

Definitions of abuse of rights (*abus de droit*) are mostly found in the domestic law of torts and of neighbours, covering instances in which someone, when exercising a right, has acted out of pure malice or spite, arbitrarily or without good reason and in rigid reliance on a rule, or in bad faith or fraudulently. In international law, a state may be thought to have 'abused' one of its rights when it exercises the right in a way that causes unjust harm to another state, or for an end that is different from the one for which the right has been granted (*détournement de pouvoir*), or against the social function of the right. It is believed that in such cases the state, although acting within the law (or, rather, in conformity with the letter of the law), incurs responsibility.[458] For abuse of rights to make sense, however, there must be a 'right' and an 'abuse' in its exercise *within* the limits of the right. Outside the limits of the right, there is no right at all that can be abused and the violation of the law derives from the *absence* of the right rather than from the *abuse* of an existing right.[459]

While often unilaterally invoked by states against other states, the abuse of rights doctrine has rarely been endorsed by international courts in the particular circumstances of the case.[460] The doctrine can easily be used to accuse adversaries of unlawful behaviour even where their behaviour has been adopted within the law. The notion that abuse of rights reflects a general principle of law recognized by civilized nations finds little support in domestic legal systems for a variety of reasons.[461] First, only a few states recognize the doctrine, typically European states, and with significant variations.[462] Secondly, abuse of rights cannot readily be transposed to international law bearing in mind that in the international legal system it is often difficult even to argue for a 'right', let alone for an abuse of a right.[463] On the other hand, if the doctrine is not

[458] For an overall analysis, see M Byers, 'Abuse of Rights: An Old Principle, a New Age' (2002) 47 McGill LJ 389.

[459] See B Elkind, 'Footnote to the Nuclear Test Cases: Abuse of Right—A Blind Alley for Environmentalists' (1976) 9 Van JTL 57, 71; BO Iluyomade, 'The Scope and Content of a Complaint of Abuse of Right in International Law' (1975) 16 Harv ILJ 47, 48.

[460] cf WTO, *United States—Import Prohibition of Certain Shrimp and Shrimp Products* (n 137 above) para 158. In his separate opinion appended to the 1997 *Gabčíkovo-Nagymaros Project* Judgment (n 140 above) 95, Judge Weeramantry included abuse of rights within the 'well-established areas of international law' from which the components of the principle of sustainable development derive.

[461] This view was first hinted at within the Advisory Committee of Jurists appointed to draft the Statute of the PCIJ by the Italian member Arturo Ricci Busatti, who referred to the principle 'which forbids the abuse of rights' as an example of such principles along with *res judicata*. cf Advisory Committee of Jurists, *Procès-verbaux* (n 75 above) 314–15, 335.

[462] The most typical provision is found in Art 2 of the *Titre préliminaire* to the Swiss Civil Code, which reads: 'Chacun est tenu d'exercer ses droits et d'exécuter ses obligations selon les règles de la bonne foi. L'abus manifeste d'un droit n'est pas protégé par la loi'.

[463] For the purely speculative, at best promotional, view that when the responsibility to protect (RtoP) doctrine applies (see Ch 8 below, section B (2)(b)), the veto in the UN Security Council may amount to an abuse of rights and should be regarded as 'legally irrelevant', if not plainly illegal, see recently A Peters, 'The Responsibility to Protect: Spelling out the Hard Legal Consequences for the

part of existing international law, it cannot be a factor in the development of international law either. Abuse of rights is not designed to affect future law since it is by definition applicable on a case-by-case basis.

The only relevant question is thus whether and to what extent abuse of rights may be taken into consideration by the courts. The better view is that it can be admitted within the limits of the discretionary power of international courts and tribunals as rooted in their ultimate mission (inherent in their very establishment) to deliver justice. What distinguishes abuse of rights from absence of rights is the fact that the former limits rights from a systemic perspective within the interpretative discretion of the courts, thus operating only when a court is seised, whereas the latter sets specific limits to *individual* rights as such. It is thus systemic reasons of justice that could inspire a judicial decision to consider the possible exercise of a right in an abusive way. Abuse of rights means the exercise of a right that leads to a perceived 'unjust' outcome according to the common sense (or 'social conscience') shared by the international community at any given moment.[464] What courts are expected to hold, properly speaking, is not so much that the state has abused its right as that the right (properly construed in the light of systemic justice and common sense) does not extend to its act. This explains why states often claim abuse of rights and courts rarely answer in such terms, but rather either accept or deny the right.

(b) Good faith

Good faith (*bona fide, bonne foi*) is rooted in ancient thinking and generally thought to be a principle found in every legal system as an expression of trust, honesty, conscientiousness, and loyalty inherent in the very concept of law. At the same time, it is invariably criticized as being too vague, ambiguous, and elusive, relating to morals rather than to law.

Good faith is expressly mentioned in several international instruments of various kinds and in quite a few international judicial decisions.[465] For example, in the 1974 *Nuclear Tests* Judgment the ICJ stated that 'One of the basic principles governing the creation and performance of legal obligations, whatever their source, is the principle of good faith' and linked it with 'the binding character of an international obligation assumed by unilateral declaration' in addition to treaties.[466] In the 1984 *Gulf of Maine* Judgment the Court ruled that the parties were not only under a duty to negotiate but also 'to do so in good faith, with a genuine intention to achieve a positive result'.[467]

UN Security Council and its Members' in U Fastenrath, R Geiger, D-E Khan, A Paulus, S von Schorlemer, and C Vedder (eds), *From Bilateralism to Community Interest: Essays in Honour of Judge Bruno Simma* (Oxford: OUP, 2011) 297, 317, 322. That the decision to cast a veto may be more difficult in RtoP situations is a different matter.

464 Of particular interest is the formulation of abuse of rights in the *Mitamura v Suzuki* case, decided on 27 June 1972, by the Supreme Court of Japan. The Court held that: 'In all cases a right must be exercised in such a fashion that the result of the exercise remains within a scope judged reasonable in the light of the prevailing social conscience . . . Thus, the person who exercises his right in such a fashion shall be held liable because his conduct constitutes *an abuse of right*'. cf 26 *Saiko Saibansho minji hanreishu*, 1067, English trans extract in K Sono and Y Fujioka, 'The Role of the Abuse of Right Doctrine in Japan' (1975) 35 Lou LR 1037, 1037 (original emphasis).

465 See R Kolb, *La bonne foi en droit international public: contribution à l'étude des principes généraux de droit* (Paris: Presses Universitaires de France, 2000).

466 ICJ, *Nuclear Tests Case (Australia v France)* (n 76 above) para 46; *Nuclear Tests Case (New Zealand v France)* (n 76 above) para 49.

467 ICJ Chamber, *Case concerning Delimitation of the Maritime Boundary in the Gulf of Maine Area (Canada/United States)* Judgment of 12 October 1984, [1984] ICJ Rep 246, para 87. See in addition

Appeals to good faith have been made also by Arbitral Tribunals[468] and frequently by WTO panels and the Appellate Body.[469]

Is good faith part of international law? Does it refer to an autonomous obligation or to the way other obligations should be observed? Good faith has been mostly regarded as a general principle of law recognized by civilized nations under Article 38(1)(c) ICJ Statute.[470] It is meant to inform other more specific principles of law such as reciprocity, acquiescence, equity, *abus de droit*, duties of information and disclosure, and even the *rebus sic stantibus* principle. In international judicial proceedings it informs the general duty of loyalty between the parties, as well as more specific procedural rules, such as abuse of process, *venire contra factum proprium* (estoppel), and *nemo ex propria turpitudine commodum capere potest*.[471] Despite the frequent charge that good faith is too vague and favours judicial activism excessively, it has been suggested that good faith 'deploys a certain kind of constitutional quality within the international law scheme' and—as a general and objective principle of international law—enables interpreters to proceed with an evolutionary and non-formalistic interpretation of treaties, while also being capable of filling gaps in the law.[472] This view stretches the concept of good faith too far: good faith may be important, but to elevate it to a 'constitutional' status, if the term 'constitution' is given a prescriptive and not a mere descriptive meaning, simply risks discrediting international law as a whole.

Significantly, in the 1988 *Border and Transborder Armed Actions* Judgment, the ICJ excluded the notion that good faith is per se a source of legal obligation in the absence of other sources.[473] This suggests that good faith is concerned with the *way* in which an obligation is carried out, a matter falling within the discretionary power impliedly conferred on international courts in order to conduct all the reasoning deemed necessary to reach a decision on the basis (and within the limits) of the applicable law.

(c) Reasonableness

Reasonableness is often depicted as inherent in law, helpful to fill the gaps and solve the antinomies of positive law, as well as to avoid *non liquet*.[474] Between two equally plausible meanings of a rule or between two values underlying two rules, reasonableness

ICJ, *North Sea Continental Shelf Cases* (n 80 above) para 85; *Case concerning Pulp Mills on the River Uruguay (Argentina v Uruguay)* Judgment of 20 April 2010, at <http://www.icj-cij.org/docket/files/135/15877.pdf>, para 145.

[468] See eg Arbitral Tribunal, *Affaire du lac Lanoux (Espagne, France)* Award of 16 November 1957, 12 RIAA 281, 305; Arbitral Tribunal for the Agreement on German External Debts, *Kingdom of Greece v Federal Republic of Germany* Award of 26 January 1972, (1974) 47 ILR 418, para 62; Arbitral Tribunal, *Filleting within the Gulf of St Lawrence between Canada and France* Award of 17 July 1986, 19 RIAA 225, para 27.

[469] See M Panizzon, *Good Faith in the Jurisprudence of the WTO: The Protection of Legitimate Expectations, Good Faith Interpretation and Fair Dispute Settlement* (Oxford: Hart, 2006).

[470] See n 166 above.

[471] R Kolb, 'General Principles of Procedural Law' in A Zimmermann, C Tomuschat, and K Oellers-Frahm (eds), *The Statute of the International Court of Justice: A Commentary* (Oxford: OUP, 2006) 793, 830.

[472] M Kotzur, 'Good Faith (Bona fide)', MP EPIL (January 2009 update) paras 25, 26, as well as paras 8, 14.

[473] ICJ, *Border and Transborder Armed Actions (Nicaragua v Honduras), Jurisdiction and Admissibility* Judgment of 20 December 1988, [1988] ICJ Rep 69, para 94. (While being 'one of the basic principles governing the creation and performance of legal obligations' the principle of good faith 'is not in itself a source of obligation where none would otherwise exist.')

[474] See Ch 3 above, section B (1)(c) and (2).

allows the interpreter to opt for the best meaning or to balance appropriately the two values in relation to the concrete case in hand with a view to preferring the outcome that appears more in accordance with reason. What is meant by 'reasonable' is difficult to grasp and has to do with social attunement.[475] The relation of reasonableness to rationality, as well as to equity and proportionality is uncertain. The ICJ held that 'What is reasonable and equitable in any given case must depend on its particular circumstances'.[476] Similarly, the ECtHR pointed out that 'reasonableness . . . must be assessed in each case according to its special features'.[477] Reasonableness is thus context-related. This contrasts with the opinion that reasonableness, by referring to reason, enhances the unity of the international legal system.

The term 'reasonable' is explicitly found in several international law rules. For example, in the law of treaties, recourse may be had to supplementary means of interpretation under Article 32 VCLT when the ordinary criteria would give rise 'to a result which is manifestly absurd or unreasonable'. In the law of human rights, the right to a hearing or to be tried, after arrest or detention on a criminal charge, 'within a reasonable time' are set out in all existing instruments and specified by monitoring bodies in a set of criteria, namely, the complexity of the case, the conduct of the applicant, and the conduct of the relevant state authorities.[478] According to the jurisprudence, non-discrimination clauses prohibit discrimination without 'an objective and reasonable justification';[479] restrictions on the exercise of rights 'necessary to a democratic society' must be 'reasonably proportionate' to the legitimate aim pursued.[480] Elections may be required to be organized 'at reasonable intervals'.[481] In the international law of the sea, the delimitation of the continental shelf should be made, as held by the ICJ in the 1969 *North Sea* Judgment, in accordance with 'a reasonable degree of proportionality' with the lengths of their respective coastlines,[482] or 'provided that, by the application of equitable principles, a reasonable result is arrived at'.[483] In the subsequent case law concerning the delimitation of maritime zones, other criteria and factors of reasonableness were devised, including the length and shape of coastline; the presence of islands, certain rocks, or headlands; and the proximity of neighbouring states. As regards prompt release, ITLOS has consistently held that any assessment of the reasonableness of a bonding or other financial guarantee depends upon such factors as 'the gravity of the alleged offences, the penalties imposed or imposable under the laws of the detaining State, the value of the detained vessel and of the cargo seized, the amount of the bond imposed by the detaining State and its

[475] See O Corten, *L'utilisation du 'raisonnable' par le juge international* (Brussels: Bruylant, 1997); O Corten, 'Reasonableness in International Law', MP EPIL (May 2006 update).

[476] ICJ, *Interpretation of the Agreement of 25 March 1951 between the WHO and Egypt* (n 111 above) para 49.

[477] cf ECtHR, *Wemhoff v Germany* Judgment of 27 June 1968, App 2122/64, Series A No 7, (1979–80) 1 EHRR 55, para 10.

[478] As constantly affirmed by monitoring bodies in relation to the interpretation of Arts 5 and 6 ECHR, as well as Art 9 ICCPR.

[479] cf eg ECtHR, *Certain Aspects of the Laws on the Use of Languages in Education in Belgium (Merits)* Judgment of 23 July 1968, App 1474/62, 1677/62, 1691/62, 1769/63, 1994/63, 2126/64, Series A No 6, section I B, para 10; *Observer and Guardian v United Kingdom* Judgment of 26 November 1991, App 13,585/88, Series A No 216, (1992) 14 EHRR 153, para 73.

[480] cf eg ECtHR, *Chorherr v Austria* Judgment of 25 August 1993, App 13,308/87, Series A No 266-B, (1994) 17 EHRR 358, para 33.

[481] Art 3 Protocol (I) to the Convention for the Protection of Human Rights and Fundamental Freedoms (signed 20 March 1952, entered into force 18 May 1954) CETS No 9.

[482] ICJ, *North Sea Continental Shelf Cases* (n 80 above) para 101 D(3).

[483] ibid 49, para 90.

form'.[484] In the law of international trade, reference is often made to 'reasonable price' or to 'reasonable compensation'. In international environmental law, a 'reasonable and equitable utilization' standard is routinely set out in treaties. A 'reasonable' amount of compensation is often awarded by international courts.[485] Finally, in international adjudication, the standard of evidence may require proof beyond 'reasonable doubt'.[486]

Reasonableness is also occasionally depicted as a general principle inherent in international law. In the 1970 *Barcelona Traction* Judgment the ICJ held that 'in the field of diplomatic protection as in all other fields of international law, it is necessary that the law be applied reasonably'.[487] *Mutatis mutandis*, in the 1986 *La Bretagne* Award, the Arbitral Tribunal observed that 'like the exercise of any authority, the exercise of a regulatory authority is always subject to the rule of reasonableness'.[488]

A 'reasonable' application of international law reflects the social expectation that courts will construe the law in accordance with the basic assumption of common sense, or 'non-absurdity', shared in the international community at any given moment. Despite the difficulty of capturing what kind of common sense prevails in a complex and hard-to-define community such as the international community, there are indeed things that can be identified by international courts and tribunals as definitely absurd in that community. Reasonableness per se is not an autonomous source of legal obligation. Rather, it concerns the 'appropriate' application of other norms and falls within the discretion conferred on courts at the time of their creation.

(d) Non liquet

It may happen that in a particular case before an international court or tribunal the law that is to be applied is uncontroversial (for example, CIL or/and a certain treaty) but the court fails to identify the specific rule needed to decide the case. The Court then faces the dilemma of either delivering a *non liquet* decision or devising an alternative strategy aimed at avoiding *non liquet*. It should be noted that the *non liquet* problem does not coincide with that concerning the completeness of law.[489] The rule capable of solving the issue may indeed exist, for example because the system is considered complete through the operation of an implied 'closing' principle, but it may not fall within the body of law applicable by the court under the terms of its statute. Conversely, the rule may not exist, because the system is considered to be incomplete, yet the court may be able to fill the gap by using its discretion in interpreting the law. *Non liquet* is not to be confused with the non-justiciability of certain disputes and other grounds for disposing of a case, such as jurisdictional and procedural grounds (for example, lack of jurisdiction, lack of plaintiff's standing, inadmissibility of the case), lack of morally or politically desirable rules, reasons of propriety, and political considerations advising the court not to make a legal finding. Unlike these grounds, *non liquet* relates to the merits viewed in the light of the law as it stands.

[484] cf ITLOS, *The 'Camouco' Case (Panama v France) (Prompt Release)* Judgment of 7 February 2000, Case No 5, at <http://www.itlos.org/index.php?id=65>, para 67.

[485] cf eg ICJ, *Corfu Channel Case (United Kingdom v Albania) (Merits)* Judgment of 9 April 1949, [1949] ICJ Rep 4, 18.

[486] ibid 18.

[487] ICJ, *Barcelona Traction, Light and Power Co Ltd (Belgium v Spain) (Second Phase)* Judgment of 5 February 1970, [1970] ICJ Rep 3, para 93.

[488] Arbitral Tribunal, *Dispute concerning Filleting within the Gulf of St Lawrence* (n 468 above) para 54.

[489] The distinction between completeness of the system and *non liquet* was aptly underscored by Judge Simma in his declaration appended to the ICJ 2010 *Kosovo* Advisory Opinion (n 149 above).

It is widely held that courts should refrain from making *non liquet* decisions. When international courts and tribunals are involved, this duty is made to anchor either in CIL or in a general principle of law recognized by civilized nations. The underlying reasons against *non liquet* are twofold. First, it is argued that *non liquet* is inconsistent with the judicial function since it allows the court not to do what it is expected to do, namely, deliver justice to the parties in the proceedings. Secondly, it is assumed that international law is a complete legal system and thus the court can always find a rule to decide the case. Advocates of *non liquet* retort that international courts (unlike domestic courts) lack legitimacy and should avoid the quasi-legislative task of filling the gaps in the law. Moreover, international law (unlike, once again, domestic law) is far from envisaging mechanisms entrusted to correct unsatisfactory rulings. They also claim that international courts should avoid intruding in political questions and a *non liquet* is a helpful tool to this end.

The prohibition of *non liquet*, just like the doctrine of the unity and completeness of international law, is inspired by the ideal that international law should regulate every possible case and limit states' freedom of action as far as possible. Common law jurists are perhaps more readily prepared to deny *non liquet* because of the wide discretion and reputation of judges in their legal systems. Legal theorists tend to deny *non liquet* on the ground that it undermines the systemic unity of law and ultimately law in its very essence. Naturalists are immediately led to see natural law as the 'background law' that automatically surfaces when positive law is wanting or defective. Positivists, on the other hand, tend to see judges as the 'the mouth of the law' and deny them any creativity beyond what the law-maker has enacted.

In international practice *non liquet* is quite unpopular. The Advisory Committee of Jurists appointed to draft the PCIJ Statute sought to avoid *non liquet* by inserting in Article 38 the general principles of law recognized by civilized nations.[490] International courts and tribunals clearly try their best to find some rule or principle to decide the case. For example, in the 1924 *Mavrommatis* Judgment, the PCIJ held that, failing a legal rule in its Statute and Rules of Court applicable to the procedure to be followed in the event of an objection being taken in *limine litis* to the Court's jurisdiction, it was 'at liberty to adopt the principle which it consider[ed] best calculated to ensure the administration of justice, most suited to the procedure before an international tribunal and most in accordance with the fundamental principles of international law'.[491] In the 1953 *Desgranges* Judgment the ILO Administrative Tribunal stated that: 'One of the fundamental tenets of all legal systems is that no court may refrain from giving judgment on the ground that the law is silent or obscure'.[492] In the 1969 *North Sea* Judgment, the ICJ emphasized the role of equity in delimiting the continental shelf in the absence of any conventional or customary rule.[493] Nevertheless, the ICJ apparently made an implicit finding of a *non liquet* in the 1996 *Nuclear Weapons* Advisory Opinion. The Court refused to 'conclude definitively whether the threat or use of nuclear weapons would be lawful or unlawful in an extreme circumstance of self-defence, in which the very survival of a State would be at stake'.[494] The ICJ did not specifically discuss the basis of this finding, nor did it attempt to reconcile

[490] See section B (1)(d) above.

[491] PCIJ, *Mavrommatis Palestine Concessions* (n 248 above) 16.

[492] ILOAT, *Desgranges v International Labour Organization* Judgment of 12 August 1953 No 11, (1957) 20 ILR 523, 530.

[493] ICJ, *North Sea Continental Shelf Cases* (n 80 above) paras 83, 88–91.

[494] ICJ, *Legality of the Threat or Use of Nuclear Weapons* (n 88 above) para 105.

its refusal to reach a definitive conclusion with the previous weight of authority against *non liquet*.[495] One way of doing so, it has been suggested, is 'to distinguish between contentious and advisory cases and to limit the prohibition on *non liquet* to the former'.[496]

Assuming that international law is far from 'complete',[497] courts may well find themselves in a situation where they have no choice but to acknowledge the lack of any rule, norm, or principle applicable to the case and, therefore, make a pronouncement similar to that of the ICJ in *Nuclear Weapons*. This is not, however, automatic. Incompleteness in the regulation of state behaviour is one thing, it is quite another for a court to find some standard in order to decide the instant case. A court may use its discretion to arrive where states in their relations cannot. Moreover, states may not be willing to create a *general rule* that is always applicable, even when they are not involved in a court proceedings, although they accept that such a standard is applied by an international court on a case-by-case basis. A court may also exercise its discretion to decide exactly at what point the absence of any standard (by which the dispute can be settled) must be acknowledged, the point in other words beyond which the court finds that it is exceeding the discretion which was conferred on it at the time of its creation. It is where *this point* is set that is crucial, and this depends on many factors, including the degree of legitimacy and prestige the court enjoys (basically) among states.

(3) Procedural discretion

It is commonplace to note that international courts and court-like institutions have proliferated impressively since the end of the Cold War.[498] This burgeoning of courts, together with the acceptance of international courts' jurisdiction by an increasing number of states, produces several remarkable effects: increasing areas of international law (such as trade, sea, and human rights) are progressively falling within international judicial control; international courts increasingly interfere in domestic constitutional issues; the 'factual' compulsoriness of international adjudication is apparently materializing since, in a globalized world, states have little choice but to accede to treaties, be subjected to international courts set up therein, and then comply with their decisions.[499] These extensive powers allegedly call for legitimacy and control of international courts.[500] The debate is, however, overstated. More courts and more decisions can only improve the articulation and effectiveness of international law and the likelihood of conflicting decisions is very low indeed. Contradictions in any law are physiological and international courts and tribunals tend to use their inherent discretion not to contradict one another. Since the question arises of whether conflicting jurisdictions and decisions may be avoided, or reduced, or better handled, a discussion of *lis alibi pendens*, *res judicata*, and *stare decisis* in international law is now helpful. It is argued that, despite the absence of coordination rules and the fact that international courts and tribunals operate each within its statutory regime,[501] the global states system itself informally presses for uniformity and coherence.

[495] cf the dissident opinion of Judge Higgins whereby 'the concept of *non liquet*... is no part of the Court's jurisprudence' (ibid 591, para 36).

[496] D Bodansky, 'Non Liquet', MP EPIL (May 2006 update) para 14.

[497] See section B (2) above.

[498] See eg Skouteris (n 5 above) 126, 159–216.

[499] V Lowe, 'Overlapping Jurisdiction in International Tribunals' (1999) 20 Aus YBIL 191, 198–200.

[500] See eg Klabbers, Peters, and Ulfstein (n 17 above) 126–52.

[501] See n 270 above.

(a) Lis alibi pendens

When a dispute is brought in two or more jurisdictions by one or more of the litigants, the question arises of whether the court subsequently seised should decline its jurisdiction because the case is under examination in the previously seised court (*lis alibi pendens, litispendance*). In domestic law *lis pendens* is usually regulated by giving exclusive jurisdiction to the court previously seised with a view to precluding two or even more (possibly contradictory) decisions on the same case and thus avoiding judicial instability. The question is whether this rule should also be operative in international law in order to reinforce its unity and coherence.

In the 1925 *Polish Upper Silesia* Judgment the PCIJ defined international *lis pendens* as the situation in which 'the judges of one State should, in the absence of a treaty, refuse to entertain any suit already pending before the courts of another State, exactly as they would be bound to do if an action on the same subject had at some previous time been brought in due form before another court of their own country' so as 'to prevent the possibility of conflicting judgments'.[502] International law rules governing *lis pendens* are found in a number of treaties. Typically, human rights treaties provide *lis pendens* among the conditions of admissibility: applications are rejected when the same case between the same parties is under way before another international court, tribunal, or monitoring body.[503]

The principle of *lis pendens* is not part of general international law.[504] It is sometimes argued that international courts and tribunals can adopt it[505] by relying on comity,[506] or on a general duty to cooperate.[507] However, the point is that while in domestic legal systems all courts form a legally unitary system, in international law no 'courts' system' exists. Each international court functions according to its own rules and these rules are tailored to the needs of each particular court. When *lis pendens* is internationally regulated, this is from the unilateral perspective of the court concerned and in accordance with a specific treaty governing its functioning, while other treaties may well provide otherwise. This complex state of affairs is no doubt unsatisfactory if observed from an ideal 'rational' viewpoint since no one would doubt that judicial stability is essential to the effectiveness of law. This stability can be improved, at least to some extent and as a matter of fact, by the courts' appropriate use of judicial discretion.

(b) Res judicata

According to the *res judicata* doctrine, a final judgment or award by a court or arbitral tribunal is not only binding between the parties (positive effect) but also conclusive and incapable of re-litigation in other courts (negative effect).[508] While the *lis pendens* doctrine discussed above prevents two or more proceedings involving the same parties

[502] PCIJ, *Certain German Interests in Polish Upper Silesia (Preliminary Objections)* Judgment of 25 August 1925, PCIJ Series A No 6, at 20. The Court acknowledged that whether the doctrine of *litis pendance* could be invoked in international relations was 'a much disputed question in the teachings of legal authorities and in the jurisprudence of the principal countries'.

[503] cf eg Art 35(2)(b) ECHR.

[504] See eg K Oellers-Frahm, 'Multiplication of International Courts and Tribunals and Conflicting Jurisdiction: Problems and Possible Solutions' (2001) 5 MP YBUNL 67, 77; J Finke, *Die Parallelität internationaler Streitbeilegungsmechanismen* (Berlin: Duncker & Humblot, 2004) 317; Shany (n 52 above) 244.

[505] Lowe (n 499 above) 203; A Reinisch, 'The Use and Limits of *Res Judicata* and *Lis Pendens* as Procedural Tools to Avoid Conflicting Dispute Settlement Outcomes' (2004) 3 LPICT 37, 48.

[506] Shany (n 52 above) 255–66.

[507] Finke (n 504 above) 318.

[508] See eg Shany (n 52 above) 22–8, 164–73, 245–55; Reinisch (n 505 above).

and the same subject-matter from being carried out by two or more courts *simultaneously*, the *res judicata* effect prevents a court from re-examining a case *already decided* by another court. This difference apart, the two doctrines pose similar problems as to the required 'identity' of the case for them to be applied.

The *res judicata* doctrine is generally followed by international courts and arbitral tribunals despite the absence of formal international law rules providing that it should be applied. According to the 1941 *Trail Smelter* Award, based on several previous arbitral tribunal and CPIJ decisions, 'That the sanctity of *res judicata* attaches to a final decision of an international tribunal is an essential and settled rule of international law' or 'a principle of international law'.[509] The formal legal basis of this 'rule' or 'principle' is in fact controversial. The prevailing view is that the doctrine reflects a general principle of law recognized by civilized nations under Article 38(1)(c) ICJ Statute.[510] In the 1954 *Effect of Awards* Advisory Opinion the ICJ held that a judgment rendered by such judicial body [UNAT] is *res judicata* and has binding force between the parties to the dispute according to 'a well-established and generally recognized principle of law'.[511] This view enjoys wide acceptance in legal doctrine.[512]

In international judicial practice, for the doctrine to apply there must be identity of the question (*petitum*, or relief sought, and *causa petendi*, or grounds) and of the parties. In his dissenting opinion in the 1927 *Interpretation of Judgments Nos 7 and 8 (The Chorzów Factory)* PCIJ Judgment, Judge Anzilotti famously recalled the 'three traditional elements for identification, persona, *petitum*, *causa petendi*'.[513] This statement has been generally affirmed by international courts and tribunals subsequently.[514] However, much depends on what is meant by 'same' parties and subject-matter. For example, as to the same-party requirement it has been denied that there is identity between a minority shareholder, albeit a controlling one, and the actual company.[515] The *res judicata* effect has been upheld when the parties to the dispute were seeking a different relief on the same grounds,[516] while it was denied when the question was considered to be 'new',[517] or non-identical,[518] or when the two decisions were based on different treaties made by different states.[519]

[509] Arbitral Tribunal, *Trail Smelter Case* (n 219 above) 1950–4.

[510] Advisory Committee of Jurists, *Procès-verbaux* (n 75 above); PCIJ, *Interpretation of Judgments Nos 7 and 8 (The Chorzów Factory)* Judgment of 16 December 1927, PCIJ Series A No 13, dissenting opinion of Judge Anzilotti, at 27, para 7.

[511] ICJ, *Effect of Awards of Compensation Made by the United Nations Administrative Tribunal* (n 235 above) 53.

[512] See eg V Lowe, '*Res Judicata* and the Rule of Law in International Arbitration' (1996) 8 RADIC 38, 41–2; Shany (n 52 above) 171, 245–6, oscillating between a general principle of law and international custom.

[513] PCIJ, *Interpretation of Judgments Nos 7 and 8* (n 510 above) 23, para 1. Similarly, cf American British Arbitration Claims Tribunal, *China Navigation Co Ltd (Great Britain) v United States (Newchwang case)* Award of 9 December 1921, 6 RIAA 64, 65.

[514] cf eg Arbitral Tribunal, *Trail Smelter Case* (n 219 above) 1952.

[515] Swedish Svea Court of Appeals, *CME Czech Republic BV v Czech Republic*, Judgment of 15 May 2003, Case No T 8735-01, (2003) 42 ILM 919, 967.

[516] cf Spanish–US Claims Commission, *Delgado Case* Award of 27 May 1881, in JB Moore (ed), *History and Digest of the International Arbitrations to which the United States Has Been a Party* (Washington, DC: Government Printing Office, 1898) vol 3, 2196, 2198–200.

[517] ICJ, *Haya de la Torre Case (Columbia v Peru) (Merits)* Judgment of 13 June 1951, [1951] ICJ Rep 71, 80.

[518] American British Arbitration Claims Tribunal, *China Navigation Co Ltd (Great Britain) v United States (Newchwang Case)* Award of 9 December 1921, 6 RIAA 64, 65, remarking that 'Whatever ... be the connection in fact between the two questions, they are not identical'.

[519] Swedish Svea Court of Appeals, *CME Czech Republic BV v Czech Republic* (n 515 above) 965.

The precluding effect of *res judicata* undoubtedly covers the *dispositif* of the previous decision on the merits. It is doubtful whether the effect extends to other parts of the decision, such as the statement of reasons and dicta, or to procedural decisions, such as those on preliminary objections. As to the reasoning, it is difficult to separate the reasons and operative part of a decision clearly, if only because the former may prove decisive to an understanding of the latter. In *Barcelona Traction*, Judge Gros stated in his separate opinion that: 'Although the force of *res judicata* does not extend to the reasoning of a judgment, it is the practice of the Court, as of arbitral tribunals, to stand by the reasoning set forth in previous decisions'.[520] The interconnection thesis was expressed as early as 1902 by the PCA in the 1902 *Pious Fund* Award,[521] and revived by Judge Anzilotti in his 1927 *Chorzów Factory* dissenting opinion, where he argued that while 'only the terms of a judgment are binding... it is almost always necessary to refer to the statement of reasons to understand clearly the operative part'.[522] It does not follow, however, that the *res judicata* effect extends to dicta. In the 1925 *Polish Postal Service in Danzig* Advisory Opinion the PCIJ, although agreeing with the *Pious Fund* Award 'that all the parts of a judgment concerning the points in disputes explain and complete each other and are to be taken into account in order to determine the precise meaning and scope of the operative portion', pointed out that 'it by no means follows that any reason given in a decision constitutes a decision' and that an unquestionably personal opinion expressed by the decision-maker 'is irrelevant to the point actually decided by him and therefore has no binding force'.[523] In the 1905 *Compagnie Générale de l'Orénoque* Award the Franco-Venezuelan Mixed Claims Commission adopted a similar position.[524] Moreover, the *res judicata* effect covers the *dispositif* of an annulment decision and not its reasoning.[525] It is straightforward that decisions on preliminary objections[526] or decisions on jurisdiction, except when they necessarily decide an identical issue later raised on the merits,[527] have no *res judicata* effect and can be re-adjudicated.

In principle, the *res judicata* doctrine concerns only the hypothesis that the two decisions involved are international. Whether the *res judicata* effect extends to domestic decisions is doubtful. In *Amco* the first tribunal excluded its power to re-examine a domestic decision,[528] while in *Azinian*, a NAFTA Chapter 11 tribunal followed the decision of a domestic court, despite its quotation of *Amco*, on the grounds that:

[520] ICJ, *Barcelona Traction, Light and Power Co Ltd* (n 487 above), separate opinion of Judge Gros, ibid 267.

[521] PCA Arbitral Tribunal, *The Pious Fund of Californias (United States v The United Mexican States)* Award of 14 October 1902, HCR 3, 5.

[522] PCIJ, *Interpretation of Judgments Nos 7 and 8* (n 510 above) 28, para 2.

[523] PCIJ, *Polish Postal Service in Danzig* Advisory Opinion of 16 May 1925, PCIJ Series B No 11, at 30.

[524] Franco-Venezuelan Mixed Claims, *Company General of The Orinoco Case* Award of 9 February and 31 July 1905, 10 RIAA 184, 186.

[525] ICSID Arbitral Tribunal, *AMCO Asia Corp et al v Republic of Indonesia* Award of 20 November 1984, Case No ARB/81/1, 1 ICSID Rep (1993) 413, 522; *AMCO Asia Corp et al v Republic of Indonesia* Decision on Jurisdiction of 10 May 1988, Case No ARB/81/1, Resubmission on jurisdiction, 1 ICSID Rep (1993) 543, paras 32–45.

[526] ICJ, *South West Africa (Ethiopia v South Africa; Liberia v South Africa) (Merits)* Judgment of 18 July 1966, [1966] ICJ Rep 6, 59, holding that 'a decision on a preliminary objection could never be preclusive of a matter appertaining to the merits, whether or not it has in fact been dealt with in connection with the preliminary objection'.

[527] NAFTA Ch 11 Arbitration Tribunal, *Waste Management Incorporated v Mexico (Mexico's Preliminary Objection concerning the Previous Proceedings)*, Decision of 26 June 2002, Case No ARB (AF)/00/3, (2002) 41 ILM 1315, para 43, arguing that 'in general, the dismissal of a claim by an international tribunal on grounds of lack of jurisdiction does not constitute a decision on the merits and does not preclude a later claim before a tribunal which has jurisdiction'.

[528] Arbitral Tribunal, *Amco Asia Corp* Award of 20 November 1984 (n 525 above) 460.

'A governmental authority surely cannot be faulted for acting in a manner validated by its courts *unless the courts themselves are disavowed at the international level.*'[529]

The judicial trend in favour of the *res judicata* effect is important as evidence of the effort made by international courts to promote the unity and coherence of international law. If different courts feel that they are operating within commonly shared principles, this attitude powerfully proves that international law is not, at the moment of adjudicating at least, fragmentary beyond recognition. It is quite another thing, however, to ask whether and to what extent international law is fragmentary when, as is generally the case, issues are not brought before an international court or tribunal. Yet another question is how far fragmentation remains even where cases are submitted to international adjudication and attempts are successfully made to avoid excessive fragmentation. The doctrine is, however, simply followed as a matter of discretion and inspired by the need of courts to appear to be 'in tune' with the social conscience of the international community.

(c) Stare decisis

The doctrine of *stare decisis* holds that a court has to follow the principles established in previously decided cases—either by itself or by other courts—of equal or higher rank, with a view to guaranteeing the coherence and predictability of the law. Its origins can be traced back to eleventh-century English law and it has later developed, in particular, in common law countries, including to some extent the United States. The question of whether the doctrine applies to international law is often posed, especially to support 'cross-fertilization' between courts, and answered negatively.

International courts and tribunals have frequently stated that they are not bound by their own previous decisions, let alone by those of other courts and tribunals.[530] Their statutes may of course provide otherwise but, as a rule, statutes are silent and courts interpret this silence as a sort of authorization (certainly not a duty) to follow their own, or other courts', precedents unless there are 'cogent reasons' not to do so. For example, the ICJ is not bound by its precedents,[531] as evidenced by Articles 38(1)(d) and 59 of its Statute.[532] It is true that the Court frequently recalls its previous, as well as the PCIJ's, case law as 'precedents' or 'settled jurisprudence',[533] and underscores the need for consistency in its decisions. However, never has it stated that it is legally bound to do so. Despite its reluctance to refer to the jurisprudence of other courts and monitoring bodies, the ICJ has recently done so in the 2004 *Wall* Advisory Opinion[534] and in the 2007 *Genocide* Judgment[535] by citing several findings of the UN Human Rights Committee, of the ICTR, and notably of the ICTY.

[529] NAFTA Ch 11 Arbitration Tribunal, *Azinian et al v Mexico* Award on Jurisdiction and Merits of 1 November 1999, Case No ARB(AF)/97/2, 5 ICSID Rep 272, (2000) 39 ILM 537, para 97 (original emphasis).

[530] See eg ICSID Arbitral Tribunal, *AES Corp v The Argentine Republic*, Decision on Jurisdiction of 26 April 2005, Case No ARB/02/17, at <http://italaw.com/documents/AES-Argentina-Jurisdiction_002.pdf>, paras 30–33; *Bayindir Insaat Turizm Ticaret ve Sanayi AŞ v Islamic Republic of Pakistan*, Decision of 14 November 2005, Case No ARB/03/29, at <http://italaw.com/documents/Bayindr-jurisdiction.pdf>, para 76.

[531] See M Shahabuddeen, *Precedent in the World Court* (Cambridge: CUP, 2007).

[532] See section B (4)(c) above.

[533] See eg ICJ, *United States Diplomatic and Consular Staff in Tehran* (n 80 above) para 33.

[534] ICJ, *Legal Consequences of the Construction of a Wall in the Occupied Palestinian Territory* Advisory Opinion of 9 July 2004, [2004] ICJ Rep 136, paras 109, 136.

[535] ICJ, *Application of the Convention on the Prevention and Punishment of the Crime of Genocide (Bosnia and Herzegovina v Serbia and Montenegro)* Judgment of 26 February 2007, [2007] ICJ Rep 43.

Other statutes and practices may be more supportive of *stare decisis* than the ICJ Statute. Article 21(2) ICC Statute stipulates that 'the Court may apply principles and rules as interpreted in its previous decisions'. The term 'may' is clearly a compromise that leaves the question open. Article 20(3) Statute SCSL expressly provides that the Court 'shall be guided by the decisions' of ICTY and ICTR. In turn, despite the silence of both its Statute and Rules of Procedure and Evidence, the ICTY Appeals Chamber explicitly endorsed *stare decisis* in the 2000 *Aleksovski* Judgment, holding that 'in the interests of certainty and predictability, the Appeals Chamber should follow its previous decisions, but should be free to depart from them for cogent reasons in the interests of justice' and 'a proper construction of the Statute requires that the *ratio decidendi* of its decisions is binding on Trial Chambers'.[536] The ICTR followed suit in the 2006 *Semanza* Judgment.[537] Trial Chambers have always followed the Appeal Chamber's decisions and when they have departed from them they have done so by distinguishing the facts, such as in *Strugar*,[538] or by giving an interpretation of the Appeal Chamber's opinion, such as in *Krajišnik*,[539] and in *Mrkšić*.[540] Unlike Trial Chambers, the Appeal Chamber is not bound to follow its earlier decisions, although it generally does so.[541] In a few cases 'cogent reasons in the interest of justice' have indeed emerged and the Appeals Chamber has departed from its own case law, as in *Kordić and Cerkez* and in *Žigić*.[542] Both the ICTY and the ICTR have also frequently referred to the case law of other courts, especially that of the ECtHR as far as the rights of the accused are concerned as evidence of CIL.[543]

The WTO Panels and Appellate Body as well have extensively relied on its own previous case law, despite the silence of the DSU. For example, in *Woven Wool Shirts and Blouses* the Appellate Body recalled previous GATT Panel reports with regard to the burden of proof in WTO adjudication as the 'law' for both the panels and the Appellate Body itself.[544] In the field of human rights, the ECtHR has held that it is not bound to follow its own decisions and that it is at liberty to depart from an earlier decision for 'cogent reasons'.[545] When this has occurred, the Court has distinguished the case,[546] or

536 ICTY, *Prosecutor v Zlatko Aleksovski*, Appeal Judgment of 24 March 2000, Case No ICTY-95-14/1-A, paras 107, 113.

537 ICTR, *Semanza v Prosecutor* Appeal Decision on Zoran Žigić's motion for reconsideration of appeals chamber judgment IT 98 30/1 A delivered on 28 February 2005, Judgment of 26 June 2006, Case No ICTR-97-20-A, para 92.

538 ICTY, *Prosecutor v Pavle Strugar* Judgment of 31 January 2005, Case No ICTY-01-42-T, paras 447–455.

539 ICTY, *Prosecutor v Momčilo Krajišnik* Judgment of 27 September 2006, Case No ICTY-00-39-T, para 706.

540 ICTY, *Prosecutor v Mile Mrkšić, Miroslav Radić and Veselin Šljivančanin* Judgment of 27 September 2007, Case No ICTY-95-13/1-T, paras 448–458.

541 ICTY, *Prosecutor v Stanislay Galić* Appeal Judgment of 30 November 2006, Case No ICTY-98-29-A, para 117.

542 ICTY, *Prosecutor v Dario Kordić and Mario Cerkez* Appeal Judgment of 17 December 2004, Case No ICTY-95-14/2 A, para 1040; *Prosecutor v Zoran Žigić* Appeal Decision of 25 August 2006, Case No ICTY-98-30/1-R.2, para 9.

543 ICTR, *Barayagwiza v Prosecutor* Decision of 3 November 1999, Case No ICTR-97-19-AR72, para 40.

544 cf WTO, *United States—Measures Affecting Imports of Woven Wool Shirts and Blouses from India* AB Report of 23 May 1997, WT/DS33, paras 16–17; *EC—Measures concerning Meat and Meat Products (Hormones)* AB Report of 16 January 1998, WT/DS26/AB/R and WT/DS48/AB/R, paras 104–109.

545 ECtHR, *Cossey v United Kingdom* Judgment of 27 September 1990, App 10843/84, Series A No 184, (1991) 13 EHRR 622, para 35; *Chapman v United Kingdom* Judgment of 18 January 2001 [GC], App 27238/95, ECtHR Rep 2001-I 41, (2001) 33 EHRR 1, para 70.

546 ECtHR, *Kopecký v Slovakia* Judgment of 7 January 2003, App 44912/98, ECtHR Rep 2004-IX 125, para 27, reversed in *Kopecký v Slovakia* Judgment of 28 September 2004 [GC], (2005) 41 EHRR 944, para 52.

has made reference to 'changing conditions' and 'evolving... standards' on the protection of human rights in order 'to maintain a dynamic and evolutive approach'.[547] ITLOS recalled ICJ holdings as legal bases for its legal definitions in *Southern Bluefin Tuna*,[548] and *Mavrommatis*.[549]

However, international courts and tribunals at times decline to follow the case law of other courts and tribunals. In *Lubanga* the ICC Pre-Trial Chamber held that the CIL definition of 'joint criminal enterprise' accepted by the ICTY was inapplicable within the statutory regime of the ICC.[550] The ICTY overtly opposed in *Tadić*[551] the 'effective control' test defended by the ICJ in *Nicaragua*[552] and *Genocide*.[553] The ICTR refused to follow as persuasive, a precedent of another court in *Karemera*.[554]

On balance, there is an undeniable trend to convergence or, at least, to provide justification when courts decide to depart from other decisions. This is a welcome trend explicable in terms of discretion inherent in the judicial function.

D. Compliance, Implementation, and Enforcement

Once it has been established that international law consists of legally binding rules and judicial or quasi-judicial decisions, its credibility depends heavily on the extent to which they are complied with, implemented by the states within their legal systems, and enforced in case of non-compliance. Needless to say, there are binding rules of international law and decisions based thereon if both the rules and the decisions do not press their addressees to compliance. This section argues that the compliance record of international law is difficult to assess and in some respects misleading and that enforcement by way of sanction is far from proving or disproving that international law is 'true' law. The credibility of international law is to a large extent dependent on how far states implement it within their legal systems on the basis on their own law.

(1) Compliance

In his famous adage 'almost all nations observe almost all principles of international law and almost all of their obligations almost all of the time', Louis Henkin assumed the distinction between compliance and enforcement.[555] The existence of a rule is different from its factual observance. Rules may exist even if they are not complied with, although the level of compliance is relevant to their credibility and effectiveness. The fact that robberies occur does not prove that they have become lawful. Different

[547] ECtHR, *Christine Goodwin v United Kingdom* Judgment of 11 July 2002 [GC], App 28957/95, ECtHR Rep 2002-VI 1, (2002) 35 EHRR 447, para 74.

[548] ITLOS, *Southern Bluefin Tuna Cases (New Zealand v Japan; Australia v Japan) (Provisional Measures)*, Order of 27 August 1999, (1999) 38 ILM 1624, para 44.

[549] PCIJ, *Mavrommatis Palestine Concessions* (n 248 above) 11.

[550] ICC, *Prosecutor v Thomas Lubanga Dyilo* Decision on the Confirmation of Charges of 29 January 2007, Case No ICC-01/04-01/06, paras 317–367.

[551] ICTY, *Prosecutor v Dusko Tadić* (n 269 above) paras 99–145.

[552] LCJ, *Case concerning Military and Paramilitary Activities* (n 87 above) para 115.

[553] LCJ, *Application of the Convention on the Prevention and Punishment of the Crime of Genocide* (n 535 above) paras 403–407.

[554] ICTR, *Prosecutor v Karemera* Decision on Interlocutory Appeal Regarding Witness Proofing of 11 May 2007, Case No ICTR-98-44-AR73.8, para 7.

[555] L Henkin, *How Nations Behave: Law and Foreign Policy* (New York: Columbia University Press, 2nd edn, 1979) 47; L Henkin, 'International Law: Politics, Values, and Functions: General Course on Public International Law' (1989) 216 RdC 1, 69.

terms have been suggested to indicate different degrees of adherence to a legal rule, such as 'coincidence', 'conformity', 'compliance', and 'obedience'.[556] Also the term 'effectiveness' can have different meanings depending on whether it refers to how rules affect a substantive issue, or to how actors comply with the rules, or to how breaches of the rules are detected and punished through sanctions.[557] For present purposes the term 'compliance' is used in a broad sense to mean that the addressees of international law voluntarily conform their behaviour to the rules and judicial decisions. There is of course no need for all rules and decisions to be complied with by all addressees at all times. Overall compliance is sufficient, although how sufficient it must be depends on the common sense shared by its particular addressees. States display a propensity for both compliance and non-compliance according to different circumstances and in regard to different legal areas. This sub-section argues that the question of compliance with international law and judicial decisions can hardly be given a univocal answer.[558]

(a) Rules

A number of international law scholars have claimed that states comply with international law because they generally have an interest in doing so and/or for other reasons.[559] Rational-choice theorists do not generally question the notion that states mostly comply with international law, but are sceptical of the assumption that compliance is inspired by the 'force' of law, arguing that compliance depends on the factual convergence of the interests of states.[560] They contend that states either agree on a rule, but then law is *useless* since they would follow the alleged rule even if it had not existed, or do not agree on the rule, in which case law is *powerless* since the alleged rule is of itself incapable of forcing them to compliance. Realists, in turn, question the very assumption that states in fact comply (or even that they should comply) with international law, insisting that failures to comply ultimately depend on the absence of centralized and effective sanctions against transgressors.[561]

Critics generally downplay the *informal* pressure of the system to compliance. And the more the system is integrated (ie strongly interlaced), the greater the pressure on powerful and weak states alike. Although such pressure is not yet 'law' and does not imply per se that law is actually working, still it explains why there is a law and this law

[556] HH Koh, 'Why Do Nations Obey International Law?' (1996–97) 106 Yale LJ 2599, 2600–11, 2613.

[557] DW Drezner, *All Politics is Global: Explaining International Regulatory Regimes* (Princeton and Oxford: Princeton University Press, 2007) 12.

[558] For the elusiveness of the concept of compliance, see B Kingsbury, 'The Concept of Compliance as a Function of Competing Conceptions of International Law' (1998) 19 Mich JIL 345, challenging 'the tendency ... to view "compliance" simply as "correspondence of behaviour with legal rules"' on the assumption that 'the concept of "compliance" with law does not have, and cannot have, any meaning except as a function of prior theories ... so that different theories lead to significantly different notions of what is meant by "compliance"' and in particular call for 'different types of empirical research design'.

[559] See eg Henkin (1979) (n 555 above) 19, 49–56, 96–7; TM Franck (n 15 above); TM Franck, *Fairness in International Law and Institutions* (Oxford: OUP, 1998); A Chayes and A Handler Chayes, *The New Sovereignty: Compliance with International Regulatory Agreements* (Cambridge, Mass: Harvard University Press, 1995); HH Koh, 'Transnational Legal Process (1996) 75 Nebraska Law Review 181; HH Koh (n 556 above); J Brunnée and SJ Toope, 'Persuasion and Enforcement: Explaining Compliance with International Law' (2002) 13 Finn YBIL 273–95; A Alkoby, 'Theories of Compliance with International Law and the Challenge of Cultural Difference' (2008) 4 Journal of International Law & International Relations 151; M Bothe, 'Compliance', MP EPIL (October 2010 update).

[560] See Ch 4 above, section B (3). [561] ibid.

does work in international society. International jurists are generally able to produce a mass of material (such as laws, judicial decisions, treaties, state statements, scholarly views, etc) corroborating compliance with international law.

There are many reasons why states comply with international law even when it would appear at first sight not to be in their interest to do so. One reason is to avoid constantly recalculating the costs and benefits of their behaviour, unless circumstances are visibly changed. Another reason is that international law is made by states and states make it according to their interests. A third reason is that domestic law may require state officials, notably judges, to apply international law. Realists tend to see international law as a sort of etiquette recommending how foreign ministries 'should' behave in their mutual relations when it is in their interest to do so. But the application of international law is in many instances required by domestic (often by constitutional) law, as discussed shortly. In turn, non-compliance may be motivated by reasons other than the will to 'violate' the rule. One reason may be the vagueness of the rule. A state may find itself in the position of seeking to discover the scope of its obligation by testing the responses of other states, without any intention of breaching the law. A second reason may be the wish of the law-breaker to promote a change in the rule. A third reason may lie in domestic law and result from the priority accorded to domestic law. A fourth reason is that the state may prove objectively incapable of complying with a positive obligation, such as taking effective preventative or repressive measures towards private individuals, especially a weak or a failed state.

(b) Judicial decisions

Few studies have been devoted to the degree of compliance with international decisions,[562] yet the question is important in order to know how effective and credible, and hence legitimate in the perception of the parties and of the entire international community, international courts and tribunals are. Compliance with judicial decisions is not only important to the parties to any particular dispute but also to all other international potential parties, which are encouraged or discouraged in their decisions on whether to resort to adjudication in proportion to the degree of expected compliance in past cases. What was noted in 1997, with regard to the ICJ,[563] is still valid, ie: 'It is ironic Court's business up to the delivery of judgment is published in lavish detail, but it is not at all easy to find out what happened afterwards'.[564] Although today information is far more available, this assessment can safely be generalized to all international courts and tribunals.

The determination of whether international judicial decisions have been complied with by states is no easy task. It depends on a variety of complex issues, such as establishing what is meant by compliance, undue delay, good faith negotiations, and

[562] For an overview, see MK Bulterman and M Kuijer (eds), *Compliance with Judgments of International Courts* (The Hague: Nijhoff, 1996); ME O'Connell, *The Power and Purpose of International Law: Insights from the Theory and Practice of Enforcement* (Oxford: OUP, 2008) 295–325; Y Shany, 'Compliance with Decisions of International Courts as Indicative of Their Effectiveness: A Goal-Based Analysis', Hebrew University of Jerusalem Faculty of Law Research Paper No 04–10, at <http://papers.ssrn.com/sol3/papers.cfm?abstract_id=1697488>.

[563] C Paulson, 'Compliance with Final Judgments of the International Court of Justice since 1987' (2004) 98 AJIL 434; C Schulte, *Compliance with Decisions of the International Court of Justice* (Oxford: OUP, 2004).

[564] R Jennings, 'Presentation' in C Peck and RS Lee (eds), *Increasing the Effectiveness of the International Court of Justice: Proceedings of the ICJ/UNITAR Colloquium To Celebrate The 50th Anniversary of The Court* (The Hague: Nijhoff, 1997) 78, 78.

changing political conditions. It also depends on the frequent uncertainty of the legal obligations flowing from the decision, the disagreement between the parties as to compliance by the other party, the ambiguity of state behaviour, the difficulties of implementation, the margin of non-compliance accepted as physiological, administrative hurdles, the availability and reliability of the sources, etc. One might find the international judicial decision compliance record satisfactory when considering some of these factors and yet unsatisfactory when considering others. Compliance itself may or may not be found, depending on the notion of compliance accepted in the first place.

It is often said that the ICJ final decisions have generally been complied with,[565] the compliance rate being 'much higher in the ICJ's first twenty years than in its last twenty'.[566] It has also been suggested that many ICJ decisions are complied with because they are self-enforcing, such as those on jurisdiction, as well as no-violation or no-liability findings.[567] The critical question is, however, whether states comply with final decisions on the merits. The fact that procedural decisions are complied with has in practice little bearing for a meaningful assessment.

There are, however, well-known cases of non-compliance. The PCIJ 1939 *Socobelge* Judgment was not complied with.[568] Albania refused to pay damages to the United Kingdom for decades as a result of the 1949 *Corfu Channel* Judgment.[569] The United States refused to pay damages to Nicaragua as a result of the ICJ 1986 *Nicaragua* Judgment.[570] Argentina refused to comply with the 1977 *Beagle Channel* Arbitral Award.[571] The European Union refused to comply with the 1999 *Bananas* WTO Panel Report,[572] just as the United States did with regard to the 2004 *Cotton Subsidies* WTO Panel Report.[573] In 1990 Ethiopia refused to implement a boundary award in favour of Eritrea.[574] In 2001 the United States executed a German citizen in defiance of an ICJ binding order to stay the execution in the *LaGrand* case,[575] and delayed implementing an ICJ Judgment in the *Avena* case.[576] Provisional measures and substantive interim measures are rarely complied with.[577] An exception was the

565 SM Schwebel, 'Commentary' in Bulterman and Kuijer (eds) (n 562 above) 42; O'Connell (n 562 above) 298.

566 Posner, *The Perils of Global Legalism* (n 454 above) 142.

567 R Jennings, 'The Judicial Enforcement of International Obligations' (1987) 47 ZaöRV 3, 4.

568 PCIJ, *Société Commerciale de Belgique* Judgment of 15 June 1939, PCIJ Series A/B No 78, 160. cf O'Connell (n 562 above) 300.

569 The case was settled in 1992 by a payment of £1.2m by Albania to the UK. See R Norton-Taylor, 'Bank Returns Looted Nazi Gold to Albania', *The Guardian*, 30 October 1996, at 15.

570 The case, however, was apparently settled in 1991, as evidenced by a letter sent by Nicaragua to the ICJ to withdraw the case as a result of 'agreements aimed at enhancing Nicaraguan economic, commercial and technical development' reached between the two countries. cf (1992) 31 ILM 103, 105.

571 Arbitral Tribunal, *Dispute between Argentina and Chile concerning the Beagle Channel (Argentina v Chile)* Award of 18 February 1977, 21 RIAA 53. The boundary dispute was eventually settled by the Treaty of Peace and Friendship between Chile and Argentina of 29 November 1984, concluded with mediation by the Vatican.

572 WTO, *EC—Regime for the Importation, Sale and Distribution of Bananas—Recourse to Arbitration by the European Communities Under Article 22.6 of the DSU-Decision by the Arbitrators*, Panel Report of 9 April 1999, WT/DS27/ARB.

573 WTO, *United States—Subsidies on Upland Cotton*, Panel Report of 8 September 2004, WT/DS267/R.

574 cf O'Connell (n 562 above) 299.

575 ICJ, *LaGrand Case (Germany v United States) (Merits)* Judgment of 27 June 2001, [2001] ICJ Rep 466.

576 ICJ, *Case concerning Avena and Other Mexican Nationals (Mexico v United States)* Judgment of 31 March 2004, [2004] ICJ Rep 12; US Supreme Court, *Medellín v Texas* Judgment of 25 March 2008, 552 US 491, stating that ICJ judgments are not subject to direct enforcement by US courts (n 677 below).

577 Schwebel (n 565 above) 39–42; O'Connell (n 562 above) 306–7.

decision of the US Congress to cut off funding for mining Nicaragua's harbours in 1984 as a measure to comply with an ICJ interim measure.[578]

A substantial number of scholars tend to place excessive trust in the quantitative analysis of compliance. The major problem with judicial decision compliance is not so much how many decisions are complied with as the fact that international adjudication is not compulsory. Since the consent of the parties to the dispute is always necessary, it is neither surprising nor particularly telling that most judicial decisions have in fact been complied with. This may give the impression (and is supposed to 'prove') that international law is effective, an impression that would be fully justified in the context of domestic courts. But international judicial decisions do not bind states against their (previously given) consent and it is the capacity of being enforced against non-consenting parties that justifies confidence in a purely numerical calculation of compliance cases—an impossible count indeed.

(2) Domestic implementation

In the absence of a universal authority superior to states, all international law rules and decisions need to be made effective by state authorities within domestic legal systems.[579] International law needs to be implemented within states through national legislation, then applied by national courts, and be enforced by national authorities endowed with sufficient effectiveness. This is not to imply that international law is 'true' law only after 'entering' domestic legal systems. International law is 'law' at the international level, but its administration as law, as distinct from 'big politics', becomes credible within states.

Today, international law is greatly concerned with the lives of people in their mutual relations and in their relations with state officials. It is no longer a sort of goodwill-based code of conduct for rulers and diplomats, useful to guide their mutual dealings with no or little impact within the states involved. The domestic implementation of international law by state organs is thus crucial.[580] There is little hope that international law will 'work' if states do not direct their organs to apply it as 'law' equal to domestic law within their legal systems. It is a fact, however, that in cases of conflict between a domestic rule and an international rule, the former is considered to be fully valid domestically by all states, the only consequence of its application being the international responsibility of the state on grounds that domestic law cannot be relied upon to justify non-compliance with international law.[581]

[578] cf O'Connell (n 562 above) 307.

[579] For a recent survey of 27 states, see D Shelton (ed), *International Law and Domestic Legal Systems: Incorporation, Transformation, and Persuasion* (Oxford and New York: OUP, 2011).

[580] See eg B Conforti, 'Cours général de droit international public' (1988-V) 212 RdC 9, 25–7, giving the application of international law within legal domestic systems the greatest weight on the practical relevance thereof; B Conforti, *International Law and the Role of Domestic Legal Systems* (Dordrecht: Nijhoff, 1993); Koh (n 556 above) 2645–58, stressing state internalization of international law in the context of the transnational legal process approach; O'Connell (n 562 above) 329; A Nollkaemper, *National Courts and the International Rule of Law* (Oxford and New York: OUP, 2011); A Roberts, 'Comparative International Law? The Role of National Courts in Creating and Enforcing International Law' (2011) 60 ICLQ 57.

[581] Art 27 VCLT, Arts 3 and 32 ILC Articles on State Responsibility. An exception is Art 46 VCLT, contemplating the manifest violation of a provision of domestic law of fundamental importance regarding competence to conclude treaties as a ground for invalidity of treaties.

The issue is often framed in terms of monism or dualism between international law and domestic law.[582] Monism generally presupposes that international law is antecedent and superior to the state. It claims that there is only one universal legal system. Dualism assumes, by contrast, that international law is created by states and states have their own autonomous legal systems. In fact, states often adopt a dualistic approach in the sense that they generally authorize their legal officials to apply international law by a domestic act of legislation, whether explicit or implied, general or ad hoc. In practice, monism holds that state officials apply international law directly, whereas dualism accepts that international law can be applied domestically only after being 'transformed' into domestic law. Apart from theory, the dualism–monism dichotomy is also used to refer to different approaches taken by the constitutions of different states as to how international law is incorporated. In 'monist' states treaties are domestically valid, ie they have the status of domestic law, immediately at the moment of ratification.[583] In 'dualist' states treaties are domestically valid after their 'incorporation' into domestic law by a specific act. Incorporation may occur by way either of formal parliamentary approval,[584] or substantive parliamentary legislation.[585] The diffused notion that monist states are more inclined to apply international law than dualist states is misleading. Courts of monist states may either decline to apply an international law rule as 'not self-executing', a term to be discussed in detail later, or accord it a hierarchical rank lower than that of statutes, whereas the same rule may be applied as 'self-executing' or be accorded a higher rank than statutes by courts of dualist states.

An important phenomenon, linked to global transgovernmentalism and the alleged erosion of the traditional separation between international law and domestic law and the need *formally* to incorporate international law in domestic law, is 'informal' transnational decision-making by state authorities and officials in either a public or a private capacity and the 'implementation' of such decisions at the domestic level through the enactment of rules based on the powers formally conferred by domestic law.[586] National parliamentarians, members of the executive at the higher or lower level, judges, central banks' officials, and sub-state authorities of different states may and do increasingly meet within a variety of permanent forums—such as IOs, 'soft international organizations',[587] including near-secret transnational or 'global' commissions—or simply adopt common guidelines of action outside any permanent forum, and make arrangements whose contents they subsequently 'pour' into formal domestic acts enacted within their powers, such as laws, judgments, and administrative acts. The formal rank of the rules adopted is

582 For a historically contexualized account of the monism–dualism debate in the 19th and 20th centuries, see JE Nijman and A Nollkaemper (eds), *New Perspectives on the Divide Between National and International Law* (Oxford: OUP, 2007) 6–10.

583 eg Belgium, France, Japan, the Netherlands, Portugal, the Russian Federation, Spain, Switzerland, most Latin American countries, and former French colonies such as Algeria, Mali, and Senegal. cf K Kaiser, 'Treaties, Direct Applicability', EPIL (September 2006 update) para 9; D Sloss (ed), *The Role of Domestic Courts in Treaty Enforcement: A Comparative Study* (Cambridge: CUP, 2009) 7; Shelton (n 579 above) 9–10.

584 eg Austria, Germany, Italy, Ukraine, the US, and several Central and Eastern European countries such as the Czech Republic, Lithuania, and Poland. cf Kaiser (n 583 above) para 9; Sloss (n 583 above) 7; Shelton (n 579 above) 9–10.

585 eg Israel, the Scandinavian countries, the UK, and several countries which used to be part of the British Commonwealth such as Australia, Canada, India, and South Africa. cf Kaiser (n 583 above) para 9; Sloss (n 583 above) 7; Shelton (n 579 above) 9–10.

586 Theoretical frameworks of international and transnational 'regulators' include constitutionalism and administrativism, see Ch 4 above, section B (7) and (8). As regards 'informal' international law, see nn 374–82 above and accompanying text.

587 For the use of this expression, see Ch 5 above, n 207.

obviously the one accorded to the domestic 'implementing' act. While such practices may be necessary to govern globalization somehow, they may also be disruptive of the state as a political unit (by disaggregating it beyond recognition) and of its basic constitutional values once these are *informally bypassed* by state officials who may show more deference to their interlocutors of other states across the world (including for personal gains) than to their fellow citizens. The state is thus eroded without proposing a credible, better alternative political organization. It is often argued that transgovernmental forums need internal democratization (ie participation, transparency, accountability, etc) to 'compensate' the ongoing process of domestic 'deconstitutionalization'.[588] The entire process appears, more often than not, to be an *escape* by powerholders from (domestic) democratic and constitutional bounds towards a 'global' sphere which is too remote to be reliably checked by most people.

How international law is formally 'received' in domestic legal systems is a matter left to national law and is often governed by constitutional law. Since a survey of all national legal systems is obviously impossible here, the focus will be on four key general questions: (a) whether, and in what circumstances, international law has the force of law within domestic legal systems; (b) whether, and in what circumstances, international law is directly enforceable in domestic courts; (c) whether, and in what circumstances, international law prevails over domestic law in case of conflict; and (d) whether, and in what circumstances, domestic courts decline to adjudicate a case on the ground that the case is non-justiciable.

(a) Reception

Domestic legal systems generally have specific provisions (whether written or implied) which give effect to international law and direct state organs to apply it. International law leaves states free to determine how international law is given effect in their legal systems, the only relevant point being that it is observed by the state as a whole.

The reception of international law may consist of either a *reproduction* of the international law rule to be given effect in a domestic act or in a *reference* (or *renvoi*) to the international law rule (or set of rules, like a treaty, or even to a class of rules, such as all treaties). The first technique is typical of treaties in the United Kingdom and other Commonwealth countries. Courts are directed to apply the domestic Act—generally by following international criteria of interpretation—regardless of the persisting existence, validity, and effect of the international rule 'reproduced'. The second technique leaves the court the power to determine whether the referred rule of international law still exists, is valid, and has effect in the international sphere. Examples concerning general international law include Article 9(1) of the Austrian Constitution, Article 25 of the German Constitution, Article 28(1) of the Greek Constitution, Article 10(1) of the Italian Constitution, and Article 8(1) of the Portuguese Constitution. As regards treaties, worthy of mention are Article 55 of the French Constitution, Article VI of the US Constitution, and Article 31 of the Argentine Constitution. A few national constitutions also provide for the implementation of IOs' binding decisions, such as Articles 93 and 94 of the Dutch Constitution and Article 8(3) of the Portuguese Constitution.

Once introduced in the domestic legal system, international law is given effect and needs to be identified and applied by state officials. Even where international law is not received in domestic law, it still matters for interpretative purposes.[589] Disbelief in

[588] See Ch 4 above, note 217.

[589] On the so-called 'Charming Betsy principle' whereby 'an act of Congress ought never to be construed to violate the law of nations if any other possible construction remains' (see US Supreme

international law makes little sense in this (often overlooked) context. Whatever one may think of the reality of international law, it is a fact that some international law must be identified and applied by state officials as a matter of domestic law.[590]

(b) *Enforceability*

State legislation may be necessary not only to give international law effect within the domestic legal system, but also to supplement it in case the international law rule involved is interpreted in such a way that it cannot be applied for want of some indispensable element, such as the establishment of a domestic body or the appropriation of the funds necessary for the implementation of the rule. The term usually used, most frequently referring to treaties, is 'self-executing'. The term was first used in the 1829 *Foster v Neilson* Judgment of the US Supreme Court, when Chief Justice Marshall stated that a treaty is self-executing when it 'operates of itself without the aid of any legislative provision'.[591] The point is that the need for further legislative or administrative provisions may depend on a variety of reasons and the term 'self-executing' is open to various meanings and abuse.

First, legislation may be necessary to make a treaty validly, as is the case when a statute is required to authorize the ratification of the treaty. This legislation affects both the constitutional and the international validity of the treaty under Article 46 VCLT.[592] Its absence makes the treaty legally non-existent in the domestic legal system. At this level, the 'further legislation' required is needed *before* the operation of the treaty in the domestic legal system; still, its enactment may be relevant because it is the condition for the international law rule to operate. For example, 'duly ratified' treaties are generally directly operative in 'monist' domestic legal systems.

Secondly, there may be either no rule or an invalid rule in domestic law providing for the reception of international law (whether customary, or treaty, or other) within the domestic legal system. It is at *this* level that monism and dualism differ. Without legislation giving international law effect domestically, in most states state officials have no choice but to apply domestic law. At the same time, in case of conflict between international and domestic law they engage the international responsibility of the state for non-application of international law, although international law may still be considered for the interpretation of the domestic law applicable. In the United Kingdom, for example, domestic law may be interpreted consistently with a treaty irrespective of the question of whether the treaty has been incorporated into domestic law.[593] On the other hand, when a valid domestic rule giving effect to international law exists in domestic law, international law becomes operative domestically and state officials have to apply it. Questions concerning the 'political' nature of international

Court, *Murray v The Charming Betsey* [1804] 6 US 64, 118), see RG Steinhardt, 'The Role of International Law As a Canon of Domestic Statutory Construction' (1990) 43 Van LR 1103.

590 The same holds true, of course, for any domestic law rule referring to international law for any other purpose than incorporating it in municipal law. For example, the US Alien Tort Claims Act (ATCA) (28 USC § 1350) refers to the 'law of nations' as a criterion of jurisdiction of US district courts in tort claims made by aliens and presupposes that such a thing as international law does exist and can be objectively identified. ('The district courts shall have original jurisdiction of any civil action by an alien for a tort only, committed in violation of the law of nations or a treaty of the United States.')

591 US Supreme Court, *James Foster and Pleasants Elam v David Neilson* [1829] 27 US 253, 314.

592 See n 581 above.

593 See eg UK Court of Appeal, *Derbyshire CC v Times Newspapers Ltd* Judgment of 15 March 1992 [1992] QB 770, 830.

law must then be left to speculations and the courts have to be able to discern international law as it stands. The term used at this level is often 'direct applicability', meaning that the international law rule is 'directly' applicable by legal officials and courts, without the need of an additional ad hoc implementing act. Reception is sufficient. The term 'direct applicability' was first introduced by the PCIJ in its 1928 *Jurisdiction of the Courts of Danzig* Advisory Opinion, where it held that 'the wording and general tenor' of an agreement which was relevant in the case 'show that its provisions are directly applicable as between the officials of the Administration'.[594] At this level, 'further legislation' is needed in order to provide international law with legal force in the domestic legal system. For example, in the 2006 *Jones* Judgment, the House of Lords defined aggression as an international crime under CIL but refrained from giving it effect in the British legal system for lack of implementing legislation.[595]

Thirdly, international law may also be given 'direct effect' and be invoked by individuals in domestic courts. Not only does international law then bind state officials, it also provides individuals with rights and obligations. This meaning was also introduced by the PCIJ, in its *Jurisdiction of the Courts of Danzig* Opinion, in which the Court famously pointed out that 'the very object of an international agreement, according to the intention of the contracting Parties, may be the adoption by the Parties of some definite rules creating individual rights and obligations enforceable by the national courts'.[596] The term was taken up by the ECJ in the 1963 *Van Gend & Loos* Judgment, when the Court concluded that Article 12 EC 'produces direct effects and creates individual rights which national courts must protect', assuming that EU law constitutes a legal order of its own distinct from both international and domestic law.[597] In its subsequent case law, the ECJ has distinguished a 'vertical' direct effect of directives (concerning individuals towards the state) from a 'horizontal' direct effect (concerning individuals *inter se*), this latter being generally denied. The direct effect may have various legal bases. It can be expressly set out in the international law rule itself (for example, EU regulations under Article 288 TFEU), or be the result of the interpretation of the international law rule, or simply be produced by the technique used to make international law have effect in the legal system (for example, a statute reproducing a treaty). In any event, when the direct effect is recognized, international law is regarded as not only creating obligations engaging states (or their officials) with each other, but also as creating rights and obligations of individuals enforceable or actionable in the courts. As noted earlier, the direct effect is key to the international 'relevance' of individuals but has little to do with their international legal personality. It only implies that individuals may have rights and obligations before national courts (as *domestic* legal persons) because of an international law rule as created by states. International law rules are, in practice, often interpreted by domestic courts as not directly enforceable, even where a limited international legal personality of individuals is recognized. In the 2006 *Varvarin* Judgment, for example, the German Constitutional

[594] PCIJ, *Jurisdiction of the Courts of Danzig* Advisory Opinion of 3 March 1928, PCIJ Series B No 15, at 18–21.

[595] UK House of Lords, *R v Jones et al* Judgment of 29 March 2006, [2006] UKHL 16, paras 29–31, observing that 'it is for those representing the people of the country in Parliament, not the executive and not the judges, to decide what conduct should be treated as lying so far outside the bounds of what is acceptable in our society as to attract criminal penalties' and 'One would need very compelling reasons for departing from that principle' (*per* Lord Bingham of Cornhill).

[596] PCIJ, *Jurisdiction of the Courts of Danzig* (n 594 above) 17–18.

[597] ECJ, Case 26/62 *Van Gend en Loos v Netherlands Inland Revenue Administration* [1963] ECR 1, 12, Judgment of 5 February 1963.

Court held that Article 3 of the 1907 Hague Land Warfare Convention (IV) and Article 91 Protocol (I) additional to the 1949 Geneva Conventions on the protection of the victims of war set out an obligation of reparation for violations of the laws of war addressed to state organs, not a right of the individual victim to obtain reparation from the foreign state in domestic courts, although the individual has a limited international legal personality.[598] IOs' binding decisions are generally not regarded as being directly actionable in national courts,[599] as evidenced, for example, by the 1973 *Bradley* judgment of the High Court of Australia,[600] the 1976 *Diggs* Judgment of the US Court of Appeals,[601] the 1993 *Barcot* Judgment of the Italian Tribunal of Trieste,[602] and the 2006 *Dumez* Judgment of the French Court of Cassation.[603] National legislation giving effect to the founding treaty which provides for its adoption is not thought to be sufficient to produce a direct effect in the municipal sphere. Such acts are regarded as legally binding as between states, not within states.[604] This practice has some justification, bearing in mind that IOs' binding decisions may be seen as executive agreements (especially if concluded by unanimity), capable of derogating from the founding treaty as *lex posterior*. The only circumstances in which such resolutions can be assumed to be subordinate to, and hence in conformity with, the founding treaty is when there is a judicial review mechanism aimed at quashing them if they diverge from the founding treaty, an occurrence found only in the European Union.[605]

Finally, legislation may be needed to supplement international law rules which are incomplete in their contents. At this level, 'further' legislation is not needed to give effect to international law in the domestic legal system, nor to transform the rule into a directly-enforceable domestic rule. The tendency in some domestic courts to state that an 'incomplete' or 'vague' international law rule is not self-executing and, therefore, cannot be given effect in the domestic legal system causes confusion and, as clarified below, may be abusively used to avoid applying unpopular rules.[606] At this level, the treaty is operative within the domestic legal system and might also be invoked by private parties in domestic courts, but cannot be applied before legislative or

[598] German Constitutional Court, *Bombing of the Bridge of Varvarin* Judgment of 2 November 2006, at <http://lexetius.com/2006,2924> (see Ch 5 above, nn 259 and 542). Against the direct effect, see further the *Markovic Case* ((note 619 below) para 3 in the 'The Law' section). For an overview and further references, see N Ronzitti, 'Compensation for Violations of the Law of War and Individual Claims' (2002) 12 It YBIL 39; P Gaeta, 'Are Victims of War Crimes Entitled to Compensation?' in O Ben-Naftali (ed), *International Humanitarian Law and International Human Rights Law* (Oxford: OUP, 2011) 305, 308–11.

[599] See CH Schreuer, 'The Relevance of United Nations Decisions in Domestic Litigation' (1978) 27 ICLQ 1.

[600] Full Court of High Court of Australia, *Bradley v Commonwealth of Australia and anor* Judgment of 10 September 1973, (1979) 52 ILR 1, 2–3.

[601] US Court of Appeals DC Cir, *Diggs v Richardson* Judgment of 17 December 1976, at <http://ftp.resource.org/courts.gov/c/F2/555/555.F2d.848.75-1775.html>, para 14.

[602] Tribunal of Trieste, *Barcot and Trojic* Judgment of 24 December 1993, (1994) 77 RDI 206; Italian Court of Cassation, *Barcot and Trojic* Judgment of 8 July 1994, (1995) 31 RDIPP 760.

[603] French Court of Cassation, *Iraqi State v Société Dumez GTM (SA)* Judgment of 25 April 2006 No 679, (2006) 110 RGDIP 950.

[604] For an exception, see Court of Assize of Rome, *Lozano* Judgment of 25 October 2007 No 21/07, (2008) 17 It YBIL 287.

[605] See Ch 5 above, n 217. For the relevance of acts of IOs within domestic legal systems, see A Reinisch (ed), *Challenging Acts of International Organizations before National Courts* (Oxford: OUP, 2010).

[606] For a critical view in the context of the US legal system, see JJ Paust, 'Self-Executing Treaties' (1988) 82 AJIL 760, arguing that the distinction between self-executing and non-self-executing treaties 'is a judicially invented notion that is patently inconsistent with express language in the Constitution' and with the predominant views of the framers. See further D Sloss, 'United States' in Sloss (n 583 above) 509.

administrative provisions are passed to specify its contents. The degree of precision required varies with the state, as a function of the organs and procedures already in place in the state. The need for specification may derive either from the insufficient contents of the international law rule, or from the insufficient contents of the domestic legal system on the matter, or from the deficiencies of both combined.

In summary, an international law rule could be called non-self-executing, and hence in need of further national legislation, for at least three different reasons: (a) to give it effect domestically; (b) to create directly enforceable rights and obligations in domestic courts; and (c) to specify and supplement it if it is 'incomplete' in content. The rule might thus be self-executing in one sense but not in another. This is sufficient reason for courts to avoid the term; they should concentrate on the substance rather than playing with the words.

(c) Rank

Once it has been established that an international law rule (or set of rules contained in one instrument, or an entire class of rules) has the force of law within a given domestic legal system, with or without direct enforceability, it remains to be seen what hierarchical status the rule has in relation to all other domestic legal rules in order to solve the question of which prevails in case of conflict. This question is not a matter of international hierarchy but of domestic hierarchy, and the two hierarchies may not coincide. As noted, there is no doubt that international law prevails over conflicting domestic law as a matter of international law (or better, domestic law cannot be invoked to justify the violation of international law),[607] yet domestic legal officials may be directed by their national law to apply only domestic law and respect this latter's hierarchy.

When international law conflicts with domestic law, what matters is their domestic 'rank' within the municipal sphere, and this depends on how international law is given effect in the domestic law of each country. If a statute is used, then international law has in principle a statutory rank, unless a higher or different rank is laid down by some other principle of domestic law. For example, in the United States treaties and CIL are often deemed to have the rank of federal law, and hence prevail over conflicting state law and give way to federal constitutional law, while in their relationship with federal law the last-in-time rule usually applies.[608] In Italy, CIL has a constitutional rank, or even a higher-than-constitutional rank when it pre-dates the entry into force of the 1948 Italian Constitution, according to the Constitutional Court,[609] whereas treaties have an intermediate rank between constitutional law and standard legislation even when, as is usually the case, they are implemented through standard legislation.[610]

(d) Non-justiciability

For 'law' to work, the administration of the courts is essential. When the courts decline to adjudicate a case on the ground that the case is not justiciable, the law is generally

[607] See n 582 above.

[608] For the view that a treaty prevails over a subsequent statute in the absence of a legislative will to the contrary, see the District Court of New York, *Attorney-General v PLO* Judgment of 29 September 1988, (1988) 27 ILM 1055, 1073. Along similar lines, cf Swiss Federal Tribunal, *Frigerio v Département fédéral des transports* Judgment of 2 November 1968, (1987) 72 ILR 679, 689, and *Wohnbau SA Giswil in liquidation v Canton d'Obwald* Judgment of 9 March 1986, (1987) 43 ASDI 153.

[609] Italian Constitutional Court, *Russel* Judgment of 18 June 1979 No 48, (1979) 62 RDI 797.

[610] Italian Constitutional Court, *EP et al v Municipality of Avellino et al* Judgment of 22 October 2007 No 349/2007, ILDC 301 (IT 2007).

weakened. International law is no exception. Domestic courts do this by invoking prudential doctrines and impediments that often relate to the internal distribution of constitutional powers in order to allow the executive freedom of manoeuvre in conducting foreign policy. Obstacles to the judicial application of international law within domestic legal systems, based on its 'diplomatic' and 'inter-state' nature, should in principle be dismissed today. International law is no longer a law governing only the 'external' relations of states, ie an inter-ruler law. While it is made, unmade, and enforced by states, it governs the lives of *individuals* within states, all the more so at a time when the right of access to court is increasingly seen as a basic human right. It is true that the question of how to maintain a proper relationship between the courts and both the legislature and the executive is certainly a sensitive matter and different answers are possible in different states. However, international law as 'law' cannot but be applied as such by the domestic courts (their rulings, of course, being limited to the instant case), and courts should do so independently of the executive.[611] Domestic courts are called upon to deliver justice and justice today includes global justice, while deference to the executive may amount to a miscarriage of justice and a violation of constitutional and international law provisions providing for the right of access to justice.[612]

Questions of non-justiciability are properly limited to those in which the court declines to exercise jurisdiction because the question pertains to inter-state relations and has no judicial or objective standard to decide it.[613] For present purposes a broader sense is adopted, including the political question, the deference of the courts to the executive, the act of state doctrine, the state secrets doctrine, and the indeterminacy of international law.

The political question doctrine is designed to avoid deciding cases which touch upon matters deemed to be delegated to the other branches of the government, such as the conduct of foreign affairs.[614] Domestic courts decline to adjudicate cases involving sensitive questions touching upon possible violations of international law by the executive.[615] The doctrine was famously applied by US courts to decline to review the legality of the Vietnam War,[616] as well as the legality of arbitrary and prolonged detention authorized by the US Attorney-General.[617] It was applied by the French Conseil d'Etat when it declined to adjudicate a case concerning the legality of French nuclear tests,[618] and recently by the Italian Court of Cassation in the 2002 *Marković* Judgment concerning an action for damages caused in the Kosovo War of 1999,[619] and

[611] For an example of questionable deference of the court to the executive, see Singapore Court of Appeal, *Civil Aeronautics Administration v Singapore* Judgment of 14 January 2004, (2008) 133 ILR 371, para 27.

[612] C Focarelli, 'Denial of Justice', MP EPIL (January 2009 update).

[613] cf eg A Aust, *Handbook of International Law* (Cambridge: CUP, 2nd edn, 2010) 146. For the view that transactions involving foreign states invite 'judicial restraint or abstention' and are non-justiciable for lack of 'judicial or manageable standards' amounting to 'a judicial no-man's land', see UK House of Lords, *Buttes Gas v Hammer* Judgment of 29 October 1981, (1982) 21 ILM 92, 107.

[614] L Henkin, 'Is There a Political Question Doctrine?' (1976) 85 Yale LJ 597.

[615] See eg US Supreme Court, *Baker v Carr* Judgment of 26 March 1962, 369 US 186, 217, indicating six categories of political questions; Court of Appeals for the Second Circuit, *Klinghoffer et al v SNC Achille Lauro et al* Judgment of 21 June 1991, (1994) 96 ILR 69, 75–6, excluding the political character of the question of whether the PLO was a state and enjoyed sovereign immunity.

[616] R Falk (ed), *The Vietnam War and International Law* (Princeton: Princeton University Press, 1968–76, 4 vols).

[617] cf (1986) 80 AJIL 913–37 and (1987) 81 AJIL 371–90.

[618] cf (1976) 103 JDI 126–7.

[619] Italian Court of Cassation, *Marković et al v Italy* Judgment of 5 June 2002, (2002) 85 RDI 800–3, ILDC 293 (IT 2002), para 2 at 'The Law'. The case was brought to the ECtHR, which did not find the judgment in breach of the right of access to justice under Art 6 ECHR: see *Marković et al v Italy* Judgment of 14 December 2006 [GC], App 1398/03, (2007) 44 EHRR 1045.

by the US Court of Appeals for the District of Columbia Circuit in the 2009 *El-Shifa* Judgment in relation to a missile strike ordered by the US President against a pharmaceutical plant in Sudan which was believed to be connected to Al Qaeda's terrorist activities.[620] Certain matters may well fall under the discretionary power of the executive and be exempted from judicial scrutiny, such as the accreditation of foreign diplomats, the ratification of a treaty, the exercise of diplomatic protection,[621] or the decision to take a certain lawful action rather than another during a conflict. However, when a state is bound by an international law rule and this rule is operative within its domestic legal system, all the organs of the state have to apply the rule and the courts should ascertain whether a violation of such a rule by the state has occurred, with effect of course being limited to the instant case. The executive may decide whether a certain lawful act of war is preferable to another, equally lawful, but cannot prefer an unlawful act of war instead of a lawful one.[622] It is another question to ask whether in particular circumstances national constitutional law (made to prevail over international law) requires the courts to abstain from reviewing the executive's decisions. A related, although distinct, question is that of the power of the executive to violate CIL with a view to transforming it.[623]

Another self-imposed limit to the autonomous application of international law by domestic courts is the need for certificates from the executive. This practice was normal in the past, but it often sounds anachronistic today at a time when international law is mostly concerned with the lives of people within states. In France the interpretation of treaties was until recently delegated by the courts to the executive.[624] In the United Kingdom, the courts refer to the executive for a variety of foreign matters.[625] In the United States, courts are inclined to ask the executive for the direct applicability of treaties.[626] In many countries, the courts ask the executive for advice in relation to the existence of a ground of termination of treaties.[627] When referrals to the executive go beyond requests for information to be freely assessed and are aimed at obtaining direction, they are a form of deference to the executive which is barely acceptable, at

620 US Court of Appeals for the District of Columbia Circuit, *El-Shifa Pharmaceutical Industries Company and Salah el Din Ahmed Mohammed Idris v United States* Judgment of 27 March 2009 at <http://pacer.cadc.uscourts.gov/common/opinions/200903/07-5174-1172578.pdf>, at 7, holding that 'it is not for the federal courts to review the President's battlefield decisions', and 'Under the Constitution, this decision is immune from judicial review'.

621 eg for the view that 'under domestic law . . . the Government has no obligation to exercise diplomatic protection against a foreign State in favour of [its] citizens' since 'the acts performed by a state in the regulation of international relations are in effect political acts, as such non-justiciable by both ordinary and administrative courts' for the award of damages, see recently Italian Council of State, *Il Tuo Viaggio srl v Presidenza del Consiglio dei ministri, Ministero delle infrastrutture e dei trasporti e Ministero degli affair esteri* Judgment of 24 December 2009 No 8719, (2010) 93 RDI 1280, para 6 (English trans by the author). For the non-existence of an international obligation placed on states to exercise diplomatic protection, see Ch 5 above, nn 272–6 and accompanying text.

622 See, *mutatis mutandis*, the 2010 *Habib* Judgment (n 632 below).

623 See JI Charney, 'The Power of the Executive Branch of the United States Government to Violate Customary International Law' (1986) 80 AJIL 913, 917, stating that: 'If the executive branch is restrained by the rule that customary international law is domestic law of the United States and that it may not be violated, U.S. participation in the international system will be handicapped'. On the transformation of customary international law, see section B (4) above.

624 D Carreau and F Marrella, *Droit international* (Paris: Pédone, 11th edn, 2012) 577–9, 586–7.

625 FA Mann, *Foreign Affairs in English Courts* (Oxford: Clarendon Press, 1986) 23–62; I Brownlie, *Principles of Public International Law* (Oxford: OUP, 7th edn, 2008) 49.

626 Y Iwasawa, 'The Doctrine of Self-Executing Treaties in the United States: A Critical Analysis' (1985–86) 26 Virg JIL 627, 666, note 175.

627 B Conforti and A Labella, 'Invalidity and Termination of Treaties: The Role of National Courts' (1990) 1 EJIL 44.

least when a proper standard by which a case can be decided exists in the law to be applied. It is true that the executive may 'know' better than courts the state of international affairs involved in the instant case, but its knowledge and assessment is (and should be) based mainly on policy considerations, while the courts have to apply the law.

The act of state doctrine prevents domestic courts from reviewing the international or constitutional legality of foreign laws or other state acts and thus espouses their validity in the forum. The doctrine has been upheld by the courts of certain states and not by others. The Supreme Court of Aden did not apply it in the 1953 *Rose Mary* Judgment,[628] and this line has also been taken by French and Dutch courts.[629] By contrast, the US Supreme Court in the 1964 *Sabbatino* Judgment endorsed the doctrine,[630] thereby triggering the enactment of the so-called 'Second Hickenlooper Amendment' requiring US courts not to apply it in cases involving foreign laws of expropriation of US property unless the executive instructs them to do so on a case-by-case basis.[631] The doctrine has been recently rejected, for very sound reasons, by the Federal Court of Australia in the 2010 *Habib* Judgment concerning a detainee in Guantanamo.[632] It is grounded in diverse rationales and policies, including the respect for international comity, separation of powers, and sovereignty of foreign states, as well as the avoidance of embarrassment to the executive in its conduct of foreign relations.[633] Given this variety in the jurisprudence, the doctrine is neither required nor prohibited by general international law.[634] Yet, as a matter of domestic law and policy, one should wonder why national courts are not to consider the international lawfulness of foreign laws and other measures and to refuse their application in the forum as a consequence of their international unlawfulness. That domestic courts are called upon to assess whether a certain act is or is not in keeping with international law is in principle an integral part of their work, as this section shows, and there is little reason to depart from this basic assumption when the question relates to whether a foreign law should be given effect in the forum.

Also the state secrets doctrine may bar domestic courts from adjudicating a case of international law concern. This question has been widely debated in relation to 'extraordinary renditions' of alleged terrorists to states where they have been tortured. US courts have relied on the doctrine to decline jurisdiction,[635] followed by other

[628] Aden Supreme Court, *Anglo-Iranian Oil Co v Jaffrate et al (The Rose Mary)* Judgment of 9 January 1953, (1953) 20 ILR 316, 322–3, holding that 'a foreign law that is contrary to international law or in flagrant violation of international comity need not be regarded'.

[629] Dutch Supreme Court, *Attorney-General of the United States v NV Bank voor Handel en Scheepvaart* Judgment of 17 October 1969, (1987) 74 ILR 150, 153. See P Weil, 'Le contrôle par les tribunaux nationaux de la licéité internationale des actes des Etats étrangers' (1971) 23 AFDI 9.

[630] US Supreme Court, *Banco Nacional de Cuba v Sabbatino* [1964] 376 US 398, 437, concluding that 'both the national interest and progress toward the goal of establishing the rule of law among nations are best served by maintaining intact the act of state doctrine in this realm of its application'.

[631] cf 22 USC § 2370.

[632] Federal Court of Australia, *Habib v Commonwealth of Australia* Judgment of 25 February 2010, [2010] FCAFC 12, para 24, holding that 'The act of state doctrine—whatever it might be—has no application where it is alleged that Commonwealth officials have acted beyond the bounds of their authority under Commonwealth law' (*per* Perram J).

[633] US Supreme Court, *Underhill v Hernandez* [1897] 168 US 250, 254, revisited in *Kirkpatrick & Co v Environmental Tectonics* [1990] 493 US 400, 409.

[634] See section B (2)(a) above. For the view that 'If international law does not prescribe use of the doctrine, neither does it forbid application of the rule even if it is claimed that the act of state in question violated international law', see US Supreme Court, *Banco Nacional de Cuba* (n 630 above) 422.

[635] See V Hansen, 'Extraordinary Renditions and the State Secrets Privilege: Keeping Focus on the Task at Hand' (2008) 33 NC JILCR 629. See additionally Ch 7 below, n 435.

courts elsewhere, including the Italian Constitutional Court.[636] The doctrine is, however, difficult to justify in states in which the rule of law is expected to prevail. It is in the interest of the whole national community, not simply of the victims, to know what the executive has done or is doing, at least when it is accused of serious violations of human rights, whatever the underlying motives.[637]

Finally, domestic courts tend to use the 'indeterminacy' and 'vagueness' of international law to decline to apply certain undesired rules for unstated considerations of policy. Indeterminacy and vagueness are relative concepts: what appears too indeterminate or vague to one court may well appear sufficiently determinate and precise to another. Only when the international law rule provides either for a discretionary power or for an obligation which cannot by any means be fulfilled without supplementing legislation, should the rule be treated as not self-executing.[638] At other times, domestic courts may decline to adjudicate because the treaty provides for an international mechanism for the settlement of disputes, as is the case with the ECJ's treatment of the GATT.[639] In yet other cases, domestic courts may decline to decide a case because of the presence in the treaty of a 'clause of implementation' stating that the state shall adopt all domestic measures to give effect to its rules, such as Article 2(2) ICCPR, Article 2(1) ICESCR, and Article 4 CRC.[640] However, implementation clauses have to be interpreted as any other treaty rule (according to the criteria codified in Articles 31 to 33 VCLT or others used in the practice) and may well be construed as simply imposing on states the obligation to take legislative or other measures 'whenever necessary' to their full application, meaning that when they are not necessary, because the specific rule of the treaty involved is self-executing according to its appropriate interpretation, the rule is directly enforceable.[641] This construction explains why *identical* rules contained in other human rights treaties, in which no implementation clause is found, are applied without hesitation as self-executing by the same courts. The function

[636] Italian Constitutional Court, Judgment of 11 March 2009 No 106, at <http://www.giurcost.org/decisioni/2009/0106s-09.html>, para 3, founding the state secrets doctrine on the 'supreme interest' in the security of the state which justifies no judicial review but only parliamentary scrutiny of the executive branch.

[637] For a recent critical stand, see COE Parliamentary Assembly Res 1838 (2011) ('Abuse of State Secrecy and National Security: Obstacles to Parliamentary and Judicial Scrutiny of Human Rights Violations') and Recommendation 1983 (2011), both of 6 October 2011, at <http://assembly.coe.int/ASP/NewsManager/EMB_NewsManagerView.asp?ID=7021>.

[638] Conforti (n 310 above) 312.

[639] cf eg ECJ, Case C-93/02 P *Biret International SA v Council of the European Union* [2003] ECR I-10497, paras 61–63, Judgment of 30 September 2003.

[640] cf eg US Court of Appeals for the Third Circuit, *Mannington Mills Inc v Congoleum Corp* Judgment of 3 April 1979, 595 F2d 1287, para 72; French Court of Cassation, Judgment of 15 July 1993, (2005) 109 RGDIP 1017; Court of Cassation, Judgment of 13 July 1994, (2005) 109 RGDIP 1017; US District Court for the District of Columbia, *Tel-Oren v Libyan Arab Republic* Judgment of 30 June 1981, 517 F Supp 542, para 180; Dutch Supreme Court, *WdK v Public Prosecutor* Judgment of 6 December 1983 No 557, 16 Neth YBIL (1985) 526, 528, but see next note for the opposite view; Italian Court of Cassation, *Armenio et al v Società Caramar* Judgment of 10 September 1993 No 9459, (1995) 78 RDI 807, 810. For a critical assessment of the US jurisprudence, see Iwasawa (n 626 above) 658–61.

[641] In this sense cf eg Court of Appeal of Turin, *Suisse v Ditta Valpreda and Ditta Promotor* Judgment of 12 November 1965, (1966) 10 RDIPP 369, 372; Supreme Court of Madagascar, *Ratsimba* Judgment of 19 April 1969, (1987) 73 ILR 388, 390; Dutch Supreme Court, *Hoogenraad v Organisation for Pure Research in the Netherlands* Judgment of 20 April 1990, 22 Neth YBIL (1991) 376, 378, para 3.2; Belgian Labour Court of Nivelles, *RF v Office Nationale des pensions* Judgment of 15 November 1991, (1994) 27 RBDI 693; Dutch Supreme Court, *Luvia Mathilda and 21 others v Roman Catholic Central School Board Foundation* Judgment of 7 May 1993, (1994) 24 Neth YBIL 510, 511, para 3.4.

of implementation clauses is in fact to place on the states parties the obligation (additional to the obligations stemming from any provision of the treaty, which may or may not be self-executing) to enact laws and other regulations capable of ensuring respect for the treaty as a matter of general application, as opposed to respect based on case-by-case decisions by executive bodies, courts, and other domestic organs.[642] They require legislation or other regulation not because the treaty provisions are non-self-executing but because legislation or other regulation may ensure a higher likelihood of compliance and uniformity in the application of the treaty by domestic organs. As a result, if a state fails to enact the required legislation, no matter how it abides by all the provisions of the treaty on a case-by-case basis through its organs, it is in breach of the implementation clause alone. This has clearly nothing to do with the self-executing or non-self-executing character of each provision of the treaty.

(3) Enforcement

While compliance refers to uncoerced abidance by the law, enforcement denotes the process of coercing the transgressor to compliance. Coercion occurs through 'sanctions'. It is dubious that in international law sanctions play a vital role and even their very availability has been questioned. The Austinian view of international law as 'positive morality', not 'law properly so called', is based on the absence in the international legal system of centralized sanctions applied by a sovereign. Kelsen's reply is that international law does have sanctions (reprisals and war), although these are decentralized. Today, sanctions include countermeasures, either armed (self-defence) or peaceful, and other measures adopted within international organizations. A few procedures exist to enforce international judicial decisions. Here again, the roles played by domestic legal courts and enforcement bodies are essential to the credibility and effectiveness of international law.

(a) Sanctions

Enforcement is typically associated with sanctions.[643] Opinions as to the necessity of sanctions in order for law in general, and for international law in particular, to qualify as law are divided.[644] The Austinian view that international law is not law 'properly so called' because of its lack of effective and centralized sanctions is widespread.[645] Kelsen's specification that international law does have sanctions, although decentralized, is open to question.[646] Some would reply to both Austin and Kelsen that sanctions are not inherent elements of law.[647] It might also be argued that sanctions are essential to law by endorsing a broad notion of sanction (including, for example, reputational sanctions directed against future behaviour) and the *prospect* of the application of sanctions.[648] The

[642] The approach here adopted differs from that which assigns to implementation clauses the mere function of obliging contracting states to make the treaty become effective within their legal systems, thereby ensuring the formal validity of the treaty domestically, as maintained eg by Conforti (n 580 above) 46–7.

[643] See JM Farrall and K Rubenstein (eds), *Sanctions, Accountability and Governance in a Globalised World* (Cambridge: CUP, 2009).

[644] See Ch 1 above, section B (3)(f).

[645] See Ch 1 above, n 64.

[646] For a critical appraisal of Kelsen's approach, see Q Wright, 'Enforcement of International Law' (1944) 38 ASIL Proc 77, 78; JL Kunz, 'Sanctions in International Law' (1960) 54 AJIL 324, 332.

[647] See Ch 1 above, n 65. Specifically referring to international law, see W Friedmann, *The Changing Structure of International Law* (London: Stevens and Sons, 1964) 81–95; Henkin (1979) (n 555 above) 49.

[648] Henkin (1979) (n 555 above) 54; O'Connell (n 562 above) 7–11.

possibility of reciprocity is important in order to prevent possible violations and induce other states to conform to the rules. In a globalized world, sanctions from individual states are in fact problematic. As noted, international sanctions can no longer be conceived of as they were in the past and should be rethought when considering that in an interconnected world 'exclusion from participation' is more and more important in comparison to 'traditional sanctions'.[649]

Defining a 'sanction' is no easy matter.[650] Domestically, a sanction is usually a means of law enforcement, a reaction to a breach of the law. Internationally, a sanction can also be a means of coercing another state to behave in a particular manner or of punishing another state for conduct which is thought to be a threat to a basic value of the system, albeit not formally unlawful. Sanctions can thus serve both preventative and repressive purposes. For example, UN sanctions adopted by the Security Council under Article 41 UN Charter, are not limited to violations of international law, not even to violations of the UN Charter, and can be undertaken also when a 'threat to the peace' occurs.[651] The same could be said of Security Council 'authorizations' of the use of force: they are 'enforcement measures' amounting to sanctions designed to target either a state or a non-state actor, although they are neither binding nor necessarily reactive to an international wrongful act.[652]

There are at least three general categories of international sanctions in current international law: those taken by individual states against individual states (individual countermeasures and self-defence), those taken individually by two or more states against individual states outside any institutional framework (collective countermeasures and self-defence), and those taken by states collectively or allegedly for a collective purpose within an international organization against individual states (so-called 'institutionalized' sanctions). One might be tempted to describe the sanctions of the first category as 'private' and those which fall into the second and third categories as 'public'.[653] However, the terms 'private' and 'public' are misleading in a law, such as international law, in which there is no universal recognized authority acting *as such* for the collective good, although one cannot exclude the possibility that states in certain circumstances do act for the collective good. The notion that law is simply enforcement through sanctions is magnified with the doctrine that also 'third' states are allowed to apply sanctions, especially against states that have breached fundamental rules contemplating obligations *erga omnes*.[654]

(b) Countermeasures

Countermeasures are per se unlawful reactions by a state to a breach by another state of any kind of international law rule.[655] As reactions to an unlawful act they are lawful, and hence a cause precluding wrongfulness.[656] They may be either individual or

[649] Friedmann (n 647 above) 81–95.

[650] MR Reiff, *Punishment, Compensation, and the Law: A Theory of Enforceability* (New York: CUP, 2005) 17–44, distinguishing physical, strategic, moral, social, automatic, and 'legal' sanctions.

[651] Conforti and Focarelli (n 32 above) 204–20.

[652] See Ch 7 below, section A (1)(d).

[653] See eg Kelsen (n 10 above) 20, defining a sanction as 'the reaction of the community, constituted by the legal order, to the evil-doer, the delinquent' and claiming that 'the individual who carries out the sanction acts as an organ of the community, constituted by the legal order'.

[654] See Ch 8 below, section B (1)(c).

[655] For the conditions required to assert the commission of an internationally unlawful act, see J Crawford, A Pellet, and S Olleson (n 401 above). Self-defence as an armed countermeasure is discussed in Ch 7 below, section A (1)(c).

[656] See n 270 above.

collective, depending on whether they are adopted by the injured state or by 'third' states (ie states intervening in assistance of the injured state), as well as either peaceful or forcible, depending on whether they involve the use of international force. The 2001 ILC Articles on State Responsibility basically focus on individual peaceful countermeasures, since forcible countermeasures are limited to self-defence (armed reprisals in peacetime being today prohibited,[657] and belligerent reprisals not being covered by the Articles) and collective countermeasures are only seen as 'lawful measures', as explained in Chapter 8. Unlike countermeasures, 'retorsions' are per se lawful measures which may be adopted, inter alia, as unfriendly reactions to an unlawful act of another state. The temporary non-performance of a treaty because of its non-performance by the other party (*inadimplenti non est adimplendum*) may be seen as a countermeasure, although the termination of the treaty on the same ground is an autonomous justification, as set out in Article 60 VCLT.[658]

Countermeasures are to be treated as lawful acts, although per se consisting in unlawful acts, on condition that they respect a set of limits. These are stated in Articles 49 to 54 ILC Articles on States Responsibility: proportionality (Article 51), temporariness (Articles 49(2), 52(3), and 53), prior request for reparation (Articles 49(1) and 52), prohibition on the threat or use of force pursuant to the UN Charter, or respect for fundamental human rights or for IHL rules prohibiting belligerent reprisals, or of 'other obligations' belonging to *jus cogens* (Article 50(1)),[659] as well as provisions relating to diplomatic immunities (Article 50(2)(b)).

The issue of proportionality deserves close scrutiny. In the 1928 *Naulilaa* Award the Arbitral Tribunal, concerned with armed acts of reprisal carried out by Germany against Portugal when Portugal was neutral in World War I, held that reprisals which are 'highly disproportionate' (*hors de toute proportion*) with the act which had motivated them were 'excessive and hence unlawful'.[660] In the 1978 *Air Services* Award, the Arbitral Tribunal articulated the condition of proportionality by observing that countermeasures must have 'some degree of equivalence with the alleged breach', this being 'a well-known rule' which both Parties had recognized and invoked in the instant case. However, in the Tribunal's view, 'judging the "proportionality" of countermeasures is not an easy task and can at best be accomplished by approximation', taking into account 'not only the injuries suffered by the companies concerned but also the importance of the questions of principle arising from the alleged breach'.[661] What was meant by 'questions of principle' is unclear; still, the Tribunal's view was unquestionably that damages alone were inadequate for an accurate assessment of proportionality. In the 1997 *Gabčíkovo-Nagymaros* Judgment the ICJ reiterated that the 'effects' of a countermeasure must be 'commensurate with the injury suffered, taking account of the rights in question'.[662] There is uncertainty as to the meaning to be attached to the concept of proportionality, as well as to the terms which are expected to be proportionate. As to the first point, 'proportion', 'equivalence', and 'reciprocity' have been evoked by different authorities with different meanings, and outcomes may obviously be different depending on the concept adopted. As to the second point, reference has

[657] See Ch 7 below, n 59.
[658] ICJ, *Gabčíkovo-Nagymaros Project* (n 140 above) para 106.
[659] See Focarelli (n 428 above) 452–4.
[660] Arbitral Tribunal, *Portugal v Germany (The Naulilaa Case)* Award of 31 July 1928, Case No 360, 2 RIAA, 1011, 1028.
[661] Arbitral Tribunal, *Case concerning the Air Service Agreement of 27 March 1946 between the United States and France* Award of 9 December 1978, 18 RIAA 417, para 83.
[662] LCJ, *Gabčíkovo-Nagymaros Project* (n 140 above) para 85.

been made in different contexts either to the 'losses', or to the 'overall effects', or to the 'gravity of the act', or to the 'amount of coercion' applied, or to the 'necessity' to attain the legitimate ends of countermeasures. More often than not, a selection of these criteria have been put forward and combined to reach a certain conclusion rather than another.[663] It is sometimes argued that retaliation in kind, ie the violation of the same rule violated by the alleged offending state, is automatically proportionate, but this is rarely the case (assuming that the correct notion of proportionality is a reasonable balance between damages) since the same violation may cause different damages to different states in different circumstances. Moreover, state practice is rather poor in (if not totally devoid of) cases in which proportionality has been invoked by the reacting state or lack of proportionality has been denounced by the targeted state. Unlike cases in which armed countermeasures have been adopted, states do not seem very interested in 'measuring' the reaction when adopting a countermeasure (for example, by ensuring that the quantity of assets frozen is proportionate to the severity of the breach committed by the alleged offending state).[664] In the jurisprudence and in legal doctrine proportionality seems quite understandably to have been dictated by common sense, perhaps by a general principle of law, but one has to acknowledge that states take little heed of proportionality when it comes to peaceful countermeasures, showing an interest only for humanitarian exceptions, which, unlike proportionality, are pre-established and independent of any 'measurement'. The taking into account of proportionality by international courts and tribunals may thus be seen as part of the justice inherent in their discretion rather than as the content of a legal rule.

Another difficult question is whether for a countermeasure to be taken a prior request for reparation, or a prior attempt at dispute settlement when available, is required. The need for a prior request for reparation was famously stated in the *Naulilaa* Award (*sommation restée infructueuse*), but the case concerned acts of armed reprisal and the requisite prior request was linked to the limit of necessity for the use of force.[665] In the *Air Services* Award countermeasures were said to be prohibited when there is a compromise between the parties prescribing the submission of their dispute to an impartial tribunal and *a fortiori* when the dispute is already *sub judice* and the court or tribunal does not have the means necessary to achieve the (legitimate) aim of countermeasures, including the aim of compelling the other party to submit without delay to adjudication and then to comply with the decision.[666] Since international courts and tribunals as a rule lack any means to enforce their decisions, as discussed in the next sub-section, the prohibition remains theoretical and the sentence may have the effect, in practice, of permitting countermeasures when the dispute is *sub judice*. The *Gabčíkovo-Nagymaros* Judgment only recalled that 'the injured State must have called upon the State committing the wrongful act to discontinue its wrongful conduct or to make reparation for it'.[667] For their part, the 2001 ILC Articles accept that the aim of countermeasures is reparation (Article 49(1)) and that when reparation is made countermeasures must cease (Article 53). Before taking a countermeasure the state must request reparation (Article 52(1)), except for urgent countermeasures (Article 52

[663] For a more detailed analysis, see C Focarelli, *Le contromisure nel diritto internazionale* (Milan: Giuffrè, 1994) 382–93.

[664] This was the result of a review of some 70 cases of alleged countermeasures in the international practice subsequent to 1945 in Focarelli (n 663 above) 396–420.

[665] Arbitral Tribunal, *Portugal v Germany (The Naulilaa Case)* (n 660 above) 1027.

[666] Arbitral Tribunal, *Case concerning the Air Service Agreement* (n 661 above) paras 84–96.

[667] ICJ, *Gabčíkovo-Nagymaros Project* (n 140 above) para 85.

(2)). The 2001 ILC Articles prohibit countermeasures when the dispute is pending before an international court or tribunal endowed with the power to issue binding decisions on the parties to the dispute (Article 52(3)(b)). However, under Article 52(4), countermeasures are permitted when the alleged responsible state fails to implement the dispute settlement procedures in good faith.

In the past, a humanitarian limitation to armed or belligerent reprisals was recognized *a fortiori* with regard to non-armed reprisals taken in time of peace.[668] In the *Naulilaa* Award the Tribunal held that a reprisal is 'limitée par les expériences de l'humanité'.[669] Today, the humanitarian limitation is often absorbed in *jus cogens*, although Article 50 2001 ILC Article has opted for separate provision in paragraphs (2)(c) and (2)(d). In international practice, countermeasures generally provide for humanitarian exceptions, such as food and medicine, and limited to the most basic human rights concerning respect for life and the prohibition on inhuman or degrading treatment.[670] In the 1980 *Hostages* Judgment the ICJ held that the detention as hostages of US citizens, including non-diplomatic persons, in the US embassy in Tehran, presented by the United States as inhumane, was unjustified under international law even assuming that it was a countermeasure against alleged unlawful acts committed by the United States against Iran.[671]

Under Article 50(2)(b) diplomatic immunities may not be violated by way of countermeasure. In the 1980 *Hostages* Judgment the ICJ famously stated that diplomatic law is a 'self-contained regime' that provides its own means of redress in case of abuse, specifically the declaration of *persona non grata* of the foreign diplomatic agents who have abused their functions and in the more serious cases the breaking off of diplomatic relations with the sending state.[672] The Court dealt with the hypothesis of the breach of diplomatic law as a reaction to the violation of rules pertaining to other fields of international law. In fact, several national legislatures provide for reciprocity in the treatment of foreign diplomats, and international practice attests that states are prepared to resort to retaliation in kind. Countermeasures against foreign diplomats cannot thus be excluded in the form of reciprocity, provided that the general humanitarian limit to countermeasures is respected.[673] By contrast, it does not seem that diplomatic law may be violated by way of countermeasure as a reaction to violations of other rules of international law.[674] The 'self-contained regime' statement of the ICJ, far from excluding the operation of countermeasures in general in the field of diplomatic law, may be understood as suggesting that diplomatic law is 'special' in that it may not be violated by way of *non-reciprocal* countermeasures under general international law.

(c) Judicial decisions

As regards the enforcement of judicial decisions, Article 94(2) UN Charter is notable.[675] It provides the winning party in proceedings before the ICJ with the power to seise the Security Council, which may 'make recommendations or decide upon measures to be taken to give effect to the judgment'. This provision gives the Council the discretion

[668] cf eg Anzilotti (n 212 above) 166–7.
[669] Arbitral Tribunal, *Portugal v Germany (The Naulilaa Case)* (n 660 above) 1026.
[670] See Focarelli (n 663 above) 495–511.
[671] LCJ, *United States Diplomatic and Consular Staff in Tehran* (n 80 above) paras 23, 91.
[672] ibid paras 85–88.
[673] See Focarelli (n 663 above) 512–22.
[674] ibid 520–1.
[675] More generally, see O Schachter, 'The Enforcement of International Judicial and Arbitral Decisions' (1960) 54 AJIL 1.

to enforce ICJ judgments and to choose whether to do so by way of non-binding recommendation or binding decision, but precludes the Council from proceeding *proprio motu*. It is unclear whether the term 'judgment' should be understood literally as excluding any other type of pronouncement by the Court, such as interim decisions, bearing in mind that Article 94(1) uses the term 'decision' instead. The rule has received no practice, except for the well-known request by Nicaragua to the Security Council—the only one thus far—to have the 1986 *Nicaragua* Judgment enforced against the United States. The response was vetoed by the United States itself.[676] In the 2008 *Medellín* Judgment the US Supreme Court stated that Article 94 UN Charter is not directly enforceable in the US domestic legal system.[677]

Other international law rules provide that judicial decisions shall be treated by the states parties like the decisions made by their national courts.[678] The Iran–US Claims Tribunal has an interesting system of enforcement based on a security account to satisfy claims of US nationals.[679] ICSID arbitral awards' pecuniary obligations are automatically enforced in domestic legal systems under Article 54(1) ICSID Convention 'as if it were a final judgment of a court in that State', while the recognition and enforcement of arbitral awards may be refused under Article V 1958 New York Recognition Convention only on proof of certain circumstances.[680] However, as a rule, international courts have no authority to enforce their own decisions, and enforcement is not provided by other bodies either. In the Council of Europe, for example, the Committee of Ministers is entrusted to 'supervise' compliance with the decisions of the ECtHR, which are not directly enforceable.[681]

[676] cf UN Docs S/18428, S/PV.2715, and S/PV.2718 October 1986. The draft, vetoed by the US on 28 October 1986, obtained 11 votes in favour and 3 abstentions (France, the UK, and Thailand).

[677] US Supreme Court, *Medellín v Texas* (n 576 above), holding that Art 94 'is not a directive to domestic courts', its words 'call[ing] upon governments to take certain action'. Of great interest, pointing in the opposite direction, is the recent (final) judgment delivered by the Tribunal of Florence, on 14 March 2012 (Case No 16410/2004), in *Paolo Toldo v Repubblica Federale di Germania*, in relation to the humanitarian exception to sovereign immunity (not yet published, on file with the author; for a discussion of the issue see Ch 7 below, section B (l)(a)). The Tribunal stated that 'Art 94 UN Charter places on UN member states an obligation to comply with the judgments of the ICJ' and, in so doing, 'it does not address to a particular state institution (Executive, Parliament), but rather to the whole of the institutions and organs which make up the state, among which courts are also included'. The Court added that Article 11 of the Italian constitution [whereby 'Italy agrees, on conditions of equality with other States, to the limitations of sovereignty that may be necessary to a world order ensuring peace and justice among the Nations' and 'promotes and encourages international organizations furthering such ends', such as the United Nations] 'elevates to constitutional rank any treaty rule which can limit our national sovereignty, including no doubt Art 94 UN Charter'. As a result, the Tribunal held that the ICJ's judgment prevails over the contrary domestic provisions binding national courts to abide by the *res judicata* effect of the previous jurisprudence of the Court of Cassation originating in the famous 2004 *Ferrini* decision (cf notes 392 and 442 above). Interestingly, the Court pointed out that, unlike domestic decisions, the judgment of the ICJ 'does not have direct effect on private relationships; however, it binds the court as a state organ' and as such trumps domestic *res judicata* (trans by the author). It is to be noted that this outcome is in part contingent on the existence and formulation of Art 11 of the Italian constitution.

[678] cf UNCLOS, at Annex III, Art 21, concerning the Seabed Chamber.

[679] cf O'Connell (n 562 above) 313–19.

[680] See S Choi, 'Judicial Enforcement of Arbitration Awards under the ICSID and New York Conventions' (1996) 28 NYU JILP 175.

[681] Art 46(2) ECHR. Art 46(4), as amended by Protocol No 14 (signed 13 May 2004, entered into force 1 June 2010) adds that if the COE Committee of Ministers considers that a state party refuses to abide by a final judgment in a case to which it is a party, 'it may, after serving formal notice on that Party and by decision adopted by a majority vote of two-thirds of the representatives entitled to sit on the Committee, refer to the Court the question whether that Party has failed to fulfil its obligation' to

Conclusion

This chapter investigated what classes of rules are believed to be international law by their addressees as a whole and in particular how they are made, integrated, reconciled, changed, applied judicially, complied with, implemented within states, and enforced. It argued that (a) the classes of rules generally recognized as international law are ultimately grounded in custom and lack formal hierarchy in terms of what is known as hierarchy in domestic legal systems; (b) these rules are systematically respected by the generality of states and, in particular, are daily applied by international and domestic courts in their task of delivering justice to individuals. Just like any other kind of law, international law is very far from contemplating all imaginable cases of life and needs integration by way of interpretation. The 'sociological' methods for ascertaining the rules based on the assumption that law works somewhat spontaneously 'from below', or to the extent that it affects behaviour, were found to be implausible. Hierarchy, heteronomy, and formalism are the hallmarks of law, including international law, in the very perception of state officials and people. International law rules are ultimately made, pressured, implemented, and (formally and informally) enforced by the states *uti universi* vis-à-vis the states *uti singuli*. Non-state actors (notably legal scholarship, public opinion, and epistemic communities) play a combined, crucial role to shape state behaviour. International courts, for their part, decide only a very limited number of disputes and their decisions still need enforcement within domestic legal systems. But when they decide a case, they enjoy an important, indeed unavoidable, margin of discretion (within the existing rules) inherent in their very creation.

abide by the judgment. Art 46(5) further states that 'if the Court finds a violation of paragraph 1, it shall refer the case to the Committee of Ministers for consideration of the measures to be taken'.

7

Values

Having discussed who believes and is believed to be part of the international community and how the recognized rules (grouped in classes) are made and applied, it is now necessary to ask what 'values' are believed to be protected, or to be worth being better protected, by the rules of international law. It is proposed to focus on five (by no means exhaustive) basic global values: security, humanity, wealth, environment, and knowledge. All point to 'justice' in the system either within the law or as a guide for the law to come. Values are diverse and tend to interact and compete with one another, thereby raising the question of whether and how separate legal rules which underlie different, even opposing, values can be coordinated. This chapter first discusses the specific rules which protect, or ought to protect, the above basic values and then investigates the interaction between rules, or groups of rules, protecting competing or conflicting values. It argues that there is much to struggle for, both in improving global justice and overcoming inconsistencies.

A. Inspiring Values

All legal rules are inspired by one or more values for the benefit of their addressees as a whole,[1] but not all values in a group are protected by legal rules. While values inspire legal rules, they are distinct from the rules. The existence of a value does not imply that there must also be a legal rule capable of protecting it, at least to the degree that is desired or necessary. Moreover, the identification of all values in a group is very difficult because values are of infinite number, differ from one sub-group to another, and enjoy different degrees of adherence. The relationship is bi-directional. On the one hand, the existence of rules helps in the identification of at least those values that the group regards as deserving legal protection. On the other hand, values as such help in the understanding of the essence of existing rules and channel the action needed to make new rules. The sphere of values is that of what 'there ought to be' both *within* existing law as flowing from the recognized sources, to the fullest extent possible, and *outside* it specifically as guidance in the struggle for a better law. In this sense values point to justice and, in the perspective here adopted, to the protection of the most vulnerable.

It is extremely difficult both to identity what is valuable to all human beings, as is inevitable when dealing with international law, and to trace a scale of priority of different values. In *A Theory of Human Motivation*, published in 1943 and refined in 1954, Abraham H Maslow famously developed a 'hierarchy of needs'.[2] This hierarchy is usually portrayed in the shape of a pyramid made up of four layers (representing physiological, safety, love and belonging, and esteem needs), with the more basic needs

[1] The ancient Roman sources suggested three basic values or precepts of law: 'live honestly, harm nobody, treat all persons with the respect due to them' ('honeste vivere, alterum non laedere, suum cuique tribuere', attributed to Ulpian). cf Justinian, *Institutes*, I, 1, 3; *Digest*, I, 1, 10, 1.

[2] AH Maslow, 'A Theory of Human Motivation' (1943) 50 *Psychological Review* 370; AH Maslow, *Motivation and Personality* (New York: Harper, 1954).

at the bottom. At the top of the pyramid lies the need for self-actualization. Physiological needs include breathing, food, water, sex, sleep, homeostasis, and excretion. They are requirements for human survival in the sense that when they are not sufficiently met the human body simply cannot continue to function. It is reasonable to assume that these needs are independent of any cultural background. Safety needs refer to security of the body, employment, financial resources, morality, the family, health, well-being, and property. They are linked to people's yearning for a predictable, orderly world in which injustice and inconsistency are under control. Love and belonging needs are social in nature, grounded in the need of human beings to feel a sense of belonging and acceptance, and include friendship, sexual intimacy, and family bonds. Esteem needs include self-esteem, confidence, achievement, respect for others, and respect from others. Finally, the need for self-actualization is grounded in the idea that 'what a man can be, he must be'. In principle, the needs which are placed higher cannot be fulfilled if the needs placed lower have not been met.[3] Maslow's ranking of needs has been criticized as lacking empirical evidence.[4] Some have more radically excluded the notion that needs are hierarchical.[5] Others have contended that the order in which the hierarchy is arranged is ethnocentric.[6] Maslow's theory has been further expanded and explained by the ERG (Existence, Relatedness and Growth) theory.[7]

The existing rules of international law, especially those of general international law or contained in multilateral treaties of universal participation, can be classified in different ways either according to the values protected or to other factors. The 2000 Millennium Development Goals (MDGs) list twelve values that are expected to be realized as a matter of global justice to a certain degree by the year 2015.[8] It is proposed here to organize the global values protected (or that ought to be protected) by international law around security, humanity, wealth, environment, and knowledge. The international community is (or is going to be) concerned with these values probably more than any others and expects international law to contribute to their realization. These are not all values protected by international law rules. Moreover, they shade off into each other with a tendency of all to converge on the core of humanity, and often overlap. There are also values that are not protected at all by international law, but rather by other tools, such as diplomatic and strategic means. The focus here is on the values that are protected, at least to some meaningful extent, by international law rules, or that ought to be legally protected as a matter of justice. It goes beyond the scope of this book to discuss in detail all pertinent rules.

(1) Security

Most people seem to value more than anything else their security from out-groups and in-groups not only at local level, but also at global level when remote events may produce significant effects locally. The notion of 'security' is indeed anything but uncontroversial. This section focuses on security understood as protection from others'

[3] Maslow (1943) (n 2 above) 370.

[4] A Wahba and L Bridgewell, 'Maslow Reconsidered: A Review of Research on the Need Hierarchy Theory' (1976) 15 OBHP 212.

[5] MA Max-Neef, A Elizalde, and M Hopenhayn, *Human Scale Development: Conception, Application and Further Reflections* (New York: Apex, 1991).

[6] G Hofstede, 'The Cultural Relativity of the Quality of Life Concept' (1984) 9 AMR 389.

[7] CP Alderfer, *Existence, Relatedness, and Growth; Human Needs in Organizational Settings* (New York: Free Press, 1972).

[8] cf <http://www.un.org/millenniumgoals>.

aggression, either from within or outside states. It raises the question of how the line between legitimate and illegitimate use of force can be drawn in international affairs, ie whether and how the 'policeman' can be distinguished from the 'delinquent' when they use force. The point of departure is the doctrine of just war developed in the Western civilization and recurrently surfacing in justifying wars of any kind. The section then proceeds by examining the existing rules which ban in general the threat and use of force in international relations, but allow it in self-defence, and the UN system of collective security. It finally focuses on the containment of transnational crime. It argues that also in the international sphere there must be a distinction between the actors who use force on behalf and for the benefit of all, at least in principle, and the actors who use force against the international community and that as regards individuals it is basically for states to protect them within their jurisdiction in coordination with one another with a view to ensuring that all humankind is protected by one or another state in every corner of the world.

(a) Just war

Security first of all means security 'from physical annihilation by war'.[9] Most people believe in the pressing need for legal rules limiting aggression from individuals and generally support collective or 'public' violence. There seems to be always a distinction between 'legitimate' and 'illegitimate' violence in any group, although the criteria for drawing it change in time and space. At its core, legitimate violence is the violence of the group against its individual members who break the rules and/or undermine the cohesion of the group as a whole. Those who use force on behalf of the group stand for the 'policeman', while the others who are seen by the former as 'deviant' stand for the 'delinquent'. This distinction is key to the international community too. If violence is to be banned, there is a need for credible counter-violence governed by legal rules so as to guarantee that this latter is for the good of all and is applied according to the law (both procedural and substantive) supported by the international community as a whole. The violence banned (or 'illegitimate') is of necessity the violence of the single state, whether strong or weak, while the violence admitted (or 'legitimate') is the violence of the international community as a whole. If we are to ban (individual) violence in international relations, we need to construct a (collective and legally regulated) counter-violence. The notion that violence will end some day without devising a collective mechanism that can use progressive measures up to an overwhelming level of violence is wishful thinking at best. The point is how to differentiate the 'policeman' from the 'delinquent' and, pre-eminently, how to avoid a situation in which the stronger unilaterally apply violence exclusively for their own benefit by unjustifiably claiming that they are acting in the name and on behalf of the entire international community. This is no doubt a very difficult task in international affairs due to the absence of any universal legitimate authority laying down the law from above. The *locus classicus* of discussion about where to draw the line is the 'just war doctrine'.[10]

[9] W Friedmann, *The Changing Structure of International Law* (London: Stevens and Sons, 1964) 63.

[10] See eg J von Elbe, 'The Evolution of the Concept of the Just War in International Law' 33 AJIL (1939) 665; JT Johnson, *Just War Tradition and the Restraint of War: A Moral and Historical Inquiry* (Princeton: Princeton University Press, 1984); M Evans (ed), *Just War Theory: A Reappraisal* (Edinburgh: Edinburgh University Press, 2005); GM Reichberg, 'Preventive War in Classical Just War Theory' (2007) 9 JHIL 5; SC Neff, *War and the Law of Nations: A General History* (Cambridge: CUP, 2008) 19–93; R Dreveskracht, 'Just War in International Law: An Argument for a Deontological Approach to Humanitarian Law' (2010) 16 Buffalo Human Rights Law Review 237.

The doctrine is found in Aristotle (*dikaios polemos*) to justify self-defence, conquest, and aggrandisement.[11] In the Latin literature, Varro makes the most ancient reference to *bellum justum* by associating it with fetial law (*ius fetiale*).[12] The main Latin sources on just war are Cicero and Livy. While some Ciceronian texts clearly refer to war in conformity with the (Roman) *procedural* law,[13] just like Livy's,[14] a few others refer to a *substantive* just cause, ie to an ethical meaning,[15] while for others the classification is more controversial.[16] The crucial problem with Cicero's texts is whether he gave the term *bellum justum* an ethical or a merely legalistic meaning limited to the Roman procedure of waging war (against a *state*, after a *warning*, and a *declaration* of war). The issue was taken up by the Fathers of the Church in relation to the question of whether a Christian had to serve as a soldier. Some Fathers, like Lactantius and Tertullian,[17] answered in the negative; others, including Augustine, answered in the affirmative provided that the war was 'just'.[18] The Church Fathers changed the Roman just war doctrine radically into a theologically inspired doctrine. The question was now about the 'just grounds' for a Christian to serve as a soldier and obey a ruler in this respect. Just grounds for war were found in the Scriptures, which actually relate many wars, some even commanded by God. The term 'just' became ethical in character and even assuming that it had ethical (Stoic) connotations also in Cicero, now it acquired a specifically Christian ethical meaning.[19] By successfully dismissing the view of the Church Fathers who had opposed war under all circumstances, Augustine took a decisive step in Western history, his thought being eventually upheld, through Isidore of Seville[20] and Gratian's Decretum,[21] by Thomas Aquinas, who systematized the doctrine by requiring the authority of the prince (*auctoritas principis*), the just cause (*justa causa*), and the right intention (*recta intentio*).[22]

Just war and natural law, as previously hinted,[23] are the two pillars of international law as shaped by the Western tradition. The former has worked as the armed arm of the latter. Both presuppose a universal order and a universal authority in charge of determining *what* is just and *who* is on the just side. In this context, 'just' war means 'legitimate' coercion from a higher authority—allegedly acting on behalf of the community—against individual transgressors of the existing legal order, that is to say, 'law enforcement'.[24] There can be no 'equal' contenders, or equality of belligerents,[25] within the just war framework at its purest. Good and Evil are set one against the other and war is but the reaction of the community, through the common authority, against a

[11] Aristotle, *Politics*, I, 6, 1255a–b, and I, 8, 1256b.

[12] Varro, *De lingua latina*, V, 15.

[13] Cicero, *De re pubblica*, II, 17, 31 ('every war which was not proclaimed and declared, was deemed to be impious and unjust'); *De officiis*, I, 12, 36 ('no war is just, unless it is entered upon after an official demand for satisfaction has been submitted or warning has been given and a formal declaration made').

[14] See, in particular, Livy, *Ab urbe condita*, I, 32 6–14, describing the Roman archaic procedure to initiate a war according to fetial law.

[15] Cicero, *De re pubblica*, III, 23, 35.

[16] Cicero, *De legibus*, III, 3, 9; *De officiis*, I, 12, 35, and I, 12, 38.

[17] Lactantius, *Divine Institutes*, VI, 6, 18; Tertullian, *On Idolatry*, XIX.

[18] Augustine, *Quaestionum in Heptateuchum*, VI, 10 *De civitate Dei*, III, 10; ibid IV, 6; ibid VII, 30; ibid XIX, 7; ibid XIX, 13, 1; ibid XXII, 6, 30; *Contra Faustum*, 22, 74–5; *Epistola (ad Bonifacium)*, 189, 6.

[19] See L Loreto, *Il* bellum iustum *e i suoi equivoci: Cicerone e una componente della rappresentazione romana del Völkerrecht antico* (Naples: Jovene, 2001); A Calore, *Forme giuridiche del* 'bellum iustum' (Milan: Giuffrè, 2003).

[20] Isidore of Seville, *Etymologiae*, XVIII, 1, 1–4.

[21] *Decretum Gratiani*, c 23.

[22] Thomas Aquinas, *Summa Theologiae*, II, q 40.

[23] See Ch 4 above, n 55 and accompanying text.

[24] See n 56 below.

[25] See n 180 below.

transgressor. The doctrine presupposes a stable and effective social and political hierarchical order, such as the medieval *Respublica Christiana* guided by the Church as a mystical body.[26] The just war doctrine implies that the contenders are not on an equal footing (one is superior and the other inferior) and that what is permitted to one (basically to kill) is prohibited to the other. One belligerent stands for the 'police' and the other for the 'delinquent'. The doctrine tends to assume that the 'unjust' belligerent, ie the delinquent, does not enjoy the rights of war (*jura belli*) simply because it is by definition, as a transgressor of the law common to all, completely subjected to the authority of the other belligerent. While the police can legally kill the delinquent, the delinquent is not allowed to kill those who serve as the police.[27] In this sense Hans Kelsen was right in defending just war as a sanction, or law enforcement, ie a collective punishment against a transgressor.[28] The *Christian* just war doctrine, unlike the Roman doctrine, presupposes One Universal Truth, and this implies that One Party is Right simply because it is the Whole and not a party (it is the Authority from which Legitimacy originates) and the Other is Wrong. It is not merely that a *given* war is right or wrong, although this is how things are presented; it is that the war conducted by the Right Party is *always* just because it is a 'punishment' against wrongdoers and those who attack the Whole Order. The *same action* is right and legitimate (as punishment against an attack to the Universal Order) when it is conducted by the Right Party and wrong and illegitimate (as an attack to the system by single individuals as 'private' violence) when it is conducted by the Wrong Party.

The just war doctrine is often viewed as a limit to violence and a means of enforcing law and ensuring peace.[29] Its proponents insist that the doctrine is concerned with preventing total war. Opponents, such as Carl Schmitt,[30] reply that just war is necessarily a total war fought to impose the Universal Good and Truth at any price. Both condemn total war, ie war without restraint, but clearly from different assumptions. Advocates of just war assume that there is (or there must be in any case) a Universal Good and Truth, while critics contend that such Universal Good and Truth

[26] See Ch 4 above, nn 53 and 54; and Ch 5 above, n 45.

[27] However, the asymmetry between the just side and the unjust side did not exclude that the latter had *some* (not *equal*) rights towards the former, which had correlative obligations with regard to the way in which law enforcement was carried out. The key obligation was 'necessity', to the effect that force by the just side was limited to what was strictly necessary to prevail. The necessity requirement was, just as it is today, ambivalent since it allowed *not more* force than was strictly necessary to prevail, but also *all* of the force that was necessary to that end (including total war). Apart from the right to respect for necessity, the unjust side (unlike the just side) did not have any right of war, such as the right to use force (although strictly personal self-defence was permitted), the right to enslave captured persons of the just side, the right to be ransomed, and the right to receive legal title to enemy property captured (see Neff (n 10 above) 62–5). Over time, wars occurred between sovereign 'equal' states, ie equal enemies (*justi hostes*), deprived of any superior authority determining which side was just. Justness was gradually assumed to be potentially on both sides, with the consequence that both had *equal* rights of war (*iura belli*) regardless of the justness of the recourse to war by one or the other. Just war as law enforcement changed into the classical concept of non-discriminatory war between equal enemies having equal rights. The necessity requirement alone was no longer satisfactory since it simply allowed both sides to annihilate each other, so that more specific rules applicable to the conduct of hostilities were devised to prevent total war (see section A (2)(b) below).

[28] H Kelsen, *General Theory of Law and State* [1945] (New Brunswick and London: Transaction Publishers, 2007) 331–41; H Kelsen, *Principles of International Law* (New York: Rinehart & Co, 1952) 33–44.

[29] ME O'Connell, *The Power and Purpose of International Law: Insights from the Theory and Practice of Enforcement* (Oxford: OUP, 2008) 19–55.

[30] For an overview and appropriate references, see G Slomp, 'Carl Schmitt's Five Arguments against the Idea of Just War' (2006) 19 CRIA 435.

is but the Good and Truth of the stronger of the day. For the former, violence is 'legitimate' (hence 'just') 'only' when certain conditions are met; for the latter, violence is inescapable and what law can do is only to pose limitations to the conduct of war for both belligerents on an equal footing. The doctrine is inherently ambivalent: while it *prohibits* war when this is unjust, it *allows* it when it is just. It delegitimizes certain wars and legitimizes others. The doctrine can be viewed at the same time as a limitation and as a promotion of war, the critical watershed being what is meant by 'just' and who is entitled to determine this.

Natural law has been used to present a particular political or legal philosophy (or legal system) as eternal and sacrosanct, capable of justifying war against the 'enemies' of such a providential order. What was called 'natural law', or the 'law common to humankind', whether Christian or not, was the perspective of the stronger. Other perspectives were possible in the abstract of what should count as the law common to humankind, but could not be successfully asserted. Departures from the dominant view were simply breaches of the law deserving 'just' punishment. The Conquest of the New World and colonialism were basically justified as a just war, and this war was 'just' because it was against those who were in breach of natural law as unilaterally conceived by the conquerors.[31] Without natural law the conquest appeared as a brutal act of force. If there were no all-embracing law, there would have been no law in common with the conquered and no legitimizing effect. Just war is by definition a *limitation* of the war *of others*, certainly a means towards *peace* but the peace *of the stronger*. Every belligerent needs not only to legitimize its action in the eyes of the other (potentially defeated) belligerent but also to provide a 'moral' self-justification capable of intellectually reinforcing the fact that it *must* be right. The whole scientific discourse on just war is *internal* to a *totalizing* vision that creates its 'other' as a projection *within* this totality. Different visions and just war doctrines from different civilizations may of course conflict with one another, giving rise to civilizational clashes.[32]

The just war doctrine has been recurrently evoked in history to pass off a genuine war between equals as law enforcement by a superior (the 'policeman' acting on behalf of the community) to an inferior ('the delinquent' threatening the community).[33] In recent decades it has been relied on to justify military interventions that were otherwise unlawful, or whose lawfulness was very doubtful,[34] using justifications such as humanitarian intervention,[35] intervention in support of national liberation wars,[36] and the use of force against terrorists.[37] In these instances the preference for the term 'war'—as in 'war on terror' and 'armed conflict [of the United States] with Al Qaeda'—aims to justify the (otherwise prohibited) killing of the enemy, whether a state official or a

[31] See Ch 4 above, section B (1).

[32] See RJ Hoffmann (ed), *The Just War and Jihad: Violence in Judaism, Christianity, and Islam* (Amherst, NY: Prometheus Books, 2006); J Kelsay, 'Just War, Jihad, and the Study of Comparative Ethics' (2010) EIA 227; N Godehardt, 'Just War Concepts: Western and Chinese Perspectives' in MD Voyame (ed), *International law, Conflict and Development: The Emergence of a Holistic Approach in International Affairs* (Leiden: Nijhoff, 2010) 443.

[33] For a classical treatment, see M Walzer, *Just and Unjust Wars* (New York: Basic Books, 1977, 4th edn, 2006).

[34] See eg E Patterson, 'Just War in the 21st Century: Reconceptualizing Just War Theory After September 11' (2005) 42 *International Politics* 116.

[35] See Ch 8 below, section B (2).

[36] See Ch 5 above, section C (4)(c).

[37] For a recent discussion of the 'war on terror' and 'new' asymmetric wars, see JB Bellinger III and VM Padmanabhan, 'Detention Operations in Contemporary Conflicts: Four Challenges for the Geneva Conventions and Other Existing Law' (2011) 105 AJIL 201.

private person, as a 'lawful military target',[38] equating him/her with the ancient figure of either the pirate (ie the deviant acting outside the legal order) or the brigand (ie the deviant acting in defiance of the law from within the legal order). Occasionally, also a war 'mandated' by the UN Security Council has been seen as 'just' and legitimate as it is allegedly backed by the international community as a whole.[39] The key point in defending the just war doctrine is that in a social order there must be some criteria to draw the line between legitimate and illegitimate use of force. However, the just war doctrine does not conform to specific rules; it is a global vision of Good and Evil. Legal rules are different, at least in the secularized approach to law prevailing today. There may be common legal rules because their addressees as a whole concur in believing in their existence and generally obey them. In today's globalized world people can hardly be deemed to share one and the same idea of Good and Evil, although they do share common *specific* rules on the use of force. What matters is not *who* is just, but *what* is legal. There is no actor who is by definition just, whatever it may do, for the sole reason that it is the 'very source' of justness, legitimacy, and legality. There are rules that apply to certain situations, whoever the actor. It is thus convenient now to turn to these rules.

(b) Ban on the threat and use of force

There have been innumerable wars in the course of history which have shaped the world as we know it. The states system is the outcome of wars that have constantly changed state borders and the number of states. Wars have not succeeded, however, in changing the anti-hegemonial structure of the system and states have remained its essential component units, none of them having been capable of dominating the whole system completely and irreversibly.[40] The trend towards legal, as opposed to ethical, limits to the threat and use of armed force peaked in 1945 with the making of the UN Charter.

Article 2(4) UN Charter outlaws the threat or use of force by member states in their international relations against the territorial integrity or political independence of any state, or in any other manner inconsistent with the purposes of the United Nations.[41] This provision must be read in combination with Article 2(3) whereby all member states shall settle their international disputes by peaceful means in such a manner that international peace and security, and justice, are not endangered. Article 51 admits as an exception the inherent right of individual and collective self-defence 'if an armed

[38] See eg the statement of US Attorney General Mr Eric Holder to the Senate Judiciary Committee made on 4 May 2011 whereby Usama Bin Laden was a 'lawful military target', equating killing him to targeting an enemy commander in the field, at <http://www.politico.com/blogs/joshgerstein/0511/Holder_Killing_of_bin_Laden_legal_as_national_selfdefense.html>. This position was reiterated after the killing of Bin Laden in Pakistan on 2 May 2011. For a leading case on targeted killings, see Israeli Supreme Court Sitting as the High Court of Justice, *The Public Committee against Torture in Israel et al v The Government of Israel et al* Judgment of 13 December 2006, at <http://elyon1.court.gov.il/files_eng/02/690/007/a34/02007690.a34.pdf>. For a dismissive approach, see US District Court for the District of Columbia, *Nasser Al-Aulaqi v Barack H Obama et al* Judgment of 25 September 2010, at <https://ecf.dcd.uscourts.gov/cgi-bin/show_public_doc?2010cv1469-31> (cf <http://www.economist.com/node/21531477> for the killing in Yemen of Anwar al-Awlaki on 30 September 2011).

[39] From a different perspective, see B Conforti, 'The Doctrine of "Just War" and Contemporary International Law' (2002) 12 It YBIL 3, suggesting that when the UN security system fails to work the use of force can only be assessed in terms of natural law and the just war doctrine.

[40] See Ch 5 above, n 152.

[41] For a detailed overview, see CD Gray, *International Law and the Use of Force* (Oxford: OUP, 3rd edn, 2008).

attack occurs against a Member' until the Security Council has taken the measures necessary to maintain international peace and security, and provided that the measures taken in self-defence are immediately reported to the Security Council. The ban on the threat and use of force is understandable as a tool to ward off the law of the jungle, but it makes sense only if, and to the extent that, states' security is ensured by other means. Chapters VII and VIII of the Charter, in particular, govern a centralized system of security operating in accordance with legal rules. Briefly, the UN Charter prohibits individual states from threatening and using force (Article 2(4)) by centralizing legitimate force in the Security Council (Chapters VII and VIII) and leaving individual states the possibility of reacting immediately in self-defence (also collectively) until the Security Council takes the necessary measures (Article 51).

All of these provisions are binding on the 193 UN member states as treaty rules. Member states are free to accede to the UN Charter and when they decide to do so they accept such obligations and are bound by them until they exit the United Nations or the Charter is amended. Since the ban on the use of force is general, it automatically applies unless an exception is proved.[42] It is widely accepted that the ban not only reflects customary international law,[43] but also belongs to *jus cogens*[44] and contemplates an obligation *erga omnes*.[45]

It has been contended, however, that the ban on the use of force is no longer 'good law', given its violation on numerous occasions to date.[46] This view is overstated. The UN Charter is still good law and Article 2(4) does reflect general international law. The persisting legal weight and general scope of the ban on the use of force may be drawn from the following data: (a) all states categorically assert that the unilateral use of force is illegal, except in self-defence; (b) when certain states resort to illegal force, all other states strongly protest; (c) even states that resort to force imply the prohibition by providing justifications;[47] (d) single violations do not abrogate the prohibition;[48] (e) states that resort to military action may be willing in certain instances to change the law, but this presupposes that, however desirable the change may be, force is used in breach of the existing law; (f) states that resort to war are aware that force in principle is illegal and limit their action as far as possible in scope, weapons, duration, purposes, and justifications in accordance with shared existing rules; (g) today states generally refrain from resorting to force, preferring peaceful methods of settlement of their disputes, in cases where in the past resort to force was routine, as was the case with gunboat diplomacy; and (h) states are generally induced to comply with the prohibition

[42] cf German Federal Administrative Court Judgment of 21 June 2005, available at <http://www.bundesverwaltungsgericht.de>, para 4.1.4.1.1, holding that 'Militärische Gewalt darf gegen den Willen des davon betroffenen Staates unter der Geltung der UN-Charta—ausnahmsweise—angewandt werden, nämlich nur wenn ein völkerrechtlicher Rechtfertigungsgrund dies im Einzelfall erlaubt', specifically intervention by the Security Council under Chapter VII and self-defence. The Court ruled that the Iraq War, as well as the contribution made by Germany thereto, carried 'grave concerns' in terms of legality under international law. For a comment, see N Schultz, 'Was the War on Iraq Illegal? The German Federal Administrative Courts's Judgment of 21st June 2005' (2005) 7 Ger LJ 25.

[43] ICJ, *Case concerning Military and Paramilitary Activities in and against Nicaragua* (*Nicaragua v United States) (Merits)* Judgment of 27 June 1986, [1986] ICJ Rep 14, paras 190–191; *Legal Consequences of the Construction of a Wall in the Occupied Palestinian Territory*, Advisory Opinion of 9 July 2004, [2004] ICJ Rep 136, para 88.

[44] See Ch 6 above, section B (4)(f).

[45] See Ch 8 below, section B (1).

[46] See eg TM Franck, 'Who Killed Article 2(4)? or: Changing Norms Governing the Use of Force by States' (1970) 64 AJIL 809; MJ Glennon, 'The UN Security Council in an Unipolar World' (2003–04) 44 Virg JIL 91.

[47] ICJ, *Case concerning Military and Paramilitary Activities* (n 43 above) para 186.

[48] ibid.

on unilateral force for several reasons, including the prospect of Mutual Assured Destruction (MAD) and the costs of today's wars compared to their benefits, domestic pressures, and constitutional constraints following a widespread culture of peace that was absent in the past and the only possibility of major wars fought 'on behalf of the global community', ie as supported by the five nuclear powers.[49] This picture is profoundly different from the state of affairs prevailing in the nineteenth century and critics of the persisting legal weight of Article 2(4) fail to explain the difference.

The meaning of the 'threat' prohibited by Article 2(4) is uncertain and the practice is rather scarce.[50] In the 1986 *Nicaragua* Judgment the ICJ pointed out that 'in international law there are no rules, other than such rules as may be accepted by the State concerned, by treaty or otherwise, whereby the level of armaments of a sovereign State can be limited',[51] thereby suggesting not only that the mere possession of arms is not internationally unlawful but also, more generally, that there may well be cases of life which are not covered by any rule of international law.[52] In the 1996 *Nuclear Weapons* Advisory Opinion the Court held that 'if the use of force itself in a given case is illegal—for whatever reason—the threat to use such force will likewise be illegal'.[53] It also held that whether the possession of nuclear weapons is illegal:

> ... depends upon whether the particular use of force envisaged would be directed against the territorial integrity or political independence of a State, or against the purposes of the United Nations or whether, in the event that it were intended as a means of defence, it would necessarily violate the principles of necessity and proportionality.[54]

More recently, in the 2007 *Guyana v Suriname* Award, a PCA Arbitral Tribunal ruled that 'the action mounted by Suriname [issuance of an order to leave Suriname waters within 12 hours directed at the oil rig and drill ship of CGX Resources Inc, a Canadian company which had been granted a concession from Guyana for oil exploration] ... seemed more akin to a threat of military action rather than a mere law enforcement activity' and concluded that 'Suriname's action therefore constituted a threat of force in contravention of the Convention [UNCLOS], the United Nations Charter and general international law'.[55] This conclusion is questionable in that Suriname was seemingly prepared to use force in order to impose public security, law, and order within its jurisdiction.[56] In any event, the 'threat' prohibited by Article 2(4) does not necessarily coincide with the 'threat' to peace under Article 39 UN Charter for the purposes of adopting measures by the Security Council, nor with the 'threat' which is required in order for anticipatory self-defence to be exercised, both of which are discussed below.

The meaning of the term 'force' in Article 2(4) has received more clarification in practice. Unlike the Covenant of the League of Nations[57] and the Briand-Kellogg

[49] L Henkin, *How Nations Behave: Law and Foreign Policy* (New York: Columbia University Press, 2nd edn, 1979) 146–51.

[50] M Roscini, 'Threats of Armed Force and Contemporary International Law' (2007) 54 Neth ILR 229; N Stürchler *The Threat of Force in International Law* (Cambridge: CUP, 2007).

[51] ICJ, *Case concerning Military and Paramilitary Activities* (n 43 above) para 269.

[52] See Ch 6 above, section B (2)(a).

[53] ICJ, *Legality of the Threat or Use of Nuclear Weapons*, Advisory Opinion of 8 July 1996, [1996] ICJ Rep 226, para 47.

[54] ibid para 48.

[55] PCA Arbitral Tribunal, *Guyana v Suriname* Award of 17 September 2007, at <http://www.pca-cpa.org/upload/files/Guyana-Suriname%20Award.pdf>, paras 438–445.

[56] See Ch 5 above, section B (4). For the notion of 'law enforcement' as 'all territorial and extraterritorial measures taken by a State to vertically impose public security, law and order, or to otherwise exercise its authority or power over individuals in any place or manner whatsoever', see N Melzer, *Targeted Killing in International Law* (Oxford: OUP, 2008) 88.

[57] Covenant of the League of Nations (adopted 28 June 1919) 225 CTS 195.

Pact,[58] it certainly extends beyond war, also covering forcible measures short of war, such as armed reprisals and naval blockades.[59] There is no doubt that the force prohibited is *armed* force, as evidenced from the drafting history of the norm, its systematic interpretation, and its application in practice. Aggression is no doubt included in the 'force' prohibited, although what 'aggression' means is disputed. UN General Assembly Resolution 3314 (XXIX) defines aggression as 'the use of armed force by a State against the sovereignty, territorial integrity or political independence of another State', specifically the 'invasion or attack by the armed forces of a State of the territory of another State, or any military occupation, however temporary', including the 'action of a State in allowing its territory... to be used by [another] State for perpetrating an act of aggression against a third State'.[60] Aggression was also considered to be an international crime by Article 6(a) IMT Statute, as a form of the 'crimes against peace' falling under the Tribunal's jurisdiction, and the Tribunal itself emphasized that a war of aggression was not only prohibited by international law (notably by the 1928 Briand-Kellogg Pact) but was also 'criminal',[61] and it is today included in an amendment to the ICC Statute adopted at Kampala in 2010.[62] However, the prohibition also 'includes others [descriptions of the use of force] which refer only to less grave forms of the use of force', and, although contrary to the ban on the use of force, do not allow self-defence.[63] It follows that the 'use of force' prohibited by Article 2(4) does not necessarily coincide with the 'attack' which allows self-defence under Article 51. While Article 2(4) clearly does not prohibit 'internal' law enforcement, doubts exist as to the meaning of 'international relations'. The term clearly refers to cross-border military operations and, presumably, also to attacks on military troops legally headquartered abroad. It does not seem to cover the force used within the territory by the legitimate government against insurgents and, probably, the force used by a state within its territory against foreign diplomats.[64] The distinction between (prohibited) 'international use of force' and (permitted) 'internal law enforcement' is particularly difficult to trace with regard to 'targeted killings'.[65]

While 'territorial integrity' and 'political independence' indisputably refer to uses of force aimed at taking either the territory or the independence of another state, the wording 'any other manner inconsistent with the purposes of the United Nations' has occasionally been invoked to justify military interventions that, although contrary to the prohibition, could be justified as 'compatible' with UN purposes.[66] Today, the

[58] General Treaty for Renunciation of War as an Instrument Of National Policy (signed 27 August 1928, entered into force 25 July 1929) 94 LNTS 57.

[59] For the general prohibition of intervention, see ICJ, *Corfu Channel (United Kingdom v Albania) (Merits)* Judgment of 9 April 1949, [1949] ICJ Rep 4, 34; for the prohibition of armed reprisals in times of peace, in contrast to belligerent reprisals (see nn 187 and 188 below), see *Legality of the Threat or Use of Nuclear Weapons* (n 53 above) para 46; PCA Arbitral Tribunal, *Guyana v Suriname* (n 55 above) para 446.

[60] UNGA Res 3314 (XXIX) of 14 December 1974, 'Definition of Aggression', GAOR 29th Session Supp 31, vol 1, 142 (Arts 1 and 3).

[61] IMT, *Trial of the Major War Criminals* Judgment of 1 October 1946, (1947) 41 AJIL 172, 220.

[62] See n 106 below.

[63] See nn 84 and 85 below.

[64] In *United States Diplomatic and Consular Staff in Tehran (United States v Iran)* Judgment of 24 May 1980, [1980] ICJ Rep 3, para 93–94, the ICJ confined itself to noting that it could not fail 'to express its concern in regard to the United States' [military] incursion into Iran' since in the circumstances the operation to rescue the persons taken hostage was of such a kind as 'to undermine respect for the judicial process in international relations'.

[65] Melzer (n 56 above). On targeted killings, see n 38 above.

[66] cf Henkin (n 49 above) 291, referring (critically) to the Cuban quarantine.

typical example is humanitarian intervention, as compatible with the protection of human rights envisaged in the UN Charter, which is discussed below.[67]

Finally, the ban on the threat and use of force has important constitutional implications that could scarcely be overstated. Many national constitutions renounce the use of armed force as a means of solving international disputes and as an instrument of national policy, such as article 9 of the Japanese constitution, article 11 of the Italian constitution, etc. Other constitutional provisions assign the declaration of war—with the consequent triggering of the state of war and the possible suspension of constitutional freedoms for emergency reasons—to both Parliaments and heads of state. The emergence of 'new' wars and the participation in UN peacekeeping missions and Security Council-authorized armed interventions abroad challenge such provisions.[68] Executives tend to depict these operations as 'actions of international police' or as 'missions of peace' radically different from traditional wars. The reconciliation of constitutional provisions banning or constraining war and practice favourable to participation in military operations abroad has raised concerns in many countries. The novelty of the 'new' wars has also caused problems with the domestic law governing troops abroad, whether the law applicable in peacetime or that applicable in wartime. No doubt the 'new' wars are different from traditional wars since they are not aimed at the annihilation of the enemy and, in this respect, escape from the constitutional provisions concerning war in the traditional sense. However, as will be shown shortly, the only new wars that can be regarded as other than traditional wars, ie as actions of 'international police' aimed at global peace and security, are those mandated by the UN Security Council not meeting with significant reactions from states as a whole.

(c) Self-defence

People's security is protected from external attacks not only by the general ban on the use of force, but also, when an attack occurs, by the right to self-defence. In the UN Charter self-defence is the only exception to the ban left to individual states. This 'exception' has always been regarded as 'inherent' in human behaviour to the point that even the just war doctrine focused on 'just grounds' for offensive wars, assuming that a defensive war is always permitted.[69] As already noted, Article 51 UN Charter allows the 'inherent' right of individual and collective self-defence 'if an armed attack occurs' ('agression armée' in the French text). While individual self-defence is the armed reaction by the victim of the attack, collective self-defence is the armed reaction of states other than the victim. In any case, since collective self-defence requires a request from the victim and does not leave third states to assess unilaterally whether the attack has occurred and whether their possible reaction is willed by the victim,[70] self-defence is an *individual* reaction even when it is 'collectively' exercised, allowed for *urgency* reasons until the UN collective security system is triggered. It has nothing to do with

[67] See Ch 8 below, section B (2).

[68] For the complaint filed by 10 bi-partisan US Representatives with the US District Court for the District of Columbia against President Obama and Secretary of Defense Robert Gates alleging that the 'Libyan operations ordered by President Obama [started on 19 March 2011] constitute "war" for the purposes of the . . . Constitution', and since Congress at no point approved the war, President Obama was violating the US Constitution; see US District Court for the District of Columbia, *Kucinich v Obama* Complaint of 15 June 2011, at <http://kucinich.house.gov/UploadedFiles/Libya_ Complaint_Master.pdf>.

[69] Neff (n 10 above) 59–62.

[70] ICJ, *Case concerning Military and Paramilitary Activities* (n 43 above) para 199.

collective force aimed at targeting states that undermine the whole global system. The security of individual states is one thing, the security of the system as a whole is quite another. While self-defence concerns the former, the UN security system is typically devised to tackle the latter. There is no doubt that Article 51 reflects customary international law.[71]

A debate constantly under way concerns the permissibility of anticipatory self-defence, ie armed action to face a threat of force. It is routinely argued that technological advances in weapons make anticipatory self-defence a matter of necessity, whatever the language of Article 51. The 2002 'Bush Doctrine', reaffirmed by the United States in its '2006 National Security Strategy', admitted anticipatory self-defence in very broad terms and linked it with the military reaction to international terrorism ('war on terror').[72] In the 1996 *Nuclear Weapons* Advisory Opinion the ICJ, noting 'the fundamental right of every State to survival, and thus its right to resort to self-defence, in accordance with Article 51 of the Charter, when its survival is at stake', observed that 'it cannot reach a definitive conclusion as to the legality or illegality of the use of nuclear weapons by a State in an extreme circumstance of self-defence, in which its very survival would be at stake'.[73] It is a fact, however, that Article 51 refers to the condition that 'an armed attack occurs' and it is the provision *thus formulated* that binds member states. The term 'inherent', far from indicating that Article 51 resumed the pre-Charter permissibility of anticipatory self-defence,[74] simply takes note that self-defence reflects the universal principle *vim vi repellere licet*. Further, a broad notion of anticipatory self-defence based on remote attacks shades off into a justification of aggression, which is unquestionably prohibited. US Secretary of State Webster's famous statement of 1842, according to which self-defence may be justified in cases where the 'necessity of that self-defence is instant, overwhelming, and leaving no choice of means, and no moment for deliberation',[75] reaffirmed by the IMT,[76] is open to several interpretations. In the 1981 *Osirak* incident, many states condemned anticipatory self-defence,[77] and they have eventually continued to do so on other occasions. In the 2004 report *A More Secure World* the UN-mandated High-Level Panel distinguished between lawful 'pre-emptive' self-defence when the attack is imminent, and unlawful (unless authorized by the Security Council) 'preventative' self-defence when the alleged attack is too remote,[78] an opinion which has apparently been endorsed by the UN Secretary-General[79] but

[71] ibid para 193.

[72] CD Gray, 'The Bush Doctrine Revisited: The 2006 National Security Strategy of the USA' (2006) 5 Chin JIL 555. The latest US National Security Strategy issued by President Barack Obama on 26 May 2010, while not ruling out striking first when necessary 'to defend our nation and our interests', makes no mention of pre-emptive attacks, expresses the intent to 'seek broad international support' and 'to adhere to standards that govern the use of force'. It also endorses the responsibility to protect doctrine (see Ch 8 below, section B (2)(b)) and humanitarian intervention, at <http://www.whitehouse.gov/sites/default/files/rss_viewer/national_security_strategy.pdf>, at 22, 48.

[73] ICJ, *Legality of the Threat or Use of Nuclear Weapons* (n 53 above) para 97. See Ch 6 above, section B (2)(a).

[74] See eg DW Bowett, *Self-Defense in International Law* (New York: Praeger, 1958) 188–92.

[75] JB Moore, *A Digest of International Law* (Washington, DC: Government Printing Office, 1906) vol 2, 409–10.

[76] See n 61 above.

[77] UN Doc SCOR, 36th year, 2280th–2283rd, 2286th and 2288th meetings, and UNSC Res 487 (1981) of 19 June 1981, adopted unanimously, condemning the attack.

[78] 'A More Secure World: Our Shared Responsibility, Report of the High-Level Panel on Threats, Challenges and Change' in UNGA 'Note by the Secretary-General', 2 December 2004, UN Doc A/59/565, 8, paras 188–192.

[79] UNSG, 'In Larger Freedom: Towards Development, Security and Human Rights for All', Report of 21 March 2005, UN Doc A/59/2005, para 124.

opposed by the Non-Aligned Movement (NAM).[80] Most states are against any kind of anticipatory self-defence simply because they fear that the permission of some form of it will defeat the ban on the use of force to the advantage of the stronger. Article 51 and its expression 'if an armed attack occurs' remain, even under the terms of the ICJ *Nuclear Weapon* Opinion, the basic parameter. The better view seems to be that in certain *specific cases* anticipatory self-defence may be justifiably necessary, although it remains unlawful as a *general* rule, according to the maxim 'hard cases make bad law'.[81] It may be condoned *ex post* by the international community on a case-by-case basis if the threat to the state proves well-founded on the basis of the knowledge and inferences which can be drawn at the moment of deliberation. This suggests that so-called anticipatory self-defence may in fact be an instance of what today is 'necessity' as a *distinct* circumstance precluding wrongfulness.[82] In any event, Article 51 applies and justifies 'interceptive' self-defence—ie a reaction to an attack already launched and at most about to strike the target even if it has not yet been hit[83]—while military intervention against a 'threat to peace' authorized by the UN Security Council, when this is permitted, is justified under Chapter VII.

If an 'armed attack' is required, there is uncertainty as to what amounts to an 'armed attack'. Possible armed attacks for self-defence purposes may range from cross-border shootings and killing of a few individuals to fully fledged military invasions. In the 1986 *Nicaragua* Judgment and the 2003 *Oil Platforms* Judgment the ICJ held that actions such as the supply of funds, arms, and logistical support to rebels in another country—although contrary to Article 2(4) as a 'less grave form' of use of force—are not 'armed attacks' which justify self-defence.[84] By contrast, indirect aggression, ie the sending of armed bands on behalf of a state into another state, justifies self-defence when its 'scale and effects' are similar to those resulting from direct aggression.[85] Lesser border incidents do not generally justify self-defence.[86] Grave doubts exist in relation to several other situations such as cyber-attacks, nuclear attacks, laying mines at sea struck by a single vessel,[87] seizure of foreign embassies,[88] the launch of a few rockets or missiles into the territory of another state, and offences against nationals abroad. Given the general ban on the use of force, the narrower view is more persuasive.[89]

The permissibility of self-defence against 'non-state' actors—in particular rebels (such as Chechen fighters operating in Georgia against Russia, anti-Uganda rebels operating in the Democratic Republic of Congo, the PKK operating in North Iraq against Turkey, and the FARC operating in Ecuador against Colombia) and alleged terrorists (such as Al Qaeda and other organizations operating in Afghanistan and in

[80] NAM Comments on the High-level Panel Report, 28 February 2005, UN Doc A/59/PV, 14–15, at <http://www.un.int/malaysia/NAM/Positionpaper280205.doc>.

[81] See L Henkin, *How Nations Behave: Law and Foreign Policy* (New York: Columbia University Press, 2nd edn, 1979) 245.

[82] cf Art 25 UN ILC 'Draft Articles on Responsibility of States for Internationally Wrongful Acts, with Commentaries' (2001) GAOR 56th Session Supp 10, 43.

[83] See Y Dinstein, *War, Aggression and Self-Defence* (Cambridge: CUP, 5th edn, 2011) 203–5.

[84] ICJ, *Case concerning Military and Paramilitary Activities* (n 43 above) para 195; *Oil Platforms (Islamic Republic of Iran v United States)* Judgment of 6 November 2003, [2003] ICJ Rep 161, para 191. See D Raab, '"Armed Attack" after the Oil Platforms case' (2004) 17 LJIL 719.

[85] ICJ, *Case concerning Military and Paramilitary Activities* (n 43 above) para 191; *Oil Platforms* (n 84 above) para 51.

[86] ICJ, *Case concerning Military and Paramilitary Activities* (n 43 above) para 195; EECC, Ius ad bellum Case, *Ethiopia's Claims 1–8* Award of 19 December 2005,, at <http://www.pca-cpa.org/showfile.asp?fil_id=158>, para 10.

[87] ICJ, *Oil Platforms* (n 84 above) para 72.

[88] See n 64 above.

[89] See Gray (n 41 above) 114–66.

Pakistan especially against the United States, the Hezbollah operating in Lebanon against Israel)—is today heatedly debated.[90] The question is whether the unwillingness or the inability of a state to control its own territory and to prevent such operations from being carried out amounts to an 'armed attack' justifying self-defence either against the state as a whole (for example, Afghanistan) or limited to the part of its territory from which the attack has been launched (as the practice of North Iraq and Lebanon suggests). Even assuming the permissibility of self-defence against non-state actors, unwillingness and inability should be kept distinct since in cases of unwillingness there may be some involvement of the state, which could in principle more readily justify self-defence against the state as a whole, while in cases of inability the state is by definition uninvolved and only a reaction targeting the sources of attack may appear justifiable. There is some support today for self-defence against non-state actors, as evidenced by the trend of viewing its critics (as well as the ICJ's jurisprudence on the matter) as 'conservative'.[91] Another similar trend consists in admitting self-defence against non-state actors as a corollary of the responsibility to protect doctrine specifically understood as a 'duty to prevent'.[92] In effect, the doctrine of self-defence against non-state actors rests at first sight on sound systemic reasons. It assumes that the global states system is premised on the trust that any state in the system is willing and able to control its territory in order to avoid harm in other states; if not, it proves unreliable in and to the system, thereby justifying the use of cross-border force to prevent harm from occurring or aggravating a situation.[93] This rationale, however, tends to overlook the historical reasons why certain states may find themselves unable (and can also partly explain why they may be unwilling) to control their own territory, such as past colonialism.[94] It also tends to justify unilateral military operations only one way from the stronger towards the weaker, including so-called 'failed', 'outlaw', and 'rogue' states, labelled as such by the stronger states, showing little or no interest in addressing the 'causes' (rather than only the undesired effects) of states' inability or unwillingness. The debate raged when in Resolution 1368 (2001) and in Resolution 1373 (2001) the UN Security Council affirmed the inherent right to self-defence without specifying whether the source of the armed attack had to be a state, apparently suggesting that the attribution requirement and the concomitant acceptance of the concept of a 'private' armed attack could be abandoned.[95] According to the Russian Federation, Resolution 1373 (2001) also covers Chechen rebels and justifies self-defence against states (such as Georgia) from the territory of which they launch their attacks.[96] Not surprisingly, the

[90] N Lubell, *Extraterritorial Use of Force against Non-state Actors* (Oxford: OUP, 2010); T Reinold, 'State Weakness, Irregular Warfare, and the Right to Self-defense Post-9/11' (2011) 105 AJIL 244.

[91] See eg Reinold (n 90 above) 245, 260, 262, 285.

[92] See Ch 8 below, n 104.

[93] See Ch 5 above, section (B)(3)(a) and (b).

[94] See Ch 5 above, n 122.

[95] See eg TM Franck, 'Terrorism and the Right of Self-Defense' (2001) 95 AJIL 839, 840; C Greenwood, 'International Law and the Pre-emptive Use of Force: Afghanistan, Al-Qaida, and Iraq' (2003) 4 SD ILJ 7, 17.

[96] The Russian Federation accused Georgia of failure to comply with UNSC Res 1373 (2001), pointing out that such failure justified self-defence under Art 51 UN Charter. According to Russia: 'If the Georgian leadership is unable to establish a security zone in the area of the Georgian–Russian border, continues to ignore United Nations Security Council resolution 1373 (2001) of 28 September 2001, and does not put an end to the bandit sorties and attacks on adjoining areas in the Russian Federation, we reserve the right to act in accordance with Article 51 of the Charter of the United Nations'. cf Statement by Russian Federation President VV Putin, Annex to Letter dated 11 September 2002 from the Permanent Representative of the Russian Federation to the United Nations Addressed to the Secretary-General, UN Doc S/2002/1012, at 2–3.

Russian position was opposed by the United States.[97] As previously noted, there must clearly be a difference between 'global' and 'local' terrorists, or more generally between different groups, on the basis of their motivations and impact at global level.[98] To argue for the extension of self-defence against non-state actors to any group called 'terrorist' by any state for any reason ultimately amounts to defending the status quo. Not only is this posture anything but 'progressive'; it is also plainly unrealistic and in contradiction with the practice of promoting *certain* groups and insurgents, such as Libyan insurgents in 2011, by the states themselves which are deeply engaged in combating terrorism.

As a rule, when private individuals or groups kill or cause the death of someone beyond the border, they are responsible for criminal offences and are supposed to be tried by the territorial state, or by other states after their lawful apprehension or extradition. It is not permitted that a state can use armed force against a state as a whole for the sole reason that some of its citizens, or in any case some private individuals acting from its territory, have caused harm in their territory.[99] There is indeed a duty of every state to prevent its territory from being used to do harm to other states,[100] but the occurrence of harm does not necessarily imply a breach thereof and even when a breach is committed it is anything but clear that this unlawful act justifies a reaction such as self-defence against another state taken as a whole. While in the 2004 *Wall* Advisory Opinion the ICJ seems to have endorsed the view that self-defence is an inter-state measure,[101] some of its judges have argued for the admissibility of self-defence against non-state actors. They have contended, first, that when taken literally, Article 51 does not exclude self-defence against non-state actors; secondly, Security Council Resolutions 1368 (2001) and 1373 (2001) adopted in the aftermath of the 9/11 attacks on the United States expressly referred to self-defence; thirdly, the denial of self-defence against non-state actors would lead to absurd results since the same action would trigger self-defence when carried out by a state and would not do so when carried out by a private group; finally, self-defence against non-state actors is all the more reasonable where governmental authority is lacking or, more generally, when the territorial state is unwilling or unable to prevent the attack from being carried out.[102] In reply it has been stated that Article 51 is to be interpreted literally in state-to-state terms, that referral by Resolutions 1368 (2001) and 1373 (2001) to self-defence is unqualified, that self-defence against non-state actors amounts to a grave violation of the sovereignty of another state, and that reasonableness is different from lawfulness. The favourable position has been in some measure endorsed by the states in the Security Council debates on Israel's attacks against Lebanon's main airport, highways, military bases, and other targets, in retaliation for attacks by Hezbollah guerrilla rockets against Israel in July 2006, at least when the state from which attacks are launched proves incapable of controlling the territory and within the limit of a reaction targeting the source of the attack (as opposed to the entire territory).[103] In contrast, a Colombian

[97] SL Myers, 'Echoing Bush, Putin Asks U.N. to Back Georgia Attack' *New York Times*, 12 September 2002, at A9; 'US Warns Russia over Georgia Strike' *BBC News*, 13 September 2002, at <http://news.bbc.co.uk/2/hi/world/europe/2254959.stm>.

[98] See Ch 5 above, section C (4)(a).

[99] See section A (1)(e) below.

[100] See nn 441–9 below.

[101] ICJ, *Legal Consequences of the Construction of a Wall* (n 43 above) para 139.

[102] ibid declaration of Judge Buergenthal, at 242, para 6, and separate opinions of Judge Higgins, at 215, para 33, and Judge Kooijmans, at 230, para 35; *Armed Activities on the Territory of the Democratic Republic of the Congo v Uganda* Judgment of 19 December 2005, [2005] ICJ Rep 168, separate opinions of Judge Kooijmans, at 6–7, paras 28–32, and Judge Simma, at 3–4, paras 11–14.

[103] cf UN Doc S/PV.5489 of 14 July 2006 and S/PV.5492 of 20 July 2006. See J Kammerhofer, 'The Armed Activities Case and Non-State Actors in Self-Defence Law' (2007) 20 LJIL 89.

raid against the FARC in the territory of Ecuador, in 2008, was condemned in the OAS Permanent Council by Resolution 930 (2008).[104] It may also be of significance that the definition of the crime of aggression adopted at the 2010 Review Conference of the ICC Statute of Kampala does not mention the harbouring of irregular forces. It only includes, by mirroring UN General Assembly Resolution 3314 (XXIX) of 14 December 1974 and in line with the ICJ *Nicaragua* Judgment,[105] the active sending of armed bands by, or on behalf of, a state to carry out acts of armed force against another state.[106]

A different question may arise when alleged terrorist groups *prepare* attacks in the territory of a state to be carried out elsewhere. The practice shows that military responses in such instances were strongly condemned before the end of the Cold War as unlawful armed reprisals or blatant acts of aggression. Typical examples include the Israeli raid on Tunis in 1985[107] and the US raid on Tripoli and Benghazi in 1986.[108] This trend partially changed on the occasion of the US bombing of Sudan and Afghanistan in 1998,[109] and in particular with the Afghanistan War in 2001.[110]

Although not expressly envisaged in Article 51 UN Charter, self-defence is permitted only if it is necessary, proportionate, and immediate.[111] There must be no alternative peaceful means to repel the attack, the reaction must be proportionate (limited, in particular, to the amount of force strictly necessary to repel the attack), and action must be taken at a point sufficiently close to the attack.[112] Another limitation, procedural in character, is the duty of all UN member states to notify any action they take in self-defence to the Security Council under Article 51 UN Charter. In the 1986 *Nicaragua* Judgment the ICJ pointed out that this duty does not reflect customary international law, although it may prove useful to know the subjective attitude of the reacting state.[113] Under Article 51 self-defence must cease if and when the Security Council intervenes. It is unclear what measures of the Security Council preclude the reacting state from continuing its action in self-defence. It seems reasonable that what is required for preclusion is measures capable of repelling the attack.

(d) UN collective security

The global system, as hinted earlier, needs to make the distinction between the 'policeman' and the 'delinquent' as clear as possible. The former acts on behalf of the

[104] OAS Permanent Council Res 930 of 6 March 2008, at <http://www.oas.org/consejo/resolutions/res930.asp>.

[105] See nn 60 and 85 above.

[106] ICC Res RC/Res 6 of 11 June 2010, Annex I, Art 8*bis* (1) and (2), at <http://www.icc-cpi.int/iccdocs/asp_docs/Resolutions/RC-Res.6-ENG.pdf>. See K Ambos, 'The Crime of Aggression after Kampala' (2011) 53 Ger YBIL 463; S Barriga, 'A Historic Breakthrough on the Crime of Aggression' (2011) 105 AJIL 517.

[107] UN Doc S/PV2611, S/PV2611, and S/PV2615, and UNSC Res 573 (1985) of 4 October 1985, adopted by 14 votes in favour and the abstention of the US, condemning the Israeli 'aggression'.

[108] UN Doc S/PV.2902, at 7–16.

[109] cf (1999) 93 AJIL 165.

[110] cf in favour of the admissibility of self-defence, <http://www.nato.int/docu/pr/2001/p01-124e.htm>, 12 September 2001, and <http://www.nato.int/docu/speech/2001/s011002a.htm>, 4 October 2001, (NATO), EU Doc SN 140/01 of 21 September 2001 (EU), UN Doc S/2001/946 of 7 October 2001 (US and UK), UN Doc UN Doc. S/7167 of 7 October 2001 (UNSC President).

[111] See eg Dinstein (n 83 above) 230–4.

[112] ICJ, *Case concerning Military and Paramilitary Activities* (n 43 above) para 194; *Legality of the Threat or Use of Nuclear Weapons* (n 53 above) paras 40–44; *Oil Platforms* (n 84 above) paras 50–51. See additionally ITLOS, *M/V 'SAIGA' (No 2) (St Vincent and the Grenadines v Guinea) (Merits)* Judgment of 1 July 1999, Case No 2, at <http://www.itlos.org/index.php?id=64&L=0>, paras 155–159.

[113] ICJ, *Case concerning Military and Paramilitary Activities* (n 43 above) para 200.

community as a whole, while the latter acts exclusively for its own benefit according to the belief of the international community. There is little doubt that the UN Security Council and the United Nations as a whole are expected to play a central role in drawing the line between the international 'policeman' and the international 'delinquent'. The global community constantly appeals to the United Nations as the centre of international legitimacy. Action that would be unlawful when taken by states acting unilaterally, or 'unilaterally united' in alliances of the willing, or in regional organizations, are believed to be lawful when mandated by the Security Council, all the more so where they enjoy considerable support from the UN General Assembly. Even strong states often seek the support of the Security Council. At the same time, the Security Council is not a universal legislative or executive authority and its determinations may be presumed to reflect the belief of the global community only when no significant protests arise.[114]

Article 42 UN Charter provides that the Security Council 'may take such action by air, sea, or land forces as may be necessary to maintain or restore international peace and security', including demonstrations, blockades, and other operations by air, sea, or land forces of UN members, when 'any threat to the peace, breach of the peace, or act of aggression' exists under Article 39. Such collective military action is permitted should the Security Council consider that measures not involving the use of armed force under Article 41—including complete or partial interruption of economic relations and of rail, sea, air, postal, telegraphic, radio, and other means of communication, and the severance of diplomatic relations[115]—would be inadequate or have proved to be inadequate. The Council may also authorize regional organizations to take enforcement measures under Article 53 in Chapter VIII. All actions amounting to 'enforcement measures' taken under Chapter VII are excluded from the 'domestic jurisdiction' of member states set out in Article 2(7). In contrast to what was originally envisaged by the UN Charter,[116] the Security Council still lacks an army at its disposal. Rather than 'taking action' directly under the terms of Article 42, the Council has created 'peacekeeping' missions and has 'authorized' states and/or regional IOs to use force on numerous occasions, especially after the end of the Cold War.

Enforcement measures under Article 42 may be taken when the Security Council has determined 'the existence of any threat to the peace, breach of the peace, or act of aggression' under Article 39. As is well known, the precondition by far most often relied upon by the Council has been the 'threat to the peace' and this, especially since the end of the Cold War, has been interpreted very broadly to include not only external attacks but also domestic situations, such as apartheid, civil war, the commission of international crimes, nuclear proliferation by non-state actors, and international terrorism. It is very difficult to set 'limits' to the action of the Security Council in this context, although the general trend is to reconstruct them by way of logic and general principles. Apart from the 'internal' limits set out in the Charter, primarily the voting requirements,[117] the discretionary power of the Council in determining the existence of any

[114] For the protests against UNSC Res 1540 (2004) of 28 April 2004, see Ch 6 above, n 160.

[115] For decisions under Art 41, see Ch 6 above, section B (1)(c). Peaceful 'smart' sanctions adopted by the Security Council are discussed in Ch 8 below, section B (3).

[116] Art 43 provides that all members states 'undertake to make available to the Security Council, on its call and in accordance with a special agreement or agreements, armed forces, assistance, and facilities, including rights of passage', agreements that had to be 'negotiated as soon as possible' but have never been concluded.

[117] eg on 12 January 2007, a draft resolution calling on Myanmar to cease military attacks against civilians was vetoed by the People's Republic of China (PRC) and the Russian Federation, affirming

threat to the peace, breach of the peace, or act of aggression is informally limited by the generalized attitude of states, notably expressed in the UN General Assembly.[118]

In a few instances peacekeeping has evolved into state-building, notably in Kosovo (UNMIK) and East Timor (UNTAET), when all state functions (executive, legislative, and judicial), and hence effective control, have been exercised over a territory by a mandated international entity or 'presence' temporarily placed under international supervision or assistance.[119] The legal basis of both is uncertain. There is nothing in the Charter that provides for peacekeeping operations as established in current practice, let alone for state-building administrations. Traditional peacekeeping is based on (a) the consent of the territorial state or at least of the factions fighting in the territory; (b) the neutrality between the conflicting parties; (c) the use of force allowed only in self-defence; and (d) the supply of military troops through ad hoc agreements between the United Nations and its members. The Charter provides, by contrast, that action may be carried out even without the consent of the territorial state, beyond the limits of neutrality and self-defence, and by troops permanently supplied by member states. Over time, peacekeeping has extended to civil tasks and, occasionally, to so-called 'peace enforcement' (UNOSOM II and UNPROFOR) without the consent of the territorial sovereign and respect for neutrality, but has failed. In the 1962 *Certain Expenses* Advisory Opinion the ICJ held that both UNEF I and ONUC had a legal basis in the Charter.[120] In fact, peacekeeping does not fall under Chapter VI in so far as it is not directed, or not exclusively directed, to the peaceful settlement of a dispute between states, nor under the suggested limbo of 'Chapter Six and a Half',[121] but neither does it fit into the coercive measures of Article 42 because, although being anything but peaceful, they require the consent of the local sovereign or of the factions fighting on the ground. It is, however, precisely because of these hybrid characteristics, or rather due to it being characterized by a 'low-level' use of force, that peacekeeping is accepted by the international community. It seems, then, that UN peacekeeping and international territorial administrations can be legally grounded in a particular permissive customary rule within Chapter VII—under which the Security Council has always acted when setting up peacekeeping missions—which has come into being and supplemented the Charter.[122] Since the peacekeeping forces are UN organs, their acts are

that the matter 'basically was an internal affair of a sovereign State' not posing a threat to international peace and security (cf <http://www.un.org/News/Press/docs/2007/sc8939.doc.htm>). Likewise, a draft resolution of 11 July 2008, intended to impose sanctions not involving the use of force against Zimbabwe, President Mugabe, and other 13 government and security officials was not adopted because of the Chinese and Russian veto (cf <http://www.un.org/News/Press/docs/2008/sc9396.doc.htm>).

[118] B Conforti and C Focarelli, *The Law and Practice of the United Nations* (Leiden and Boston: Nijhoff, 4th rev edn, 2010) 215–17.

[119] See B Knoll, *The Legal Status of Territories Subject to Administration by International Organisations* (Cambridge: CUP, 2008); C Stahn, *The Law and Practice of International Territorial Administration* (Cambridge: CUP, 2008); R Wilde, *International Territorial Administration: How Trusteeship and the Civilizing Mission Never Went Away* (Oxford: OUP, 2008).

[120] ICJ, *Certain Expenses of the United Nations (Article 17, Paragraph 2, of the Charter)* Advisory Opinion of 20 July 1962, [1962] ICJ Rep 151, 170–3.

[121] The term was introduced by Secretary-General Dag Hammarskjold and seems to have been shared by Secretary-General B Boutros-Ghali in the often cited *An Agenda for Peace* Report (at <http://www.un.org/Docs/SG/agpeace.html>, para 46), where peacekeeping operations were defined as an 'invention' of the UN, even though it is not clear whether the 'invention' falls under 'Chapter Six and a Half' or under a specific customary norm that has come into being under Chapter VII, or outside the Charter altogether.

[122] Conforti and Focarelli (n 118 above) 267–9.

attributed to the organization. This does not necessarily exclude the joint responsibility of the states that have sent peacekeepers, and, in general, the view held by a number of scholars and recently endorsed by the Court of Appeal of The Hague in the 2011 *Nuhanovic* Judgment and by the ECtHR in the 2011 *Al-Jedda* Judgment,[123]—that the acts of peacekeepers should be attributed both to the state and to the organization, according to the aspects over which each exercises effective control—deserves support.[124]

Although Article 42 stipulates that the Security Council itself 'may take action' directly, not having an army at its disposal it has authorized states and IOs to use force or to take other enforcement measures.[125] The basic assumption of authorizations from the Security Council is that the states which take up the authorization act lawfully, although their action would be unlawful if taken without the authorization. This idea is generally accepted, yet many questions remain unanswered. One is that in many cases the action taken by the authorized states is, at least at first sight, already internationally lawful. This has occurred when the targeted state had given its consent to the action,[126] or when the action was justified as collective self-defence.[127] No doubt the existence of an 'authorization' may help governments to belittle constitutional and parliamentary concerns about the employment of national military forces abroad by claiming that the operation has an 'international police' character. The permissibility of certain operations, when carried out unilaterally, may also be doubtful and an authorization from the Security Council may ensure that the action is lawful in any case. It has been suggested, for example, that Resolution 1816 (2008) and Resolution 1846 (2008) authorizing counter-piracy operations in the Somali territorial sea provide authority for those states that do not recognize the Somali Transitional Federated Government (TFG).[128] A second problem is that while in certain instances authorizations referred to fully fledged military operations, in others the activities authorized were essentially of internal law enforcement or were civil in nature. A third, particularly critical problem is that there is little certainty as to the extent of the 'legalizing' effect of authorizations. Resolutions authorizing the use of force no doubt render lawful the (otherwise unlawful) resort to force by states, but it is unclear whether they render lawful also other acts connected with the use of force, such the violation of any rule of international humanitarian law, or human rights, or treaties binding the targeted state and the states which take up the authorization. The instinctive answer is in the negative, but once it has been accepted that the Security Council has the power to 'legalize' otherwise illegal acts, then in principle this effect is either unlimited or proof must be given of the limit.

[123] Ch 5 above, nn 240 and 243.

[124] See eg L Condorelli, 'Le statut des forces de l'ONU et le droit international humanitaire' 78 (1995) RDI 881; G Verdirame, *The UN and Human Rights: Who Guards the Guardians?* (Cambridge: CUP, 2011) 112–3, 200–1.

[125] See Conforti and Focarelli (n 118 above) 271–87. For critical analysis from diverse perspectives, see P Picone, 'Le autorizzazioni all'uso della forza tra sistema delle Nazioni Unite e diritto internazionale generale' (2005) 88 RDI 5; L-A Sicilianos, 'Entre multilatéralisme et unilatéralisme: l'autorisation par le Conseil de sécurité de recourir à la force' (2008) 339 RdC 9; TL Chapman, *Securing Approval: Domestic Politics and Multilateral Authorization for War* (Chicago: University of Chicago Press, 2011).

[126] cf UNSC Res 1816 (2008) of 2 June 2008, Res 1846 (2008) of 2 December 2008, Res 1851 (2008) of 16 December 2008, renewed by Res 1897 (2009) of 30 November 2009, and Res 2020 (2011) of 22 November 2011 authorizing the repression of piracy off the coasts of Somalia expressly based on the consent of the Somali Transitional Government (whose representativeness and effectiveness is, however, rather questionable), and Res 1950 (2010) of 23 November 2010, renewing prior authorizations. For a thorough discussion of recent piracy off Somalia, see JA Roach, 'Countering Piracy off Somalia: International Law and International Institutions' (2010) 104 AJIL 397.

[127] cf UNSC Res 678 (1990) of 29 November 1990 in relation to the 1991 Gulf War.

[128] Roach (n 126 above) 401.

A fourth problem is that the action authorized increasingly tends to overlap with peacekeeping or state-building missions, thus creating a complex network of authorizations of UN organs, states, and regional IOs which may be hard to disentangle in order to know who is empowered or bound to do what. A fifth problem is that an authorization leaves a discretionary power to states as to whether to take up the authorization while apparently imposing a set of mandatory duties on them to be met once the authorization has been taken up. A sixth problem, which overlaps with the scope of Article 103 UN Charter,[129] is to whom the acts performed by the participating states are legally attributed and who accounts for the unlawful conduct which is not covered by the authorization, notably for violations of human rights.[130]

A useful distinction to make in attempting an answer is between recommendations, authorizations, and delegations of the Security Council. The Council 'recommends' when it *exhorts* states to adopt a conduct in itself *lawful*; it 'authorizes' when it *makes lawful* a specified conduct outside its powers under the Charter that, if held by a member state, would otherwise be *unlawful*, without necessarily suggesting that the state should pursue it; it 'delegates' when it *transfers* one of its powers under the Charter (or customary rules emerged to supplement or to derogate from it) to the states, thus submitting their whole regime to the norms which apply to the Council rather than to those that otherwise would apply to states.[131] It follows that a recommendation is simply to indicate to the individual states what lawful conduct, according to the Council, it is desirable that they take, states still remaining free not to pursue it.[132] An authorization has the effect of making lawful otherwise unlawful conduct, the states remaining free not to behave in the manner authorized, but knowing that if they do the authorization exempts them from any responsibility which they would otherwise incur, and presumably entails a set of duties. When the Council authorizes or recommends it is not necessary for the conduct recommended or authorized to fall within its powers and if an act were to 'recommend' states to adopt a wrongful act, making it lawful, it would be an authorization which also contains an exhortation.[133] But when the Council 'delegates' a power, then the delegated conduct must fall within its powers, otherwise the delegation risks being *ultra vires*, and the states may be seen, within the powers conferred by the delegation, as 'decentralized organs' of the Council: the legal regime is therefore the one applicable to the Council that carries out directly the delegated function, while the attribution of the conduct to the states or the Council (or both) in case of an unlawful act depends on the 'effective control' test.[134] In this sense 'authorizations' of the Council to carry out per se lawful acts—such as measures of collective self-defence or actions carried out with the consent of the local sovereign—

[129] See Ch above 6, section B (3)(d).

[130] See Ch 5 above, nn 240 and 243.

[131] See ICJ, *Application for Review of Judgment No. 158 of the United Nations Administrative Tribunal* Advisory Opinion of 12 July 1973, [1973] ICJ Rep 1973 166, para 20.

[132] cf UNSC Res 84 (1950) of 7 July 1950 adopted in relation to the Korean War, in which the Council 'recommends' that 'all Member States providing military forces and other assistance . . . make such forces and other assistance available to a unified command under the United States' and 'authorizes' use of the UN flag.

[133] cf UNSC Res 221 (1966) of 9 April 1966, which 'calls upon . . . and empowers' the UK prevent 'by the use of force if necessary' the arrival at the port of Beira of oil destined to proceed overland to Rhodesia, thus enforcing an embargo decided earlier.

[134] *Agim Behrami and Bekir Behrami v France and Ruzhdi Saramati v France, Germany and Norway* Decision of admissibility of 2 May 2007 [GC], Apps 71412/01 and 78166/01, 45 EHRR SE10, para 43, distinguishing between authorizations and delegations. Framing the case in terms of 'delegation' (paras 129, 133–134, 141), the Court concluded that 'the challenged action [of KFOR] was, in principle, [exclusively] attributable to the United Nations'.

may well amount to 'delegations' *by the United Nations* conducted pursuant to the rules of the Charter, regardless of whether the states could have lawfully carried them out independently. It is as if the Council intends to 'authorize' states to act on its behalf, which technically amounts to a delegation. It is presumably in this latter sense that the 'authorization' of the Security Council is to be understood when it is necessary for the actions of regional organizations in order to preserve the peace under Article 53 UN Charter.

The question is indeed difficult to untangle and hair-splitting arguments or general explanation models, as sometimes advanced in legal doctrine, especially when these proliferate, tend to overintellectualize a practice which does not (and should arguably not) fit into any pre-conceived, 'rationally irresistible' pattern. Each authorization has its own story, presuppositions, and consequences. The UN Security Council ostensibly works as the authority which decides what is best in any given situation. It may be right or wrong in its deliberations and omissions, and 'disobedience' to its decisions by the states may work as appreciable (even necessary) containing factors.[135] The only connecting thread in all authorizations is that the conduct authorized is lawful while it would otherwise not be so. While the practice tends to bring to mind the model of a 'delegation' of powers, as known in domestic legal systems and general jurisprudence, it is in fact more reflective of a pattern of mere authorizations, with the least possible (yet not totally absent) degree of 'institutionalization'. There is in fact a general consensus that authorizations of the Security Council work as an 'external' circumstance precluding wrongfulness of the recourse to force under general international law.[136] The function of the authorization is to 'legalize' certain otherwise illegal acts within the limits of the authorization, rather than to allow the exercise of delegated powers of the Security Council. This minimal level of institutionalization does not exclude that the authorized entities act under a Security Council's mandate supposedly in the interest of the international community as a whole. It is, however, from the support of the generality of states, rather than from the powers conferred on the Security Council by the Charter, that the legalizing effect derives. The Council thus remains under the bounds of general international law (as supported by the states as a whole), and when it authorizes states to deviate from general international law, as in the case of authorizations of an otherwise unlawful use of force, it does so on the basis of a (distinct) general international law rule (or exception). As to their legal basis, in the absence of a specific rule in the Charter and given that virtually all existing states are members of the United Nations, authorizations may be thought to be also 'internally' justified by virtue of an ad hoc particular permissive customary rule emerging within the organization in derogation from (or supplementing) Chapter VII UN Charter.[137]

Under both general international law and the UN particular customary rule, for the authorization to produce the desired effects both 'externally' and 'internally', certain conditions have to be met. First, there must be an express formulation. No resolution of the Council can be interpreted as implicitly providing an authorization if it does not state this clearly.[138] Secondly, the illegality of the use of force cannot be removed by a

[135] For disobedience to the Security Council's sanctions, see A Tzanakopoulos, *Disobeying the Security Council: Countermeasures against Wrongful Sanctions* (Oxford: OUP, 2011).

[136] As defined in general, without mentioning authorizations of the Security Council to use force, by Arts 20–27 UN ILC 'Draft Articles on Responsibility of States for Internationally Wrongful Acts, with Commentaries' (2001) GAOR 56th Session Supp 10, 43.

[137] For this view, see Conforti and Focarelli (n 118 above) 280–3.

[138] ECtHR, *Behrami* (n 134 above) para 134, emphasizing that the delegation of UNSC Res 1244 which had set up UNMIK 'was neither assumed, nor implicit, but rather prior and explicit'.

subsequent (implicit) ratification, for example by resolutions that provide for post-conflict measures. In international practice states have often criticized possible implicit authorizations and/or post hoc authorizations.[139] Finally, the Security Council should retain 'control' over the authorized operations through various expedients, ranging from limited duration to the provision of informative reports, although in individual operations the degree of effective control exercised by the Council has been highly variable.[140] This control is not necessarily to be understood as evidence of a 'delegation', as is often maintained, but rather as a limit to the 'legalizing' effect implied in the authorization and as a measure of the 'effective control' exercised by the United Nations for attribution purposes.[141] It follows that the conduct of the authorized operations can be evaluated, whenever this is possible, by domestic and international courts in terms of the rules applicable to the states or IOs which have taken up the authorization. These latter may well be judicially found in breach of the applicable international law if their otherwise unlawful action has gone beyond the terms of the authorization, such as, just to mention a recent case, the purpose of protecting the civilian population in the 2011 Libyan crisis.[142]

(e) Transnational crime

People's security is also ensured by states, both individually and in cooperation with one another, combating crime, in particular transnational organized crime. A great many treaties, either bilateral or multilateral, have been concluded both general in scope, for instance the 2000 Palermo Convention on Transnational Organized Crime,[143] and specifically dealing with a certain crime or class of crimes, ranging from money laundering to cybercrime, corruption, currency counterfeiting, child prostitution and pornography, migrant smuggling, pollution, maritime piracy, and terrorism or terrorism-related crimes, as well as illicit trafficking in narcotic drugs and psychotropic substances, in human beings, in endangered species of wild fauna and flora, in cultural property, in nuclear material, in firearms, and in counterfeit goods.[144]

In a globalized world transnational crime is particularly powerful and threatens both states and people.[145] Criminals take advantage of the partition of the world into a multiplicity of states, however borderless in other respects, and act where states are unable or unwilling to extend their jurisdictional power or do not cooperate enough (or seriously enough) with one another. Cross-border crime is facilitated by the advances and reduced costs of transport and communication as well as by the decreased ability of states to control transboundary operations, also as a consequence of massive use of the internet.[146] Globalization encourages jurisdictional shopping and criminal groups

[139] See Conforti and Focarelli (n 118 above) 281–2.

[140] cf the statement by the President of the Security Council of 30 November 1998 whereby 'in general operations should have a clear mandate, including a statement of objectives, rules of engagement, a well-developed plan of action, a time-frame for disengagement, and arrangements for regular reporting to the Council', UN Doc S/PRST/1998/35, at 2.

[141] Ch 5 above, nn 240 and 243.

[142] Ch 8 below, n 114.

[143] United Nations Convention against Transnational Organized Crime (signed 12–15 December 2000, entered into force 29 September 2003) 2225 UNTS 209. See JD McClean, *Transnational Organized Crime: A Commentary on the UN Convention and its Protocols* (Oxford: OUP, 2007).

[144] For a recent overview, see T Obokata, *Transnational Organised Crime in International Law* (Oxford and Portland: Hart, 2010).

[145] UNDOC, *The Globalization of Crime: A Transnational Organized Crime Threat Assessment* (Vienna: United Nations Office on Drugs and Crime, 2010).

[146] See Ch 5 above, section B (3)(c).

compete with one another to select the most advantageous state in which to commit crimes, or more likely parts thereof. They may also commit the crime instantly and virtually in all states through the internet. In turn, states tend to compete with one another, overtly or covertly, in order to attract criminal groups (in particular 'white-collar' groups) by offering offshore spaces of convenience and great benefits through social, environmental, fiscal, and criminal legislation.

It is in principle for each state to protect people from crime, whether this is internal or transnational, within its territory. Treaties on transnational crime share a number of key features. First and foremost, they set out the principle of sovereign equality and the territorial integrity of states: repression of crimes is permitted only by each state within its territory by its organs. States are not allowed to intervene, either by force or any other means, in another state without this latter's consent in order to apprehend a criminal, however grave the crime may be.[147] They may ask other states for investigative and judicial assistance and, in cases where the criminal has been captured by another state, they may ask for the extradition of the alleged criminal, extradition which may be compulsory on the basis of a treaty binding the two states subject to certain conditions. This legal regime presupposes a high degree of mutual trust in the ability and willingness of states to combat crime. However, states are often unable or unwilling to fully enforce treaties and have (but also give) little reason to trust others. Secondly, all transnational crime treaties stipulate a number of typical obligations, such as the obligation to criminalize in domestic law the conducts prohibited, the obligation to introduce in the domestic legal system effective sanctions against such conduct, the obligation to set up domestic mechanisms of management, monitoring, and cooperation with analogous mechanisms in other contracting states, and the obligation to cooperate with one another in investigative and judiciary assistance, including extradition, the carrying out of which is generally facilitated with a view to reducing impunity. Thirdly, treaties always contain a clause which allocates jurisdiction among the contracting states, usually reflecting the criteria established by customary international law,[148] but also providing for other criteria, such as the residence of either the perpetrator and/or of the victim, depending on the treaty and the crime involved. Fourthly, treaties occasionally contemplate the functioning of a conference or assembly of the parties which may help to administer the implementation of the treaty. Fifthly, a subordination clause governing the relationship between these treaties and others on the same subject-matter is frequently found.[149] Finally, while treaties often provide for the functioning of domestic bodies entrusted to cooperate with one another, they rarely establish international monitoring bodies, and when they do such bodies have little if any decision-making power.

While the existence of so many treaties is a good sign, the regime is, all in all, weaker than expected and needed. Leaving aside the Palermo Convention, every other treaty deals with a specific crime (or class of crimes), the legal regime of each being independent of the others. There may well be two or even more treaties on the same crime, with the risk of different and incompatible legal regimes, and no treaty at all for another (possibly even graver) crime. Moreover, failing a customary international law regime, every treaty binds only its parties, and parties vary depending on the treaty. As a rule, regional treaties (such as those concluded within the Council of Europe or the Organization of American States) work better than universal treaties, but they maintain

[147] See Ch 5 above, n 178.
[148] See Ch 5 above, section B (4)(a).
[149] See Ch 6 above, section B (3)(c).

continental (rather than state) fragmentation. On the other hand, universal treaties, such as those concluded within the United Nations, are far from being acceded to by all states and the circle of acceding states may vary markedly from one treaty to another. It is true that IOs are increasingly engaged in combating transnational crime, but it is also true that their effectiveness is weakened by the above shortcomings. At a time of globalization when a universal regime is crucial to the effectiveness of the rules, this objective and subjective fragmentation is indeed discouraging and calls for a redoubling of efforts. It should also be noted that even when a treaty binds states, its full domestic implementation is often problematic and delayed, inter alia, as a result of the absence of international monitoring or supervisory bodies. Finally, transnational crime treaties are often formulated in broad terms, in order to meet different legal realities in the potential parties, and are thus open to divergent (although equally plausible) interpretations and diverse implementation in different states. Unfortunately, not only are states relatively impotent in exercising their legislative and enforcement jurisdiction at a time of globalization, but they (or, rather, their rulers) are often reluctant to adopt effective measures against transnational crime. They can have a personal interest in avoiding the repression of certain crimes, or may even be involved in them.

At least the most serious transnational crimes ought to be seen as international crimes or breaches of human rights, ie the other side of the coin in relation to the existing formal legal regimes concerning such matters, thus enjoying the most effective guarantees provided by these latter rules. In this respect, protection of security shades off into protection of humanity.

(2) Humanity

While the most basic meaning of security refers to survival, it has been noted that 'The greater the level of security enjoyed, the more individuals and groups... can have an existence beyond the instinctual animal struggle merely to survive'.[150] Security can indeed be defined from the starting point of insecurity and fear as 'survival-plus', not just being alive but living.[151] As Thomas Hobbes himself observed: 'By safety one should understand not mere survival in any condition, but a happy life so far as that is possible'.[152] Accordingly, the concept of 'human security'—first mentioned in the Palme Commission's 1982 *Common Security: A Blueprint for Survival* report,[153] and later recurrently endorsed in international practice—may be taken on as a bridge from security to humanity.[154]

Human security reinterprets the traditional notion of national security (understood as a defence of the borders with weapons) 'beyond the protection of borders, ruling elites and exclusive state interests to include the protection of people' from new threats, such as diseases, urban crime, food insecurity, environmental degradation, unemployment, terrorism, and natural disasters.[155] The core idea of human security is that individuals are 'no longer consubstantial to the state'.[156] The debate was unleashed

[150] K Booth, *Theory of World Security* (Cambridge: CUP, 2007) 4.

[151] ibid 98, 102–7.

[152] Thomas Hobbes, *De Cive*, XIII, 4.

[153] Independent Commission on Disarmament and Security Issues, *Common Security: A Blueprint for Survival* (New York, 1982).

[154] The concept of humanity has already been touched upon, see Ch 5 above, section A (3)(b), discussing the notion of international community.

[155] Commission on Global Governance, *Our Global Neighborhood* (Oxford: OUP, 1995), at <http://www.sovereignty.net/p/gov/ogn-front.html>.

[156] S Tadjbakhsh and AM Chenoy, *Human Security: Concepts and Implications* (Abingdon and New York: Routledge, 2007) 13.

after the collapse of the Soviet Union, the reduced threat of a major-power war, and the concomitant outbreak of many local, internal conflicts across the world. The new concept appeared promising, while also being somehow derided as 'hot air'[157] and as a questionable justification for humanitarian intervention.[158] In fact the term 'security' attracts public attention, urgency in mobilization, priority over other goals, and financial resources. For its part, the term 'human' allows the project to be presented as universal, non-discriminatory, benefiting all without distinctions of nationality or other factors, and morally sound.[159]

After discussing the concept of humanity, this section examines the key features of the international legal regimes restraining warfare, prohibiting international crimes, and promoting human rights and cultural diversity. It argues that humanity is a sense of empathic closeness and emotional attunement with other sentient beings rather than an abstract concept, that international crimes do capture a core of common humanity beyond cultural diversity, and that human rights are historical and relative, in need of being shouldered by other people than the persons who benefit from them and of being defended by society, although their precise aim is to protect the individual from the overwhelming might of society.

(a) Defining humanity

The most diffused idea of 'humanity' today reproduces the Western view of what counts as 'human'. It is difficult to say that, for example, the world system is converging towards a Himalayan Buddhist notion of humanity. The West has monopolized the notion of humanity and injected it into the law, beginning with ancient Greek philosophy and the tradition of natural law.

The term 'humanity', however, has various meanings even within Western civilization. It may refer, first, to the perfected form, the ideal, or the 'spirit of Man'. In this sense, the ancients used the term *humanitas* (corresponding to the Greek *paideia*), hence humanism and humanities, and Wilhelm von Humboldt regarded 'the realization of the idea of humanity' as the purpose (*Ziel*) or end of history.[160] Secondly, humanity may denote the 'essence of Man', as illustrated by Thomas Aquinas who held, in Aristotelian terms, that 'humanity is the essence of man . . . the essential principles of the species'.[161] Thirdly, humanity may indicate the 'human race', ie the human species as a biological entity, as is the case in discussions on the history or the biological evolution of humanity. Fourthly, humanity may be seen as the hypostatized synthesis of the 'history and tradition of Man' in Auguste Compte's sense.[162] Fifthly, humanity may refer to the reasonable nature of Man as endowed with 'dignity' and worth being treated as an end in itself according to Immanuel Kant's second formulation of his categorical imperative: 'Act in such a way that you treat humanity, whether in your own person or in the person of any other, never merely as a means to an end,

[157] R Paris, 'Human Security: Paradigm Shift or Hot Air?' (2001) 26(2) *International Security* 87.

[158] See Ch 8 below, section B (2).

[159] See B von Tigerstrom, *Human Security and International Law: Prospects and Problems* (Oxford and Portland: Hart, 2007).

[160] W von Humboldt, 'Ueber die Aufgabe des Geschichtschreibers' in *Wilhelm von Humboldts Gesammelte Schriften* [1905] (Berlin: Walter de Gruyter, 1968) vol 4, 55, noting that 'Das Ziel der Geschichte kann nur die Verwirklichung der durch die Menschheit darzustellenden Idee seyn'.

[161] Thomas Aquinas, *Contra Gentiles*, IV, 81, 10.

[162] A Compte, *Système de politique positive ou traité de sociologie, instituant la religion de l'humanité* (Paris: Librairie scientifique-industrielle de L Mathias,1852) IV, 30.

but always at the same time as an end'.[163] Sixthly, humanity may denote the attitude of 'understanding and sympathy towards the others', as defined, once again, by Kant as follows:

> ... *humanity* [*Humanität*] signifies ... the universal *feeling of sympathy*, and, on the other, the faculty of being able to *communicate* universally one's inmost self-properties constituting in conjunction the befitting *social character* of mankind, in contradistinction to the narrowly constricted life of animals.[164]

Finally, humanity may be seen as a fiction for domination due to its intrinsic totalizing scope.[165]

Human dignity, for its part, originates in Stoic philosophy (notably in Cicero) developed in Christian theology (reflecting human nature as *imago Dei*),[166] and in modern secular thinking, exemplarily in Pico della Mirandola[167] and, as already noted, in Immanuel Kant. The notion of human dignity is alluded to in the preamble to the UN Charter, in various human rights instruments adopted after the end of World War II,[168] including the EU Charter of Fundamental Rights,[169] as well as in international jurisprudence[170] and in a few national constitutions, famously in Article 1 of the federal German Constitution.[171] This induces one to assume that the concept has a legal bearing beyond philosophical speculation. However, since it is used either in non-binding acts or in the preambles to treaties, and is generally combined with other more specific human rights, the question of its autonomous legal meaning is open. While some contend that human dignity is today envisaged by customary international law and/or a general principle of law recognized by civilized nations, others argue that human dignity only provides a symbolic foundation for more specific human rights.[172] The thesis favouring autonomy is indeed problematic since it justifies multiple, opposing answers.[173]

[163] See I Kant, *Grundlegung zur Metaphysik der Sitten* [1785] (Hamburg: Meiner, 1962) II, 37, English trans *Grounding for the Metaphysics of Morals* (Indianapolis and Cambridge: Hackett, 1981) 36; I Kant, *Metaphysik der Sitten* [1797] (Hamburg: Meiner, 1959) II, §§ 37–40, 320–3, English trans *The Metaphysics of Morals* (Cambridge: CUP, 1996) 209–10. On Kant's ideas about humanity, see DG Sussman, *The Idea of Humanity: Anthropology and Anthroponomy in Kant's Ethics* (New York and London: Routledge, 2001).

[164] I Kant, *Kritik der Urteilskraft* [1790] (Hamburg: Meiner, 1959) § 60, 215–17, English trans *The Critique of Judgement* (Oxford: OUP, 2007) 182 3 (original emphasis).

[165] C Schmitt, *Der Begriff des Politischen* [1932] (Berlin: Duncker & Humblot, 1991) 55, English trans *The Concept of the Political* (New Brunswick: Rutgers University Press, 1976) 54, referring to P-J Proudhon's saying, 'Wer Menschheit sagt, will betrügen' ('Whoever invokes humankind wants to cheat').

[166] See MJ Perry, *The Idea of Human Rights: Four Inquiries* (Oxford: OUP, 1998).

[167] See GP della Mirandola, *Oratio de hominis dignitate* (Bologna: Benedetto Faelli, 1496, English trans *Discourse on the Dignity of Man*, at <http://www.cscs.umich.edu/~crshalizi/Mirandola>.

[168] See O Schachter, 'Human Dignity as a Normative Concept' (1983) 77 AJIL 848; D Kretzmer and E Klein (eds), *The Concept of Human Dignity in Human Rights Discourse* (Leiden: Brill, 2002).

[169] Art 1 ('Human dignity is inviolable. It must be respected and protected') [2000] OJ C364/1.

[170] C McCrudden, 'Human Dignity and Judicial Interpretation of Human Rights' (2008) 19 EJIL 655.

[171] 'Die Würde des Menschen ist unantastbar' ('The dignity of man is inviolable').

[172] The well-known view of the Yale Law School that human dignity (specified as the base values of well-being, affection, respect, power, wealth, enlightenment, skill, and rectitude) is the ultimate goal of the international legal order is open to criticism (see Ch 4 above, n 144).

[173] For the ambivalence of the concept when applied to euthanasia, see C Focarelli, 'Euthanasia', MP EPIL (June 2009 update). A well-known example is the case raised by the ban on 'dwarf tossing'. In two identical orders of 27 October 1995 (Nos 136727 and 143578) the French Council of State had found that an administrative authority could legally prohibit dwarf tossing on grounds that it did not respect human dignity and was contrary to public order. The UNHRC, *Wackenheim v France* Views of 15 July 2002, Comm No 854/1999, UN Doc A/57/40, vol II, 179, paras 4, 7.4, and 7.5,

For present purposes humanity can be taken as a feeling of empathic closeness to other sentient beings. Its basic hallmark is to feel a unison vibration and natural attraction in one's own emotional life with that of the other. It is proposed that this sense of sympathy could be seen as the foundation of the rules of international law inspired by humanitarian considerations rather than (or in addition to) the more ambiguous idea of human dignity. It is in this sense, in particular, that the expression 'elementary considerations of humanity' should be understood in broad terms.[174]

(b) Restraints on armed conflict

Since time immemorial, belligerents have appeared to accept the idea that there must be some legal restraints even during war. A set of legal rules *common* to belligerents *despite* and *within* the conflict, in contrast to the adage *inter arma silent leges*, have thus been created over time, especially since the second half of the nineteenth century.[175] The underlying reasons are manifold, including reciprocity—any belligerent is aware that the *sine qua non* (albeit not always sufficient) condition for respect of the rules by the other belligerent is its own respect for those rules in the first place—and a sense of self-restraint that can also be inspired by a feeling of humanity towards other individual human beings occasionally serving as soldiers in the enemy army.

Once an armed conflict breaks out, many fundamental rules of the international law of peace—prominently the rule on respect for state sovereignty—cease to apply and others, forming the body of international humanitarian law (IHL), take over.[176] Also in domestic law the applicable rules change and what in peacetime is a crime (typically, murder), in wartime, when committed against enemy combatants, normally becomes a lawful act. At least in this minimal (but indeed critical) sense war has been inextricably intertwined with law from time immemorial: any community needs to know when murder and other very serious offences become lawful under certain circumstances and when this exceptional state of affairs will cease.[177] Since the change is triggered when an 'armed conflict' breaks out, the crucial point is how armed conflict, either international or non-international, is defined. In the 1995 *Tadić* Decision the ICTY held that 'an armed conflict exists whenever there is a resort to armed force between States or protracted armed violence between governmental authorities and organized armed groups or between such groups within

seised by one of the dwarfs involved who claimed that it was actually the Council of State that discriminatorily had impaired his dignity by depriving him of his work and means of subsistence, held that 'the ban on dwarf tossing as practised by the author did not constitute an abusive measure but was necessary in order to protect public order, which brings into play considerations of human dignity' and was not discriminatory under Art 26 ICCPR. For a comment, see M Levinet, 'Dignité contre dignité. L'épilogue de l'affaire du "lancer de nains" devant le Comité des droits de l'homme des Nations Unies' (2003) 55 RTDH 1017. More generally, see R Andorno, 'The Paradoxical Notion of Human Dignity' (2001) 78 RIFD 151.

[174] For the view that they can specifically amount to general principles of law recognized by civilized nations, see Ch 6 above, n 173.

[175] For the ancient practices, see DJ Bederman, *International Law in Antiquity* (Cambridge: CUP, 2001) 242–66; J Keegan, *A History of Warfare* (London: Pimlico, 2nd edn, 2004).

[176] ICJ, *Legality of the Threat or Use of Nuclear Weapons* (n 53 above) para 75, noting that two traditional branches of *jus in bello*, the 'Hague Law' governing the conduct of hostilities and neutrality and the 'Geneva Law' specifically dealing with the protection of the victims of war, today form IHL as one single complex system.

[177] For the ancient practice, see Neff (n 10 above) 25–9.

a State'.[178] A conflict generally requires a sufficiently *high level* use of force. Low-level clashes between states are not armed conflicts. The notion that terrorism in itself, regardless of any involvement with a state, constitutes 'armed conflict'—often with a view to killing presumed terrorists as lawful military targets wherever they are[179]—finds little or no support in practice. Conflicts started under a UN Security Council authorization are generally not seen as 'war' for domestic (especially constitutional) purposes, although they may well be (and indeed generally are) armed conflicts for IHL purposes. The rules of IHL governing armed conflict (*jus in bello*) apply independently of the rules on recourse to force (*jus ad bellum*) equally to all belligerents.[180]

International law protects the security of people during both international and internal conflict, including belligerent occupation, to the fullest extent possible in the circumstances. By 'people' is meant first and foremost the 'civilians', ie those who do not or no longer take part in the hostilities, but in some measure also 'combatants'—although, unlike civilians, combatants are lawful military targets—to the extent that the conduct of hostilities is subject to legal restraints and belligerents are not allowed to behave as they wish against the enemy. IHL is thus aimed at 'humanizing' the conflict in the sense that people are to be protected for the sole reason that they are human beings, whatever their flag and cause for war.[181] The basic rules of IHL specifically protecting civilians provide that only enemy combatants are lawful military targets and may be hit (principle of distinction), that when civilians are hit as a 'collateral' effect of hitting a lawful military target the loss of civilian lives must be proportionate to the military advantage pursued (principle of proportionality), and that precautions are to be taken in advance to avoid hitting civilians (principle of precaution).[182] What is prohibited is basically gratuity, ie those violent acts that are unnecessary (or manifestly out of proportion) to the objective of hostilities and immediately appear inhumane, such as the killing of those who are not (or are no longer) taking part in the hostilities, for example wounded and sick combatants, health personnel, civilians, and prisoners of war (POWs).[183] Under IHL what is 'inhumane' is not, and may not be, the killing or wounding of others, which is the quintessence of armed conflict, but rather killing or wounding that is unnecessary in order to win. IHL also prohibits the use of weapons against enemy combatants that cause 'superfluous injury or unnecessary suffering', not any weapon. In recent decades the kernel of IHL, in particular the legal regime of war crimes, has been extended to internal conflict, which was in the past reserved to the domestic jurisdiction of states.[184] The whole body of IHL is thus essentially aimed at

[178] cf ICTY, *Prosecutor v Tadić*, Decision on the Defence Motion for Interlocutory Appeal on Jurisdiction of 2 October 1995, Case No ICTY-94-1, para 70.

[179] See n 38 above.

[180] H Meyrowitz, *Le principe de l'égalité des belligérants devant le droit de la guerre* (Paris: Pédone, 1970); M Mandel, 'Aggressors' Rights: The Doctrine of "Equality between Belligerents" and the Legacy of Nuremberg' (2011) 24 LJIL 627. For the development of the principle in the just war context, see n 27 above.

[181] cf Saint Petersburg Declaration Renouncing the Use, in Time of War, of Explosive Projectiles under 400 Grammes Weight of 29 November/11 December 1868, famously aimed at fixing 'the technical limits at which the necessities of war ought to yield to the requirements of humanity', with a view to 'alleviating as much as possible the calamities of war', on the assumption that 'the only legitimate object which States should endeavour to accomplish during war is to weaken the military forces of the enemy', at <http://www.icrc.org/ihl.nsf/WebART/130-60001?OpenDocument>.

[182] For a general overview, see D Fleck (ed), *The Handbook of International Humanitarian Law* (New York: OUP, 2nd edn, 2008).

[183] cf Art 35(2) Geneva Protocol I.

[184] ICJ, *Case concerning Military and Paramilitary Activities* (n 43 above) para 218; ICTY, *Prosecutor v Tadić*, Decision on the Defence Motion for Interlocutory Appeal on Jurisdiction of 2 October 1995

the protection of a minimum standard of humanity in all circumstances. The underlying 'principle of humanity' is generally expressed in the Martens Clause found in a few IHL treaties,[185] and thought to apply all the more so in peacetime.[186]

Respect for IHL in the midst of a conflict is understandably difficult, given the overwhelming need of all belligerents to prevail at any price, but not as rare as one might suppose. Since it is basically grounded in reciprocity, IHL may be enforced by way of belligerent reprisal—although there are various exceptions and such reprisals are subject to a number of conditions,[187] in principle they are permitted.[188] Other means designed to reduce the likelihood of breaches of IHL have been devised, such as the Protecting Powers system, the establishment of fact-finding commissions, the reparation of damages, but have had little success. More effective, but subject to various limitations and shortcomings that will be discussed in Chapter 8, is the prosecution of perpetrators of war crimes by international criminal tribunals.

Unlike the rules found in human rights treaties, most IHL rules, as noted, protect people on the basis of reciprocity. A few IHL rules, however, are not based on reciprocity and apply to any person in all circumstances.[189] In the 1996 *Nuclear Weapons* Advisory Opinion the ICJ held that 'a great many rules of humanitarian law applicable in armed conflict are so fundamental to the respect of the human person and "elementary considerations of humanity"' that they 'are to be observed by all States whether or not they have ratified the conventions that contain them, because they constitute intransgressible principles of international customary law'.[190] In the 2004 *Wall* Advisory Opinion the Court specified that such principles 'incorporate obligations which are essentially of an *erga omnes* character'.[191] Human rights rules, although generally created for use in peacetime, also apply in time of war as *lex generalis*, the IHL being *lex specialis ratione materiae*,[192] even extraterritorially and in occupied territories,[193] unless a derogation clause is invoked.[194] It is noteworthy, in such instances,

(n 178 above) para 98, and Judgment of 7 May 1997, para 611, holding that Common Article 3 Geneva Conventions [and Additional Protocol II] reflects customary international law. See E La Haye, *War Crimes in Internal Armed Conflicts* (Cambridge: CUP, 2008).

[185] T Meron, 'The Martens Clause, Principles of Humanity, and Dictates of Public Conscience' (2000) 94 AJIL 78. For the view that the Martens Clause authorizes the interpreter to give more weight to *opinio juris* than to *usus* in ascertaining ICL, see A Cassese, 'The Martens Clause: Half a Loaf or Simply Pie in the Sky?' (2000) 11 EJIL 187, 214. On this approach and a different view, see Ch 6 above, nn 110, 174.

[186] For this *a fortiori* argument, see ICJ, *Corfu Channel* (n 59 above) 22, noting that the obligation of Albania to warn the approaching British warships of the minefield in time was grounded in 'elementary considerations of humanity, even more exacting in peace than in war'.

[187] ICTY, *Prosecutor v Martić* Trial Chamber Judgment of 12 June 2007, Case No IT-95-11, paras 465–467; *Prosecutor v Kupreškić* Trial Chamber Judgment of 14 January 2000, Case No IT-95-16, paras 515–536, holding that under customary international law reprisals are also prohibited in internal conflicts, a position opposed by F Kalshoven, 'Reprisals and the Protection of Civilians: Two Recent Decisions of the Yugoslavia Tribunal' in LC Vohrah, F Pocar, Y Featherstone, O Fourmy, C Graham, J Hocking, and N Robson (eds), *Man's Inhumanity to Man: Essays on International Law in Honour of Antonio Cassese* (The Hague: Kluwer, 2003) 481, 496–505.

[188] C Focarelli, 'Common Article 1 of the 1949 Geneva Conventions: A Soap Bubble?' (2010) 21 EJIL 125, 160–3.

[189] Y Dinstein, *The Conduct of Hostilities under the Law of International Armed Conflict* (Cambridge: CUP, 2nd edn, 2010) 20–5.

[190] ICJ, *Legality of the Threat or Use of Nuclear Weapons* (n 53 above) para 79.

[191] ICJ, *Legal Consequences of the Construction of a Wall* (n 43 above) paras 157–158. On this point, see further Ch 8 below, section B (1).

[192] ibid para 106; *Legality of the Threat or Use of Nuclear Weapons* (n 53 above) para 25; *Armed Activities* (n 102 above) para 216.

[193] See section A (2)(d) below.

[194] See section B (2)(a) above.

that human rights rules apply regardless of reciprocity and that international monitoring bodies (generally absent in IHL) are available to the victims against states. IHL may also overlap with international criminal law when war crimes are involved, in which case the key consequence is that perpetrators may be criminally prosecuted.

The rules of IHL clearly uncover a 'principle of humanity' in that even war is thought to have to 'halt' in the face of the humanity of single, extremely vulnerable individuals, which does not differ in essence from the instinctively 'right act' of allowing an ambulance to 'breach the rules' of road traffic to rush to the hospital and save the life of the unknown occupant. The gist is that however 'right' one may be, there is never a justification for compromising the other sentient being in her/his individual uniqueness, ie there is no stance right enough to be worth defending regardless of the costs.

(c) International crimes

Humanity means that there is something in common to all human beings, but this 'common core' is hard to detect in the variety of cultural backgrounds prevailing today. In quest thereof, the category of international crimes is undoubtedly promising. It is difficult to see how such acts as extermination and torture could be justified on cultural or other grounds, with their repression simply being seen as an unjustifiable act of unilateral, if not imperialistic in Schmitt's sense,[195] force. The avoidance of selective practices of repression and double standards is equally imperative, but even one-way justice is still justice if the convicted individual has actually perpetrated the crime and all procedural guarantees have been ensured, as will be further discussed in Chapter 8. Excruciating physical and psychological pain is dependent on the biological structure of any human being. The suffering of a mother forced to witness the torture of her children, or their brutal killing, may hardly be said to be contingent on cultural backgrounds varying in time and place.

It is, however, no easy matter to define what an international crime is. Yet, a definition is essential in order for national courts to know when the special regime allegedly attached to international crimes under general international law applies, if only as required by the principle of strict legality in criminal matters. Article 6 IMT Statute famously listed crimes against peace, war crimes, and crimes against humanity as those within its jurisdiction. In the 1948 *List* Judgment the US Military Tribunal at Nuremberg held that: 'An international crime is such act universally recognized as criminal, which is considered a grave matter of international concern and for some valid reason cannot be left within the exclusive jurisdiction of the State that would have control over it under ordinary circumstances'.[196] A myriad refinements have since been introduced in the statutes and jurisprudence of the subsequently established international criminal tribunals (ICTs) and hybrid criminal tribunals (HCTs), notably by the ICTY and the ICTR, as well as in several treaties. Criteria for a definition of international crimes have been proposed in legal doctrine, in order to distinguish them from traditional transnational crimes—such as their object of protecting the fundamental values of the international community as a whole,[197] or

[195] See n 165 above.

[196] US Military Tribunal At Nuremberg, *List et al* Judgment of 19 February 1948, (1953) ADRPILC Year 1948 (Case No 15) 632, 636.

[197] MC Bassiouni, *Introduction to International Criminal Law* (New York: Transnational Publishers, 2003) 114–17, referring to the transnational implications of international crimes.

a set of cumulative requirements[198]—but the issue remains unsettled.[199] ICTs and HCTs, although bound to conform to their statutes,[200] are often called upon to identify and apply customary international law, and for domestic courts the characterization of a particular crime as an international crime is generally for the purposes of universal jurisdiction, denial of functional immunity, irrelevance (or limited relevance) of superior orders, and non-operation of the statute of limitations under customary international law.[201]

The doctrine of universal jurisdiction provides that the courts of all states may exercise criminal—and presumably also civil[202]—jurisdiction over alleged perpetrators of an international crime even where neither the perpetrator nor the victim is a national of the prosecuting state and the crime has not been committed in this state (often, however, provided that the suspect is found in its territory).[203] The doctrine has been expressly endorsed, or at least implied, in international legal practice, for example by the Israeli Supreme Court in the 1962 *Eichmann* Judgment,[204] the US Court of Appeals for the Second Circuit in the 1984 *Filártiga* Judgment,[205] the US Court of Appeals for the Sixth Circuit in the 1985 *Demjanjuk* Judgment,[206] the Austrian Supreme Court in the 1994 *Cvetkovic* Judgment,[207] the Spanish National Court in the 1998 *Pinochet* Judgment,[208] the ICTY in the 1998 *Furundžija* Judgment,[209] the UK House of Lords in the 1999 *Pinochet* Judgment,[210] and the German Federal Court in the 2001

[198] A Cassese, *International Criminal Law* (Oxford: OUP, 2003) 23–5, suggesting that international crimes are (a) violations of ICL; (b) intended to protect values considered important by the whole international community as spelled out in several international instruments; (c) subjected to universal jurisdiction; and (d) barring perpetrators from claiming functional immunity in cases where they have acted on behalf of a state. As a result, international crimes do not include piracy (for lack of requirement (b)), transnational crimes and apartheid (for lack of requirement (a)), although apartheid is listed in the crimes falling under the jurisdiction of the ICC under Art 7(1)(j) as defined in Art 7(1)(j) ICC Statute.

[199] eg for the question of why the dumping of toxic wastes, clearly a mass crime, is not included in the category 'international crimes', see B Rajagopal, *International Law from Below: Development, Social Movements and Third World Resistance* (Cambridge: CUP, 2003) 196.

[200] See Ch 6 above, n 269.

[201] See eg WA Schabas and N Bernaz (eds), *Routledge Handbook of International Criminal Law* (London: Routledge, 2011).

[202] DF Donovan and A Roberts, 'The Emerging Recognition of Universal Civil Jurisdiction' (2006) 100 AJIL 142.

[203] cf IDI, Res on universal criminal jurisdiction with regard to the crime of genocide, crimes against humanity and war crimes of 26 August 2005, at <http://www.idi-iil.org/idiE/resolutionsE/2005_kra_03_en.pdf>; UNSG, 'The Scope and Application of the Principle of Universal Jurisdiction', Report of 29 July 2010, UN Doc A/65/181.

[204] Israeli Supreme Court, *Attorney-General of the Government of Israel v Adolf Eichmann* Judgment of 29 May 1962, (1962) 36 ILR 277, para 12.

[205] US Court of Appeals for the Second Circuit, *Filártiga v Peña-Irala* Judgment of 30 June 1980, 630 F 2d 876, holding that 'the torturer has become like the pirate and slave trader before him *hostis humani generis*, an enemy of all mankind'.

[206] US Court of Appeals for the Sixth Circuit, *Demjanjuk v Petrovsky* Judgment of 31 October 1985, (1989) 79 ILR 534, paras 63–73, holding that they were 'common enemies of all mankind and all nations have an equal interest in their apprehension and prosecution'.

[207] Austrian Supreme Court, *Dusko Cvetkovic* Judgment of 13 July 1994, at <http://www.ris.bka.gv.at>.

[208] Spanish National Court, *Pinochet* Judgment of 5 November 1998, (2002) 119 ILR 331, 335–6.

[209] ICTY, *Prosecutor v Furundžija*, Trial Chamber Judgment of 10 December 1998, Case No IT-95-17/I-T, (1999) 38 ILM 317, para 156 (as 'one of the consequences of the *jus cogens* character bestowed by the international community upon the prohibition of torture').

[210] UK House of Lords, *R v Bow Street Metropolitan Stipendiary Magistrate, ex p Pinochet* Judgment of 24 March 1999, (1999) 38 ILM 581, 589, stating that 'The jus cogens nature of the international

Sokolovic Judgment.[211] On occasion, universal jurisdiction has been inferred from the *erga omnes* character of the obligation prohibiting the crime, such as in the 2000 *Jorgic* Judgment of the German federal Constitutional Court, later to be upheld by the ECtHR.[212] The 1949 Geneva Conventions set out the rule *aut dedere aut judicare* by assuming that prosecution of 'grave breaches' is permitted regardless of the nationality of the perpetrator.[213] This rule is commonly understood as obliging the state where the alleged perpetrator is found either to bring the perpetrator to trial (regardless of any contact with the forum) or to extradite them to a state willing to do so. A few recent national legislatures—notably those of Belgium, Canada, Germany, the Netherlands, Spain, and Switzerland[214]—in principle allow universal jurisdiction and have provided the legal basis for asserting universal jurisdiction in most of the above-mentioned cases, although they contemplate universal jurisdiction for crimes or categories of crimes which partly differ from one legislation to another and subject to a number of restrictions (for example, universal jurisdiction is generally excluded when the accused is an official of another state entitled to diplomatic immunity). While frequently hailed, universal jurisdiction has also attracted severe criticisms.[215] It has been argued that the rule is no longer justified at a time when ICTs and HCTs exist and can prosecute perpetrators; that it functions only in one direction, from Western states towards all others, never the other way round; that non-Western states may not meet a sufficient standard of procedural fairness in the trials; and, finally, that trials may well be driven by political considerations, if not by a destabilizing intent from foreign states. Some courts have denied universal jurisdiction over international crimes, including genocide, such as the Court of Appeal of Paris in the 1994 *Javor* Judgment[216] and a Danish Court of Appeal in the 2011 *Mbarushimana* Judgment.[217] The overall picture is thus far from clear. First, national laws providing for universal jurisdiction are *few* in number and come only from *Western* states. Secondly, even Western states, such as the United States, have strongly criticized universal jurisdiction when their officials stand accused. Thirdly, existing legislation provides for universal jurisdiction with regard to partly different crimes. Fourthly, they let prosecutors and the executive branch exert variable influence on the cases to be decided based on a number of exceptions which are

crime of torture justifies states in taking universal jurisdiction over torture wherever committed' (*per* Lord Browne-Wilkinson).

211 German Federal Court, *Maksim Sokolovic* Judgment of 21 February 2001, No 3 StR 373/00, at <http://www.icrc.org>, para 25.

212 ECtHR, *Jorgic v Federal Republic of Germany* Judgment of 12 July 2007, App 74613/01, ECtHR Rep 2007-IX, paras 20, 68.

213 Arts 49–50; 50–51; 129–130; 146–147 of the respective 1949 Geneva Conventions.

214 For a detailed analysis of national legislation and its application, see M Langer, 'The Diplomacy of Universal Jurisdiction: The Political Branches and the Transnational Prosecution of International Crimes' (2011) 105 AJIL 1–49, 11–41.

215 From a realist perspective, see HA Kissinger, 'The Pitfalls of Universal Jurisdiction' (July/August 2001) 80 *Foreign Affairs* 86.

216 Tribunal de Grande Instance de Paris, *Javor et al* Order of lack of jurisdiction of 6 May 1994, (2005) 127 ILR 126, basically affirmed by the Court of Appeal of Paris, Judgment of 24 November 1994, and by the Court of Cassation, Judgment of 26 March 1996. All decisions are available in French at <http://competenceuniverselle.wordpress.com/en-france>. For a comment, see B Stern, case report (1999) 93 AJIL 525.

217 Danish Court of Appeal, *Emmanuel Mbarushimana* Judgment of 24 October 2011, at <http://allafrica.com/stories/201110270626.html>, affirming a Judgment of 31 May 2011 by the Court of Roskilde to the effect that there was 'no legal basis in Denmark to prosecute foreigners charged with genocide in another country', at <http://www.loc.gov/lawweb/servlet/lloc_news?disp3_l205402700_text>.

arguably designed to avoid prosecutions against 'high-cost' defendants,[218] as evidenced by the dismissal of several 'sensitive cases' (for example, those concerning US former President George W Bush and Secretary of State Donald Rumsfeld in Belgian courts), even with retroactive effect.[219] Fifthly, a look at cases shows that those convicted for international crimes on the basis of universal jurisdiction are *few* in number and come from a few *weak* states. Sixthly, domestic courts often inaccurately label as universal jurisdiction what is properly (ordinarily admitted) termed extra-territorial personal jurisdiction.[220] Seventhly, reliance on obligations *erga omnes* by some international and domestic courts is neither necessary to conclude in favour of universal jurisdiction (as evidenced by the reference in *Eichmann* merely to the old customary international law rule on piracy)[221] nor sufficient to draw logical inferences in so far as obligations *erga omnes* pertain to international remedies, not to domestic jurisdiction.[222] Eighthly, although connected, universal jurisdiction and the rule *aut dedere aut judicare* are not co-extensive, the latter being found also in treaties which do not concern international crimes. Finally, even assuming that universal jurisdiction over international crimes is permitted under general international law, the fact is that states are extremely reluctant to exercise it, especially against high- and mid-cost defendants, as also occurs with piracy.[223] All this, particularly the one-way argument, suggests that universal jurisdiction is not part of current customary international law. For a rule of customary international law to emerge, practice from the *generality* of states should be proved, a few cases from a few Western states clearly not being enough.

The functional immunity of the perpetrators is generally excluded by the statutes of ICTs and HCTs to the effect that state officials accused of international crimes cannot invoke their official position to evade responsibility.[224] There is a tendency to transplant the legal regime of functional immunity operating in ICTs and HCTs to the domestic sphere. However, the provisions found in the statutes of ICTs and HCTs cannot be automatically extended to domestic courts. They are to be read in their own context, which differs from one to another, and do not apply to third-party states. Their 'extension' to domestic courts is only plausible with regard to states parties as between themselves and in so far as the removal of immunity is necessary for cooperation with the ICTs or HCTs concerned. In the 2002 *Arrest Warrant* Judgment the ICJ seems to have implied that from the operation of the immunity rule in proceedings before 'certain' ICTs 'where they have jurisdiction' it does not follow that the rule also applies in domestic courts,[225] attracting strong criticism.[226] Of course, domestic courts may deny functional immunity whenever this is prescribed by a treaty rule, such as Article IV of the 1948 Genocide Convention and Article III of the 1973 Apartheid Convention. The question is, however, about the existence of a CIL rule lifting functional immunity, whereas the personal

[218] Langer (n 214 above) 2–3. [219] ibid 26–32 for a summary of the Belgian saga.

[220] See Ch 5 above, section B (4)(a).

[221] For the ECtHR and IACtHR jurisprudence, see Ch 8 below, nn 35, 66.

[222] See Ch 8 below, nn 68–69.

[223] See E Kontorovich and S Art, 'An Empirical Examination of Universal Jurisdiction for Piracy' (2010) 104 AJIL 436.

[224] cf Art 7 IMT Statute, Art IV Genocide Convention, Art 7(2) ICTY Statute, Art 6(2) ICTR, Art 6(2) SCSL, Art 27 ICC Statute.

[225] ICJ, *Arrest Warrant of 11 April 2000 (Democratic Republic of the Congo v Belgium)* Judgment of 14 February 2002, [2002] ICJ Rep 3, para 61. This reasoning was explicitly adopted by the Court when dealing with the *personal* immunity of *incumbent* state officials (ibid para 58). See further n 545 below and accompanying text.

[226] A Cassese, 'When May Senior State Officials Be Tried for International Crimes? Some Comments on the Congo v Belgium Case' (2002) 13 EJIL 853.

immunity of certain incumbent state officials is invariably recognized by domestic courts regardless of the crimes allegedly committed.[227] In the *Eichmann* Judgment the Israeli Supreme Court held that functional immunity cannot be relied upon to evade liability for international crimes.[228] Famously, the UK House of Lords upheld the irrelevance of functional immunity in the *Pinochet* case, although mainly relying on the 1984 Torture Convention.[229] The ICTY has stated that Article 7(2) ICTY Statute and Article 6(2) ICTR Statute 'are indisputably declaratory of customary international law'.[230] But it is unclear whether the denial of functional immunity by domestic courts is an exception to a general rule prescribing immunity, as is often contended assuming that in principle the conduct of the organ is attributable to the state,[231] or simply reflects the absence of any obligation to accord the immunity to most state officials regardless of the fact that they have committed an international crime. Domestic courts have frequently tried foreign state officials, especially military officers.[232] On balance, state practice seems to favour the second alternative, suggesting that functional immunity with certainty only applies under CIL (a) to diplomatic and consular agents and high-ranking state officials;[233] (b) who have acted in the exercise of their (typical or 'normal') official functions.[234] It is only within this margin that a CIL rule lifting immunity is necessary and does exist, in all other cases there being no immunity at all, whatever the crime.[235]

It is unclear whether 'superior orders' operates as a defence when one considers the difficulties in balancing the efficiency of the military apparatus, based on the execution

[227] See n 546 below.

[228] Israeli Supreme Court, *Attorney-General of the Government of Israel v Adolf Eichmann* (n 204 above) para 14.

[229] UK House of Lords, *R v Bow Street Metropolitan Stipendiary Magistrate, ex p Pinochet* (n 210 above) 152 (*per* Lord Hope), 171–9 (*per* Lord Millet), and 189–90 (*per* Lord Phillips of Worth Matravers), arguing for a CIL rule. See in addition nn 541 and 544 below.

[230] cf eg ICTY, *Prosecutor v Furundžija* (n 209 above) para 140.

[231] See Israeli Supreme Court, *Attorney-General of the Government of Israel v Adolf Eichmann* (n 204 above) para 14; ICTY, *Prosecutor v Tihomir Blaskic* Judgment on the request of the Republic of Croatia for review of the Decision of Trial Chamber II of 18 July 1997, Case No IT-95-14-AR108, 110 ILR (1997) 607, paras 38 and 41.

[232] See P De Sena, *Diritto internazionale e immunità funzionale degli organi statali* (Milan: Giuffrè, 1996); M Frulli, *Immunità e crimini internazionali: l'esercizio della giurisdizione penale e civile nei confronti degli organi statali sospettati di gravi crimini internazionali* (Turin: Giappichelli, 2007); R Nigro, 'La disciplina dei militari impegnati all'estero in missioni umanitarie: in margine al caso Lozano' (2009) 3 *Diritti Umani e Diritto Internazionale* 565–90.

[233] See ICJ, *Arrest Warrant of 11 April 2000* (n 225 above) para 51, stating in general terms that 'in international law it is firmly established that, as also diplomatic and consular agents, certain holders of high-ranking office in a State, such as the Head of State, Head of Government and Minister for Foreign Affairs, enjoy immunities from jurisdiction in other States, both civil and criminal'. See further ICJ, *Certain Questions of Mutual Assistance in Criminal Matters (Djibouti v France)* Judgment of 4 June 2008, [2008] ICJ Rep 117, para 170.

[234] The common view, whereby non-immunity for international crimes invariably constitutes an 'exception' to the *general* rule prescribing immunity to any act attributable to the state, is grounded in the co-extensiveness of the acts of the organ benefiting from immunity with the acts of the state, but there is no necessary coincidence between the two for the purposes of functional immunity. What matters in state practice is neither attribution of the conduct to the state per se nor the 'official' character of the conduct per se, much less the *jure imperii* character of the act for state immunity purposes, but rather the type of *functions* performed. Only certain functions (of certain organs acting in an official capacity, whether *jure imperii* or *jure gestionis* for state immunity purposes) enjoy immunity.

[235] The class of 'official acts' includes also acts in breach of international law and, in particular, international crimes. The thesis that international crimes cannot intrinsically be 'sovereign' or 'official' acts is untenable, as correctly argued by D Akande and S Shah, 'Immunities of State Officials, International Crimes, and Foreign Domestic Courts' (2010) 21 EJIL 815, 828–32, 850. Nor can *jus cogens*, let alone 'implied waiver', be relied upon to overcome immunity (ibid 832–8), as is further discussed in section B (1)(a) below.

of orders, against the need to avoid impunity. In the statutes of most ICTs and IHTs superior orders are relevant only as a mitigating factor, not as a defence.[236] Not surprisingly, however, national legislation tends to excuse crimes committed in execution of superior orders when the crime is not 'manifestly' recognizable as such or when the perpetrator is not aware of its unlawfulness.[237] A compromise is found in Article 33 ICC Statute which requires, for the purposes of invoking superior orders as a defence, that a duty of obedience exists (as is generally the case with war crimes), that the order is 'manifestly illegal', and that the perpetrator is not aware of the illegality. No defence is permitted, however, under Article 33 when it comes to genocide and crimes against humanity. An adjustment to the rule has been introduced by certain courts when they have accepted 'necessity' or 'duress' to justify in part the perpetrator,[238] in particular when the harm inflicted is not greater than the harm avoided.[239] This qualification seems to be quite reasonable.

Whether international crimes involve the non-operation of statutes of limitation is also unclear. While prescribed by Article II(5) of Law No 10 of 20 December 1945 and by Article 29 ICC Statute, the rule has not been included in the statutes of any other ICTs and HCTs. The 1968 UN Convention on Non-Operation of the Statutes of Limitations has been ratified by fifty-four states,[240] whereas the 1974 European Convention has been ratified by only seven states (as of 8 April 2012).[241] All other treaties on acts that are commonly viewed as international crimes, such as the 1984 Torture Convention[242] and the 1973 Apartheid Convention,[243] do not provide for the

[236] cf Art 8 IMT Statute, Art 6 IMTFE, Art 2(4)(b) Law No 10 of 20 December 1945, Art 7(4) ICTY Statute, Art 6(4) ICTR, Art 33 ICC Statute.

[237] For the view that superior orders cannot be invoked to evade responsibility for international crimes when (as in the instant case) they 'inherently and ontologically' present the signs of 'the manifest, macroscopic, sensational, and *ictu oculi* recognizable criminosity of mass extermination', see Italian Court of Cassation, *Hass and Priebke* Judgment of 1 December 1998, (1999) 82 RDI 822, 838 (English trans by the author).

[238] ICTY, *Prosecutor v Erdemović* Judgment of 29 November 1996, Case No IT-96-22-T, at <http://www.icty.org/x/cases/erdemovic/tjug/en/erd-tsj961129e.pdf>, paras 14–20, finding that Erdemović's reliance on moral duress 'may also be regarded as a defence for the criminal conduct which might go so far as to eliminate the mens rea of the offence and therefore the offence itself' (para 14) provided that certain conditions are met, including proportionality (para 17), but concluding that 'proof of the specific circumstances which would fully exonerate the accused of his responsibility has not been provided' (para 20); ICTY, *Prosecutor v Erdemović*, Appeals Judgment of 7 October 1997, Case No IT-96-22-A, at <http://www.icty.org/x/cases/erdemovic/acjug/en/erd-aj971007e.pdf>, para 19, holding, Judge Cassese and Judge Stephen dissenting, that 'duress does not afford a complete defence to a soldier charged with a crime against humanity and/or a war crime involving the killing of innocent human beings'. Of special interest is the separate and dissenting opinion of Judge Cassese, contending that 'Law is based on what society can reasonably expect of its members' and 'should not set *intractable* standards of behaviour which require mankind to perform acts of martyrdom, and brand as criminal any behaviour falling below those standards', at <http://www.icty.org/x/cases/erdemovic/acjug/en/erd-adojcas971007e.pdf>, especially para 47 (original emphasis).

[239] Art 31(d) ICC. A similar view was taken by the Italian Court of Cassation in the 1998 *Hass and Priebke* Judgment (n 237 above) 839–40, excluding that in the instant case the crimes committed by the Nazi officials were proportionate to the penalties provided for failure to execute the order.

[240] Convention on the Non-Applicability of Statutory Limitations to War Crimes and Crimes against Humanity (adopted 26 November 1968, entered into force 11 November 1970) 154 UNTS 73.

[241] European Convention on the Non-Applicability of Statutory Limitation to Crimes against Humanity and War Crimes (opened for signature 25 January 1974, entered into force 27 June 2003) CETS 82.

[242] Convention against Torture and Other Cruel, Inhuman or Degrading Treatment or Punishment (adopted on 10 December 1984, entered into force 26 June 1987) 1465 UNTS 85.

[243] International Convention on the Suppression and Punishment of the Crime of Apartheid (opened for signature 30 November 1973, entered into force 18 July 1976) 1015 UNTS 243.

non-operation of statutes of limitation. The rule, originally contained in Article 17 of the 1996 Draft Code of Crimes against the Peace and Security of Mankind,[244] was later deleted due to the protests of numerous states which contended that statutes of limitation may contribute to national reconciliation and that reconciliation may be of more immediate concern than the punishment of this or that perpetrator of international crimes. The principle was upheld in some well-known decisions, including the 1984 *Barbie* Judgment of the French Court of Cassation (although only concerning crimes against humanity),[245] and the 1997 *Priebke* Judgment of the Italian Military Tribunal of Rome,[246] the 1998 *Furundžija* Judgment,[247] and the 2001 *Barrios Altos* Judgment of the IACtHR.[248] In the 2008 *Menéndez* Judgment the Argentine Tribunal of Córdoba upheld the rule even retroactively, maintaining that it definitely exists today in customary international law and belongs to *jus cogens*.[249] Other courts, however, have decided otherwise and national legislation diverges on the categories of international crimes which are subject to statutory limitations.[250] All in all, it is difficult to conclude that the rule is part of current customary international law, let alone of *jus cogens*. It is of course quite a different matter to campaign for it to become a rule as soon as possible.

The present categories of 'international crimes' have actually emerged at different times and for different purposes. War crimes were first introduced by states in their domestic law to subject their own military, who had committed certain grave offences during hostilities, to criminal jurisdiction, as was the case with the low-ranking officials' offences punished by the 1863 Lieber Code of the United States.[251] Crimes against humanity were first mentioned in 1915 to condemn the Ottoman Empire for the massacre of the Armenians and to try the perpetrators, notably officials of the Empire.[252] The notion that state officials, including heads of state, could be tried and held personally responsible on the basis of international law was famously affirmed in Article 227 of the 1919 Treaty of Versailles with regard to William II of Hohenzollern, formerly the German Emperor, 'for a supreme offence against international morality

[244] UN ILC, 'Draft Code of Crimes against the Peace and Security of Mankind', (1996) GAOR 51st Session, Supp 10, 9.

[245] French Court of Cassation, *Fédération Nationale des Déportés et Internés Résistants et Patriotes et al v Barbie* Judgment of 20 December 1985, (1998) 78 ILR 136, 136–7.

[246] Italian Military Tribunal of Rome, *Priebke* Judgment of 22 July 1997 (1998) 38 *Cassazione Penale* 668, 690–1, holding that 'the principle of non-application of statutory limitation to war crimes and crimes against humanity objectively assumes the character of "jus cogens" since it is aimed to protect general interests of international society' (English trans by the author). See too, more recently, Italian Tribunal of Turin, *De Guglielmi v Repubblica Federale di Germania, Presidenza del Consiglio dei Ministri* Judgment of 20 May 2010 No 3464, (2010) 46 RDIPP 1006, arguing for the existence of a retroactive rule of customary international law prescribing the non-application of statutory limitation to the crimes committed by the Nazis During World War II; Tribunal of Bologna, *G and A v Repubblica Federale di Germania, Repubblica Italiana* Judgment of 11 January 2009 (2010) 46 RDIPP 992.

[247] ICTY, *Prosecutor v Furundžija* (n 209 above) para 157.

[248] IACtHR, *Chumbipuma Aguirre et al v Peru (Barrios Altos Case)* Judgment of 14 March 2001, at <http://www.corteidh.or.cr/docs/casos/articulos/seriec_75_ing.pdf>, para 41.

[249] Argentine Tribunal for Federal Crimes No 1, *Menéndez et al* Judgment of 24 July 2008, File 40/M/2008, at <http://www.pjn.gov.ar>, at 352. See G Chavez Tafur, 'Using International Law to By-pass Domestic Legal Hurdles: On the Applicability of the Statute of Limitations in the *Menéndez et al* Case' (2008) 6 JICJ 1061.

[250] See Cassese (n 198 above) 319.

[251] F Lieber, *Instructions for the Government of Armies of the United States in the Field* (Washington, DC: Government Printing Office, 1898).

[252] Cassese (n 198 above) 67–8.

and the sanctity of treaties', adding that a special tribunal would have been constituted (but was never actually constituted) to try the Emperor.[253] Crimes against peace were first introduced in 1945 in the IMT[254] and IMTFE Statutes[255] to try major Nazi and Japanese officials for breach, inter alia, of the 1928 Briand-Kellogg Pact on the renunciation of war.[256] The fresh memory of the holocaust soon induced states to conclude the 1948 Genocide Convention in which the contracting states 'confirmed' that genocide was a 'crime under international law', whether committed in time of peace or in time of war.[257] Several provisions of the 1949 Geneva Conventions refer to 'grave breaches' of the Conventions against 'protected persons', thus suggesting that such breaches coincide with war crimes.[258]

The different origins of international crimes affect the definition of the key categories and their relationships. War crimes are 'grave breaches' of IHL (both Hague Law and Geneva Law),[259] or other 'serious' violations of IHL,[260] even if they are isolated, and are committed either in international or in non-international armed conflict.[261] They require a 'nexus' with an armed conflict,[262] although both the perpetrator and the victim may be civilians.[263] Offences committed by servicemen against their own military, whatever their nationality, do not qualify as war crimes.[264] Grave breaches are specified in the Geneva Conventions and Additional Protocol I,[265] and may be expressly listed in the statutes of ICTs and HCTs.[266] In contrast, crimes against humanity are widespread or systematic attacks (not necessarily military in character, and hence any 'attack', including ill-treatment) on the civilian population. While Article 6 IMT Statute required their commission during an armed conflict for the Tribunal to have jurisdiction, and this condition is also contemplated by Article 5 ICTY Statute, there is no need today for any such nexus under general international law, nor is a persecutory intent required (although Article 3 ICTR Statute does require

[253] cf <http://avalon.law.yale.edu/imt/partvii.asp>.

[254] Charter of the Nuremberg International Military Tribunal (proclaimed on 8 August 1945) in United Nations, 'The Charter and Judgment of the Nürnberg Tribunal: History and Analysis', 3 March 1949, UN Doc A/CN.4/5 (New York: United Nations Publications, 1949).

[255] Charter of the International Military Tribunal for the Far East TIAS No 1589 (signed on 19 January 1946).

[256] See n 58 above.

[257] Convention on the Prevention and Punishment of the Crime of Genocide (adopted 9 December 1948, entered into force 12 January 1951) 78 UNTS 277.

[258] MD Öberg, 'The Absorption of Grave Breaches into War Crimes Law' (2009) 91 IRRC 163.

[259] ICTY, *Prosecutor v Tadić* (n 178 above) para 94; Italian Court of Cassation, *Lozano* Judgment No of 24 July 2008 No 31171, (2009) 18 It YBIL 346, ILDC 1085 (IT 2008).

[260] cf Art 8(2)(b)–(e) ICC Statute.

[261] For their application to non-international conflicts, ICTY, *Prosecutor v Tadić* (n 178 above) paras 97–137; cf Art 8(2)(c)–(f) ICC Statute. See E La Haye (n 184 above).

[262] Italian Court of Assize of Santa Maria Capua Venere, *Lehnigh and Schuster* Judgment of 25 October 1994, at <http://www.giustiziamilitare.difesa.it>, excluding that the accused could be found responsible for war crimes in the absence of a nexus with a conflict.

[263] See Swiss Military Court of Appeal, *Prosecutor v F Niyonteze* Judgment of 26 May 2000, at <http://www.icrc.org>, ch 3, section D(2).

[264] Dutch Martial Court [Temporary Court Martial at Amboina, Netherlands East Indies], *Re Motosuke* Judgment of 28 January 1948, (1953) ADRPILC Year 1948 (Case No 220) 682; Dutch Special Court of Cassation, *Re Pilz* Judgment of 5 July 1950, (1956) ADRPILC Year 1950 (Case No 123) 391.

[265] Arts 49–50, 50–51, 129–130, and 146–147 respectively of the 1949 Geneva Conventions and Art 85 Protocol I.

[266] cf Art 2 ICTY Statute and Art 8(2)(a) ICC Statute. See in addition Art 4 ICTR Statute and Art 3 SCSL Statute for a list of 'serious violations' of Art 3 common to the Geneva Conventions and of Additional Protocol II, as well as Art 4 SCSL Statute for 'other serious violations' of IHL.

this). Unlike war crimes, the attack must be 'widespread or systematic' and the targeted 'civilian population' may include both fellow citizens of the perpetrator and stateless persons. The irrelevance of nationality and reciprocity approximates crimes against humanity to breaches of international human rights, although these latter may consist, unlike the former, of isolated acts. The term 'civilian' must evidently be given a different meaning in the absence of an armed conflict than when one deals with war crimes.[267] The idea underlying crimes against humanity is that they, although physically committed against one or more specific persons, are deemed to attack all human beings.[268] Genocide is carefully defined in the 1948 Convention and has received extensive application in the international jurisprudence of both the ICTY and the ICTR, as well as by the ICJ.[269] As noted earlier, aggression has recently been introduced in the ICC Statute on several conditions.[270] For the moment, the prospects that the ICC will prosecute perpetrators of aggression remain remote.

Briefly, international criminal law is an intricate patchwork of rules and judicial decisions that strongly collides with the principles of criminal justice developed in the Western tradition of the rule of law, such as strict legality. At the same time, one has to appreciate the efforts made by existing ICTs and HCTs to construct a 'system' of rules coherent enough, and not manifestly unfair in the way justice is delivered, to assist local communities and the international community as a whole to make perpetrators account for their misdeeds. Their key role is the identification of a common core of humanity in legal terms, regardless of the author's descent and cause, acceptable to and accepted by all peoples. Once this minimum threshold is set, the next fundamental step is to insist that double standards are intolerable.

(d) Human rights

Human rights are rooted in the theoretical notion of humanity and human dignity, but take on a practical connotation when they are protected by law. The concepts of human rights and of human dignity may not necessarily be seen as coincident. It has been noted, for example, that while all societies possess a conception of human dignity, human rights—understood as rights inherent in human nature[271]—specifically express a (Western) 'liberal' conception of life.[272] Communitarian societies, by giving priority to the community over the individual, 'regard their members as worthy of concern and respect, but only as members of society performing prescribed roles'.[273]

Basically, human rights as currently conceived of imply a limitation to the power of the sovereign, whether a monarch or an assembly, which may extend up to a right of resistance. Their purpose is to safeguard individuals from the overwhelming might

[267] A Roberts, 'The Civilian in Modern War' (2010) 12 YBIHL 13.

[268] cf Israeli Supreme Court, *Attorney-General of the Government of Israel v Adolf Eichmann* (n 204 above) para 11.

[269] ICJ, *Application of the Convention on the Prevention and Punishment of the Crime of Genocide (Bosnia and Herzegovina v Serbia and Montenegro)* Judgment of 26 February 2007, [2007] ICJ Rep 43.

[270] See n 106 above. See further C Kreß and L von Holtzendorff, 'The Kampala Compromise on the Crime of Aggression' (2010) 8 JICJ 1179.

[271] For different conceptions of human nature, see L Stevenson and DL Haberman, *Ten Theories of Human Nature* (New York: OUP, 5th edn, 2009).

[272] See RE Howard and J Donnelly, 'Human Dignity, Human Rights, and Political Regimes' (1986) 80 APSR 801.

[273] ibid 808.

of society.[274] As individual rights, they differ from collective rights to a certain form of government (such as democracy) or to become a state by virtue of the right of self-determination.[275] They are typically conceived of as 'quintessential' to human life and inherent in human nature,[276] pre-dating and superior to societies and any political organization.[277] Despite the rhetoric of 'beyondness' and intrinsic 'intangibility', human rights are more often than not abused and the victims find it difficult, if not simply impossible, to obtain justice unless the surrounding social and political context is being changed, whether by peaceful or violent means. Human rights are systematically presented and promoted as inherent in human nature, but, in fact, they historically emerge only when needed and are the rights which their holders succeed in obtaining at any given point in time.[278] Human rights are protected if the group supports them. A 'right' is a claim in need of assistance by society. Individuals have little or no power against the group as a whole and their claim to 'rights' is simply destined to remain *flatus vocis* unless that claim is upheld by society or at least by an influential part thereof. Whatever the merit of human rights as 'moral' or 'inherent' rights, the point is that without the support and force of society they remain a dead letter.[279] The most vulnerable are to be protected by struggling *within society* for their rights rather than by proclamations and appeals to human nature. Of course, the rhetoric of human rights as innate and universal, pre-dating (and hence prevailing over) statehood and society, and only susceptible to be 'recognized' by the state, may be instrumental and helpful to the struggle. But it is with the force of the state (or any other political

[274] For the well-known thesis that 'Individuals have rights and there are things no person or group may do to them (without violating their rights)' and that only a 'minimal state' (ie a state 'limited to the narrow functions of protection against force, theft, fraud, enforcement of contracts, and so on') is justified, 'any more extensive state [violating] persons' rights not to be forced to do certain things', see R Nozick, *Anarchy, State, and Utopia* (Oxford: Blackwell, 1974) ix.

[275] J Crawford (ed), *The Rights of Peoples* (Oxford: Clarendon Press, 1988).

[276] See R Tuck, *Natural Rights Theories: Their Origin and Development* (Cambridge: CUP, 1979); B Tierney, *The Idea of Natural Rights: Studies on Natural Rights, Natural Law and Church Law, 1150–1625* (Atlanta, GA: Scholars Press, 1997).

[277] cf Art 1 UDHR ('All human beings are born free and equal in dignity and rights'), clearly inspired by Art 1 of the 1789 Declaration of the Rights of Man and of the Citizen ('Men are born and remain free and equal in rights') and by the 1776 US Declaration of Independence ('We hold these truths to be self-evident, that all men are created equal, that they are endowed by their Creator with certain unalienable Rights, that among these are Life, Liberty and the pursuit of Happiness' and that 'to secure these rights, Governments are instituted among Men, deriving their just powers from the consent of the governed' so that 'whenever any Form of Government becomes destructive of these ends, it is the Right of the People to alter or to abolish it and to institute new Government'); the idea of there being a supreme law before any written law of any state which is grounded in nature and from which every law dates back notably to Cicero, *On the Laws*, I, 19–20. For its extension to international human rights, see eg the dissident opinion of ICJ Judge Tanaka in the 1966 *South West Africa* Judgment, [1966] ICJ Rep 6, 296. For the critical view that the concept of natural rights is 'a conception of individuals both stripped of all social status and yet bearers of rights' and that 'What was originally both in Roman and canon law *jus*, a norm governing the relationships of individuals within a structure of community, has become a *right*, something possessed by an individual as he or she is alone, prior to any communal relationships', see A MacIntyre, *Are There Any Natural Rights?* (Portland: Anthoensen, 1983) 13–14 (original emphasis).

[278] See N Bobbio, *L'età dei diritti* (Turin: Einaudi, 1990) xiii–xvi, English trans *The Age of Rights* (Cambridge: Polity Press, 1996) x–xii.

[279] For the different view that the link between human rights and law (although justified in terms of conceptualization, language, and practice towards legislative recognition of human rights by their advocates) is misleading and 'foundationally mistaken', see A Sen, 'Human Rights and the Limits of Law' (2006) 27 CLR 2913.

organization) and, more importantly, of the surrounding society that they may be legally protected.[280]

Human rights instruments have been made, especially following World War II, at both universal and regional level. Their creation has extended the protection of individuals to the human person as such (unlike in the past when individuals were protected by international law only as nationals of another state), often drawing from the rights of minorities already envisaged in the post-World War I treaties and, ultimately, from the freedom of religion typical of treaties entered into after the Reformation and the religious wars in Europe. A key step in the process was the abolition of the slave trade in the nineteenth century sustained for a variety of reasons by Great Britain.[281] The international human rights instruments typically list a number of rights of 'any person' or of 'everyone' to be respected and protected within the territory and/or jurisdiction of the states parties, but fail to clarify how a 'human right' can be identified and appropriately construed.[282] For example, Article 1 UDHR takes human rights for granted and proceeds by solemnly enunciating them.[283] History shows that claims of any sort have been presented as inherent in human nature and hence universal, leaving the interpreter to solve difficult practical problems as to their interrelation, balancing, and conflict. Most if not all asserted human rights, although conceptually differentiated from 'standard' rights by their 'absolute' character, are generally limited by various considerations, ranging from collective imperatives—such as national security, public morality, financial cost, and abuse[284]—to the operation of other human rights of either the same person or other persons.[285] The question of whether there is a hierarchy of human rights is variously addressed by appealing to rights listed in treaty derogation clauses, to *jus cogens*, and to the priority of certain rights (such as security and subsistence rights) for the enjoyment of others. The issue, however, remains highly uncertain and contentious in terms of which human rights should be given priority.[286]

Human rights are to be secured 'within the jurisdiction' of the states parties to human rights treaties.[287] While it is certain that jurisdiction is primarily territorial and in exceptional cases extraterritorial,[288] it remains unclear when exactly it extends

[280] Bobbio (n 278 above) 3–11, arguing that 'Every attempt at an absolute principle [of human rights, at the irrefutable argument whose reasoning no one could deny] has proved groundless' and that 'The fundamental problem concerning human rights today is not so much how to justify them, but how to protect them', this problem being 'political, not philosophical'.

[281] See Ch 8 below, n 83.

[282] L Hunt, *Inventing Human Rights: A History* (New York and London: WW Norton and Co, 2007) 26, arguing that 'The claim of self-evidence relies ultimately on an emotional appeal; it is convincing if it strikes a chord within each person' or 'when we feel horrified by its violation'.

[283] For the view that this silence is deliberate, see M Ignatieff, *Human Rights as Politics and Idolatry* (Princeton and Oxford: Princeton University Press, 2001) 77–8.

[284] cf eg Art 30 UDHR and Art 17 ECHR, as well as section B (2) and (4) below.

[285] See section B (2) and (4) below.

[286] K Teraya, 'Emerging Hierarchy in International Human Rights and Beyond: From the Perspective of Non-derogable Rights' (2001) 12 EJIL 917.

[287] cf eg Art 2(1) ICCPR, Art 1 ECHR, Art 1(1) ACHR. See M Gibney and S Skogly (eds), *Universal Human Rights and Extraterritorial Obligations* (Philadelphia: University of Pennsylvania Press, 2010); M Milanovic, *Extraterritorial Application of Human Rights Treaties: Law, Principles and Policy* (Oxford: OUP, 2011); R Nigro, 'The Notion of "Jurisdiction" in Article 1: Future Scenarios for the Extra-Territorial Application of the European Court of Human Rights' (2011) 20 It YBIL 11.

[288] In addition to the ECtHR cases cited elsewhere in this section, with regard to Art 2(1) ICCPR, see UNHRC, *Lilian Celiberti de Casariego v Uruguay*, Views of 29 July 1981, Comm No 56/1979, CCPR/C/13/D/56/1979, paras 10.1 and 10.3; UNHRC, *Sergio Ruben Lopez Burgos v Uruguay*, Views of 29 July 1981, Comm No 52/1979, CCPR/C/13/D/52/1979, paras 12.1 and 12.3; UNHRC, *Mabel Pereira Montero v Uruguay*, Views of 31 March 1983, Comm No 106/1981, CCPR/C/18/D/106/1981, paras 5 and 9.4; UNHRC, *Mohammad Munaf v Romania*, Views of 21 August 2009,

outside the territory.[289] Classical examples of extraterritorial jurisdiction include acts performed by officials of a state party either in its embassies abroad or on board vessels and aircraft beyond territorial waters and airspace registered in the state party or flying its flag, or under the control of the state.[290] The jurisprudence of the ECtHR plays a leading role in this respect. In the 1996 *Loizidou* Judgment the Court held that Turkey exercised jurisdiction over the Northern part of Cyprus which had been under its military occupation since 1974, because the Turkish army's stable presence proved an 'effective' form of 'overall control' in the area, and found Turkey responsible for the violation of the Convention.[291] In the 2001 *Bankovic* Decision the Court denied that the nineteen NATO states participating in the bombing of the Federal Republic of Yugoslavia (FRY) during the Kosovo War in 1999 exercised jurisdiction over the territory bombed and declared the application inadmissible *ratione loci*.[292] According to the Court, in particular, 'jurisdiction' could not extend to the 'legal space' outside the territories of the states parties (the FRY was actually not a party) since the Convention was essentially regional in character.[293] In the 2004 *Issa* Judgment the Court found that a six-week Turkish cross-border military operation in the territory of Northern Iraq against Kurdish alleged terrorists fell within Turkey's jurisdiction because of Turkey's control over the *individuals* who were victims of the incursions, there being evidence of state involvement 'beyond a reasonable doubt', and regardless of the fact that Iraq was outside the 'legal space' of the states parties.[294] The 'extra-regional' application of the

Comm No 1539/2006, CCPR/C/96/D/1539/2006, para 14.2. With regard to Article 1(1) ACHR, see IACommHR, *Coard et al v United States*, Report of 29 September 1999 No 109/99, Case No 10.951, at <http://www.cidh.org/annualrep/99eng/Merits/UnitedStates10.951.htm>, para 37; IACommHR, *Armando Alexandre Jr, Carlos Cost, Mario de la Pena, and Pabro Morales v Cuba*, Report of 29 September 1999 No 86/99, Case No 11.589, at <http://www.cidh.org/annualrep/99eng/Merits/Cuba11.589.htm>, para 23; IACommHR, *Victor Saldaño v Argentina*, Report of 11 March 1999 No 38/99, Petition, OEA/Ser.L/V/II.95, Doc 7 Rev 289, para 17. See further note 304 below.

[289] Jurisdiction over extraterritorial acts (such as killings by the officials of a state committed in the territory of another state) must be kept distinct from jurisdiction over intra-territorial acts which have extraterritorial effects (such as the expulsion, extradition, or *refoulement* of a person decided in the territory of a state towards another state in which the person risks being subjected to serious violations of human rights, as classically stated by the ECtHR in the *Soering v United Kingdom and Germany (intervening)* Judgement of 7 July 1989, App No 14038/88, (1989) 11 EHRR 439, para 86). Yet another distinction is between intra-territorial acts with extraterritorial effects on persons initially under the control of a state (such as the above-mentioned cases of expulsion, extradition, or *refoulement*) and those having effects on persons who are in the territory and under the control of another state (such as the poor living in developing countries in relation to possible duties for richer states to assist poorer states in implementing human rights, including economic, social, and cultural rights). While there is no doubt that human rights obligations may extend to extraterritorial acts and to intra-territorial acts with extra-territorial effects on persons found in the territory of the acting state, their extension also to intra-territorial acts with extra-territorial effects on persons found in the territory of another state is rather dubious, despite several attempts made in this direction by the UN bodies concerned with human rights and some international law scholars in the name of global justice and with regard to the fulfilment of basic needs (see section A(3)(a) below). See M Salomon, *Global Responsibility for Human Rights* (Oxford: OUP, 2007).

[290] ECtHR, *Bankovic et al v Belgium et al* Decision of 12 December 2001 [GC], App 52207/99, ECtHR Rep 2001-XII 333, para 61; ICJ, *Legal Consequences of the Construction of a Wall* (n 43 above) para 109; *Armed Activities* (n 102 above) para 216.

[291] ECtHR, *Loizidou v Turkey (Merits)* Judgment of 18 December 1996, ECtHR Rep 1996-VI 2216, (1996) 23 EHRR 513, paras 52 and 56. Along the same lines, see ECtHR, *Ilaşcu et al v Moldova and Russia* Judgment of 8 July 2004 [GC], App 48787, ECtHR Rep 2004-VII 179, (2005) 40 EHRR 1030, para 392.

[292] ECtHR, *Bankovic* (n 290 above) para 82. [293] ibid para 80.

[294] ECtHR, *Issa et al v Turkey* Judgment of 16 November 2004, App 31821/96, (2005) 41 EHRR 27, para 74; *Isaak et al v Turkey*, Decision of 24 June 2008, App 44587/98, section (2)(b)(ii) The Law.

ECHR was expressly affirmed by the Court in the 2007 *Pad* Judgment.[295] In the 2004 *Ilascu* Judgment the Court found that the lack of effective control over the territory could not exclude jurisdiction by Moldova in so far as this state was in a position to take positive measures to secure for the applicants the rights enshrined in the Convention.[296] In the 2007 *Behrami* Decision the Court asserted that the 'international presences' set up by UN Security Council Resolution 1244 (1999)[297] exercised powers similar to those of a state, thus adumbrating that a UN-mandated multinational force administering a foreign territory (presumably any UN peacekeeping mission) may exercise jurisdiction for the purposes of applying (and hence of respecting) human rights.[298] This jurisprudence was applied by the UK House of Lords in the 2007 *Al-Skeini* Judgment to hold that the United Kingdom, as an occupying power in Iraq in 2004, exercised jurisdiction within a prison but not outside it in the territory occupied.[299] This view was reiterated by the UK Supreme Court in the 2010 *Smith* Judgment, this time concerning a military base, with the victim being a British soldier.[300] The ECtHR, however, found the United Kingdom in breach of the Convention in the 2011 *Al-Skeini* Judgment, holding that the United Kingdom also exercised jurisdiction (in the sense of 'the exercise of physical power and control over the person') outside the prison.[301] Other difficulties have arisen in relation to push-backs of migrants on the high seas, apart from the relatively unproblematic case of migrants aboard,[302] in cases where the migrants are not taken aboard or are escorted.[303] In a 2010 report the IACommHR confirmed the *Issa* jurisprudence concerning an 11-hour Colombian cross-border military operation in the territory of Ecuador aimed at killing members of the allegedly terrorist group FARC, a case that is also relevant to self-defence against non-state actors.[304] This jurisprudence is rather liberal and suggests that jurisdiction for human rights purposes extends extraterritorially everywhere the state is de facto normally in a position to avoid a violation of human rights. This may imply that the scope of jurisdiction varies, even in the same case and with respect to the same provision, depending on the obligation at issue since a state may not have the power to take a certain measure to prevent a human rights abuse, such as a killing, yet be fully in power in terms of carrying out an investigation into this same abuse.

Existing human rights instruments, while generous in rights, rarely mention duties.[305] Yet, as was rightly noted, 'it is essential to a right that it is a demand upon others'.[306] There can be no rights of someone without correlative duties of someone else. The question is,

[295] ECtHR, *Pad et al v Turkey*, Decision of 27 June 2007, App 60167/00, para 54.

[296] ECtHR, *Ilaşcu* (n 291 above) paras 333–335. See Ch 5 above, n 277.

[297] UNSC Res 1244 (1999) of 10 June 1999.

[298] ECtHR, *Behrami* (n 134 above) paras 69–70.

[299] UK House of Lords, *Al-Skeini et al v Secretary of State for Defence* Judgment of 13 June 2007, para 132 (*per* Lord Brown).

[300] UK Supreme Court, *R (on the application of Smith) v Secretary of State for Defence and another* Judgment of 30 June 2010, at <http://www.supremecourt.gov.uk/decided-cases/docs/UKSC_2009_0103_Judgment.pdf>, paras 60, 92.

[301] ECtHR, *Al-Skeini et al v United Kingdom* Judgment of 7 July 2011 [GC], App 55721/07, paras 136, 149–150.

[302] ECtHR, *Hirsi Jamaa et al v Italy* Judgment of 23 February 2012 [GC], App 27765/09, paras 81, 178, extending the prohibition of collective expulsion under Article 4 of Protocol No 4 of the ECHR to Italy's extraterritorial maritime push-backs of migrants at sea.

[303] ECtHR, *Medvedyev v France* Judgment of 29 March 2010 [GC], App 3394/03, paras 66–67.

[304] IACommHR, *Ecuador v Colombia* Report No 112/10 of 21 October 2010, Inter-State Petition IP-02, at <http://www.cidh.oas.org/casos/10.eng.htm>.

[305] Two meaningful exceptions are Art 29(1) UDHR and Arts 28 and 29 ACHPR.

[306] H Shue, *Basic Rights: Subsistence, Affluence, and U.S. Foreign Policy* (Princeton: Princeton University Press, 2nd edn, 1996) 16, 51–5, identifying a duty to prevent (from depriving), a duty to protect (from deprivation), and duty to aid (the deprived).

then, *what* legal obligations on *whom* correspond with the rights envisaged in international instruments. It may of course be presumed that the states parties are the bearers of obligations, both negative and positive. It is states that are expected to accord rights through the imposition of correlative duties on others. The rights of workers to higher wages correspond to a duty of employers to lose a part of their profit and of society at large (in particular taxpayers) to fund such rights. The struggle for human rights is a struggle of certain groups against others within a given society. All rights taken for granted today are the outcome of a successful political struggle in favour of certain interests and groups against others. The human rights strategy is 'universalistic' by showing that the protection of such rights is for the benefit of all on grounds that they are 'by definition' inherent in human nature, but in fact it inevitably favours a group and imposes on others the correlative costs. Absolute human rights for all at all times in all parts of the globe are impossible. A choice is needed and a struggle will be engaged by different groups to have *their* rights, invariably presented as universal and protected, while balancing obligations are in fact shouldered by the others. At stake is who pays for the benefits to those who are accorded rights. In this sense, human rights underlie a constant struggle for the shift of some measure of power from the stronger to the most vulnerable. A society which endorses human rights is a society in which the stronger are prepared to yield some power to the weaker, somehow in contrast with their lust for power. As rightly noted, 'taking rights seriously means taking duties seriously', the problem being that while many are prepared to take rights seriously very few are prepared to take the correlative duties equally seriously.[307] Human rights instruments and rhetoric invariably 'conceal' the duty dimension of rights. They list rights as though unlimited rights were freely available to all and do not require any duty on the part of anyone. Faced with this ambiguity, in a world where there are apparently rights for all and duties for no one, the stronger tend to appropriate the human rights discourse and exploit it to the detriment rather than for the benefit of the weaker, with the result that human rights constantly risk converting into their opposite.[308]

The notion that human rights correspond to a tripartite duty of states to respect, to protect, and to fulfil their obligations is widespread.[309] In particular, not only have states a negative obligation to respect human rights, they also have a positive obligation to protect people by taking affirmative action against encroachment from sources other than states, including private individuals, under human rights treaties and, perhaps, customary international law.[310] The duty to protect is of utmost importance in relation to the ability of states to govern their populations decently. The duty extends to the protection of people from crime, including transnational crime,[311] natural disasters,[312] and abuses of MNEs.[313] The state is supposed to do everything in its power to prevent

[307] H Shue, (n 306 above) 167.

[308] See eg D Joyce, 'Human Rights and the Mediatization of International Law' (2010) 23 LJIL 507, 523, noting that 'the field of human rights . . . has rapidly professionalized and turned to increasingly sophisticated communication and marketing strategies'.

[309] cf UN CESCR, 'General Comment No 12: The Right to Adequate Food' (11 May 1999) ESCOR [2000] Supp 2, 102, para 15.

[310] Against the view that the duty to protect is a *general* obligation under *customary international law* and in favour of ascertaining it on a case-by-case basis, see the letter of the UK Legal Adviser, Mr Bethlehem, dated 9 July 2009, at <http://www.reports-and-materials.org/UK-Foreign-Office-letter-to-Ruggie-9-Jul-2009.pdf>.

[311] See section A (1)(e) above.

[312] C Focarelli, 'Duty to Protect in Cases of Natural Disasters', MP EPIL (March 2010 update).

[313] See eg O De Schutter (ed), *Transnational Corporations and Human Rights* (Oxford: OUP, 2006); R McCorquodale and P Simons, 'Responsibility Beyond Borders: State Responsibility for Extraterritorial Violations by Corporations of International Human Rights Law' (2007) 70 MLR 598.

a violation of human rights either through one of its *de jure* or *de facto* organs, or private entities exercising elements of governmental authority (typically outsourced entities), or natural or juridical persons acting privately. As regards private entities to which public services have been outsourced, state responsibility for their supervision has been recurrently affirmed by human rights monitoring bodies, such as the ECtHR,[314] the UNHRC,[315] and the IACtHR,[316] in line with Article 5 of the 2001 ILC Articles on State Responsibility,[317] while the operation of the state's duty to protect as a due diligence obligation to prevent abuses of MNEs acting as private entities, has been emphasized by the UN Special Representative at the Human Rights Council in his reports on the matter, stressing in particular the broad meaning of the term 'ensure' found in several human rights treaties.[318] Concerning the critical question of whether the duty to protect extends extraterritorially, the Special Representative noted in his last 2011 report that 'States are not generally required under international human rights law to regulate the extraterritorial activities of businesses domiciled in their territory and/or jurisdiction', nor 'are they generally prohibited from doing so, provided there is a recognized jurisdictional basis'.[319] As a result, the duty to protect people from MNEs' abuses seems to be mostly up to host states, many of which are notoriously unwilling or unable to fulfil it.

On balance, human rights have profoundly affected the vision of international affairs and how rulers have to govern their populations. However, judicial practice shows different degrees of development and enforcement. The jurisprudence, even when it works, as is the case with the ECtHR, addresses individual cases and findings of breaches are borne by the collectivity.[320] It appears that rulers and state officials are generally unimpressed by the consequences of possible breaches of human rights. Finally, what is perhaps worse, the economic, social, and cultural rights directed to fulfil the basic needs of the most vulnerable in the world are almost exclusively the subject-matter of innocuous reports, studies, and talk, with little effective jurisprudence and impact on people.

(e) Cultural identity

A right to cultural identity is attributed by international treaties to groups living within states, notably to minorities and indigenous peoples. A number of ad hoc treaty provisions have been ratified by a few states and hardly prove a customary international law right to cultural identity. The UNHRC has stressed that the states parties to the ICCPR have a duty to protect minorities under Article 27 and to accord them the right

[314] ECtHR, *Costello-Roberts v United Kingdom* Judgment of 25 March 1993, App 13134/87, Series A No 247-C, (1994) 19 EHRR 112, para 27; *Woś v Poland* Decision of 1 March 2005, App 22860/02, para 60; *Storck v Germany* Judgment of 16 June 2005, App 61603/00, (2006) 43 EHRR 96, para 103.

[315] UNHRC, *Cabal and Pasini Bertran v Australia* Views of 7 August 2003, CCPR/C/78/1020/2001, para 7.2.

[316] IACtHR, *Ximenes Lopes v Brazil, Lopes et al (on behalf of Ximenes Lopes) v Brazil (Merits, Reparations and Costs)* Judgment of 4 July 2006, IACtHR Series C No 149, paras 86–87, 90, 96–97; and the opinion of Judge Sergio García-Ramírez, paras 26–28.

[317] See n 82 above.

[318] cf UN Doc A/HRC/4/035, 9 February 2007, para 10, stating that 'international law firmly establishes that states have a duty to protect against non-state human rights abuses within their jurisdiction, and that this duty extends to protection against abuses by business entities. The duty to protect exists under the core United Nations human rights treaties as elaborated by the treaty bodies, and is also generally agreed to exist under customary international law' (notes omitted). Along the same lines, see A/HRC/8/5, 7 April 2008, para 18, and more recently, A/HRC/17/31, 21 March 2011, at 6–13.

[319] ibid 7. For the 'neither required nor prohibited' qualification, see Ch 6 above, section B (2)(a).

[320] See Ch 8 below, section B (4).

to enjoy their own culture, especially when issuing permits in favour of MNEs to exploit local resources.[321] A right to cultural diversity is set out, in very elusive terms, in Article 22 EU Charter of Fundamental Rights.[322] The right is not, in any event, absolute, as held in the 2001 *Chapman* Judgment by the ECtHR, holding that it yields to the environmental rights of the community.[323] The 2005 UNESCO Cultural Diversity Convention also excludes fundamental rights, although it does not clarify which human rights are 'fundamental' for its purposes.[324] The matter is often addressed by national constitutions, in which the courts detect the fundamental rights which cannot be overcome by invoking, in civil and criminal domestic proceedings, any cultural exception as a defence.

National minorities, as discussed earlier,[325] do not have a right to self-determination, but both bilateral and multilateral treaties provide them with several rights to be enjoyed within states. The 1995 European National Minorities Convention actually fails to define national minorities and accord rights only to 'persons' belonging thereto rather than to national minorities as such.[326] Among the rights to cultural identity provided are the right 'freely to choose to be treated or not to be treated as such', specifying that persons belonging to national minorities may exercise their rights 'individually as well as in community with others' (Article 3). The Convention imposes on the states parties not only the obligation to guarantee the right of equality before the law and of equal protection of the law, but also to adopt adequate measures in order to promote, in all areas of economic, social, political and cultural life, full and effective equality between persons belonging to a national minority and those belonging to the majority (Article 4). It prohibits, in particular, 'policies or practices aimed at assimilation of persons belonging to national minorities against their will' and obliges states 'to promote the conditions necessary for persons belonging to national minorities to maintain and develop their culture, and to preserve the essential elements of their identity, namely their religion, language, traditions and cultural heritage' (Article 5). Article 10 provides persons belonging to national minorities with the right to use freely and without interference their minority language, in private and in public, orally and in writing.

Similar provisions are made by treaties governing the status of tribal and indigenous peoples, such as the 1989 ILO Indigenous and Tribal Peoples Convention.[327] Article 5 provides that 'the social, cultural, religious and spiritual values and practices of these peoples shall be recognised and protected' and 'the integrity of the values, practices and institutions of these peoples shall be respected'. Under Article 6 the states parties shall 'consult the peoples concerned, through appropriate procedures and in particular through their representative institutions' and:

[321] See eg HRC, *Ominayak, Chief of the Lubicon Lake Band v Canada* Views of 26 March 1990, Comm No 167/1984, GAOR 45th Session, Supp 40, vol 2, 1, para 33; *Ilmari Länsman et al v Finland* Comm No 511/1992, Report of 26 October 1994, CCPR/C/52/D/511/1992, paras 9.5, 9.8.

[322] Charter of Fundamental Rights of the European Union, 2000/C 364/01.

[323] ECtHR, *Chapman v United Kingdom* Judgment of 18 January 2001 [GC], App 27238/95, ECtHR Rep 2001-I 41, (2001) 33 EHRR 1, para 96.

[324] UNESCO Convention on the Protection and Promotion of the Diversity in Cultural Expressions (adopted 20 October 2005, entered into force 18 March 2007).

[325] See Ch 5 above, section C (4)(e).

[326] COE, Framework Convention for the Protection of National Minorities (opened for signature 1 February 1995, entered into force 1 February 1998) 2151 UNTS 243.

[327] ILO Convention (No 169) concerning Indigenous and Tribal Peoples in Independent Countries (signed 27 June 1989, entered into force 5 September 1991).

> ... establish means by which these peoples can freely participate, to at least the same extent as other sectors of the population, at all levels of decision-making in elective institutions and administrative and other bodies responsible for policies and programmes which concern them.

Under Article 9 'The methods customarily practised by the peoples concerned for dealing with offences committed by their members shall be respected' and their customs 'in regard to penal matters shall be taken into consideration'. Similar provisions are found in the 2007 Declaration on the Rights of Indigenous Peoples.[328]

(3) Wealth

Humanity is better protected if material wealth is also taken care of and extreme poverty eradicated. Meeting basic needs is the bridge from humanity to a minimum, life-sustaining level of wealth.[329] However, once this threshold has been met, poverty is a relative concept. It exists for some people when there are others who are far wealthier. At *this* level, the problem is not poverty per se, but the *gap* between the poor and the wealthy. The gap actually means a gap in power. There is no reason why people cannot live in (voluntary) poverty better than in opulence.[330] The pursuit of wealth makes people more dependent on the *immediate* fulfilment of *material* needs and hence on those who provide them, who become stronger and have an obvious interest in keeping people under a state of 'infantilist ethos' disguised as freedom.[331] Freedom from want *itself* is different from freedom from want of this or that good, just as freedom of the adult is different from freedom as the instant satisfaction of the infant. The current global trend assumes that wealth is *the* value to be pursued and that all other values, such as those embodied in human rights, are deemed to follow. It is indeed recurrently argued that the pursuit of wealth may help to protect human rights.[332] However, in so far as the problem is the gap rather than poverty per se, the alleged increasing level of wealth of the poor globally (assuming that it reflects realities) makes little sense unless and until the gap is narrowed. If the wealthy become wealthier at a higher speed than the poor become less poor, then the problem is simply exacerbated to the advantage of the wealthy. Moreover, wealth typically refers to people in the aggregate and in the long term, while human rights pertain to justice here and now for single individuals in the flesh. Wealth may well improve human rights in the long term for people in the aggregate but often it worsens the human rights of many individuals at present. Finally, if wealth is successfully spurred by hard-to-control strategies designed to manufacture needs and encourage regression through illusionistic strategies, then human rights are sold just like any other commodity (or as a powerful vehicle to sell yet other commodities) and end up being used to increase dependency and vulnerability rather than to work in the opposite direction.

A dense network of international law rules is in place to regulate the economy and wealth of people at global level, providing guidance to global trade, finance, and aid to

[328] cf eg Art 8(2)(a), Art 11(1), and Art 16(2) UN Declaration on the Rights of Indigenous Peoples (13 September 2007) UN Doc A/Res/61/295.

[329] See eg CR Beitz and RE Goodin, *Global Basic Rights* (Oxford: OUP, 2009).

[330] For a comparative analysis of poverty across cultures, see M Rahnema, 'Global Poverty: A Pauperizing Myth' (1992) 24 *Interculture* 4–51.

[331] For the excesses of consumerism and the pernicious effects of creeping libertarianism, although rather repetitive and populist in tone, see BR Barber, *Consumed: How Markets Corrupt Children, Infantilize Adults, and Swallow Citizens Whole* (New York and London: WW Norton & Co, 2007).

[332] See eg J Harrison, *The Human Rights Impact of the World Trade Organisation* (Oxford: Hart, 2007) 37.

developing countries. These rules are generally framed in terms of the free flow of goods, services, capital, and investment. Critics insist that such rules hardly solve the problem at its roots, but rather worsen it by widening the gap. Besides, in several sensitive areas (such as global concentrations of economic power and state bankruptcy) there are virtually no international law rules at all at global level, leaving total freedom of action or diversion from one particular regime to another to states. There is ample scope for struggle in the years to come for better rules aimed at bringing the poorest people in the world (whose lives critically depend today on a global economy in which they have little or no say, and no longer on local lifestyles) to meet their basic needs.

This section explores the existing rules on global wealth concerning basic needs, trade, aid, foreign investment, and sovereign debt. Here more than elsewhere the focus must be not only on international law as it stands but also and perhaps primarily on international law as it may or ought to be in the future. It is argued that global poverty is more often than not a problem of bridging the gap between the poor and the wealthy than one of bringing all peoples to levels of wealth predetermined by the wealthier and useful to these latter to become wealthier at a faster speed than the speed at which the poor become less poor. At the same time, the wealthier (being also the stronger) push the poorer to respect and ensure respect for human rights and force them into a 'double bind' dilemma.[333] Weaker states and peoples are requested (having been historically forced into statehood and the global states system) to meet human rights standards without creating the conditions which allow them to live up to such standards. Even where poor peoples are willing to respect human rights, they may be unable to do so for global economic reasons. And when they fail to fulfil humanitarian needs, the spectre of a 'reeducative', in fact punitive, external humanitarian intervention (possibly assorted with other sanctions) surfaces. The double bind then translates into what may be felt as an 'impossible triptych' demanding global market, human rights, and humanitarian policing. The current global economic system also constantly generates—quite inevitably in the absence of a legitimate and effective global political authority—a never-ending race to the bottom of all actors, including states, which worsens human rights and environmental standards in several areas of the globe, while other areas (including formerly developing, now emerging economies) profit therefrom and become wealthier. Overall statistical indices may be optimistic, but improving statistics can hardly satisfy those who suffer. International law is indeed expected to establish an effective and absolute threshold within which competition is regulated so as to ensure equal access and beyond which competition is prohibited to all. If law has any function, this function is indeed to prohibit unjust and general free-riding. This, however, is very far from coming true in the near future, while the world is rushing towards new abysses and few if any are capable of seeing a way out.

(a) Basic needs

Fundamental human rights are those which fulfil the 'basic needs' of people concerning their very biological subsistence, such as the right to food, to water, to health, and to

[333] For the 'double bind' theory, especially associated with the mother–child relationship, as a situation (deriving from conflicting injunctions) in which 'no matter what a person does, he "can't win"' and develops schizophrenic symptoms, see G Bateson, *Steps to an Ecology of Mind* [1972] (Chicago and London: University of Chicago Press, 2000) 201–27, 271–8.

shelter.[334] Closely linked with 'human' development, the 'basic needs' discourse emerged in the 1970s in the context of campaigns for 'another development',[335] more human- or people-centred than mere economic development as understood up to then, locally orientated and endogenous. It was stressed that empowerment of the poor could be achieved through, inter alia, political participation and enjoyment of human rights. The question of the identification of the 'basic needs', and hence of 'basic rights', has remained open. Today it is closely linked with the 'poverty question' and with 'global justice' studies.[336] The theoretical assumption is that rulers who arbitrarily deprive people of basic needs can no longer be considered 'legitimate', whatever the consent they may enjoy among their own populations, and, in particular, that the misappropriation of aid funds, corruption, and widespread extreme poverty, should not go unpunished.

The basic rights to food, water, health, and shelter are generally viewed as less important than 'civil and political' rights. They are regulated in international instruments to be subject to progressive introduction, depending on state resources, and are often regarded as non-justiciable. In fact, the treaty obligations to fulfil such rights are not always subject to progressive introduction (in any event this implies a clear prohibition of regressive measures) and nothing prevents the courts from adjudicating them.[337] Their abuse should be treated as being of equal importance to international crimes. The objection that international crimes and international criminal justice are Western tools to change unaligned regimes is difficult to avoid,[338] but it cannot serve as a justification for abusers.

The right to food is recognized in several treaties and non-binding instruments. It is defined by the CESCR 1999 General Comment No 12 as the right to have 'physical and economic access at all times to adequate food or means for its procurement', implying the availability of food in a quantity and of quality sufficient to satisfy the dietary needs of individuals, free from adverse substances, and acceptable within a given culture, and the accessibility of such food in ways that are sustainable and that do not interfere with the enjoyment of other human rights.[339] It includes the right to food security, recently seen by the UN special rapporteur on the right to food as being potentially undermined by the WTO trade regime, as part of the post-global food crisis

[334] See D Bilchitz, *Poverty and Fundamental Rights: The Justification and Enforcement of Socio-Economic Rights* (Oxford: OUP, 2007); T Pogge (ed), *Freedom from Poverty as a Human Right: Who Owes What to the Very Poor?* (Oxford: OUP, 2007). For the theory of extraterritorial human rights obligations to the people in other states, notably in developing countries, which prove unable to discharge their primary duty to fulfil the basic needs of their populations and to implement human rights as a result, inter alia, of the current global economic system, see n 289 above.

[335] See eg R Chambers, *Rural Development: Putting the Last First* (London: Longman, 1983).

[336] See Ch 2 above, n 117; and Ch 5 above, note 192 and accompanying text.

[337] For this position, see Constitutional Court of South Africa, *Ex p Chairperson of the Constitutional Assembly: Re Certification of the Constitution of the Republic of South Africa* Judgment of 6 September 1996, 1996-IV SALR 744, para 78, stating that 'The fact that socio-economic rights will almost inevitably give rise to [budgetary] implications does not seem to be a bar to their justiciability'.

[338] For the view that human rights support the etatization (ie Westernization) of the world, hence the necessity for repressive measures by the state to secure preconceived ends such as 'development' (including the 'right to a better standard of living' and the 'right to employment'), understood as a 'catching up' project with the Western standard, asking then 'What sort of living standards are being talked about, whose living standards are they and what are they measured against?', see Rajagopal (n 199 above) 195, 201.

[339] UN CESCR, 'General Comment No 12: The Right to Adequate Food' (n 309 above) paras 6, 8. See eg S Joseph, *Blame It on the WTO?: A Human Rights Critique* (Oxford: OUP, 2011) 181–213.

agenda aimed at managing price and income volatility for poor rural households, especially in developing countries.[340]

In the UN 2000 Millennium Declaration states have resolved 'by the year 2015, . . . to halve the proportion of people who are unable to reach or to afford safe drinking water'.[341] The right to water includes the right to access water without discrimination in the quantity and quality sufficient to meet vital human needs (drinking, food production, and sanitation) within safe physical reach affordable for all, a right corresponding to obligations of states (both negative and positive) to respect, protect, and ensure it within their jurisdiction. With some exceptions, the right to water is not expressly mentioned in most human rights treaties and is then inferred by international monitoring bodies from the right to life, the right to health, and the right to an adequate standard of living. In its 2002 General Comment No 15 the CESCR regarded the right to water as falling 'within the category of guarantees essential for securing an adequate standard of living, particularly since it is one of the most fundamental conditions for survival', and as such 'inextricably related' to the right to the highest attainable standard of health and the rights to adequate housing and adequate food.[342] However, the international case law, unlike the national jurisprudence, which is basically grounded in constitutional rules, remains rather poor. The ACommHPR has produced some significant (although non-binding) reports which are worth mentioning. In the 1996 *Free Legal Assistance Group v Nigeria* Report the ACommHPR found that Zaire had failed to provide basic services necessary for a minimum standard of health, such as safe drinking water and electricity, and that there was a shortage of medicine in breach of Article 16 ACHPR.[343] In its 2001 *Ogoniland* Report, the Commission held that Nigeria had violated Articles 16 and 24 ACHRP by allowing the contamination of water resources in Ogoniland.[344]

The right to life entails a right to health and medical care.[345] This right is sanctioned by several human rights treaties, both universal and regional, including Article 25(1) UDHR, Article 12 ICESCR, and Article 16 ACHPR. Article 55 UN Charter provides that the United Nations shall promote 'solutions of . . . health, and related problems'. The UN 2000 Millennium Declaration contemplates the improvement of maternal and child health and the fight against HIV/AIDS, malaria, and other major diseases, and calls for cooperation with pharmaceutical companies in order to provide access to affordable essential drugs in developing countries.[346] The right to health is assumed to

[340] See 'The World Trade Organization and the Post-Global Food Crisis Agenda: Putting Food Security First in the International Food System', report submitted in November 2011 by the UN special rapporteur on the right to food, at <http://www.wto.org/english/news_e/news11_e/deschutter_2011_e.pdf>, and the critical response on 14 December 2011 by the WTO Director-General, at <http://www.wto.org/english/news_e/news11_e/agcom_14dec11_e.htm>, stressing that 'international trade is part of the package of solutions to achieve food security'. For the international trade regime and its tensions with human rights, see respectively section A (3)(b) and section B (3) below.

[341] UNGA Res 55/2 of 8 September 2000, 'UN Millennium Declaration', GAOR 55th Session, Supp 49, vol 1, 4. See in addition, more recently, HR Council, Res A/HRC/15/L.14 of 24 September 2009 and UNGA Res 64/292 of 28 July 2010.

[342] UN CESCR, 'General Comment No 15: The Right to Water (Arts 11 and 12)' of 26 November 2002, ESCOR [2003] Supp 2, 120, para 3.

[343] ACommHPR, *World Organisation Against Torture, Lawyers' Committee for Human Rights, Jehovah Witnesses, Inter-African Union for Human Rights v Zaire*, Report of March 1996, Comm Nos 25/89, 47/90, 56/91, 100/93, (1995) 4 IHRR 89, para 47.

[344] ACommHPR, *The Social and Economic Rights Action Center and the Center for Economic and Social Rights v Nigeria*, Report of 13–27 October 2001, Comm No 155/96, at <http://www.achpr.org/english/Decison_Communication/Nigeria/Comm.155-96.pdf>, paras 52–54.

[345] J Tobin, *The Right to Health in International Law* (Oxford: OUP, 2012).

[346] See n 341 above.

embody, inter alia, the right to control one's health and body, including sexual and reproductive freedoms, the right to be free from non-consensual medical treatment and experimentation, and the right to a system of health protection which produces equality of opportunity for people to enjoy the highest attainable level of health.[347] According to CESCR General Comment No 14, Article 12 ICESCR imposes three levels of obligations for states parties, namely, an obligation to 'respect' (requiring 'States to refrain from interfering directly or indirectly with the enjoyment of the right to health'), an obligation to 'protect' (requiring 'States to take measures that prevent third parties from interfering with Article 12 guarantees'), and an obligation to 'fulfil' (which contains obligations to 'facilitate, provide and promote').[348] In the 1996 *Free Legal Assistance Group v Zaire* Report,[349] in the 1998 *International Pen* Report,[350] and in the 2001 *Ogoniland* Report,[351] the ACommHPR held that failure to ensure the availability of a minimum standard of health was in violation of Article 16 ACHPR. In the 2003 *Purohit and Moore* Report the Commission ordered the Gambian government to repeal national legislation regulating the treatment of mentally ill persons and to provide new legislation compatible with international standards.[352] The right to medical care has been held by the Supreme Court of South Africa as implying that prices of medicine and medical services must be made accessible and more affordable.[353] The WHO is key to setting international health standards for the promotion and protection of the right to health.[354] Noteworthy are WHA 1978 Resolution 31.32 ('Action Programme on Essential Drugs'),[355] and WHA 2005 Resolution 58.3 ('Revision of International Health Regulations').[356]

The right to housing implies a positive obligation on the state to provide its population with a habitable space which is affordable, accessible, and has basic amenities such as access to running water, electricity, and a drainage system.[357] The right is envisaged in several treaties. In the 2001 *Ogoniland* Report the ACommHPR held that the rights to life and physical well-being include the right to adequate housing.[358]

Finally, the right to life makes sense when life is worth living and this entails a right also to an adequate standard of living. What constitutes an 'adequate standard' at global level probably varies with the lifestyles of different people. What counts as the basics of life and assurance of survival in one place at a certain point in time may not be so elsewhere or in another moment. Article 25(1) UDHR, Article 11 ICESCR, and

347 UN CESCR, 'General Comment No. 14' of 11 May 2000, ESCOR [2001] Supp 2, 128, para 8.

348 ibid para 33. 349 See n 343 above.

350 ACommHPR, *International Pen, Constitutional Rights Project, Interights on behalf of Ken Saro-Wiwa Jr And Civil Liberties Organisation v Nigeria* Report of 31 October 1998, Comm Nos 137/94, 139/94, 154/96, and 161/97, (1998) 7 IHRR 274, para 112.

351 See n 344 above.

352 ACommHPR, *Purohit and Moore v The Gambia* Report of 15–29 May 2003, Comm No 241/ 2001, at <http://www.achpr.org/english/Decison_Communication/Gambia/Comm.%20241-2001.pdf>, paras 77–85.

353 Constitutional Court of South Africa, *Minister of Health v New Clicks South Africa (PTY) Ltd* Judgment of 30 September 2005, at <http://www.saflii.org/za/cases/ZACC/2005/14.pdf>.

354 WHO, Constitution of the World Health Organization (signed 22 July 1946, entered into force 7 April 1948) 14 UNTS 185.

355 WHA, Res 31.32, 'Action Programme on Essential Drugs' of 23 May 1978, 31st World Health Assembly Official Records 247 Part I, 20.

356 WHA, Res 58.3, 'Revision of the International Health Regulations' (adopted 23 May 2005, entered into force 15 June 2005).

357 UN CESCR, 'General Comment No 4: The Right to Adequate Housing (Art. 11(1))' of 13 December 1991, ESCOR [1991] Supp 3, 114, para 6.

358 ACommHPR, *The Social and Economic Rights Action Center* (n 344 above) paras 60–63.

Article 27 CRC expressly provide for the right and the UN Charter stipulates that member states and the United Nations undertake to promote 'higher standards of living'. The right is assumed to include the right to food, to adequate housing, special care and assistance in motherhood and childhood, clothing, medical care, and social security. It is, in short, a synthesis of the rights to the fulfilment of basic needs.

Few if any would deny that the right to the fulfilment of basic needs is at the very heart of humanity and emotional attunement with those who suffer. Economic growth appears to be a satisfactory strategy by which to accumulate resources while the commitment to human rights and the rule of law is a guarantee against local rulers who abuse their power. At the same time, one should be mindful that it is precisely because of their unsolicited inclusion in the global state and economic system that many people cannot fulfil their basic needs and find it extremely difficult (if not impossible) to win the competition with all other actors.

(b) Trade

The exchange of goods, services, capital, and investment between different peoples has always been a catalyst for economic growth and human intercourse. The founders of international law included in their *jus gentium*, based on natural law, a right to trade grounded in the unity and brotherhood of all human beings despite the partition of the world into different states.[359] Classic economists, such as David Ricardo, developed the theory of comparative advantage to hold that national specialization in the most competitively produced goods and mutual exchange reduce production costs, increase the quality of the goods exchanged, and enrich all partner states.[360] The result of autarchic policies pursued in Europe in the inter-war period proved the need for generalized obligations on states progressively to reduce or eliminate barriers to trade (tariffs, quotas, subsidies, currency controls, etc) and for a globally interrelated system in which goods, services, capital, and investment could flow freely across political borders. The World Bank for Reconstruction and Development (IBRD) and the International Monetary Fund (IMF) were set up at Bretton Woods in 1944.[361] At the time, the establishment of the International Trade Organization (ITO) failed, but a part thereof was 'provisionally' applied as the General Agreement on Tariffs and Trade (GATT).[362] In 1994 the World Trade Organization (WTO) was set up, providing a complex body of rules and a powerful Dispute Settlement Body (DSB).[363] The information revolution in recent years has made an enormous contribution to the global economic interconnectedness of all peoples, while political borders remain formally unaffected.

The big problem with global economic interconnectedness and competition is the prospect of a global, unregulated, race to the bottom. All actors, state and non-state actors alike, are pressed to compete with one another and to exploit any possible

[359] See Ch 4 above, note 64.

[360] R Torrens, *An Essay on the External Corn Trade* [1815] (London: Longman, Rees, Orme, Brown, and Green, 3rd edn, 1826); D Ricardo, *On the Principles of Political Economy and Taxation* (London: John Murray, 1817). For a classical analysis, see PA Samuelson, 'The Gains from International Trade' (1939) 5 Can JEPS 195.

[361] Articles of Agreement of the International Bank for Reconstruction and Development (done and entered into force 27 December 1945) 2 UNTS 134; Articles of Agreement of the International Monetary Fund (signed and entered into force 27 December 1945) 2 UNTS 39.

[362] General Agreement on Tariffs and Trade (adopted 30 October 1947, entered into force 1 January 1948) 55 UNTS 187.

[363] Marrakesh Agreement Establishing the World Trade Organization (adopted 15 April 1994, entered into force 1 January 1995) 1867 UNTS 154.

strategy to stay in the market and survive. Given the dependence of states on their resources and budgets, the free flow of capital, now instant in cyberspace, has notably accelerated the need for states to win the competition (not only with other states, but also) with powerful private actors, such as MNEs. People are at the same time the winning and losing parties in this struggle for existence. Some people gain from trade liberalization while others (in other states or in the very same state) lose. They may gain as consumers, but lose as taxpayers or as producers, or the reverse. Different outcomes affect not only different classes of people, but also one and the same person depending on whether he or she is considered as a consumer (or a consumer of a certain good rather than another), or a producer, or a taxpayer, or an home investor, or a transnational investor, and so forth. The whole is very intricate and it is extremely difficult to give a trustworthy account of the entire picture. There are countless data supporting virtually every thesis, and the suspicion that those behind them are biased is sensible. What is lacking is a legal mechanism capable of avoiding the 'tragedy' of any actor compelled to free ride to the fullest extent possible so as not to be thrown out of existence. The system is structured constantly to force all to exploit any opportunity so as to 'precede' competitors in the race and destroy any common concern. If one entity wisely renounces a bad practice, others will not, in the absence of common and effective (deterrent) rules. Only rules common to all can avoid this, but rules work only if people believe in them, as this book suggests. There is no hope that justice will descend from heaven for free in a world where all feel compelled to win simply to avoid obliteration.

The WTO system is based on the principle of non-discrimination among products. This is thought to avoid protectionist laws, either explicit or disguised, the alteration of competition against like foreign products or certain foreign products in relation to less competitive like products from another foreign state, escalating commercial wars, and ultimately to be for the benefit of consumers, taxpayers, the most efficient producers, and people in general. The basic distinction between protectionist and non-protectionist national measures is difficult to make in many instances and they may well protect important local values, even some which are of global import. The most-favoured-nation (MFN) principle ensures the 'external parity' of 'like products' by prohibiting states from imposing on a product from one state tariffs higher (in fact or in law) than those applied to a like product from another state (Article I GATT), with exceptions being made, inter alia, for free exchange zones or regional customs unions (Article XXIV GATT) and the operation of the 'enabling clause' which allows preferences for developing countries. The national-treatment principle (in the sense of non-less-favourable treatment) ensures the 'internal parity' of 'like products' by prohibiting states from imposing taxes or other measures concerning the sale to like products from another state higher than those applied to like national products (Article III GATT). The assessment of when two products are 'like' under Articles I and III for the purposes of applying the non-discrimination principles is critical. In the 1996 *Taxes on Alcoholic Beverages* Report the Appellate Body held that the concept of likeness is relative and to be interpreted, as least in relation to Article III(2) GATT, narrowly.[364] In the 2001 *Asbestos* Report the Appellate Body pointed out that likeness is to be understood

[364] WTO, *Japan—Taxes on Alcoholic Beverages*, AB Report of 1 November 1996, WT/DS8/AB/R, WT/DS10/AB/R, WT/DS11/AB/R, at 21, noting that 'The concept of likeness is a relative one that evokes the image of an accordion' which 'stretches and squeezes in different places as different provisions of the *WTO Agreement* are applied' and concluding that 'in Article III:2, first sentence of the GATT 1994, the accordion of "likeness" is meant to be narrowly squeezed'.

differently in the context of Article III(4) and to be ascertained by four criteria.[365] It is unclear whether two products which differ only in terms of the process and production method (PPM) are classified as 'like' for GATT purposes and fall within the non-discrimination regime.[366]

The above principles are limited, inter alia, by a number of general and security exceptions (Articles XX and XXI GATT). The security exceptions are intended to justify national measures aimed at preventing the disclosure of information that the state considers contrary to its essential security interests; or taking action which it considers necessary for the protection of its essential security interests relating to fissionable materials and the traffic in arms, or taken in time of war or other emergency in international relations; or taking action in pursuance of the state's obligations under the UN Charter for the maintenance of international peace and security. In practice, it justifies measures to protect national security and to enforce UN Security Council mandated embargos. General exceptions cover a number of 'legitimate protective aims' concerning non-economic matters, such as public morals, health, and the environment. Such exceptions justify national measures (otherwise contrary to GATT) which are 'necessary' or 'relating to' the legitimate goals listed, but not protectionist measures disguised under the *chapeau* of Article XX. They are discussed in the next section of this chapter.

There seems to be perhaps no doubt, at least in theory, that in the aggregate free trade increases the quantity and quality of goods and services, and hence choice and wealth. Nor is there any doubt that wealth may contribute much to extreme poverty eradication. At the same time free trade entails costs which can be hard to grasp in terms of economic efficiency and short-term physical well-being. Trade leads people to believe that what matters in human life is price (ie the balance between demand and supply, whatever the commodity sold) and the capacity of those goods used as money to exchange everything for everything.[367] A 'free trade world' is shaped as a place in which all is interchangeable and can be purchased by offering more. Every method, including illusionistic strategies under the control of a few media conglomerates, is in principle allowed to any entity in order to keep demand higher than supply and *its own* price as high as possible, no matter what this entails for society as a whole. In such a world people may easily believe themselves to be in the market for every moment of their (also intimate) lives, in the grip ultimately of selling themselves at the highest possible price. Their uniqueness is merely a brand to attract better (ie wealthier) purchasers. This dependence on the day-to-day tastes of purchasers (hence on the stronger who have the *money*) incurs very high costs indeed. It leaves the weaker either to remain at the mercy of the stronger or to enter the struggle and gain the purchasing power which allows them to have others at their mercy. *Tertium non datur*. Since current international law does little to reduce such costs, a struggle is worth engaging to enhance a sense of sobriety and non-interchangeability. The system should encourage people to think of themselves as unique, non-marketable, and should, in particular, strengthen the conditions in which they are left free enough to be able to resist major pressures for surviving and living as merchandise.

[365] WTO, *EC—Measures Affecting Asbestos and Asbestos-Containing Products*, AB Report of 12 March 2001, WT/DS135/AB/R, paras 97–98, 108.

[366] For a discussion of this issue, see Christiane R. Conrad, *Processes and Production Methods (PPMs) in WTO Law: Interfering Trade and Social Goals* (Cambridge: CUP, 2011). See further n 642 below.

[367] For a recent, insightful analysis, see D Satz, *Why Some Things Should Not Be for Sale: The Moral Limits of Markets* (Oxford: OUP, 2010).

(c) Aid and development

The economic gap between North and South, to use a simplistic terminology, is rooted in the inequality of states despite their legal equality. Historically, the gap is rooted, inter alia, in colonialism and subjugation by the European powers of the rest of the world and in the following process of decolonization (ie the etatization of former colonies) which took place especially during the post-World War II period. Developing states then denounced the injustice inherent in the Western-driven capitalist economic system, while developed states took on in part a responsibility towards developing countries which takes several forms. A key channel for development is commercial protectionism (or, rather, preferential treatment) in accordance with the nascent-industry theory. Capital flows into developing countries include aid, debt, and foreign investment. Grants, bank loans and government and corporate bonds, as well as foreign (direct and portfolio) investment are especially needed in cases where internal savings are insufficient or scarcely reinvested. Neo-liberal circles have in recent years maintained that foreign aid, debt, and portfolio equity investment do not work, these latter due to their volatility, and that foreign direct investment (FDI) is the best vehicle for development.

An international law of development emerged in the 1960s and peaked in 1974 with the adoption by the UN General Assembly of a number of resolutions embodying the New International Economic Order (NIEO), notably the 'Charter of Economic Rights and Duties of States'.[368] In 1965, Part IV on 'trade and development' was added to the GATT 1947 as evidence of the conviction that trade (not only aid) was essential to development. Article XXXVI(8) provided that the developed parties 'd[id] not expect reciprocity for commitments made by them in trade negotiations to reduce or remove tariffs and other barriers to the trade of less-developed contracting parties'. In the 1970 'Agreed Conclusions' of the UNCTAD Special Committee on Preferences, preferential tariff treatment accorded under a generalized scheme of preferences was recognized, expressly requiring a GATT waiver with respect to the MFN obligation in Article I(1).[369] As a result, in 1971 the states parties to the GATT adopted a Waiver Decision for a ten-year period.[370] In 1979 an Enabling Clause was adopted by another decision expanding the authorization provided by the Waiver Decision to cover additional preferential measures and making the authorization permanent. In 1994 the Enabling Clause was incorporated into the GATT 1994.[371] A 'special and differentiated treatment' for developing states is also envisaged in provisions such as Article 10(2) of the Agreement on Sanitary and Phytosanitary Measures (SPS Agreement) and Articles 65 and 66 TRIPS (contemplating the postponement of the application of these treaties to developing states), and Articles 4 and 8 of the Agreement on Technical Barriers to Trade (TBT Agreement) (stipulating provisional derogations from general obligations benefiting developing states).[372] Article 11(2) Marrakesh Agreement establishing the

[368] UNGA Res 3281 (XXIX) of 12 December 1974, 'Charter of Economic Rights and Duties of States', GAOR 29th Session Supp 31, 50.

[369] UNCTAD, Agreed Conclusions, 1970, at <http://www.wto.org/english/tratop_e/dispu_e/246r_e_e.doc>.

[370] GATT, Decision of 25 June 1971, L/3545 (28 June 1971).

[371] GATT, Decision of 28 November 1979, L/4903 (3 December 1979). cf Annex 1A to the WTO Agreement incorporating the GATT 1994 into the WTO Agreement, para 1(b)(iv). On the interpretation of the Enabling Clause, see WTO *EU—Conditions for the Granting of Tariff Preferences to Developing Countries*, AB Report of 7 April 2004, WT/DS246/AB/R (see ch 6 above, n 259).

[372] Agreement on Technical Barriers to Trade (signed 15 April 1994, entered into force 1 January 1995) 1186 UNTS 120.

WTO expressly provides that the least-developed countries will only be required to undertake commitments and concessions 'to the extent consistent with their individual development, financial and trade needs or their administrative and institutional capabilities'. Today, development is informed by principles including the sovereignty of developing states over their natural resources, relative solidarity between developing and developed countries, sustainable development, and the human right to development.

The development priorities of developing countries have been financed through lending by the World Bank Group and the IMF, and today also by private banks and export credit agencies. The World Bank lends resources to member states, their political subdivisions, and private enterprises operating in their territory provided that they are controlled by the government, to cope with the need for foreign currency for the realization of development projects, such as infrastructure, food and social safety, school and professional training. These long-term, low-interest loans—together with interest-free credits from the International Development Association (IDA) within the World Bank Group—are said to favour developing countries, which cannot normally repay the debt in the short term and can borrow money in international markets only at high interest rates at best. The loans concession is contingent on the solvency of the requesting state and on other parameters which guarantee coherence, economic viability, and efficiency in the implementation of the financed projects. The IMF provides financial assistance to states encountering temporary balance of payment difficulties through 'structural adjustment programmes' (SAPs) on condition that they reform their economic policies according to its requests. The IMF thus plays a major role in influencing national balance of payments and currency exchange rates, hence in supervising economic policies and governmental priorities.[373] Conditionality has been strongly criticized for its adverse environmental and social effects.[374] The Global Environmental Facility (GEF) was established in 1991 to meet four global environmental priorities: climate change, biodiversity conservation, protection of international waters, and ozone depletion. As is well known, the voting in both organizations is weighted and few states control the decision-making process.

Most developing countries are strongly dependent on the export of raw materials and primary commodities.[375] They are interested in an increase in, or at least in the stabilization of, prices. Developed countries, as importing states, are interested in decreases in prices, but generally share with developing countries an interest in stable prices. International Commodity Agreements (ICAs) between exporting and importing countries are specifically aimed at ensuring stable production and prices. They are often administered by IOs, such as the International Coffee Organization (ICO), the International Cocoa Organization (ICCO), the International Sugar Organization (ISO), and the International Tropical Timber Organization (ITTO). Stability of supply and prices is realized through a variety of mechanisms. One is the introduction of import and export quotas which, although contrary to Article XI GATT, are justified under Article XX(h) GATT, specifically devoted to commodity agreements. Quotas, however, are of little use in terms of reducing the dependency of exporting countries on a few commodities (if not on just one) since they

[373] See recently CD Zimmermann, 'Exchange Rate Misalignment and International Law' (2011) 105 AJIL 423.

[374] R Saner and R Guilherme, 'The International Monetary Fund's Influence on Trade Policies of Low-income Countries: A Valid Undertaking?' (2007) 41 JWT 931–81; RW Stone, 'The Scope of IMF Conditionality' (2008) 62 *International Organization* 589.

[375] For a recent overview, see MG Desta, 'Commodities, International Regulation of Production and Trade', MP EPIL (March 2010 update). For the connected topic of food security, see n 340 above.

discourage import diversification. A second mechanism is market intervention through the purchase of commodities by the administering IOs when the supply rises, thus avoiding a fall in the world price. The problem with market intervention is the management of buffer stocks and the risk of the IOs involved going bankrupt. A third mechanism, prevalent today, is consultation and information exchange. While ICAs are concluded between importing and exporting countries, commodity cartels, such as the Organization of the Petroleum Exporting Countries (OPEC),[376] are concluded between exporting states with a view to controlling production in such a way as to keep prices remunerative.

The question of whether a human right to development (together with others belonging to the 'third-generation' rights category, such as the rights to peace and to a healthy environment)[377] is now part of international law is much debated.[378] In 1986 the UN General Assembly adopted the Declaration on the Right to Development,[379] first recognized in 1981 in Article 22 ACHPR as an individual and collective right, and later reaffirmed by Principle 3 of the 1992 Rio Environment and Development Declaration,[380] Article 10 of the 1993 Vienna Declaration and Programme of Action,[381] and Article 23 of the 2007 Declaration on the Rights of Indigenous Peoples.[382] Article 1(1) of the UN Declaration defines the right to development as 'an inalienable human right' by virtue of which 'every human person and all peoples' are entitled to participate in, contribute to, and enjoy economic, social, cultural and political development, in which all human rights and fundamental freedoms can be fully realized. Articles 3(1) and 4(1) impose on states 'the primary responsibility for the creation of national and international conditions favourable to the realization of the right to development' and 'the duty to take steps, individually and collectively' to formulate international development policies with a view to facilitating the full realization of the right to development. As is apparent, the Declaration, which was adopted with the contrary vote of the United States and eight abstentions from developed states, is rather indeterminate; moreover, it is non-binding and hardly reflects customary international law. Grave uncertainties remain as to who has the right (whether individuals or people, or both), what is the conduct required, and who is required (whether only developed states or also developing states) to take action. The key question is about 'human' and 'sustainable' development, ie about development which is not confined simply to *more wealth* for the *present* generation only.[383]

The measures taken in favour of developing countries are often viewed as 'humanitarian'. However, the key problem of development is global distributive justice and considerations of humanity are to be kept distinct from this. There is an industry of assistance to developing countries which in the name of humanity widens the gap and worsens distributive justice. The wealthier obviously need the poor and are inclined to assist them to the extent that the latter remain poorer and purchase the products and

376 See <http://www.opec.org/home>.

377 See section A (4)(a) below.

378 See R Sarkar, *International Development Law: Rule of Law, Human Rights, and Global Finance* (Oxford: OUP, 2009).

379 UNGA Res 41/128 of 4 December 1986, 'Declaration on the Right to Development', GAOR 41st Session, Supp 53, 186.

380 UN Conference on Environment and Development, 'Rio Declaration on Environment and Development' of 14 June 1992, UN Doc A/CONF.151/26/Rev 1 vol I, 3.

381 UN World Conference on Human Rights, 'Vienna Declaration and Programme of Action' of 25 June 1993, IUN Doc A/CONF.157/23.

382 UNGA Declaration on the Rights of Indigenous Peoples of 13 September 2007, UN Doc A/Res/61/295.

383 On sustainable development, see section A (4) below.

services of the North. Unsurprisingly, the wealthier show no sign of being prepared to become less wealthy in order to reduce the gap with the poorer and improve distributive justice. Rather, they accept the granting of aid to the poorer provided that this will make them wealthier.[384] As a result, to the surprise of some observers, distributive injustice increases at the same pace as humanitarian aid.[385] The very idea of 'development' takes on the standard of the wealthier as a yardstick, beginning with the wealth standard itself,[386] and instils a sense of transcendent 'never-ending lack' and dependence while promising salvation by duly meeting the standards required.[387] There is room for a struggle in favour of improving distributive justice rather than promoting crowd-pleasing humanitarian aid and of shaping international law accordingly.

(d) Foreign investment

The question of whether foreign investment has positive or negative effects on the wealth and development of the host state, as well as in the economy of the home state of the investor, is contentious. Positive effects of direct investment in host states include growing levels of employment, internal revenue, and national wealth, and an improvement in technological standards due to the transfer of technology and know-how (when the foreign investor is technologically more advanced than local investors) as well as in labour conditions and product quality. As to adverse effects, foreign investment may weaken the national identity of the host state (due to being progressively taken over by a standardized world culture) and of local enterprises (which are likely to be incapable of competing with global MNEs), as well as, at least in the weaker host states, a strong dependence of their political power on foreign investors and the exploitation of labour (including forms of slavery), and damage to the environment. Opposite effects may be produced, on the other hand, in the home state of the investor, such as a fall in employment, demand, internal revenue, and a worsening of long-term technological advancement. In turn, positive effects for the home state include access to foreign markets and new opportunities for the export of national products, which raise foreign demand, hence national supply, employment, and internal revenue. Portfolio investment, for its part, can increase the supply of foreign currency in the host state, hence demand, employment, and national production, but can also have adverse effects when it is short-term and purely speculative, in which case the availability of money can wane abruptly. The net effect in the host state and in the home state is extremely difficult to assess and varies with the state, the circumstances, the time, and other factors. Generally, while positive effects benefit certain groups in the home and/or in the host state, adverse effects hit others in the same state, and internal conflicts arise between different groups. The effects of foreign direct investment (FDI) on development are also uncertain. While there is little doubt that FDI may have positive short-term

[384] See H-J Chang, *Bad Samaritans: The Guilty Secrets of Rich Nations and the Threat to Global Prosperity* (London: Business Books, 2007) 15–16, asking 'Why don't the rich countries recommend to today's developing countries the [protectionist] strategies that served them so well?' in the past, and claiming that developed countries have kicked away the ladder they have climbed up.

[385] For the distinction, see B Barry, 'Humanity and Justice in Global Perspective' (1982) 24 *Nomos* 219–52; K-C Tan, *Justice Without Borders: Cosmopolitanism, Nationalism and Patriotism* (Cambridge: CUP, 2004) 21–9.

[386] For a critique from the TWAIL perspective, see Rajagopal (n 199 above) 24–36, 216–30. More recently, see S Pahuja, *Decolonising International Law: Development, Economic Growth and the Politics of Universality* (Cambridge: CUP, 2011).

[387] For the Christian metaphysics of development, see JL Beard, *The Political Economy of Desire: International Law, Development and the Nation State* (Oxon: Routledge-Cavendish, 2006).

(especially spill-over) developmental effects driven by foreign levels of productivity, still development rests on long-term national productive capabilities which may be impaired by the *medio tempore* throwing out of the market of the less competitive local enterprises by MNEs and the mobility of MNEs themselves.[388]

Foreign investment is governed by the rules of customary international law applicable to the treatment of aliens and their property. It was disputed in the past whether the standard to be ensured was 'national' (treating aliens not less favourably than nationals) or 'international' (guaranteeing a minimum below which the host state was not allowed to go whatever the standard applied to its citizens). It seems that by the end of the twentieth century the international standard prevailed. This standard requires that investors be recognized as having legal personality and some basic rights, including the right to a fair trial and to equality before the law in domestic courts, the right to compensation in case of expropriation or nationalization, and a prohibition against the confiscation of foreign property without a public goal or with discrimination. Human rights rules may apply also to aliens, notably the right to property in cases where this right is set out in an applicable treaty.[389]

Especially since the end of the Cold War, most foreign investment has been governed by an impressive number of bilateral investment treaties (BITs). Their precursors are the treaties of friendship, commerce and navigation (FCN) concluded since the end of the eighteenth century, which also regulated investment to some extent and may still apply today in the absence of a specific treaty.[390] The first BIT was concluded in 1959 between Germany and Pakistan, and since then some 2,500 BITs have been entered into between developed and developing states or between developed states. They typically define what is meant by 'investment' and establish a legal regime which includes 'fair and equitable' treatment, prohibits discrimination among investors, regulates expropriations and currency flows, and provides for the recourse to arbitral procedures in case a dispute arises between the investor and the host state. Similar provisions are also contained in regional multilateral treaties such as NAFTA,[391] CAFTA,[392] and the Energy Charter.[393]

A general multilateral treaty governing foreign investment, let alone an ad hoc international organization, is lacking. The draft of a Multilateral Agreement on Investment (MAE), developed in the period 1995–98, failed for a variety of reasons including criticisms from developing countries and NGOs.[394] Provisions on particular aspects of foreign investment are found in the WTO framework, such as TRIMS,[395] GATS,[396] and TRIPS.[397] TRIMs applies to investment related to trade, stipulating national

[388] For the view (against neo-liberals) that FDI should follow growth and not the other way round, see Chang (n 384 above) 99.

[389] cf eg Art 1 of Protocol No 1 additional to ECHR.

[390] See ICJ Chamber, *Case concerning Elettronica Sicula SpA (ELSI) (United States v Italy)* Judgment of 20 July 1989, [1989] ICJ Rep 15.

[391] North American Free Trade Agreement (adopted 17 December 1992, entered into force 1 January 1994), (1993) 32 ILM 289.

[392] Central America Free Trade Agreement (CAFTA) (done 5 August 2004), at <http://www.ustr.gov/trade-agreements/free-trade-agreements/cafta-dr-dominican-republic-central-america-fta/final-text>.

[393] Energy Charter Treaty (signed 17 December 1994, entered into force 16 April 1998) [1994] OJ L380/24.

[394] See eg SJ Canner, 'The Multilateral Agreement on Investment' (1998) 31 Corn ILJ 657.

[395] Agreement on Trade-Related Investment Measures (signed 1 April 1995, entered into force 1 January 1995) 1868 UNTS 186.

[396] General Agreement on Trade in Services (adopted 15 April 1994, entered into force 1 January 1995) 1869 UNTS 183.

[397] Agreement on Trade-Related Aspects of Intellectual Property Rights, Including Trade in Counterfeit Goods (signed 15 April 1994, entered into force 1 January 1995) 1869 UNTS 299.

treatment, non-discrimination, and a ban on quantitative restrictions. GATS applies to the 'commercial presence' abroad, this being a foreign investment linked to the exchange of services, contemplating the most-favoured-nation treatment, access to the market, and (as part of specific commitments) national treatment. TRIPS protects foreign investors' intellectual property rights. In the IBRD framework, ICSID operates for the settlement of disputes between states and investors by way of conciliation or arbitration according to pre-existing rules of procedure,[398] while MIGA insures foreign investment in developing countries against non-commercial risks, such as restrictions on currency flows, expropriations, non-performance of contract, and war.[399]

Against this inter-state background, investors also generally conclude contracts with the host state, typically concerning the building of infrastructure or the exploitation of raw materials, such as oil extraction. These contracts generally provide for obligations on the investor (basically the obligation to perform what is established in the contract) and obligations on the state (such as the obligation to provide the authorizations necessary to the performance of the contract, a guarantee against expropriation and nationalization, the stabilization of national legislation, and a commitment not to change its legislation). The question of whether these contracts are 'treaties' governed by international law is disputed. In the *Anglo-Iranian Oil Company* Judgment the ICJ held that a contract of concession between a UK company and Iran was not a source of international law.[400] The opposite view was taken in the 1977 *Texaco* Arbitral Award.[401] In addition, the relationship between contracts and applicable treaties gives rise to doubts.

The key problem with foreign investment is how to reconcile the economic sovereignty of the host state with the protection of the investment. The latter is possible only when the host state admits the investor and its property within its borders. The host state's freedom to admit foreign investors is formally unbound, except for treaty limitations. Once admitted, investors are subject to the local fiscal, social, labour, and environmental legislation. Local laws generally ensure the stability of the investment and profits, so as to attract investors, as well as requirements that magnify positive effects (such as the reinvestment of profit in the host state) and limit adverse effects (often through fiscal measures). However, the investor is often an MNE that is more powerful than the host state. The investor can thus have a massive impact on the economy, law, society, and cultural identity of the host state. MNEs can move to another state in search of higher profits from local legislation which allows them a greater freedom in dealing with workers and the environment (thus giving rise to social and environmental dumping) or because the host state is unwilling or unable to enforce the law, even as a result of the investor's pressure. Investors may thus easily behave in ways which clash with international standards by simply moving to states in which such conduct is lawful (or unlawful but tolerated) and the state is free from international obligations (or is actually bound by international obligations, but tolerates or even encourages violations of these). On the other hand, foreign investment takes place because there are convergent interests between the host state and the foreign investor, for the former in terms of capital inflows and technological innovation, and for the

[398] Convention on the Settlement of Investment Disputes between States and Nationals of Other States (opened for signature 18 March 1965, entered into force 14 October 1966) 575 UNTS 159.

[399] Convention establishing the Multilateral Investment Guarantee Agency (done 11 October 1985, entered into force 12 April 1988) 1508 UNTS 99.

[400] ICJ, *Anglo-Iranian Oil Co Case* (*United Kingdom v Iran*) *(Preliminary Objection)* Judgment of 22 July 1952, [1952] ICJ Rep 93, 112.

[401] Sole Arbitrator Dupuy, *Texaco Overseas Petroleum Co/California Asiatic Oil Co v Government of the Libyan Arab Republic* Award on the Merits of 19 January 1977, (1979) 53 ILR 422, para 47.

latter in the making of profit. This problem contemplates a series of sub-problems, including the traditional question of the admissibility of expropriations and nationalizations, non-discrimination, access to market, and protection from national legislation depreciating the worth of the investment.

Foreign investment is perhaps an area of international law which is more susceptible of enforcement. The parties, notably the investor, normally have the right to submit disputes to arbitration and are bound by the ensuing award without the intercession of the home state or the exhaustion of domestic remedies. This differs from what is required by the rules on the treatment of aliens or human rights, which similarly provide for the functioning of international courts delivering binding decisions. Unlike investment treaties, however, human rights treaties allow petitions against a state by its own nationals. In cases where the dispute is submitted to ICSID the award is to be recognized as binding and pecuniary obligations are to be enforced like final domestic judgments in all states parties to the ICSID Convention under Article 54(1), although under Article 55 the obligation to enforce the award does not affect the immunity from execution that the defendant state may enjoy under international law.[402]

(e) State debt and bankruptcy

Free and instant capital outflows, competition with powerful MNEs, increases in public debt to sustain governmental services together with financial global crises with devastating recessive effects, ageing populations and falling of the birthrates (with the ensuing strain on pension schemes), tax evasion and recourse to tax havens, as well as widespread corruption, increasingly combine to render statehood prone to bankruptcy. Politics seems more and more involved in individual long-term gains and short-term marketing strategies to seize power, just like the rest of human life informed by the present 'post-ideological' economic global system, with little or no interest at all in the well-being of the communities (and notably of the most vulnerable) who grant them power. The global states system appears to be going adrift, incapable of behaving 'responsibly' and sustaining collective life and genuine protection of the other, especially the weak. Massive state debt and the risk of bankruptcy, especially in the leading economies, threatens the global states system (including its ability to protect human rights) far more than 'old-style' terrorism, whether local or global, and, indeed, one should ask if it should be considered for inclusion in the legal concept of international terrorism (and/or international crimes) as an extraordinarily serious attack on the well-being of billions of people on earth.

There are no international law rules, whether customary international law or treaty law, governing state bankruptcy as such, ie the lasting failure of a state to comply with its financial obligations, in particular to repay its debt.[403] Nor is there any international mechanism entrusted to investigate the financial reliability of a state and to authoritatively declare its state of bankruptcy. While prompt coercive solutions have been

[402] See Ch 6 above, n 680 and accompanying text.

[403] See M Waibel, *Sovereign Defaults Before International Courts and Tribunals* (Cambridge: CUP, 2011); MC Malaguti, 'Sovereign Insolvency and International Legal Order' (2009) 11 ICLR 307. For the current European sovereign debt crisis, see all the references cited at <http://en.wikipedia.org/wiki/European_sovereign_debt_crisis>. See further, German Constitutional Court, Judgment of 6 September 2011, rejecting a series of lawsuits aimed at blocking the participation of Germany in emergency loan packages, in particular EU Greek and Irish bail-outs, provided that the government obtained the approval of parliament's budget committee before granting such aid, Press release in English at <http://www.bundesverfassungsgericht.de/en/press/bvg11-055en.html>.

rapidly devised against 'failed' (in fact weak) states, no effective rules have been adopted against the insolvency of developed states, although their breaking down is much more disruptive for the survival of large portions of humanity. Private rating agencies are influential, whereas third states' assessments may amount to unlawful intervention in the domestic affairs of the state involved. The number and weight of financial duties which the state fails to service (or those possibly leading to a large-scale domino effect as a result, inter alia, of 'cross-default clauses', whereby failure to service a debt in time triggers maturity of other bonds) in order for it to be considered internationally bankrupt is uncertain, except perhaps when there is no absolute doubt that the state is unable to escape from its insolvency by its own effort. There is actually no 'bankrupt statehood' status in international law. What is known as 'state failure', apart from its own uncertainties, is not necessarily coincident with financial bankruptcy. Failed states may easily be bankrupt, but bankrupt states may well not be (yet at least) failed or failing. It has been suggested that the term 'state insolvency' means the existence of formal proceedings to deal with state bankruptcy at international level, despite the fact that there is no formal international procedure to address state bankruptcy similar to those existing in domestic legal systems, if only because states cannot be dissolved by authority and liquidated.[404] Even assuming that such a procedure existed, however, neither its initiation nor its results could presumably be imposed on the debtor state without its consent, given the whole structure of international law as it stands. In any event, a bankrupt state is likely to be incapable of complying with basic human rights (of any sort, given the costs of all rights, whether civil and political or economic, social, and cultural) and other rules of international law. The inability to comply with basic human rights has been regarded as a threshold marking the 'bankruptcy' or 'severe crisis' level of statehood.

Financial obligations may be owed by the state to other states, IOs, or private actors (especially banks and bondholders). Failure to comply with international financial obligations owed to other states or IOs amounts to a breach thereof and engages international responsibility. Failure to comply with private law obligations, by contrast, gives rise to private law responsibility of the state. While unwillingness to comply ('opportunistic default') is generally unlawful, it is debated whether (at both the private law and international level) necessity may be invoked to justify the inability to comply. The state of necessity operates as a justification of an internationally unlawful act according to Article 25 ILC Article on State Responsibility in state-to-state relations.[405] In the 1912 *Indemnité russe* Award the Arbitral Tribunal held that the Ottoman Empire was entitled in the abstract to invoke its financial distress (as a case of *force majeure* rather than necessity) against a Russian claim for interest payments due under sovereign bonds given to Russian citizens,[406] confirmed by the PCIJ in the 1939 *Socobel* Judgment.[407] The ILC held that a severe economic crisis may cause a state of necessity under the terms of Article 25.[408] The question is whether it operates as such also when a state is no longer able or willing to repay the debt towards private subjects, such as private banks, under private law contracts. A case in point is the Argentine Debt Crisis in late 2001. Many

[404] A Mugasha, 'Solutions for Developing-Country External Debt: Insolvency or Forgiveness?' (2007) 13 LBRA 859, 882.

[405] See n 82 above.

[406] Arbitral Tribunal, *Affaire de l'indemnité russe (Russia v Turkey)* Award of 11 November 1912, 11 RIAA 421, 443.

[407] PCIJ, *Société Commerciale de Belgique* Judgment of 15 June 1939, PCIJ Series A/B No 78, 177–8.

[408] UN ILC, (1980) II UN YBILC, part 1, 22–3, 50–1; part 2, 36–7.

legal proceedings have been initiated in various countries, with different outcomes. In the 2005 *Borri* Judgment the Italian Court of Cassation accorded Argentina sovereign immunity assuming that the issuance of the bonds was an act performed *jure imperii*, observing that the human rights of the Argentine people had to be balanced against the loss of the Italian creditor.[409] Two ICSID Tribunals excluded the invocability of the state of necessity on grounds that Argentina had contributed to the crisis,[410] while another held the opposite view with regard to the period from 1 December 2001 to 26 April 2003.[411] Lately, in the 2011 *Abaclat* Decision an ICSID Arbitral Tribunal unprecedentedly found, Arbitrator Abi-Saab dissenting, for its jurisdiction to hear an investment treaty claim (alleging breach of the 1990 Italy–Argentina BIT) brought by a class of 60,000 holders of defaulted Argentine debt, admitting mass proceedings in the silence of the BIT and thus allowing the bondholders' claims to proceed to the merits with Argentina likely to re-invoke necessity.[412] In the 2007 *R* Judgment the German Federal Constitutional Court excluded, Judge Lübbe-Wolff dissenting, the invocability of the state of necessity in private law contract relationships governed by German law failing both *usus* and *opinio juris* in favour of the extension to such relations of the rule applying in inter-state relations.[413] In any case, even admitting the necessity objection, it would only temporarily suspend the obligation to service the debt.

Debt relief or remission requires the consent of both the debtor state and its creditors, typically to be realized through a treaty, while a moratorium provides the debtor state with the (unilateral or agreed-upon) power or duty to suspend temporarily its payment in cases where it can invoke a state of necessity. Relief implies a renegotiation of the debt through conversion into another type of debt or a postponement of the loan maturity. States cannot unilaterally relieve themselves of their debt, except perhaps for 'odious debts' inherited from predecessors,[414] nor can creditors do so since relief may adversely affect the future creditworthiness and ratings of the debtor state against its will. Debt relief or reduction is envisaged by the 'Heavily Indebted Poor Countries Initiative' (HIPC), launched as early as 1996 by the World Bank Group and endorsed by the G8 since 1999. In order to qualify for HIPC debt relief the debtor state must fall within the scope of the International Development Association (IDA) and be eligible

[409] Italian Court of Cassation, *Borri v Argentine Republic* Judgment of 27 May 2005 No 6532, ILDC 296 (IT 2005).

[410] ICSID Arbitral Tribunal, *CMS Gas Transmission Co v Republic of Argentina* Award of 12 May 2005, Case No ARB/01/8, (2005) 44 ILM 1205, paras 304–394; *Enron Corp and Ponderosa Assets, LP v Argentine Republic* Award of 22 May 2007, Case No ARB/01/3, at <http://ita.law.uvic.ca/documents/Enron-Award.pdf>, paras 288–345.

[411] ICSID Arbitral Tribunal, *LG&E Energy Corp, LG&E Capital Corp and LG&E International Inc v Republic of Argentina* Award of 3 October 2006, Case No ARB/02/1, (2007) 46 ILM 40, paras 201–266.

[412] ICSID Arbitral Trbunal, *Abaclat et al (Case formerly known as Giovanna and Beccara et al) v Argentine Republic* Decision on Jurisdiction and Admissibility of 4 August 2001, Case No ARB/07/5, at <http://italaw.com/documents/AbaclatDecisiononJurisdiction.pdf>. For the opposite view by a domestic court, see US Supreme Court, *Stolt-Nielsen SA v AnimalFeeds International Corp*, Judgment of 27 April 2010, 130 S Ct 1758 (2010) at 1776, holding that 'the differences between bilateral and class-action arbitration are too great for arbitrators to presume . . . that the parties' mere silence on the issue . . . constitutes consent to resolve their disputes in class proceedings', at <http://www.law.cornell.edu/supct/html/08-1198.ZO.html#10>. On 15 September 2011, ICSID suspended the proceeding on the merits in response to Argentina's proposal for disqualification of the two arbitrators who favoured the tribunal's decision upholding jurisdiction. On 21 December 2011, after the third dissenting arbitrators had resigned, the proposal for disqualification of two arbitrators was declined.

[413] German Constitutional Court, *K* Judgment of 8 May 2007, 117 BVerfGE 124.

[414] S Ludington and M Gulati, 'A Convenient Untruth: Fact and Fantasy in the Doctrine of Odious Debts' (2007–08) 48 Virg JIL 595.

for the IMF's 'Poverty Reduction and Growth Facility' (PRGF), reserved to states with a very low per capita income; its debt burden must be too high for conventional debt-restructuring mechanisms to apply; and the state debtor must seriously endeavour to bring about political and economic reform, as provided for by the IMF and the IDA, and present a Poverty Reduction Strategy Paper (PRSP). As of November 2011, forty states have been listed in the HIPC. In 2005 the G8 introduced the 'Multilateral Debt Relief Initiative' (MDRI), limited, unlike HIPC, to state-to-state debt.[415] Although they do not require beneficiary states to be bankrupt, these initiatives have been regarded as international 'insolvency regimes'.[416] However, debt remission may be a (temporary) solution when the debt is state-to-state, but debt is frequently owed to private subjects. Debt restructuring, ie conversion into new loans, is negotiated in the London Club with private banks and in the Paris Club with states, and processed in the IMF through an initial 'letter of intent' aimed at obtaining a 'condition precedent'. However, even restructuring cannot avoid the vicious circle of debt. In 2002 the IMF launched the 'Sovereign Debt Restructuring Mechanism' (SDRM), a procedure for the international management of state debt addressed, unlike HIPC, to all bankrupt countries and binding on both debtor and creditor states, and possibly also on non-state creditors.[417] The project, however, failed due to the resistance of several states, including the United States.

New market-orientated mechanisms have been introduced in the past few decades to relieve both the debt overhang of developing countries and the financial exposure of commercial banks, notably debt-equity swaps, ie debt-for-equity conversions, but with little success.[418]

Increasing levels of public debt make states, including Western states, less capable of providing services to their own citizens, let alone aid to poorer peoples. There can hardly be adequate respect for human rights in states which, even where they are willing to observe them, cannot simply afford it. The human rights discourse translates into a business for survival at best. States are forced to privatize services and to depend on global MNEs for their own survival. The spectre of a global default, with costs especially spreading to the most vulnerable, seems to be around the corner and there is little sign of either adequate control by any institution or of any will to make and abide by effective global rules. Hopes in wise decisions from above are difficult to cherish. It is simply in the nature of the things that either people responsibly push decision-makers, both public and private, to more satisfactory solutions or humanity can only expect further global crises and disasters striking the vulnerable far more than any others.

(4) Environment

If the wealthy become wealthier at a higher speed than the poor become less poor, and if the system encourages a global race to the bottom, not only is the problem of poverty simply exacerbated to the advantage of the wealthy, except for a number of people who

[415] For the status of implementation, impact, and costs of the HIPC Initiative and the MDRI as of 14 September 2010, see <http://www.imf.org/external/np/pp/eng/2010/091410.pdf>.

[416] JA Kämmerer, 'State Bankruptcy', MP EPIL (September 2009 update) para 15.

[417] IMF, 'The Design of the Sovereign Debt Restructuring Mechanism—Further Considerations', 27 November 2002, at <http://www.imf.org/external/np/pdr/sdrm/2002/112702.pdf>.

[418] SM Wallenstein and JR Silkenat, 'Investment Funds and Dept-Equity Swaps: Broadening the Base of a New Financial Tool' (1988–89) 12 Ford ILJ 8.

succeed in overtaking the minimum threshold of survival, but the trend also leads to the progressive disruption of the 'human house' through the depletion of the environment in which all human beings spend their lives. The protection of the environment from massive degradation is today key to human survival and well-being, involving, inter alia, the responsibility of present generations for future generations, ie 'sustainable development'.[419] This emergency has often been underscored by both international and national courts, as is the case with the ICJ in the 1996 *Nuclear Weapons* Advisory Opinion,[420] in the 1997 *Gabčíkovo-Nagymaros* Judgment[421] and in the 2010 *Pulp Mills* Judgment,[422] as well as with the Supreme Court of the Philippines, to name just one significant national case, in the 1993 *Minors Oposa* Judgment.[423] In its 1996 Draft Articles on State Responsibility, the ILC included among 'international crimes' of states 'a serious breach of an international obligation of essential importance for the safeguarding and preservation of the human environment, such as those prohibiting massive pollution of the atmosphere or of the seas'.[424] This section examines first the protection of individuals from pollution in the context of human rights, then the rules of neighbouring states which govern cross-border pollution and a number of guiding principles of global environmental policy which have not yet hardened into general international law, and finally the major treaties on global ecological degradation. It argues that existing rules are notable for their ineffectiveness, which is hardly surprising given the structure of the current world economic system and the political background supporting it.

(a) Right to a healthy environment

A right to a healthy environment—first hinted at in Principle 1 of the 1972 Stockholm Declaration[425]—is expressly mentioned only in Article 24 ACHPR, as a collective right attributed to 'all peoples' and (with only a limited procedural meaning) in the preamble to the 1998 Aarhus Convention.[426] In the 2001 *Ogoniland* Report the ACommHR found that Nigeria had breached, inter alia, Article 24 towards the Ogoni people as a result of the government's failure to prevent oil pollution and ecological degradation.[427]

Other human rights treaties, such as the ECHR, being silent on the matter, have been interpreted in such a way that the right to private life, or to life, implies a positive obligation of the states parties to take all reasonable and appropriate measures to secure a healthy environment, including avoiding failure to regulate private industry and to enforce environmental laws. For instance, the ECtHR, while taking note that 'Neither

[419] World Commission on Environment and Development, *Our Common Future* (Oxford: OUP, 1987) (Brundtland Report) 43, defining sustainable development as 'development that meets the needs of the present without compromising the ability of future generations to meet their own needs'.

[420] ICJ, *Legality of the Threat or Use of Nuclear Weapons* (n 53 above) para 29.

[421] ICJ, *Gabčíkovo-Nagymaros Project (Hungary/Slovakia)* Judgment of 25 September 1997, [1997] ICJ Rep 7, paras 53, 140.

[422] ICJ, *Case concerning Pulp Mills on the River Uruguay (Argentina v Uruguay)* Judgment of 20 April 2010, at <http://www.icj-cij.org/docket/files/135/15877.pdf>, paras 75–76.

[423] Supreme Court of the Philippines, *Oposa et al v Fulgencio S Factoran, Jr et al* Judgment of 30 July 1993, at <http://www.elaw.org/node/1343>, para 20.

[424] UN LLC, 'Draft Articles on State Responsibility', GAOR (1996) 51st Session Supp 10, 125.

[425] See n 452 below.

[426] Convention on Access to Information, Public Participation in Decision-Making and Access to Justice in Environmental Matters (done 25 June 1998, entered into force 30 October 2001) 2161 UNTS 447.

[427] ACommHPR, *The Social and Economic Rights Action Center* (n 344 above) para 52.

Article 8 nor any of the other Articles of the [European] Convention are specifically designed to provide general protection of the environment as such',[428] insisted that 'severe environmental pollution may affect individuals' well-being and prevent them from enjoying their homes in such a way as to affect their private and family life adversely, without, however, seriously endangering their health'.[429] In the Court's view, however, 'the adverse effects of environmental pollution must attain a certain minimum level if they are to fall within the scope of Article 8' concerning the right to private life.[430] The Court has systematically balanced the right to private property under Article 1 Protocol (I) ECHR against the restricting measures adopted in pursuit of the public interest in the protection of the environment,[431] including the collective economic interest in development,[432] some form of environmental impact assessment before making decisions capable of infringing individuals' rights,[433] and the establishment of an effective and accessible procedure to provide those involved with relevant information[434] or directly to provide essential information.[435] It has found no violation of the ECHR where a state has taken all measures in its power to avoid a risk to the life, private life, health, or property of the individuals within its jurisdiction.[436]

A similar approach has also been taken by other human rights monitoring bodies, including the UNHRC[437] and the IACtHR,[438] concerning in particular threats to the ability of indigenous peoples and other minorities to enjoy their own way of life and culture.[439] Both the IACommHR and the UNHRC have excluded, however, that the

[428] ECtHR, *Kyrtatos v Greece* Judgment of 22 May 2003, App 41666/98, ECtHR Rep 2003-VI 257, (2005) 40 EHRR 390, para 52.

[429] ECtHR, *López Ostra v Spain* Judgment of 9 December 1994, App 16798/90, Series A No 303-C, (1995) 20 EHRR 277, para 51; *Guerra et al v Italy* Judgment of 9 February 1998, App 14967/89, ECtHR Rep 1998-I 210, (1998) 26 EHRR 357, paras 57 and 60; *Öneryildiz v Turkey* Judgment of 30 November 2004 [GC], App 48939/99, ECtHR Rep 2004-XII 79, (2005) 41 EHRR 325, paras 90; *Taskin v Turkey* Judgment of 10 November 2004, App 46117/99, ECtHR Rep 2004-X 179, (2006) 42 EHRR 1127, paras 113, 119.

[430] ECtHR, *Fadeyeva v Russia* Judgment of 9 June 2005, App 55723/00, ECtHR Rep 2005-IV 255, (2007) 45 EHRR 295, para 69.

[431] ECtHR, *Fredin v Sweden* Judgment of 18 February 1991, App 12033/86, Series A No 192, (1991) 13 EHRR 784, para 54; *Pine Valley Developments Ltd et al v Ireland* Judgment of 29 November 1991, App 12742/87, Series A No 222, (1992) 14 EHRR 319, paras 57–59; *Matos e Silva, Lda et al v Portugal* Judgment of 16 September 1996, App 15777/89, ECtHR Rep 1996-IV 1092, para 92; *Katsoulis et al v Greece* Judgment of 8 July 2004, App 66742/01, paras 30–35.

[432] ECtHR, *Hatton v United Kingdom* Judgment of 8 July 2003 [GC], App 36022/97, (2003) 37 EHRR 611, para 126.

[433] ECtHR, *Taskin v Turkey* (n 429 above) para 119.

[434] ECtHR, *McGinley and Egan v United Kingdom* Judgment of 9 June 1998, App 23414/94, ECtHR Rep 1998-III 1334, (1999) 27 EHRR 1, paras 97, 101.

[435] ECtHR, *Guerra et al v Italy* (n 429 above) para 60.

[436] ECtHR, *LCB v United Kingdom* Judgment of 9 June 1998, App 23413/94, ECtHR Rep 1998-III 1390, (1998) 27 EHRR 212, para 36.

[437] UNHRC, *Bordes et al v France* Views of 22 July 1996, Comm No 645/1995, GAOR 51st Session, Supp 40, vol 2, 267, concluding, however, that there was no evidence of serious risk to life deriving from French nuclear tests in the Pacific.

[438] IACtHR, *Mayagna (Sumo) Awas Tingni Community v Nicaragua* Judgment of 31 August 2001, IACtHR Series C No 79, paras 106–114.

[439] UNHRC, *Ominayak, Chief of the Lubicon Lake Band v Canada* Views of 26 March 1990, Comm No 167/1984, GAOR 45th Session, Supp 40, vol 2, 1, para 32.2; *Länsman et al v Finland* Views of 26 October 1994, Comm No 511/1992, GAOR 50th Session, Supp 40, vol 2, 66, paras 9.4, 9.5; *Mahuika et al v New Zealand* Views of 27 October 2000, Comm No 547/1993, GAOR 56th Session, Supp 40, vol 2, 11, para 9.8; IACommHR, *Yanomami Indians v Brazil* Report of 5 March 1985 No 12/85, Case No 7615, OEA/Ser L/V/II.66 doc.10 Rev 1 (1984–85) 24, paras 7, 10(d); IACommHR, *Maya Indigenous Community of the Toledo District v Belize* Case 12.053, Report of 12 October 2004, No 40/04 OEA/Ser.L/V/II.122 Doc. 5 rev 1, vol 2 (2004) 727, paras 150, 154–155.

human rights set out in the ACHR and in the UN Covenants, respectively, apply when their holders are not sufficiently affected by environmental loss.[440]

(b) Transboundary pollution

It was a commonplace in the past that states were allowed to use their territory as they pleased, except for the prohibition against using their territory or allowing private persons to use it in such a way as to cause cross-border damage (*sic utere tuo ut alienum non laedas*). In recent decades this general principle has been extended to damages deriving from environmental pollution. As famously held in the 1941 *Trail Smelter* Award:

> ... under the principles of international law ... no State has the right to use or permit the use of its territory in such a manner as to cause injury by fumes in or to the territory of another or the properties or persons therein, when the case is of serious consequence and the injury is established by clear and convincing evidence.[441]

Similar dicta had already been made, in relation to the utilization of international watercourses, by a PCA Arbitral Tribunal in the 1928 *Island of Palmas* Award[442] and by the PCIJ in the 1929 *Oder River Commission* Judgment,[443] despite some isolated attempts veering in the opposite direction, such as the well-known 'Hamron doctrine' enunciated in 1895 in favour of the absolute sovereign power of the United States to use for agricultural purposes within its territory the water of the Rio Grande before the river entered the territory of Mexico.[444] The principle was later restated by the ICJ in general terms in the 1949 *Corfu Channel* Judgment in terms of 'every State's obligation not to allow knowingly its territory to be used for acts contrary to the rights of other States',[445] and, specifically referring to environmental protection, in the 1996 *Nuclear Weapons* Advisory Opinion,[446] in the 1997 *Gabčíkovo-Nagymaros* Judgment,[447] and in the 2010 *Pulp Mills* Judgment,[448] as well as in Article 3 of the 1992 Biodiversity Convention.[449]

Another general international law rule on the protection of the environment which has emerged during the past few decades relates to international cooperation. As held in the 1957 *Lac Lanoux* Award, relating again to the utilization of shared waters and stressing that 'territorial sovereignty ... must bend before all international obligations', neighbouring riparian states have a procedural obligation to consult and to negotiate in good faith an agreement (as opposed to an obligation to reach an agreement) that

[440] IACommHR, *Metropolitan Nature Reserve v Panama* Report of 22 October 2003 No 88/03, Case 11.533, OEA/Ser.L/V/II.118 doc.70 rev 2, vol 1 (2003) 524, para 34; UNHRC, *Brun v France* Views of 18 October 2006, Comm No 1453/2006, GAOR 62nd Session Supp 40, vol 2, 629, para 6.3.

[441] Arbitral Tribunal, *Trail Smelter Case (United States v Canada)* Award of 11 March 1941, 3 RIAA 1905, 1965.

[442] PCA Arbitral Tribunal, *Island of Palmas Case (Netherlands v United States)* Award of 4 April 1928, 2 RIAA 829–71, at 839.

[443] PCIJ, *Territorial Jurisdiction of the International Commission of the River Oder* Judgment of 10 September 1929, PCIJ Series A No 23, at 27.

[444] Moore (n 75 above) vol 1, 654.

[445] ICJ, *Corfu Channel* (n 59 above) 22.

[446] ICJ, *Legality of the Threat or Use of Nuclear Weapons* (n 53 above) para 29, ruling that the principle 'is now part of the corpus of international law relating to the environment'.

[447] ICJ, *Gabčíkovo-Nagymaros Project* (n 421 above) paras 53, 140.

[448] ICJ, *Case concerning Pulp Mills on the River Uruguay* (n 422 above) para 101, holding that 'the principle of prevention, as a customary rule, has its origins in the due diligence that is required of a State in its territory' and reiterating what the Court had already stated in the 2006 Order (ICJ, *Case concerning Pulp Mills on the River Uruguay (Argentina v Uruguay), Provisional Measures* Order of 13 July 2006, [2006] ICJ Rep 113, para 72).

[449] Convention on Biological Diversity (concluded 5 June 1992, entered into force 29 December 1993) 1760 UNTS 79.

reconciles their opposing interests.[450] In the 2010 *Pulp Mills* Judgment the ICJ articulated the treaty relationship between procedural obligations to cooperate and environmental substantive obligations, concluding that Uruguay had violated its treaty procedural obligation to inform the other party to the dispute as necessary to fulfil the customary obligation of prevention.[451] The obligation to cooperate for the reduction of (under way or imminent) transboundary damage to the environment has been inserted in non-binding instruments, such as Principle 21 of the 1971 Stockholm Declaration,[452] Principle 21(d) of the 1982 World Charter for Nature,[453] and Principle 24 of the 1992 Rio Declaration,[454] as well as in treaty provisions. It should be noted that the existence of an international procedural obligation to supply information does not necessarily entail a right of the private victims of cross-border pollution to compensation in the domestic courts of their state. In the 1987 *Contamination of a Garden* Judgment the District Court of Bonn held, in relation to the Chernobyl incident, that general international law provides for an obligation on the state in whose territory the contamination occurred 'to provide other states with information' and that the failure to inform may give rise to an obligation to compensate 'only directly between subjects of international law', ie only between the two states involved.[455]

(c) Guidelines of global policy

While there is enough evidence and agreement that today the two rules referred to above are part of general international law, much less evidence exists when it comes to other 'principles'—the term is often used to exclude the notion that they reflect true 'rules', although they have some normative implications—embodied in multilateral environmental agreements (MEAs) and soft law instruments, namely, sustainable development, common but differentiated responsibilities, a precautionary approach, and the 'polluter pays'. These principles may (indeed should) serve as a guidance to specify present and future rules. They are directives of global policy and are not per se legally binding as part of general international law.

The sustainable development concept, originated in the 1970s, was set out, inter alia, in Principles 3 and 4 Rio Declaration. It goes hand in hand with the principle of state inter- and intra-generational responsibility. It also has at its core the notion of human development whereby, in the words of Principle 1 Rio Declaration: 'Human beings are at the centre of concerns for sustainable development'. However, there is no certainty about how developmental and environmental needs should be balanced one against the

[450] Arbitral Tribunal, *Affaire du lac Lanoux (Espagne, France)* Award of 16 November 1957, 12 RIAA 281, at 306–7, recognizing that states have a right to use their natural resources but have to reconcile it with the conflicting interests of other states. The Tribunal pointed out that it would apply the relevant treaties, but if their interpretation was necessary because of lack of clarity, then it would have turned, inter alia, to the 'rules of common international law' and 'certain rules of customary international law' (para 2).

[451] ICJ, *Case concerning Pulp Mills on the River Uruguay* (n 422 above) paras 95, 111.

[452] UN Conference on the Human Environment, 'Stockholm Declaration of the United Nations Conference on the Human Environment' of 16 June 1972, UN Doc A/CONF.48/14/Rev 1, 3.

[453] UNGA Res 37/7 of 28 October 1982, 'World Charter for Nature', GAOR 37th Session Supp 51, 17.

[454] UN Conference on Environment and Development, 'Rio Declaration on Environment and Development' of 14 June 1992, UN Doc A/CONF.151/26/Rev 1, vol I, 3.

[455] District Court of Bonn, *Contamination of a Garden* Judgment of 29 September 1987, (1989) 80 ILR 378, 382. For the question of direct enforceability of treaty obligations, see Ch 6 above, section D (2)(b).

other, nor did the 2002 Johannesburg World Summit on Sustainable Development Report clarify the point.[456] Despite the optimism of some writers,[457] while others have attempted to view it as a 'meta-principle' tantamount to an 'interstitial norm',[458] and despite mention of it in the international case law,[459] it is difficult to see the principle as part of customary international law. The concept of inter-generational responsibility, while no doubt crucial to the protection of totally vulnerable people since they do not even exist yet, is to be seen within the law as it stands, and with a view to the present generation adopting it.

The common but differentiated responsibilities concept is found in Principles 6 and 7 of the Rio Declaration, stating that 'The special situation and needs of developing countries, particularly the least developed and most environmentally vulnerable, shall be given special priority' and that 'In view of the different contributions to global environmental degradation, States have common but differentiated responsibilities'. The principle is not mentioned in most MEAs, an important exception being Article 3 (1) Climate Change Framework Convention.[460] It is, however, variously specified in individual MEA provisions, such as those allowing developed states a grace period before having to comply with the treaty, or providing obligations only for certain states or classes of states, or making implementation by developing states conditional on a transfer of technology and funds, or containing special substantive rules favouring developing states, or finally providing for assistance in case of non-compliance.[461]

The precautionary principle has been adopted in several instruments, including Article V(7) SPS Agreement,[462] although with various meanings.[463] According to Principle 15 of the Rio Declaration 'where there are threats of serious or irreversible damage, lack of full scientific certainty shall not be used as a reason for postponing cost-effective measures to prevent environmental degradation'. While the principle is generally accepted, the details which are needed for its practical implementation remain unclear. In the 1998 *Hormones* Report the WTO Appellate Body cautiously stated that 'Whether it has been widely accepted by [WTO] Members as a principle of *general* or *customary international law* [as the European Communities claimed] appears less than clear' and, at least outside the field of international environmental law, 'still awaits authoritative formulation'.[464] Although increasingly appealed to in various areas of

[456] World Summit on Sustainable Development (Johannesburg Summit), 'Report' (26 August–4 September 2002) UN Doc A/CONF.199/20.

[457] PJ Sands, *Principles of International Environmental Law* (Cambridge: CUP, 2nd edn, 2003) 254.

[458] V Lowe, 'Sustainable Development and Unsustainable Arguments' in AE Boyle and D Freestone (eds), *International Law and Sustainable Development: Past Achievements and Future Challenges* (Oxford: OUP, 1999) 19–37.

[459] See nn 421–3 above.

[460] UN Framework Convention on Climate Change (with Annexes) (adopted 9 May 1992, entered into force 21 March 1994) 1771 UNTS 107.

[461] See CD Stone, 'Common but Differentiated Responsibilities in International Law' (2004) 98 AJIL 276.

[462] Agreement on the Application of Sanitary and Phytosanitary Measures (signed 15 April 1994, entered into force 1 January 1995) 1867 UNTS 493.

[463] A Trouwborst, *Precautionary Rights and Duties of States* (Leiden: Nijhoff, 2006); CE Foster, *Science and the Precautionary Principle in International Courts and Tribunals: Expert Evidence, Burden of Proof and Finality* (Cambridge: CUP, 2011).

[464] WTO, *EC—Measures concerning Meat and Meat Products (Hormones)*, AB Report of 16 January 1998, WT/DS26/AB/R and WT/DS48/AB/R, para 123 (original emphasis). The Appellate Body also considered it 'unnecessary, and probably imprudent . . . in this appeal to take a position on this important, but abstract, question'. It also pointed out that, although reflected in certain SPS Agreement rules, the principle does not operate to justify SPS measures otherwise inconsistent with the SPS Agreement.

international law, including IHL as applied to cyber war and pre-emptive self-defence,[465] there is still only nebulous evidence in the practice as to its content.

The 'polluter pays' principle, originally developed by the OECD in the 1970s and inserted later in several treaties, is defined in Principle 16 Rio Declaration as the principle whereby 'the polluter should, in principle, bear the cost of pollution, with due regard to the public interest and without distorting international trade and investment'. The non-binding character of the Rio Declaration and the term 'should' suggest that the principle was not intended to reflect the law. It has actually been implemented diversely by states, through taxation, charges, the responsibility of polluters for the clean-up costs and restoration after accidents, and liability laws. None of these methods has proved adequate in ensuring that polluters, rather than taxpayers and victims, bear the costs. The ILC 2006 Draft Principles defines the principle in terms of the domestic civil liability of the polluter, not of international responsibility.[466] In the 2004 *Rhine River* Award a PCA Arbitral Tribunal denied that the principle is part of general international law.[467]

(d) Global environmental disruption

The focus on the global environment (notably on global warming, climate change, depletion of the ozone layer, and loss of biodiversity) increased considerably following the end of the Cold War and sparked the conclusion of several MEAs. To what extent they reflect customary international law is the subject of lively debate.

Global warming and climate change is governed by the 1992 Climate Change Convention (FCCC) and the 1997 Kyoto Protocol. Article 1 of the Convention defines climate change as a 'a change of climate which is attributed directly or indirectly to human activity that alters the composition of the global atmosphere and which is in addition to natural climate variability observed over comparable time periods'. The objective of the Convention is to stabilize the amount of greenhouse gases in the atmosphere at a level that could prevent dangerous man-made climate changes. It provides that such a level should be achieved within a time frame sufficient to allow ecosystems to adapt naturally to climate change, to ensure that food production is not threatened and to enable economic development to proceed in a sustainable manner (Article 2). The Convention expressly refers, in exhortatory terms ('should'), to the principles of sustainable development, common but differentiated responsibilities, and precaution (Article 3), and provides for a set of obligations concerning exchange of information and domestic measures aimed at preventing or reducing man-made greenhouse gas emissions (Article 4). Greenhouse gases (GHG) are defined by Article 1 as 'those gaseous constituents of the atmosphere, both natural and anthropogenic, that absorb and re-emit infrared radiation'.[468] Unlike the FCCC, the Kyoto Protocol sets binding targets applied from 2008 to 2012. Under its terms, thirty-seven industrialized

[465] JM Conde Jiminián, 'The Principle of Distinction in Virtual War: Restraints and Precautionary Measures under International Humanitarian Law' (2010) 15 *Tilburg Law Review* 69; E Louka, 'Precautionary Self-defense and the Future of Preemption in International Law', in MH Arsanjani (ed), *Looking to the Future: Essays on International Law in Honor of W. Michael Reisman* (Leiden: Nijhoff, 2011) 951.

[466] UN LLC, 'Draft Principles on Allocation of Loss in the Case of Transboundary Harm Arising out of Hazardous Activities', GAOR (2006) 61st Session Supp 10, 106.

[467] PCA Arbitral Tribunal, *Case concerning the Auditing of Accounts between the Kingdom of the Netherlands and the French Republic pursuant to the Additional Protocol of 25 September 1991 to the Convention on the Protection of the Rhine against Pollution by Chlorides of 3 December 1976 (Netherlands/France)* Award of 12 March 2004, para 103.

[468] UN Framework Convention on Climate Change (with Annexes) (adopted 9 May 1992, entered into force 21 March 1994) 1771 UNTS 107.

countries plus the EU as a whole, listed in Annex I, have pledged to reduce their emissions of greenhouse gases by 5 per cent on average from the 1990 level. The Protocol contemplates three flexibility mechanisms that can be used by 'Annex I countries' to meet their GHG emission limitations by purchasing GHG emission reductions credits from other countries, namely, International Emissions Trading (IET), the Clean Development Mechanism (CDM), and Joint Implementation (JI). IET allows Annex I countries to trade their emissions. CDM and JI generate emission reductions from projects in non-Annex I countries and in Annex I countries, respectively. States are still divided while a new binding treaty replacing the Kyoto Protocol is awaited.[469] The impact of the Protocol has been far from satisfactory. The 'emission trade' approach is not bad in itself, but there can be little hope for a true protection of the global environment solely on commercial grounds.

The protection of the ozone layer in the stratosphere (10 to 15 kilometres above the earth) from depletion is regulated by the 1985 Vienna Convention on the Protection of the Ozone Layer (VCPOL)[470] and the 1987 Montreal Protocol on Substances that Deplete the Ozone Layer (MP).[471] The ozone layer is defined as 'the layer of atmospheric ozone above the planetary boundary layer' (Article 1 VCPOL). The Convention imposes on states an obligation to take 'appropriate measures' to protect human health and the environment against adverse effects resulting or likely to result from human activities which modify or are likely to modify the ozone layer, in particular by cooperating in information exchange and by adopting legislative and administrative measures within their jurisdiction (Article 2). States may take more stringent measures than those required by the Convention. The Montreal Protocol aims at reducing and phasing out Ozone Depleting Substances (ODSs) worldwide according to a time schedule based on periodic scientific assessment in keeping with technical and economic feasibility. Its regime has apparently been quite successful thus far.[472]

While essential to support human life on the planet, the global diversity of natural resources has been depleting alarmingly in recent decades due to over-exploitation (for example, through hunting and unsustainable agricultural practices), over-population, and (air, soil, and water) pollution, including climate change, desertification, and deforestation. Since the second half of the twentieth century, many rules have been adopted, nationally and internationally, to slow down biodiversity loss, but with little success. States retain their sovereignty over the natural resources in their territories and their cooperation is needed in spaces outside national jurisdiction (such as in Antarctica, on the high seas, and in the international seabed area) as well as with regard to straddling and highly migratory species. The 1992 Biodiversity Convention, completed by the Cartagena Protocol on Biosafety,[473] is aimed at 'the conservation of biological

[469] Kyoto Protocol to the United Nations Framework Convention on Climate Change (adopted 10 December 1997, entered into force 16 February 2005), (1998) 37 ILM 32.

[470] Vienna Convention for the Protection of the Ozone Layer (adopted 22 March 1985, entered into force 22 September 1988) 1513 UNTS 324.

[471] Montreal Protocol on Substances that Deplete the Ozone Layer (adopted 16 September 1987, entered into force 1 January 1989) 1522 UNTS 3.

[472] See UNEP 'Synthesis Report of the 2006 Assessments of the Scientific Assessment Panel, the Environmental Effects Assessment Panel and the Technology and Economic Assessment Panel' of 22 February 2007, UN Doc UNEP/OzL.Pro.WG.1/27/3, 3–4, noting that 'The Montreal Protocol is working. There is clear evidence of a decrease in the atmospheric burden of ozone-depleting substances in the lower atmosphere and in the stratosphere; some early signs of the expected stratospheric ozone recovery are also evident.... Assuming continuing compliance with the Protocol, it is estimated that the global ozone levels (60°S–60°N) will recover to the pre–1980 values around 2050'.

[473] Cartagena Protocol on Biosafety to the Convention on Biological Diversity (done 29 January 2000, entered into force 11 September 2003), (2000) 39 ILM 1027.

diversity, the sustainable use of its components and the fair and equitable sharing of the benefits arising out of the utilization of genetic resources' (Article 1), meaning by biodiversity 'the variability among living organisms from all sources including, inter alia, terrestrial, marine and other aquatic ecosystems and the ecological complexes of which they are part; this includes diversity within species, between species and of ecosystems' (Article 2). This definition includes genetic diversity, species diversity, and ecosystem diversity, and is not confined, as in the typical 1970s treaties,[474] to species diversity understood as protection of certain species from threats or extinction. The Convention extends the traditional conservation approach to include sustainable use. It applies, in relation to each state party, in the case of components of biological diversity, not only in areas within its national jurisdiction, but also, in the case of processes and activities carried out under its jurisdiction or control 'regardless of where their effects occur' even beyond the limits of national jurisdiction (Article 4). The states parties have a general obligation to cooperate (Article 5) and to take measures for the conservation and sustainable use of biological diversity 'in accordance with [their] particular conditions and capabilities' (Article 6). In situ conservation is preferred—including the rehabilitation of ecosystems and the eradication of alien species (Article 8)—to ex situ conservation, for example through botanical gardens and zoos (Article 9). Access to genetic resources is left by Article 15 to state negotiations. Article 22 contains a particular conflict clause providing for the prevalence of other treaties, significantly 'except where the exercise of those rights and obligations would cause a serious damage or threat to biological diversity'.

(5) Knowledge

If law depends on what people believe and beliefs depend on what people know, then the reliability of the knowledge available to people is critical to international law.[475] At the same time people expect law to control the media rather than the other way round. The previous analysis has shown that knowledge—understood here in broad terms to include information provided by education systems and the media—is today more critical than ever. Both states and global non-state actors compete to shape people's beliefs. Sellers and purchasers of truths naturally abound, while the ability to detect what is fabricated dwindles. The point is who controls the global media, including the internet, and hence global reality? This section provides a few succinct insights into education and the media by discussing the international law rules on the rights to education and to freedom of expression. It argues that critical knowledge, albeit one of the most valuable of all values, is scarcely promoted and protected by international law.

(a) Education

Education plays a key role in shaping the beliefs of people, and hence has an influence on what they are prepared to struggle for. Whoever controls education also controls, in significant measure, the behaviour of the mass of people and their impact on local and

[474] cf Convention for the Protection of the World Cultural and Natural Heritage (adopted 16 November 1972, entered into force 17 December 1975) 1037 UNTS 151; Convention on Wetlands of International Importance Especially as Waterfowl Habitat (signed 2 February 1971, entered into force 21 December 1975) 996 UNTS 245.

[475] The question here addressed, although connected, is different from the one concerning the communication of international law through the media discussed already (see Ch 4 above, section C).

global affairs. What really matters is not only information, or technical information, but rather the capacity of critical judgment *on* information. Not only are information in itself and critical judgment on information distinct; they may even be opposed when the former is allowed to flow, or more precisely to overflow, and actually impede the latter. Elites and businesses in the education sector have little or no interest at all in people who are capable of critical judgment. They prefer people who are flooded by information in proportion to their control of the flow thereof.

Historically, it was with the advent of the modern secular state in Europe, concomitant with the Enlightenment, that education became a matter of state responsibility. Today, all major human rights treaties establish the right to education and impose on the states parties a number of obligations.[476] They generally require states to provide free and compulsory primary education as well as progressive access to secondary education and higher education on the basis of merit or capacity. A basic principle is equality of opportunity for all in education, referring to the marginalized and underprivileged, both in developed and in developing countries, including girls, tribal and indigenous peoples, cultural and linguistic minorities, disadvantaged groups, and persons with disabilities.[477] States not only have the negative obligation not to impair the right to education, but also positive obligations to take steps towards promoting education and, in particular, a duty to protect people from impairment by private persons and entities.[478] However, it has been noted that 'Governments are failing to address the root causes of marginalization in education'.[479] The prospects of achieving Millennium Development Goals (MDGs) 2 and 3 are bleak[480] and the 'Education for All' project (EFA) is falling behind.[481] States are proving either unwilling or simply unable to reach minimum thresholds of equal access to education, let alone advancing critical judgment.

The current worldwide trend towards the commodification of knowledge, under the pressure of international economic institutions and rules, has shifted from pursuing in good conscience 'truth' to deliberately pursuing 'profit'. In the quest for profit the system is destined to reproduce itself uncritically without being able to see its own functioning and ultimate direction.[482] Structural adjustment policies by international financial institutions have required the privatization of social services, including education, often causing an increase in school fees and the transfer of costs (from the community, in particular the wealthier) to families. While enrolment in schools in many countries is expanding, fewer and fewer resources are provided by states to ensure the right to education. The inclusion of education (notably higher education as far as critical judgment is concerned) in the services which are subject to liberalization under

[476] KD Beiter, *The Protection of the Right to Education by International Law: Including a Systematic Analysis of Article 13 of the International Covenant on Economic, Social and Cultural Rights* (Nijhoff: Leiden, 2006).

[477] cf UNESCO Convention against Discrimination in Education (adopted 14 December 1960, entered into force 22 May 1962) 429 UNTS 93.

[478] HR Council, 'The promotion of equality of opportunity in education', Report of 18 April 2011, UN Doc A/HRC/17/29, paras 19, 46–47, at <http://www2.ohchr.org/english/issues/education/rapporteur>, pointing out that states have obligations not only to respect, but also to protect, and to fulfil (ie to facilitate and to provide).

[479] UNESCO, *EFA Global Monitoring Report 2010: Reaching the Marginalized* (Paris: Unesco, 2010) 5 (Summary).

[480] See n 8 above.

[481] HR Council, 'The promotion of equality of opportunity in education' (n 478 above).

[482] See MC Nussbaum, *Not for Profit: Why Democracy Needs the Humanities* (Princeton and Oxford: Princeton University Press, 2010).

the GATS has reinforced this trend, despite the flexibility of the GATS.[483] The pursuit of 'efficiency', whether purely economic or other, in educational matters is often disruptive and actually meets with stiff resistance, although not powerful enough.[484] It constrains the intellectual and emotional development of a mass of people into standards (and increasingly into 'global' standards which reflect the cultural traditions and preferences of the global stronger) suited to match the market demand, ie the purchasing power of the wealthier (who are not necessarily the wiser, let alone the most vulnerable), thereby taking for granted the world 'as it is' as the best of all possible worlds. It is, in fact, the task of education, knowledge, and critical judgement to imagine new (previously completely unimaginable) better worlds, however good the present world may be, and all the more so where the present world is not so good for too many people. In present circumstances, humanities are deemed valuable only in so far as they 'sell' thought and art on the market, without taking seriously that sales hinge on strong demand from the purchasers and it may be precisely the purchasers (among others) who need to take a more critical glimpse at life. Masses of uncritical people, including people who are 'well-educated' according to uncritical global standards or to standards encouraging the *sale* of 'critical' attitudes to uncritical purchasers, may prove efficient at the workplace, just as slaves may be for the master, but there can be no real democracy when the 'demos' apparently managing the 'cratos' is actually unable (and even left to feel unwilling) constantly to unmask the strategies of the elite in power, whether this elite is relatively fixed in time or changes through elections.

Human rights treaties and monitoring bodies are still pre-eminently construed as being based on states' willingness to comply with existing treaties.[485] They place several obligations on states, including a duty to protect, without providing for powers to meet with their positive obligations. For example, a UN Comment on the right to education has suggested that states are, inter alia, under an obligation to ensure the 'academic freedom of staff and students',[486] without considering that this freedom may actually be largely contingent on private financing and that the alternative to less freedom is no freedom at all. Moreover, the right to education is systematically limited to the individual and the social benefits of education are confined within the local and national communities, especially in terms of informed political participation,[487] with little attention being paid to what is to be done to ensure critical judgement in assessing global realities. The content of education is generally left unaddressed.[488] It is also

[483] See eg LE Weber and JJ Duderstadt (eds), *The Globalization of Higher Education* (London, Paris, and Geneva: Economica, 2008); VV Mishra, 'Liberalisation of Higher Education Services under the GATS Regime: Implications for a Developing Country' (2009) 42 *Comparative and International Law Journal of Southern Africa* 387–421; A Verger, *WTO/GATS and the Global Politics of Higher Education* (New York and Abingdon: Routledge, 2010).

[484] See D Hill (ed), *Contesting Neoliberal Education Public Resistance and Collective Advance* (New York and Abingdon: Routledge, 2008); M Novelli and A Ferus-Comelo (eds), *Globalization, Knowledge and Labour: Education for Solidarity within Spaces of Resistance* (New York and Abingdon: Routledge, 2009).

[485] See K Tomasevski, 'Globalizing What: Education as a Human Right or as a Traded Service?' (2005) 12 Ind JGLS 1–78.

[486] See CESCR, 'General Comment No. 13: The Right to Education (Art 13 of the Covenant)' of 8 December 1999, UN Doc E/C.12/1999/10, para 38.

[487] ibid, para 1, referring to the education of people as giving them a 'means to participate fully in their community' and as 'one of the best financial investments States can make', as well as 'one of the joys and rewards of human existence'.

[488] HR Council, 'The promotion of equality of opportunity in education' (n 478 above) para 6, for the view that 'the form and substance of education, including curricula and teaching methods, have to be acceptable (e.g. relevant, culturally appropriate and of good quality) to students and, in appropriate

difficult to see how critical knowledge may be subject to 'quality standards', which are tailored to training and getting information for specific ends, such as how a job is to be done efficiently, according to the standard 'the less critical, the more efficient'.

(b) Media

The well-known MacBride Report, approved by UNESCO in 1980 for a New World Information and Communication Order (NWICO), introduced information- and communication-related issues to the global agenda for the first time.[489] The eighty-two recommendations submitted, insisting on the democratization of communications, were favourably received by Third World countries but not by Western states. The former denounced the distortions of Third World realities by the world information system controlled by the West, thereby perpetuating inequality and dependence, whereas the latter complained about the use of national or local media by Third World leaders to divert attention from abuse of power and atrocities. Western states contended that their media were free from political power and thus necessary in order to 'free' oppressed people in the Third World. In fact the report remained a dead letter.

Media power is today concentrated in a few large MNEs as a result of the convergence of both media (newspapers, magazines, books, radio, broadcast television, cable systems and programming, movies, music recordings, video recordings and online services, etc) and technologies (satellite, cable, the internet, bandwidth, fixed and mobile networks, content digitalization, etc), as well as of vertical integration, mergers, and acquisitions which have occurred over the past two decades.[490] Few doubt that Western corporations and states, led by the United States, dominate the world's entertainment and information networks and that the Western lifestyle is in the process of becoming globalized.[491] Risks of manufactured consent and fabricated information,[492] including scientific information, as well as diversion of attention from sensitive issues through convenient entertainment policies, along the lines of the Roman *panem et circenses* ('bread and circuses'),[493] are likely and are difficult to keep under control. Those who control information and entertainment are also in control of the psychology and expectations of workers, consumers, taxpayers, investors, and speculators, in short of households, markets, and stock exchanges. Self-fulfilling prophecies may relatively easily be triggered to manufacture realities on the basis of any news, whether true or untrue. In international law, manipulated information broadcast worldwide about alleged acts of brutal repression by a given government may be used to mobilize people and trigger the action of international bodies, such as a mandate from the UN Security Council to use military force.

No doubt all states work hard to control the hearts and minds of people in other states. States use the media both to shield the information space within their boundaries, and protect their national identity and cohesion, and to influence the information space of other states.[494] Media liberalization entails a fall of the national borders with

cases, parents'. Nowhere does the Comment specify what is meant by 'acceptable' or from whose viewpoint the assessment is made.

[489] At <http://unesdoc.unesco.org/images/0004/000400/040066eb.pdf>.

[490] See CE Baker, *Media Concentration and Democracy: Why Ownership Matters* (Cambridge: CUP, 2007).

[491] DK Thussu, *International Communication* (London: Hodder Education, 2nd edn, 2006) 111, 141.

[492] ES Herman and N Chomsky, *Manufacturing Consent: The Political Economy of the Mass Media* (New York: Pantheon, new edn, 2002); MD Alkyne, *Global Lies? Propaganda, the United Nations and World Order* (London: Palgrave Macmillan, 2003).

[493] Juvenal, *Satires*, 10, 77–81.

[494] ME Price, *Media and Sovereignty: The Global Information Revolution and the Challenge to State Power* (Cambridge, Mass: The MIT Press, 2002) 3–29.

regard to information in- and outflows and a comparative advantage for those states which have more opportunity and power to affect the information policy of others, in particular by profiting from its language (today English) as the world *lingua franca*. Such liberalization also entails a massive entry of private media conglomerates in the market. As a result, the states in which these conglomerates are based have an additional (indirect) source of control of the internal cohesion of other states and all 'messages' (whether private or public) are forced to pass through, and be screened out by, one or another private conglomerate. The net result is that a few states, and private conglomerates linked to these states, tend to control all the knowledge on the planet and what is in the minds of people worldwide, thus shaping their preferences and votes.

The right to freedom of expression and information set out in all major human rights treaties places on the states parties not only an obligation not to control information from the government through monopolies or oligopolies and to ensure pluralism of the sources, but also a positive obligation to prevent excessive concentration of media ownership in private media conglomerates.[495] National and regional antitrust regulations are indeed in place but prove hardly capable of keeping the issue at bay, while a global, legitimate, and effective anti-trust authority is missing. The prevention of concentrations of media ownership should be attained through the adoption of measures aimed at ensuring the 'impartial allocation of resources as well as equitable access to such media', and 'anti-trust legislation regulating mass media'.[496] The CCPR has recently referred to the obligation of states 'to ensure that persons are protected from any acts of private persons or entities that would impair the enjoyment of the freedoms of opinion and expression' and 'to prevent undue media dominance or concentration by privately controlled media groups in monopolistic situations that may be harmful to a diversity of sources and view'.[497]

Typical measures contrary to the right of expression and information are the impairment of basic rights on the basis of actual, perceived, or supposed opinions of whoever, whether political, scientific, historic, moral, or religious in nature, as well as the criminalization of the holding of a given opinion, the harassment, intimidation, or stigmatization of persons, including arrest, detention, trial or imprisonment, because of the opinions they may hold, and any form of effort to coerce the holding or rejection of any opinion. States are required to ensure the free communication of information and ideas about public and political issues between citizens, candidates, and elected representatives.[498] A free and uncensored press or other media is of 'paramount importance' in a democratic society, including 'the right of individuals to criticize or openly and publicly evaluate their Governments without fear of interference or punishment'.[499] All forms of expression and means for their dissemination are covered, in principle, including spoken, written, and sign language and such non-verbal expression as images and art, books, newspapers, pamphlets, posters, banners, dress, and legal

[495] IACtHR, *Compulsory Membership in an Association Prescribed by Law for the Practice of Journalism (Articles 13 and 29 American Convention on Human Rights)*, Advisory Opinion of 13 November 1985 No OC-5/85, IACtHR Series A No 5, para 56; COE, Parliamentary Assembly, Resolution 428 (1970) containing a 'Declaration on Mass Communication Media and Human Rights', para 8.

[496] cf UNHRC, 'Concluding Observations on Italy of 3 August 1994', UN Doc CCPR/C/79/Add.37, paras 10, 17.

[497] UNHRC, 'General comment No 34 (Article 19: Freedoms of opinion and expression)' of 21 July 2011, in UN Doc CCPR/C/GC/34, 21 July 2011, paras 7, 14, 40.

[498] ibid paras 9–11.

[499] UNHRC, *Marques de Morais v Angola* Views of 18 April 2005, Comm No 1128/2002, paras 6.7, 6.8, UN Doc CCPR/C/83/D/1128/2002.

submissions.[500] States are also required to take all necessary steps to foster the independence of the new mass media intermediaries, including internet- and mobile-based electronic information dissemination systems, and to ensure that individuals have access to these.[501] They must ensure that public broadcasting services operate in an independent manner by guaranteeing, in particular, their independence and editorial freedom.[502] All of these obligations are limited only by two sets of legitimate restrictions (to be construed narrowly, however), ie (a) the safeguarding of the rights or reputations of others; and (b) the protection of national security or of public order (*ordre public*) or of public health or morals.[503]

This legal regime is largely unsatisfactory in terms of what is needed to promote and protect critical knowledge at the global level. First, existing rules focus on limiting state powers, but at the same time, quite schizophrenically, require states to do everything in their power to prevent private actors from abusing freedom of expression. What states could do against private abuse is often prohibited by the same rules. Secondly, no provision is made to combat the censorship inherent in the functioning of the free market. In a free market environment the best goods and services are those which are sold, ie which are purchased by those who can afford it, and these are the wealthier, ie the stronger. All goods and services which do not attract 'sufficient' purchasers to recoup the costs and make a profit are censored. When media service providers select what information is to be given (in the news, in advertisements,[504] etc), they cannot but choose what consumers want to be told, and, since the media firms basically sell media products to audiences and sell audiences to advertisers, the greater the number of purchasers of entertainment and information, the higher the profits from the sale of advertising.[505] This 'upstream', hidden censorship, which profoundly affects people's beliefs, is rarely explicitly discussed. What is extensively debated is the need for pluralism *within* the market environment in which today the state also finds itself. Thirdly, nothing is provided by human rights rules to counter the pluralism fabricated just like any commercial strategy of product diversification by the same covert firm. There is today perhaps less opportunity for overt monopolies, but hidden monopolies abound behind apparent pluralism. Pluralism itself may be sold in the market as a 'brand' like any other. Finally, the private actors operating in the media are a few global conglomerates and existing rules do not adequately address the impact of their dimensions and the resulting effects on local communities.[506]

B. Competing Values

The values inspiring the rules of international law not only partially overlap, they are also often in competition with one another. This causes tensions between different legal regimes and a pressing need to reconcile the rules involved. The most efficient method of overcoming legal conflicts is no doubt the operation of hierarchically superior rules

[500] UNHRC, 'General comment No 34' (n 497 above) para 12. [501] ibid para 15.
[502] ibid para 16. [503] ibid paras 21–36.
[504] For the view that freedom of expression can in principle be restricted to prevent untrustworthy or misleading advertising, see ECtHR, *Casado Coca v Spain* Judgment of 24 February 1994, App 15450/89, Series A No 285-A, 18 (1994) EHRR 1, para 51.
[505] For the 'special nature' of media products and the view that the standard model of economics (whatever the validity of general critiques thereof) applies particularly badly to such products, see CE Baker, *Media, Markets, and Democracy* (Cambridge: CUP, 2002) 7–14.
[506] For an extensive survey of the ECtHR and comparative (especially British) case law, see A Nicol, G Millar, and A Sharland, *Media Law and Human Rights* (Oxford: OUP, 2nd edn, 2009).

which give priority to one of the conflicting values and displace the other. *Jus cogens* has the potential to be viewed as the key to this end. However, for the reasons already stated, *jus cogens* should be seen as a catalyst for new rules *over time* rather than overriding rules *of higher rank* here and now. This section explores, by way of illustration, a few value tensions of current international law concerning order versus humanity, wealth versus humanity, and humanity versus humanity. It argues that, in the absence of general formal methods to resolve these conflicts, when the techniques of prioritization already discussed and the discretion of the courts (provided that there is one seised with a particular case) fail, the only way out is to struggle for the values and the corresponding rules favouring the most vulnerable in the circumstances. In legal terms, this struggle is designed to induce states to make better rules and, for the time being, to induce both states and courts to interpret existing rules in a way which favours the values protective of the most vulnerable rather than the others.[507]

(1) Order versus justice

Although order is protected by any legal rule, certain rules are particularly tailored to this end, such as those which prohibit aggression. The inter-state order, as a world order devoid of a universal authority superior to states, is especially protected by the rules providing for non-interference and the jurisdictional immunity of states, foreign states' officials, and IOs in foreign domestic courts. While protecting the equality of states, including their officials and associations as distinct from their members, these rules limit the individual's right of access to court. This right today amounts to a human right as set out in both international treaties and national constitutions,[508] although yielding when necessary to the pursuit of 'legitimate aims' which include international jurisdictional immunities.[509] This section explores two emerging exceptions to jurisdictional immunities, namely, the possibility for domestic courts to deny immunity either to states and state officials accused of international crimes or to IOs which do not offer intra-organizational complaints mechanisms capable of ensuring a level of judicial protection approximately equivalent to that offered by the municipal courts. It argues

[507] ICJ, *Case concerning the Continental Shelf (Tunisia/Libyan Arab Jamahirya) (Merits)* Judgment of 24 February 1982, [1982] ICJ Rep 18, para 71, stating that 'when applying positive international law, a court may choose among several possible interpretations of the law the one which appears, in the light of the circumstances of the case, to be closest to the requirements of justice'.

[508] See EU CFI, Case T-315/01 *Kadi v Council of the European Union and Commission of the European Communities and United Kingdom (intervening)* [2005] ECR II-3649, para 288, Judgment of 21 September 2005, and Case T-306/01 *Yusuf and Al Barakaat International Foundation v Council of the European Union and Commission of the European Communities and United Kingdom (intervening)* [2005] ECR II-3533, para 343, Judgment of 21 September 2005, stating that the right of access to justice, albeit not absolute, is guaranteed by *jus cogens*. Both decisions were set aside by the ECJ (Grand Chamber) in Case C-402/05 P *Kadi v Council of the European Union and Commission of the European Communities* [2008] ECR I-6351, para 329, Appeal Judgment of 3 September 2008, affirming that the rights of defence and to an effective legal remedy are fundamental rights forming an integral part of the general principles of European Community law and refraining from examining the *jus cogens* ground of appeal. For the view that the right of access to courts is established under customary international law and amounts to *jus cogens* and/or to an obligation *erga omnes*, see in addition IACtHR, *Goiburú et al v Paraguay* Judgment of 22 September 2006, IACtHR Series C No 153, para 131; *La Cantuta v Peru* Judgment of 29 November 2006, IACtHR Series C No 162, para 160; STL, *El Sayed* Order of 15 April 2010, Case No CH/PRES/2010/01, paras 29–32.

[509] See M Kloth, *Immunities and the Right of Access to Court under Article 6 of the European Convention on Human Rights* (Leiden and Boston: Nijhoff, 2010) 132–53.

that these trends, whatever their merit, meet with several difficulties and cannot been upheld unconditionally.

(a) Humanitarian exception to jurisdictional immunities

In recent decades a trend towards the denial of immunity when the defendant is accused of egregious violations of human rights or of international crimes amounting to breaches of *jus cogens*—a sort of 'humanitarian exception' to international jurisdictional immunities—has taken hold in legal doctrine and has been asserted in a few judicial decisions. A good number of scholars have argued that in such instances the balance between the value of inter-state 'order' and the value of individual 'justice' should be struck in favour of the latter. Other scholars have insisted that the humanitarian exception to international immunities is not (or not yet) part of international law.[510] The importance of the point can scarcely be overstated and deserves close scrutiny.

The first ever final judicial decision exclusively based on international law that has denied jurisdictional immunity to a foreign state accused of alleged international crimes amounting to violations of *jus cogens* is the *Ferrini* Judgment delivered by the Italian Court of Cassation in 2004.[511] The Court held that states accused of international crimes amounting to violations of *jus cogens* do not enjoy immunity from civil jurisdiction in the courts of other states under customary international law. It thus denied jurisdictional immunity to the Federal Republic of Germany (FRG) for having allegedly committed international crimes (deportation and forced labor) during World War II against Italian citizens. Such acts had no doubt been performed *jure imperii* and, according to the Court, would have otherwise entailed immunity. The key argument in *Ferrini* was that non-immunity flows from the higher-ranking rules on international crimes which trump the 'ordinary' immunity rule. Eventually, other similar (although not identical) decisions followed from the same Court, including the 2005 *Borri* Judgment,[512] the 2008 *Mantelli* Order and the twelve other decisions issued on the same day,[513] the 2008 *Milde* Judgment,[514] the 2008 *Lozano* Judgment,[515] and the 2011 *Autogestione prefettizia di Vojotia* Judgment.[516] Since the Italian legal system has

[510] See recently S Knuchel, 'State Immunity and the Promise of *Jus Cogens*' (2011) 9 Nw JIHR 149.

[511] Italian Court of Cassation, *Ferrini v Federal Republic of Germany* Judgment of 11 March 2004 No 5044, (2004) 128 ILR 658. For a comment, see C Focarelli, 'Denying Foreign State Immunity for Commission of International Crimes: The *Ferrini* Decision' (2005) 54 ICLQ 951.

[512] Italian Court of Cassation, *Borri v Argentine Republic* Judgment of 27 May 2005 No 6532, ILDC 296 (IT 2005).

[513] Italian Court of Cassation, *Federal Republic of Germany v Giovanni Mantelli et al* Order of 29 May 2008 No 14201, (2009) 17 It YBIL 292, ILDC 1037 (IT 2008). The *Mantelli* Order was one of 13 orders (12 of which are mostly identical in wording) concerned with actions for damages brought by the victims or their heirs in various Italian lower courts. For a comment, see C Focarelli, 'Federal Republic of Germany v. Giovanni Mantelli and Others, Order No. 14201' (2009) 103 AJIL 122.

[514] Italian Court of Cassation, *Milde* Judgment of 21 October 2008 No 1072, (2009) 18 It YBIL 325, ILDC 1085 (IT 2008). For a comment, see C Focarelli, 'Diniego dell'immunità alla Germania per crimini internazionali: la Suprema Corte si fonda su valutazioni 'qualitative' (2009) 92 RDI 363–410.

[515] Italian Court of Cassation, *Lozano* (n 259 above).

[516] Italian Court of Cassation, *Repubblica Federale di Germania v Autogestione prefettizia di Vojotia* Judgment of 12 January 2011 No 11163, at <http://www.europeanrights.eu/index.php?funzione=S&op=2&id=2242>, holding that the *Ferrini* jurisprudence 'has constituted an unquestionable *progress* on the matter of the alignment of the immunity rule to the *new* international order and therefore deserves to be affirmed here' (para 28, emphasis added). It is apparent that the Court affirmed the *Ferrini* jurisprudence as a progressive step towards a presumably better future international law, not as existing law.

no statute on foreign states' immunity, Italian courts routinely apply to state immunity claims the rule *par in parem non habet jurisdictionem* as general international law under article 10(1) of the Italian Constitution.[517] In all of these decisions the Court oscillated between giving weight to superior humanitarian 'values' rather than to positive rules and stating that the alleged *jus cogens* rule authorizing the denial of immunity was in the process of emerging.[518]

The major problem with the humanitarian exception to sovereign immunity is that, at least at the moment, practice suggests otherwise.[519] All national and international final decisions exclusively based on international law have hitherto invariably affirmed the immunity rule even in cases of alleged international crimes amounting to breaches of *jus cogens*. The international legal practice is strongly in favour of immunity, as attested by the 2002 *Distomo* Judgment of the Greek Special Supreme Court[520] and the 2003 *Distomo* Judgment of the German Federal Court,[521] the 2001 *Al-Adsani* Judgment and the 2002 *Kalogeropoulou* admissibility Decision of the ECtHR,[522] the 2002 *Bouzari* Judgment of the Ontario Superior Court of Justice,[523] the 2003 *Bucheron* Judgment of the French Court of Cassation,[524] the 2006 *Jones* Judgment of the House

517 'The Italian legal system shall conform to the generally recognized norms of international law.'

518 A number of lower courts, to which the cases decided by the Court of Cassation were referred back, while following the Court of Cassation in accepting jurisdiction, have dismissed the case on the grounds that the statute of limitations barred the action and there is no rule of customary international law today to the contrary, let alone in the period of World War II when the alleged crimes had been committed. See Italian Tribunal of Arezzo, *Ferrini Luigi v Repubblica Federale di Germania* Judgment of 13 March 2007 No 316; Tribunal of La Spezia, *Rita Bartoli e Laura Poli v Repubblica Federale di Germania* Judgment of 16 October 2008 No 1077; Tribunal of Turin, *Allasio et al v Repubblica Federale di Germania et al* Judgment of 19 October 2009 No 7137; Tribunal of Catania, *Pennisi Maria et al v Repubblica Federale di Germania* Judgment of 4 October 2010 No 63; Tribunal of Rossano, *Curia Serafino et al v Repubblica Federale di Germania and al*, Judgment of 16 September 2011; Court of Appeal of Turin, *Allasio et al v Repubblica Federale di Germania et al* Judgment of 19 October 2011 (all unreported, on file with the author). What remains unclear in these decisions is why *jus cogens* has an overriding retrospective effect on jurisdiction (this point being unhesitatingly endorsed) but does not have a similarly overriding effect on the rule on the statute of limitations itself. Such selectivity suggests that reliance on *jus cogens* cannot have unlimited special effects, as discussed above, (Ch 6, section B (4)(f)), and is simply unwarranted in both hypotheses. Other lower courts, by contrast, have held the opposite and condemned Germany (n 246 above).

519 The Italian Court of Cassation itself has more recently noted, in a dictum found in the 2009 *United States v Tissino et al* Judgment of 25 February 2009 No 4461, that 'the international legal system itself—through customary and treaty rules virtually accepted by all domestic and supranational courts in decisions made also after the 2004 *Ferrini* [decision]—has constantly reaffirmed as "fundamental" the need to admit immunity from territorial jurisdiction of foreign states . . . even in case of breach of peremptory norms of international law' (ILDC 1262 (IT 2009) para 16).

520 The Greek Supreme Court had denied immunity to the FRG in the *Distomo* decision of 4 May 2000 No 11, (2001) 54 RHDI 590; see M Gavouneli and E Bantekas, 'Prefecture of Voiotia v Federal Republic of Germany' (2001) 95 AJIL 198. This decision was overruled by the Greek Special Supreme Court, however, on 17 September 2002, (2003) 56 RHDI 199; see E Vournas, 'Prefecture of Voiotia v. Federal Republic of Germany: Sovereign Immunity and the Exception for *Jus Cogens* Violations' (2002) 21 New York Law School Journal of International and Comparative Law 648–9.

521 *The Distomo Massacre Case (Greek Citizens v Federal Republic of Germany)* Judgment of 26 June 2003, (2003) 42 ILM 1030.

522 ECtHR, *Al-Adsani v United Kingdom* Judgment of 21 November 2001 [GC], App 35763/97, ECtHR Rep 2001-XI 79, (2002) 34 EHRR 273; *Kalogeropoulou v Greece* Decision on admissibility of 12 December 2002, App 59021/00, ECtHR Rep 2002-X 389.

523 Ontario Superior Court of Justice, *Bouzari v Iran* Judgment of 1 May 2002, at <http://www.ccij.ca/uploads/Bouzari-Superior%20Court%20of%20Justice.pdf>, affirmed by the Court of Appeal of Ontario on 30 June 2004, at <http://www.ccij.ca/uploads///Bouzari-Court%20of%20Appeal.pdf>.

524 French Court of Cassation, *Bucheron v Federal Republic of Germany* Judgment of 16 December 2003 No 258, (2003) I(258) *Bulletin des Arrêts Chambres civiles* 206, 108 RGDIP (2008) 259.

of Lords,[525] the 2008 *Mothers of Srebrenica* Judgment of the District Court in The Hague, this latter also excluding the exception with regard to IOs,[526] the 2010 *Natoniewski* Judgment of the Polish Supreme Court,[527] and the 2011 *La Réunion aérienne* Judgment of the French Court of Cassation.[528] Even the Italian Avvocatura dello Stato, led by the Attorney General, pleaded the immunity rule be applied in the course of the *Mantelli* and other proceedings, stating that the *Ferrini* decision 'is a *unicum* in the panorama of domestic and international jurisprudence', it was not 'in line with the current *status* of international law' and 'constitute[ed] a case completely incapable of creating a rule of international law'.[529] True, some of these decisions (notably *Al-Adsani*, *Bouzari*, and *Jones*) have stressed that the rule violated (prohibiting torture) was peremptory, but denied that this allowed the denial of immunity. In other words, certain international rules may be peremptory, but it does not follow that their alleged violation by one state allows courts of another state to deny immunity to the former—especially when practice supporting the non-immunity rule is lacking or uncertain. The underlying assumption is that *jus cogens* may not in itself replace the absence of state practice,[530] and no other technique exists in international law to reach the desired end. This shows that *jus cogens*, far from being a *static* matter of what (hierarchically superior) law exists at a given moment, as is routinely depicted, is rather a *dynamic* tool capable of generating new (hopefully better) law.[531]

There appears to be no way to explain the *Ferrini* jurisprudence other than assuming that the Italian Court of Cassation is willing to operate as a pace-setter, as it did in the second half of the nineteenth century in respect of acts *jure gestionis* (the so-called commercial exception).[532] Customary international law cannot be changed except through a process involving the unilateral, non-conforming actions of state authorities, including domestic courts; by domestic courts in particular when the subject-matter concerns the exercise of jurisdiction. And, of course, customary international law cannot avoid being subject to change. In this sense exception could be taken to the view expressed by Lord Hoffmann in *Jones* whereby: 'It is not for a national court to

[525] UK House of Lords, *Jones v Ministry of Interior Al-Mamlaka Al-Arabiya AS Saudiya (the Kingdom of Saudi Arabia) et al* Judgment of 14 June 2006, [2006] UKHL 26, reported by E Steinerte and R Wallace (2006) 100 AJIL 901.

[526] District Court of The Hague, *Association of Citizens 'Mothers of Srebrenica' v State of the Netherlands and the United Nations* Judgment of 4 July 2008, Case No 295247/HA ZA 07–2973, (2008) 55 Neth ILR 428, para 5.20.

[527] Polish Supreme Court, *Natoniewski v Federal Republic of Germany* Judgment of 29 October 2010, reported by E Dąbrowska (2010) 30 Pol YBIL 299.

[528] French Court of Cassation, *La Réunion aérienne, Groupement d'intérêt économique et al v Jamahiriya Arabe populaire et socialiste* Judgment of 9 March 2011 No 247, at <http://www.courdecassation.fr/jurisprudence_2/premiere_chambre_civile_568/247_9_19167.html>.

[529] The statement, submitted at the hearing of 6 May 2008, is not mentioned in the 2008 orders; it is unpublished but is lodged with the Italian Ministry of Foreign Affairs. A critical stance against *Ferrini* was also publicly taken by the Italian Minister of Foreign Affairs in an interview released to the Swiss newspaper *Süddeutsche Zeitung*, published on 20 June 2008, where the Minister termed the *Ferrini* jurisprudence 'dangerous' and confirmed that Italy had an interest in maintaining sovereign immunity since it could be sued by the victims of the Italian wars in the Balkans, in Libya, and in Ethiopia.

[530] cf Lord Bingham's view in the *Jones* decision whereby 'since the rule on immunity is well-understood and established, and no relevant exception is generally accepted, the rule prevails', although Saudi Arabia was accused of torture and the prohibition of torture was undisputably regarded as *jus cogens*.

[531] See Ch 6 above, section B (4)(f). For further details, see C Focarelli, 'Immunité des Etats et *Jus Cogens*. La dynamique du droit international et la fonction du *jus cogens* dans le processus de changement de la règle sur l'immunité juridictionnelle des Etats étrangers' (2008) 112 RGDIP 761.

[532] See eg Court of Cassation of Naples, *Typaldos Console di Grecia v Manicomio di Aversa* Judgment of 16 March 1886, 38 (1886) I(1) *Giurisprudenza Italiana* 228.

"develop" international law by unilaterally adopting a version of that law which, however desirable, forward-looking and reflective of values it may be, is simply not accepted by other states'.[533] The court's 'deviating' conduct is necessarily (a) an internationally unlawful act; and (b) based on domestic values and/or rules which are internally made to prevail over existing international law.[534] This does not in itself exclude the pursuit of global values, a point to be empirically tested against the subsequent attitude of the other states. In this sense courts do participate in the process of formation and transformation of customary international law. It is therefore crucial for courts to elaborate their reasons for any departure as clearly as possible—and in an effort to explain why the divergence should be acceptable to the generality of states. The rule thus promoted must also be shown to be capable of two-way functioning, so that it can be invoked not only by, but also against the particular state which promotes it and also by non-democratic states against democratic ones. Needless to say, grave violations of human rights may be committed by *any* state, including democratic countries, as has been proved by the practice of extraordinary renditions.[535]

How likely is the formation of a rule excluding immunity in case of egregious violations of human rights? Whether the exception will emerge depends on the practice of the generality of states (not just on aspects of the practice of a group of states, such as Western states, let alone from one single state) and so far states have refrained from joining the *Ferrini* jurisprudence. The 'tort exception' envisaged by Article 12 of the 2005 Jurisdictional Immunities Convention seems to be of little use and is confined to torts committed in the forum.[536] The fact that most existing states have in the past committed what today are regarded as international crimes and fear a flood of compensation claims which would be very hard, if not impossible, to manage by way of judicial litigation, clearly militates against the humanitarian exception.[537] For example, would the United States contemplate the possibility—as a new rule of customary international law or as an effect of *jus cogens*—that it might be sued by Japanese victims in Japanese courts for the Nagasaki and Hiroshima bombing in 1945, or by Iraqis in Iraqi courts for the ill-treatment (amounting to 'torture' according to the ICRC) of Iraqi prisoners in Abu-Ghraib in 2003, or by detainees in Guantanamo Bay in their national courts for serious violations of human rights? Would a European State, such as Italy or the United Kingdom, allow an exception meaning that it could be sued by an Arab citizen in Saudi Arabia's courts for inhuman and degrading treatment when such serious violation of human rights has been established by the ECtHR? Would former colonial European states accept that they might be sued in their courts or in the United States or elsewhere for slavery (a crime today generally viewed as belonging to *jus cogens*) committed during their colonial age?[538] Serious doubts seem reasonable. The ICJ, seised by Germany in

533 UK House of Lords, *Jones* (n 525 above) para 63.

534 See Ch 6 above, n 623.

535 For instance, Sweden was condemned by both the UN CAT on 20 May 2005, in the *Agiza v Sweden* case (Comm No 233/2003, UN Doc CAT/C/34/D/233/2003) and the UNHRC on 25 October 2006, in *Alzery v Sweden* (Comm No 1416/2005, UN Doc CCPR/C/88/D/1416/2005) for breach of Art 3 Torture Convention and of Art 7 ICCPR, respectively. For an important recent judicial condemnation of extraordinary renditions, see Tribunal of Milan, *Public Prosecutor v Adler et al* Judgment of 1 February 2010 No 12428/09, ILDC 1492 (IT 2010), and the comment thereon by L Cinti.

536 Convention on Jurisdictional Immunities of States and their Property (adopted 2 December 2004), (2005) 44 ILM 803. For the irrelevance of Art 12 of the 2005 Jurisdictional Immunities Convention, as well as of other treaty rules, see the recent *Jurisdictional Immunities of the State* Judgment of the ICJ (n 539 below), paras 64–78.

537 See C Tomuschat, 'L'immunité des Etats en cas de violations graves des droits de l'homme' (2005) 109 RGDIP 51.

538 See RM Spitzer, 'The African Holocaust: Should Europe Pay Reparations to Africa for Colonialism and Slavery?' (2002) 35 Virg JTL 1319, 1341.

2008, recently confirmed the above analysis in its *Jurisdictional Immunities of the State* Judgment of 3 February 2012, concluding that under customary international law, 'as it presently stands', 'a State is not deprived of immunity by reason of the fact that it is accused of serious violations of international human rights law or the international law of armed conflict'.[539] While the *Ferrini* jurisprudence has proved an understandable promotional attempt to change the law, the self-professed 'progressive' scholars who have been insisting on the humanitarian exception to state immunity without qualifications by using all possible strategies found in the professional toolkit appear to have been driven sometimes by a somewhat simplistic (if not moralistic) attitude in ignoring the elementary fact that most existing states, whether Western (including Italy) or non-Western, have committed during their history, often at the very moment of becoming a state, plenty of acts which today constitute international crimes. Advocates of the humanitarian exception have paid little attention to wonder what kind of impact the heralded rule would have had should it have become a general rule. An understanding of *jus cogens*, in particular, as a tool capable of producing a special retrospective effect going backwards in time without limits would have had the potential to subvert the current world political structure without introducing an alternative structure. It would also have called for identical overriding effects with regard to many other, if not all, existing rules of international law, including a retrospective non-application of the statute of limitations, which few if any states and courts are prepared to uphold. In practice, it would have allowed floods of compensatory claims in the domestic courts of virtually every state from people throughout the world in respect of events occurred everywhere at any point in time. This clearly makes no sense. The struggle for global justice to be engaged is towards a qualified admissibility of the exception, for example only with regard to *present* and *future* acts as an integral part of the legal regime of *specified* international crimes, especially where no alternative forum exists.[540]

A few years before the *Ferrini* Judgment, the UK House of Lords had denied jurisdictional immunity to Mr Augusto Pinochet, as a former Chilean head of state, essentially on the basis of the operation of the 1984 Torture Convention within the British legal system in proceedings concerning his extradition to Spain, which was connected to the crime of torture committed when he was in office.[541] Following this decision, in particular, the view has often been held that former state officials cannot

[539] ICJ, *Jurisdictional Immunities of the State (Germany v Italy: Greece intervening)* Judgment of 3 February 2012, at <http://www.icj-cij.org/docket/files/143/16883.pdf>, para 91. After a judicial mortgage had been imposed on Villa Vigoni, a cultural German-Italian centre located in Italy, on 17 June 2007, fearing a flood of compensation claims, on 23 December 2008 the FRG instituted proceedings against Italy before the ICJ claiming that 'Italian judicial bodies have repeatedly disregarded the jurisdictional immunity of Germany as a foreign state' (cf ICJ Press Release No 2008/44 of 23 December 2008, at <http://www.icj-cij.org/docket/files/143/14925.pdf>.) The Court found that Italy violated its obligation to respect the immunity of the FRG under international law 'by allowing civil claims to be brought against it based on violations of international humanitarian law committed by the German Reich between 1943 and 1945', as well as its obligation to respect the immunity of the FRG under international law 'by taking measures of constraint against Villa Vigoni' and to respect the immunity of the FRG under international law 'by declaring enforceable in Italy decisions of Greek courts based on violations of international humanitarian law committed in Greece by the German Reich' (para 139). For the 'domestic effect' of the ICJ judgment, see Ch 6 above, note 677.

[540] An outcome which *somehow* comes close to the one suggested in the text seems to have been reached by the Italian courts, which have dismissed the cases under their review by applying the statute of limitations after having followed the *Ferrini* jurisprudence on the matter of jurisdiction (n 518 above).

[541] UK House of Lords, *R v Bow Street Metropolitan Stipendiary Magistrate, ex p Pinochet* Judgment of 24 March 1999, (1999) 38 ILM 581.

rely on functional (or *ratione materiae*) jurisdictional immunity before foreign courts when they are accused of international crimes amounting to violations of *jus cogens* committed in an official capacity while in office. As discussed earlier, the irrelevance of functional immunity of state officials accused of international crimes is basically envisaged in ICTs' and HCTs' statutes and the fact that these apply in ICTs and HCTs does not necessarily mean that they also apply in domestic courts, as the ICJ pointed out in the 2002 *Arrest Warrant* Judgment.[542] The humanitarian exception to immunity in respect of former state officials is much more strongly supported than that in respect of states themselves. The jurisprudence is, however, far from unanimous. For example, the 2004 *Jiang Zemin* Judgment of the US Court of Appeals for the Seventh Circuit confirmed the immunity to the former President of the People's Republic of China, although on grounds of a suggestion of immunity made by the Executive,[543] and the UK House of Lords specified in the *Jones* Judgment that the denial of immunity in *Pinochet* was exclusively based on the interpretation of the 1984 Torture Convention.[544] In the *Arrest Warrant* Judgment the ICJ admitted the denial of immunity of former foreign ministers—apart from the unlikely hypotheses of trials in their own state's courts and waiver of immunity—only before 'certain' ICTs, 'where they have jurisdiction', and (after the minister has ceased to hold the office) the courts of other states, inter alia, 'in respect of acts committed during that period of office in a private capacity', thereby excluding their official acts performed when in office and apparently upholding functional immunity also for international crimes.[545] In any event, no doubt the immunity does not apply in domestic courts when the foreign state official is incumbent, as implied, for example, in the 2001 *Gaddafi* Judgment by the French Court of Cassation,[546] and clearly asserted by the ICJ in the *Arrest Warrant* Judgment.[547] Whether state immunity and state official immunity should be subject to the same rule is unclear. Although both protect foreign states, the better view is that they are to be treated distinctly to the effect that the legal regime of one does not necessarily apply to the other.[548] States as a whole may be differently inclined towards the two issues, in view of the fact that a proceeding against a natural person (former state official) may be

542 See nn 224 and 225 above and accompanying text.

543 US Court of Appeals for the Seventh Circuit, *Ye et al v Zemin and Falun Gong Control Office* Judgment of 8 September 2004, ILDC 683 (US 2004), arguing that 'The Executive Branch's determination that a foreign leader should be immune from suit even when the leader is accused of acts that violate *jus cogens* norms is established by a suggestion of immunity' and 'We are no more free to ignore the Executive Branch's determination than we are free to ignore a legislative determination concerning a foreign state'. For the deference of domestic courts to the Executive, see Ch 6 above, section D (2)(d).

544 UK House of Lords, *Jones* (n 525 above) para 19 (*per* Lord Bingham of Cornhill), para 49 (*per* Lord Hoffmann).

545 See nn 225 and 226 above.

546 French Court of Cassation, *Gaddafi* Judgment, Decision of 13 March 2001 No 64, Appeal No 00-87215, ILDC 774 (FR 2001). For further analysis, see eg Akande and Shah (n 235 above) 818–20.

547 ICJ, *Arrest Warrant of 11 April 2000* (n 225 above) para 58.

548 For the distinction between the immunity of the *state* from *civil* jurisdiction and the immunity of *state officials* from *criminal* jurisdiction, and in particular for the irrelevance of the UK *Pinochet* Judgment (n 541 above) for the purposes of state jurisdictional immunity, see ICJ, *Jurisdictional Immunities of the State* (n 539 above) paras 87, 91, 100. For the view that 'as a matter of international law, the same immunity against suit in a foreign domestic court which protects the state itself also protects the individuals for whom the state is responsible', following Lord Bingham' holding 'the distinction between criminal proceedings (which were the subject of universal jurisdiction under the Torture Convention) and civil proceedings (which were not)' as 'fundamental to [the Pinochet] decision', see UK House of Lords, *Jones* (n 525 above) para 32 (*per* Lord Bingham) and para 66 (*per* Lord Hoffmann).

less intrusive than a proceeding against the state itself, if only because the official may no longer be in any way associated with the government in power.[549]

(b) Equivalent protection of alternative forums

Recently, the reconciliation between jurisdictional immunity and the right of access to court as an aspect of the right to a fair trial has been addressed on the basis of the 'equivalent protection' doctrine.[550] Domestic courts have denied jurisdictional immunity to IOs, in furtherance of the essential right of access to court established either in constitutional or in international norms when the plaintiff has had no opportunity to obtain justice in any alternative forum (such as an administrative tribunal within the IO), granting an approximately 'equivalent' procedural protection to that guaranteed domestically.[551] This trend was followed, for example, by the Swiss Labour Tribunal of Geneva in the 1993 *ZM* Judgment,[552] by the Italian Court of Cassation in the 1994 *Nacci* Judgment,[553] in the 2005 *Pistelli* Judgment,[554] and in the 2007 *Drago* Judgment,[555] by the French Court of Cassation in the 2005 *Haas* Judgment,[556] and by the Belgian Court of Cassation in the 2009 *Siedler*, *Lutchmaya*, and *BD* Judgments.[557] By contrast, in the 2008 *Mothers of Srebrenica* Judgment the District Court of The Hague denied that the equivalent protection doctrine applied to the United Nations in a case

[549] Moreover, immunity from criminal jurisdiction of the organ does not necessarily entail immunity from civil jurisdiction of the state for which it has acted (since the rules applicable are different, those concerning state immunity reflecting the distinction between acts *jure gestionis* and acts *jure imperii*, as recently stated by the ICJ in the 2012 *Jurisdictional Immunities of the State* (n 539 above), para 59), the individual who has acted as an organ is not subject to 'succession' as may occur with states, and certain individuals acting as state organs enjoy personal immunity in respect of acts carried out in a private capacity until in office while the state can be suited immediately for acts *jure gestionis*. See Nigro (n 232 above) 587. The distinction also holds for functional immunity. For example, a state organ may act in an official capacity and within its 'normal' functions (thus enjoying functional immunity under the prescribed conditions) in relation to an act which, while no doubt attributable to the state, is an act *jure gestionis* of the state (this latter thus enjoying no immunity). In reverse, a state may enjoy immunity for acts *jure imperii* (including alleged commission of international crimes) while the official who has acted on behalf of it does not, as the ICJ seems somehow to imply (or at least not to exclude) in *Jurisdictional Immunities of the State* (para 91).

[550] For the doctrine as a basis—at least in its original formulation—for the exercise of judicial scrutiny over state acts transferring constitutional (or 'sovereign') powers to IOs with regard to the protection of fundamental rights at a level comparable to what would be available domestically, see Ch 5 above, n 242.

[551] C Ryngaert, 'The Immunity of International Organizations Before Domestic Courts: Recent Trends' (2010) 7 IOLR 121.

[552] Swiss Labour Court of Geneva, *ZM v Permanent Delegation of the League of Arab States to the United Nations* Judgment of 17 November 1993, (2000) 116 ILR 643, 645–6.

[553] Italian Court of Cassation, *Nacci v Istituto di Bari del Centre international de hautes études agronomiques méditerranéennes* Judgment of 8 June 1994 No 5565, (1994) 77 RDI 838.

[554] Italian Court of Cassation, *Pistelli v European University Institute* Judgment of 28 October 2005 No 20995, ILDC 297 (IT 2005).

[555] Italian Court of Cassation, *Drago v International Plant Genetic Resources Institute (IPGRI)* Judgment of 19 February 2007 No 3718, ILDC 827 (IT 2007).

[556] French Court of Cassation, *African Development Bank v Mr X* Judgment of 25 January 2005, Appeal No 04-41012, at <http://www.sfdi.org/actualites/cass.fr.25.01.05.pdf> and <http://www.oxfordlawreports.com>, ILDC 778 (FR 2005).

[557] Belgian Court of Cassation, *Western European Union v Siedler* Judgment of 21 December 2009 No S.04.0129.F.; *General Secretariat of the ACP Group v Lutchmaya* Judgment of 21 December 2009 No C.03.0328.F.; *General Secretariat of the ACP Group v BD* Judgment of 21 December 2009 No C.07.0407.F. All of these decisions are available at <http://www.belgiumlex.be>. For a comment, see J Wouters, C Ryngaert, and P Schmitt, 'Case Report' (2011) 105 AJIL 560.

relating to peacekeeping.[558] For its part, in the 1999 *Waite and Kennedy* and *Beer and Regan* Judgments,[559] the ECtHR held that when alternative equivalent means of redress are available within an IO (as was found in the instant cases), the grant of jurisdictional immunity by national courts not only pursues a 'legitimate aim' (as established in international law) but is also proportionate to the aim pursued. It seems to be assumed *a contrario* that in the reverse case the grant of immunity is disproportionate and hence in breach of the right of access to a court set out in Article 6 ECHR.[560]

This practice does not per se imply that the denial of immunity is justified under international law when no alternative equivalent forums exist, but only that a conflict between different international law rules or between international law rules and constitutional rules arises. If the conflict is between international law rules, then a solution in favour of the denial of immunity may be justified simply as a result of the application of rule conflict techniques such as *lex posterior* and *lex specialis*. If not, the denial of immunity may represent a new 'exception' to the immunity rule rather than a breach thereof, provided that the practice is sufficiently settled. As a strategy to secure the right of access to court to the fullest extent possible without dispensing with the immunity rule altogether, the doctrine is welcome. However, domestic courts generally avoid specifying the reasons why the right of access to court trumps the immunity rule (apart from the intuitive perception that justice must be done), whether on international or domestic grounds, and often appear incoherent, especially in the different assessments provided by different courts (and even by the same court in different cases) as to the equivalence of the procedural guarantees offered by the alternative forums.

(2) Security versus humanity

Human rights are designed to trump security considerations (or '*ragion di stato*') but this is not possible in absolute terms. In certain circumstances it is security that prevails over humanity (or, to put it another way, it is the alleged protection of the basic rights of the community that overrides that of individuals), even within the framework of human rights treaties. Human rights are obviously inspired by the need to protect the individual from the overwhelming might of the collectivity, but this cannot be pushed to the point of making the collectivity collapse. Typical situations requiring the primacy of security are 'national emergencies', notably armed conflict and terrorism. The 'derogatory clauses' contained in a few human rights treaties allow contracting states to derogate from the rights guaranteed by the treaty (except for a 'core' of rights which are non-derogable in any circumstances) provided that a given procedure is followed. A relative prevalence of security over humanity may derive from the legitimate restrictions to specific human rights based on public interest issues or social priorities, such as safety, order, morals, and others. This section will succinctly focus on terrorism, as a typical ground for justifying behaviour otherwise contrary to human rights rules, and on other public interest-based restrictions to human rights.

[558] District Court of The Hague, Judgment of 4 July 2008, *Association of Citizens 'Mothers of Srebrenica'* (n 526 above) para 5.24.

[559] ECtHR, *Waite and Kennedy v Germany* Judgment of 18 February 1999, App 26083/94, ECtHR Rep 1999-I 393, paras 68, 72–73; *Beer and Regan v Germany* Judgment of 18 February 1999, App 28934/95, ECtHR Rep 1999-I, paras 58, 62–63.

[560] See Kloth (n 509 above) 132–53.

(a) Terrorism

Especially after the 9/11 attacks on the United States, several states—also in furtherance of UN Security Council resolutions, including 'smart sanctions'[561]—introduced extraordinary counter-terrorism measures which appear to be incompatible with basic human rights. While, in principle, binding Security Council resolutions prevail over human rights treaties under Article 103 UN Charter, the Council itself has routinely stipulated in recent years that counter-terrorism measures adopted by UN member states in furtherance of its resolutions must comply with their other international obligations, 'in particular international human rights, refugee, and humanitarian law',[562] and in the 2011 *Al-Jedda* Judgment the ECtHR argued for a presumption under the UN Charter that Security Council resolutions are consistent with human rights and the ECHR.[563] National counter-terrorism legislation (depending on the state considered) provides for such measures as prolonged detention without trial, wide-scale wire-tapping and other forms of invasion of privacy, the criminalization of terrorist-sympathetic speech and 'glorification' of terrorism, more liberal evidence admissibility (including evidentiary presumptions, use of secret evidence, coercive interrogation of suspects, and even use of evidence extracted by torture or torture-like acts), special courts or chambers, and restrictions on the right of the accused to meet with their legal representatives, as well as limitations to immigration laws. These measures have had significant adverse effects on individual liberties and have eroded judicial controls to the advantage of the executive and at the expense of other branches of government, raising in particular concerns about the spillover of restrictions initially addressed to alleged terrorists to other members of society.

National and international courts have been seised on grounds of inconsistency of counter-terrorism measures with international and constitutional human rights, with success in a number of cases. In the 2008 *Kadi* Judgment, the ECJ held that the EU regulation implementing UN Security Council 'smart sanctions' was in breach of EU fundamental principles and could not be given effect in the European Union,[564] soon to be followed by the EU Court of First Instance in the 2009 *Sison* Judgment[565] and by the UNHRC in the 2008 *Sayadi and Vinck* Views.[566] The US Supreme Court ruled in the 2006 *Hamdan* Judgment that the Military Commission procedures set up to try alleged terrorists were in breach of international due process guarantees.[567] In the 2008

[561] See Ch 8 above, section B (3).

[562] See eg UNSC Res 1456 (2003) of 20 January 2003 (para 6) and, more recently, UNSC presidential statements PRST/2010/19 of 27 September 2010 and S/PRST/2011/9 of 2 May 2011.

[563] ECtHR, *Al-Jedda v United Kingdom* Judgment of 7 July 2011 [GC], App 27021/08, para 102. See Ch 6 above, n 295.

[564] ECJ, *Kadi v Council of the European Union and Commission of the European Communities* (n 508 above) paras 281, 283–284, 291, 294, 298–300, 326, 372.

[565] EU CFI, Case T-341/07 *Jose Maria Sison v Council of the European Union* [2009] ECR II-3625, para 134, Judgment of 30 September 2009, noting that it had 'not been established, or even alleged, that [the involved] murders or attempted murders, even if they could be ascribed to the applicant, may be regarded as acts of terrorism, for the purpose of Article 1(3) of [EU] Common Position 2001/931'.

[566] UNHRC, *Nabil Sayadi and Patricia Vinck v Belgium* Views of 22 October 2008, Comm No 1472/2006, UN Doc CCPR/C/94/D/1472/2006 (2008), paras 10.7–10.8, 10.12–10.13, finding Belgium responsible for a breach of Arts 12 and 17 ICCPR since, in implementing the Security Council's sanctions, the imposition of the travel ban was not necessary to protect national security or public order and the accessibility of the personal information to the whole world through the internet constituted an attack on their honour and reputation. On 20 July 2009, Mr Sayadi and Ms Vinck were removed from the 1267 terrorist list (cf <http://www.un.org/News/Press/docs/2009/sc9711.doc.htm>).

[567] US Supreme Court, *Hamdan v Rumsfeld* Judgment of 29 June 2006, 548 US 557.

Boumediene Judgment the same Court ruled that the Combatant Status Review procedures were also in breach of constitutional due process standards.[568] In the 2004 *A* Judgment, the UK House of Lords asserted the inconsistency with the ECHR of indefinite detention of foreign terror suspects pending their deportation from the United Kingdom.[569] In the 2007 *Charkaoui* Judgment the Supreme Court of Canada struck down a system of prolonged detention without trial based on immigration laws.[570] In the 2009 *Abdelrazik* Judgment a Canadian Federal Court found that the Canadian authorities, by denying the return to Canada of a Canadian citizen in furtherance of a travel ban imposed by Res 1267 (1999) of the Security Council, had breached the applicant's right to enter Canada contrary to subsection 6(1) of the Canadian Charter of Rights and Freedom and directed the respondent authorities to issue the applicant an emergency passport in order to enable him to return to and enter Canada.[571] Also the Israeli Supreme Court struck down several governmental measures authorizing detention without trial,[572] or judicial review,[573] deportation of family members of alleged terrorists,[574] and the use of coercive interrogation techniques.[575] Admittedly, other decisions have been less successful and even those that have achieved success have often been late in coming and/or not fully carried through by the executive.

The difficult balance between security and humanity, particularly the question of the extent to which counter-terrorist measures inconsistent with human rights may be justified on security grounds, is addressed in general, apart from the specific restrictions to individual human rights on a case-by-case basis examined below, in major human rights treaties through derogatory clauses which allow contracting states to derogate temporarily from the rights guaranteed therein in cases of emergency threatening 'the life of the nation' (including armed conflict, subversion, natural disasters, severe economic crises, etc)[576] as a sort of treaty substitute for necessity under general international

[568] US Supreme Court, *Boumediene v Bush* Judgment of 12 June 2008, 553 US 723.

[569] UK House of Lords, *A v Secretary of State for the Home Dept* Judgment of 16 December 2004, [2004] UKHL 54, essentially affirmed by the ECtHR, *A et al v United Kingdom* Judgment of 19 February 2009 [GC], App 3455/05, (2009) 49 EHRR 29, paras 126, 190, observing that 'Even in the most difficult of circumstances, such as the fight against terrorism, and irrespective of the conduct of the person concerned, the Convention prohibits in absolute terms torture and inhuman or degrading treatment and punishment' and concluding for a non-violation of Art 3 ECHR and a violation of Art 5 (1) ECHR on grounds that 'the derogating measures were disproportionate in that they discriminated unjustifiably between nationals and non-nationals'.

[570] Supreme Court of Canada, *Charkaoui v Canada (Citizenship and Immigration)* Judgment of 23 February 2007, [2007] 1 SCR 350, at <http://scc.lexum.org/en/2007/2007scc9/2007scc9.html>, para 28, relying on: 'The overarching principle of fundamental justice' whereby 'before the state can detain people for significant periods of time, it must accord them a fair judicial process'.

[571] Federal Court of Canada, *Abousfian Abdelrazik v the Minister of Foreign Affairs and the Attorney General of Canada* Judgment of 4 June 2009, at <http://reports.fja.gc.ca/eng/2010/2009fc580.html>, para 51, holding the Security Council's 1267 Committee 'as a denial of basic legal remedies and as untenable under the principles of international human rights'.

[572] Israeli Supreme Court, *Anonymous (Lebanese citizens) v Minister of Defence* Judgment of 12 April 2000, ILDC 12 (IL 2000).

[573] Israeli Supreme Court, *Marab et al v Israel Defence Force Commander in the West Bank and anor* Judgment of 5 February 2003, HCJ 3239/02, (2008) 133 ILR 332–64.

[574] Israeli Supreme Court, *Ajuri v IDF Commander in West Bank*, Judgment of 3 September 2002, at <elyon1.court.gov.il/files_eng/02/150/070/a15/02070150.a15.pdf>.

[575] Israeli Supreme Court, *Public Committee Against Torture in Israel and ors v State of Israel, General Security Service et al* Judgment of 13 December 2006, HCJ 5100/94, 4054/95, 6536/95, 5188/96, 7563/97, 7628/97, and 1043/99, 133 ILR (2008) 283–313.

[576] UNHRC, 'General Comment No 29 (Derogations from Provisions of the Covenant during a State of Emergency)' of 24 July 2001, GAOR 56th Session, Supp 40, vol 1, 202, para 3.

law.[577] Human rights treaties do not mention threats to 'global security', according to today's view, involving international terrorism, as opposed to local terrorism.[578] On the other hand, the determination of the Security Council that international terrorism is a 'threat to the peace' under Article 39 UN Charter has no direct bearing on the interpretation of derogation clauses. Treaties which do not contain a derogatory clause do not apparently permit derogations in any circumstance, as the ACommHPR has reiterated in several reports.[579]

According to derogation clauses, the state of emergence must be officially proclaimed and the proclamation must be internationally notified to relevant authorities; the derogation from human rights must be proportionate, ie limited to the extent strictly required by the exigencies of the situation; and the extraordinary measures adopted must be ended when the exceptional circumstances no longer exist. However, certain enumerated rights, which vary in part with the treaties and are not necessarily peremptory in character,[580] may not be derogated from even in states of emergency. Their explicit enumeration is not even necessarily exhaustive, since also rights not expressly listed may be considered non-derogable when they are 'essential' for the protection of the enumerated non-derogable rights,[581] as held in relation to the right to personal liberty[582] and the right to a fair trial.[583] The operation of a derogatory clause allows what would otherwise be a breach of the human rights set out in the treaty but does not justify other breaches of international law, including IHL in situations of armed conflict, nor may such clauses be discriminatory on grounds of race, colour, sex, language, religion, or social origin.[584]

(b) Other public interests

Human rights must usually be reconciled with a number of restrictions based on collective considerations. Restriction clauses are found in all major human rights treaties and raise difficult balancing issues for monitoring bodies. A general clause encompassing all human rights is contained in Article 29(2) UDHR.[585] Treaty restriction clauses pertain to specific rights, such as the right to respect for private life; the right to freedom of thought, conscience, and religion; the right to freedom of opinion and expression; and the right to freedom of association and assembly.[586] Others may be

[577] cf Art 4 ICCPR, Art 25 ECHR, Art 27 ACHR, and Part V, Art F European Social Charter.

[578] See Ch 5 above, section C (4)(a).

[579] ACommHPR, *Commission Nationale des Droits de l'Homme et des Libertés v Chad* Report of October 1995, Comm No 74/92, (2000) AHRLR 66, para 21; ACommHPR, *Malawi Africa Association, Amnesty International, Ms Sarr Diop, Union Interafricaine des Droits de l'Homme and RADDHO, Collectif des Veuves et Ayants-Droit, Association Mauritanienne des Droits de l'Homme* Report of 11 May 2000, Comm Nos 54/91, 61/91, 98/93, 164–196/97, 210/98, (2000) AHRLR 149, para 84; *Media Rights Agenda v Nigeria* Report of 6 November 2000, Comm No 224/98, (2000) AHRLR 227, para 67.

[580] UNHRC, 'General Comment No 29' (n 576 above) para 11.

[581] ibid paras 6, 13, 15–16.

[582] IACtHR, *Habeas Corpus in Emergency Situations (Arts. 27(2), 25(1) and 7(6) of the American Convention on Human Rights* Advisory Opinion of 30 January 1987 No OC-8/87, IACtHR Series A No 8, paras 31, 42; UNHRC, 'General Comment No 29' (n 576 above) para 16.

[583] IACtHR, *Judicial Guarantees in States of Emergency (Arts 27[2], 25 and 8 of the American Convention on Human Rights* Advisory Opinion of 6 October 1987 No OC-9/87, IACtHR Series A No 9, para 41.

[584] UNHRC, 'General Comment No 29' (n 576 above) paras 8–9.

[585] UNGA Res 217 A (III) of 10 December 1948, 'Universal Declaration of Human Rights', GAOR 3rd Session Part I 71.

[586] See eg para 2 of Arts 8–11 ECHR.

inserted in particular provisions, such as the limitations to the right to life or the right to a fair trial.[587] The focus here is on the restrictions grounded in the demands of public interest especially concerning the community as such, while those based on demands of respect for the rights of other individuals are discussed below.[588]

A restriction to human rights is generally permitted when it is prescribed by law, pursues a legitimate aim, and is necessary in order to attain the purpose of the treaty in a democratic society. Restrictions are prescribed by law when they are laid down in legislation, or in unwritten law, or in judicial practice. They must be adequately accessible and formulated with sufficient precision.[589] The legitimate aims that can be pursued vary not only with the treaty but also with the right involved, ranging from the protection of national security,[590] public health,[591] morals,[592] economic well-being,[593] territorial integrity,[594] public safety,[595] prevention of disorder or crime,[596] disclosure of information received in confidence,[597] and maintenance of the authority and impartiality of the judiciary.[598] The restriction must be required by a 'pressing social need', rather than due

[587] See eg ibid Arts 2, 6.

[588] This distinction, although 'somewhat artificial', as noted by RCA White and C Ovey, *The European Convention on Human Rights* (Oxford: OUP, 2010) 311, may still be helpful to a first approximation, as suggested by S Greer, *The Exceptions to Articles 8 to 11 of the European Convention on Human Rights* (Strasbourg: Council of Europe Publishing, 1997) 18.

[589] ECtHR, *Sunday Times v United Kingdom* Judgment of 26 April 1979, App 6538/74, Series A No 30, (1979–80) 2 EHRR 245, para 40.

[590] cf ECtHR, *Klass v Germany* Judgment of 6 September 1978, App 5029/71, Series A No 28, (1979–80) 2 EHRR 214, para 46; *Zana v Turkey* Judgment of 25 November 1997, App 18954/91, (1999) 27 EHRR 667, para 49; *Rekvényi v Hungary* Judgment of 20 May 1999, App 25390/94), (2000) 30 EHRR 519, para 41.

[591] cf ECtHR, *Eriksson v Sweden* Judgment of 22 June 1989, App 11373/85, Series A No 156, (1990) 12 EHRR 183, para 67; *Laskey, Jaggard and Brown v the United Kingdom* Judgment of 19 February 1997, Apps 21627/93, 21826/93, 21974/93, (1997) 24 EHRR 39, para 50.

[592] cf ECtHR, *Handyside v United Kingdom* Judgment of 7 December 1976, App 5493/72, Series A No 24, (1979–80) 1 EHRR 737, para 46; *Dudgeon v United Kingdom* Judgment of 22 October 1981, App 7525/76, Series A No 45, (1982) 4 EHRR 149, para 46 ('morals in the sense of moral standards obtaining in Northern Ireland'); *Müller et al v Switzerland* Judgment of 24 May 1988, App 10737/84, Series A No 132, (1991) 13 EHRR 212, para 30. In ECtHR, *A, B and C v Ireland* Judgment of 16 December 2010 [GC], App 25579/05, para 226, the Court held that the impugned restrictions to abortion in Ireland in the instant case 'were based on profound moral values concerning the nature of life which were reflected in the stance of the majority of the Irish people against abortion during the 1983 referendum and which have not been demonstrated to have relevantly changed since then', concluding that they 'pursued the legitimate aim of the protection of morals of which the protection in Ireland of the right to life of the unborn was one aspect'.

[593] ECtHR, *Gillow v United Kingdom* Judgment of 24 November 1986, App 9063/80, Series A No 109, (1986) 11 EHRR 355, para 54; *Berrehab v Netherlands* Judgment of 21 June 1988, App 10730/84, Series A No 138, (1989) 11 EHRR 322, para 26; *Miailhe v France* Judgment of 25 February 1993, App 12661/87, Series A No 256-C, (1993) 16 EHRR 332, para 33; *Funke v France* Judgment of 25 February 1993, App 10828/84, Series A No 256-A, (1993) 16 EHRR 297, para 52; *Hatton v United Kingdom* (n 432 above) para 126.

[594] cf ECtHR, *Zana v Turkey* (n 590 above) para 49.

[595] cf ECtHR, *Rekvényi v Hungary* (n 590 above) para 41; *Metropolitan Church of Bessarabia v Moldova* Judgment of 14 December 2001, App 45701/99, (2002) 35 EHRR 306, para 113; *Leela Förderkreis EV v Germany* Judgment of 6 November 2008, App 58911/00, (2009) 49 EHRR 117, para 94.

[596] cf ECtHR, *Klass v Germany* (n 590 above) para 46; *S and Marper v United Kingdom* Judgment of 4 December 2008 [GC], Apps 30562/04 and 30566/04, (2009) 48 EHRR 1169, para 100 (retention of fingerprint and DNA information).

[597] cf ECtHR, *Autronic AG v Switzerland* Judgment of 22 May 1990, App 12726/87, Series A No 178, (1990) 12 EHRR 485, para 59.

[598] cf ECtHR, *Schöpfer v Switzerland* Judgment of 20 May 1998, App 25405/94, (2001) 33 EHRR 845, para 24; *News Verlags GmbH and Co.KG v Austria* Judgment of 11 April 2000, App 31457/96, (2001) 31 EHRR 246, para 45.

to idiosyncratic policy preferences, and has to be proportionate to the aim sought. Social priorities can override individual human rights only when this is necessary in a democratic society. The use of restrictions to abuse rights and bring about an undemocratic regime is prohibited. Since the restrictions are exceptions to the full enjoyment of human rights, their enumeration is exhaustive and they have to be interpreted narrowly.[599] The burden of proof is on the defendant state.

The above discussion shows that human rights are by no means absolute and cannot avoid yielding to community demands. However, since their raison d'être is precisely to protect the individual from the might of the community, they make a difference in that their yielding is in principle excluded and when it is exceptionally permitted it is subject to the fulfilment of procedural and substantive standards.

(3) Wealth versus humanity

The urge to enjoy the greatest wealth possible tends to lead people to weaken respect for humanity. Resources are scarce and somebody's wealth is somebody else's poverty. It is highly difficult to strike a fair balance between wealth and humanity,[600] or between the right to trade and property of those who benefit from the pursuit of wealth and the rights of all others who do not enjoy the same benefits (or suffer from adverse effects) at least in the short term.[601] Advocates of free trade insist that exchange is beneficial to all the partners involved, but critics retort that the quest for wealth at any cost marketizes everything, including basic needs. It is counter-objected that free trade treaties do not make free trade an end in itself. They always contain clauses which allow exceptions when important non-trade matters are involved, such as morality and health. The preamble to the WTO Agreement, for example, makes reference to global standards of living, sustainable development, and environment preservation. Article XX GATT, together with similar clauses in other WTO Agreements,[602] is said to 'sound in human rights law', although states never expressly invoke human rights in WTO disputes to justify their measures. Moreover, the WTO's Appellate Body has interpreted WTO rules, from its inception, not 'in clinical isolation' but rather in the light of customary international law, including the rules on the interpretation of treaties codified in the VCLT.[603] This section briefly discusses a few issues (among many others) in which the

599 cf eg ECtHR, *Sidiropoulos et al v Greece* Judgment of 10 July 1998, App 26695/95, (1999) 27 EHRR 633, para 38.

600 For a general overview, see D Kinley, *Civilising Globalisation: Human Rights and the Global Economy* (Cambridge and New York: CUP, 2009) 37–92. For a critique of the tendency to assume that the regimes of international trade and human rights rest on disconnected, opposite, monolithic, and fixed ideologies, see A Lang, *World Trade Law After Neoliberalism: Re-Imagining the Global Economic Order* (Oxford: OUP, 2011).

601 For the debate about a human right to trade, see the impeccable observations of Joseph (n 339 above) 32–55. For the terms of the debate, see (among many other writings) E-U Petersmann, 'The WTO Constitution and Human Rights' (2000) 3 JIEL 19; the critique of P Alston, 'Resisting the Merger and Acquisition of Human Rights by Trade Law: A Reply to Petersmann' (2002) 13 EJIL 815, and the reply of E-U Petersmann, 'Taking Human Dignity, Poverty and Empowerment of Individuals More Seriously: Rejoinder to Alston' (2002) 13 EJIL 845; E-U Petersmann, 'Human Rights, International Economic Law and "Constitutional Justice"' (2008) 19 EJIL 769; and the critique of R Howse, 'Human Rights, International Economic Law and Constitutional Justice: A Reply' (2008) 19 EJIL 945.

602 For the possible extension of Art XX to WTO Agreements which do not contain a similar clause, see Y Ngangjoh-Hodu, 'Relationship of GATT Article XX Exceptions to other WTO Agreements' (2011) 80 Nord JIL 219.

603 See SJ Powell, 'The Place of Human Rights in World Trade Organization Rules' (2004) 16 Flo JIL 219.

tension between wealth and humanity is apparent: the exceptions to free trade based on public morals, food safety, access to essential medicine, environmental protection, cultural expression, and respect for the needs of local populations from abusive foreign investment.[604] It argues that in the absence of satisfactory rule conflict principles, as well as of principles to balance the conflicting values beyond the judicial discretion inherent in international bodies, such as WTO Panels and the Appellate Body, the question concerns not so much the law as it stands but rather the law which ought to be brought about as a result of engaging in a struggle in favour of the most vulnerable in the circumstances. It is social change that can spur both new interpretations of existing rules and changes in the law. Any term of Article XX GATT, such as 'public morals' and 'human, animal or plant life or health', can be understood as being more in favour of non-commercial values, without 'forcing' the law, or triggering a formal change in the law, if people change their attitudes in their daily life and demand interpretations and new rules more in line with the reality thus changed.

(a) *Public morals*

The question of whether a morally motivated trade measure adopted by a state is incompatible with international trade rules relates, as has been observed, to a wide variety of issues, including trade in slaves, heroin, alcohol, cigarettes, abortion-inducing drugs, lottery tickets, gambling, goods made by forced or indentured child labour, trafficking in human organs, blasphemous cartoons and movies, sex-related products, child pornography, Buddha images, non-kosher meat products, anti-Moslem articles, skins of baby seal pups, animal pelts, plumage of birds, meat produced according to various slaughtering methods, marine mammals captured in a inhumane manner, leghold traps, fur, wild animals and birds transported in unhealthly conditions, goods originating in states accused of breaching human rights, in particular core labour rights, and so forth. The meaning to be attached to 'morals' is contentious. It may be country-specific or involving the global dimension. Also, it may or may not be the same as the meaning attached to the word 'morals' used in human rights treaties as a legitimate aim to restrict their enjoyment.[605] Needless to say, what is moral to some may not be so to others, even within the same community.

Relevant to these issues is the 'moral exception' in Articles XX(a) GATT, XIV(a) GATS, and in other WTO Agreements, such as Articles XXIII GPA and 27(2) TRIPS Agreement.[606] The WTO adjudicating bodies had the first opportunity to address the question in the 2004 *Gambling Services* Report in relation to Article XIV(a) GATS.[607] The Panel considered that public morals, on the basis of the *Shorter Oxford English Dictionary*, 'denotes standards of right and wrong conduct maintained by or on behalf of a community or nation' and that 'the content of these concepts for Members c[ould] vary in time and space, depending upon a range of factors, including prevailing social, cultural,

[604] See T Cottier, J Pauwelyn, and E Bürgi (eds), *Human Rights and International Trade* (Oxford: OUP, 2005).

[605] See n 592 above.

[606] See MA Gonzalez, 'Trade and Morality: Preserving "Public Morals" Without Sacrificing the Global Economy' (2006) 39 Van JTL 939–72; JC Marwell, 'Trade and Morality: The WTO Public Morals Exception After Gambling' (2006) 81 NYU LR 802; NF Diebold, 'The Morals and Order Exceptions in WTO Law: Balancing the Toothless Tiger and the Undermining Mole' (2008) 11 JIEL 43.

[607] WTO, *United States—Measures Affecting the Cross-Border Supply of Gambling and Betting Services* Panel Report of 10 November 2004, WT/DS285/R; WTO, *United States—Measures Affecting the Cross-Border Supply of Gambling and Betting Services* AB Report of 20 April 2005, WT/DS285/AB/R.

ethical and religious values'.[608] The Panel added that WTO Members 'should be given some scope to define and apply for themselves the concepts of "public morals" . . . in their respective territories, according to their own systems and scales of values'.[609] Building on this national, country-specific notion of public morals (as opposed to an international or WTO standard) and relying on some international practice, ECJ judicial precedents, as well as comparative legislation specifically concerning lottery and gambling, the Panel concluded that national measures prohibiting gambling and betting services, including their supply by the internet, as those in force in the United States in the instant case, could fall within the scope of Article XIV(a) if they were enforced in pursuance of policies aimed to protect public morals or to maintain public order.[610]

A WTO Panel had a second opportunity to address the question, this time in relation to Article XX(a) GATT, in the 2009 *Publications and Audiovisual Entertainment Products* Report.[611] The Panel saw no reason to depart from the interpretation previously given to Article XIV(a) GATS,[612] but applied a strict standard to determine whether the invocation of public morals by China was 'necessary'. It concluded that China failed to meet the 'necessity' test since other, less trade-restrictive means to achieve the objective of protecting public morals were available.[613] In its 2009 report, the Appellate Body affirmed that, because there was at least one other reasonably available alternative, China's measures were not 'necessary' within the meaning of Article XX(a).[614]

This jurisprudence suggests that public morals is primarily defined according to national standards, but the necessity test is stringent. While the moral exception can be (too) readily invoked by relying on national moral standards, its endorsement by the DSB is ruled out whenever less trade-restrictive means to achieve its objectives are available.

(b) Food safety

As regards health, Article XX(b) GATT allows national measures necessary to protect 'human, animal or plant life or health'. This provision, together with the Agreement on Sanitary and Phytosanitary Measures (SPS Agreement), which is an integral part of WTO law, allows in principle both national sanitary measures (aimed at protecting human or animal life or health) and phytosanitary measures (aimed at protecting plant life or health), even when they are not discriminatory and have a restrictive effect on trade.[615]

Under Article 2(4) SPS Agreement, a national measure designed to protect against pests or diseases, additives, contaminants, or toxins in food, beverages, or feedstuffs which conforms to the SPS Agreement is presumed to comply with GATT, which means in practice a shift of the burden of proof (that in the instant case the measure is incompatible with GATT) to the complaining party.[616] National SPS measures are

608 ibid (Panel Report) paras 6.465, 6.461.

609 ibid para 6.461.

610 ibid para 6.465. The Panel's finding was upheld in general terms by the Appellate Body (para 299).

611 WTO, *China—Measures Affecting Trading Rights and Distribution Services for Certain Publications and Audiovisual Entertainment Products*, Panel Report of 12 August 2009, WT/DS363/R.

612 ibid para 7.759.

613 ibid paras 7.908, 7.911–7.912.

614 WTO, *China—Measures Affecting Trading Rights and Distribution Services* (n 611 above) AB Report of 21 December 2009, WT/DS363/AB/R, para 337.

615 E Dowler and CJ Finer (eds), *Welfare of Food: Rights and Responsibilities in a Changing World* (Oxford: Blackwell, 2003); E Gillman, 'Making WTO SPS Dispute Settlement Work: Challenges and Practical Solutions' (2011) 31 Nw JILB 439. For food security as part of the human right to food, see n 340 above.

616 WTO, *EC—Measures concerning Meat and Meat Products (Hormones)* (n 464 above) para 98.

allowed, under Article 2(1) and (2) SPS Agreement, if they are 'necessary' to the purpose of protecting human, animal, or plant life or health and if they are 'based on scientific criteria', 'within the territory' of the regulating state. PPM regulations of the importing state are thus allowed but only when aimed at protecting health within its territory. SPS national measures are also allowed, under Article 3(1) SPS Agreement, when grounded in 'international norms, directives, or recommendations'. When they conform to the Codex Alimentarius, a non-binding FAO and WHO instrument, they are presumed legitimate under Article 3(2) SPS Agreement. In the 1998 *Hormones* Report the Appellate Body aptly noted that the reference to international standards does not imply an obligation on member states to conform thereto.[617] Article 5 SPS Agreement requires a risk assessment when a standard other than an international standard is used. In the 2000 *Salmon* Report, the Appellate Body established three risk assessment requirements to be met.[618] Article 5(7) SPS Agreement mentions the precautionary principle so as to allow, on certain conditions, provisional measures where scientific evidence is insufficient on the basis of available information. In the 1998 *Hormones* Report, the Appellate Body avoided taking a position on the question of whether the principle had become a general principle of international law.[619]

The SPS Agreement, uniquely in the WTO system, makes the lawfulness of national SPS measures predominantly dependent on science. This 'turn' to science-based truth has been criticized for ignoring the political and cultural dimensions of risk. Science is often as uncertain or questionable among the scientists themselves as non-science, and in any event can hardly be properly handled within a non-scientific institution like the WTO. In the approach taken here, when science is also uncertain, as is often the case, and in the absence of any standard, consumers in principle should be protected, as the most vulnerable, and the precautionary principle should be taken seriously.

(c) Access to medicine

Another question surrounding wealth and health concerns the effects of the TRIPS Agreement on access to medicine.[620]

Under Article 27 TRIPS Agreement, WTO member states (except, however, for LDCs until 2016) are under a general obligation to make patents available 'for any inventions, whether products or processes, in all fields of technology', arguably including pharmaceutical products and process patents, and to provide for a twenty-year protection term (Article 33). Patents for the use of drugs in the treatment of such diseases as HIV/AIDS determine monopoly pricing (far higher than marginal cost) by patent-holders (typically MNEs), normally to recoup research and development costs, and such high prices may prove unaffordable for many patients, and health budgets, especially in thepoorer countries. Moreover, private markets have generally no incentive in developing unrewarding research in drugs for neglected diseases (which are widespread in developing countries) or in cures and vaccines rather than mere symptom relief. Article 8(1)

[617] WTO, *EC—Measures concerning Meat and Meat Products (Hormones)* (n 464 above) para 170.

[618] WTO, *Australia—Measures Affecting Importation of Salmon* AB Report of 18 February 2000, WT/DS18/RW, para 121.

[619] See n 464 above.

[620] H Hestermeyer, *Human Rights and the WTO: The Case of Patents and Access to Medicines* (Oxford: OUP, 2007); C Ho, *Access to Medicine in the Global Economy: International Agreements on Patents and Related Rights* (Oxford: OUP, 2011); FM Abbott and G Dukes, *Global Pharmaceutical Policy: Ensuring Medicines for Tomorrow's World* (Cheltenham and Northampton: Edward Elgar, 2011); Joseph (n 339 above) 214–44.

specifies, as one of the 'basic principles' of the TRIPS, that member states may adopt measures 'necessary to protect public health' and 'to promote the public interest in sectors of vital importance' to their socio-economic and technological development, 'provided that such measures are consistent' with the TRIPS. Exceptions found in Article 27 itself do not cover access to medicine as such,[621] the 'limited exceptions' in Article 30 are uncertain in scope,[622] and the 'security exception' in Article 73 may apply only to extreme situations, such as grave pandemics. For its part, Article 6 has no impact on the 'exhaustion' of IP rights and on parallel importations, while Article 31 allows states to issue compulsory licenses on certain conditions in respect of the generic manufacture of patented goods without the consent of the patent-holder. At the same time, most states bound by the TRIPS Agreement are also parties to both the ICCPR, whose Article 6 protects the right to life and, presumably, the right of access to life-saving medicine, as well as to the ICESCR, whose Articles 12 and 15(1)(b) provide, respectively, for the right to health (arguably including a right of access to medicine) and the right to enjoy the benefits of scientific progress.[623] While the states parties to ICCPR have an immediate obligation to respect and ensure respect of Article 6, the states parties to Articles 12 and 15(1)(b) ICESCR have an obligation to achieve these rights progressively under Article 2(1), although they are required to take immediate steps to the maximum of their available resources to respect, protect, and fulfil such rights. From these provisions an obligation may be placed on states to prevent private MNEs from charging excessively high prices for drugs, in which case a rule conflict arises.[624]

Possible ways of resolving the conflict such as the insertion of a human rights exception in the TRIPS, or an express reference to human rights treaties, or a broad interpretation of the word 'security' in Article 73 (in terms of 'human security')[625] are unlikely. The 2001 DOHA Declaration on TRIPS and public health, affirming that the TRIPS Agreement 'should be interpreted and implemented in a manner supportive of WTO Members' right to protect public health and, in particular, to promote access

[621] cf Art 27(2) (*ordre public*, morality, 'including to protect human, animal or plant life or health or to avoid serious prejudice to the environment'), Art 27(3)(a) ('diagnostic, therapeutic and surgical methods for the treatment of humans or animals'), Art 27(3)(b) ('plants and animals other than micro-organisms, and essentially biological processes for the production of plants or animals other than non-biological and microbiological processes'), as well as Art 65(4) (transition period), and Art 70(8).

[622] For the view that testing generic drugs prior to the expiry of a patent, unlike their stockpiling, is a 'limited exception' under Article 30 on the basis of a narrow interpretation of the exception, see WTO, *Canada—Patent Protection of Pharmaceutical Products*, Panel Report of 17 March 2000, WT/DS114/R, paras 7.30, 7.33–7.35, 7.45.

[623] See CESCR, 'General Comment No 14: The right to the highest attainable standard of health (Art. 12)' of 11 August 2000, UN Doc E/C.12/2000/4; UNGA, 'Report of the Special Rapporteur on the right of everyone to the enjoyment of the highest attainable standard of physical and mental health' of 13 September 2006, UN Doc A/61/338; HR Council, 'Access to Medicine in the context of the right of to the enjoyment of the highest attainable standard of physical and mental health' of 12 October 2009, UN Doc A/HRC/RES/12/24.

[624] It is worth noting that the conflict may also be seen as one between different human rights if one considers that IP rights can be regarded as aspects of the right to property and, more specifically, of the right of everyone 'to benefit from the protection from the moral and material interests resulting from any scientific, literary or artistic production of which he is the author' (cf Art 15(1)(c) ICESCR). It is also often argued that IP rights may have a positive effect on development and human rights in general by encouraging technology transfer, foreign direct investment, and local innovation. However, for the distinction between Art 15(1)(c) rights and IP rights, see CESCR, 'General Comment No 17: The right of everyone to benefit from the protection of the moral and material interests resulting from any scientific, literary or artistic production of which he or she is the author (article 15, paragraph 1 (c)' of 12 January 2006, UN Doc E/C.12/GC/17.

[625] See nn 153–9 above and accompanying text.

to medicines for all',[626] as implemented by a Decision adopted in 2003,[627] has led to the 2005 Amendment to the TRIPS Agreement designed to transform the 2003 Decision into a new Article 31*bis*, but the amendment is not yet in force.[628] Other proposals include price caps and interventions by the public sector,[629] the Health Impact Fund,[630] a new treaty to be included under the rubric of WTO commitments to fund 'global public goods',[631] and 'the de-linkage of the costs of research and development and the price of health products and methods for tailoring the optimal mix of incentives to a particular condition or product with the objective of addressing diseases that disproportionately affect developing countries'.[632] To some extent states may succeed in avoiding breaches of human rights by utilizing the exceptions and flexibilities of the TRIPS as much as possible.[633] For their part, Panels and the Appellate Body are required to apply the TRIPS Agreement, although they might in some measure take account of human rights rules when applying the TRIPS 'not in isolation' from the whole body of international law.[634] There is also a trend in Free Trade Agreements (FTAs) and Bilateral treaties (BITs) which pulls in the direction of placing 'TRIPS-plus' obligations even stricter than TRIPS, then extending to all WTO member states on the basis of MFN obligations for those states which accept them, or as conditions to accede to the WTO, thereby weakening the flexibility of the TRIPS itself.

The approach taken here suggests that, rather than hair-splitting speculation on the available legal texts to force them into the desired meaning, a struggle is to be engaged for an international law that favours the sick of the moment as manifestly more

[626] WTO, Ministerial Conference 'Declaration on the TRIPS Agreement and Public Health' of 14 November 2001, WT/MIN(01)/DEC/2, recognizing to WTO member states 'the right to grant compulsory licenses and the freedom to determine the grounds upon which such licenses are granted' and 'the right to determine what constitutes a national emergency or other circumstances of extreme urgency', it 'being understood that public health crises, including those relating to HIV/AIDS, tuberculosis, malaria and other epidemics, can represent a national emergency or other circumstances of extreme urgency' under Art 31, and leaving each of them 'free to establish its own regime [for the] exhaustion [of intellectual property rights] without challenge' for the purposes of parallel imports.

[627] cf WTO, 'Implementation of Paragraph 6 of the DOHA Declaration on the TRIPS Agreement and Public Health', Decision by the General Council of 30 August 2003, WT/L/540, waiving in certain circumstances and on several conditions the territorial restriction on compulsory licenses in Article 31(f) TRIPS whereby licenses must be issued 'predominantly for the supply of the domestic market', thus encouraging the issuance of compulsory licenses in countries which have the capacity to manufacture generic drugs for exports to developing countries. As of 31 January 2012, only Rwanda has notified the WTO (on 17 July 2007) of an intention to use the waiver as an importing state and only Canada has notified an intention (on 8 October 2007) to use the waiver as an exporting state (cf WTO, IP/N/9/RWA/1 and IP/N/10/CAN/1).

[628] WTO, 'Amendment of the Trips Agreement', Decision by the General Council of 6 December 2005, WT/L/641. The 2003 Decision will remain in force until the Amendment is approved by two-thirds of the WTO members, at which time it will take effect in such members and replace the 2003 Decision in their relations while for each of the remaining members the waiver will continue to apply until each of them accepts the Amendment. As of 31 January 2012, 42 WTO member states have accepted the Amendment (cf <http://www.wto.org/english/tratop_e/trips_e/amendment_e.htm>).

[629] See Joseph (n 339 above) 238–9.

[630] See T Pogge and W Menko (eds), *Incentives for Global Public Health: Patent Law and Access to Essential Medicines* (Cambridge: CUP, 2010).

[631] Knowledge Ecology International (KEI), 'KEI Proposal: A WTO Agreement on the Supply of Knowledge as a Global Public Good', at <http://keionline.org/wtoandpublicgoods>.

[632] WHA, 'Global Strategy and plan of action on public health, innovation and intellectual property', WHO doc WHA61.21 of 24 May 2008, at <http://apps.who.int/gb/ebwha/pdf_files/A61/A61_R21-en.pdf>, para 4.

[633] For this approach, see HR Council, 'Report of the Special Rapporteur on the right of to the enjoyment of the highest attainable standard of physical and mental health' of 31 March 2009, UN Doc A/HRC/11/12.

[634] See Ch 6 above, section B (3)(e).

vulnerable in comparison with patent-holders, if necessary with measures of compensation from collective funds. The wealth, and hence also the availability of resources to be allocated to health, that patents may guarantee in the long term is welcome but hardly cures those who suffer now.

(d) Healthy environment

Free trade produces both positive and negative effects on the environment which vary in place and time. According to neo-liberal economists, positive effects are far stronger, including a more efficient use of resources, the diffusion of cleaner technologies, and greater availability of resources for environmental protection. Neo-Malthusians and environmentalists retort that harmful effects are devastating, including relocalization of polluting industries to states with lower environmental standards in order to take advantage of lower costs of production, and ensuing state competition and a race to the bottom to attract foreign investment.[635] When negative effects are produced, a conflict arises between the WTO regime and the environmental regime. National trade-related environmental measures (TREMs) tend to be in conflict with the WTO regime, and in particular with the aim of prohibiting all restrictions on trade other than tariffs under Article XI GATT. MEAs may expressly provide for a ban on the import of environmentally harmful products from non-party states, as is the case with Article 4 of the 1987 Montreal Protocol on Substances that Deplete the Ozone Layer.[636]

In recent years the WTO jurisprudence has shown signs of some greater deference to environmental measures restricting trade. Before the establishment of the WTO, in the 1991 *Tuna I* Report the prohibition on imports of tuna fished using nets which endangered dolphins under the US Marine Mammal Protection Act (MMPA) was found to be an impermissible quantitative restriction under Article XI(1) GATT 1947 not justifiable under Article XX(b), (d), or (g), and also because it had an extraterritorial reach since it applied to fishing carried on outside the territory of the United States.[637] In the 1994 *Tuna II* Report (unadopted) Article XX(b), (d), or (g) exceptions were equally rejected.[638] After the establishment of the WTO, in the 1996 *Gasoline* Report[639] and notably in the 1998 *Shrimps/Turtles* Report, the Appellate Body construed the 'exhaustible natural resources' exception under Article XX(g) to be more in favour of environmental concerns, inter alia, as a result of an evolutionary interpretation of the term 'exhaustible' to be understood today also to include 'renewable' resources exposed to extinction, such as endangered animal species capable of reproducing, such as sea turtles,[640] although the national measures challenged were found in the end to be contrary to the chapeau of Article XX.[641] The Appellate Body has also

[635] For a collection of essays discussing the relationship between justice, fairness, and environmental protection, see J Ebbesson and PN Okowa (eds), *Environmental Law and Justice in Context* (Cambridge: CUP, 2009).

[636] See n 471 above; eg pursuant to Art 4(1) 'As of 1 January 1990, each party shall ban the import of the [ozone depleting] controlled substances in Annex A from any State not party to this Protocol'.

[637] WTO, *Restrictions on Import of Tuna (No 1) (Mexico v United States)* Panel of 3 September 1991, WT/DS21/R, BISD/39S/155, (1991) 30 ILM 1594, paras 5.18, 5.27–5.28, 5.32–5.33, 5.40.

[638] GATT 1947, *Restrictions on Import of Tuna (No 2) (European Economic Community v United States)* Panel Report of 16 June 1994, WT/DS29/R, (1994) 33 ILM 842, paras 5.27, 5.39, 5.40, 6.1.

[639] GATT 1947, *United States—Standards for Reformulated and Conventional Gasoline*, AB Report of 29 April 1996, WTO Doc WT/DS2/AB/R, section III (b).

[640] WTO, *United States—Import Prohibition of Certain Shrimp and Shrimp Products*, AB Report of 12 October 1998, WT/DS58/AB/R, paras 128–134.

[641] ibid paras 160–184.

taken a more nuanced approach over time to 'likeness' and PPMs going beyond the physical characteristics of the product, with some possibility of seeing as unlike products not falling within the non-discriminatory WTO regime two products which are like in terms of their physical characteristics but are unlike due to the process by which they are made, without any need for reliance on an Article XX exception.[642] Finally, in the 2001 *Shrimps (Article 21.5)* Report, the Appellate Body upheld the US import ban after the United States had pursued good faith negotiations with the other states concerned to reach agreement on measures to be taken to conserve sea turtles.[643]

The recent WTO jurisprudence is welcome in its effort to strike a balance between the two relevant values without giving forced readings of existing rules. This, in fact, has occurred because of the struggle for less pursuit of profit at any cost engaged by non-state actors and proves that the meaning to be given to rules, including the notion of 'likeness' ultimately rests on social attitudes and efforts made towards a greater protection of the most vulnerable.

(e) Core labour standards

The fierce competition among businesses in a globalized world and their ability to relocate in another, more profitable state often causes a race to the bottom in labour conditions, affecting 'core labour standards' and encouraging child and forced labour, if not slavery.[644] In the absence of any provision in WTO law to prevent social dumping, developed states and trade unions have reacted in defence of workers and children worldwide.[645] Their proposals include a 'social clause' to be inserted in WTO law (following the NAFTA example)[646] which would reward the states which protect the basic rights of workers while penalizing those which fail to do so. However, proposals for social clauses have been opposed by developing countries, low labour costs representing for them a major comparative advantage in world trade. In the 1996 Singapore Declaration states have committed to core labour standards, reserving this concern to the ILO.[647] In the framework of the ILO, core labour standards, as regulated by several ILO Conventions and soft law instruments, have been stated in the 1998 Copenhagen Declaration[648] and reasserted in the 2008 Declaration.[649] They include the rights to

[642] See WTO, *EC—Measures Affecting Asbestos and Asbestos-Containing Products* (n 365 above) paras 101–103. See in addition n 366 above.

[643] WTO, *United States—Import Prohibition of Certain Shrimp and Shrimp Products, Recourse to Article 21.5 of the DSU by Malaysia* AB Report of 22 October 2001, WT/DS58/AB/RW, paras 134, 152–153.

[644] See eg C Granger and J-M Siroën, 'Core Labour Standards in Trade Agreements: From Multilateralism to Bilateralism' (2006) 40 JWT 813.

[645] For the sanctions adopted by the European Union against Myanmar and Belarus and their doubtful effectiveness, see W Zhou and L Cuyvers, 'Linking International Trade and Labour Standards: The Effectiveness of Sanctions under the European Union's GSP' (2011) 45 JWT 63.

[646] C Summers, 'NAFTA's Labor Side Agreement and International Labor Standards' (1999) 3 JSESBL 173. Social clauses have also been included in a number of commodities agreements.

[647] WTO, Ministerial Conference 'Singapore Ministerial Declaration' (13 December 1996) WT/MIN(96)/DEC.

[648] ILO, Declaration on Fundamental Principles and Rights at Work (done 19 June 1998), (1998) 37 ILM 1233, listing in para 2: (a) freedom of association and the effective recognition of the right to collective bargaining; (b) the elimination of all forms of forced or compulsory labour; (c) the effective abolition of child labour; and (d) the elimination of discrimination in respect of employment and occupation.

[649] ILO, Declaration on Social Justice for a Fair Globalization (done 10 June 2008) in *International Labour Organization: ILO Declaration on Social Justice for a Fair Globalization* (Geneva: ILO Publications, 2008) 5, stating that 'the violation of fundamental principles and rights at work cannot be

association,[650] collective bargaining,[651] equal remuneration,[652] non-discrimination,[653] and the prohibition of forced labour.[654]

Within the WTO, national measures aimed at prohibiting imports of goods allegedly produced by abusing the core rights of workers or children are in principle contrary to the principles of GATT, notably the most-favoured-nation and national treatment standards. Such measures can hardly be regarded as dumping under Article VI GATT or subsidies under Article XVI GATT, nor do they fall within the safeguard clause found in Article XIX GATT. One could argue that 'likeness' under Articles I and III includes PPM likeness and that two otherwise like products are not like for GATT purposes when they are produced by abusing core labour standards. Developing countries insist, however, that likeness should be given a narrow meaning and the jurisprudence thus far, apart some recent openness in environmental matters, is not prepared to accept too broad a notion of like products lest this would defeat the entire system.

The question is then whether national measures aimed at discouraging abuse of core labour standards extra-jurisdictionally can be justified under Article XX GATT. In fact, none of the exceptions provided therein expressly mentions the protection of labour conditions, but in the abstract the exceptions concerning public morals, human, animal or plant life or health, and products of prison labour may be relevant. The exception based on public morals, understood in a country-specific sense,[655] might match social dumping, but it would open the system to an unpredictable flood of morality-based claims. Its reading in terms of 'universal public morality', on the other hand, is not supported by the practice and is reminiscent of the 'moralizing' or 'civilizing' mission of Western powers in the past. The 'life or health' exception refers in principle to the life and health of the people coming into contact with the product within the importing country, not of those who have produced the good abroad. The 'prison labour' exception may presumably be reasonable only as regards extreme forms of forced labour. A solution may be to interpret Article XX and extend by analogy the jurisprudence on environmental matters to social dumping, making appeal in particular to the reference made by the *Shrimps/Turtles* AB Report to the interpretation of Article XX(g) 'in the light of contemporary concerns of the community of nations'.[656] This, however, seems a rather weak argument bearing in mind that it would justify virtually every national measure (only) from the states whose basic values are those of the international community.

Another solution is to address the question 'from outside' the WTO and endorse the permissibility of collective countermeasures against abuses of core labour standards.

invoked or otherwise used as a legitimate comparative advantage and that labour standards should not be used for protectionist trade purposes'.

[650] ILO Convention (No 87) concerning Freedom of Association and Protection of the Right to Organise (adopted 9 July 1948, entered into force 4 July 1950) 68 UNTS 17.

[651] ILO Convention (No 98) concerning the Application of the Principles of the Right to Organize and to Bargain Collectively (adopted 1 July 1949, entered into force on 18 July 1951) 96 UNTS 258.

[652] ILO Convention (No 100) concerning Equal Remuneration for Men and Women Workers for Work of Equal Value (adopted 29 June 1951, entered into force 23 May 1953) 165 UNTS 303.

[653] ILO Convention (No 111) concerning Discrimination in Respect of Employment and Occupation (adopted 25 June 1958, entered into force 15 June 1960] 362 UNTS 31).

[654] ILO Convention (No 29) concerning Forced or Compulsory Labour (adopted 28 June 1930, entered into force 1 May 1932) 39 UNTS 55; Convention (No 105) concerning the Abolition of Forced Labour (adopted 25 June 1957, entered into force 17 January 1959) 320 UNTS 291. Forced labour is also prohibited by all major human rights treaties, both universal and regional: see eg Art 4 UDHR, Art 8(3) ICCPR, Art 6(1) ICESCR, Art 4(2) ECHR, Art 1(2)(II) European Social Charter.

[655] See section B (3)(a) above.

[656] WTO, *United States—Import Prohibition of Certain Shrimp and Shrimp Products* (n 640 above) para 129.

This presupposes that the WTO is not a self-contained regime with its own exclusive, institutional system of countermeasures. However, while it is true that the WTO is not self-contained,[657] it is still contentious that collective countermeasures are permitted under general international law.[658] Apart from the *general* question of the permissibility of collective countermeasures, it is unclear on what basis such countermeasures should be permitted where most states, notably developing states, are in fact *specifically* contrary to any derogation from the principles of free trade in this respect. Even assuming *arguendo* that the generality of states is in favour of collective countermeasures, it is only developed states that would be in favour of them when core labour rights are involved.

Briefly, there is room for a struggle to change 'from below' the *meanings* attached to the expressions found in Article XX, bringing them more into line with notions of justice. This rule does not specify the meaning of 'public morals' or 'prison labour' and adjudicators cannot but turn to society for the meaning of such words through a process of social attunement. It is at this level that the law can be changed in favour of the most vulnerable (both workers and communities in general who make a living, by means of acceptable lower labour standards), even when it is not formally changed and it is even satisfactory as it is (loosely) formulated at the moment. Human rights standards may indeed improve when wealth increases, but there are non-extreme situations in which reasonable but worse labour conditions than the average Western standard may be vital to the most vulnerable in their social, economic, and cultural context.

(f) Cultural expression

The question of whether cultural objects—including films, TV programmes, the internet, books, newspapers, magazines, etc—are merchandise just like any other is at the core of the debate over an alleged 'McDonaldization' of world culture, threatening local and national identities.[659]

The issue arose following World War I when European states introduced screen quotas to protect their film industries from the influx of films from the United States. Eventually, Articles III(10) and IV GATT 1947 provided for an exception to the prohibition on quantitative restrictions of imports under Article XI in relation to national treatment for films. During the Uruguay Round the question of whether audiovisual media were to be treated as merchandise and subjected to goods and services free trade was heatedly discussed, the United States pushing for their liberalization. The view that cultural goods and services fall under WTO law, at least in principle, gained currency. GATT 1994 confirmed in Articles I, III, and XI the MFN principle, the national treatment, and the prohibition on quantitative restrictions of imports. Since GATS did the same in Articles III, XVII, and XVI, many WTO members, including EU members, Canada, and Switzerland have refrained from making any commitments in the audiovisual sector, and some fifty WTO members have listed MFN exemptions in this sector. GATT provides for a 'cultural exception' in Article IV, as regards screen quotas, and Article XX(f), limited to 'national treasures of historic, artistic, or archaeological value'.

[657] See Ch 6 above, section B (3)(b).
[658] See Ch 8 below, section B (1)(c).
[659] See eg CB Graber and M Burri-Nenova (eds), *Governance of Digital Game Environments and Cultural Diversity: Transdisciplinary Enquiries* (Cheltenham: Edward Elgar, 2010). For the need for resistance to free trade in educational services, see nn 484 and 485 above and accompanying text.

WTO Panels and the Appellate Body have been slow to accept the cultural exception thus far. In the 1997 *Periodicals* Reports, they found certain measures adopted by Canada in favour of Canadian periodicals, allegedly to protect cultural identity under Article XX(d), to be in breach of GATT.[660] In the 2009 *Publications and Audiovisual Entertainment Products* Reports, as seen earlier, they found that the 'moral exception' raised by China to justify the protection of its culture and traditional values did not apply since the Chinese measures were not necessary for this purpose.[661] In the 2009 *Intellectual Property Rights* Report a WTO Panel found that China's copyright law, which protected certain publications allegedly designed, inter alia, to protect social ethics or fine Chinese cultural traditions, was inconsistent with Article 5(1) Berne Convention,[662] as referred to by Article 9(1) TRIPS,[663] without considering the relevance of any cultural justification.

As a sort of 'external' corrective, after the adoption in 2001 of the Universal Declaration on Cultural Diversity,[664] the 2005 UNESCO Convention on Cultural Diversity (CCD) was concluded.[665] By assuming that cultural goods and services have a 'dual nature', since 'they convey identities, values and meanings, and must therefore not be treated as solely having commercial value', as stated in recital 18 of the Preamble and in Article 1(g), the Convention provides a series of 'rights' aimed at allowing national measures of protection of local culture that could very likely be contrary to WTO obligations if, or to the extent that, the goods and services protected are covered by WTO law. The few obligations found in the CCD are of minor importance and suggest that its purpose was to correct the law of the WTO 'from outside' with rights conferred on states against WTO obligations. Unsurprisingly the Convention has been accused of being an anti-WTO, protectionist instrument in disguise, contrary, inter alia, to freedom of expression and information.[666] Article 20 CCD contains a rather ambiguous conflict rule stipulating that the 'Parties recognize that they shall perform in good faith . . . all other treaties to which they are parties' and, accordingly, 'without subordinating this Convention to any other treaty', they shall foster mutual supportiveness between the CCD and the other treaties to which they are parties, and in particular they 'shall take into account the relevant provisions of this Convention'. This clause leaves open whether, in case of conflict, WTO law or the CCD prevails, but suggests that WTO law should be interpreted in the light of the CCD—a clear message to WTO Panels and the Appellate Body.

[660] WTO, *Canada—Certain Measures concerning Periodicals* Panel Report of 14 March 1997, WT/DS31/R, paras 3.5, 5.45, ruling that 'the ability of any Member to take measures to protect its cultural identity was not at issue in the present case'; AB Report of 30 June 1997, WT/DS31/AB/R, not addressing the issue but 'leav[ing] intact the findings and conclusions of the Panel that were not the subject of this appeal'.

[661] WTO, *China—Measures Affecting Trading Rights and Distribution Services* (n 611 above) Panel Report of 12 August 2009, paras 4.314–4.324, 7.724–7.914, concluding that, while 'it is undoubtedly the case that the protection of public morals ranks among the most important values or interests pursued by Members as a matter of public policy' (para 7.817), China had not demonstrated that its measures were 'necessary' under Art XX(a) (paras 7.908, 7.911–7.912).

[662] Berne Convention for the Protection of Literary and Artistic Works of 9 September 1886.

[663] WTO, *China—Measures Affecting the Protection and Enforcement of Intellectual Property Rights* Panel Report of 26 January 2009, WT/DS362/R.

[664] UNESCO, Universal Declaration on Cultural Diversity of 2 November 2001, Records of the General Conference 31st Session, vol 1, 61.

[665] See n 324 above.

[666] For a re-definition of the trade–culture relationship in the digital networked environment, see M Burri-Nenova, 'Trade versus Culture in the Digital Environment: An Old Conflict in Need of a New Definition' (2009) 12 JIEL 17.

(g) Local basic needs

Of great importance today is the complex relationship between foreign investment by MNEs and human rights.[667] Both international investment law (IIL) and international human rights law (IHRL) have individuals (mostly foreign juridical persons in the case of the former, and natural persons in the latter) at their heart. IIL is basically aimed at protecting the right to property of foreign investors, a right often treated as a fundamental right since the 1789 French Declaration on the Rights of Man and the Citizen.[668] At a time of global privatization, foreign investors are in any case usually outsourced by the states to supply formerly public services affecting local people's basic needs. While the rights conferred on foreign investors by investment treaties may be regarded to some extent as human rights, ranging from the right to property to the rights included in 'fair and equitable' treatment, the host state has to respect basic human rights for its citizens, including the positive obligation to take all the measures in its power to prevent human rights violations within its jurisdiction perpetrated by private foreign investors.

Like a number of human rights treaties, IIL grants private foreign investors direct access to international tribunals, but, unlike IHRL, investment arbitral tribunals' applicable law includes various classes of rules which are specified in the compromissory clause, including international law (hence arguably also IHRL),[669] and access to justice is normally provided without prior exhaustion of local remedies, this allowing investors to avoid relying on the goodwill of their home state to exercise diplomatic protection (which is permitted, inter alia, only when local remedies have been exhausted).[670] Unlike human rights treaties, IIL as a rule grants access to arbitration only to nationals of the states parties to the investment treaty.

Although in the abstract both investors and host states might invoke human rights in investment disputes, they rarely do so. Investors find that the human rights standard is generally lower than that provided by investment treaties. Host states may refrain from invoking breaches of human rights by investors to avoid being found in complicity with investors or in breach of their duty to protect from investors' abuses. For their part, arbitral tribunals are reluctant to address questions involving human rights,[671] except for hearing *amici curiae*,[672] and tend to focus on standards of transparency and public interest. Local populations may successfully file complaints with available human rights monitoring bodies.[673] On balance, remedies available to local populations are still few and have little effect.

(4) Humanity versus humanity

Not only do human rights often have to be balanced against imperative demands of public interest; they frequently also have to be balanced against one another. Here the

[667] See P-M Dupuy, F Francioni, and E-U Petersmann (eds), *Human Rights in International Investment Law and Arbitration* (Oxford: OUP, 2009).

[668] cf Art 17 UDHR, Art 16 CEDAW, Art 15 CMW, Art 1 Protocol No 1 to the ECHR, Art 21 ACHR, and Art 14 ACHPR. Neither the ICCPR nor the ICESCR contains a provision protecting the right to property.

[669] cf Art 42 ICSID Convention, Art 1131 NAFTA, and Art 26(6) Energy Charter Treaty.

[670] cf Art 26(1) ICSID Convention.

[671] cf Arbitral Tribunal, *Biloune and Marine Drive Complex Ltd v Ghana Investments Centre and the Government of Ghana* Award on Jurisdiction and Liability of 27 October 1989, (1994) 95 ILR 184, 203.

[672] See Ch 5 above, section C (3)(a).

[673] cf eg IACtHR, *Mayagna (Sumo) Awas Tingni Community v Nicaragua* Judgment of 31 August 2001, IACtHR Series C No 79.

value of humanity is unhelpful as guidance. International and national courts use various techniques to reconcile these tensions when the law in itself fails to give any reasonable clue. The key criterion should be to favour the human right of the most vulnerable in the circumstances and in proportion to the relative vulnerability of the persons and entities involved. This section cites a few cases, among very many, in which a balance has been struck by a human rights monitoring body between the competing human rights of different people. It then presents the various legal frameworks of humanitarian concern in current international law, showing the difficulties involved in their coordination. The bottom line is that humanity is a galaxy of innumerable possible meanings, capable of leading to a wide variety of different conclusions.

(a) Rights of others

Restrictions to human rights are not only envisaged to protect social priorities, as discussed earlier, but also to protect the rights and freedoms of others. Admittedly, restrictions justified for public interest reasons can also be seen as designed to protect the rights of others. For example, a restriction of the right to freedom of association for safety reasons may be seen as designed to protect the rights of the persons whose safety is in danger. However, certain restrictions expressly refer to certain specific persons or classes of persons. In such instances there is not so much a balance to be struck between an individual and the community as between individuals whose rights are in principle equally worthy of protection, and protection meets with no significant restriction based on the very survival of the community as such.

The 'protection of the rights and freedoms of others' is expressly envisaged in human rights treaties as a legitimate aim which may justify a restriction (proportionate to the aim pursued) of a certain right, notably the right for respect of private life, freedom of thought, conscience, and religion, freedom of expression, and freedom of association. For example, in the 1996 *Johansen* Judgment the ECtHR found, on the assumption that 'a fair balance ha[d] to be struck between the interests of the child in remaining in public care and those of the parent in being reunited with the child', that the taking into care of a child, the refusal to terminate the care, and the deprivation of her parental rights and access, served the purpose of protecting the rights and freedoms of others (the child in the instant case) under Article 8(2).[674] In the 2001 *Pretty* Judgment the ECtHR balanced the right of the applicant to respect for private life, specifically an alleged right to assisted suicide of a terminally ill person, against the rights of others of protection from abuse by third persons.[675] In the 2005 *Şahin* Judgment the ECtHR found that a prohibition against wearing the Islamic headscarf in the University of Istanbul was justified, inter alia, in the interests of the rights and freedoms of others.[676] Similar issues arise when it comes to 'the protection of the reputation or rights of others'

[674] ECtHR, *Johansen v Norway* Judgment of 7 August 1996, App 17383/90, (1997) 23 EHRR 33, para 61.

[675] ECtHR, *Pretty v United Kingdom* Judgment of 29 April 2002, App 2346/02, ECtHR Rep 2002-III, (2002) 35 EHRR 1, para 74.

[676] ECtHR, *Şahin v Turkey* Judgment of 10 November 2005, App 44774/98, ECtHR Rep 2005-XI, para 99. For an insightful analysis, see R Nigro, 'The Margin of Appreciation Doctrine and the Case-law of the European Court of Human Rights on the Islamic Veil' (2010) 11 HRR 531. For a case previously decided by the UNHRC finding a violation of Art 18(2) ICCPR, which prohibits any coercion that would impair the individual's freedom to have or adopt a religion, 'in the absence of any justification provided by the State party', see UNHRC, *Raihon Hudoyberganova v Uzbekistan* Views of 5 November 2004, Comm No 931/2000, UN Doc CCPR/C/82/D/931/2000, para 6.2.

as a legitimate aim with regard to freedom of expression, especially in defamation cases where a balance has to be struck between the right of writers and publishers to circulate information or ideas about other persons and the right of the latter to protect their reputations.[677]

Different human rights expressly envisaged in a treaty might be invoked by different persons pointing in diverging directions and thus requiring an appropriate balancing as to the proportionality of the restriction of one right in favour of the other. For example, concerning freedom of expression and freedom of religion, the ECtHR held in the 1994 *Otto-Preminger-Institut* Judgment that the prohibition under the Austrian Penal Code against publicly showing a film allegedly offending the Catholic faith (as 'intended to suppress behaviour directed against objects of religious veneration that is likely to cause "justified indignation"') served to protect 'the right of citizens not to be insulted in their religious feelings by the public expression of views of other persons' and was therefore justified under Articles 9 and 10(2) ECHR combined.[678] Often a difficult balance is to be struck between press freedom and the right to privacy. In the 2005 *Von Hannover* Judgment the ECtHR held that there was no justification for the constant media intrusion into the private life of Princess Caroline of Monaco since the photos portraying the Princess were published only to satisfy 'public curiosity' and the Princess, although a public figure, exercised no official functions and was to be considered a private person.[679] In the 2008 *Armonienė* Judgment the ECtHR found that 'the publication of [an] article about the state of health of the applicant's husband, namely that he was HIV-positive, as well as the allegation that he was the father of two children by another woman who was also suffering from AIDS' was an 'outrageous abuse of press freedom', thus once again striking the balance between press freedom and the right to privacy in favour of the latter and finding a breach of Article 8 ECHR.[680] In contrast, the ECtHR ruled in the 2007 *Hachette Filipacchi* that an order directing a publisher to publish a statement to the effect that the family of a murdered politician had found deeply distressing the publication of a photo (picturing the body of the victim) without their consent was 'proportionate to the legitimate aim pursued'.[681] With regard to the tension between freedom of expression and freedom of association, the 2003 *Refah Partisi* Judgment is worthy of mention, in which the ECtHR found that the dissolution of the Refah Partisi political party by the Turkish Constitutional Court was justified on grounds of protection of the rights and freedoms of others, in addition to protection of national security and public safety and prevention of disorder or crime, because of the Islamic fundamentalism of the party dissolved.[682]

[677] cf ECtHR, *News Verlags GmbH and Co.KG v Austria* (n 598 above) para 45; *Lindon, Otchakovsky-Laurens and July v France* Judgment of 22 October 2007 [GC], Apps 21279/02 and 36448/02, (2008) 46 EHRR 761, para 44.

[678] ECtHR, *Otto-Preminger-Institut v Austria* Judgment of 20 September 1994, App 13470/87, Series A No 295-A, 19 (1995) EHRR 34, paras 46–48.

[679] ECtHR, *Von Hannover v Germany* Judgment of 24 June 2004, App 59320/00, (2005) 40 EHRR 1, paras 59, 79, specifying that 'the decisive factor in balancing the protection of private life against freedom of expression should lie in the contribution that the published photos and articles make to a debate of general interest'.

[680] ECtHR, *Armonienė v Lithuania* Judgment of 25 November 2008, App 36919/02, paras 42, 47.

[681] ECtHR, *Hachette Filipacchi Associés v France* Judgment of 14 June 2007, App 71111/01, (2009) 49 EHRR 515, para 63.

[682] ECtHR, *Refah Partisi (Welfare Party) et al v Turkey* Judgment of 13 February 2003 [GC], Apps No 41340/98, 41342/98, 41343/98, and 41344/98, ECtHR Rep 2003-II, (2003) 37 EHRR 1, para 67.

In other cases one and the same human right may be invoked in diverging directions by different persons and the balancing test is to be struck within opposite aspects or effects of this sole right. For example, as discussed earlier, the IACtHR has held that the right to property in Article 21 ACHR applies both to private and communal property, in particular to the communal property of indigenous peoples, to their ancestral lands and resources, and the right of property of other persons.[683] In the 2007 *Evans* Judgment the ECtHR was called upon to strike a balance between the right to respect for private life of a woman and the same right of her partner in the specific sense of respect for the decision to become or not to become genetic parents through *in vitro* fertilization. The Court ruled that the right of the woman's partner not to have a genetically related child with her (in the absence of his consent after having withdrawn it according to UK legislation) could not yield to (and thus prevailed over) her right to become a mother.[684]

(b) Coordinating the puzzle

Beyond single rules, humanitarian considerations puzzlingly compete with one another and call for coordination across entire legal frameworks designed to protect humanity. These frameworks give rise to different 'branches' of international law, often emerging at different points in time and for different purposes, namely, international human rights law (IHRL), crimes under international law (ICs), international humanitarian law (IHL), and arguably also transnational criminal law (TCL). The combination of these rules and branches generates a variegated picture which is hard to disentangle.

The relationship between human rights and international crimes is complex. First, both branches deal with individuals, but the former use a right language, the latter a duty language.[685] Secondly, while human rights treaties 'normally' apply in time of peace and exceptionally also in wartime unless a derogation clause has been invoked and the rights involved are derogable in time of national emergency, war crimes (but not other international crimes) can be committed only within (or in relation to) an armed conflict. Thirdly, most crimes against humanity amount to violations of human rights; however, the former require 'a widespread or systematic attack directed against any civilian population' that is not required by the latter. In other words, international crimes must meet specific requirements which are not necessarily required when seen as breaches of international human rights. Finally, human rights courts adjudicate the conduct of states, and may condemn states to pay compensation to the victims or to take other measures, whereas international criminal tribunals adjudicate the conduct of individuals, and may sentence them to prison and to reparation.

The relationship between crimes under international law, human rights, and transnational crimes is also intricate. Unlike international crimes, transnational crimes are deemed not to target the international community as a whole (but only the direct victims) and are not governed by customary international law (but only by treaties), nor are they prosecuted by international courts and tribunals (but only by domestic courts

[683] See Ch 5 above, n 454.

[684] ECtHR, *Evans v United Kingdom* Judgment of 10 April 2007 [GC], App 6339/05, (2008) 46 EHRR 34, paras 73, 89–92, posing the question as follows: 'The dilemma central to the present case is that it involves a conflict between the Article 8 rights of two private individuals: the applicant and J. Moreover, each person's interest is entirely irreconcilable with the other's, since if the applicant is permitted to use the embryos J. will be forced to become a father, whereas if J.'s refusal or withdrawal of consent is upheld the applicant will be denied the opportunity of becoming a genetic parent'.

[685] See Ch 5 above, section C (2)(a).

under domestic law as receptive of applicable treaties binding the state). The lack of availability of international courts and tribunals differentiates transnational crimes also from the violation of human rights treaties establishing international monitoring bodies. Certain transnational crimes may amount to international crimes, like human trafficking, as well as violations of human rights treaties, but with different consequences. For example, human trafficking as a transnational crime may be prosecuted only by the courts of the states having a jurisdictional link, with the effects set out in applicable treaties and in domestic law (notably, the criminal responsibility of the perpetrator).[686] As an international crime, human trafficking is exposed to prosecution by the courts of any state regardless of any (or most) jurisdictional links and possibly by international criminal tribunals when it falls within their jurisdiction, with the effects set out in applicable treaties (notably ICTs statutes) or in domestic law prescribing the criminal responsibility of the perpetrator.[687] As a human rights violation, human trafficking may be adjudicated by a human rights international court, which can condemn the state to pay compensation to the victim, or by domestic courts, with the effects set out in domestic law including the rules of international law incorporated in the domestic legal system.[688]

In addition, the relationship between international human rights law and international humanitarian law is puzzling as well.[689] They have in common the protection of human dignity,[690] but do not have the same scope of applicability. IHL presupposes an international or non-international 'armed conflict',[691] while IHRL presupposes state 'jurisdiction'.[692] IHL does not apply in times of peace or in any case when no conflict is under way, while IHRL applies also in 'armed conflict', except by operation of a derogation clause. Some IHRL rules reflect customary international law, just as some IHL rules do, but the respective rules reflecting customary international law do not necessarily have the same content. While IHRL and IHL may apply concurrently (for instance, both ensure protection against torture), they normally apply exclusively, and there may be situations in which neither applies. Even when they apply concurrently, their application may be based on different preconditions, provide different remedies, and lead to different results. As the ICJ has held, IHL is 'special' relative to IHRL. The prevailing meaning of this speciality is that both branches apply in armed conflict and IHL prevails in case of collision with IHRL.[693] Against this view, certain states, such as the United States and Israel, have argued for a 'mutual exclusivity' doctrine to the effect that when IHL applies, ie in armed conflict, IHRL does not apply at all.[694] The gist of this approach is that in armed conflicts life may be taken or people may be detained without trial, with no need to respect human rights, but with the only obligation to respect IHL, which is obviously far less stringent and more prone to 'flexible' interpretation and application (if only for lack of ad hoc international monitoring bodies). Speciality cannot, in fact, be understood in terms of exclusivity,[695] although it cannot

[686] See section A (1)(e) above.

[687] As noted earlier, universal jurisdiction over international crimes is a matter of controversy at the very least, but occasionally the courts of a few states adopt it (see section A (2)(c) above).

[688] See ECtHR, *Rantsev v Cyprus and Russia* Judgment of 7 January 2010, App 25965/04, para 282, equating human trafficking with enslavement expressly prohibited by Art 4 ECHR.

[689] For a recent general treatment, see O Ben-Naftali (ed), *International Humanitarian Law and International Human Rights Law* (Oxford: OUP, 2011).

[690] ICTY, *Prosecutor v Furundžija* (n 209 above) para 183.

[691] See section A (2)(b) above.

[692] See section A (2)(d) above.

[693] See nn 192 and 194 above.

[694] Melzer (n 56 above) 79–80.

[695] See Ch 6 above, section B (3)(a).

be conceived of in terms of a subset of IHRL either. While both regimes apply in armed conflict, it is for IHL to determine what acts of war are 'legitimate', and hence permitted acts of deprivation of human life in keeping with human rights treaties.[696] From the perspective of remedies, while in IHRL international courts and monitoring bodies are often open to individual petitions, IHL lacks international courts and tribunals, except for war crimes when these fall (as they usually do) within the jurisdiction of an ICT or HCT.

The temptation either to call for a 'rationalization' of these frameworks or to conclude that international law is anything but a 'system' is strong but has to be resisted. While international law is to some extent a puzzle, it embodies and reflects the international community as it is. Contrary to a widespread idea, law may work even in a fragmented condition, and sometimes it works precisely *because* of fragmentation (faithfully mirroring the international community and its real conflicting interests and views), the alternative being no rules at all.

Conclusion

Having discussed players and rules in the previous two chapters, the present chapter focused on the values which inspire the rules. The international community not only believes in certain rules, but also in certain 'values' underlying these rules capable of both orientating their interpretation and generating better rules. The constructionist approach here adopted suggests that the law which exists today is the result of past struggles and the law which will exist tomorrow is the result of the struggles to be engaged today. Values make sense of existing rules and provide guidance for the rules to come. They convey a sense of justice, which is the key component of law. This chapter grouped the rules of international law into five basic values which already are, or ought to be, protected by international law: security, humanity, wealth, environment, and knowledge. It argued (a) for the rules as they stand, according to the recognized criteria of identification and interpretation of international law; and (b) for new rules towards improving justice and achieving more consistency in cases where no clear rule exists to resolve conflicts.

[696] cf eg ECHR, Art 15(2) stating that the right to life is non-derogable even in time of emergency 'except in respect of deaths resulting from lawful acts of war'.

8

Remedies

The previous discussion on players, rules, and values emphasized that contemporary international law is marked by the need for states which protect people within their jurisdiction, inter alia, as a result of the pressure exerted by non-state actors. This chapter explores the remedies against major breaches of international law, as described thus far, in terms of sovereignty as responsibility. It is primarily for states to protect the basic rights of their populations, and when they fail to do so it is for the international community to intervene, in particular by collective and personal measures. The 'responsibility' of the international community is a consequence of the 'One World' now in the making. Collective measures, which include collective standing in international courts, universal jurisdiction in domestic courts, collective countermeasures, and humanitarian intervention, are often based on the existence of obligations *erga omnes*. This chapter argues that it is difficult to draw definite legal conclusions from this concept and that humanitarian intervention is not permitted within the responsibility to protect doctrine (RtoP) unless mandated on a case-by-case basis by the UN Security Council. Personal measures include targeted sanctions and criminal responsibility in international and hybrid courts, these latter being the best tools (despite their shortcomings) to combat abuse of power by rulers and to bring more justice in and to the system.

A. Sovereignty as Responsibility

In *Sovereignty as Responsibility*, Francis M Deng, Sadikiel Kimaro, Terrence Lyons, Donald Rothchild, and I William Zartman discussed conflict management in Africa in terms of responsible sovereignty.[1] Their basic contention was that 'in order to be legitimate, sovereignty must demonstrate responsibility' to both domestic and international constituencies, this implying in practice 'at the very least . . . providing for the basic needs of its people'. It was assumed that where governments prove unable or unwilling to discharge this responsibility, it was the international community that was 'expected to step in to provide the needed remedies'.[2] While focusing on the post-decolonized Africa, the concept of sovereignty as responsibility—drawn from the *droit d'ingérence* doctrine worked out in the 1980s by French scholars, activists, and political leaders[3]—had the potential to be extended to all states as well as to preventative extraterritorial use of force and natural disasters. In 1999 the UN Secretary-General, Kofi Annan, contrasted 'two concepts' of sovereignty, old and new, and insisted that the state should be perceived as a servant of its people, not vice versa.[4]

[1] FM Deng, S Kimaro, T Lyons, D Rothchild, and IW Zartman, *Sovereignty as Responsibility. Conflict Management in Africa* (Washington, DC: The Brookings Institution, 1996).

[2] ibid xvii–xviii.

[3] M Bettati and B Kouchner (eds), *Le devoir d'ingérence* (Paris: Denoël, 1987); M Bettati, 'Un droit d'ingérence?' (1991) 95 RGDIP 639; M Bettati, *Le droit d'ingérence. Mutation de l'ordre international* (Paris: Editions Odile Jacob, 1996).

[4] KA Annan, 'Two Concepts of Sovereignty' *The Economist*, 16 September 1999, at <http://www.economist.com/node/324795>; UN Docs SG/SM/7136 and GA/9596, 20 September 1999.

His vision was soon expanded by the International Commission on Intervention and State Sovereignty (ICISS), set up by the Canadian government, in the 2001 report on the responsibility to protect (RtoP).[5] The report's central idea was that in today's globalized world, sovereignty as control, which is deemed to be typical of the so-called Westphalian system, must give way to sovereignty as responsibility, both external (towards other states) and internal (towards citizens),[6] as a result of the dramatically growing impact of international norms on human rights and of the concept of human security.[7]

(1) Implications of sovereignty as responsibility

Although the gist of sovereignty as responsibility is ultimately that rulers who conquer or purchase statehood to gain impunity can no longer be tolerated, to embrace this concept does not necessarily mean, as explained below in greater detail, that certain measures against irresponsible sovereigns are automatically permitted. However, sovereignty as responsibility has at least four major implications that are worth briefly resuming and clarifying.

First, sovereignty is indispensable today at a time when a return to tribes is impossible and forms of political organization which are better than states are not in sight. Sovereignty means statehood and statehood means globalization, ie the imposition of this form of government on all peoples worldwide. In this sense, one can use the expression 'a globalized world of states', although 'global' is often associated with non-state actors and set against the 'international', or state-centred, system established with the 1648 Peace of Westphalia. To say that sovereignty is indispensable today is not to suggest that this is the best form of human political organization. Sovereignty was created and imposed by the West on all peoples, concomitant with the colonization and subjugation of the globe, forcing most of them (typically tribal and indigenous peoples), for the sake of the global 'order' which benefited Western peoples, to live embedded in one or another state and adapt their lifestyles accordingly.[8] The existing world inter-state order is the result of injustice according to current perceptions, but this injustice cannot be corrected by eliminating the states system as it stands. Other means within the system and projects for new orders need to be pursued. Moreover, many non-Western peoples would now, *ex post facto*, be unwilling to renounce this organization of the world, although they might be ready to change it for the better. In this sense sovereignty is at the moment inevitable. The issue is not 'if' but 'how' sovereignty is to be exercised.

Secondly, sovereignty must be exercised 'responsibly', the term responsibility having here two different, albeit interconnected, meanings.[9] In the first sense, responsibility means that those who exercise *pro tempore* (either because of the limit in time of their office or because of death where their office is for life) state sovereignty must behave in such a way that (at the very minimum) the basic needs of their populations are fulfilled, statehood is not essentially used for personal gain, power is not abused, and international law is generally complied with. In the second sense, responsibility means that

[5] ICISS, *The Responsibility to Protect* (Ottawa: International Development Research Center, 2001), at <http://www.iciss.ca/report-en.asp>.

[6] ibid para 2.14.

[7] See Ch 7 above, section A (2)(a) and (d).

[8] P Keal, *European Conquest and the Rights of Indigenous Peoples: The Moral Backwardness of International Society* (Cambridge: CUP, 2003); A Anghie, *Imperialism, Sovereignty and the Making of International Law* (Cambridge: CUP, 2005).

[9] For the ambivalence of the term 'responsibility', see HLA Hart, 'Postscript: Responsibility and Retribution' in *Punishment and Responsibility. Essays in the Philosophy of Law* (Oxford: Clarendon Press, 1968; 2nd edn, 2008) 210, 211.

when those responsible in the first sense fail to fulfil their duties, then they breach international law and face the consequences of internationally unlawful acts. In the first sense, responsibility refers to duties prescribed by 'primary' rules, notably by human rights and IHL rules prescribing a positive duty to protect and by the rules governing international crimes, whereas in the second sense reference is made to sanctions provided by 'secondary' rules. There is a widespread confusion between the two meanings. The fact that a primary rule provides a set of duties does not necessarily imply that failure to fulfil these duties entails the consequences set out in general in the secondary rules. For example, human rights treaties provide for remedies against alleged violations of the rights guaranteed therein, such as the possibility to file a complaint with monitoring bodies. The permissibility of other measures (including military intervention) is then to be tested against general international law and may or may not follow.[10] Moreover, the fact that responsibility in the second sense entails the personal responsibility of state officials does not imply that the state as such, and hence indirectly its population, becomes internationally irresponsible.[11]

Thirdly, it is up to 'responsible' non-state actors to push for the greater responsibility of any and all states, whether Western or other. Non-state actors cannot (nor can they claim to) replace states, although they may perform public services on behalf of states. Non-state actors need states at any stage of their life to accomplish their missions. What they do, and should do, is to oversee states and their populations and engage in a struggle for responsible states in every part of the world. This struggle 'from below'—even to support IOs in using their powers 'from above' towards member states—is not just indispensable but rather the 'normal' way to guide rulers and other state officials. There would be no tyrants if there were no people available to give them support. Both abuses of and checks on power come from below. Nor can there be any responsible state or ruler, or any working law and justice, when most people 'wait and see', hoping that something good may come from heaven overnight. No global agreement on climate change can be achieved without creating the conditions that make states recalculate their interests and arrive at the conclusion that it is convenient to foster and enter into the agreement, and to implement it domestically. People also have the power to change the very meaning of 'calculation' and of 'interest' of states in order to achieve a responsible outcome.[12] Since law is a social construction, nothing prevents people from constructing a better and more effective international law in a more responsible world. Unless a sense of global responsibility grows 'from below' in the midst of all of us, no law will work, whatever the legal theory endorsed. Without a common mythology of responsibility in everyday life belief in law is hopeless. The point is what we do for justice, not what justice does for us.

Finally, when sovereignty is exercised irresponsibly a number of remedies are available. Here the point is what kind of responsibility arises according to 'secondary' rules of international law when sovereignty is exercised irresponsibly in breach of the international law 'primary' rules. Since the concept of international responsibility refers to any form of breach of international law, the 'traditional' remedies still apply. As noted earlier, the responsibility of rulers and state officials cannot be completely detached from that of their populations and state practice attests that there is still a collective responsibility of peoples. The novelty is the 'targeted' remedies against those responsible regardless of (or in addition to) the international responsibility of the state.

[10] On this distinction, see C Focarelli, 'Duty to Protect in Cases of Natural Disasters', MP EPIL (March 2010 update) para 27.

[11] See nn 17–20 below.

[12] See Ch 5 above, n 153.

(2) Defining responsible sovereignty

When is sovereignty exercised 'responsibly' under current international law? The 2001 ICISS report argued that sovereignty should be exercised responsibly both externally (towards other states) and internally (towards citizens). The external and internal components of sovereignty as responsibility are largely, but not necessarily, coincident. Coincidence exists based on the increasing number and impact of international rules on human rights, IHL, and international crimes. States are required to comply with these rules and when they fail to do so their international responsibility arises. In this context, the question is what is legally required and with reference to whom. Obligations change from one treaty to another, including the remedies provided, and different treaties bind different groups of states. It is difficult to draw a common line applying to all states below which sovereignty is exercised 'irresponsibly' on the basis of these rules. There is, however, a core on which states today seem to agree concerning international crimes according to general international law. But if it is true that irresponsible sovereignty typically means a breach of international law, it is also true that sovereignty may be considered 'irresponsible' even without the breach of any existing international law rules. This occurs when the UN Security Council determines that a certain situation within a state constitutes a 'threat to the peace' and decides on enforcement measures or authorizes the use of force under Chapter VII UN Charter.

A state may exercise sovereignty 'responsibly' under different meanings and, therefore, be regarded as responsible under one and not under another meaning: (a) by taking account of the bounds of international law on its sovereignty, whatever such bounds may be; (b) by coordinating itself with all other states to exercise jurisdiction according to the allocation thereof under international law; (c) by protecting the basic rights of its population as embodied in international human rights rules, otherwise being subject to measures from other states ranging from criminal prosecution of its officials, to the imposition of sanctions, and ultimately to external intervention; and (d) by managing key resources, such as the environment or cultural treasures, in its territory for the benefit of all humanity in accordance with international law. In *all* these meanings a state has a responsibility *towards all other states* to comply with certain rules of *international law*. What varies is the content of the rules involved. When invoking 'sovereignty as responsibility' reference is normally made only to meaning (c). Under this meaning 'responsible sovereignty' means that all *rulers* must act for the *ruled* according to *international law*. A ruler is thus held to be irresponsible in cases of brutal repression, failure to fulfil the basic needs of the population, use of statehood for private ends, and abuse of power. It is assumed that today there is an international standard that rulers must respect at any cost, even against the will of the population when it is the population itself that wants these acts to be committed. On the other hand, the concept lends itself to serving as an ideological ground for neo-colonialist intervention directed to setting aside even the popular will, as expressed in elections, when the outcome of the election is unwelcome to major powers. One should not overlook the fact that in most cases 'irresponsibility' derives from past subjugation and is measured by the standard of the subjugators. The risk of abuse on the part of powerful states can be reduced if only a *core* of guidelines about ruling are to be conformed to, such as the fulfilment of basic needs and the prevention of international crimes. This meaning of responsible sovereignty does not imply a requirement for democratic government.

In a broad sense, all of the meanings (a) to (d) set out above are compatible with the term 'responsible sovereignty' in the sense that states under meaning (a) are always responsible, unless they deny international law altogether; and states under meaning (b) have usually been responsible, as a condition *sine qua non* for participating in the system. Becoming a state has *always* implied a set of responsibilities. All states are vigilant with regard to how any corner of the planet is managed by all other states. Under this meaning sovereignty is supposed to be exercised in the service of the whole states system and of all peoples. The novelty of sense (c) is twofold: (i) states are required to be responsible towards their own citizens, as established by international law; and (ii) third states are empowered to take measures in case the local state fails to provide such protection. Novelty (i) is clearly found in all international human rights rules, while novelty (ii) is not found in the substantive rules and does not necessarily follow from novelty (i). The novelty of sense (d) is that states are not only responsible for the way in which they treat their own citizens, but also for their management of resources essential to humanity which are found in their territory, thus apparently operating as managers or trustees of humankind.

It should be noted that once people are placed at the core of international law, all rules thereof can be seen as rules which require rulers to govern people in a certain way. For example, the prohibition of war may be seen as a human right of people not to get involved in a war, except for self-defence, and bear its costs in terms of loss of lives, physical and psychological suffering, taxes, and so on. Treaty rules on free trade may be seen as conferring on people the human right to participate in the wealth generated by trade.[13] If international law limits sovereignty, it basically limits rulers in the way they rule people in their daily lives, whether in domestic or foreign policy. International law as a whole may be seen as a set of rules aimed at establishing how all humanity 'must be ruled', ie how sovereignty must be exercised 'responsibly' by all states.

B. Collective and Personal Remedies

In the 'traditional' law of international responsibility, once it has been ascertained that an act has been committed which is contrary to substantive rules of international law attributable to a state,[14] and that there are no justifications,[15] the wrongdoing state has to account by making reparation to the injured state and by being exposed to individual countermeasures or self-defence.[16] In the classical regime of international responsibility, therefore, only the injured state is entitled to obtain reparation and to take countermeasures, and the costs of the unlawful act (linked to reparation and countermeasures) are borne by the community of the wrongdoing state rather than personally by the state officials who have physically performed the act. Today, this type of situation tends to be taken over by the imposition of 'new', allegedly more effective, consequences for internationally wrongful acts which allow remedies by *third* states and give rise to the *personal* responsibility of the state officials responsible for the unlawful act. There is often a nexus between the collective and personal components of these remedies, as exemplified by a humanitarian intervention in an authoritarian state aimed at capturing the alleged tyrant in order to have him tried by an international criminal tribunal. It is often said in such cases, with a view to reducing the impact of an intervention which in principle is capable of targeting the entire community, that

[13] For the view that there exists in current international law a WTO 'human right to trade', see Ch 7 above, n 601.

[14] For some observations on the attribution to a state of private acts in the exercise of governmental powers, see Ch 7 above, section A (2)(d).

[15] For some hints at necessity, see Ch 7 above, section A (3)(e).

[16] See Ch 6 above, section D (3)(a), and Ch 7 above, section A (1)(c).

military force is used 'surgically' to hit the tyrant and those who support him, not the population in general. In particular, the question of who is to bear the costs of reparation and of sanctions and possibly of making rulers and state officials (as opposed to the state as a whole and hence people) responsible for violations of international law has been extensively discussed in recent years,[17] notably by moral philosophers.[18] The better view is that new forms of collective and personal responsibility have (and should) not displace the 'old' forms,[19] although this may encourage states (or rather, state officials) to 'behave badly'.[20] This section focuses on the permissibility and effectiveness of these newly devised remedies, beginning with collective measures based on the concept of obligations *erga omnes*.

(1) Obligations *erga omnes*

The concept of obligations *erga omnes* became popular following the ICJ 1970 *Barcelona Traction* Judgment. The Court famously held that an 'essential distinction' had to be drawn between the 'obligations of a state towards the international community as a whole', and those 'arising vis-à-vis another state in the field of diplomatic protection', the former being 'by their very nature' the 'concern of all states' so that 'In view of the importance of the rights involved, all States can be held to have a legal interest in their protection'. The Court referred to them as 'obligations *erga omnes*'.[21] The Court went on to specify that in contemporary international law such obligations 'derive, for example, from the outlawing of acts of aggression, and of genocide, as also from the principles and rules concerning the basic rights of the human person, including protection from slavery and racial discrimination' and that while 'some of the corresponding rights of protection have entered into the body of general international law . . . others are conferred by international instruments of a universal or quasi-universal character'.[22]

The concept was far from novel, and can be traced back to the Christian-Western idea of a universal mystical community (*corpus mysticum Christi*), in which what happens to the limbs reverberates through the whole body,[23] to the notion that pirates are 'enemies of humankind' who may be prosecuted by the judges of any state, and to the just war doctrine, especially when used to justify humanitarian intervention by foreign states in cases of tyranny.[24] Even in the international jurisprudence the notion had been previously adumbrated in Triepel's theory of law-making treaties revived by

[17] For the view that, given the primitive character of international law, when a state breaches international law it is the whole national collectivity that bears responsibility, see eg A Cassese, *International Law* (Oxford: OUP, 2005, 2nd edn) 241.

[18] See eg D Miller, *National Responsibility and Global Justice* (Oxford: OUP, 2007) 111–34. For the plausibility of attributing collective responsibility for the acts of the Third Reich to all Germans, including those born after 1945, see R Dworkin, *Law's Empire* (Cambridge, Mass: Harvard University Press, 1986) 167–75. Along similar lines, see DJ Goldhagen, *Hitler's Willing Executioners: Ordinary Germans and the Holocaust* (London: Abacus, 1997).

[19] See J Crawford and J Watkins, 'International Responsibility' in S Besson and J Tasioulas (eds), *The Philosophy of International Law* (Oxford: OUP, 2010) 283–98; partially critical is L Murphy, 'International Responsibility' ibid 299–315, 301–3.

[20] P Allott, 'State Responsibility and the Unmaking of International Law' (1988) 29 Harv ILJ 16.

[21] ICJ, *Barcelona Traction, Light and Power Co Ltd (Belgium v Spain) (Second Phase)* Judgment of 5 February 1970, [1970] ICJ Rep 3, para 33.

[22] ibid para 34. [23] See Ch 4 above, nn 53 and 54, and Ch 5 above, n 45.

[24] CJ Tams, *Enforcing Obligations* Erga Omnes *in International Law* (Cambridge: CUP, 2005) 48–9. See further T Meron, 'Common Rights of Mankind in Gentili, Grotius and Suarez' (1991) 85 AJIL 110.

the ICJ in the 1951 *Genocide* Advisory Opinion, later to be taken up by human rights monitoring bodies,[25] and by Gerald Fitzmaurice when working on the codification of the law of treaties leading to Article 60 VCLT.[26] In 1967 the Ambassador to the United Nations, Mr Arvid Pardo, launched the concept of a 'common heritage of mankind' in the UN General Assembly, again alluding to certain basic values and resources shared (or to be shared) by the international community as a whole.[27] In 1969 the Vienna Conference endorsed *jus cogens*, which had in common with obligations *erga omnes* a 'justice' and pro-Third World (or anti-colonialist) connotation. In the same period the ILC included in the codification work on state responsibility 'international crimes' of states, as violations of the basic rules of international law approximately coincident with those regarded as peremptory and contemplating obligations *erga omnes*.[28] Since that time, the concept of obligations *erga omnes* has been relied on in numerous judicial decisions and has sparked a massive doctrinal debate touching upon the structure of international law, well beyond international responsibility. Obligations *erga omnes* were understood as the key to a 'new', value-based, constitutional, globalization-friendly international law.

Eventually, the ICJ mentioned obligations *erga omnes* in the 1995 *East Timor* Judgment,[29] in the 1996 *Genocide Convention (Preliminary Objections)* Judgment,[30] in the 2004 *Wall* Advisory Opinion,[31] in the 2006 *Armed Activities* Judgment,[32] and in the 2007 *Genocide Convention* Judgment.[33] Other international courts—operating as human rights monitoring bodies or as international criminal tribunals—have upheld the existence of the obligations, such as the ICTY in the 2000 *Kupreskić* Judgment[34] and the ECtHR in the 2007 *Jorgic* Judgment,[35] as well as domestic courts.[36] In these

25 See Ch 6 above, nn 122–6.

26 ILC, 'Second Report by G.G. Fitzmaurice, Special Rapporteur' (1957) II UN YBILC 30, 35–6, 54, 68; 'Third Report' (1958) II UN YBILC 27, 41, 44; 'Fourth Report' (1959) II UN YBILC 45, 66, 70.

27 A Pardo, *The Common Heritage: Selected Papers on Oceans and World Order 1967–1974* (Malta: Malta University Press, 1975).

28 Art 19 1996 UN ILC 'Draft Articles on State Responsibility' (1996) GAOR 51st Session, Supp 10, 125.

29 ICJ, *East Timor (Portugal v Australia)* Judgment of 30 June 1995, [1995] ICJ Rep 90, para 29.

30 ICJ, *Application of the Convention on the Prevention and Punishment of the Crime of Genocide (Bosnia and Herzegovina v Serbia and Montenegro) (Preliminary Objections)* Judgment of 11 July 1996, [1996] ICJ Rep 595, para 31, noting that 'the rights and obligations enshrined by the [Genocide] Convention are rights and obligations *erga omnes*' and that 'the obligation each State thus has to prevent and to punish the crime of genocide is not territorially limited by the Convention'.

31 *Legal Consequences of the Construction of a Wall in the Occupied Palestinian Territory*, Advisory Opinion of 9 July 2004, [2004] ICJ Rep 136, paras 155–157.

32 ICJ, *Case concerning Armed Activities on the Territory of the Congo (New Application: 2002) (Democratic Republic of the Congo v Rwanda)* Judgment of 3 February 2006, [2006] ICJ Rep 6, paras 64, 125.

33 ICJ, *Application of the Convention on the Prevention and Punishment of the Crime of Genocide (Bosnia and Herzegovina v Serbia and Montenegro)* Judgment of 26 February 2007, [2007] ICJ Rep 43, paras 147, 185.

34 ICTY, *Prosecutor v Kupreškić* Trial Chamber Judgment of 14 January 2000, Case No IT-95-16, paras 517–520. See further *Prosecutor v Furundžija* Trial Chamber Judgment of 10 December 1998, Case No IT-95-17/I-T, (1999) 38 ILM 317, paras 151–152.

35 ECtHR, *Jorgic v Federal Republic of Germany* Judgment of 12 July 2007, App No 74613/01, ECtHR Rep 2007-IX, para 68. See in addition IACtHR, *Peace Community of San José de Apartadó*, Order of 18 June 2002, paras 10–11, at <http://www.unhcr.org/refworld/docid/4268c86f4.html>; *Matter of the Communities of Jiguamiandó and Curbaradó*, Order of 7 February 2006, paras 4 and 6, at <http://www.corteidh.or.cr/docs/medidas/jiguamiando_se_04_ing.doc>.

36 Domestic courts generally take for granted a complete overlap of obligations *erga omnes* with *jus cogens* as to the norms and the values concerned. See eg Spanish High Court, *Public Prosecutor's Office v Scilingo Manzorro* Judgment of 19 April 2005 No 16/2005, ILDC 136 (ES 2005); more clearly UK

decisions various international obligations have been regarded as *erga omnes* (such as self-determination of peoples and the prohibition of torture) and the concept has been associated with a variety of legal effects. In its 2001 Articles on State Responsibility the ILC accepted that certain international obligations are 'owed to the international community as a whole' or 'to all parties in a multilateral treaty having that character'.[37] One major problem that the ILC has left open is the relationship between obligations *erga omnes* and *jus cogens* as defined in Article 53 VCLT.[38] Broadly speaking, both concepts relate to international law rules aimed at protecting the basic values of the international community as a whole, the former by allowing collective responses to their violation (such as ICJ proceedings or countermeasures), the latter by elevating the rule to a higher than ordinary, overriding rank. While the ILC underlined that 'there is at the very least substantial overlap between them',[39] a widespread view is that all peremptory rules are *erga omnes*, whereas not all obligations *erga omnes* are necessarily peremptory,[40] although Article 65 VCLT excludes third states from invoking the invalidity of a treaty on grounds of conflict with *jus cogens*.

There are at least three key reasons why the concept of obligations *erga omnes* is valuable. First, weak states injured by the unlawful acts of stronger states can hardly respond to the wrongdoer, but with the introduction of obligations *erga omnes* they might count on the possible help of other states. Secondly, even where there is no injured state—as is the case with violations by a state of the human rights of its own citizens—international responsibility might be invoked by other states. Thirdly, the possibility of invoking international responsibility by virtually all states and even non-state actors—as occurs with the violation of human rights treaties which also entitle individuals to seise an international body—in cases where the most fundamental obligations have been violated makes international law more effective and credible. Yet obligations *erga omnes* as a general legal pattern, although today in vogue, are not immune from noteworthy criticism.

The basic assumption of obligations *erga omnes* is invariably that certain (treaty or customary) international law rules are so important (and/or of common concern) that all of their addressees have a legal interest in compliance. The consequence is generally drawn that all addressees have a legal interest or a right, if not an obligation, to demand compliance. From a 'common interest' in the protection of the underlying values a 'legal interest' of all states in compliance is drawn.[41] But what particular course of action is allowed (if not imposed) in pursuance of the 'legal interest' in compliance remains obscure. While a wide range of measures are conceivable in the abstract, not all collective measures may be permitted under the same circumstances (for example, countermeasures might not be permitted in cases in which appeal may be made to the

House of Lords, *A (FC) et al (FC) v Secretary of State for the Home Department, A et al (FC) v Secretary of State for the Home Department (joined appeals)* Judgment of 8 December 2005, ILDC 363 (UK 2005).

[37] Art 48 UN ILC 'Draft Articles on Responsibility of States for Internationally Wrongful Acts, with Commentaries' (2001) GAOR 56th Session Supp 10, 43.

[38] See Ch 6 above, section B (4)(f).

[39] cf RJ Crawford, *The International Law Commission's Articles on State Responsibility: Introduction, Text and Commentaries* (Cambridge: CUP, 2002) 244, para 7.

[40] See eg M Ragazzi, *The Concept of International Obligations* Erga Omnes (Oxford: Clarendon Press, 1997) 190–210; Tams (n 24 above) 141–53. On this point, see P Picone, 'The Distinction between *Jus Cogens* and Obligations *Erga Omnes*' in E Cannizzaro (ed), *The Law of Treaties beyond the Vienna Convention* (Oxford: OUP, 2011) 411–24; and more generally, P Picone, *Comunità internazionale e obblighi 'erga omnes': Studi critici di diritto internazionale* (Naples: Jovene, 2006).

[41] The passage from 'importance' and 'common concern' to a 'legal interest' in compliance is (inter alia) found in the *Barcelona Traction* Judgment (n 21 above).

ICJ, or other international bodies) and not all possible measures may rest on the same standing requirements (for example, a state may be entitled in a given situation to institute proceedings before the ICJ, or other international bodies, but not to adopt countermeasures). One might think that the particular 'legal interest' to respond relevant to each case depends on existing rules and/or on the practice prevailing in the area of the law at hand, whether it is the ICJ's jurisdiction or the power to adopt countermeasures. But it is difficult to see, then, what purposes the general category of obligations *erga omnes* may serve: the *erga omnes* effects would be derived from existing law and/or practice on a case-by-case basis. That is, the effect sought is produced, but it does not depend on the *erga omnes* structure of the rule. If obligations *erga omnes* as a general category are to be given a univocal meaning, it seems that they should *automatically*—ie without any possible differentiation either in their effects or in their standing requirements—produce all possible *erga omnes* effects, a conclusion which stretches the concept very far indeed and actually has little evidential foundation. And if the *erga omnes* category is construed as producing a variety of different effects in diverse contexts, then a further criterion is still needed (indeed a *decisive* criterion) to identify these different legal regimes.

The line of reasoning often followed for both obligations *erga omnes* and *jus cogens* seems to proceed in three logical stages: first, an urgent common 'need' for certain legal rules (producing *erga omnes* and/or peremptory effects) is detected in order for the international community as a whole to see its most fundamental values adequately protected; secondly, this need generates a 'legal interest' to see such a need fulfilled; thirdly, the existence of an *erga omnes* and/or overriding legal rule capable of fulfilling such a need is inferred. In so doing, what is at best a need for a rule may easily become a 'legal interest' (in seeing the desired rule complied with) and, finally, an *erga omnes* and/or an overriding rule capable of producing effects which all other rules do not produce. If the two extremes of this reasoning are directly connected, what emerges is a syllogistic transformation of a *need* for a rule into an existing *erga omnes* and/or even overriding *rule*. This allows the interpreter to create a generic *erga omnes* effect or to *bypass any existing rule* simply by elaborating on the *need* for the *erga omnes* effect or for a 'superior' opposite rule. No doubt, this process may be important and even unavoidable in order to *change* existing law in the direction of needs and values which are felt to be vital to humankind, but this cannot justify mistaking a legal need for the law in force at a given moment. Underlying this approach is after all the unintended notion that international law is an *instrument* to be used in the struggle towards desirable goals, a notion which is typically advanced by major powers. But the law as it stands is one thing, the struggle for a better law is quite another. If one accepts that a pressing need for certain rules (or for rules contemplating obligations *erga omnes* in particular) can *ipso facto* generate such rules, even providing them (as peremptory in particular) with an overriding force, the ultimate end is a denial of international law as a sufficiently objective legal system common to all, since every rule—despite its being in fact accepted by the generality of states as an existing legal rule—would constantly be open to being set aside by any need for a different rule (either structurally contemplating obligations *erga omnes* or substantively producing special peremptory effects), and the only relevant needs in practice are inevitably those of the strongest.

Obligations *erga omnes* tend to be used to justify various misleading equations and inferences between distinct legal concepts. By way of example, advocates of sovereignty as responsibility suggest that human rights treaties, conferring rights on individuals allegedly towards any other subject capable of redressing abuses, permit collective responses also by third states when the state primarily responsible proves unable or unwilling to comply with the treaty.[42] However, human rights treaties usually stipulate only the possibility for any contracting state and (at least some of them) for the victims of the alleged violation of filing a complaint with an international monitoring body. This 'collective' response is different from others equally plausible in the abstract, such as permitting third states to seise another international court when the same obligation is involved or to take countermeasures against the violation of such obligation. The inference from one expressly permitted response to another response not expressly envisaged by the treaty and purportedly having a general effect is simply arbitrary, however desirable. One could also suggest that non-compliance with a binding decision of a human rights monitoring body implies a 'fall-back' to general international law and to the possibility of taking collective countermeasures.[43] This, though, should be proved on the basis of what each treaty stipulates, either expressly or impliedly, as well as of general international law. Once again, there is no automaticity in the *erga omnes* nature of human rights treaty rules for drawing the conclusion that collective countermeasures are allowed against the defiant state. Another suggestion is that because human rights treaties often provide for third states and individuals the possibility of seising an international monitoring body, then the same possibility should be assumed in respect of any other international court by any state. Although this issue is specifically discussed below, it should be noted here that there is no reason why such a pseudo-logical conclusion should be drawn. Certain states may accept certain monitoring bodies functioning within certain treaties, but states as a whole (including those which have concluded those treaties) may not accept at all that the same applies as a general rule. Evidence thereof is precisely that only a *few* treaties are so devised, and even these differ from one another, while many others provide otherwise. An even stronger assertion in the same direction is that the possibility in human rights treaties for third states or individuals to seise a monitoring body entails the permissibility of unilateral countermeasures. But countermeasures may or may not be permitted as a matter of general international law, depending on what this prescribes, regardless of any particular treaty. Finally, when collective sanctions are mandated by the United Nations, rather than being taken unilaterally, their permissibility depends on what the UN Charter provides, independently of the *erga omnes* nature of the rule allegedly violated. The United Nations itself is not obliged to decide or authorize such sanctions, its decision (and hence the presumed *erga omnes* character of the rule violated) depending on the majorities of the day. An obligation that is or is not *erga omnes* as a function of the majorities at the UN Security Council is a rather curious thing. It simply is not *erga omnes*, and perhaps not even an obligation before the Security Council decides to impose it on the states.

In the 2004 *Wall* Advisory Opinion the ICJ pronounced itself on the consequences of a violation of obligations *erga omnes*.[44] Here the Court held that rules of humanitarian law constituting 'intransgressible principles of international customary law', as referred to in the 1996 *Nuclear Weapons* Advisory Opinion,[45] 'incorporate obligations which are essentially of an *erga omnes* character',[46] specifying that under Article 1 of the Fourth Geneva Convention

[42] See n 1 above.

[43] The term 'fall-back' was used extensively by the ILC in the report 'Fragmentation of International Law: Difficulties Arising From the Diversification And Expansion of International Law', *Report of the study group on the fragmentation of international law, finalized by Martti Koskenniemi*, UN Doc. A/CN.4/L.682, 13 April 2006, paras 186–190.

[44] ICJ, *Legal Consequences of The Construction of A Wall* (n 31 above) paras 157–159.

[45] ICJ, *Legality of the Threat or Use of Nuclear Weapons* Advisory Opinion of 8 July 1996, [1996] ICJ Rep 226, para 79.

[46] ICJ, *Legal Consequences of The Construction of A Wall* (n 31 above) para 157.

'every party...whether or not it is a party to a specific conflict, is under an obligation to ensure that the requirements of the instruments in questions are complied with'.[47] Finding Israel in breach of obligations *erga omnes*, the Court spelled out the consequences to be attached to their violation, namely the obligation of all states 'not to recognise the illegal situation resulting from the construction of the wall' and 'not to render aid or assistance in maintaining the situation created by such construction'.[48] As is well known, these consequences are those provided for in Article 41 of the 2001 ILC Articles on State Responsibility in relation to serious violations of international peremptory norms.[49] The Court avoided mentioning the possibility of taking countermeasures and allowing all states to bring a case before it, or in any case any other *positive* measures against the transgressor. The Court did recall that 'certain participants in the proceedings contended that the states parties to the Fourth Geneva Convention are *obliged* to take measures to ensure compliance with the Convention', that they are 'under an *obligation* to prosecute or extradite the authors' of breaches of the Convention and that 'the United Nations Security Council *should* consider flagrant and systematic violation of international law norm[s]..., particularly...international humanitarian law, and take all necessary measures to put an end [to] these violations'.[50] However, apart from recommending the UN General Assembly and Security Council to 'consider further action' and to 'take due account' of the *Wall* Advisory Opinion itself,[51] the Court carefully abstained from discussing such a contention.[52]

In short, the need for greater compliance—no doubt a paramount need in the international (as well as in any) legal system—cannot automatically and logically generate obligations *erga omnes* solely because a higher degree of compliance is, rightly or wrongly, believed to follow. As mentioned, even when an obligation is proved *erga omnes*, this obligation does not necessarily entail a commitment of all states to take all possible and imaginable measures capable of inducing transgressor states to compliance. This conclusion can be concisely tested against three major alleged effects or manifestations of the obligations *erga omnes*, ie *actio popularis*, universal jurisdiction over international crimes, and collective countermeasures.

(a) Actio popularis

Obligations *erga omnes* are often thought of in terms of *actio popularis*, ie of the possibility for non-injured states to seise an international court or tribunal when

[47] ICJ, *Legal Consequences of The Construction of A Wall* (n 31 above) para 158.

[48] ibid para 159.

[49] See n 37 above.

[50] ibid para 146; emphasis added. For a comment, see V Kattan, 'The Wall, Obligations *Erga Omnes* and Human Rights: The Case for Withdrawing the European Community's Terms of Preferential Trade with Israel' (2004–05) 13 Pal YBIL 71.

[51] ICJ, *Legal Consequences of The Construction of A Wall* (n 31 above) para 160.

[52] In their individual opinions Judges Higgins and Kooijmans explained why they could not join the majority on this point. In Judge Higgins' view, 'That an illegal situation is not to be recognized or assisted by third parties is self-evident, requiring no invocation of the uncertain concept of "*erga omnes*"' (para 38) and common Art 1 'is simply a provision in an almost universally ratified multilateral Convention' (para 39). Judge Kooijmans, after stating that the duty to cooperate referred to in Art 41 (1) of the 2001 ILC Articles 'does not refer to individual obligations of third States' (para 42) and that 'the duty not to recognize an illegal fact...amounts...to an obligation without real substance' (para 44), concluded that a duty of abstention—such as the obligation 'not to encourage' breaches of the Geneva Conventions mentioned by the ICJ in the *Nicaragua* case ((n 93 below) para 220)—'is completely different from a positive duty to ensure compliance with the law' (para 49). He failed 'to see what kind of positive action, resulting from this obligation [as supposedly envisaged by common Art 1], may be expected from individual States, apart from diplomatic demarches' (para 50).

'a common interest' of the international community is involved.[53] The violation of an obligation *erga omnes* is thought to confer on 'third' states, having no direct interest in the dispute, the power to institute proceedings before an international court or tribunal, thereby making more likely the adjudication of the case and possibly the finding of a presumed serious violation of a fundamental rule of international law. This question is distinct from requiring the consent of all the parties to the dispute in order for a court to adjudicate, although the rationale may be similar.[54] Jurisdiction and standing (*jus standi* or *intérêt à agir*) are different. In fact, the derogatory effect on the jurisdictional requirement because of the *erga omnes* character of the obligation allegedly violated was clearly denied by the ICJ in the 1995 *East Timor* Judgment,[55] in the 2006 *Armed Activities* Judgment,[56] and in 2007 *Genocide* Judgment.[57] The special collective effect on standing because of the *erga omnes* character of the obligation allegedly violated was denied by the ICJ in the 1966 *South West Africa* Judgment, when the Court rejected the notion than an *actio popularis* was permitted by international law for the protection of fundamental common interests, such as in that particular case the cessation of South Africa's trustee mandate over Namibia.[58]

In *Barcelona Traction*, the ICJ concluded that Belgium did not have legal standing to bring the action, assuming that it was Canada that had a 'legal interest' in the action (as the national state of the company) and Belgium could not invoke a 'more general' interest in the action. In fact, Belgium had not invoked the violation of an obligation *erga omnes* and the denial of justice attributed to Spain was not *erga omnes* by any standard proposed to identify obligations *erga omnes*.[59] One might be led to presume that, had Spain been accused of a violation of an obligation *erga omnes*, in the Court's view also Belgium (although the company was not its national) could have had legal standing in the proceedings.

Human rights treaties usually provide for the filing of complaints from states parties and individuals with international monitoring bodies regardless of any 'injured' state. A contracting state may accuse another contracting state of having violated a treaty vis-à-vis a person who is not its national and may well be a national of the accused state itself, and even of a state not party to the treaty (provided that the abuse occurred within the jurisdiction of the accused state).[60] Such mechanism suggests that treaty obligations are not 'reciprocal' but 'objective' and that the treaty admits a sort of *actio popularis*.[61] However, this is the case only in part. The treaty binds the states, and each

[53] See K Kawasaki, 'The "Injured State" in the International Law of State Responsibility' (2000) 28 Hitotsubashi Journal of Law and Politics 17; Tams (n 24 above) 158–97.

[54] In the *Armed Activities* case, for example, the Democratic Republic of Congo (DRC) suggested that if an obligation is *erga omnes*, and/or belonging to *jus cogens*, then the consent requirement for jurisdiction of the Court falls (n 32 above), paras 56 and 73.

[55] ICJ, *Case concerning East Timor* (n 29 above) para 29.

[56] ICJ, *Case concerning Armed Activities on the Territory of the Congo* (n 32 above) paras 64, 125.

[57] ICJ, *Application of the Convention on the Prevention and Punishment of the Crime of Genocide* (n 33 above) paras 147, 185.

[58] ICJ, *South West Africa (Ethiopia v South Africa; Liberia v South Africa) (Merits)* Judgment of 18 July 1966, [1966] ICJ Rep 6, para 88.

[59] ICJ, *Case concerning Barcelona Traction* (n 21 above) para 91. For the view that 'by recognizing the legal interest of all States in seeing obligations *erga omnes* observed, the Court intended to confer upon them standing to institute judicial proceedings' and that, therefore, 'Where jurisdiction is established, all States can institute proceedings against States principally responsible for violations of obligations *erga omnes*', see Tams (n 24 above) 163–5, 196–7.

[60] On 'jurisdiction' in the context of human rights treaties, see Ch 7 above, section A (2)(d).

[61] For the view that the right of *actio popularis* was recognized as part of international law long before 1966, but relying only on treaty regimes, see E Schwelb, 'The "Actio Popularis" and International Law' (1972) 2 Is YBHR 46–56, 50–1.

state party expects that each of the others will comply with it, although the obligations whose performance is expected concern the treatment of individuals falling within the jurisdiction of the accused state regardless of their nationality. Within these terms, obligations *erga omnes* raise little question, but one might wonder whether they are needed at all as a conceptual pattern. What if a contracting state fails to observe the decision of the monitoring body, in cases where there is one and its decisions are binding? Are *all* contracting states allowed to take countermeasures against the wrongdoer despite the fact that the victim is not assumed to be one of their nationals? Treaties are generally silent on this question and the answer should be sought in general international law, unless the silence in the treaty is construed as a prohibition of countermeasures capable of overriding any possibly contrary rule provided by general international law as between the parties. The problem arises in any treaty regime, such as those of WTO Agreements and EU law, as a result of their potentially 'self-contained' character.[62] There are, thus, two distinct issues: (a) what the treaty stipulates, expressly or impliedly; (b) what general international law provides as to the possible 'fall-back' to itself by the treaty. The first is to be solved on a treaty-by-treaty basis, taking into account in particular its language and subsequent application. The second requires a comprehensive analysis of the international practice, including general treaty practice.[63]

The concept of *actio popularis*, drawn from national public (notably criminal) justice, just like obligations *erga omnes* in general, is rather problematic. If *actio popularis* is permitted when the allegedly breached obligation is *erga omnes*, then *all* states (having accepted the jurisdiction of the court seised) should be allowed to sue the transgressor before *all* existing courts having jurisdiction, not only before the ICJ. There is no reason to confine the collective standing to one or another court if the effect derives from the character *erga omnes* of the 'primary' rule allegedly breached. On the other hand, if collective standing depends on the statute of each court, then one and the same obligation may be *erga omnes* (in the specific sense of collective standing) in one court and not in another. This simply means that the category is pointless, although its desired effects may well be produced on the basis of the statute and its reading by a particular court. One should not overlook that, unlike in domestic legal systems, international adjudication is not formally organized in a unitary set of courts having compulsory jurisdiction.[64] The 'collective effect' would be produced only in respect of states which have consented to the jurisdiction of any particular court seised. To allow *all* states to institute proceedings in *all* courts in such a judicial 'system' is open to abuse by states and to destabilization of the judicial function. Some accommodation is clearly necessary, such as perhaps applying the abuse of process doctrine as a counter-weight.[65] But there is no significant guidance in the practice. Even such an accommodation, in any event, would make the concept of obligations *erga omnes* pointless, since the judicial regime would be based on the statute and margin of discretion of each court, and 'cross-fertilization' among the courts will be a matter of fact, not of law. An obligation may be *erga omnes*, yet a particular court may not feel that seisure should be allowed to third states, while the same court or other courts may accept a different notion or different degrees of 'direct interest' and allow seisure by third states in certain cases and not in others when the interest of the applicant appears approximately the same.

[62] L Gradoni, Regime Failure *nel diritto internazionale* (Padua: Cedam, 2009).
[63] See n 43 above, and Ch 6 above, n 271.
[64] See Ch 6 above, section C (1)(c).
[65] See C Brown, *A Common Law of International Adjudication* (Oxford: OUP, 2007) 245–50.

(b) Universal jurisdiction

A similar logic seems to inform the notion of universal jurisdiction over piracy and international crimes. In recent times international and domestic courts have appealed to the concept of obligations *erga omnes* to uphold universal jurisdiction over international crimes committed by individuals. For example, in the *Jorgic* case both German courts and the ECtHR argued that Article 1 Genocide Convention contemplates an obligation *erga omnes* which allows universal jurisdiction over genocide, although universal jurisdiction was rejected when the Convention was drafted.[66] There seems to be a necessary connection between universal jurisdiction and obligations *erga omnes*, assuming that a violation of international law towards all states gives all of them an exceptional title to exercise their criminal jurisdiction without any further jurisdictional link being necessary (or only the *forum deprehensionis* link being required).

However, universal jurisdiction can be asserted, on the one hand, even without relying on obligations *erga omnes* and, on the other hand, the latter may not produce the effect of universal jurisdiction. Universal jurisdiction over piracy and even over international crimes has been judicially asserted in the past, when international law was allegedly only an inter-ruler law, without any need for obligations *erga omnes*.[67] Moreover, the breach of an obligation *erga omnes* may allow a collective response (for example, countermeasures) against the wrongdoer but not universal jurisdiction. It is the practice that can help to find out the law, and practice may or may not reflect (or may not fully reflect) the logical inferences which are often drawn from obligations *erga omnes*. Article 1 Genocide Convention may be *erga omnes* in one sense (for example, by allowing standing before an international court) but not in another (for example, by failing to allow universal jurisdiction in domestic courts). States may converge on the permissibility of an *actio popularis* in certain international courts, operating according to their statutes and guarantees, yet diverge on universal jurisdiction in the domestic courts of all states, including those which do not offer adequate procedural guarantees. The *Barcelona Traction* Judgment itself was not concerned with universal jurisdiction, but with diplomatic protection, and there is no inherent necessity that from the possible admissibility of the latter by third states the admissibility of the former automatically follows.[68] An inter-state reaction is one thing, a title of jurisdiction of domestic courts is quite another. Nor was Article 19 ILC Draft on State Responsibility concerned with universal jurisdiction, but instead with the international responsibility deriving from the commission of state international crimes.[69]

[66] ECtHR, *Jorgic v Federal Republic of Germany* (n 35 above) paras 54, 68, recalling the Judgment of the Spanish National Court of 5 November 1998 in the *Pinochet Case* ((2002) 119 ILR 331, 335–6), whereby 'The fact that the Contracting Parties have not agreed on universal jurisdiction over the crime for their respective national jurisdictions does not preclude the establishment, by a State which is a party to the Convention, of such jurisdiction over a crime which involves the whole world and affects the international community and indeed all of humanity directly, as stated in the Convention itself'). See V Thalmann, 'National Criminal Jurisdiction over Genocide' in P Gaeta (ed), *The UN Genocide Convention: A Commentary* (Oxford: OUP, 2009) 231–58.

[67] See eg Israeli Supreme Court, *Attorney-General of the Government of Israel v Adolf Eichmann* Judgment of 29 May 1962, (1962) 36 ILR 277, para 12.

[68] cf R Higgins, *Problems and Process: International Law and How we Use it* (Oxford: Clarendon Press, 1994) 57.

[69] It is worth noting that the 1996 ILC Draft included apartheid in the list of international crimes and that Art IV(b) of the 1973 Apartheid Convention does provide for universal jurisdiction by placing on the states parties the obligation: 'To adopt legislative, judicial and administrative measures to prosecute, bring to trial and punish in accordance with their jurisdiction persons responsible for, or accused of, the acts defined in article II of the present Convention, whether or not such persons reside in the territory of the State in which the acts are committed or are nationals of that State or of some

Universal jurisdiction over piracy, in particular, has always been the consequence of a convergence in state practice with no need of the general concept of obligations *erga omnes*. In any event, it is difficult to conclude that general international law permits universal jurisdiction over international crimes in the first place, and even in respect of piracy the practice shows the extreme reluctance of states to engage in prosecutions.[70] But if this is true, once again, what is the usefulness of obligations *erga omnes*? The rule on universal jurisdiction is to be ascertained in the practice, it is not to be extracted from the concept of obligations *erga omnes*, and the practice may pull in any direction, whatever the theoretical potentialities of obligations *erga omnes*.

(c) Collective countermeasures

May 'third' states take countermeasures against a state that has violated an obligation *erga omnes*?[71] Article 19 1996 ILC Articles defined an 'international crime' of states as 'the breach by a State of an international obligation so essential for the protection of fundamental interests of the international community that its breach is recognized as a crime by that community as a whole' and provided a list of crimes including aggression, colonial domination, slavery, genocide, apartheid, and massive pollution of the atmosphere or of the seas. Article 40 specified that, in case of an international crime, 'all other States' were 'injured' and Articles 51 to 53 indicated the further specific consequences of crimes.[72] Article 19 and the term 'crime' were deleted in the 2001 ILC Articles as a result of the strong objections from states.

However, the notion of obligations *erga omnes* has remained, and the expression 'international crimes of states' has recently gained currency in international legal practice, especially in the context of the 'humanitarian exception' to sovereign immunity.[73] Article 48 2001 ILC Articles provides that any state other than the 'injured state' may 'invoke' the responsibility of another state for a breach of an obligation *erga omnes* and, consequently, 'may claim' cessation of the international wrongful act, and assurances and guarantees of non-repetition, as well as performance of the obligation of reparation in the interest of the injured state or of the beneficiaries of the obligation breached. Article 54 stipulates that non-injured states may adopt 'lawful measures'. The Commentary to Article 54 takes a very cautious approach to the possibility that 'lawful measures' include countermeasures as opposed to mere retorsions, pointing out that 'there appears to be no clearly recognised entitlement of States referred to in Article 48 to take countermeasures in the collective interest' and for this very reason Article 54 'speaks of "lawful measures" rather than "countermeasures"'.[74] A decidedly stronger position in favour of collective countermeasures was adopted in 2005 by the IDI in a resolution on obligations and rights *erga omnes* in international law. Article 5(c) of the Resolution provides that 'should a widely acknowledged grave breach of an *erga omnes* obligation occur, all the States to which the obligation is owed . . . are entitled to take

other State or are stateless persons'. This is clearly a case in which the two notions of universal jurisdiction and international crimes overlap, but it is far from proving in general that whatever was included in the ILC Draft for state responsibility purposes is automatically to be taken as authorizing (or even imposing) universal jurisdiction, let alone that this (possible, but not inevitable) equation is evidence of the relevance of the category of obligations *erga omnes*.

[70] See Ch 5 above, nn 279–84 and accompanying text, and Ch 7 above, section A (2)(c).

[71] For individual countermeasures taken by the injured state, see Ch 6 above, section D (3)(b).

[72] See n 28 above.

[73] See Ch 7, section B (2)(a).

[74] Crawford (n 39 above) 302–5, paras 6–7, and 276–80.

non-forcible counter-measures under conditions analogous to those applying to a State specially affected by the breach'.[75] There is, in fact, some practice in favour of collective countermeasures, but this practice is selective and comes predominantly, although not exclusively, from Western states. States have been generally critical of collective countermeasures and for this reason the ILC refrained from endorsing such measures in the 2001 Articles.[76]

What measures otherwise unlawful are allowed to third states remains obscure. Writers rarely distinguish between discretionary and mandatory measures,[77] binding and exhortatory, per se unlawful and unfriendly although lawful measures, measures adopted by or under the UN Security Council or other UN bodies' authorization and unilateral measures, peaceful and armed measures. Many measures adoptable by third states are per se *lawful* and need no special title to be allowed. A mere demand for cessation or non-repetition of the breach or a request for reparation on behalf of the injured state by a third state is not an unlawful act. And it hardly violates the principle of non-interference in the domestic affairs of the alleged wrongdoing state.[78] The term 'invoke' used in Article 48 2001 ILC Articles is inherently ambiguous. The Commentary to Article 48 uses, as synonyms, 'request', 'claim', and 'demand', but this may simply refer to means of compliance already provided for by any treaty, such as the possibility of appealing to monitoring bodies expressly provided by a human rights treaty, or to a mere verbal protest. Retorsions may of course be adopted by third states, but they are adoptable in any case. Their only possible relevance arises when arguing that as a reaction to the violation of an obligation *erga omnes* they change from discretionary to mandatory. There is, however, no support for this. Also an *obligation* on third states to take countermeasures finds no support in international legal practice. On the other hand, if admitted, it would entail the rather extravagant consequence that for *each* violation of an obligation *erga omnes* there would be some 200 or so violations of this obligation by all states (given their well-known reluctance to respond) which will not take countermeasures against the wrongdoer. This explains why Common Article 1 1949 Geneva Conventions[79] cannot be construed as a 'quasi-constitutional' rule incorporating a general obligation *erga omnes* to 'respect and ensure respect' of the Geneva Conventions.[80] The same applies to Article 41, which sets out certain *obligations* concerning serious violations of *jus cogens* and may thus envisage an obligation to take per se lawful measures. Article 48, for its part, implies that states other than the injured state have a discretionary power (as opposed to an obligation) to 'invoke' the responsibility of the transgressor state, as evidenced by terms like 'entitled' and 'may'. Measures adopted by third states on the basis of an obligation, a recommendation, or an authorization of a UN body are lawful or unlawful depending on the UN Charter, without any need for the concept of obligations *erga omnes*. As already noted, collective self-defence cannot be considered to be a manifestation of obligations *erga omnes* since

[75] At <http://www.idi-iil.org/idiE/resolutionsE/2005_kra_01_en.pdf>.

[76] An accurate, but not fully convincing, analysis in favour of countermeasures taken by all states as a response to breaches of obligations *erga omnes* has been developed, on the basis of state practice, by Tams (n 24 above) 198–251.

[77] See Ch 6 above, section A (2)(c).

[78] cf Art 1 of the IDI Res of 13 September 1989 on the Protection of Human Rights and the Principle of Non-intervention in Internal Affairs of States, at <http://www.idi-iil.org/idiE/resolutionsE/1989_comp_03_en.PDF>.

[79] 'The High Contracting Parties undertake to respect and to ensure respect for the present Convention in all circumstances.'

[80] C Focarelli, 'Common Article 1 of the 1949 Geneva Conventions: A Soap Bubble?' (2010) 21 EJIL 125.

it requires the request of the attacked state, that is to say, third states are not entitled to determine whether a certain state has been attacked and whether an armed reaction is to be carried out.[81] Humanitarian intervention, by contrast, is rooted in the concept of obligations *erga omnes* but, as explained below, today it is permitted only when it is authorized by the UN Security Council, hence on the basis of the UN Charter. The issue of countermeasures taken by third states is thus confined to peaceful, unilateral, and discretionary countermeasures.

Being the issue confined to unilateral and discretionary countermeasures, one might wonder whether the liberty conferred on the stronger to *select* the cases in which they decide *unilaterally* to respond by way of an otherwise *unlawful act* is a wise legal answer as a matter of policy. Especially to scholars attracted to authoritarian and totalizing foundations of law, the *erga omnes* answer sounds promising. But doubts are far from unreasonable. The suspicion that obligations *erga omnes* are enforced on the basis of double standards and for purposes of power politics is hard to avoid. The conviction that the stronger will really unilaterally act 'on behalf of the international community as a whole', especially when this occurs outside an institutional framework, sounds like a fairy tale. It is a fact that in recorded history great powers have always justified their actions in the name of the 'public good' but, of course, never to their disadvantage.[82] While this is simply obvious, the fact remains that what major powers claim in their own interest (as possibly coinciding with the global interest) is one thing, but what the law states is quite another. The basic assumption underlying obligations *erga omnes* historically derives from both universal jurisdiction over piracy and (especially in its humanitarian armed version) the Christian notion that rulers should intervene in other states within Christendom, and possibly elsewhere, to enforce a right of resistance to the tyrant. This claim was possible within the universalistic vision of the Christian faith, based on the common brotherhood of the human race under the only God, as sons of the same Father, ie from Christian monotheism, and on the autonomy of the Church from any particular universal emperor or local ruler. In the nineteenth century the rule of universal jurisdiction was extended, on the initiative of Great Britain, to the slave trade. It was, inter alia, a strategic move aimed at patrolling the oceans, under the pretext of overseeing the slave trade, implying that the trade was 'quasi-piracy' which deserved the same legal treatment.[83] In fact, the rationale is different: the universal repression of piracy is obvious in a world of states since all states are strongly interested in repressing such individuals when there is no state able and willing to punish them for their misdeeds. The same does not hold true for those who engage in the slave trade or other grave abuses of human rights but do have an effective national state which can actually punish them or in any case account on the international plane. Unsurprisingly, while slave trading on the high seas was prohibited by the end of the nineteenth

[81] See Ch 7 above, n 70.

[82] cf EH Carr, *Twenty Years' Crisis (1919–1939): An Introduction to the Study of International Relations* [1939] (Houndmills and New York: Palgrave, 2001) 74–6.

[83] For (excessive) emphasis on this, see WG Grewe, *Epochen der Völkerrechtsgeschichte* (Baden-Baden: Nomos, 1984) 651–72, English trans *The Epochs of International Law* (Berlin and New York: Walter de Gruyter, 2000) 554–69. The equation of the slave trade with piracy was not always upheld by the courts; eg in the 1817 landmark *Le Louis* Judgment the British High Court of Admiralty held that unlike pirates slave traders did not engage in the 'act of freebooters, enemies of the human race, renouncing every country, and ravaging every country in its coasts and vessels indiscriminately, and thereby creating an universal terror and alarm; but of persons confining their transactions (reprehensible as they may be) to particular countries, without exciting the slightest apprehension in others' (see British High Court of Admiralty, *Le Louis* Judgment of 15 December 1817, in Dodson, *Reports*, 210, 247).

century, slavery continued to be admitted until the early decades of the twentieth century.[84]

Finally, even assuming that collective countermeasures are permitted, a further unavoidable question remains as to whether the requirements of individual countermeasures apply unaltered. It would be reasonable to expect that at least in some respects requirements should suffer some alterations (for example, proportionality and the 'repartition' of the response among all those states which decide to take countermeasures), but no indication whatsoever exists in the practice.

(2) Humanitarian intervention

Perhaps the most far-reaching purported implication of obligations *erga omnes* is humanitarian intervention, ie the military intervention in another state to protect its own population, or more likely a part thereof, from gross violations of human rights committed by their own government. It sounds logical that if international law protects the human rights of people from their own government, then it must also provide the means to react against this government when it massively violates human rights, including by armed force if need be. However, state practice shows that states are extremely reluctant to intervene in other states on humanitarian grounds and when they intervene they do so because they have a gain in sight. This finding has not substantially changed after the restyling of humanitarian intervention in terms of responsibility to protect (RtoP). However, a distinction should be made between human interventions that are carried out unilaterally by individual states or coalitions of the willing (including regional organizations, such as NATO) and those which are authorized by the UN Security Council. Current international law permits the latter, but not the former. This section is devoted to a succinct analysis of the issue by focusing on unilateral intervention and on the RtoP doctrine.

(a) Unilateral intervention

Western states are in principle in favour of humanitarian intervention since the humanitarian 'standard of civilization' to be complied with is simply theirs. No humanitarian intervention has ever been devised for cases where a social or political organization proves unable or unwilling to live according to the humanitarian standard of a tribe. Non-Western states view humanitarian intervention with understandable suspicion. Historically, this kind of military intervention was often carried out by Western powers to 'rescue' Christians who lived under non-Western rulers, such as the Ottoman Empire.[85] Humanitarian intervention is by definition an altruistic enterprise and few if any would believe that a state is really prepared to sacrifice its own resources and presumably the lives of its military to rescue someone unknown somewhere in the world. The only reason for intervention to take place is because the intervening states find it profitable or are compelled to intervene, inter alia, because of a popular push, whatever their sincere humanitarian feelings may be. One possible reason, among many, to intervene is in order to destabilize another state, which it is feared might jeopardize the national security of the intervening state, simply by ousting its political

[84] cf Slavery Convention (adopted 25 September 1926, entered into force 9 March 1927) 60 LNTS 253; Supplementary Convention on the Abolition of Slavery, the Slave Trade, and Institutions and Practices Similar to Slavery (adopted 7 September 1956, entered into force 30 April 1957) 266 UNTS 3.

[85] For a list of 18th-century cases, see Grewe (n 83 above) 487–96.

leadership under the pretext of acting against a tyrant. Humanitarian intervention is by its very nature basically contingent on civilizational stakes.

Several theories have been elaborated to justify unilateral humanitarian intervention. One is that the prohibition of gross violations of human rights is *erga omnes* and 'therefore' an appropriate reaction in the form of military intervention is permitted. However, as previously seen, obligations *erga omnes* are not sufficient to infer any automatic consequence. Another theory is that the UN Charter not only prohibits the use of force but also promotes human rights, and 'therefore' the use of force to promote human rights—or the use of force being not 'inconsistent with the purposes of the United Nations' in the words of Article 2(4) UN Charter[86]—is lawful. The problem with this theory is that the Charter does prohibit the use of force and nowhere provides for a humanitarian exception. The claim that human rights are today *jus cogens* meets with the objection that also the prohibition of the use of force is seen as peremptory and there is no certainty as to why the former should prevail over the latter. It is also a fact that humanitarian intervention, while justified in terms of avoiding humanitarian catastrophes, inevitably causes other serious breaches of human rights. The mechanical reasoning based on the priority of humanitarian needs or the supremacy of *jus cogens* leads to inextricable problems. Yet another theory is based on necessity, as envisaged in Article 25 of the 2001 ILC Articles. It is somehow assumed that when a humanitarian catastrophe is under way the maxim 'necessity knows no law' applies.[87] But while necessity may indeed apply in certain circumstances (which is different from saying that humanitarian intervention is lawful as such), it applies as a legal tool and within the law, not outside it. If a humanitarian intervention takes place under necessity outside the law, then it is simply unlawful, however morally desirable. Humanitarian intervention has also been justified by referring to the idea of 'human security',[88] more precisely as 'human security in action' trumping state sovereignty.[89] To some, human security is 'interventionist by nature' for cosmopolitan goals.[90] The theory has been rightly criticized, especially as a form of neo-colonialism.[91] In fact, human security may also be invoked against humanitarian intervention.[92]

International practice militates against the permissibility of unilateral humanitarian intervention. In the 1986 *Nicaragua* Judgment the ICJ denied that military measures could be justified as a response to alleged violations of human rights.[93] The very few cases of humanitarian intervention which occurred during the Cold War were generally condemned.[94] The position taken by the United Kingdom since 1992 in favour of

[86] See Ch 7 above, section A (1)(b).

[87] cf the speech given by UK Prime Minister Tony Blair in Sedgefield on 5 March 2004, arguing that: 'It may well be that under international law as presently constituted, a regime can systematically brutalise and oppress its people and there is nothing anyone can do . . . This may be the law, but should it be?', at <http://www.guardian.co.uk/politics/2004/mar/05/iraq.iraq>.

[88] See Ch 7 above, section A (2).

[89] B von Tigerstrom, *Human Security and International Law: Prospects and Problems* (Oxford and Portland: Hart, 2007) 96.

[90] G Oberleitner, 'Human Security: A Challenge to International Law?' (2005) 11 *Global Governance* 185, 194.

[91] P Upadhyaya, 'Human Security, Humanitarian Intervention, and Third World Concerns' (2004) 33 Den JILP 71.

[92] Tigerstrom (n 89 above) 108–11.

[93] ICJ, *Case concerning Military and Paramilitary Activities in and against Nicaragua (Nicaragua v United States of America) (Merits)* Judgment of 27 June 1986, [1986] ICJ Rep 14, para 268.

[94] For the (few) relevant cases during the Cold War, see M Newman, *Humanitarian Intervention: Confronting the Contradictions* (London: Hurst and Co, 2009) 28–36.

humanitarian intervention 'in extreme circumstances' has remained isolated.[95] The bombing of the Federal Republic of Yugoslavia (FRY) in 1999 by NATO, allegedly on grounds of humanity, was not authorized by the UN Security Council and was strongly condemned by most states.[96] The humanitarian argument made, among others, by the United States to justify the 2003 Iraq War was unsubstantiated.[97] The invocation of humanitarian grounds by the Russian Federation in the 2008 Georgia conflict was strongly criticized and proves, whatever the soundness of the criticisms in the particular circumstances, that humanitarian intervention is open to manipulation.[98] Even Israel hinted, inter alia, at humanitarian grounds to justify its three-week Operation 'Cast Lead' started on 27 December 2008 at the UN Security Council when its representative stated that 'the Hamas regime . . . brutally seized control of Gaza, murdering scores of fellow Palestinians . . . Its only interest is in establishing a regime of tyranny for Gazans and of terror for Israelis' so that Israel had 'no choice' but to defend itself 'not from the Palestinian people, but from the terrorists who have taken them hostage'.[99] Lately, in the 2011 Libyan UN-authorized intervention, states were not prepared to intervene unilaterally, not even within a coalition of the willing, despite their presumable interest in doing so, without the authorization of the Security Council.[100]

(b) *Responsibility to protect*

The doctrine of the responsibility to protect (RtoP), introduced by the 2001 ICISS report,[101] was born with a view to finding a positive solution—legally acceptable and compatible with state sovereignty—to the traditional problem of humanitarian intervention, and more precisely to the question posed by the then UN Secretary-General Kofi Annan, who asked 'if humanitarian intervention is, indeed, an unacceptable assault on sovereignty, how should we respond to a Rwanda, to a Srebrenica—to gross and systematic violations of human rights that affect every precept of our common humanity?'[102] From then on the doctrine has been extensively discussed both in legal doctrine and in international practice,[103] with positions that range from enthusiastic acceptance, through relative indifference as a mere political catchword, to rejection, and even extend to international security[104] and

[95] cf the Statement of the Legal Adviser to the Foreign and Commonwealth Office of 2 December 1992, (1992) 63 BYBIL 828.

[96] ME O'Connell, *The Power and Purpose of International Law: Insights from the Theory and Practice of Enforcement* (Oxford: OUP, 2008) 97, 180, 224–5. For a comprehensive insightful analysis, see P Picone, 'La "guerra del Kosovo" e il diritto internazionale generale' (2000) 83 RDI 309. See further Ch 6 above, n 18.

[97] O'Connell (n 96 above) 146–7, 227.

[98] cf UN Doc S/PV.5953, at 8.

[99] UN Doc S/PV.6061, at 6–7.

[100] See n 114 below.

[101] See n 5 above.

[102] *We the Peoples: The Role of the United Nations in the 21st Century*, Millennium Report of the Secretary-General of the United Nations, September 2000, 48.

[103] See eg A Orford, *International Atrocities and the Responsibility to Protect* (Cambridge: CUP, 2011); J Genser and I Cotler (eds), *The Responsibility to Protect, The Promise of Stopping Mass Atrocities in Our Time* (Oxford and New York: OUP, 2012); C Focarelli, 'Ahead to the past? Responsibility to Protect and the Global System' (2012) I GroJIL I, also at <www.grojil.org>.

[104] L Feinstein and A-M Slaughter, 'A Duty to Prevent' (2004) 83 *Foreign Affairs* 136. The attempt to apply the RtoP to security threats, especially terrorism, is today relatively frequent in legal doctrine and also the practice of justifying the military response as self-defence against non-state actors (see section C 7 section (A)(1)(C) above). In 2008 Israel observed that states have a duty 'to ensure that intentional [terrorist] attacks against civilians' in other states are not launched from their territory, hence a duty of the targeted states 'to protect their civitions' (cf UN Doc S/PV.5898 (Resumption 1), 27 May 2008, at 7). It is assumed that military action by the targeted state is permissible for the 'protection' of *its own* citizens as distinct from the citizens of the state which is unable or unwilling to control its territory from which attacks have been launched. It is true that states have a customary obligation of prevention (see Ch 7 above, nn 441–9), undoubtedly covering the use of force against

natural disasters.[105] The notion that the RtoP is an 'emerging norm', as the ICISS's report in 2001 suggested, is unsubstantiated. There has never been an international law norm, not even emerging, allowing RtoP in the specific sense of justifying otherwise unlawful unilateral measures taken by individual states. It is one thing to understand RtoP as a guide for political mediation, it is quite another to use it as a justification for otherwise internationally unlawful acts, especially military intervention. While the first aspect is straightforward, the second is highly questionable.

The RtoP was grounded by the ICISS in the idea of sovereignty as responsibility, articulated in three pillars (to prevent, to protect, and to rebuild), permitted in a few extreme circumstances possibly under the UN mandate, and subject to a number of conditions extracted from the just war theory.[106] The ICISS did not exclude unilateral intervention,[107] but presupposed a priority—which tended towards an exclusive competence—of the UN Security Council. It also envisaged the possibility of a mandate of the General Assembly under the terms of the 1950 'Uniting for Peace' resolution,[108] or even of regional IOs, in cases where the Security Council had reached an impasse because of the veto of its permanent members. RtoP was endorsed, although somewhat diluted, in 2005 by the UN Secretary-General[109] and the General Assembly,[110] in 2006 by the Security Council (although in general terms),[111] and again in 2009 by the Secretary-General[112] and General Assembly.[113] Finally it was loosely applied by the Security Council with the adoption of Resolution 1973 (2011) on Libya without meeting with significant protests.[114] This confirms that humanitarian intervention authorized by the Security Council is lawful. However, the partial endorsement of the doctrine by the Security Council does not mean that this latter will necessarily follow its own example in future cases, even less that it will do so on the basis of 'egalitarian' and 'just' global policy considerations. The UN Security Council has no

neighbouring states, but there is little certainty that its violation always justifies armed reaction. In fact, the permissibility of the RtoP doctrine, as discussed in the text, is highly contentious even in its original version and there is no evidence that it may be further extended to the protection of people abroad. Foreign military intervention to protect the people of the territorial state and foreign military intervention to protect one's own people from attacks launched by private actors abroad are different issues and do not necessarily admit identical legal conclusions.

105 TR Saechao, 'Natural Disasters and the Responsibility to Protect: From Chaos to Clarity' (2007) 32 Brooklyn JIL 663. The UN Secretary-General expressed the view that RtoP should not extend to natural disaster (n 112 below).

106 For a critical analysis and further references, see C Focarelli, 'The Responsibility to Protect Doctrine and Humanitarian Intervention: Too Many Ambiguities for a Working Doctrine' (2008) 13 JCSL 191.

107 For a remarkable report on the RtoP from the perspective of the US, see Genocide Prevention Task Force, *Preventing Genocide: A Blueprint for U.S. Policymakers* (released on 8 December 2008) at <http://www.ushmm.org/genocide/taskforce/report.php>. For the endorsement of the doctrine in the 2010 US National Security Strategy, see Ch 7 above, n 72.

108 UNGA Res 377 (V) of 3 November 1950, 'Uniting for Peace', UN Doc A/1775, 10.

109 UNSG, 'In Larger Freedom: Towards Development, Security and Human Rights for All', Report of 21 March 2005, UN Doc A/59/2005, paras 132, 135.

110 UNGA Res 60/1 of 24 October 2005, 'World Summit Outcome' document, UN Doc A/RES/60/1, limiting the hypotheses under which states are 'prepared' to react to genocide, war crimes, ethnic cleansing, and crimes against humanity (paras 138–139).

111 UNSC Res 1674 (2006) of 28 April 2006, para 4, and, more recently, UN Docs/PV.6650 (Presumption 1).

112 UNSG 'Implementing the Responsibility to Protect', Report of 12 January 2009, UN Doc A/63/677, pointing out that RtoP applies only to 'genocide, war crimes, ethnic cleansing and crimes against humanity', and should not extend to 'other calamities, such as HIV/AIDS, climate change or the response to natural disasters' (para 10(b)).

113 UNGA Res 63/308 of 14 September 2009, and, more recently, <http://gadebate.un.org>.

114 UNSC Res 1973 (2011) of 13 March 2011. For a brief comment, see C Focarelli, 'Libya: a Turning Point for the Responsibility to Protect Doctrine?', at <http://www.e-ir.info/?p=8091>.

obligation to apply RtoP.[115] The doctrine remains grounded in a case-by-case assessment by the Council and dependent on the majorities of the day. It also, quite inevitably, will depend on a great many other factors such as urgency, prospects of success, military costs, possible benefits, foreseeable reaction, new alliances, risks of escalation, surrounding local environment, likelihood that military operations will end as early as possible, local political destabilization, cross-border spill-over effects, outflows of refugees, state-building prospects, and so forth.

(3) Smart sanctions

Especially after the end of the Cold War, the UN Security Council has imposed 'comprehensive' economic sanctions, contemplating some 'humanitarian exemptions', under Article 41 UN Charter. Problems soon arose not only with regard to their effectiveness, as in the past, but also their 'collateral effects', ie adverse and harmful consequences, on both the civilian population of the targeted state and on third states with traditional trading links with the targeted state. In certain cases sanctions were adopted against states deemed to have violated civil and political human rights, while other economic, social, and cultural human rights were violated by the sanctions themselves.[116]

Faced with strong criticisms, notably by just-war theorists,[117] the Security Council began to adopt 'targeted' or 'smart' sanctions,[118] either individual- and/or sector-specific, and to target either incumbent state officials (for example, of Eritrea,[119] Iraq,[120] Liberia,[121] Sudan,[122] Somalia,[123] Syria and Lebanon,[124] Iran,[125] North Korea,[126] and Libya[127]) or non-state actors, such as rebels fighting against the legitimate government (in Angola,[128] Sierra Leone,[129] Liberia,[130] Ivory Coast,[131] and the

[115] For the opposite view, see Ch 6 above, n 463.

[116] For this 'schizophrenic role' of economic sanctions, see A Howlett, 'Getting "Smart": Crafting Economic Sanctions that Respect All Human Rights' (2004–05) 73 Ford LR 1199.

[117] See eg A Winkler, 'Just Sanctions' (1999) 21 HRQ 133.

[118] For plenty of information, see <http://www.smartsanctions.se>.

[119] UNSC Res 1907 (2009) of 23 December 2009.

[120] UNSC Res 1483 (2003) of 22 May 2003.

[121] UNSC Res 1343 (2001) of 7 March 2001, Res 1521 (2003) of 22 December 2003, and Res 1532 (2004) of 12 March 2004.

[122] UNSC Res 1591 (2005) of 29 March 2005, Res 1672 (2006) of 25 April 2006.

[123] UNSC Res 2002 (2011) of 29 July 2011.

[124] UNSC Res 1636 (2005) of 31 October 2005. It should be noted that, although Res 1636 (2005) imposed individual measures, no persons have actually been named by the Sanctions Committee established pursuant to Res 1636 itself.

[125] UNSC Res 1737 (2006) of 23 December 2006, Res 1747 (2007) of 24 March 2007, Res 1803 (2008) of 3 March 2008, and Res 1929 (2010) of 9 June 2010.

[126] UNSC Res 1718 (2006) of 14 October 2006, and Res 1874 (2009) of 12 June 2009.

[127] UNSC Res 1970 (2011) of 26 February 2011, Res 1973 (2011) of 17 March 2011, and Res 2016 (2011) of 27 October 2011.

[128] UNSC Res 864 (1993) of 15 September 1993, Res 1127 (1997) of 28 August 1997, Res 1173 (1998) of 12 June 1998, Res 1237 (1999) of 7 May 1999, Res 1295 (2000) of 18 April 2000, Res 1412 (2002) of 17 May 2002 (suspending previous sanctions), Res 1448 (2002) of 9 December 2002 (suspending previous sanctions).

[129] UNSC Res 1132 (1997) of 8 October 1997, and Res 1171 (1998) of 5 June 1998. By Res 1940 (2010) of 29 September 2010 the Security Council decided to terminate the measures set forth in Res 1171 (1998) and to dissolve the Committee established by Res 1132 (1997).

[130] See n 121 above.

[131] UNSC Res 1572 (2004) of 15 November 2004, Res 1584 (2005) of 1 February 2005, Res 1643 (2005) of 15 December 2005, Res 1975 (2011) of 30 March 2011, and Res 1980 (2011) of 28 April 2011.

Democratic Republic of Congo[132]) or 'terrorist' organizations (the Taliban and Al Qaeda[133]), or also individuals acting in violation of an arms embargo (for example, Somalia),[134] providing for humanitarian exemptions mainly covering the funds necessary for foodstuffs, rent and mortgage, medicines, and medical treatment. Another element of 'smartness' is the insertion since 2000 in resolutions imposing sanctions of a 'sunset clause' which specifies a time-limit, usually 12 months, thereby causing sanctions to be lifted automatically when not renewed.[135] Like traditional 'blunt' sanctions, smart sanctions include embargos on specific classes of items, such as arms, oil, or diamonds, the freezing of assets, and travel bans. The 'smart trend' has been followed by other IOs, such as the European Union,[136] and unilaterally by states, including the United States,[137] the United Kingdom,[138] Australia,[139] and New Zealand.[140]

Smart sanctions are clearly inspired by the notion that governments should rule responsibly for the benefit of their people, who are generally—although not necessarily—the victims of oppressing rulers.[141] Different rationales, however, lie behind different targets. When rulers are targeted the problem is generally linked to violations of human rights and the exercise of irresponsible sovereignty by the incumbent government. By contrast, when terrorists are targeted the problem is generally linked to terrorist attacks against foreign citizens and property. Depending on the definition of 'terrorism', terrorists so defined in the state may be regarded as rebels defending people against an oppressor government. If so, it is unclear how targeted sanctions against terrorists could assist people. As clarified earlier, it is generally the Security Council that determines who is the 'legitimate' government and who is 'legitimately' fighting against the government in power.[142]

When adopted unilaterally by individual states, smart sanctions may be retorsions, countermeasures, or simply unlawful acts devoid of any justification under international law. When adopted by the Security Council the addressees of the resolutions imposing smart sanctions are UN member states, not necessarily the targeted entities.

[132] UNSC Res 1493 (2003) of 28 July 2003, Res 1596 (2005) of 3 May 2005, Res 1649 (2005) of 21 December 2005, Res 1698 (2006) of 31 July 2006, Res 1771 (2007) of 10 August 2007, Res 1807 (2008) of 31 March 2008, Res 1857 (2008) of 22 December 2008, and Res 1952 (2010) of 29 November 2010.

[133] UNSC Res 1267 (1999) of 15 October 1999, Res 1333 (2000) of 19 December 2000, Res 1390 (2002) of 28 January 2002, Res 1526 (2004) of 30 January 2004, Res 1617 (2005) of 29 July 2005, Res 1735 (2006) of 22 December 2006, Res 1822 (2008) of 30 June 2008, Res 1904 (2009) of 17 December 2009, Res 1988 (2011) of 17 June 2011, and Res 1989 (2011) of 17 June 2011.

[134] UNSC Res 1844 (2008) of 20 November 2008, Res 1916 (2010) of 19 March 2010, and Res 1972 (2011) of 17 March 2011.

[135] UNSC Res 1298 (2000) of 17 May 2000, paras 16–17.

[136] cf <http://eeas.europa.eu/cfsp/sanctions/docs/measures_en.pdf>.

[137] The Sanctions Programs of the US government are available at <http://www.treasury.gov/about/organizational-structure/offices/Pages/Office-of-Foreign-Assets-Control.aspx> at 'Resources'.

[138] The Financial Sanctions of the UK government are available at <http://www.hm-treasury.gov.uk/fin_sanctions_index.htm>.

[139] Australia's Autonomous Sanctions Regime is available at <http://www.dfat.gov.au/un/unsc_sanctions/aasb.html>.

[140] cf eg the targeted sanctions adopted by New Zealand following the 2006 coup in Fiji, available at <http://mfat.govt.nz/Foreign-Relations/Pacific/0-Fiji-FAQ.php>.

[141] cf P Clawson, 'Sanctions as Punishment, Enforcement, and Prelude to Further Action' (1993) 7 EIA 17, 20–1, arguing that 'Absolving the local population of responsibility for the actions of the government can have nefarious effects' since otherwise 'they would have no moral encouragement for taking the risks inherent in overthrowing a brutal dictator'. For the opposite view, see J Galtung, 'On the Effects of International Economic Sanctions: With Examples from the Case of Rhodesia' (1967) 19 *World Politics* 378.

[142] See Ch 5 above, nn 397 and 400.

To be 'targeted' is different from being the 'addressee' of a Security Council resolution. It is member states that are required to take measures against the targeted entities indicated by the Council. This provision is different from that in which the Security Council imposes obligations directly on non-state entities, such as factions struggling in a territory for its control. Smart sanctions have not been significantly contested by the states. If mandatory, they prevail over any other agreement binding on UN member states under Article 103 UN Charter.[143] Their implementation at national (or EU) level is decisive.[144]

Although smart sanctions have been devised to overcome the breach of human rights (of civilian populations) by past 'blunt' sanctions, they have also raised anxieties about respect for human rights (of the targeted persons), in particular the right to a fair trial.[145] Targeted persons and entities, designated by the Security Council or by sanction committees and inserted in public 'black lists', have little or no possibility to challenge sanctions before the courts. Some commentators have suggested that this practice amounts to a sort of 'judicial activity' of the Security Council.[146] However, both the listing and the delisting procedures are subjected to the political assessment of the Security Council, without any judicial review of the charges, and the targeted persons have little or no effective opportunity to defend themselves. To call this procedure 'judicial' or 'quasi-judicial' is inappropriate and misleading. In any event, a good number of cases have been brought before national courts by the targeted persons and entities,[147] and the Security Council has been forced to change its strategy and provide some mechanisms allowing sanctions to be challenged and delisting sought. As noted earlier, the Security Council first responded with some palliatives[148] and, lately, with the establishment of an Ombudsperson.[149]

The debate is still on concerning how to make smart sanctions even 'smarter', ie how to devise sanctions less prone to abuse of human rights and, at the same time, effective and capable of avoiding the destabilization of the state as a whole, with cross-border spill-over effects, without a new stable regime being installed (let alone simply ousting undesirable rulers). Different notions of 'smartness' lie behind human rights protection and goal-attainment maximization. Moreover, measuring the effectiveness of sanctions is extremely difficult,[150] and views diverge profoundly between optimists[151] and

[143] See Ch 6 above, section B (3)(d). [144] See Ch 6 above, section D (2).

[145] I Cameron, 'UN Targeted Sanctions, Legal Safeguards and the European Convention on Human Rights' (2003) 72 Nord JIL 159; G Lysen, 'Targeted UN Sanctions: Application of Legal Sources and Procedural Matters' (2003) 72 Nord JIL 291.

[146] See Ch 6 above, n 161.

[147] R Kolb, 'Le contrôle de Résolutions contraignantes du Conseil de sécurité des Nations Unies sous l'angle du respect du *jus cogens*' (2008) 18 *Schweizerische Zeitschrift für internationales und europäisches Recht* 401.

[148] UNSC Res 1730 (2006) of 19 December 2006 and Res 1735 (2006) of 22 December 2006.

[149] UNSC Res 1904 (2009) of 17 December 2009. The Ombudsperson presented his first report on 28 February 2011 (cf <http://www.un.org/News/Press/docs/2011/sc10189.doc.htm>). More recently, in Res 1988 (2011) and Res 1989 (2011) of 17 June 2011 the Security Council decided to separate the sanctions regime on the two groups by creating an additional mechanism to manage the new regime and extended existing ones for an additional 18 months. See DL Tehindrazanarivelo, 'Targeted Sanctions and Obligations of States on Listing and De-listing Procedures' in L Boisson De Chazournes (ed), *International Law and the Quest for its Implementation* (Leiden: Brill, 2010) 127.

[150] WM Reisman, 'When are Economic Sanctions Effective? Selected Theorems and Corollaries' (1995–96) 2 IISA JICL 587.

[151] IM Petrescu, 'Rethinking Economic Sanctions Success: Sanctions as Deterrent' (Washington, DC: AEI, 2008), at <http://www.aei.org/docLib/111009sanctions.pdf>.

pessimists.[152] Sanctions, either smart or dumb, are always blind enough from a legal perspective in the absence of a universally legitimate and effective authority. All arguments against any kind of sanctions converge in suggesting that international courts should be set up instead and sanctions should be under constant *judicial* scrutiny.

(4) Criminal responsibility

In *Peace Through Law*, published in 1944 when the end of World War II was approaching, Hans Kelsen suggested that the world needed first an international court with compulsory jurisdiction rather than a universal legislator or enforcer, and made a case for international criminal justice.[153] Following the end of the Cold War international criminal justice has witnessed spectacular achievements, with the creation of the ICTY and the ICTR, whose jurisprudence has considerably enriched and articulated the legal perception of intolerable evil at any latitude, and, most importantly, the ICC at global level.

One of the key defects of international human rights law is that international monitoring bodies find against the state rather than against the authors of the violation personally. This was a major step in the past, but today is becoming inadequate since state officials take less and less care to avoid violating human rights treaties (and may even feel encouraged to violate them in exchange for some personal gain) knowing that the consequences of the violation will fall on the state, ie on the people as taxpayers. The media may have no capacity to prove, or any interest in exposing, such behaviour, and even people may have little interest—with the possible exception of a few front-page cases—in learning that the state has been condemned somewhere in Strasbourg or in New York for the violation of human rights towards this or that unknown complainant. International criminal justice is, in this respect, far more effective, although confined for the moment to *extreme* violations of human rights. International criminal tribunals (ICTs) and hybrid tribunals (HCTs) ensure uniformity and often provide greater credibility than the fragmented and frequently politically motivated jurisprudence of domestic courts.

However, the practice is still very far from ensuring that the officials of *any* state are prosecuted, and double standards are routine. Since the establishment of the International Military Tribunal (IMT) at Nuremberg, ICTs have invariably been accused of delivering the 'justice of the victor', ie a 'political justice' against the enemy. The 'internal' legal accuracy of proceedings is said to be a façade of law since it is the victor (or anyway the stronger) that determines who will appear as the accused and who will appear as the judge on an ad hoc basis. The IMT, in particular, was made up of members drawn from the victors and also adjudicated acts which were arguably not international crimes at the time they were committed. It is rather intuitive to feel that had World War II been won by the Nazis, then the same banner of 'justice' would have led to exactly the opposite outcomes. It is true that much has been done to improve international criminal justice since. But doubts remain. The legal basis of the ICTY and the ICTR, set up by Security Council Resolution 827 (1993) and Resolution 955 (1994) under Chapter VII UN Charter, was the subject of heated debate until the Tribunals themselves anchored their legal basis, with difficulty, in Article 41 UN

[152] DA Baldwin and RA Pape, 'Evaluating Economic Sanctions' (1998) 23 *International Security* 189.

[153] H Kelsen, *Peace Through Law* (Chapel Hill: University of Carolina Press, 1944).

Charter.[154] The Council thus imposed the tribunals on all member states. The ICTY has also been allowed to prosecute crimes committed before its establishment (from 1 January 1991), when the perpetrators had no knowledge that they would be tried by this Tribunal for what they were doing. The ICC has overcome many objections, but certainly not all of them. It is a pre-existing, permanent court, allowed to prosecute only crimes committed after the entry into force of its Statute (1 July 2002). It has been created by treaty, not by Security Council resolution, it binds only the states which have voluntarily acceded to its Statute, and may not resort to broad interpretation or to analogy.[155] However, the separation of powers is only loosely implemented and the Court has been accused of political bias from opposite sides. Thus far, the Court has only investigated African situations and few believe in its capacity also to prosecute the officials of stronger states. The Court seems weak and its prospects remain uncertain.

All of these criticisms are no doubt disturbing since they are invariably also advanced by the accused in order to avoid being tried, when in fact they clearly deserve to be tried for their heinous acts. Yet, the objections against international criminal justice should be carefully assessed to dispel criticisms and generate more acceptance and effectiveness. All efforts should be made, in particular, towards: (a) avoiding any suspicion, from any side, that international criminal justice is the justice of 'one side', whatever the side; (b) respecting the principle of strict legality and all other basic principles of criminal justice, such as non-retroactivity, *nulla poena sine lege*, and transparency to the fullest extent possible; (c) reducing selectivity and double standards, although this should not per se discourage (well-founded) prosecutions, since obviously one has to start somewhere; (d) strictly banning every sort of show trial; (e) prosecuting any attempt to use trials instrumentally to fight and delegitimize adversaries and enemies; (f) remaining detached from pressure from both states and non-state actors; (g) ensuring the highest reputation of the judges; (h) progressively getting popular support in order to try also Western leaders and non-state perpetrators. Unless all such conditions (at the very minimum) are met, international criminal justice is destined to remain suspect and to raise healthy scepticism. Only when ICTs also try officials of the stronger states, including Western states, and only when they do so for crimes and 'irresponsible behaviour' which may be committed by *all* states—such as extensive pollution, tax evasion, and crimes related to debt and state bankruptcy in developed countries to the detriment of the global economy and general well-being—will international criminal justice cease to appear to be merely another way to dominate the world and inspire a sense of genuine global justice. This may sound like science fiction, but much has already been done and the reality is in the making. The key point is clearly not to have this or that political leader behind bars, but to instil and disseminate a global sense of respect for, and commitment to, legality and justice towards the most vulnerable. It is in society that law has to work, and it will not work unless society believes in it and refrains from blindly supporting undeserving rulers. By changing society law also changes. International criminal justice can help to spread a sense of legality and accountability in the people and deter political leaders anywhere from seizing power exclusively for their personal gain. It is time collectively to believe in a world in which lust for power and arrogance meets resistance and does not pay at any level.

[154] ICTY, *Prosecutor v Tadić*, Decision on the Defence Motion for Interlocutory Appeal on Jurisdiction of 2 October 1995, Case No ICTY-94-1, paras 34–36; ICTR, *Prosecutor v Kaniabashi*, Decision on the Defence Motion on Jurisdiction of 18 June 1997, Case No ICTR-96-15-T, para 27.

[155] cf Art 22(2) ICC Statute.

Despite all its imperfections, international criminal justice is the preferable path to the punishment of rulers and other state officials for their gravest misdeeds, without affecting the state as such. The state is an institution, common to the whole population, expected to protect people. When a state degenerates into an instrument for the private gain and pleasures of the rulers and other state officials in power, then it is no longer a state but a gang of criminals.[156] The gradual shift from statehood into criminal conspiracy may be difficult to discern and expose, yet this remains essential. When the degeneration occurs, the problem is not the state, as an institution, but those *pro tempore* in power who *use* it for their private gain. It is thus the rulers and all other state officials that are the problem, not the state. When the state as an institution is taken hostage by a gang of unscrupulous men and women who use manipulation and force to silence the population, then the state is incapable of curing itself. People witness with impotence the brutality of the gang. Successful revolts are exceptional. Remedies can then come only from outside and they should strike rulers and state officials, leaving the state intact as much as possible in the circumstances. No political leader is indispensable. International criminal justice helps to do justice by offering the accused all the guarantees necessary to reduce the likelihood of vengeance, inaccurate convictions, double standards, and political and cultural bias, as well as partially overcoming the fragmentation, politicization, inconsistency, and uncertainty of national courts. It does so not only when rulers and state officials are accused, but also when the accused are private persons. Rulers and state officials are not only supposed to refrain from committing gross abuse of power, they are also supposed to protect people by both preventing and repressing gross abuse committed by private individuals and groups.

It is to be hoped that international justice with regard to individuals, while by no means displacing traditional inter-state courts and methods (such as political and diplomatic tools), will be extended to include other serious breaches of international law, not necessarily amounting to international crimes at the moment, such as extensive pollution and other global crimes committed by MNEs against present and future generations, through the setting up of courts like the ICC or the expansion of the scope of their substantive jurisdiction. The more international law breaches come under judicial scrutiny and global public attention, the more international law works as law. This is not to imply a 'rule of the judges', let alone their 'tyranny', because courts are thought to remain confined to adjudicating specific unlawful acts or omissions on a case-by-case basis, while the rest remains at the political discretion of the rulers. The selection of international judges is critical and adequate mechanisms have to be devised to ensure their integrity, competence, and legitimacy.[157] The point is not so much to create new rules as to struggle for reliable global institutions that can, as impartially as possible, administer law and justice. Nor is it to establish one single universal Court with compulsory jurisdiction, as Kelsen proposed. Both proposals of one single court and compulsory jurisdiction are too remote in prospect and arguably not even desirable. International courts exercising jurisdiction over individuals should be (at least in part) extended to IHRL and IHL, as well as to transnational organized crime, especially 'white collar' crime. Transnational crime, just like ordinary crime within each state, should cease to be a low-profile annex of international law, if human security is to be guaranteed. It should be seen as the other side of human rights protection, especially in

[156] cf Augustine, *De Civitate Dei*, IV, 4 ('Justice being taken away then, what are kingdoms but great robberies?').

[157] R Mackenzie, *Selecting International Judges: Principle, Process, and Politics* (Oxford: OUP, 2010).

terms of the duty to protect of states and their positive obligations towards their own populations and every human being within their jurisdiction.

Is all this a dream? Perhaps. Realists have plenty of arguments to challenge this dream or any other. They may be right. However, the world is what we make of it and we can create the conditions for the impossible to become possible by struggling for its reality. There is much to do and some results are far from unachievable, whatever realists may think. Realists follow realities as they are, but we need (possibly with their help, since they also need) to construct the realities of tomorrow, as no one really knows what lies ahead.

Conclusion

This final chapter examined remedies against the breach of international law in terms of sovereignty as responsibility. The concept of sovereignty as responsibility implies that it is primarily for states to protect the basic rights of their populations, and when they fail to do so, it is the international community that should intervene. Collective and personal measures are particularly suited to meeting responsible sovereignty's requirements. Collective measures of various kinds—including collective standing in international courts, universal jurisdiction in domestic courts, collective countermeasures, and humanitarian military intervention—are often based on the notion of obligations *erga omnes*, but it is difficult to draw definite legal conclusions from this concept. Unilateral humanitarian intervention is not permitted even within the responsibility to protect doctrine, unless it is mandated by the UN Security Council. Personal measures include targeted sanctions and criminal responsibility before international or hybrid courts. The case was finally made for the operation of international courts as the best tool available, despite their shortcomings, to combat the abuse of power by rulers and bring more justice in and to the system.

EPILOGUE

Epilogue

From infancy, fear and wonder inspire human life and behaviour. Fear of losing vital physical and emotional resources in a world where life needs action to sustain itself could hardly be overstated. This sense of dependence advises people that keeping control is the key to survival and well-being. Invulnerability, wealth, and the capacity to generate apparently irrefutable logical arguments are carefully pursued, while applied science and technology are most valued. The others are seen either as useful tools for one's own satisfaction or obstacles to one's own pre-defined plans. Fear presses human beings to bend inward and tactlessly defend themselves against whatever stands in their way, either human or other. The division between 'I' and 'others', 'we' and 'them', reigns. Because of fear, the 'other' is systematically obliterated or treated as contaminating or defiling. The 'humanization' of the opponent is experienced as equivalent to giving up the fight and losing. Class, prestige, fame, profits, career, and any other source of well-being are felt to be constantly threatened by potentially greedy competitors. Fear warns that force and hierarchy are the key ingredients of social life against conflict and violence. This fear renders people cynical, suspicious. Authoritarian and paternalistic methods are preferred as the only effective means to control 'real' (rather than utopianly conceived) human life. Truth is thought not to be within reach of most people. It should thus be managed by a few who offer security. A more equal world could be dreamed of, but in fact it will turn out to cause even worse conflict and violence.

At the same time human beings feel the uniqueness, the unspeakable beauty of their and others' lives. As soon as they outgrow infantile narcissism, they cultivate concern for others. Wonder and curiosity towards the outside world often overwhelm their lives. They learn that they can place themselves in the shoes of other persons and feel that dialogue with them is not only possible but emotionally rewarding. Empathy, compassion, attunement, and sympathy, even sacrifice, for the life of others are not only a priceless component of individual life but also an intrinsic part of social life. The others are not lived as threatening, but as journey fellows in a world ultimately mysterious to all. This shared sense of mystery and curiosity produces a need for solidarity with the whole creation, whether human or other. Contemplation and self-examination, poetry, and the humanities are most treasured. Without fear life appears overwhelmingly unspeakable just 'as it is'. Wonder presses people to open up, cost what it may, since life is worth living (no matter how short) by experiencing its innerness. No one and nothing is an enemy, and there is nothing to compete for, each occurrence in life being a chance to feel what 'actually' occurs in oneself and in any other sentient being. Wonder advises people that love is the key to life. Non-authoritarian, cooperative, and truth-loving attitudes are then esteemed. People are in principle trustful and sympathetic. The pursuit of truth, about self and others, whatever the truth and its implications, is valued more than anything else, just like the urge to detect one's own fallacies. As respect naturally extends to anyone, this sense of solidarity proves contagious and expands to humankind, nourishing a cosmopolitan, even sacred sense of humanity.

Both fear and wonder are engines of human life in all people, although differently combined in different people or in the same person at different moments, and both urge the creation and cultivation of law to provide some order and solve problems in society. Fear-inspired people call for law as a tool to apply force when necessary, to reinforce hierarchies, and to give each his due according to the 'right' position which reflects what each member is deemed to be worth in society. Wonder-inspired people call for law as a tool to reinforce equality and compassionate concern for others, vulnerability, dissenting voices, and the idea that law itself cannot govern in the name of the community every aspect of human life. In a sense, fear is typical of the infant and wonder arises in adults, although wonder is also a typical attitude of the child before the world. But the infant is incapable of reconciling itself to its vulnerability, while the adult has the potential to realize and act upon this ultimate truth. Most adults fail, however, to do so and societies require law to govern fearful people of any age. Many would like to adopt a wonder-inspired approach, if only this were possible, but just a few cultivate wonder rather than letting fear grow. Widespread competition suggests that most people are extremely fearful that their vital resources might be taken away from them by others. Law is destined to work in society and societies are made up of many different people, most (perhaps all) of whom have good reason to expect law to provide reassurance and cure their fears. Wonder-inspired people usually fear that fear-inspired people might prevail. They then expect law—together with other factors, such as family, education, and so on—to instil and spread in society compassionate concern for the 'other' and ultimately for the creation as such.

It is in this complex, fascinating dynamic that law, including international law, is expected to operate. This book has argued for law as a social construct, meaning, first, that law is *created and sustained by society* as a form of collective (and hence 'public' *latu sensu*) violence against individual violence, ie violence of all individuals *uti universi* against violence of all individuals *uti singuli*. It is one thing to contemplate the individual vis-à-vis the *whole* of other individuals, it is quite another to consider the individual vis-à-vis *any* other individual in the group. Law is basically violence, but it is *collective* violence in a group in relation to (and as a counter-strategy to contain) individual violence. It is imposed by the stronger on the weaker as a precarious, yet recognizable and relatively stable, form of 'balance of balances' between different individuals and groups engaged in safeguarding their lives. The reality of law cannot be separated from hierarchy, heteronomy, and objectivity. Hierarchy means that law is lived by any of its addressees as imposed 'from above' by an overarching force, the one of the group as a whole. Heteronomy means that law is lived by any of its addressees as dictated by others 'from outside', rather than being merely the result of individual autonomous determination. Objectivity means that law is lived by any of its addressees as existing and ascertainable independently of individual preferences. Law is not just the result of social pressure or social practices 'from below'. Legal pluralism fails to explain the collective (or 'public' *latu sensu*) origin and nature of law. There is a difference between a group and a gunman giving commands. Law is not what individuals simply 'do' together, but what in their view as a whole each of them *must* do. It is an 'ought' from the group towards the 'is' of any of its members.

Secondly, the quality of law, ie its possible differences from other norms, depends on what its addressees as a whole in *any* particular society *believe*. Law 'as such' rests on belief and belief is ultimately grounded in myth. There is always a shared mythic belief in law, no matter what kind of myth (either authoritarian or democratic, obscurantist or enlightened, backward- or forward-looking, scientific or emotional, and so forth). Law is so imbued with myth that when it is demythologized on certain grounds, it is instantly remythologized on other grounds. Law cannot work without myth. The most effective (although not necessarily the most just) law is the one which enjoys greater mythic adherence.

Thirdly, law is *not like a mountain*, ie an empirically observable fact open to scientific verification or falsification. Relationships between human beings are part of the process of the making and unmaking of law. Humans are not mere 'impartial spectators' attending at law as a 'fixed' entity inherently distinct from their beliefs and acts. Human beings make law real and effective (or less real and effective) by *commitment*, *promotion*, and *action* (or lack thereof): commitment to the law that 'there must be' *right now* in order for a community to survive; promotion of a better, more just law for the *future*; and action towards taking the *right side* when acting. Thus understood, law is the result of a daily struggle which is a struggle for a just law, ie for justice. It is the inner, personal sense of justice and injustice that works as the engine of the construction of social, objective justice, and possibly law. Law is not a scientific enterprise, nor are jurists mere scientists. Law operates in any particular group when the group recognizes it as 'its' law. This marks a key difference between law and political science. The latter pursues true propositions to be used for either descriptive or prescriptive purposes, while the former requires a commitment. Political scientists who treat law exclusively as a subject of scientific inquiry, with which they are familiar in their discipline, are far away from law. Law demands of people commitment, promotion, and action, besides analysis. One cannot simply 'find' that the law is unsatisfactory. If law is unsatisfactory, then something has to be done to improve it, unless one is against law. Law falls within the perspective of practical (rather than theoretical) reason, social attunement, and prudence. Arguments which are too subtle or complicated, or excessive levels of abstraction and speculation, while apparently helpful to clarify obscurities, may push away from law. Nor does overintellectualizing law necessarily help to make it more effective, even where the theory advanced aims to explain how law could be more effective. Theoretical engagement is a sophisticated attempt to control an ultimately uncontrollable world. Far from offering a 'grand theory', this book cautions against all theories or, perhaps, theorizes that theorizing (or too much theorizing) is not always appropriate when dealing with law, notably with international law. Social attunement may be much more appropriate.

Fourthly, law must *work in practice*, whatever its contents and abstract plausibility. In a group of the mad only a law congenial to the mad can work. If it works, then *this* is their law, although it may appear absurd to outsiders or to an isolated insider. Law works in practice when it meets a number of requirements which vary with societies (certainty, legitimacy, expediency, etc). What matters with law is its practical working, not its 'truth', and its working depends on the underlying mythic belief of individuals in law.

On this general theoretical framework, the book adopts a stance on international law which is different from other scholarly approaches. Against deconstructionists, the argument adopted might be called the 'in the meantime objection'. Deconstructionist reasoning is very skilled at finding defects without asking what people should do 'in the meantime', before a sufficiently satisfactory argument has finally been devised or before the demonstration has been given that no possible argument will ever be satisfactory. In the meantime people live and have to live somehow, with or without well-founded theories or arguments. This means, at the *cognitive* level, that 'in the meantime' people need to identify a set of legal rules, no matter how irrational or indeterminate they may turn out to be, the key point being that they work in people's perception. One can also note that, at the *pragmatic* level, 'in the meantime' people have to act, ie to decide what to do next, which side to take, and which justice (according to their inner sense of justice) they should pursue. Deconstructionists avoid considering the urge of people to live right now and their need to have some rules rather than none, while law is still (or will even always be) indeterminate or flawed. The fact is that there will always be some working law 'in the meantime' and some meaningful degree of commitment to law, however rough or incongruous, in any society. The point becomes self-evident if only the reference point is moved from the minds of deconstructionists to societies themselves. Then one can readily realize that what does not work in the mind of an enlightened individual, can actually work well enough in society, and vice versa.

Against the sociologists the book proceeds by objecting, first, that the opposition between solidaristic society and abusive state authority is anachronistic, unrealistic, and ultimately unfounded since society is often not as solidaristic as expected, nor is state authority necessarily abusive. On the other hand, abuse of power is more often than not much more rooted in society and among the people (who support abusive rulers and other state officials) than in authorities as such. Secondly, social 'spontaneism' reflects social reality only in part. True, people often want to be left alone and at times succeed in self-governing in some rudimentary way without any formal authority. However, people also want authority, protection from authority, hierarchy of authority over transgressors, and legal certainty. To say that law is a social construct is not to say that people are always right and states are always wrong, if only because states are generally the expression of their peoples. Nor does it mean that existing law is bad and all that we should do is to fight for a 'better' law. Existing law is the result of social construction in exactly the same way as any possible future law. It might also be better, however defective, than other rules that could be created for the future. As noted, law is not simply the result of 'social pressure' or 'social practice', as is often believed among legal sociologists, but also promotion, commitment, and action by individuals, as well as hierarchy and heteronomy (although not necessarily expressed by a formal superior authority).

Realists are also criticized in the book because, first, realism often fails to reflect the 'reality' that many see. Their 'rational actors' often act far less rationally than expected, by their own standards, and in any case their view of 'rationality' is often an economistic, means-to-an-end reasoning that is very far from being followed by most people and states. Secondly, realism ends up realizing self-fulfilling prophecies and inciting cynicism, even when truly reflecting reality. What realists record as real, objective facts, often work—either within or beyond their intentions—as a sort of encouragement to be cynical in a cynical world, and this contagious process results in the generation of more fragile societies. No law can work when this kind of contagion has spread to most people in a community. In this sense realists, by their scientific anchoring in the 'reality as it is', weaken the law and 'take note' of the weakness of the law *while* contributing to its weakening. For the sake of 'truth' law is being sacrificed. This is a very high cost for a community and realists should always ponder whether they want law and, if yes, how they can reconcile their scientific truths about 'realities' and the commitment demanded by law (in addition to, and even) beyond any truth.

Finally, against the third-worldist the book argues, first, that law (not only international law, as they seem to imply) is *always* the product of the stronger and it is hardly surprising that international law is no exception. Secondly, while the struggle for a new international law advocated by third-worldists may be shared, the fact still remains that *in the meantime* the law is what it is here and now according to the generally prevailing criteria for its identification. It is *this* law that must be regarded as existing international law, no matter what other better ideas third-worldist theorists may have in their minds and whatever the merits of the law promoted. After all, if it is true that existing international law is the law of the stronger, it is also true that the possible future (allegedly better) law advocated by the third-worldist would also reflect the will of the stronger were the third-worldists to prevail. The point is clearly whether one is prepared to struggle for their cause, a question profoundly different from asking what is the international law in force at the moment.

The key message of this book is that international law is the law of the states making up the global system as shaped by non-state actors, both domestically and transnationally. Today international law extensively regulates how states must behave within their jurisdiction at the inter-individual level. It is an inter-state law for inter-individual justice. This is quite different from either an inter-state law governing only the external relations between states or an inter-individual (or global) law directly governing all individuals living on earth. Nor does this entail that international law is inevitably undergoing an irreversible transition from the former to the latter. States are fundamental, and most people count on their protection and legitimacy every day. States per se are neither bad nor good. They are not fixed entities, but what people make of them. States are better if people shape them better. Better states make a better international law, and a better international law forces single states to behave better. The point of departure is people and what they believe in and are prepared to struggle for. How people construct social reality is at the heart of international law.

What should be believed in and struggled for? If law is a social construct and we are part of its reality and effectiveness rather than detached observers, then we need to know both what law has been constructed thus far (ie the law 'as it stands') and what law is to be constructed for the future (ie the 'just' law). This book suggests that the right direction for belief and struggle is towards the protection of the most vulnerable. As a matter of principle, children, women, the sick, minorities, future generations, weak states, animals, and other organic life forms (such as plants and the greater environment) are more vulnerable than adults, men, the healthy, majorities, the present generation, strong states, and human beings. Justice is to be improved in *this* world, namely, within a global states system in which states are essential and their sovereignty is to be exercised responsibly as prescribed by common rules created by the system itself. The tendency to present as already existing law, or as already 'superior' law, the values that are deemed to protect the most vulnerable is a promotional strategy that may be successful, but rests on anticipating (and hence also on betraying) reality. It constructs a suprastructural 'better law' in the hope that facts will follow. But it is at odds with legal certainty, another important value to most people, and with a realistic vision of why things are as they are and not otherwise. Law works when it is felt to be real among its addressees as a whole, not when it is thought of as real by a circle of specialists or proclaimed in solemn acts devoid of sufficient espousal. The risk is to build castles in the air. The struggle is for the *reality* of the law—presumably shared by most people—as it is, however uncomfortable, and then for *action* towards a better law in favour of the most vulnerable.

If the global system is irreversible and can be neither changed nor improved overnight, it is a fact that in the meantime some order and justice, rather than none, have to be ensured. International law is the law which is expected to help to preserve this order and justice in the hope that *we* show to ourselves the capacity to live in a better world, with a better law, in which the most vulnerable are protected from the predatory urges of too many of us.

Bibliography

Abbott, FM and Dukes, G, *Global Pharmaceutical Policy: Ensuring Medicines for Tomorrow's World* (Cheltenham and Northampton: Edward Elgar, 2011).

Abelard, P, *Dialogus inter philosophum, judaeum et christianum*, English trans 'Dialogue between a Philosopher, a Jew and a Christian', *Abélard's* Collationes: *Text and Translation* (Oxford: Clarendon Press, 2001).

Abi-Saab, G, 'Whither the International Community?' (1998) 9 EJIL 248–65.

Abu-Lughod, JL, *Before European Hegemony: The World System A.D. 1250–1350* (New York and Oxford: OUP, 1989).

Acharya, UD, 'War on Terror or Terror Wars: The Problem in Defining Terrorism' (2009) 37 Duke JILP 653–79.

Achenwall, G, *Jus Naturae in Usum Auditorium* [1752] (Göttingen: Sumtibus Victorini Bossigelii, 7th edn, 1774), at <http://catalog.hathitrust.org/Record/003867738>.

Acheson, D, 'Remarks by Honorable Dean Acheson' (1963) 57 ASIL Proc 13–14.

——, 'The Arrogance of International Lawyers' (1968) 2 International Lawyer 591–9.

Ackerman, B, 'The Rise of World Constitutionalism' (1997) 83 Virg LR 771–97.

Adamson, FB, 'International Terrorism, Non-State Actors, and Transnational Political Mobilization: A Perspective from International Relations' in Biersteсker, TJ, Spiro, PJ, Sriram, CL, and Raffo, V (eds), *International Law and International Relations: Bridging Theory and Practice* (London and New York: Routledge, 2007) 79–92.

Adler, E, 'The Emergence of Cooperation: National Epistemic Communities and the International Evolution of the Idea of Nuclear Arms Control' (1992) 46 *International Organization* 101–45.

—— and Haas, PM, 'Conclusion: Epistemic Communities, World Order, and the Creation of a Reflective Research Program' (1992) 46 *International Organization* 367–90.

Ago, R, *Scienza giuridica e diritto internazionale* (Milan: Giuffrè, 1950).

——, 'Positive Law and International Law' (1957) 51 AJIL 691–733.

——, 'Positivism', MP EPIL, 1st edn, 1984, vol. 7, 385–93.

Akande, D and Shah, S, 'Immunities of State Officials, International Crimes, and Foreign Domestic Courts' (2010) 21 EJIL 815–52.

Akehurst, M, 'Custom as a Source of International Law' (1974–75) 47 BYBIL 1–53.

Alderfer, CP, *Existence, Relatedness, and Growth; Human Needs in Organizational Settings* (New York: Free Press, 1972).

Alexander, L and Sherwin, E, *Demystifying Legal Reasoning* (Cambridge: CUP, 2008).

Alexandrowicz, CH, 'Kautilyan Principles and the Law of Nations' (1965–66) 41 BYBIL 301–20.

Alexy, R, 'A Defence of Radbruch's Formula' in Dyzenhaus, D (ed), *Recrafting the Rule of Law: The Limits of Legal Order* (Oxford: Hart Publishing, 1999) 15–39.

——, *Begriff und Geltung des Rechts* [1992] (Freiburg and Munich: Alber Karl, 2nd edn, 2002), English trans *The Argument from Injustice: A Reply to Legal Positivism* (Oxford: Clarendon Press, 2002).

——, *Theorie der Grundrechte* (Frankfurt: Suhrkamp, 3rd edn, 1996), English trans *A Theory of Constitutional Rights* (Oxford: OUP, 2002).

Alkoby, A, 'Theories of Compliance with International Law and the Challenge of Cultural Difference' (2008) 4 Journal of International Law & International Relations 151–98.

——, 'Three Images of "Global Community": Theorizing Law and Community in a Multicultural World' (2010) 12 ICLR 35–79.

Alleyne, MD, *Global Lies? Propaganda, the United Nations and World Order* (London: Palgrave Macmillan, 2003).

Allison, HE, *Kant's Transcendental Idealism: An Interpretation and Defense* (New Haven: Yale University Press, rev expanded edn, 2004).
Allott, P, 'Language, Method and the Nature of International Law' (1971) 45 BYBIL 79–135.
——, 'State Responsibility and the Unmaking of International Law' (1988) 29 Harv ILJ 16–24.
——, *Eunomia: New Order for a New World* [1990] (Oxford: OUP, 2001).
——, *The Health of Nations: Society and Law beyond the State* (Cambridge: CUP, 2004).
——, 'International Law and International Revolution: Reconceiving the World' in P Allott, *The Health of Nations: Society and Law beyond the State* (Cambridge: CUP, 2004).
Alston, P, 'Resisting the Merger and Acquisition of Human Rights by Trade Law: A Reply to Petersmann' (2002) 13 EJIL 815–44.
Altheide, DL, 'The Mass Media, Crime and Terrorism' (2006) 4 JICJ 982–97.
Alvarez, A, *La codification du droit international: ses tendances, ses bases* (Paris: Pédone, 1912).
Alvarez, JE, *International Organizations as Law-Makers* (Oxford and New York: OUP, 2005).
Ambos, K, 'The Crime of Aggression after Kampala' (2011) 53 Ger YBIL 463–509.
Ambrose, *In Epistolam Beati Pauli Ad Romanos*, at <http://www.documentacatholicaomnia.eu/02m/0339-0397_Ambrosius_In_Epistolam_Beati_Pauli_Ad_Romanos_MLT.pdf>.
Anaya, SJ, *Indigenous Peoples in International Law* (Oxford: OUP, 2nd edn, 2004).
Anderson, B, *Imagined Communities: Reflections on the Origin and Spread of Nationalism* (London and New York: Verso, rev edn, 1991).
Anderson, G, *Constitutional Rights after Globalization* (Oxford: Hart, 2005).
Andorno, R, 'The Paradoxical Notion of Human Dignity' (2001) 78 RIFD 151–68.
Anghie, A, *Imperialism, Sovereignty and the Making of International Law* (Cambridge: CUP, 2005).
—— and Chimni, BS, 'Third World Approaches to International Law and Individual Responsibility in Internal Conflict' (2003) 77 Chin JIL 77–103.
——, Chimni, BS, Mickelson, K, and Okafor, O (eds), *The Third World and International Legal Order: Law, Politics and Globalization* (Leiden: Nijhoff, 2003).
Anholt, S, *Competitive Identity: The New Brand Management for Nations, Cities and Regions* (Houndmills: Palgrave Macmillan, 2007).
Annan, KA, 'Two Concepts of Sovereignty', *The Economist*, 16 September 1999, at <http://www.economist.com/node/324795>.
Anzilotti, D, *Corso di diritto internazionale* [1928] (Padua: Cedam, 1964).
Aquinas, Thomas, *Summa Theologiae*, English trans *The 'Summa Theologica' of St Thomas Aquinas* (London: Burns, Oates & Washburne, 1916–37).
——, *Contra Gentiles*, English trans *On the Truth of the Catholic Faith: Summa Contra Gentiles* (Notre Dame: University of Notre Dame Press, 1955–57).
Arangio-Ruiz, G, 'On the Nature of the International Personality of the Holy See' (1996) 29 RBDI 354–69.
——, 'The "Federal Analogy" and UN Charter Interpretation: A Crucial Issue' (1997) 8 EJIL 1–28.
Araujo, RJ, 'Objective Meaning of Constituent Instruments and Responsibility of International Organisations' in M Ragazzi (ed), *International Responsibility Today: Essays in Memory of Oscar Schachter* (Leiden: Nijhoff, 2005) 343–54.
Arendt, H, 'The Image of the Hell' [1946], in *Essays in Understanding, 1930–1954: Formation, Exile, and Totalitarianism* (New York: Schocken Books, 1994) 197–205.
Aristotle, *De anima*, English trans at <http://classics.mit.edu/Aristotle/soul.html>.
——, *De somno et vigilia*, English trans at <http://classics.mit.edu/Aristotle/sleep.html>.
——, *Historia Animalium*, English trans at <http://classics.mit.edu/Aristotle/history_anim.html>.
——, *Metaphysics*, English trans at <http://classics.mit.edu/Aristotle/metaphysics.html>.

Aristotle, *Nicomachean Ethics*, English trans at <http://classics.mit.edu/Aristotle/nicomachaen.html>.

——, *On Sophistical Refutations*, English trans at <http://classics.mit.edu/Aristotle/sophist_refut.html>.

——, *Physics*, English trans at <http://classics.mit.edu/Aristotle/physics.html>.

——, *Politics*, English trans at <http://classics.mit.edu/Aristotle/politics.html>.

——, *Prior Analytics*, English trans at <http://classics.mit.edu/Aristotle/prior.html>.

——, *Rhetoric*, English trans at <http://classics.mit.edu/Aristotle/rhetoric.html>.

Atias, C, *Epistémologie juridique* (Paris: Dalloz-Sirey, 2002).

Augustine, *Commentary on the Sermon on the Mount*, English trans <http://www.newadvent.org/fathers/1601.htm>.

——, *Confessiones*, English trans at <http://www.newadvent.org/fathers/1101.htm>.

——, *Contra Faustum*, English trans at <http://www.newadvent.org/fathers/1406.htm>.

——, *De Civitate Dei*, English trans at <http://www.newadvent.org/fathers/1201.htm>.

——, *Epistola (ad Bonifacium)*, English trans at <http://www.newadvent.org/fathers/1102189.htm>.

——, *Epistolae*, English trans at <http://www.newadvent.org/fathers/1102.htm>.

——, On *Eighty-Three Diverse Questions* (Washington, DC: The Catholic University of America Press, 1982).

——, *On Order* (*De Ordine*), (St Augustine's Press, 2007).

——, *On the Trinity*, English trans at <http://www.newadvent.org/fathers/1301.htm>.

——, *Quaestionum in Heptateuchum Libri VII* (New York: Johnson Reprint, 1970).

——, *Sermons* (Brooklyn, NY: New City Press, 1990)

——, *On the Free Choice of the Will, On Grace and Free Choice, and Other Writings* (Cambridge and New York: CUP, 2010).

Aust, A, *Modern Treaty Law and Practice* (Cambridge: CUP, 2nd edn, 2007).

——, *Handbook of International Law* (Cambridge: CUP, 2nd edn, 2010).

Austin, J, *Lectures on Jurisprudence or the Philosophy of Positive Law* (London: John Murray, 5th edn, 1885).

——, *The Province of Jurisprudence Determined* [1832] (Cambridge: CUP, 1995).

Avant, DD, Finnemore, M, and Sell, SK (eds), *Who Governs the Globe?* (Cambridge: CUP, 2010).

Avicenna, *Liber de anima seu sextus de naturalibus* (Leiden: Simone van Riet, 1972).

Bacon, F, *Novum Organum* [1620], English trans *The New Organon* (Cambridge: CUP, 2000).

Bakan, J, *The Corporation: The Pathological Pursuit of Profit and Power* (London: Constable and Robinson Ltd, 2004).

Baker, CE, *Media, Markets, and Democracy* (Cambridge: CUP, 2002).

——, *Media Concentration and Democracy: Why Ownership Matters* (Cambridge: CUP, 2007).

Barber, BR, *Consumed: How Markets Corrupt Children, Infantilize Adults, and Swallow Citizens Whole* (New York and London: WW Norton & Co, 2007).

Baldwin, DA and Pape, RA, 'Evaluating Economic Sanctions' (1998) 23 *International Security* 189–98.

Barker, E, *Traditions of Civility: Eight Essays* (Cambridge: CUP, 1948).

Barkun, M, *Law without Sanctions: Order in Primitive Societies and the World Community* (New Haven and London: Yale University Press, 1968).

Barriga, S, 'A Historic Breakthrough on the Crime of Aggression' (2011) 105 AJIL 517–33.

Barry, B, 'Humanity and Justice in Global Perspective' (1982) 24 *Nomos* 219–52.

Bartelson, J, *A Genealogy of Sovereignty* (Cambridge: CUP, 1995).

——, *Visions of World Community* (Cambridge: CUP, 2009).

Bassiouni, MC, *Introduction to International Criminal Law* (New York: Transnational Publishers, 2003).

Bateson, G, *Steps to an Ecology of Mind* [1972] (Chicago and London: University of Chicago Press, 2000).
Batstone, D, *From Conquest to Struggle: Jesus of Nazareth in Latin America* (Albany: State University of New York Press, 1991).
Baumeister, RF and Leary, MR, 'The Need to Belong—Desire for Interpersonal Attachments as a Fundamental Human Motivation' (1995) 117 *Psychological Bulletin* 497–529.
Bautista, J, and Khek Gee Lim, F (eds), *Christianity and the State in Asia: Complicity and Conflict* (London and New York: Routledge, 2009).
Beard, JL, *The Political Economy of Desire: International Law, Development and the Nation State* (Oxon: Routledge-Cavendish, 2006).
Beccaria, C, *Dei delitti e delle pene* [1764] (Milan: Feltrinelli, 2008), English trans *On Crimes and Punishments* (Indianapolis: Hackett, 1986).
Bederman, DJ, *International Law in Antiquity* (Cambridge: CUP, 2001).
——, *The Spirit of International Law* (Athens: University of Georgia Press, 2002).
——, 'The Unique Legal Status of the Bank for International Settlements Comes into Focus' (2003) 16 LJIL 787–94.
——, *Globalization and International Law* (New York: Palgrave Macmillan, 2008).
——, *Custom as a Source of Law* (Cambridge: CUP, 2010).
Beiter, KD, *The Protection of the Right to Education by International Law: Including a Systematic Analysis of Article 13 of the International Covenant on Economic, Social and Cultural Rights* (Nijhoff: Leiden, 2006).
Beitz, R, *Political Theory and International Relations* (Princeton: Princeton University Press, 1999).
—— and Goodin, E, *Global Basic Rights* (Oxford: OUP, 2009).
Bellinger III JB and Padmanabhan, VM, 'Detention Operations in Contemporary Conflicts: Four Challenges for the Geneva Conventions and Other Existing Law' (2011) 105 AJIL 201–43.
Ben-Naftali, O (ed), *International Humanitarian Law and International Human Rights Law* (Oxford: OUP, 2011).
Benvenisti, E, 'The Conception of International Law as a Legal System' (2007) 50 Ger YBIL 393–405.
Berger, PL and Luckmann, T, *The Social Construction of Reality: A Treatise in the Sociology of Knowledge* (New York: Anchor Books, 1966).
Bergson, H, *Ecrits et paroles* [1895] (Paris: Presses universitaires de France, 1957).
Berman, HJ, 'World Law' (1995) 18 Ford ILJ 1617 22.
——,'World Law: An Ecumenical Jurisprudence of the Holy Spirit', Emory Public Law Research Paper No 05–4 (February 2005), at <http://papers.ssrn.com/sol3/papers.cfm?abstract_id=666143>.
Berman, PS, 'Global Legal Pluralism' (2007) 80 S Cal LR 1155–238.
Berner, BK, *The World According to Al Qaeda* (New Delhi: Peacock Books, 2006).
Bernhardt, R, 'Article 103' in Simma, B (ed), *The Charter of the United Nations: A Commentary* (New York: OUP, 1994) 1116–25.
——, 'Article 103' in Simma, B (ed), *The Charter of the United Nations: A Commentary* (New York: OUP, 2nd edn, 2002) vol 2, 1292–302.
Besson, S, 'The Authority of International Law: Lifting the State Veil' (2009) 31 Sydney Law Review 343–80.
—— and Tasioulas, J (eds), *The Philosophy of International Law* (Oxford: OUP, 2010).
Bettati, M, 'Un droit d'ingérence?' (1991) 95 RGDIP 639–70.
——, *Le droit d'ingérence. Mutation de l'ordre international* (Editions Odile Jacob: Paris, 1996).
—— and Kouchner, B (eds), *Le devoir d'ingérence* (Denoël: Paris, 1987).
Bettelheim, B, *Surviving and Other Essays* (New York: Alfred A Knopf, 1979) 48–83.
Bierstecker, TJ, and Weber, C, *State Sovereignty as Social Construct* (Cambridge: CUP, 1996).

Bierstecker, TJ, and Weber, C, *Grundprobleme und Methoden des Völkerrechts* (Freiburg: Albert Bleckmann, 1982).

——, Spiro, PJ, Sriram, CL, and Raffo, V (eds), *International Law and International Relations: Bridging Theory and Practice* (London and New York: Routledge, 2007).

Bilchitz, D, *Poverty and Fundamental Rights: The Justification and Enforcement of Socio-Economic Rights* (Oxford: OUP, 2007).

Billig, M, *Banal Nationalism* (London: Sage, 1995).

Bix, B, 'Robert Alexy, Radbruch's Formula, and the Nature of Legal Theory' (2006) 37 *Rechtstheorie* 139–49.

Blankenburg, W, 'Ansatze zu einer Psychopathologie des "common sense"' (1969) 12 *Confinia Psychiatrica* 144–63.

——, *Der Verlust der natürlichen Selbstverständlichkeit: ein Beitrag zur Psychopathologie symptom-armer Schizophrenien* (Stuttgart: Enke, 1971).

Bleckmann, A, 'Analogie im Völkerrecht' (1977–78) 17 AdV 161–80.

——, *Grandprobleme und Methoden des Völkerrects* (Freiburg: Alber, 1982) 241–3.

Blumenberg, H, *Arbeit am Mythos* (Frankfurt am Main: Suhrkamp Verlag, 1979), English trans *Work on Myth* (Cambridge, Mass and London: MIT Press, 1988).

Bob, C, 'Packing Heat: Pro-Gun Groups and the Governance of Small Arms' in Avant, DD, Finnemore, M, and Sell, SK (eds), *Who Governs the Globe?* (Cambridge: CUP, 2010) 183–201.

Bobbio, N, *L'età dei diritti* (Turin: Einaudi, 1990), English trans *The Age of Rights* (Cambridge: Polity Press, 1996).

Bodansky, D, 'Non Liquet', MP EPIL (May 2006 update).

Bodin, J, *Les six livres de la République* [1576] (Paris: Fayard, 1986), English trans *Six Books of The Commonwealth*, at <http://www.constitution.org/bodin/bodin_.htm>.

Boisson de Chazournes, L (ed), *International Law and the Quest for its Implementation* (Leiden: Brill, 2010).

Bolton, JR, 'Is There Really "Law" in International Affairs?' (2000) 10 TLCP 1–48.

Booth, K, *Theory of World Security* (Cambridge: CUP, 2007).

Borgen, CJ, 'Resolving Treaty Conflicts', 37 Geo Wash ILR (2005) 573–648.

Bos, M, *A Methodology of International Law* (Amsterdam: North-Holland, 1984).

Bossche, P van den, 'NGO Involvement in the WTO: A Comparative Perspective' (2008) 11 JIEL 717–49.

Bothe, M, 'The Role of National Law in the Implementation of International Humanitarian Law' in Swinarski, C (ed), *Studies and Essays on International Humanitarian Law and Red Cross Principles in Honour of Jean Pictet* (Dordrecht: Nijhoff, 1984) 301–12.

——'Compliance', MP EPIL (October 2010 update).

Boulding, KE, 'The Economics of the Coming Spaceship Earth' in Jarrett, H (ed), *Environmental Quality in a Growing Economy* (Baltimore: John Hopkins University Press, 1966) 3–14.

Bourquin, M, 'Règles générales du droit de la paix' (1931-I) 35 RdC 5–229.

Bovet, P and Parnas, J, 'Schizophrenic Delusions: A Phenomenological Approach', 19 *Schizophrenia Bulletin* (1993) 579–97.

Bowden, B, 'The Colonial Origins of International Law: European Expansion and the Classical Standard of Civilization' (2005) 7 JHIL 1–23.

——, *The Empire of Civilization: The Evolution of an Imperial Idea* (Chicago: University of Chicago Press, 2009).

Bowett, DW, *Self-Defense in International Law* (New York: Praeger, 1958).

Boyle, A and Chinkin, C, *The Making of International Law* (Oxford: OUP, 2007).

Bozeman, AB, *The Future of Law in a Multicultural World* (Princeton: Princeton University Press, 1971).

Breycha-Vauthier, AC and Potulicki, M, 'The Order of St John in International Law: A Forerunner of the Red Cross' (1954) 48 AJIL 554–63.

Bridge, FR and Bullen, R, *The Great Powers and the European States System 1815–1914* (London and New York: Longman, 2nd edn, 2005).
Brierly, JL, 'Le fondement du caractère obligatoire du droit international' (1928) 23 RdC 467–549.
——, 'Règles générales du droit de la paix' (1936-IV) 58 RdC 5–237.
——, 'The Covenant and the Charter' (1946) 23 BYBIL 83–94.
——, *The Basis of Obligation in International Law and Other Papers* (Oxford: Clarendon Press, 1958).
——, *The Law of Nations: An Introduction to the International Law of Peace* (Oxford: Clarendon Press, 6th edn, 1968).
Brölmann, CM, 'Law-Making Treaties: Form and Function in International Law' (2005) 74 Nord JIL 383–404.
Brown, C, *A Common Law of International Adjudication* (Oxford: OUP, 2007).
Brown Scott, J, 'The Legal Nature of International Law' (1907) 1 AJIL 831–66.
—— (ed), *The Hague Court Reports* (New York: OUP, 1916).
——, *The Spanish Origin of International Law: Francisco de Vitoria and his Law of Nations* (London: Humphrey Milford, 1934).
Brownlie, I, 'The Reality and Efficacy of International Law' (1981) 52 BYBIL 1–8.
——, 'International Law at the Fiftieth Anniversary of the United Nations: General Course on Public International Law' (1995) 255 RdC 13–227.
——, *Principles of Public International Law* (Oxford: OUP, 7th edn, 2008).
Brunnée, J and Toope, SJ, 'International Law and Constructivism: Elements of an International Theory of International Law' (2000) 39 Col JTL 19–74.
—— and Toope, SJ, 'Persuasion and Enforcement: Explaining Compliance with International Law' (2002) 13 Finn YBIL 273–95.
——, ——, *Legitimacy and Legality: An Interactional Account* (Cambridge: CUP, 2010).
Buchanan, A, *Justice, Legitimacy, and Self-Determination: Moral Foundations for International Law* (Oxford: OUP, 2004).
Bull, H, *The Anarchical Society: A Study of Order in World Politics* (Houndmills and New York: Palgrave, 3rd edn, 2002).
—— and Watson, A (eds), *The Expansion of International Society* (Oxford: OUP, 1983).
Bulterman, MK and Kuijer, M (eds), *Compliance with Judgments of International Courts* (The Hague: Nijhoff, 1996).
Burge, T, *Origins of Objectivity* (Oxford: Clarendon Press, 2010).
Burgess, Y, *The Myth of Progress* (Glasgow: The Cromwell Press, 1996).
Burri-Nenova, M, 'Trade versus Culture in the Digital Environment: An Old Conflict in Need of a New Definition' (2009) 12 JIEL 17–62.
Bury, JB, *The Idea of Progress: An Inquiry Into Its Origin and Growth* (London: Macmillan, 1920).
Buxton, R (ed), *From Myth to Reason? Studies in the Development of Greek Thought* (Oxford: OUP, 2001).
Buzan, B and Little, R, *International Systems in World History: Remaking the Study of International Relations* (Oxford: OUP, 2000).
Byers, M, 'Abuse of Rights: An Old Principle, a New Age' (2002) 47 McGill LJ 389–431.
—— and Nolte, G (eds), *United States Hegemony and the Foundations of International Law* (Cambridge: CUP, 2003).
Byrne, RMJ, Evans, JStBT, and Newstead, ST, *Human Reasoning: The Psychology of Deduction* (Hove: Lawrence Erlbaum Associates, 1993).
Calore, A, *Forme giuridiche del* 'bellum iustum' (Milan: Giuffrè, 2003).
Cameron, I, 'UN Targeted Sanctions, Legal Safeguards and the European Convention on Human Rights (2003) 72 Nord JIL 159–214.
Campbell, E, 'Thomas Hobbes and the Common Law' (1958) 1 Tas ULR 20–45.

Cançado Trindade, AA, *International Law for Humankind: Towards a New* Jus Gentium (Leiden and Boston: Nijhoff, 2010).
Cane, P (ed), *The Hart-Fuller Debate in the Twenty-first Century* (Oxford: Hart, 2010).
Canner, SJ, 'The Multilateral Agreement on Investment' (1998) 31 Corn ILJ 657–81.
Cannizzaro, E (ed), *The Law of Treaties beyond the Vienna Convention* (Oxford: OUP, 2011).
Carr, EH, *Twenty Years' Crisis (1919–1939): An Introduction to the Study of International Relations* [1939] (Houndmills and New York: Palgrave, 2001).
Carreau, S, and Marrella, F, *Droit international* (Paris: Pédone, 11th edn, 2012).
Carty, A, *The Decay of International Law? A Reappraisal of the Limits of Legal Imagination in International Affairs* (Manchester: Manchester University Press, 1986).
——, 'Distance and Contemporaneity in Exploring State Practice: The British Archives in Relation to the 1957 Oman and Muscat Incident' in Craven, M, Fitzmaurice, M, and Vogiatzi, M (eds), *Time, History and International Law* (Leiden: Nijhoff, 2007) 231–46.
——, 'Sociological Theories of International Law', MP EPIL (March 2008 update).
Cass, DZ, *The Constitutionalization of the World Trade Organization* (Oxford, OUP, 2005).
Cassese, A, *Self-Determination of Peoples: A Legal Reappraisal* (Cambridge: CUP, 1995).
——, 'The Martens Clause: Half a Loaf or Simply Pie in the Sky?' (2000) 11 EJIL 187–216.
——, 'When May Senior State Officials Be Tried for International Crimes? Some Comments on the Congo v Belgium Case' (2002) 13 EJIL 853–75.
——, *International Criminal Law* (Oxford: OUP, 2003).
——, *International Law* (Oxford: OUP, 2nd edn, 2005).
——, 'The Multifaceted Criminal Notion of Terrorism in International Law' (2006) 4 JICL 933–58.
Cassirer, E, *An Essay on Man: An Introduction to a Philosophy of Human Culture* [1944] (New Haven and London: Yale University Press, 1972).
——, *The Myth of the State* [1946] (New Haven and London: Yale University Press, 1977).
——, *Philosophie der symbolischen Formen. Zweiter Teil: Das mythische Denken* [1925] (Hamburg: Meiner, 2010), English trans *Philosophy of Symbolic Forms: Volume 2: Mythical Thought* (New Haven and London: Yale University Press, 1955).
Castberg, F, 'La méthodologie du droit international public' (1933-I) 43 RdC 313–83.
Catry, J, 'La liberté du commerce international d'après Vitoria, Suarez et les Scholastiques' (1932) 39 RGDIP 193–218.
Cavaglieri, A, 'Règles générales du droit de la paix' (1929) 26 RdC 315–583.
Chambers, R, *Rural Development: Putting the Last First* (London: Longman, 1983).
Chang H-J, *Bad Samaritans: The Guilty Secrets of Rich Nations & and the Threat to Global Prosperity* (London: Business Books, 2007).
Chapman, TL, *Securing Approval: Domestic Politics and Multilateral Authorization for War* (Chicago: University of Chicago Press, 2011).
Charney, JI, 'The Persistent Objector Rule and the Development of Customary International Law' (1985) 56 BYBIL 1–24.
——, 'The Power of the Executive Branch of the United States Government to Violate Customary International Law' (1986) 80 AJIL 913–22.
Charnovitz, S, 'Two Centuries of Participation: NGOs and International Governance' (1997) 18 Mich JIL 183–286.
——, 'Nongovernmental Organizations and International Law' (2006) 100 AJIL 348–72.
Chavez-Tafur, G, 'Using International Law to Bypass Domestic Legal Hurdles: On the Applicability of the Statute of Limitations in the Menéndez et al. Case' (2008) 6 JICL 1061–75.
Chayes, A and Handler Chayes, A, *The New Sovereignty: Compliance with International Regulatory Agreements* (Cambridge, Mass: Harvard University Press, 1995).
Checkel, JT, 'The Constructivist Turn in International Relations Theory' (1998) 50 *World Politics* 324–48.

Cheng, B, 'United Nations Resolutions on Outer Space: "Instant" International Customary Law?' (1965) 23 Indian JIL 23–48.

Chibundu, M, 'The Other in International Law: Community and International Legal Order', SSRN (University of Maryland Working Paper Series No 2004–03), at <http://papers.ssrn.com/sol3/papers.cfm?abstract_id=504782>.

Chimni, BS, 'International Institutions Today: An Imperial Global State in the Making' (2004) 15 EJIL 1–37.

——, 'Third World Approaches to International Law: A Manifesto' (2006) 8 ICLR 3–27.

——, 'The Past, Present and Future of International Law: A Critical Third World Approach' (2007) 8 Mel JIL 499–515.

——, 'Is there an Asian Approach to International Law?' (Tokyo: ASIL Conference, 2009), at <http://asiansil.web.fc2.com/PlenarySessionI/chmni.pdf>.

——, 'Prolegomena to a Class Approach to International Law' (2010) 21 EJIL 57–82.

Chinkin, C, '*Jus Cogens*, Article 103 of the UN Charter and Other Hierarchical Techniques of Conflict Solution' (2006) 17 Finn YBIL 63–82.

Choi, S, 'Judicial Enforcement of Arbitration Awards under the ICSID and New York Conventions' (1999) 28 NYU JILP 175–215.

Cicero, *De Partitione Oratoria*, English trans *De Oratore, Together with De Fato, Paradoxa Stoicorum, De Partitione Oratoria* (Cambridge, Mass and London: Harvard University Press and Heinemann, 1967–1968.

——, *Tusculanae Disputationes*, English trans *Tusculan Disputations* (London: Heinemann, 1950).

——, *De legibus*, English trans *The Republic and The Laws* (Oxford: OUP, 1998).

——, *De Finibus, Bonorum et Malorum*. English trans *On Moral Ends* (Cambridge: CUP, 2001).

——, *De oratore*, English trans *On the Ideal Orator* (Oxford: OUP, 2001).

——, *De Natura Deorum*. English trans *De Natura Deorum* (Cambridge: CUP, 2003).

——, *De officiis*, English trans <http://www.perseus.tufts.edu/hopper/text?doc=Perseus:text:2007.01.0048>.

Cimiotta, E, *I tribunali penali misti* (Padua: Cedam, 2009).

——, 'Immunità personali dei Capi di Stato dalla giurisdizione della Corte penale internazionale e responsabilità statale per gravi illeciti internazionali' (2011) 94 RDI 1083–175.

Claessen, HJM and Skalnik, P (eds), *The Early State* (The Hague: Mouton, 1978).

—— and Oosten, JG (eds), *Ideology and the Formation of Early States* (Leiden: Brill, 1996).

Clapham, C, *Africa and the International System: The Politics of State Survival* (Cambridge: CUP, 1996).

Clark, I, *International Legitimacy and World Society* (Oxford: OUP, 2007).

Clawson, P, 'Sanctions as Punishment, Enforcement, and Prelude to Further Action' (1993) 7 EIA 17–37.

Cochetti, S, *Mythos und "Dialektik der Aufklärung"* (Königstein: Taunus, 1985).

Cohen, PS, 'Theories of Myth' (1969) 4 *Man* 337–53.

Collins, R and White, ND (eds), *International Organizations and the Idea of Autonomy: Institutional Independence in the International Legal Order* (Abingdon and New York: Routledge, 2011).

Commission on Global Governance, *Our Global Neighbourhood* (Oxford: OUP, 1995) at <http://www.sovereignty.net/plgov/ogn-front.html>.

Compte, A, *Système de politique positive ou traité de sociologie, instituant la religion de l'humanité* (Paris: Librairie scientifique-industrielle de L Mathias, 1852) IV.

Condorelli, L, 'Le statut des forces de l'ONU et le droit international humanitaire' (1995) 78 RDI 881–906.

—— and Boisson de Chazournes, L, 'Common Article 1 of the Geneva Conventions Revisited: Protecting Collective Interest' (2000) 82 IRRC 67–87.

——, La Rosa, A-M, and Scherrer, S (eds), *The United Nations and International Humanitarian Law* (Paris: Pédone, 1996).
Conforti, B, 'Cours général de droit international public' (1988-V) 212 RdC 9–210.
——, 'Sui privilegi e le immunità dell'Ordine di Malta' (1990) I Il Foro Italiano 2597–604.
——, *International Law and the Role of Domestic Legal Systems* (Dordrecht: Nijhoff, 1993).
——, 'The Doctrine of "Just War" and Contemporary International Law' (2002) 12 It YBIL 3–11.
——, *Diritto internazionale* (Naples: Editoriale Scientifica, 8th edn, 2010).
—— and Focarelli, C, *The Law and Practice of the United Nations* (Leiden and Boston: Nijhoff, 4th rev edn, 2010).
—— and Labella, A, 'Invalidity and Termination of Treaties: The Role of National Courts' (1990) 1 EJIL 44–66.
Conrad, CR. *Processes and Production Methods (PPMS), in WTO Law: Interfacing Trade and Social Goals* (Cambridge: CUP, 2011).
Cooper, AA, Earl of Shaftesbury, *Characteristics of Men, Manners, Opinions, Times* [1711] (Cambridge: CUP, 1999) 29, note A.
Corbett, PE, 'The Consent of States and the Sources of the Law of Nations' (1925) 6 BYBIL 20–30.
——, *Law and Society in the Relations of States* (New York: Harcourt Brace & Co, 1951).
——, 'Social Basis of a Law of Nations' (1954) 85 RdC 471–543.
Corten, O, *L'utilisation du 'raisonnable' par le juge international* (Brussels: Bruylant, 1997).
——, 'Reasonableness in International Law', MP EPIL (May 2006 update).
——, *Méthodologie du droit international public* (Brussels: Editions de l'Université de Bruxelles, 2009).
Corthay, E, 'Le concept de terrorisme ou la définition d'un monstre polycéphale', ONU (Issue 20–21, 2006) 111–44.
Cot, J-P, Pellet, A, and Forteau, M (eds), *La Charte des Nations Unies: Commentaire article par article* (Paris: Economica, 3rd edn, 2005) 2 vols.
Cotterrell, R, *The Sociology of Law: An Introduction* (Oxford: OUP, 1992).
——, 'Sociology of Law' in ELS (Thousand Oaks: SAGE, 2007).
——, 'The Struggle for Law: Some Dilemmas of Cultural Legality' (2008) 4 IJLC 373–84.
Cottier, T, Pauwelyn, J, and Bürgi, E (eds), *Human Rights and International Trade* (Oxford: OUP, 2005).
Cox, N, 'The Acquisition of Sovereignty by Quasi-States: The Case of the Order of Malta' (2002) 6 *Mountbatten Journal of Legal Studies* 26–47.
Craig, C, 'The Resurgent Idea of World Government' (2008) 22 EIA 133–42.
Craig, TW, 'Public Management as Interagency Cooperation: Testing Epistemic Community Theory at the Domestic Level' (1997) 2 JPART 221–46.
Crates, fr 18 in Mette HJ, *Sphairopoiia. Untersuchungen zur Kosmologie des Krates von Pergamon. Mit einem Anhang: Texte* (Munich: Beck, 1936).
Craven, M, Fitzmaurice, M, and Vogiatzi, M (eds), *Time, History and International Law* (Leiden: Nijhoff, 2007).
Crawford, RJ, *The Rights of Peoples* (Oxford: Clarendon Press, 1988).
——, *International Law as an Open System: Selected Essays* (London: Cameron May, 2002).
——, *The International Law Commission's Articles on State Responsibility: Introduction, Text and Commentaries* (Cambridge: CUP, 2002).
—— (ed), *The Creation of States in International Law* (Oxford: Clarendon Press, 2nd edn, 2006).
—— and Olleson, S, 'The Continuing Debate on a UN Convention on State Responsibility' (2005) 54 ICLQ 959–71.
—— and Watkins, J, 'International Responsibility' in Besson, S and Tasioulas, J (eds), *The Philosophy of International Law* (Oxford: OUP, 2010) 283–98.

——, Pellet, A, and Olleson, S, *The Law of International Responsibility* (Oxford: OUP, 2010).
Creveld, M van, *The Rise and Decline of the State* (Cambridge: CUP, 1999).
Cronin, B, *Community Under Anarchy: Transnational Identity and the Evolution of Cooperation* (New York: Columbia University Press, 1999).
Crossette, B, 'Media' in Weiss, TG and Daws, S (eds), *The Oxford Handbook on the United Nations* (Oxford: OUP, 2007) 275–84.
Culver, K and Giudice, M, *Legality's Borders: An Essay in General Jurisprudence* (Oxford and New York: OUP, 2010).
Cutler, AC, Haufler, V, and Porter, T (eds), *Private Authority and International Affairs* (Albany: State University of New York Press, 1999).
D'Amato, A, 'Is International Law Really "Law"?' (1985) 79 NwU LR 1293–314.
D'Aspremont, J, 'Hart et le positivisme postmoderne en droit international' (2009) 113 RGDIP 635–54.
——, *Formalism and the Sources of International Law: A Theory of the Ascertainment of Legal Rules* (Oxford: OUP, 2011).
——, 'In Defense of the Hazardous Tool of Legal Blogging' (2011), at <http://www.ejiltalk.org/in-defense-of-the-hazardous-tool-of-legal-blogging>.
—— (ed), *Participants in the International Legal System: Multiple Perspectives on Non-state Actors in International Law* (London: Routledge, 2011).
Damasio, A, *Descartes' Error: Emotion, Reason and the Human Brain* (London: Vintage Books, rev edn, 2006).
——, *Self Comes to Mind: Constructing the Conscious Brain* (New York: Pantheon Books, 2010).
David, E, *Principes de droit des conflits armées* (Brussels: Bruylant, 3rd edn, 2002).
Dawson, C (ed), *The Mongol Missions: Narratives and Letters of the Franciscan Missionaries in Mongolia and China in the Thirteenth and Fourteenth Centuries* (New York: Sheed and Ward, 1955).
De Búrca, G and Weiler, JHH (eds), *The Worlds of European Constitutionalism* (Cambridge: CUP, 2011).
D'Entrèves, AP, 'Legality and Legitimacy' (1963) 16 RM 687.
De Schutter, O (ed), *Transnational Corporations and Human Rights* (Oxford: OUP, 2006).
De Secondat, C-L, Baron de la Brède et de Montesquieu, De l'esprit des lois [1748] (Paris: Gallimard, 1995–1999) 2 vols, English trans The Spirit of the Laws (New York: MacMillan 1949).
De Sena, P, *Diritto internazionale e immunità funzionale degli organi statali* (Milan: Giuffrè, 1996).
De Visscher, C, *Théories et réalités en droit international public* (Paris: Pédone, 4th edn, 1970), English version *Theory and Reality in International Law* (Princeton: Princeton University Press, 1968).
De Waal, F, *The Age of Empathy: Nature's Lessons for a Kinder Society* (New York: Harmony Books, 2009).
Del Vecchio, A, 'In maiore stat minus: A Note on the EEZ and the Zones of Ecological Protection in the Mediterranean Sea' (2008) 39 ODIL 287–97.
Deleuze, G, *Différence et répétition* (Paris: Presses Universitaires de France, 1968), English trans *Difference and Repetition* (New York: Columbia University, 1994).
Deng, FM, Kimaro, S, Lyons, T, Rothchild, D, and Zartman, IW, *Sovereignty as Responsibility. Conflict Management in Africa* (Washington, DC: The Brookings Institution, 1996).
Derian, J Der, *Virtuous War: Mapping the Military–Industrial–Media–Entertainment Network* (New York and London: Routledge, 2nd edn, 2009).
Descartes, R, *Principia Philosophiae* [1644], preface to French edn, English trans *The Philosophical Writings of Descartes* (Cambridge: CUP, 1985) vol 1.

Descartes, R, *Discours de la méthode: Pour bien conduire sa raison, et chercher la vérité dans les sciences* [1637] (Paris: Flammarion, 2000), English trans *Discourse on the Method of Rightly Conducting the Reason, and Seeking Truth in the Sciences* (Oxford: OUP, 2008).

Desta, MG, 'Commodities, International Regulation of Production and Trade', MPEPIL (March 2010 update).

Deudney, DH, *Bounding Power: Republican Security Theory from the Polis to the Global Village* (Princeton: Princeton University Press, 2006).

Dewey, J, 'Logical Method and Law' (1924–25) 10 Corn LQ 17–27.

——, *Logic: The Theory of Inquiry* (New York: Holt, Rinehart and Winston, 1938).

Diani, M, 'The Concept of Social Movement' (1992) 40 *Sociological Review* 1–25.

Díaz-Barrado, CM, 'The Definition of Terrorism and International Law' in Fernández Sánchez, PA (ed), *International Legal Dimension of Terrorism* (Leiden: Nijhoff, 2009) 27–41.

Dickinson, ED, 'The Analogy between Natural Persons and International Persons in the Law of Nations' (1917) 26 Yale LJ 564–91.

Diebold, NF, 'The Morals and Order Exceptions in WTO Law: Balancing the Toothless Tiger and the Undermining Mole' (2008) 11 JIEL 43–74.

Diels, H and Kranz, W, *Die Fragmente der Vorsokratiker* (Zurich: Weidmann, 1985).

Dinnie, K (ed), *Nation Branding: Concepts, Issues, Practice* (Oxford: Butterworth-Heinemann, 2008).

——, 'The Impact on Country Image of the North Africa and Middle East Uprisings' (2011) 6 PBPD 79–80.

Dinstein, Y, 'International Law as a Primitive Legal System', 19 NYU JILP (1986–87) 1–32.

——, 'Terrorism as an International Crime'(1989) 19 Is YBHR 55–73.

——, *The Conduct of Hostilities under the Law of International Armed Conflict* (Cambridge: CUP, 2nd edn, 2010).

——, *War, Aggression and Self-Defence* (Cambridge: CUP, 5th edn, 2011).

Diogenes Laertius, *Lives of Eminent Philosophers*, VII, 1, *Zeno*, 125–6.

D'Olivier Farran, C, 'The Sovereign Order of Malta in International Law' (1954) 3 ICLQ 217.

Domarus, E von, 'The Specific Laws of Logic in Schizophrenia' in Kasanin, JS (ed), *Language and Thought in Schizophrenia* (New York: Norton, 1944).

Domingo, R, *The New Global Law* (Cambridge: CUP, 2010).

——, 'Gaius, Vattel, and the New Global Law Paradigm' (2011) 22 EJIL 627–47.

Dominicé, C, 'La personnalité juridique internationale du CICR' in Swinarski, C (ed), *Studies and Essays on International Humanitarian Law and Red Cross Principles in Honour of Jean Pictet* (Dordrecht: Nijhoff, 1984) 663–73.

——, 'L'article 103 de la Charte des Nations Unies et le droit international humanitaire' in Condorelli, L, La Rosa, A-M, and Scherrer, S (eds), *The United Nations and International Humanitarian Law* (Paris: Pédone, 1996) 175–92.

——, 'Methodology of International Law', MP EPIL, 1st edn, 1984, vol 7, 334–9.

Donovan, DF and Roberts, A, 'The Emerging Recognition of Universal Civil Jurisdiction' (2006) 100 AJIL 142–63.

Dörr, O, 'Privatisierung des Völkerrechts' (2005) 60 JZ 905–16.

Douzinas, C and Gearey, A, *Critical Jurisprudence: The Political Philosophy of Justice* (Oxford: Hart, 2005).

Dowler, E and Finer, CJ (eds), *Welfare of Food: Rights and Responsibilities in a Changing World* (Oxford: Blackwell, 2003).

Downey, TW, book review (1988) 69 IJP 139–40.

Dreher, A, Gaston, N, and Martens, P, *Measuring Globalisation: Gauging its Consequences* (New York: Springer, 2008).

Dreveskracht, R, 'Just War in International Law: An Argument for a Deontological Approach to Humanitarian Law' (2010) 16 Buffalo Human Rights Law Review 237–88.

Drezner, DW, *All Politics is Global: Explaining International Regulatory Regimes* (Princeton and Oxford: Princeton University Press, 2007).
Du Pasquier, C, *Introduction à la théorie générale et à la philosophie du droit* (Neuchâtel and Paris: Delachaux et Niestlé, 1948).
Dubouchet, D, *Droit et épistémologie: L'Organon du droit* (Paris: L'Harmattan; 2008).
Dugard, JR, *Recognition and the United Nations* (Cambridge: CUP, 1987).
Duguit, L, *L'Etat, le droit objectif et la loi positive* (Paris: Fontemoing, 1901).
——, *Traité de droit constitutionnel* (Paris: Fontemoing, 2nd edn, 1921) vol 1.
Dunant, H, *A Memory of Solferino* (Geneva: ICRC, 1986).
Dundes, A (ed), *Sacred Narrative: Readings in the Theory of Myth* (Berkeley, Los Angeles, and London: University of California Press, 1984).
Dunn, M, Krishna-Hensel, SF, and Mauer, V (eds), *The Resurgence of the State: Trends and Processes in Cyberspace Governance* (Haldershot: Ashgate, 2007).
Dunoff, JL, 'International Legal Scholarship at the Millennium' (2000) 1 Chic JIL 85–92.
—— 'The Politics of International Constitutions: The Curious Case of the World Trade Organization' in Dunoff, JL and Trachtman, JP (eds), *Ruling the World? Constitutionalism, International Law, and Global Governance* (Cambridge: CUP, 2009) 178–205.
—— and Trachtman, JP, 'Economic Analysis of International Law' (1999) 24 Yale JIL 1–59.
—— and —— (eds), *Ruling the World? Constitutionalism, International Law, and Global Governance* (Cambridge: CUP, 2009).
Duns Scotus, *Opus Oxoniense*, in *Opera omnia* (Lyon: Wadding, 1639) 12 vols (repr Paris: Vives, 1891–95).
Dupuy, P-M, 'The Constitutional Dimension of the Charter of the United Nations Revisited' (1997) 1 MP YBUNL 1–33.
——, 'Les "considérations élémentaires d'humanité" dans la jurisprudence de la Cour internationale de justice' in Dupuy, R-J (ed), *Mélanges en l'honneur de Nicolas Valticos. Droit et justice* (Paris: Pédone, 1999) 117–30.
——, 'L'unité de l'ordre juridique international: Cours général de droit international public' (2002) 297 RdC 9–489.
—— and Vierucci, L (eds), *NGOs in International Law: Efficiency and Flexibility* (Northampton: Edward Elgar, 2008).
——, Francioni, F, and Petersmann, E-U (eds), *Human Rights in International Investment Law and Arbitration* (Oxford: OUP, 2009).
Dupuy, R-J (ed), *Mélanges en l'honneur de Nicolas Valticos. Droit et justice* (Paris: Pédone, 1999).
Durkheim, E, *Les formes élémentaires de la vie religieuse: le système totémique en Australie* [1912] (Paris: Les Presses universitaires de France, 1968), English trans *The Elementary Forms of Religious Life* (Mineola, NY: Dover Publications, 2008).
Duxbury, A, *The Participation of States in International Organisations: The Role of Human Rights and Democracy* (Cambridge: CUP, 2011).
Duxbury, N, *Random Justice: On Lotteries and Legal Decision-Making* (Oxford: OUP, 2002).
Dwertmann, E, *The Reparation System of the International Criminal Court: Its Implementation, Possibilities and Limitations*, (Leiden: Nijhoff, 2010).
Dworkin, R, *Taking Rights Seriously* (London: Duckworth, 1978).
——, *Law's Empire* (Cambridge, Mass: Harvard University Press, 1986).
Dyzenhaus, D, 'Why Positivism is Authoritarian' (1992) 37 AJJ 83–112.
——, *Legality and Legitimacy: Carl Schmitt, Hans Kelsen, and Hermann Heller in Weimar* (Oxford: OUP, 1997).
—— (ed), *Recrafting the Rule of Law: The Limits of Legal Order* (Oxford: Hart, 1999).
Ebbesson, J and Okowa, PN (eds), *Environmental Law and Justice in Context* (Cambridge: CUP, 2009).
Eckhard, F (ed), *Speaking for the Secretary-General—A History of the UN Spokesman's Office* (New York: United Nations, 2005).

Ehrlich, E, *Grundlegung der Soziologie des Rechts* (Munich and Leipzig: Duncker & Humblot, 1913), English trans *Fundamental Principles of Sociology of Law* (New Brunswick, NJ: Transaction Reprint, 2002).
——, 'The Sociology of Law' (1922) 36 Harv LR 130–45.
Einstein, A and Freud, S, *Warum Krieg?* (Paris: Internationales Institut für Geistige Zusammenarbeit, 1933), English trans 'Why War?' [1933], in Strachey, J (ed), *The Standard Edition of the Complete Psychological Works of Sigmund Freud* (London: Vintage, 1953) vol 22, 199–215.
Elbe, J von, 'The Evolution of the Concept of the Just War in International Law' (1939) 33 AJIL 665–88.
Eliade, M, *The Sacred and the Profane: The Nature of Religion* (New York: Harper and Row, 1961).
——, *Myth and Reality* (New York: Harper and Row, 1963).
——, *The Quest: History and Meaning in Religion* (Chicago: University of Chicago Press, 1969).
Elkind, B, 'Footnote to the Nuclear Test Cases: Abuse of Right—A Blind Alley for Environmentalists' (1976) 9 Van JTL 57–98.
Elshtain, JB, 'The Just War Tradition and Natural Law' (2005) 28 Ford ILJ 742–55.
Emmerich-Fritsche, A, *Vom Völkerrecht zum Weltrecht* (Berlin: Duncker & Humblot, 2007).
Emon, AM, 'Natural Law and Natural Rights in Islamic Law' (2004–05) 20 JLR 351–95.
——, *Islamic Natural Law Theories* (Oxford: OUP, 2010).
Epicurus, *Letter to Menoeceus*, English trans at <http://classics.mit.edu/Epicurus/menoec.html>.
Esser, J, *Vorverständnis und Methodenwahl in der Rechtsfindung: Rationalitäts-Garantien der Richterlichen Entscheidungspraxis* (Frankfurt am Main: Athenäum-Fischer-Taschenbuch-Verlag, 2nd edn, 1970).
Evans, M (ed), *Just War Theory: A Reappraisal* (Edinburgh: Edinburgh University Press, 2005).
Etzioni, A, *From Empire to Community: A New Approach to International Relations* (New York and Houndmills: Palgrave Macmillan, 2004).
Falk, R, (ed), *The Vietnam War and International Law* (Princeton: Princeton University Press, 1968–76) 4 vols.
——, *Law in an Emerging Global Village: A Post-Westphalian Perspective* (Ardsley, NY: Transnational Publishers, 1998).
——, book review (2010) 104 AJIL 543–8.
Farrall, JM and Rubenstein, K (eds), *Sanctions, Accountability and Governance in a Globalised World* (Cambridge: CUP, 2009).
Fassbender, B, 'The United Nations Charter as Constitution of the International Community' (1998) 36 Col JTL 529–619.
——, *The United Nations Charter and the Constitution of the International Community* (Leiden and Boston: Nijhoff, 2009).
Fastenrath, U, Geiger, R, Khan, D-E, Paulus, A, Schorlemer, S von, and Vedder, C (eds), *From Bilateralism to Community Interest: Essays in Honour of Judge Bruno Simma* (Oxford: OUP, 2011).
Feinstein, L and Slaughter, A-M, 'A Duty to Prevent' (2004) 83 *Foreign Affairs* 136–50.
Feldman, N, *The Fall and Rise of the Islamic State* (Princeton and Oxford: Princeton University Press, 2008).
Ferrari Bravo, L, 'Méthodes de recherche de la coutume internationale dans la pratique des états' (1985-III) 192 RdC 233–330.
Feyerabend, P, *Against Method* (London: New Left Books, 1975) ch 18, at <http://www.marxists.org/reference/subject/philosophy/works/gefeyerabe.htm>.
——, *Against Method* (London: Verso, 4th edn, 2010).
Findlay, R and O'Rourke, KH, *Power and Plenty: Trade, War, and the World Economy in the Second Millennium* (Princeton and Oxford: Princeton University Press, 2007).

Finke, J, *Die Parallelität internationaler Streitbeilegungsmechanismen* (Berlin: Duncker & Humblot, 2004).
Finkelstein, L, 'What is Global Governance?' (1995) 1 *Global Governance* 367–72.
Finnemore, M, *National Interests in International Society* (New York: Cornell University Press, 1996).
—— and Sikkink, K, 'International Norm Dynamics and Political Change' (1998) 52 *International Organization* 887–917.
Finnis, J, *Natural Law and Natural Rights* (Oxford and New York: Clarendon Press, 2nd edn, 2011).
Fischer-Lescano, A and Teubner, G, 'Regime Collisions: The Vain Search for Legal Unity in the Fragmentation of Global Law' (2004) 25 Mich JIL 999–1046.
——, *Regime-Kollisionen: zur Fragmentierung des globalen Rechts* (Frankfurt am Main: Suhrkamp, 2006).
Fitzmaurice, GG, 'The Foundations of the Authority of International Law and the Problem of Enforcement' (1956) 19 MLR 1–13.
——, 'Some Problems Regarding the Formal Sources of International Law' in *Symbolae Verzijl* (The Hague: Martinus Nijhoff, 1958) 153–76.
——, 'The Contribution of the Institute of International Law to the Development of International Law' (1973) 138 RdC 203–60.
Fitzpatrick, P, *The Mythology of Modern Law* (London and New York: Routledge, 1992).
Flauss, F, 'Vers un aggiornamento des conditions d'exercice de la protection diplomatique', in Flauss, F, *La protection diplomatique: Mutations contemporaines et pratiques nationales* (Brussels: Bruylant, 2003) 29–61.
Fleck, D (ed), *The Handbook of International Humanitarian Law* (New York: OUP, 2nd edn, 2008).
Fletcher, GP, 'The Indefinable Concept of Terrorism' (2006) 4 JICJ 894–911.
Flory, T, 'Article 103' in Cot, J-P and Pellet, A (eds), *La Charte des Nations Unies: Commentaire article par article* (Paris: Economica, 2nd edn, 1991) 1381–8.
Focarelli, C, *Le contromisure nel diritto internazionale* (Milan: Giuffrè, 1994).
——, 'The Legal Nature of the Acts Adopted Under Article IX of the Antarctic Treaty and their Implementation in Italy' in Francioni, F and Scovazzi, T, (eds), *International Law for Antarctica* (The Hague: Kluwer, 1996) 505–77.
——, 'Denying Foreign State Immunity for Commission of International Crimes: The *Ferrini* Decision' (2005) 54 ICLQ 951–8.
——, 'Customary Foundations of *jus gentium* in Francisco Suárez's Thought and the Concept of International Community in Contemporary International Law' (2006) 16 It YBIL 41–56.
——, 'Immunité des Etats et *Jus Cogens*. La dynamique du droit international et la fonction du *jus cogens* dans le processus de changement de la règle sur l'immunité juridictionnelle des Etats étrangers' (2008) 112 RGDIP 761–93.
——, 'Promotional *Jus Cogens*: A Critical Appraisal of *Jus Cogens*' Legal Effects' (2008) 77 Nord JIL 429–59.
——, 'The Responsibility to Protect Doctrine and Humanitarian Intervention: Too Many Ambiguities for a Working Doctrine' (2008) 13 JCSL 191–213.
——, 'Tanto rumore (quasi) per nulla: lo status del Kosovo e la strategia argomentativa della Corte Internazionale di giustizia nel parere del 22 luglio 2010' (2011) 76 *Il Politico* 59.
——, book review (2009) 11 JHIL 357–63.
——, 'Denial of Justice', MP EPIL (January 2009 update).
——, 'Diniego dell'immunità alla Germania per crimini internazionali: la Suprema Corte si fonda su valutazioni "qualitative"' (2009) 92 RDI 363–410.
——, 'Euthanasia', MP EPIL (June 2009 update).
——, 'Federal Republic of Germany v Giovanni Mantelli and Others, Order No 14201' (2009) 103 AJIL 122–31.

——, book review (2010) 104 AJIL 557–64.
——, 'Common Article 1 of the 1949 Geneva Conventions: A Soap Bubble?' (2010) 21 EJIL 125–71.
——, 'Duty to Protect in Cases of Natural Disasters', MP EPIL (March 2010 update).
——, 'Costituzionalismo internazionale e costituzionalizzazione della "global governance": Alla ricerca del diritto globale' (2011) 42 *Politica del diritto* 207–37.
——, 'Tanto rumore (quasi) per nulla: lo status del Kosovo e la strategia argomentativa della Corte Internazionale di giustizia nel parere del 22 luglio 2010' (2011) 76 *Il Politico* 59–80.
——, '*Le jus gentium*' dans la pensée d'Alberico Gentili' in P Haggenmacher, V Mainetti, and D Campanelli (eds), *Alberico Gentili and International Law* (Leiden and Boston: Nijhoff, forthcoming 2012).
——, 'Libya: a Turning Point for the Responsibility to Protect Doctrine?', (2011) at <http://www.e-ir.info/?p=809>.
——, 'Ahead to the Past?' Responsibility to Protect and the Global System (2012) I GroJIL I, also at <www.grojil.org>.
Foot, R, Gaddis, JL, and Hurrell, A (eds), *Order and Justice in International Relations* (Oxford: OUP, 2003).
Forsythe, DP, *The Humanitarians: The International Committee of the Red Cross* (New York: CUP, 2005).
—— and Rieffer-Flanagan BAJ, *The International Committee of the Red Cross: A Neutral Humanitarian Actor* (Abingdon and New York: Routledge, 2007).
Foster CE, *Science and the Precautionary Principle in International Courts and Tribunals: Expert Evidence, Burden of Proof and Finality* (Cambridge: CUP, 2011).
Francione, GL and Garner, R, *The Animal Rights Debate: Abolition or Regulation?* (New York: Columbia University Press, 2010).
Francioni, F, 'Of War, Humanity and Justice: International Law after Kosovo' (2000) 4 MP YBUNL 107–26.
—— and Scovazzi, T, (eds), *International Law for Antarctica* (The Hague: Kluwer, 1996).
Franck, TM, 'Who Killed Article 2(4)? or: Changing Norms Governing the Use of Force by States' (1970) 64 AJIL 809–37.
——, *The Power of Legitimacy Among Nations* (Oxford: OUP, 1990).
——, *Fairness in International Law and Institutions* (Oxford: OUP, 1998).
——, 'Terrorism and the Right of Self-Defense' (2001) 95 AJIL 839–43.
——, *The Empowered Self: Law and Society in the Age of Individualism* (Oxford: OUP, 2001).
——, 'Preface: International Institutions: Why Constitutionalize?' in Dunoff JL and Trachtman, JP (eds), *Ruling the World? Constitutionalism, International Law, and Global Governance* (Cambridge: CUP, 2009) xi–xiv.
Frangipane, M, *La nascita dello Stato nel Vicino Oriente: Dai lignaggi alla burocrazia nella Grande Mesopotamia* (Roma-Bari: Laterza, 2nd edn, 2005).
Frank, J, 'Aristotle on Constitutionalism and the Rule of Law Critical Modernities: Politics and Law beyond the Liberal Imagination' (2007) 8 Theoretical Inquiries in Law 37–50.
Frankenberg, G, 'Critical Theory', MP EPIL (October 2010 update).
Frazer, JG, *Folklore in the Old Testament* (London: Macmillan, 1918) 3 vols.
Freeman, MDA, *Lloyd's Introduction to Jurisprudence* (London: Sweet & Maxwell, 7th edn, 2001).
Freud, S, *Totem und Taboo* (Leipzig and Vienna: Heller, 1913), English trans 'Totem and Taboo: Some Points of Agreement between the Mental Lives of Savages and Neurotics' in Strachey, J, *The Standard Edition of the Complete Psychological Works of Sigmund Freud* (London: Vintage, 1955) vol 13, 1–161.
——, *Massenpsychologie und Ich-Analyse* (Leipzig, Vienna and Zurich: Internationaler Psychoanalytischer Verlag, 1921), English trans 'Group Psychology and the Analysis of the Ego' in Strachey, J, *The Standard Edition of the Complete Psychological Works of Sigmund Freud* (London: Vintage, 1955) vol 18, 69–143.

——, *Der Mann Moses und die monotheistische Religion: Drei Abhandlungen* (Amsterdam: Verlag Allert de Lange, 1939), English trans 'Moses and Monotheism: Three Essays' in Strachey, J, *The Standard Edition of the Complete Psychological Works of Sigmund Freud* (London: Vintage, 1955) vol 23, 1–137.

——, 'Zur Einführung der Narzissmus' (1914) 6 *Jahrbuch der Psychoanalyse* 1–24, English trans 'On Narcissism: An Introduction' in Strachey, J, *The Standard Edition of the Complete Psychological Works of Sigmund Freud* (London: Vintage, 1957) vol 14, 67–102.

——, 'Zeitgemäßes über Krieg und Tod' (1915) 4 *Imago* 1–21, English trans 'Thoughts for the Times on War and Death' in Strachey, J, *The Standard Edition of the Complete Psychological Works of Sigmund Freud* (London: Vintage, 1957) vol 14, 275–300.

——, *Das Unbehagen in der Kultur* (Vienna: Internationaler Psychoanalytischer Verlag, 1930), English trans 'Civilization and Its Discontents' in Strachey, J (ed), *The Standard Edition of the Complete Psychological Works of Sigmund Freud* (London: Vintage, 1964) vol 21, 64–145.

Friedman, J, 'Indigeneity: Anthropological Notes on a Historical Variable' in Minde, H (ed), *Indigenous Peoples: Self-determination Knowledge Indigeneity* (Delft: Eburon, 2008) 29–48.

Friedman, LM, *The Legal System: A Social Science Perspective* (New York: Russell Sage Foundation, 1975).

Friedman, RB, 'On the Concept of Authority in Political Philosophy' in Raz, J (ed), *Authority* (New York: New York University Press, 1990) 56–91.

Friedmann, W, *The Changing Structure of International Law* (London: Stevens and Sons, 1964).

——, 'The "Reality" of International Law—A Reappraisal' (1971) 10 Col JTL 46–60.

Friel, H and Falk, R, *The Record of the Paper: How the New York Times Misreports US Foreign Policy* (London and New York, Verso, 2004).

Fromm, E, *The Anatomy of Human Destructiveness* (London: Pimlico, 1973).

Fruehwald, ES, *Law and Human Behavior: A Study in Behavioral Biology, Neuroscience, and the Law* (Lake Mary: Vandeplas Publishing LLC, 2011).

Frulli, M, *Immunità e crimini internazionali: l'esercizio della giurisdizione penale e civile nei confronti degli organi statali sospettati di gravi crimini internazionali* (Turin: Giappichelli, 2007).

Fulford, R, *Globe and Mail*, 5 June 1999, at <http://www.robertfulford.com/Paradigm.html>.

Fuller, LL, 'Positivism and Fidelity to Law: A Reply to Professor Hart' (1958) 71 Harv LR 630–72.

——, *The Anatomy of Law* (Westport, Conn: Greenwood Press, 1968).

——, *The Morality of Law* (New Haven and London: Yale University Press, rev edn, 1969).

Fusinato, G, 'La personalità giuridica dell' Instituto internazionale d'Agricoltura' (1914) 3 ROI 149.

Gadamer, H-G, *Wahrheit und Methode: Grundzüge einer philosophischen Hermeneutik* (Tübingen: JCB Mohr, rev edn 1975, 1960), English trans *Truth and Method* (London and New York: Continuum, rev translation, 2004).

Gaeta, P (ed), *The UN Genocide Convention: A Commentary* (Oxford: OUP, 2009).

——, 'Are Victims of War Crimes Entitled to Compensation?' in Ben-Naftali, O (ed), *International Humanitarian Law and International Human Rights Law* (Oxford: OUP, 2011) 305–27.

Ganeri, J, 'The Hindu Syllogism: Nineteenth-Century Perceptions of Indian Logical Thought' (1996) 46 PEW 1–16.

Gaius, *Institutes*, English trans *The Institutes of Gaius* (London: Duckworth, 2001).

Galtung, J, 'On the Effects of International Economic Sanctions: With Examples from the Case of Rhodesia' (1967) 19 *World Politics* 378–416.

Gamble, JK and Dirling, NL, 'Mass Media Coverage of International Law: (Benign) Neglect?, Distortion?' (2006) 18 Flo JIL 211–300.

Gargani, A, 'Introduzione' in Wittgenstein, L, *Della certezza. L'analisi filosofica del senso comune* (Turin: Einaudi, 1978).
Garner, R, *The Political Theory of Animal Rights* (Manchester: Manchester University Press, 2005).
Gasser, H-P, 'International Committee of the Red Cross (ICRC)', MP EPIL (April 2009 update).
Gavouneli, M and Bantekas, E, 'Prefecture of Voiotia v Federal Republic of Germany' (2001) 95 AJIL 198–204.
Gazzini, T, 'The Relationship between International Legal Personality and Institutional Autonomy' in Collins, R and White, ND (eds), *International Organizations and the Idea of Autonomy: Institutional Independence in the International Legal Order* (Abingdon and New York: Routledge, 2011) 196–212.
Gellius, Aulus Cornelius, *Noctes Atticae*, English trans *A. Gellii Noctes Atticae* (Oxford: OUP, 1990) 2 vols.
Genser, J and Cotler, I, *The Responsibility to Protect* (Oxford and New York: OUP, 2012).
Gentili, A, *De Iure Belli Libri Tres* [1598], English trans *Three Books On The Law Of War* (Oxford and London: Clarendon Press and Humphrey Milford, 1933).
Gény, F, *Méthode d'interprétation et sources du droit positif* (Paris: Librairie générale de droit et de jurisprudence, 1899; 2nd edn, 1919).
George, RP (ed), *Natural Law Theory: Contemporary Essays* (Oxford and New York: Clarendon Press, 1992).
Gert, B, 'The Definition of Morality' in Stan EP, at <http://plato.stanford.edu/archives/fall2008/entries/morality-definition>.
Gerth, HH and Mills, CW (eds), *From Max Weber: Essays in Sociology* (New York: OUP, 1958).
Gewirth, A, 'The Rationality of Reasonableness' (1983) 57 *Synthèse* 225–47.
Gibney, M, and Skogly, S (eds), *Universal Human Rights and Extraterritorial Obligations* (Philadelphia: University of Pennsylvania Press, 2010).
Gierke, O von, *Political Theories of the Middle Ages* (Boston: Beacon Press, 1958).
Gies, L, *Law and the Media: The Future of an Uneasy Relationship* (Abingdon and New York: Routledge-Cavendish, 2008).
Gilbert, NW, *Renaissance Concepts of Method* (New York: Columbia University Press, 1960).
Gilboa, E, 'The CNN Effect: The Search for a Communication Theory of International Relations' (2005) 22 *Political Communication* 27–44.
Gilissen, J, *Les sources du droit en Europe occidentale (XIIe–XX siècle)* (Brussels: Presses Universitaires de Bruxelles, 1978).
Gill, S, *American Hegemony and the Trilateral Commission* (Cambridge: CUP, 1990).
Gillman, E, 'Making WTO SPS Dispute Settlement Work: Challenges and Practical Solutions' (2011) 31 Nw JILB 439–77.
Giovanoli, M and Devos, D (eds), *International Monetary and Financial Law: The Global Crisis* (Oxford: OUP, 2010).
Girard, R, *La violence et le sacré* (Paris: Grasset, 1972), English trans *Violence and the Sacred* (Baltimore: Johns Hopkins University Press, 1977).
Giuliano, M, 'Il problema dell'analogia nell'ordinamento giuridico internazionale' (1941) 20 RDI 69–121.
——, Scovazzi, T, and Treves, T, *Diritto internazionale, Parte generale* (Milan, Giuffrè, 2nd edn, 1983).
Glenn, HP, *Legal Traditions of the World: Sustainable Diversity in Law* (Oxford: OUP, 4th edn 2010).
Glennon, MJ, 'The UN Security Council in an Unipolar World' (2003–04) 44 Virg JIL 91–112.

Godehardt, N, 'Just War Concepts: Western and Chinese Perspectives' in Voyame, MD (ed), *International Law, Conflict and Development: The Emergence of a Holistic Approach in International Affairs* (Leiden: Nijhoff, 2010) 443–63.

Godwin, W, *Enquiry Concerning Political Justice and Its Influence on Modern Morals and Happiness* (Harmondsworth: Penguin, 1976).

Goldhagen, DJ, *Hitler's Willing Executioners: Ordinary Germans and the Holocaust* (London: Abacus, 1997).

Goldsmith, J, 'Remarks' in 'Scholars in the Construction and Critique of International Law' (2000) 94 ASIL Proc 317–20.

——, 'Sovereignty, International Relations Theory, and International Law: Sovereignty: Organized Hypocrisy' (2000) 52 Stan LR 959–86.

—— and Posner, EA, *The Limits of International Law* (Oxford: OUP, 2005).

Goleman, DP, *Emotional Intelligence: Why It Can Matter More Than IQ* (New York: Bantam Books, 1997).

Gommer, H, 'From the "Is" to the "Ought"' (2010) 96 ARS 449.

—— *A Biological Theory of Law: Natural Law Theory Revisited* (Seattle: CreateSpace, 2011).

Gong, GW, *The Standard of 'Civilization' in International Society* (Oxford: Clarendon Press, 1984).

Gonzalez, MA, 'Trade and Morality: Preserving "Public Morals" Without Sacrificing the Global Economy' (2006) 39 Van JTL 939–72.

Goodrich, LM and Hambro, E, *Charter of the United Nations: Commentary and Documents* (New York: Columbia University Press, 3rd edn, 1969).

Gowers, A, 'The Power of Two' (2002) 132 *Foreign Policy* 32–3.

Graber, CB and Burri-Nenova, M (eds), *Governance of Digital Game Environments and Cultural Diversity: Transdisciplinary Enquiries* (Cheltenham: Edward Elgar, 2010).

Gradoni, L, Regime Failure *nel diritto internazionale* (Padua: Cedam, 2009).

Graham, RA, *The Rise of the Double Diplomatic Corps in Rome: A Study in International Practice (1870–1875)* (The Hague: Nijhoff, 1952).

Granger, C and Siroën, J-M, 'Core Labour Standards in Trade Agreements: From Multilateralism to Bilateralism' (2006) 40 JWT 813–36.

Grant, M, *Myths of the Greeks and Romans* (London: Weidenfeld and Nicolson, 1962).

Gray, CD, 'The Bush Doctrine Revisited: The 2006 National Security Strategy of the USA' (2006) Chin JIL 555–78.

——, *International Law and the Use of Force* (Oxford: OUP, 3rd edn, 2008).

Gray, JC, *The Nature and Sources of the Law* (New York: Columbia University Press, 1909).

Green, LC and Dickason, OP, *The Law of Nations and the New World* (Edmonton: University of Alberta Press, 1989).

Greenwalt, K, *Law and Objectivity* (New York and Oxford: OUP, 1992).

Greenwood, C, 'International Law and the Pre-emptive Use of Force: Afghanistan, Al-Qaida, and Iraq' (2003) 4 SD ILJ 7–37.

Greer, S, *The Exceptions to Articles 8 to 11 of the European Convention on Human Rights* (Strasbourg: Council of Europe Publishing, 1997).

Grewe, WG, *Epochen der Völkerrechtsgeschichte* (Baden-Baden: Nomos, 1984), English trans *The Epochs of International Law* (Berlin and New York: Walter de Gruyter, 2000).

Griffin, DR, 'Objections to World Government Considered', at <http://www.dwfed.org/pp_objections_world%20govt_considered.htm>.

Grotius, H, *De Jure Belli ac Pacis Libri Tres* [1625], English trans *On the Law of War and Peace Three Books* (Washington, DC, Oxford, and London: Carnegie Institution, Clarendon Press, and Humphrey Milford, 1925).

Gunning, IR, 'Modernizing Customary International Law: The Challenge of Human Rights' (1991) 31 Virg JIL 211–47.

Gutman, RW, 'Spotlight on Violations of International Humanitarian Law: The Role of the Media' (1998) 80 IRRC 619–25.
Guyer, P, *Kant and the Claims of Knowledge* (Cambridge: CUP, 1987).
Guzman, AT, *How International Law Works: A Rational Choice Theory* (Oxford and New York: OUP, 2008).
Haas, PM, 'Do Regimes Matter? Epistemic Communities and Mediterranean Pollution' (1989) 43 *International Organization* 377–403.
——, 'Epistemic Communities and International Policy Coordination' (1992) 46 *International Organization* 1–35.
Habermas, J, *Theorie des kommunikativen Handelns* (Frankfurt am Main: Suhrkamp, 1981), English trans *Theory of Communicative Action* (Boston: Beacon Press, 1984–87) 2 vols.
——, *Moralbewußtsein und kommunikatives Handeln* (Frankfurt am Main: Suhrkamp, 1983), English trans *Moral Consciousness and Communicative Action* (Cambridge, Mass: MIT Press, 1990).
——, *Die gespaltene Westen* (Frankfurt am Main: Suhrkamp, 2004), English trans *The Divided West* (Cambridge: Polity Press, 2006).
Hacking, I, *The Social Construction of What?* (Cambridge: Harvard University Press, 1999).
Hafner, G, 'Is the Topic of Responsibility of International Organizations Ripe for Codification?' in Fastenrath, U, Geiger, R, Khan, D-E, Paulus, A, Schorlemer, S von, and Vedder, C (eds), *From Bilateralism to Community Interest: Essays in Honour of Judge Bruno Simma* (Oxford: OUP, 2011) 695–717.
Haggenmacher, P, *Grotius et la doctrine de la guerre juste* (Paris: Presses Universitaires de France, 1983).
Hakimi, M, 'The Media as Participants in the International Legal Process' (2006) 16 Duke JCIL 1–33.
Haldermann, F, 'Gustav Radbruch vs. Hans Kelsen: A Debate on Nazi Law' (2005) 18 Ratio Juris 162.
Hall, RB and Bierstecker, TJ, (eds), *The Emergence of Private Authority in Global Governance* (Cambridge: CUP, 2002).
Hall, WE, *A Treatise on International Law* (Oxford: Clarendon Press, 8th edn, 1924).
Handeyside, H, 'The Lotus Principle in ICJ Jurisprudence: Was the Ship Ever Afloat?' (2007–08) 29 Mich JIL 71–94.
Hansen, V, 'Extraordinary Renditions and the State Secrets Privilege: Keeping Focus on the Task at Hand' (2008) 33 NC JILCR 629–55.
Hardt, M and Negri, A, *Empire* (Cambridge, Mass: Harvard University Press, 2002).
Harland, C, 'The Impact of the Media on International Law and Relations' (1995) 89 ASIL Proc 119–27.
Harrison, J, *The Human Rights Impact of the World Trade Organisation* (Oxford: Hart, 2007).
Hart, HLA, 'Positivism and the Separation of Law and Morals' (1958) 71 Harv LR 593–629.
——, 'Postscript: Responsibility and Retribution' in *Punishment and Responsibility. Essays in the Philosophy of Law* (Oxford: Clarendon Press, 1968; 2nd edn, 2008) 210–37.
——, *The Concept of Law* (Oxford: OUP, 1994, 2nd edn).
Harvey, D, A brief History of Neoliberalism (Oxford and New York: OUP, 2007).
Hayashi, M, 'The Information Revolution and the Rules of Jurisdiction in Public International Law' in Dunn, M, Krishna-Hensel, SF, and Mauer, V (eds), *The Resurgence of the State: Trends and Processes in Cyberspace Governance* (Aldershot: Ashgate, 2007) 59–83.
Heeren, AHL, *Handbuch der Geschichte der Staaten des Alterthums, mit besonderer Rücksicht auf ihre Verfassungen, ihren Handel und ihre Colonien* (Göttingen: Rower, 1809), English trans from the 5th German edn *A Manual of the History of the Political System of Europe and its Colonies, from its Formation at the Close of the Fifteenth Century, to its Re-establishment upon the Fall of Napoleon* (Oxford: Talboys, 1834).

Hegel, GWF, *Grundlinien der Philosophie des Rechts* [1821] (Berlin: Akademie Verlag, 2005), English trans *Elements of the Philosophy of Right* (Cambridge: CUP, 1991).
——, *Phänomenologie des Geistes*, in *Werke* (Hamburg: Meiner, 1980), English trans *Phenomenology of Spirit* (Oxford: Clarendon Press, 1977).
Heidegger, M, *Sein und Zeit* [1927] (Frankfurt am Main: Klostermann, 1977), English trans *Being and Time* (Oxford: Blackwell Publishing, 2005).
Heinegg, WH von, 'Die weiteren Quellen des Völkerrechts' in Ipsen, K (ed), *Völkerrecht* (Munich: Beck, 5th edn, 2004) 210–56.
Held, V, *How Terrorism Is Wrong: Morality and Political Violence* (Oxford and New York, OUP, 2008).
Heller-Roazen, D, *The Enemy of All: Piracy and the Law of Nations* (New York: Zone Books, 2009).
Helman, GB and Ratner, SR, 'Saving Failed States' (1992–93) 89 *Foreign Policy* 3–20.
Henkin, L, 'Is There a Political Question Doctrine?' (1976) 85 Yale LJ 597–622.
——, *How Nations Behave: Law and Foreign Policy* (New York: Columbia University Press,2nd edn, 1979).
——, 'International Law: Politics, Values, and Functions: General Course on Public International Law' (1989) 216 RdC 1–416.
Heraclitus, *Fragments* (London: Penguin, 2003).
Herbst, J, *States and Power in Africa: Comparative Lessons in Authority and Control* (Princeton: Princeton University Press, 2000).
Herman, ES and Chomsky, N, *Manufacturing Consent: The Political Economy of the Mass Media* (New York, Pantheon Books, 2002).
Herodotus, *The History*, English trans *The History* (Chicago: University of Chicago Press, 1988), at <http://classics.mit.edu/Herodotus/history.html>.
Hestermeyer, H, *Human Rights and the WTO. The Case of Patents and Access to Medicines* (Oxford: OUP, 2007).
Higgins, AP, *The Binding Force of International Law* (Cambridge: CUP, 1910).
Higgins, R, *Problems and Process: International Law and How we Use it* (Oxford: Clarendon Press, 1994).
Hill, D (ed), *Contesting Neoliberal Education Public Resistance and Collective Advance* (New York and Abingdon: Routledge, 2008).
Hirsch, M, 'The Sociology of International Law: Invitation to Study International Rules in their Social Context', 55 UTLJ (2005) 891–939.
Hirschman, A, *The Rhetoric of Reason: Perversity, Futility, Jeopardy* (Cambridge, Mass and London: The Belknap Press of Harvard University Press, 1991).
Ho, C, *Access to Medicine in the Global Economy: International Agreements on Patents and Related Rights* (Oxford: OUP, 2011).
Hobbes, T, *De Cive* [1642], *On the Citizen* (Cambridge: CUP, 1998).
——, *Leviathan, or the matter, forme and power of a commonwealth ecclesiasticall and civill* [1651], *Leviathan* (New York and Oxford: OUP, 2009).
Hoebel, EA, *The Law of Primitive Man: A Study in Comparative Legal Dynamics* (Cambridge, Mass: London, 1954).
Hoffmann, RJ (ed), *The Just War and Jihad: Violence in Judaism, Christianity, and Islam* (Amherst, NY: Prometheus Books, 2006).
Hofmann, H, *Legitimität gegen Legalität: Der Weg der politischen Philosophie Carl Schmitts* (Berlin: Hermann Luchterhand, 1964).
Hofstede, G, 'The Cultural Relatively of the Quality of Life Concept' (1984) 9 AMR 389–98.
Holland, TE, *Studies in International Law* (Oxford: Clarendon Press, 1898).
Holmes, AF, 'Moore's Appeal to Common Sense' (1961) 58 JPh 197–207.
Holmes, OW, *The Common Law* (Boston: Little Brown, 1881).
Hoof, GJH van, *Rethinking the Sources of International Law* (Deventer: Kluwer, 1983).
Hooke, SH (ed), *Myth and Ritual* (Oxford: OUP,1933).

Horkheimer, M, *Eclipse of Reason* (New York: OUP, 1947), eventually published in German as *Zur Kritik der instrumentellen Vernunft* (Frankfurt am Main: S Fischer, 1967).

——, and Adorno, TW, *Dialektik der Aufklärung* (Amsterdam: Querido, 1947), English trans *Dialectic of Enlightenment* (Stanford: Stanford University Press, 2002).

Horsman, M and Marshall, A, *After the Nation State: Citizens, Tribalism and the New World Disorder* (London: Harper Collins, 1994).

Hostiensis, *Lecture quinque decretalium* [1512], in Muldoon, J, (ed), *The Expansion of Europe. The First Phase* (Philadelphia: University of Pennsylvania Press, 1977).

Howard, RE and Donnelly, J, 'Human Dignity, Human Rights, and Political Regimes' (1986) 80 APSR 801–17.

Howlett, A, 'Getting "Smart": Crafting Economic Sanctions that Respect All Human Rights' (2004–05) 73 Ford LR 1199–237.

Howse, R, 'Human Rights, International Economic Law and Constitutional Justice: A Reply' (2008) 19 EJIL 945–53.

Huber, M, 'Die soziologischen Grundlagen des Völkerrechts' in Huber, M, *Gemischte Schriften: Gesellschaft und Humanität* (Zürich: Atlantis, 1948) vol 3, 49–162.

Hudson, WD, *The Is–Ought Question: A Collection of Papers on the Central Problem in Moral Philosophy* (London: Macmillan, 1969).

Hufetau, Y-L, *Le référé législatif et les pouvoirs du juge de silence de la loi* (Paris: Presses universitaires de France, 1965).

Humboldt, W von, 'Ueber die Aufgabe des Geschichtschreibers' in *Wilhelm von Humboldts Gesammelte Schriften* [1905] (Berlin: Walter de Gruyter, 1968).

Hume, D, *A Treatise of Human Nature* [1739] (Oxford and New York: Clarendon Press, 2007).

Hunt, L, *Inventing Human Rights: A History* (New York and London: WW Norton and Co, 2007).

Hurrell, A, *On Global Order: Power, Values, and the Constitution of International Society* (Oxford: OUP, 2007).

Hutchenson, F, *A System of Moral Philosophy* [1755] (London and New York: Thoemmes Continuum, 2006).

Ibrahim, R, *The Al Qaeda Reader: The Essential Texts of Osama Bin Laden's Terrorist Organization* (New York: Broadway Books, 2007).

Ignatieff, M, *Human Rights as Politics and Idolatry* (Princeton and Oxford: Princeton University Press, 2001).

Iluyomade, BO, 'The Scope and Content of a Complaint of Abuse of Right in International Law' (1975) 16 Harv ILJ 47–92.

Innocent IV, *Dei Patris Immensa*, 5 March 1245, at <http://en.wikisource.org/wiki/Dei_Patris_Immensa>.

——, *Cum non solum*, 13 March 1245, at <http://en.wikisource.org/wiki/Cum_non_solum>.

——, *Viam Agnoscere Veritatis*, 22 November 1248, at <http://en.wikisource.org/wiki/Viam_agnoscere_veritatis>.

——, *Commentaria doctissima in Quinque Libros Decretalium* [1581], in J Muldoon, *The Expansion of Europe: The First Phase* (Philadelphia: University of Pennsylvania Press, 1977) 191–2.

Ipsen, K (ed), *Völkerrecht* (Munich: Beck, 5th edn, 2004).

Isidore of Seville, *Etymologies*, English trans *The Etymologies of Isidore of Seville* (Cambridge: CUP, 2010).

Iwasawa, Y, 'The Doctrine of Self-Executing Treaties in the United States: A Critical Analysis' (1985–86) 26 Virg JIL 627–92.

Jackson, RH, *Quasi-states. Sovereignty, International Relations and the Third World* (Cambridge: CUP, 1990).

Jagers, NMCP and Heijden, M-J van der, 'Corporate Human Rights Violations: The Feasibility of Civil Recourse in the Netherlands' (2007–08) 33 Brooklyn JIL 833–70.

James, W, 'Pragmatism: A New Name for some Old Ways of Thinking' in James, W, *Writings 1902–1910* (New York: The Library of America, 1987) 479–624.

——, *Writings 1902–1910* (New York: The Library of America, 1987).

Jarrett, H (ed), *Environmental Quality in a Growing Economy* (Baltimore. John Hopkins University Press, 1966).

Jaspers, K, 'Myth and Religion' in H-W Bartsch, (ed), *Kerygma and Myth: A Theological Debate* (London: ET, 1962).

Jeannet, S, 'Recognition of the ICRC's Long-Standing Rule of Confidentiality' (2000) 82 IRRC 403–25.

Jellinek, G, *Allgemeine Staatslehre* (Berlin: O Häring, 3rd edn, 1914).

——, *Die Rechtliche Natur Der Staatenverträge: Ein Beitrag Zur Juristischen Construction Des Völkerrechts* [1880] (Whitefish: Kessinger, 2010).

Jenks, CW, *The Common Law of Mankind* (London: Stevens and Sons, 1958).

Jennings, J, *The Business of Abolishing the British Slave Trade, 1783–1807* (Abingdon and New York: Routledge, 1997).

Jennings, R, 'The Judicial Enforcement of International Obligations' (1987) 47 ZaöRV 3–16.

——, 'Presentation' in Peck, C and Lee, RS (eds), *Increasing the Effectiveness of the International Court of Justice: Proceedings of the ICJ/UNITAR Colloquium To Celebrate The 50th Anniversary of The Court* (The Hague: Nijhoff, 1997) 78–85.

—— and Watts, A, *Oppenheim's International Law* (Harlow: Longman, 9th edn, 1992).

Jessup, PC, 'The Reality of International Law' (1939–40) 18 *Foreign Affairs* 244–53.

——, 'The Subjects of a Modern Law of Nations' (1947) 45 Mich LR 383–408.

Jhering, R von, *Der Kampf ums Recht* [1872] (Frankfurt am Main: Klostermann, 2003), English trans *The Struggle for Law* (Chicago: Callaghan and Co, 1915).

——, *Der Zweck im Recht* (Leipzig : Breitkopf und Härtel, 1877–1883, 2 vols), English trans of the first volume, originally published in 1877, of the 4th German edition published in 1903, *Law as a Means to an End* (Kila: Kessinger, 1914).

——, *Scherz und Ernst in der Jurisprudenz Eine Weihnachtsgabe für das juristische Publikum* (Göttingen: Breitkopf und Härtel, 1884).

Jiminián, JMC, 'The Principle of Distinction in Virtual War: Restraints and Precautionary Measures under International Humanitarian Law' (2010) 15 Tilburg Law Review 69–91.

Johnson, JT, *Just War Tradition and the Restraint of War: A Moral and Historical Inquiry* (Princeton: Princeton University Press, 1984).

Johnston, D, *A Brief History of Justice* (Chichester: Wiley-Blackwell, 2011).

Johnston, DM, *The Historical Foundations of World Order: The Tower and the Arena* (Leiden and Boston: Nijhoff, 2008).

Johnstone, I, 'Legislation and Adjudication in the UN Security Council: Bringing down the Deliberative Deficit' (2008) 102 AJIL 275–308.

Jørgensen, NHB, *The Responsibility of States for International Crimes* (Oxford: OUP, 2000).

Joseph, S, *Blame It on the WTO?: A Human Rights Critique* (Oxford: OUP, 2011).

Jouannet, E, 'French and American Perspectives on International Law: Legal Cultures and International Law' (2006) 58 Maine Law Review 291–335.

Joyce, D, 'Human Rights and the Mediatization of International Law' (2010) 23 LJIL 507–27.

Jung, CG, *Memories, Dreams and Reflection* (London: ET, 1963).

Justinian, *Justinian's Institutes* (Ithaca: Cornell University Press, 1987).

——, *The Digest of Justinian* (Philadelphia: University of Pennsylvania Press, 1997) 2 vols.

Juvenal, *Satirae*, English trans *The Sixteen Satires* (London: Penguin, 1999).

Kafka, F, *Der Prozeß*, 1 *Gesammelte Werke* (Frankfurt am Mein: S Fischer, 1950), English trans *The Trial* (Oxford: OUP, 2009).

Kahn, CH, 'Sensation and Consciousness in Aristotle's Psychology' (1966) 48 AGP 41–82.

——, 'Aristotle on Thinking' in Nussbaum, MCand Rorty, AO (eds), *Essays On Aristotle's* De Anima (Oxford: Clarendon Press, 1992) 343–79.

Kaiser, K, 'Treaties, Direct Applicability', EPIL (September 2006 update).

Kaldor, M, *Global Civil Society: An Answer to War* (Cambridge: Polity Press, 2003).

——, *Human Security: Reflections on Globalization and Intervention* (Cambridge: Polity, 2007).

Kalshoven, F, 'Reprisals and the Protection of Civilians: Two Recent Decisions of the Yugoslavia Tribunal' in Vohrah, LC, Pocar, F, Featherstone, Y, Fourmy, O, Graham, C, Hocking, J, and Robson, N (eds), *Man's Inhumanity to Man: Essays on International Law in Honour of Antonio Cassese* (The Hague: Kluwer, 2003).

Kämmerer, JA, 'State Bankruptcy', MP EPIL (September 2009 update).

Kammerhofer, J, 'The Armed Activities Case and Non-State Actors in Self-Defence Law' (2007) 20 LJIL 89–113.

Kamminga, MT, 'What Makes an NGO "Legitimate" in the Eyes of States?' in Vedder, V (ed), *The Involvement of NGOs in International Governance and Policy: Sources of Legitimacy* (Leiden: Nijhoff, 2007) 175–95.

————and Scheinin, M, (eds), *The Impact of Human Rights Law on General International Law* (Oxford: OUP, 2009).

Kant, I, *Grundlegung zur Metaphysik der Sitten* [1785] (Hamburg: Meiner, 1962), English trans *Grounding for the Metaphysics of Morals* (Indianapolis and Cambridge: Hackett, 1981).

——, *Metaphysik der Sitten* [1797] (Hamburg: Meiner, 1959), English trans *The Metaphysics of Morals* (Cambridge: CUP, 1996).

——, *Zum ewigen Frieden. Ein philosophischer Entwurf* [1795] (Stuttgart: Reclam, 1984), English trans *To Perpetual Peace: A Philosophical Sketch* (Indianapolis, Hackett, 2003).

——, *Kritik der reinen Vernunft* [1781] (Berlin: De Gruyter, 1968), English trans *Critique of Pure Reason* (London: Penguin, 2007).

——, *Kritik der Urteilskraft* [1790] (Hamburg: Meiner, 1959), English trans *The Critique of Judgement* (Oxford: OUP, 2007).

——, *Prolegomena zu einer jeden künftigen Metaphysik, die als Wissenschaft wird auftreten können* [1783] (Hamburg: Meiner, 1957), English trans *Prolegomena to Any Future Metaphysics* (Forgotten Books, 2008), also available at <http://philosophy.eserver.org/kant-prolegomena.txt>.

Kantorowicz, H (under pseudonym of Gnaeus Flavius), *Der Kampf um die Rechtswissenschaft* [1906] (Baden-Baden: Nomos, 2002).

Kaplow, L, 'Rules versus Standards: An Economic Analysis' (1992) 42 Duke LJ 557–629.

Kasanin, JS (ed), *Language and Thought in Schizophrenia* (New York: Norton, 1944).

Kattan, V, 'The Wall, Obligations *Erga Omnes* and Human Rights: The Case for Withdrawing the European Community's Terms of Preferential Trade with Israel' (2004–05) 13 Pal YBIL 71–89.

Kawasaki, K, 'The "Injured State" in the International Law of State Responsibility' (2000) 28 Hitotsubashi Journal of Law and Politics 17–31.

——, 'A Brief Note on the Legal Effects of *Jus Cogens* in International Law' (2006) 34 Hitotsubashi Journal of Law and Politics 27–43.

Keal, P, *European Conquest and the Rights of Indigenous Peoples: The Moral Backwardness of International Society* (Cambridge: CUP, 2003).

Keane, J, *Global Civil Society?* (Cambridge: CUP, 2003).

Kearney, RD and Dalton, RE, 'The Treaty on Treaties' (1987) 64 AJIL 495–561.

Keegan, J, *A History of Warfare* (London: Pimlico) 2nd edn, 2004).

Kelly, G, *The Psychology of Personal Constructs* (New York: Norton, 1955) 2 vols.

Kelly, JP, 'The Twilight of Customary International Law' (1999–2000) 40 Virg JIL 449–543.

Kelsay, J, 'Just War, Jihad, and the Study of Comparative Ethics' (2010) EIA 227–38.

Kelsen, H, 'La naissance de l'Etat et la formation de sa nationalité: les principes; leur application au cas de la Tchécoslovaquie' (1929) 4 RDI 613–41.

——, 'Théorie générale du droit international public: problèmes choisis' (1932-IV) 42 RdC 121–351.
——, *Reine Rechtslehre: Einleitung in die rechtswissenschaftliche Problematik* (Leipzig: Deuticke, 1934).
——, 'Théorie du droit international coutumier' (1939) 1 RITD 253–74.
——, *Peace Through Law* (Chapel Hill: University of Carolina Press, 1944).
——, *The Law of the United Nations: A Critical Analysis of its Fundamental Problems* (London: Stevens and Sons, 1950, with supplement 1951).
——, *Principles of International Law* (New York: Rinehart & Co, 1952).
——, 'Théorie du droit international public' (1953-III) 84 RdC 1–201.
——, *Was ist Gerechtigkeit?* (Vienna: Franz Deuticke, 1953).
——, *What is Justice?: Justice, Law, and Politics in the Mirror of Science* (Berkeley and Los Angeles: University of California Press, 1957).
——, *Principles of International Law* (New York: Holt, 2nd edn, 1967).
——, *Allgemeine Theorie der Normen* (Vienna: Manz, 1979), English trans *General Theory of Norms* (Oxford: Clarendon Press, 1991).
——, *General Theory of Law and State* [1945] (New Brunswick and London: Transaction Publishers, 2007).
Kennan, GF, *American Diplomacy, 1900–1951* (Chicago: University of Chicago Press, 1951).
Kennedy, David, *International Legal Structures* (Baden-Baden: Nomos Verlag, 1987).
——, 'The Disciplines of International Law and Policy' (1999) 12 LJIL 9–133.
——, *The Dark Sides of Virtue: Reassessing International Humanitarianism* (Princeton and Oxford: Princeton University Press, 2004).
——, 'The Mystery of Global Governance' in Dunoff, JL and Trachtman, JP (eds), *Ruling the World? Constitutionalism, International Law, and Global Governance* (Cambridge: CUP, 2009) 37–68.
Kennedy, Duncan, 'Form and Substance in Private Law Adjudication' (1976) 89 Harv LR 1685–778.
Kent, J, *Commentaries on American Law* [1826–30] (New York: Da Capo Press, 1971).
Kepel, G and Milelli, J-P (eds), *Al Qaeda in Its Own Words* (Cambridge, Mass: Belknap Press of Harvard University Press, 2010).
Kerferd, GB, *The Sophistic Movement* (Cambridge and New York: CUP, 1981).
Kiernan, B, *Blood and Soil: A World History of Genocide and Extermination from Sparta to Darfur* (New Haven and London: Yale University Press, 2007).
Kim, B, 'Social Constructivism', at <http://projects.coe.uga.edu/epltt/index.php?title=Social_Constructivism>.
Kingsbury, B, 'The Concept of Compliance as a Function of Competing Conceptions of International Law' (1998) 19 Mich JIL 345–72.
——, 'The Concept of "Law" in Global Administrative Law' (2009) 20 EJIL 23–57.
——, 'Indigenous Peoples', MP EPIL (July 2011 update).
——, Krisch, N, and Stewart, RB, 'The Emergence of Global Administrative Law' (2005) 68 LCP 15–61.
Kinley, D, *Civilising Globalisation: Human Rights and the Global Economy* (Cambridge and New York: CUP, 2009) 37–92.
Kiss, A and Shelton, D, 'Systems Analysis of International Law: A Methodological Inquiry' (1986) 17 Neth YBIL 45–74.
Kissinger, HA, 'The Pitfalls of Universal Jurisdiction' (July/August 2001) 80 *Foreign Affairs* 86–96.
Klabbers, J, 'Institutional Ambivalence by Design: Soft Organizations in International Law' (2001) 70 Nord JIL 403–21.
——, *An Introduction to International Institutional Law* (Cambridge: CUP, 2002).

——, '(I Can't Get No) Recognition: Subjects Doctrine and the Emergence of Non-state Actors' in Petman, J and Klabbers, J (eds), *Nordic Cosmopolitanism: Essays in International Law for Martti Koskenniemi* (Leiden: Nijhoff, 2003) 351–69.

——, 'The Concept of Legal Personality', 11 *Ius Gentium* (2005) 35.

——, Peters, A, and Ulfstein, G, *The Constitutionalization of International Law* (Oxford: OUP, 2009).

Klein, E, 'Self-contained Regime', MP EPIL (November 2006 update).

Kloth, M, *Immunities and the Right of Access to Court under Article 6 of the European Convention on Human Rights* (Leiden and Boston: Nijhoff, 2010).

Knoll, B, *The Legal Status of Territories Subject to Administration by International Organisations* (Cambridge: CUP, 2008).

Knuchel, S, 'State Immunity and the Promise of *Jus Cogens*' (2011) 9 Nw JIHR 149–83.

Kocs, SA, 'Explaining the Strategic Behaviour of States: International Law as a Systems Structure' (1994) 38 ISQ 535–54.

Koh, HH, 'Transnational Legal Process' (1996) 75 Nebraska Law Review 181–207.

——, 'Why Do Nations Obey International Law?' (1996–97) 106 Yale LJ 2599–659.

Kolb, R, *La bonne foi en droit international public: contribution à l'étude des principes généraux de droit* (Paris: Presses Universitaires de France, 2000).

——, *Théorie du* ius cogens *international: Essai de relecture du concept* (Genève: Presses Universitaires de France, 2001).

——, 'Does Article 103 of the Charter of the United Nations Apply Only to Decisions or Also to Authorizations Adopted by the Security Council?' (2004) 64 ZaöRV 21–35.

——, 'General Principles of Procedural Law' in Zimmermann, A, Tomuschat, C, and Oellers-Frahm, K, (eds), *The Statute of the International Court of Justice: A Commentary* (Oxford: OUP, 2006) 793–835.

——, 'Le contrôle de Résolutions contraignantes du Conseil de sécurité des Nations Unies sous l'angle du respect du *jus cogens*' (2008) 18 *Schweizerische Zeitschrift für internationales und europäisches Recht* 401–11.

Komarow, G, 'Individual Responsibility under International Law: The Nuremberg Principles in Domestic Legal Systems' (1980) 29 ICLQ 21–37.

Kontorovich, E and Art, S, 'An Empirical Examination of Universal Jurisdiction for Piracy' (2010) 104 AJIL 436–53.

Koppell, JGS, *World Rule: Accountability, Legitimacy, and the Design of Global Governance* (Chicago: University of Chicago Press, 2010).

Korten, DC, *When Corporations Rule the World* (Sterling and San Francisco: Kumarian Press and Berrett-Koeler Publisher, 2nd edn, 2001).

Koskenniemi, M, *From Apology to Utopia: The Structure of International Legal Argument* (Helsinki: Lakimiesliiton Kustannus, 1989).

——, 'Letter to the Editors of the Symposium' in Slaughter, A-M, and Ratner, SR (eds), 'Symposium on Method in International Law' (1999) 93 AJIL 351–361.

——, *From Apology to Utopia. The Structure of International Legal Argument* (Cambridge: CUP, reissue with new epilogue, 2005).

——, 'International Legislation Today: Limits and Possibilities' (2005) 23 Wisc ILJ 61–92.

——, 'Constitutionalism as Mindset: Reflections on Kantian Themes about International Law and Globalization' (2007) 8 Theoretical Inquiries in Law 9–36.

——, 'Constitutionalism, Managerialism and the Ethos of Legal Education' (2007) 4 EJLS, at <http://www.ejls.eu/1/3UK.pdf>.

——, 'Methodology of International Law', MP EPIL (November 2007 update).

——, 'The Fate of Public International Law: Between Technique and Politics' (2007) 70 MLR 1–30.

——, 'The Politics of International Law—20 Years Later' (2009) 20 EJIL 7–19.

Kotzur, M, 'Good Faith (Bona fide)', MP EPIL (January 2009 update).

Krabbe, H, *Die moderne Staats-Idee* (Haag: Nijhoff, 2nd edn, 1919).
Kramer, MH, *Where Law and Morality Meet* (Oxford: OUP, 2004).
——, *Objectivity and the Rule of Law* (Cambridge: CUP, 2007).
Krasner, SD, *Sovereignty: Organized Hypocrisy* (Princeton: Princeton University Press, 1999).
Kratochwil, F, *Rules, Norms and Decisions: On the Conditions of Practical and Legal Reasoning in International Relations and Domestic Affairs* (Cambridge: CUP, 1989).
Kreß, C, and von Holtzendorff, L von, 'The Kampala Compromise on the Crime of Aggression' (2010) 8 JICJ 1179–217.
Kretzmer, Dand Klein, E, (eds), *The Concept of Human Dignity in Human Rights Discourse* (Leiden: Brill, 2002).
Krisch, N, *Beyond Constitutionalism: The Pluralist Structure of Postnational Law* (Oxford and New York: OUP, 2010).
—— and Kingsbury, B, 'Introduction: Global Governance and Global Administrative Law in the International Legal Order' (2006) 17 EJIL 1–13.
Kritsiotis, D, 'Imagining the International Community' (2002) 13 EJIL 961–92.
Kubota, T, 'Regulation of Rating Agencies: Current and Future' in Giovanoli, M and Devos, D (eds), *International Monetary and Financial Law: The Global Crisis* (Oxford: OUP, 2010) 251–61.
Kuhn, TS, *The Structure of Scientific Revolutions* [1962] (Chicago and London: University of Chicago Press, 3rd edn, 1996).
Kunz, JL, 'The Swing of the Pendulum: From Overestimation to Underestimation of International Law' (1950) 44 AJIL 135–40.
——, 'Roberto Ago's Theory of a "Spontaneous" International Law' (1958) 52 AJIL 85–91.
——, 'Sanctions in International Law' (1960) 54 AJIL 324–47.
Kuper, A, 'The Return of the Native' (2003) 44 *Current Anthropology* 389–95.
——, 'Discussion' (2006) 14 *Social Anthropology* 21–2.
Kuyper, PJ 'Introduction to the Symposium on Responsibility of International Organizations and of (Member) States' (2010) 7 IOLR 9–33.
La Haye, E, *War Crimes in Internal Armed Conflicts* (Cambridge: CUP, 2008).
Lactantius, *Divine Institutes*, English trans *Divine Institutes* (Liverpool: Liverpool University Press, 2004).
Lagrange, E, 'Retour sur un classique: A. Verdross, Die Verfassung der Völkerrechtsgemeinschaft, 1926' (2008) 112 RGDIP 973–84.
Landheer, B, 'Contemporary Sociological Theories and International Law' (1957) 91 RdC1.
Lang, A, *World Trade Law After Neoliberalism: Re-Imagining the Global Economic Order* (Oxford: OUP, 2011).
Langer, M, 'The Diplomacy of Universal Jurisdiction: The Political Branches and the Transnational Prosecution of International Crimes' (2011) 105 AJIL 1–49.
Lauterpacht, E, 'The Development of the Law of International Organization by the Decisions of International Tribunals' (1976–IV) 152 RdC 377, 403.
Lauterpacht, H, *Private Law Sources and Analogies (With Special Reference to International Arbitration)* (London and New York: Longmans, Green and Co, 1927).
——, 'The Covenant as the "Higher Law"' (1936) 17 BYBIL 54–65.
——, 'The Grotian Tradition of International Law' (1946) 23 BYBIL 1–53.
——, 'The Subjects of the Law of Nations' (1947) 63 LQR 438–60.
Lavalle, R, 'A Politicized and Poorly Conceived Notion Crying Out for Clarification: The Alleged Need for a Universally Agreed Definition of Terrorism' (2007) 67 ZaöRV 89–117.
Le Bon, G, *La psychologie des foules* (Paris: F Alcan, 1895), English trans *The Crowd: A Study of the Popular Mind* (Mineola, NY: Dover Publications, 2002).
Le Fur, L, 'La théorie du droit naturel depuis le XVIIIe siècle et la doctrine moderne' (1927-III) 18 RdC 263–441.

Lehmann, IA, *Peacekeeping and Public Information: Caught in the Crossfire* (London: Frank Cass, 1999).

Leibniz, GW, *Nova Methodus Discendae Docendaeque Jurisprudentiae* [1667] (Francofurti: Zunnerus, 1667).

——, *Codex Juris Gentium Diplomaticus* [1693], English trans '*Codex Iuris Gentium (Praefatio)*' in Riley, P (ed), *Leibniz: Political Writings* (Cambridge: CUP, 2nd edn, 1988) 165–75.

Leiter, B (ed), *Objectivity in Law and Morals* (Cambridge: CUP, 2001).

Lepard, BD, *Customary International Law: A New Theory with Practical Applications* (Cambridge: CUP, 2010).

Lesaffer, R, 'The Grotian Tradition Revisited: Change and Continuity in the History of International Law' (2002) 73 BYBIL 103–39.

Levack, BP, *The Witch-hunt in Early Modern Europe* (Harlow: Pearson Education Ltd, 3rd edn, 2006).

Levi, W, *Contemporary International Law: A Concise Introduction* (Boulder, San Francisco, and Oxford: Westview Press, 2nd edn, 1979).

Levinet, M, 'Dignité contre dignité. L'épilogue de l'affaire du "lancer de nains" devant le Comité des droits de l'homme des Nations Unies' (2003) 55 RTDH 1017–42.

Lévi-Strauss, C, 'The structural study of Myth' in *Structural Anthropologg* (New York: Basic Books, 1963).

——, 'The Story of Asdiwal' in Leach, E (ed), *The Structural Study of Myth and Totemism* (London: Tavistock Publications, 1967).

Lévy-Bruhl, L, *L'âme primitive* [1927] (Paris: Les Presses universitaires de France, 1963), English trans *The 'Soul' of the Primitive* (New York: Macmillan, 1928).

——, *La mentalité primitive* [1922] (Paris: Les Presses universitaires de France, 1960), English trans *Primitive Mentality* (New York: AMS Press, 1978).

Leys, C, *Market Driven Politics: Neoliberal Democracy and the Public Interest* (London: Verso, 2001).

Lieber, F, *Instructions for the Government of Armies of the United States in the Field* (Washington, DC: Government Printing Office, 1898).

Liivoja, R, 'The Scope of the Supremacy Clause of the United Nations Charter' (2008) 57 ICLQ 583–612.

Linderfalk, U, 'Who are "the Parties"? Article 31, Paragraph 3(c) of the 1969 Vienna Convention and the "Principle of Systemic Integration" Revisited' (2008) 55 Neth ILR 343–64.

——, 'State Responsibility and the Primary–Secondary Rules Terminology: The Role of Language for an Understanding of the International Legal System' (2009) 78 Nord JIL 53–72.

——, 'The Creation of *Jus Cogens*: Making Sense of Article 53 of the Vienna Convention' (2011) 71 ZaöRV 359–78.

Lindroos, A, 'Addressing Norm Conflicts in a Fragmented Legal System: The Doctrine of *Lex Specialis*' (2005) 74 Nord JIL 27–66.

—— and Mehling, M, 'Dispelling the Chimera of "Self-contained Regimes" International Law and the WTO' (2005) 16 EJIL 857–77.

Livy, *Ab urbe condita*, English trans *The History of Rome*, at <http://classics.mit.edu/Livy/liv.html>.

Loreto, L, *Il* bellum iustum *e i suoi equivoci: Cicerone e una componente della rappresentazione romana del Völkerrecht antico* (Naples: Jovene, 2001).

Loughlin, M, 'The Functionalist Style in Public Law' (2005) 55 UTLJ 361–403.

—— and Walker, N, *The Paradox of Constitutionalism: Constituent Power and Constitutional Form* (Oxford: OUP, 2007).

Louka, E, 'Precautionary Self-defense and the Future of Preemption in International Law', in Arsanjani, MH (ed), *Looking to the Future: Essays on International Law in Honor of W. Michael Reisman* (Leiden: Nijhoff, 2011) 951–87.

Lowe, V, *Res Judicata* and the Rule of Law in International Arbitration' (1996) 8 RADIC 38–50.

——, Overlapping Jurisdiction in International Tribunals' (1999) 20 Aus YBIL 191–204.
——, Sustainable Development and Unsustainable Arguments' in Boyle, AE and Freestone, D (eds), *International Law and Sustainable Development: Past Achievements and Future Challenges* (Oxford: OUP, 1999) 19–37.
——, 'Corporations as International Actors and International Law Makers' (2004) 14 It YBIL 23–38.
——, *International Law* (Oxford: Clarendon Press, 2007).
Lu, C, 'World Government', Stan EP, at <http://plato.stanford.edu/entries/world-government>.
Lubell, N, *Extraterritorial Use of Force against Non-state Actors* (Oxford: OUP, 2010).
Ludington, S and Gulati, M, 'A Convenient Untruth: Fact and Fantasy in the Doctrine of Odious Debts' (2007–08) 48 Virg JIL 595–639.
Luhmann, N, *Das Recht der Gesellschaft* (Frankfurt am Main: Suhrkamp, 1993), English trans *Law As a Social System* (Oxford: OUP, 2004).
Lysen, G, 'Targeted UN Sanctions: Application of Legal Sources and Procedural Matters' (2003) 72 Nord JIL 291–304.
McClean, JD, *Transnational Organized Crime: A Commentary on the UN Convention and its Protocols* (Oxford: OUP, 2007).
MacCormick, N, *Legal Reasoning and Legal Theory* (Oxford: Clarendon Press, 1978).
——, 'In Praise of Theory' (1997) 29 Ariz SLJ 353–76.
——, *Rhetoric and the Rule of Law: A Theory of Legal Reasoning* (Oxford: OUP, 2005).
McCorquodale, R, 'An Inclusive International Legal System' (2004) 17 LJIL 477–504.
—— and Simons, P, 'Responsibility Beyond Borders: State Responsibility for Extraterritorial Violations by Corporations of International Human Rights Law' (2007) 70 MLR 598–625.
McCrudden, C, 'Human Dignity and Judicial Interpretation of Human Rights' (2008) 19 EJIL 655–724.
McDougal, MS, 'International Law, Power, and Policy: A Contemporary Conception' (1953) 82 RdC 137–259.
McGrady, B, 'Fragmentation of International Law or "Systemic Integration" of Treaty Regimes: EC-biotech Products and the Proper Interpretation of Article 31(3)(c) of the Vienna Convention on the Law of Treaties' (2008) 42 JWT 589–618.
McIlwain, CH, *Constitutionalism, Ancient and Modern* (Ithaca, NY: Cornell University Press, 1940).
MacIntyre, A, *Are There Any Natural Rights?* (Portland: Anthoensen, 1983).
——, *Whose Justice? Which Rationality?* (London: Duckworth, 1988).
Mackenzie, R, *Selecting International Judges: Principle, Process, and Politics* (Oxford: OUP, 2010).
McLachlan, C, 'The Principle of Systematic Integration and Article 31(3)(C) of the Vienna Convention' (2005) 54 ICLQ 279–320.
McNair, AD, *The Law of Treaties* (Oxford: Clarendon Press, 2nd edn, 1961).
Magee, GA, *Hegel and the Hermetic Tradition* (Ithaca: Cornell University Press, 2001).
Malaguti, MC, 'Sovereign Insolvency and International Legal Order' (2009) 11 ICLR 307–26.
Mali, J, *The Rehabilitation of Myth: Vico's 'New Science'* (Cambridge: CUP, 1992).
Malinowski, B, 'Myth in Primitive Psychology' in *Magic, Science and Religion and Other Essays 1948* (Boston: Beacon Press, 1948).
Mallon, R, 'Naturalistic Approaches to Social Construction', Stan EP, at <http://plato.stanford.edu/entries/social-construction-naturalistic/index.html>.
Mandel, M, 'Aggressors' Rights: The Doctrine of "Equality between Belligerents" and the Legacy of Nuremberg' (2011) 24 LJIL 627–50.
Manktelow, K and Chung, M-C (eds), *Psychology of Reasoning: Theoretical and Historical Perspectives* (Hove and New York: Psychology Press, 2004).
Mann, FA, 'The Doctrine of Jurisdiction in International Law' (1964) 111 RdC 1–162.

——, 'The Doctrine of International Jurisdiction Revisited After Twenty Years' (1984) 186 RdC 9–116.
——, *Foreign Affairs in English Courts* (Oxford: Clarendon Press, 1986).
Manner, G, 'The Object Theory of the Individual in International Law' (1952) 46 AJIL 428–49.
Manzoni, A, *I promessi sposi* [1840–42] (Roma: Newton Compton, 2004), English trans *The Betrothed* (London and New York: Penguin Books, 1972).
Mapel, DR and Nardin, T (eds), *International Society: Diverse Ethical Perspectives* (Princeton: Princeton University Press, 1999).
Marks, S (ed), *International Law on the Left: Re-examining Marxist Legacies* (Cambridge: CUP, 2008).
Marston, G, 'Armed Intervention in the 1956 Suez Canal Crisis: The Legal Advice Tendered to the British Government' (1988) 37 ICLQ 773–817.
Martini, C, '"States" Control over New International Organization' (2006) 6 GJA 1–25.
Marwell, JC, 'Trade and Morality: The WTO Public Morals Exception After Gambling' (2006) 81 NYU LR 802–42.
Maslow, AH, 'A Theory of Human Motivation' (1943) 50 *Psychological Review* 370–96.
——, *Motivation and Personality* (New York: Harper, 1954).
Masters, RD and Gruter, M (eds), *The Sense of Justice: Biological Foundations of Law* (Nesbury Park, London, and New Delhi: Sage Publications, 1992).
Mattingly, G, *Renaissance Diplomacy* (Boston: Houghton Mifflin, 1955; repr New York: Dover Publications, 1988).
Matz-Luck, N, 'Harmonization, Systemic Integration, and "Mutual supportiveness" as Conflict-solution Techniques: Different Modes of Interpretation as a Challenge to Negative Effects of Fragmentation?' (2008) 17 Finn YBIL 39–53.
Max-Neef, MA, Elizalde, A, and Hopenhayn, M, *Human Scale Development: Conception, Application and Further Reflections* (New York: Apex, 1991).
Mearsheimer, JJ, *The Tragedy of Great Power Politics* (New York and London: WW Norton and Co, 2001).
Melissaris, E, *Ubiquitous Law: Legal Theory and the Space for Legal Pluralism* (Farnham and Burlington: Ashgate, 2009).
Melzer, AM, Weinberger, J, and Zinman, MR (eds), *History and the Idea of Progress* (Ithaca, NY: Cornell University Press, 1995).
Melzer, N, *Targeted Killing in International Law* (Oxford: OUP, 2008).
Mendelson, MH, 'The Subjective Element in Customary International Law' (1995) 66 BYBIL 177–208.
——, 'The Formation of Customary International Law' (1998) 272 RdC 155–410.
Menon, PK, 'The Legal Personality of Individuals' (1994) 6 Sri Lanka JIL 127–56.
Meron, T, 'Common Rights of Mankind in Gentili, Grotius and Suarez' (1991) 85 AJIL 110–16.
——, 'The Martens Clause, Principles of Humanity, and Dictates of Public Conscience' (2000) 94 AJIL 78–89.
Meyrowitz, H, *Le principe de l'égalité des belligérants devant le droit de la guerre* (Paris: Pédone, 1970).
Michailakis, D, 'Review: Law as an Autopoietic System' (1995) 38 *Acta Sociologica* 323–37.
Midgley, M, *The Myths We Live By* (London and New York: Routledge, 2004).
Miéville, C, *Between Equal Rights: A Marxist Theory of International Law* (London: Pluto Press, 2006).
Milanoric, M, *Extraterritorial Application of Human Rights Treahess: Law Principles and Policy* (Oxford: OUP, 2011).
Miller, D, *National Responsibility and Global Justice* (Oxford: OUP, 2007).
Miller, RA and Bratspies, RM (eds), *Progress in International Law* (Leiden: Nijhoff, 2008).

Minde, H (ed), *Indigenous Peoples: Self-determination Knowledge Indigeneity* (Delft: Eburon, 2008).

Mingers, J, 'Can Social Systems be Autopoietic? Assessing Luhmann's Social Theory' (2002) 50 *Sociological Review* 278–99.

Mirandola, GP della, *Oratio de hominis dignitate* (Bologna: Benedetto Faelli, 1496, English trans *Discourse on the Dignity of Man*, at <http://www.cscs.umich.edu/~crshalizi/Mirandola>.

Mishra, VV, 'Liberalisation of Higher Education Services under the GATS Regime: Implications for a Developing Country' (2009) 42 *Comparative and International Law Journal of Southern Africa* 387–421.

Moghaddam, FM, *From the Terrorists' Point of View: What They Experience and Why They Come to Destroy* (Westport and London: Praeger Security International, 2006).

Monazahian, D, *Vergleich der UNO-Charta mit Immanuel Kant's "Zum ewigen Frieden" und John Rawls "Das Recht der Völker"* (Hamburg: Diplomica Verlag, 2008).

Montesquieu, C-L, baron de La Brède et de Secondat, *De l'esprit des lois* [1748] (Paris: Gallimard, 1995–99) 2 vols, English trans *The Spirit of the Laws* (New York: Macmillan, 1949).

Moore, GE, 'A Defence of Common Sense' in Muirhead, JH (ed), *Contemporary British Philosophy (2nd series)* (London: Allen and Unwin, 1925) 193–223.

——, *Principia Ethica* [1903] (Cambridge: CUP, rev edn, 1993).

Moore, J B (ed), *History and Digest of the International Arbitrations to which the United States Has Been a Party* (Washington, DC: Government Printing office, 1898) vol 3, 2196, 2198–2.

——, *A Digest of International Law* (Washington, DC: Government Printing Office, 1906) vol 2.

Moretti, M, *Le Droit international public et les peoples nomades* (Paris: Editions Publibook, 2006).

Morgan, KA, *Myth and Philosophy from the Presocratic to Plato* (Cambridge: CUP, 2000).

Morgenthau, H, 'Diplomacy' (1946) 55 Yale LJ 1067–80.

——, *Scientific Man vs Power Politics* (Chicago: University of Chicago Press, 1946).

——, *Politics among Nations: The Struggle for Power and Peace* (New York: Knopf, 5th edn, 1973).

Mosler, H and Bernhardt, R (eds), *Judicial Settlement of International Disputes: International Court of Justice, Other Courts and Tribunals, Arbitration and Conciliation: An International Symposium* (Heidelberg and New York: Springer, 1974).

Muchlinski, PT, *Multinational Enterprises and the Law* (Oxford: OUP, 2007).

Mugasha, A, 'Solutions for Developing-Country External Debt: Insolvency or Forgiveness?' (2007) 13 LBRA 859–83.

Muirhead, JH (ed), *Contemporary British Philosophy (2nd series)* (London: Allen and Unwin, 1925).

Muldoon, J, *The Expansion of Europe. The First Phase* (Philadelphia: University of Pennsylvania Press, 1977).

—— (ed), *Popes, Lawyers, and Infidels: The Church and the Non-Christian World, 1250–1550* (Philadelphia: University of Pennsylvania Press, 1979).

Müllerson, RA, *Ordering Anarchy: International Law in International Society* (The Hague: Nijhoff, 2000).

Murphy, L, 'International Responsibility' in Besson, S and Tasioulas, J (eds), *The Philosophy of International Law* (Oxford: OUP, 2010) 299–315.

Myera, SL, 'Echoing Bush, Putin Asks U. N. to Back Georgia Attack' *New York Times*, 12 September, 2002.

Nagel, T, 'The Problem of Global Justice' (2005) 33 *Philosophy and Public Affairs* 113–47.

Nathan, O and Norden H (eds), *Einslein on Peace* (New york: Schocken Books, 1960).

Nederman, CJ, 'Nature, Sin and the Origins of Society: The Ciceronian Tradition in Medieval Political Thought' (1988) 49 JHI 3–26.

Neff, SC, *War and the Law of Nations: A General History* (Cambridge: CUP, 2008).

Nelken, D, 'Eugen Ehrlich, Living Law, and Plural Legalities' (2008) 9 Theoretical Inquiries in Law 443–72.

Nerlich, V, 'Core Crimes and Transnational Business Corporations' (2010) 24 JICJ 895–908.

Newman, M, *Humanitarian Intervention: Confronting the Contradictions* (London: Hurst and Co, 2009).

Ngangjoh-Hodu, Y, 'Relationship of GATT Article XX Exceptions to other WTO Agreements' (2011) 80 Nord JIL 219–34.

Nicol, A, Millar, G, and Sharland, A, *Media Law and Human Rights* (Oxford: OUP, 2nd edn, 2009).

Nietzsche, FW, *Unzeitgemässe Betrachtungen*, II, *Vom Nutzen und Nachteil der Historie für das Leben* (Leipzig: EW Fritzsch, 1874), English trans *Untimely Meditations* (also translated as *Unfashionable Observations*) (Stanford: Stanford University Press, 1995, annotated edn).

Nigro, R, 'La disciplina dei militari impegnati all'estero in missioni umanitarie: in margine al caso Lozano' (2009) 3 *Diritti Umani e Diritto Internazionale* 565–90.

——, 'The Margin of Appreciation Doctrine and the Case-law of the European Court of Human Rights on the Islamic Veil' (2010) 11 HRR 531–64.

——, 'The Notion of "Jurisdiction" in Article 1: Future Scenarios for the Extra-Territorial Application of the European Court of Human Rights' (2011) 20 It YBIL 11–30.

Nijman, JE, *The Concept of International Legal Personality. An Inquiry into the History and Theory of International Law* (The Hague: TMC Asser Press, 2004).

—— and Nollkaemper, A (eds), *New Perspectives on the Divide Between National and International Law* (Oxford: OUP, 2007).

Nollkaemper, A, 'Dual Attribution: Liability of the Netherlands for Removal of Individuals from the Compound of Dutchbat', 2011, at <http://www.sharesproject.nl/dual-attribution-liability-of-the-netherlands-for-removal-of-individuals-from-the-compound-of-dutchbat>.

——, *National Courts and the International Rule of Law* (Oxford and New York: OUP, 2011).

Norman, R, 'Criteria of Justice: Desert, Needs And Equality' (2001) 7 *Res Publica* 115–36.

Norton-Taylor, R, 'Bank Returns Looted Nazi Gold to Albania', *The Guardian*, 30 October 1996.

Novelli, M and Ferus-Comelo, A (eds), *Globalization, Knowledge and Labour: Education for Solidarity within Spaces of Resistance* (New York and Abingdon: Routledge, 2009).

Nowrot, K, 'New Approaches to the International Legal Personality of Multinational Corporations: Towards a Rebuttable Presumption of Normative Responsibilities', 2005, at <http://www.esil-sedi.eu/fichiers/en/Nowrot_513.pdf>.

——, *Normative Ordnungsstruktur und private Wirkungsmacht: Konsequenzen der Beteiligung transnationaler Unternehmen an der Rechtssetzungsprozessen im internationalen Wirtschaftssystem* (Berlin: Berliner Wissenschaftsverlag, 2006).

Nozick, R, *Anarchy, State, and Utopia* (Oxford: Blackwell, 1974) ix.

Nussbaum, A, *A Concise History of the Law of Nations* (New York: Macmillan, 1954).

Nussbaum, MC, *Upheavals of Thought: The Intelligence of Emotions* (Cambridge: CUP, 2001).

——, *Not for Profit: Why Democracy Needs the Humanities* (Princeton and Oxford: Princeton University Press, 2010).

—— and Rorty, AO (eds), *Essays on Aristotle's* De Anima (Oxford: Clarendon Press, 1992).

O'Connell, DP, *State Succession in Municipal Law and International Law* (Cambridge: CUP, 1967).

——, *International Law* (London: Stevens and Sons, 2nd edn, 1970).

O'Connell, ME, 'Crying War' in Bierstecker, TJ, Spiro, PJ, Sriram, CL, and Raffo, V (eds), *International Law and International Relations: Bridging Theory and Practice* (London and New York: Routledge, 2007) 93–110.

——, *The Power and Purpose of International Law: Insights from the Theory and Practice of Enforcement* (Oxford: OUP, 2008).

O'Neill, O, *Constructions of Reason: Explorations of Kant's Practical Philosophy* (Cambridge: CUP, 1990).

Öberg, MD, 'The Absorption of Grave Breaches into War Crimes Law' (2009) 91 IRRC 163–83.

Oberleitner, G, 'Human Security: A Challenge to International Law?' (2005) 11 GG 185–203.

Obokata, T, *Transnational Organised Crime in International Law* (Oxford and Portland: Hart, 2010).

Ochoa, C, 'The Individual and Customary International Law Formation' (2007–08) 48 Virg JIL 119–86.

Odugbemi, Sand Lee, T (eds), *Accountability through Public Opinion: From Inertia to Public Action* (Washington, DC: The World Bank, 2010).

Oellers-Frahm, K, 'Multiplication of International Courts and Tribunals and Conflicting Jurisdiction: Problems and Possible Solutions' (2001) 5 MP YBUNL 67–104.

Oetinger, MFC, *Die Wahrheit des sensus communis oder des allgemeinen Sinnes, in den nach dem Grundtext erklärten Sprüchen und Prediger Salomo oder das beste Haus- und Sittenbuch für Gelehrte und Ungelehrte* (Stuttgart: Ehmann, 1861).

——, *Inquisitio in sensum commune et rationem* [1753] (Stuttgart: Bad Cannstatt, 1964).

Ohmae, K, *The End of the Nation-State: The Rise of Regional Economies* (New York: Simon and Schuster, 1995).

——, *The Borderless World: Power and Strategy in the Interlinked Economy* [1991] (New York: HarperCollins, rev ed, 1999).

Olufemi, E, 'The Relationship Between General and Particular Customary International Law' (1996) 8 AJICL 67–88.

Onuf, NG, *World of Our Making: Rules and Rule in Social Theory and International Relations* (Columbia, SC: University of South Carolina Press, 1989).

Onuma, Y, 'Eurocentrism in the History of International Law' in Onuma, Y (ed), *A Normative Approach to War: Peace, War and Justice in Hugo Grotius* (Oxford: Clarendon Press, 1993) 371–86.

——, 'When Was the Law of International Society Born? An Inquiry of the History of International Law from an Intercivilizational Perspective' (2000) 2 JHIL 1–66.

——, *A Transcivilizational Perspective on International Law: Questioning Prevalent Cognitive Frameworks in the Emerging Multi-polar and Multi-civilizational World of the Twenty-first Century* (Leiden: Nijhoff, 2010).

Oppenheim, LFL *International Law: A Treatise* (London: Longmans, 1st edn, 1905).

——, *International Law* (London and New York: Longmans, 3rd edn, 1920).

Orakhelashvili, A, *Peremptory Norms in International Law* (Oxford: OUP, 2006).

——, 'Natural Law and Justice', MP EPIL (August 2007 update).

—— (ed), *Research Handbook on the Theory and History of International Law* (Cheltenham: Elgar, 2011).

——, 'The Idea of European International Law' (2006) 17 EJIL 315–47.

Orford, A (ed), *International Law and Its Others* (Cambridge: CUP, 2006).

——, *International Authority and the Responsibility to Protect* (Cambridge: CUP, 2011).

Osiander, A, *The States System of Europe, 1640–1990: Peacemaking and the Conditions of International Stability* (Oxford: Clarendon Press, 1994).

——, *Before the State: Systemic Political Change in the West from the Greeks to the French Revolution* (Oxford and New York: OUP, 2007).

Pahuja, S, *Decolonising International Law: Development, Economic Growth and the Politics of Universality* (Cambridge: CUP, 2011).

Panizzon, M, *Good Faith in the Jurisprudence of the WTO: The Protection of Legitimate Expectations, Good Faith Interpretation and Fair Dispute Settlement* (Oxford: Hart, 2006).

Pardo, A, *The Common Heritage: Selected Papers on Oceans and World Order 1967–1974* (Malta: Malta University Press, 1975).

Paris, R, 'Human Security: Paradigm Shift or Hot Air?' (2001) 26(2) *International Security* 87–102.

Parlett, K, *The Individual in the International Legal System: Continuity and Change in International Law* (Cambridge: CUP, 2011).

Parnas, J, Bovet, P, and Zahavi, D, 'Schizophrenic Autism: Clinical Phenomenology and Pathogenetic Implications' (2002) 1 *World Psychiatry* 131–6.

Passerin D'Entrèves, A, 'Legality and Legitimacy' (1963) 16 Review of Metaphysics 687–702.

——, *Natural Law: An Introduction to Legal Philo*sophy [1951] (New Brunswick and London: Transaction Publishers, 1994).

Patterson, E, 'Just War in the 21st Century: Reconceptualizing Just War Theory After September 11' (2005) 42 *International Politics* 116–34.

Paulson, C, 'Compliance with Final Judgments of the International Court of Justice since 1987' (2004) 98 AJIL 434–61.

Paulson, SL, 'On the Background and Significance of Gustav Radbruch's Post-War Papers' (2006) 26 OJLS 17–40.

Paulus, AL, *Die internationale Gemeinschaft im Völkerrecht: Eine Untersuchung zur Entwicklung des Völkerrechts im Zeitalters der Globalisierung* (Munich: Beck, 2001).

——, 'Potential and Limits of the Economic Analysis of International Law: A View from Public International Law' (2009) 165 JITE 170–84.

——, 'The International Legal System as a Constitution' in Dunoff, JL and Trachtman, JP (eds), *Ruling the World? Constitutionalism, International Law, and Global Governance* (Cambridge, CUP, 2009) 69–109.

Paust, JJ, 'Self-Executing Treaties' (1988) 82 AJIL 760–83.

——, 'Terrorism's Proscription and Core Elements of an Objective Definition' (2010) 8 *Santa Clara* JIL 51–67.

Pauwelyn, J, 'The Role of Public International Law in the WTO: How Far Can We Go?' (2001) 95 AJIL 535–78.

Payandeh, M, 'The Concept of International Law in the Jurisprudence of H.L.A. Hart' (2010) 21 EJIL 967–95.

Pearson, Z, 'NGOs and International Law: New Mechanisms for Governance?' (2004) 23 Aus YBIL 73–103.

Peck, C and Lee, RS (eds), *Increasing the Effectiveness of the International Court of Justice: Proceedings of the ICJ/UNITAR Colloquium To Celebrate The 50th Anniversary of The Court* (The Hague: Nijhoff, 1997).

Perelman, C, *Logique juridique, nouvelle rhétorique* (Paris: Dalloz, 1976).

—— and Olbrechts-Tyteca, L, *Traité de l'argumentation. La nouvelle rhétorique* (Paris: Presses universitaires de France, 1958), English trans *The New Rhetoric: A Treatise on Argumentation* (Notre Dame: University of Notre Dame Press, 1991).

Pergantis, V, 'Towards a "Humanization" of Diplomatic Protection?' (2006) 66 ZaöRV 351–97.

Perreau-Saussine, A and Murphy, JB (eds), *The Nature of Customary Law: Legal, Historical and Philosophical Perspectives* (Cambridge: CUP, 2007).

Perry, MJ, *The Idea of Human Rights: Four Inquiries* (Oxford: OUP, 1998).

Peters, A, 'Compensatory Constitutionalism: The Function and Potential of Fundamental International Norms and Structure' (2006) 19 LJIL 579–610.

——, 'Treaty-Making Power', MP EPIL (March 2009 update).

——, 'Does Kosovo Lie in the Lotus-Land of Freedom?' (2011) 24 LJIL 95–108.

——, 'The Responsibility to Protect: Spelling out the Hard Legal Consequences for the UN Security Council and its Members' in Fastenrath, U, Geiger, R, Khan D-E, Paulus, A, Schorlemer, S von, and C. Vedder (eds), *From Bilateralism to Community Interest: Essays in Honour of Judge Bruno Simma* (Oxford: OUP, 2011) 297–325.

Peters, E, *Torture* (Philadelphia: University of Pennsylvania Press, exp edn 1996).

Petersmann, E-U, 'The WTO Constitution and Human Rights' (2000) 3 JIEL 19–26.

——, 'Taking Human Dignity, Poverty and Empowerment of Individuals More Seriously: Rejoinder to Alston' (2002) 13 EJIL 845–51.

——, 'Human Rights, International Economic Law and "Constitutional Justice"' (2008) 19 EJIL 769–98.

Petman, J and Klabbers, J, (eds), *Nordic Cosmopolitanism: Essays in International Law for Martti Koskenniemi* (Leiden: Nijhoff, 2003).

Petrescu, IM, 'Rethinking Economic Sanctions Success: Sanctions as Deterrent' (Washington, DC: AEI, 2008) at <http://www.aei.org/docLib/111009sanctions.pdf>.

Phillipson, R, 'Lingua franca or lingua frankensteinia? English in European Integration and Globalisation' (2008) 27 *World Englishes* 250–67.

Picone, P, 'La "guerra del Kosovo" e il diritto internazionale generale' (2000) 83 RDI 309–60.

——, 'Le autorizzazioni all'uso della forza tra sistema delle Nazioni Unite e diritto internazionale generale' (2005) 88 RDI 5–75.

——, *Comunità internazionale e obblighi* 'erga omnes': *Studi critici di diritto internazionale* (Naples: Jovene, 2006).

——, 'The Distinction between *Jus Cogens* and Obligations *Erga Omnes*' in Cannizzaro, E (ed), *The Law of Treaties beyond the Vienna Convention* (Oxford: OUP, 2011) 411–24.

Pildes, RH, 'Conflicts Between American and European Views of Law: The Dark Side of Legalism' (2003–04) 44 Virg JIL 145–67.

Plant, R, *The Neo-liberal State* (Oxford and New York: OUP, 2009).

Plato, *Gorgias*, English trans at <http://classics.mit.edu/Plato/gorgias.html>.

——, *Laws*, English trans at <http://classics.mit.edu/Plato/laws.html>.

——, *Protagoras*, English trans at <http://classics.mit.edu/Plato/protagoras.html>.

——, *Statesman*, English trans at <http://classics.mit.edu/Plato/stateman.html>.

——, *Symposium*, English trans at <http://classics.mit.edu/Plato/symposium.html>.

——, *The Republic*, English trans at <http://classics.mit.edu/Plato/republic.html>.

——, *Theaetetus*, English trans at <http://classics.mit.edu/Plato/theatu.html>.

——, *Timaeus*, English trans at <http://classics.mit.edu/Plato/timaeus.html>.

Plotinus, *The Six Enneads*, English trans at <http://classics.mit.edu/Plotinus/enneads.html>.

Plotkin, HC, *Evolution in Mind: An Introduction to Evolutionary Psychology* (London: Penguin, 1997).

Plutarch, *Alexander*, English trans *The Life of Alexander the Great* (New York and Toronto: Modern Library, 2004), at <http://classics.mit.edu/Plutarch/alexandr.html>.

——, *De Gloria Atheniensium*, English trans *On the Fame of Athenians*, at <http://penelope.uchicago.edu/Thayer/E/Roman/Texts/Plutarch/Moralia/De_gloria_Atheniensium*.html#copyright>.

Pogge, T (ed), *Freedom from Poverty as a Human Right: Who Owes What to the Very Poor?* (Oxford: OUP, 2007).

—— and Menko, W (eds), *Incentives for Global Public Health: Patent Law and Access to Essential Medicines* (Cambridge: CUP, 2010).

—— and Moellendorf, D (eds), *Global Justice: Seminal Essays* (St Paul: Paragon House, 2008) vol 1.

Poggi, G, *The Development of the Modern State: A Sociological Introduction* (London: Hutchinson, 1978).

——, *The State, Its Nature, Development and Prospects* (Cambridge: Polity Press, 1990).

Politis, N, *Les nouvelles tendances du droit international* (Paris: Hachette, 1927).

——, *The New Aspects of International Law* (Washington, DC: Carnegie Endowment for International Peace, 1928).

Portmann, R, *Legal Personality in International Law* (Cambridge: CUP, 2010).

Posner, EA, *The Perils of Global Legalism* (Chicago and London: University of Chicago Press, 2009).

Postema, GJ, 'Implicit Law' (1994) 13 Law and Philosophy 361–87.

Pound, R, 'Mechanical Jurisprudence' (1908) 8 Col LR 605–23.

——, 'The Scope and Purpose of Sociological Jurisprudence' (1911) 25 Harv LR 489–516.

Powell, SJ, 'The Place of Human Rights in World Trade Organization Rules' (2004) 16 Flo JIL 219–31.
Price, ME, *Media and Sovereignty: The Global Information Revolution and the Challenge to State Power* (Cambridge, Mass: MIT Press, 2002).
Prost, M, *The Concept of Unity in Public International Law* (Oxford: Hart, forthcoming).
Pufendorf, S, *De Systematibus Civitatum*, in *Dissertationae Accademicae Selectiores* (Upsaliae: [s.n.], 1677).
—— [Severino da Monzambano], *De Statu Imperii Germanici* (1667, rev edn 1684), English trans *The Present State of Germany, or an Account of the Extent, Rise, Form, Wealth, Strength, Weaknesses and Interests of that Empire* (London: Chiswell, 1690).
——, *Elementa Jurisprudentiae Universalis Libri Duo* [1660], English trans *The Elements of Universal Jurisprudence Two Books* (Oxford and London: Clarendon Press and Humphrey Milford, 1931).
——, *De Iure Naturae et Gentium Libri Octo* [1672], English trans *Of the Law Of Nature And Nations, Eight Books* (Oxford and London: Clarendon Press and Humphrey Milford, 1934).
Purvis, N, 'Critical Legal Studies in Public International Law' (1991) 32 Harv ILJ 81–127.
Quackenbush, SL, 'The Rationality of Rational Choice Theory' (2004) 30 *International Interactions* 87–107.
Quadri, R, 'Le fondement du caractère obligatoire du droit international public' (1952-I) 80 RdC 579–633.
——, *Diritto internazionale pubblico* (Naples: Liguori, 5th edn, 1968).
Quintilian, *Institutes of Oratory*, English trans *Quintilian's Institutes of Oratory: Or, Education of an Orator*, at <http://rhetoric.eserver.org/quintilian>.
Raab, D, '"Armed Attack" after the Oil Platforms Case' (2004) 17 LJIL 719–35.
Rabkin, JA, *Law without Nations?: Why Constitutional Government Requires Sovereign States* (Princeton: Princeton University Press, 2005).
Rabo, A and Utas, B (eds), *The Rule of the State in West Asia* (Stockholm: Swedish Research Institute in Istanbul, 2005).
Radbruch, G. 'Gesetzliches Unrecht und übergesetzliches Recht' (1946) *Süddeutsche Juristen-Zeitung* 105–8, Englishmans 'Statutory Laudessness and Supra-Statutory Law (1946)' (2006) 26 OJLS 1, 7.
Rae, H, *State Identities and the Homogenisation of Peoples* (Cambridge: CUP, 2002).
Ragazzi M, *The Concept of International Obligations* Erga Omnes (Oxford: Clarendon Press, 1997).
—— (ed), *International Responsibility Today: Essays in Memory of Oscar Schachter* (Leiden: Nijhoff, 2005).
Rahnema, M, 'Global Poverty: A Pauperizing Myth' (1992) 24 *Interculture* 4–51.
Rajagopal, B, 'International Law and Social Movements: Challenges of Theorizing Resistance', (2003) 41 Col JTL 397–433.
——, *International Law from Below: Development, Social Movements and Third World Resistance* (Cambridge: CUP, 2003).
Rama-Montaldo, M, 'International Legal Personality and Implied Powers of International Organizations' (1970) 44 BYBIL 111–55.
Rasulov, A, 'Revisiting State Succession to Humanitarian Treaties: Is There a Case for Automaticity?' (2003) 14 EJIL 141–70.
Ratner, SR, 'Law Promotion Beyond Law Talk: The Red Cross, Persuasion, and the Laws of War' (2011) 22 EJIL 459–506.
Rawls, J, 'Kantian Constructivism in moral Theory' (1980) 77 JPB 515.
Rawls, J, *A Theory of Justice* (Cambridge, Mass: The Belknap Press of Harvard University Press, rev edn, 1999).
——, *The Law of Peoples* (Cambridge, Mass, and London: Harvard University Press, 1999).

Raz, J, *The Concept of a Legal System: An Introduction to the Theory of Legal Systems* (Oxford: Clarendon Press, 2nd edn, 1980).
—— (ed), *Authority* (New York: New York University Press, 1990).
——, *The Authority of Law: Essays on Law and Morality* (Oxford: OUP, 2009).
Rebasti, E, 'Beyond Consultative Status: Which Legal Framework for an Enhanced Interaction Between NGOs and Intergovernmental Organizations?' in Dupuy, P-M and Vierucci, L (eds), *NGOs in International Law: Efficiency and Flexibility* (Northampton: Edward Elgar, 2008) 21–70.
Reed, L, 'The Media's Portrayal of International Law' (2001) 95 ASIL Proc 216–17.
Reichberg, GM, 'Preventive War in Classical Just War Theory' (2007) 9 JHIL 5–34.
Reid, T, *An Inquiry Into the Human Mind* [1794] (Edinburgh: Edinburgh University Press, 2010).
Reiff, MR, *Punishment, Compensation, and the Law: A Theory of Enforceability* (New York: CUP, 2005).
Reinisch, A. *International Organizations Before National Courts* (Cambridge: CUP, 2000).
——, 'The Use and Limits of *Res Judicata* and *Lis Pendens* as Procedural Tools to Avoid Conflicting Dispute Settlement Outcomes' (2004) 3 LPICT 37–77.
—— (ed), *Challenging Acts of International Organizations before National Courts* (Oxford: OUP, 2010).
Reinold, T, 'State Weakness, Irregular Warfare, and the Right to Self-defense Post-9/11' (2011) 105 AJIL 244–86.
Reisman, WM, 'When are Economic Sanctions Effective? Selected Theorums and Corollaries' (1995–96) 2 ILSA JICL 587.
—— (ed), *Jurisdiction in International Law* (Aldershot: Ashgate, 1999).
Rescher, N, *Value Matters: Studies in Axiology* (Frankfurt: Ontos Verlag, 2005).
Reuter, P, 'La personnalité juridique internationale du Comité international de la Croix-Rouge' in Swinarski, C (ed), *Studies and Essays on International Humanitarian Law and Red Cross Principles in Honour of Jean Pictet* (Dordrecht: Nijhoff, 1984) 783–91.
Reynolds, J, 'Common Sense and Philosophical Methodology: Some Metaphilosophical Reflections on Analytic Philosophy and Deleuze' (2010) 41 *Philosophical Forum* 231–58.
Ricardo, D, *On the Principles of Political Economy and Taxation* (London: John Murray, 1817).
Riedel, B, *The Search for Al Qaeda: Its Leadership, Ideology, and Future* (Washington, DC: Brookings Institution Press, 2nd edn, 2010).
Rieff, D, *A Bed for the Night: Humanitarianism in Crisis* (New York: Simon & Schuster, 2002).
Riley, P (ed), *Leibniz: Political Writings* (Cambridge: CUP, 2nd edn, 1988).
Roach, JA, 'Countering Piracy off Somalia: International Law and International Institutions' (2010) 104 AJIL 397–416.
Roberts, A, 'The Civilian in Modern War' (2010) 12 YBIHL 13–52.
——, 'Comparative International Law? The Role of National Courts in Creating and Enforcing International Law' (2011) 60 ICLQ 57–92.
Robertson, J, 'Empire and Union: Two Concepts of the Early Modern European Political Order' in Robertson, J (ed), *A Union for Empire: Political Thought and the British Union of 1707* (Cambridge: CUP, 1995) 3–36.
Robinson, P, 'The CNN Effect: Can the News Media Drive Foreign Policy?' (1999) 25 RIS 301–9.
Rodrik, O, *The Globalization Paradox: Why Global Markets, States, and Denocracy Cant Coexist* (Oxford and New York: OUP, 2011).
Rolfe, JC, *Cicero and His Influence* (New York: Longmans, Green & Co, 1928).
Romano, C, 'PICT Synoptic Chart', at <http://www.pict-pcti.org>.
Romano, S, *Corso di diritto internazionale* (Padua: Cedam, 4th edn, 1939).
——, *L'ordinamento giuridico* (Florence: Sansoni, 2nd edn, 1962).
Rona, G, 'The ICRC Privilege not to Testify: Confidentiality in Action' (2002) 84 IRRC 207–19.

Ronzitti, N, 'Compensation for Violations of the Law of War and Individual Claims' (2002) 12 It YBIL 39–50.
Root, E, 'The Need of Popular Understanding of International Law' (1907) 1 AJIL 1–3.
Rosati, CS, 'Some Puzzles about the Objectivity of Law' (2004) 23 *Law and Philosophy* 273–323.
Roscini, M, 'Threats of Armed Force and Contemporary International Law' (2007) 54 Neth ILR 229–77.
Rosenau, JN, 'Governance, Order, and Change in World Politics' in Rosenau, JN and Czempiel, E-O (eds), *Governance Without Government: Order and Change in World Politics* (Cambridge: CUP, 1992) 1–29.
——, 'Toward an Ontology for Global Governance' in Hawson, M and Sinclair, T (eds), *Approaches to Global Governance Theory* (Albany: State University of New York Press, 1999) 287–301.
—— and Czempiel E-O (eds), *Governance Without Government: Order and Change in World Politics* (Cambridge: CUP, 1992).
Rosenne, S, *Practice and Methods of International Law* (London: Oceana Publications, 1984).
Ross, A, *On Law and Justice* (London: Stevens and Sons, 1958).
Rubin, AP, *Ethics and Authority in International Law* (Cambridge: CUP, 1997).
——, *The Law of Piracy* (Irvington-on-Hudson, NY: Transnational Publishers, 2nd edn, 1998).
Ruggie, JG, 'Territoriality and Beyond: Problematizing Modernity in International Relations' (1993) 47 *International Organization* 139–74.
——, 'What Makes the World Hang Together? Neo-utilitarianism and the Social Constructivist Challenge' (1998) 52 *International Organization* 855–85.
Rundle, K, 'The Impossibility of an Exterminatory Law: Law and the Holocaust' (2009) 59 UTLJ 65–125.
Ryngaert, C, *Jurisdiction in International Law* (Oxford: OUP, 2008).
——, 'The Immunity of International Organizations Before Domestic Courts: Recent Trends' (2010) 7 IOLR 121–48.
Sabel, R, *Procedure at International Conferences* (Cambridge: CUP, 2nd edn, 2006).
Saechao, TR, 'Natural Disasters and the Responsibility to Protect: From Chaos to Clarity' (2007) 32 Brooklyn JIL 663–707.
Salmon, J (ed), 'Positivisme Juridique', *Dictionnaire de droit international public* (Brussels: Bruylant, 2001).
Salomon, M, *Global Responsibility for Human Rights* (Oxford: OUP, 2007).
Samuel, G, *Epistemology and Method in Law* (Aldershot: Ashgate, 2003).
Samuelson, PA, 'The Gains from International Trade' (1939) 5 Can JEPS 195–205.
Sánchez, PAF (ed), *International Legal Dimension of Terrorism* (Leiden: Nijhoff, 2009).
Sandel, MJ, *Justice: What's the Right Thing to Do?* (New York: Ferrar, Straus and Giroux, 2009).
Sandoz, Y, *International Committee of the Red Cross: The International Committee of the Red Cross as Guardian of International Humanitarian Law* (Geneva: ICRC, 1998).
Sands, PJ, *Principles of International Environmental Law* (Cambridge: CUP, 2nd edn, 2003).
—— and Klein, P, *Bowrett's Law of International Institutions* (London: Sweet & Maxwell, 6th edn, 2009) 476.
Saner, R and Guilherme, R, 'The International Monetary Fund's Influence on Trade Policies of Low-income Countries: A Valid Undertaking?' (2007) 41 JWT 931–81.
Sarkar, R, *International Development Law: Rule of Law, Human Rights, and Global Finance* (Oxford: OUP, 2009).
Satz, D, *Why Some Things Should Not Be for Sale: The Moral Limits of Markets* (Oxford: OUP, 2010).
Saul, B, *Defining Terrorism in International Law* (Oxford: OUP, 2006).
Scelle, G, 'La doctrine de L. Duguit et les fondements du droit des gens' (1932) 2 *Archives de Philosophie du Droit et de Sociologie Juridique* 83–119.
——, *Précis de droit des gens: principes et systématique* (Paris: Sirey, 1932–34).

——, *Théorie du gouvernement international* (Paris: Presses Universitaires de France, 1934).
——, *Manuel élémentaire de droit international public* (Paris: Domat-Montchrestien, 1943).
——, *Manuel de droit international public* (Paris: Domat-Montchrestien, 1948).
——, 'Le phénomène juridique du dédoublement fonctionnel' in Schätzel, W and Schlochauer, H-J (eds), *Rechtsfragen der internationalen Organisation: Festschrift für Hans Wehberg zu seinem 70. Geburtstag* (Frankfurt am Main: Klostermann, 1956) 324–42.
Schabas, WA and Bernaz, N (eds), *Routledge Handbook of International Criminal Law* (London: Routledge, 2011).
Schachter, O, 'The Enforcement of International Judicial and Arbitral Decisions' (1960) 54 AJIL 1–24.
——, 'Towards a Theory of International Obligation' (1968) 8 Virg JIL 300–322.
——, 'The Invisible College of International Lawyers' (1977) 72 NwU LR 217–26.
——, 'Human Dignity as a Normative Concept' (1983) 77 AJIL 848–54.
Scheler, M, *Wesen und Formen der Sympathie: Die Deutsche Philosophie der Gegenwart* [1923] (Bern and Munich: Francke, 1973), English trans *The Nature of Sympathy* (New Brunswick and London: Transaction Publishers, 2008).
Schelling, FWJ von, *Philosophie der Mythologie—in drei Vorlesungsnachschriften* [1842] (Munich: Fink 1996), English trans *Historical-Critical Introduction to the Philosophy of Mythology* (Albany: State University of New York Press, 2007).
Schmid, A, 'Terrorism: The Definitional Problem' (2004) 36 CWR JIL 375–419.
Schmitt, C, *Der Begriff des Politischen* [1932] (Berlin: Duncker & Humblot, 1991), English trans *The Concept of the Political* (New Brunswick: Rutgers University Press, 1976).
——, 'Der Gegensatz von Parlamentarismus und moderner Massendemokratie' in Schmitt, C, *Positionen und Begriffe im Kampf mit Weimar—Genf—Versailles 1923–1939* [1926] (Berlin: Duncker & Humblot, 1988).
——, *Legalität und Legitimität* (Munich: Duncker & Humblot, 1932), English trans *Legality and Legitimacy* (Durham and London: Duke University Press, 2004).
Schofield, M, *The Stoic Idea of the City* (Chicago and London: University of Chicago Press, 1999).
Schreuer, CH, 'The Relevance of United Nations Decisions in Domestic Litigation' (1978) 27 ICLQ 1–17.
——, 'The Waning of the Sovereign State: Towards a New Paradigm for International Law?' (1994) 4 EJIL 447–71.
Schuett, R, *Political Realism, Freud, and Human Nature in International Relations: The Resurrection of the Realist Man* (London: Palgrave Macmillan, 2010).
Schulte, C, *Compliance with Decisions of the International Court of Justice* (Oxford: OUP, 2004).
Schultz, N, 'Was the War on Iraq Illegal? The German Federal Administrative Court's Judgment of 21st June 2005' (2005) 7 Ger LJ 25–44.
Schutz, A, 'Common-sense and Scientific Interpretation in Human Action' (1953) 14 PPR 1–38.
——, *Collected Papers* (The Hague: Nihjoff, 1973).
Schwarzenberger, G, 'Jus Pacis Ac Belli?: Prolegomena to a Sociology of International Law' (1943) 37 AJIL 460–479.
——, 'International Law and Society' (1947) 1 YBWA 159–77.
——, *International Law as Applied by International Courts and Tribunals* (London: Stevens and Sons, 3rd edn, 1957).
Schwebel, SM, 'Commentary' in Bulterman, MK and Kuijer, M (eds), *Compliance with Judgments of International Courts* (The Hague: Nijhoff, 1996) 39–42.
Schwelb, E, 'The "Actio Popularis" and International Law' (1972) 2 Is YBHR 46–56.
Schwietzke, J, 'Fourteen Points of Wilson (1918)', MP EPIL (March 2007 update).
Scicluna, HP, *A Short History of the Knights Hospitaller of St. John, of Jerusalem, of Rhodes, and of Malta* (Floriana, Malta: Catholic Institute, 1970).

Searle, JR, *The Construction of Social Reality* (New York: The Free Press, 1995).
——, *Making the Social World: The Structure of Human Civilization* (Oxford: OUP, 2010).
Sebenius, JK, 'Challenging Conventional Explanations of International Cooperation: Negotiation Analysis and the Case of Epistemic Communities' (1992) 46 *International Organization* 323–65.
Sen, A, 'Human Rights and the Limits of Law' (2006) 27 Card LR 2913–27.
Seneca, *Epistulae morales ad Lucilium*, at <http://www.intratext.com/X/LAT0230.HTM>, English trans at <http://www.archive.org/stream/adluciliumepistu01seneuoft#page/n7/mode/2up>.
Seyersted, F, 'International Personality of Intergovernmental Organizations: Do Their Capacities Really Depend upon Their Constitutions?' (1964) 4 Indian JIL 1–74.
——, *Common Law of International Organizations* (Leiden: Nijhoff, 2008).
Shaftesbury, AAC, Earl of, *Characteristics of Men, Manners, Opinions, Times* [1711] (Cambridge, CUP, 1999).
Shahabuddeen, M, *Precedent in the World Court* (Cambridge: CUP, 2007).
Shany, Y, 'Compliance with Decisions of International Courts as Indicative of Their Effectiveness: A Goal-Based Analysis', Hebrew University of Jerusalem Faculty of Law Research Paper No 04–10, at <http://papers.ssrn.com/sol3/papers.cfm?abstract_id=1697488>.
——, *The Competing Jurisdictions of International Courts and Tribunals* (Oxford: OUP, 2003).
Shapiro, SJ, *Legality* (Cambridge, Mass and London: Harvard University Press, 2011).
Shelton, D, *Commitment and Compliance: The Role of Non-binding Norms in the International Legal System* (Oxford: OUP, 2000).
——, 'Normative Hierarchy in International Law' (2006) 100 AJIL 291–321.
—— (ed), *International Law and Domestic Legal Systems: Incorporation, Transformation, and Persuasion* (Oxford and New York: OUP, 2011).
Shue, H, *Basic Rights: Subsistence, Affluence, and U.S. Foreign Policy* (Princeton: Princeton University Press, 2nd edn, 1996).
Sicilianos, L-A, 'Entre multilatéralisme et unilatéralisme: l'autorisation par le Conseil de sécurité de recourir à la force' (2008) 339 RdC 9–436.
Simma, B, 'The Antarctic Treaty as a Treaty Creating an "Objective Regime"' (1985–86) 19 Corn ILJ 189–209.
—— and Alston, P, 'The Sources of Human Rights Law: Custom, *Jus Cogens* and General Principles' (1988–89) 12 Aus YBIL 81–108.
—— and Paulus, AL, 'The "International Community": Facing the Challenge of Globalization' (1998) 9 EJIL 266–77.
—— and Paulus, AL, 'The Responsibility of Individuals for Human Rights Abuses in Internal Conflicts: A Positivist View' (1999) 93 AJIL 302–16.
—— and Pulkowski, D, 'Of Planets and the Universe: Self-contained Regimes in International Law' (2006) 17 EJIL 483–529.
Sinclair, IR, *The Vienna Convention on the Law of Treaties* (Manchester: Manchester University Press, 2nd edn, 1984).
Sire, HJA, *The Knights of Malta* (New Haven and London: Yale University Press, 1994).
Skinner, Q, 'The State', in T Ball, J Farr, and RL Hanson (eds), *Political Innovation and Conceptual Change* (Cambridge: Cup, 1989).
Skouteris, T, *The Notion of Progress in International Law Discourse* (The Hague: TMC Asser Press, 2010).
Slaughter, A-M, *A New World Order* (Princeton and Oxford, Princeton University Press, 2004).
—— and Burke-White, W, 'An International Constitutional Moment' (2002) 43 Harv ILJ 1–22.
—— and Ratner, SR (eds), 'Symposium on Method in International Law' (1999) 93 AJIL 291–423.
Slomp, G, 'Carl Schmitt's Five Arguments against the Idea of Just War' (2006) 19 CRIA 435–47.

Sloss, D, *The Role of Domestic Courts in Treaty Enforcement: A Comparative Study* (Cambridge: CUP, 2009).
—— (ed), 'United States' in Sloss, D (ed), *The Role of Domestic Courts in Treaty Enforcement: A Comparative Study* (Cambridge: CUP, 2009).
Slye, RC, 'Corporations, Veils, and International Criminal Liability' (2007–08) 33 Brooklyn JIL 955–73.
Soeteman, A, *Logic in Law: Remarks on Logic and Rationality in Normative Reasoning, Especially in Law* (Dordrecht: Kluwer, 1989).
Sonnenfeld, R, *Resolutions of the United Nations Security Council* (Dordrecht: Nijhoff, 1987).
Sono, K and Fujioka, Y, 'The Role of the Abuse of Right Doctrine in Japan' (1975) 35 Lou LR 1037.
Sophocles, *Antigone* (Clayton: Prestwick House, 2005).
Sørensen, M, 'Principes de droit international public: cours général' (1960-III) 101 RdC 6–254.
Sousa Santos, B de, *Toward a New Legal Common Sense* (London: Butterworths, 2nd edn, 2002).
Spitzer, RM, 'The African Holocaust: Should Europe Pay Reparations to Africa for Colonialism and Slavery?' (2002) 35 Van JTL 1319–47.
Spruyt, H, *The Sovereign State and Its Competitors* (Princeton: Princeton University Press, 1994).
Staggenborg, S, *Social Movements* (New York and Oxford: OUP, 2010).
Stahn, C, *The Law and Practice of International Territorial Administration* (Cambridge: CUP, 2008).
——, Olásolo, H, and Gibson, K, 'Participation of Victims in Pre-trial Proceedings of the ICC' (2006) 4 JICJ 219–38.
Stair, J, *Institutions of the Law of Scotland* [1893] (New Haven: Yale University Press, 1981).
Stanghellini, G, 'At Issue: Vulnerability to Schizophrenia and Lack of Common Sense' (2000) 26 *Schizophrenia Bulletin* 775–87.
——, *Disembodied Spirits and Deanimated Bodies: The Psychopathology of Common Sense* (Oxford: OUP, 2004).
Stavropoulos, N, *Objectivity in Law* (Oxford and New York: Clarendon Press, 1996).
Steinerte, E and Wallace, R, 'Jones v. Ministry of Interior of the Kingdom of Saudi Arabia' (2006) 100 AJIL 901–8.
Steinhardt, RG, 'The Role of International Law As a Canon of Domestic Statutory Construction' (1996) 43 Van LR 1103.
——, 'Soft Law, Hard Markets: Competitive Self-Interest and the Emergence of Human Rights Responsibilities for Multinational Corporations'(2007–08) 33 Brooklyn JIL 933–53.
Steinitz, M, '"The *Milošević* Trial—Live!": An Iconical Analysis of International Law's Claim of Legitimate Authority' (2005) 2 JICJ 103–23.
Stern, B, case report (1999) 93 AJIL 525–9.
Stern, DN, *The Interpersonal World of the Infant* (New York: Basic Books, 1985).
Stevens, J, 'Sigmund Freud and International Law' (2006) 2 LCH 201–17.
Stevenson, L and Haberman, DL, *Ten Theories of Human Nature* (New York: OUP, 5th edn, 2009).
Stiglitz, JE, *Freefall: Free Markets and the Sinking of the Global Economy* (New York: Norton, 2010).
Stobaeus, *Eclogarum Physicarum et Ethicarum Libri Duo*, English trans *Physical and Moral Extracts (Eclognis')*, I, 50. (Lipsiae: Teubner, 1860–64).
Stone, CD, 'Common but Differentiated Responsibilities in International Law' (2004) 98 AJIL 276–301.
Stone, J, 'Problems Confronting Sociological Enquiries Concerning International Law' (1956) 89 RdC 65–179.
Stone, RW, 'The Scope of IMF Conditionality' (2008) 62 *International Organization* 589–620.

Strange, S, *The Retreat of the State: The Diffusion of Power in the World Economy* (Cambridge: CUP, 1996).

Strauss, S, 'Darfur and the Genocide Debate' (2005) 84 *Foreign Affairs* 123–33.

Strayer, JR, *On the Medieval Origins of the Modern State* (Princeton and Oxford: Princeton University Press, 1970).

Strupp, K, 'Les règles générales du droit de la paix' (1934) 47 RdC 263–595.

Stürchler, N, *The Threat of Force in International Law* (Cambridge: CUP, 2007).

Suárez, F, *De Legibus ac Deo Legislatore* [1612], English trans in *Selections from Three Works of Francisco Suarez* (Oxford: Clarendon Press, 1944).

——, *De Triplici Virtute Theologica* [1621], in *Selections from Three Works of Francisco Suarez* (Oxford: Clarendon Press, 1944).

Summers, C, 'NAFTA's Labor side Agrement and International Labor Standards' (1999) 3 JSESBL 173.

Summers, J, 'Relativizing Sovereignty: Remedial Secession and Humanitarian Intervention in International Law' (2010) 6 SAIR 16–36.

Sunstein, CR and Nussbaum, MC (eds), *Animal Rights: Current Debates and New Directions* (Oxford and New York: OUP, 2004).

Sussman, DG, *The Idea of Humanity: Anthropology and Anthroponomy in Kant's Ethics* (New York and London: Routledge, 2001).

Sweet, AS, 'Constitutionalism, Legal Pluralism, and International Regimes' (2009) 16 Ind JGLS 621–45.

Swinarski, C (ed), *Studies and Essays on International Humanitarian Law and Red Cross Principles in Honour of Jean Pictet* (Dordrecht: Nijhoff, 1984).

'Symposium: The Hart-Fuller Debate At Fifty' (2008) 83 NYU LR 993–1212.

Szondi, G, *Public Diplomacy and Nation Branding: Conceptual Similarities and Differences* (The Hague: Netherlands Institute of International Relations, 2008).

Tadjbakhsh, S and Chenoy, AM, *Human Security: Concepts and Implications* (Abingdon and New York: Routledge, 2007).

Talmon, S, 'The Legal Character of Statements by the President of the Security Council' (2003) 2 Chin JIL 419–67.

——, 'The Security Council as World Legislature' (2005) 99 AJIL 175–93.

——, 'Recognition of the Libyan National Transitional Council' (16 June 2011) 15 ASIL Insights, at <http://www.asil.org/insights110616.cfm>.

Tamanaha, BZ, *A General Jurisprudence of Law and Society* (Oxford: OUP, 2001).

——, *Law as a Means to an End: Threat to the Rule of Law* (Cambridge: CUP, 2006).

Tammes, AJP, 'Decisions of International Organs as a Source of International Law' (1958) 94 RdC 265–363.

Tams, CJ, *Enforcing Obligations* Erga Omnes *in International Law* (Cambridge: CUP, 2005).

Tan, K-C, *Justice Without Borders: Cosmopolitanism, Nationalism and Patriotism* (Cambridge: CUP, 2004).

Tancredi, A, 'Neither Authorized nor Prohibited? Secession and International Law after Kosovo, South Ossetia and Abkhazia' (2009) 18 It YBIL 37–62.

Tarrow, SG, *Power in Movement: Social Movements, Collective Action and Politics* (Cambridge: CUP, 1994).

Tehindrazanarivelo, DL, 'Targeted Sanctions and Obligations of States on Listing and Delisting Procedures' in Boisson de Chazournes, L (ed), *International Law and the Quest for its Implementation* (Leiden: Brill, 2010) 127–71.

Teraya, K, 'Emerging Hierarchy in International Human Rights and Beyond: From the Perspective of Non-derogable Rights' (2001) 12 EJIL 917–41.

Tertullian, *On Idolatry* (Whitefish: Kessinger Publishing, 2004).

Tesón, F, *A Philosophy of International Law* (Boulder, CO: Westview Press, 1998).

Teubner, G (ed), *Law as an Autopoietic System* (Cambridge, Mass and Oxford: Blackwell, 1993).

——, '"Global Bukowina": Legal Pluralism in the World Society' in Teubner, G (ed), *Global Law Without a State* (Aldershot: Dartmouth, 1997) 3–22.
—— (ed), *Global Law Without a State* (Aldershot: Dartmouth, 1997).
Thalmann, V, 'National Criminal Jurisdiction over Genocide' in Gaeta, P (ed), *The UN Genocide Convention: A Commentary* (Oxford: OUP, 2009) 231–58.
Thiele, LP, *The Heart of Judgment: Practical Wisdom, Neuroscience, and Narrative* (Cambridge: CUP, 2006).
Thomson, JE, *Mercenaries, Pirates, & Sovereigns: State Building and Extraterritorial Violence in Early Modern Europe* (Princeton: Princeton University Press, 1994).
Thornton, MT, 'Aristotelian Practical Reason' (1982) 41 *Mind* 57–76.
Thouvenin, J-M, 'Article 103' in Cot, J-P, Pellet, A, and Forteau, M (eds), *La Charte des Nations Unies: Commentaire article par article* (Paris: Economica, 3rd edn, 2005) vol 2, 2133–47.
Thucydides, *History of the Peloponnesian War* (Chicago: University of Chicago Press, 1989).
Thussu, DK, *International Communication* (London: Hodder Education, 2nd edn, 2006).
Tierney, B, *The Idea of Natural Rights: Studies on Natural Rights, Natural Law and Church Law, 1150–1625* (Atlanta, GA: Scholars Press, 1997).
Tietje, C, *Internationalisiertes Verwaltungshandeln* (Berlin: Duncker & Humblot, 2001).
Tigerstrom, B Von, *Human Security and International Law: Prospects and Problems* (Oxford and Portland: Hart, 2007).
Tilly, C (ed), *The Formation of National States in Western Europe* (Princeton: Princeton University Press, 1975).
——, 'Reflection on the History of European State-Making' in Tilly, C (ed), *The Formation of National States in Western Europe* (Princeton: Princeton University Press, 1975) 70.
——, *Coercion, Capital, and European States, A.D. 990–1992* (Cambridge: Blackwell, 1990).
—— and Wood, LJ, *Social Movements, 1768–2008* (Boulder: Paradigm Publishers, 2nd edn, 2009).
Tobin, J, *The Right to Health in International Law* (Oxford: OUP, 2012).
Tomasevski, K, 'Globalizing What: Education as a Human Right or as a Traded Service?' (2005) 12 Ind JGLS 1–78.
Tomuschat, C, 'International Courts and Tribunals with Regionally Restricted and/or Specialized Jurisdiction' in Mosler, M and Bernhardt, R (eds), *Judicial Settlement of International Disputes: International Court of Justice, Other Courts and Tribunals, Arbitration and Conciliation: An International Symposium* (Heidelberg and New York: Springer, 1974).
——, 'L'immunité des Etats en cas de violations graves des droits de l'homme' (2005) 109 RGDIP 51–74.
——, 'World Order Models: A Disputation with B.S. Chimni and Yasuaki Onuma' (2006) 8 ICLR 71–9.
Tönnies, F, *Gemeinschaft und Gesellschaft: Grundbegriffe der reinen Soziologie* [1887] (Darmstadt: Wissenschaftliche Buchgesellschaft, 2005), English trans *Community and Society: Gemeinschaft und Gesellschaft* (Minneapolis: Michigan State University Press, 1957).
Torrens, R, *An Essay on the External Corn Trade* [1815] (London: Longman, Rees, Orme, Brown, and Green, 3rd edn, 1826).
Toublanc, A, 'L'article 103 et la valeur juridique de la Charte des Nations Unies' (2004) 108 RGDIP 439–62.
Toyoda, T, 'Influence of Public Opinion on International Law in the Nineteenth Century', 46 Alb LR (2009) 1099–113.
Treves, T, Frigessi Di Rattalma, M, Tanzi, A, Fodella, A, Pitea, C, and Rani, C (eds), *Civil Society, International Courts and Compliance Bodies* (The Hague: TMC Asser Press, 2005).
Trevor-Roper, HR, *The European Witch Craze of the Sixteenth and Seventeenth Centuries* (London: Penguin, 1967).
Triepel, H, *Völkerrecht und Landesrecht* (Leipzig: Hirschfeldt, 1899).

Trimble, PR, 'A Revisionist View of Customary International Law' (1986) 33 UCLA LR 665–732.
Trone, J, 'Sovereign Immunity of the Member States of a Federation' (2008) 11 International Trade and Business Law Review 279–86.
Trouwborst, A, *Precautionary Rights and Duties of States* (Leiden: Nijhoff, 2006).
Truyol Y Serra, A, *Doctrines sur le fondement du droit des gens* (Paris: Pédone, 2007, rev edn by Kolb, R).
Tuck, R, *Natural Rights Theories: Their Origin and Development* (Cambridge: CUP, 1979).
Tunkin, GI, 'The Legal Nature of the United Nations' (1966-III) 119 RdC 6–66.
Twining, W, *Globalisation and Legal Theory* (London, Edinburgh, and Dublin: Butterworths, 2000).
——, 'A Post-Westphalian Conception of Law' (2003) 37 Law and Society Review 199–258.
——, *General Jurisprudence: Understanding Law from a Global Perspective* (Cambridge: CUP, 2009).
Tylor, EB, *The Origins of Culture* (New York: Harper, 1958).
Tzanakopoulos, A, *Disobeying the Security Council: Countermeasures against Wrongful Sanctions* (Oxford: OUP, 2011).
Tzevelekos, VP, 'The Use of Article 31(3)(C) of the VCLT in the Case Law of the ECtHR: An Effective Anti-fragmentation Tool or Selective Loophole for the Reinforcement of Human Rights Teleology? Between Evolution and Systemic Integration' (2009–10) 31 Mich JIL 621–90.
Unger, RM, *Knowledge and Politics* (New York: The Free Press, 1975).
United Nations Development Programme (UNDP), *Human Development Report 1999* (Oxford and New York: OUP, 1999) 8.
Untersteiner, M, *I sofisti* [1949] (Milan: Bruno Mondadori, 1996), English trans *The Sophists* (Oxford: Basil Blackwell, 1954).
Upadhyaya, P, 'Human Security, Humanitarian Intervention, and Third World Concerns' (2004) 33 Den JILP 71–91.
Vajic, N, 'Some Concluding Remarks on NGOs and the European Court of Human Rights' in Treves, T, Frigessi di Rattalma, M, Tanzi, A, Fodella, A, Pitea, C, and Rani, C (eds), *Civil Society, International Courts and Compliance Bodies* (The Hague: TMC Asser Press, 2005) 179–93.
Van Doan, T, *Reason, Rationality, and Reasonableness* (Washington, DC: The Council for Research in Values and Philosophy, 2001).
Varro, *De lingua latina*, English trans *On the Latin Language* (Cambridge, Mass and London: Harvard University Press, 1951).
Vassalli, G, *Formula di Radbruch e diritto penale: note sulla punizione dei delitti di Stato nella Germania postnazista e nella Germania postcomunista* (Milan: Giuffrè, 2001).
Vattel, E De, *Droit des gens; ou, Principes de la loi naturelle appliqués à la conduite et aux affaires des nations et des souverains* [1758] (Boston: Adamant Media, 2001), English trans *The Law of Nations or the Principles of Natural Law Applied to the Conduct and to the Affairs of Nations and of Sovereigns* (Washington, DC: Carnegie Institution, 1916).
Vedder, A (ed), *The Involvement of NGOs in International Governance and Policy: Sources of Legitimacy* (Leiden: Nijhoff, 2007).
Verdirame, G, '"The Divided West": International Lawyers in Europe and America' (2007) 18 EJIL 553–80.
——, *The UN and Human Rights: Who Guards the Guardians?* (Cambridge: CUP, 2011).
Verdross, A, *Die Einheit des rechtlichen Weltbildes auf Grundlage der Völkerrechtsverfassung* (Tübingen: JCB Mohr, 1923).
——, *Die Verfassung der Völkerrechtsgemeinschaft* (Vienna: Springer, 1926).
Verger, A, *WTO/GATS and the Global Politics of Higher Education* (New York and Abingdon: Routledge, 2009).

Vernant, J-P, *Mythe et société en Grèce ancienne* (Paris: Librairie François Maspero, 1974), English trans *Myth and Society in Ancient Greece* (New York: Zone Books, 1990).
Vico, G, *New Science: Principles of the New Science Concerning the Common Nature of Nations, Third edition Thoroughly Corrected, Revised, and Expanded by the Author* [1744] (London: Penguin Books, 2001).
Vismara, G, '"Impius Foedus": Le origini della Respublica Christiana' in *Scritti di storia giuridica. 7. Comunità e Diritto Internazionale* (Milan: Giuffrè, 1989).
Vitoria, F de *De Indis et De Jure Belli Relectiones* [1539], *The Reflections in Moral Theology of the Very Celebrated Spanish Theologian, Franciscus De Victoria* (Washington, DC: Carnegie Institution, 1917).
Voneky, S, 'Analogy in International LAw', Mp EPIL (February 2008 update) para 21.
Voyame, MD (ed), *International law, Conflict and Development: The Emergence of a Holistic Approach in International Affairs* (Leiden: Nijhoff, 2010) 443–63.
Vournas, E, 'Prefecture of Voiotia v. Federal Republic of Germany: Sovereign Immunity and the Exception for *Jus Cogens* Violations' (2002) 21 New York Law School Journal of International and Comparative Law 648–9.
Wahba, A and Bridgewell, L, 'Maslow Reconsidered: A Review of Research on the Need Hierarchy Theory' (1976) 15 OBHP 212–40.
Waibel, M, *Sovereign Defaults Before International Courts and Tribunals* (Cambridge: CUP, 2011).
Vöneky, S, 'Analogy in International Law', MP EPIL (February 2008 update).
Walker, N, 'Reframing EU Constitutionalism' in Dunoff, Jl and Trachtman, JP (eds), *Ruling the World? Constitutionalism, International Law, and Global Governance* (Cambridge: CUP, 2009) 149–76.
Wallace, RJ, 'Practical Reason' in Stan EP, at <http://plato.stanford.edu/entries/practical-reason>.
Wallenstein, SM and Silkenat, JR, 'Investment Funds and Dept-Equity Swaps: Broadening the Base of a New Financial Tool' (1988–89) 12 Ford ILJ 8–42.
Wallerstein, I, *World-Systems Analysis: An Introduction* (Durham and London: Duke University Press, 2004).
Walter, C, 'Subjects of International Law', MP EPIL (May 2007 update).
Walzer, M, *Just and Unjust Wars* (New York: Basic Books, 1977, 4th edn 2006).
Ward, RP, *An Enquiry into the Foundation and History of the Law of Nations in Europe from the Time of the Greeks and Romans to the Age of Grotius* (London: Strahan and Woodfall, 1795) xiii–xv.
Watson, A, *The Evolution of International Society: A Comparative Historical Analysis* (London and New York: Routledge, 1992).
Weber, LE and Duderstadt, JJ (eds), *The Globalization of Higher Education* (London, Paris, and Geneva: Economica, 2008).
Weber, M, 'Politics as a Vocation', repr in Gerth, HH and Wright Mills, C (eds), *From Max Weber. Essays in Sociology* (New York: OUP, 1958) 77–128.
——, *Economy and Society: An Outline of Interpretive Sociology* (Berkeley: University of California Press, 1978) 2 vols.
Weil, E and Labadie, JG, 'Good Sense or Philosophy' (1955) 3 *Diogenes* 29–49.
Weil, P, 'Le contrôle par les tribunaux nationaux de la licéité internationale des actes des Etats étrangers' (1971) 23 AFDI 9–52.
——, 'Le judaïsme et le développement du droit international' (1976-III) 151 RdC 253–335.
——, 'Towards Relative Normativity in International Law' (1983) 77 AJIL 413–42.
Weiler, J. 'Demyslifying the EJIL Selection and Editorial Process: How Does one Get Publish-eed in EJIL?' (2011) 22 EJIL 1.
Weinreb, LL, *Legal Reason: The Use of Analogy in Legal Argument* (Cambridge: CUP, 2005).
Weiss, L, *The Myth of the Powerless State* (Ithaca, NY: Cornell University Press, 1998).

Weiss, TG and Daws, S (eds), *The Oxford Handbook on the United Nations* (Oxford: OUP, 2007).
Weller, M (ed), *Universal Minority Rights: A Commentary on the Jurisprudence of International Courts and Treaty Bodies* (Oxford: OUP, 2007).
Wendehorst, CC, 'The State as a Foundation of Private Law Reasoning' (2008) 56 AJCL 567–604.
Wendt, A, 'The Agent-Structure Problem in International Relations Theory' (1987) 41 *International Organization* 335–70.
——, 'Anarchy is What States Make of It: The Social Construction of Power Politics' (1992) 46 *International Organization* 391–425.
——, *Social Theory of International Politics* (Cambridge: CUP, 1999).
——, 'Why a World State Is Inevitable' (2003) 9 European Journal of International Relations 491–542.
Wessel, RA, 'Informal International Law-Making as a New Form of World Legislation?' (2011) 8 IOLR 253–65.
Westlake, J, *Chapters on the Principles of International Law* (Cambridge: CUP, 1894).
Wheatley, S, *The Demociatic Legitimacy of International Law* (Oxford: Hart, 2010).
White, AR, 'Moore's Appeal To Common Sense' (1958) 33 *Philosophy* 221–39.
White, N, *The Law of International Organisations* (Manchester: Manchester University Press, 2nd edn, 2005).
White, PD, 'Philosophy and Law: Some Observations on MacCormick's Legal Reasoning and Legal Theory' (1979–80) 78 Mich LR 736–42.
White, RCA and Overy, C, *The European Convention Human Rights* (Oxford: OUP, 2010).
WHO, *Tobacco Company Strategies to Undermine Tobacco Control Activities of the World Health Organization Report of the Committee of Experts on Tobacco Industry Document* (Geneva, 2000).
Whitehead, AN, *The Organization of Thought: Educational and Scientific* (London: Williams and Norgate, 1929).
Wight, M, *Systems of States* (Leicester: Leicester University Press, 1977).
Wilde, R, *International Territorial Administration: How Trusteeship and the Civilizing Mission Never Went Away* (Oxford: OUP, 2008).
Williams, JF, 'The Legal Character of the Bank for International Settlements' (1930) 24 AJIL 665–73.
Williams, M, *Problems of Knowledge: A Critical Introduction to Epistemology* (Oxford: OUP, 2001).
Williams, OF (ed), *Peace through Commerce: Responsible Corporate Citizenship and the Ideals of the United Nations Global Compact* (Notre Dame: University of Notre Dame Press, 2008).
Williams, RA, *The American Indian in Western Legal Thought: The Discourses of Conquest* (New York and Oxford, OUP, 1990).
Williamson, M, *Terrorism, War and International Law* (Aldershot: Ashgate, 2009).
Willoughby, WW, 'The Legal Nature of International Law' (1908) 2 AJIL 357–65.
Wilson, A, 'The Nature of Legal Reasoning: A Commentary with Special Reference to Professor MacCormick's Theory' (1982) 2 *Legal Studies* 273–85.
Winkler, A, 'Just Sanctions' (1999) 21 HRQ 133–55.
Wittgenstein, L, *Über Gewissheit*, English trans *On Certainty* (Oxford: Basil Blackwell, 1969).
——, *Della certezza. L'analisi filosofica del senso comune* (Turin: Einaudi, 1978).
Wolff, C von, *Ius Gentium Methodo Scientifica Perpetractatum* [1749], English trans *The Law of Nations Treated According to a Scientific Method* (Oxford and London: Clarendon Press and Humphrey Milford, 1934).
——, *Philosophia Practica Universalis, Methodo Scientifica Pertracta* [1738–1739] (Hildesheim and New York: Georg Olms, 1979).

Wolff, RP, 'The Conflict between Authority and Autonomy', in Raz, J (ed), *Authority* (New York: New York University Press, 1990) 20–31.

Wolterstorff, N, *Justice: Rights and Wrongs* (Princeton and Oxford: Princeton University Press, 2008).

Wouters, J, Ryngaert, C, and Schmitt, P, case report (2011) 105 AJIL 560–7.

Wright, Q, 'Enforcement of International Law' (1944) 38 ASIL Proc 77–86.

Wróblewski, J, 'Kelsen, The Is–Ought Dichotomy and Naturalistic Fallacy' (1981) 35 RIP 508–17.

Xenophanes of Colophon, *Fragments* (Toronto, Buffalo, and London: University of Toronto Press, 2001).

Xenophon, *Memorabilia*, English trans *Memorabilia. Oeconomicus. Symposium. Apologia* (Harvard, Mass and London: Harvard University Press, 1923).

Yablo, S, 'Intrinsicness', at <http://www.mit.edu/~yablo/intrinsicness.html>.

Yack, B, 'Myth and Modernity: Hans Blumenberg's Reconstruction of Modern Theory' (1987) 15 *Political Theory* 244–61.

Yan, J, 'Branding and the International Community' (2003) 10 JBM 447–56.

Young, R, 'Defining Terrorism: The Evolution of Terrorism as a Legal Concept in International Law and its Influence on Definition in Domestic Legislation' (2006) 29 Boston Coll ICLR 23–105.

Zagrebelsky, G, *Intorno alla legge: Il diritto come dimensione del vivere comune* (Turin: Einaudi, 2009).

Zeidan, S, 'Desperately Seeking Definition: The International Community's Quest for Identifying the Specter of Terrorism' (2003–04) 36 Corn ILJ 491–6.

Zhou, W and Cuyvers, L, 'Linking International Trade and Labour Standards: The Effectiveness of Sanctions under the European Union's GSP' (2011) 45 JWT 63–83.

Ziegert, KA, 'The Sociology behind Eugen Ehrlich's Sociology of Law' (1979) 7 IJSL 225–73.

Zimmermann, A, Tomuschat, C, and Oellers-Frahm, K (eds), *The Statute of the International Court of Justice: A Commentary* (Oxford: OUP, 2006).

Zimmermann, CD, 'Exchange Rate Misalignment and International Law' (2011) 105 AJIL 423–76.

Zimmern, A. *The League of Nations and the Rule of Law (1918–1935)* (London: Macmillan, 1936) 98.

Zouche, R, *Iuris et Iudicii Fecialis, sive, Iuris Inter Gentes, et Quaestionum de Eodem Explicatio* [1650], English trans *An Exposition of Fecial Law and Procedure, or of Law Between Nations and Questions Concerning the Same* (Washington, DC: Carnegie Institution, 1911).

Name Index

Subject Index

The manufacturer's authorised representative in the EU for product safety is Oxford University Press España S.A. of El Parque Empresarial San Fernando de Henares, Avenida de Castilla, 2 - 28830 Madrid (www.oup.es/en or product.safety@oup.com). OUP España S.A. also acts as importer into Spain of products made by the manufacturer.
Printed and bound by CPI Group (UK) Ltd, Croydon, CR0 4YY
14/09/2026
02216306-0016